MW01625965

THE NAVARRE BIBLE

MAJOR PROPHETS

VOLUMES IN THIS SERIES

Standard Edition

NEW TESTAMENT

St Matthew's Gospel
St Mark's Gospel
St Luke's Gospel
St John's Gospel
Acts of the Apostles
Romans and Galatians
Corinthians
Captivity Letters
Thessalonians and Pastoral Letters
Hebrews
Catholic Letters
Revelation

OLD TESTAMENT

The Pentateuch
Joshua–Kings [Historical Books 1]
Chronicles–Maccabees [Historical Books 2]
The Psalms and the Song of Solomon
Wisdom Books
Major Prophets
Minor Prophets

Reader's (Omnibus) Edition

The Gospels and Acts
The Letters of St Paul
Revelation, Hebrews and Catholic Letters

Single-volume, large-format New Testament

THE NAVARRE BIBLE

Major Prophets

The Books of Isaiah, Jeremiah, Lamentations,
Baruch, Ezekiel and Daniel
in the Revised Standard Version and New Vulgate
with a commentary by members of the
Faculty of Theology of the University of Navarre

FOUR COURTS PRESS • DUBLIN
SCEPTER PUBLISHERS • NEW YORK

Typeset by Carrigboy Typesetting Services for
FOUR COURTS PRESS LTD
7 Malpas Street, Dublin 8, Ireland
www.fourcourtspress.ie
and in North America for
SCEPTER PUBLISHERS, INC.
P.O. Box 211, New York, NY 10018–0004
www.scepterpublishers.org

Original title: *Sagrada Biblia: Antiguo Testamento: Libros proféticos* [part only]

Nihil obstat: Jerome McCarthy, *censor deputatus*
Imprimi potest: Dermot, Archbishop of Dublin, 1 September 2004

First published 2005; reprinted 2007, 2012, 2016, 2018.

The translation of introductions and commentary was made by Michael Adams and Coilín Ó hAodha.

A catalogue record for this title is available from the British Library.

ISBN 978–1–85182–872–2 (Four Courts Press)
ISBN 978–1–594170–23–2 (Scepter Publishers)

Library of Congress Cataloging-in-Publication Data [for first volume in this series]

Bible. O.T. English. Revised Standard. 1999.
The Navarre Bible. – North American ed.
p. cm
"The Books of Genesis, Exodus, Leviticus, Numbers, Deuteronomy in the Revised Standard Version and New Vulgate with a commentary by members of the Faculty of Theology of the University of Navarre."
Includes bibliographical references.
Contents: [1] The Pentateuch.
ISBN 1–889334–21–9 (hardback: alk. paper)
I. Title.
BS891.A1 1999.P75 99–23033
221.7'7—dc21 CIP

ACKNOWLEDGMENTS
Quotations from Vatican II documents are based on the translation in *Vatican Council II: The Conciliar and Post Conciliar Documents*, ed. A. Flannery, OP (Dublin 1981).

Printed and bound in England by TJ Books Limited, Padstow, Cornwall.

Contents

Preface and Preliminary Notes

The project of a new Spanish translation of the Bible, with commentary, was originally entrusted to the faculty of theology at the University of Navarre by St Josemaría Escrivá, the founder of Opus Dei and the university's first chancellor.

The main feature of the English edition, *The Navarre Bible*, is the commentary, that is, the notes and introductions provided by the editors; rarely very technical, these are designed to elucidate the spiritual and theological message of the Bible. Quotations from commentaries by the Fathers, and excerpts from other spiritual writers, not least St Josemaría, are provided to show how they read Scripture and made it meaningful in their lives. This edition also carries the Western Church's official Latin version of the Bible, the *editio typica altera* of the New Vulgate (1986).

For the English edition we consider ourselves fortunate in having the Revised Standard Version as the translation of Scripture and wish to record our appreciation for permission to use that text.[1]

PRELIMINARY NOTES

The headings in the biblical text have been provided by the editors (they are not taken from the RSV); this is true also of the cross references in the marginal notes. These headings are also listed together at the end of the book, to act as a sort of index.

References in the margin of the biblical text or its headings point to parallel passages or other passages which deal with the same theme. With the exception of the New Testament and Psalms, the marginal references are to the New Vulgate, that is, they are not normally adjusted to the RSV.

Some headings carry an asterisk; this means there is an asterisked note below, more general than the normal and one which examines the structure or content of an entire passage. To get an overview of each book, the reader may find it helpful to read the asterisked notes before reading the biblical text and the more specific notes. An asterisk *inside the RSV text* refers the reader to the Explanatory Notes at the end of the book.

1. Integral to which are the RSV footnotes, which are indicated by superior letters.

Table of Kings and Prophets

KINGS OF ISRAEL AND JUDAH
from the death of Solomon onwards

Kingdom of Israel		*Kingdom of Judah*		*Prophets*
928–907	Jeroboam	931–911	Rehoboam	
		911–908	Abijam	
		908–867	Asa	
907–906	Nadab			
906–883	Baasha			
883–882	Elah			
882	Zimri			
882–871	OMRI			
873–852	AHAB			
		870–846	JEHOSHAPHAT	
852–851	Ahaziah			
851–842	Joram	851–843*	Jehoram	
		843–842	Ahaziah	
842–814	Jehu	842–836	Athaliah	
		836–798	Joash	
817–800	Jehoahaz (Joahaz)			
800–784	(Jehoash)			
		798–769	Amaziah	
788–747*	JEROBOAM II			AMOS
		785–733*	AZARIAH (UZZIAH)	
747	Zechariah			HOSEA
747	Shallum			
747–737	Menahem			
737–735	Pekahiah			
735–732	Pekah	759–743*	Jotham	
				ISAIAH
732–724	Hoshea	743–727	Ahaz	
		727–698	HEZEKIAH	MICAH
		698–642	Manasseh	
				NAHUM
		641–640	Amon	
		639–609	JOSIAH	ZEPHANIAH
				JEREMIAH
		609	Jehoahaz	
		608–598	Jehoiakim	EZEKIEL
				HABAKKUK
		597	Jehoiachin	
		596–587	Zedekiah	
			Post-exile	ZECHARIAH, HAGGAI
				MALACHI

Note: The biblical books listed on the right contain references to the period of the kings mentioned in the other columns, although some of those books were written later.

The more important kings' names are given in capital letters.

An asterisk indicates that the regnal years include years of regency.

For the dating of prophets Daniel, Joel, Obadiah, Jonah, see the introductions to these books.

Abbreviations

1. BOOK OF HOLY SCRIPTURE

Acts	Acts of the Apostles
Amos	Amos
Bar	Baruch
1 Chron	1 Chronicles
2 Chron	2 Chronicles
Col	Colossians
1 Cor	1 Corinthians
2 Cor	2 Corinthians
Dan	Daniel
Deut	Deuteronomy
Eccles	Ecclesiastes (Qoheleth)
Esther	Esther
Eph	Ephesians
Ex	Exodus
Ezek	Ezekiel
Ezra	Ezra
Gal	Galatians
Gen	Genesis
Hab	Habakkuk
Hag	Haggai
Heb	Hebrews
Hos	Hosea
Is	Isaiah
Jas	James
Jer	Jeremiah
Jn	John
1 Jn	1 John
2 Jn	2 John
3 Jn	3 John
Job	Job
Joel	Joel
Jon	Jonah
Josh	Joshua
Jud	Judith
Jude	Jude
Judg	Judges
1 Kings	1 Kings
2 Kings	2 Kings
Lam	Lamentations
Lev	Leviticus
Lk	Luke
1 Mac	1 Maccabees
2 Mac	2 Maccabees
Mal	Malachi
Mic	Micah
Mk	Mark
Mt	Matthew
Nah	Nahum
Neh	Nehemiah
Num	Numbers
Obad	Obadiah
1 Pet	1 Peter
2 Pet	2 Peter
Phil	Philippians
Philem	Philemon
Ps	Psalms
Prov	Proverbs
Rev	Revelation (Apocalypse)
Rom	Romans
Ruth	Ruth
1 Sam	1 Samuel
2 Sam	2 Samuel
Sir	Sirach (Ecclesiasticus)
Song	Song of Solomon
1 Thess	1 Thessalonians
2 Thess	2 Thessalonians
1 Tim	1 Timothy
2 Tim	2 Timothy
Tit	Titus
Wis	Wisdom
Zech	Zechariah
Zeph	Zephaniah

2. RSV ABBREVIATIONS

In the notes indicated by superior *letters* in the biblical text, the following abbreviations are used:

Cn	a correction made where the text has suffered in transmission and the versions provide no satisfactory restoration but the RSV Committee agrees with the judgment of competent scholars as to the most probable reconstruction of the original text
Heb	the Hebrew of the consonantal Masoretic Text of the Old Testament
Gk	Septuagint, Greek Version of the Old Testament
Lat	Latin Version of Tobit, Judith, and 2 Maccabees
Ms	manuscript
Mss	manuscripts
MT	the Hebrew of the pointed Masoretic Text of the Old Testament
Sam	Samaritan Hebrew text of the Old Testament
Syr	Syriac Version of the Old Testament
Tg	Targum
Vg	Vulgate, Latin Version of Old Testament

N.B. In the biblical text, the word LORD, when spelled with capital letters, stands for the divine name, Yhwh.

3. OTHER ABBREVIATIONS

ad loc.	*ad locum*, commentary on this passage
AAS	*Acta Apostolicae Sedis*
Apost.	Apostolic
can.	canon
chap.	chapter
cf.	*confer*, compare
CCC	*Catechism of the Catholic Church*
Const.	Constitution
Decl.	Declaration
Dz-Sch	Denzinger-Schönmetzer, *Enchiridion Biblicum* (4th edition, Naples & Rome, 1961)
Enc.	Encyclical
Exhort.	Exhortation
f	and following (*pl.* ff)
ibid.	*ibidem*, in the same place
in loc.	*in locum*, commentary on this passage
loc.	*locum*, place or passage
par.	parallel passages
Past.	Pastoral
RSV	Revised Standard Version
RSVCE	Revised Standard Version, Catholic Edition
SCDF	Sacred Congregation for the Doctrine of the Faith
sess.	session
v.	verse (*pl.* vv.)

The Prophetical Books of the Old Testament

There are sixteen prophetical books in the biblical canon—four "major" (Isaiah, Jeremiah, Ezekiel and Daniel) and twelve "minor" works, a distinction referring only to their length: whereas each of the "major prophets" comprises an entire parchment roll, all the others take up only one—the Roll of the Twelve Prophets. In the Hebrew canon, the books of Deuteronomic history (Joshua, Judges, 1 & 2 Samuel, 1 & 2 Kings) are called "Earlier Prophets", and the name "Later Prophets" covers all the others (Isaiah, Jeremiah, Ezekiel and the Roll of the Twelve Prophets). Also, because it regards the prophetical books as teaching or commentary on the Law (the Pentateuch), the Hebrew canon places them immediately after the Pentateuch and before the books known as the "Writings". The book of Daniel, which was written after the "Prophets" collection was assembled, is included among the "Writings".[1] However, the Christian canon, which focuses on the *history of salvation*, sees the later prophets as being largely oriented towards a hopeful future that finds its fulfilment in Jesus Christ; hence it puts the prophetical books at the end of the canon and includes among them the book of Daniel, given its eschatological concerns. That is the order followed in the Navarre Bible, in line with the Septuagint Greek and the Latin versions. [The RSV places the two last historical books, 1 & 2 Maccabees, after the prophets.]

Both Jewish and Christian traditions hold the books of the prophets in high regard, because prophecy was an integral part of the religious heritage of ancient Israel and these books record the word of God addressed to his people through the oracles of the prophets.

1. PROPHETS AND PROPHETICAL BOOKS

The word "prophet" comes from the Greek *pro-phetes*, which means "to speak on behalf of someone," especially a god. It therefore has nothing to do with predicting the future, an activity described in Greek as *mantis*. The Hebrew word for *pro-phetes* is *nabî*, and its reference, too, is religious. *Nabî* came to mean "one chosen by God to speak in his name". The prophet is referred to in other ways in the Bible, in addition to *nabî*—for example, "man of God" (Josh 14:6; 1 Kings 17:18; 2 Kings 4:7), "man of the spirit" (Hos 9:7), "servant of

1. Cf. *The Navarre Bible: Psalms* and *Wisdom Books*, Introduction, p. 11.

the Lord" (2 Kings 9:7), all of which refer more to aspects of the prophet's personality.

a) In the Bible, the word "prophet" and its derivatives (prophecy, prophesying etc.) have quite a broad meaning, but all, primarily, refer to the idea of "speaking in the name of God", being his spokesman. We can see this, for example, in the opening words of the Letter to the Hebrews: "In many and various ways God spoke of old to our fathers by the prophets ..." (Heb 1:1). The New Testament also describes as prophetical all those passages that refer to the future Messiah, be they in the Pentateuch, the Prophets or the Psalms, and it even goes so far as to consider the entire Old Testament as being prophetical (cf. Mt 2:23; Lk 18:13; Rom 1:2). The Church has inherited this way of speaking when she professes her faith in the Holy Spirit "who has spoken through the prophets" (Nicene-Constantinopolitan Creed).

Using this broad sense of the word, the Bible gives the title of "prophet" to Abraham (Gen 20:7), to Mary, the sister of Moses and Aaron (Ex 15:20), to the seventy elders of the people (Num 11:25–29), to Deborah, who judged Israel in the time of the judges (Judg 4:4), and, of course, to Moses, the very prototype of the prophet (Deut 18:15–18). Indeed, of him it goes so far as to say that "there has not arisen a prophet in Israel like Moses, whom the Lord knew face to face" (Deut 34:10).

People can receive messages in a variety of ways—some quite exceptional, such as visions, dreams, ecstasies etc.; others ordinary, such as incidents in the prophet's life, his alertness to see the significance of quite small things, etc. St Thomas Aquinas, who studied prophecy in depth, distinguishes four types of it in terms of the manner in which the prophet receives the message (the "species", in Thomistic language)—intellectually, by means of the imagination, by infused sight, or by natural sight. He regards the last-mentioned mode as the least perfect because it involves the least degree of direct intervention by God. He also deduces that the gift of prophecy is something transitory, unlike that of sanctifying grace; a person can be chosen to enunciate a specific oracle and never again speak in the name of God.[2]

b) As an institution proper to Israel, prophecy began during the very early days of the monarchy, at the shrines to which the Israelites went for answers to their questions and to discover what the Lord's will demanded of them. Samuel, a prophet in the temple of Shiloh (cf. 1 Sam 3:19–21), is considered to have been the earliest of the prophets (1 Sam 3:20) and later tradition raised him to the rank of intercessor (Ps 99:6; Acts 13:20), one who passed on the word of God (2 Chron 35:18), an upholder of the institutions of Israel (Sir 46:13–20) and the first herald of messianic times (Acts 3:24). Samuel is a prophet because he interprets God's will for the entire people, or for an individual chosen by God to undertake some important assignment: it is he

2. Cf. *Quodlib.*, 12,1.7, a. 26.

who anoints Saul and David; he spells out how the monarchy should operate; etc. From Samuel onwards, the prophet will have a public role in Israel, to make known God's will at key moments in the history of the people.

There were also "groups of prophets" associated with the shrines (though they often operated beyond their confines). These were communities of people who would enter into ecstatic trances by means of music, dancing and exaggerated gestures (1 Sam 10:5, 10–13). The Bible gives very little information about these groups, but they seem to have had some sort of internal structure and to have in general acted as a group. We know, for example, that at one point, when Saul had sent men to arrest David, Saul himself and his messengers actually took part in the ceremonies of a company of prophets that owed allegiance to Samuel (1 Sam 19:18–24).

In addition to what it has to say about temple prophets, the Bible also tells us about a number of individuals who, on occasion, acted as prophets. For example, Balaam spoke oracles (cf. Num 23:7–10; 18–24; 24:3–9, 15–25), even though he did not belong to the chosen people. Others, like Gad (1 Sam 22:5; 2 Sam 24:11–14, 18–19) and Nathan (2 Sam 7; 12:1–15) lived at court and were prophets of King David. Others, such as Abijah of Shiloh (1 Kings 11:29–39), Jehu (1 Kings 16:1–2) and Micaiah, son of Imlah (1 Kings 22:8–28), were court prophets in the Northern kingdom, where this type of prophetic office was more in evidence. Moreover, prophecy was an established ministry in the shrines at Jericho (2 Kings 2:4–5), Gilgal (2 Kings 4:38) and Bethel (1 Kings 13:11–24). Special mention should be made of the so-called charismatic prophets; these had no particular connexion with court or temple but they were very influential in the life of the people of Israel. Outstanding among these were Elijah (1 Kings 17–19; 2 Kings 1–2) and Elisha (2 Kings 1–13), who operated as prophets in the ninth century BC and had very considerable influence on the politics of the period and on the reform of religious life in Israel. To a greater or lesser extent, the Bible tells us about oracles or interventions by these men, but it does not attribute any written books or texts to them. They are prophets because the Bible tells us that they acted or transmitted their message in the name of God. After the fall of Samaria (722 BC) there were no prophets who were not also writers, or, if there were, they were not particularly influential.

c) The "writer prophets", that is, those who figure in the biblical canon, were, like those mentioned above, men who were conscious of being spokesmen of God; but what distinguishes them is the fact that their visions, oracles and careers, are recorded in writing. Strictly speaking, one should talk not of prophets but of "prophetical literature" or "prophetical books", meaning those writings which are attributed to a particular prophet and which have been handed down as such in the biblical canon. Many of these people exercised their prophetical office in the same way as the prophets mentioned earlier; others, perhaps, never actually preached, and there may even have been one prophet, Malachi, whose name was given to the book by a writer using a pseudonym. Be that as it may, the prophetical books (like the rest of Holy Scripture) are authoritative "on the grounds that, written under the inspiration of the Holy Spirit, they have God as their author, and have been handed on as such to the Church herself".[3]

In this edition, unless it is specifically stated to the contrary, when we speak of "prophets" and "prophetical books", we mean the same thing. As regards when the prophets lived: Amos, Hosea, Isaiah, and Micah belong to the eighth century BC; Nahum, Zephaniah, Habakkuk and Jeremiah, seventh to sixth century; Ezekiel, sixth century. Haggai, Zechariah and Malachi belong to the Persian period; Joel, Obadiah and Jonah are of a later period (it is difficult to be more specific). The book of Daniel was probably written a little before 165 BC.

d) In the New Testament, Jesus is the greatest and last messenger of God, and the eternal Word of the Father (Heb 1:1), although St Luke alone (and then only obliquely) applies to him the title of prophet (Lk 4:24; 13:33; cf. 7:16, 39; 9:8–19). The Church expresses her belief in this regard as follows: "Christ is the great prophet who proclaimed the kingdom of the Father both by the testimony of his life and by the power of his word. Until the full manifestation of his glory, he fulfills the prophetic office ...".[4]

For their part, the first people to embrace faith in Christ shared the conviction, widespread at the time, that prophecy would be a feature of the messianic age. Thus, we find them applying the title of prophet to such people as Anna, the prophetess in the temple (Lk 2:36), and John the Baptist (cf. Mt 11:9–11), who had a prominent role in signalling the dawning of the messianic age. In the aftermath of Pentecost, there were quite a number of Christians who "prophesied". These included Agabus (Acts 11:27–28; 21:10–11), the prophets of Antioch, among them Barnabas (Acts 13:2), the daughters of Philip (Acts 21:9), and many more whose names we do not know. In fact, St Paul praises the gift of prophecy that manifested itself in liturgical assemblies (1 Cor 11:4–5), and he pointed out that it was a gift to aspire to possess (1 Cor 14:1) because it helped to build up the whole Christian community (cf. 1 Cor 14:2–5). However, for that very reason, in order to protect the true charism of prophecy, the leaders of those communities were on their guard against false prophets (cf. 1 Jn 4:1–3) who might introduce erroneous teachings by claiming the authority of spokesmen of God.

The gift of prophecy survives in the Church, for "all the holy people of God shares also in the Church's prophetic office: it spreads abroad a living witness to him, especially by a life of faith and love and by offering to God a sacrifice of praise, the tribute of lips which praise his name (cf. Heb 13:15)".[5]

3. Vatican II, *Dei Verbum*, 11. **4.** Vatican II, *Lumen gentium*, 35. **5.** Ibid., 12.

2. HOW THE PROPHETICAL BOOKS CAME INTO BEING

The prophetical books, like many other books in ancient times, were not written all at one go. Like most of the books of the Bible, they went through an editing process over a period of time, until they reached the final stage and became part of the canon. Still, each book has a lot to do with the figure whose name it bears: first, because it contains the main elements of his teaching, but also because we know that some sections were written by the prophet himself (cf. Is 30:8), or by his amanuensis, as in the case of Baruch, who took dictation from Jeremiah. It will never be easy, or for that matter necessary, to work out which words of a book are the original words of the prophet, his *ipsissima verba*, but without doubt each book, as a whole, can be attributed to the original prophet or his circle of disciples.

Scholars usually point to there being three "layers" in the editorial compilation of these books, which correspond to three specific stages. Generally speaking (because the history of each book is different), we can say that one layer can be attributed to the prophet, one to the contribution of disciples, with the third layer, the literary structure, being the work of an editor who came later. The entire process was carried out under the inspiration of the Holy Spirit, who is the principal author of these books and of all Holy Scripture.

In general, the poetical sections of the books are attributed to the prophet himself, specifically those parts which are most expressive, such as, for example, the oracles against the neighbouring countries in Amos (Amos 1:3—2:8); the "confessions" of Jeremiah (Jer 12:1–6; 15:15–21; 20:7–18); the greater part of the Book of the Immanuel in Isaiah (Is 6–12); and many others to which we will draw attention in the commentaries.

The main work involved in creating the book is ascribed to the prophet's disciples—collecting and selecting the most significant oracles, giving them a literary form, writing the biographical sections in the third person, writing down the visions and details of the symbolic actions of the prophet. The disciples would have been responsible for the greater part of each book, given that it could take a lot of time and effort to do all that work. However, it is not always possible to work out the "itinerary" of an oracle from when it was first spoken by the prophet: maybe in the first instance it was transmitted among his immediate followers by being memorized and repeated orally, and was then linked up with other passages in the same tone or with similar content, and then, later still, found its way into small written collections or perhaps larger blocs of writings, until the book as we now know it was eventually produced.

Scholars see the final editor or redactor as being responsible for the book as such and for its final updating. For example, the oracles against the nations in Amos end with the prophecy pronounced against Israel (Amos 2:6–16), but the final redactor must have inserted a similar prophecy against Judah (Amos 2:4–5), because, once the Northern kingdom collapsed, only the people of the

South were in a position to receive the book by the prophet from Teko. In some cases, the final redactor collected and rearranged oracles which, though not those of the original prophet, did carry a message consistent with that in earlier texts; this could have occurred in the case of the book of Isaiah, which includes oracles from different periods but which are arranged in such a way that they make up a coherent book with a particular specific literary character to it. This last redactor played a very important role, because in addition to putting all the various elements together he gave them a unified style and a distinctive doctrinal focus. So, commentators are right to say, as they often do, that he performed the role of an author. To him also must be attributed the heading or title given to each book and the insertion of most of the references to when events took place.

From the literary point of view, prophetical books are different from others in that they retain the features of a public proclamation of the message. The prophet would normally address people in a speech, to move their hearts and to exhort them to mend their ways. Therefore, the most common form of prophetical expression is the oracle, that is, a solemn statement made in the name of God involving either denunciation or a promise of salvation. In the strict sense, an oracle is not a prediction of concrete events, but rather a proclamation of God's plan, which will always be realized. It is addressed to a particular individual (Amos 7:16–17) or, more often, a group of people or the whole nation (cf. Amos 4:1–3; 9–12). Oracles of salvation include the messianic and most of the eschatological oracles. There are also oracles expressed in the form of legal suits (*rîb:* see the notes on Is 1:10–20 and 1:2–31) between God and the people, designed to spell out the reasons for the punishment imposed by God (cf. Hos 2:4–10). In addition to oracles, the prophetical books contain songs (Is 5:1–2), hymns (Is 44:23), letters (Jer 29), wisdom teachings (Amos 5:21–24; Is 8:11–15), etc. The oracles are found side by side with narrative sections, such as accounts of the prophet's calling (Is 6:1–13; Jer 1:4–10), visions (Jer 1:11–14), dreams (Zech 1:7–17) and many other biographical or autobiographical references. Special mention should be made of symbolic actions, that is, "acted-out" oracles. These have nothing to do with magic performed to produce some desired result; they are simply designed to show by signs something that will happen in the future. For example, when Elijah poured water over the burnt offerings at Mount Carmel, he did not cause rainfall, but was imploring God to send it (cf. 1 Kings 18:25, 34–35); and when Jeremiah put the yoke around his neck (cf. Jer 27:2–22), this did not have the effect of plunging the people into slavery (in Babylon); it was an action he did to signal the slavery that awaited them. Almost all the writer prophets use this sort of oracle to help explain their message: Hosea made his matrimonial life a sign of God's love for his people (Hos 1–3), and Isaiah used the symbolic names of his sons (Is 7:3; 8:3) and that of Immanuel (Is 7:14) to proclaim the salvation that was to come. Jeremiah, for his part, employed symbolic actions of this sort more than his predecessors had done: among the examples we find in his work are the spoiled piece of linen (Jer 13:1–11), the broken flask (Jer 19), the yoke around his neck (Jer 27; 28:10), the purchase of the field (Jer 32), the foundation of the throne of Nebuchadnezzar (Jer 43:8–13) and the book thrown into the Euphrates (Jer 51:59–64). Still, the greatest number of symbolic actions is to be found in Ezekiel, although, due to his style, it is not always easy to work out what they symbolize—his temporary loss of speech (Ezek 3:24–27; cf. 4:1–3); his acting-out of the siege of Jerusalem (Ezek 4:1–17); cutting his hair and beard (Ezek 5:1–3); venturing out with an exile's baggage (Ezek 12:1–16); eating bread with quaking (Ezek 12:17–20); not mourning the death of his wife (Ezek 24:15–27); the two sticks in his hand (Ezek 37:15–28); etc. New Testament prophets, too, carried out symbolic actions (as when Agabus predicted St Paul's imprisonment: Acts 21:11), but it must have occurred very seldom, because the Christian message has more to do with the proclamation of past events than with prophesying future ones (cf. Rom 10:14–18).

3. CONTENT

The message contained in the prophetical books covers all aspects of Israelite faith, but each prophet underlines and develops points of teaching that were of particular relevance to his contemporaries. This makes it difficult to summarize and synthesize the teaching of the prophets as a whole, for their writings extend over more than four centuries. The immediate concerns of Amos in the seventh century BC were different from those of Haggai and Zechariah (who lived towards the end of the sixth century) or those of Daniel (second-century). Even so, there are three points, that all the prophets stressed, more or less—belief in one God, the future messianic age, and ethical and social teaching.

a) *Monotheism* is the primary subject of the prophetical oracles. This involves not only the promotion of a single form of worship but also belief in the one, true God: there is no God but the Lord. The main points in their teaching in this regard are:

—God is the sovereign Lord of all human affairs. The God of Israel does not reside in a special *place*, where one must go to find him (in a pantheon, so to speak); nor is he essentially "the god of nature", whose seasons and fertility testify to his presence. Like the wise men (cf. Ps 29; 96; etc.) the prophets acknowledge the Lord (*Yhwh*) to be the ruler of the created universe, and, above all, the one who guides the course of history. It is he who determines victory or defeat, political success or exile, and everything is geared towards encouraging his people to "return" to him (cf. Amos 4:4–12).

—God has a special relationship with Israel. In the book of Amos he is described as being a fellow wayfarer who reveals his secrets to his servants, the prophets (Amos 3:3–8), and in Hosea (eight century BC) we find the first mention of the Covenant in the books of the prophets (Hos 2:20; 6:7; 8:2). It is Hosea, too, who depicts the God-man relationship as being spousal (Hos 1–3) and that of father-and-son (Hos 11:1–14)—imagery that finds its way, via later prophetical books (cf. Jer 2:2), into the New Testament (cf. Mt 9:15; Rev 21:2).

—God is holy. Even though God has a close relationship with his people, he is not like them; he cannot be treated as being on a par with them; He cannot be "manipulated", not even by means of sacrifices and offerings. God stands above everything; he is the Most High—as Isaiah stresses so much (cf. Is 6:3). The holiness of the people, therefore, derives from their participating in the holiness of their God: their belief and its ethical demands mark them out as being different from other nations. God is the "Holy One of Israel" (Is 5:19–24), because, without ceasing to be the Most High, he has drawn near to his people.

—Punishment is interpreted as part of God's relationship with his people. If they fail to live up to the demands of their special calling, if their behaviour is no better than that of other nations, there is nothing for it but for God to chastise them (cf. Amos 3:2). That is the only way they can be brought back to the path of righteousness. God "visits" his people (that is, makes them pay the just price of their sins) in order to re-establish a proper relationship with them. That is what the prophets mean when they speak of the "day of the Lord" (cf. Amos 5:18–19; Zeph 1:7–18).

b) *Messianic hope* forms the very backbone of the prophetical books. Those from the pre-exilic period, as indeed the Psalms (Ps 2; 89) use Nathan's prophecy (2 Sam 7:14) to get across the idea that salvation will come through a descendant of David (*royal messianism*). But they never adopt a sycophantic attitude towards the king or use courtly forms of address or bestow divine titles on him or envision that he shall reign forever. The notion they have of the Messiah looks to the future, so that the reigning monarch pales into insignificance; they encourage the people to place their hopes in "the Lord's anointed", who is soon to come. Isaiah is the prophet who most often mentions the Davidic dynasty (cf. Is 7:13–17; 9:5–6; 11:1–5), and yet he never mentions the king by name. He applies grandiose, unheard-of titles to him, but in doing so he exalts the Lord's wondrous works more than the individual whom the Lord places at their centre. Micah, too, refers to the Davidic line without mentioning the king's name (Mic 5:1–5). And Jeremiah, who produced only one oracle about the future king, proclaims the coming of a descendant in the line of David who will rule with the justice and righteousness of the Lord (Jer 23:5–6). The king that all the prophets look forward to is someone who will live a life befitting a true son of God—not at all the sort of king they were familiar with.

The prophets of the exile period hardly ever speak in terms of royal Messiah: Ezekiel will not even give the title of "king" to the prince who will rule over a restored Israel and whom he sees as being a new "David" (Ezek

34:23–24). And in the years just before the return from exile we find it being said that God himself will bring salvation, without using intermediaries (Is 41:14)—a *messianism without a Messiah.* And sometimes we find the title of Messiah being given to any person who, acting in God's name, brings deliverance to Israel—even if he be a foreigner, as the Persian king Cyrus was (Is 45:1). But salvation will come about, primarily, through the people, or through someone born into it, a servant of the Lord who will achieve full freedom for himself and his fellow countrymen.

Among the last prophets, those of the period after the Exile, we find a spiritualization of messianism, which fits in very well with their teaching about the last days. This "eschatology" refers to their conviction that God will, in due course, save man once and for all, by means of Israel, his chosen people, who have a special role to play in the advent of salvation. Israel will judge the nations—in a scenario that prefigures God's last judgment (*the day of the Lord*) which will cover both Israel and all other nations. In the last of the prophetical books, things to do with the End take second place: the main emphasis is on the Messiah. According to Zechariah, God himself will come to rule over all the earth (cf. Zech 13:9), and the book of Daniel, where we find the figure of the "son of man", attests to the hope that God will give a humble person (read "the chosen people") a kingdom that will last forever and will encompass the whole world (Dan 7:13—14:27). In the New Testament we recognize Jesus to be the true Messiah, with all the features (and more) that the prophets attributed to the Messiah: he is the descendant of King David; he judges and redeems the world; he is the son of Man; and he takes on the features of Isaiah's Servant of the Lord in order to bring enduring salvation to all mankind.

c) *Ethical and social teaching*. The prophets, especially those prior to the Exile, lay much stress on the social implications of the faith. As heralds of God's teaching about his choice of Israel and about the Covenant, they exhort the people to obedience time and again. And because their contemporaries are losing their old ideals, exploiting the weaker members of society and adopting Gentile lifestyles, the prophets are not slow to reproach them for "forgetting God" (cf. Hos 2:13; Jer 2:32) and becoming like other peoples (cf. Hos 9:1).

Oppressive rulers come in for the severest criticism, and the prophets are at pains to stress divine preference for the "humble and lowly" (Zeph 3:12–13). In line with the thinking of the entire Old Testament, the prophets never consider material poverty as something desirable, much less as being an ideal. Poor people are not virtuous because they lack resources, but God has a special love for them because their poverty is often caused by the injustice of powerful, wealthy people. It is that type of poverty, the result of injustice, that the prophets seek to eliminate. Hence their continual insistence on the fact that justice and holiness are inescapable demands deriving from the Covenant.

The moral precepts preached by the prophets are those to be found in the Law, but the prophets are at pains to point out that good conduct must come from the heart. A clean heart is more imporant than external conformity to the Law (cf. Is 2:16–17; Ezek 11:19; 36:26); and from Jeremiah (cf. Jer 31:29–30) and Ezekiel (Ezek 18:1–4) onwards, great stress is laid on individual reponsibility: a person has to take responsibility for his own sins and not blame them on his forebears.

Finally, the prophets' message also stresses the importance of religious worship: it has to be performed properly, in the right spirit, as befitting the reverence due to God. They constantly criticize an external formalism in the practice of religion, and stress that there needs to be continuity between the worship rendered to God and the people's ethical and social life. A people that brings offerings to the Lord and professes faith in him in the sphere of the liturgy must make sure that it does not then turn around and deny him by misconduct and corruption in everyday life.

4. HISTORICAL BACKGROUND

The writer-prophets, from Amos down to Malachi, exercised their ministry over a long period of time—from the eighth century BC to the fourth century, or right into the second if one includes the book of Daniel. These were eventful years for Israel, as we know from the historical books of the Bible,[6] a period in which its fortunes changed radically. The Northern kingdom was dominant at first, under Omri and his successors, until it eventually decayed and then collapsed at the hands of the Assyrians (722 BC). Then came the heyday of the kingdom of Judah, in the reign of Hezekiah, and the religious reform led by Josiah (662 BC). But everything stopped abruptly with the invasion by Nebuchadnezzar. The king and all the most prominent members of the community were deported to Babylon (587 BC)—an exile that lasted fifty years; the exiles were allowed to return, thanks to King Cyrus' decree, but the country no longer had independence. Soon it came under the sway of the Persians (537–333 BC), and these were followed by the Greeks—the Lagid and the Seleucid kings (333–70 BC). From the time of the Babylonian captivity onwards, the Jews were never again independent, but they managed to maintain a strong religious life. All this is borne out in the prophetical books, which set out in an explicit way the historical background of each prophet. Being men of their time (and insightful interpreters of events), their writings contain many historical references, explicit and implicit, and these are very useful for dating an oracle or a book or part of a book.

a) *The prophets, interpreters of events.* The prophetical books tell us quite a lot about Israel's contacts with the peoples round about. We can see this in a literary genre found in all the main prophetical works—the "oracles against

6. Cf. *The Navarre Bible: Joshua–Kings*, Introduction, pp 14–18.

the nations" (Amos 1–2; Is 13–23; Zeph 2:4–15; Ezek 25–32; etc.); but there are frequent references also to the pagan nations in the minor prophets—for example, Nahum's oracles concerning Nineveh, and those of Obediah to do with Edom. All these oracles help to show the prophets' great interest in Israel's relationship with its pagan neighbours.

However, the prophets did not confine themselves to preaching about events in which they themselves played leading roles or which impinged on themselves more or less directly: they reflected deeply on all events and on the personalities involved, and pointed out the direction that history was taking. Their interpretation of events was based on three basic ideas—monotheism, God's election of Israel, and that the salvation he promised would apply to all mankind.

Because there is only one God, all human life and history is under his sway; he is in control of everything that happens. He guides the course of events; he is behind all the great and terrible events of history. Even so, people's faith in God can falter, especially at times of crisis, when some defeat or an invasion seems to be imminent, or actually takes place. When Israel is in difficulties (which is when it seeks protection from foreign nations or from foreign gods), a prophet is raised up to confirm them in the true faith: "'Do not seek Bethel and do not enter into Gilgal or cross over to Beer-sheba, for Gilgal shall surely go into exile, and Bethel shall come to naught.' Seek the Lord and live, lest he break out like fire in the house of Joseph, and it devour, with none to quench it for Bethel" (Amos 5:5–6).

Assyria, Babylon and Egypt are the main oppressors: these are evil and idolatrous nations, and yet everything goes well for them. If this is so, how can one say that the fate of nations is being determined by the Lord, the only God? It would seem, on the contrary, that the gods, the protectors of those nations, were getting the better of the Lord. However, the prophets do not agree at all: they tell us that God himself is behind those nations, he is using them to punish Israel as its sins deserve: "I will raise up against you a nation, O house of Israel, [says the Lord, the God of hosts], and they shall oppress you from the entrance of Hamath to the Brook of the Arabah" (Amos 6:14). In the oracles against the nations, as in other oracles, the prophets do not always predict specific future events but, rather, proclaim God's will, which is fulfilled in different ways at different times.

God in his wisdom shows special favour to the people of Israel. But this election does not mean that he isolates them from the rest of mankind or that he gives them special political privileges or a false security (cf. Amos 9:7); Israel should not think it is the greatest of nations (cf. Amos 7:2–5) or the richest (cf. Amos 6:2) or the strongest (cf. Amos 2:9). Israel is called to lead all the nations to share in the blessings and benefits that God bestows: "'Come, let us go up to the mountain of the Lord, to the house of the God of Jacob; that he may teach us his ways and that we may walk in his paths.' For out of Zion shall go forth the law, and the word of the Lord from Jerusalem" (Is 2:3 and

Mic 4:2). Israel is not the object of God's choice for its own benefit alone; that choice looks to all mankind, to all the nations. This idea comes across more clearly after the exile, when their experiences led them to reflect on the implications of their election by God. At that point we find God's relationship with his people being described in terms of an intimate and loving bond: "You, Israel, my servant, Jacob, whom I have chosen, the offspring of Abraham, my friend; you whom I took from the ends of the earth, and called from its farthest corners, saying to you, 'You are my servant, I have chosen you and not cast you off'; fear not for I am with you, be not dismayed, for I am your God" (Is 41:8–9).

Moreover, Israel has a close solidarity with the rest of mankind. In one of Zechariah's oracles of salvation, we are told how the history of the chosen people will impinge on others: "As you have been a byword of cursing among the nations, O house of Judah and house of Israel, so will I save you and you shall be a blessing. [...] In those days ten men from the nations shall take hold of the robe of a Jew, saying, 'Let me go with you, for we have heard that God is with you'" (Zech 8:13, 23).

b) *Apocalyptic writing*. When it seems that the voice of the prophets can be heard no more, the word of God begins to express itself in a new way. In the darkest days of the Maccabees, after a long period that had seen no prophet in Israel, the book of Daniel came to be written. Although that book does link up with the earlier prophets, whom it explicitly cites (cf. Dan 9:2) or whom it copies when it comes to heavenly visions (cf. Ezek 1:3–4; Dan 8:2–3; etc.), its message and literary form are similar to what we find in other Jewish writings of the same period, or even earlier, which have not found their way into the Bible. It is an instance of what is called "apocalyptic" literature, two of whose features are that world history is seen as a continuum involving successive epochs, and the end of the world is nigh—the point when a new world will come into being and when even the dead (through resurrection) will live again. The book of Daniel is structured by real events, but the interpretation it offers of them is unlike that of earlier prophets, who concerned themselves with the fortunes of other nations only to the degree that they impacted on Israel at a particular juncture: the book of Daniel surveys the panorama of world history, which it divides into epochs and assesses from the standpoint of the final outcome—the establishment of the kingdom of God. The narratives in Daniel 2–7 show us the main periods of history, from Nebuchadnezzar to Antiochus IV Epiphanes, bringing in a new and hitherto unknown element as far as the Old Testament is concerned – the advent of the kingdom of God. The vision of the image or of the statue in chapter 2 is a superb description of the succession of empires—first, the Babylonian (gold), then that of the Medes (silver), followed by the Persian (bronze); then comes Alexander and the Greek empire, which, due to the continuous rivalry between Lagids and Seleucids, is depicted as iron mixed with clay. The final or eschatological stage is described in terms of a stone cut from a mountain: "The God of heaven will set up a kingdom which shall never be destroyed, [...] and it shall stand forever" (Dan 2:44). In chapter 7, where the visions of Daniel start, the author gives another description of the series of empires, from the Babylonian to the Seleucid, using wild beasts as imagery. It will all come to an end, and the climax will be the arrival of that "son of man", representing "the people of the saints of the Most High" who will be given "an everlasting kingdom, and all dominions shall serve and obey them" (Dan 7:27).

Daniel's prophecy, then, follows a historical schema, a highly stylized one consisting of three stages—past history (from Nebuchadnezzar to Antiochus), current events (a description of the persecution instigated by Antiochus, in great detail), and the definitive events at the End (a short account of the death of the oppressive king and the establishment of the Kingdom of God): see Daniel 7:17–23; 11:8–36; 11:40—12:3.

To sum up: although historical events provide the framework within which earlier modes of prophecy developed, the interpretation of history forms the literary base of apocalyptic writings. Earlier prophets buoyed up their listeners' hopes by means of oracles of denunciation and salvation, using contemporary events as a pretext for what they had to say. Apocalyptic writing achieves the same objective by proclaiming the catastrophe that will befall the whole world at the end of time—and which will be followed by salvation for those "written in the book", a salvation in which Gentiles and Israelites will share.

The focus of prophetical and apocalyptic writing on events of human history opens the way to a point in time when it will find fulfilment—when the New Testament will bear out everything found in the Old. The advent of the Messiah will mark the beginning of that fulfilment, the start of the last stage of history.

5. THE PROPHETS IN THE LIGHT OF THE NEW TESTAMENT

Apart from the Psalms, the prophetical books are, of all the Old Testament books, those that are to be found most often in the New, be it by way of explicit quotation or easily identifiable reference, or (as sometimes happens) allusions that are difficult to pin down.

As the *Catechism of the Catholic Church* explains, the prophetical books contain a message of hope and proclaim the ultimate salvation of all mankind: "Through the prophets, God forms his people in the hope of salvation, in the expectation of a new and everlasting Covenant intended for all ... (cf. Is 2:2–4; Jer 31:31–34; Heb 10:16). The prophets proclaim a radical redemption of the People of God, purification from all their infidelities (cf. Ezek 36), a salvation which will include all the nations (cf. Is 49:5–6; 53:11)."[7] In the New

7. *Catechism of the Catholic Church*, 64.

Testament we can see these expectations finding fulfilment in Jesus Christ—in his person and in his life and teaching, as St Matthew bears witness: "all this has taken place, that the scriptures of the prophets might be fulfilled" (Mt 26:56). The Gospels and the Letters of the apostles are well aware of the prophets and point out the ways their oracles find fulfilment: they show that they were referring to the present time; and that events have borne out what they predicted; and they use words of the prophets to confirm people in their faith in Jesus.

a) *The Christian meaning of the prophetic oracles.* As we know from biblical commentaries or pesarim discovered at Qumran, Jews of Jesus' time used to read the prophetical books in the light of events happening around them. The commentary in the book of Habakkuk (1 Qp Hab.), for example, does so, to explain Roman invasion and oppression (the Romans being the *Kittim* mentioned in Habbakuk). Similarly, the New Testament explains some passages by applying them to Jesus: in the synagogue of Nazareth, Jesus, after reading out Isaiah 61:1–2, openly says, "Today this scripture has been fulfilled in your hearing" (Lk 4:21). The book of the Acts tells us that the eunuch from the court of the Ethiopian queen asked Philip about the meaning of the fourth song of the Servant (Is 53:7–8), "and beginning with this scripture (Philip) told him the good news of Jesus" (Acts 8:35).

b) *The fulfilment of prophecies.* The New Testament writers never tried to prove that things contained in the prophetical writings were carried out to the last letter in the life of Jesus, as if the gift of prophecy was a form of magical foresight or fortune-telling. Rather, they saw Jesus as being the climax of salvation history: in him the ancient promises found fulfilment; the salvation which the prophets could only ever vaguely see had now come about in all its fullness.

The accounts of Christ's passion and infancy were, respectively, perhaps the first and last to be consigned to writing—the passion, death, and resurrection, because these underpinned the Christian faith; the birth and childhood of Christ, because they showed that Jesus was the Son of God. Various accounts contain references to the prophets in the repeated observation, "so that the scriptures might be fulfilled".

Apropos of Jesus' passion and death, we find the Gospels using the prophets to explain such episodes as his entry into Jerusalem on a donkey (Jn 12:14–15), the fact that his disciples fled from the garden of olives (Mt 26:30–31), the purchase of the potter's field with the thirty pieces of silver (Mt 27:7–10), the soldiers' dividing out Christ's garments (Jn 19:24), his side being pierced by a lance (Jn 19:36–37); and the whole sordid process of the passion (cf. Acts 3:18–24). Also, we quite often find puzzling events commented on through quotations from the prophets—for example, the reason for Christ's sentence, that is, the fact that he says he is the son of Man (Mt 26:64) the mention of his being "reckoned with transgressors" (Lk 22:37), the lament of the women of Jerusalem (Lk 23:26–30) and many little things that take on great significance when seen in the light of the Old Testament. Indeed, as Jesus himself told the disciples at Emmaus, the sufferings he underwent were necessary for the Messiah to enter into his glory, in keeping with what the prophets had said (Lk 24:25–26).

The infancy accounts of Matthew and Luke also carry many quotations from the prophets. Perhaps the most important one is that of the Immanu-el (Is 7:14), used to confirm the virginal conception and Person of Jesus, defining him, as it does, as "God with us" (cf. Mt 1:22–23 and Lk 1:30–31). St Matthew uses explicit quotations to justify, among other things, the fact that Bethlehem was the Messiah's birthplace (Mt 2:5), the flight into Egypt and the return from there (Mt 2:15), the slaughter of the innocents (Mt 2:17), and the return to Nazareth (Mt 2:23). St Luke prefers allusions and general references—in the announcement to Zechariah (Lk 1:17), in the *Magnificat* (Lk 1:47) and the *Benedictus* (Lk 1:76, 79), in the angels' hymn (Lk 2:14), and in that of Simeon (Lk 2:30–31).

The narrative of Jesus' public life also contains quotations from and references to the prophets, bearing out what Jesus himself said: "You search the scriptures [...] and it is they that bear witness to me" (Jn 5:39). And so, for example, a passage from Jeremiah is used by Jesus to justify his driving the merchants out of the temple (Mt 21:13), and he refers to Isaiah to explain why he speaks in parables (Mt 13:14) and to denounce the hypocrisy of the Pharisees (Mt 15:8).

c) *Confirmation of Christians in the faith*. The early Christians would have subscribed to the old adage that "What is not in the Torah [in the Bible] is not in the world".[8] They felt a need to support their belief in Christ, who died and rose from the dead, with passages from the Bible and particularly from the prophets. In the skeletal creed to be found in St Paul's First Letter to the Corinthians (it is probably the earliest of the creeds), we find the same refrain being repeated: "that Christ died *in accordance with the scriptures*, that he was buried, that he was raised on the third day *in accordance with the scriptures*" (1 Cor 15:3–4). The scriptures confirmed that Jesus rose from the dead in line with what the prophets, including Hosea and Isaiah, had announced (1 Cor 15:54–55). This way of reading the prophetical writings might sometimes seem to us to be not particularly "scholarly", but it shows the authority that the scriptures had for the early Christians (and for the Jews)—and how convinced early Christian communities were that the prophets' message about definitive salvation found its fulfilment in Christ Jesus, the Messiah and Saviour of all mankind.

The Fathers of the Church read the Bible in the same sort of way, and used the prophets as a source for their theology of Christ and the Church. St Irenaeus of Lyons, for example, who lived in the second century BC, makes a

8. Cf. *Mishnah, Abbot*, 5, 22.

subtle distinction between promise and prophecy. A promise is bound by the words in which it is expressed: the words are to be taken literally; whereas a prophecy goes beyond the confines of the meaning of the words and, referring as it does to Christ and the Church, it attains its full meaning when the events it describes take place. "If you wonder what changes the Lord effected when he came, know that everything was made new by his becoming present among us as it was foretold. For it was prophesied that the author of great change would come to renew and revitalize all mankind. The coming of a king is announced by servants sent out before him to prepare the people to receive their Lord. When the king stands before his subjects, they will be filled with the joy that was foretold and they will enjoy the freedom that comes from him and they will partake of his vision and listen to his preaching and rejoice in his gifts, and they will no longer wonder what changes the king will effect: for he brings himself and will grant to men all the gifts that have been foretold, gifts that the angels desire to know."[9]

9. *Adversus haereses*, 4, 34, 1.

ISAIAH

Introduction

The authorship of this book has been attributed by Jewish and Christian tradition to the great prophet Isaiah. We are told in the book of Sirach that he lived in the time of Hezekiah, king of Judah (716–687 BC), and that "he saw the last things, and comforted those who mourned in Zion", that is, those exiled to Babylon (cf. Sir 48:22–25). A Hebrew text of Isaiah forms part of the Qumran documents; these contain in fact a complete copy of the text (1 Q Is[a]) and another document that includes passages from almost all parts of the book (1 Q Is[b]); both of these documents date from the first century BC. The Greek version of Isaiah in the Septuagint is, in terms of content, the same as that in the Masoretic text tradition.

In the Christian Bible, the book of Isaiah is the first of the major prophets, not just because Isaiah himself predates the other writer-prophets but also because his book is the longest and perhaps the most important of all the prophetical books. The Hebrew Bible also places him first among the "later prophets", that is, ahead of Jeremiah and Ezekiel and the twelve minor prophets.

As well as for its length and where it is placed in the Bible, the book of Isaiah is important because it is the Old Testament book most quoted in the New Testament. This means that it is the prophetical book that most clearly announces Jesus Christ and the Christian economy of salvation: "This prophet, through the censures he issues and the teachings he offers and in the warnings he makes to the sinful people concerning future times, prophesied many more things about Christ and the Church [...] than the other (prophets) did. So much so that some say he is an evangelist, not a prophet".[1]

1. STRUCTURE AND CONTENT

At the start of the book we are told that the visions and oracles of the prophet took place in the reigns of the kings of Judah from Uzziah to Hezekiah (cf. 1:1). At other parts in the book we find brief accounts of the prophet's relations with kings Ahaz and Hezekiah, and descriptions of the historical context in which he speaks his oracles (cf. 7:1–17; 36:1—39:8). However, the tone of the book changes from chapter 40 on. There we find exhortations by God to the people in which he offers them consolation and raises their hopes (cf. chaps.

1. St Augustine, *De civitate Dei*, 18, 29, 1.

40–55) and urges them to act virtuously in response to all the wonderful things God has done to restore Jerusalem (chaps. 56–66). These exhortations are no longer attributed to Isaiah, nor do they form part of the book's descriptions of the historical context; in fact they reflect contexts other than those of the monarchy period. The exhortations presuppose the exile to Babylon and the return therefrom.

For these reasons the book of Isaiah can be taken as having three parts, in line with the content and the historical background of each part.

FIRST PART. This covers chapters 1–39. It has to do with the times of the kings of Judah, and records visions and oracles of the eighth-century prophet. It is usually seen as having six sections to it: 1. Oracles addressed to the people of God (chaps. 1–12). 2. Oracles concerning foreign nations (chaps.13–23). 3. The "Apocalypse of Isaiah" (chaps. 24–27). 4. Warnings addressed to Judah and Jerusalem (chaps. 28–33). 5. "Lesser Apocalypse" (chaps. 34–35). 6. Historical appendix (chaps. 36–39).

SECOND PART. This covers chapters 40–55. There are grounds for thinking that these chapters were not written by Isaiah. Some of these grounds are historical in character: Jerusalem has fallen, in line with the prophecy in 1:20, and hope is placed on the return of the exiles thanks to the decree of Cyrus, king of Persia (described as the Lord's "anointed": 45:1) and on the rebuilding of Jerusalem (44:26–28; 49:14–23); the oracles are addressed to the exiles in Babylon (43:14; 48:20); the Davidic dynasty is mentioned only once, and then only to say that its attributes have been transferred to the people as a whole. Other arguments against Isaian authorship have more to do with the literary matters: the threatening tone of the oracles in the earlier part of the book gives way to oracles of consolation announcing a future restoration; there are no more biographical references to the prophet; the concise, forthright, pointed and insightful style of the first part gives way, largely, to a more ornate, formal style; the prophetic denunciations of the people of Jerusalem, who put their trust in their own resources and a relatively prosperous way of life, is replaced by the depiction of a depressed people who have been punished for their sins and who now need to be consoled and encouraged to look forward to a hopeful future that still lies beyond their horizon.

This part of the book is usually seen as having two sections to it, after a short prologue (40:1–11). The historical background to the first section (40:12—48:22) is the Babylonian captivity, the mission that God gives Cyrus, and the release of the exiles and their return to the promised land. This section, usually called the "Book of the Consolation of Israel", contains the "first song of the Servant".

The second section (49:1—55:13) proclaims divine salvation and the restoration of Zion after the return from exile. The three other "songs of the Servant" are to be found here.

THIRD PART. This covers chapters 56–66. One can see that it was written against the background of problems that arose in Judah, and particularly in Jerusalem, on the return from exile. The initial enthusiasm of the returned exiles was quickly punctured by harsh realities: the land of Judah was in ruins; those who returned and those who had never been exiled had different priorities, and tensions developed between the two groups; and although Persian rule was tolerant and ensured law and order, it was in the last analysis ruled by foreigners. The message of this part of the book is geared to encouraging the people to stay faithful to God and to be sincere in their religious practice; it also looks forward in hope to a wonderful restoration of Jerusalem and the whole world.

It is not easy to say what occasioned the oracles in this part of the book, or to date them exactly. Moreover, the structure of chapters 56–66 is not easy to work out; it is not clear to what degree they form a unit. Chapters 56–59 are usually interpreted as being a sort of introduction, wide-ranging in theme—on invalid criteria for membership of the people of God (56:1–8); corruption among leaders, and condemnation of the idolatry that is still in evidence (56:9—57:21); a religion of lip-service (58:1–14); and denunciation of sin (59:1–15a). Chapters 60–62, which form the central section, carry the main message of this part of the book—the predominant theme being the sending of the Spirit of the Lord upon the prophet (61:1–11). The third and last section (chapters 62–66) acts as a conclusion not just to this part but to the whole book. It consists of a series of oracles: judgments against various nations (63:1–6); remembrance of God's kindness towards Israel and a desire for him to reveal himself again (63:7—64:11); the judgment that will take place at the End, the new creation and messianic peace (chap. 65); an oracle about the temple, religious worship and divine judgment (66:1–6), and another about the new people that will come into being (66:7–17); and finally, an eschatological discourse proclaiming that all the nations will come as pilgrims to Jerusalem (66:18–24).

2. COMPOSITION AND HISTORICAL BACKGROUND

Given the historical contexts referred to or hinted at different points in the book, it is reasonable to suppose that it was composed and edited over a period of more than two centuries, from 733 BC (the year when King Uzziah died and when Isaiah began his prophetic ministry) to the years following the return of the Babylonian exiles, that is, around 525 BC. Thus, scholars no longer go along with the old idea that all the oracles contained in the book were spoken by the prophet Isaiah—in other words, that he was able to foresee in detail events that happened more than a hundred years after his death.

However, there is a clear unity to the book: not just in the sense that it is all attributed to Isaiah, but because, internally, from the point of view of the book's structure, chapters 2 and 66 constitute a sort of framework for the content of the book, with chapter 1 acting as an introduction or prologue to everything that follows.

Theories as to how the text took shape

In recent times scholars have put forward a number of theories as to how the book of Isaiah as we know it came into being. These theories are basically along the three lines indicated below:

1) One theory has it that there was an original nucleus (chapters 1–39) dating from the time of Isaiah, to which chapters 40–45 were added, during the Babylonian exile, to update the earlier chapters; after the return from exile, in the Persian period, chapters 56–66 were added to round the book off, and the whole book substantially re-edited.

2) The second theory is that of scholars who speak of there being two or three "Isaiahs", that is, that originally there were separate books by distinct prophets which were later combined to form one. According to this theory, the book as we now have it is clearly the work of at least two authors (the historical Isaiah and Second Isaiah) and maybe even three, implying a Third Isaiah. This view links up with the first theory, which divides the book into three parts (chaps. 1–39; 40–55; 56–66). The first part, or at least most of its passages, would be attributable to Isaiah himself; the second would be by an unknown "prophet" (Second Isaiah) and the third the work of Third Isaiah. This theory, of there having been two or three Isaiahs, is a very elaborate one, backed by sound reasons, yet it involves serious difficulties. For one thing there are no documents to support it—no sign in Israelite tradition of a "Second" or "Third" Isaiah. Also, it does put the unity of the book at risk. Therefore, we feel that this explanation is too detached from what we know of the history of Israel, being based more on conjecture than on the reality as we know it.

3) The third theory is that of those who are inclined to give the whole book a later date: They argue that it was composed after the exile, from material that existed in another form, some of which could date back as far as the eighth century. The proponents of this theory have tried to identify the central core of the book—but without reaching agreement; some see it as being the second part (chaps. 40–55), to which chapters 1–39 would have been added as an extensive introduction, with the third part (chaps. 56–66) added as an elaborate conclusion. Others see the third as being the main part, to which everything else was added later.

Stages in the redaction of the book

Taking into account the most significant elements of these various theories, we could say that the book of Isaiah came to be written at different stages but its guiding spirit was always that which guided Isaiah in his time; and the writer always sought to apply Isaiah's message to the contemporary situation. Of course, this whole process took place under the action of the Holy Spirit, ensuring that the entire work is inspired. The main junctures in the formation of the book would have been as follows:

1) The first stage was the lifetime of the prophet Isaiah himself, of whom little is known other than the information provided by chapters 1–39 of the book. He was the son of Amoz (1:1)—not to be confused with the prophet Amos—and all the indications are that he was born around 760 in Jerusalem, for that was where he preached and it must have been there that he acquired his very considerable literary and religious culture; it would have been difficult for him to get it anywhere else. He would have grown up during the reign of Uzziah/Azariah (885–733), the king who contracted leprosy and who was succeeded first by Jotham (759–743), and then by Ahaz (743–727). God called Isaiah to the prophetical ministry in the last year of the reign of Uzziah, approximately 733 BC, by means of a vision of the glory of the Lord in the temple. The account of his calling (6:1–13) is important because it includes four themes that echo right through his teaching—the holiness of God, the prophet's conviction that sin is uncleanness and profanation, the imminence of divine punishment from which there can be no escape, and hope of salvation. Shortly after the start of his ministry, Isaiah married the "prophetess" (8:3; the name may derive from the fact that she was married to the prophet), by whom he had at least two sons to whom he gave symbolic names (7:3 and 8:3)—Shear-jashub ("a remnant shall return": see RSV footnote **h**) and Ma-her-shalal-hash-baz ("the spoil speeds, the prey hastens").

His career began at the time of the ruthless expansion of the Assyrian empire, which began under Teglat-pileser III (745–727), and continued under Shalmaneser V (726–722), Sargon II (721–705) and Sennacherib (704–681). In 735 the kings of Syria and Israel entered the territory of Judah to support an alliance against Assyria and, with help promised by Egypt, to bring Assyria's advance to a halt. Isaiah persuaded Ahaz, king of Judah (743–727) not to join that alliance (7:1–16). Assyria overran Syria and Israel; it did not invade Judah, but did impose tribute on it. In the regency that followed the death of Ahaz, during the minority of Hezekiah (727–698), Samaria, the capital of Israel, was overrun by Assyria, which then adopted a policy of ethnic cleansing and deported all the upper classes and replaced them with foreigners. Meanwhile, Egypt continued to foment opposition to Assyria in the countries on the Mediterranean coast. With the death of Sargon II, an insurrection against Assyria began: Isaiah was totally opposed to Israel's involvement, as we can see from his outspoken oracles. But his words went unheeded, and in 701, under Sennacherib, Judah was invaded and laid waste by the Assyrians, who came very close to Jerusalem. However, Isaiah proclaimed that the city of David was under God's protection and would not fall (chap. 37)—and that was what happened: the besiegers unexpectedly withdrew (37:36–38). This surprising escape on Jerusalem's part happened around the year 700. The years that followed were relatively peaceful for Judah until the pressure from Assyria eventually eased.

In this historical context, Isaiah was a very influential religious figure who made an impact on events in the kingdom of Judah over the course of four decades. His message was a profound one, and wide-ranging, and his oracles and interventions were seen to be accurate—with the result that, as a person and as a prophet, Isaiah came to have immense prestige. To this must be added the sheer beauty of his language and the power of his visions and imagery—all of which soon made him the premier poet of Hebrew literature. Hence, his enduring popularity, and the development of an Isaian "school" of disciples (not necessarily people who actually knew him) that passed on his great body of teaching.

Isaiah must have died around the start of the seventh century, although we do not know for certain. In the apocryphal book *The Ascension of Isaiah*, 5:1, there is a Jewish tradition, with no great grounds to it, that Isaiah was put to death by Manasseh (698–642); according to that tradition, the king gave orders for him to be sawn in two, for having compared Jerusalem to Sodom and Gomorrah (1:10; cf. Heb 11:37).

The original core of the book (mainly, chaps. 1–11 and 28–32) must have soon become joined to a collection of "oracles against the nations" (chaps. 13–23), also substantially the work of the prophet himself. Chapters 34–35 (the oracle against Edom, and oracle on the salvation of Zion) probably date from the last years of Isaiah's life.[2] The various historical appendixes (covering the last years of the reign of Hezekiah and the first of Manasseh), taken together with 2 Kings 18:3—20:19 also include words attributable to Isaiah. Chapters 24–27 came later; these are known as the "Apocalypse of Isaiah" and they deal with divine judgment and the messianic banquet provided in Jerusalem for all the nations. All these chapters account for the first part of the book of Isaiah as we know it.

2) Another important juncture in the redaction of the book is the Babylonian captivity. The exiles were restless, full of hope that they would soon be able to return to the land of Israel. This is the context of chapters 40–55, which refer to a period more than one hundred years after the first part of the book—as the mention of Cyrus the Great shows.

When the Israelites had already been thirty years in exile, news began to circulate about the dramatic victories of the Persian king, Cyrus (559–530). In the year 553 Cyrus defeated Astyages, king of the Medes; in 550 the Median capital, Ecbathana, fell, and Cyrus became king of the Medes and the Persians. In 546 Cyrus defeated Croesus, king of Lydia, taking its capital, Sardis. The net effect of all this was that Babylon was encircled by Persia—and this at a time of internal strife (the last Babylonian king, Nabonid, 555–539, was at

2. That is, the final years of Hezekiah's reign and the early years of Manasseh's.

loggerheads with the nation's priesthood). The exiled Jews in Babylonia became decidedly uneasy: Was the prospect of a Persian takeover likely to favour their release? The last time there had been a change in hegemony (from Assyria to Babylon), things had only got worse. This is the historical background to the second book of Isaiah, and in some passages we can see that the exiles are losing hope (cf. 40:27; 49:14). There may even have been those who were tempted to think that the Lord had turned his back on the Covenant, as is implied perhaps by the references in 50:1 to the bill of divorce and to the creditor's receipt.

The situation is such that God feels he should console his people. They were so downhearted that they needed to hear new arguments, new reasons for hope. The prophet, at God's inspiration, must explain God's reason for doing what he did: first, he delivered Israel from slavery in Egypt; then he allowed them to be made captives once more; but now, the prophet tells them, hope is on the horizon: they are going home; there will be a new exodus. The writer approaches the situation in the same spirit as Isaiah himself would and, in effect, "updates" Isaiah's message, trying even to keep the prophet's superb writing style. Scholars surmise that this part of the book was written by a prophet whose name we do not know, or by an "Isaian" prophetical school. However, it must be admitted that it is not at all clear how and when this part came to be written; the question has so far defeated scholars, and may never be settled in a definitive way. We can certainly say that in general (with some exceptions here and there) it has a majesty, a richness of content and a literary perfection that can be compared justly with the visions and oracles in the first part of the book.

So, the second part of the book offers further explanations for the devastating state of affairs created by the exile. But its message extends beyond the boundaries of a particular point in history. That exile can be interpreted as the way a person or a people can feel when their life seems to have fallen apart, when there seem to be no grounds for hope and when God seems to have turned his back on them. Hence the great value of this part of the book: it carries a message of light and of hope in God that can dispel the darkness of human anguish.

3) Chapters 56–66 reflect another juncture in Jewish history—the situation in Judah when the exiles returned. Once again the Lord sends them a message through his prophets.

Babylon collapsed unexpectedly quickly, and in the year 539 Cyrus the Great, the king of the Persians, issued a decree allowing the exiles to go free—and those who so wished to return to Judah and rebuild the temple of Jerusalem (cf. the text of the decree in Ezra 1:2–4 and 6:2–5). However, once they arrived back, the returnees ran into all sorts of difficulties. The country was in ruins, and those who were living there (including Jews who had not suffered exile) felt threatened by the newcomers, fearing for their property rights and concerned about whether the country could support the increase in population. The books of Ezra, Nehemiah, Haggai and Zechariah tell us about these difficulties. To begin with, the returned exiles were very enthusuastic, but their ardour soon cooled when they saw that an entire nation needed to be rebuilt—and not just its towns and farms.

Most of the third part of Isaiah fits into that historical framework—as can be seen from its oracles, songs, laments, denunciations and prophetical visions spelling hope and describing the restoration of the glories of Zion. Alongside prophetical condemnations of unfaithfulness, vice, and merely perfunctory religious practice, we find passages full of hope and encouragement that urge perseverance, despite external difficulties (settlers planted in Judah in Babylonian times; difficulties in dealing with Persian authorities, who were foreigners when all was said and done, although they were generally well-meaning), and also internal ones (rivalries, demoralization). The oracles of "Third Isaiah" increasingly direct people towards horizons that transcend those of human history, and that look forward to "new heavens and a new earth" (65:17), presided over by "the glory of the Lord" (60:1) in the new Jerusalem (60:4–22), to whose light the nations of the earth shall throng (60:3).

These magnificent oracles, presented so well in literary terms, and the influence of the true Isaiah on the teaching contained in them, are further reasons for thinking that an "Isaian school" was continuing to operate. Scholars concur that the doctrinal core of this third part of the book is to be found in chapters 60–62, which deal with the visions of the glorious new Jerusalem and the "anointing" of the "prophet". Along with this we find (in passages in chapters 65 and 66) the notion of a salvation that is not attainable by human effort but which will be a gift from God and which opens up the way to the fullness of revelation in the New Testament. However, one can see also that in addition to taking the core message of Isaiah and updating it (tying it in with changed circumstances), it has worked this in with other themes from the creed of Israel—such as the revelation of the creative and provident power of God; belief in his holiness, oneness and sovereignty, in his loving-kindness and his fidelity in the Covenant, and in the special care that he takes of his people. As well as all this, there is a universality in the writer's outlook, extending much further than the narrow nationalism of other Old Testament writings.

So, the third part of Isaiah extends the perspective to the End times. The prophetical promises contained in these last chapters of the book often remind one of the last book of the Bible, the Revelation of St John. Like John's, Isaiah's visions will find fulfilment in the second coming of Jesus Christ, the Son of God.

The book of Isaiah has a unity to it

We do not know when the book of Isaiah took on the form that it now has in the Bible, but, given that the latest historical content discernible in the book refers to the period following the return from exile, it seems reasonable to suppose that the book must have been compiled around the end of the sixth century BC. This was, besides, a time when prophetic oracles containing messages of hope were prevalent—as we can see from the books of Haggai, Zechariah and Malachi. Later, with the reform instituted by Ezra around the middle of the fifth century, the religious focus tended to be more on the Law of God and its interpretation (the general attitude being that the spirit of prophecy had ceased to operate and would not do so again until the messianic era: cf. Zech 13:3–6; Mal 4:4–6). Since Isaiah was the prophet who, in his time, spoke most clearly and vigorously about the coming of the Messiah, son of David (cf. Is 7:3–14), it is reasonable to attribute also to him oracles which, written in the spirit of the prophet (Isaiah), are designed to console Israel (cf. 40:1–20) and which tell of how the Lord will come and renew all things, creating new heavens and a new earth (cf. 66:18–24).

Although we can detect different stages in the book's formation, in order to understand the different passages it helps to remember the historical context in which they were written. The reader needs to take the book as a single unit, in order to see the continuity running through it, and to do justice to the shape that God chose it to have in the Bible. There is no denying that reading the book from start to finish is somewhat disorienting, with all sorts of ups and downs—oracles announcing punishment of the nations for their sins, or punishment of the people of God themselves; other oracles promising salvation, followed again by predictions of gloom and doom, and then further prospects of hope. At first, it seems to be all disarray, like a pack of cards newly shuffled. Still, that apparent disorder is a sign of something much deeper. The book of Isaiah reflects the paradoxes of the history of the chosen people of God, a history that could also represent that of any nation and, even, of any individual—a wayfarer on his or her way to a destination, and experiencing the ups and downs of life. Fidelity to God, and infidelity; success and misadventure—all this forms the fabric of a person's life on earth. The prophetic message recalled in this book arose in a context of two centuries of war and devastation, of reconstruction and hope—a scenario not unlike that in which Christians have lived over the centuries. But in every age Isaiah's message of hope remains valid and is an inspiration.

3. MESSAGE

Of all the books of the Old Testament, the book of Isaiah is one of the most important from the doctrinal point of view—as regards the great themes of God, man and salvation. In a sense, it is a compendium of Old Testament belief, and it opens a wide window onto the fullness of Revelation in the New Testament. In his introduction to Isaiah, for example, St Jerome had this to say: "This book is as it were a compendium of all the Scriptures," and, in line with the example of the Fathers of the Church, one could cite passages from Isaiah in support of almost every point of Christian teaching. However, if one had to say what the main strengths of Isaiah are, one would have to choose two motifs that run throughout the book—the transcendence of God, and the grave offence that man's sin causes him—and then a specific motif for each of the book's three sections—1) the Messiah that is to come; 2) salvation for the whole world; 3) hope in regard to the End time.

The God revealed in Isaiah

Isaiah, who lived some decades after Amos and Hosea, writes about the holiness of God—the fact that he is above all created things, visible and invisible. He is sovereign lord of all things, wrapped in, hidden by, the radiance of his glory. In his presence, created beings (angels and human beings) can but tremble in fear and reverence. There is no doubt but that this message can be traced back to Isaiah's own experience in the temple, when he received his calling in a vision of the Lord seated in majesty (6:1–3). The Lord, the "Holy One of Israel" (5:19, 24; 12:6; 17:7; 30:11, 12, 15 etc.) appears to him seated on a throne, raised on high and surrounded by the seraphim who render him supreme worship, crying, "Holy, holy, holy is the Lord of hosts." God is above all things, there is none that can resist him (cf. 6:5), and he reveals himself by all kinds of wondrous works that amaze the people and evidence his glory (cf. 29:14; 35:2).

But this God, the Lord who reveals himself to Israel as being almighty and above all things, the author of creation and of human history, is not an abstract being: he is a personal being, having attributes and qualities that can be described in human terms: for example, in the oracles we find references to God's "eyes" (1:15, 16; 37:17; 38:3; 43:4; 49:5; etc.) his "hands" (1:25; 9:11, 16, 20: etc.), his "breath" that cleanses (30:33; cf. 11:15), his "spirit" (11:2) that gives wisdom, understanding, counsel, fortitude, knowledge and the fear of the Lord. The Lord is a God who enters into dialogue with man.

The sins of Jerusalem and Judah

The counterpart of God's majesty is man's lowliness—especially when he sins. From his very first vision, Isaiah sees man as being a weak and sinful creature when compared with God, who transcends everything. Man ought to humbly acknowledge God as his master, but instead he rebels against him. Sin is not a trivial fault: it is rebellion against God (1:2, 4), an insult to God (3:8–9; 5:4–6, 24; 8:6; 28:12; 29:15–16; 30:9–13); it makes a mockery of God (5:18–19). The vanity of women (3:16), religious indifference (5:19), attachment to wealth (2:7), reliance on military fortifications (17:3; 22:5–11) and force of arms (2:7; 22:6; 31:1), and coalitions with foreigners (30:1) are in fact signs of distrust in God. Therefore, the worst sin of all is pride and self-sufficiency (2:6—4:1; 9:7—10:4, 12–19; 13:11–22; 23:9; etc.).

Divine punishment, therefore, should involve a humiliation for man, and "the day of the Lord" will involve precisely that (2:11–17). The proud and rebellious must be laid low; all haughtiness and pride fall before the glory of God.

A future Messiah

The core of Isaiah's teaching, which is to be found in the first part of the book, is the promise that God makes about David and Jerusalem. The kingdom of Israel disappeared in 722 BC when it was over-run by the Assyrians, and part of Judah went too, but Isaiah teaches that a "remnant" will be saved which will become the nucleus for the revival of the nation's fortunes. Only "a tenth" will remain, but from that stump or root will spring the branch of the Lord, the survivors of Israel (cf. 4:2–3).

Although Isaiah does not use the term "Messiah", he is the prophet who best represents "royal messianism", which depicts the future saviour as having the character of a king. This magnificent person he calls "Wonderful Counsellor, Mighty God, Everlasting Father, Prince of Peace" (9:5).

Jerusalem, where those who put their faith in God (10:20; 30:18; 33:2) huddle for shelter during the invasion, will also be a source of messianic peace for all the nations (2:1–5); they will flock there, to partake of the messianic banquet—those of Ethiopia (18:7), Tyre (23:17–18), Egypt and Assyria (19:18–25), that is, all the nations.

All the promises are concentrated in the Immanu-el (7:14): he will reign over his country (8:8); he will be the one who restores the Davidic monarchy, which has become reduced to a "stump"; he will be the eternal king promised by God, drawing together in his person all the main springs of Israel's hope—dynastic-royal (7:14; 8:8), prophetical (9:7; 11:2), paradisiacal (11:6–9) and eschatological (11:7).

The universal scope of salvation

During the Babylonian captivity, Israel reflected, perhaps more than ever before, on what its life and history and traditions meant. The second part of the book, which was compiled during the exile, focuses on the role of Israel among the nations, particularly at three important stages, each with its special leader—the patriarchal period, with Abraham; the exodus, with Moses; and the monarchy, with David. And, whereas earlier prophets depicted the empires (Assyria and Babylon) as God's instruments for punishing Israel, now we are told that Cyrus, a pagan king, is an instrument of salvation used in the hands of God—so much so that he merits the title of "anointed" (cf. 45:1–6).

Down through its history, Israel has seen God intervene on its behalf; and it senses that it, too, is an instrument of salvation. Like their forebears in times gone by, and like Cyrus too (who has a role to play between God and Israel), the people of God have a mission to be a mediator between God and all other nations.

Nowhere else does the Bible speak so touchingly about God's choice of his people: "I have called you by name, you are mine" (43:1; cf. 41:9–14). Israel knows that the Lord made the world in his great wisdom (40:18–26; 43:8–12; 45:6–8; 46:5–11), and by means of that wisdom and power performed all the wonderful things to do with the exodus (43:14–21; 51:9–10), thereby extending his very first act of salvation (creation itself); he chose Abraham (51:2) and made him his friend (41:8). On account of that election, God will stay true to his people—caring for them even better than a mother does for her child (49:14–16).

However, the book shows that the fact that Israel is God's most favoured nation is something that redounds also to the benefit of other nations. Election implies mission: Israel is to be the channel through which salvation reaches all mankind. Therefore, the restoration which God will bring about within his people will not be confined within its frontiers: it will extend to the whole world: "all flesh shall know that I am the Lord your Saviour" (49:26). The radiance of God and his salvation will reach out to the ends of the earth (42:10–12), and even inanimate nature will rejoice (55:12–13).

The personality and mission of Israel are summed up in the figure of the "servant of the Lord" (cf. 42:1–4; 49:1–6; 50:4–11; 52:13—53:12). This person, so vilified and yet so very close to God, symbolizes the entire nation and stands for the Messiah who, by atoning for the sins of others, will obtain salvation for all the nations.

The new Jerusalem and a glorious future

One cannot say that the third part of the book carries one unequivocal message, given the diversity of its oracles and the contexts in which they were written. But certainly the whole book does have an eschatological and salvific focus. Divine intervention, we learn from the text, will not be limited to miracles similar to those reported in the accounts of the exodus; God will guide his people until they acknowledge the special love he harbours for them.

As has been pointed out already, this part of the book was addressed to Israelites who had come back from exile but were beginning to think that the rebuilding of Jerusalem was beyond them. The prophet encourages them to discover a glorious new Jerusalem, to which all nations will have recourse, because it is "the City of the Lord, the Zion of the Holy One of Israel" (60:14); its walls will be called "Salvation" and its gates "Praise" (60:18). The epithets applied to the city by the prophet are always spiritual ones (cf. 62:4, 12; 65:18), to convince his listeners that the capital he is referring to is a new Jerusalem not only in a geographical or political sense but also in the sense that it belongs to an entirely new order of being.

The prophet ends the book on a note of hope in a glorious future, which goes far beyond a renewal of the old order: an entirely new creation will take place, a joy never before known will be discovered. The poems contained in 65:17–25 and 66:7–14 point to a final, definitive period of life, free from tears and strife.

This joy and hope in a more promising future, about which the prophet speaks, cannot be measured in terms of human institutions—not in the monarchy, or armies, or human authorities; not even in religious worship, for its precepts (fasting) will be cleansed of any type of formalism (58:1–14). Even the construction of the temple, the focus of the returnees' enthusiasm (60:7,13) is not their ultimate objective, for the true throne of God is in heaven (66:1–2). But righteousness must be established once and for all (61:8–11) so that the whole people attain salvation with no need of intermediaries (62:1–12).

These ideas open a window on a new, enduring state of affairs—in no sense limited to the frontiers of Israel or to the present time: what we have here is an eschatological vision, which will also be found in the books of Haggai and Zechariah.

4. THE BOOK OF ISAIAH IN THE LIGHT OF THE NEW TESTAMENT

The prophetical books of the Old Testament (like all the books of the Bible) are read in the Church not merely as records of times past that had relevance for a particular time and situation only. As the Church sees it, the prophets preached a message that was open to later developments in salvation history that will reach their climax in the Saviour Jesus Christ. That was how St Jerome saw the prophetical books when he wrote: "I will interpret the book of Isaiah, showing him to be not only a prophet but an evangelist and apostle as well. Isaiah says, referring to himself and to the other evangelists: *How lovely are the feet of him who brings good news!* And God speaks to him as an apostle when he asks: *Whom shall I send? Who shall go to this people?* And he replies: *Here I am, send me* [...]. Let no one think that I intend to summarize the content of this book, for it encompasses all the mysteries of the Lord: Isaiah speaks of the Immanuel who will be born of the Virgin, who will perform great works and marvels, who will die and be buried, and who will rise again from the dead to be the Saviour of all mankind."[3]

The book of Isaiah is quoted explicitly ninety times in the New Testament—and as many as four hundred times implicitly. The reason for this high incidence has probably to do with the way that Jesus applies the prophet's words to events in his own life. At the start of his preaching, in the synagogue of Nazareth, he applied to himself the words of Isaiah 61:1–2: "The Spirit of the Lord is upon me, because he has anointed me ..." (Lk 4:16–18). And throughout his public ministry, our Lord noticed certain circumstances as bearing out the words of the prophet: this happens, for example, in connexion with the authorities' failure to understand his parables (Mk 13:14ff and par.), and the rupture between formal religious worship and religion of the heart (Mt 15:7ff and par.), etc. But it is particularly in the events of his passion that Jesus depicts himself as the son of Man who "came not to be served but to serve, and to give his life as a ransom for many" (Mt 20:28), that is to say, as the suffering servant whom the book of Isaiah describes as bearing on his shoulders the transgressions of the chosen people and of the whole world (cf. Is 53:4–5).

3. St Jerome, *Commentarii in Isaiam*, Prologue.

After Christ's death and resurrection, the apostles realized that all these oracles about the servant of the Lord found fulfilment in Jesus. St Matthew actually says that, and he quotes Isaiah 42:1–4 when recording the things Jesus did, curing all the people and not displaying his glory (cf. Mt 12:15–21). Similarly, when reporting the passion of our Lord, the evangelists seem to be very conscious of the poems of the suffering servant and how they help to show the expiatory value of the death of Christ (cf. Mt 26:63; 27:13, 14 and Is 53:7; Mt 27:38 and Is 53:12).

The New Testament evocation of Isaiah does not end with the Gospels: the book of the Acts, for example, attests to how the early Christians used Isaiah to justify their belief (cf. Acts 7:49–50; 8:32–33; 13:34, 47; 14:15; 15:18; 28:26–27; etc.); and St Paul reads Isaiah as prophesying the rejection of Israel and the extension of salvation to all nations (cf. Rom 9:1—11:36). Similarily, the author of the Apocalypse describes the hope of future salvation by using passages from the prophet.

Patristic tradition follows this route marked out by the New Testament writers. In controversies with Jewish writers, Christian apologists (St Justin, St Irenaeus, Tertullian) use Isaiah and the Gospels to explain that in Jesus, and in no other, the prophet's words find fulfilment. However, the main use they make of Isaiah is in doctrinal instruction. True, there are Fathers who comment on the entire book or on parts of it (for example, Origen, St Cyril of Alexandria, St John Chrysostom, Theodoret of Cyrus, St Jerome, etc.), but it is more usual to find quotations from Isaiah being used in support of Christian teaching about the properties of God and about Christ's work of salvation.

This recurrent presence of Isaiah in Christian teaching goes right back to Jesus himself and to the apostles; and it can be seen also in the liturgy. Second only to Psalms, Isaiah is the Old Testament book most quoted in Christian liturgy. At some points in the liturgical cycle (Advent and Christmas) Isaiah accounts for three quarters of the quotations from Old Testament prophets. So, it is not surprising that the iconography of Christmastide uses elements taken from this book (the ox and the ass: Is 1:3) which are not mentioned in the New Testament: for Christians, the book speaks, above all, of Christ.

Christian readers find in the book of Isaiah the same attitude of faith and fidelity to God as Isaiah and other prophets had in their lifetimes—which are a prelude to and preparation for Christians' faith and fidelity. So, Isaiah is not a book whose significance is confined to two long centuries of Jewish history. When we read it, we are helped to deepen our faith, to strengthen our commitment to pursue the ideals we share with the rest of mankind, and to have a more continuous dialogue with God, the supreme Lord of creation and of human affairs.

Title

1 [1]The vision of Isaiah the son of Amoz, which he saw Mic 1:11
concerning Judah and Jerusalem in the days of Uzziah, Jotham,
Ahaz, and Hezekiah, kings of Judah.

1:1. According to the title, Isaiah's prophetic visions about the meaning of what was happening around him took place over a period of some forty years —from the reign of Uzziah (885–733) to that of Hezekiah (727–698).

These were times when the Assyrian empire was pursuing an expansionist policy across wide stretches of the Middle East, establishing sovereignty over many kingdoms, from each of which it exacted heavy tribute, and which it then denuded by a series of deportations. The entire region lived in fear of the Assyrian armies, and some kingdoms formed coalitions in an attempt to keep them at bay. Judah, too, was under threat, and it was in two minds whether to enter into alliances against Assyria or put its trust in the Lord. In the year 722 BC, the Assyrians conquered Samaria, marking the end of Judah's neighbouring kingdom, Israel. During the last years of the century, pressure mounted on Judah, the Southern kingdom, until eventually, in 701, Sennacherib laid waste the great part of Judah, and Jerusalem found itself under siege and on the point of being attacked.

***1:2—39:8.** The first part of the book of Isaiah is usually described as "First Isaiah". It includes prophetic passages that have as their background the threat posed by the Assyrians to Judah and Jerusalem during the second half of the eighth century BC. At the start and conclusion of this part, Jerusalem is referred to as a "besieged city" and as "overthrown by aliens" (1:7–8; 36:1ff).

The sacred text links the people of Judah's distress and uneasiness with the fact that they have distanced themselves from God; they live without reference to him, forgetful of all he has done for them. The future looks bleak, for there is no sign of their heeding the prophet's call to conversion. However, there is still some cause for hope, for a remnant of Israel has kept faith with God, and from it a new, reformed people will emerge. In various ways a contrast is drawn between those (like King Ahaz: cf. 7:1–17) who clearly do not put their trust in God, relying only on human prudence to deal with the situation, and others (like King Hezekiah: 36:1—38:22) who have recourse to the Lord and make every effort to remedy things; they are confident that God will come to their aid and deliver them from danger.

The first part of the book contains prophetic passages that differ in style and origin. The oldest of them reflect the fear caused by the sheer might of Assyria, which is depicted as a rod or staff wielded by the Lord in his anger (cf. 10:5). All nations in the region felt threatened by Assyria, whose armies

[1] [1]Visio Isaiae filii Amos, quam vidit super Iudam et Ierusalem in diebus Oziae, Ioatham, Achaz, Ezechiae regum Iudae. [2]Audite, caeli, et auribus percipe, terra, / quoniam Dominus locutus est: / «Filios

PART ONE*

1. ORACLES ADDRESSED TO ISRAEL AND JUDAH*

A. THE LORD COMPLAINS THAT THE PEOPLE HAVE FORSAKEN HIM

Deut 4:26; 32:1,5–6 Bar 4:8 Mic 1:2

General denunciation

2Hear, O heavens, and give ear, O earth;
for the LORD has spoken:

---

reached the very gates of Jerusalem when Sennacherib besieged the city. (That siege marks the end of this part of the book.)

These words of prophecy fall into six sections. The first deals with the threat hanging over Israel and Judah (1:2—12:6); and the second contains oracles to do with foreign nations (13:1—23:18). The third, which in a way contains the theological basis of all the teaching found in First Isaiah, and which is known as the "Apocalypse of Isaiah", deals with the sentence passed on the nations by the Lord (he is supreme, and nothing escapes his justice); still, the light of salvation is always on the horizon (24:1—27:13). Then we hear more about the misfortunes that threaten Jerusalem on account of its sins—and further reason to hope that all is not lost (28:1—33:24). After returning to the theme of divine judgment and rallying the people to hope in salvation, in a section known as the "Little Apocalypse" (34:1—35:10), First Isaiah ends with a narrative section dealing with the havoc caused in Judah by Sennacherib's forces, although, for a while at least, a small remnant is spared—those who take refuge in Jerusalem alongside Hezekiah the king (36:1—39:8).

***1:2—12:6.** Isaiah's ministry as a prophet must have begun in the years prior to the war, when the kingdoms of Syria and Ephraim (Israel), with Egypt's encouragement, joined forces and took to the field in campaigns aimed at stemming the advance of the Assyrians. The kings of Syria and Israel tried to persuade Ahaz of Judah to join their alliance. Ahaz refused to get involved and, instead, sought to ingratiate himself with Assyria in order to save his country. In 734 BC Assyria overran Syria, most of Israel and the Lebanon, the Philistine coast and the Transjordan, and in the years that followed it consolidated its grip on the region. After the fall of Samaria (722 BC), much of the population of Israel was deported and replaced by foreigners.

The kingdom of Judah was not invaded, but it was forced to pay heavy

enutrivi et exaltavi, / ipsi autem spreverunt me. / 3Cognovit bos possessorem suum, / et asinus praesepe domini sui; / Israel non cognovit, / populus meus non intellexit». / 4Vae genti peccatrici, / populo gravi

"Sons have I reared and brought up,
but they have rebelled against me.
3The ox knows its owner,
and the ass its master's crib;
but Israel does not know,
my people does not understand."

Jer 8:7

---

tribute and became a state dependent on Assyria. At the cost of many concessions, an uneasy peace prevailed. Religious life and the rule of law deteriorated. This was the background to the earliest of the oracles contained in these twelve chapters.

The section begins with a general denunciation of the forsaking of the Lord; no specific events are mentioned. It is a time of crisis, with Judah laid waste and Jerusalem under siege (1:2–20); clearly there is need for a call to conversion, to atone for sins and infidelities (1:21–31). After a few verses that strike a note of hope (in time, Jerusalem will be raised on high), there follow oracles that describe how the people have been laid low on account of their pride (2:6–22). However, amid all the uncleanness, a seed of beauty remains, offering hopes of rebirth (3:1—4:6). One could say that the core of the whole section is the "Song of the vineyard" (5:1–7), a lovely allegory about the care that the Lord lavishes on his people, and about their failure to appreciate it.

After this we begin to find references to specific times in what is called the "Book of Immanuel" (7:1—12:6), which begins with an account of the calling of Isaiah, whom the Lord has commissioned to explain the meaning of what is happening and to show that there are grounds for hope (6:1–13). In line with this, the prophet approaches Ahaz to encourage him to trust in the Lord (7:1–17) in the face of threatened invasion (7:18–25). Assyria is about to close in on Israel and Judah (8:1–22), but there is still hope of deliverance (8:23—9:6). Punishment does await Israel and Judah (9:7—10:4), but Assyria will not escape it either (10:5–19). Meanwhile, the "remnant" of Israel will grow in its appreciation of the Lord and will find peace (10:20—11:9). The section ends with a song of joy and praise to the Lord for saving and renewing his people (11:10—12:6).

1:2–31. The first oracles are couched in the language of a lawsuit (*rîb*). This is a style of writing often found in the prophetical literature of Israel, which shares similar modes of expression with other writings of the ancient Middle East (see the note on Is 1:10–20). However, other people resort to that legal style when they seek to justify the punishment inflicted on a vassal by an aggrieved overlord, whereas when prophetical texts denounce a fault it is in order to evince an immediate change of heart. The Lord takes no pleasure in

iniquitate, / semini nequam, filiis sceleratis! / Dereliquerunt Dominum, / blasphemaverunt Sanctum Israel, / abalienati sunt retrorsum. / 5Super quo percutiemini vos ultra, / addentes praevaricationem? /

A sinful nation

Lev 17:1
Is 30:9
Jer 2:13

4Ah, sinful nation,
a people laden with iniquity,
offspring of evildoers,
sons who deal corruptly!
They have forsaken the LORD,
they have despised the Holy One of Israel,
they are utterly estranged.

---

punishing people; he very much wants to forgive transgressors and reestablish friendship with them.

The passage begins by calling on heaven and earth to see how wickedly the people have acted, and by accusing them of forsaking the Lord (vv. 2–3). It then inveighs against those who have turned away from the Lord and show no inclination to react, even though misfortune has overtaken them (vv. 4–9), and it denounces the hypocrisy of a people that goes through the motions of religious worship without having the right dispositions (vv. 10–15). A call to conversion follows (vv. 16–17). The Lord is ready to argue his point against his people, to reward them if they mend their ways or punish them if they persist in their sins (vv. 18–20). They are in a bad way, such is their sinfulness (vv. 21–23). Their punishment will be very harsh; so they should respond now and be faithful, as they were in earlier times (vv. 24–31).

This oracle brings in all the main theological themes found in the history of the chosen people of the Old Testament —their divine election; God's offer of a Covenant; the people's transgression of the Covenant; God's punishment for their infidelity. Even so, it shows that theirs is a merciful God, ever ready to forgive offences; he never turns his back on those whom he has loved.

1:3. An apocryphal text from the seventh or eighth century AD reads these words as a prophecy that came true when Jesus was born and the only ones to adore him were an ox and an ass (*Gospel of Pseudo-Matthew*, 14)—meaning that the people's rejection of the Lord, about which the prophet complains, could be seen in the fact that the Blessed Virgin and St Joseph could find no accommodation (cf. Lk 2:7). This interpretation led to the traditional depiction of Jesus as born in a cave that housed an ox and an ass; St Gregory the Great interprets the scene symbolically: "The ox stands for the people of Israel, subject to the yoke of the Law; the ass refers to the Gentiles, who are violent and consumed by their passions" (*Moralia in Iob,* 35, 16, 39).

1:4–9. The prophet bemoans the desolation and pain that those who neglect God can experience, and he upbraids them for turning away from God. Good Shepherd that he is (cf.

Omne caput languidum, / et omne cor maerens. / 6A planta pedis usque ad verticem / non est in eo sanitas; / vulnus et livor et plaga tumens / non est circumligata / nec curata medicamine neque fota oleo.

[5]Why will you still be smitten,
that you continue to rebel?
The whole head is sick,
and the whole heart faint.
[6]From the sole of the foot even to the head,
there is no soundness in it,
but bruises and sores
and bleeding wounds;
they are not pressed out, or bound up,
or softened with oil.

Jer 5:3
Lev 26:14–33
Amos 4:6–12

Jer 30:12–15
Lk 10:34

[7]Your country lies desolate,
your cities are burned with fire;
in your very presence
aliens devour your land;
it is desolate, as overthrown by aliens.

Gen 19:1
Deut 28:51–52

1:2), God looked after his people, but received only ingratitude. When they forsook God, everything went wrong for them. Judah laid waste, and Jerusalem besieged by the armies of Assyria, should make them consider their position and lead them to the right conclusions. That is the first message of the prophet. He wants to bring about a change of heart. All is not lost; there are still some survivors (v. 9); they can still mend their ways and have hope of salvation. In Romans 9:27–29, St Paul quotes v. 9 in the context of insisting that God will never revoke his election of Israel; in spite of all the people's sins, God will keep a faithful remnant safe.

The people's sin, their rebellion against God, lay not so much in a deliberate intention to offend him as in their "not knowing", "not understanding" (cf. 1:3) that everything they had came from the goodness of the Lord; they could not claim personal credit for it.

Time and again, we fail to realize our good fortune and be grateful for it. But, thanks to the Redemption wrought by Christ "when the time had fully come" (Gal 4:4), it is always possible to triumph over evil and sin. "The prophets often announce not only the terrible punishment that sinners will suffer but also the punishment that sins deserve, so that when the day of reckoning comes the people will rejoice and give thanks to God, for his punishment is much less than they deserve [...]. Paul conveys the same idea, in a more subdued tone than the prophet uses here: he shows that, just as in the days of the prophet, if the mercy of God were not so great, all would be destroyed. If grace had not been made manifest with the coming of Christ, all would have suffered a more terrible fate" (St John Chrysostom, *In Isaiam*, 1, 4).

/ [7]Terra vestra deserta, / civitates vestrae succensae igni; / regionem vestram coram vobis alieni devorant, / et desolabitur sicut in vastitate hostili. / [8]Et derelinquetur filia Sion / ut umbraculum in

[8]And the daughter of Zion is left
like a booth in a vineyard,
like a lodge in a cucumber field,
like a besieged city.

Gen 18:16–33; 19:1–29 · 2 Kings 19:4 · Is 4:3 · *Rom 9:27–29*

[9]If the LORD of hosts
had not left us a few survivors,
we should have been like Sodom,
and become like Gomorrah.

Is 29:13–14

Religion without soul

Deut 32:32 [10]Hear the word of the LORD,
you rulers of Sodom!
Give ear to the teaching of our God,
you people of Gomorrah!

1 Sam 15:22 · Amos 5:21

[11]"What to me is the multitude of your sacrifices?
says the LORD;

1:10–20. These verses, too, in some ways form a literary unit in line with the "lawsuit" (*rîb*) style often found in prophetical literature: the charge-sheet (vv. 10–15) is set against a list of good works, given here in the form of an exhortation (vv. 16–17), and then comes to the sentence at the end, seen here in the attitude of the judge, who is God (vv. 18–20).

Harsh words (v. 10) are used: the people of Judah are identified with those of Sodom and Gomorrah, the epitome of sin and rejection of God. The transgressions of which they are accused are against acts of worship (vv. 11–15), listed one after the other—sacrifices, incense offerings, festivals, entreaties. The accusation is not against acts of worship in themselves, for these are laid down in the book of Leviticus and therefore are right and proper. What the prophet is inveighing against is religious formalism and the dichotomy between performance and intention, as can be seen from the verses that follow. What God desires is sincerity of heart, virtue, protection for the weak—in other words, proper treatment of others. In laying down the law here, the Lord shows his readiness to forgive, while still holding out the threat of punishment (vv. 18–20).

Some passages of the section are read in the Liturgy during Lent (Tuesday of the Second Week) to help people check whether they have given God the worship due to him, and as a call to a sincere change of heart. Christian writers have used this passage from Isaiah (and other texts from the Scriptures) to explain that true religion and com-

vinea, / sicut tugurium in cucumerario, / sicut civitas, quae obsessa est. / [9]Nisi Dominus exercituum reliquisset nobis semen, / quasi Sodoma fuissemus / et quasi Gomorra similes essemus. / [10]Audite verbum Domini, / principes Sodomorum; / percipite auribus legem Dei nostri, populus Gomorrae. / [11]«Quo mihi multitudinem victimarum vestrarum?, / dicit Dominus. / Plenus sum holocaustis arietum

I have had enough of burnt offerings of rams
and the fat of fed beasts;
I do not delight in the blood of bulls,
or of lambs, or of he-goats.

12 "When you come to appear before me,
who requires of you
this trampling of my courts?
13 Bring no more vain offerings; 1 Chron 32:31
incense is an abomination to me.
New moon and sabbath and the calling of assemblies—
I cannot endure iniquity and solemn assembly.
14 Your new moons and your appointed feasts
my soul hates;
they have become a burden to me,
I am weary of bearing them.
15 When you spread forth your hands, Is 59:2–3
I will hide my eyes from you; Jer 2:34; 14:12
even though you make many prayers, Mic 3:4
I will not listen;
your hands are full of blood.

Call to conversion

16 Wash yourselves; make yourselves clean; Amos 5:14–15
remove the evil of your doings

---

passion begin in a person's heart and then express themselves in actions. For example, one of the apostolic Fathers writes: "Inspired by the Holy Spirit, the ministers of God's grace will speak of penance. And the Lord of all things himself spoke of penance, and swore an oath: I do not desire the death of the wicked man, but that he should change his ways; and he adds: *Cease to do evil, learn to do good;* [...] *though your sins are like scarlet, they shall be as white as snow; though they are red like crimson, they shall become like wool.* The Lord desires that all whom he loves would repent, and he affirms it by his all-powerful will. Let us be obedient, then, to his glorious plan, and, by imploring his mercy and kindness, let us return to his goodness and be converted, leaving aside all our vain works, the disputes and jealousies that lead to death" (St Clement of Rome, *Ad Corinthios*, 8, 1–9, 1).

/ et adipe pinguium; / et sanguinem vitulorum / et agnorum et hircorum nolui. / [12]Cum veneritis ante conspectum meum, / quis quaesivit haec de manibus vestris, / ut ambularetis in atriis meis? / [13]Ne afferatis ultra sacrificium vanum; / abominatio mihi incensum, / neomenia et sabbatum et conventus; / non feram scelus cum coetu sollemni; / [14]calendas vestras et sollemnitates vestras odivit anima mea, / facta sunt mihi molesta, laboravi sustinens. / [15]Et cum extenderitis manus vestras, / avertam oculos

from before my eyes;
Ex 22:21–22 cease to do evil,
Jer 22:3 17 learn to do good;
seek justice,
correct oppression;
defend the fatherless,
plead for the widow.

Ps 32:1; 51:9 **The people must decide—obedience or rebellion**
Is 43:26 18 "Come now, let us reason together,
says the LORD:
though your sins are like scarlet,
they shall be as white as snow;
though they are red like crimson,
Lev 26:3–12 they shall become like wool.
Deut 28:1–14 19 If you are willing and obedient,
you shall eat the good of the land;
Lev 26:14–39 20 But if you refuse and rebel,
Deut 28:15 you shall be devoured by the sword;
Is 40:5; 58:14 Mic 4:4 for the mouth of the LORD has spoken."

1:17. "Learn to do good": in order to lead the sort of lives that God wants, we need to be properly schooled. St Basil comments: "Since moral understanding is neither self-evident nor clear to all, we must learn to do good deeds through our study of sound doctrine" (*Enarratio in Isaiam*, 1, 40). As well as calling for sound doctrine, holiness of life requires the practice of virtue, day after day, consistently, in whatever circumstances we find ourselves. The "human virtues are [...] the foundation for the supernatural ones. These in turn provide us with constant encouragement to behave in a noble way. But it is not sufficient merely to want to have these virtues: we must learn how to practise them. *Discite benefacere* (Is 1:17), learn to do good. We need to make a habit of exercising each virtue, by actually being sincere, truthful, balanced, calm, and patient ... —for love is proved by deeds and we cannot love God only by word, but 'with deeds and in truth' (1 Jn 3:18)" (St Josemaría Escrivá, *Friends of God*, 91).

1:21–31. Elaborating on God's judgment, the prophet laments the sorry

meos a vobis; / et cum multiplicaveritis orationem, / non exaudiam: / manus enim vestrae sanguine plenae sunt. / [16]Lavamini, mundi estote, / auferte malum cogitationum vestrarum ab oculis meis; / quiescite agere perverse, / [17]discite benefacere: / quaerite iudicium, subvenite oppresso, / iudicate pupillo, defendite viduam. / [18]Et venite, et iudicio contendamus, / dicit Dominus. / Si fuerint peccata vestra ut coccinum, / quasi nix dealbabuntur; / et, si fuerint rubra quasi vermiculus, / velut lana erunt. / [19]Si volueritis et audieritis, / bona terrae comedetis; / [20]quod si nolueritis et me ad iracundiam provocaveritis, / gladius devorabit vos, / quia os Domini locutum est». / [21]Quomodo facta est meretrix

Infidelity and injustice

[21] How the faithful city
has become a harlot,
she that was full of justice!
Righteousness lodged in her,
but now murderers.
[22] Your silver has become dross,
your wine mixed with water.
[23] Your princes are rebels
and companions of thieves.
Every one loves a bribe
and runs after gifts.
They do not defend the fatherless,
and the widow's cause does not come to them.

Jer 2:20
Ezek 16; 23
Rev 17:1

Jer 6:29
Ezek 22:18
Hos 9:4
Mic 3:11
Zech 7:10

Punishment and purification

[24] Therefore the Lord says,
the LORD of hosts,
the Mighty One of Israel:
"Ah, I will vent my wrath on my enemies,
and avenge myself on my foes.
[25] I will turn my hand against you
and will smelt away your dross as with lye
and remove all your alloy.
[26] And I will restore your judges as at the first,
and your counsellors as at the beginning.
Afterward you shall be called the city of righteousness,
the faithful city."

Is 1:21
Zech 8:3

---

state of Jerusalem (vv. 21–23) and proclaims that a restoration will take place (vv. 24–31). Purification is the main idea here: "I … will smelt away your dross as with lye" (v. 25)—a simile that makes it perfectly clear that what the Lord seeks is not the sinner's ruin, but his conversion and rehabilitation: "He does not punish in order to destroy; rather, he teaches in order to restore" (St Basil, *Enarratio in Isaiam*, 1, 55).

/ civitas fidelis, plena iudicii? / Iustitia habitavit in ea, / nunc autem homicidae. / [22]Argentum tuum versum est in scoriam, / vinum tuum mixtum est aqua; / [23]principes tui infideles, socii furum: / omnes diligunt munera, sequuntur retributiones, / pupillo non iudicant, et causa viduae non ingreditur ad illos. / [24]Propter hoc ait Dominus, Deus exercituum, Fortis Israel: / «Heu, consolabor super hostibus meis / et vindicabor de inimicis meis. / [25]Et convertam manum meam ad te / et excoquam ad purum scoriam tuam / et auferam omne stannum tuum. / [26]Et restituam iudices tuos, ut fuerunt prius, / et consiliarios tuos sicut antiquitus; / post haec vocaberis Civitas iustitiae, Urbs fidelis». / [27]Sion in iudicio redimetur / et, qui in ea reversi sunt, in iustitia. / [28]Erit autem ruina scelestis et peccatoribus simul; / et, qui

[27] Zion shall be redeemed by justice,
and those in her who repent, by righteousness.
[28] But rebels and sinners shall be destroyed together,
and those who forsake the LORD shall be consumed.
[29] For you shall be ashamed of the oaks
in which you delighted;
and you shall blush for the gardens
which you have chosen.
[30] For you shall be like an oak
whose leaf withers,
and like a garden without water.
[31] And the strong shall become tow,
and his work a spark,
and both of them shall burn together,
with none to quench them.

B. IDOLATRY CONDEMNED*

The glory of Zion and peace among the nations

Is 56:6–8; 60:11–14 Mic 4:1–3 Zech 8:20; 14:16 Lk 24:47

2 [1]The word which Isaiah the son of Amoz saw concerning
Judah and Jerusalem.
[2]It shall come to pass in the latter days
that the mountain of the house of the LORD
shall be established as the highest of the mountains,

***2:1—4:6.** This section opens with a new "dispute" (*rîb*) in which we find echoes of the teaching about the "day of the Lord" (2:12; cf. Amos 5:18–20). Previously, the people were accused of forsaking God (cf. 1:2–3); now we are told why God has forsaken them (cf. 2:6): it was on account of their arrogance and their idolatry (cf. 2:6—4:1). However, it is not really the case that God has forsaken his people; his "forsaking" them is a way of describing the punishment he inflicts on them on account of their sins. When the Lord's sentence is revealed, human arrogance will be brought low, and the Lord will be exalted (cf. 2:9, 11, 17).

Oracles about the splendour that will be Zion's on that day introduce (cf. 2:1–5) and round off (4:2–6) this "dispute".

2:1–5. Despite the sins of the people and the disastrous situation in Judah

dereliquerunt Dominum, consumentur. / [29]Confundemini enim terebinthis, in quibus delectati estis, / et erubescetis super hortis, quos elegistis. / [30]Nam eritis velut quercus, defluentibus foliis, / et velut hortus absque aqua; / [31]et erit fortitudo vestra ut favilla stuppae, / et opus eius quasi scintilla, / et succendetur utrumque simul, et non erit qui exstinguat. **[2]** [1]Verbum, quod vidit Isaias filius Amos super Iudam et Ierusalem. [2]Et erit in novissimis diebus / praeparatus mons domus Domini in vertice montium, / et elevabitur super colles; / et fluent ad eum omnes gentes. / [3]Et ibunt populi multi et dicent:

and shall be raised above the hills;
and all the nations shall flow to it,
3and many peoples shall come, and say: Mic 4:2 Jn 4:22
"Come, let us go up to the mountain of the LORD,
to the house of the God of Jacob;
that he may teach us his ways
and that we may walk in his paths."
For out of Zion shall go forth the law,
and the word of the LORD from Jerusalem.
4He shall judge between the nations, Is 9:6; 11:6–9
and shall decide for many peoples; Hos 2:20 Joel 4:9–11
and they shall beat their swords into ploughshares, Zech 9:9–10
and their spears into pruning hooks;
nation shall not lift up sword against nation,
neither shall they learn war any more.*
5O house of Jacob, Is 60:1–3
come, let us walk
in the light of the LORD.

---

that is described in this first part of the book, from the very start a glimmer of hope is provided in this vision of messianic and eschatological restoration which shows that the salvation of the world centres on Zion, "the mountain of the Lord", that is, Jerusalem.

All the nations will converge on the holy city, but not to despoil it of its wealth: they will come in peace to hearken to the word of the Lord and receive instruction in his law. This note of hope, struck, strategically, at the very start of the book, and at its end (66:18–24), constitutes one of its most important messages.

The prophecy in vv. 2–5 (found also, with slight variations, in Micah 4:1–3) links the Law with the temple, the spiritual centre of Jerusalem after the national reconstruction that took place when the exiles returned from Babylon.

In contrast with the strife and desolation that sin brings in its wake (cf. 1:2–9), peace is the outcome of reverence for God and readiness to obey his precepts, of the practice of virtue and of love of neighbour. The weapons of war become tools for development and agriculture: "Insofar as men are sinful, the threat of war hangs over them, and hang over them it will until the return of Christ. But insofar as men vanquish sin by a union of love, they will vanquish violence as well and make these words come true: 'They shall turn their swords into plough-shares, and their spears into sickles. Nation shall not lift up sword against nation, neither shall they learn

/ «Venite, et ascendamus ad montem Domini, / ad domum Dei Iacob, / ut doceat nos vias suas, / et ambulemus in semitis eius»; / quia de Sion exibit lex, / et verbum Domini de Ierusalem. / 4Et iudicabit gentes / et arguet populos multos; / et conflabunt gladios suos in vomeres / et lanceas suas in falces; / non levabit gens contra gentem gladium, / nec exercebuntur ultra ad proelium. / 5Domus Iacob, venite,

The day of the Lord

Deut 18:14 6 For thou hast rejected thy people,
the house of Jacob,
because they are full of diviners[a] from the east
and of soothsayers like the Philistines,
and they strike hands with foreigners.
Deut 17: 16–17 Ps 20:8 7 Their land is filled with silver and gold,
and there is no end to their treasures;
their land is filled with horses,
and there is no end to their chariots.
8 Their land is filled with idols;
they bow down to the work of their hands,
to what their own fingers have made.
Is 5:15 9 So man is humbled,
and men are brought low—
forgive them not!
Hos 10:8 2 Thess 1:9 Rev 6:16 10 Enter into the rock,
and hide in the dust

---

war any more' (Is 2:4)" (*Gaudium et spes*, 78).

These words of Isaiah announcing God's salvific intervention in the fullness of time will come true with the birth of Christ, who will open up an era of perfect peace and reconciliation. The Church uses this text in the liturgy of the first Sunday in Advent, encouraging us to look forward to the second coming of Christ as we prepare to recall his first coming at Christmas.

2:6–22. Men show their arrogance in their reliance on their treasures, their armies and those they seek advice from (and who tell them what they want to hear). However, this overweening pride is defeated when they have to appear before God: those who trusted in themselves will be brought low by the majesty of God.

The poem is a challenging call to the people of Judah and Jerusalem to review their values and put their trust in God, the only one who is of any account (cf. v. 22). This is a message that never goes out of date, and it needs to be heeded by those who are so confident in the potential of science and technology, so content with their standard of living, that they forget about those in need and give no thought to God. All of their apparent successess and posses-

/ et ambulemus in lumine Domini. / 6 Proiecisti enim populum tuum, domum Iacob, / quia repleti sunt hariolis orientalibus / et augures habuerunt ut Philisthiim / et manus alienis porrigunt. / 7 Repleta est terra eius argento et auro, / et non est finis thesaurorum eius; / 8 et repleta est terra eius equis, / et innumerabiles quadrigae eius; / et repleta est terra eius idolis: / opus manuum suarum adoraverunt, / quod fecerunt digiti eorum. / 9 Et incurvavit se homo, / et humiliatus est vir: / ne dimittas eis. / 10 Ingredere in petram, abscondere in pulvere / a facie timoris Domini et a gloria maiestatis eius. /

a. Cn: Heb lacks *of diviners*

from before the terror of the LORD,
and from the glory of his majesty.
11 The haughty looks of man shall be brought low,
and the pride of men shall be humbled;
and the LORD alone will be exalted
in that day.

12 For the LORD of hosts has a day
against all that is proud and lofty,
against all that is lifted up and high;[b]
13 against all the cedars of Lebanon,
lofty and lifted up;
and against all the oaks of Bashan;
14 against all the high mountains,
and against all the lofty hills;
15 against every high tower,
and against every fortified wall;
16 against all the ships of Tarshish,
and against all the beautiful craft.
17 And the haughtiness of man shall be humbled,
and the pride of men shall be brought low;
and the LORD alone will be exalted in that day.

Amos 5:18–20

1 Kings 10:22
Ps 48:8

sions will be of no avail when the "day of the Lord" comes (v. 12), "that day" (v. 11) when he will hand down sentence against which there is no appeal. Commenting on v. 9, St Jerome writes: "We can say that all human thinking that runs contrary to the truth leads man to build and worship idols: *man is humbled, and men are brought low*, and they will not be able to raise themselves up for they will be bound by the devil, unless the Lord releases them. They will be like the woman who suffered under Satan's power for eighteen years: she could not look up to heaven but could only see the ground beneath her feet" (*Commentarii in Isaiam*, 2, 9).

"That day" (vv. 11, 17, 20): a phrase that appears here for the first time, and that is used throughout the book to introduce an eschatological oracle, usually with reference to the "day of the Lord". It marks the point when God will be definitively exalted.

[11]Oculi sublimes hominis humiliabuntur, / et incurvabitur altitudo virorum; / exaltabitur autem Dominus solus in die illa. / [12]Quia dies Domini exercituum / super omnem superbum et excelsum / et super omnem arrogantem, et humiliabitur; / [13]et super omnes cedros Libani sublimes et erectas / et super omnes quercus Basan / [14]et super omnes montes excelsos / et super omnes colles elevatos / [15]et super omnem turrim excelsam / et super omnem murum munitum / [16]et super omnes naves Tharsis / et super omnia navigia pulchra. / [17]Et incurvabitur sublimitas hominum, / et humiliabitur altitudo virorum;

b. Cn Compare Gk: Heb *low*

Jer 10:11–15 [18] And the idols shall utterly pass away.
Is 2:10 [19] And men shall enter the caves of the rocks
and the holes of the ground,
from before the terror of the LORD,
and from the glory of his majesty,
when he rises to terrify the earth.

Is 31:7 [20] In that day men will cast forth
their idols of silver and their idols of gold,
which they made for themselves to worship,
to the moles and to the bats,
[21] to enter the caverns of the rocks
and the clefts of the cliffs,
from before the terror of the LORD,
and from the glory of his majesty,
when he rises to terrify the earth.
Gen 2:7; 6:3 [22] Turn away from man
Job 27:3; 34:14 in whose nostrils is breath,
Jer 17:5 for of what account is he?

Downfall of Judah and Jerusalem

Lev 26:26 3 [1]For, behold, the Lord, the LORD of hosts,
is taking away from Jerusalem and from Judah
stay and staff,
the whole stay of bread,
and the whole stay of water;

3:1–15. This oracle, which begins and ends by speaking of the Lord of "hosts" (or "armies"), proclaims the Lord's sentence on Judah and Jerusalem on account of their pride and self-sufficiency.

The scenario painted here is one of anarchy, a society in which no one is ready to enforce justice and the rule of law. It seems to refer to a time of transition, when a regency operated (cf. vv. 4 and 12)—possibly the time when King Uzziah (Azariah) contracted leprosy, and Jotham began to take on the responsibilities of government (cf. 2 Kings 15:5).

Once again a moral message is being preached—addressed to society as a whole and to the individual: all

/ et elevabitur Dominus solus in die illa, / [18]et idola penitus conterentur. / [19]Et introibunt in speluncas petrarum / et in voragines terrae / a facie formidinis Domini et a gloria maiestatis eius, / cum surrexerit percutere terram. [20]In die illa proiciet homo idola sua argentea et simulacra sua aurea, quae fecerat sibi, ut adoraret, ad talpas et vespertiliones. [21]Et ingredietur scissuras petrarum et cavernas saxorum a facie formidinis Domini et a gloria maiestatis eius, cum surrexerit percutere terram. [22]Quiescite ergo ab homine, cuius spiritus in naribus eius. Quanti enim aestimabitur ipse? **[3]** [1]Ecce enim Dominator, Dominus exercituum, / aufert a Ierusalem et a Iuda robur et praesidium, / omne robur panis et omne

[2]the mighty man and the soldier,
the judge and the prophet,
the diviner and the elder,
[3]the captain of fifty
and the man of rank,
the counsellor and the skilful magician
and the expert in charms.
[4]And I will make boys their princes,
and babes shall rule over them.
[5]And the people will oppress one another,
every man his fellow
and every man his neighbour;
the youth will be insolent to the elder,
and the base fellow to the honourable.

2 Kings 15:5
Eccles 10:16

[6]When a man takes hold of his brother
in the house of his father, saying:
"You have a mantle;
you shall be our leader,
and this heap of ruins
shall be under your rule";
[7]in that day he will speak out, saying:
"I will not be a healer;
in my house there is neither bread nor mantle;
you shall not make me
leader of the people."
[8]For Jerusalem has stumbled,
and Judah has fallen;

---

will be judged; the righteous will be rewarded, the wicked punished (cf. vv. 10–11).

The pejorative references to women (here in v. 12 and elsewhere in the book—19:16; 32:9; 54:6; etc.) are in line with people's thinking at the time when the book was written. It was one when women had a lower standing than men in the eyes of the law, being dependent on their father or husband in all matters.

robur aquae, / [2]fortem et virum bellatorem, / iudicem et prophetam et hariolum et senem, / [3]principem super quinquaginta et honorabilem vultu / et consiliarium et sapientem magum / et prudentem incantatorem. / [4]Et dabo pueros principes eorum; / et infantes dominabuntur eis. / [5]Et irruet populus, vir ad virum, / unusquisque ad proximum suum: / tumultuabitur puer contra senem, / et ignobilis contra nobilem. / [6]Apprehendet enim vir fratrem suum / in domo patris sui: / «Vestimentum tibi est, / princeps esto noster, / ruina autem haec sub manu tua». / [7]Clamabit in die illa dicens: / «Non sum medicus, / et in domo mea non est panis neque vestimentum; / nolite constituere me principem populi». / [8]Ruit enim Ierusalem, et Iudas concidit, / quia lingua eorum et adinventiones eorum contra Dominum, / ut provocarent oculos maiestatis eius. / [9]Procacitas vultus eorum accusat eos, / et peccatum suum quasi

because their speech and their deeds are against the LORD,
defying his glorious presence.

Gen 18:20–21; 19:4–11 9 Their partiality witnesses against them;
they proclaim their sin like Sodom,
they do not hide it.
Woe to them!
For they have brought evil upon themselves.
Eccles 8:12 10 Tell the righteous that it shall be well with them,
for they shall eat the fruit of their deeds.
11 Woe to the wicked! It shall be ill with him,
for what his hands have done shall be done to him.
2 Kings 15:5 12 My people—children are their oppressors,
and women rule over them.
O my people, your leaders mislead you,
and confuse the course of your paths.

Mic 6:1–5 Hos 4:1–5 13 The LORD has taken his place to contend,
he stands to judge his people.[d]
Is 5:1–7 14 The LORD enters into judgment
with the elders and princes of his people:
"It is you who have devoured the vineyard,
the spoil of the poor is in your houses.
Amos 2:7 15 What do you mean by crushing my people,
by grinding the face of the poor?" says the Lord GOD of hosts.

3:16—4:1. The prophet now adopts the language of dramatic irony to describe the desolation into which Judah will be plunged: the haughtiness and luxurious lifestyle of the women of Jerusalem will be turned into humiliation and torment (3:16–24), and they will not be able to find husbands because so many of their menfolk will have died in battle (3:25—4:1).

These oracles must remind the reader of what happened when Jerusalem fell to the forces of Nebuchadnezzar, and deportees and their families filed out of the city on their way to exile in Babylon. Those who had led empty-headed,

Sodoma / praedicaverunt nec absconderunt; / vae animae eorum, / quoniam reddita sunt eis mala! / [10]Dicite iusto: «Bene!», / quoniam fructum adinventionum suarum comedet. / [11]Vae impio in malum: / retributio enim manuum eius fiet ei! / [12]Populum meum opprimit infans, / et mulieres dominantur ei. / Popule meus, qui te beatum dicunt, ipsi te decipiunt / et viam gressuum tuorum dissipant. / [13]Surgit ad arguendum Dominus / et stat ad iudicandos populos. / [14]Dominus ad iudicium veniet / cum senibus populi sui et principibus eius: / «Vos enim depasti estis vineam, / et rapina pauperis in domibus vestris. / [15]Quare atteritis populum meum / et facies pauperum commolitis?», / dicit Dominus, Deus exercituum. / [16]Et dixit Dominus: / «Pro eo quod elevatae sunt filiae Sion / et ambulaverunt extento

d. Gk Syr: Heb *judge peoples*

A warning to the women of Jerusalem

16 The LORD said: Is 32:9–14
Amos 4:1–3
Because the daughters of Zion are haughty
and walk with outstretched necks,
glancing wantonly with their eyes,
mincing along as they go,
tinkling with their feet;
17 the Lord will smite with a scab
the heads of the daughters of Zion,
and the LORD will lay bare their secret parts.

18 In that day the Lord will take away the finery of the anklets,
the headbands, and the crescents; 19 the pendants, the bracelets,
and the scarfs; 20 the headdresses, the armlets, the sashes, the
perfume boxes, and the amulets; 21 the signet rings and nose rings;
22 the festal robes, the mantles, the cloaks, and the handbags; 23 the
garments of gauze, the linen garments, the turbans, and the veils.
24 Instead of perfume there will be rottenness; Amos 8:10
and instead of a girdle, a rope;
and instead of well-set hair, baldness;
and instead of a rich robe, a girding of sackcloth;
instead of beauty, shame.[e]
25 Your men shall fall by the sword
and your mighty men in battle.
26 And her gates shall lament and mourn; Lam 2:10
ravaged, she shall sit upon the ground.

4 1 And seven women shall take hold of one man in that day,
saying, "We will eat our own bread and wear our own clothes,
only let us be called by your name; take away our reproach."

---

frivolous lives, giving no heed to the Lord, could not see that their pleasures were gossamer things and their joys had no depth—and were to be replaced by suffering and privation.

4:2–6. In the midst of all that distress, there is still some reason to hope that the Lord will come back and shelter his people again. These verses fill out the vision we found in 2:1–5. Mount Zion

collo et nutibus oculorum, / parvis passibus incedebant / et catenulis pedum tinniebant, / 17 decalvabit
Dominus verticem filiarum Sion / et Dominus crinem earum nudabit». / 18 In die illa auferet Dominus
/ ornamentum calceamentorum et torques / 19 et lunulas et inaures / et armillas et mitras, /
20 discriminalia et periscelidas / et fascias et olfactoriola / 21 et anulos et ornamenta narium, / 22 mutatoria
et palliola / et linteamina et marsupia, / 23 specula et sindones / et vittas et pallia. / 24 Et erit pro suavi
odore foetor, / et pro zona funiculus, / et pro crispante crine calvitium, / et pro fascia pectorali cilicium,
/ stigma pro pulchritudine. / 25 Viri tui gladio cadent, / et fortes tui in proelio, / 26 et maerebunt atque

e. One ancient Ms: Heb lacks *shame*

Jer 23:5–6
Zech 3:8; 6:12
Lk 1:42
Is 52:1; 60:21
Dan 12:1
Zeph 3:13
Ex 13:21–22; 24:16
Joel 4:17–21
Is 25:4–5
Rev 7:15–16
21:3–4

A holy remnant in Jerusalem

2In that day the branch of the LORD shall be beautiful and glorious, and the fruit of the land shall be the pride and glory of the survivors of Israel. 3And he who is left in Zion and remains in Jerusalem will be called holy, every one who has been recorded for life in Jerusalem, 4when the Lord shall have washed away the filth of the daughters of Zion and cleansed the bloodstains of Jerusalem from its midst by a spirit of judgment and by a spirit of burning. 5Then the LORD will create over the whole site of Mount Zion and over her assemblies a cloud by day, and smoke and the shining of a flaming fire by night; for over all the glory there will be a canopy and a pavilion. 6It will be for a shade by day from the heat, and for a refuge and a shelter from the storm and rain.

2 Sam 12:1–15
Ps 80:9–19
Is 27:2–5
Jer 2:21; 5:10; 6:9; 12:10
Ezek 15:1–8; 17:3–10; 19:10–14

C. FAILURE TO RESPOND TO THE LORD

The song of the vineyard

5 1*Let me sing for my beloved
a love song concerning his vineyard:

---

refers above all to the assembly of the remnant of Israel gathered in the temple; these will enjoy the Lord's protection as in the days in the wilderness when, after being delivered from Egypt, they made their way towards the promised land guided by the pillar of cloud and the pillar of fire (cf. Ex 13:21–22).

The "branch of the Lord" (v. 2) is a title belonging to the king in the line of David (cf. 11:1). It is not only the "remnant" of Israel that will survive and see the glory of the purified Jerusalem, but also the Messiah, David's son. For this reason, a later Christian writer, commenting on Elizabeth's greeting to Mary ("Blessed are you among women, and blessed is the fruit of your womb": Lk 1:42), says: "Isaiah speaks of this fruit when he says: *In that day ... the fruit of the land shall be the pride and glory of the survivors of Israel.* What can this fruit be, if not the Holy One of Israel, who is at the same time the seed of Abraham, the shoot of the Lord, the flower that springs from the root of

---

lugebunt portae eius, / et desolata in terra sedebit. **[4]** 1Et apprehendent septem mulieres / virum unum in die illa dicentes: / «Panem nostrum comedemus / et vestimentis nostris operiemur, / tantummodo vocetur nomen tuum super nos: / aufer opprobrium nostrum». / 2In die illa erit germen Domini in splendorem et gloriam, / et fructus terrae sublimis et exsultatio / his, qui salvati fuerint de Israel. / 3Et erit: omnis, qui relictus fuerit in Sion, / et residuus in Ierusalem, sanctus vocabitur, / omnis, qui scriptus est ad vitam in Ierusalem. / 4Cum abluerit Dominus sordem filiarum Sion / et sanguinem Ierusalem laverit de medio eius / spiritu iudicii et spiritu ardoris, / 5et creabit Dominus super omnem locum montis Sion / et super coetum eius / nubem per diem / et fumum et splendorem ignis flammantis in nocte: / super omnem enim gloriam protectio, / 6et tabernaculum erit in umbraculum diei ab aestu / et in securitatem et absconsionem a turbine et a pluvia. **[5]** 1Cantabo dilecto meo / canticum amici mei de vinea sua: / Vinea facta est dilecto meo / in colle pingui; / 2et saepivit eam / et lapides elegit ex

My beloved had a vineyard
on a very fertile hill. Mt 21:33–44 Jn 15:1–2
[2]He digged it and cleared it of stones,
and planted it with choice vines;
he built a watchtower in the midst of it,
and hewed out a wine vat in it;
and he looked for it to yield grapes,
but it yielded wild grapes.

[3]And now, O inhabitants of Jerusalem Mic 6:1–5
and men of Judah,
judge, I pray you, between me
and my vineyard.
[4]What more was there to do for my vineyard, Jer 2:4–7
that I have not done in it?
When I looked for it to yield grapes,
why did it yield wild grapes?

[5]And now I will tell you
what I will do to my vineyard.
I will remove its hedge,
and it shall be devoured;

Jesse, the life-giving fruit of which we all partake?" (Baldwin of Canterbury, *De salutatione angelica*).

5:1–7. The "song of the vineyard" is a masterpiece of Hebrew poetry, full of symbolism and carrying an important message. In the figure of heartbroken farmer, we can see our Lord Jesus Christ and his sorrow at finding that his people yield such a poor crop of righteousness. In vv. 1–2 the author assumes the role of God's friend; in vv. 3–6 the lover speaks, describing all the care he has taken of his people, and then in v. 7 the author speaks again. It is a simple story that does not take long to tell; to begin with, the author keeps us in suspense as to what he is getting at (rather as Nathan does, in the parable he tells David: cf. 2 Sam 12:1–15), but then he tells us: the vineyard is "the house of Israel" (v. 7); despite all the care God has taken of it, it failed to yield the expected fruit, giving "wild grapes" instead. Israel needs to admit its fault. So, the lyrical tone now ceases, and a series of woes follows. The song

illa / et plantavit in ea vites electas / et aedificavit turrim in medio eius / et torcular exstruxit in ea; / et exspectavit, ut faceret uvas, / et fecit labruscas. / [3]Nunc ergo, habitator Ierusalem / et vir Iudae, / iudicate inter me et vineam meam. / [4]Quid est quod debui ultra facere vineae meae / et non feci ei? / Cur exspectavi, ut faceret uvas, / et fecit labruscas? / [5]Et nunc ostendam vobis / quid ego faciam vineae meae: / auferam saepem eius, / et erit in direptionem; / diruam maceriam eius, / et erit in conculcationem. / [6]Et ponam eam desertam: / non putabitur et non fodietur, / et ascendent vepres et

I will break down its wall,
  and it shall be trampled down.
6 I will make it a waste;
  it shall not be pruned or hoed,
  and briers and thorns shall grow up;
I will also command the clouds
  that they rain no rain upon it.
7 For the vineyard of the LORD of hosts
  is the house of Israel,
and the men of Judah
  are his pleasant planting;
and he looked for justice,
  but behold, bloodshed;
for righteousness,
  but behold, a cry!

Is 32:13
2 Sam 1:21
Is 27:2–5
Jer 2:21; 6:9; 12:10
Ezek 15:1–8; 17:3–10; 19:10,14
Hos 10:1
Mt 21:33–46
Mk 12:1–12
Lk 20:9–19

Laments about sinners

8 Woe to those who join house to house,
  who add field to field,

Ezek 7:5–26
Amos 6:1–7
Mic 2:1–5
Hab 2:6–20
Mt 23
Lk 6:24–26
Jas 5:1–5

---

contains many plays on words, impossible to render in translation.

The prophet Hosea, earlier, used the simile of a vine to describe Israel (Hos 10:1). Isaiah himself will use it again (27:2–5) and it recurs in Jeremiah (2:21; 5:10; 6:9; 12:10) and in Ezekiel (Ezek 15:1–8; 17:3–10; 19:10, 14); and there are traces of it in Psalm 80:8–18 and in the "Song of Moses" (Deut 32: 32–33). For his part, Sirach compares divine wisdom to a vine (cf. Sir 24:23–30). Finally, it appears in our Lord's parable of the wicked tenants of a vineyard, a parable that is a kind of compendium of salvation history, including his own experiences with the Jewish authorities (Mt 21:33–46; Mk 12:1–12; Lk 20:9–19).

As the heir of ancient Israel, the Church, too, is prefigured in the story of the vineyard. The Second Vatican Council remarks on this when it comments on the metaphors that the Bible uses for the Church: "The Church is a piece of land to be cultivated, the field of God (1 Cor 3:9). On that land the ancient olive tree grows whose holy roots were the patriarchs and in which the reconciliation of Jews and Gentiles has been brought about and will be brought about (Rom 11:13–26). That land, like a choice vineyard, has been planted by the heavenly Husbandman (Mt 21:33–43 and par.; cf. Is 5:1–7). The true vine is Christ who gives life, and the power to bear abundant fruit, to the branches, that is, to us, who through

spinae; / et nubibus mandabo, ne pluant super eam imbrem. / 7Vinea enim Domini exercituum domus Israel est, / et vir Iudae germen eius delectabile; / et exspectavi, ut faceret iudicium, et ecce iniquitas, / et iustitiam, et ecce nequitia. / 8Vae, qui coniungunt domum ad domum / et agrum agro copulant usque

until there is no more room,
and you are made to dwell alone
in the midst of the land.
9 The LORD of hosts has sworn in my hearing:
"Surely many houses shall be desolate,
large and beautiful houses, without inhabitant.
10 For ten acres of vineyard shall yield but one bath, Is 7:23
and a homer of seed shall yield but an ephah."

11 Woe to those who rise early in the morning, Wis 2:7–9
that they may run after strong drink, Is 22:13; 28:1,7–8; 56:12
who tarry late into the evening Amos 4:1
till wine inflames them! Mic 2:11; Joel 1:5
12 They have lyre and harp, Ps 28:5
timbrel and flute and wine at their feasts;
but they do not regard the deeds of the LORD,
or see the work of his hands.

13 Therefore my people go into exile for want of knowledge;
their honoured men are dying of hunger,
and their multitude is parched with thirst.
14 Therefore Sheol has enlarged its appetite
and opened its mouth beyond measure,

---

the Church remain in Christ, without whom we can do nothing (Jn 15:1–5)" (*Lumen gentium*, 6).

5:8–30. The poem consists of six woes or laments (vv. 8–10, 11–17, 18–19, 20, 21 and 22–24) which close with the threat of a punishment even harsher than they have suffered so far (vv. 25–30). The prophet denounces six kinds of sin committed by the people of Judah and Jerusalem and which will bring divine punishment upon them; it is another way of lamenting the behaviour criticized earlier in the parable of the vineyard.

The first lament (vv. 8-10) is aimed at those who selfishly build up their wealth, without giving any thought to others (cf. Jas 5:1–5). The punishment that God will impose for this will be extreme penury, described quite dramatically here. The Hebrew text literally says: "For ten acres of vineyard shall yield only one *bath*, and a *homer* of seed shall yield only one *ephah*." An

ad terminum loci! / Numquid habitabitis vos soli in medio terrae? / 9 In auribus meis iuravit Dominus exercituum: / «Certe domus multae desertae erunt, / grandes et pulchrae absque habitatore». / 10 Decem enim iugera vinearum facient lagunculam unam, / et triginta modii sementis facient modios tres. / 11 Vae, qui consurgunt mane ad ebrietatem sectandam / et ad potandum usque ad vesperam, / ut vinum inflammet eos! / 12 Cithara et lyra / et tympanum et tibia / et vinum in conviviis eorum, / et opus Domini non respiciunt, / nec opera manuum eius considerant. / 13 Propterea captivus ductus est populus meus,

and the nobility of Jerusalem[f] and her multitude go down,
her throng and he who exults in her.
Is 2:9,11 15 Man is bowed down, and men are brought low,
and the eyes of the haughty are humbled.
Is 1:26; 6:3 16 But the LORD of hosts is exalted in justice,
and the Holy God shows himself holy in righteousness.
Is 7:25 17 Then shall the lambs graze as in their pasture,
fatlings and kids[g] shall feed among the ruins.

18 Woe to those who draw iniquity with cords of falsehood,
who draw sin as with cart ropes,
2 Pet 3:4 19 who say: "Let him make haste,
let him speed his work
that we may see it;
let the purpose of the Holy One of Israel draw near,
and let it come, that we may know it!"

"acre" (*semed*) was the area that a team of oxen could plough in a day, and a *bath* is a dry measure of 45 litres (10 gallons). A *homer*, another dry measure, is the equivalent of about 200 kilograms (32 stone), and an *ephah* is one tenth of a *homer*. What the prophet is saying is that the land will not even yield as much as the amount of seed sown in it: in fact, it will return only a tenth of it.

The other laments clearly show the moral decadence of the ruling class, who are interested only in feasting, frivolity and deception, and have no time for righteousness or the Law. Here we find invective directed against people whose only interest is in having a good time (vv. 11–17), and against those who challenge the truth of the prophet's message (vv. 18–19). The emphasis is put on people's attachment to sin, symbolized by the reference to "drawing sin as with cart ropes". Then the prophet turns on those who deny objective moral truth (v. 20), those who think they are wise (v. 21), people who drink too much (v. 22), and venal judges (v. 23). Punishment awaits them, they are all told (v. 24). The description given of the punishments to befall Judah and Jerusalem include all sorts of misfortunes: some are natural catastrophes, such as the destructive earthquake (v. 25) that happened in the reign of Uzziah (cf. Amos 1:1; Zech 14:5); others are the

/ quia non habuit scientiam, / et nobiles eius interierunt fame, / et multitudo eius siti exaruit. / 14Propterea dilatavit infernus fauces suas / et aperuit os suum absque ullo termino; / et descendunt fortes Ierusalem, et populus eius, / et sublimes et tripudiantes in ea. / 15Et incurvabitur homo, et humiliabitur vir, / et oculi sublimium deprimentur; / 16et exaltabitur Dominus exercituum in iudicio, / et Deus sanctus sanctificabitur in iustitia, / 17et pascentur agni iuxta ordinem suum velut in prato suo, / et alieni comedent in ruinis pinguium. / 18Vae, qui trahunt iniquitatem in funiculis vanitatis / et quasi vinculum plaustri peccatum! / 19Qui dicunt: «Festinet / et cito veniat opus eius, ut videamus; / et

f. Heb *her nobility* **g.** Cn Compare Gk: Heb *aliens*

[20] Woe to those who call evil good
and good evil,
who put darkness for light
and light for darkness,
who put bitter for sweet
and sweet for bitter!
[21] Woe to those who are wise in their own eyes,
and shrewd in their own sight!
[22] Woe to those who are heroes at drinking wine,
and valiant men in mixing strong drink,
[23] who acquit the guilty for a bribe,
and deprive the innocent of his right!

Prov 17:15
Mt 23:13

Jn 9:40–41
Rom 1:21–22

[24] Therefore, as the tongue of fire devours the stubble,
and as dry grass sinks down in the flame,
so their root will be as rottenness,
and their blossom go up like dust;

---

effect of war (vv. 26–29), like the havoc wreaked by Assyrian forces all over Judah and which worsened as those forces were regularly replenished.

5:20. Among lamentations provoked by the actions of the wicked, this denunciation of falsehood stands out: these people have no interest in the truth; so frivolous are they, that inevitably they will become decadent and spread decadence. It is an attitude often found. John Paul II points out that the martyrs, "by witnessing fully to the good, are a living reproof to those who transgress the law (cf. Wis 2:12), and they make the words of the Prophet echo ever afresh: 'Woe to those who call evil good and good evil, who put darkness for light and light for darkness, who put bitter for sweet and sweet for bitter!' (Is 5:20). Although martyrdom represents the high point of the witness to moral truth, and one to which relatively few people are called, there is nonetheless a consistent witness which all Christians must daily be ready to make, even at the cost of suffering and grave sacrifice. Indeed, faced with the many difficulties which fidelity to the moral order can demand, even in the most ordinary circumstances, the Christian is called, with the grace of God invoked in prayer, to a sometimes heroic commitment. In this he or she is sustained by the virtue of fortitude, whereby—as Gregory the Great teaches—one can actually 'love the difficulties of this world for the sake of eternal rewards'" (*Veritatis splendor*, 93).

appropiet et veniat consilium Sancti Israel, / et sciemus illud!». / [20]Vae, qui dicunt malum bonum et bonum malum, / ponentes tenebras in lucem et lucem in tenebras, / ponentes amarum in dulce et dulce in amarum! /[21]Vae, qui sapientes sunt in oculis suis / et coram ipsis prudentes! / [22]Vae, qui potentes sunt ad bibendum vinum, / et viri fortes ad miscendam ebrietatem! / [23]Qui absolvunt impium pro muneribus / et iustitiam iusti auferunt ab eo! / [24]Propter hoc, sicut devorat stipulam lingua ignis, / et palea flamma

for they have rejected the law of the LORD of hosts,
Is 9:11,16,20; 10:4; Amos 1,1; Zech 14:13
   and have despised the word of the Holy One of Israel.
25 Therefore the anger of the LORD was kindled against his people,
   and he stretched out his hand against them and smote them,
   and the mountains quaked;
and their corpses were as refuse
   in the midst of the streets.
For all this his anger is not turned away
   and his hand is stretched out still.
Jer 5:15–17; 6:22–30
26 He will raise a signal for a nation afar off,
   and whistle for it from the ends of the earth;
lo, swiftly, speedily it comes!
27 None is weary, none stumbles,
   none slumbers or sleeps,
not a waistcloth is loose,
   not a sandal-thong broken;
28 their arrows are sharp,
   all their bows bent,
their horses' hoofs seem like flint,
   and their wheels like the whirlwind.
Hos 5:14 Amos 3:12
29 Their roaring is like a lion,
   like young lions they roar;
they growl and seize their prey,
   they carry it off, and none can rescue.
Is 8:20–22
30 They will growl over it on that day,
   like the roaring of the sea.
And if one look to the land,
   behold, darkness and distress;
and the light is darkened by its clouds.

---

consumitur, / sic radix eorum quasi tabes erit, / et flos eorum sicut putredo ascendet; / abiecerunt enim
legem Domini exercituum / et eloquium Sancti Israel blasphemaverunt. / 25 Ideo exarsit furor Domini
in populum suum, / et extendit manum suam super eum et percussit eum, / et conturbati sunt montes;
/ et facta sunt morticina eorum quasi stercus in medio platearum. / In his omnibus non est aversus furor
eius, / sed adhuc manus eius extenta. / 26 Et levabit signum nationibus procul; / et sibilabit ad eum de
finibus terrae; / et ecce festinus velociter veniet. / 27 Non est deficiens neque laborans in eo, / non
dormitabit neque dormiet; / neque solvetur cingulum renum eius, / nec rumpetur corrigia calceamenti
eius. / 28 Sagittae eius acutae, et omnes arcus eius extenti; / ungulae equorum eius ut silex reputantur,
/ et rotae eius quasi impetus tempestatis. / 29 Rugitus eius ut leonis: / rugiet ut catuli leonum et frendet;
/ et arripiet praedam et in tuto collocabit, / et non erit qui eruat. / 30 Et sonabit super eum in die illa sicut
sonitus maris. / Aspiciet in terram: et ecce tenebrae tribulationis, / et lux obtenebrata est in caligine eius.
[6] 1 In anno, quo mortuus est rex Ozias, vidi Dominum edentem super solium excelsum et elevatum;
et fimbriae eius replebant templum. 2 Seraphim stabant iuxta eum; sex alae uni et sex alae alteri: duabus
velabat faciem suam et duabus velabat pedes suos et duabus volabat. 3 Et clamabat alter ad alterum et
dicebat: «Sanctus, Sanctus, Sanctus Dominus exercituum; / plena est omnis terra gloria eius». 4 Et
commota sunt superliminaria cardinum a voce clamantis, et domus repleta est fumo. 5 Et dixi: «Vae

The Lord calls Isaiah

6 1 *In the year that King Uzziah died I saw the Lord sitting upon
a throne, high and lifted up; and his train filled the temple.
2 Above him stood the seraphim; each had six wings: with two he
covered his face, and with two he covered his feet, and with two
he flew. 3 And one called to another and said:
"Holy, holy, holy is the LORD of hosts;
the whole earth is full of his glory."
4 And the foundations of the thresholds shook at the voice of him
who called, and the house was filled with smoke. 5 And I said:
"Woe is me! For I am lost; for I am a man of unclean lips, and I
dwell in the midst of a people of unclean lips; for my eyes have
seen the King, the LORD of hosts!"
6 Then flew one of the seraphim to me, having in his hand a
burning coal which he had taken with tongs from the altar. 7 And
he touched my mouth, and said: "Behold, this has touched your
lips; your guilt is taken away, and your sin forgiven." 8 And I heard

2 Kings 15:7
Rev 4:2
Ezek 1:11; 10:21
Num 14:21
Rev 4:8
Ex 19:16; 40:34–35; 1 Kings 8:10–12; Jn 12:41
Ex 3:6; 4:10; 6:30; 33:20
Judg 6:22; 13:22; Jer 1:6
Jer 1:9; Dan 10:16; Rev 8:3
Ex 4:10–13
Jer 1:6

6:1–13. As an introduction to what is called the "Book of Immanuel" (7:1—12:6) we get this account of how the Lord called Isaiah to be a prophet, sending him to his people at the time of the Syrian–Ephraimite coalition to explain to them what is going on and how they should act.

The account begins with a theophany (vv. 1–4), which is one of the key points in this book's message. God manifests himself seated in the manner of eastern kings, surrounded by his angelic court (the "seraphim"), who extol the holiness of the Lord: he clearly is Lord of all. In this vision, God is depicted as the thrice holy (v. 3), the highest form of superlative available in Hebrew. Being holy implies standing apart—standing above everything else. God stands far above all other beings, and he is their creator. In Hebrew "holy" includes the idea of "sacred". It means that God has none of the limitations and imperfections that created beings have.

The holiness and majesty of God fill Isaiah with a sense of his own uncleaness and that of his people (v. 5). Typically, visions of God in biblical history induce feelings of fear in the seer; we even see this in the angel's announcement to Mary (cf. Lk 1:30): "Do not be afraid, Mary, for you have found favour with God." "Faced with God's fascinating and mysterious presence, man discovers his own insignificance. Before the burning bush, Moses takes off his sandals and veils his face (cf. Ex 3:5–6) in the presence of God's

mihi, quia perii! / Quia vir pollutus labiis ego sum / et in medio populi polluta labia habentis ego habito / et regem, Dominum exercituum, vidi oculis meis». 6 Et volavit ad me unus de seraphim, et in manu eius calculus, quem forcipe tulerat de altari, 7 et tetigit os meum et dixit: «Ecce tetigit hoc labia tua, / et auferetur iniquitas tua, / et peccatum tuum mundabitur». 8 Et audivi vocem Domini dicentis: «Quem mittam? Et quis ibit nobis?». Et dixi: «Ecce ego, mitte me». / 9 Et dixit: «Vade, et dices populo huic:

Mt 13:14–15 par.; Jn 12:40 Acts 28:26–27

the voice of the Lord saying, "Whom shall I send, and who will go
for us?" Then I said, "Here am I! Send me." [9]And he said, "Go,
and say to this people:

'Hear and hear, but do not understand;
see and see, but do not perceive.'

---

holiness. Before the glory of the thrice-holy God, Isaiah cries out: 'Woe is me! I am lost; for I am a man of unclean lips' (Is 6:5). Before the divine signs wrought by Jesus, Peter exclaims: 'Depart from me, for I am a sinful man, O Lord' (Lk 5:8). But because God is holy, he can forgive the man who realizes that he is a sinner before him: 'I will not execute my fierce anger ... for I am God and not man, the Holy One in your midst (Hos 11:9)'" (*Catechism of the Catholic Church*, 208).

Isaiah is cleansed and consoled as soon as he humbly acknowledges his unworthiness and insignificance before God (vv. 6–7). His instinctive sense of fear is immediately replaced by a generous and trusting response on the prophet's part: he is ready to do what God wants (v. 8). "In their 'one to one' encounters with God the prophets draw light and strength for their mission. Their prayer is not flight from this unfaithful world, but rather attentiveness to the Word of God. At times their prayer is an argument or a complaint, but it is always an intercession that awaits and prepares for the intervention of the Saviour God, the Lord of history (cf. Amos 7:2, 5; Is 6:5, 8, 11; Jer 1:6; 15:15–18; 20:7–18)" (*Catechism of the Catholic Church*, 2584).

Finally, the Lord entrusts him with his mission. The message he is to deliver is hard-hitting and full of paradoxes (vv. 9–10). The task given him is not, as one might at first think, to render the people incapable of hearing and understanding the word of God that could move their hearts. It is, rather, to tell them that if they fail to listen to the word of God, their hearts will be blinded: they will not be able to see things right and, because of that, the sinner will feel no need to take stock of his position and be converted. The Synoptic Gospels interpret Jesus' preaching as a fulfilment of what is said here in vv. 9–10 (Mt 13:13–15; Mk 4:11–12). The Gospel of St John sees these same words as anticipating what will happen to those who reject Jesus' message: "Therefore they could not believe. For Isaiah again said, 'He has blinded their eyes and hardened their heart, lest they should see with their eyes and perceive with their heart, and turn for me to heal them.' Isaiah said this because he saw his glory and spoke of him" (Jn 12:27–41). And St Paul also uses vv. 9–10 to reproach the Jews of Rome for rejecting the Good News of salvation in Christ which he is proclaiming to them (cf. Acts 28:23–28).

The people's hardness of heart will merit severe punishment; cities and houses will be laid waste, but all will not be lost: a holy seed will remain and from it the tree will grow back again (vv.

"Audientes audite et nolite intellegere, / et videntes videte et nolite cognoscere". / [10]Pingue redde cor populi huius / et aures eius aggrava / et oculos eius excaeca, / ne forte videat oculis suis / et auribus suis

10 Make the heart of this people fat,
and their ears heavy,
and shut their eyes;
lest they see with their eyes,
and hear with their ears,
and understand with their hearts,
and turn and be healed."
11 Then I said, "How long, O Lord?" And he said:
"Until cities lie waste
without inhabitant,
and houses without men,
and the land is utterly desolate,
12 and the LORD removes men far away,
and the forsaken places are many in the midst of the land.
13 And though a tenth remain in it,
it will be burned again,

11–13). These verses carry a message for people in all ages. Isaiah approaches God in all humility, showing him every reverence, and at the same time he puts his trust in God. For his part, the Lord cleanses his chosen ones and sends them out to help in his work of salvation. Origen, who commented on this passage a number of times, points out: "May burning coals be brought from the altar of heaven to burn my lips. If the burning coals of the Lord touch my lips, they will be purified; and when they are purified and cleansed of all sin, [...] my mouth will be opened to the Word of God and I will not utter another impure word [...]. The seraphim who was sent to purify the prophet's lips did not purify the lips of the people [...]; therefore, they continued to live in sin, and now they deny the Lord Jesus Christ and curse him from their unclean mouths. For my part, I pray that the seraphim will come to cleanse my lips" (*Homiliae in Isaiam*, 1, 4). All we need is the same humble docility that Isaiah had: "Having received the grace of God, he did not want it to be a gift granted to him to no avail, without being put to work in everything that needed to be done. Seeing the seraphim and the Lord of hosts seated on high, on his throne of glory, he said: 'Woe is me ...'. By speaking thus and making himself 'unworthy', he received the help of God because He took into account his humility" (ibid., 6:2). And St John Chrysostom, commenting on Isaiah's response to God, says that the prophet shows readiness to carry out his mission to the people because "since the saints are friends of God, they, too, love all men dearly" (*In Isaiam*, 6, 5).

audiat / et corde suo intellegat et convertatur / et sanetur». 11Et dixi: «Usquequo, Domine?». Et dixit: «Donec desolentur / civitates absque habitatore, / et domus sine homine, / et terra relinquatur deserta». / 12Et longe adducet Dominus homines, / et magna erit desolatio in medio terrae; / 13et adhuc in ea

like a terebinth or an oak,
whose stump remains standing
when it is felled."
The holy seed is its stump.

D. THE BOOK OF IMMANU-EL*

The sign of Immanu-el

2 Kings 16:1–6 **7** [1]In the days of Ahaz the son of Jotham, son of Uzziah, king of
Judah, Rezin the king of Syria and Pekah the son of Remaliah
the king of Israel came up to Jerusalem to wage war against it, but
they could not conquer it. [2]When the house of David was told,
"Syria is in league with Ephraim," his heart and the heart of his
people shook as the trees of the forest shake before the wind.
2 Kings 20:20–21 [3]And the LORD said to Isaiah, "Go forth to meet Ahaz, you and
Shear-jashub[h] your son, at the end of the conduit of the upper pool
on the highway to the Fuller's Field, [4]and say to him, 'Take heed,

---

***7:1—12:6.** This series of oracles and narratives is usually known as the "Book of Immanuel", because its climax is taken to be the mysterious announcement of a Messiah-Saviour, called "Immanu-el", which means "God-with-us" (7:14). This "book" is one of the most interesting parts of First Isaiah. Some scholars include in the "book", as its introduction, the prophet's vision of God in majesty, and the account of Isaiah's calling (6:1–13).

The Immanuel prophecy begins with the announcement of a God-given "sign" of salvation—the "virgin" who will conceive and bear a "son" (7:1—8:22). The "son" is described in such a way that he seems to be no ordinary human child (8:23—9:6). Paradoxically, the joy of salvation that has just been proclaimed is then immediately clouded by announcements about the wrath of God, the collapse of Samaria and the Assyrian threat to Jerusalem (9:7—10:19). But, as often happens in Isaiah, we are told that a "remnant" will be saved, a "shoot from the stump of Jesse" (11:1), that is, a descendant of David on whom "the Spirit of the Lord will rest" (11:2), and that a kingdom of righteousness and peace will emerge and the exiles will return home (10:20—11:16). This leads the prophet to intone a short psalm of thanksgiving (12:1–6).

decimatio, / et rursus excisioni tradetur / sicut terebinthus et sicut quercus, / in quibus deiectis manebit aliquid stabile. / Semen sanctum erit id quod steterit in ea. **[7]** [1]Et factum est in diebus Achaz filii Ioatham filii Oziae regis Iudae, ascendit Rasin rex Syriae et Phacee filius Romeliae rex Israel in Ierusalem ad proeliandum contra eam; et non potuerunt debellare eam. [2]Et nuntiaverunt domui David dicentes: «Requievit Syria super Ephraim». Et commotum est cor eius et cor populi eius, sicut moventur ligna silvarum a facie venti. [3]Et dixit Dominus ad Isaiam: «Egredere in occursum Achaz, tu et Seariasub (id est Reliquiae revertentur) filius tuus, ad extremum aquaeductus piscinae superioris in viam agri fullonis; [4]et dices ad eum: Vide, ut sileas; noli timere, et cor tuum ne formidet a duabus

h. That is *A remnant shall return*

be quiet, do not fear, and do not let your heart be faint because of
these two smouldering stumps of firebrands, at the fierce anger of
Rezin and Syria and the son of Remaliah. [5]Because Syria, with
Ephraim and the son of Remaliah, has devised evil against you,
saying, [6]"Let us go up against Judah and terrify it, and let us
conquer it for ourselves, and set up the son of Tabe-el as king in
the midst of it," [7]thus says the Lord GOD:

It shall not stand,
and it shall not come to pass.
[8]For the head of Syria is Damascus,
and the head of Damascus is Rezin.
(Within sixty-five years Ephraim will be broken to pieces so
that it will no longer be a people.)
[9]And the head of Ephraim is Samaria, Is 28:16;
and the head of Samaria is the son of Remaliah. 30:15
If you will not believe,
surely you shall not be established.'"

7:1–9. After the account of Isaiah's vocation, where we heard that a hardened heart is unable to hear the word of the Lord (cf. 6:9–10), we are now given evidence to that effect. Isaiah has a meeting with King Ahaz, in which the king is in two minds as to what to do in the face of pressure to join the coalition against the Assyrians made up of Israel (here also called Ephraim), whose capital was Samaria, and Syria (Aram), the capital of which was Damascus. Verse 6 mentions Tabe-el, about whom nothing more is known; he may have been a senior official in the Southern kingdom who was in favour of joining the coalition. The prophet's message warns Judah that it should put its trust in God, believing in his word, and not try to take refuge in any political alliance, be it with the Syrians and Ephraimites, or with Assyria. It ends abruptly with the threat that if Ahaz and his supporters fail to listen, their downfall will soon follow (vv. 7–9). The narrative says that a son of Isaiah is present at his exchange with Ahaz—Shear-jashub (v. 3), a name full of symbolism, for it means "a remnant shall return". The presence of this son implies, in some way, that God will ensure the permanent survival of the people: there will always be some, a remnant, who will come back to the Lord and recover what has been lost (cf. 10:20–22).

caudis titionum fumigantium istorum, ob ardorem irae Rasin et Syriae et filii Romeliae, [5]eo quod consilium malum inierit contra te Syria, Ephraim et filius Romeliae dicentes: [6]"Ascendamus ad Iudam et terrorem iniciamus ei et avellamus eum ad nos et ponamus regem in medio eius filium Tabeel"». [7]Haec dicit Dominus Deus: «Non stabit et non erit! / [8]Caput enim Syriae Damascus, / et caput Damasci Rasin; / et adhuc sexaginta et quinque anni / et desinet Ephraim esse populus; / [9]et caput Ephraim Samaria, / et caput Samariae filius Romeliae. / Si non credideritis, non permanebitis». [10]Et

2 Kings 19:29 [10]Again the LORD spoke to Ahaz, [11]"Ask a sign of the LORD
Deut 6:16 your God; let it be deep as Sheol or high as heaven." [12]But Ahaz
said, "I will not ask, and I will not put the LORD to the test." [13]And
Is 9:5 he said, "Hear then, O house of David! Is it too little for you to
Mic 5:2 weary men, that you weary my God also? [14]Therefore the Lord
Mt 1:23 himself will give you a sign. Behold, a young woman[i*] shall
Lk 1:27–31 conceive and bear[j] a son, and shall call his name Immanu-el.[k]
Is 7:22 [15]He shall eat curds and honey when he knows how to refuse the
Deut 1:39 evil and choose the good. [16]For before the child knows how to
1 Kings 3:9 refuse the evil and choose the good, the land before whose two
kings you are in dread will be deserted. [17]The LORD will bring
upon you and upon your people and upon your father's house such
days as have not come since the day that Ephraim departed from
Judah—the king of Assyria."

7:10–17. Even though the king did not listen, the Lord offers him a sign that he has no reason to fear the threats made by the kings of Israel and Syria: a maiden will conceive and bear a son, who will be called Immanuel; within a few years, before the boy reaches the age of reason, the two kingdoms that Ahaz fears will be laid low, and Judah will enjoy even greater prosperity than it had prior to the Assyrian threat.

The prophet's words, which at the time and taken literally would have been easy enough for the protagonists to understand, can have further significance: and as Revelation develops this becomes clearer. Verse 14 has three elements in it which, taken separately and together, can be read as a sign of peace and salvation—the mother, the child, and his name, "Immanuel". The mother is a maiden, that is, a young woman who has had no children previously. This could refer to the young wife of Ahaz or to some other young woman. In any event, by setting her pregnancy in the context of a sign given to the king, the point is that something quite important is involved. It is not surprising, therefore, that, to stress this, later interpreters, particularly those who translated the text into Greek in the second century BC, translated the Hebrew word for "young woman" into the Greek word for "virgin". Later, the evangelists St Matthew (Mt 1:23) and St Luke (Lk 1:26–31) indicated that the virginity of Mary was the sign that her son was the Messiah, the true God with us, who brings salvation.

adiecit Dominus loqui ad Achaz dicens: [11]«Pete tibi signum a Domino Deo tuo in profundum inferni
sive in excelsum supra». [12]Et dixit Achaz: «Non petam et non tentabo Dominum». [13]Et dixit: «Audite
ergo, domus David; numquid parum vobis est molestos esse hominibus, quia molesti estis et Deo meo?
[14]Propter hoc dabit Dominus ipse vobis signum. Ecce, virgo concipiet et pariet filium et vocabit nomen
eius Emmanuel; [15]butyrum et mel comedet, ut ipse sciat reprobare malum et eligere bonum. [16]Quia
antequam sciat puer reprobare malum et eligere bonum, desolabitur terra, cuius tu formidas duos reges;
[17]adducet Dominus super te et super populum tuum et super domum patris tui dies, qui non venerunt a
diebus separationis Ephraim a Iuda, regem Assyriorum».

i. Or *virgin* **j.** Or *is with child and shall bear* **k.** That is *God is with us*

The child, the son, is the most significant part of the sign. If the prophecy refers to the son of Ahaz, the future King Hezekiah, it would be indicating that his birth will be a sign of divine protection, because it will mean that the dynasty will continue. If it refers to another child, not yet known, the prophet's words would mean that the child's birth could manifest hope that "God was going to be with us", and his reaching the age of discretion (v. 16) would indicate the advent of peace; the child's birth would, then, be the sign that "God is with us". In the New Testament, the deeper meaning of these words find fulfilment: Mary is Virgin and Mother, and her Son is not a symbol of God's protection but God himself who dwells among us.

The word "Immanuel" is a prophetic indication of the revelation that the child's birth implies, just as the names of Isaiah's sons also contain revelation—Shear-jashub, which means "a remnant shall return" (7:3), and Maher-shalal-hash-baz, meaning "the spoil speeds, the prey hastens" (8:1–3). In the New Testament, the name conveys the joyful news that Jesus is truly "God with us".

Christian tradition has treated this Isaian oracle with great reverence: "Learn from the prophet himself how all this could come to pass. Does it, perhaps, follow the laws of nature? Absolutely not, replies the prophet: *Behold, a virgin....* What a miracle! A virgin will become a mother and remain a virgin! [...] It is fitting that he who enters into human life to save all mankind [...] should be born of a woman of perfect integrity who has given herself wholly to Him" (St Gregory of Nyssa, *In diem natalem Christi*, 1136).

Therefore, expounding the Church's interpretation, the Second Vatican Council has this to say: "The Holy Scriptures of both the Old and the New Testament, as well as ancient Tradition, show the role of the Mother of the Saviour in the economy of salvation in an ever clearer light and draw attention to it. The books of the Old Testament describe the history of salvation, by which the coming of Christ into the world was slowly prepared. These earliest documents, as they are read in the Church and are understood in the light of a further and full revelation, bring the figure of the woman, Mother of the Redeemer, into a gradually clearer light. When it is looked at in this way, she is already prophetically foreshadowed in the promise of victory over the serpent which was given to our first parents after their fall into sin (cf. Gen 3:15). Likewise she is the Virgin who shall conceive and bear a son, whose name will be called Immanuel (Is 7:14; Mic 5:2–3; Mt 1:22–23). She stands out among the poor and humble of the Lord, who confidently hope for and receive salvation from Him. With her the exalted Daughter of Sion, and after a long expectation of the promise, the times are fulfilled and the new economy established, when the Son of God took a human nature from her, that He might in the mysteries of His flesh free man from sin" (*Lumen gentium*, 55).

The fact that the oracle was spoken in a specific historical context does not

Threat of invasions

[18]In that day the LORD will whistle for the fly which is at the sources of the streams of Egypt, and for the bee which is in the land of Assyria. [19]And they will all come and settle in the steep

mean that it does not have a more transcendental, that is, messianic meaning; in the light of salvation history, past events should be read as part of God's plan of salvation and of its climax, the advent of Jesus Christ. Only by adopting this viewpoint can we see that what happened in the Old Testament, taken as a whole, and many of the stages in it, are a prophecy of New Testament events, a "preparation for the Gospel". Therefore, a Christian reading of the text, which in a way enjoys "hindsight" and gives a messianic interpretation to the Immanuel oracle, is perfectly compatible with its literal meaning.

The words of the prophet, which find fulfilment in Christ, have been given many lovely spiritual interpretations: "This Immanuel, born of the Virgin, eats curds and honey, and asks each of us to provide him with the curds that he eats [...]. Our good deeds, our sweet and noble words, are the honey eaten by the Immanuel, born of the Virgin [...]. For truly he consumes our good words and intentions and actions, and feeds us, in turn, with a spiritual food that is greater and divine. As soon as we realize that to welcome the Saviour is a blessing, and open wide the doors of our hearts, we will prepare for him the 'honey' and all his feast, and he will bring us to the great feast of the Father in the kingdom of heaven, that is in Christ Jesus" (Origen, *Homiliae in Isaiam*, 2, 2).

7:18–25. Four oracles beginining with the words "In that day" are positioned here, perhaps because they refer to themes connected with this section of the book They probably refer to the Assyrian campaigns that laid waste the land of Judah, leading eventually to a siege of Jerusalem.

The first oracle (vv. 18–19) speaks of the threat of devastation by foreign armies. This may refer to constant harassment by Egypt or, more likely, the imminent attack by Assyria.

In the second (v. 20) Assyria is compared to a "hired razor"—a sarcastic reference to the help sought by Ahaz from that quarter (cf. 2 Kings 16:8). "The River" is the Euphrates.

However, the third oracle (vv. 21–22) is a call to rely totally on the Lord. It speaks of "curds and honey" (v. 22) as the Immanuel prophecy does (cf. 7:15). Despite the food shortage caused by the devastation of farmland, the Lord will provide plenty of delicious food for the "remnant" left in the land; the country will be built up again by these people.

The fourth oracle (vv. 23–25) paints a bleak picture of the havoc that the Assyrian armies will cause.

[18]Et erit in die illa: / sibilabit Dominus muscae, / quae est in extremo fluminum Aegypti, / et api, quae est in terra Assur; / [19]et venient et requiescent omnes / in vallibus praeruptis / et in cavernis petrarum / et in omnibus frutetis / et in omnibus pascuis. / [20]In die illa radet Dominus / in novacula conducta e

ravines, and in the clefts of the rocks, and on all the thornbushes,
and on all the pastures.
[20]In that day the Lord will shave with a razor which is hired
beyond the River—with the king of Assyria—the head and the
hair of the feet, and it will sweep away the beard also.
[21]In that day a man will keep alive a young cow and two sheep;
[22]and because of the abundance of milk which they give, he will
eat curds; for every one that is left in the land will eat curds and
honey.
[23]In that day every place where there used to be a thousand Is 5:10
vines, worth a thousand shekels of silver, will become briers and
thorns. [24]With bow and arrows men will come there, for all the
land will be briers and thorns; [25]and as for all the hills which used Is 5:17
to be hoed with a hoe, you will not come there for fear of briers
and thorns; but they will become a place where cattle are let loose
and where sheep tread.

Assyria conspires against Israel and Judah

8 [1]Then the LORD said to me, "Take a large tablet and write upon 2 Kings
it in common characters, 'Belonging to Maher-shalal-hash- 16:10–16;
baz.'"[l] [2]And I got reliable witnesses, Uriah the priest and 18:2

8:1–20. The Assyrian threat continues to concern the inhabitants of Jerusalem. There are some who favour joining the alliance formed by Rezin of Damascus and the king of Samaria, but the prophet warns that that will be no protection against the Assyrians (vv. 5–8). Pacts made by men will fail, unless they take account of God (vv. 8c–10). On the other hand, nothing will go wrong if they put all their trust in the Lord: he is the only one to dread and reverence (vv. 11–15). Verse 14 will be used by St Paul to make the point that if Israel did not find righteousness it was because it did not seek it through faith in God, but instead relied on its own efforts (cf. Rom 9:31–33). The Letter to the Hebrews (Heb 2:13) applies the words of vv. 17–18, according to the Greek text, to Jesus Christ, who bore in his flesh his own sufferings and those of the rest of men, whom he can therefore call his brothers. All these considerations are

regione trans flumen / —in rege Assyriorum— / caput et pilos pedum / et barbam quoque abradet. / [21]Et erit in die illa: / nutriet homo vitulam et duas oves / [22]et prae ubertate lactis / comedet butyrum; / butyrum enim et mel manducabit omnis, / qui relictus fuerit in medio terrae. / [23]Et erit in die illa: / omnis locus, ubi fuerint mille vites mille argenteis, / spinae et vepres erunt. / [24]Cum sagittis et arcu ingredientur illuc, / vepres enim et spinae erit universa terra. / [25]Et in omnes montes, qui in sarculo sarriebantur, / nemo veniet prae terrore spinarum et veprium, / et erit in pascua bovis et in conculcationem pecoris. **[8]** [1]Et dixit Dominus ad me: «Sume tibi tabulam grandem et scribe in ea stilo hominis: Maher Salal Has Baz (*id est Velociter spolia detrahe, cito praedare*). [2]Et adhibui mihi

l. That is *The spoil speeds, the prey hastes*

Zechariah the son of Jeberechiah, to attest for me. 3And I went to
the prophetess, and she conceived and bore a son. Then the LORD
Is 7:16 said to me, "Call his name Maher-shalal-hash-baz; 4for before the
child knows how to cry 'My father' or 'My mother,' the wealth of
Damascus and the spoil of Samaria will be carried away before
Is 7:1–2 the king of Assyria."
Neh 3:15 Jn 9:7 5The LORD spoke to me again: 6"Because this people have
refused the waters of Shiloah that flow gently, and melt in fear
Rev 12:15 before[m] Rezin and the son of Remaliah; 7therefore, behold, the
Lord is bringing up against them the waters of the River, mighty
and many, the king of Assyria and all his glory; and it will rise
Is 7:14 over all its channels and go over all its banks; 8and it will sweep
on into Judah, it will overflow and pass on, reaching even to the
neck; and its outspread wings will fill the breadth of your land, O
Immanu-el."

9Be broken, you peoples, and be dismayed;
give ear, all you far countries;
gird yourselves and be dismayed;
Is 7:14 gird yourselves and be dismayed.
Mt 1:23 10Take counsel together, but it will come to nought;
speak a word, but it will not stand,
for God is with us.[x]

---

set within narrative passages (vv. 1–4 and 16–20). The first (vv. 1–4) has to do with a symbolic action of Isaiah's—writing down at the Lord's bidding the name of "Maher-shalal-hash-baz", which means "the spoil speeds, the prey hastens", and giving this name to one of his sons, the meaning being that those who pressure the king of Judah to join the alliance against Assyria will soon fall prey to the Assyrians. The second narrative section (vv. 16–20) has to do with the prophet himself asserting the authority of his testimony, which is the equivalent of his vouching for the word of God that promises the survival of the people and of Jerusalem; witness, in particular, the names, the meaning of the names of Isaiah's two sons (v. 18; cf. 7:3). God is faithful, and he cannot disappoint his own by failing to keep his promises; it would be

testes fideles, Uriam sacerdotem et Zachariam filium Barachiae; 3et accessi ad prophetissam, et concepit et peperit filium». Et dixit Dominus ad me: «Voca nomen eius Maher Salal Has Baz, 4quia antequam sciat puer clamare: "Pater mi" et "Mater mea", afferentur opes Damasci et spolia Samariae coram rege Assyriorum». 5Et adiecit Dominus loqui ad me adhuc dicens: 6«Pro eo quod abiecit populus iste aquas Siloae, / quae vadunt cum silentio, / et defecit coram Rasin et filio Romeliae, / 7propter hoc ecce Dominus adducet super eos / aquas Fluminis fortes et multas, / regem Assyriorum et omnem gloriam eius, / et ascendet super omnes rivos eius / et fluet super universas ripas eius; / 8et ibit

m. Cn: Heb *rejoices in* **x.** Heb *immanu el*

11For the LORD spoke thus to me with his strong hand upon me,
and warned me not to walk in the way of this people, saying:
12"Do not call conspiracy all that this people call conspiracy, and *1 Pet 3:14,15*
do not fear what they fear, nor be in dread. 13But the LORD of
hosts, him you shall regard as holy; let him be your fear, and let
him be your dread. 14And he will become a sanctuary, and a stone *Rom 9:33* 1 Pet 2:8
of offence, and a rock of stumbling to both houses of Israel, a trap
and a snare to the inhabitants of Jerusalem. 15And many shall
stumble thereon; they shall fall and be broken; they shall be snared
and taken."

16Bind up the testimony, seal the teaching among my disciples.
17I will wait for the LORD, who is hiding his face from the house of Is 1:26; 7:3;
Jacob, and I will hope in him. 18Behold, I and the children whom the 8: 3–4
LORD has given me are signs and portents in Israel from the LORD of *Heb 2:13*
hosts, who dwells on Mount Zion. 19And when they say to you,
"Consult the mediums and the wizards who chirp and mutter,"
should not a people consult their God? Should they consult the
dead on behalf of the living? 20To the teaching and to the testimony! Surely for this word which they speak there is no dawn.

---

absurd, as well as idolatrous, to have recourse to mediums and wizards, as pagans do (vv. 19–20).

8:21–22. The fear caused by news of Assyria's growing strength increased even more once Judah began to feel its effects. This passage seems to refer to the deportation of the Galileans by Tiglath-pileser III in 732. Very succinctly it describes the distress of those who make their way into exile and can see for themselves the havoc caused by their enemies all over their country. This depressing panorama will be offset by the joyful oracle that follows.

per Iudam inundans et diffluens, / usque ad collum veniet. / Et erit extensio alarum eius / implens
latitudinem terrae tuae, o Emmanuel». / 9Clamorem tollite, populi, et consternemini; / et audite,
universae procul terrae: / accingimini et perterremini, / accingimini et perterremini. / 10Inite consilium,
et dissipabitur; / loquimini verbum, et non fiet, / quia nobiscum Deus. 11Haec enim ait Dominus ad me,
cum apprehendit me manu et monuit, ne irem in via populi huius, dicens: 12«Ne vocetis coniurationem,
/ quodcumque populus iste vocat coniurationem, / et timorem eius ne timeatis neque paveatis». /
13Dominum exercituum ipsum sanctificate: / ipse pavor vester, et ipse terror vester; / 14et erit in
sanctuarium, / in lapidem offensionis et in petram scandali / duabus domibus Israel, / in laqueum et
in insidias habitantibus Ierusalem. / 15Et offendent ex eis plurimi / et cadent et conterentur / et
irretientur et capientur. 16Liga testimonium, signa legem in discipulis meis. 17Et exspectabo Dominum,
qui abscondit faciem suam a domo Iacob, et praestolabor eum. 18Ecce ego et pueri, quos dedit mihi
Dominus in signum et in portentum Israel a Domino exercituum, qui habitat in monte Sion. 19Et cum
dixerint ad vos: «Quaerite a pythonibus et a divinis, qui susurrant et murmurant; numquid non populus
a deo suo requiret, pro vivis a mortuis?». 20Ad legem et ad testimonium! Quod si non dixerint iuxta
verbum hoc, non erit eis matutina lux. 21Et transibit per eam afflictus et esuriens; / et, cum esurierit,
irascetur / et maledicet regi suo et deo suo / et suspiciet sursum / 22et ad terram intuebitur: / et ecce
tribulatio et tenebrae, / caligo opprimens et obscuritas diffusa. / 23Non erit enim amplius caligo, / ubi

Anguish caused by early defeats

21They will pass through the land,[n] greatly distressed and hungry;
and when they are hungry, they will be enraged and will curse[o]
their king and their God, and turn their faces upward; 22and they
will look to the earth, but behold, distress and darkness, the gloom
of anguish; and they will be thrust into thick darkness.

The prince of Peace

Mt 4:13–16 9[p] 1But there will be no gloom for her that was in anguish. In
the former time he brought into contempt the land of Zebulun
and the land of Naphtali, but in the latter time he will make
glorious the way of the sea, the land beyond the Jordan, Galilee of
the nations.

Mt 4:13–16 2[q]The people who walked in darkness
LK 1: 79 have seen a great light;
Jn 8:12 those who dwelt in a land of deep darkness,
Eph 5:8,14 on them has light shined.

9:1–17. At this point, though not yet very clearly, we begin to see the figure of King Hezekiah, who, unlike his father Ahaz, was a pious man who put all his trust in the Lord. After Galilee was laid waste by Tiglath-pileser III of Assyria, and its population subsequently deported (cf. 8:21–22), Hezekiah of Judah would reconquer that region, which would recover its splendour for a period. All this gave grounds for hope again.

This oracle may have a connexion with the Immanuel prophecy (7:1–17), and the child with messianic prerogatives that has been born (cf. 9:6–7) could be the child that Isaiah prophesied about (cf. 7:14). For this reason, 9:1–7 is seen as the second oracle of the Immanuel cycle. This "child" that is born, the son given to us, is a gift from God (9:6), because it is a sign that God is present among his people. The Hebrew text attributes four qualities to the child which seem to embrace all the typical features of Israel's illustrious forebears—the wisdom of Solomon (cf. 1 Kings 3: "Wonderful Counsellor"), the prowess of David (cf. 1 Sam 7: "Mighty God"), the administrative skills of Moses (cf. Ex 18:13–26) as liberator, guide and father of the people (cf. Deut 34:10–12), ("Everlasting Father"), and the virtues of the early patriarchs, who made peace pacts (cf. Gen 21:22–34; 26:15–35; 23:6), ("Prince of peace"). In the old Latin Vulgate, the translation gave six features ("*Admirabilis, Consiliarius, Deus, Fortis, Pater futuri saeculi,*

erat oppressio. Primo tempore contemptibilem reddidit terram Zabulon et terram Nephthali; et novissimo glorificavit viam maris, trans Iordanem, Galilaeam gentium. **[9]** 1Populus, qui ambulabat in tenebris, / vidit lucem magnam; / habitantibus in regione umbrae mortis / lux orta est eis. / 2Multiplicasti exsultationem / et magnificasti laetitiam; / laetantur coram te / sicut laetantes in messe,

n. Heb *it* **o.** Or *curse by* **p.** Ch 8:23 in Heb **q.** Ch 9:1 in Heb

[3]Thou hast multiplied the nation,
thou hast increased its joy;
they rejoice before thee
as with joy at the harvest,
as men rejoice when they divide the spoil.
[4]For the yoke of his burden,
and the staff for his shoulder,
the rod of his oppressor,
thou hast broken as on the day of Midian.
[5]For every boot of the tramping warrior in battle tumult
and every garment rolled in blood
will be burned as fuel for the fire.
[6]For to us a child is born,
to us a son is given;
and the government will be upon his shoulder,
and his name will be called
"Wonderful Counsellor, Mighty God,
Everlasting Father, Prince of Peace."*

Ps 126

Is 10:25–26; 14:25
Judg 7:15–25

Gen 3:15; 49:10
Num 24:17
Deut 34:10–12
2 Sam 7:12–16
Judg 13:18
Mt 28:18
Lk 2:11; Mic 5:1–3
Zech 9:9

Princeps pacis"); these have found their way into the liturgy. The New Vulgate has reverted to the Hebrew text. Either way, what we have here are titles that Semite nations applied to the reigning monarch; but, taken together, they go far beyond what befitted Hezekiah or any other king of Judah. Therefore, Christian tradition has interpreted them as being appropriate only for Jesus. St Bernard, for example, explains the justification for these names as follows: "He is *Wonderful* in his birth, *Counsellor* in his preaching, *God* in his works, *Mighty* in the Passion, *Everlasting Father* in the resurrection, and *Prince of Peace* in eternal happiness" (*Sermones de diversis*, 53, 1).

Because these names are applied to Jesus, the short-term conquest of Galilee by Hezekiah is seen as being only an announcement of the definitive salvation brought about by Christ. In the Gospels we find echoes of this oracle in a number of passages that refer to Jesus. When Luke narrates the Annunciation by the angel to Mary (Lk 1:31–33) we hear that the son that she will conceive and give birth to will receive "the throne of his father David and he will reign over the house of Jacob for ever; and of his kingdom there shall be no end" (Lk 1:32b–33; cf. Is 9:7). And in the account about the shepherds of Bethlehem, they are told that "to you is born this day in the city

/ sicut exsultant, quando dividunt spolia. / [3]Iugum enim oneris eius / et virgam umeri eius / et sceptrum exactoris eius / fregisti, sicut in die Madian. / [4]Quia omnis caliga incedentis cum tumultu / et vestimentum mixtum sanguine / erit in combustionem, cibus ignis. / [5]Parvulus enim natus est nobis, / filius datus est nobis; / et factus est principatus super umerum eius; / et vocabitur nomen eius / admirabilis Consiliarius, Deus fortis, / Pater aeternitatis, Princeps pacis. / [6]Magnum erit eius imperium, / et pacis non erit finis / super solium David et super regnum eius, / ut confirmet illud et corroboret in

Jer 23:5 Lk 1:32–33; 2:11–12: 14

[7]Of the increase of his government and of peace
there will be no end,
upon the throne of David, and over his kingdom,
to establish it, and to uphold it
with justice and with righteousness
from this time forth and for evermore.
The zeal of the LORD of hosts will do this.

The pride of the people of Ephraim

Is 55:10–11

[8]The Lord has sent a word against Jacob,
and it will light upon Israel;
[9]and all the people will know,
Ephraim and the inhabitants of Samaria,
who say in pride and in arrogance of heart:
[10]"The bricks have fallen,
but we will build with dressed stones;
the sycamores have been cut down,
but we will put cedars in their place."

---

of David a Saviour, who is Christ the Lord ..." (Lk 2:11–12; cf. Is 9:6). St Matthew sees the beginning of Jesus' ministry in Galilee (Mt 4:12–17) as the fulfilment of this Isaian oracle (cf. Is 9:1): the lands that in the prophet's time were laid waste and saw ethnic cleansing and transplantation were the first to receive the light of salvation from the Messiah.

9:8—10:4. This is an uncompromising oracle against Israel, the Northern kingdom. The lands of Ephraim and Manasseh, and their capital Samaria, were being harassed by the Assyrians, but that was only the start of a chain of events that led to the utter destruction of the kingdom.

Each stanza ends with the same refrain: "For all this his anger is not turned away and his hand is stretched out still" (9:12, 17, 21; 10:4), to make the point that what befalls them is due to their impiety and to the fact that they have not turned back to God. The oracle begins with a reference to the people's arrogance, for which they are castigated by an invasion by Syrians and Philistines (9:8–12), and it goes on to describe the obduracy of the country's leaders: not even those without resources (whom at other times God's mercy and love protect) will escape punishment now (9:13–17). In the wake of this come anarchy and civil strife (9:18–21). The oracle ends by decrying unjust lawgivers and those who sin against social justice (10:1–4).

iudicio et iustitia / amodo et usque in sempiternum: / zelus Domini exercituum faciet hoc. / [7]Verbum misit Dominus in Iacob, et cecidit in Israel. / [8]Et sciet omnis populus Ephraim et habitantes Samariam / in superbia et magnitudine cordis dicentes: / [9]«Lateres ceciderunt, sed quadris lapidibus aedificabimus; / sycomori succisae sunt, sed cedris commutabimus». / [10]Et elevavit Dominus hostes super eum / et inimicos eius excitavit, / [11]Syriam ab oriente et Philisthim ab occidente, / qui

11 So the LORD raises adversaries[r] against them,
and stirs up their enemies.
12 The Syrians on the east and the Philistines on the west
devour Israel with open mouth.
For all this his anger is not turned away
and his hand is stretched out still.

Prov 30:14
Jer 10:25; Mic 3:3; Hab 1:13

13 The people did not turn to him who smote them,
nor seek the LORD of hosts.
14 So the LORD cut off from Israel head and tail,
palm branch and reed in one day—
15 the elder and honoured man is the head,
and the prophet who teaches lies is the tail;
16 for those who lead this people lead them astray,
and those who are led by them are swallowed up.
17 Therefore the Lord does not rejoice over their young men,
and has no compassion on their fatherless and widows;
for every one is godless and an evildoer,
and every mouth speaks folly.
For all this his anger is not turned away
and his hand is stretched out still.

Is 5:25
Jer 5:3–6
Amos 4:6–11
Hos 7:10–15

18 For wickedness burns like a fire,
it consumes briers and thorns;
it kindles the thickets of the forest,
and they roll upward in a column of smoke.
19 Through the wrath of the LORD of hosts
the land is burned,
and the people are like fuel for the fire;
no man spares his brother.
20 They snatch on the right, but are still hungry,
and they devour on the left, but are not satisfied;

---

devoraverunt Israel toto ore. / In omnibus his non est aversus furor eius, / sed adhuc manus eius extenta.
/ 12Et populus non est reversus ad percutientem se, / et Dominum exercituum non inquisierunt. / 13Et
succidit Dominus ab Israel caput et caudam, / palmam et arundinem die una: / 14longaevus et
honorabilis vultu ipse est caput, / et propheta docens mendacium ipse est cauda; / 15rectores populi
istius seducentes / et, qui regebantur, perierunt. / 16Propter hoc super adulescentulis eius non laetabitur
Dominus / et pupillorum eius et viduarum non miserebitur, / quia omnis impius est et nequam, / et
universum os loquitur stultitiam. / In omnibus his non est aversus furor eius, / sed adhuc manus eius
extenta. / 17Succensa est enim quasi ignis impietas, / veprem et spinam vorat, / et succenditur in
densitate saltus, / et convolvuntur columnae fumi. / 18In ira Domini exercituum incenditur terra; / et est
populus quasi esca ignis: / vir fratri suo non parcit. / 19Et devorat ad dexteram et esurit / et comedit ad
sinistram et non saturatur; / unusquisque carnem proximi sui vorat: / 20Manasses Ephraim, et Ephraim

r. Cn: Heb *the adversaries of Rezin*

each devours his neighbour's[s] flesh,
Mic 7:2,6 21 Manasseh Ephraim, and Ephraim Manasseh,
and together they are against Judah.
For all this his anger is not turned away
and his hand is stretched out still.

10 [1]Woe to those who decree iniquitous decrees,
Ex 22:21 and the writers who keep writing oppression,
Is 1:17,23; [2]to turn aside the needy from justice
3:14; 5:23 and to rob the poor of my people of their right,
that widows may be their spoil,
Jer 5:31 and that they may make the fatherless their prey!
Hos 9:7 [3]What will you do on the day of punishment,
Lk 19:44 in the storm which will come from afar?
To whom will you flee for help,
and where will you leave your wealth?
[4]Nothing remains but to crouch among the prisoners
or fall among the slain.
For all this his anger is not turned away
and his hand is stretched out still.

Assyria condemned

Is 14:24–27 [5]Ah, Assyria, the rod of my anger,
the staff of my fury![t]

10:5–19. The prophet sees the Assyrians' doings as evidence of God's control over the fate of nations: Assyria is the rod that the Lord uses to punish his people for their unfaithfulness (cf. vv. 5–6). The *Catechism of the Catholic Church* uses this passage from Isaiah, and others from Holy Scripture, to point out that "we see the Holy Spirit, the principal author of Sacred Scripture, often attributing actions to God without mentioning any secondary causes. This is not a 'primitive mode of speech', but a profound way of recalling God's primacy and absolute Lordship over history and the world (cf. Is 10:5–15; 45:5–7; Deut 32:39; Sir 11:14)" (no. 304). However, Assyria went beyond its brief,

Manassen, / simul ipsi contra Iudam. / In omnibus his non est aversus furor eius, / sed adhuc manus eius extenta. **[10]**[1]Vae, qui condunt leges iniquas / et scribentes iniustitiam scribunt, / [2]ut opprimant in iudicio pauperes / et vim faciant causae humilium populi mei, / ut fiant viduae praeda eorum, / et pupillos diripiant! / [3]Quid facietis in die visitationis / et calamitatis de longe venientis? / Ad cuius confugietis auxilium / et ubi derelinquetis gloriam vestram? / [4]Nam incurvabimini subter captivos / et infra occisos cadetis. / In omnibus his non est aversus furor eius, / sed adhuc manus eius extenta. / [5]Vae Assur, virga furoris mei / et baculus in manu mea, indignatio mea! / [6]Ad gentem impiam mitto eum /

s. Tg Compare Gk: Heb *the flesh of his arm* **t.** Heb *a staff it is in their hand my fury*

[6]Against a godless nation I send him,
and against the people of my wrath I command him,
to take spoil and seize plunder,
and to tread them down like the mire of the streets.
[7]But he does not so intend,
and his mind does not so think;
but it is in his mind to destroy,
and to cut off nations not a few;
[8]for he says:
"Are not my commanders all kings?
[9]Is not Calno like Carchemish?
Is not Hamath like Arpad?
Is not Samaria like Damascus?
[10] As my hand has reached to the kingdoms of the idols
whose graven images were greater than those of Jerusalem
and Samaria,
[11] shall I not do to Jerusalem and her idols
as I have done to Samaria and her images?"

Is 47:6
Jer 34:22
Zech 1:15

2 Kings 18:34
Is 36:18–20

[12]When the Lord has finished all his work on Mount Zion and
on Jerusalem he[u] will punish the arrogant boasting of the king of

2 Kings 19:35–37

---

by treating Judah the same way it did pagan nations: it did not realize that its strength was on loan from God, and it took pride in its own might: v. 9 carries a list of important cities captured by the Assyrians (vv. 7–11). So, in due course, God will judge and humble their pride (vv. 12–18); Assyria will be reduced to a shadow of its former glory.

There is a call here to acknowledge that God is Lord of human affairs, and to be docile to his purposes (cf. vv. 15–16). The sin of pride is denounced, for it involves arrogating to oneself what belongs to God, and putting oneself in God's place. Therefore, reading the spiritual meaning of the passage, Origen notices that it applies to every sinner: "Every evildoer makes an idol of what he desires, and serves his sin; by melting down the work of a craftsman's hands and sculpting the idol in secret, he becomes subject to its curse. We make many idols in the depths of our hearts when we sin" (*Homiliae in Isaiam*, 8, 1).

et contra populum furoris mei mando illi, / ut auferat spolia et diripiat praedam / et ponat illum in conculcationem / quasi lutum platearum. / [7]Ipse autem non sic arbitratur, / et cor eius non ita existimat; / sed in corde suo ad conterendum / et ad internecionem gentium non paucarum. / [8]Dicet enim: «Numquid non principes mei omnes reges sunt? / [9]Numquid non ut Charcamis sic Chalano? / Numquid non ut Arphad sic Emath? / Numquid non ut Damascus sic Samaria? / [10]Quomodo apprehendit manus mea regna idololatra, / quorum simulacra plura sunt quam in Ierusalem et in Samaria, / [11]numquid non sicut feci Samariae et idolis eius, / sic faciam Ierusalem et simulacris eius?» [12]Et erit: cum impleverit

u. Heb *I*

Assyria and his haughty pride. 13For he says:
Deut 8:17 "By the strength of my hand I have done it,
and by my wisdom, for I have understanding;
I have removed the boundaries of peoples,
and have plundered their treasures;
like a bull I have brought down those who sat on thrones.
14 My hand has found like a nest
the wealth of the peoples;
and as men gather eggs that have been forsaken
so I have gathered all the earth;
and there was none that moved a wing,
or opened the mouth, or chirped."

Is 45:9 Rom 9:20–21 15 Shall the axe vaunt itself over him who hews with it,
or the saw magnify itself against him who wields it?
As if a rod should wield him who lifts it,
or as if a staff should lift him who is not wood!
16 Therefore the Lord, the LORD of hosts,
will send wasting sickness among his stout warriors,
and under his glory a burning will be kindled,
like the burning of fire.
Is 37:36 17 The light of Israel will become a fire,
and his Holy One a flame;
and it will burn and devour
his thorns and briers in one day.
18 The glory of his forest and of his fruitful land
the LORD will destroy, both soul and body,
and it will be as when a sick man wastes away.
19 The remnant of the trees of his forest will be so few
that a child can write them down.

Dominus cuncta opera sua in monte Sion et in Ierusalem, visitabo super fructum superbiae cordis regis
Assyriae et super arrogantiam altitudinis oculorum eius. 13Dixit enim: «In fortitudine manus meae feci
/ et in sapientia mea, prudens sum enim; / et abstuli terminos populorum / et scrinia eorum depraedatus
sum / et detraxi quasi potens in sublimi sedentes; / 14et apprehendit quasi nidum manus mea
fortitudinem populorum; / et sicut colliguntur ova derelicta, / sic universam terram ego congregavi, / et
non fuit qui moveret pennam aut aperiret os et ganniret». / 15Numquid gloriabitur securis / contra eum,
qui secat in ea? / Aut exaltabitur serra / contra eum, qui trahit eam? / Quomodo si agitet virga elevantem
eam, / et exaltet baculus eum, qui non est lignum. / 16Propter hoc mittet Dominator, Dominus
exercituum, / in pingues eius tenuitatem; / et subtus gloriam eius / ardor ardebit quasi combustio ignis.
/ 17Et erit Lumen Israel ignis, / et Sanctus eius flamma; / et succendetur et devorabit spinas eius / et
vepres in die una. / 18Et gloriam saltus eius et horti eius / ab anima usque ad carnem consumet, / et erit
sicut aeger tabescens; / 19et reliquiae ligni saltus eius / tam paucae erunt, / ut puer scribat ea. / 20Et erit
in die illa: / non adiciet residuum Israel / et, qui effugerint de domo Iacob, / inniti super eo, qui percutit
eos, / sed innitentur super Dominum, / Sanctum Israel, in veritate. / 21Reliquiae revertentur, / reliquiae,
inquam, Iacob, ad Deum fortem. / 22Si enim fuerit populus tuus, Israel, quasi arena maris, / reliquiae

The remnant of Israel

20In that day the remnant of Israel and the survivors of the house Is 7:3
of Jacob will no more lean upon him that smote them, but will 2 Chron 30:6
lean upon the LORD, the Holy One of Israel, in truth. 21A remnant Is 4:3
will return, the remnant of Jacob, to the mighty God. 22For though *Rom 9:27*
your people Israel be as the sand of the sea, only a remnant of
them will return. Destruction is decreed, overflowing with
righteousness. 23For the Lord, the LORD of hosts, will make a full
end, as decreed, in the midst of all the earth.
24Therefore thus says the Lord, the LORD of hosts: "O my Is 14:24–27; 30:27–33;
people, who dwell in Zion, be not afraid of the Assyrians when 31:4–9;
they smite with the rod and lift up their staff against you as the 37:22–29
Egyptians did. 25For in a very little while my indignation will Ex 14:16,
come to an end, and my anger will be directed to their destruction. 26–27; Judg
26And the LORD of hosts will wield against them a scourge, as 7:25; 20:45–47 Is 9:3
when he smote Midian at the rock of Oreb; and his rod will be Mic 1:10–15
over the sea, and he will lift it as he did in Egypt. 27And in that

---

10:20–34. Unlike the insignificant remnant of Assyria (cf. 10:19), the "remnant" of Israel will be saved and restored to vitality (cf. 4:3; 7:3). It is not a remainder which will eventually disappear, but a pruned vine which, at the right time, will grow again and bear much fruit .

There is, of course, no escaping what the prophet is saying; he is warning Judah of what awaits them—an exemplary punishment (vv. 20–23); the only ones to survive it will be those who rely on the Lord and who do not expect any succour from those who inflict the punishment (v. 20); that is, the survivors will be those who listen to the warning that the Lord gave Ahaz through Isaiah: "If you will not believe, surely you shall not be established," that is, shall not survive (7:9). The Assyrians are moving down from the north and levelling every city in their path between Samaria and Jerusalem (vv. 27–32), but Judah must bear with all this, because it will not go on for long and God will intervene on behalf of his people, just as he came to the rescue of their ancestors in earlier times of crisis (vv. 33–34).

Verse 22 (Septuagint) is quoted explicitly by St Paul in Romans 9:27 to support what he has to say about the election of Israel and the call of the Gentiles to salvation in the context of the mystery of predestination.

revertentur ex eo; / consummatio decreta redundat in iustitia: / 23interitum enim, qui decretus est, / Dominus, Deus exercituum, faciet in medio omnis terrae. / 24Propter hoc haec dicit Dominus, Deus exercituum: «Noli timere, populus meus habitator Sion, ab Assur; in virga percutiet te et baculum suum levabit super te sicut Aegyptus. 25Adhuc enim paululum modicumque, et consummabitur indignatio et furor meus ad destructionem eorum». 26Et suscitabit super eum Dominus exercituum flagellum iuxta plagam Madian in Petra Oreb et virgam suam super mare et levabit eam sicut in Aegypto. 27Et erit in die illa: / auferetur onus eius de umero tuo, / et iugum eius de collo tuo. / Et vastator ascendit a

day his burden will depart from your shoulder, and his yoke will
be destroyed from your neck."
He has gone up from Rimmon,[v]
1 Sam 14:5 28 he has come to Aiath;
he has passed through Migron,
at Michmash he stores his baggage;
1 Sam 1:19; 14:2,16; 15:34 29 they have crossed over the pass,
at Geba they lodge for the night;
Ramah trembles,
Gibe-ah of Saul has fled.
Jer 1:1 30 Cry aloud, O daughter of Gallim!
Hearken, O Laishah!
Answer her, O Anathoth!
31 Madmenah is in flight,
the inhabitants of Gebim flee for safety.
1 Sam 21:2 32 This very day he will halt at Nob,
he will shake his fist
at the mount of the daughter of Zion,
the hill of Jerusalem.

33 Behold, the Lord, the LORD of hosts
will lop the boughs with terrifying power;
the great in height will be hewn down,
and the lofty will be brought low.
34 He will cut down the thickets of the forest with an axe,
and Lebanon with its majestic trees[w] will fall.

Num 11:17 Judg 3:10 1 Sam 16:13 1 Kings 5:26 Ps 72:1; Is 9:5; 42:1–12 Jer 23:5; Mt 3:16; Rom 15:12; Rev 22:16

The new descendant of David

11 1 *There shall come forth a shoot from the stump of Jesse,
and a branch shall grow out of his roots.

11:1–9. This passage, which is regarded as the third Immanuel oracle, has two parts to it. The first (vv. 1–5) announces that the shoot will spring from the stump of Jesse (David's father) at some future date. The second (vv. 6–9)

Remmon. / 28 Veniet in Aiath, transibit per Magron, / apud Machmas deponit sarcinas suas; / 29 transeunt vadum cursim; in Geba pernoctabimus; / trepidat Rama, Gabaa Saulis fugit. / 30 Hinni voce tua, Bathgallim; / attende, Laisa; responde, Anathoth. / 31 Migrat Medemena, habitatores Gabim fugiunt; / 32 hodie in Nob stabit: / agitabit manum suam ad montem filiae Sion, / collem Ierusalem. / 33 Ecce Dominator, Dominus exercituum, / amputat ramos in terrore, / et extrema acumina succiduntur, / et sublimes humiliantur; / 34 et caeduntur condensa saltus ferro, / et Libanus cum excelsis suis cadet. **[11]** 1 Et egredietur virga de stirpe Iesse, / et flos de radice eius ascendet; / 2 et requiescet super eum

v. Cn: Heb *and his yoke from your neck, and a yoke will be destroyed because of fatness* **w.** Cn Compare Gk Vg: Heb *with a majestic one*

[2]And the Spirit of the LORD shall rest upon him,
the spirit of wisdom and understanding,
the spirit of counsel and might,
the spirit of knowledge and the fear of the LORD.*
[3]And his delight shall be in the fear of the LORD.

Ex 31:3
Deut 34:9
Jn 3:34
1 Pet 4:14

Jn 7:24

He shall not judge by what his eyes see,
or decide by what his ears hear;
[4]but with righteousness he shall judge the poor,
and decide with equity for the meek of the earth;
and he shall smite the earth with the rod of his mouth,
and with the breath of his lips he shall slay the wicked.
[5]Righteousness shall be the girdle of his waist,
and faithfulness the girdle of his loins.

Ps 2:9; 72:2
Mic 4:6
2 Thess 2:8
Rev 19:11–15

Eph 6:14

---

describes the good things associated with his reign, using imagery to do with messianic peace: creation will be restored to its state of original justice.

The first part is a formal announcement of the accession of a new king in the line of David—humble, because he comes from a tree that has been pruned yet has all the vitality of a tender shoot. It refers to a future king ("there shall come …") and not the reigning monarch. The new king will be endowed with exceptional qualities that equip him to rule, thanks to the Holy Spirit who will descend upon him. The divine Spirit is an inner strength, a gift that God gives to key figures in salvation history to enable them to accomplish a difficult and dangerous mission—Moses (cf. Num 11:17), the judges (cf. 3:10; 6:34) and David (1 Sam 16:13). The new descendent of David will rule over the people not in a heavy-handed way like the kings of the time, but with a charismatic dynamism that comes from God. Six gifts of the Spirit are mentioned, in pairs—wisdom and understanding, referring to the skill and prudence that ensure that he will judge rightly; counsel and fortitude, the characteristics of an astute strategist like David; knowledge and the fear of the Lord, which have to do with the religious sphere, for the king must not forget that he is God's representative.

The second part describes very beautifully the messianic peace that will flower with this new "shoot". It paints a panorama of the harmony that reigned at the dawn of creation, only to be broken by sin. Even among wild beasts violence will disappear. No longer will man in his pride desire to be "like God, knowing good and evil" (Gen 3:5); instead he will be filled with the divine gift of the "knowledge of the

spiritus Domini: / spiritus sapientiae et intellectus, / spiritus consilii et fortitudinis, / spiritus scientiae et timoris Domini; / [3]et deliciae eius in timore Domini. / Non secundum visionem oculorum iudicabit / neque secundum auditum aurium decernet; / [4]sed iudicabit in iustitia pauperes / et decernet in aequitate pro mansuetis terrae; / et percutiet terram virga oris sui / et spiritu labiorum suorum interficiet impium. / [5]Et erit iustitia cingulum lumborum eius, / et fides cinctorium renum eius. / [6]Habitabit lupus

Is 65:25 [6]The wolf shall dwell with the lamb,
and the leopard shall lie down with the kid,
and the calf and the lion and the fatling together,
and a little child shall lead them.
[7]The cow and the bear shall feed;
their young shall lie down together;
and the lion shall eat straw like the ox.
[8]The sucking child shall play over the hole of the asp,
and the weaned child shall put his hand on the adders den.
Job 5:23 [9]They shall not hurt or destroy
Is 2:4; 40:5 in all my holy mountain;
Jer 31,33–34 for the earth shall be full of the knowledge of the LORD
Hab 2:14 as the waters cover the sea.

Lord" (v. 9). The "child", mentioned twice (vv. 6, 8) is not directly connected with the child-king of the oracle found in 9:6 or with the Immanuel (7:14); however, in the mind of the prophet they must have had many points of contact, given the reference to the child having a leadership role (v. 6).

The image of the "shoot" from the royal line who will bring peace has been interpreted in Christian tradition as finding fulfilment in Jesus Christ. St Thomas Aquinas read this passage as referring to Christ, who brought about the restoration of mankind; he points out: "First, the birth of Christ the 'restorer', is spoken of (v. 1); then, his holiness (vv. 2–9) and his dignity (v. 10) are described" (*Expositio super Isaiam*, 11). And John Paul II comments: "Alluding to the coming of a mysterious personage, which the New Testament revelation will identify with Jesus, Isaiah connects his person and mission with a particular action of the Spirit of God—the Spirit of the Lord. These are the words of the Prophet: "There shall come forth a shoot from the stump of Jesse, and a branch shall grow out of his roots. And *the Spirit of the Lord shall rest upon him*, the spirit of wisdom and understanding, the spirit of counsel and might, the spirit of knowledge and the fear of the Lord. And his delight shall be the fear of the Lord" (Is 11:1–3). This text is important for the whole pneumatology of the Old Testament, because it constitutes a kind of bridge between the ancient biblical concept of 'spirit,' understood primarily as a 'charismatic breath of wind', and the 'Spirit' as a person and as a gift, a gift for the person. The Messiah of the lineage of David ('from the stump of Jesse') is precisely that person upon whom the Spirit of the Lord 'shall rest'. It is obvious that in this case one cannot yet speak of a revelation of the Paraclete.

---

cum agno, / et pardus cum haedo accubabit; / vitulus et leo simul saginabuntur, / et puer parvulus minabit eos. / [7]Vitula et ursus pascentur, / simul accubabunt catuli eorum; / et leo sicut bos comedet paleas. / [8]Et ludet infans ab ubere / super foramine aspidis; / et in cavernam reguli, / qui ablactatus fuerit, manum suam mittet. / [9]Non nocebunt et non occident / in universo monte sancto meo, / quia

The return of the exiles

[10]In that day the root of Jesse shall stand as an ensign to the peoples; him shall the nations seek, and his dwellings shall be glorious. Rom 15:12 Rev 5:5; 22:16

[11]In that day the Lord will extend his hand yet a second time to recover the remnant which is left of his people, from Assyria, from Egypt, from Pathros, from Ethiopia, from Elam, from Shinar, from Hamath, and from the coastlands of the sea.

However, with this veiled reference to the figure of the future Messiah there begins, so to speak, the path towards the full revelation of the Holy Spirit in the unity of the Trinitarian mystery, a mystery which will finally be manifested in the New Covenant" (*Dominum et Vivificantem*, 15).

A Christian reading of these words finds in them a reference to the action of the Holy Spirit in souls; the "spirits" that repose in the Messiah; are stable "gifts" through which the Holy Spirit acts. There are six of these gifts, according to the Hebrew text (which the New Vulgate and the RSV follow). The Greek translation of the Septuagint and the Vulgate divide the gift of fear into two—piety and fear of the Lord. That is why catechesis and theology speak of there being seven gifts: "The seven *gifts* of the Holy Spirit are wisdom, understanding, counsel, fortitude, knowledge, piety and fear of the Lord. They belong in their fullness to Christ, Son of David (cf. Is 11:1–2). They complete and perfect the virtues of those who receive them. They make the faithful docile in readily obeying divine inspirations" (*Catechism of the Catholic Church*, 1831).

11:10—12:6. The first big section of the book of Isaiah (1:2—12:6), which began by describing a time of deep crisis, with Judah brought to ruin and Jerusalem under siege (1:2–23), ends now with words of joy and praise to the Lord, who saves and restores his people. After the times of crisis, the people's infidelities, stern warnings from the prophet, and the fear and destruction sown by the armies of Assyria, a "remnant" will return in triumph and joy to the land that God gave them. The four stanzas in this passage look forward to "that day" (cf. 11:10, 11; 12:1, 4), thereby setting the glorious fulfilment of the promises of salvation in an eschatological context. The first two stanzas may be an addition inserted in the Persian period (fifth century BC), when the Babylonian exiles had already returned but there were still many Jews scattered abroad.

The Lord, who had stretched out his hand to punish their infidelities (cf. 5:26; 9:12, 17, 21; 10:4), will extend it once more in order to rescue his people (11:11) from all the countries where they were dispersed and reunite all the tribes (Pathros refers to Upper Egypt; Elam, to an area in south-eastern Iran; Shinar, to Babylon; Hamath, to a city in

plena erit terra scientia Domini, sicut aquae mare operiunt. / [10]In die illa radix Iesse / stat in signum populorum; / ipsam gentes requirent, / et erit sedes eius gloriosa. / [11]Et erit in die illa: rursus extendet

Is 5:26; 27:13 Jer 49:36

12 He will raise an ensign for the nations,
and will assemble the outcasts of Israel,
and gather the dispersed of Judah
from the four corners of the earth.

Syria; and the coastlands were islands in the Aegean Sea, mainly). As they make their way home, they will sense that God is with them, just as their ancestors did when they left Egypt and journeyed to the promised land (cf. 11:11–16).

The Church sees herself in this "remnant" who have experienced God's salvation and she feels called to bear witness to her joy before all mankind. "Therefore," says Vatican II, "all sons of the Church should have a lively awareness of their responsibility to the world; they should foster in themselves a truly catholic spirit; they should spend their forces in the work of evangelization. And yet, let everyone know that their first and most important obligation for the spread of the Faith is this: to lead a profoundly Christian life. For their fervor in the service of God and their charity toward others will cause a new spiritual wind to blow for the whole Church, which will then appear as a sign lifted up among the nations (cf. Is. 11:12), 'the light of the world' (Matt. 5:14) and 'the salt of the earth' (Matt. 5:13)" (*Ad gentes*, 36).

Christians are very conscious of the fact that the Church and her children come under God's protection: "The strength and the power of God light up the face of the earth. The Holy Spirit is present in the Church of Christ for all time, so that it may be, always and in everything, a sign raised up before all nations, announcing to all men the goodness and the love of God. In spite of our great limitations, we can look up to heaven with confidence and joy: God loves us and frees us from our sins. The presence and the action of the Holy Spirit in the Church are a foretaste of eternal happiness, of the joy and peace for which we are destined by God" (St Josemaría Escrivá, *Christ Is Passing By*, 128).

Verses 12–16 are really a little psalm of thanksgiving and praise to God, an appropriate colophon to the prophecies in the "Book of Immanuel" (7:1—12:6). At the centre of the hymn we find the "salvation" (vv. 2, 3) promised by God the Holy One of Israel (v. 6; cf. 6:3) in these chapters. St Jerome writes: "The one who was called Immanuel, first, now strips himself of all his wealth and hastens to hand over all the spoils of war that he has won, and he is given other names, too, so that it can be seen that he is none other than the one of whom Gabriel spoke in his annunciation to the Virgin (cf. Lk 1:31). He is called Saviour, and all must drink the waters that flow from his source" (*Commentarii in Isaiam*, 12, 1). In his commentary, St Cyril of Alexandria

Dominus manum suam / ad possidendum residuum populi sui, / quod relictum erit ab Assyria et ab Aegypto / et a Phatros et ab Aethiopia / et ab Elam et a Sennaar / et ab Emath et ab insulis maris; / [12]et levabit signum in nationes / et congregabit profugos Israel / et dispersos Iudae colliget a quattuor plagis

[13] The jealousy of Ephraim shall depart,
and those who harass Judah shall be cut off;
Ephraim shall not be jealous of Judah,
and Judah shall not harass Ephraim.
[14] But they shall swoop down upon the shoulder of the Philistines in the west, Jer 49:2
and together they shall plunder the people of the east.
They shall put forth their hand against Edom and Moab,
and the Ammonites shall obey them.

---

identified these springs of water with the person of Christ: "The water is the life-giving word of God, the springs are the apostles and the evangelists and the prophets themselves; but, above all, Christ is the source of salvation" (*Commentarius in Isaiam*, 12, 3) The words of v. 3 were used as the title of Pius XII's encyclical on devotion to the Sacred Heart of Jesus: "The words with which Isaiah symbolically foretells the many, great gifts that the messianic era would produce in the world spring immediately to our lips if we cast our minds back over the one hundred years since our predecessor Pius IX, in response to the desires of the multitude of Catholics everywhere, commanded that the feast of the Sacred Heart of Jesus be celebrated in the Church throughout the world. The adoration of Christ's Sacred Heart is the source of innumerable graces: it purifies the soul, fills it with supernatural consolation, moves it to strive to attain all the virtues. In considering the words of St James, *Every good endowment and every perfect gift is from above, coming down from the Father of lights* (Jas 1:17), we are given cause to remember how much this worship of the inestimable gift of the Incarnate Word, our divine Saviour and the only Mediator of grace between God the Father and his children, which is universal and ever more fervent, and which was given by God to the Church, His mystical Spouse, has helped her to overcome great difficulties in the many trials she has suffered over the course of recent centuries. It is thanks to this great gift that the Church can show more fully her love for her Divine Founder, and fulfill more faithfully the exhortation that St John the evangelist recorded from the lips of our Lord Jesus Christ himself: *On the last day of the feast, the great day, Jesus stood up and proclaimed, 'If any one thirst, let him come to me and drink. He who believes in me, as the scripture has said, "'Out of his heart shall flow rivers of living water.*"' Now this he said about the Spirit, which those who believed in him were to receive (Jn 7:37–39)" (*Haurietis aquas*, 1).

terrae. / [13]Et auferetur zelus Ephraim, / et hostes Iudae abscindentur; / Ephraim non aemulabitur Iudam, et Iudas non pugnabit contra Ephraim. / [14]Et volabunt in umeros Philisthim ad mare, / simul praedabuntur filios orientis: / in Edom et Moab extendent manus suas, / et filii Ammon oboedient eis.

Zech 10:11 15 And the LORD will utterly destroy
the tongue of the sea of Egypt;
and will wave his hand over the River
with his scorching wind,
and smite it into seven channels
that men may cross dryshod.
Ex 14:22 16 And there will be a highway from Assyria
Is 35:8 for the remnant which is left of his people,
as there was for Israel
when they came up from the land of Egypt.

12 1 You will say in that day:
"I will give thanks to thee, O LORD,
for though thou wast angry with me,
thy anger turned away,
and thou didst comfort me.

Ex 15:2 2 "Behold, God is my salvation;
I will trust, and will not be afraid;
for the LORD GOD is my strength and my song,
and he has become my salvation."

Is 55:1
Jn 4:1 3 With joy you will draw water from the wells of salvation.
Ps 105:1 4 And you will say in that day:
"Give thanks to the LORD,
call upon his name;
make known his deeds among the nations,
proclaim that his name is exalted.

5 "Sing praises to the LORD, for he has done gloriously;
let this be known[x] in all the earth.
6 Shout, and sing for joy, O inhabitant of Zion,
for great in your midst is the Holy One of Israel."

/ 15 Et exsiccabit Dominus linguam maris Aegypti / et levabit manum suam super flumen in fortitudine spiritus sui / et percutiet illud in septem rivos, / ita ut transire faciat eos calceatos. / 16 Et erit via residuo populo meo, / qui relinquetur ab Assyria, / sicut fuit Israeli in die illa, / qua ascendit de terra Aegypti. **[12]** 1 Et dices in die illa: / «Confitebor tibi, Domine, / quoniam cum iratus eras mihi, / conversus est furor tuus, et consolatus es me. / 2 Ecce Deus salutis meae; / fiducialiter agam et non timebo, / quia fortitudo mea et laus mea Dominus, / et factus est mihi in salutem». / 3 Et haurietis aquas in gaudio de fontibus salutis. / 4 Et dicetis in die illa: / «Confitemini Domino et invocate nomen eius, / notas facite in populis adinventiones eius; / mementote quoniam excelsum est nomen eius. / 5 Cantate Domino, quoniam magnifice fecit; / notum sit hoc in universa terra. / 6 Exsulta et lauda, quae habitas in Sion, /

x. Or *this is made known*

2. ORACLES CONCERNING FOREIGN NATIONS*

Oracle against Babylon

Is 21:1–10; 47:1–15 Jer 50–51 Rev 17–18

13 [1]The oracle concerning Babylon which Isaiah the son of Amoz saw.

[2]On a bare hill raise a signal,
cry aloud to them;
wave the hand for them to enter
the gates of the nobles.
[3]I myself have commanded my consecrated ones, Joel 2:11
have summoned my mighty men to execute my anger,
my proudly exulting ones.

***13:1—23:18.** The second section of the first part of the book of Isaiah comprises a collection of oracles addressed to foreign nations. In the form which it has come down to us, it has a definite unity of style. The oracles are not arranged in chronological order but, instead, are grouped according to nation.

This section has many parallels in other prophetical books, especially Amos, Jeremiah and Ezekiel. The events that the oracles deal with in fact occurred over a considerable period of time (some two centuries), reaching down to when the Babylonian empire was overrun by Cyrus the Great, king of the Medes and Persians.

The oracles are addressed to Babylon (13:1—14:23), Assyria (14:24–27), the Philistines (14:28–32), Moab (15:1—16:14), Damascus and Ephraim (17:1–4), Ethiopia (18:1–7), Egypt (19:1—20:6), Babylon again (21:1–10) and finally Dumah (21:1–12), and Arabia (21:13–17). There is also an oracle against Jerusalem itself (22:1–14), and another, exceptionally, against an individual, Shebna (22:15–25). At the end comes an oracle against Tyre (23:1–18).

The theological message of this section is a clear one: God is the Lord of human affairs. Sometimes he uses the nations as an instrument of his wrath to punish the chosen people for their rebellions and sins. But he also judges and denounces the various foreign nations for the cruelty and arrogance with which they have carried out God's purposes. Despite all their sins and all the misfortunes his people meet, God will save them; and what is more, and seemingly impossible, he will bring about the conversion of the nations (cf. 19:12–25).

13:1—14:23. The first two oracles are directed against Babylon (13:1–22 and 14:4–23). They are later in time than many other oracles in this section, but they are put first perhaps because the Babylonian exile was the worst mis-

quia magnus in medio tui Sanctus Israel». **[13]** [1]Oraculum Babylonis, quod vidit Isaias filius Amos. / [2]Super montem decalvatum levate signum, / exaltate vocem, levate manum, / et ingrediantur portas ducum. / [3]Ego mandavi sanctificatis meis / et vocavi fortes meos ad iram meam, / exsultantes in gloria

[4]Hark, a tumult on the mountains
as of a great multitude!
Hark, an uproar of kingdoms,
of nations gathering together!
The LORD of hosts is mustering
a host for battle.
[5]They come from a distant land,
from the end of the heavens,
the LORD and the weapons of his indignation,
to destroy the whole earth.

---

fortune to befall Judah—and the one that had most far-reaching consequences. These pieces must date from around the end of the Babylonian empire, when Babylon still enjoyed the glory (13:19) that it would later lose forever (13:20–22). The two oracles are separated by a short prose passage meant to explain them: the Lord will have mercy on his people, he will grant them peace, and the people of Israel will come to rule those who oppressed them (14:1–3).

Chapter 13:1–22 is an oracle about the destruction of Babylon at the hands of the Medes (13:17), a people that joined forces with the Persians to attack that empire. The prophet predicts that the Medes will be used by God to lay waste to Babylon. He paints an appalling picture of the "day of the Lord" (13:6), that is, the day when this will happen. After announcing that this day will come, the oracle says that even the stars in the sky will play their part (vv. 9–13) and Babylon will meet a terrible end (vv. 14–22).

Verses 4–23 of chapter 14 are a satirical poem against the (already vanquished: 13:5–21) king of Babylon including a colophon in prose (vv. 22–23). Both passages could refer to any king of Babylon. The "mount of assembly" and the "far north" are allusions to the Babylonian mythical notion of the dwelling-place of the gods.

In 14:12 Isaiah refers to the king of Babylon as "Day Star". The Latin, following the Greek, has "lucifer", "the bearer of light", that is, the planet Venus. Jesus' words in Luke 10:18, "I saw Satan fall like lightning from heaven," may be an allusion to this passage of Isaiah, meaning the downfall of the devil that results from the establishment of the Kingdom of God. For this reason, the Fathers of the Church saw in these two texts (Is 14: 12 and Lk 10:18) a sign that the devil fails in his rebellion against God. Ever since the middle ages "Lucifer" has been used as a name for the devil. In line with this interpretation, which takes "Sheol" (14:15) to be the place of the damned, St Bernard reflects on how terrible hell is, in order to move people to conversion while there is still time: "Lord! What a difference there is between a cloak of precious jewels and one of

mea. / [4]Vox multitudinis in montibus quasi populi ingentis, / vox sonitus regnorum gentium congregatarum. / Dominus exercituum recenset militiam belli; / [5]veniunt de terra procul a termino caeli,

[6]Wail, for the day of the LORD is near;
as destruction from the Almighty it will come!
[7]Therefore all hands will be feeble,
and every man's heart will melt,
[8]and they will be dismayed.
Pangs and agony will seize them;
they will be in anguish like a woman in travail.
They will look aghast at one another;
their faces will be aflame.

Ezek 20:2–3
Joel 1:15
Amos 5:18
Zeph 1:17
Rev 6:17

Is 21:3; 26:17
Jer 4:31

[9]Behold, the day of the LORD comes,
cruel, with wrath and fierce anger,
to make the earth a desolation
and to destroy its sinners from it.
[10]For the stars of the heavens and their constellations
will not give their light;
the sun will be dark at its rising
and the moon will not shed its light.
[11]I will punish the world for its evil,
and the wicked for their iniquity;
I will put an end to the pride of the arrogant,
and lay low the haughtiness of the ruthless.
[12]I will make men more rare than fine gold,
and mankind than the gold of Ophir.
[13]Therefore I will make the heavens tremble,
and the earth will be shaken out of its place,

Mic 4:1

Ezek 32,7
Joel 3:4; 4:15
Amos 8:9
Mt 24:29
Mk 13:24

Lam 1:12
Hag 2:6

---

worms, between the delights of paradise and the misery of hell! I know that hell is reserved for the devil and his servants, and for all men who become like them; hell is an eternal unmaking, an endless death, an unbearable torment. Descend, now, in this life, into hell; open the eyes of your soul to the den of pain, and flee then from the sin and vice that cause the eternal death of sinners and evildoers. Learn to hate sin and to love the Law of the Lord; from the terrifying stall [of hell] buy your hatred of sin" (*Sermones de diversis*, 42, 6).

/ Dominus et vasa furoris eius, / ut disperdat omnem terram. / [6]Ululate, quia prope est dies Domini; / quasi vastitas a Domino veniet. / [7]Propter hoc omnes manus dissolventur, / et omne cor hominis tabescet. / [8]Perterrebuntur. / Torsiones et dolores tenebunt eos, / quasi parturiens dolebunt; / unusquisque ad proximum suum stupebit: / facies combustae vultus eorum. / [9]Ecce dies Domini venit, / crudelis et indignationis plenus / et irae furorisque, / ad ponendam terram in solitudinem, / et peccatores eius conteret de ea. / [10]Quoniam stellae caeli et sidera eius / non expandent lumen suum; / obtenebratus est sol in ortu suo, / et luna non splendebit in lumine suo. / [11]Et visitabo super orbem propter mala / et super impios propter iniquitatem eorum; / et quiescere faciam superbiam protervorum / et arrogantiam fortium humiliabo. / [12]Pretiosior erit vir auro, / et homo mundo obryzo. / [13]Super hoc

at the wrath of the LORD of hosts
in the day of his fierce anger.
Jer 50:16 14 And like a hunted gazelle,
or like sheep with none to gather them,
every man will turn to his own people,
and every man will flee to his own land.
Jer 51:20–23 15 Whoever is found will be thrust through,
and whoever is caught will fall by the sword.
Hos 10:14 16 Their infants will be dashed in pieces
Nahum 3:10 before their eyes;
Zech 14:2 their houses will be plundered
and their wives ravished.

17 Behold, I am stirring up the Medes against them,
who have no regard for silver
and do not delight in gold.
18 Their bows will slaughter the young men;
they will have no mercy on the fruit of the womb;
their eyes will not pity children.
19 And Babylon, the glory of kingdoms,
the splendour and pride of the Chaldeans,
will be like Sodom and Gomorrah
Is 34:10–17 when God overthrew them.
Jer 50:3; 20 It will never be inhabited
51:29 or dwelt in for all generations;
no Arab will pitch his tent there,
no shepherds will make their flocks lie down there.
21 But wild beasts will lie down there,
and its houses will be full of howling creatures;
there ostriches will dwell,
and there satyrs will dance.
22 Hyenas will cry in its towers,
and jackals in the pleasant palaces;
its time is close at hand
and its days will not be prolonged.

---

caelum turbabo, / et movebitur terra de loco suo / in indignatione Domini exercituum / et in die irae furoris eius. / 14Et erit quasi damula fugiens et quasi ovis, / et non erit qui congreget; / unusquisque ad populum suum convertetur, / et singuli ad terram suam fugient. / 15Omnis, qui inventus fuerit, occidetur, / et omnis, qui captus fuerit, cadet in gladio; / 16infantes eorum allidentur in oculis eorum, / diripientur domus eorum, / et uxores eorum violabuntur. / 17Ecce ego suscitabo super eos Medos, / qui argentum non quaerant nec aurum velint; / 18sed arcus pueros prosternent / et fructui uteri non miserebuntur. / 19Et erit Babylon, splendor regnorum, / inclita superbia Chaldaeorum, / sicut cum subvertit Dominus Sodomam et Gomorram. / 20Non habitabitur usque in finem / et non fundabitur usque ad generationem et generationem, / nec ponet ibi tentoria Arabs, / nec pastores accubare facient ibi, / 21sed accubabunt

14 1The LORD will have compassion on Jacob and will again Is 60:4; 61:5
choose Israel, and will set them in their own land, and Zech 1:17
aliens will join them and will cleave to the house of Jacob. 2And Zeph 2:9
the peoples will take them and bring them to their place, and the Zech 2:13
house of Israel will possess them in the LORD'S land as male and
female slaves; they will take captive those who were their captors,
and rule over those who oppressed them.

3When the LORD has given you rest from your pain and turmoil
and the hard service with which you were made to serve, 4you will Jer 50:23–24
take up this taunt against the king of Babylon: Mic 2:4; Hab 2:6

"How the oppressor has ceased, Rev 18:9–19
the insolent fury[y] ceased!
5The LORD has broken the staff of the wicked,
the sceptre of rulers,
6that smote the peoples in wrath
with unceasing blows,
that ruled the nations in anger
with unrelenting persecution.
7The whole earth is at rest and quiet; Jer 51:48
they break forth into singing. Rev 18:20; 19:1–2
8The cypresses rejoice at you,
the cedars of Lebanon, saying,
'Since you were laid low,
no hewer comes up against us.'
9Sheol beneath is stirred up Num 16:33
to meet you when you come, Ezek 32:18–32
it rouses the shades to greet you,
all who were leaders of the earth;
it raises from their thrones
all who were kings of the nations.

---

ibi bestiae, / et replebunt domus eorum ululae, / et habitabunt ibi struthiones, / et pilosi saltabunt ibi; / 22et respondebunt ibi hyaenae in aedibus eius, / et thoes in delubris voluptatis. / Prope est ut veniat tempus eius, / et dies eius non elongabuntur. **[14]** 1Miserebitur enim Dominus Iacob / et eliget adhuc de Israel / et requiescere eos faciet super humum suam; / adiungetur advena ad eos / et adhaerebit domui Iacob. / 2Et tenebunt eos populi / et adducent eos in locum suum; / et possidebit eos domus Israel / super terram Domini in servos et ancillas; / et erunt capientes eos, qui se ceperant, / et subicient exactores suos. / 3Et erit in die illa: / cum requiem dederit tibi Dominus / a labore tuo et a concussione tua / et a servitute dura, qua ante servisti, / 4proferes parabolam istam contra regem Babylonis et dices: / «Quomodo cessavit exactor, quievit oppressio? / 5Contrivit Dominus baculum impiorum, / virgam dominantium, / 6caedentem populos in indignatione plaga sine remissione, / subicientem in furore gentes persecutione sine fine. / 7Conquievit et siluit omnis terra, / gavisa est, et exsultaverunt. / 8Abietes quoque laetatae sunt super te, et cedri Libani: / "Ex quo dormisti, non ascendit, qui succidat nos". / 9Infernus subter conturbatus est / in occursum adventus tui; / suscitat tibi umbras, omnes principes

y. One ancient Ms Compare Gk Syr Vg: The meaning of the Hebrew word is uncertain

[10] All of them will speak
and say to you:
'You too have become as weak as we!
You have become like us!'
[11] Your pomp is brought down to Sheol,
the sound of your harps;
maggots are the bed beneath you,
and worms are your covering.

Lk 10:18
Jn 12:31 [12] "How you are fallen from heaven,
Rev 8:10; 9:1; 12:9 O Day Star, son of Dawn!
How you are cut down to the ground,
you who laid the nations low!
Ps 48:3
Mt 11:23 [13] You said in your heart,
Lk 10:15 'I will ascend to heaven;
Dan 8:10 above the stars of God
I will set my throne on high;
I will sit on the mount of assembly
Gen 3:5 in the far north;
Ezek 28:2
Dan 10:13; [14] I will ascend above the heights of the clouds,
11:36 I will make myself like the Most High.'
2 Thess 2:4 [15] But you are brought down to Sheol,
to the depths of the Pit.
[16] Those who see you will stare at you,
and ponder over you:
'Is this the man who made the earth tremble,
who shook kingdoms,
[17] who made the world like a desert
and overthrew its cities,
who did not let his prisoners go home?'
[18] All the kings of the nations lie in glory,
each in his own tomb;
Jer 22:19 [19] but you are cast out, away from your sepulchre,

---

terrae / surgere fecit de soliis suis, / omnes reges nationum. / [10]Universi respondebunt et dicent tibi: / "Et tu vulneratus es sicut nos, / nostri similis effectus es". / [11]Detracta est ad inferos superbia tua, / sonitus nablorum tuorum; / subter te sternitur tinea, / et operimentum tuum sunt vermes. / [12]Quomodo cecidisti de caelo, lucifer, fili aurorae? / Deiectus es in terram, qui deiciebas gentes, / [13]qui dicebas in corde tuo: / "In caelum conscendam, / super astra Dei exaltabo solium meum, / sedebo in monte conventus / in lateribus aquilonis; / [14]ascendam super altitudinem nubium, / similis ero Altissimo". / [15]Verumtamen ad infernum detractus es, / in profundum laci. / [16]Qui te viderint, te intuentur / teque prospicient: / "Numquid iste est vir, qui conturbavit terram, / qui concussit regna, / [17]qui posuit orbem desertum / et urbes eius destruxit, / vinctis eius non aperuit carcerem? / [18]Omnes reges gentium universi dormiunt in gloria, / vir in domo sua; / [19]tu autem proiectus es de sepulcro tuo / quasi stirps

like a loathed untimely birth,[z]
clothed with the slain, those pierced by the sword,
who go down to the stones of the Pit,
like a dead body trodden under foot.
20 You will not be joined with them in burial,
because you have destroyed your land,
you have slain your people.

"May the descendants of evildoers
nevermore be named!
21 Prepare slaughter for his sons
because of the guilt of their fathers,
lest they rise and possess the earth,
and fill the face of the world with cities."

22"I will rise up against them," says the LORD of hosts, "and Is 4:3
will cut off from Babylon name and remnant, offspring and
posterity, says the LORD. 23And I will make it a possession of the
hedgehog, and pools of water, and I will sweep it with the broom
of destruction, says the LORD of hosts."

Oracle against Assyria Is 10:24

24 The LORD of hosts has sworn:
"As I have planned,
so shall it be,
and as I have purposed,
so shall it stand,

14:24–27. The short oracle against Assyria is in line with other denunciations of that nation in chapters 7–12: the Lord will destroy it. The Assyrian empire should have been simply the "rod of the Lord's anger" (10:5), but its cruelty has overstepped the limits, and it has arrogated to itself credit for its achievements (cf. 10:12–24). It has failed to acknowledge God's sover-

abominabilis, / obvolutus cum his, qui interfecti sunt gladio / et descenderunt ad lapides sepulcri, / quasi cadaver conculcatum. / 20Non habebis consortium cum eis in sepultura; / tu enim terram tuam disperdidisti, / tu populum tuum occidisti: / non vocabitur in aeternum semen malefactorum. / 21Praeparate filios eius occisioni / ob iniquitatem patrum suorum; / ne consurgant, ut hereditent terram, / neque impleant faciem orbis civitatum"». / 22«Et consurgam contra eos, / dicit Dominus exercituum; / et perdam Babylonis nomen et reliquias / et germen et progeniem, dicit Dominus; / 23et ponam eam in possessionem ericii / et in paludes aquarum, / et scopabo eam in scopa destructionis», / dicit Dominus exercituum. / 24Iuravit Dominus exercituum dicens: / «Profecto, ut putavi, ita erit; / et

z. Cn Compare Tg Symmachus: Heb *a loathed branch*

Is 9:3 [25] that I will break the Assyrian in my land,
and upon my mountains trample him under foot;
and his yoke shall depart from them,
and his burden from their shoulder."
[26] This is the purpose that is purposed
concerning the whole earth;
and this is the hand that is stretched out
over all the nations.
[27] For the LORD of hosts has purposed,
and who will annul it?
His hand is stretched out,
and who will turn it back?

Oracle against the Philistines

2 Kings 16:20 [28] In the year that King Ahaz died came this oracle:
Jer 47:1–7 [29] "Rejoice not, O Philistia, all of you,
that the rod which smote you is broken,

eignty over the world, and, instead, has sought to supplant him: that is its sin, and the reason why it is punished.

Irrespective of the circumstances in which it was spoken, this oracle is always valid and it is a warning that we must take account of God in all that we intend to do. "If we were the 'mountains' of God (cf. v. 25), his foundations would be set within us, so that the word of truth could be fixed in our hearts and the good works of faith built up. We must truly renounce all sin, so that the yoke of the Assyrians will be lifted from our shoulders and we may become the servants [lit. 'donkeys'] of Christ. We cannot bear two yokes, the Assyrians' and Christ's" (St Basil, *Enarratio in Isaiam*, 14, 284).

14:28–32. Now comes the turn of the Philistines, who occupied the lands on the Mediterranean coast (territory that never formed part of the kingdoms of Israel and Judah, and whose inhabitants had shown hostility to the Israelites ever since the time of the Judges). The book of Jeremiah, too, contains oracles against the Philistines (Jer 47:1–7). According to its heading, this oracle dates from the year when King Ahaz died (727 BC), when Isaiah was at the height of his prophetical ministry. It warns the Philistines that they should take no pleasure at the death of the king in the context of the Syrian-Ephraimite war against Assyria (Ahaz was a vassal of that empire and had been able to make life very difficult for the Philistines:

quomodo mente tractavi, sic eveniet. / [25]Conteram Assyrium in terra mea / et in montibus meis conculcabo eum; / et auferetur ab eis iugum eius, / et onus illius ab umero eorum tolletur». / [26]Hoc consilium, quod initum est / super omnem terram, / et haec est manus extenta / super universas gentes. / [27]Dominus enim exercituum decrevit, / et quis poterit infirmare? / Et manus eius extenta, / et quis avertet eam? / [28]In anno, quo mortuus est rex Achaz, factum est oraculum istud: / [29]«Ne laeteris, Philisthaea omnis tu, / quoniam comminuta est virga percussoris tui; / de radice enim colubri egredietur

for from the serpent's root will come forth an adder,
and its fruit will be a flying serpent.
30 And the first-born of the poor will feed,
and the needy lie down in safety;
but I will kill your root with famine,
and your remnant I[a] will slay.
31 Wail, O gate; cry, O city; Is 20:1
melt in fear, O Philistia, all of you! Jer 1:13
For smoke comes out of the north,
and there is no straggler in his ranks."

32 What will one answer the messengers of the nation?
"The LORD has founded Zion,
and in her the afflicted of his people find refuge."

Oracle against Moab Gen 19:30–37
15 [1]An oracle concerning Moab. Jer 16:6–10; 48:32–33
Because Ar is laid waste in a night Ezek 25:8–11
Moab is undone; Amos 2:1–3 Jer 48:37–38

14:29a). There is a mysterious prediction about a successor to the king of Assyria who will protect his own (14:29b–30a). This will spell more danger for the Philistines: troops will come from the north, from Assyria, and inflict defeat on them, while the poor and needy of the Lord's people will be able to find refuge in Jerusalem (14:30b–32). And in fact, in his campaign in 701 BC, during the reign of the devout King Hezekiah, the son of Ahaz, Sennacherib laid waste the fertile plains of Philistea and besieged Jerusalem, but he had to raise the siege before its inhabitants came to any harm (cf. 36:1ff; 2 Kings 18:13ff).

15:1—16:14. Moab was a traditional enemy of Judah. It was a nation made up of nomadic tribes that marauded east of the Jordan and the Dead Sea. The Moabites, who had blood-ties with the Israelites (cf. Gen 19:30–37), sometimes took advantage of Judah's weakness or misfortunes to attack it and encroach on its territory. This explains why Moab appears in oracles against the nations in Amos (Amos 2:1–3), Jeremiah (48:1–47) and Ezekiel (Ezek 25:8–11).

regulus, / et semen eius draco volans. / [30]Et pascentur primogeniti egenorum, / et pauperes fiducialiter requiescent; / et interire faciam in fame radicem tuam / et reliquias tuas interficiam. / [31]Ulula, porta! Clama, civitas! / Contremisce, Philisthaea omnis; / ab aquilone enim fumus venit, / et non est fugitivus in agminibus eius». / [32]Et quid respondebitur nuntiis gentis? / «Quia Dominus fundavit Sion, / et in ipsam confugiunt pauperes populi eius». **[15]** [1]Oraculum Moab. / Quia nocte vastata est Ar moab, conticuit; / quia nocte vastata est Cirmoab, conticuit. / [2]Ascendit filia Dibon ad excelsa in planctum; /

a. One ancient Ms Vg: Heb *he*

because Kir is laid waste in a night
Moab is undone.
[2]The daughter of Dibon[b] has gone up
to the high places to weep;
over Nebo and over Medeba
Moab wails.
On every head is baldness,
every beard is shorn;
[3]in the streets they gird on sackcloth;
on the housetops and in the squares
every one wails and melts in tears.
Num 21:23 Jer 48:34 [4]Heshbon and Ele-aleh cry out,
their voice is heard as far as Jahaz;
therefore the armed men of Moab cry aloud;
his soul trembles.
Gen 19:22 Jer 48:34,36 [5]My heart cries out for Moab;
his fugitives flee to Zoar,
to Eglath-shelishiyah.
For at the ascent of Luhith
they go up weeping;
on the road to Horonaim
they raise a cry of destruction;
[6]the waters of Nimrim
are a desolation;

The one here, like that in Jeremiah, is a long poem. It begins by showing the land of the Moabites laid waste, including all its main mountains (Nebo), strongholds and cities (15:1–9). The Moabites, in vain, seek refuge in Judah when they are invaded by Assyrian troops (16:1–5). Then comes a lamentation about the dire straits that Moab will find itself in—and recourse to its idolatrous shrines will bring its people no respite (16:6–12). The oracle ends with a short prose passage announcing the imminent downfall of Moab (16:13–14).

Some of the things said in the oracle appear again in similar terms in Jeremiah (16:6–10 and Jer 48:29–33; 15:2b–3 and Jer 48:37–38). And, as in the Jeremiah oracles (Jer 48:47), the final passage says that a remnant of Moab, a small one, will survive (16:14).

super Nabo et super Medaba Moab ululavit; / in cunctis capitibus eius calvitium, omnis barba rasa. / [3]In triviis eius accincti sunt sacco; / super tecta eius et in plateis eius / omnes ululant, prorumpunt in fletum. / [4]Clamat Hesebon et Eleale, / usque Iasa auditur vox eorum; / super hoc expediti Moab fremunt, / anima eius fremit sibi. / [5]Cor meum super Moab clamat, / vectes eius usque ad Segor, Eglatselisiam; / per ascensum enim Luith flentes ascendunt / et in via Oronaim clamorem contritionis levant. / [6]Aquae enim Nemrim desertae erunt, / quia aruit herba, defecit germen, / viror omnis interiit.

b. Cn: Heb *the house and Dibon*

the grass is withered, the new growth fails,
the verdure is no more.
[7]Therefore the abundance they have gained
and what they have laid up
they carry away
over the Brook of the Willows.
[8]For a cry has gone
round the land of Moab;
the wailing reaches to Eglaim,
the wailing reaches to Beer-elim.
[9]For the waters of Dibon[c] are full of blood;
yet I will bring upon Dibon even more,
a lion for those of Moab who escape,
for the remnant of the land.

16 [1]They have sent lambs
to the ruler of the land,
from Sela, by way of the desert,
to the mount of the daughter of Zion.
[2]Like fluttering birds,
like scattered nestlings,
so are the daughters of Moab
at the fords of the Arnon.
[3]"Give counsel,
grant justice;
make your shade like night
at the height of noon;
hide the outcasts,
betray not the fugitive;
[4]let the outcasts of Moab
sojourn among you;
be a refuge to them
from the destroyer.

/ [7]Ideo supellectiles colligunt, copias divitiarum suas / trans torrentem Salicum ducunt. / [8]Quoniam circuivit clamor terminum Moab; / usque ad Eglaim ululatus eius, / et usque ad Beerelim clamor eius. / [9]Quia aquae Dimon repletae sunt sanguine; / ponam enim super Dimon additamenta / his, qui fugerint de Moab leonem, et reliquiis terrae. **[16]** [1]Emittite agnum dominatori terrae / de Petra deserti ad montem filiae Sion. / [2]Et erit: sicut avis fugiens, / et pulli de nido avolantes, / sic erunt filiae Moab / ad vada Arnon. / [3]Affer consilium, fac iudicium; / pone quasi noctem umbram tuam in meridie, / absconde fugientes et vagos ne prodas. / [4]Habitent apud te profugi Moab; / esto latibulum eorum a facie vastatoris; / finitus est enim exactor, / consummata est devastatio, / defecit calcator a terra. / [5]Et firmabitur in misericordia solium; / et sedebit super illud in veritate, / in tabernaculo David, iudicans et

c. One ancient Ms Vg Compare Syr: Heb *Dimon*

When the oppressor is no more,
and destruction has ceased,
and he who tramples under foot
has vanished from the land,
[5]then a throne will be established in steadfast love
and on it will sit in faithfulness
in the tent of David
one who judges and seeks justice
and is swift to do righteousness."

Jer 48: 29–33 [6]We have heard of the pride of Moab,
how proud he was;
of his arrogance, his pride, and his insolence—
his boasts are false.
[7]Therefore let Moab wail,
let every one wail for Moab.
Mourn, utterly stricken,
for the raisin-cakes of Kir-hareseth.

[8]For the fields of Heshbon languish,
and the vine of Sibmah;
the lords of the nations
have struck down its branches,
which reached to Jazer
and strayed to the desert;
its shoots spread abroad
and passed over the sea.
[9]Therefore I weep with the weeping of Jazer
for the vine of Sibmah;
I drench you with my tears,
O Heshbon and Ele-aleh;
for upon your fruit and your harvest
the battle shout has fallen.
[10]And joy and gladness are taken away
from the fruitful field;

---

quaerens iudicium / et velociter reddens, quod iustum est. / [6]Audivimus superbiam Moab / —superbus est valde— / superbiam eius et arrogantiam eius et indignationem eius / et iactantiam eius non rectam. / [7]Idcirco ululabit Moab super Moab, / omnes ululabunt; / super placentas Cirhareseth / lamentantur percussi. / [8]Quoniam suburbana Hesebon deserta sunt et vinea Sabama; / dominos gentium perdiderunt uvae eius; / usque ad Iazer pervenerunt, / erraverunt in deserto: / propagines eius diffusae sunt, / transierunt mare. / [9]Super hoc plorabo in fletu Iazer vineam Sabama; / inebriabo te lacrima mea, Hesebon et Eleale, / quoniam super vindemiam tuam et super messem tuam / clamor cecidit. / [10]Et ablata est laetitia et exsultatio de hortis, / et in vineis non exsultant neque iubilant. / Vinum in torculari

and in the vineyards no songs are sung,
  no shouts are raised;
no treader treads out wine in the presses;
  the vintage shout is hushed.[d]
11 Therefore my soul moans like a lyre for Moab,
  and my heart for Kir-heres.

12And when Moab presents himself, when he wearies himself
upon the high place, when he comes to his sanctuary to pray, he
will not prevail.

13This is the word which the LORD spoke concerning Moab in
the past. 14But now the LORD says, "In three years, like the years
of a hireling, the glory of Moab will be brought into contempt, in
spite of all his great multitude, and those who survive will be very
few and feeble."

Is 4:3
Jer 48:47

Oracle against Damascus and Ephraim

17 1An oracle concerning Damascus.
  Behold, Damascus will cease to be a city,
  and will become a heap of ruins.
2Her cities will be deserted for ever;[e]
  they will be for flocks,
  which will lie down, and none will make them afraid.

Jer 49:23–27
Amos 1:3–5

17:1–14. The reason why the oracles against Damascus (the capital of Syria) and Ephraim (that is, Israel, the Northern kingdom) are combined has to do with the coalition that those kingdoms formed against Judah (in what is known as the Syrian-Ephraimite war) to force it to join them in their attempt to stem Assyrian invasion (cf. 2 Kings 16:5–9).

First comes an oracle against Damascus which includes invective against Ephraim (vv. 1–6). Then there is a short prose passage which, as in other groups of oracles against the nations, sums up the main ideas: those who have forsaken the Lord will suffer desolation, which will cause them to react and to return to their Maker (vv. 7–9). The passage ends with new oracles announcing a foreign invasion that will spell the end of the kingdom of Israel (vv. 10–14).

non calcabit, qui calcare consueverat; / clamor cessavit. / 11Ideo venter meus super Moab quasi cithara fremit, / et viscera mea super Cirhareseth. / 12Et erit: cum apparuerit / et laboraverit Moab super excelsis, / ingredietur ad sancta sua, ut obsecret, / et non valebit. 13Et hoc verbum, quod locutus est Dominus ad Moab ex tunc; 14nunc autem loquitur Dominus dicens: «In tribus annis, quasi anni mercennarii, auferetur gloria Moab cum omni populo multo, et residuum parvum et modicum nequaquam ingens erit». **[17]** 1Oraculum Damasci. / «Ecce Damascus desinet esse civitas / et erit sicut acervus ruinarum. / 2Derelictae civitates Aroer gregibus erunt; / et requiescent ibi, et non erit qui

d. Gk: Heb *I have hushed* **e.** Cn Compare Gk: Heb *the cities of Aroer are deserted*

Is 4:3 3 The fortress will disappear from Ephraim,
and the kingdom from Damascus;
and the remnant of Syria will be
like the glory of the children of Israel, says the LORD of hosts.

4 And in that day
the glory of Jacob will be brought low,
and the fat of his flesh will grow lean.
Jer 51:33 5 And it shall be as when the reaper gathers standing grain
Josh 18:16 and his arm harvests the ears,
and as when one gleans the ears of grain
in the Valley of Rephaim.
6 Gleanings will be left in it,
as when an olive tree is beaten—
two or three berries
in the top of the highest bough,
four or five
on the branches of a fruit tree, says the LORD God of Israel.

7 In that day men will regard their Maker, and their eyes will
Ex 34:13 look to the Holy One of Israel; 8 they will not have regard for the
altars, the work of their hands, and they will not look to what their
own fingers have made, either the Asherim or the altars of incense.
9 In that day their strong cities will be like the deserted places of
the Hivites and the Amorites,[f] which they deserted because of the
children of Israel, and there will be desolation.

Deut 32:4 10 For you have forgotten the God of your salvation,
Is 44:8 and have not remembered the Rock of your refuge;
therefore, though you plant pleasant plants
and set out slips of an alien god,

---

exterreat. / 3 Et auferetur munimentum ab Ephraim / et regnum a Damasco, / et reliquiae Syriae sicut gloria filiorum Israel erunt, / dicit Dominus exercituum. / 4 Et erit in die illa: attenuabitur gloria Iacob, / et pinguedo carnis eius marcescet; / 5 et erit, sicut cum messor arripit culmos, / et brachium eius spicas legit; / et erit, sicut cum quis quaerit spicas in valle Raphaim. / 6 Et relinquetur in eo racemus, / et sicut cum excutitur olea: / duae vel tres olivae in summitate rami / sive quattuor aut quinque in cacuminibus arboris fructiferae», / dicit Dominus Deus Israel. / 7 In die illa attendet homo ad factorem suum, / et oculi eius ad Sanctum Israel respicient; / 8 et non attendet ad altaria, / quae fecerunt manus eius, / et quae operati sunt digiti eius; / non respiciet lucos et thymiateria. / 9 In die illa erunt civitates fortitudinis eius derelictae, / sicut civitates, quas dereliquerunt Hevaei et Amorraei / a facie filiorum Israel; / et erit desolatio, / 10 quia oblita es Dei salutis tuae / et petrae fortitudinis tuae non es recordata: / propterea

f. Cn Compare Gk: Heb *the wood and the highest bough*

11 though you make them grow on the day that you plant them,
and make them blossom in the morning that you sow;
yet the harvest will flee away
in a day of grief and incurable pain.

12 Ah, the thunder of many peoples,
they thunder like the thundering of the sea!
Ah, the roar of nations,
they roar like the roaring of mighty waters!
13 The nations roar like the roaring of many waters,
but he will rebuke them, and they will flee far away,
chased like chaff on the mountains before the wind
and whirling dust before the storm.
14 At evening time, behold, terror!
Before morning, they are no more!
This is the portion of those who despoil us,
and the lot of those who plunder us.

Oracle against Ethiopia

18 1 Ah, land of whirring wings
which is beyond the rivers of Ethiopia;
2 which sends ambassadors by the Nile,
in vessels of papyrus upon the waters!

18:1–7. The earlier oracles were directed against powers to the north, east and west. Now the prophet directs his attention to the peoples of the south—Ethiopia and Egypt (18:1—20:6). In translations of the Bible, the original Kûsh (Cush) is often given as *Ethiopia* (v.1); but Kûsh was the ancient name of an extensive region (also known as Nubia) covering much of present-day Sudan and Ethiopia. Shabaka, king of Kûsh (710–696 BC), conquered Egypt and founded a new dynasty (the 25th dynasty) there, which was Nubian. He sent ambassadors to Jerusalem, proposing an alliance against Assyria. The embassy must have been impressive—tall, very dark men, bearing gifts and with a great reputation that preceded them, for they were conquerors of Egypt. The information given here indicates that this oracle against the Egyptians was spoken in Isaiah's time.

plantabis plantationes iucundas / et germen alienum seminabis. / 11In ipso die plantationis tuae saepies eas / et mane semen tuum florere facies; / evanescet messis in die penuriae, / et dolor insanabilis erit. / 12Heu!, strepitus populorum multorum; / strepunt quasi strepitu maris, / et tumultus turbarum / quasi sonitu aquarum sonabunt. / 13Sonabunt populi sicut sonitus aquarum inundantium, / et increpabit eum, et fugiet procul; / et rapietur sicut pulvis montium a facie venti / et sicut turbo coram tempestate. / 14In tempore vespere, et ecce turbatio, / ante matutinum non subsistet: / haec est pars eorum, qui vastaverunt nos, / et sors diripientium nos. **[18]** 1Vae terrae alarum strepitantium, / quae est trans flumina Aethiopiae! / 2Quae mittit in mari legatos / et in vasis papyri super aquas: / «Ite, nuntii veloces, / ad gentem proceram et lucidam, / ad populum terribilem, / prope et procul, / gentem robustam et

Go, you swift messengers,
to a nation, tall and smooth,
to a people feared near and far,
a nation mighty and conquering,
whose land the rivers divide.

Joel 2:1 [3]All you inhabitants of the world,
you who dwell on the earth,
when a signal is raised on the mountains, look!
When a trumpet is blown, hear!
[4]For thus the LORD said to me:
"I will quietly look from my dwelling
like clear heat in sunshine,
like a cloud of dew in the heat of harvest."
[5]For before the harvest, when the blossom is over,
and the flower becomes a ripening grape,
he will cut off the shoots with pruning hooks,
and the spreading branches he will hew away.
[6]They shall all of them be left
to the birds of prey of the mountains
and to the beasts of the earth.
And the birds of prey will summer upon them,
and all the beasts of the earth will winter upon them.

[7]At that time gifts will be brought to the LORD of hosts
from a people tall and smooth,
from a people feared near and far,
a nation mighty and conquering,
whose land the rivers divide,
to Mount Zion, the place of the name of the LORD of hosts.

---

conculcantem, / cuius flumina scindunt terram». / [3]Omnes habitatores orbis / et in terra commorantes, / cum elevatum fuerit signum in montibus, videbitis / et, cum clanguerit tuba, audietis. / [4]Quia haec dixit Dominus ad me: / «Quiescam et considerabo in loco meo, / sicut calor torrens orta iam luce / et sicut nubes roris in aestu messis». / [5]Etenim ante vindemiam, cum consummatus fuerit flos, / et uva germinans maturescens erit, / praecidet ramusculos falcibus / et propagines abscindet et proiciet; / [6]et relinquentur simul avibus montium / et bestiis terrae; / et aestate erunt super ea volucres, / et omnes bestiae terrae super illa hiemabunt. [7]In tempore illo deferetur munus Domino exercituum a populo procero et lucido, a populo terribili, prope et procul, a gente robusta et conculcante, cuius terram flumina scindunt, ad locum nominis Domini exercituum, montem Sion. **[19]** [1]Oraculum Aegypti. / Ecce Dominus vehitur super nubem levem / et ingreditur Aegyptum; / et commovebuntur simulacra Aegypti a facie eius, / et cor Aegypti tabescet in medio eius. / [2]«Et concurrere faciam Aegyptios adversus Aegyptios; / et pugnabit vir contra fratrem suum, / et vir contra amicum suum, / civitas adversus civitatem, / regnum adversus regnum. / [3]Et dirumpetur spiritus Aegypti in visceribus eius, / et consilium eius confundam; / et interrogabunt simulacra et divinos / et pythones et hariolos. / [4]Et tradam

Oracle against Egypt

19 [1]An oracle concerning Egypt. Jer 46ff Ezek 29–32
Behold, the LORD is riding on a swift cloud
and comes to Egypt;
and the idols of Egypt will tremble at his presence,
and the heart of the Egyptians will melt within them.
[2]And I will stir up Egyptians against Egyptians,
and they will fight, every man against his brother
and every man against his neighbour,
city against city, kingdom against kingdom;
[3]and the spirit of the Egyptians within them will be emptied out,
and I will confound their plans;
and they will consult the idols and the sorcerers,
and the mediums and the wizards;
[4]and I will give over the Egyptians
into the hand of a hard master;
and a fierce king will rule over them,
says the Lord, the LORD of hosts.

[5]And the waters of the Nile will be dried up,
and the river will be parched and dry;
[6]and its canals will become foul,

19:1–25. The thought of Ethiopia (cf. 18:1–7) may have led the prophet to turn his attention to Egypt. This oracle contains many geographical, religious and cultural references to the country on the Nile—to some cities (Zoan, vv. 11, 13 better known as Tanis, in the Nile delta; Memphis, v. 13; the City of the Sun, v. 18, that is, Heliopolis, whose majestic ruins can be seen today in the suburbs of Cairo); to the canals and branches of the Nile and the cultivation in the delta; to Egypt's sages, idols, priests and sorcerers.

The first oracle (vv. 1–15) makes fun of the proverbial Egyptian wisdom (vv. 11–13) and draws a picture of a country that is disintegrating and receiving no protection from its idols.

Attached to this prophecy are six short prose oracles, in a different tone, each beginning with the words "In that day" (vv. 16–17, 18, 19–20, 21–22, 23, 24–25). These show the universal reach of the salvation offered by the Lord, involving the reconciliation of Egypt, Assyria and Israel with God, who will send his blessing on all three. It is a very moving message: God is Lord of all nations and all times. He uses the events of human history to effect his purposes: everything converges to provide a peaceful and happy end when all the nations will worship him as the true God in his chosen place, "Israel my heritage" (v. 24).

Aegyptios in manu domini crudelis, / et rex fortis dominabitur eorum», / ait Dominus, Deus exercituum. / [5]Et arescet aqua de mari, / et fluvius desolabitur atque siccabitur, / [6]et putrida fient

and the branches of Egypt's Nile will diminish and dry up,
reeds and rushes will rot away.
7 There will be bare places by the Nile,
on the brink of the Nile,
and all that is sown by the Nile will dry up,
be driven away, and be no more.
8 The fishermen will mourn and lament,
all who cast hook in the Nile;
and they will languish
who spread nets upon the water.
9 The workers in combed flax will be in despair,
and the weavers of white cotton.
10 Those who are the pillars of the land will be crushed,
and all who work for hire will be grieved.

Num 13:2 11 The princes of Zoan are utterly foolish;
the wise counsellors of Pharaoh give stupid counsel.
How can you say to Pharaoh,
"I am a son of the wise,
a son of ancient kings"?
12 Where then are your wise men?
Let them tell you and make known
what the LORD of hosts has purposed against Egypt.
13 The princes of Zoan have become fools,
and the princes of Memphis are deluded;
those who are the cornerstones of her tribes
have led Egypt astray.
1 Sam 16:14; 1 Kings 22:19–23; Is 29:10
14 The LORD has mingled within her
a spirit of confusion;
and they have made Egypt stagger in all her doings
as a drunken man staggers in his vomit.
Is 9:13 15 And there will be nothing for Egypt
which head or tail, palm branch or reed, may do.

---

flumina; / attenuabuntur et siccabuntur rivi Aegypti, / calamus et iuncus marcescent; / 7nudabuntur ripae
Nili, / et omnis planta Nili siccabitur; / arescet et non erit. / 8Et maerebunt piscatores, / et lugebunt
omnes mittentes in flumen hamum; / et expandentes rete super faciem aquarum languebunt. /
9Confundentur, qui operantur linum, / pectentes et texentes byssum. / 10Et opifices eius deprimentur,
/ omnes mercennarii omnino deficient. / 11Quam stulti principes Taneos! / Sapientes consiliarii
pharaonis dederunt consilium insipiens; / quomodo dicetis pharaoni: / «Filius sapientium ego, filius
regum antiquorum»? / 12Ubi nunc sunt sapientes tui? / Annuntient tibi et indicent / quid cogitaverit
Dominus exercituum super Aegyptum. / 13Stulti facti sunt principes Taneos, / decepti sunt principes
Mempheos, / deceperunt Aegyptum anguli tribuum eius. / 14Dominus miscuit in medio eius spiritum
vertiginis, / et errare fecerunt Aegyptum in omni opere suo, / sicut errat ebrius in vomitu suo; / 15et non

[16]In that day the Egyptians will be like women, and tremble Jer 51:30
with fear before the hand which the LORD of hosts shakes over Nahum 3:13
them. [17]And the land of Judah will become a terror to the
Egyptians; every one to whom it is mentioned will fear because of
the purpose which the LORD of hosts has purposed against them.

[18]In that day there will be five cities in the land of Egypt which
speak the language of Canaan and swear allegiance to the LORD of
hosts. One of these will be called the City of the Sun.

[19]In that day there will be an altar to the LORD in the midst of
the land of Egypt, and a pillar to the LORD at its border. [20]It will be
a sign and a witness to the LORD of hosts in the land of Egypt;
when they cry to the LORD because of oppressors he will send
them a saviour, and will defend and deliver them. [21]And the LORD
will make himself known to the Egyptians; and the Egyptians will
know the LORD in that day and worship with sacrifice and burnt
offering, and they will make vows to the LORD and perform them.
[22]And the LORD will smite Egypt, smiting and healing, and they
will return to the LORD, and he will heed their supplications and
heal them.

[23]In that day there will be a highway from Egypt to Assyria,
and the Assyrian will come into Egypt, and the Egyptian into
Assyria, and the Egyptians will worship with the Assyrians.

[24]In that day Israel will be the third with Egypt and Assyria, a
blessing in the midst of the earth, [25]whom the LORD of hosts has
blessed, saying, "Blessed be Egypt my people, and Assyria the
work of my hands, and Israel my heritage."

---

erit Aegypto opus, / quod faciat, caput vel cauda, palma vel arundo. [16]In die illa erunt Aegyptii quasi
mulieres et stupebunt et timebunt a facie commotionis manus Domini exercituum, quam ipse movebit
super eam. [17]Et erit terra Iudae Aegypto in pavorem: omnis, qui illius fuerit recordatus, pavebit a facie
consilii Domini exercituum, quod ipse cogitavit super eam. [18]In die illa erunt quinque civitates in terra
Aegypti loquentes lingua Chanaan et iurantes per Dominum exercituum. Civitas Solis vocabitur una.
[19]In die illa erit altare Domino in medio terrae Aegypti, et titulus iuxta terminum eius Domino. [20]Et erit
in signum et in testimonium Domino exercituum in terra Aegypti. Clamabunt enim ad Dominum a facie
tribulantium, et mittet eis salvatorem et propugnatorem, qui liberet eos. [21]Et cognoscetur Dominus ab
Aegypto, et cognoscent Aegyptii Dominum in die illa; et colent eum in hostiis et in muneribus et vota
vovebunt Domino et solvent. [22]Et percutiet Dominus Aegyptum plaga et sanabit; et revertentur ad
Dominum, et placabitur eis et sanabit eos. [23]In die illa erit via de Aegypto in Assyriam; et intrabit
Assyrius Aegyptum, et Aegyptius in Assyriam, et servient Aegyptii cum Assyriis. [24]In die illa erit Israel
tertius cum Aegypto et Assyria; benedictio in medio terrae, [25]cui benedicet Dominus exercituum dicens:
«Benedictus populus meus Aegyptius, et opus manuum mearum Assyrius, et hereditas mea Israel».
[20] [1]In anno quo ingressus est Tharthan in Azotum, cum misisset eum Sargon rex Assyriorum, et
pugnasset contra Azotum et cepisset eam, [2]in tempore illo locutus est Dominus in manu Isaiae filii
Amos dicens: «Vade et solve saccum de lumbis tuis et calceamenta tua tolle de pedibus tuis». Et fecit
sic, vadens nudus et discalceatus. [3]Et dixit Dominus: «Sicut ambulavit servus meus Isaias nudus et
discalceatus tribus annis signum et portentum super Aegyptum et super Aethiopiam, [4]sic minabit rex

Isaiah, a sign against Egypt and Ethiopia

2 Kings 18:17 **20** 1In the year that the commander in chief, who was sent by
Sargon the king of Assyria, came to Ashdod and fought
against it and took it,—2at that time the LORD had spoken by
Isaiah the son of Amoz, saying, "Go, and loose the sackcloth from
your loins and take off your shoes from your feet," and he had
done so, walking naked and barefoot—3the LORD said, "As my
servant Isaiah has walked naked and barefoot for three years as a
2 Sam 10:4 sign and a portent against Egypt and Ethiopia, 4so shall the king
of Assyria lead away the Egyptians captives and the Ethiopians
exiles, both the young and the old, naked and barefoot, with
Is 30:3–7 buttocks uncovered, to the shame of Egypt. 5Then they shall be
dismayed and confounded because of Ethiopia their hope and of
Egypt their boast. 6And the inhabitants of this coastland will say
in that day, 'Behold, this is what has happened to those in whom
we hoped and to whom we fled for help to be delivered from the
king of Assyria! And we, how shall we escape?'"

Oracle concerning the fall of Babylon

Is 13–14; 47:1ff **21** 1The oracle concerning the wilderness of the sea.
Jer 50–51 As whirlwinds in the Negeb sweep on,
Rev 17–18 it comes from the desert,
Jer 51:36 from a terrible land.

20:1–6. The original text mentions "the Tartan", the title or rank of a high official of the Assyrian army, possibly the commander-in-chief. We have here an instance of a symbolic action (other prophets performed symbolic actions, but this is the only one in the book of Isaiah: cf. "Introduction", pp. 16–17, above); it occurs on the occasion when Sargon II took the fortress of Ashdod (711 BC). This was at a time when Judah was relying on support from Egypt and Ethiopia to keep the Assyrians at bay. The prophet mimics the action of a prisoner of war being led into captivity —a warning of what will happen at the hands of the Assyrians to those who put their trust in Egypt and Ethiopia. The whole passage is a warning to the people not to seek refuge in foreign alliances but to put all their trust in God.

21:1–10. The oracle begins with a vision of the assault on Babylon by the

Assyriorum captivos Aegypti et exsules Aethiopiae, iuvenes et senes, nudos et discalceatos, discoopertis natibus ad ignominiam Aegypti. 5Et timebunt et confundentur ab Aethiopia spe sua et ab Aegypto gloria sua. 6Et dicet habitator maritimae regionis huius in die illa: "Ecce, haec erat spes nostra, quo confugimus in auxilium, ut liberaremur a facie regis Assyriorum; et quomodo effugere poterimus nos?"». **[21]** 1Oraculum deserti maris. / Sicut turbines per austrum transeuntes, / de deserto venit, de terra horribili. / 2Visio dura nuntiata est mihi: / praedo praedatur, / et vastator vastat. / Ascende, Elam; / obside, Media; / omnem gemitum eius cessare feci. / 3Propterea repleti sunt lumbi mei tremore, /

[2]A stern vision is told to me; Rev 17:3
the plunderer plunders,
and the destroyer destroys.
Go up, O Elam,
lay siege, O Media;
all the sighing she has caused
I bring to an end.
[3]Therefore my loins are filled with anguish;
pangs have seized me,
like the pangs of a woman in travail;
I am bowed down so that I cannot hear,
I am dismayed so that I cannot see.
[4]My mind reels, horror has appalled me;
the twilight I longed for
has been turned for me into trembling.
[5]They prepare the table, Dan 5
they spread the rugs,
they eat, they drink.
Arise, O princes,
oil the shield!
[6]For thus the Lord said to me:
"Go, set a watchman,
let him announce what he sees.

Elamites and the Medes, who occupied the area of present-day Iran and created the great Persian empire. It probably dates from a little before 539 BC.

The attack takes the Babylonian rulers completely unaware (vv. 1–5). The vision shows that they took no steps to defend their empire and instead lived a life of ease and luxury, even when the enemy was at the gates. Suddenly, the alarm is raised: "Arise, O princes"; they must ready themselves for battle and "oil the shield", the better to deflect the weapons of the enemy. But it is far too late.

As well as this, the prophet is told to be watchful (vv. 6–9), ready to hear the news that the word of God has been put into effect. He must keep an ear out, question every caravan, in case it brings news of the fall of Babylon. At last the news is brought by two horsemen (v. 9); it is a message that will later be taken up in the Revelation of John, to proclaim the end of the Babylon that symbolized Rome (Rev 14:8; 18:2).

The fall of Babylon brings joy to Israel, here called "my threshed and winnowed one" (v. 10); a reference to

angustia possedit me sicut angustia parientis; / corrui, cum audirem; / conturbatus sum, cum viderem. / [4]Vacillat cor meum, / pavor invadit me: / crepusculum optatum / posuit mihi in terrorem. / [5]Ponunt mensam, / stragulum pandunt, comedunt, bibunt. / Surgite, principes, / ungite clipeum. / [6]Haec enim dixit mihi Dominus: / «Vade et pone speculatorem; / quodcumque viderit, annuntiet. / [7]Si viderit

[7]When he sees riders, horsemen in pairs,
riders on asses, riders on camels,
let him listen diligently,
very diligently."
[8]Then he who saw[g] cried:
"Upon a watchtower I stand, O Lord,
continually by day,
and at my post I am stationed
whole nights.
Rev 14:8; 18:2 [9]And, behold, here come riders,
horsemen in pairs!"
And he answered,
"Fallen, fallen is Babylon;
and all the images of her gods
he has shattered to the ground."
[10]O my threshed and winnowed one,
what I have heard from the LORD of hosts,
the God of Israel, I announce to you.

Jer 49:7–22
Ezek 25:12–14; 35:1–15
Obad 1–9

Oracle concerning Dumah

[11]The oracle concerning Dumah.
One is calling to me from Seir,
"Watchman, what of the night?
Watchman, what of the night?"

---

those people of Judah and Jerusalem who had been deported to those regions (vv. 8–10).

21:11–12. Dumah is an oasis in the north of Arabia, the territory of the Ishmaelite tribe that bears that name (cf. Gen 25:14; 1 Chron 1:30). But it is more likely that this Dumah is a variant of the name of Edom, the land across the Jordan which is the subject of oracles in Jeremiah (Jer 49:7–22), Ezekiel (Ezek 25:12–14; 35:1–15) and Obadiah (Obad 1–9). In fact, the mountain of Seir referred to in this oracle (v. 11) is in the region of Edom. The Greek version reads: "Oracle concerning Idumea", that is, Edom.

In the Bible, the darkness of night symbolizes misadventure, whereas the light of day stands for salvation. The watchman's mysterious reply is a threat:

currum, bigam equitum, / ascensorem asini et ascensorem cameli, / intueatur diligenter multo intuitu». / [8]Et clamavit speculator: / «Super specula, Domine, / ego sum stans iugiter per diem, / et super custodiam meam / ego sum stans totis noctibus. / [9]Ecce, huc venit agmen virorum, / biga equitum». / Et respondit et dixit: / «Cecidit, cecidit Babylon, / et omnia sculptilia deorum eius / contrita sunt in terram». / [10]Tritura mea et fili areae meae, / quae audivi a Domino exercituum, Deo Israel, / annuntiavi vobis. / [11]Oraculum Duma. / Ad me clamat ex Seir: / «Custos, quid de nocte? / Custos, quid de nocte?».

g. One ancient Ms: Heb *a lion*

12 The watchman says:
"Morning comes, and also the night.
If you will inquire, inquire;
come back again."

Oracle concerning Arabia

13 The oracle concerning Arabia. Gen 10:7; 25:3
In the thickets in Arabia you will lodge, Jer 49:8
O caravans of Dedanites.
14 To the thirsty bring water,
meet the fugitive with bread,
O inhabitants of the land of Tema.
15 For they have fled from the swords,
from the drawn sword,
from the bent bow,
and from the press of battle.

16 For thus the Lord said to me, "Within a year, according to the Is 16:14
years of a hireling, all the glory of Kedar will come to an end;
17 and the remainder of the archers of the mighty men of the sons Jer 49:28
of Kedar will be few; for the LORD, the God of Israel, has spoken."

---

even though a time of peace and victory (morning) comes first, punishment (night) will eventually fall (cf. v. 12).

The exhortation to vigilance ("Watchman, what of the night") has also been interpreted as a call on Christians to be watchful to make sure that others do not go astray: "Although I must guard my own conscience and that of my neighbour, neither is well-known to me: each contains inscrutable depths. Nevertheless I am called to be the guardian of both, and they cry out: *Watchman, what of the night?*" (St Bernard, *Sermones in adventu Domini*, 3, 6). Hence St Josemaría Escrivá's teaching: "*Custos, quid de nocte?*—Watchman, how goes the night? May you acquire the habit of having a day on guard once a week, during which to increase your self-giving and loving vigilance over little details, and to pray and mortify yourself a little more" (*Furrow*, 960).

21:13–17. The oracle about Arabia mentions famous tribes and places of ancient Transjordan—Dedan (cf. Gen 10:6–7; 25:3; Jer 49:8; Ezek 25:12–13), Tema (cf. Gen 25:15) and Kedar (cf. 42:11; Jer 2:10; 49:28). Those tribes of northern Arabia were at times a thorn in the side of Judah. They too will feel the fierce effects of war.

/ 12 Dixit custos: / «Venit mane, sed etiam nox; / si quaeritis, quaerite, / revertimini, venite». / 13 Oraculum in solitudine. / In saltu, in solitudine dormietis, / turmae Dedanim. / 14 Occurrentes sitienti ferte aquam, / qui habitatis terram Thema; / cum panibus occurrite fugienti: / 15 a facie enim gladiorum fugerunt, / a facie gladii nudati, / a facie arcus extenti, / a facie gravis proelii. 16 Quoniam haec dicit Dominus ad me: «Adhuc anno sicut anni mercennarii, et auferetur omnis gloria Cedar; 17 et reliquiae numeri arcuum fortium filiorum Cedar imminuentur; Dominus enim, Deus Israel, locutus est».

Oracle concerning the valley of vision

22 [1]The oracle concerning the valley of vision.
What do you mean that you have gone up,
all of you, to the housetops,
[2]you who are full of shoutings,
tumultuous city, exultant town?
Your slain are not slain with the sword
or dead in battle.

22:1–14. In the form in which it has come down to us, the book of Isaiah inserts chapter 22 among the oracles against the nations. It contains oracles against Jerusalem itself (vv. 1–14), and against a person called Shebna (22:15–25), a high official at the court of King Hezekiah of Judah. It is inserted here perhaps because it must refer to events that occurred around 710 BC, towards the end of Isaiah's ministry.

The oracle about Jerusalem (vv. 1–14) reproaches it for excessive rejoicing at the raising of the siege and the departure of Sennacherib's army in 701 BC. The inhabitants of the city soon forgot that they owed their deliverance to the Lord. As Isaiah sees it they have learned nothing: they failed to see that God saved them this time in order to have them repent of their sins; instead, they carry on as before. The prophet expected more of them; now he senses that this new dawn will soon turn to lamentation. The reference to Edam and Kir is explained by the fact that those regions of Persia and northern Arabia, respectively, supplied mercenaries to the Assyrian armies. In v. 11 there is a reference to Hezekiah's building scheme to supply water to Jerusalem during the siege (cf. 2 Kings 20:20 and 2 Chron 32:27ff), including a tunnel that is still extant.

There is no valley known as the "valley of vision" (vv. 1, 5). This may be a symbolic name; in any case, it would have been on the outskirts of Jerusalem. The "House of the Forest" (v. 8) was a large hall in the palace of Solomon (cf. 1 Kings 7:1–12).

The second part of v. 13 ("Let us eat and drink ...") is quoted by St Paul in 1 Corinthians 15:32b to epitomize the attitude that people might adopt if there were no resurrection of the dead. In other words, God is just and he will reward those who hope in him (cf. Heb 11:6). And so, St John Damascene, commenting on this verse, says: "The day of resurrection will dawn, for God is just and will reward all those who hope in him (cf. Heb 11:6). If the soul alone had striven for virtue, it alone would be rewarded; or if the soul alone had yielded to sin, it alone would be punished. But since the soul cannot give itself to virtue or to vice without the body, both soul and body will be rewarded or chastised" (*De fide orthodoxa*, 4, 27).

[22] [1]Oraculum vallis Visionis. / Quidnam tibi est, / quia ascendisti omnis in tecta, / [2]clamoris plena, urbs tumultuans, / civitas exsultans? / Interfecti tui non interfecti gladio / nec mortui in bello; / [3]cuncti principes tui fugerunt / simul sine arcu capti; / omnes, qui inventi sunt, capti sunt simul, / procul

3 All your rulers have fled together, 2 Kings 25:2–11
without the bow they were captured.
All of you who were found were captured,
though they had fled far away.[h]
4 Therefore I said:
"Look away from me,
let me weep bitter tears;
do not labour to comfort me
for the destruction of the daughter of my people."

5 For the Lord GOD of hosts has a day
of tumult and trampling and confusion
in the valley of vision,
a battering down of walls
and a shouting to the mountains.
6 And Elam bore the quiver
with chariots and horsemen,[i]
and Kir uncovered the shield.
7 Your choicest valleys were full of chariots,
and the horsemen took their stand at the gates.
8 He has taken away the covering of Judah. 1 Kings 7:2–5

In that day you looked to the weapons of the House of the
Forest, 9 and you saw that the breaches of the city of David were 2 Sam 5:9
many, and you collected the waters of the lower pool, 10 and you
counted the houses of Jerusalem, and you broke down the houses
to fortify the wall. 11 You made a reservoir between the two walls 2 Kings 20:20
for the water of the old pool. But you did not look to him who did 2 Chron 32:10 Neh 3:16
it, or have regard for him who planned it long ago.

12 In that day the Lord GOD of hosts
called to weeping and mourning,
to baldness and girding with sackcloth;

---

fugerunt. / 4 Propterea dixi: «Recedite a me, / amare flebo; / nolite incumbere, ut consolemini me / super vastitate filiae populi mei». / 5 Dies enim confusionis / et conculcationis et fletus / Domino, Deo exercituum, in valle Visionis, / eversio murorum et vociferatio ad montem. / 6 Et Elam sumpsit pharetram, / in agmine hominum equitum, / et Cir nudavit clipeum. / 7 Et electae valles tuae / plenae sunt quadrigarum, / et equites ponunt sedes suas in porta. / 8 Et revelatum est operimentum Iudae, / et respexisti in die illa armamentarium domus Saltus; / 9 et scissuras civitatis David vidistis, / quia multiplicatae sunt; / et congregastis aquas piscinae inferioris. / 10 Et domos Ierusalem numerastis / et destruxistis domos / ad muniendum murum; / 11 et lacum fecistis inter duos muros / pro aqua piscinae veteris; / sed non suspexistis ad eum, qui fecit haec, / et eum, qui haec de longe formavit, non vidistis. / 12 Et vocavit Dominus, Deus exercituum, in die illa / ad fletum et ad planctum, / ad calvitium et ad

h. Gk Syr Vg: Heb *from far away* **i.** The Hebrew of this line is obscure

Wis 2:7–9 13 and behold, joy and gladness,
Is 5:11 slaying oxen and killing sheep,
1 Cor 15:32 eating flesh and drinking wine.
"Let us eat and drink,
for tomorrow we die."
14 The LORD of hosts has revealed himself in my ears:
"Surely this iniquity will not be forgiven you
till you die,"
says the Lord GOD of hosts.

Oracle concerning Shebna

2 Kings 18:18,26,37 15 Thus says the Lord GOD of hosts, "Come, go to this steward, to
Is 36:3,11,22 Shebna, who is over the household, and say to him: 16 What have
you to do here and whom have you here, that you have hewn here
a tomb for yourself, you who hew a tomb on the height, and carve
a habitation for yourself in the rock? 17 Behold, the LORD will hurl
you away violently, O you strong man. He will seize firm hold on
you, 18 and whirl you round and round, and throw you like a ball into
a wide land; there you shall die, and there shall be your splendid

---

22:15–25. Shebna had a high position in the royal court, and he is mentioned in other passages (36:3, 11, 22; 37:2; and 2 Kings 18:26, 37; 19:2). He may have been a foreigner who, after occupying a senior position in Hezekiah's palace, was replaced by Eliakim. Isaiah reproaches Shebna for being ostentatious (v. 16) and he tells him he will be dismissed from office (vv. 17–19, 25). His successor, Eliakim, son of Hilkiah (vv. 20–24), will be the official who, during the Assyrian siege of Jerusalem, heads a royal embassy charged with negotiating peace (cf. 2 Kings 18:18—19:2).

Irrespective of the historical context in which the oracle was spoken, the words of v. 22 find significant resonance in the New Testament. The first part of the verse is reminiscent of what Jesus says to Peter when giving him the "keys of the kingdom" (Mt 16:19). In this connexion it is no harm to remember that the king's high steward, as his representative, opened and closed the official court business of the day. The text of the second part of this same verse is applied in the book of Revelation to the Messiah, "the holy one, the true, who has the key of David" (Rev 3:7), because Jesus, the Messiah, as the new

cingendum saccum; / 13 et ecce gaudium et laetitia, / occidere boves et iugulare pecus, / comedere carnes et bibere vinum: / «Comedamus et bibamus, / cras enim moriemur». / 14 Et revelatum est in auribus meis / a Domino exercituum: / «Certe non dimittetur iniquitas haec vobis, donec moriamini!», / dicit Dominus, Deus exercituum. / 15 Haec dicit Dominus, Deus exercituum: / «Vade, ingredere ad procuratorem istum, / ad Sobnam praepositum palatii: / 16 "Quid tibi hic? Aut quis tibi hic, / quia excidisti tibi hic sepulcrum?". / Effodiens in excelso sepulcrum suum, / excavabat in petra tabernaculum sibi. / 17 Ecce Dominus vehementer proiciet te, homo, / violenter te apprehendens. / 18 In

chariots, you shame of your master's house. [19]I will thrust you 2 Kings 16,9
from your office, and you will be cast down from your station. 2 Kings
[20]In that day I will call my servant Eliakim the son of Hilkiah, 18:18,26
[21]and I will clothe him with your robe, and will bind your girdle Is 36:3,11,22
on him, and will commit your authority to his hand; and he shall
be a father to the inhabitants of Jerusalem and to the house of
Judah. [22]And I will place on his shoulder the key of the house of Mt 16:19
David; he shall open, and none shall shut; and he shall shut, and Rev 3:7
none shall open. [23]And I will fasten him like a peg in a sure place, Ezek 26–28
and he will become a throne of honour to his father's house. [24]And Amos 1:9–10
they will hang on him the whole weight of his father's house, the Zech 9:2–4
offspring and issue, every small vessel, from the cups to all the
flagons. [25]In that day, says the LORD of hosts, the peg that was
fastened in a sure place will give way; and it will be cut down and
fall, and the burden that was upon it will be cut off, for the LORD
has spoken."

Oracle concerning Tyre

Ezek 26–28
Amos 1:9–10
Zech 9:2–4
Ps 48:8; Is 2:16

23 [1]The oracle concerning Tyre.
Wail, O ships of Tarshish,
for Tyre is laid waste, without house or haven!
From the land of Cyprus
it is revealed to them.

David opens the doors of heaven. The Church's liturgy, in the famous "O" antiphons prior to Christmas, extols Christ, giving him this messianic title: "Key of David and sceptre of the house of Israel, you, who reign over the whole world, come and free those who wait for you in darkness" (*Divine Office*, Antiphon at Vespers, 20 December).

23:1–18. The last oracle against the nations has to do with Tyre, the main city of Phoenicia. Sidon, which is also mentioned (vv. 2, 4, 12), is another important Phoenician city, located 35 km. (22 miles) to the north of Tyre. This prophecy may be a combination of two separate oracles about these cities, or perhaps the name of Sidon is being used

globum te convolvet glomerans; / quasi pilam mittet te / in terram latam et spatiosam: / ibi morieris, / et ibi erunt currus gloriae tuae, / ignominia domus domini tui. / [19]Et expellam te de statione tua / et de ministerio tuo deponam te. / [20]Et erit in die illa: / vocabo servum meum Eliachim filium Helciae / [21]et induam illum tunicam tuam / et cingulo tuo cingam eum / et potestatem tuam dabo in manu eius; / et erit in patrem habitantibus Ierusalem / et domui Iudae. / [22]Et dabo clavem domus David / super umerum eius; / et aperiet, et non erit qui claudat; / et claudet, et non erit qui aperiat. / [23]Et figam illum paxillum in loco securo, / et erit in solium gloriae domui patris sui. [24]Et suspendent super eum omnem gloriam domus patris sui, propagines et stirpes, omne vas parvulum, a pelvibus ad amphoras. [25]In die illa, dicit Dominus exercituum, auferetur paxillus, qui fixus fuerat in loco securo, et frangetur et cadet; et peribit, quod pependerat in eo, quia Dominus locutus est». **[23]** [1]Oraculum Tyri. / Ululate, naves Tharsis, / quia vastatum est refugium vestrum; / cum redirent de terra Cetthim, revelatum est eis. / [2]Obstupescite,

[2]Be still, O inhabitants of the coast,
O merchants of Sidon;
your messengers passed over the sea[j]
[3]and were on many waters;
your revenue was the grain of Shihor,
the harvest of the Nile;
you were the merchant of the nations.
[4]Be ashamed, O Sidon, for the sea has spoken,
the stronghold of the sea, saying:
"I have neither travailed nor given birth,
I have neither reared young men
nor brought up virgins."
[5]When the report comes to Egypt,
they will be in anguish over the report about Tyre.
[6]Pass over to Tarshish,
wail, O inhabitants of the coast!

---

in a generic sense, to mean the whole Phoenician region: that is how the Septuagint interprets it in v. 2. Tyre, although it was besieged by Assyrians and Babylonians, managed to resist them (later it was taken by Alexander the Great), thanks to its strategic position on two rocky promontories. This geographical feature explains why the prophet refers to Tyre as an island (vv. 2, 4). It is not easy to work out which attacks the oracle is referring to; but it certainly manages to give an idea of the commercial and seafaring life of those prosperous cities.

"Tarshish" (vv. 1, 6, 10): no one knows for sure where this was. Some scholars have thought it could be Tartesos, on the west coast of Andalucia in Spain; but it may refer to some other region of the distant west (cf. Ps 72:10; Jon 1:3; Ezek 27:12). The "ships of Tarshish" (vv. 1, 14; cf. 2:16; 60:9; 1 Kings 10:22) could mean ships built there, but it became a stock description of big ships that operated on commercial routes.

"Cyprus" (vv. 1, 12): in Hebrew "Kittim", a word that originally referred to the people of Cyprus, but over time came to be applied also to the peoples of the Aegean Sea (cf. Jer 2:10; Ezek 27:6), to the Macedonians (1 Mac 1:1; 8:5) and even to the Romans (Dan 11:30).

"Shihor" (v. 3): probably the name of a branch of the Nile delta, used here to mean the river itself (cf. Jer 2:18; Josh 13:3).

qui habitatis in insula; / negotiatores Sidonis / transfretantes mare repleverunt te. / [3]In aquis multis semen Nili, / messis fluminis fruges eius; / et facta est negotiatio gentium. / [4]Erubesce, Sidon, ait enim mare, / fortitudo maris, dicens: / «Non parturivi et non peperi; / et non enutrivi iuvenes / nec virgines educavi». / [5]Cum auditum fuerit in Aegypto, / dolebunt cum audierint de Tyro. / [6]Transite ad Tharsis, /

j. One ancient Ms: Heb *who passed over the sea, they replenished you*

[7]Is this your exultant city
whose origin is from days of old,
whose feet carried her
to settle afar?
[8]Who has purposed this Rev 18:23
against Tyre, the bestower of crowns,
whose merchants were princes,
whose traders were the honoured of the earth?
[9]The LORD of hosts has purposed it,
to defile the pride of all glory,
to dishonour all the honoured of the earth.
[10]Overflow your land like the Nile,
O daughter of Tarshish;
there is no restraint any more.
[11]He has stretched out his hand over the sea,
he has shaken the kingdoms;
the LORD has given command concerning Canaan
to destroy its strongholds.
[12]And he said:
"You will no more exult,
O oppressed virgin daughter of Sidon;
arise, pass over to Cyprus,
even there you will have no rest."

[13]Behold the land of the Chaldeans! This is the people; it was
not Assyria. They destined Tyre for wild beasts. They erected their
siegetowers, they razed her palaces, they made her a ruin.[k]
[14]Wail, O ships of Tarshish,
for your stronghold is laid waste.
[15]In that day Tyre will be forgotten for seventy years, like the days
of one king. At the end of seventy years, it will happen to Tyre as
in the song of the harlot:

---

ululate, qui habitatis in insula. / [7]Estne vestra haec, quae gloriabatur? / A diebus pristinis antiquitas eius. / Ducebant eam pedes sui longe / ad peregrinandum. / [8]Quis cogitavit hoc / super Tyrum quondam coronatam, / cuius negotiatores principes, / institores eius incliti terrae? / [9]Dominus exercituum cogitavit hoc, / ut detraheret superbiam omnis gloriae / et viles faceret universos inclitos terrae. / [10]Excole terram tuam sicut litus Nili, / filia Tharsis, iam non est portus. / [11]Manum suam extendit super mare, / conturbavit regna. / Dominus mandavit adversus Chanaan, / ut contereret munimenta eius, / [12]et dixit: «Non adicies ultra ut glorieris, / violata virgo filia Sidonis; / in Cetthim consurgens transfreta: / ibi quoque non erit requies tibi». / [13]Ecce terra Chaldaeorum: / talis populus non fuit; / Assyria fundavit eam pro feris. / Erexerunt turres suas; / suffoderunt domos eius, / posuerunt eam in ruinam. / [14]Ululate, naves Tharsis, / quia devastatum est praesidium vestrum. [15]Et erit in die illa: in oblivione erit Tyrus

k. The Hebrew of this verse is obscure

16"Take a harp,
go about the city,
O forgotten harlot!
Make sweet melody,
sing many songs,
that you may be remembered."
17At the end of seventy years, the LORD will visit Tyre, and she
will return to her hire, and will play the harlot with all the
kingdoms of the world upon the face of the earth. 18Her
merchandise and her hire will be dedicated to the LORD; it will not
be stored or hoarded, but her merchandise will supply abundant
food and fine clothing for those who dwell before the LORD.

3. THE APOCALYPSE OF ISAIAH*

The earth shall be laid waste

24 1Behold, the LORD will lay waste the earth and make it
desolate, and he will twist its surface and scatter its
inhabitants.
2And it shall be, as with the people, so with the priest;

***24:1—27:13** The third section of part one of the book of Isaiah contains texts of different sorts, but mainly visions and eschatological oracles. Many scholars call this section the "Apocalypse of Isaiah", or the "Great Apocalypse" as distinct from a later, shorter section (34:1—35:10) of a similar type, usually called the "Little Apocalypse". The "Great Apocalypse" is made up of a collection of eschatological oracles that was given its present form after the Babylonian exile. They announce the sentence that the Lord will pass on the whole world, describing in great detail the cataclysms of the "day of the Lord". At the very end, after a catastrophe of cosmic proportions, God will reward the righteous with the messianic banquet that marks the definitive victory of the righteous scattered throughout the nations. Interspersed among these oracles are lyrical poems in praise of God's special providence towards his people and their victory over enemies and oppressors.

septuaginta annis, sicut dies regis unius. Post septuaginta autem annos erit Tyro iuxta canticum
meretricis: 16«Sume citharam, circui civitatem, / meretrix oblivioni tradita; / bene cane, frequenta
canticum, / ut memoria tui sit». 17Et erit: post septuaginta annos visitabit Dominus Tyrum, et redibit
ad mercedes suas et rursum fornicabitur cum universis regnis terrae super faciem terrae. 18Et erunt
negotiatio eius et merces eius sanctificatae Domino; non condentur neque reponentur, quia his, qui
habitaverint coram Domino, erit negotiatio eius, ut manducent in saturitate et vestiantur splendide.
[24] 1Ecce Dominus dissipat terram et frangit eam / et conturbat faciem eius / et dispergit habitatores
eius. / 2Et erit sicut populus sic sacerdos, / et sicut servus sic dominus eius, / sicut ancilla sic domina
eius, / sicut emens sic ille qui vendit, / sicut fenerator sic is qui mutuum accipit, / sicut qui repetit sic

as with the slave, so with his master;
as with the maid, so with her mistress;
as with the buyer, so with the seller;
as with the lender, so with the borrower;
as with the creditor, so with the debtor.
3The earth shall be utterly laid waste and utterly despoiled;
for the LORD has spoken this word.

4The earth mourns and withers, Hos 4:3
the world languishes and withers;
the heavens languish together with the earth.
5The earth lies polluted Gen 9:16
under its inhabitants;
for they have transgressed the laws,
violated the statutes,
broken the everlasting covenant.

24:1–23. The oracles addressed to the nations (13:1—23:18) revealed God's judgment against each nation; now, this terrible oracle announces a chastisement that will affect the whole cosmos. It speaks of the entire population of the world being destroyed (vv. 1–3); of the effects of this on all living things (vv. 4–16a); and of the ultimate destruction of the earth and all that it contains (vv. 16b–23).

The oracle speaks of a cosmic catastrophe affecting the entire earth and even the heavens (v. 4)—all because men have transgressed the laws and broken the "everlasting covenant" (v. 5). This latter probably means the covenant with Noah (Gen 9:8–17); because men have failed to keep it, it weighs as a curse that will bring down upon them all kinds of misfortune, from which only a small remnant will escape (v. 6).

As we already saw (in the accounts of the origins of the world), when mankind went about its business without reference to God, it was scattered across the face of the earth (cf. Gen 11:1–9). Here, too, the city is emptied and left desolate (vv. 8–12). Even so, in the midst of universal desolation, there are those who joyfully sing of their deliverance (vv. 13–20), as happened in the exodus after the crossing of the Red Sea. On "that day", too, as at the time of the Flood, the Lord will reveal his power by punishing sinners, while also manifesting his glory as he reigns from Jerusalem (vv. 21–23).

The "west" (v. 14), in Hebrew the "Sea", means the Mediterranean and by extension the west. The "host of heaven" (v. 21) refers to the stars, regarded as gods in the Assyrian-Babylonian myths.

qui debet. / 3Dissipatione dissipabitur terra / et direptione praedabitur: / Dominus enim locutus est verbum hoc. / 4Luget, languet terra, / marcescit, languet orbis, / marcescit altitudo simul cum terra. / 5Et terra infecta est sub habitatoribus suis, / quia transgressi sunt leges, / violaverunt mandatum, / dissipaverunt foedus sempiternum. / 6Propter hoc maledictio voravit terram, / et poenas exsolverunt

[6]Therefore a curse devours the earth,
and its inhabitants suffer for their guilt;
therefore the inhabitants of the earth are scorched,
and few men are left.
[7]The wine mourns,
the vine languishes,
all the merry-hearted sigh.
Jer 7:34; 16:9; 25:10 [8]The mirth of the timbrels is stilled,
Ezek 26:13 the noise of the jubilant has ceased,
Rev 18:22 the mirth of the lyre is stilled.
[9]No more do they drink wine with singing;
strong drink is bitter to those who drink it.
[10]The city of chaos is broken down,
every house is shut up so that none can enter.
[11]There is an outcry in the streets for lack of wine;
all joy has reached its eventide;
the gladness of the earth is banished.
[12]Desolation is left in the city,
the gates are battered into ruins.
Is 17:6 [13]For thus it shall be in the midst of the earth
among the nations,
as when an olive tree is beaten,
as at the gleaning when the vintage is done.

[14]They lift up their voices, they sing for joy;
over the majesty of the LORD they shout from the west.

[15]Therefore in the east give glory to the LORD;
in the coastlands of the sea, to the name of the LORD, the God of Israel.
[16]From the ends of the earth we hear songs of praise,
of glory to the Righteous One.
But I say, "I pine away,
I pine away. Woe is me!

---

habitatores eius; / ideoque imminuti sunt cultores eius, / et relicti sunt homines pauci. / [7]Luget mustum, / emarcuit vitis, / ingemiscunt omnes, qui laetabantur corde. / [8]Cessavit gaudium tympanorum, / quievit sonitus laetantium, / cessavit gaudium citharae; / [9]cum cantico non bibent vinum, / amara erit potio bibentibus illam. / [10]Attrita est civitas inanitatis, / clausa est omnis domus, ut nemo introeat; / [11]clamor est super vino in plateis, / occidit omnis laetitia, / translatum est gaudium terrae. / [12]Relicta est in urbe solitudo, / et in ruinam confracta est porta; / [13]quia haec erunt in medio terrae, / in medio populorum, / quomodo si olivae excutiantur, / et finita vindemia colligantur racemi. / [14]Hi levabunt vocem suam, / laudabunt maiestatem Domini, / hinnient de mari. / [15]Propter hoc in regionibus lucis glorificate Dominum, / in insulis maris nomen Domini, Dei Israel. / [16]A finibus terrae laudes audivimus: / «Gloria iusto». / Et dixi: «Secretum meum mihi, / secretum meum mihi. / Vae mihi!». / Praevaricantes

For the treacherous deal treacherously,
the treacherous deal very treacherously."

17 Terror, and the pit, and the snare Jer 48:43–44
are upon you, O inhabitant of the earth!
18 He who flees at the sound of the terror Gen 7:11 Amos 8:9
shall fall into the pit;
and he who climbs out of the pit
shall be caught in the snare.
For the windows of heaven are opened,
and the foundations of the earth tremble.
19 The earth is utterly broken, Is 2:10
the earth is rent asunder,
the earth is violently shaken.
20 The earth staggers like a drunken man,
it sways like a hut;
its transgression lies heavy upon it,
and it falls, and will not rise again.

21 On that day the LORD will punish Gen 6:13–8:22
the host of heaven, in heaven,
and the kings of the earth, on the earth.
22 They will be gathered together
as prisoners in a pit;
they will be shut up in a prison,
and after many days they will be punished.
23 Then the moon will be confounded, Ex 24:9–11,16
and the sun ashamed; Ps 47:1 Mt 24:29
for the LORD of hosts will reign Rev 4:4,10–11
on Mount Zion and in Jerusalem
and before his elders he will manifest his glory.

---

praevaricati sunt / et praevaricatione praevaricantium praevaricati sunt. / 17 Formido et fovea et laqueus
super te, / habitator terrae. / 18 Et erit: qui fugerit a voce formidinis, cadet in foveam; / et, qui ascenderit
de fovea, / tenebitur laqueo, / quia cataractae de excelsis apertae sunt, / et concussa sunt fundamenta
terrae. / 19 Confractione confracta est terra, / contritione contrita est terra, / commotione commota est terra,
/ 20 agitatione agitabitur terra sicut ebrius / et fluctuabit quasi tabernaculum; / et gravis erit super eam
iniquitas eius, / et corruet et non adiciet ut resurgat. / 21 Et erit in die illa: / visitabit Dominus super militiam
caeli in excelso / et super reges terrae super terram; / 22 et congregabuntur et vincientur in lacu / et
claudentur in carcere; / et post multos dies visitabuntur. / 23 Et erubescet luna, et confundetur sol, / quia
regnavit Dominus exercituum in monte Sion et in Ierusalem / et in conspectu senum suorum glorificabitur.
[25] 1 Domine, Deus meus es tu; / exaltabo te, confitebor nomini tuo, / quoniam fecisti mirabilia, /
cogitationes antiquas, fideles, veraces. / 2 Quia posuisti civitatem in tumulum, / urbem munitam in
ruinam: / arx superborum non amplius est civitas, / in sempiternum non reaedificabitur. / 3 Super hoc
glorificabit te populus fortis, / civitas gentium robustarum timebit te; / 4 quia factus es fortitudo pauperi,

Hymn of thanksgiving

Ps 31:15 **25** [1]O LORD, thou art my God;
I will exalt thee, I will praise thy name;
for thou hast done wonderful things,
plans formed of old, faithful and sure.
[2]For thou hast made the city a heap,
the fortified city a ruin;
the palace of aliens is a city no more,
it will never be rebuilt.
[3]Therefore strong peoples will glorify thee;
cities of ruthless nations will fear thee.
Is 4:5–6 [4]For thou hast been a stronghold to the poor,
Ao 7:15–16 a stronghold to the needy in his distress,
a shelter from the storm and a shade from the heat;
for the blast of the ruthless is like a storm against a wall,
5 like heat in a dry place.
Thou dost subdue the noise of the aliens;
as heat by the shade of a cloud,
so the song of the ruthless is stilled.

Mt 8:11 **The Lord's banquet**

Prov 9:2 [6]On this mountain the LORD of hosts will make for all peoples a
Mt 22:4
Lk 14:16 feast of fat things, a feast of wine on the lees, of fat things full of
Jn 6:51,54 marrow, of wine on the lees well refined. [7]And he will destroy on
this mountain the covering that is cast over all peoples, the veil

---

25:1–5. After reflecting on the just judgment of God who has caused the entire world to tremble and has chosen Jerusalem as the place to manifest his glory (cf. 24:23), the text now moves into a vibrant song of thanksgiving and praise to the Lord; the arrogant city he has defeated and turned into a place of refuge for the poor and needy (v. 4). It is not clear what city has been reduced to ruins (v. 2). It may be Babylon, but in any event and over and above any particular point in history, the song expresses the joy felt by someone who exalts the Lord at any time, in any place, rejoicing that he protects the weak and casts down the proud of heart.

25:6–8. The Lord has prepared a special feast for all the nations on Mount Zion. There he will provide succulent food and fine wine—a symbolic refer-

/ fortitudo egeno in tribulatione sua, / protectio a turbine, / umbraculum ab aestu: / spiritus enim robustorum / quasi imber hiemalis. / [5]Sicut aestus in arida / tumultum superborum humiliabis; sicut aestus in umbra nubis / canticum fortium reprimes. / [6]Et faciet Dominus exercituum / omnibus populis in monte hoc / convivium pinguium, / convivium vini meri, / pinguium medullatorum, / vini deliquati. / [7]Et praecipitabit in monte isto / faciem vinculi colligati super omnes populos / et telam, quam orditus

that is spread over all nations. [8]He will swallow up death for ever, Hos 13:14
and the Lord GOD will wipe away tears from all faces, and the *1 Cor 15:26,54–55*
reproach of his people he will take away from all the earth; for the *Rev 7:17; 21:4*
LORD has spoken.

Songs of salvation

[9]It will be said on that day, "Lo, this is our God; we have waited for him, that he might save us. This is the LORD; we have waited for him; let us be glad and rejoice in his salvation."

---

ence to the divine fare that God will provide and which surpasses anything that man could imagine.

These words prefigure the eucharistic banquet, instituted by Jesus in Jerusalem, in which he provides divine nourishment, his own Body and Blood, which strengthens the soul and is a pledge of future glory: "To share in 'the Lord's Supper' is to anticipate the eschatological feast of the 'marriage of the Lamb' (Rev 19:9). Celebrating this memorial of Christ, risen and ascended into heaven, the Christian community waits 'in joyful hope for the coming of our Saviour, Jesus Christ'" (John Paul II, *Dies Domini*, 38). The saints often encourage us to bear this in mind when we receive the Eucharist: "It is an eternal pledge to us; it assures us of a place in heaven; it is a guarantee that one day heaven will be our home. Moreover, Jesus Christ will raise up our bodies in glory, in accordance with how often and with what dignity we have received his Body in Holy Communion" (St John Baptist Mary Vianney, *Sermon on Holy Communion*).

"Death" (v. 8) is a metaphor for the definitive destruction of Israel: God gives an assurance that it will never happen. Also, St Paul quotes this verse when he rejoices that the resurrection of Christ marks the definitive victory over death (1 Cor 15:54–55), and it appears also in the book of Revelation, when it proclaims the salvation that has been wrought by the Lamb who has died and risen again: "he will wipe away every tear from their eyes, and death shall be no more, neither shall there be mourning nor crying nor pain anymore, for the former things have passed away" (Rev 21:4; cf. also Rev 7:17). The Church, too, speaks in similar vein in its prayer for the dead, beseeching God to receive them into his Kingdom "There we hope to share in your glory when every tear will be wiped away. On that day we shall see you, our God, as you are. We shall become like you and praise you forever through Christ our Lord, from whom all good things come" (*Roman Missal*, Eucharistic Prayer III).

est super omnes nationes. / [8]Praecipitabit mortem in sempiternum / et absterget Dominus Deus lacrimam ab omni facie / et opprobrium populi sui auferet de universa terra, / quia Dominus locutus est. / [9]Et dicetur in die illa: «Ecce Deus noster iste, / exspectavimus eum, ut salvaret nos; / iste Dominus, sustinuimus eum: / exsultabimus et laetabimur in salutari eius. / [10]Quia requiescet manus Domini in monte isto». / Et triturabitur Moab in loco suo, / sicuti teruntur paleae in sterquilinio; / [11]et

10 For the hand of the LORD will rest on this mountain, and
Moab shall be trodden down in his place, as straw is trodden down
in a dung-pit. 11 And he will spread out his hands in the midst of it
as a swimmer spreads his hands out to swim; but the LORD will
Is 60:18 lay low his pride together with the skill[l] of his hands. 12 And the
high fortifications of his walls he will bring down, lay low, and
cast to the ground, even to the dust.

26 1 In that day this song will be sung in the land of Judah:
"We have a strong city;
he sets up salvation
Ps 118:19–20 as walls and bulwarks.
2 Open the gates,
that the righteous nation which keeps faith
may enter in.
3 Thou dost keep him in perfect peace,
whose mind is stayed on thee,
Deut 32:4 because he trusts in thee.
4 Trust in the LORD for ever,
for the LORD GOD
is an everlasting rock.
5 For he has brought low
the inhabitants of the height,
the lofty city.
He lays it low, lays it low to the ground,
casts it to the dust.
6 The foot tramples it,
the feet of the poor,
the steps of the needy."

25:9—26:6. After the celebration of the banquet prepared by God, two hymns are intoned that will be sung "on that day". The first praises the Lord: he is faithful; those who put their hope of salvation in him will never be disappointed, whereas Moab will be laid low on account of its pride (25:9–12). The

extendet manus suas in medio eius, / sicut extendit natans ad natandum; / et humiliabitur superbia eius / cum allisione manuum eius. / 12 Et firmum munimentum murorum tuorum evertit, / deiecit, prostravit in terram usque ad pulverem. **[26]** 1 In die illa cantabitur canticum istud in terra Iudae: / «Urbs fortis nobis in salutem; / posuit muros et antemurale. / 2 Aperite portas, et ingrediatur gens iusta, / quae servat fidem. / 3 Propositum eius est firmum; / servabis pacem, / quia in te speravit. / 4 Sperate in Dominum in saeculis aeternis, / Dominus est petra aeterna. / 5 Quia evertit habitantes in excelso, / civitatem sublimem humiliabit; / humiliabit eam usque ad terram, / detrahet eam usque ad pulverem. / 6 Conculcabit eam

l. The meaning of the Hebrew word is uncertain

The righteous call on the Lord

7The way of the righteous is level;
thou[m] dost make smooth the path of the righteous.
8In the path of thy judgments,
O LORD, we wait for thee;
thy memorial name
is the desire of our soul.
9My soul yearns for thee in the night, Ps 42:2
my spirit within me earnestly seeks thee.
For when thy judgments are in the earth,
the inhabitants of the world learn righteousness.
10 If favour is shown to the wicked,
he does not learn righteousness;
in the land of uprightness he deals perversely
and does not see the majesty of the LORD.
11 O LORD, thy hand is lifted up,
but they see it not.

---

second hymn returns (cf. 25:1–5) to the theme of praise of the Lord for giving refuge to the poor and needy (26:1–6).

26:7–19. Now comes a personal dialogue with God in the form of a prayer or sapiential psalm (vv. 7–10). Here the greatness of the Lord is not being described to third parties nor are his works being praised: the prophet is addressing him directly, to tell him that he trusts in Him (vv. 7–8), to express his innermost feelings (v. 9a; cf. Ps 42), to ask him to reveal his righteousness (vv. 9b–10) and intervene (v. 11) and bring peace (v. 12), and to celebrate enduring fidelity to the Lord (vv. 13–19). Verse 19 is a ray of hope in personal resurrection, although here, as in 25:8, it refers to the resurgence of the nation, as in the vision of the bones restored to life in the book of Ezekiel (cf. Ezek 37:1–14). Daniel 12:1–3 clearly predicts the resurrection of people from the dead. Commenting on v. 10, St Bernard addresses God, saying: "Father of mercies, may your anger be roused against me—the anger that chastens a soul who has lost his way, not the wrath by which you seal off the path of righteousness" (*In Cantica Canticorum*, 42, 4).

pes, pedes pauperis, / gressus egenorum. / 7Semita iusti recta est; / rectum callem iusti complanas. / 8Et in semita iudiciorum tuorum, Domine, speravimus in te; / ad nomen tuum et ad memoriale tuum desiderium animae. / 9Anima mea desiderat te in nocte, / sed et spiritu meo in praecordiis meis te quaero. / Cum resplenduerint iudicia tua in terra, / iustitiam discent habitatores orbis. / 10Fit misericordia impio, / non discet iustitiam; / in terra probitatis inique gerit / et non videt maiestatem Domini. / 11Domine, exaltata est manus tua, et non vident; / videant confusi zelum tuum in populum, / et ignis hostium tuorum devorabit eos. / 12Domine, dabis pacem nobis; / omnia enim opera nostra

m. Cn Compare Gk: Heb *thou (that art) upright*

Let them see thy zeal for thy people, and be ashamed.
    Let the fire for thy adversaries consume them.
12 O LORD, thou wilt ordain peace for us,
    thou hast wrought for us all our works.
2 Tim 2:19 13 O LORD our God,
    other LORDS besides thee have ruled over us,
    but thy name alone we acknowledge.
14 They are dead, they will not live;
    they are shades, they will not arise;
to that end thou hast visited them with destruction
    and wiped out all remembrance of them.
15 But thou hast increased the nation, O LORD,
    thou hast increased the nation; thou art glorified;
    thou hast enlarged all the borders of the land.

16 O LORD, in distress they sought thee,
    they poured out a prayer[n]
    when thy chastening was upon them.
Is 13:8;37:3 17 Like a woman with child,
Hos 13:3 who writhes and cries out in her pangs,
    when she is near her time,
so were we because of thee, O LORD;
18 we were with child, we writhed,
    we have as it were brought forth wind.

26:20—27:13. The "Great Apocalypse" (24:1—27:13) culminates in a call to witness the judgment of the Lord, when all mankind will be called to account (26:20–21; cf. Rev 3:10; 6:10). We have here four oracles, each beginning with a formal reference to "that day" (27:1, 2, 12, 13).

The first is a symbolic description of the punishment that will overtake the nations that have oppressed Israel. "Leviathan" according to the ancients, was a sea monster, a kind of serpent or dragon; it personified the raging chaos of the sea and forces hostile to God (cf. Job 3:8). The first "Leviathan" refers to Assyria; the second, probably to Babylon; and the sea dragon to Egypt.

In contrast with that oracle the second one (27:2–11) is favourable to

operatus es nobis. / [13]Domine Deus noster, possederunt nos domini absque te; / tantum in te recordemur nominis tui. / [14]Mortui non reviviscent, / defuncti non resurgent; / propterea visitasti et contrivisti eos et perdidisti omnem memoriam eorum. / [15]Auxisti gentem, Domine, / auxisti gentem, glorificatus es; / elongasti omnes terminos terrae. / [16]Domine, in angustia quaesierunt te, / fuderunt incantationem, castigatio tua in eis. / [17]Sicut quae concipit, cum appropinquaverit ad partum / dolens clamat in doloribus suis, / sic facti sumus a facie tua, Domine. / [18]Concepimus et parturivimus, / quasi peperimus

n. Heb uncertain

We have wrought no deliverance in the earth,
and the inhabitants of the world have not fallen.
19 Thy dead shall live, their bodies[o] shall rise.
O dwellers in the dust, awake and sing for joy!
For thy dew is a dew of light,
and on the land of the shades thou wilt let it fall.

Ezek 37
Dan 12:1–3
Hos 13:14
Eph 5:14

The Lord hands down judgment

20 Come, my people, enter your chambers,
and shut your doors behind you;
hide yourselves for a little while
until the wrath is past.
21 For behold, the LORD is coming forth out of his place
to punish the inhabitants of the earth for their iniquity,
and the earth will disclose the blood shed upon her,
and will no more cover her slain.

Job 14:13–15
Mt 6:6
Heb10:37

Job 16:18
Mt 1:3
Rev 3:10; 6:10

27 1 In that day the LORD with his hard and great and strong sword will punish Leviathan the fleeing serpent, Leviathan the twisting serpent, and he will slay the dragon that is in the sea.

Job 3:8; 40:25

Israel; it uses the simile of the vineyard, already seen in 5:1–7. Unlike that earlier song which complained that the vineyard was unproductive despite all the care that the Lord had given it, now we find it in good working order; the Lord will protect it, and it will yield fruit even though it will have to go through a painful cleansing process (27:6–11). St Paul uses 27:9 to announce the ultimate salvation of Israel (cf. Rom 11:25–27).

The last two oracles announce the happy future that awaits Israel (27:12–13). The passage contains two references to the call addressed to the people of Israel scattered across the world, including deportees; they will come and worship the Lord in Jerusalem. "From the river Euphrates to the Brook of Egypt": the original says "From the River ...": this means just as the RSV says, the Euphrates. The Brook must be Wadi-al-Arish which flows out of the northern coast of the Sinai peninsula. These were seen as being the true, ideal, frontiers of Israel.

ventum. / Salutes non fecimus in terra, / ideo non nati sunt habitatores terrae. / 19Reviviscent mortui tui, interfecti mei resurgent. / Expergiscimini et laudate, qui habitatis in pulvere, / quia ros lucis ros tuus, / et terra defunctos suos edet in lucem. / 20Vade, populus meus, intra in cubicula tua, / claude ostia tua super te, / abscondere modicum ad momentum, / donec pertranseat indignatio. / 21Ecce enim Dominus egredietur de loco suo, / ut visitet iniquitatem habitatoris terrae contra eum; / et revelabit terra sanguinem suum / et non operiet ultra interfectos suos». **[27]** 1In die illa visitabit Dominus / in gladio suo duro et forti et grandi / super Leviathan serpentem fugacem / et super Leviathan serpentem

o. Cn Compare Syr Tg: Heb *my body*

Is 5:1–7 [2]In that day:
"A pleasant vineyard, sing of it!
[3] I, the LORD, am its keeper;
every moment I water it.
Lest any one harm it,
I guard it night and day;
[4] I have no wrath.
Would that I had thorns and briers to battle!
I would set out against them,
I would burn them up together.
[5]Or let them lay hold of my protection,
let them make peace with me,
let them make peace with me."

[6]In days to come[q] Jacob shall take root,
Israel shall blossom and put forth shoots,
and fill the whole world with fruit.

[7]Has he smitten them as he smote those who smote them?
Or have they been slain as their slayers were slain?
[8]Measure by measure,[r] by exile thou didst contend with them;
he removed them with his fierce blast in the day of the east wind.
Ex 34:13 [9]Therefore by this the guilt of Jacob will be expiated,
2 Kings 23:6–14 and this will be the full fruit of the removal of his sin:
Is 17:8 when he makes all the stones of the altars
Rom 11:25–27 like chalkstones crushed to pieces,
no Asherim or incense altars will remain standing.
[10] For the fortified city is solitary,
a habitation deserted and forsaken, like the wilderness;
there the calf grazes,
there he lies down, and strips its branches.

---

tortuosum / et occidet draconem, qui in mari est. / [2]In die illa vinea erit iucunda; / cantate ei. / [3]Ego Dominus, qui servo eam; / per singula momenta irrigabo eam. / Ne forte visitetur contra eam, / nocte et die servo eam. / [4]Indignatio non est mihi. / Quis dabit mihi spinam et veprem? / In proelio gradiar super eam, / succendam eam pariter, / [5]nisi forte protectionem meam apprehendat, / faciat pacem mecum, / pacem faciat mecum. / [6]Diebus futuris radices mittet Iacob, / florebit et germinabit Israel, / et implebunt faciem orbis fructibus. / [7]Numquid iuxta plagam percutientis eum percussit eum? / Aut, sicut occiduntur occisi eius, occisus est? / [8]In mensura punit eum deiciens eum, / impellit in spiritu suo duro, tempore quo spirat eurus. / [9]Idcirco super hoc dimittetur iniquitas Iacob, / et hic erit omnis fructus ablationis peccati eius: / ut scilicet ponat omnes lapides altaris / sicut lapides calcis comminutos, / ne exstent luci et thymiateria. / [10]Civitas enim munita desolata est, / habitaculum derelictum et dimissum quasi desertum; / ibi pascetur vitulus et ibi accubabit / et consumet arbusta eius. / [11]In siccitate frondes

q. Heb *Those to come* **r.** Compare Syr Vg Tg: The meaning of the Hebrew word is unknown

11 When its boughs are dry, they are broken;
women come and make a fire of them.
For this is a people without discernment;
therefore he who made them will not have compassion on them,
he that formed them will show them no favour.

12 In that day from the river Euphrates to the Brook of Egypt the
LORD will thresh out the grain, and you will be gathered one by
one, O people of Israel. 13 And in that day a great trumpet will be — Num 10:1–2
blown, and those who were lost in the land of Assyria and those — Is 2:2; 18:3; Joel 2:1,15
who were driven out to the land of Egypt will come and worship — Zech 14:6
the LORD on the holy mountain at Jerusalem.

4. OBDURACY OF ISRAEL AND JUDAH*

Lamentation concerning the rulers of the people — Amos 4:1; 6:4–6; Hos 7:5; Is 5:11–13

28 1 Woe to the proud crown of the drunkards of Ephraim,
and to the fading flower of its glorious beauty,
which is on the head of the rich valley of those overcome
with wine!
2 Behold, the LORD has one who is mighty and strong;
like a storm of hail, a destroying tempest,
like a storm of mighty, overflowing waters,
he will cast down to the earth with violence.

***28:1—33:24.** We now come to the fourth section of the first part of the book of Isaiah. God, the Lord of all the world, now passes sentence on the nations for the evil they have done, and he prepares the way for Israel and Judah, once their exiles have returned, to share in his glory. However (and this is the theme of the section), the chosen people are not ready. And so we find a tone of complaint about those whose lifestyle is in fact opposed to God's plans of salvation.

The section is made up of six units, known as the "woes" of Isaiah because each begins on that note of lamentation (28:1; 29:1, 15; 30:1; 31:1; 33:1).

28:1–29. The first "woe" is directed at the rulers of the people. Like drunken men, out of their minds, they fail to discern the works and purposes of God.

illius conterentur; / mulieres venient et comburent eas. / Ipse enim non est populus sapiens, / propterea non miserebitur eius, qui fecit eum, / et, qui formavit eum, non parcet ei. / 12 Et erit: in die illa percutiet spicas Dominus / a Flumine usque ad torrentem Aegypti; / et vos congregabimini / unus et unus, filii Israel. / 13 Et erit: in die illa clangetur in tuba magna; / et venient, qui perditi fuerant de terra Assyriorum, / et qui eiecti erant in terra Aegypti, / et adorabunt Dominum / in monte sancto in Ierusalem. **[28]** 1 Vae coronae superbiae ebriorum Ephraim / et flori decidenti gloriae maiestatis eius,

[3]The proud crown of the drunkards of Ephraim
will be trodden under foot;
[4]and the fading flower of its glorious beauty,
which is on the head of the rich valley,
will be like a first-ripe fig before the summer:
when a man sees it, he eats it up
as soon as it is in his hand.

[5]In that day the LORD of hosts will be a crown of glory,
and a diadem of beauty, to the remnant of his people;
Is 4:3; 11:2–4 [6]and a spirit of justice to him who sits in judgment,
and strength to those who turn back the battle at the gate.

There are two denunciations here—one of the Northern kingdom (vv. 1–6), and another, more elaborate, of the Southern (vv. 7–29).

The first piece (vv. 1–6) is a judgment against Ephraim, which stands for all the Northern kingdom. As other prophets had done previously (cf. Amos 4:1; 6:4–6 and Hos 7:5), Isaiah upbraids its inhabitants for being drunk with self-confidence. He warns them of impending invasion by Assyria. The "one who is mighty and strong" (v. 2) may be the Assyrian king, Sargon, who captured Samaria and put an end to the kingdom of Israel. Isaiah contrasts the "crown" that drunkards don in their pride (vv. 1, 3) with the "crown of glory" (v. 5) that the Lord will be for the "remnant" that stays faithful to him.

The second piece (vv. 7–20) is a judgment against Jerusalem, spelt out in three diatribes. The first is against priests and false prophets who deceive the people (vv. 7–13). Isaiah mocks them (v. 10) by describing how their words sound to the people—like the babbling of children who are beginning to speak, or the senseless talk of drunkards (the RSV translates the Hebrew literally, but the words are probably meant to imitate inarticulate sounds). God will laugh at them and he will also speak to them in their own unintelligible language (cf. v. 13). St Paul uses v. 11 to warn Christians against abusing the gift of tongues (cf. 1 Cor 14:20–22).

The second diatribe (vv. 14–19) is aimed at bad rulers and counsellors. They think that lies will protect them but they will only lead them to their deaths. By contrast, the Lord has laid a cornerstone in Zion, a sure foundation —law and righteousness (cf. vv. 16–17). From very early on, the precious stone, "a tested stone", was interpreted as a reference to the Messiah. In the Qumran texts found near the Dead Sea, this

/ qui erant in vertice vallis pinguissimae, / errantes a vino! / [2]Ecce validus et fortis Domino / sicut impetus grandinis, turbo confringens, / sicut impetus aquarum multarum inundantium, / et deiciet in terram violenter. / [3]Pedibus conculcabitur / corona superbiae ebriorum Ephraim; / [4]et erit flos decidens gloriae maiestatis eius, / qui est super verticem vallis pinguium, / quasi ficus praecox ante messem, / quam quis, ut viderit, / manu statim arreptam devorabit. / [5]In die illa erit Dominus exercituum / corona gloriae / et sertum maiestatis / residuo populi sui / [6]et spiritus iudicii / sedenti ad iudicandum / et

[7]These also reel with wine
and stagger with strong drink;
the priest and the prophet reel with strong drink,
they are confused with wine,
they stagger with strong drink;
they err in vision,
they stumble in giving judgment.
[8]For all tables are full of vomit,
no place is without filthiness.

Prov 20:1
Is 5:11–13; 19:14; 59:10
Hos 4:11

[9]"Whom will he teach knowledge,
and to whom will he explain the message?
Those who are weaned from the milk,
those taken from the breast?
[10]For it is precept upon precept, precept upon precept,
line upon line, line upon line,
here a little, there a little."

Jer 6:10

---

stone is the community; in the *targum* or Aramaic version it is the Messiah King. In the New Testament we find many references to the Christological meaning of the cornerstone—sometimes citing Psalm 118:22 (Mt 21:42), sometimes when explaining that the Church is God's building (1 Pet 2:4–8). St Peter in the same letter (1 Pet 2:8) refers to its being a stumbling block, and in Romans 9:33 it occurs in connexion with the scandal that St Paul's preaching provoked in some Jews.

The third diatribe (vv. 20–29) refers to the entire people; it has an exceptionally serious tone and warns that when the Lord acts, it is not a time to make jokes: he must be heeded. The prophet compares God's way of acting with that of a farmer—methodical, undramatic, but effective. God sometimes treats his people roughly, just as a farmer can be hard on the land when preparing it for cultivation. The passage is a lesson in divine providence: God grooms his people by means of teachings, rewards and punishment. It is also a reflection on the "signs of the times", which we must always read even though it becomes more difficult to do so when some misfortune overtakes us that we cannot or do not want to understand. Agricultural work is often used as a simile for God's method of working—as, for example, in the New Testament parable of the sower (Mt 13:1–23 and par.).

fortitudo / vertentibus proelium usque ad portam. / [7]Verum hi quoque prae vino vacillant / et prae ebrietate nutant; / sacerdos et propheta vacillant prae ebrietate, / absorpti sunt a vino, / nutant in ebrietate, / vacillant in visione, / fluctuant in iudicio. / [8]Omnes enim mensae repletae sunt vomitu sordiumque, / ita ut non esset ultra locus. / [9]Quem docebit scientiam? / Et quem intellegere faciet auditum? / Ablactatos a lacte, / avulsos ab uberibus. / [10]Etenim praeceptum ad praeceptum, praeceptum ad praeceptum, / regula ad regulam, regula ad regulam, / modicum ibi, modicum ibi. / [11]Balbis enim labiis et lingua altera / loquetur ad populum istum, / [12]cui dixerat: «Haec requies, reficite lassum; / et

Jer 5:15
1 Cor 14:21

11 Nay, but by men of strange lips
and with an alien tongue
the LORD will speak to this people,
12 to whom he has said,
"This is rest;
give rest to the weary;
and this is repose";
yet they would not hear.
13 Therefore the word of the LORD will be to them
precept upon precept, precept upon precept,
line upon line, line upon line,
here a little, there a little;
that they may go, and fall backward,
and be broken, and snared, and taken.

14 Therefore hear the word of the LORD, you scoffers,
who rule this people in Jerusalem!

Wis 1:16
Sir 14:12
Jer 5:12
Amos 9:10

15 Because you have said, "We have made a covenant with death,
and with Sheol we have an agreement;
when the overwhelming scourge passes through
it will not come to us;
for we have made lies our refuge,
and in falsehood we have taken shelter";

Gen 49:24
Ps 118:22–23
Is 1:26; 7:9
Mt 16:18; 21:42
Rom 9:33
1 Cor 3:11
Eph 3:20
1 Pet 2:6

16 therefore thus says the Lord GOD,
"Behold, I am laying in Zion for a foundation
a stone, a tested stone,
a precious cornerstone, of a sure foundation:
'He who believes will not be in haste.'

Is 28:15

17 And I will make justice the line,
and righteousness the plummet;
and hail will sweep away the refuge of lies,
and waters will overwhelm the shelter."
18 Then your covenant with death will be annulled,
and your agreement with Sheol will not stand;

---

hoc est refrigerium». / Et noluerunt audire. / 13Et erit eis verbum Domini: / «Praeceptum ad praeceptum, praeceptum ad praeceptum, / regula ad regulam, regula ad regulam, / modicum ibi, modicum ibi», / ut vadant et cadant retrorsum et conterantur / et illaqueentur et capiantur. / 14Propter hoc audite verbum Domini, / viri illusores, qui dominamini super populum meum, / qui est in Ierusalem. / 15Dixistis enim: «Percussimus foedus cum morte / et cum inferno fecimus pactum; / flagellum inundans cum transierit, / non veniet super nos, / quia posuimus mendacium spem nostram / et in fallacia absconditi sumus». / 16Idcirco haec dicit Dominus Deus: / «Ecce ego fundamentum ponam in Sion, lapidem, / lapidem probatum, angularem, pretiosum, fundatum; / qui crediderit, non turbabitur. / 17Et ponam iudicium tamquam normam / et iustitiam tamquam perpendiculum; / et subvertet grando spem mendacii, / et latibulum aquae inundabunt. / 18Et delebitur foedus vestrum cum morte, / et pactum

when the overwhelming scourge passes through
you will be beaten down by it.
19 As often as it passes through it will take you;
for morning by morning it will pass through,
by day and by night;
and it will be sheer terror to understand the message.
20 For the bed is too short to stretch oneself on it,
and the covering too narrow to wrap oneself in it.
21 For the LORD will rise up as on Mount Perazim, 2 Sam 5:17–25
he will be wroth as in the valley of Gibeon;
to do his deed—strange is his deed!
and to work his work—alien is his work!
22 Now therefore do not scoff,
lest your bonds be made strong;
for I have heard a decree of destruction
from the Lord GOD of hosts upon the whole land.

23 Give ear, and hear my voice; Mt 13:19
hearken, and hear my speech.
24 Does he who ploughs for sowing plough continually?
does he continually open and harrow his ground?
25 When he has leveled its surface,
does he not scatter dill, sow cummin,
and put in wheat in rows
and barley in its proper place,
and spelt as the border?
26 For he is instructed aright;
his God teaches him.

27 Dill is not threshed with a threshing sledge,
nor is a cart wheel rolled over cummin;
but dill is beaten out with a stick,
and cummin with a rod.

---

vestrum cum inferno non stabit; / flagellum inundans cum transierit, / eritis ei in conculcationem. /
19Quandocumque pertransierit, tollet vos; / quoniam mane diluculo pertransibit, / in die et in nocte, / et
erit tantummodo horrendum intellegere auditum». / 20Coangustatum est enim stratum, ut quis se
extendat, / et pallium brevius, ut quis se operire possit. / 21Sicut enim in monte Pharasim stabit
Dominus, / sicut in valle, quae est in Gabaon, irascetur, / ut faciat opus suum, novum opus suum, / ut
operetur operationem suam, / peregrinam operationem suam. / 22Et nunc nolite illudere, / ne forte
constringantur vincula vestra; / decretum enim destructionis audivi / a Domino, Deo exercituum, / super
universam terram. / 23Auribus percipite et audite vocem meam, / attendite et audite eloquium meum.
/ 24Numquid tota die arat arans, ut serat, / proscindit et sarrit humum suam? / 25Nonne, cum
adaequaverit faciem eius, / spargit nigellam et serit cuminum, / ponit triticum et hordeum / et far in
finibus suis? / 26Erudit enim illum recte, / Deus suus docet illum. / 27Non enim in serris trituratur

28 Does one crush bread grain?
No, he does not thresh it for ever;
when he drives his cart wheel over it
with his horses, he does not crush it.
29 This also comes from the LORD of hosts;
he is wonderful in counsel,
and excellent in wisdom.

Lamentation over Ariel

2 Sam 5:9
Ezek 43:15–16

29 1 Ho Ariel, Ariel,
the city where David encamped!
Add year to year;
let the feasts run their round.

Is 33:7; 36:1–2; 37:33–37

2 Yet I will distress Ariel,
and there shall be moaning and lamentation,
and she shall be to me like an Ariel.

29:1–14. This lamentation is addressed to Jerusalem, here given the symbolic name of Ariel, which was also used for the upper part of the altar of sacrifice in the temple (cf. Ezek 43:15; see the note on Ezek 43:13–17). The oracle concerns the siege of the holy city by the Assyrian army in 701 BC (vv. 1–4), a siege that would be mysteriously lifted a few months later (vv. 5–8). However, all this is simply a call to the people of Jerusalem: their hard-heartedness is preventing them from understanding the words of the Lord. The prophet complains about Jerusalem's blindness, its failure to "read" the message that God is sending in the events around them (vv. 9–11). The passage ends by denouncing religious formalism—lip-service offered by people whose hearts are far from God (vv. 13–14).

Hardness of heart or a disinclination to see the hand of God in events, taking refuge in mere religious conformism, was something about which Jesus had harsh things to say: "For the sake of your tradition you have made void the word of God. You hypocrites! Well did Isaiah prophesy of you, when he said: 'This people honours me with their lips, and their heart is far from me; in vain do they worship me, teaching as doctrines the precepts of men'" (Mt 15:6b–9; cf. Mk 7:6–8).

In the Letter to the Romans, St Paul uses words from v. 10 when discussing Israel's role in God's plan of salvation: "God gave them a spirit of stupor, eyes that should not see and ears that should not hear, down to this very day" (Rom 11:8). He says, in effect, that Jewish failure to believe in Christ was part of

nigella, / nec rota plaustri super cuminum circuit; / sed in virga excutitur nigella, / et cuminum in baculo. / [28]Numquid comminuitur triticum? / Verum non in perpetuum triturans triturabit illum, / neque vexabit eum rota plaustri, / nec ungulis suis comminuet eum. / [29]Et hoc a Domino, Deo exercituum, exivit; / mirabile fecit consilium, / magnificavit sapientiam. **[29]** [1]Vae Ariel, Ariel, civitas, / quam circumdedit David! / Addite annum ad annum, / sollemnitates evolvantur; / [2]et circumvallabo Ariel, /

[3]And I will encamp against you round about, Lk 19:43
and will besiege you with towers
and I will raise siegeworks against you.
[4]Then deep from the earth you shall speak,
from low in the dust your words shall come;
your voice shall come from the ground like the voice of a ghost,
and your speech shall whisper out of the dust.

[5]But the multitude of your foes[s] shall be like small dust,
and the multitude of the ruthless like passing chaff.
And in an instant, suddenly,
[6]you will be visited by the LORD of hosts Ex 13:22; 19:16
with thunder and with earthquake and great noise,
with whirlwind and tempest, and the flame of a devouring fire.
[7]And the multitude of all the nations that fight against Ariel,
all that fight against her and her stronghold and distress her,
shall be like a dream, a vision of the night.
[8]As when a hungry man dreams he is eating
and awakes with his hunger not satisfied,
or as when a thirsty man dreams he is drinking
and awakes faint, with his thirst not quenched,
so shall the multitude of all the nations be
that fight against Mount Zion.

God's plan. And in the Letter to the Corinthians, in connexion with the wisdom of the cross, he quotes v. 14b: "For the word of the cross is folly to those who are perishing, but to us who are being saved it is the power of God. For it is written, 'I will destroy the wisdom of the wise, and the cleverness of the clever I will thwart'" (1 Cor 1:18–19). At the time of Sennacherib's invasion, God confounded the human prudence that favoured an alliance with Egypt; and he also confounds the human wisdom that sees the cross of Christ as being folly: "The wisdom of wise men founders when what they say can never come to pass does come to pass; and the knowledge of prudent men is overthrown when God, whom they believe to be far away, intervenes in what they think are the foolish affairs of men" (Ambrosiaster, *Ad Corinthios*, 1, 19).

et erit maeror et maestitia, / et erit mihi quasi Ariel. / [3]Et circumdabo te quasi sphaeram / et iaciam contra te aggerem / et munimenta ponam in obsidionem tuam. / [4]Humiliaberis, de terra loqueris, / et de pulvere vix audietur eloquium tuum, / et erit quasi pythonis de terra vox tua, / et de humo eloquium tuum mussitabit. / [5]Et erit sicut pulvis tenuis multitudo superborum tuorum, / et sicut palea volans multitudo fortium. / Eritque repente confestim, / [6]a Domino exercituum visitaberis / in tonitruo et commotione terrae, / magno fragore, turbine et tempestate / et flamma ignis devorantis. / [7]Et erit sicut

s. Cn: Heb *strangers*

9 Stupefy yourselves and be in a stupor,
blind yourselves and be blind!
Be drunk, but not with wine;
stagger, but not with strong drink!

1 Sam 16:14 / Is 19:14 / Rom 11:8

10 For the LORD has poured out upon you
a spirit of deep sleep,
and has closed your eyes, the prophets,
and covered your heads, the seers.

Is 8:16 / Dan 12:4,9 / 2 Cor 3:14–15 / Rev 5:1–3

11 And the vision of all this has become to you like the words of
a book that is sealed. When men give it to one who can read,
saying, "Read this," he says, "I cannot, for it is sealed." 12 And
when they give the book to one who cannot read, saying, "Read
this," he says, "I cannot read."

Amos 5:21 / *Mt 15:8–9* / Is 1:10–20

13 And the LORD said:
"Because this people draw near with their mouth
and honour me with their lips,
while their hearts are far from me,
and their fear of me is a commandment of men learned by rote;

Jer 49:7 / Obad 8 / *1 Cor 1:19*

14 therefore, behold, I will again
do marvellous things with this people,
wonderful and marvellous;
and the wisdom of their wise men shall perish,
and the discernment of their discerning men shall be hid."

Against those who hide from the Lord

Job 22:13 / Ps 10:4

15 Woe to those who hide deep from the LORD their counsel,
whose deeds are in the dark,

29:15–24. The third "woe" marks the start of the third lamentation. First, it describes the ridiculous situation of someone who thinks he can escape divine judgment (vv. 15–16). The simile of the clay and the potter (cf. the note

somnium visionis nocturnae / multitudo omnium gentium, quae dimicant contra Ariel, / et omnes, qui pugnant contra eam et contra munimenta eius et oppressores eius; / 8 Et sicut somniat esuriens, et ecce comedit, / cum autem fuerit expergefactus, vacua est anima eius; / et sicut somniat sitiens, et ecce bibit / et, postquam fuerit expergefactus, lassus adhuc sitit, / et anima eius vacua est, / sic erit multitudo omnium gentium / dimicantium contra montem Sion. / 9 Obstupescite et admiramini, / excaecamini et caeci estote, / inebriamini et non a vino, / vacillate et non ab ebrietate. / 10 Quoniam miscuit vobis Dominus spiritum soporis, / clausit oculos vestros / et capita vestra operuit. 11 Et erit vobis visio omnis sicut verba libri signati; quem cum dederint scienti litteras dicentes: «Lege istum», respondebit: «Non possum, signatus est enim». 12 Et dabitur liber nescienti litteras diceturque ei: «Lege», et respondebit: «Nescio litteras». 13 Et dixit Dominus: «Eo quod appropinquat populus iste ore suo / et labiis suis glorificat me, / cor autem eius longe est a me, / et est timor eorum erga me / velut mandatum hominum perceptum, / 14 ideo ecce ego addam ut admirationem faciam / populo huic miraculo grandi et stupendo: / peribit sapientia sapientium eius, / et prudentia prudentium eius abscondetur». / 15 Vae, qui profunde

and who say, "Who sees us? Who knows us?"
16 You turn things upside down!
Shall the potter be regarded as the clay;
that the thing made should say of its maker,
"He did not make me";
or the thing formed say of him who formed it,
"He has no understanding"?

Wis 12:12
Sir 33:13
Is 45:9; 64:7
Jer 18:1–6;
19:1–13
Rom 9:20–21

17 Is it not yet a very little while
until Lebanon shall be turned into a fruitful field,
and the fruitful field shall be regarded as a forest?
18 In that day the deaf shall hear
the words of a book,
and out of their gloom and darkness
the eyes of the blind shall see.

Is 35:5
Mt 11:5
Lk 7:22

---

on Jer 18:1–12) shows how senseless it is to deny that man has a "Maker", or to try to tell God that he doesn't know what he is doing. The prophet denounces the folly shown by the people of Judah who have wandered away from God. In Romans 9:20–21, St Paul will use the argument of v. 16 to show that God is free to do as he wishes with nations and individuals (cf. 45:9).

However, things will change (vv. 17–24). The Lord is going to take action and when he does, no one will be able to evade him: the deaf will hear, the blind will see, there will be no more oppression or hardness of heart.

Cure of illnesses, specifically release from deafness and blindness (vv. 18–19; cf. 35:5), is a feature of messianic times; it will be the signal that the kingdom has been reconstituted. St Matthew says that when Jesus was told about the questions asked by the disciples of John—was Jesus he who was to come, or should they wait for another—he replied: "Go and tell John what you hear and see: the blind receive their sight and the lame walk, lepers are cleansed and the deaf hear, and the dead are raised up, and the poor have good news preached to them. And blessed is he who takes no offence at me" (Mt 11:4–6; cf. Is 26:19; 35:5–6; 61:1–3). Thus, by referring to these actions of his, Jesus is showing that he is the Messiah, whose mission is to establish the Kingdom of God, just as Isaiah had prophesied.

The last promise (vv. 22–24) is deeply rooted in patriarchal tradition. The vocation of Abraham (this is the only place in the Bible where he is described as "redeemed") and the story of Jacob who managed to survive all kinds of dangers, form the foundation for all hope of an enduring deliverance and salvation.

a Domino / consilium abscondunt, / quorum sunt in tenebris opera, et dicunt: / «Quis videt nos, et quis novit nos?». / [16]Perversa cogitatio vestra! / Numquid quasi lutum reputabitur figulus, / ut dicat opus factori suo: / «Non fecisti me»; / et figmentum dicat fictori suo: / «Non intellegis»? / [17]Nonne adhuc in modico et in brevi convertetur Libanus in hortum, / et hortus in saltum reputabitur? / [18]Et audient in die

1 Sam 2:5ff
Is 6:3
19 The meek shall obtain fresh joy in the LORD,
and the poor among men shall exult in the Holy One of Israel.
20 For the ruthless shall come to nought and the scoffer cease,
and all who watch to do evil shall be cut off,
21 who by a word make a man out to be an offender,
and lay a snare for him who reproves in the gate,
and with an empty plea turn aside him who is in the right.

Is 41:8; 51:2 22 Therefore thus says the LORD, who redeemed Abraham,
concerning the house of Jacob:
"Jacob shall no more be ashamed,
no more shall his face grow pale.
Mt 6:9 23 For when he sees his children,
the work of my hands, in his midst,
they will sanctify my name;
they will sanctify the Holy One of Jacob,
and will stand in awe of the God of Israel.
24 And those who err in spirit will come to understanding,
and those who murmur will accept instruction."

Lamentation over rebellious children

Jer 2:18 30 1 "Woe to the rebellious children," says the LORD,
"who carry out a plan, but not mine;
and who make a league, but not of my spirit,
that they may add sin to sin;

30:1–33. The fourth lamentation is aimed at those who waste their time in a vain search for Egyptian help against the Assyrians; they should be counting on God and relying completely on him. It begins by warning them that they are going to be punished, but then the tone changes, to the point that we are told that God is going to be kind to his people and will show them what they must do to free themselves from the Assyrian threat (vv. 18–33).

To begin with (vv. 1–17) the main point being made is that it is sheer rebellion, it makes no sense, to draw up plans that don't take account of God: it makes no sense to seek protection from Egypt; it is too weak to help anyone.

illa surdi verba libri, / et de tenebris et caligine oculi caecorum videbunt. / [19]Et addent mites in Domino laetitiam, / et pauperrimi hominum in Sancto Israel exsultabunt; / [20]quoniam defecit, qui praevalebat, / consummatus est illusor, / et succisi sunt omnes, qui vigilabant super iniquitatem, / [21]qui peccare faciebant homines in verbo / et arguentem in porta supplantabant / et deiecerunt inanibus verbis iustum. / [22]Propter hoc haec dicit Dominus / ad domum Iacob, qui redemit Abraham: / «Non modo confundetur Iacob, / nec modo vultus eius erubescet; / [23]sed, cum viderit opera manuum mearum, / in medio sui sanctificabunt nomen meum / et sanctificabunt Sanctum Iacob / et Deum Israel pavebunt, / [24]et scient errantes spiritu sapientiam, / et mussitatores discent doctrinam». **[30]** [1]«Vae, filii desertores, dicit Dominus, / eo quod facitis consilium et non ex me, / et pactum statuitis et non per spiritum meum, / ut

[2]who set out to go down to Egypt,
  without asking for my counsel,
 to take refuge in the protection of Pharaoh,
  and to seek shelter in the shadow of Egypt!
[3]Therefore shall the protection of Pharaoh turn to your shame,
  and the shelter in the shadow of Egypt to your humiliation.
[4]For though his officials are at Zoan
  and his envoys reach Hanes,
[5]every one comes to shame
  through a people that cannot profit them,
 that brings neither help nor profit,
  but shame and disgrace."

Is 20:5; 36:5–9
Jer 37:5,7

The Lord denounces the distrust of God implicit in overtures to Egypt (vv. 1–7). The prophet must warn the people who obstinately refuse to obey God's Law and have no time for prophets (vv. 8–11): an alliance with Egypt (vv. 12–14) will lead to disaster; it is progressively described as troublesome or dangerous (v. 6), worthless (v. 7), and absolutely perverse (vv. 12–14). They could have avoided punishment if they had had recourse to the Lord, but they have trusted in their own strength, thinking to find help in their allies' horses (vv. 15–17). Zoan (Tanis) and Hanes (Hierapolis), mentioned in v. 4, are Egyptian cities in the Nile Delta (cf. the note on 19:1–25). Rahab (v. 7) was a sea monster in Eastern mythology, and is sometimes used as a name for Egypt (cf. Job 9:13; 26:12; Ps 87:4; 89:11).

The second part of the lamentation (vv. 18–33) consists of a number of oracles which contain promises that Jerusalem will be delivered, and threats that Assyria will be punished. It begins by describing how happy the people will be if they turn back to their God (vv. 18–22). The Lord eagerly awaits their return, for he is full of kindness and mercy towards those who trust in him (v. 18).

As soon as they return, they will enjoy great contentment—described here in terms of a material abundance greater than anything they could imagine (vv. 23–26). Assyria, on the other hand, will be severely punished by God (vv. 27–33). The "Topheth" (v. 33, note t), literally "a burning place", was the site in the valley of Ben-Hinom (or Ge-ben-Hinnôn, Gehenna) on the outskirts of Jerusalem where, at one time, children were sacrificed to the Canaanite god Moloch (see the note on Jer 7:21—8:3; cf. Jer 19:5; 32:35). It came to mean a place of damnation and divine retribution for sinners. There the might of Assyria will meet its fate.

addatis peccatum super peccatum! / [2]Qui ambulatis, ut descendatis in Aegyptum, / et os meum non interrogastis, / sperantes auxilium in fortitudine pharaonis / et habentes fiduciam in umbra Aegypti. / [3]Et erit vobis fortitudo pharaonis in confusionem, / et fiducia sub umbra Aegypti in ignominiam. / [4]Cum fuerint enim in Tani principes tui, / et nuntii tui usque ad Hanes pervenerint, / [5]omnes confundentur / super populo, qui eis prodesse non potest; / non erit in auxilium et in utilitatem sed in

Num 21:4–9 / Deut 8:14–15 / Is 14:29
6 An oracle on the beasts of the Negeb.
Through a land of trouble and anguish,
from where come the lioness and the lion,
the viper and the flying serpent,
they carry their riches on the backs of asses,
and their treasures on the humps of camels,
to a people that cannot profit them.
Job 9:13; 26:12 / Ps 87:4; 89:11
7 For Egypt's help is worthless and empty,
therefore I have called her
"Rahab who sits still."

8 And now, go, write it before them on a tablet,
and inscribe it in a book,
that it may be for the time to come
as a witness for ever.
Deut 32:20 / Is 1:2–4
9 For they are a rebellious people,
lying sons,
sons who will not hear
the instruction of the Lord;
1 Sam 9:9 / 1 Kings 22:8–27 / Amos 2:12; 7:13 / Mic 2:6
10 who say to the seers, "See not";
and to the prophets, "Prophesy not to us what is right;
speak to us smooth things,
prophesy illusions,
11 leave the way, turn aside from the path,
let us hear no more of the Holy One of Israel."
Ps 62:11
12 Therefore thus says the Holy One of Israel,
"Because you despise this word,
and trust in oppression and perverseness,
and rely on them;
Ezek 13:11–13
13 therefore this iniquity shall be to you
like a break in a high wall, bulging out, and about to collapse,
whose crash comes suddenly, in an instant;

---

confusionem et opprobrium». / 6 Oraculum iumentorum Nageb. / In terra tribulationis et angustiae, /
leaenae et leonis rugientis, / viperae et draconis volantis / portant super umeros iumentorum divitias
suas / et super gibbum camelorum thesauros suos / ad populum, qui eis prodesse non poterit. /
7 Aegyptus enim frustra et vane auxiliabitur; / ideo vocavi Rahab otiosam. / 8 Nunc ingredere, scribe
coram eis super buxum / et in libro diligenter exara illud, / et erit in posterum / in testimonium usque
in aeternum. / 9 Populus enim rebellis est, / et filii mendaces, / filii nolentes audire legem Domini; / 10 qui
dicunt videntibus: «Nolite videre» / et aspicientibus: «Nolite aspicere nobis ea, quae recta sunt; /
loquimini nobis placentia, aspicite nobis illusiones. / 11 Recedite a via, declinate a semita, / tollite a facie
nostra Sanctum Israel». / 12 Propterea haec dicit Sanctus Israel: / «Pro eo quod reprobastis verbum hoc
/ et sperastis in perversitatem et in perfidiam / et innixi estis super eis, / 13 propterea erit vobis iniquitas
haec / sicut interruptio cadens, locus tumens in muro excelso, / cuius confractio subito, dum non
speratur, / venit improviso; / 14 et comminuetur, sicut conteritur lagoena figuli, / contritione absque

[14] and its breaking is like that of a potter's vessel
which is smashed so ruthlessly
that among its fragments not a sherd is found
with which to take fire from the hearth,
or to dip up water out of the cistern."

[15] For thus said the LORD GOD, the Holy One of Israel, Is 6:3; 7:9
"In returning and rest you shall be saved;
in quietness and in trust shall be your strength."
And you would not, [16]but you said, Hos 1:7
"No! We will speed upon horses,"
therefore you shall speed away;
and, "We will ride upon swift steeds,"
therefore your pursuers shall be swift.
[17] A thousand shall flee at the threat of one, Deut 32:30
at the threat of five you shall flee,
till you are left
like a flagstaff on the top of a mountain,
like a signal on a hill.

[18] Therefore the LORD waits to be gracious to you; Ps 2:12
therefore he exalts himself to show mercy to you. Is 54:8
For the LORD is a God of justice; Rom 3:26
blessed are all those who wait for him.
[19]Yea, O people in Zion who dwell at Jerusalem; you shall
weep no more. He will surely be gracious to you at the sound of

---

30:18. In a few simple words this verse manages to catch God's attitude towards man, and the tone of man's response. God "waits", hoping to forgive man; this "waiting" St Paul calls "divine forbearance" (Rom 3:26); but the time will come when he will "show mercy": the Hebrew word implies maternal feelings (cf. 14:1; 49:10, 13, 15; etc.; and see the note on 49:15). God acts as he does because he is the "God of justice", that is, the God who saves. Really, God is only waiting for man to turn to him, and he will forgive him. A person who realizes this, who is convinced of this, has every reason to persevere in hope. God's patience elicits from man hope in Him.

misericordia, / et non invenietur de fragmentis eius testa, / in qua capiatur igniculus de incendio, / aut hauriatur aqua de fovea». / [15]Quia haec dixit Dominus Deus, Sanctus Israel: / «In conversione et quiete salvi eritis; / in silentio et in spe erit fortitudo vestra». / Et noluistis [16]et dixistis: / «Nequaquam, sed super equis fugiemus», / ideo fugietis; / et: «Super veloces ascendemus», / ideo veloces erunt, qui persequentur vos. / [17]Mille pavebunt a facie terroris unius, / et a facie terroris quinque fugietis, / donec relinquamini / quasi malus in vertice montis / et quasi signum super collem. / [18]Propterea exspectat Dominus, ut misereatur vestri, / et ideo exaltabitur parcens vobis, / quia Deus iudicii Dominus; / beati omnes, qui exspectant eum. / [19]Nam, popule Sion, qui habitas in Ierusalem, / plorans nequaquam

your cry; when he hears it, he will answer you. 20And though the
LORD give you the bread of adversity and the water of affliction,
yet your Teacher will not hide himself any more, but your eyes
shall see your Teacher. 21And your ears shall hear a word behind
you, saying, "This is the way, walk in it," when you turn to the
right or when you turn to the left. 22Then you will defile your
silver covered graven images and your gold-plated molten images.
You will scatter them as unclean things; you will say to them,
"Begone!"

23And he will give rain for the seed with which you sow the
ground, and grain, the produce of the ground, which will be rich
and plenteous. In that day your cattle will graze in large pastures;
24and the oxen and the asses that till the ground will eat salted
provender, which has been winnowed with shovel and fork. 25And
upon every lofty mountain and every high hill there will be brooks
running with water, in the day of the great slaughter, when the
towers fall. 26Moreover the light of the moon will be as the light
of the sun, and the light of the sun will be sevenfold, as the light
of seven days, in the day when the LORD binds up the hurt of his
people, and heals the wounds inflicted by his blow.

27 Behold, the name of the LORD comes from far,
burning with his anger, and in thick rising smoke;
his lips are full of indignation,
and his tongue is like a devouring fire;
Wis 5:23 28 his breath is like an overflowing stream
that reaches up to the neck;
to sift the nations with the sieve of destruction,
and to place on the jaws of the peoples a bridle that leads astray.

---

plorabis: / miserans miserebitur tui ad vocem clamoris tui; / statim ut audierit, respondebit tibi. / 20Et
dabit vobis Dominus / panem angustiae et aquam afflictionis, / sed non amplius avolabit a te doctor
tuus; / et erunt oculi tui videntes praeceptorem tuum, / 21et aures tuae audient verbum post tergum
monentis: / «Haec via, ambulate in ea», / si declinaveritis ad dexteram vel ad sinistram. / 22Et
contaminabis laminas sculptilium argentorum tuorum / et vestimentum conflatilis aurei tui; / disperges
ea sicut immunditiam menstruatae. / «Egredere» dices ei. / 23Et dabit pluviam semini tuo, / quod
seminaveris in terra, / et panis frugum terrae erit uberrimus et pinguis; / pascetur pecus tuum in die illo,
agnus in pascuis spatiosis, / 24et boves tui et asini, qui operantur terram, / commixtum migma comedent
/ ventilatum in pala et ventilabro. / 25Et erunt super omnem montem excelsum / et super omnem collem
elevatum / rivi currentium aquarum / in die interfectionis multorum, / cum ceciderint turres. / 26Et erit
lux lunae sicut lux solis, / et lux solis erit septempliciter sicut lux septem dierum / in die, qua alligaverit
Dominus vulnus populi sui / et percussuram plagae eius sanaverit. / 27Ecce nomen Domini venit de
longinquo, / ardens furor eius, et gravis eius fragor; / labia eius repleta sunt indignatione, / et lingua
eius quasi ignis devorans. / 28Spiritus eius velut torrens inundans, / usque ad collum pertingens, / ad
cribrandas gentes in cribro funesto, / et frenum dolosum in maxillis populorum. / 29Canticum erit vobis
/ sicut nox sanctificatae sollemnitatis, / et laetitia cordis / sicut eius, qui ad sonum tibiae pergit / in

[29]You shall have a song as in the night when a holy feast is
kept; and gladness of heart, as when one sets out to the sound of
the flute to go to the mountain of the LORD, to the Rock of Israel.
[30]And the LORD will cause his majestic voice to be heard and the Ex 19:16
descending blow of his arm to be seen, in furious anger and a Ps 29: 1ff
flame of devouring fire, with a cloudburst and tempest and
hailstones. [31]The Assyrians will be terror-stricken at the voice of
the LORD, when he smites with his rod. [32]And every stroke of the
staff of punishment which the LORD lays upon them will be to the
sound of timbrels and lyres; battling with brandished arm he will
fight with them. [33]For a burning place[t] has long been prepared; Jer 7:21–8:3; 19:5; 32:35
yea, for the king[u] it is made ready, its pyre made deep and wide,
with fire and wood in abundance; the breath of the LORD, like a
stream of brimstone, kindles it.

Lamentation over those who put their trust in Egypt

31 [1]Woe to those who go down to Egypt for help Is 6:3 30:1–7
and rely on horses, Hos 1:7
who trust in chariots because they are many
and in horsemen because they are very strong,

31:1—32:20. The fifth lamentation maintains the same line of argument as the previous one. As before, the first verses (31:1–9) are addressed to those who trusted in Egypt's support, forgetting about the Lord, who is really the only one in a position to help them against the Assyrians. The Lord mocks their empty plans.

The second part, however, looks ahead, to when the Kingdom of God will be established and peace will reign in Zion (32:1–20). This passage is a poem, in a more sapiential tone, providing a prophetic vision of the messianic future, whereas the previous oracles referred to historical events: the king and his ministers will be just men (32:1–5), whom the Lord will use to free his people from the knaves (32:6–8) and vain women of Jerusalem (32:9–14). When the Spirit is poured out from on high (v. 15), messianic justice and peace will reign.

31:1–9. These verses repeat, in brief, the ideas contained in the previous chapter: Egypt can provide no help

---

montem Domini, / ad petram Israel. / [30]Et auditam faciet Dominus / gloriam vocis suae / et terrorem brachii sui / ostendet in comminatione furoris / et flamma ignis devorantis, / in turbine et in imbre et in lapide grandinis. / [31]A voce enim Domini pavebit / Assyrius virga percussus. / [32]Et erit omnis ictus baculi percutientis, / quem requiescere faciet Dominus / super eum in tympanis et citharis, / et in bellis agitatis expugnabit eos. / [33]Praeparata est enim ab heri Topheth, / praeparata, profunda et dilatata, / in pyra eius ignis et ligna multa; / flatus Domini sicut torrens sulphuris / succendit eam. **[31]** [1]Vae, qui descendunt in Aegyptum ad auxilium, / in equis sperantes / et habentes fiduciam super quadrigis, quia

t. Or *Topheth* **u.** Or *Molech*

but do not look to the Holy One of Israel
or consult the LORD!
2 And yet he is wise and brings disaster,
he does not call back his words,
but will arise against the house of the evildoers,
and against the helpers of those who work iniquity.
Ex 14:26 3 The Egyptians are men, and not God;
Ezek 28:9 and their horses are flesh, and not spirit.
When the LORD stretches out his hand,
the helper will stumble, and he who is helped will fall,
and they will all perish together.

Hos 11:10 4 For thus the LORD said to me,
Amos 1:2 As a lion or a young lion growls over his prey,
and when a band of shepherds is called forth against him
is not terrified by their shouting
or daunted at their noise,
so the LORD of hosts will come down
to fight upon Mount Zion and upon its hill.
Deut 32:11 5 Like birds hovering, so the LORD of hosts
Ps 36:8 will protect Jerusalem;
he will protect and deliver it,
he will spare and rescue it.

6 Turn to him from whom you[v] have deeply revolted, O people
Is 2:20 of Israel. 7 For in that day every one shall cast away his idols of

---

(vv.1–3); Assyria, despite its expansion, will end up defeated (vv. 4–9). The people must put all their trust in the Lord, for he will protect Jerusalem (v. 5). Here, too, the same point is made: the Lord lays down the condition that his people must give up idolatry (vv. 6–7) and return to him if he is to deliver them from their enemies (vv. 8–9).

multae sunt, / et super equitibus, quia praevalidi nimis, / et non intendunt in Sanctum Israel / et Dominum non requirunt! / 2 Tamen et ipse sapiens adducit malum / et verba sua non retractat; / et consurget contra domum pessimorum / et contra auxilium operantium iniquitatem. / 3 Aegyptius homo et non Deus, / et equi eorum caro et non spiritus; / et Dominus inclinabit manum suam, / et corruet auxiliator, / et cadet, cui praestatur auxilium, / simulque omnes consumentur. / 4 Quia haec dicit Dominus ad me: / «Quomodo si rugit leo et catulus leonis super praedam suam, / cum occurrerit ei multitudo pastorum, / a voce eorum non formidabit et a multitudine eorum non pavebit, / sic descendet Dominus exercituum, ut proelietur super montem Sion et super collem eius. / 5 Sicut aves volantes, / sic proteget Dominus exercituum Ierusalem, / protegens et liberans, / parcens et salvans». / 6 Convertimini ad eum, a quo penitus recesseratis, / filii Israel. / 7 In die enim illa abiciet vir / idola argentea sua et idola aurea sua, / quae fecerunt vobis manus vestrae in peccatum; / 8 et cadet Assyria in gladio non viri, / et

v. Heb *they*

silver and his idols of gold, which your hands have sinfully made
for you.
[8]"And the Assyrian shall fall by a sword, not of man;
and a sword, not of man, shall devour him;
and he shall flee from the sword,
and his young men shall be put to forced labour.
[9]His rock shall pass away in terror,
and his officers desert the standard in panic,"
says the LORD, whose fire is in Zion,
and whose furnace is in Jerusalem.

32 [1]Behold, a king will reign in righteousness, Is 11:3–4
and princes will rule in justice. Jer 23:5–6
[2]Each will be like a hiding place from the wind,
a covert from the tempest,
like streams of water in a dry place,
like the shade of a great rock in a weary land.
[3]Then the eyes of those who see will not be closed, Is 30:10
and the ears of those who hear will hearken.

32:1–20. This oracle opens up a messianic horizon for the inhabitants of Jerusalem—the promise of a peace that will endure. The future king, surely the same person as is announced in the "Book of Immanuel" (7:1—12:6), will ensure justice and protection against enemies (vv. 1–8; cf. 9:6; 11:4). The holy city will suffer misfortune: its ancient fortifications will be levelled; its vain women (a symbol of a society that relies on its own resources and has no regard for God: cf. Amos 4:1–3) will do penance—a signal that a new era has begun (vv. 9–14). And, at last, the Spirit will be poured out on everyone (vv. 15–20), including the future king (as announced in 11:2)—a guarantee that peace and security will endure, for they are grounded on justice (v.17; cf. v. 1): "Peace is not merely the absence of war; nor can it be reduced solely to the maintenance of a balance of power between enemies; nor is it brought about by dictatorship. Instead, it is rightly and appropriately called an enterprise of justice. Peace results from that order structured into human society by its divine Founder, and actualized by men as they thirst after ever greater justice. The common good of humanity finds its ultimate meaning in the eternal law. But since the concrete demands of this common good are constantly changing as time goes on, peace is never attained once and for all, but must be built up ceaselessly" (Vatican II, *Gaudium et spes*, 78).

gladius non hominis vorabit eum, / et fugiet a facie gladii, / et iuvenes eius vectigales erunt. / [9]Et fortitudo eius prae terrore transibit, / et pavebunt signum principes eius, / dixit Dominus, cuius ignis est in Sion, / et caminus eius in Ierusalem. **[32]** [1]Ecce in iustitia regnabit rex, / et principes in iudicio praeerunt. / [2]Et erit vir sicut latibulum a vento / et refugium a tempestate, / sicut rivi aquarum in sitiente

4The mind of the rash will have good judgment,
and the tongue of the stammerers will speak readily and distinctly.
Is 5:20 5The fool will no more be called noble,
nor the knave said to be honourable.
Ps 14:1 Eccles 10:13 6For the fool speaks folly,
and his mind plots iniquity:
to practise ungodliness,
to utter error concerning the LORD,
to leave the craving of the hungry unsatisfied,
and to deprive the thirsty of drink.
Ps 10:2,7–11 7The knaveries of the knave are evil;
he devises wicked devices
to ruin the poor with lying words,
even when the plea of the needy is right.
8But he who is noble devises noble things,
and by noble things he stands.

Is 3:16–24 Amos 4:1–3 9Rise up, you women who are at ease, hear my voice;
you complacent daughters, give ear to my speech.
10In little more than a year
you will shudder, you complacent women;
for the vintage will fail,
the fruit harvest will not come.
11Tremble, you women who are at ease,
shudder, you complacent ones;
strip, and make yourselves bare,
and gird sackcloth upon your loins.
12Beat upon your breasts for the pleasant fields,
for the fruitful vine,
13for the soil of my people
growing up in thorns and briers;

---

terra / et umbra petrae magnae in terra arida. / 3Non caligabunt oculi videntium, / et aures audientium diligenter auscultabunt, / 4et cor stultorum intelleget scientiam, / et lingua balborum velociter loquetur et plane. / 5Non vocabitur ultra is, qui insipiens est, nobilis, / neque fraudulentus appellabitur maior; / 6stultus enim fatua loquitur, / et cor eius cogitat iniquitatem, / ut perficiat impietatem / et loquatur contra Dominum errores / et vacuam faciat animam esurientem / et potum sitienti auferat. / 7Fraudulenti fraudes pessimae sunt; / ipse enim cogitationes concinnat / ad perdendos mites in sermone mendaci, / etiam quando pauper iudicium vindicat. / 8Nobilis vero consilia nobilia dat / et ipse ad nobilia assurget. / 9Mulieres vanae, surgite, audite vocem meam; / filiae confidentes, percipite auribus eloquium meum. / 10Post dies enim et annum / vos pavebitis confidentes; / consummata est enim vindemia, / collectio ultra non veniet. / 11Obstupescite, vanae; / pavete, confidentes, / exuite vos et nudate vos, / accingite lumbos vestros. / 12Super ubera plangite, / super regione desiderabili, / super vinea fertili. / 13Super

yea, for all the joyous houses
in the joyful city.
[14] For the palace will be forsaken,
the populous city deserted;
the hill and the watchtower
will become dens for ever,
a joy of wild asses,
a pasture of flocks;
[15] until the Spirit is poured upon us from on high,
and the wilderness becomes a fruitful field,
and the fruitful field is deemed a forest.
[16] Then justice will dwell in the wilderness,
and righteousness abide in the fruitful field.
[17] And the effect of righteousness will be peace, Is 11:6
and the result of righteousness, quietness and trust for ever.
[18] My people will abide in a peaceful habitation,
in secure dwellings, and in quiet resting places.
[19] And the forest will utterly go down,[w]
and the city will be utterly laid low.
[20] Happy are you who sow beside all waters,
who let the feet of the ox and the ass range free.

Lamentation concerning destroyers and traitors

33 [1]Woe to you, destroyer,
who yourself have not been destroyed;
you treacherous one,
with whom none has dealt treacherously!

33:1–24. This chapter, beginning with the word "woe", is the sixth lamentation. It brings this section (chap. 28–33) to a close, and sums up the ideas contained in it. It begins with a passage about the "destroyer who will be destroyed" (vv. 1–6)—a reference to the invader, although he is not explicitly named. Jerusalem's fears will be stemmed by a divine intervention (vv. 10–16) which will restore Zion and bring back its exiles (vv. 17–24).

humum populi mei / spinae et vepres ascendent, / super omnes domos gaudii, / super civitatem exsultantem. / [14]Domus enim dimissa est; / multitudo urbis relicta est, / Ophel et Bahan erunt speluncae / usque in aeternum, / gaudium onagrorum, / pascua gregum, / [15]donec effundatur super nos / spiritus de excelso. / Et erit desertum in hortum, / et hortus in saltum reputabitur, / [16]et habitabit in solitudine iudicium, / et iustitia in horto sedebit; / [17]et erit opus iustitiae pax, / et cultus iustitiae silentium, / et securitas usque in sempiternum. / [18]Et sedebit populus meus in habitatione pacis / et in tabernaculis fiduciae / et in locis securis. / [19]Et penitus cadet saltus, / et profunde deprimetur civitas. / [20]Beati, qui seminatis super omnes aquas, / immittentes pedem bovis et asini. **[33]** [1]Vae, qui praedaris, cum nemo te praedatus sit; / qui devastas, cum nemo te devastaverit! / Cum consummaveris depraedationem,

w. Cn: Heb *And it will hail when the forest comes down*

When you have ceased to destroy,
you will be destroyed;
and when you have made an end of dealing treacherously,
you will be dealt with treacherously.

Ps 32: 10; 33:22; 46:2 [2]O LORD, be gracious to us; we wait for thee.
Be our arm every morning,
our salvation in the time of trouble.
Num 10:35 Ps 46:7; 5–8; 68:2 [3]At the thunderous noise peoples flee,
at the lifting up of thyself nations are scattered;
[4]and spoil is gathered as the caterpillar gathers;
as locusts leap, men leap upon it.

Ps 57:6; 83:19; 97:9 [5]The LORD is exalted, for he dwells on high;
he will fill Zion with justice and righteousness;
[6]and he will be the stability of your times,
abundance of salvation, wisdom, and knowledge;
the fear of the LORD is his treasure.

The sound health that is promised (cf. v. 24) is a sign of the salvation that the Lord grants his people. Here, as elsewhere in the Old and New Testaments, we find a link between health and salvation, sin and sickness. "It is the experience of Israel that illness is mysteriously linked to sin and evil, and that faithfulness to God according to his law restores life: 'For I am the Lord, your healer' (Ex 15:26). The prophet intuits that suffering can also have a redemptive meaning for the sins of others (cf. Is 53:11). Finally Isaiah announces that God will usher in a time for Zion when he will pardon every offence and heal every illness (cf. Is 33:24)" (*Catechism of the Catholic Church*, 1502).

33:1–6. The destroyer (v. 1) must be Assyria, although it could apply to Babylon, Persia or any other power that oppressed the chosen people over the course of history. Verses 2–5 are a heartfelt prayer confessing the sovereignty of God; he stands above all things (v. 5). The prayer asks that the qualities and gifts of the Spirit (v. 6), which are those of the Messiah King (cf. 11:2), should be given to all the faithful dwelling in Jerusalem, now restored.

depraedaberis; / cum perfeceris devastationem, te devastabunt. / [2]Domine, miserere nostri, / te enim exspectavimus; / esto brachium nostrum in mane / et salus nostra in tempore tribulationis. / [3]A voce fragoris fugerunt populi, / ab exaltatione tua dispersae sunt gentes. / [4]Et congregabuntur spolia, sicut colligitur bruchus; / sicut discurrunt locustae, ad ea discurritur. / [5]Sublimis est Dominus, quoniam habitat in excelso; / implet Sion iudicio et iustitia. / [6]Et erit firmitas in temporibus tuis; / divitiae salutis sapientia et scientia: / timor Domini ipse est thesaurus eius. / [7]Ecce praecones clamabunt foris, / angeli pacis amare flebunt. / [8]Dissipatae sunt viae, cessavit transiens per semitam; / irritum fecit pactum, / reiecit testes, / non reputavit homines. / [9]Luget et elanguescit terra, / confusus est Libanus et obsorduit,

7Behold, the valiant ones[y] cry without; Is 29:1
the envoys of peace weep bitterly.
8The highways lie waste,
the wayfaring man ceases.
Covenants are broken,
witnesses[z] are despised,
here is no regard for man.
9The land mourns and languishes; Amos 1:2
Lebanon is confounded and withers away;
Sharon is like a desert;
and Bashan and Carmel shake off their leaves.

33:7–24. Divine judgment, expressed here in sapiential language (vv. 7–16), precedes a magnificent hymn celebrating a glorious Jerusalem (vv. 17–24). The effects of divine punishment are to be seen in the desolation felt by the inhabitants of Jerusalem and other parts of the country (Lebanon, Sharon, Bashan and Carmel), famous for their wealth and fertility (vv. 7–9; cf. 35:2). However, only sinners have to fear in Zion (v. 14), for the virtuous will be saved (vv. 15–16). This text gives an inkling of the doctrine of individual retribution, which will be spelt out more clearly in Jeremiah and Ezekiel. Still, the main theme has to do with a restoration of the country, most clearly to be seen in Jerusalem. The prophet gives his imagination free rein and describes a huge country, ruled directly by the Lord (v. 17), a country serene, at peace, devoid of pride. Jerusalem will be a luxuriant place, well-watered, where everything will function properly, because the Lord will be its governor (v. 22).

Commenting on v. 22 in the light of the Gospel, St Cyril speaks of the trust we should place in the Lord against the snares of the devil: "When we have been redeemed by Christ and have begun to live in his holy tent—that is, the Church—we will reap many rewards from the words of the Gospels and the apostles, and we will overcome the one who previously had power over us, because Christ will guard our hearts [...]. We should take heart! Because God is great, and he will never abandon us; that is, Satan shall never again be lord over us. We will never again be ground down under his feet, for the Lord is our judge, the Lord is our master, the Lord is our king: he will save us. Once we take upon ourselves the saving yoke of the Gospel, we have a judge and master and king, the Lord, the Son, and he will save us" (*Commentarius in Isaiam*, 33, 22).

/ et factus est Saron sicut desertum, / et exaruerunt Basan et Carmelus. / 10«Nunc consurgam, dicit Dominus, / nunc exaltabor, nunc sublevabor. / 11Concipietis fenum, parietis stipulam; / spiritus meus ut ignis vorabit vos. / 12Et erunt populi fornaces calcis: / spinae congregatae igne comburentur. / 13Audite, qui longe estis, quae fecerim, / et cognoscite, vicini, fortitudinem meam». / 14Conterriti sunt

y. The meaning of the Hebrew word is uncertain **z.** One ancient Ms: Heb *cities*

Ps 12:6 10 "Now I will arise," says the LORD,
"now I will lift myself up;
now I will be exalted.
11 You conceive chaff, you bring forth stubble;
your breath is a fire that will consume you.
12 And the peoples will be as if burned to lime,
like thorns cut down, that are burned in the fire."

13 Hear, you who are far off, what I have done;
and you who are near, acknowledge my might.
14 The sinners in Zion are afraid;
trembling has seized the godless:
"Who among us can dwell with the devouring fire?
Who among us can dwell with everlasting burnings?"
Ps 15 15 He who walks righteously and speaks uprightly,
who despises the gain of oppressions,
who shakes his hands, lest they hold a bribe,
who stops his ears from hearing of bloodshed
and shuts his eyes from looking upon evil,
16 he will dwell on the heights;
his place of defence will be the fortresses of rocks;
his bread will be given him, his water will be sure.

17 Your eyes will see the king in his beauty;
they will behold a land that stretches afar.
1 Cor 1:20 18 Your mind will muse on the terror:
"Where is he who counted, where is he who weighed the tribute?
Where is he who counted the towers?"
Is 28:11 19 You will see no more the insolent people,
the people of an obscure speech which you cannot comprehend,
stammering in a tongue which you cannot understand.
Is 54:2 20 Look upon Zion, the city of our appointed feasts!
Your eyes will see Jerusalem,

---

in Sion peccatores, / possedit tremor impios. / Quis poterit habitare de vobis cum igne devorante? / Quis habitabit ex vobis cum ardoribus sempiternis? / 15Qui ambulat in iustitiis et loquitur aequitates, / qui reicit lucra ex rapinis / et excutit manus suas, ne munera accipiat, / qui obturat aures suas, ne audiat sanguinem, / et claudit oculos suos, ne videat malum: / 16iste in excelsis habitabit, / munimenta saxorum refugium eius; / panis ei datus est, aquae eius fideles sunt. / 17Regem in decore suo videbunt oculi tui, / cernent terram longinquam. / 18Cor tuum cum timore inquiret: / «Ubi est scriba? Ubi ponderator? / Ubi computator turrium?». / 19Populum impudentem non videbis, / populum profundi sermonis, ininterpretabilis, / linguae barbarae absque intellegentia. / 20Respice Sion civitatem sollemnitatum nostrarum! / Oculi tui videbunt Ierusalem, / habitationem securam, / tabernaculum quod

a quiet habitation, an immovable tent,
whose stakes will never be plucked up,
nor will any of its cords be broken.
21 But there the LORD in majesty will be for us
a place of broad rivers and streams,
where no galley with oars can go,
nor stately ship can pass.
22 For the LORD is our judge, the LORD is our ruler,
the LORD is our king; he will save us.

23 Your tackle hangs loose;
it cannot hold the mast firm in its place,
or keep the sail spread out.
Then prey and spoil in abundance will be divided;
even the lame will take the prey.
24 And no inhabitant will say, "I am sick";
the people who dwell there will be forgiven their iniquity.

5. VENGEANCE AND SALVATION PROMISED*

Oracle against Edom

34 [1]Draw near, O nations, to hear,
and hearken, O peoples!
Let the earth listen, and all that fills it;
the world, and all that comes from it.

Deut 32:1
Num 20:14–21
Is 63:1–6
Jer 49: 7–22
Ezek 35:1–15

***34:1—35:10.** The fifth section of the first part of Isaiah is often called the "Little Apocalypse", as against the "Great Apocalypse", the third section (24:1—27:13). Due to similarities in style to the "Book of Consolation" (40:1—48:22), these chapters are thought to date from the time of the exile or even later still. The first verses (34:1–17) are a series of oracles against Edom (Edomites moved into Jerusalem to fill the vacuum left by those sent into exile in Babylon). There follows (35:1–10) a description of the destruction of Edom and a new liberation of Israel, depicted as a new exodus.

nequaquam transferri poterit; / nec auferentur clavi eius in sempiternum, / et omnes funiculi eius non rumpentur. / [21]Quia ibi potens Dominus pro nobis / loco fluviorum, rivorum late patentium; / non transibit ibi navis remigum, / neque navis magna transgredietur eum. / [22]Dominus enim iudex noster, Dominus legifer noster, / Dominus rex noster: ipse salvabit nos. / [23]Laxati sunt funiculi tui / nec sustinent malum suum, / ut dilatare velum non queant. / Tunc divident caeci praedam multam; / claudi diripient rapinam. / [24]Nec dicet incola: «Elangui». / Populus, qui habitat in ea, / auferetur ab eo iniquitas. **[34]** [1]Accedite, gentes, ad audiendum; / et populi, attendite. / Audiat terra et plenitudo eius, / orbis et omne germen eius. / [2]Quia indignatio Domini super omnes gentes, / et furor super universam

[2]For the LORD is enraged against all the nations,
and furious against all their host,
he has doomed them, has given them over for slaughter.
Joel 2:20 [3]Their slain shall be cast out,
and the stench of their corpses shall rise;
the mountains shall flow with their blood.

This section is a sort of diptych, contrasting the ruin towards which the nations (symbolized by Edom) are headed with the hope that the people of God should always harbour.

34:1–17. Edom, the nation descended from Esau, tried to block the Israelites' route to the promised land during the Exodus (cf. Num 20:14–21). The rivalry between the Edomites (or Idumeans) and the Israelites is explained in the story of Esau and Jacob (Gen 25:19ff) and it seems to have continued down the centuries. The Idumeans took advantage of the destruction of Jerusalem in 597 BC and the deportation of the Jews to Babylon to occupy the southern part of Judah. This chapter probably refers to those events, while not losing sight of the previous rivalry that existed. It begins with a call to all the nations: the whole world must hear God's sentence against the Edomites. It is a severe one, similar to that in Ezekiel 35:1–15. The language is vivid and evocative: the killing of lambs and goats (v. 6) suggests that the destruction of Edom is a sort of burnt offering in honour of the Lord; the fire and brimstone (v. 9) are reminiscent of the destruction of Sodom and Gomorrah (Gen 19:24–28). The chaos (v. 11) echoes that which preceded creation (Gen 1:2). The wild beasts (vv. 14–15) symbolize a scene of devastation. "The night hag" ("Lilit" in Hebrew) is the name of a demon in Babylonian mythology, depicted as having the head and trunk of a woman and the wings and feet of a bird.

The cosmic confusion described in v. 4 was interpreted by many Fathers of the Church in an eschatological sense, as having to do with the second coming of Christ and the last judgment: "Our Lord Jesus Christ will come down from heaven; he will bring the glory of the end of the world on the last day [...]. Corruption, robbery, adultery, sins of every kind have spread everywhere, and blood is mingled with blood of the earth. And so that this place may no longer be tainted by sin, this world will pass away, and a new and better world will be brought into being. Do you need proof of this from the Scriptures? Listen to Isaiah: *All the host of heaven shall rot away, and the skies roll up like a scroll. All their host shall fall, as leaves fall from the vine, like leaves falling from the fig tree*" (St Cyril of Jerusalem, *Catecheses ad illuminandos*, 15, 3).

militiam eorum: / ad interitum devovit eos et dedit eos in occisionem. / [3]Interfecti eorum proicientur, / et de cadaveribus eorum ascendet foetor; / dissolventur montes sanguine eorum. / [4]Et tabescet omnis militia caelorum, / et complicabuntur sicut liber caeli, et omnis militia eorum defluet, / sicut defluit folium de vinea et arida frons de ficu. / [5]Quoniam inebriatus est in caelo gladius meus: / ecce super

4All the host of heaven shall rot away,
and the skies roll up like a scroll.
All their host shall fall,
as leaves fall from the vine,
like leaves falling from the fig tree.

Mt 24: 29 par.
Rev 6:14

5For my sword has drunk its fill in the heavens;
behold, it descends for judgment upon Edom,
upon the people I have doomed.

Is 63:1–6
Jer 46:10; 49:7
Mal 1:4

6The LORD has a sword; it is sated with blood,
it is gorged with fat,
with the blood of lambs and goats,
with the fat of the kidneys of rams.
For the LORD has a sacrifice in Bozrah,
a great slaughter in the land of Edom.
7Wild oxen shall fall with them,
and young steers with the mighty bulls.
Their land shall be soaked with blood,
and their soil made rich with fat.

Is 63:1–6

8For the LORD has a day of vengeance,
a year of recompense for the cause of Zion.
9And the streams of Edom[a] shall be turned into pitch,
and her soil into brimstone;
her land shall become burning pitch.
10Night and day it shall not be quenched;
its smoke shall go up for ever.
From generation to generation it shall lie waste;
none shall pass through it for ever and ever.

Gen 19:24–28
Job 18:15
Rev 14:10–11

11But the hawk and the porcupine shall possess it,
the owl and the raven shall dwell in it.
He shall stretch the line of confusion over it,
and the plummet of chaos over[b] its nobles.

2 Kings 21:13
Is 13:20–22
Lam 2:8

Edom descendet / et super populum interfectionis meae ad iudicium. / 6Gladius Domini repletus est sanguine, / incrassatus est adipe, / de sanguine agnorum et hircorum, de adipe viscerum arietum; / victima enim Domini in Bosra, / et interfectio magna in terra Edom. / 7Cadunt bubali cum eis, / iuvenci cum tauris; / inebriabitur terra eorum sanguine, / et humus eorum adipe pinguium, / 8quia dies ultionis Domini, / annus retributionum ad vindicandam Sion. / 9Et convertentur torrentes eius in picem, / et humus eius in sulphur, / et erit terra eius in picem ardentem. / 10Nocte et die non exstinguetur, / in sempiternum ascendet fumus eius, / a generatione in generationem desolabitur, / in saecula saeculorum non erit transiens per eam. / 11Et possidebunt illam onocrotalus et ericius, / noctua et corvus habitabunt

a. Heb *her streams* **b.** Heb lacks *over*

Is 13:21 Zeph 2:14 Rev 18:2

12 They shall name it No Kingdom There,
and all its princes shall be nothing.

13 Thorns shall grow over its strongholds,
nettles and thistles in its fortresses.
It shall be the haunt of jackals,
an abode for ostriches.
14 And wild beasts shall meet with hyenas,
the satyr shall cry to his fellow;
yea, there shall the night hag alight,
and find for herself a resting place.

15 There shall the owl nest and lay
and hatch and gather her young in her shadow;
yea, there shall the kites be gathered,
each one with her mate.
16 Seek and read from the book of the LORD:
Not one of these shall be missing;
none shall be without her mate.
For the mouth of the LORD has commanded,
and his Spirit has gathered them.
17 He has cast the lot for them,
his hand has portioned it out to them with the line;
they shall possess it for ever,
from generation to generation they shall dwell in it.

Mt 11:2–6

Promise of redemption

Is 41:19

35 1 The wilderness and the dry land shall be glad,
the desert shall rejoice and blossom;

Is 60:13

like the crocus 2 it shall blossom abundantly,
and rejoice with joy and singing.

35:1–10. The focus now changes with this hymn celebrating Zion, the holy city. It presents a picture of the restored Jerusalem in language reminiscent of that of chapters 11 and 12. God, who manifested his presence and protection

in ea; / et extendet super eam mensuram solitudinis / et perpendiculum desolationis. / [12]Nobiles eius non erunt, / nec regnum proclamabunt; / et omnes principes eius erunt in nihilum. / [13]Et orientur in domibus eius spinae, / urticae et paliurus in munitionibus eius; / et erit cubile draconum / et pascua struthionum. / [14]Et occurrent hyaenae thoibus, / et pilosus clamat ad amicum suum; / ibi cubat lamia / et invenit sibi requiem. / [15]Ibi nidificat serpens ovaque deponit / et circumfodit et fovet in umbra eius; / illuc congregantur milvi alter ad alterum. / [16]Requirite in libro Domini et legite: / unum ex eis non deest, / alter alterum exspectare non debet; / quia os Domini praecepit, / et spiritus eius ipse congregavit ea. / [17]Et ipse misit eis sortem, / et manus eius divisit terram illis in mensura; / usque in aeternum possidebunt eam, / in generatione et generatione habitabunt in ea. **[35]** [1]Laetentur deserta et invia,

The glory of Lebanon shall be given to it,
the majesty of Carmel and Sharon.
They shall see the glory of the LORD,
the majesty of our God.

3 Strengthen the weak hands, Is 40:29–31
and make firm the feeble knees. Heb 12:12
4 Say to those who are of a fearful heart, Is 40:10
"Be strong, fear not!
Behold, your God
will come with vengeance,
with the recompense of God.
He will come and save you."

---

during the exodus, when Israel came up out of Egypt, will do so again in wonderful ways as the redeemed flock back home to Zion. He will show them the route and give them a highway and be with them in a sort of solemn procession to where he dwells (v. 8). Just as in Babylon there was a "Holy Way" lined with statues of lions and dragons that led to the temple of Marduk, the redeemed will have a truly "Holy Way" to take them to the house of the Lord in Jerusalem. The joy of the returnees is compounded by the instant cure of the blind, deaf and lame (cf. 29:18–19), which is an anticipation of what will happen in the messianic era.

The miracles worked by Jesus demonstrate that the moment of true redemption foreseen indistinctly by the prophets has come to pass (cf. Mt 11:2–6). St Justin, showing the Jew Tryphon that this prophecy found fulfilment in Christ, points out: "Christ is the stream of living water that flows from God; he sprang up in the desert wastes of ignorance of God; that is, in the parched earth of all the nations. He, who was born among your people, cured those who were blind from birth, and the deaf and the lame: by his word alone, they leapt and heard and saw once more. He raised the dead and gave them new life, and by all his good works prompted men to see Him for who he is. [...] He did all these things to convince those who were to believe in him, whatever bodily defects they might have, that if they obeyed the teachings that he gave them, he would raise them up again at his Second Coming and make them whole and perfect and immortal as He is" (*Dialogus cum Tryphone*, 69, 6).

The Church uses this passage from Isaiah in the Advent liturgy (3rd Sunday, Cycle A) to encourage the faithful in joyous hope that God will come and bring salvation.

/ et exsultet solitudo et floreat quasi lilium. / [2]Germinet et exsultet / laetabunda et laudans. / Gloria Libani data est ei, / decor Carmeli et Saron; / ipsi videbunt gloriam Domini, / maiestatem Dei nostri. / [3]Confortate manus dissolutas / et genua debilia roborate. / [4]Dicite pusillanimis: / «Confortamini, nolite timere! / Ecce Deus vester, / ultio veniet, retributio Dei; / ipse veniet et salvabit vos». / [5]Tunc aperientur

Mt 9: 6–7, 27–30; 11:5 Mk 7:32–35 Lk 7:22 Is 41:18; 43:20; 48:21 Jn 4:1 Acts 3:8

5 Then the eyes of the blind shall be opened,
and the ears of the deaf unstopped;
6 then shall the lame man leap like a hart,
and the tongue of the dumb sing for joy.
For waters shall break forth in the wilderness,
and streams in the desert;
7 the burning sand shall become a pool,
and the thirsty ground springs of water;
the haunt of jackals shall become a swamp,[c]
the grass shall become reeds and rushes.

Is 40:3–5; 43:19 Joel 3:17

8 And a highway shall be there,
and it shall be called the Holy Way;
the unclean shall not pass over it,[d]
and fools shall not err therein.
9 No lion shall be there,
nor shall any ravenous beast come up on it;
they shall not be found there,
but the redeemed shall walk there.

Ps 126 Is 51:11

10 And the ransomed of the LORD shall return,
and come to Zion with singing;
everlasting joy shall be upon their heads;
they shall obtain joy and gladness,
and sorrow and sighing shall flee away.

2 Kings 18:13–20:19

6. HEZEKIAH IN THE FACE OF A THREAT FROM ASSYRIA*

2 Kings 18:30–37 Is 37:10f

Sennacherib's first embassy

36 1 In the fourteenth year of King Hezekiah, Sennacherib king
of Assyria came up against all the fortified cities of Judah

***36:1—39:8.** This sixth section marks the end of the first part of the book of Isaiah (1:1—39:8). Here, as in the oracles at the start, Jerusalem is depicted as a city under siege in the midst of a land laid waste by foreigners (cf. 1:7–8;

oculi caecorum, / et aures surdorum patebunt. / 6 Tunc saliet sicut cervus claudus, / et exsultabit lingua mutorum, / quia erumpent in deserto aquae, / et torrentes in solitudine. / 7 Et terra arida erit in stagnum, / et sitiens in fontes aquarum; / in cubilibus, in quibus dracones habitabant, / erit locus calami et iunci. / 8 Et erit ibi semita et via; / et via sancta vocabitur: / non transibit per eam pollutus; / et erit eis directa via, / ita ut stulti non errent per eam. / 9 Non erit ibi leo, / et rapax bestia non ascendet per eam / nec

c. Cn: Heb *in the haunt of jackals is her resting place* **d.** Heb *it and he is for them a wayfarer*

and took them. [2]And the king of Assyria sent the Rabshakeh from
Lachish to King Hezekiah at Jerusalem, with a great army. And he
stood by the conduit of the upper pool on the highway to the
Fuller's Field. [3]And there came out to him Eliakim the son of Is 7:3; 22:20
Hilkiah, who was over the household, and Shebna the secretary,
and Joah the son of Asaph, the recorder.

[4]And the Rabshakeh said to them, "Say to Hezekiah, 'Thus
says the great king, the king of Assyria: On what do you rest this
confidence of yours? [5]Do you think that mere words are strategy
and power for war? On whom do you now rely, that you have

36:1–22). It recounts three important events in Jewish history that bolster the faith of the people—first, the confrontation between the devout King Hezekiah and Sennacherib who is determined to take the city (chaps. 36 and 37); then, Hezekiah's grave illness and his miraculous cure thanks to Isaiah's intercession (chap. 38); and, finally, the sentence passed on Hezekiah for having made a pact with the king of Babylon (chap. 39). The description of events overlaps quite a bit with that in 2 Kings 15–20 and 2 Chronicles 26–32. In fact, Isaiah 36–39 transcribes 2 Kings 18:13—20:19 but with two significant differences: it omits 2 Kings 18:14–16, which deals with Hezekiah's submission to the king of Assyria, and it adds the poem of the king of Judah (Is 38:9–20), spoken after his cure from illness; in other words, this book presents the king in a more positive light. These various texts help to show the importance of Isaiah as a prophet, a counseller to the king and a man of prestige in the nation; they also show clearly that Hezekiah is blessed when he is docile to God, and condemned when he disobeys him.

36:1–22. Sennacherib, king of Assyria (704–681 BC) overran the fortified cities of Judah in 701 and sent his Rabshaken as an envoy to Hezekiah to pressure him to surrender. ("Rabshaken", an Assyrian title, is usually translated as "chief cupbearer"; it denotes a general of high rank.) The envoy's tone is insulting to the king of Judah and to the God of Israel. The meeting takes place exactly where, years earlier, Isaiah warned King Ahaz to put his trust in the Lord (cf. 7:3): Ahaz failed to do so, and soon regretted it. Unlike his father, Hezekiah is a prudent man and does rely on the Lord (cf. 37:1–20); this will cause the danger to disappear, and the siege of Jerusalem will be lifted (cf. 37:36–37).

invenietur ibi; / et ambulabunt, qui liberati fuerint, / [10]et redempti a Domino revertentur. / Et venient in Sion cum laude, / et laetitia sempiterna super caput eorum: / gaudium et laetitiam obtinebunt, / et fugiet maeror et gemitus. **[36]** [1]Et factum est in quarto decimo anno regis Ezechiae, ascendit Sennacherib rex Assyriorum super omnes civitates Iudae munitas et cepit eas. [2]Et misit rex Assyriorum Rabsacen de Lachis in Ierusalem ad regem Ezechiam in manu gravi, et stetit in aquaeductu piscinae superioris in via agri fullonis. [3]Et egressus est ad eum Eliachim filius Helciae, qui erat super domum, et Sobna scriba et Ioah filius Asaph a commentariis. [4]Et dixit ad eos Rabsaces: «Dicite Ezechiae: Haec dicit rex magnus, rex Assyriorum: Quae est ista fiducia, qua confidis? [5]Dixisti: "Verbum labiorum est consilium

Is 30:3 rebelled against me? 6Behold, you are relying on Egypt, that broken reed of a staff, which will pierce the hand of any man who leans on it. Such is Pharaoh king of Egypt to all who rely on him. 7But if you say to me, "We rely on the LORD our God," is it not he whose high places and altars Hezekiah has removed, saying to Judah and to Jerusalem, "You shall worship before this altar"? 8Come now, make a wager with my master the king of Assyria: I will give you two thousand horses, if you are able on your part to set riders upon them. 9How then can you repulse a single captain among the least of my master's servants, when you rely on Egypt for chariots and for horsemen? 10Moreover, is it without the LORD that I have come up against this land to destroy it? The LORD said to me, Go up against this land, and destroy it.'"

11Then Eliakim, Shebna, and Joah said to the Rabshakeh, "Pray, speak to your servants in Aramaic, for we understand it; do not speak to us in the language of Judah within the hearing of the people who are on the wall." 12But the Rabshakeh said, "Has my master sent me to speak these words to your master and to you, and not to the men sitting on the wall, who are doomed with you to eat their own dung and drink their own urine?"

13Then the Rabshakeh stood and called out in a loud voice in the language of Judah: "Hear the words of the great king, the king of Assyria! 14Thus says the king: 'Do not let Hezekiah deceive you, for he will not be able to deliver you. 15Do not let Hezekiah make you rely on the LORD by saying, "The LORD will surely deliver us; this city will not be given into the hand of the king of Assyria." 16Do not listen to Hezekiah; for thus says the king of Assyria: Make your peace with me and come out to me; then

---

et fortitudo ad bellum". Nunc super quem habes fiduciam, quia recessisti a me? 6Ecce confidis super baculum arundineum confractum istum, super Aegyptum; cui si innixus fuerit homo, intrabit in manum eius et perforabit eam: sic pharao rex Aegypti omnibus, qui confidunt in eo. 7Quod si responderis mihi: "In Domino Deo nostro confidimus"; nonne ipse est, cuius abstulit Ezechias excelsa et altaria et dixit Iudae et Ierusalem: "Coram altari isto adorabitis"? 8Et nunc sponde domino meo regi Assyriorum, et dabo tibi duo milia equorum, si poteris ex te praebere ascensores eorum. 9Et quomodo averteris faciem unius ex servis domini mei minoribus? Et tamen confidis in Aegypto, in quadriga et in equitibus; 10et nunc, numquid sine Domino ascendi ad terram istam, ut disperderem eam? Dominus dixit ad me: "Ascende super terram istam et disperde eam"». 11Et dixit Eliachim et Sobna et Ioah ad Rabsacen: «Loquere ad servos tuos Aramaice; intellegimus enim. Ne loquaris ad nos Iudaice in auribus populi, qui est super murum». 12Et dixit Rabsaces: «Numquid ad dominum tuum et ad te misit me dominus meus, ut loquerer omnia verba ista? Et non potius ad viros, qui sedent in muro, ut comedant stercora sua et bibant urinam suam vobiscum?». 13Et stetit Rabsaces et clamavit voce magna Iudaice et dixit: «Audite verba regis magni, regis Assyriorum: 14Haec dicit rex: Non seducat vos Ezechias, quia non poterit eruere vos. 15Et non vobis tribuat fiduciam Ezechias super Domino dicens: "Eruens liberabit nos Dominus; non dabitur civitas ista in manu regis Assyriorum". 16Nolite audire Ezechiam. Haec enim dicit rex Assyriorum: Facite mecum benedictionem et egredimini ad me; et comedite unusquisque

every one of you will eat of his own vine, and every one of his
own fig tree, and every one of you will drink the water of his own
cistern; 17until I come and take you away to a land like your own
land, a land of grain and wine, a land of bread and vineyards.
18Beware lest Hezekiah mislead you by saying, "The LORD will
deliver us." Has any of the gods of the nations delivered his land
out of the hand of the king of Assyria? 19Where are the gods of Is 10:8
Hamath and Arpad? Where are the gods of Sepharvaim? Have
they delivered Samaria out of my hand? 20Who among all the
gods of these countries have delivered their countries out of my
hand, that the LORD should deliver Jerusalem out of my hand?'"

21But they were silent and answered him not a word, for the
king's command was, "Do not answer him." 22Then Eliakim the
son of Hilkiah, who was over the household, and Shebna the
secretary, and Joah the son of Asaph, the recorder, came to
Hezekiah with their clothes rent, and told him the words of the
Rabshakeh.

Isaiah is insulted

37 1When King Hezekiah heard it, he rent his clothes, and 2 Kings 19:1–7
covered himself with sackcloth, and went into the house of
the LORD. 2And he sent Eliakim, who was over the household, and

---

37:1–38. King Hezekiah, raging but full of faith and trust in the Lord, goes up to the temple to pray, and sends his counsellors to consult Isaiah. Speaking on the Lord's behalf, the prophet gives them reassurances (vv. 6–7). Sennacherib sends another ambassador, who makes the same threats, adding words dismissive of Hezekiah's faith in the Lord—as if the God of Israel were on the same level as the gods of other nations that Assyria had conquered (vv. 8–13). Once again Hezekiah goes up to the temple, where he makes a pious entreaty (vv. 14–20), in which he acknowledges that there is only one true God, the creator of all things, and explains how those nations came to be defeated: it was because they did not belong to the true God. We can hear an echo of

vineam suam et unusquisque ficum suam, et bibite unusquisque aquam de cisterna sua, 17donec veniam
et tollam vos ad terram, quae est ut terra vestra, terram frumenti et vini, terram panis et vinearum. 18Ne
illudat vos Ezechias dicens: "Dominus liberabit nos". Numquid liberaverunt dii gentium unusquisque
terram suam de manu regis Assyriorum? 19Ubi sunt dii Emath et Arphad? Ubi sunt dii Sepharvaim?
Numquid liberaverunt Samariam de manu mea? 20Quinam ex omnibus diis terrarum istarum eruerunt
terram suam de manu mea? Numquid eruet Dominus Ierusalem de manu mea?». 21Et siluerunt et non
responderunt ei verbum; mandaverat enim rex dicens: «Ne respondeatis ei». 22Et ingressus est Eliachim
filius Helciae, qui erat super domum, et Sobna scriba et Ioah filius Asaph a commentariis ad Ezechiam
scissis vestibus; et nuntiaverunt ei verba Rabsacis. **[37]** 1Et factum est cum audisset rex Ezechias,
scidit vestimenta sua et obvolutus est sacco et intravit in domum Domini; 2et misit Eliachim, qui erat
super domum, et Sobnam scribam et seniores de sacerdotibus opertos saccis ad Isaiam filium Amos

Shebna the secretary, and the senior priests, clothed with sack-
Hos 13:13 cloth, to the prophet Isaiah the son of Amoz. 3They said to him,
"Thus says Hezekiah, 'This day is a day of distress, of rebuke, and
of disgrace; children have come to the birth, and there is no
Is 4:3 strength to bring them forth. 4It may be that the LORD your God
2 Kings 19:8–9 heard the words of the Rabshakeh, whom his master the king of
Assyria has sent to mock the living God, and will rebuke the
words which the LORD your God has heard; therefore lift up your
prayer for the remnant that is left.'"

5When the servants of King Hezekiah came to Isaiah, 6Isaiah
said to them, "Say to your master, 'Thus says the LORD: Do not be
afraid because of the words that you have heard, with which the
servants of the king of Assyria have reviled me. 7Behold, I will put
a spirit in him, so that he shall hear a rumor, and return to his own
land; and I will make him fall by the sword in his own land.'"

2 Kings 19:9–19 8The Rabshakeh returned, and found the king of Assyria
fighting against Libnah; for he had heard that the king had left
Lachish.

Hezekiah's prayer in that of the Christians of Jerusalem gathered round the apostles, as recounted by St Luke (Acts 4:24–26). Isaiah then takes the initiative and sends the king a message from God in which he confirms to him that the Assyrians will not enter Jerusalem (vv. 21–35). And, indeed, Sennacherib soon decamps and retreats because a divine intervention has left his army in tatters (v. 36). We are also told about the king's death, which ocurred in 681 BC. The whole account depicts Hezekiah as a model king who gives priority to God's purposes over and above his personal plans.

Isaiah's beautiful oracle (vv. 21–35), which links up with vv. 6–7, dismisses and satirizes the pride of the Assyrian king, and makes it clear that God is the protector of Jerusalem (cf. vv. 22, 33–35). After a brief reference to the holy city, which Sennacherib has mocked (v. 22), the oracle is directed against that king, without specifically naming him. It denounces his blasphemy against "the Holy One of Israel" and his pride in claiming to be as great as God, the only one who can truly "dry" the streams of Egypt (vv. 23–25). It goes on to say that, in his arrogance, Sennacherib failed to realize that the

prophetam, 3et dixerunt ad eum: «Haec dicit Ezechias: Dies tribulationis et correptionis et contumeliae dies haec, quia venerunt filii usque ad partum, et virtus non est pariendi. 4Forsitan audiet Dominus Deus tuus verba Rabsacis, quem misit rex Assyriorum, dominus suus, ad blasphemandum Deum viventem, et puniet sermones, quos audivit Dominus Deus tuus; leva ergo orationem pro reliquiis, quae repertae sunt». 5Et venerunt servi regis Ezechiae ad Isaiam; 6et dixit ad eos Isaias: «Haec dicetis domino vestro: Haec dicit Dominus: Ne timeas a facie verborum, quae audisti, quibus blasphemaverunt pueri regis Assyriorum me. 7Ecce ego dabo ei spiritum, et audiet nuntium et revertetur ad terram suam, et corruere eum faciam gladio in terra sua». 8Reversus est autem Rabsaces et invenit regem Assyriorum

Sennacherib's second embassy

[9]Now the king heard concerning Tirhakah king of Ethiopia, "He
has set out to fight against you." And when he heard it, he sent
messengers to Hezekiah, saying, [10]"Thus shall you speak to
Hezekiah king of Judah: 'Do not let your God on whom you rely
deceive you by promising that Jerusalem will not be given into the
hand of the king of Assyria. [11]Behold, you have heard what the
kings of Assyria have done to all lands, destroying them utterly.
And shall you be delivered? [12]Have the gods of the nations
delivered them, the nations which my fathers destroyed, Gozan,
Haran, Rezeph, and the people of Eden who were in Tel-assar?
[13]Where is the king of Hamath, the king of Arpad, the king of the
city of Sepharvaim, the king of Hena, or the king of Ivvah?'"

[14]Hezekiah received the letter from the hand of the messengers,
and read it; and Hezekiah went up to the house of the LORD, and
spread it before the LORD. [15]And Hezekiah prayed to the LORD:
[16]"O LORD of hosts, God of Israel, who art enthroned above the *Acts 4:24–26*
cherubim, thou art the God, thou alone, of all the kingdoms of the
earth; thou hast made heaven and earth. [17]Incline thy ear, O LORD,
and hear; open thy eyes, O LORD, and see; and hear all the words
of Sennacherib, which he has sent to mock the living God. [18]Of a

---

victories he won were all part of God's plan (cf. 10:5); God misses nothing (vv. 26–28). Therefore, the time has come for Assyria to be punished: she will be forced into submission as a bull or a wild horse is tamed (v. 29). Then the direction of the oracle changes—to focus on Hezekiah and all the people of Jerusalem; these are offered a sign of the goodness of God: a time of trial will be replaced by one of prosperity (v. 30), in which God will see to it that a "surviving remnant" will continue the work of salvation (vv. 31–32). Finally, the oracle confirms that Sennacherib will fail to take the city—this, in honour of God and his servant, David (v. 35; cf. 2 Sam 7:4–16; Ps 132:10–12). Thus, Jerusalem's role as an instrument of salvation is stressed.

proeliantem adversus Lobnam; audierat enim quia profectus esset de Lachis. [9]Et audivit de Tharaca rege Aethiopiae dicentes: «Egressus est, ut pugnet contra te». Quod cum audisset, misit nuntios ad Ezechiam dicens: [10]«Haec dicetis Ezechiae regi Iudae loquentes: Non te decipiat Deus tuus, in quo tu confidis, dicens: "Non dabitur Ierusalem in manu regis Assyriorum". [11]Ecce tu audisti omnia, quae fecerunt reges Assyriorum omnibus terris, quas ad interitum devoverunt, et tu poteris liberari? [12]Numquid eruerunt eos dii gentium, quos subverterunt patres mei, Gozan et Charran et Reseph et filios Eden, qui erant in Thelassar? [13]Ubi est rex Emath et rex Arphad et rex urbis Sepharvaim, Ana et Ava?». [14]Et tulit Ezechias epistulam de manu nuntiorum et legit eam. Et ascendit in domum Domini et expandit eam Ezechias coram Domino. [15]Et oravit Ezechias ad Dominum dicens: [16]«Domine exercituum, Deus Israel, qui sedes super cherubim, tu es Deus solus omnium regnorum terrae, tu fecisti caelum et terram. [17]Inclina, Domine, aurem tuam et audi; aperi, Domine, oculos tuos et vide et audi omnia verba Sennacherib, quae misit ad blasphemandum Deum viventem. [18]Vere enim, Domine,

truth, O LORD, the kings of Assyria have laid waste all the nations
and their lands, [19]and have cast their gods into the fire; for they
were no gods, but the work of men's hands, wood and stone;
therefore they were destroyed. [20]So now, O LORD our God, save us
from his hand, that all the kingdoms of the earth may know that
thou alone art the LORD."

2 Kings 19:20–28

Isaiah's oracle concerning Sennacherib

[21]Then Isaiah the son of Amoz sent to Hezekiah, saying, "Thus
says the LORD, the God of Israel: Because you have prayed to me
concerning Sennacherib king of Assyria, [22]this is the word that the
LORD has spoken concerning him:

'She despises you, she scorns you—
the virgin daughter of Zion;
she wags her head behind you—
the daughter of Jerusalem.

[23] 'Whom have you mocked and reviled?
Against whom have you raised your voice
and haughtily lifted your eyes?
Against the Holy One of Israel!
[24] By your servants you have mocked the Lord,
and you have said, With my many chariots
I have gone up the heights of the mountains,
to the far recesses of Lebanon;
I felled its tallest cedars,
its choicest cypresses;
I came to its remotest height,
its densest forest.
[25] I dug wells
and drank waters,
and I dried up with the sole of my foot
all the streams of Egypt.

---

dissipaverunt reges Assyriorum gentes et regiones earum [19]et dederunt deos earum igni: non enim erant dii, sed opera manuum hominum, lignum et lapis; et comminuerunt eos. [20]Et nunc, Domine Deus noster, salva nos de manu eius; et cognoscant omnia regna terrae quia tu, Domine, es solus Deus». [21]Et misit Isaias filius Amos ad Ezechiam dicens: «Haec dicit Dominus, Deus Israel: Pro quibus rogasti me de Sennacherib rege Assyriorum, [22]hoc est verbum, quod locutus est Dominus super eum: Despexit te, subsannavit te virgo filia Sion; / post te caput movit filia Ierusalem. / [23]Cui exprobrasti et quem blasphemasti? / Et super quem exaltasti vocem / et levasti altitudinem oculorum tuorum? / Contra Sanctum Israel! / [24]In manu servorum tuorum exprobrasti Domino / et dixisti: "In multitudine quadrigarum mearum / ego ascendi altitudinem montium, iuga Libani; / et succidi excelsa cedrorum eius / et electas abietes illius / et introivi altitudinem summitatis eius, / silvam condensam. / [25]Ego fodi et bibi aquam alienam / et exsiccavi vestigio pedis mei / omnes rivos Aegypti". / [26]Numquid non

26 'Have you not heard
that I determined it long ago?
I planned from days of old
what now I bring to pass,
that you should make fortified cities
crash into heaps of ruins,
27 while their inhabitants, shorn of strength, Ps 139:2–3
are dismayed and confounded,
and have become like plants of the field
and like tender grass,
like grass on the housetops,
blighted[e] before it is grown.

28 'I know your sitting down
and your going out and coming in,
and your raging against me.
29 Because you have raged against me
and your arrogance has come to my ears,
I will put my hook in your nose
and my bit in your mouth,
and I will turn you back on the way
by which you came.'

30"And this shall be the sign for you: this year eat what grows Lev 25:5,11 1 Sam 14:10
of itself, and in the second year what springs of the same; then in
the third year sow and reap, and plant vineyards, and eat their
fruit. 31And the surviving remnant of the house of Judah shall
again take root downward, and bear fruit upward; 32for out of
Jerusalem shall go forth a remnant, and out of Mount Zion a band Deut 4:24
of survivors. The zeal of the LORD of hosts will accomplish this.
33"Therefore thus says the LORD concerning the king of Assyria:
He shall not come into this city, or shoot an arrow there, or come

---

audisti? / A saeculo feci illud; a diebus antiquis / ego plasmavi illud et nunc adduxi, / ut fiat in eradicationem, / in lapides eversos civitates munitae. / 27Habitatores earum breviata manu / contremuerunt et confusi sunt; / facti sunt sicut fenum agri / et gramen viride et herba tectorum, quae exaruit a facie austri. / 28Sessionem tuam / et egressum tuum et introitum tuum cognovi / et insaniam tuam contra me. / 29Cum fureris adversum me, / et superbia tua ascenderit in aures meas, / ponam circulum in naribus tuis / et frenum in labiis tuis / et reducam te in viam, / per quam venisti. / 30Tibi autem hoc erit signum: / Comedantur hoc anno, quae colligi poterunt, / et in anno secundo, quae sponte nascuntur; / in anno autem tertio seminate et metite / et plantate vineas et comedite fructum earum. / 31Et mittet id, quod salvatum fuerit de domo Iudae, / quod reliquum est, radicem deorsum / et faciet fructum sursum. / 32Quia de Ierusalem exibit residuum, / et, quod salvum fuerit, de monte Sion. / Zelus Domini exercituum faciet istud. / 33Propterea haec dicit Dominus de rege Assyriorum: / Non introibit

e. With 2 Kings 19:26: Heb *field*

before it with a shield, or cast up a siege mound against it. [34]By
2 Sam 7:12–17 1 Kings 11:13 the way that he came, by the same he shall return, and he shall not
Is 31:5 come into this city, says the LORD. [35]For I will defend this city to
Hos 1:7 save it, for my own sake and for the sake of my servant David."

2 Kings 19:35–37

Death of Sennacherib

[36]And the angel of the LORD went forth, and slew a hundred and
eighty-five thousand in the camp of the Assyrians; and when men
arose early in the morning, behold, these were all dead bodies.
[37]Then Sennacherib king of Assyria departed, and went home and
dwelt at Nineveh. [38]And as he was worshiping in the house of
Nisroch his god, Adrammelech and Sharezer, his sons, slew him
with the sword, and escaped into the land of Ararat. And Esar-
haddon his son reigned in his stead.

2 Kings 20:1–11

Illness and cure of Hezekiah

38 [1] In those days Hezekiah became sick and was at the point
of death. And Isaiah the prophet the son of Amoz came to
him, and said to him, "Thus says the LORD: Set your house in
order; for you shall die, you shall not recover." [2]Then Hezekiah
turned his face to the wall, and prayed to the LORD, [3]and said,
"Remember now, O LORD, I beseech thee, how I have walked
before thee in faithfulness and with a whole heart, and have done
what is good in thy sight." And Hezekiah wept bitterly. [4]Then the
word of the LORD came to Isaiah: [5]"Go and say to Hezekiah, Thus

---

38:1–22. Hezekiah's faith and devotion were tested during the siege of Jerusalem; now comes a further test: the king falls gravely ill, even though he is still a young man. This time, too, he turns to God, and his prayer is answered. Isaiah's intervention (vv. 4–8) assures the king that his health will be restored; the defence of the city requires it.

Here we are given a further example of Hezekiah's trust in the Lord as against Ahaz's lack of faith. The Lord

civitatem hanc / et non iaciet ibi sagittam / et non opponet ei clipeum / et non mittet contra eam aggerem. / [34]In via, qua venit, per eam revertetur, / et civitatem hanc non ingredietur, dicit Dominus. / [35]Et protegam civitatem istam, ut salvem eam / propter me et propter David servum meum». [36]Egressus est autem angelus Domini et percussit in castris Assyriorum centum octoginta quinque milia; et surrexerunt mane, et ecce omnes illi cadavera mortuorum. [37]Et egressus est et abiit; et reversus est Sennacherib rex Assyriorum et habitavit in Nineve. [38]Et factum est, cum adoraret in templo Nesroch dei sui, Adramelech et Sarasar filii eius percusserunt eum gladio fugeruntque in terram Ararat. Et regnavit Asarhaddon filius eius pro eo. **[38]** [1]In diebus illis aegrotavit Ezechias usque ad mortem. Et introivit ad eum Isaias filius Amos propheta et dixit ei: «Haec dicit Dominus: "Dispone domui tuae, quia morieris tu et non vives"». [2]Et convertit Ezechias faciem suam ad parietem et oravit ad Dominum [3]et dixit: «Obsecro, Domine; memento, quaeso, quomodo ambulaverim coram te in veritate et in corde perfecto et, quod bonum est in oculis tuis, fecerim». Et flevit Ezechias fletu magno. [4]Et factum est verbum Domini ad Isaiam dicens: [5]«Vade et dic Ezechiae: "Haec dicit Dominus, Deus David patris tui:

says the LORD, the God of David your father: I have heard your prayer, I have seen your tears; behold, I will add fifteen years to your life. [6]I will deliver you and this city out of the hand of the king of Assyria, and defend this city.

[7]"This is the sign to you from the LORD, that the LORD will do this thing that he has promised: [8]Behold, I will make the shadow cast by the declining sun on the dial of Ahaz turn back ten steps." So the sun turned back on the dial the ten steps by which it had declined.[f]

[9]A writing of Hezekiah king of Judah, after he had been sick and had recovered from his sickness: Ps 116

[10]I said, In the noontide of my days
    I must depart;
  I am consigned to the gates of Sheol
    for the rest of my years.
[11]I said, I shall not see the LORD Ps 27:13
    in the land of the living;

---

offers him a sign (just as he did his father) that He will keep his word (vv. 7–8; cf. 7:14). After this, Hezekiah's canticle is inserted (vv. 9–20)—a passage which does not appear in the parallel texts in 2 Kings and 2 Chronicles, and which has features of the sapiential writing style. The poem takes the form of a thanksgiving psalm spoken by the king. When all seemed lost (vv. 10–12), he had recourse to the Lord in humble and trusting prayer (vv. 13–16), and God saved him from death (v. 17). Therefore, the psalmist expresses his great desire to worship the Lord in the temple (cf. v. 22) along with the rest of the community (vv. 18–20). Verses 21–22 fit in better (as St Jerome points out) after vv. 6–7, which is where they appear in the parallel account (2 Kings 20:7).

38:8. From the text of the book of Isaiah found at Qumran we know that Ahaz had built a flight of steps that worked as a sundial, so that the time could be told depending on which steps were in shadow. "Turning the sun back" meant extending the day by a few hours—a sign that God would grant the king some more years of life.

Audivi orationem tuam, vidi lacrimas tuas; ecce ego adiciam super dies tuos quindecim annos [6]et de manu regis Assyriorum eruam te et civitatem istam et protegam hanc civitatem". [7]Hoc autem tibi erit signum a Domino quia faciet Dominus verbum hoc, quod locutus est: [8]Ecce ego reverti faciam umbram graduum, per quos descenderat in horologio Achaz in sole retrorsum decem gradibus». Et reversus est sol decem gradibus per gradus, quos descenderat. [9]Scriptura Ezechiae regis Iudae, cum aegrotasset et convaluisset de infirmitate sua: [10]«Ego dixi: In dimidio dierum meorum / vadam ad portas inferi; / quaesivi residuum annorum meorum. / [11]Dixi: Non videbo Dominum Deum in terra viventium, / non

f. The Hebrew of this verse is obscure

I shall look upon man no more
among the inhabitants of the world.
Job 4:20; 7:6 Ps 90:5–6 12 My dwelling is plucked up and removed from me
2 Cor 5:1–4 like a shepherd's tent;
2 Pet 1:13–14 like a weaver I have rolled up my life;
he cuts me off from the loom;
from day to night thou dost bring me to an end;[g]
Job 10:16 13 I cry for help[h] until morning;
like a lion he breaks all my bones;
from day to night thou dost bring me to an end.[g]

Ps 69:4; 121:1 14 Like a swallow or a crane[i] I clamour,
I moan like a dove.
My eyes are weary with looking upward.
O Lord, I am oppressed; be thou my security!
15 But what can I say? For he has spoken to me,
and he himself has done it.
All my sleep has fled[j]
because of the bitterness of my soul.

16 O Lord, by these things men live,
and in all these is the life of my spirit.[k]
Oh, restore me to health and make me live!
Ps 103:3–4 17 Lo, it was for my welfare
that I had great bitterness;
but thou hast held back[l] my life
from the pit of destruction,
for thou hast cast all my sins
behind thy back.
Ps 6:6 18 For Sheol cannot thank thee,
Sir 17:27 Bar 2:17 death cannot praise thee;
those who go down to the pit cannot hope
for thy faithfulness.

---

aspiciam hominem ultra / inter habitatores orbis. / 12Habitaculum meum ablatum est et abductum longe
a me / quasi tabernaculum pastorum; / convolvit sicut textor vitam meam; / de stamine succidit me. /
De mane usque ad vesperam confecisti me. / 13Prostratus sum usque ad mane, / quasi leo sic conterit
omnia ossa mea; / de mane usque ad vesperam confecisti me. / 14Sicut pullus hirundinis, sic mussitabo,
/ meditabor ut columba; / attenuati sunt oculi mei / suspicientes in excelsum. / Domine, vim patior, /
sponde pro me. / 15Quid dicam, aut quid respondebit mihi? / Ipse fecit! / Incedam per omnes annos
meos / in amaritudine animae meae. / 16Domine, in te sperat cor meum; / vivat spiritus meus, / sana me
et vivifica me; / 17ecce in pacem versa est amaritudo mea. / Tu autem eruisti animam meam / a fovea
consumptionis, / proiecisti enim post tergum tuum / omnia peccata mea. / 18Quia non infernus

g. Heb uncertain **h.** Cn: Heb obscure **i.** Heb uncertain **j.** Cn Compare Syr: Heb *I will walk slowly all my years* **k.** Heb uncertain **l.** Cn Compare Gk Vg: Heb *loved*

19 The living, the living, he thanks thee, Deut 4:9
as I do this day;
the father makes known to the children
thy faithfulness.

20 The LORD will save me,
and we will sing to stringed instruments[m]
all the days of our life,
at the house of the LORD.

21 Now Isaiah had said, "Let them take a cake of figs, and apply
it to the boil, that he may recover." 22 Hezekiah also had said,
"What is the sign that I shall go up to the house of the LORD?"

Embassy from the king of Babylon 2 Kings 20:12–19

39 1 At that time Merodach-baladan the son of Baladan, king of
Babylon, sent envoys with letters and a present to

39:1–8. This short account brings to an end the first part of the book of Isaiah. Hezekiah we knew as a devout man, loyal to God; but he has changed, and his failure now to rely on God will bring a terrible punishment upon Judah—the Babylonian exile, which provides the historical context of the oracles found in the second part of the book, which announces the consolation of Israel.

Merodach-baladan reigned in Babylon from 721 to 711 BC when he was deposed by Sargon II, king of Assyria (721–705). After Sargon's death, he became king again for a short while (703–702). Merodach-baladan's embassy must have sought to forge an alliance with Judah against Assyria. Hezekiah acts imprudently, by allowing his visitors to see the resources available to him for fighting Assyria; for this, he is criticized by Isaiah and told what lies ahead—defeat and exile (as happened in 587 BC). The passage carries an implicit lesson: merely human calculations designed to make things work out as one wants them to are quite pointless: one must believe in and obey what God says, he is the Lord of history.

The Fathers read this passage as meaning that Hezekiah sinned through pride by wanting to show off and boast, and they warn against the misuse of wealth: "The vices that stem from wealth are also denounced in the Gospel: *Woe betide the rich!* because

confitebitur tibi, / neque mors laudabit te; / non exspectabunt, qui descendunt in lacum, / veritatem tuam. / 19 Vivens, vivens ipse confitebitur tibi, / sicut et ego hodie; / pater filiis notam faciet veritatem tuam. / 20 Domine, salvum me fac, / et ad sonum citharae cantabimus / cunctis diebus vitae nostrae / in domo Domini». 21 Et iussit Isaias, ut tollerent massam de ficis et cataplasmarent super vulnus, et sanaretur. 22 Et dixit Ezechias: «Quod erit signum quia ascendam in domum Domini?». **[39]** 1 In tempore illo misit Merodachbaladan filius Baladan rex Babylonis litteras et munera ad Ezechiam;

m. Heb *my stringed instruments*

Hezekiah, for he heard that he had been sick and had recovered.
2And Hezekiah welcomed them; and he showed them his treasure house, the silver, the gold, the spices, the precious oil, his whole armoury, all that was found in his storehouses. There was nothing in his house or in all his realm that Hezekiah did not show them.
3Then Isaiah the prophet came to King Hezekiah, and said to him, "What did these men say? And whence did they come to you?" Hezekiah said, "They have come to me from a far country, from Babylon." 4He said, "What have they seen in your house?" Hezekiah answered, "They have seen all that is in my house; there is nothing in my storehouses that I did not show them."

5Then Isaiah said to Hezekiah, "Hear the word of the LORD of hosts: 6Behold, the days are coming, when all that is in your house, and that which your fathers have stored up till this day, shall be carried to Babylon; nothing shall be left, says the LORD.
7And some of your own sons, who are born to you, shall be taken away; and they shall be eunuchs in the palace of the king of Babylon." 8Then said Hezekiah to Isaiah, "The word of the LORD which you have spoken is good." For he thought, "There will be peace and security in my days."

---

you have already received your consolation in this life, in the human glory and riches and earthly goods that you possess. As it is written in the book of Deuteronomy: *Take heed lest you forget the Lord your God,* [...] *when you have eaten and are full, and have built goodly houses and live in them, and when your herds and flocks multiply, and your silver and gold is multiplied* (Deut 8:11–13). King Hezekiah, who gloried in his treasures, boasted of them, not in God, to the Persian ambassadors, and he was reproved by Isaiah for his sin" (Tertullian, *Adversus Marcionem*, 4, 15).

audierat enim quod aegrotasset et convaluisset. 2Laetatus est autem super eis Ezechias et ostendit eis cellam thesauri sui et argentum et aurum et aromata et oleum optimum et omnes apothecas supellectilis suae et universa, quae inventa sunt in thesauris eius. Nihil fuit, quod non ostenderet eis Ezechias in domo sua et in omni potestate sua. 3Introivit autem Isaias propheta ad Ezechiam regem et dixit ei: «Quid dixerunt viri isti et unde venerunt ad te?». Et dixit Ezechias: «De terra longinqua venerunt ad me, de Babylone». 4Et dixit: «Quid viderunt in domo tua?». Et dixit Ezechias: «Omnia, quae in domo mea sunt, viderunt; non fuit res, quam non ostenderim eis in thesauris meis». 5Et dixit Isaias ad Ezechiam: «Audi verbum Domini exercituum: 6Ecce dies venient, et auferentur omnia, quae in domo tua sunt, et quae thesaurizaverunt patres tui usque ad diem hanc, in Babylonem; non relinquetur quidquam, dicit Dominus. 7Et de filiis tuis, qui exibunt de te, quos genueris, tollent, et erunt eunuchi in palatio regis Babylonis» 8Et dixit Ezechias ad Isaiam: «Bonum verbum Domini, quod locutus est». Et dixit: «Dummodo fiat pax et securitas in diebus meis».

PART TWO*

1. THE BOOK OF THE CONSOLATION OF ISRAEL*

Prologue: promise of deliverance

Is 52:7–11

40 [1]*Comfort, comfort my people,
says your God.
[2]Speak tenderly to Jerusalem,
and cry to her
that her warfare[n] is ended,
that her iniquity is pardoned,
that she has received from the LORD'S hand
double for all her sins.

***40:1—55:13.** These chapters make up the second part of the book of Isaiah, also known as "Second Isaiah" or "Deutero-Isaiah". Almost everything here refers to a period of history one or two centuries later than that of "First Isaiah". The oppressor is no longer Assyria but Babylon, which conquered Jerusalem in 587–586 BC, and then began a series of deportations that sent the upper classes of Jerusalem and Judah into exile. Many years later (539 BC), Cyrus, king of the Persians, conquered the Babylonians and issued a decree allowing those deportees who so wished to return home. These events are echoed in Second Isaiah's oracles, songs, lamentations and denunciations, and the prophetic visions of the final, enduring deliverance and restoration of the chosen people and the city of Zion.

The various literary units in this part of the book are grouped into two sections more or less by subject. The first (40:1—48:22) implies that the Jews are still held against their will in Babylon. Their deliverance is announced, thanks to the power of the Lord, who rules the world and determines the course of human affairs; he has chosen Cyrus, king of Persia, called here his "anointed", his messiah, to redeem Israel from exile (44:24—45:25).

This section, too, contains the announcement that God will choose a "servant", whom he will send empowered by the Spirit to establish law and justice (42:1–9, the first "song of the Servant").

The second section celebrates the glorious restoration of the people of God on Zion; in this, too, the "Servant of the Lord" will play the key role; the section contains the last three "songs of the Servant" (49: 1–6; 50:4–9; 52:13—53:12).

[40] [1]Consolamini, consolamini populum meum, / dicit Deus vester. / [2]Loquimini ad cor Ierusalem / et clamate ad eam, / quoniam completa est militia eius, / expiata est iniquitas illius; / suscepit de manu

n. Or *time of service*

Is 45:2 Sir 48:10 Mal 3:23–24 *Mt 3:3 and par.* Lk 1:76 *Lk 3:4–6*

[3]A voice cries:
"In the wilderness prepare the way of the LORD,
make straight in the desert a highway for our God.
[4]Every valley shall be lifted up,
and every mountain and hill be made low;
the uneven ground shall become level,
and the rough places a plain.

Ex 24:16 Is 1:20; 58:8,14; 60:1

[5]And the glory of the LORD shall be revealed,
and all flesh shall see it together,
for the mouth of the LORD has spoken."

***40:1—48:22.** The historical background to these chapters is the time immediately after the return of the exiles from Babylon, which is depicted as a "new exodus". The exodus from Egypt was the prototype of all God's interventions on his people's behalf: now we hear of another one, "new" because the power with which God, the Creator of all things, acts now surpasses that to be seen in the exodus. The news that deliverance is at hand greatly consoles the people: we are told this at the start, and it is repeated in the oracles that follow. For this reason, this part of the book of Isaiah is usually called the "Book of Consolation", and it has been interpreted as an anticipation of the consolation that Christ will bring: "The true consolation, balm and release from all human ills is the Incarnation of our God and Saviour" (Theodoret of Cyrrhus, *Commentaria in Isaiam*, 40, 3)

The section opens with a song of joy over the imminent release of the exiles (40:1–11). After this a number of oracles are grouped together which describe the reason why the people should hope in the Lord, who is mighty and desires to save, who is ready to do so (42:1–25), to manifest himself as the Redeemer of Israel (43:1—44:23) and bring salvation to Jerusalem (44:24—48:19). The section ends with a prophecy of the redemption of his people and a call to leave Babylon (48:20–22).

40:1–11. The section begins on a formal note with an anonymous voice proclaiming the Lord's consolation (vv. 1–5). The same voice calls on the prophet himself to proclaim that the word of God and his message of salvation will endure forever (vv. 6–11).

The oracles are addressed to those people of Jerusalem who have been deported to Babylon. When they were first spoken, many decades had passed since these people and the previous generation were forced to leave the holy city. Those years of suffering and exile have more than atoned for their sins. The time comes for them, with the Lord's help, to set out on the return journey. That journey is mentioned throughout this section. The vioce

Domini / duplicia pro omnibus peccatis suis. / [3]Vox clamantis: / «In deserto parate viam Domini, / rectas facite in solitudine / semitas Dei nostri. / [4]Omnis vallis exaltetur, / et omnis mons et collis humilietur; / et fiant prava in directa, / et aspera in plana: / [5]et revelabitur gloria Domini, / et videbit

[6]A voice says, "Cry!"
And I said, "What shall I cry?"
All flesh is grass,
and all its beauty is like the flower of the field.
[7]The grass withers, the flower fades,
when the breath of the LORD blows upon it;
surely the people is grass.
[8]The grass withers, the flower fades;
but the word of our God will stand for ever.

Job 14:2
Ps 37:2; 90:5
Is 51:12
Jas 1:10–11
1 Pet 1:24–25

Ps 119:89
Mt 24:35
Jn 1:1–2

---

speaking in the name of the Lord boosts their morale: it won't be a difficult journey; they will find a way opened up for them which will bring them to the glory of the Lord. As in the exodus from Egypt, on the "way" from Babylon to Jerusalem they will see wonderful evidence of the power of God. The words spoken by the mysterious voice, inviting them to set out, fills the returnees with hope. The four Gospels see these words fulfilled in the ministry of John the Baptist, who is the voice crying in the wilderness, "Prepare the way of the Lord" (cf. v. 3). And, indeed, John, with his call to personal conversion and his baptism of repentance, does prepare the way for people to find Jesus (cf. Mt 3:3; Mk 1:3; Lk 3:4; Jn 1:23), whom the Gospels confess to be "the Lord" (cf. v. 3). John the Baptist is his herald, the "precursor": "The voice commands that a way be opened for the Word of God, the path smoothed and all obstacles removed: when our God comes, he will be able to walk without hindrance. *Prepare the way of the Lord*: this means to preach the gospel and to offer consolation to his people, with the desire that the salvation of God embrace all mankind" (Eusebius of Caesarea, *Commentaria in Isaiam*, 40, 366). Hence, in Christian tradition, "John the Baptist is 'more than a prophet' (Lk 7:26). In him, the Holy Spirit concludes his speaking through the prophets. John completes the cycle of prophets begun by Elijah (cf. Mt 11:13–14). He proclaims the imminence of the consolation of Israel; he is the 'voice' of the Consoler who is coming (Jn 1:23; cf. Is 40:1–3)" (*Catechism of the Catholic Church*, 719).

In the second part of the oracle, the anonymous voice asks the prophet to speak in the name of the Lord (vv. 6–8). Merely human plans can only go so far; but the word of God stands forever. In the things that the voice says there must be an allusion to the might of Babylon, which withers like the "flower of the field" when the "breath of the Lord blows upon it", because it challenged the goodness of God. The message to be given to the people speaks of trusting in the power of God, who comes not to lay waste but to protect and recompense those in his

omnis caro pariter / quod os Domini locutum est». / [6]Vox dicentis: «Clama!». / Et dixi: «Quid clamabo?». / Omnis caro fenum, / et omnis gloria eius quasi flos agri; / [7]exsiccatum est fenum, et cecidit flos, / quia spiritus Domini sufflavit in eo. Vere fenum est populus. / [8]Exsiccatum est fenum,

[9]Get you up to a high mountain,
O Zion, herald of good tidings;[o]
lift up your voice with strength,
O Jerusalem, herald of good tidings,[p]
lift it up, fear not;
say to the cities of Judah,
"Behold your God!"
Is 62:11 [10] Behold, the Lord GOD comes with might,
and his arm rules for him;
behold, his reward is with him,
and his recompense before him.
Deut 32:11 Ps 23:4 Jer 23:3 Ezek 34:1 Lk 15:5 [11] He will feed his flock like a shepherd,
he will gather the lambs in his arms,
he will carry them in his bosom,
and gently lead those that are with young.

God, Creator and ruler of all*

Job 28:23–27; 38:4–5 Prov 30:4 [12] Who has measured the waters in the hollow of his hand
and marked off the heavens with a span,
enclosed the dust of the earth in a measure
and weighed the mountains in scales

---

care (vv. 9–11). Here we find for the first time the simile of the "flock" being applied to the people of God, one of a number of figures of speech used in Holy Scripture to describe God's tender care of his people (cf. Jer 23:3; Ezek 34:1ff; Ps 23:4) and which Christian tradition uses to explain the mystery of the Church: "The Church is a sheepfold whose one and indispensable door is Christ (Jn 10:1–10). It is a flock of which God himself foretold he would be the shepherd (Is 40:11; Ezek 34:11–31), and whose sheep, although ruled by human shepherds, are nevertheless continuously led and nourished by Christ himself, the Good Shepherd and the Prince of the shepherds (cf. Jn 10:11; 1 Pet 5:4), who gave his life for the sheep (cf. Jn 10:11–15)" (Vatican II, *Lumen gentium*, 6).

The words of vv. 6–8 will later be used in the First Letter of St Peter to confirm the validity of the precept of brotherly love (1 Pet 1:24–25).

***40:12—41:29.** The message of hope at the start of the second part of Isaiah

et cecidit flos; / verbum autem Dei nostri manet in aeternum. / [9]Super montem excelsum ascende, / tu, quae evangelizas Sion; / exalta in fortitudine vocem tuam, / quae evangelizas Ierusalem; / exalta, noli timere; / dic civitatibus Iudae: / «Ecce Deus vester, / [10]ecce Dominus Deus in virtute venit, / et brachium eius dominatur: / ecce merces eius cum eo, / et praemium illius coram illo. / [11]Sicut pastor gregem suum pascit, / in brachio suo congregat agnos / et in sinu suo levat; / fetas ipse portat». / [12]Quis mensus est pugillo aquas / et caelos palmo disposuit, / modio continuit pulverem terrae / et libravit in

o. Or *O herald of good tidings to Zion* **p.** Or *O herald of good tidings to Jerusalem*

and the hills in a balance?
13 Who has directed the Spirit of the LORD,
or as his counsellor has instructed him?
14 Whom did he consult for his enlightenment,
and who taught him the path of justice,
and taught him knowledge,
and showed him the way of understanding?

Job 15:8; 21:22; 36:22–26; 38:2–21
Prov 8:22–31
Jer 23:18
Rom 11:34
1 Cor 2:16

---

is not the product of naïve credulity nor is it a dream that can never come true. These verses outline the logical basis of that hope: first, the immense power of God, to be seen in creation (40:12–31); and second, the sovereignty of God, who rules over the destiny of human beings and desires to save his people, and who raises up Cyrus to do that very thing (41:1–29).

40:12–31. These verses deal with the first of the arguments to justify hope. A series of ironical questions, vividly worded, conveys the omnipresence and transcendence of God (similar to what happens in Job 38:2–21): the Lord made all things and there is nothing, no one, to compare with him (vv. 12–26). In v. 26, the "host"is a reference to the heavenly bodies. In Babylonian religion and cosmology, these were considered to be gods. The sacred writer demythologizes them, making them mere creatures of God.

But the Lord does not confine himself to heaven, away from the cares of men, heedless of what is happening to his people. He, who is author of everything that exists, of life, of the rulers of the earth, is infinitely good, and in his providence he supports and strengthens those who trust in him (vv. 27–31). The image of the eagle (v. 31) is reminiscent of Psalm 103:5: "Your youth is renewed like the eagle's." St Augustine, commenting on these words, points out that in ancient times it was thought that when an eagle grew old it was unable to eat food because its beak got too big and, "finding itself in such difficulty, it is said that the eagle, driven by natural instinct and the need to recover its youth, strikes the upper part of it beak against a rock, because the beak has grown too large and prevents it from eating. The beak is worn down by the rock and the eagle eats easily again, and its whole body is restored. Having been old, the eagle is made young and strong again: the sheen returns to its feathers, and power to its wings. It soars to the heights once more, and experiences in that way a type of resurrection" (*Enarrationes in Psalmos*, 102, 9). And so, Christian preaching has used this simile in a spiritual sense as a call to renew one's efforts, trusting in God. If we hope in him, we can cope with difficulties without getting tired, for, as St Bernard points out, "*ubi autem amor est, labor non est, sed sapor*": "where there is love, there is no suffering, but rather savouring" (*In Cantica Canticorum*, 85, 8).

pondere montes / et colles in statera? / 13Quis direxit spiritum Domini? / Aut quis consilium suum / ostendit illi? / 14Cum quo iniit consilium, et instruxit eum / et docuit eum semitam iustitiae / et erudivit

Sir 10:16–17 15 Behold, the nations are like a drop from a bucket,
Wis 11:22 and are accounted as the dust on the scales;
behold, he takes up the isles like fine dust.
16 Lebanon would not suffice for fuel,
nor are its beasts enough for a burnt offering.
Ps 62:10 Dan 4:32 17 All the nations are as nothing before him,
they are accounted by him as less than nothing and emptiness.

Acts 17:29 18 To whom then will you liken God,
or what likeness compare with him?
Ps 115:3–8 19 The idol! a workman casts it,
Wis 13:11–19 and a goldsmith overlays it with gold,
Bar 6 Is 41:6–7; and casts for it silver chains.
44:9–20 20 He who is impoverished[q] chooses for an offering
Jer 10:1–6; wood that will not rot;
51:15–19 he seeks out a skilful craftsman
to set up an image that will not move.

21 Have you not known? Have you not heard?
Has it not been told you from the beginning?
Have you not understood from the foundations of the earth?
Ps 104:2 Is 44:24 22 It is he who sits above the circle of the earth,
Dan 4:32 and its inhabitants are like grasshoppers;
who stretches out the heavens like a curtain,
and spreads them like a tent to dwell in;
Job 34: 18–19 23 who brings princes to nought,
Ps 2:2–5 and makes the rulers of the earth as nothing.

Is 17:13–14 24 Scarcely are they planted, scarcely sown,
scarcely has their stem taken root in the earth,
when he blows upon them, and they wither,
and the tempest carries them off like stubble.

---

eum scientiam / et viam prudentiae ostendit illi? / 15Ecce gentes quasi stilla situlae / et quasi momentum pulveris in statera reputantur; / ecce insulae quasi pulvis exiguus. / 16Et Libanus non sufficiet ad succendendum, / et animalia eius non sufficient ad holocaustum. / 17Omnes gentes, quasi non sint, coram eo; / quasi nihilum et inane reputantur ab eo. / 18Cui ergo similem facitis Deum? / Aut quam imaginem ponitis ei? / 19Sculptile conflat faber, / et aurifex auro figurat illud, / et laminis argenteis argentarius. / 20Nimis pauper, ut offerat lignum imputribile: / exquirit sibi sapientem artificem, / ut statuat simulacrum, / quod non moveatur. / 21Numquid non scitis? Numquid non audistis? / Numquid non annuntiatum est vobis ab initio? / Numquid non intellexistis fundamenta terrae? / 22Qui sedet super gyrum terrae, / et habitatores eius sunt quasi locustae; / qui extendit sicut velum caelos / et expandit eos sicut tabernaculum ad inhabitandum; / 23qui redigit in nihilum principes, / iudices terrae velut inane facit. / 24Et quidem neque plantatus neque satus / neque radicatus in terra truncus eorum; / repente flavit

q. Heb uncertain

[25] To whom then will you compare me, Is 6:3
that I should be like him? says the Holy One.
[26] Lift up your eyes on high and see: Gen 15:5
who created these? 1 Sam 1:3
He who brings out their host by number, Ps 147:4
calling them all by name; Bar 3:34–35
by the greatness of his might,
and because he is strong in power
not one is missing.

[27] Why do you say, O Jacob, Is 49:14–16
and speak, O Israel,
"My way is hid from the LORD,
and my right is disregarded by my God"?
[28] Have you not known? Have you not heard? Gen 21:33
The LORD is the everlasting God, Rom 11:34
the Creator of the ends of the earth.
He does not faint or grow weary,
his understanding is unsearchable.
[29] He gives power to the faint,
and to him who has no might he increases strength.
[30] Even youths shall faint and be weary,
and young men shall fall exhausted;
[31] but they who wait for the LORD shall renew their strength, Ps 103,5
they shall mount up with wings like eagles,
they shall run and not be weary,
they shall walk and not faint.

---

in eos, et aruerunt, / et turbo quasi stipulam aufert eos. / [25]«Et cui assimilabitis me, / quasi aequalis ei sim ego?», / dicit Sanctus. / [26]Levate in excelsum oculos vestros / et videte: Quis creavit haec? / Qui educit in numero militiam eorum / et omnes ex nomine vocat; / prae multitudine fortitudinis et roboris virtutisque eius / neque unum deest. / [27]Quare dicis, Iacob, / et loqueris, Israel: / «Abscondita est via mea a Domino, / et a Deo meo iudicium meum transit?». / [28]Numquid nescis? Aut non audisti? / Deus sempiternus Dominus, / qui creavit terminos terrae; / non deficiet neque laborabit, / nec est investigatio sapientiae eius. / [29]Qui dat lasso virtutem / et invalido robur multiplicat. / [30]Deficient pueri et laborabunt, / et iuvenes lapsu labentur; / [31]qui autem sperant in Domino, / mutabunt fortitudinem, / assument pennas sicut aquilae, / current et non laborabunt, / ambulabunt et non deficient.

Is 45:1–8 **The Lord will raise up a deliverer**

41 [1]Listen to me in silence, O coastlands;
let the peoples renew their strength;
let them approach, then let them speak;
let us together draw near for judgment.

[2]Who stirred up one from the east
whom victory meets at every step?
He gives up nations before him,
so that he tramples kings under foot;
he makes them like dust with his sword,
like driven stubble with his bow.
[3]He pursues them and passes on safely,
by paths his feet have not trod.
Is 44:6 [4]Who has performed and done this,
calling the generations from the beginning?
I, the LORD, the first,
and with the last; I am He.

[5]The coastlands have seen and are afraid,
the ends of the earth tremble;
they have drawn near and come.
Is 40:19–20 [6]Every one helps his neighbour,
and says to his brother, "Take courage!"

41:1–7. The God of Israel, the Lord of creation, also governs the affairs of man. Using the literary device of legal pleading (cf. 1:10–20), the poem calls on the nations to state their case. The historical background to this passage is the campaigns of Cyrus the Great, king of Persia, who swept across the whole region after his victory over Cresus of Lydia in 546 BC (although Cyrus is not explicitly named here); however, it does not refer to his conquest of Babylon, which did not happen until about ten years later.

The prophet plays the part of God and explains what these events mean: it is the Lord who raises up Cyrus and gives him victory over the nations (vv. 1–5). Craftsmen rush to produce idols (vv. 6–7), thinking they will fend off the conquerer: it is all in vain, because God, who is lord of all, determines what Cyrus will accomplish.

[41] [1]Taceant ante me insulae, / et gentes renovent fortitudinem; / accedant et tunc loquantur, / simul ad iudicium propinquemus. / [2]Quis suscitavit ab oriente eum, / cuius gressum sequitur iustitia? / Dabit in conspectu eius gentes / et subiciet ei reges, / quos reddet quasi pulverem gladius eius, / sicut stipulam vento raptam arcus eius. / [3]Persequetur eos, transibit in pace; / semita sub pedibus eius non apparebit. / [4]Quis operatus est et fecit, / vocans generationes ab exordio? / Ego Dominus, primus / et cum novissimis ego sum. / [5]Viderunt insulae et timuerunt, / extrema terrae obstupuerunt, / appropinquaverunt et accesserunt. / [6]Unusquisque proximo suo auxiliabitur / et fratri suo dicet: «Confortare». /

[7]The craftsman encourages the goldsmith,
and he who smooths with the hammer him who strikes the anvil,
saying of the soldering, "It is good";
and they fasten it with nails so that it cannot be moved.

God's special love for his people Is 43:1–7

[8]But you, Israel, my servant, Deut 7:6
Jacob, whom I have chosen, Jas 2:23
the offspring of Abraham, my friend;

41:8–20. The reason why God raises up this new deliverer, Cyrus, is his tender love for his people, who are still suffering the humiliation of exile. This first oracle of the "Book of Consolation" uses expressions that reveal unsuspected tenderness on the Lord's part: "my servant" is a technical expression describing someone chosen for an important mission, as we shall see later in the songs of the Servant. Here it applies to the entire people, Israel, and not to an individual. The words "fear not" (vv. 10, 13, 14) call them to trust in the Lord even though the situation seems hopeless; the same words occur elsewhere in the Bible, addressed to people picked for a dangerous mission—for example, Jacob (Gen 46:3) or Joshua (Josh 1:9; 8:1; etc.) in the Old Testament, and the Blessed Virgin Mary, the Mother of Jesus (Lk 1:30) in the New. Other significant titles used here are: "offspring of Abraham, my friend" (v. 8), reminding them of their noble origin, and "you worm Jacob", a reference to the sorry state in which the exiles find themselves.

Even more significant than the names used to describe Israel are the actions that God takes and the titles given him. These actions are always positive: "to take from the ends of the earth", "to call" (v. 9), "to strengthen", "to help", "to uphold" (v. 10). The titles are titles of affection: "your God" (vv. 10, 13), "your Lord" and, above all, "your Redeemer" (v. 14), an expression that appears no less than fourteen times in this part of the book. A redeemer (*goel*, in Hebrew) was a person's next-of-kin, whose duty it was to ensure that family rights were not abused—whether in respect of property, good name or even life itself (cf. the note on Job 19:25).

God's special love for Israel, his people, so beautifully expressed by the prophet, should also be the basis of the hope felt by members of the new people of God: "Our Lord keeps close watch over the footsteps and progress of his children; that is, those who have love in their souls walk in his sight, and he stretches out his hand to steady them in times of difficulty. For that is what Isaiah says: *I am your God, who takes you by the hand and tells you: Do not be afraid, I will help you.* As well as taking heart from this conviction, we should also have a deep trust in God

[7]Confortabit faber aurificem, / percutiens malleo eum, qui cudit, / dicens de glutino: «Bonum est»; / et roborat eum clavis, / ut non moveatur. / [8]Tu autem, Israel, serve meus, / Iacob, quem elegi, / semen

[9]you whom I took from the ends of the earth,
and called from its farthest corners,
saying to you, "You are my servant,
I have chosen you and not cast you off";
Is 8:10 [10]fear not, for I am with you,
be not dismayed, for I am your God;
I will strengthen you, I will help you,
I will uphold you with my victorious right hand.

Is 45:24 [11]Behold, all who are incensed against you
shall be put to shame and confounded;
those who strive against you
shall be as nothing and shall perish.
[12]You shall seek those who contend with you,
but you shall not find them;
those who war against you
shall be as nothing at all.
[13]For I, the LORD your God,
hold your right hand;
it is I who say to you, "Fear not,
I will help you."

Is 6:3; 28:27; 40:25 [14]Fear not, you worm Jacob,
you men of Israel!
I will help you, says the LORD;
your Redeemer is the Holy One of Israel.
[15]Behold, I will make of you a threshing sledge,
new, sharp, and having teeth;
you shall thresh the mountains and crush them,
and you shall make the hills like chaff;

---

and in his help: if we do not spurn the grace he gives us, he will complete the good work of salvation that he has begun" (St Francis de Sales, *Treatise on the Love of God*, 3, 4).

The last section gives a graphic description of the restoration of Israel, using the simile of a wilderness that is turned into fertile, leafy terrain (cf. 44:3; 51:3).

Abraham amici mei, / [9]quem apprehendi ab extremis terrae, / et a longinquis eius vocavi te / et dixi tibi: «Servus meus es tu; / elegi te et non abieci te». / [10]Ne timeas, quia ego tecum sum; / ne declines, quia ego Deus tuus: / confortabo te et auxiliabor tibi / et sustentabo te dextera iustitiae meae. / [11]Ecce confundentur et erubescent / omnes, qui irascuntur adversum te; / erunt quasi non sint / et peribunt viri, qui contradicunt tibi. / [12]Quaeres eos et non invenies / viros, qui rixantur tecum; / erunt quasi non sint et veluti nihilum, / viri bellantes adversum te. / [13]Quia ego Dominus Deus tuus / apprehendens manum tuam / dicensque tibi: «Ne timeas; / ego auxiliabor tibi. / [14]Noli timere, vermis Iacob, / homines ex Israel. / Ego auxiliabor tibi», dicit Dominus / et redemptor tuus, Sanctus Israel. / [15]Ecce posui te quasi

[16] You shall winnow them and the wind shall carry them away,
and the tempest shall scatter them.
And you shall rejoice in the LORD;
in the Holy One of Israel you shall glory.

[17] When the poor and needy seek water,
and there is none,
and their tongue is parched with thirst,
I the LORD will answer them,
I the God of Israel will not forsake them.
[18] I will open rivers on the bare heights,
and fountains in the midst of the valleys;
I will make the wilderness a pool of water,
and the dry land springs of water.
[19] I will put in the wilderness the cedar,
the acacia, the myrtle, and the olive;
I will set in the desert the cypress,
the plane and the pine together;
[20] that men may see and know,
may consider and understand together,
that the hand of the LORD has done this,
the Holy One of Israel has created it.

Ps 114:8
Is 35:6–7;
43:20; 48:21

The Lord is mightier than idols

[21] Set forth your case, says the LORD;
bring your proofs, says the King of Jacob.

Ps 43:8–13;
44:7–11

41:21–29. The text returns to the theme of legal pleading (*rîb*, in Hebrew), indicating that all of chapter 41 forms a single poem-oracle. Here again the idols of the pagan nations are ridiculed, in a sort of challenge, to show that they are ignorant of past events, and have nothing to tell about the future (vv. 22–23, 26, 28); they are "nothing", "empty wind" (v. 29).

The Lord, however, not only knows everything: he shapes events and guides their protagonists (vv. 25–27). Everything the prophet says is designed to bolster the spirits of the oppressed.

plaustrum triturans novum, / habens rostra serrantia. / Triturabis montes et comminues / et colles quasi pulverem pones. / [16]Ventilabis eos, et ventus tollet eos, / et turbo disperget eos; / et tu exsultabis in Domino, / in Sancto Israel laetaberis. / [17]Egeni et pauperes quaerunt aquas, et non sunt, / lingua eorum siti aruit. / Ego, Dominus, exaudiam eos, / Deus Israel non derelinquam eos. / [18]Aperiam in decalvatis collibus flumina / et in medio vallium fontes; / ponam desertum in stagna aquarum / et terram aridam in rivos aquarum. / [19]Plantabo in deserto cedrum, / acaciam et myrtum et lignum olivae; / ponam in solitudine abietem, / ulmum et cupressum simul, / [20]ut videant et sciant / et recogitent et intellegant pariter / quia manus Domini fecit hoc, / et Sanctus Israel creavit illud. / [21]Proferte causam vestram, dicit

[22] Let them bring them, and tell us
what is to happen.
Tell us the former things, what they are,
that we may consider them,
that we may know their outcome;
or declare to us the things to come.
[23] Tell us what is to come hereafter,
that we may know that you are gods;
do good, or do harm,
that we may be dismayed and terrified.
Is 41:29 [24] Behold, you are nothing,
and your work is nought;
an abomination is he who chooses you.

[25] I stirred up one from the north, and he has come,
from the rising of the sun, and he shall call on my name;
he shall trample[r] on rulers as on mortar,
as the potter treads clay.
[26] Who declared it from the beginning, that we might know,
and beforetime, that we might say, "He is right"?
There was none who declared it, none who proclaimed,
none who heard your words.
[27] I first have declared it to Zion,[s]
and I give to Jerusalem a herald of good tidings.
[28] But when I look there is no one;
among these there is no counsellor
who, when I ask, gives an answer.
Is 41:24 [29] Behold, they are all a delusion;
their works are nothing;
their molten images are empty wind.

Dominus; / afferte, si quid firmum habetis, dixit Rex Iacob. / [22]Accedant et nuntient nobis, quaecumque ventura sunt. / Priora, quae fuerunt, nuntiate, / ut ponamus cor nostrum et sciamus novissima eorum; / et, quae ventura sunt, indicate nobis. / [23]Annuntiate, quae ventura sunt in futurum, / ut sciamus quia dii estis vos; / bene quoque aut male facite, / ut inspiciamus et videamus simul. / [24]Ecce vos estis nihilum, / et opus vestrum nihil valet; / abominatio est, qui eligit vos. / [25]Suscitavi ab aquilone, / et venit ab ortu solis; / vocavi eum nomine; / et conculcabit potentes quasi lutum / et velut plastes calcans humum. / [26]Quis annuntiavit ab exordio, ut sciamus, / et a principio, ut dicamus: «Iustum est»? / Non est neque annuntians neque praedicens / neque audiens sermones vestros. / [27]Primus ad Sion: Ecce adsunt; / et Ierusalem laeta nuntiantem do. / [28]Et vidi, et nemo erat, / ex istis nullus consiliator, / ut, si eos interrogarem, / responderent verbum. / [29]Ecce omnes iniquitas, / vana opera eorum; / ventus et inane / simulacra eorum.

r. Cn: Heb *come* **s.** Cn: Heb *first to Zion, Behold, behold them*

First song of the Servant of the Lord

42 [1]*Behold my servant, whom I uphold,
my chosen, in whom my soul delights;
I have put my Spirit upon him,
he will bring forth justice to the nations.

Is 11:1–10; 43:10; 49:7; 61:1
Zech 3:8
Mt 3:16,17; *12:18–21*
Jn 1:32–34; 3:34
Phil 2:7

42:1–9. The Lord, who revealed his power by creating the world (40:12–31) and showed his determination to save mankind by his interventions in history (41:1–29), now announces a new stage in his plans (v. 9). To advance them he will give a special mission to the "servant of the Lord"; in the prophetic text, this personage plays the key role in making known and putting into effect the salvific plans of God. Four passages over the course of chapters 42–55 speak of the servant and his mission; these passages may originally have made up a poem of their own. These oracles are usually called the "Songs of the Servant". Most biblical scholars see 42:1–9 as being the first song or, rather, the first stanza of that poem. The other three passages are: 49:1–6; 50:4–11; and 52:13—53:12. They combine to make a very beautiful poem, but they raise difficult questions as to style and content. They have been the subject of a great deal of commentary, and the identity of the "servant" is still a matter of debate. Those who consider the four passages to be parts of the one poem take it that the "servant" in each is one and the same person and has one and the same mission. Scholars who do not regard the four passages as originally part of a single poem interpret the person and mission of the servant as being different in each.

There are basically three theories as to who the servant is. One theory is that he is a particular individual—a king of the house of Judah, or the prophet himself or, of course, a future Messiah, who will redeem Israel. The second theory is that the servant is a collectivity: he stands for Israel, or for some group within Israel. The third theory argues that the servant is meant to be depicted ambiguously—that is, in a way that allows him to be interpreted in both of the ways mentioned previously —as a person of significance but someone who can symbolize all Israel.

In this first song (vv. 1–9), the "servant" certainly comes across as a figure of mystery: v. 1 gives him very special, universal, transcendental attributes. Verses 2–3a show his humility, but they are followed immediately by verses saying that he is someone able to "establish justice in the earth", to be "a light to the nations", someone who can "bring light to the nations" and "open the eyes that are blind and set captives free ...". The "servant" can do all this because the Lord has "put his Spirit on him" (cf. v. 1), that is, he is someone chosen by God, and he has the help of the Spirit of the Lord to carry out his mission to teach his Law to the very

[42] [1]Ecce servus meus, suscipiam eum; / electus meus, complacet sibi in illo anima mea; / dedi spiritum meum super eum, / iudicium gentibus proferet. / [2]Non clamabit neque vociferabitur, / nec

[2]He will not cry or lift up his voice,
or make it heard in the street;
Jn 8: 45; 14:16 [3]a bruised reed he will not break,
and a dimly burning wick he will not quench;
he will faithfully bring forth justice.

---

ends of the earth. So, these words could be describing the prophet's own conviction that he has a mission to perform—to proclaim the word of God; a mission that he did not seek but, rather, had given to him. But the servant could also stand for the whole people of Israel (cf. 41:8)—for in the same way were the people chosen by God to bear witness to him before all mankind concerning the Law they had received from the Lord.

The Gospels and the Acts of the Apostles, without attempting to discover exactly who this servant was originally (or whom he was meant to stand for) interpreted the main features of the servant as being a prophecy about Jesus, in whom the Father is most pleased, and who, in the unity of the Holy Spirit, is truly the light for all nations and the liberation of all the oppressed. For example, in the accounts of the baptism of Jesus in the Jordan and of the Transfiguration, the voice of the Father refers to those features: "This is my beloved Son, with whom I am well pleased" (Mt 3:17); "This is my Son, my Chosen; listen to him!" (Lk 9:35). The Gospel of Matthew, which makes a point of showing that the Scriptures find fulfilment in Jesus, explicitly quotes vv. 2–4 of this oracle of Isaiah to show that in Jesus is fulfilled the prophecy of the servant, who was rejected by the leaders of the people and whose quiet and kindly teaching would bring the light of truth to the world (Mt 12:15–21). And later in his Gospel, when St Matthew recounts the passion and death of our Lord (cf. Mt 27:30), he again makes the link between Christ and the servant.

The expression "light to the nations" (v. 6) seems to find an echo in what Jesus says about his being "the light of the world" (Jn 8:12; 9:5) and also in the *Benedictus* of Zechariah (Lk 1:78–79). There is an evocation of v. 7 in Jesus' reply to the messengers from John the Baptist who ask him whether he is "he who is to come" (cf. Mt 11:4–6; Lk 7:18–22); cf. the note on 29:15–24. And so St Justin will say, commenting on vv. 6–7: "Everything that is said here, my friends, refers to Christ and to the peoples who have been enlightened by his presence" (*Dialogus cum Tryphone*, 122, 2).

The Church, in the Second Vatican Council, acknowledges her duty to strive to use every opportunity to show that Christ is truly the "light of the nations" (v. 6): "Christ is the Light of nations. Because this is so, this Sacred Synod gathered together in the Holy Spirit eagerly desires, by proclaiming the Gospel to every creature, to bring

audietur vox eius foris. / [3]Calamum quassatum non conteret / et linum fumigans non exstinguet; / in veritatem proferet iudicium. / [4]Non languebit nec frangetur, / donec ponat in terra iudicium; / et legem

[4]He will not fail[t] or be discouraged[u]
till he has established justice in the earth;
and the coastlands wait for his law.
[5]Thus says God, the LORD,
who created the heavens and stretched them out,
who spread forth the earth and what comes from it,
who gives breath to the people upon it
and spirit to those who walk in it:
[6]"I am the LORD, I have called you in righteousness,
I have taken you by the hand and kept you;
I have given you as a covenant to the people,
a light to the nations,
[7]to open the eyes that are blind,
to bring out the prisoners from the dungeon,
from the prison those who sit in darkness.
[8]I am the LORD, that is my name;
my glory I give to no other,
nor my praise to graven images.
[9]Behold, the former things have come to pass,
and new things I now declare;
before they spring forth
I tell you of them."

Is 49:6,8; 51:4; 60:1–3; Lk 2:32; Jn 8:12

Ps 107:10
Lk 1:70,79; 4,19; 7:18–22
Jn 8:32
2 Tim 2:26

Heb 2:14
Is 48:11

A new song

[10] Sing to the LORD a new song,
his praise from the end of the earth!
Let the sea roar[v] and all that fills it,
the coastlands and their inhabitants.
[11] Let the desert and its cities lift up their voice,
the villages that Kedar inhabits;

Ps 96:1; 98:1; Rev 5:1–7, 9–10

Ps 120:5
Song 1:5
Is 21:16

---

the light of Christ to all men, a light brightly visible on the countenance of the Church" (*Lumen gentium*, 1).

42:10–13. The announcement of the "new things" (42:9) that the Lord will do occasions great joy—expressed in

eius insulae exspectant. / [5]Haec dicit Dominus Deus, / creans caelos et extendens eos, / firmans terram et quae germinant ex ea, / dans flatum populo, qui est super eam, / et spiritum calcantibus eam: / [6]«Ego, Dominus, vocavi te in iustitia / et apprehendi manum tuam; / et formavi te et dedi te / in foedus populi, in lucem gentium, / [7]ut aperires oculos caecorum / et educeres de conclusione vinctum, / de domo carceris sedentes in tenebris. / [8]Ego Dominus: hoc est nomen meum; / et gloriam meam alteri non dabo / et laudem meam sculptilibus. / [9]Quae prima fuerunt, ecce venerunt; / nova quoque ego annuntio: / antequam oriantur, audita vobis faciam». / [10]Cantate Domino canticum novum, / laus eius ab extremis terrae; / qui descenditis in mare, et plenitudo eius, / insulae et habitatores earum. / [11]Exsultent desertum

t. Or *burn dimly* **u.** Or *bruised* **v.** Cn Compare Ps 96:11; 98:7: Heb *Those who go down to the sea*

let the inhabitants of Sela sing for joy,
let them shout from the top of the mountains.
12 Let them give glory to the LORD,
and declare his praise in the coastlands.
Num 10:35 13 The LORD goes forth like a mighty man,
Judg 5:4 like a man of war he stirs up his fury;
Zeph 1:14 he cries out, he shouts aloud,
he shows himself mighty against his foes.

Further acts of salvation by the Lord

14 For a long time I have held my peace,
I have kept still and restrained myself;

---

the "new song" (v. 10) in which all creation, heaven and earth, and all living things and even people in the most faraway places will praise and glorify the Lord. These verses are a solemn hymn that echoes things that are to be found in some of the psalms (cf. Ps 96:1; 98:1).

"Kedar" (v. 11) was a nomadic Arabian tribe (cf. 21:16; Ps 120:5; Song 1:5). "Sela", which in Hebrew means "rock" and can be translated into Greek and Latin as "Petra", may refer to the present-day city in Jordan bearing that name, a city famous for its narrow entrances; if it does not refer to the city, then it means the whole barren area east of the Jordan.

In the book of Revelation, the triumph of the Lamb, the only one worthy to take "the scroll and to open its seals" (cf. Rev 5:1–10), leads to the singing of the definitive new song (v. 10; Rev 5:9).

Commenting on v. 10, St Jerome wrote "Who ought to sing the new song? The words of Scripture answer: *Let the sea roar and all that fills it, the coastlands and their inhabitants.* Jesus saw the apostles mending their nets on the shore of Lake Genesareth, and he sent them out to other wider seas, making fishers of men of fishermen. They preached the Gospel in Greece and Spain, and held sway for a short time over the great power in the city of Rome. They will go down to the shores of the sea and cross the water, braving all the storms and persecutions of this world; and like them, too, the inhabitants of the coastlands and the islands, all the peoples, and the many churches" (*Commentarii in Isaiam*, 42, 10).

42:14–25. Once again the prophet tries to raise the spirits of the exiles by announcing that God is going to act in a spectacular way (vv. 15–17). For a long time he has been silent—but that now changes. The simile of the woman in childbirth (v. 14) graphically indicates that the restoration of Israel will soon come about.

et civitates eius, / vici, quos habitat Cedar. / Iubilent habitatores Petrae, / de vertice montium clament. / 12Ponant Domino gloriam / et laudem eius in insulis nuntient. / 13Dominus sicut fortis egredietur, / sicut vir proeliator suscitabit zelum; / vociferabitur et conclamabit, / super inimicos suos praevalebit. / 14«Tacui semper, silui, patiens fui; / sicut parturiens ululabo, / gemam et fremam simul. / 15Desertos

now I will cry out like a woman in travail,
I will gasp and pant.
15 I will lay waste mountains and hills, Ps 107:33
and dry up all their herbage; Is 44:27; 50:2
I will turn the rivers into islands,
and dry up the pools.
16 And I will lead the blind Is 6:9–10;
in a way that they know not, 42:19
in paths that they have not known
I will guide them.
I will turn the darkness before them into light,
the rough places into level ground.
These are the things I will do,
and I will not forsake them.
17 They shall be turned back and utterly put to shame,
who trust in graven images,
who say to molten images,
"You are our gods."

18 Hear, you deaf; Mt 11:5
and look, you blind, that you may see! Lk 7:22
19 Who is blind but my servant, Is 41:8
or deaf as my messenger whom I send? Mt 13:9
Who is blind as my dedicated one,

The prophet warns Israel not to think that its God is blind and deaf, that he does not realize the plight of his people. It is Israel that is blind and deaf, for it has failed to understand and failed to learn the lesson implied in the punishment that God has sent it: its purpose is to make them turn to him and be saved (vv. 18–25). Up to this, the people, whom he has chosen to be his servant and messenger, has not understood the Lord's purposes. They must open their eyes and their ears. The Lord is ready to take action, to set them free and punish their oppressors (v. 17). "Let us rejoice", says St Augustine, commenting on this passage, "in the mercy of the Lord, and be fearful of his justice. He forgives, but he does not remain silent. If he is silent now, he will not be silent forever. Listen to him in the silence and do not speak, so that when the time of justice comes you will be able to hear him" (*Sermones*, 9, 1).

faciam montes et colles / et omne gramen eorum exsiccabo; / et ponam flumina in insulas / et stagna arefaciam. / 16Et ducam caecos in viam, quam nesciunt, / et in semitis, quas ignoraverunt, ambulare eos faciam; / ponam tenebras coram eis in lucem / et prava in recta. / Haec verba faciam eis / et non dereliquam eos». / 17Conversi sunt retrorsum; / confundantur confusione, qui confidunt in sculptili, / qui dicunt conflatili: / «Vos dii nostri». / 18Surdi, audite; / et caeci, intuemini ad videndum. / 19Quis caecus sicut servus meus, / et surdus sicut nuntius, quem ego mittam? / Quis caecus sicut qui restitutus

or blind as the servant of the LORD?
[20] He sees[w] many things, but does not observe them;
his ears are open, but he does not hear.
[21]The LORD was pleased, for his righteousness' sake,
to magnify his law and make it glorious.
[22] But this is a people robbed and plundered,
they are all of them trapped in holes
and hidden in prisons;
they have become a prey with none to rescue,
a spoil with none to say, "Restore!"
[23] Who among you will give ear to this,
will attend and listen for the time to come?
[24] Who gave up Jacob to the spoiler,
and Israel to the robbers?
Was it not the LORD, against whom we have sinned,
in whose ways they would not walk,
and whose law they would not obey?
Is 9:17–18 Amos 4:6 [25] So he poured upon him the heat of his anger
and the might of battle;
it set him on fire round about, but he did not understand;
it burned him, but he did not take it to heart.

Is 41:8,14; 42:2

The Lord's tender care of Israel*

43 [1]But now thus says the LORD,
he who created you, O Jacob,
he who formed you, O Israel:

***43:11—44:5.** God chose Israel and he has special love for his people (cf. 43:1–13). Just as in the past he acted in ways that showed he had not forgotten them, not least by releasing them from Egypt and guiding them through the wilderness, he will show equal power and kindness by bringing them out of Babylon (cf. 43:14–21). The provident care that he takes of them is not a reward that the people has earned; it stems entirely from his mercy; he is

est? / Et quis caecus sicut servus Domini? / [20]Multa vidisti, sed non servas; / aures aperuisti, sed non audis. / [21]Dominus voluit propter iustitiam suam / magnificare legem et extollere. / [22]Ipse autem populus direptus et vastatus; / in foveis conclusi omnes, / et in domibus carcerum absconditi sunt. / Facti sunt in rapinam, nec est qui eruat; / in direptionem, nec est qui dicat: «Redde!». / [23]Quis est in vobis, qui audiat hoc, / attendat et auscultet futura? / [24]Quis dedit in direptionem Iacob / et Israel vastantibus? / Nonne Dominus ipse, cui peccavimus? / Et noluerunt in viis eius ambulare / et non audierunt legem eius. / [25]Et effudit super eum indignationem furoris sui / et forte bellum. / Et combussit eum in circuitu, et non cognovit; / et succendit eum, et non intellexit. **[43]** [1]Et nunc haec dicit Dominus, / qui creavit te, Iacob, et formavit te, Israel: / «Noli timere, quia redemi te / et vocavi te

w. Heb *you see*

"Fear not, for I have redeemed you;
I have called you by name, you are mine.
2When you pass through the waters I will be with you;
and through the rivers, they shall not overwhelm you;
when you walk through fire you shall not be burned,
and the flame shall not consume you.

Ps 91
1 Kings 10:1
Dan 3:25,27
1 Cor 3:15

---

steadfast in his love for them, despite all their faults (43:22—44:5). His people have more than enough reason to be tranquil and unconcerned, for the Lord, who has special love for them, is the one true God and there is nothing, no one, to match him (cf. 44:6–23). So, this group of oracles ends with shouts of joy, acknowledging the redemption that God brings (cf. 44:23).

43:1–13. As in 41:8–20, this oracle proclaims God's special love for his people. The words used to describe them—my sons, my daughters (v. 6), everyone who is called by my name (v. 7), my witnesses, my servant whom I have chosen (v. 10); the titles of the Lord—the Holy One of Israel, the Saviour, the Lord your God (vv. 3, 11); and, above all, the actions of God—creation, redemption (v. 1), ransoming (v. 3), etc.: all make this one of the most moving passages in the book—most tender in its language, and very explicit about God's love. "In the course of its history, Israel was able to discover that God had only one reason to reveal himself to them, a single motive for choosing them from among all peoples as his special possession: his sheer gratuitous love (cf. Deut 4:37; 7:8; 10:15). And thanks to the prophets Israel understood that it was again out of love that God never stopped saving them (cf. Is 43:1–7) and pardoning their unfaithfulness and sins (cf. Hos 2)" (*Catechism of the Catholic Church*, 218).

Many saints have been moved by the opening words of this oracle (v. 1). St Josemaría Escrivá liked to repeat them, savouring the tender love that God the Father has for every one of his children: "Go over, calmly, that divine admonition which fills the soul with disquiet and which at the same time tastes as sweet as honey from the comb: *redemi te, et vocavi te, nomine tuo: meus es tu:* I have redeemed you and called you by your name: you are mine! Let us not steal from God what belongs to him. A God who has loved us to the point of dying for us, who has chosen us from all eternity, before the creation of the world, so that we may be holy in his presence; and who continually offers us opportunities to purify our lives and give ourselves to him" (*Friends of God*, 312). And he often found in them a motive for conversion and gratitude: "he helps me, he reassures me, and I hear him repeat slowly in the depths of my heart, *meus es tu* ('you are mine'). I know the way you are, as I have always known it. Press on!" (ibid., 215).

nomine tuo; meus es tu. / 2Cum transieris per aquas, tecum ero, / et flumina non operient te; / cum ambulaveris in igne, non combureris, / et flamma non ardebit in te, / 3quia ego Dominus Deus tuus, /

[3]For I am the LORD your God,
the Holy One of Israel, your Saviour.
I give Egypt as your ransom,
Ethiopia and Seba in exchange for you.
[4]Because you are precious in my eyes,
and honoured, and I love you,
I give men in return for you,
peoples in exchange for your life.
Is 8:10; 41:21–29 42:18; 44:7–11 [5]Fear not, for I am with you;
I will bring your offspring from the east,
and from the west I will gather you;
[6]I will say to the north, Give up,
and to the south, Do not withhold;
bring my sons from afar
and my daughters from the end of the earth,
Is 63:19; 65:1 Eph 2:10 [7]every one who is called by my name,
whom I created for my glory,
whom I formed and made."

[8]Bring forth the people who are blind, yet have eyes,
who are deaf, yet have ears!
[9]Let all the nations gather together,
and let the peoples assemble.
Who among them can declare this,
and show us the former things?
Let them bring their witnesses to justify them,
and let them hear and say, It is true.
Is 41:8; 44:6 Jn 8:24,28; 15:16 Acts 1:8 [10]"You are my witnesses," says the LORD,
"and my servant whom I have chosen,
that you may know and believe me
and understand that I am He.
Before me no god was formed,
nor shall there be any after me.

Sanctus Israel, salvator tuus: / dedi propitiationem tuam Aegyptum, / Aethiopiam et Saba pro te. / [4]Quoniam pretiosus factus es in oculis meis / et gloriosus, ego diligo te / et dabo homines pro te / et populos pro anima tua. / [5]Noli timere, quoniam ego tecum sum: / ab oriente adducam semen tuum / et ab occidente congregabo te. / [6]Dicam aquiloni: "Da" / et austro: "Noli prohibere; / affer filios meos de longinquo / et filias meas ab extremis terrae. / [7]Omnem, qui vocatur nomine meo, / in gloriam meam creavi eum, / formavi eum et feci eum". / [8]Educ foras populum caecum, et oculos habentem, / surdos, et aures eis sunt. / [9]Omnes gentes congregentur simul, / et colligantur nationes: / quis in eis annuntiabit istud / et priora audire nos faciet? / Dent testes suos et iustificentur / et audiant et dicant: "Vere"./ [10]Vos testes mei, dicit Dominus, / et servus meus, quem elegi, / ut sciatis et credatis mihi / et intellegatis quia ego ipse sum; / ante me non est formatus Deus / et post me non erit. / [11]Ego, ego sum Dominus, / et non

[11] I, I am the LORD,
and besides me there is no saviour.
[12] I declared and saved and proclaimed,
when there was no strange god among you;
and you are my witnesses," says the LORD.
[13] "I am God, and also henceforth I am He;
there is none who can deliver from my hand;
I work and who can hinder it?"

Deut 32:39
Is 45:21
Hos 13:4
Acts 4:12

Is 42:8

Announcement of a new exodus

[14] Thus says the LORD,
your Redeemer, the Holy One of Israel:
"For your sake I will send to Babylon
and break down all the bars,

Ex 14:21–29
Lev 17:1
Is 6:3; 40:3

43:14–21. This oracle is part of the doctrinal core of the "Book of Consolation" (40:1—48:22), where we can see the exodus from Egypt as the prototype of every instance of liberation brought about by the Lord. Its most direct reference would be to the return of those exiled in Babylon. The original exodus from Egypt was quite remarkable and well worth pondering; but this exodus is truly "new", surpassing what happened in former times (cf. vv. 18–19). This prophecy is very carefully constructed. It first acknowledges God by giving an impressive list of divine titles, repeated several times: Lord, Redeemer, Holy One of Israel, Creator, King (vv. 14–15); then comes the announcement of the new exodus based on traditions to do with the first exodus, without mentioning it specifically (vv. 16–21); it recalls, with sadness, yet serenity, the people's infidelities (vv. 22–24); and it ends with God asserting his forgiveness in the context of a *rîb*, that is, a "legal hearing" (vv. 25–28).

The prophet's words are designed to fill the people with hope that they will soon be able to return home, and also with the energy to undertake the religious restoration of Israel. But they are also a reminder to people at all times that God never abandons his chosen ones, and a constant encouragement to renew their fervour. The only proviso is that they must have recourse to the mercy of God and sincerely admit their sins. Thus, we find St Gregory the Great interpreting the "suit" in v. 26 as describing the examination of conscience that leads to the confession of sins: "The conscience accuses, reason judges, fear binds, and suffering tortures" (*Moralia in Job*, 25, 7, 12–13).

---

est absque me salvator. / [12]Ego, annuntiavi et salvavi; / auditum feci, et non fuit in vobis alienus; / et vos testes mei, dicit Dominus, / et ego Deus, / [13]iam ab initio ego ipse. / Et non est qui de manu mea eruat; operabor, et quis avertet illud?». / [14]Haec dicit Dominus, redemptor vester, / Sanctus Israel: / «Propter vos misi in Babylonem / et detraxi fugitivos universos / et Chaldaeos in navibus suis

and the shouting of the Chaldeans will be turned to
lamentations.[x]
15 I am the LORD, your Holy One,
the Creator of Israel, your King."
16 Thus says the LORD,
who makes a way in the sea,
a path in the mighty waters,
17 who brings forth chariot and horse,
army and warrior;
they lie down, they cannot rise,
they are extinguished, quenched like a wick:
18 "Remember not the former things,
nor consider the things of old.
2 Cor 5:17 19 Behold, I am doing a new thing;
Rev 21:5 now it springs forth, do you not perceive it?
I will make a way in the wilderness
and rivers in the desert.
Ex 17:1–7 20 The wild beasts will honour me,
Is 35:6–7 the jackals and the ostriches;
for I give water in the wilderness,
rivers in the desert,
to give drink to my chosen people,
1 Pet 2:9 21 the people whom I formed for myself
that they might declare my praise.

Mic 6:3 22 "Yet you did not call upon me, O Jacob;
Mal 1:13 but you have been weary of me, O Israel!
Amos 5:25 23 You have not brought me your sheep for burnt offerings,
or honoured me with your sacrifices.
I have not burdened you with offerings,
or wearied you with frankincense.
24 You have not bought me sweet cane with money,
or satisfied me with the fat of your sacrifices.

---

gloriantes. / 15Ego Dominus, Sanctus vester, / creans Israel, rex vester». / 16Haec dicit Dominus, / qui dedit in mari viam / et in aquis torrentibus semitam; / 17qui eduxit quadrigam et equum, / agmen et robustum; / simul iacuerunt nec resurgent, / contriti sunt quasi linum et exstincti sunt. / 18«Ne memineritis priorum / et antiqua ne intueamini: / 19ecce ego facio nova, / et nunc orientur: nonne cognoscitis ea? / Utique ponam in deserto viam / et in invio flumina. / 20Glorificabit me bestia agri, / dracones et struthiones, / quia dedi in deserto aquas, / flumina in invio, / ut darem potum populo meo, electo meo. / 21Populum istum formavi mihi; / laudem meam narrabunt. / 22Non me invocasti, Iacob; / immo taedio mei affectus es, Israel. / 23Non obtulisti mihi agnos holocausti tui / et victimis tuis non glorificasti me; / non te gravavi in oblatione / nec laborem tibi praebui in ture. / 24Non emisti mihi

x. Heb obscure

But you have burdened me with your sins,
you have wearied me with your iniquities.

25 "I, I am He
who blots out your transgressions for my own sake,
and I will not remember your sins.
26 Put me in remembrance, let us argue together;
set forth your case, that you may be proved right.
27 Your first father sinned,
and your mediators transgressed against me.
28 Therefore I profaned the princes of the sanctuary,
I delivered Jacob to utter destruction
and Israel to reviling.

Gen 27:36
Is 47:6
Jer 9:3
Lam 2:2

Hos 12:4

God is faithful, despite Israel's sin

44 1"But now hear, O Jacob my servant,
Israel whom I have chosen!
2Thus says the LORD who made you,
who formed you from the womb and will help you:
Fear not, O Jacob my servant,
Jeshurun whom I have chosen.
3For I will pour water on the thirsty land,
and streams on the dry ground;
I will pour my Spirit upon your descendants,
and my blessing on your offspring.
4They shall spring up like grass amid waters,[y]
like willows by flowing streams.

Is 41:8

Deut 32:15; 33:5,26
Is 43:1,5; 44:24

Is 11:2,42:1

44:1–5. Israel sinned, burdened the Lord with its faults, but God's love is so great that he does not take these offences into account: in spite of everything, he is faithful to the choice he made. In fact, he continues to treat his people tenderly. "Jeshurun" (v. 2) is a poetic and affectionate name for Israel, found only here and in Deuteronomy 32:15; 35:5, 26; the root of the word is ysr, meaning upright or just. There is a play on words here with the name Israel.

argento calamum / et adipe victimarum tuarum non inebriasti me; / verumtamen servire me fecisti in peccatis tuis, / praebuisti mihi laborem in iniquitatibus tuis. / 25Ego, ego sum ipse, qui deleo iniquitates tuas propter me / et peccatorum tuorum non recordabor. / 26Memorem me redde, iudicium agamus simul: / narra, ut iustificeris. / 27Pater tuus primus peccavit, / et interpretes tui praevaricati sunt in me; / 28et contaminavi principes sanctuarii, / dedi ad internecionem Iacob / et Israel in opprobrium». **[44]** 1Et nunc audi, Iacob serve meus, / et Israel, quem elegi. / 2Haec dicit Dominus, qui fecit te / et formavit te ab utero, / auxiliator tuus: / «Noli timere, serve meus Iacob, / et dilecte, quem elegi. / 3Effundam enim aquas super terram sitientem / et fluenta super aridam; / effundam spiritum meum super semen tuum / et benedictionem meam super stirpem tuam: / 4et germinabunt inter herbas / quasi

y. Gk Compare Tg: Heb *They shall spring up in among grass*

[5]This one will say, 'I am the LORD'S,'
another will call himself by the name of Jacob,
and another will write on his hand, 'The LORD'S,'
and surname himself by the name of Israel."

Is 41:4,14, 21–29; 42:8; 43:8–13; 48:12 Rev 1:8,17; 21:6; 22:13 Is 48:17

There is no God but the Lord. Rejection of idols

[6]Thus says the LORD, the King of Israel
and his Redeemer, the LORD of hosts:
I am the first and I am the last;
besides me there is no god.

Deut 32:39 Is 41:23; 43:10

[7]Who is like me? Let him proclaim it,
let him declare and set it forth before me.
Who has announced from of old the things to come?[z]
Let them tell us[a] what is yet to be.

44:6–23. This whole passage is an assertion that the Lord is the only God; there is no one or nothing to compare with him. Other so-called "gods" have no existence. The sort of "legal pleading" (*rîb)* to be found often in this part of the book is used here too. There are four stages in the argument: a confession of faith in the one, true God is the subject at issue (v. 6); then comes a challenge to compare him with other gods (vv. 7–8), and a ridiculing of graven images (vv. 9–20); and the final verses (vv. 21–22) are an exhortation to acknowledge the Lord as the author of history. Recognition of God and of his special love for Israel has practical implications: it involves personal conversion, a return to him (v. 22).

"Rock" (v. 8) is one of God's titles, often found in Hebrew poetry (cf. 17:10; 26:4; Ps 18:3, 47; 19:15; 28:1; etc.). The satirical passage about the uselessness of idols (vv. 9–20) is similar to Jeremiah 2:26–28; 10:1–16; and Wisdom 13:10–12. In all these passages, but particularly in Isaiah, the fabrication of idols is treated very dismissively; worshipping idols is like eating ashes (v. 20; cf. Prov 15:14; Hos 12:2).

Verse 23, a hymn, can be taken as an independent piece, rather like the hymn in 42:10–13. The whole world, indeed the whole cosmos, shares in the joy of Israel's liberation. Once again we can see that the notion of universality is the key to the message of the "Book of Consolation".

The *Catechism of the Catholic Church* refers to v. 6 (cf. 41:4; 48:12; Rev 1:8) when it notes that "our profession of faith begins with *God*, for God is the First and the Last (cf. Is 44:6), the beginning and the end of everything" (no. 198).

salices iuxta praeterfluentes aquas. / [5]Iste dicet: "Domini ego sum", / et ille vocabit se nomine Iacob; / et hic scribet manu sua: "Domino", et inscribetur nomine Israel». / [6]Haec dicit Dominus, rex Israel / et redemptor eius, Dominus exercituum: / «Ego primus et ego novissimus, / et absque me non est Deus. / [7]Quis similis mei? Conclamet et annuntiet / et exponat mihi, / ex quo constitui populum antiquum; /

z. Cn: Heb *from my placing an eternal people and things to come* **a.** Tg: Heb *them*

8Fear not, nor be afraid; Deut 32:4
have I not told you from of old and declared it? Is 17:10;
And you are my witnesses! 45:21
Is there a God besides me?
There is no Rock; I know not any."

9All who make idols are nothing, and the things they delight in do Jer 2:26–28;
not profit; their witnesses neither see nor know, that they may be put 10:1–16
to shame. 10Who fashions a god or casts an image, that is profitable
for nothing? 11Behold, all his fellows shall be put to shame, and the
craftsmen are but men; let them all assemble, let them stand forth,
they shall be terrified, they shall be put to shame together.
12The ironsmith fashions it[b] and works it over the coals; he Is 49:10
shapes it with hammers, and forges it with his strong arm; he Jer 10:3–10
becomes hungry and his strength fails, he drinks no water and is Hobad 2:18
faint. 13The carpenter stretches a line, he marks it out with a pencil;
he fashions it with planes, and marks it with a compass; he shapes it
into the figure of a man, with the beauty of a man, to dwell in a
house. 14He cuts down cedars; or he chooses a holm tree or an oak
and lets it grow strong among the trees of the forest; he plants a
cedar and the rain nourishes it. 15Then it becomes fuel for a man; Wis 13:11–19
he takes a part of it and warms himself, he kindles a fire and bakes
bread; also he makes a god and worships it, he makes it a graven
image and falls down before it. 16Half of it he burns in the fire;
over the half he eats flesh, he roasts meat and is satisfied; also he
warms himself and says, "Aha, I am warm, I have seen the fire!"
17And the rest of it he makes into a god, his idol; and falls
down to it and worships it; he prays to it and says, "Deliver me,
for thou art my god!"

---

ventura et, quae futura sunt, annuntiet nobis. / 8Nolite timere neque conturbemini; / nonne ex tunc
audire te feci et annuntiavi? / Vos estis testes mei. / Numquid est Deus absque me / aut Petra, quam ego
non noverim?». 9Plastae idoli omnes nihil sunt, et pretiosa eorum non proderunt eis; testes eorum non
vident neque intellegunt, ut confundantur. 10Quis formavit deum et sculptile conflavit lucrum non
quaerens? 11Ecce omnes participes eius confundentur; fabri enim sunt ex hominibus: conveniant omnes,
stent; pavebunt, confundentur simul. 12Faber ferrarius securim operatur in prunis et in malleis format
illam et polit eam in brachio fortitudinis suae; esurit et deficit, non bibit aquam et lassescit. 13Artifex
lignarius extendit normam, describit illud stilo, operatur illud scalpellis et circino describit illud quasi
imaginem viri, quasi speciosum hominem, qui resideat in domo. 14Succidit sibi cedros et arripit ilicem
et quercum, quae steterat inter ligna saltus; plantavit pinum, quam pluvia nutrivit. 15Homini facta sunt
ad comburendum; sumit ex eis, ut calefaciat, et succendit et coquit panes. De reliquo autem operatur
deum et adorat; facit sculptile et curvatur ante illud. 16Medium eius comburit igne et medio eius carnes
assat, manducat assaturam et saturatur et calefit et dicit: «Vah, calefactus sum, vidi focum». 17Reliquum
autem eius deum fecit, sculptile sibi; curvatur ante illud et adorat illud et obsecrat dicens: «Libera me,

b. Cn: Heb *an axe*

18They know not, nor do they discern; for he has shut their eyes,
so that they cannot see, and their minds, so that they cannot understand. 19No one considers, nor is there knowledge or discernment to
say, "Half of it I burned in the fire, I also baked bread on its coals,
I roasted flesh and have eaten; and shall I make the residue of it an
abomination? Shall I fall down before a block of wood?"
Ps 144:8 Hos 4:12 Rom 1:21,25 20He feeds on ashes; a deluded mind has led him astray, and he
cannot deliver himself or say, "Is there not a lie in my right hand?"

21 Remember these things, O Jacob,
  and Israel, for you are my servant;
I formed you, you are my servant;
  O Israel, you will not be forgotten by me.
22 I have swept away your transgressions like a cloud,
  and your sins like mist;
return to me, for I have redeemed you.

23 Sing, O heavens, for the LORD has done it;
  shout, O depths of the earth;
break forth into singing, O mountains,
  O forest, and every tree in it!
For the LORD has redeemed Jacob,
  and will be glorified in Israel.

The Lord chooses Cyrus to effect his will*

Is 44:2 24 Thus says the LORD, your Redeemer,
  who formed you from the womb:

***44:24—48:22.** The argument developed through the sequence of oracles in the second part of Isaiah reaches a climax here—the announcement that the Lord, the Redeemer of Israel (cf. 43:1—44:23), is going to take direct action to release his people from exile in Babylon. To this purpose he raises up Cyrus, the king of the Persians, a man of immense power, who, even though he is unaware of being the object of God's choice to carry out the

quia deus meus es tu». 18Nescierunt neque intellexerunt; nam clausit oculos eorum, ne videant et ne intellegant corde suo. 19Non recogitant in corde suo, scientia et intellegentia carent, ut dicant: «Medietatem eius combussi igne et coxi super carbones eius panes, coxi carnes et comedi et de reliquo eius abominationem faciam; ante truncum ligni procidam?». 20Cinere vescitur; cor insipiens decepit eum, et non liberabit animam suam neque dicet: «Nonne mendacium est in dextera mea?». 21Memento horum, Iacob, / et Israel, quoniam servus meus es tu; / formavi te, servus meus es tu, / Israel, non decipies me. / 22Delevi ut nubem iniquitates tuas / et quasi nebulam peccata tua; / revertere ad me, / quoniam redemi te. / 23Exsultate, caeli, quoniam hoc fecit Dominus; / iubilate, fundamenta terrae, / resonate, montes, laudationem, / saltus et omne lignum eius, / quoniam redemit Dominus Iacob / et in Israel glorificabitur. / 24Haec dicit Dominus, redemptor tuus et formator tuus ex utero: / «Ego sum

"I am the LORD, who made all things,
who stretched out the heavens alone,
who spread out the earth—Who was with me?[c]—
25 who frustrates the omens of liars, Deut 18:14
and makes fools of diviners;
who turns wise men back,
and makes their knowledge foolish;
26 who confirms the word of his servant,
and performs the counsel of his messengers;
who says of Jerusalem, 'She shall be inhabited,'
and of the cities of Judah, 'They shall be built,
and I will raise up their ruins';
27 who says to the deep, 'Be dry, Is 42:15
I will dry up your rivers';
28 who says of Cyrus, 'He is my shepherd, Is 45:1; 2 Chron 36:22; Ezekra 1:1–3 Neh 2:5f
and he shall fulfil all my purpose';
saying of Jerusalem, 'She shall be built,'
and of the temple, 'Your foundation shall be laid.'"

---

mission (cf. 45:5), is going to be Israel's deliverer (44:24—45:13). Once the holy city is restored, all the nations will acknowledge the universal sovereignty of the Lord and will make their way to Zion to worship him (45:14–25). Then the Lord's victory will be made manifest (46:1–13) and Babylon, which had Judah under its heel, will at last be humbled by the Lord (47:1–15). He is the one, true God and he must be obeyed (48:1–18) when he issues his call to leave Babylon and experience redemption (48:20–22).

44:24–28. This oracle, spoken in the first person singular, maintaining the style of a legal pleading (*rîb*) or sapiential dispute, teaches that God is the main player in creation (v. 24) and in the history of Israel (he has no time for "wise men": v. 25), as the words of the prophets and the evidence of the exodus of old show (v. 27); but the main aim of the oracle is to show that God raises up Cyrus to advance his purposes (v. 28). This is the first time that the Persian king is explicitly mentioned (cf. the note on 41:1–7) and he is called "shepherd", that is, one who guides the people on God's instructions. The mention of the order to rebuild Jerusalem must refer to the decree issued by Cyrus (cf. 2 Chron

Dominus, qui feci omnia, / extendi caelos solus, / expandi terram; et quis mecum? / [25]Qui irrita facio signa divinorum / et hariolos stultos reddo; / compello sapientes retrorsum / et scientiam eorum vanam facio; / [26]qui suscito verbum servi mei / et consilium nuntiorum meorum compleo. / Qui dico Ierusalem: "Habitaberis" et civitatibus Iudae: "Aedificabimini" / et deserta eius suscitabo; / [27]qui dico profundo: "Desolare, / et flumina tua arefaciam"; / [28]qui dico de Cyro: "Pastor meus est / et omnem voluntatem meam complebit"; / qui dico Ierusalem: "Aedificaberis", / et templo: "Fundaberis"».

c. Another reading is *who spread out the earth by myself*

Cyrus' mission

Is 13:3; 44:28; 45:1–5 **45** [1]Thus says the LORD to his anointed, to Cyrus,
whose right hand I have grasped,
to subdue nations before him
and ungird the loins of kings,
to open doors before him
that gates may not be closed:
Ps 107:16 Is 40:4 [2]"I will go before you
and level the mountains,[d]
I will break in pieces the doors of bronze
and cut asunder the bars of iron,
[3]I will give you the treasures of darkness
and the hoards in secret places,

36:23; Ezra 1:24; Neh 2:5ff) that allowed the exiles to return home and rebuild the cities of Judah and the temple of Jerusalem. The prophet wants to make it quite clear that the new empire's control of affairs is not in any sense a punishment for the Jews; God has chosen to save his people by means of this "outsider" shepherd.

45:1–13. This poetic statement is a message designed to raise the spirits of the exiles by announcing the sending of a liberator, Cyrus of Persia, whom God will use to implement his plans of salvation for Israel. The formal, very considered, mention of Cyrus, a foreign king, reveals the universal scope of God's salvific plans—which did not at all fit in with the people's own exclusive, nationalistic mentality. The prophecy can be read as an investiture oracle that maybe never reached the ears of Cyrus yet filled the exiles with hope. St Thomas comments: "Having raised the hope of the people in the divine promises (chaps. 40–44), he lists and details the promises in order to console them: first he promises freedom from all ills (chaps. 45–55), and then the restoration of all goods (chaps. 56–66)" (*Expositio super Isaiam*, 59).

Cyrus was a foreign king who did not know the God of the chosen people, and yet, surprisingly, has been given the title of "anointed", a title reserved to the kings of Israel. Moreover, the oracle says that the mission and conquest of this Persian king are attributable to special divine providence: God has chosen this man to deliver Israel from oppression by other nations (vv. 1–5). This message must have truly amazed those who heard the oracle. Even many centuries later it makes us realize that God's plans can involve historical events that at first sight can seem disconcerting or at odds with those plans.

[45] [1]Haec dicit Dominus de uncto suo Cyro: / «Apprehendi dexteram eius, / ut subiciam ante faciem eius gentes / et dorsa regum vertam / et aperiam coram eo ianuas; / et portae non claudentur. / [2]Ego ante te ibo / et montes humiliabo; / portas aereas conteram / et vectes ferreos confringam. / [3]Et dabo tibi

d. One ancient Ms Gk: Heb *the swellings*

that you may know that it is I, the LORD,
the God of Israel, who call you by your name.
4For the sake of my servant Jacob, Is 41:8
and Israel my chosen,
I call you by your name,
I surname you, though you do not know me.
5I am the LORD, and there is no other, 2 Sam 7:22 Is 44:6
besides me there is no God;
I gird you, though you do not know me,
6that men may know, from the rising of the sun
and from the west, that there is none besides me;
I am the LORD, and there is no other.
7I form light and create darkness, Sir 11:14 Amos 3:6; 4:13
I make weal and create woe,
I am the LORD, who do all these things.

The expression "ungird the loins of kings" means disarming them, for the sword was slung from the belt.

45:6–7. When these verses were written they may have been designed to counter dualism (very prevalent among the Persians and their neighbours), which held that two counterposed principles existed—good and evil; hence the emphasis on the fact that the Lord is the only God, the creator of all things, of light and of darkness. That would explain why God is described as the maker of "weal" and "woe", whereas because God is infinite goodness he cannot properly be called the author of evil. However, because Christian readers could find the statement (in v. 2) disconcerting, exegetes have commented on it. Origen, quite early on, gave this explanation: "Evil, in the absolute sense of the word, was not created by God [...]. If we speak of evil in a loose sense, meaning physical and natural evils, then we can say that God created it in order to convert men by their suffering. What is strange about this teaching? We refer to the punishments meted out by parents and teachers, and even the prescriptions and operations carried out by doctors and surgeons, as evils and sufferings, without blaming or condemning them. And that is how we should read the verse: *I form light and create darkness, I make weal and woe* (Is 45:7)" (*Contra Celsum*, 6, 55–56). And St Gregory the Great comments: "*I make weal and woe*: the peace of God is offered to us precisely in the moment when created things, which are good in themselves, though not always desired or sought with rectitude of heart, become the source of suffering

thesauros absconditos / et divitias occultas, / ut scias quia ego Dominus, / qui vocavi te nomine tuo, Deus Israel. / 4Propter servum meum Iacob / et Israel electum meum, / et vocavi te nomine tuo; / designavi te, et non cognovisti me. / 5Ego Dominus, et non est amplius: / extra me non est Deus. / Accinxi te, et non cognovisti me, / 6ut sciant ab ortu solis et ab occidente / quoniam absque me nullus est. / Ego Dominus, et non est alter, / 7formans lucem et creans tenebras, / faciens pacem et creans

Deut 32:2 Ps 85:11–12 Is 51:5; 56:1; 61:11

8"Shower, O heavens, from above,
and let the skies rain down righteousness;
let the earth open, that salvation may sprout forth,[e]
and let it cause righteousness to spring up also;
I the LORD have created it.

Is 29:16 Rom 9:20

9"Woe to him who strives with his Maker,
an earthen vessel with the potter![f]

---

and disgrace. Our union with God is broken by sin; it is fitting, therefore, that we return to him along the path of suffering. When any created thing, which is good in itself, causes us to suffer, it is an instrument for our conversion, so that we will return humbly to the source of peace" (*Moralia in Job*, 3, 9, 15).

45:8. The terms translated as "righteousness" and "salvation" correspond to three Hebrew abstract nouns. The first and third ("righteousness") mean the same thing. The New Vulgate translates them as "iustitia" and "salvatio". But the Vulgate of St Jerome interpreted the first two as adjectives—"righteous" and "saving", reading them as having more direct reference to the Messiah, the "Just (One)", the "Saviour" and giving rise to a text that is used in the Advent liturgy: "Rorate coeli desuper, et nubes pluant iustum; aperiatur terra et germinet Salvatorem, et iustitia oriantur simul" ("Let the clouds rain down the Just One, and the earth bring forth a Saviour …"). A sermon attributed to St Augustine sees these words as finding fulfilment in the birth of Christ: "Today this prophecy is fulfilled: *Shower, O heavens, from above, and let the skies rain down righteousness; let the earth open, that salvation may sprout forth.* The Creator became a creature, so that the one who was lost would be found. This is what we read in the psalms: *Before I was brought low, I sinned.* Man sinned and became a criminal; God was made man so that the criminal could be set free. Man fell, but God descended [from heaven]; man fell into misery, but God came down in his mercy; man fell through his pride, God came with his grace" (*Sermones*, 128). And St Proclus of Constantinople, reading these words as a figure of the virginal birth of Jesus, says: "*The skies rain down righteousness*: the sin of Eve has been undone and destroyed by the purity of the Virgin and by the One who was born of her, God and man. On this day, man is set free from the prison of sin and the burden of darkness that weighed him down is lifted from him" (*De Navitate Domini*, 1).

45:9–13. These words call to order those who did not believe that the Lord could implement his salvific plans in

malum: / ego Dominus faciens omnia haec. / [8]Rorate, caeli, desuper, et nubes pluant iustitiam; / aperiatur terra / et germinet salvationem; / et iustitia oriatur simul: / ego Dominus creavi eam». / [9]Vae,

e. One ancient Ms: Heb *that they may bring forth salvation* **f.** Cn: Heb *potsherds* or *potters*

Does the clay say to him who fashions it, 'What are you making'?
or 'Your work has no handles'?
10 Woe to him who says to a father, 'What are you begetting?'
or to a woman, 'With what are you in travail?'"
11 Thus says the LORD,
the Holy One of Israel, and his Maker:
"Will you question me[g] about my children,
or command me concerning the work of my hands?
12 I made the earth,
and created man upon it;
it was my hands that stretched out the heavens,
and I commanded all their host.
13 I have aroused him in righteousness,
and I will make straight all his ways;
he shall build my city
and set my exiles free,
not for price or reward,"
says the LORD of hosts.

The Lord rules over all

1 Kings 10:1
1 Cor 14:25

14 Thus says the LORD:
"The wealth of Egypt and the merchandise of Ethiopia,
and the Sabeans, men of stature,
shall come over to you and be yours,

---

the person of a foreigner, the Persian king Cyrus. This fact may make the passage easier to understand. The prophetic text uses colourful arguments to show the error made by those who question the plans of almighty God. The simile of the potter and the clay occurs here again (v. 9; cf. 29:16)—one which St Paul will evoke (Rom 9:20–21).

45:14–25. Repeatedly the point is made that the Lord is the only God, there is no other (cf. vv. 14–15, 18, 21, 22). Only God can save. And so, all the nations are invited to acknowledge his sovereignty and worship him on Zion (vv. 22–24). Although at the start of the passage the language has resonances of war (implications of plunder and taking strong men prisoner: vv. 14–17), this is

qui contradicit fictori suo, / testa de vasis fictilibus terrae! / Numquid dicet lutum figulo suo: «Quid facis?» / et «Opus tuum absque manibus est»? / [10]Vae, qui dicit patri: «Quid generas?» / et mulieri: «Quid parturis?». / [11]Haec dicit Dominus, / Sanctus Israel, plastes eius: / «Numquid ventura interrogatis me super filios meos / et super opus manuum mearum mandatis mihi? / [12]Ego feci terram / et hominem super eam creavi ego; / manus meae tetenderunt caelos, / et omni militiae eorum mandavi. / [13]Ego suscitavi eum in iustitia / et omnes vias eius dirigam; / ipse aedificabit civitatem meam / et captivitatem meam dimittet / non in pretio neque in muneribus», / dicit Dominus exercituum. / [14]Haec dicit

g. Cn: Heb *Ask me of things to come*

they shall follow you;
they shall come over in chains and bow down to you.
They will make supplication to you, saying:
'God is with you only, and there is no other,
no god besides him.'"
15 Truly, thou art a God who hidest thyself,
O God of Israel, the Saviour.
16 All of them are put to shame and confounded,
the makers of idols go in confusion together.
17 But Israel is saved by the LORD
with everlasting salvation;
you shall not be put to shame or confounded
to all eternity.

---

only a graphic way of speaking. In fact, the passage has to do with liberation from idolatry and with allowing oneself be captivated by the truth of that God who is hidden but who is the only God and true Saviour.

The words "Truly, though art a God who hidest thyself" (v. 15) is a prophetic reflection on the nature of God, a being who is unfathomable, a mystery to the mind of man, who ordinarily acts through persons and events in history, without letting himself be seen. This idea, which has profound and universal philosophical and theological implications, is very much in line with the historical circumstances—the election of Cyrus as the person God uses to advance his plans. This whole chapter is imbued with a universalist outlook, very different from the attitudes of the people before.

The Fathers saw in Cyrus a figure of Christ. God acted in a hidden way through Cyrus to bring about the salvation of the Jews; even more so was the Godhead hidden in Jesus. The Septuagint translates "Truly, thou art a God who hidest thyself" as "Thou art God and we did not know it" which some Fathers read as a reference to the divinity of Christ: "The Son of God has always been present, though he hid who he was. When he was revealed in his glory after the resurrection, the people confessed: *You are God, and we did not know it*. And when the one who is seen according to the Law as a mere Angel and the captain of the Lord's host is recognized finally as the Son of God, the people give thanks, saying: *You are God, and we did not know it*. What is meant by this is that He is the one who appeared to the patriarchs, the one who was made man and was not recognized by men" (Ambrosiaster, *Ad Romanos*, 2, 22).

Verse 23b is reminiscent of Philippians 2:10–11, which attributes to Jesus Christ qualities that the Old Testament applied only to God.

Dominus: / «Labor Aegypti et negotiatio Aethiopiae / et Sabaim viri sublimes / ad te transibunt et tui erunt; / post te ambulabunt, / vincti manicis pergent et te adorabunt / teque deprecabuntur: / "Tantum in te est Deus, / et non est absque te Deus!"». / [15]Vere tu es Deus absconditus, / Deus Israel, salvator. / [16]Confusi sunt et erubuerunt omnes, / simul abierunt in confusionem fabricatores idolorum. / [17]Israel

18 For thus says the LORD,
who created the heavens
(he is God!),
who formed the earth and made it
(he established it;
he did not create it a chaos,
he formed it to be inhabited!):
"I am the LORD, and there is no other.
19 I did not speak in secret,
in a land of darkness;
I did not say to the offspring of Jacob,
'Seek me in chaos.'
I the LORD speak the truth,
I declare what is right.

Deut 30:11–14
Jn 18:20
Acts 26:26

20 "Assemble yourselves and come,
draw near together,
you survivors of the nations!
They have no knowledge
who carry about their wooden idols,
and keep on praying to a god
that cannot save.
21 Declare and present your case;
let them take counsel together!
Who told this long ago?
Who declared it of old?
Was it not I, the LORD?
And there is no other god besides me,
a righteous God and a Saviour;
there is none besides me.

Ps 18:32
Is 41:22;
43:9–12; 44:8;
48:5

22 "Turn to me and be saved,
all the ends of the earth!
For I am God, and there is no other.

---

salvatus est in Domino salute aeterna; / non confundemini et non erubescetis / usque in saeculum saeculi. / [18]Quia haec dicit Dominus, / qui creavit caelos, ipse Deus, / qui formavit terram et fecit eam, ipse fundavit eam; / non ut vacua esset, creavit eam, / ut habitaretur, formavit eam: / «Ego Dominus, et non est alius. / [19]Non in abscondito locutus sum, / in loco terrae tenebroso; / non dixi semini Iacob: / "Frustra quaerite me". / Ego Dominus loquens iustitiam, / annuntians recta. / [20]Congregamini et venite et accedite simul, / qui salvati estis ex gentibus. / Nescierunt, qui levant lignum sculpturae suae / et rogant deum non salvantem. / [21]Annuntiate et venite et consiliamini simul. / Quis auditum fecit hoc ab initio, / ex tunc praedixit illud? / Numquid non ego Dominus, / et non est ultra Deus absque me? / Deus iustus et salvans non est praeter me. / [22]Convertimini ad me et salvi eritis, / omnes fines terrae, / quia ego Deus, et non est alius. / [23]In memetipso iuravi: / Egressa est de ore meo iustitia, / verbum, quod non

Rom 14:11 Phil 2:10–11 23 By myself I have sworn,
from my mouth has gone forth in righteousness
a word that shall not return:
'To me every knee shall bow,
every tongue shall swear.'
Is 41:11 24 "Only in the LORD, it shall be said of me,
are righteousness and strength;
to him shall come and be ashamed,
all who were incensed against him.
25 In the LORD all the offspring of Israel
shall triumph and glory."

The Lord topples false gods

Jer 50:2 46 1 Bel bows down, Nebo stoops,
their idols are on beasts and cattle;
these things you carry are loaded
as burdens on weary beasts.
2 They stoop, they bow down together,
they cannot save the burden,
but themselves go into captivity.

46:1–13. The exiles were impressed by the veneration shown by the Babylonians to their idols, and there was a serious risk of their falling into idolatry. This oracle (in the style of a sapiential dispute) contrasts the greatness of the Lord with the worthlessness of idols. It starts by taking pleasure at (and even mocking) the destruction of the Assyrian-Babylonian gods—Bel (the god of the heavens) and Nebo (the god of wisdom): they are useless things, incapable of saving anyone, and in need of beasts and drivers to move from place to place (vv. 1–2). In marked contrast to idols, who are carried around by their devotees, the God of Israel "carries" his faithful (vv. 3–7). This passage, like other oracles in this part of Isaiah, makes mention of the return of the Babylonian exiles to the land of Judah; that "new exodus" will be set in motion by the same God as did the "former things" (v. 9), that is, delivered the people out of slavery in Egypt. The prophet emphasizes the power of the Lord, the only God, who accomplishes his purposes (vv. 8–13) through the "man of my counsel", called the "bird of prey from the east" (v. 11), that is, Cyrus of Persia (cf. 45:1).

revertetur; / quia mihi curvabitur omne genu, / et iurabit omnis lingua». / [24]«Tantum in Domino» dicent / «sunt iustitiae et robur!». / Ad eum venient et confundentur / omnes, qui repugnant ei; / [25]in Domino iustificabitur et laudabitur / omne semen Israel. **[46]** [1]Concidit Bel, incurvavit se Nabo; / fuerunt simulacra eorum bestiis et iumentis. / Statuae vestrae portantur, onera lassis. / [2]Se incurvaverunt et conciderunt simul; / non potuerunt salvare onus / et ipsi in captivitatem ibunt. / [3]Audite me, domus Iacob / et omne residuum domus Israel, / qui portamini ab utero, / qui gestamini a vulva. / [4]Usque ad

3 "Hearken to me, O house of Jacob,
all the remnant of the house of Israel,
who have been borne by me from your birth,
carried from the womb;
4 even to your old age I am He,
and to gray hairs I will carry you.
I have made, and I will bear;
I will carry and will save.

Ex 19:4
Ps 22:11
Is 63:9

5 "To whom will you liken me and make me equal,
and compare me, that we may be alike?
6 Those who lavish gold from the purse,
and weigh out silver in the scales,
hire a goldsmith, and he makes it into a god;
then they fall down and worship!
7 They lift it upon their shoulders, they carry it,
they set it in its place, and it stands there;
it cannot move from its place.
If one cries to it, it does not answer
or save him from his trouble.

Is 44:7

Is 40:20

8 "Remember this and consider,
recall it to mind, you transgressors,
9 remember the former things of old;
for I am God, and there is no other;
I am God, and there is none like me,
10 declaring the end from the beginning
and from ancient times things not yet done,
saying, 'My counsel shall stand,
and I will accomplish all my purpose,'
11 calling a bird of prey from the east,
the man of my counsel from a far country.
I have spoken, and I will bring it to pass;
I have purposed, and I will do it.

Is 44:21

Ps 33:11
Is 41:26–27;
45:21
Eph 1:11

Is 41:2,5;
45:13

---

senectam ego ipse / et usque ad canos ego portabo; / et ego feci et ego feram, / ego portabo et salvabo. / 5Cui assimilatis me et adaequatis / et comparatis me, et erimus similes? / 6Qui effundunt aurum de sacculo / et argentum statera ponderant, / conducunt aurificem, ut faciat deum, / et procidunt et adorant. / 7Portant illum in umeris gestantes / et ponentes in loco suo; / et stabit ac de loco suo non movebitur; / sed et si quis clamat ad eum, non respondet; / de tribulatione eius non salvabit eum. / 8Mementote istud et confundamini; / redite, praevaricatores, ad cor. / 9Recordamini prioris saeculi, / quoniam ego sum Deus, / et non est ultra Deus, / nec est similis mei. / 10Annuntians ab exordio novissimum / et ab initio, quae necdum facta sunt, / dicens: «Consilium meum stabit, / et omnem voluntatem meam faciam». / 11Vocans ab oriente avem rapacem / et de terra longinqua virum consilii mei; / et locutus sum

[12] "Hearken to me, you stubborn of heart,
you who are far from deliverance:
[13] I bring near my deliverance, it is not far off,
and my salvation will not tarry;
I will put salvation in Zion,
for Israel my glory."

Is 13 **Oracle concerning the downfall of Babylon**
Rev 18 **47** [1]Come down and sit in the dust,
O virgin daughter of Babylon;
sit on the ground without a throne,
O daughter of the Chaldeans!
For you shall no more be called
tender and delicate.
[2]Take the millstones and grind meal,
put off your veil,
strip off your robe, uncover your legs,
pass through the rivers.
Jer 13:22 [3]Your nakedness shall be uncovered,
Hos 2:5 and your shame shall be seen.
I will take vengeance,
and I will spare no man.

47:1–15. These verses are an impressive satire against Babylon, carefully constructed as a sort of dirge; it is very graphic and quite daring, and it uses sophisticated language (over forty words occur here that are not found elsewhere in the Bible). The gods of Babylon are powerless; they can do nothing to prevent the ruin and humiliation of the city. Babylon was charged to inflict punishment on Israel, but it went beyond its brief (vv. 6–7). Therefore, the prophet, who announces its well-deserved destruction, underlines the differences between its previous state and what it will become (vv. 1–11): from being a "virgin" (v. 1), (probably because it never suffered under a foreign yoke), and a "mistress" in the better sense of the word (vv. 5, 7), it will become a slave; its pride will be brought low most shamefully; there is no way it can escape this fate. Babylon used to boast of its wisdom, knowledge and magic arts. Its reputation for astrology spread all over the Near East. But these things will be of no avail; they can do nothing to fend off the calamity that is imminent (vv. 12–15).

et adducam illud, / decrevi et faciam illud. / [12]Audite me, duri corde, / qui longe estis a iustitia. / [13]Prope feci iustitiam meam, non elongabitur; / et salus mea non morabitur: / et dabo in Sion salutem / et Israeli gloriam meam. **[47]** [1]Descende, sede in pulvere, / virgo filia Babylon; / sede in terra sine solio, / filia Chaldaeorum, / quia ultra non vocaberis / mollis et tenera. / [2]Tolle molam et mole farinam; / depone velum tuum, / subleva stolam, revela crura, / transi flumina. / [3]Revelabitur ignominia tua, / et

[4]Our Redeemer—the LORD of hosts is his name—
is the Holy One of Israel. Is 41:14

[5]Sit in silence, and go into darkness,
O daughter of the Chaldeans;
for you shall no more be called
the mistress of kingdoms.
[6]I was angry with my people, Is 10:6 Zech 1:15
I profaned my heritage;
I gave them into your hand,
you showed them no mercy;
on the aged you made your yoke
exceedingly heavy.
[7]You said, "I shall be mistress for ever," Deut 32:28–29
so that you did not lay these things to heart
or remember their end.

[8]Now therefore hear this, you lover of pleasures, Rev 18:7–8 Zeph 2:15
who sit securely,
who say in your heart,
"I am, and there is no one besides me;
I shall not sit as a widow
or know the loss of children":
[9]These two things shall come to you Rev 18:23
in a moment, in one day;
the loss of children and widowhood
shall come upon you in full measure,
in spite of your many sorceries
and the great power of your enchantments.

[10]You felt secure in your wickedness,
you said, "No one sees me";
your wisdom and your knowledge
led you astray,

---

videbitur opprobrium tuum. / «Ultionem capiam, / nemini parcam», / [4]dicit Redemptor noster, Dominus exercituum nomen illius, / Sanctus Israel. / [5]Sede tacens et intra in tenebras, / filia Chaldaeorum, / quia non vocaberis ultra / Domina regnorum. / [6]Iratus sum super populum meum, / contaminavi hereditatem meam / et dedi eos in manu tua; / non posuisti eis misericordias, / super senem aggravasti iugum tuum valde / [7]et dixisti: «In sempiternum ero domina». / Non posuisti haec super cor tuum / neque recordata es novissimi tui. / [8]Et nunc audi haec, delicata, / quae habitas confidenter / et dicis in corde tuo: / «Ego, et praeter me non est altera, non sedebo vidua et orbitatem ignorabo». / [9]Venient tibi duo haec / subito in die una, / orbitas et viduitas; / repente venerunt super te / propter multitudinem maleficiorum tuorum, / propter abundantiam incantationum tuarum. / [10]Et fiduciam habuisti in malitia tua / et dixisti: «Non est qui videat me». / Sapientia tua et scientia tua, / haec decepit te. / Et dixisti in corde tuo: / «Ego, et

and you said in your heart,
"I am, and there is no one besides me."
11 But evil shall come upon you,
for which you cannot atone;
disaster shall fall upon you,
which you will not be able to expiate;
and ruin shall come on you suddenly,
of which you know nothing.

12 Stand fast in your enchantments
and your many sorceries,
with which you have laboured from your youth;
perhaps you may be able to succeed,
perhaps you may inspire terror.
13 You are wearied with your many counsels;
let them stand forth and save you,
those who divide the heavens,
who gaze at the stars,
who at the new moons predict
what[h] shall befall you.

14 Behold, they are like stubble,
the fire consumes them;
they cannot deliver themselves
from the power of the flame.
No coal for warming oneself is this,
no fire to sit before!
15 Such to you are those with whom you have laboured,
who have trafficked with you from your youth;
they wander about each in his own direction;
there is no one to save you.

---

praeter me non est altera». / 11Veniet super te malum, / et nescies avertere; / et irruet super te calamitas, / quam non poteris expiare; / veniet super te repente / miseria, quam nescies. / 12Sta cum incantationibus tuis / et cum multitudine maleficiorum tuorum, / in quibus laborasti ab adulescentia tua: / forte poteris iuvari, forte terrebis. / 13Defecisti in multitudine consiliorum tuorum; / stent et salvent te, qui metiuntur caelum, / qui contemplantur sidera / et annuntiant singulis noviluniis / ventura tibi. / 14Ecce facti sunt quasi stipula, / ignis combussit eos. / Non liberabunt seipsos / de manu flammae; / non sunt prunae, quibus calefiant, / nec focus, ut sedeant ad eum. / 15Sic fiunt tibi incantatores tui, / in quibuscumque laborasti ab adulescentia tua; / unusquisque in via sua errat, / non est qui salvet te.

h. Gk Syr Compare Vg: Heb *from what*

Exhortation to heed the Lord

Jer 5:2
Amos 5:21

48 [1]Hear this, O house of Jacob,
who are called by the name of Israel,
and who came forth from the loins[i] of Judah;
who swear by the name of the LORD,
and confess the God of Israel,
but not in truth or right.
[2]For they call themselves after the holy city,
and stay themselves on the God of Israel;
the LORD of hosts is his name.

[3]"The former things I declared of old,
they went forth from my mouth and I made them known;
then suddenly I did them and they came to pass.
[4]Because I know that you are obstinate, Ex 32:9
and your neck is an iron sinew
and your forehead brass,

48:1–16. By way of conclusion, this passage is a rather jumbled summary of the teaching contained in the "Book of Consolation": God is the Creator (vv. 7, 12, 13), the ruler of the world (v. 13), the one who brought about the exodus (v. 3), who revealed his word through the prophets (vv. 3, 15, 16): the people, for whom he has special love and whom he chose (vv. 1, 12), have been disloyal and sinful (v. 8); they have been punished, but not annihilated (vv. 9–11), and they are destined to bear witness to God before the nations (v. 6); Cyrus, who is not explicitly named, was chosen to advance the Lord's plans of salvation (vv. 14–15). God has spoken clearly (v. 16) and the exiles, when they reflect on all these things, should feel greatly consoled. Later readers, too, will rejoice in the hope of enduring salvation.

Verse 16, which in the Latin translation of the Vulgate was given as "the Lord God hath sent me, and his spirit", has been interpreted in Christian tradition as a veiled revelation of the Holy Trinity, because the Son is sent by the Father and his Spirit to redeem men: "If some say that the Holy Spirit, too, sent the Son, as He himself says through the prophet: *And now the Lord God has sent me …*, we should understand that the verse refers to the Word made flesh, who came into the world in order to redeem it, according to the will and desire of the Father and the Holy Spirit" (St Anselm, *De processione Spiritus Sancti*, 9).

[48] [1]Audite hoc, domus Iacob, / qui vocamini nomine Israel / et de aquis Iudae existis, / qui iuratis in nomine Domini / et Deum Israel invocatis / non in veritate neque in iustitia. / [2]De civitate enim sancta vocati sunt / et super Deum Israel constabiliti sunt; / Dominus exercituum nomen eius. / [3]Priora ex tunc annuntiavi, / et ex ore meo exierunt, / et audita feci ea; / repente operatus sum, et venerunt. / [4]Scivi enim quia durus es tu, / et nervus ferreus cervix tua, / et frons tua aerea. / [5]Praedixi tibi ex tunc;

i. Cn: Heb *waters*

[5]I declared them to you from of old,
before they came to pass I announced them to you,
lest you should say, 'My idol did them,
my graven image and my molten image commanded them.'

[6]"You have heard; now see all this;
and will you not declare it?
From this time forth I make you hear new things,
hidden things which you have not known.
[7]They are created now, not long ago;
before today you have never heard of them,
lest you should say, 'Behold, I knew them.'
Is 1:2 [8]You have never heard, you have never known,
from of old your ear has not been opened.
For I knew that you would deal very treacherously,
and that from birth you were called a rebel.

[9]"For my name's sake I defer my anger,
for the sake of my praise I restrain it for you,
that I may not cut you off.

48:17–19. Now, by way of conclusion, the text deals with a theme closely connected with listening to the Lord's message (cf. 48:16). It is the theme of divine instruction: the Lord "teaches you to profit", that is, for your benefit, and "leads you in the way you should go" (v. 17)—words reminiscent of Deuteronomy 8:2. Divine "teaching" is not something purely abstract: it is based on real-life experience, on salvific events in the history of the chosen people, especially from the exodus from Egypt onwards. Just as liberation from Egypt carries a message for Israel, so too does this new exodus from Babylon.

The passage goes on to warn Judah that its punishment was due to its having closed its ears to the Lord (vv. 18–19). Leaving aside the historical context of the exile, this oracle is a "teaching" that applies in every age, and is valid for all nations and every individual: everyone must be converted and follow the way of the Lord.

/ antequam venirent, indicavi tibi, / ne forte diceres: «Idolum meum operatum est haec, / et sculptile meum et conflatile mandaverunt ista». / [6]Quae audisti, vide omnia; / vos autem num annuntiabitis? / Audita facio tibi nova ex nunc / et occulta, quae nescis. / [7]Nunc creata sunt et non ex tunc, / et ante eorum diem, et non audisti ea, / ne forte diceres: «Ecce ego cognovi ea». / [8]Neque audisti neque cognovisti, / neque ex tunc aperta est auris tua; / scio enim quia praevaricans praevaricaris / et transgressor ex utero vocaris. / [9]Propter nomen meum longe faciam furorem meum / et propter laudem meam infrenabo me super te, / ne perdam te. / [10]Ecce excoxi te, sed non quasi argentum; / probavi te in camino paupertatis. / [11]Propter me, propter me faciam, / ut non blasphemer; / et gloriam meam alteri non dabo. / [12]Audi me, Iacob, / et Israel, quem ego vocavi; / ego, ego primus / et ego novissimus. / [13]Manus mea fundavit terram, / et dextera mea expandit caelos; / ego voco eos, et stant simul. /

10 Behold, I have refined you, but not like[j] silver; Ps 66:10
I have tried you in the furnace of affliction. Is 1:2–5
11 For my own sake, for my own sake, I do it, Is 42:8
for how should my name[k] be profaned? Ezek 36:22
My glory I will not give to another.

12 "Hearken to me, O Jacob, Is 44:6
and Israel, whom I called!
I am He, I am the first,
and I am the last.
13 My hand laid the foundation of the earth, Rom 4:17
and my right hand spread out the heavens;
when I call to them,
they stand forth together.

14 "Assemble, all of you, and hear!
Who among them has declared these things?
The LORD loves him;
he shall perform his purpose on Babylon,
and his arm shall be against the Chaldeans.
15 I, even I, have spoken and called him,
I have brought him, and he will prosper in his way.
16 Draw near to me, hear this: Is 41:14
from the beginning I have not spoken in secret,
from the time it came to be I have been there."
And now the Lord GOD has sent me and his Spirit.

A lesson about history

17 Thus says the LORD, Deut 8:2
your Redeemer, the Holy One of Israel: Is 41:14
"I am the LORD your God,
who teaches you to profit,
who leads you in the way you should go.
18 O that you had hearkened to my commandments!

14Congregamini, omnes vos, et audite: / Quis de eis annuntiavit haec? / Dominus dilexit eum; / faciet voluntatem suam in Babylone / et brachium suum in Chaldaeis. / 15Ego, ego locutus sum et vocavi eum; / adduxi eum, et prospera fuit via eius. / 16Accedite ad me et audite hoc: / Non a principio in abscondito locutus sum; / ex tempore, antequam fieret, ibi eram; / et nunc Dominus Deus misit me cum spiritu suo. / 17Haec dicit Dominus, / redemptor tuus, Sanctus Israel: / Ego Dominus Deus tuus docens te utilia, / gubernans te in via, qua ambulas. / 18Utinam attendisses mandata mea! / Facta fuisset sicut flumen pax tua, / et iustitia tua sicut gurgites maris; / 19et fuisset quasi arena semen tuum, / et stirps

j. Cn: Heb *with* **k.** Gk Old Latin: Heb lacks *my name*

Then your peace would have been like a river,
and your righteousness like the waves of the sea;
Gen 15:5; 22:17 19 your offspring would have been like the sand,
and your descendants like its grains;
their name would never be cut off
or destroyed from before me."

The order is given for a new exodus

Is 41:8 Jer 50:8; 51:6,45 Rev 18:4 20 Go forth from Babylon, flee from Chaldea,
declare this with a shout of joy, proclaim it,
send it forth to the end of the earth;
say, "The LORD has redeemed his servant Jacob!"
Ex 17:1–7 Is 40:3 21 They thirsted not when he led them through the deserts;
he made water flow for them from the rock;
he cleft the rock and the water gushed out.
Is 57:21 22 "There is no peace," says the LORD, "for the wicked."

2. ZION RESTORED TO GLORY*

Is 42:1 **Second song of the Servant of the Lord**

Ps 2:7; Is 41:1 Jer 1:5,10 Gal 1:15 49 1 Listen to me, O coastlands,
and hearken, you peoples from afar.

48:20–22. The return from exile is described as being like a new exodus. Thus, the experience of slavery in Egypt and exile in Babylon merge to form a lesson that the chosen people and every member of it should never forget. God's order is unambiguous: just as he told them to leave Egypt, now he orders them to "go forth" from Babylon.

The fall of Babylon, described so dramatically in 47:1–15, and this call to leave the city, are echoed in the vision in the book of Revelation about the fall of Rome, the symbol of all sins and sinfulness, where another order to go forth is issued: "Come out of her, my people, lest you take part in her sins, lest you share in her plagues; for her sins are heaped high as heaven, and God has remembered her iniquities" (Rev 18:4–5).

***49:1—55:13.** Chapter 49 marks the start of the second section of the second part of Isaiah. The first section (40:1—48:22) dealt with the release of the Jews from exile in Babylon on the

uteri tui ut lapilli eius; / non interisset et non fuisset attritum / nomen eius a facie mea. / [20]Egredimini de Babylone, fugite a Chaldaeis, / in voce exsultationis annuntiate; / auditum facite hoc, efferte illud usque ad extrema terrae, / dicite: «Redemit Dominus servum suum Iacob». / [21]Non sitierunt, cum per desertum duceret eos; / aquam de petra produxit eis / et scidit petram, et fluxerunt aquae. / [22]Non est pax impiis, dicit Dominus. **[49]** [1]Audite me, insulae, et attendite, populi de longe; / Dominus ab utero vocavit me, / de ventre matris meae recordatus est nominis mei; / [2]et posuit os meum quasi gladium

The LORD called me from the womb,
  from the body of my mother he named my name.
[2]He made my mouth like a sharp sword,
  in the shadow of his hand he hid me;
he made me a polished arrow,
  in his quiver he hid me away.

Jer 1:9
Heb 4:12–13
Rev 1:16;
2:12; 19:15

---

orders of the Lord, the ruler of the world and of all nations. This second section sings of the restoration of Zion and the renewal of the people.

Almost all the oracles here presuppose that Babylon has fallen and the exiles have returned home (although neither event is explicitly referred to). Nor is there mention of the universal scope of salvation: the focus is mainly on future hopes and on Jerusalem.

Most of the oracles in this section were probably proclaimed between the years 515 and 500 BC. If that was the case, then they were addressed to a disillusioned people: the enthusiasm that came with the return from exile and the efforts made to rebuild Jerusalem failed to produce the desired results: there are still class differences, greed is plain to see, and huge sectors of society are experiencing poverty. The kind of Jerusalem that the exiles dreamed of had not come about: it bore no relationship to what they were experiencing; nor did it fit the image of Jerusalem found in many texts of the Priestly tradition (cf. "Introduction to the Pentateuch", in *The Navarre Bible: Pentateuch* (p. 20). These oracles are designed to dispel discouragement and to raise people's hopes by telling them about the liberator that God is going to send, the servant of the Lord, and by proclaiming that the holy city (now given the sacred name of Zion) will very soon be restored. In fact, the section can be divided into alternating poems on the servant and on Zion: 49:1–13, the *servant* (second oracle); 49:14—50:3, *Zion*; 50:4–11, the *servant*, (third oracle and exhortation); 51:17—52:12, *Zion*; 52:13—53:12, the *servant* (fourth oracle); 54:1–17, *Zion* (Jerusalem). Verses 1–13 of chapter 55 are an exhortaion to commit oneself to the new Covenant.

49:1–6. In the first Song of the Servant of the Lord (42:1–9) we meet the "servant" for the first time and we are told of his mission to liberate the exiles. In this second song, the servant himself speaks. He addresses the "coastlands", "peoples from afar", and he is conscious of having been chosen by God from his mother's womb to carry out God's plans of salvation even in those distant parts (cf. vv. 1–3). Here we are told about two aspects of his mission, which we will hear more about in the oracles that follow. First, he is to play a leading role in the recovery of the tribes and the repatriation of the exiles (v. 5); second, he will extend salvation to the ends of the earth (cf. v. 6).

acutum, / in umbra manus suae protexit me / et posuit me sicut sagittam electam, / in pharetra sua abscondit me / [3]et dixit mihi: «Servus meus es tu, / Israel, in quo gloriabor». / [4]Et ego dixi: «In vacuum

Mt 3:17

[3]And he said to me, "You are my servant,
Israel, in whom I will be glorified."

Is 53:10–12
Phil 2:8–11
Jn 17:5

[4]But I said, "I have laboured in vain,
I have spent my strength for nothing and vanity;
yet surely my right is with the LORD,
and my recompense with my God."

This poem contains things that the servant has to say about himself (vv. 1–4), and things that God says about the servant (vv. 5–6). The servant is well aware that he was called by God, even from his mother's womb, (like Jeremiah; cf. Jer 1:5) and has been charged with preaching to the pagan peoples ("the coastlands") or at least to his compatriots in the diaspora (cf. v. 1; cf. Jer 1:1–10; 25:13–38); he has been endowed with qualities that enable him to speak out, with words that find their mark like arrows, even if that creates divisions (v. 2; cf. Jer 1:10); and also, despite the divine protection given him, he feels depressed and disappointed, as happened to Jeremiah (vv. 3–4; cf. Jer 1:7; 8:18–20). Everything that the servant does is grounded on what the Lord has told him: "You are my servant, Israel" (v. 3). Some commentators are of the view that "Israel" here is a later interpretation, put in to support the collectivist interpretation of the servant that soon became widespread; but there is little evidence to support that: the word "Israel" is missing only in one manuscript, and not an important one at that. The mention of Israel does not argue against the servant's being an individual rather than a collectivity, for in poetry a person can be addressed by his own name or by his family name. In fact, both in biblical Israel and nowadays we often find people using their place of birth as a surname.

In vv. 5–6 the Lord spells out the servant's mission: it is to renew the people in such a way that even non-Israelites can see the light and attain salvation. Although the universal mission of the servant is not clearly defined here, for his work is meant to be confined to the tribes of Jacob, still the achievement of this objective (the re-assembling of Israel) will be a kind of light to help the pagan nations see and acknowledge God. The expression "light to the nations" (v. 6) already occurred in the earlier poem (42:6); there it could be taken in a social sense—to bring about the liberation of the exiles and captives; here, the religious meaning is clear: salvation will spread to all the nations.

To sum up, the servant of the Lord (be he an individual or a collectivity, or more likely both) has been chosen by God, who loves him most specially; he has all the main qualities of a prophet; and he must influence his compatriots so as to enlighten those from outside, and bring them salvation.

The messianic interpretation of the servant figure, based on this second

laboravi, / sine causa et vane fortitudinem meam consumpsi; / verumtamen iudicium meum cum Domino, / et merces mea cum Deo meo». / [5]Et nunc dicit Dominus, / qui formavit me ex utero servum

[5]And now the LORD says,
who formed me from the womb to be his servant,
to bring Jacob back to him,
and that Israel might be gathered to him,
for I am honoured in the eyes of the LORD,
and my God has become my strength—
[6]he says:
"It is too light a thing that you should be my servant
to raise up the tribes of Jacob

Lk 2:32
Acts 13:47

---

song, was widespread among the Jews of Alexandria who made the Septuagint Greek translation; it was also held by members of the Qumran community and by some authors of the period between the Old and New Testaments (the author of the *Book of Enoch*, for example). All these interpreted the servant as standing for the entire people of Israel. Christians, from the beginning, applied the songs of the servant to Jesus, and saw them as finding fulfilment in his life. Thus, although the image of the "sharp sword" (v. 2) refers to the effectiveness of the word of God, in Hebrews 4:12–13 we find it used with reference to Revelation as a whole which is fully and perfectly manifested in Jesus Christ (cf. also Rev 1:16 and 2:12). We find the expression, "light to the nations" or "light to the peoples" being applied by Simeon to Jesus (Lk 2:32). Indeed, in the Acts of the Apostles it is applied to those who, in line with Jesus' teaching and as cooperators in his work of salvation, are setting out to preach to the Gentiles, as the words Paul and Barnabas speak in the synagogue of Psidian Antioch testify: "It was necessary that the word of God should be spoken first to you. Since you thrust it from you, and judge yourselves unworthy of eternal life, behold, we turn to the Gentiles. For so the Lord has commanded us, saying, 'I have set you to be a light for the Gentiles, that you may bring salvation to the uttermost parts of the earth'" (Acts 13:46–47). Hence the Church sees her mission as spreading the truth about Jesus, the light that enlightens everyone: "The light of God's face shines in all its beauty on the countenance of Jesus Christ, 'the image of the invisible God' (Col 1:15), the 'reflection of God's glory' (Heb 1:3), 'full of grace and truth' (Jn 1:14). Christ is 'the way, and the truth, and the life' (Jn 14:6). [...] Jesus Christ, the 'light of the nations', shines upon the face of his Church, which he sends forth to the whole world to proclaim the Gospel to every creature (cf. Mk 16:15). Hence the Church, as the people of God among the nations, while attentive to the new challenges of history and to mankind's efforts to discover the meaning of life, offers to everyone the answer which comes from the truth about Jesus Christ and his Gospel" (John Paul II, *Veritatis splendor*, 2).

sibi, / ut reducerem Iacob ad eum, / et Israel ei congregaretur; / et glorificatus sum in oculis Domini, / et Deus meus factus est fortitudo mea. / [6]Et dixit: «Parum est ut sis mihi servus / ad suscitandas tribus

and to restore the preserved of Israel;
I will give you as a light to the nations,
that my salvation may reach to the end of the earth."

The Lord's aid to the returning exiles

Is 41:14; 60:10 7Thus says the LORD,
the Redeemer of Israel and his Holy One,
to one deeply despised, abhorred by the nations,
the servant of rulers:
"Kings shall see and arise;
princes, and they shall prostrate themselves;
because of the LORD, who is faithful,
the Holy One of Israel, who has chosen you."

Is 42:6 *2 Cor 6:2* 8Thus says the LORD:
"In a time of favour I have answered you,
in a day of salvation I have helped you;
I have kept you and given you

49:7–13. The Lord, who has chosen his servant and commissioned him to re-unite the scattered tribes, shows special kindness to those who have come back from exile or who are on the point of doing so. This important teaching comes across very clearly in this somewhat heterogenous passage.

It starts (v. 7) by contrasting the love of God and the humiliation of the chosen people, who will eventually be exalted (cf. 52:13–15); some commentators see the verse as part of the second Song of the Servant. The following stanza (vv. 8–9a) is addressed to those who have already returned home but who are depressed by the terrible state of the country: the Lord cannot but be faithful and he will grant salvation "in a time of favour" (v. 8). St Paul will apply this "time of favour" to the coming of Christ (cf. 2 Cor 6:2). The final stanza (vv. 9b–13), addressed to the repatriates, is a further attempt to raise the spirits of people who have already returned home from all points of the compass (v. 12): "from afar" probably means Mesopotamia and therefore the east; "the west", literally, "the Sea", often used with that meaning (cf. 24:14); "Syene" or "Sinim", that is, natives of Syene, a city in the extreme south of Egypt, symbolizes the south in general. Once again, the joy of the new exodus is mentioned, and the passage ends with a brief but intense hymn of praise to God (v. 13). The point is made repeatedly that God gives his beloved people special protection.

Iacob / et reliquias Israel reducendas: / dabo te in lucem gentium, / ut sit salus mea usque ad extremum terrae». / 7Haec dicit Dominus, / redemptor Israel, Sanctus eius, / ad contemptum in anima, / ad abominatum in gente, / ad servum dominorum: / «Reges videbunt et consurgent, / principes quoque et adorabunt, / propter Dominum, quia fidelis est, / Sanctum Israel, qui elegit te». / 8Haec dicit Dominus:

as a covenant to the people,
to establish the land,
to apportion the desolate heritages;
9saying to the prisoners, 'Come forth,' — Is 42:7
to those who are in darkness, 'Appear.'
They shall feed along the ways,
on all bare heights shall be their pasture;
10they shall not hunger or thirst, — Is 4:5–6; 25:4–5; Jn 4:1 *Rev 7:16*
neither scorching wind nor sun shall smite them,
for he who has pity on them will lead them,
and by springs of water will guide them.
11And I will make all my mountains a way, — Is 40:3–4
and my highways shall be raised up.
12Lo, these shall come from afar,
and lo, these from the north and from the west,
and these from the land of Syene."[l]
13Sing for joy, O heavens, and exult, O earth; — Is 40:1
break forth, O mountains, into singing!
For the LORD has comforted his people,
and will have compassion on his afflicted.

The restoration of Zion — Ps 22:2–3; Is 40:27; 54:8; Hos 11:8–9
14But Zion said, "The LORD has forsaken me,
my Lord has forgotten me."

49:14—50:3. After the oracles concerning the servant, the prophet now focuses on Zion, the city beloved of the Lord, to which people will come from all over the diaspora, to settle there. It will be a genuine miracle. The first verses speak very movingly of God's love for his people (49:14–20). The passage goes on, in a didactic style, to stress that the Lord will bring about the liberation of Jerusalem (49:21–26). It draws two comparisons—that of an eastern kingdom (49:22–23) and that of mighty warrior (49:24–26); each ends with an assertion reminiscent of Ezekiel's message: "And you will know that I am the Lord" (cf. "Introduction to Ezekiel", p. 595, below). Finally

/ «In tempore beneplaciti exaudivi te / et in die salutis auxiliatus sum tui; / et servavi te et dedi te in foedus populi, / ut suscitares terram / et distribueres hereditates dissipatas; / 9ut diceres his, qui vincti sunt: "Exite", / et his, qui in tenebris: "Revelamini". / Super vias pascentur, / et in omnibus collibus decalvatis pascua eorum; / 10non esurient neque sitient, / et non percutiet eos aestus vel sol, / quia miserator eorum reget eos / et ad fontes aquarum adducet eos. / 11Et ponam omnes montes meos in viam, / et semitae meae exaltabuntur. / 12Ecce isti de longe venient, / et ecce illi ab aquilone et mari, / et isti de terra Sinim». / 13Laudate, caeli, et exsulta, terra; / iubilate, montes, laudem, / quia consolatur Dominus populum suum / et pauperum suorum miseretur. / 14Et dixit Sion: «Dereliquit me Dominus,

l. Cn: Heb *Sinim*

Is 44:21 15 "Can a woman forget her sucking child,
that she should have no compassion on the son of her womb?
Even these may forget,
yet I will not forget you.

(50:1–3), the sense of abandonment felt by those in Jerusalem (cf. v. 14) is answered from another angle. Using the wedding imagery first used by Hosea (cf. Hos 1–3), the prophet puts words in the Lord's mouth to the effect that the exile was not meant to be forever; it was not irrevocable. There was no document written to terminate the marriage (cf. Deut 24:1–2, Jer 3:8); nor was the sale contract ever closed. Exile was a punishment that had to happen; it was a temporary thing, provoked by the people's sins. But God keeps his promises; he will restore Zion; he is as mighty now as he was at the time of the exodus, as he will demonstrate.

In the fullness of time, when Jesus brings salvation, this oracle will have even greater significance: "In Jesus Christ God has established a new and everlasting covenant with mankind. He has placed his almighty power at the service of our salvation. When his creatures lose confidence and are afraid through lack of faith, we hear once again the voice of Isaiah who speaks out in the name of the Lord: 'Is my hand too short to redeem? Have I not strength to save?'" (St Josemaría Escrivá, *Friends of God*, 190).

49:15–16. The image of the mother who can never forget her children (v. 15) is one of the most beautiful metaphors used in the Bible to describe the love that God has for his people; it has been echoed by spiritual writers down the ages. Pope John Paul II applies it with reference to the merciful love that God shows his own—the *rahamin* in Hebrew, a word that derives from maternal love (*rehem* means motherly embrace). Like a mother, God has borne mankind, and especially the chosen people, in his womb; he has given birth to it in pain, has nourished and consoled it (cf. 42:14; 46:3–4): "From the deep and original bond—indeed the unity—that links a mother to her child there springs a particular relationship to the child, a particular love. Of this love one can say that it is completely gratuitous, not merited, and that in this aspect it constitutes an interior necessity: an exigency of the heart. It is, as it were, a 'feminine' variation of the masculine fidelity to self expressed by hesed. Against this psychological background, rahamim generates a whole range of feelings, including goodness and tenderness, patience and understanding, that is, readiness to forgive. [...] This love, faithful and invincible thanks to the mysterious power of motherhood, is expressed in the Old Testament texts in various ways: as salvation from dangers, especially from enemies; also as for-

/ et Dominus oblitus est mei». / [15]Numquid oblivisci potest mulier infantem suum, / ut non misereatur filio uteri sui? / Et si illa oblita fuerit, / ego tamen non obliviscar tui. / [16]Ecce in manibus meis descripsi

[16] Behold, I have graven you on the palms of my hands; Is 60:10
your walls are continually before me.
[17] Your builders outstrip your destroyers, Is 60:4
and those who laid you waste go forth from you.
[18] Lift up your eyes round about and see;
they all gather, they come to you.
As I live, says the LORD,
you shall put them all on as an ornament,
you shall bind them on as a bride does.

[19] "Surely your waste and your desolate places
and your devastated land—
surely now you will be too narrow for your inhabitants,
and those who swallowed you up will be far away.
[20] The children born in the time of your bereavement Is 54:1–3
will yet say in your ears:
'The place is too narrow for me;
make room for me to dwell in.'
[21] Then you will say in your heart: Is 65:23 Jer 31:27 Zech 2:8
'Who has borne me these?
I was bereaved and barren,
exiled and put away,
but who has brought up these?
Behold, I was left alone;
whence then have these come?'"

---

giveness of sins—of individuals and also of the whole of Israel; and finally in readiness to fulfill the (eschatological) promise and hope, in spite of human infidelity" (*Dives in misericordia*, note 52; cf. *Mulieris dignitatem*, 8).

The first words of v. 16 are another graphic description of the love of God; and so we find John Paul II using them in an exhortation on that subject: "Dear young people, receive the love that God first gives you (cf. 1 Jn 4:19). Hold fast to this certainty, the only one that can give meaning, strength and joy to life: his love will never leave you, his covenant of peace will never be removed from you (cf. Is 54:10). He has stamped your name on the palms of his hands (cf. Is 49:16)" (*World Youth Day*, 6 January 1997).

te; / muri tui coram me semper. / [17]Festinant structores tui; / destruentes te et dissipantes a te exibunt. / [18]Leva in circuitu oculos tuos et vide: / omnes isti congregati sunt, venerunt tibi. / «Vivo ego, dicit Dominus, / quia omnibus his velut ornamento vestieris / et circumdabis tibi eos quasi sponsa». / [19]Quia ruinae tuae et solitudines tuae / et terra eversa: / nunc angusta eris prae habitatoribus; / et longe erunt, qui devorabant te. / [20]Adhuc dicent in auribus tuis / filii orbitatis tuae: / «Angustus est mihi locus; / fac spatium mihi, ut habitem». / [21]Et dices in corde tuo: / «Quis genuit mihi istos? / Ego orbata et non pariens, / transmigrata et captiva; / et istos quis enutrivit? / Ecce ego relicta eram sola; / et isti ubi

Is 60:4,9 Bar 5:6 22 Thus says the LORD GOD:
"Behold, I will lift up my hand to the nations,
and raise my signal to the peoples;
and they shall bring your sons in their bosom,
Ps 25:3 and your daughters shall be carried on their shoulders.
Is 60:14,16 23 Kings shall be your foster fathers,
and their queens your nursing mothers.
With their faces to the ground they shall bow down to you,
and lick the dust of your feet.
Then you will know that I am the LORD;
those who wait for me shall not be put to shame."

24 Can the prey be taken from the mighty,
Jer 31:11 or the captives of a tyrant[m] be rescued?
Lk 11:21–22 25 Surely, thus says the LORD:
"Even the captives of the mighty shall be taken,
and the prey of the tyrant be rescued,
for I will contend with those who contend with you,
and I will save your children.
Is 9:19; 41:14; 60:16 26 I will make your oppressors eat their own flesh,
Rev 16:6 and they shall be drunk with their own blood as with wine.
Then all flesh shall know
that I am the LORD your Saviour,
and your Redeemer, the Mighty One of Jacob."

Deut 24:1–4 Is 52:1,3 Jer 3:6–8 Hos 2:4–9 Bar 4:6 **50** 1 Thus says the LORD:
"Where is your mother's bill of divorce,
with which I put her away?

50:4–9. The second song dealt with the servant's mission (cf. 49:6); the third song focuses on the servant himself. The term "servant" as such does not appear here, and therefore some commentators read the passage as being a description of a prophet and not part of the songs. Still, the context (cf. 50:10)

erant?». / 22 Haec dicit Dominus Deus: / «Ecce levabo ad gentes manum meam / et ad populos exaltabo signum meum; / et afferent filios tuos in ulnis, / et filiae tuae super umeros portabuntur. / 23 Et erunt reges nutricii tui, / et reginae nutrices tuae; / vultu in terram demisso adorabunt te / et pulverem pedum tuorum lingent. / Et scies quia ego Dominus: / non confundentur, qui sperant in me». / 24 Numquid tolletur a forti praeda, / aut, quod captum fuerit, a robusto salvari poterit? / 25 Quia haec dicit Dominus: / «Equidem et captivus a forti tolletur, / et, quod ablatum fuerit a robusto, salvabitur; / cum his, qui contendebant tecum, ego contendam / et filios tuos ego salvabo. / 26 Et cibabo hostes tuos carnibus suis, / et quasi musto sanguine suo inebriabuntur; / et sciet omnis caro quia ego Dominus salvator tuus, / et redemptor tuus Fortis Iacob». **[50]** 1 Haec dicit Dominus: / «Ubinam est liber repudii matris vestrae,

m. One ancient Ms Syr Vg: Heb *righteous man*

Or which of my creditors is it
to whom I have sold you?
Behold, for your iniquities you were sold,
and for your transgressions your mother was put away.

---

does suggest that the protagonist is the servant. The poem is neatly constructed in three stanzas, each beginning with the words, "The Lord God" (vv. 4, 5, 7), and it has a conclusion containing that same wording (v. 9). The first stanza emphasizes the servant's docility to the word of God; that is, he is not depicted as a self-taught teacher with original ideas, but as an obedient disciple. The second (vv. 5–6) speaks of the suffering that that docility has brought him, without his uttering a word of complaint. The third (vv. 7–8) shows how determined the servant is: if he suffers in silence, it is not out of cowardice but because God helps him and makes him stronger than his persecutors. The conclusion (v. 9) is like the verdict of a trial: when all is said and done, the servant will stand tall, and all his enemies will be struck down.

The evangelists saw the words of this song as finding fulfilment in Jesus—especially what the song has to say about the suffering and silent fortitude of the servant. The Gospel of John, for example, quotes Nicodemus' acknowledgment of Christ's wisdom: "Rabbi, we know that you are a teacher come from God; for no one can do these signs that you do, unless God is with him" (Jn 3:21). But the description of the servant's sufferings was the part that most impressed the early Christians; that part of the song was recalled when they meditated on the passion of Jesus and how "they spat in his face; and struck him; and some slapped him" (Mt 26:67) and later how the Roman soldiers "spat upon him, and took the reed and struck him on the head" (Mt 27:30; cf. also Mk 15:19; Jn 19:3). St Paul refers to v. 9 when applying to Christ Jesus the role of intercessor on behalf of the elect in the suit pressed constantly against them by the enemies of the soul: "Who shall bring any charge against God's elect?" (Rom 8:33).

St Jerome sees the servant's docility as a reference to Christ: "His self-discipline and wisdom enabled him to communicate to us the knowledge of the Father. And he was obedient unto death, death on the cross; he offered his body to the blows they struck, his shoulders to the lash; and though he was wounded on the chest and on his face, he did not try to turn away and escape their violence" (*Commentarii in Isaiam*, 50, 4).

This passage is used in the liturgy of Palm Sunday (along with Psalm 22 and St Paul's hymn in the Letter to the Philippians 2:6–11), before the reading of our Lord's passion.

/ quo dimisi eam? / Aut quis est creditor meus, / cui vendidi vos? / Ecce in iniquitatibus vestris venditi estis, / et in sceleribus vestris dimissa est mater vestra. / [2]Cur veni, et non erat vir, / vocavi, et non erat qui responderet? / Numquid abbreviata est manus mea, / ut non possim redimere? / Aut non est in me virtus ad liberandum? / Ecce in increpatione mea exsiccabo mare, / ponam flumina in siccum; /

Num 11:2:23; Ps 106:9; 107:33; Is 65:12; 66:4; Nahum 1:4; Rev 3:20

2 Why, when I came, was there no man?
When I called, was there no one to answer?
Is my hand shortened, that it cannot redeem?
Or have I no power to deliver?
Behold, by my rebuke I dry up the sea,
I make the rivers a desert;
their fish stink for lack of water,
and die of thirst.
3 I clothe the heavens with blackness,
and make sackcloth their covering."

Is 42:1

Third song of the Servant of the Lord

Jn 3:2,11; 19:3

4 The Lord GOD has given me
the tongue of those who are taught,
that I may know how to sustain with a word
him that is weary.
Morning by morning he wakens,
he wakens my ear
to hear as those who are taught.

Is 52:13–53:12

5 The Lord GOD has opened my ear,
and I was not rebellious,
I turned not backward.

Mt 26:27; 27:30; Mk 15:19

6 I gave my back to the smiters,
and my cheeks to those who pulled out the beard;
I hid not my face
from shame and spitting.

Ps 25:3; Ezek 3:8–9

7 For the Lord GOD helps me;
therefore I have not been confounded;
therefore I have set my face like a flint,
and I know that I shall not be put to shame;

Rom 8:31–33

8 he who vindicates me is near.
Who will contend with me?
Let us stand up together.
Who is my adversary?
Let him come near to me.

---

computrescent pisces sine aqua / et morientur in siti. / 3 Induam caelos luctu / et saccum ponam operimentum eorum». / 4 Dominus Deus dedit mihi linguam eruditam, / ut sciam sustentare eum, qui lassus est, verbo; / excitat mane, mane excitat mihi aurem, / ut audiam quasi discipulus. / 5 Dominus Deus aperuit mihi aurem; / ego autem non rebellavi, retrorsum non abii. / 6 Dorsum meum dedi percutientibus / et genas meas vellentibus: / faciem meam non averti / ab increpationibus et sputis. / 7 Dominus Deus auxiliator meus; / ideo non sum confusus, / ideo posui faciem meam ut petram durissimam / et scio quoniam non confundar. / 8 Iuxta est qui iustificat me; / quis contradicet mihi?

[9]Behold, the Lord GOD helps me;
who will declare me guilty?
Behold, all of them will wear out like a garment;
the moth will eat them up.

Job 13:28
Is 51:8
Hos 5:12

Prophetic exhortation

[10] Who among you fears the LORD
and obeys the voice of his servant,
who walks in darkness
and has no light,
yet trusts in the name of the LORD
and relies upon his God?
[11] Behold, all you who kindle a fire,
who set brands alight![n]
Walk by the light of your fire,
and by the brands which you have kindled!
This shall you have from my hand:
you shall lie down in torment.

Ex 23:20–21
Is 42:16
Jn 3:11

Ps 7:14

An exhortation by the Servant

51 [1]"Hearken to me, you who pursue deliverance,
you who seek the LORD;

Mt 5:6; 6:33
Rom 9:30

50:10–11. The prophet, or the editor who positioned the third Song of the Servant here, inserts an exhortation (v. 10) to listen to the servant, and issues a severe warning to any who would dare to oppose him and thereby scandalize the weak (v. 11). This is probably a reference to repatriates who were a bad influence on their fellow citizens: the imagery of fiery brands graphically describes the harm done by scandal.

51:1–8. Comforted by divine help, the servant begins his preaching, fearless in the face of the difficulties his words might provoke. He speaks first to those who sincerely seek the Lord, inviting them to remember their roots, the history of the mercy that God showed Abraham and Sarah (vv. 1–2): this will give them hope in the power of the Lord and in his ability to turn the heap of ruins that is Jerusalem (thanks to its

Stemus simul. / Quis est adversarius meus? Accedat ad me. / [9]Ecce Dominus Deus auxiliator meus; / quis est qui condemnet me? / Ecce omnes quasi vestimentum conterentur, / tinea comedet eos. / [10]Quis ex vobis timet Dominum, / audiens vocem servi sui? / Qui ambulavit in tenebris, / et non est lumen ei, / speret in nomine Domini / et innitatur super Deum suum. / [11]Ecce vos omnes, qui accenditis ignem, / accincti sagittis, / ambulate in lumine ignis vestri / et in sagittis, quas succendistis. / De manu mea factum est hoc vobis; / in doloribus recumbetis. **[51]** [1]Audite me, qui sequimini iustitiam, / qui quaeritis Dominum; / attendite ad petram, unde excisi estis, / et ad cavernam laci, de qua praecisi estis. / [2]Attendite ad Abraham patrem vestrum / et ad Saram, quae peperit vos; / quia unum vocavi eum / et

n. Syr: Heb *gird yourselves with brands*

look to the rock from which you were hewn,
and to the quarry from which you were digged.

Gen 12:1–3; 24:1–35
Ezek 33:24
Rom 4:1
Heb 11:11,12

2Look to Abraham your father
and to Sarah who bore you;
for when he was but one I called him,
and I blessed him and made him many.

Gen 2:8–17; 13:10
Ezek 36: 35
Rev 2:7; 22: 1–2

3For the LORD will comfort Zion;
he will comfort all her waste places,
and will make her wilderness like Eden,
her desert like the garden of the LORD;
joy and gladness will be found in her,
thanksgiving and the voice of song.

4"Listen to me, my people,
and give ear to me, my nation;
for a law will go forth from me,
and my justice for a light to the peoples.

Is 46:13

5My deliverance draws near speedily,
my salvation has gone forth,
and my arms will rule the peoples;
the coastlands wait for me,
and for my arm they hope.

Ps 102:26–27
Is 56:1
2 Pet 3:7–12
Rev 20:11

6Lift up your eyes to the heavens,
and look at the earth beneath;
for the heavens will vanish like smoke,
the earth will wear out like a garment,
and they who dwell in it will die like gnats;[o]

Babylonian conquerers) into a peaceful place where they can enjoy the favours bestowed by the Lord (v. 3). Having raised their spirits by those words, he invites them to trust in the Lord (vv. 4–6) and pay no heed to those who mock them (vv. 7–8). The exhortation is mainly about docility ("Listen": vv. 1 and 7), instruction, which is what the "law" refers to here (vv. 4 and 7), and salvation, also called "righteousness" (v. 7).

benedixi ei et multiplicavi eum. / 3Consolatur enim Dominus Sion, / consolatur omnes ruinas eius; / et ponit desertum eius quasi Eden / et solitudinem eius quasi hortum Domini. / Gaudium et laetitia invenietur in ea, / gratiarum actio et vox laudis. / 4Attendite ad me, popule meus; / et nationes, me audite, / quia lex a me exiet, / et iudicium meum in lucem populorum statuam. / 5Prope est iustitia mea, / egressa est salus mea, / et brachia mea populos iudicabunt; / in me insulae sperabunt / et ad brachium meum attendent. / 6Levate in caelum oculos vestros / et inspicite in terram deorsum, / quia caeli sicut fumus liquescent, / et terra sicut vestimentum atteretur, / et habitatores eius sicut haec interibunt. / Salus autem mea in sempiternum erit, / et iustitia mea non deficiet. / 7Audite me, qui scitis iustitiam, / popule,

o. Or *in like manner*

but my salvation will be for ever,
and my deliverance will never be ended.

7 "Hearken to me, you who know righteousness,
the people in whose heart is my law;
fear not the reproach of men,
and be not dismayed at their revilings.
8 For the moth will eat them up like a garment, Job 13:28
and the worm will eat them like wool; Is 50:9
but my deliverance will be for ever,
and my salvation to all generations."

Appeal to the Lord

9 Awake, awake, put on strength, Ex 14:5–31
O arm of the LORD; Job 3:8; 7:12
awake, as in days of old, Is 30:7; 63:13
the generations of long ago.
Was it not thou that didst cut Rahab in pieces,
that didst pierce the dragon?
10 Was it not thou that didst dry up the sea,
the waters of the great deep;
that didst make the depths of the sea a way
for the redeemed to pass over?
11 And the ransomed of the LORD shall return, Is 35:10
and come to Zion with singing;

51:9–16. Now come three pressing calls which begin with similar words: "Awake, awake" (vv. 9; 52:1) and "Rouse yourself" (v. 17). The first is addressed to the Lord, and it reminds him of the great things he did in past times—and which he must surely repeat now that the exiles have returned (vv. 9–11). Then the prophet stops speaking and God replies, upbraiding the people for their lack of faith (vv. 12–13) but still promising that their deliverance is nigh (vv. 14–16).

"Rahab" (v. 9) is a monster of eastern mythology, the personification of primeval chaos; in the Old Testament it sometimes stands for Egypt (cf. 30:7; Job 9:13; Ps 87:4). The dragon (v. 9) in Hebrew, *Tannin*, is a mythological sea-monster (cf. 27:1), which is also sometimes a symbol for Egypt (cf. Ezek 29:3; 32:2).

in cuius corde est lex mea: / nolite timere opprobrium hominum / et blasphemias eorum ne metuatis. / 8 Sicut enim vestimentum sic comedet eos vermis, / et sicut lanam sic devorabit eos tinea; / iustitia autem mea in sempiternum erit, / et salus mea in generationes generationum. / 9 Consurge, consurge, induere fortitudinem, / brachium Domini; / consurge sicut in diebus antiquis, / in generationibus saeculorum. / Numquid non tu percussisti Rahab, / vulnerasti draconem? / 10 Numquid non tu siccasti mare, / aquam abyssi vehementis, / qui posuisti profundum maris viam, / ut transirent liberati? / 11 Et

everlasting joy shall be upon their heads;
they shall obtain joy and gladness,
and sorrow and sighing shall flee away.

12 "I, I am he that comforts you;
who are you that you are afraid of man who dies,
of the son of man who is made like grass,
Deut 32:5,15 13 and have forgotten the LORD, your Maker,
who stretched out the heavens
and laid the foundations of the earth,
and fear continually all the day
because of the fury of the oppressor,
when he sets himself to destroy?
And where is the fury of the oppressor?
14 He who is bowed down shall speedily be released;
he shall not die and go down to the Pit,
neither shall his bread fail.
Jer 31:35 15 For I am the LORD your God,
who stirs up the sea so that its waves roar—
the LORD of hosts is his name.
Is 49:2–3; 59:21 16 And I have put my words in your mouth,
and hid you in the shadow of my hand,
stretching out[p] the heavens
and laying the foundations of the earth,
and saying to Zion, 'You are my people.'"

Ps 75:9; Is 52:1 Jer 25:15–29 Ezek 23: 31–34 Hab 2:16 Mt 20:22

An urgent call addressed to Jerusalem

17 Rouse yourself, rouse yourself,
stand up, O Jerusalem,
you who have drunk at the hand of the LORD

51:17–23. The oracles in 51:17—52:12 all hinge on Jerusalem, giving it that name first, and then the name of "Zion". The second pressing call made by the prophet ("Rouse yourself, rouse yourself": v. 17) is addressed to the

redempti a Domino revertentur / et venient in Sion laudantes; / et laetitia sempiterna super capita eorum, / gaudium et laetitiam obtinebunt; / fugiet dolor et gemitus. / 12Ego, ego ipse consolator vester. / Quis tu, ut timeas ab homine mortali / et a filio hominis, qui quasi fenum ita arescet? / 13Et oblitus es Domini factoris tui, / qui tetendit caelos et fundavit terram; / et formidasti iugiter tota die / a facie furoris eius, qui te tribulabat, / cum parabat ad perdendum. / Ubi nunc est furor tribulantis? / 14Cito captivus liberabitur / et non morietur in fovea, / nec deficiet panis eius. / 15Ego enim sum Dominus Deus tuus, / qui conturbo mare, / et intumescunt fluctus eius; / Dominus exercituum nomen eius. / 16Posui verba mea in ore tuo / et in umbra manus meae protexi te, / cum extendebam caelos et

p. Syr: Heb *plant*

the cup of his wrath,
who have drunk to the dregs
the bowl of staggering.
18 There is none to guide her
among all the sons she has borne;
there is none to take her by the hand
among all the sons she has brought up.
19 These two things have befallen you— Jer 15:5
who will condole with you?— Nahum 3:7
devastation and destruction, famine and sword;
who will comfort you?[q]
20 Your sons have fainted, Lam 2:11
they lie at the head of every street
like an antelope in a net;
they are full of the wrath of the LORD,
the rebuke of your God.

21 Therefore hear this, you who are afflicted, Lam 3:15
who are drunk, but not with wine:
22 Thus says your Lord, the LORD,
your God who pleads the cause of his people:
"Behold, I have taken from your hand the cup of staggering;
the bowl of my wrath
you shall drink no more;
23 and I will put it into the hand of your tormentors,
who have said to you,

---

holy city, which had been laid waste and many of its people sent into exile. After its people have drunk the "cup" of God's wrath and suffered exile for their sins (vv. 17–20), the Lord will give a worse cup of anger to their oppressors (vv. 21–23). The symbol of the cup of wrath is used in other prophetical books (Hab 2:16; Jer 25:15–29; Ezek 23:31–33) to mean the trials and misfortunes permitted by God in the hope of eliciting repentance.

fundabam terram / et dicebam ad Sion: «Populus meus es tu». / [17]Elevare, elevare, consurge, Ierusalem, / quae bibisti de manu Domini calicem irae eius; / poculum soporis bibisti, / epotasti. / [18]Non est qui sustentet eam / ex omnibus filiis, quos genuit; / et non est qui apprehendat manum eius / ex omnibus filiis, quos enutrivit. / [19]Duo sunt quae occurrerunt tibi; / quis contristabitur super te? / Vastitas et contritio et fames et gladius; / quis consolabitur te? / [20]Filii tui defecerunt, / iacent in capite omnium viarum / sicut oryx illaqueatus, / pleni indignatione Domini, / increpatione Dei tui. / [21]Idcirco audi hoc, paupercula / et ebria, sed non a vino. / [22]Haec dicit dominator tuus, / Dominus et Deus tuus, qui contendit pro populo suo: / «Ecce tuli de manu tua calicem soporis, / poculum indignationis meae; / non adicies, ut bibas illum ultra. / [23]Et ponam illum in manu eorum, qui te humiliaverunt / et dixerunt tibi: "Incurvare, ut transeamus"; / et ponebas ut terram dorsum tuum / et quasi viam transeuntibus».

q. One ancient Ms Gk Syr Vg: Heb *how may I comfort you*

'Bow down, that we may pass over';
and you have made your back like the ground
and like the street for them to pass over."

A new call to Zion

Is 35:8; 51:9
Neh 11:1
Rev 21:27

52 1Awake, awake,
put on your strength, O Zion;
put on your beautiful garments,
O Jerusalem, the holy city;
for there shall no more come into you
the uncircumcised and the unclean.
2Shake yourself from the dust, arise,
O captive[r] Jerusalem;
loose the bonds from your neck,
O captive daughter of Zion.

3For thus says the LORD: "You were sold for nothing, and you
shall be redeemed without money. 4For thus says the Lord GOD:
My people went down at the first into Egypt to sojourn there, and
Ezek 36:20–22 the Assyrian oppressed them for nothing. 5Now therefore what
have I here, says the LORD, seeing that my people are taken away
for nothing? Their rulers wail, says the LORD, and continually all
Rom 2:24 the day my name is despised. 6Therefore my people shall know
my name; therefore in that day they shall know that it is I who
speak; here am I."

1 Chron 16:31
Ps 47:9; 93:1; 96:10; 97:1
Nahum 2:1
Mk 16: 15–16
Rom 10:5

The messenger of peace

7How beautiful upon the mountains
are the feet of him who brings good tidings,

52:1–6. The third call ("Awake, awake": v. 1) is addressed again to Jerusalem, this time "Zion"; the time has come for its reconstruction and renewal. Freedom stands at its gates (vv. 1–2): just as God previously set the Israelites free from Egypt and then from the Assyrians, now they will be liberated from Babylon, and will see that there is no other God but the Lord (vv. 3–6).

52:7–12. Salvation is approaching; it has reached the gates of Zion, and its

[52] 1Consurge, consurge, / induere fortitudine tua, Sion; / induere vestimentis gloriae tuae, / Ierusalem, civitas sanctitatis, / quia non adiciet ultra, ut pertranseat per te / incircumcisus et immundus. / 2Excutere de pulvere, consurge, / captiva Ierusalem; / solve vincula colli tui, / captiva filia Sion. 3Quia haec dicit Dominus: «Gratis venumdati estis et sine argento redimemini». 4Quia haec dicit Dominus Deus: «In Aegyptum descendit populus meus in principio, ut colonus esset ibi; et Assur sine causa oppressit eum.

r. Cn: Heb *sit*

who publishes peace, who brings good tidings of good,
who publishes salvation,
who says to Zion, "Your God reigns."

---

herald is the messenger "who publishes salvation" (v. 7), proclaiming that the Lord is returning to his holy city, like a victorious king coming back with his men, having redeemed them from their captors (vv. 7–8). This victory parade includes songs of joy extolling the salvation brought about by the Lord, and also a pressing call to purification, to ensure that those who welcome the Lord are worthy to form part of his holy company (vv. 11–12). These verses form the famous poem of the "messenger of peace" who "brings good tidings". The ideas of the first oracle of this second part of the book (40:1–11) are repeated here very beautifully. The messenger's feet are praised—a symbol of his speed and surefootedness when crossing the mountains, which is where important news comes from (cf. 40:9). His message (v. 7) is described very significantly as involving "peace", which in Isaiah means safety in Israel after the hardships of exile; "good tidings" or, more literally, "news of goodness and well-being", that is, genuine material and spiritual prosperity; and "salvation", which is permanent renewal on all levels. The three words read together mean the highest degree of happiness imaginable. The core of this message is the enthronement of God: "Your God reigns," similar to 40:9: "Behold your God." What is new about this poem is that it depicts God as the king of Zion (cf. 24:23). The kingdom of God is sublime, and only analogically is it comparable to earthly kingdoms, as can be seen in the psalms of divine kingship (Ps 47:8; 93:1; 96:10; 97:1), and, much more fully, in the New Testament, which records Jesus' preaching centred on the Kingdom of God.

As in a stage play, the arrival of the messenger, which is really the same thing as the arrival of God as king on Zion, causes the watchmen to raise shouts of joy that resound across the city (v. 8). Those whose job it was to give warning of any threat now provoke unconfined joy because of the "return of the Lord to Zion" (v. 8; Ezek 43:1–5).

In a beautiful personification, the "waste places of Jerusalem" are called to join in the watchmen's song (v. 9). The restoration has come, and the credit must go to the Lord, for he has "bared his holy arm", a symbol of vigorous action, as in the time of the exodus (v. 10; cf. 40:10, 51:9; Ps 98:1).

The short hymn at the end (vv. 11–12) is an exhortation to be cleansed from every trace of Babylonian idolatry and to follow the Lord's path, who, in the early trek through the wilderness (cf. Ex 13:21–22), travels at the head of the company and is also its rearguard.

St Paul quotes the words of v. 7 in Romans 10:15 when he is making the

---

[5]Et nunc quid mihi est hic, dicit Dominus, quoniam ablatus est populus meus gratis? Dominatores eius ululant, dicit Dominus, et iugiter tota die nomen meum blasphematur. [6]Propter hoc sciet populus meus nomen meum in die illa, quia ego ipse, qui loquebar: "Ecce adsum"». [7]Quam pulchri super montes /

Ex 33:20
Ezek 43:1–5

8Hark, your watchmen lift up their voice,
together they sing for joy;
for eye to eye they see
the return of the LORD to Zion.
9Break forth together into singing,
you waste places of Jerusalem;
for the LORD has comforted his people,
he has redeemed Jerusalem.

Ps 98:1–3
Mt 28:19

10The LORD has bared his holy arm
before the eyes of all the nations;
and all the ends of the earth shall see
the salvation of our God.

2 Cor 6:17
Jer 51:45
2 Tim 2:21
Rev 18:4

11Depart, depart, go out thence,
touch no unclean thing;
go out from the midst of her, purify yourselves,
you who bear the vessels of the LORD.

Ex 12:31–34,39

12For you shall not go out in haste,
and you shall not go in flight,
for the LORD will go before you,
and the God of Israel will be your rear guard.

---

point that preaching is necessary if the Gospel is to be spread. So, they are an abiding call to apostolate.

The words of this oracle (especially v. 11) have also been applied by Christian tradition to those who have pastoral responsibilities: "A pastor should be a man whose thoughts are pure and purified. No stain should mar the character of the man who holds the office of pastor; thus shall he be able to cleanse the impurity of those in his care. The one whose work it is to purify stains must have clean hands, to ensure that, when he seeks to cleanse, he does not soil his charges more. The prophet says: *purify yourselves, you who bear the vessels of the Lord.* Those who are entrusted with leading souls along the path of faith to their eternal home bear the vessels of the Lord. Consider carefully, then, how pure they must be who have devoted themselves to the task of bearing living vessels to the eternal Temple" (St Gregory the Great, *Regula pastoralis*, 2, 2).

pedes annuntiantis, praedicantis pacem, / annuntiantis bonum, praedicantis salutem, / dicentis Sion: "Regnavit Deus tuus!". / 8Vox speculatorum tuorum: levaverunt vocem, / simul exsultabunt, / quia oculo ad oculum videbunt, / cum redierit Dominus ad Sion. / 9Gaudete et exsultate simul, / deserta Ierusalem, / quia consolatus est Dominus populum suum, / redemit Ierusalem. / 10Nudavit Dominus brachium sanctum suum / in oculis omnium gentium; / et videbunt omnes fines terrae / salutare Dei nostri. / 11Recedite, recedite, exite inde, / pollutum nolite tangere; / exite de medio eius, mundamini, / qui fertis vasa Domini. / 12Quoniam non in festinatione exibitis / nec in fuga properabitis; / praecedet

Fourth song of the Servant of the Lord

[13] Behold, my servant shall prosper,
he shall be exalted and lifted up,
and shall be very high.

Ps 22; Is 42:1
Wis 2:12–24
Lk 24:25f; Jn 12: 32;
Rom 4:24; Eph 1:20–21
Phil 2:6–11; Ps 22:7

52:13—53:12. This fourth Song of the Servant is one of the most commented on passages in the Bible, as regards both its literary structure and its content. From the point of view of structure, it interrupts the hymn-style of chapter 52 (which is taken up again in chapter 54); the style here is more reflective; the theme, the value of suffering. In terms of content, the song is unusual in that it shows the servant triumphing through his humiliation and suffering. Even more than that—he makes the pains and sins of others his own, in order to heal them and set them free. Prior to this, the idea of "vicarious expiation" was unknown in the Bible. The passage is original even in its vocabulary: it contains forty words that are not to be found elsewhere in the Bible.

The poem, which is very carefully composed, divides into three stanzas: the first (52:13–15) is put on the Lord's lips and it acts as a kind of overture to what follows—taking in the themes of the triumph of the servant (v. 13), his humiliation and suffering (v. 14), and the stunning effect that this has on his own people and on strangers.

The second stanza (53:1–11a) celebrates the servant's trials and the good effects they produce. This is spoken in the first person plural, standing for the people and the prophet: both feel solidarity with the servant of the Lord. This stanza has four stages to it: first (53:1–3) it describes the servant's noble origins (he grew up before the Lord like a young plant: cf. v. 2) and the low esteem in which he is held as a "man of sorrows". Then we learn that all this suffering is atonement for the sins of others (53:4–6). Traditionally, suffering was interpreted as being a punishment for sins, but here it is borne on behalf of others. This is the first lesson to be learned by those who see him "stricken, smitten by God, and afflicted", and it marks the climax of the poem. Thirdly (53:7–9), the point is made again that he has freely accepted suffering and meekly offers himself as a sacrifice of atonement (he is like a lamb, like a sheep). His death is as ignominous as the suffering that precedes it. Finally (vv. 10–11a) we are told how fruitful all this suffering is: like the patriarchs of old (the text seems to imply) the servant will have many offspring and a long life and be a man of great wisdom.

In the third stanza (53:11b–12) the Lord speaks again, finally acknowledging that his servant's sacrifice is truly efficacious: he will cause many to be accounted "righteous", that is, he will win their salvation (v. 11) and will share in the Lord's spoils (v. 12).

The fourth song of the servant of the Lord was from very early on interpreted as having a current application. When the Jews of Alexandria made the Greek translation of the Old Testment

enim vos Dominus, / et colliget vos Deus Israel. / [13]Ecce prospere aget servus meus; / exaltabitur et elevabitur et sublimis erit valde. / [14]Sicut obstupuerunt super eum multi, / sic deformis erat, quasi non

Is 53:2–3 Mt 27:29–31 Jn 19:5 *Rom 15:21*

14 As many were astonished at him[s]—
his appearance was so marred, beyond human semblance,
and his form beyond that of the sons of men—

(the Septuagint) around the second century BC, they tinkered a little with the text to indicate that the servant in the poem stood for the people of Israel in the diaspora. Those Jews, who encountered huge obstacles in their effort to maintain their identity in that Hellenistic and polytheistic environment, found comfort in the hope that they would emerge enhanced, just like the servant.

Jews of Palestine identified the victorious servant with the Messiah, but they reinterpreted the sufferings described here to apply them to the pagan nations. The Dead Sea Scrolls interpret this song in the light of the ignominy experienced by the Teacher of Righteousness, the probable founder of the group that established itself at Qumran.

Jesus revealed his redemptive mission to be that of the suffering servant prophesied by Isaiah here. He referred to him on a number of occasions—in his reply to the request made by the sons of Zebedee ("the Son of man came not to be served but to serve, and to give his life as a ransom for many": Mt 20:28 and par.); at the Last Supper, when he announced his ignominious death among transgressors, quoting 53:12 (Lk 22:37); in some passages in the fourth Gospel (Jn 12:32, 37–38); etc. He also seems to refer to it in his conversation with the disciples of Emmaus (Lk 24:25ff) to explain his passion and death. Therefore, the first Christians interpreted Jesus' death and resurrection in terms of this poem; evidence of this is the expression "in accordance with the scriptures" in 1 Corinthians 15:3; the words "for our trespasses" (Rom 4:25; 1 Cor 15:3–5); the Christological hymn in the Letter to the Philippians (Phil 2:6–11); and expressions used in the First Letter of Peter (1 Pet 2:22–25) and in other New Testament passages (Mt 8:17; 27:29; Acts 8:26–40; Rom 10:16; etc.).

Patristic tradition reads the song as a prophecy that found fulfilment in Christ (cf. St Clement of Rome, *Ad Corinthios*, 16:1–14; St Ignatius Martyr, *Epistula ad Polycarpum*, 1, 3; the so-called *Letter of Barnabas*, 5, 2 and *Epistula ad Diognetum*, 9, 2; etc.). The Church uses it in the Good Friday liturgy.

52:14. "Beyond human semblance": this phrase sums up the description given in 53:2–3 and shows the intense pain reflected in the servant's face: the description is so graphic that Christian ascetical writing, with good reason, reads it as anticipating the passion of our Lord: "The prophet, who has rightly been called 'the Fifth Evangelist', presents in this Song an image of the sufferings of the Servant with a realism as acute as if he were seeing them with

esset hominis species eius, / filiorum hominis aspectus eius, / [15]sic disperget gentes multas. / Super ipsum continebunt reges os suum, / quia, quae non sunt narrata eis, viderunt / et, quae non audierunt,

s. Syr Tg: Heb *you*

15 so shall he startle[t] many nations; Is 49:7,23
kings shall shut their mouths because of him;
for that which has not been told them they shall see,
and that which they have not heard they shall understand.

53 [1]Who has believed what we have heard? *Jn 12:38*
And to whom has the arm of the LORD been revealed? *Rom 10,16*
[2]For he grew up before him like a young plant,
and like a root out of dry ground;
he had no form or comeliness that we should look at him,
and no beauty that we should desire him.
[3]He was despised and rejected[u] by men; Ps 22:7–8
a man of sorrows,[v] and acquainted with grief;[w] Mk 8:12
Heb 4:15
and as one from whom men hide their faces
he was despised, and we esteemed him not.

[4]Surely he has borne our griefs[x] *Mt 8:17*
and carried our sorrows;[y] Heb 2:10

---

his own eyes: the eyes of the body and of the spirit. […] The Song of the Suffering Servant contains a description in which it is possible, in a certain sense, to identify the stages of Christ's Passion in their various details: the arrest, the humiliation, the blows, the spitting, the contempt for the prisoner, the unjust sentence, and then the scourging, the crowning with thorns and the mocking, the carrying of the Cross, the crucifixion and the agony" (John Paul II, *Salvifici doloris*, 17; cf. idem, *Dives in misericordia*, 7).

53:1. St Paul cites this verse to prove the need for preaching (Rom 10:16). The verse also underlines the extraordinary degree of undeserved suffering endured by the Servant. It is sometimes interpreted as a further sign of the humility of Christ, who, being divine, took on the form of a servant: "Christ is a man of humble thought and feeling, unlike those who attack his flock. The heart of God's majesty, the Lord Jesus Christ, did not come with loud cries of arrogance and pride; he came in humility, as the Holy Spirit said of him: *Who has believed what we have heard?*" (St Clement of Rome, *Ad Corinthios*, 16, 1–3).

53:4–5. "He has borne our griefs [or, pains]": the servant's sufferings are not due to his own personal sins; they are

contemplati sunt. **[53]** [1]«Quis credidit auditui nostro, / et brachium Domini cui revelatum est? / [2]Et ascendit sicut virgultum coram eo / et sicut radix de terra sitienti. / Non erat species ei neque decor, ut aspiceremus eum, / et non erat aspectus, ut desideraremus eum. / [3]Despectus erat et novissimus virorum, / vir dolorum et sciens infirmitatem, / et quasi abscondebamus vultum coram eo; / despectus, unde nec reputabamus eum. / [4]Vere languores nostros ipse tulit / et dolores nostros ipse portavit; / et

t. The meaning of the Hebrew word is uncertain **u.** Or *forsaken* **v.** Or *pains* **w.** Or *sickness* **x.** Or *sicknesses* **y.** Or *pains*

yet we esteemed him stricken,
smitten by God, and afflicted.
Rom 4:25 / 1 Cor 15:3–5 / 2 Cor 5:21 / Gal 3:13 / *1 Pet 2:24*
5 But he was wounded for our transgressions,
he was bruised for our iniquities;
upon him was the chastisement that made us whole,
and with his stripes we are healed.
Ezek 34 / 2 Cor 5:21 / *1 Pet 2:25*
6 All we like sheep have gone astray;
we have turned every one to his own way;
and the LORD has laid on him
the iniquity of us all.*

Jer 11:19 / Mt 26:62–63 / Jn 1:29 / *Acts 8:32–33* / 1 Pet 2:23
7 He was oppressed, and he was afflicted,
yet he opened not his mouth;
like a lamb that is led to the slaughter,
and like a sheep that before its shearers is dumb,
so he opened not his mouth.
8 By oppression and judgment he was taken away;
and as for his generation, who considered
that he was cut off out of the land of the living,
stricken for the transgression of my people?
Mt 27:38; 60:66 / *1 Pet 2:22*
9 And they made his grave with the wicked
and with a rich man in his death,

---

atonement for the sins of others. "The sufferings of our Saviour are our cure" (Theodoret of Cyrrhus, *De incarnatione Domini*, 28). He suffered on account of the sins of the entire people, even though he was not guilty of them. By bearing the penalty for those sins, he expiated the guilt involved. St Matthew, after recounting some miraculous cures and the casting out of devils, sees the words of v. 4a fulfilled in Christ (Mt 8:17). He interprets Jesus Christ as being the servant foretold by the prophet, who will cure the physical suffering of people as a sign that he is curing the root cause of all types of evil, that is, sin, iniquity (v. 5). The miracles worked by Jesus for the sick are therefore a sign of Redemption: "Christ's whole life is a mystery of *redemption*. Redemption comes to us above all through the blood of his cross (cf. Eph 1:7; Col 1:13–14; 1 Pet 1:18–19), but this mystery is at work throughout Christ's entire life" (*Catechism of the Catholic Church*, 517).

nos putavimus eum quasi plagatum, / percussum a Deo et humiliatum. / 5 Ipse autem vulneratus est propter iniquitates nostras, / attritus est propter scelera nostra; / disciplina pacis nostrae super eum, / et livore eius sanati sumus. / 6 Omnes nos quasi oves erravimus, / unusquisque in viam suam declinavit; / et posuit Dominus in eo / iniquitatem omnium nostrum». / 7 Afflictus est et ipse subiecit se / et non aperuit os suum; / sicut agnus, qui ad occisionem ducitur, / et quasi ovis, quae coram tondentibus se obmutuit / et non aperuit os suum. / 8 Angustia et iudicio sublatus est. / De generatione eius quis curabit? / Quia abscissus est de terra viventium; / propter scelus populi mei percussus est ad mortem. / 9 Et posuerunt sepulcrum eius cum impiis, / cum divitibus tumulum eius, / eo quod iniquitatem non

although he had done no violence,
and there was no deceit in his mouth.

10 Yet it was the will of the LORD to bruise him;
he has put him to grief;[z]
when he makes himself[a] an offering for sin,
he shall see his offspring, he shall prolong his days;
the will of the LORD shall prosper in his hand;
11 he shall see the fruit of the travail of his soul and be satisfied; Rom 3:26
by his knowledge shall the righteous one, my servant,
make many to be accounted righteous;
and he shall bear their iniquities.

12 Therefore I will divide him a portion with the great, Ps 2:8
and he shall divide the spoil with the strong; Mk 10:45; 15:28; 20:28
because he poured out his soul to death, Lk 22:37
and was numbered with the transgressors; Jn 1:29
yet he bore the sin of many, Col 2:15
and made intercession for the transgressors. *1 Pet 2:24*

A glorious new Jerusalem

Gen 16:1; 1 Sam 2:5; Ps 113:9; Jer 10:20; *Gal 4:27*

54 1"Sing, O barren one, who did not bear;
break forth into singing and cry aloud,
you who have not been in travail!

54:1–17. After the Song of the Servant, the sacred writer turns his attention again to Zion in a beautiful hymn celebrating the glory and restoration of Jerusalem. By inserting it immediately after the fourth song, he seems to indicate that this will be the first outcome of the servant's work. This hymn is an oracle of consolation and hope after the humiliations of exile. The content of the fourth song was quite new; not so this hymn: it uses traditional Old Testament imagery—the barren wife who becomes fruitful again (v. 1; cf. 1 Sam 2:5; Ps 113:9), the unfaithful and repudiated wife who is taken back (v. 4; cf. Hos 1:16–22). Zion will have far more offspring than she had before the exile (v. 3). The Lord of hosts will be her Maker and her

fecerit, / neque dolus fuerit in ore eius. / [10]Et Dominus voluit conterere eum infirmitate. / Si posuerit in piaculum animam suam, / videbit semen longaevum, / et voluntas Domini in manu eius prosperabitur. / [11]Propter laborem animae eius / videbit lucem, saturabitur in scientia sua. / Iustificabit iustus servus meus multos / et iniquitates eorum ipse portabit. / [12]Ideo dispertiam ei multos, / et cum fortibus dividet spolia, / pro eo quod tradidit in mortem animam suam / et cum sceleratis reputatus est; / et ipse peccatum multorum tulit / et pro transgressoribus rogat. **[54]** [1]Exsulta, sterilis, quae non peperisti, / laetare, gaude, quae non parturisti, / quoniam multi sunt filii desertae / magis quam filii nuptae, dicit

z. Heb *made him sick* **a.** Vg: Heb *thou makest his soul*

For the children of the desolate one will be more
than the children of her that is married, says the LORD.
Is 33:20; 49:20 [2]Enlarge the place of your tent,
and let the curtains of your habitations be stretched out;
hold not back, lengthen your cords
and strengthen your stakes.
Is 26:15; 55:5; 61:9 [3]For you will spread abroad to the right and to the left,
and your descendants will possess the nations
and will people the desolate cities.

Husband (vv. 5–6). He forsook her for a short while (vv. 7–9) but now he will make a new Covenant with her, sealed with love (v. 10). He will rebuild Zion's walls with precious stones, and peace will prevail (vv. 11–15). But the figure of Zion now accomodates not just the city's inhabitants: it comes to stand for the homeland of all the Lord's servants.

As the poem develops, so does God's tenderness towards his city and his people: the first stanza (vv. 1–3) sees the city as a woman who was once barren and now has many children: she is the new Sarah (Gen 16:1), the new Rachel (Gen 29:31), the new Hannah (1 Sam 1:2). This will be so, for so "says the Lord" (v. 1). The second stanza (vv. 4–6) stresses the titles of her husband—Maker, Lord of hosts, Redeemer, the Holy One of Israel, etc; and it confirms this by a slight change in wording: "says your God" (v. 6). The third stanza (vv. 7–10) describes the husband's tender affection: he forsook Israel "for a brief moment", but his love is everlasting: as in the days of Noah she was disgraced for a while, but he has sworn to be angry no longer, and not to rebuke her. The oracular formula is now: "says the Lord, your Redeemer" (v. 8b) and "says the Lord who has compassion on you" (v. 10b), which is etymologically the eqivalent of "who loves you tenderly".

The second part of the poem consists of two oracles of restoration: the first (vv. 11–15) shows the city constructed with precious stones (*abanim*, in Hebrew; v. 11) and full of sons (*banim*, in Hebrew) who will be docile to the Lord; the second part (vv. 16–17) confirms that God himself, mighty and just, guarantees the splendour and permanence of Zion.

A Christian reading sees the poem as explaining that the Church is the continuation and culmination of the ancient people of God, especially in its eschatological stage when tribulation will be a thing of the past: "The cry in scripture, *Sing, O barren one*, refers to us, because our Church was barren until children were born to it. *Break forth into singing and cry aloud, you who have not been in travail:* our singing is the prayers we should offer to God, without ceasing, without fail; those who live apart from God will fail. And Scripture adds, *the children of the desolate one will be more than the*

Dominus. / [2]Dilata locum tentorii tui / et pelles tabernaculorum tuorum extende, ne parcas; / longos fac funiculos tuos / et clavos tuos consolida. / [3]Ad dexteram enim et ad laevam penetrabis, / et semen tuum

[4]"Fear not, for you will not be ashamed;
be not confounded, for you will not be put to shame;
for you will forget the shame of your youth,
and the reproach of your widowhood you will remember no more.
[5]For your Maker is your husband, Hos 1:2
the LORD of hosts is his name;
and the Holy One of Israel is your Redeemer,
the God of the whole earth he is called.
[6]For the LORD has called you Is 49:14–15
like a wife forsaken and grieved in spirit,
like a wife of youth when she is cast off,
says your God.
[7]For a brief moment I forsook you,
but with great compassion I will gather you.
[8]In overflowing wrath for a moment Ps 30:6
I hid my face from you,
but with everlasting love I will have compassion on you,
says the LORD, your Redeemer.

[9]"For this is like the days of Noah to me: Gen 9:11
as I swore that the waters of Noah

---

children of her that is married, so that we will see how, though we seemed to have been abandoned by the Lord in the beginning, we are now more fruitful than ever, and more numerous even than the people who believed that God was their God alone" (Pseudo-Clement, *Epistula II ad Corinthios*, 2).

Verses 11–12 will inspire the vision of the heavenly Jerusalem in Revelation 21:18–21. Verse 13 is applied to Jesus' disciples in John 6:45 to indicate that God himself guarantees' faith of believers in Jesus Christ.

The Church reads part of this passage (vv. 5–14) during the Easter Vigil, because the death and resurrection of Jesus is, for the new people of God, the fulfilment of this promise made by God, that he would enter into a new and definitive Covenant in which Christ unites himself permanently to his Church, the beloved spouse for whom he sacrifices himself.

hereditabit gentes, / quae civitates desertas inhabitabunt. / [4]Noli timere, quia non confunderis, / neque erubescas, quia non te pudebit; / nam confusionis adulescentiae tuae oblivisceris / et opprobrii viduitatis tuae non recordaberis amplius. / [5]Qui enim fecit te, erit sponsus tuus, / Dominus exercituum nomen eius; / et redemptor tuus Sanctus Israel, / Deus omnis terrae vocabitur. / [6]Quia ut mulierem derelictam et maerentem spiritu / vocavit te Dominus, / et uxorem ab adulescentia abiectam / dixit Deus tuus. / [7]Ad punctum in modico dereliqui te / et in miserationibus magnis congregabo te. / [8]In momento indignationis / abscondi faciem meam parumper a te / et in misericordia sempiterna misertus sum tui, / dixit redemptor tuus Dominus. / [9]Sicut in diebus Noe istud mihi est, / cui iuravi, ne inducerem aquas

should no more go over the earth,
so I have sworn that I will not be angry with you
and will not rebuke you.
Rom 11:29 10 For the mountains may depart
and the hills be removed,
but my steadfast love shall not depart from you,
and my covenant of peace shall not be removed,
says the LORD, who has compassion on you.

Is 60:17–18 Rev 21:2, 10–27 11 "O afflicted one, storm-tossed, and not comforted,
behold, I will set your stones in antimony,
and lay your foundations with sapphires.[b]
12 I will make your pinnacles of agate,
your gates of carbuncles,
and all your wall of precious stones.
Jer 31:33–34 *Jn 6:45* 13 All your sons shall be taught by the LORD,
and great shall be the prosperity of your sons.
14 In righteousness you shall be established;
you shall be far from oppression, for you shall not fear;
and from terror, for it shall not come near you.
15 If any one stirs up strife,
it is not from me;
whoever stirs up strife with you
shall fall because of you.
16 Behold, I have created the smith
who blows the fire of coals,
and produces a weapon for its purpose.
I have also created the ravager to destroy;
17 no weapon that is fashioned against you shall prosper,
and you shall confute every tongue that rises against you in judgment.
This is the heritage of the servants of the LORD
and their vindication from me, says the LORD."

Noe ultra supra terram; / sic iuravi, ut non irascar tibi / et non increpem te. / 10 Montes enim recedent, /
et colles movebuntur, / misericordia autem mea non recedet a te, / et foedus pacis meae non movebitur,
/ dixit miserator tuus Dominus. / 11 Paupercula, tempestate convulsa absque ulla consolatione, / ecce
ego sternam super carbunculos lapides tuos / et fundabo te in sapphiris; / 12 et ponam iaspidem
propugnacula tua / et portas tuas in lapides pretiosos / et omnes terminos tuos in lapides desiderabiles.
/ 13 Universi filii tui erunt discipuli Domini, / et magna erit pax filiis tuis; / 14 in iustitia fundaberis. /
Procul eris ab oppressione, quia non timebis. / et a pavore, quia non appropinquabit tibi. / 15 Ecce, si
impetus fiet, non erit ex me; qui impetum fecerit in te, cadet contra te. / 16 Ecce, ego creavi fabrum /
sufflantem in igne prunas / et proferentem vas in opus suum; / et ego creavi etiam vastatorem ad

b. Or *lapis lazuli*

Epilogue: Invitation to partake of the banquet of the Lord's Covenant

55 [1]"Ho, every one who thirsts,
come to the waters;
and he who has no money,
come, buy and eat!
Come, buy wine and milk
without money and without price.

Ex 24:5–11
Jn 4:1
Rev 21:6;
22:17

55:1–13. The invitation to the Covenant banquet acts as the epilogue to the second part of the book of Isaiah, and picks up on themes in chapter 40, which is its prologue. The two chapters help to give literary and thematic unity to this part of the book. The oracle in chapter 55 sums up in a way the teachings contained in the preceding chapters—the invitation to the Covenant banquet (vv. 1–3), reminiscent of that celebrated by Moses at Mount Sinai (Ex 24:5, 11); the renewal of the Covenant with David on Zion (vv. 4–5); the transcendence of God, who is unaffected by the sins of men (vv. 8–9); the power of the word of God (vv. 10–11); and, as a final synthesis, the promise of a new exodus, a sign of God's everlasting salvation.

These oracles are a call for conversion, a call to take advantage of the salvific gifts so generously offered: "Come to the waters" (v. 1), "Come to me" (v. 3), "Seek the Lord" (v. 6), "Let the wicked forsake his way" (v. 7). Originally, it was a call to those exiled in Babylon to return to Jerusalem; but it is a call that is made at all times, to everyone. The reference to an everlasting Covenant, in keeping with promises made to David (cf. v. 3), can be read by Christians as an invitation to share in the new and eternal Covenant sealed with the Blood of our Lord Jesus Christ, a pledge of salvation for all mankind. In the Eucharist, the banquet of the New Testament, the words of the prophet come true in the complete sense in the words spoken by our Lord when he instituted that sacrament: "Take and eat" (cf. v. 1) the true bread of life, the very finest food, which money cannot buy (vv. 1–3). Therefore, the invitation extended by the prophet is a call to Christians to partake of the Blessed Eucharist. Paul VI, urging the faithful to take part in the Sunday celebration of the Euchrist, wrote: "How could we fail to take part in this encounter, to partake of the banquet that Christ has lovingly prepared for us? Our participation should be dignified and filled with joy. Christ, crucified and glorified, comes among his disciples to draw them all into the power of his resurrection. It is the pinnacle, here on earth, of the Covenant of love between God and his people: the sign and source of Christian joy, the preparation for the eternal banquet in heaven" (*Gaudete in Domino*, 322). Verses 1–11, like

disperdendum. / [17]Omne vas, quod fictum est contra te, frustra erit. / Et omnem linguam insurgentem tibi in iudicio confutabis: / haec est hereditas servorum Domini / et iustitia eorum ex me, dicit Dominus. **[55]** [1]Heu! Omnes sitientes, venite ad aquas; / et, qui non habetis argentum, properate, / emite et comedite, venite, emite absque argento / et absque ulla commutatione vinum et lac. / [2]Quare

Prov 9:3–6 Sir 24:19–22 Jn 6:35

[2]Why do you spend your money for that which is not bread,
and your labour for that which does not satisfy?
Hearken diligently to me, and eat what is good,
and delight yourselves in fatness.

2 Sam 7,1 *Acts 13:34* Rev 1:5

[3]Incline your ear, and come to me;
hear, that your soul may live;
and I will make with you an everlasting covenant,
my steadfast, sure love for David.

Jn 18:37 Rev 1:5

[4]Behold, I made him a witness to the peoples,
a leader and commander for the peoples.
[5]Behold, you shall call nations that you know not,
and nations that knew you not shall run to you,
because of the LORD your God, and of the Holy One of Israel,
for he has glorified you.

Deut 4:7 Ps 145:18 Hos 5:6

[6]"Seek the LORD while he may be found,
call upon him while he is near;

54:5–14, are read in the liturgy of the Easter Vigil, which celebrates Christ's victory over sin and which invites the faithful to partake of the banquet of the Covenant sealed by his death and resurrection: "On the feasts of the Lord, when the faithful receive the Body of the Son, they proclaim to one another the Good News that the first fruits of life have been given, as when the angel said to Mary Magdalene, 'Christ is risen!' Now too are life and resurrection conferred on whoever receives Christ" (Fanqîth, *Brevarium iuxta ritum Ecclesiae Antiochenae Syrorum*, in *Catechism of the Catholic Church*, 1391).

55:6–9. The Israelites are called to conversion. In order to return to their homeland, they must return to God, must "seek" him (vv. 6–7). And the Lord, who allows himself to be found and who does not judge in the way that men do, is willing and able to grant forgiveness (vv. 8–9). In other words, the call to repentance is grounded on the goodness of God who "will abundantly pardon" (v. 7). Man, for his part, should grasp this opportunity that God offers him. So, the words in this passage are a constant encouragement to begin and begin again in the pursuit of virtue: "To be converted means to ask for forgiveness and to seek out the strength of God in the Sacrament of reconciliation, and thus begin again, advancing step by step every day, learning to overcome ourselves, to win the spiritual

appenditis argentum non in panibus / et laborem vestrum non in saturitate? / Audite, audientes me, et comedite bonum, / ut delectetur in crassitudine anima vestra. / [3]Inclinate aurem vestram et venite ad me; / audite, ut vivat anima vestra, / et feriam vobiscum pactum sempiternum, / misericordias David fideles. / [4]Ecce testem populis dedi eum, / ducem ac praeceptorem gentibus. / [5]Ecce gentem, quam nesciebas, vocabis, / et gentes, quae te non cognoverunt, ad te current, / propter Dominum Deum tuum / et Sanctum Israel, quia glorificavit te. / [6]Quaerite Dominum, dum inveniri potest; / invocate eum, dum

[7]let the wicked forsake his way,
and the unrighteous man his thoughts;
let him return to the LORD, that he may have mercy on him,
and to our God, for he will abundantly pardon.
[8]For my thoughts are not your thoughts,
neither are your ways my ways, says the LORD.
[9]For as the heavens are higher than the earth,
so are my ways higher than your ways
and my thoughts than your thoughts.

Zech 1:3; Mt 5:25; Lk 15:20
Jn 7:34
2 Cor 6:2
Heb 3:13

Ps 103:11

[10]"For as the rain and the snow come down from heaven,
and return not thither but water the earth,
making it bring forth and sprout,
giving seed to the sower and bread to the eater,
[11]so shall my word be that goes forth from my mouth;
it shall not return to me empty,

Deut 32:2
2 Cor 9:10

Wis 18:14–15
Zech 1:5–6
Jn 1:1

---

battles that we face, and to give of ourselves joyfully, 'for God loves a cheerful giver' (2 Cor 9:7)" (John Paul II, *Novo incipiente,* 8 April 1979). And St Augustine, apropos of conversion, wrote: "Do not say: 'Tomorrow, I will be converted; tomorrow, I will give thanks to God; and all my sins, today's and yesterday's, will be forgiven'. It is true that God promises forgiveness for your conversion; but He does not promise tomorrow for your delays" (*Enarrationes in Psalmos*, 144, 11).

The words of v. 8 are echoed by St Paul in Romans 11:33, and are a reminder to us of just how narrow-minded we can be and how we can fail even to imagine the great things that God has in store for us.

55:10–11. The prophet uses comparisons that are particularly meaningful to those who live in the arid countries of the East, to describe how very powerful the word of God is: it actually delivers the salvation that it promises. The personified word of God (cf. Wis 8:4; 9:9–10; 18:14–15) is a figure of the incarnation of Jesus Christ, the eternal Word of the Father, who comes down to save mankind. "The word of God, he says, will not return to him empty and barren; rather, it will flourish in all things, nourished by the good deeds of those who obey and fulfil his teachings. The word is fulfilled when it is put into practice; if it is not put into practice, it remains barren and withered and starved. Listen carefully, then, when he

prope est. / [7]Derelinquat impius viam suam, / et vir iniquus cogitationes suas; / et revertatur ad Dominum, et miserebitur eius, / et ad Deum nostrum, quoniam multus est ad ignoscendum. / [8]Non enim cogitationes meae cogitationes vestrae, / neque viae vestrae viae meae, dicit Dominus. / [9]Quia sicut exaltantur caeli a terra, / sic exaltatae sunt viae meae a viis vestris, / et cogitationes meae a cogitationibus vestris. / [10]Et quomodo descendit imber et nix de caelo / et illuc ultra non revertitur, / sed inebriat terram et infundit eam / et germinare eam facit / et dat semen serenti et panem comedenti, / [11]sic erit verbum meum, quod egredietur de ore meo: / non revertetur ad me vacuum, / sed faciet,

but it shall accomplish that which I purpose,
and prosper in the thing for which I sent it.

12 "For you shall go out in joy,
and be led forth in peace;
the mountains and the hills before you
shall break forth into singing,
and all the trees of the field shall clap their hands.
Is 41:19; 44:3–4 13 Instead of the thorn shall come up the cypress;
instead of the brier shall come up the myrtle;
and it shall be to the LORD for a memorial,
for an everlasting sign which shall not be cut off."

PART THREE*

1. PROSPECT OF SALVATION FOR THE WHOLE WORLD*

Worship open to all

Is 46:13; 51:6,8 56 1*Thus says the LORD:
"Keep justice, and do righteousness,
for soon my salvation will come,

---

tells of the food that nourishes him: *My food is to do the will of him who sent me* (Jn 4:34)" (St Bernard, *In Cantica Canticorum*, 71, 12–13).

***56:1—66:24.** These chapters make up the third part of the book of Isaiah, sometimes called "Third Isaiah". It consists of prophetic visions and oracles about the new Zion and the nations of the earth. The variety of style and content here makes it difficult to identify any clear structure: the sacred writer seems to have drawn these oracles together, apparently content that they are all to do with the End and all refer to the whole world and not just to Israel. But he has carefully positioned chapter 61 in the middle, making it the high-point of these chapters. Also, 56:1–8 and 66:18–24, which stress the universality of justice and worship, are very appropriately positioned at start and finish. To make this part easier to read, we have divided it into three sections in this edition. The first (56:1—59:21) is a series of oracles that show salvation being extended to all

quaecumque volui, / et prosperabitur in his, ad quae misi illud. / [12]Quia in laetitia egrediemini / et in pace deducemini; / montes et colles cantabunt coram vobis laudem, / et omnia ligna regionis plaudent manu. / [13]Pro vepribus ascendet cupressus, / et pro urtica crescet myrtus; / et erit Domino in gloriam, / in signum aeternum, quod non auferetur. **[56]** [1]Haec dicit Dominus: / «Custodite iudicium et facite

[2]Blessed is the man who does this,
and the son of man who holds it fast,
who keeps the sabbath, not profaning it,
and keeps his hand from doing any evil."

Ex 20:8
Is 58:13

mankind, even though the sins of the people of God will cause delays. In the second (60:1—64:11), the salvation that the Lord will provide is proclaimed to all the nations from Jerusalem. And the third section (65:1—66:24) has as its theme the judgment of God, handed down to each according to his or her merits, be it punishment for sin, or salvation.

Historically, the oracles have to do with the years following the return from exile after Cyrus issued his decree of repatriation (539 BC). It was for Judah a time for "beginning again". God sent messages of hope to raise the Jews' spirits during their years in exile and on their return, when they were confronted by a scene of devastation. They cannot fail to see that, from now on, peace and salvation are linked with a return to God, conversion, the practice of righteousness, and holiness.

This means that the horizon of divine salvation extends to include the whole world, extending beyond the narrow limits of Jewish nationalism. When the prophetic texts speak of Zion, they see it as the centre of a new view of mankind, as a source of light for all nations. The new Jerusalem stands for a new order, as it will in the Revelation to John. Although all the energies of repatriates are focussed on the rebuilding of the temple (60:7–13), the message here is that the ultimate goal is not material reconstruction, for the throne of God is to be found in heaven, and the earth is only his footstool (66:1–2). Hope in a glorious future is not measured in terms of external institutions—in the monarchy (which does not exist), or in any other human authority, or in force of arms. Even divine worship, and the rules and regulations to do with fasting and sacrifices, will be cleansed of the old formalism (58:1–14). God will act directly to save his people (62:2–12). The new horizon opened up by "Third Isaiah" has its parallel in Haggai and Zechariah, and, above all, it prepares the way for the still-distant eschatological vision found in the Revelation to John.

***56:1—59:21.** The new section looks forward to a salvation that is open to everyone who practises righteousness (56:1–12). However, the first announcement of this is put on hold, as it were, due to the sins of the people of God; these delay the manifestation of God's salvific power, for he refuses to hearken to the prayers of the ungodly (57:1–21). Therefore, first and foremost, the prophet issues a call to conversion (58:1–14), while promising that the Lord, who is faithful to his Covenant, will reward people according to their actions: he will punish those who are faithless and redeem those who return to him (59:1–21).

/ iustitiam, / quia iuxta est salus mea, ut veniat, / et iustitia mea, ut reveletur». / [2]Beatus vir, qui facit hoc, / et filius hominis, qui apprehendit istud, / custodiens sabbatum, ne polluat illud, / custodiens

Ex 12:48 3Let not the foreigner who has joined himself to the LORD say,
"The LORD will surely separate me from his people";
and let not the eunuch say,
"Behold, I am a dry tree."
Lev 22:25 4For thus says the LORD:
Deut 23:2–9
Wis 3:14–15 "To the eunuchs who keep my sabbaths,
who choose the things that please me
and hold fast my covenant,
1 Sam 1:8 5I will give in my house and within my walls
Rev 2:17; 3:5
a monument and a name
better than sons and daughters;
I will give them an everlasting name
which shall not be cut off.

6"And the foreigners who join themselves to the LORD,
to minister to him, to love the name of the LORD,
and to be his servants,

56:1–8. In the restored Jerusalem, the temple will begin to open its doors to all peoples. What we were told at the start of the book (cf. 2:2–5) would happen "in the latter days" is beginning to happen: the temple of the Lord will be a house of prayer for those who previously could not enter it; it will be open to all peoples.

The old rulings (Lev 22:25; Deut 23:2–9) did not permit eunuchs or foreigners to take part in the assembly of Israel (a similar approach is found in Ezra 9:1–12 and Nehemiah 9:1–2); but this oracle displays a much more open and universalist attitude (cf. Wis 3:14): there is no objection to eunuchs and foreigners provided that they observe the sabbath and the Covenant (cf. vv. 2, 4, 6). Blood ties are no longer the criteria for membership of the community of the people of God: now it suffices that a person keep to the moral teaching laid down in the old Covenant, and worship the true God.

The mission of the temple, rebuilt by the exiles after their return, with its open invitation to all without exception to come and worship God as part of his people, will reach its fullness in the redemption wrought by Christ Jesus. When he cleanses the temple (Mt 21:12–13 and par.), appealing to the words of v. 6 (along with Jeremiah 7:11; cf. note on same), this prophecy will be fulfilled.

manum suam, ne faciat omne malum. / 3Et non dicat filius advenae, qui adhaeret Domino, / dicens: «Separatione dividet me Dominus a populo suo». / Et non dicat eunuchus: / «Ecce, ego lignum aridum». / 4Quia haec dicit Dominus eunuchis: / «Qui custodierint sabbata mea / et elegerint, quae ego volui, / et tenuerint foedus meum, / 5dabo eis in domo mea et in muris meis / locum et nomen melius a filiis et filiabus: / nomen sempiternum dabo eis, / quod non peribit. / 6Et filios advenae, qui adhaerent Domino, / ut colant eum, / ut diligant nomen Domini, / ut sint ei in servos, / omnes custodientes

every one who keeps the sabbath, and does not profane it,
and holds fast my covenant—
[7]these I will bring to my holy mountain,
and make them joyful in my house of prayer;
their burnt offerings and their sacrifices
will be accepted on my altar;
for my house shall be called a house of prayer
for all peoples.
[8]Thus says the Lord GOD,
who gathers the outcasts of Israel,
I will gather yet others to him
besides those already gathered."[c]

Ps 15:1
1 Kings 8: 41–43
Mt 21:13 par.

Unworthiness of the rulers of Israel

[9]All you beasts of the field, come to devour—
all you beasts in the forest.

56:9–12. The prophet, on behalf of God, has invited foreign nations to come to the Lord's house of prayer (56:1–8), and he will also call others "besides those already gathered" (56:8) because the first to be convoked, that is, the Israelites in the diaspora, were led astray by their pastors. The indolence of those who should have looked after the ordinary people earns them severe reproach (cf. v.10).

"Dumb dogs, they cannot bark" (v. 10): Pope St Gregory the Great, meditating on these words, is reminded of the irresponsibility of Church pastors who fail to denounce errors: "Some imprudent prelates and pastors hesitate to speak clearly because they fear their words will cost them the respect of their people. As the Truth tells us, they are not true shepherds to their flocks; they act like mercenaries, because to fall silent or to dissemble when sins and defects are obvious is the same as running away when wolves appear. The Lord reproves those pastors, when he speaks through the prophet's mouth: *they are all dumb dogs, they cannot bark*" (*Regula pastoralis*, 2, 4). And St Boniface says: "May we not be dumb dogs or silent watchmen, or mercenaries who flee from the wolf, but good shepherds who care for Christ's flock, announcing God's plans to the great and to the humble, to men of all ages and states in life, using all the strength that God gives us, in season and out of season, just as St Gregory wrote in his book on the pastors of the Church" (*Epistolae*, 63).

sabbatum, ne polluant illud, / et tenentes foedus meum, / [7]adducam eos in montem sanctum meum / et laetificabo eos in domo orationis meae: / holocausta eorum et victimae eorum / placebunt mihi super altari meo, / quia domus mea domus orationis / vocabitur cunctis populis». / [8]Ait Dominus Deus, qui congregat dispersos Israel: / «Adhuc congregabo ad eum praeter congregatos eius». / [9]Omnes bestiae

c. Heb *his gathered ones*

Is 3:12; 9:15 10 His watchmen are blind,
they are all without knowledge;
they are all dumb dogs,
they cannot bark;
dreaming, lying down,
loving to slumber.
Jer 10:21; 12:10; 23:1–2 Ezek 34:2 11 The dogs have a mighty appetite;
they never have enough.
The shepherds also have no understanding;
they have all turned to their own way,
each to his own gain, one and all.
Is 5:11; 28:1,7–8 Amos 4:1 Joel 1:5 12 "Come," they say, "let us[d] get wine,
let us fill ourselves with strong drink;
and tomorrow will be like this day,
great beyond measure."

Idolatry denounced

Wis 4:11 57 1 The righteous man perishes,
and no one lays it to heart;
devout men are taken away,
while no one understands.

57:1–13. It is odd to find this oracle here: the sins that it denounces fit in better with the early years of Isaiah's preaching (from 740 BC on). Maybe the reason why it is put here is that it contains criticism of leaders that links up with and fills out what was said in the previous oracle (56:9–12). The words of the oracle are very hard-hitting (v. 3), reminiscent of earlier prophets like Amos. People don't realize that they should urgently entreat the Lord to help them; they act as if he did not exist (v. 11b): they engage in monstrous practices such as the immolation of children (v. 5) and in idol-worship (v. 7), maybe even sacred prostitution ("nakedness", v. 8). Even though the oracle is very crude in its language, ironically it reminds people that idols can do them no service whereas the Lord certainly helps those who are devoted to him (v. 13b). So, for those who stay loyal to the Lord it is in fact an oracle of consolation and hope.

agri, venite ad devorandum, / universae bestiae saltus. / 10 Speculatores eius caeci, omnes nescierunt; / universi sunt canes muti non valentes latrare, / insanientes, cubantes, amantes soporem; / 11 et canes voraces nescierunt saturitatem, / ipsi pastores ignoraverunt intellegentiam: / omnes in viam suam declinaverunt, / unusquisque ad avaritiam suam, / a summo usque ad novissimum. / 12 «Venite, sumam vinum, et impleamur ebrietate; / et cras erit sicut hodie / et multo amplius». **[57]** 1 Iustus perit, et non est qui recogitet in corde suo; / et viri misericordiae colliguntur, / tamen non est qui intellegat: / a facie

d. One ancient Ms Syr Vg Tg: Heb *me*

For the righteous man is taken away from calamity,
2 he enters into peace;
they rest in their beds
who walk in their uprightness.
3 But you, draw near hither,
sons of the sorceress,
offspring of the adulterer and the harlot.
4 Of whom are you making sport?
Against whom do you open your mouth wide
and put out your tongue?
Are you not children of transgression,
the offspring of deceit,
5 you who burn with lust among the oaks, Lev 18:21
under every green tree; Deut 12:2
who slay your children in the valleys, Jer 2:20
under the clefts of the rocks?
6 Among the smooth stones of the valley is your portion;
they, they, are your lot;
to them you have poured out a drink offering,
you have brought a cereal offering.
Shall I be appeased for these things?
7 Upon a high and lofty mountain Deut 23:19
you have set your bed,
and thither you went up to offer sacrifice.
8 Behind the door and the doorpost Ezek 16:15
you have set up your symbol;
for, deserting me, you have uncovered your bed,
you have gone up to it,
you have made it wide;
and you have made a bargain for yourself with them,
you have loved their bed,
you have looked on nakedness.[e]
9 You journeyed to Molech[f] with oil Lev 18:21

---

enim malitiae collectus est iustus. / [2]In pacem ingreditur, requiescit in cubili suo, / qui ambulat in directione sua. / [3]Vos autem accedite huc, filii auguratricis, / semen adulteri et fornicariae. / [4]Super quem luditis? / Super quem dilatatis os et eicitis linguam? / Numquid non vos filii scelesti, semen mendax, / [5]qui exardescitis in terebinthis / subter omne lignum frondosum, / immolantes parvulos in vallibus / subter scissuras petrarum? / [6]In partibus vallis pars tua, / hae sunt sors tua; / et ipsis effundisti libamen, obtulisti sacrificium. / Numquid super his consolabor? / [7]Super montem excelsum et sublimem posuisti cubile tuum, / et illuc ascendisti, ut immolares hostias. / [8]Et post ostium et postem posuisti memoriale tuum; / nam longe a me discooperuisti et ascendisti, / dilatasti cubile tuum, / et pepigisti cum eis foedus; / dilexisti stratum eorum, manum respexisti. / [9]Et ingressa es ad regem cum

e. The meaning of the Hebrew is uncertain **f.** Or *the king*

and multiplied your perfumes;
you sent your envoys far off,
and sent down even to Sheol.
10 You were wearied with the length of your way,
but you did not say, "It is hopeless";
you found new life for your strength,
and so you were not faint.

11 Whom did you dread and fear,
so that you lied,
and did not remember me,
did not give me a thought?
Have I not held my peace, even for a long time,
and so you do not fear me?
12 I will tell of your righteousness and your doings,
but they will not help you.
Ps 37:9 Is 56:7; 60:21; 65:9
13 When you cry out, let your collection of idols deliver you!
The wind will carry them off,
a breath will take them away.
But he who takes refuge in me shall possess the land,
and shall inherit my holy mountain.

Salvation for the humble

14 And it shall be said,
"Build up, build up, prepare the way,
remove every obstruction from my people's way."

57:14–21. This oracle of consolation evokes themes already found in earlier passages of the book: the new exodus (v. 14) is described in words similar to those in 40:1–3; God is depicted as standing above all things but he is also close to those who are humble (v. 15; cf. Ps 51:7): this is reminiscent of the theophany in 6:1–3; the interpretation of the exile as a temporary punishment (v. 17) is in line with the explanation given in 54:8, although here we are told that what drove God to send the people into exile was their covetousness. However, what really grieves the prophet here, as in the previous oracle, is the fact that some of the people are unfaithful to God; he describes them as

unguento / et multiplicasti pigmenta tua; / misisti legatos tuos procul / et humiliata es usque ad inferos. / [10]In multitudine viae tuae laborasti; / non dixisti: «Vanum est!». / Vitam manus tuae invenisti, / propterea non aegrotasti. / [11]Pro quo sollicita timuisti, / quia mentita es et mei non es recordata / neque cogitasti in corde tuo? / Nonne, quia ego tacui et longo tempore, / me non times? / [12]Ego annuntiabo iustitiam tuam / et opera tua, quae non proderunt tibi. / [13]Cum clamaveris, liberent te lucra tua; / et omnia illa auferet ventus, tollet aura. / Qui autem fiduciam habet in me, hereditabit terram / et possidebit montem sanctum meum. / [14]Et dicent: «Sternite, sternite, / parate viam, auferte offendicula

[15] For thus says the high and lofty One
who inhabits eternity, whose name is Holy:
"I dwell in the high and holy place,
and also with him who is of a contrite and humble spirit,
to revive the spirit of the humble,
and to revive the heart of the contrite.
[16] For I will not contend for ever,
nor will I always be angry;
for from me proceeds the spirit,
and I have made the breath of life.
[17] Because of the iniquity of his covetousness I was angry,
I smote him, I hid my face and was angry;
but he went on backsliding in the way of his own heart.
[18] I have seen his ways, but I will heal him;
I will lead him and requite him with comfort,
creating for his mourners the fruit of the lips.
[19] Peace, peace, to the far and to the near, says the LORD;
and I will heal him.
[20] But the wicked are like the tossing sea;
for it cannot rest,
and its waters toss up mire and dirt.
[21] There is no peace, says my God, for the wicked."

Lev 17:1
Ps 51:19
Is 54:8
Ex 15:26
Is 61:2–3
Jer 3:22
Acts 2:39
Eph 2:17
Heb 13:15
Is 48:22

"wicked", and they earn the same condemnation as that given in 48:20: for them "there is no peace" (v. 21).

The sacred author of this part of the book is not trying to be original in what he says, but he is updating teaching already known, to console those who are faithful and encourage them to persevere—and to try to get self-centred and impious people to see where they have gone wrong and to change their lives.

Verse 19 is quoted by St Paul in Ephesians 2:17–18, when he teaches that Christ's work of Redemption has brought Jews and Gentiles together in peace, and has reconciled them all to God.

de via populi mei». / [15]Quia haec dicit Excelsus et Sublimis, / habitans aeternitatem, et sanctum nomen eius: / «Excelsus et sanctus habito / et cum contrito et humili spiritu, / ut vivificem spiritum humilium / et vivificem cor contritorum. / [16]Non enim in sempiternum litigabo / neque usque ad finem irascar, / quia spiritus a facie mea deficeret, / halitus, quem ego feci. / [17]Propter iniquitatem avaritiae eius iratus sum et percussi eum, / abscondi faciem meam et indignatus sum; / et abiit vagus in via cordis sui. / [18]Vias eius vidi et sanabo eum et reducam eum / et reddam consolationes ipsi et lugentibus eius. / [19]Creo fructum labiorum pacem; / pacem ei, qui longe est et qui prope, dixit Dominus, / et sanabo eum». / [20]Impii autem quasi mare fervens, / quod quiescere non potest, / et redundant fluctus eius in limum et lutum. / [21]Non est pax impiis, dicit Deus meus.

Misguided fasting denounced

58 [1]"Cry aloud, spare not,
lift up your voice like a trumpet;
declare to my people their transgression,
to the house of Jacob their sins.

58:1–14. This new denunciation, very much in the style of this part of the book, criticizes fasting done in the wrong spirit; it is uncompromising (vv. 1–7) but it ends with words of encouragement. The Lord cannot go along with the hypocrisy of a purely external religion—with people going through the motions of religious observance while being unjust in their dealings with others and ignoring those in need. Those who act in this way cannot know much about God: this is why the prophet feels compelled to speak out and use every opportunity to correct them.

"They seek me daily" (v. 2), that is, they are keen to hear the oracles spoken by the prophets, to learn what God is saying, but they do not act on them—which shows that they do not really know what religion is all about. Conversion to God is not a matter of engaging in many external acts of worship and fasting, while being unjust, exploiting workers and neglecting the poor. It is not surprising that God ignores fasts if those who perform them commit sins against justice and charity (vv. 3–6). In this poem different people's voices are heard at different points: first God tells the prophet to keep on condemning hypocrisy (vv. 1–2); then men speak, complaining that God ignores their fasting (v. 3); and at the end God teaches and reproaches: he will have nothing to do with the hypocrisy of those who perform fasts but behave wickedly (vv. 4–7); whereas he will certainly listen to prayers if they are accompanied by acts of justice and charity (vv. 8–14).

The works of mercy recommended in this oracle are echoed in Jesus' discourse on the Last Judgment in Matthew 25:23–45. Christian spirituality has always stressed that love of neighbour and works of mercy are clear proof of a person's love of God and are a touchstone of true religion, for "... works of mercy are proof of a truly holy life". Rabanus Maurus, recorded by St Thomas Aquinas in the *Catena Aurea*). And St Leo the Great taught: "Let each of the faithful examine his own conscience, seeking out his deepest desires; if he finds the fruits of love within his soul, he will know that God is with him, and he should strive even harder to be worthy of so great a guest, being ever more generous in his works of mercy" (*Sermones*, 48, 3).

58:1. "Cry out, spare not": these words, addressed to the prophet to have him denounce sins, are a call to all whose responsibility it is to guide souls: they should work diligently and without pause. And, in times of difficulties or special need or upheaval, pastors as well as faithful would do

[58] [1]Clama fortiter, ne cesses; / quasi tuba exalta vocem tuam / et annuntia populo meo scelera eorum / et domui Iacob peccata eorum. / [2]Me etenim de die in diem quaerunt et scire vias meas volunt, / quasi

[2]Yet they seek me daily,
and delight to know my ways,
as if they were a nation that did righteousness
and did not forsake the ordinance of their God;
they ask of me righteous judgments,
they delight to draw near to God.
[3]'Why have we fasted, and thou seest it not? Mal 3:14
Why have we humbled ourselves, and thou takest no
knowledge of it?'
Behold, in the day of your fast you seek your own pleasure,[g]
and oppress all your workers.
[4]Behold, you fast only to quarrel and to fight
and to hit with wicked fist.
Fasting like yours this day
will not make your voice to be heard on high.
[5]Is such the fast that I choose,
a day for a man to humble himself?
Is it to bow down his head like a rush,
and to spread sackcloth and ashes under him?
Will you call this a fast,
and a day acceptable to the LORD?

Jer 34:8–9
Amos 5:21
Mt 25:34–40

[6]"Is not this the fast that I choose:
to loose the bonds of wickedness,
to undo the thongs of the yoke,
to let the oppressed go free,
and to break every yoke?

---

well to remember this message, seeking guidance and praying more intensely.

"If you feel no devotion and your heart is dry, continue to pray: call and cry without ceasing until your prayer wins a scrap or drop of grace to restore you; you need Me; I do not need you" (Thomas à Kempis, *De imitatione Christi*, 12, 3).

gens, quae iustitiam fecerit / et iudicium Dei sui non dereliquerit. / Rogant me iudicia iustitiae, / appropinquare Deum volunt. / [3]«Quare ieiunavimus, et non aspexisti, / humiliavimus animam nostram, et nescisti?». / Ecce, in die ieiunii vestri agitis negotia / et omnes operarios vestros opprimitis. / [4]Ecce, ad lites et contentiones ieiunatis / et percutitis pugno impie. / Nolite ieiunare sicut hodie, / ut audiatur in excelso clamor vester. / [5]Numquid tale est ieiunium, quod elegi, / dies, quo homo affligit animam suam? / Numquid contorquere quasi iuncum caput suum / et saccum et cinerem sternere? / Numquid istud vocabis ieiunium / et diem acceptabilem Domino? / [6]Nonne hoc est ieiunium, quod elegi: / dissolvere vincula iniqua, / solvere funes iugi, / dimittere eos, qui confracti sunt, liberos, / et omne

g. Or *pursue your own business*

7 Is it not to share your bread with the hungry,
and bring the homeless poor into your house;
Is 52:12 when you see the naked, to cover him,
and not to hide yourself from your own flesh?
8 Then shall your light break forth like the dawn,
and your healing shall spring up speedily;
your righteousness shall go before you,
the glory of the LORD shall be your rear guard.
9 Then you shall call, and the LORD will answer;
you shall cry, and he will say, Here I am.

Jn 8:12 "If you take away from the midst of you the yoke,
the pointing of the finger, and speaking wickedness,
10 if you pour yourself out for the hungry
and satisfy the desire of the afflicted,
Jn 4:14 then shall your light rise in the darkness
and your gloom be as the noonday.
11 And the LORD will guide you continually,
and satisfy your desire with good things,[h]
and make your bones strong;
and you shall be like a watered garden,
like a spring of water,
whose waters fail not.
Is 61:4 12 And your ancient ruins shall be rebuilt;
Neh 3ff you shall raise up the foundations of many generations;
you shall be called the repairer of the breach,
the restorer of streets to dwell in.

Is 56:2 13 "If you turn back your foot from the sabbath,
from doing your pleasure[i] on my holy day,
and call the sabbath a delight
and the holy day of the LORD honourable;

---

iugum dirumpere? / 7Nonne frangere esurienti panem tuum, / et egenos, vagos inducere in domum? / Cum videris nudum, operi eum / et carnem tuam ne despexeris. / 8Tunc erumpet quasi aurora lumen tuum, / et sanatio tua citius orietur; / et anteibit faciem tuam iustitia tua, / et gloria Domini colliget te. / 9Tunc invocabis, et Dominus exaudiet; / clamabis, et dicet: «Ecce adsum». / Si abstuleris de medio tui iugum / et desieris extendere digitum / et loqui iniquitatem; / 10si effuderis esurienti animam tuam / et animam afflictam satiaveris, / orietur in tenebris lux tua, / et caligo tua erit sicut meridies. / 11Et te ducet Dominus semper, / et satiabit in locis aridis animam tuam / et ossa tua firmabit; / et eris quasi hortus irriguus / et sicut fons aquarum, / cuius non deficient aquae. / 12Et reaedificabit gens tua ruinas antiquas; / fundamenta generationis et generationis suscitabis: / et vocaberis restitutor ruinarum, / instaurator viarum, ut habitentur. / 13Si averteris a sabbato pedem tuum, / facere negotia tua in die

h. The meaning of the Hebrew word is uncertain **i.** Or *business*

if you honour it, not going your own ways,
or seeking your own pleasure,[j] or talking idly;
14 then you shall take delight in the LORD, Deut 32:13
and I will make you ride upon the heights of the earth; Is 1:20; 40:5
I will feed you with the heritage of Jacob your father,
for the mouth of the LORD has spoken."

Salvation for those who admit their sin

59 1 Behold, the LORD's hand is not shortened, that it cannot Is 50:2
save,
or his ear dull, that it cannot hear;
2 but your iniquities have made a separation Deut 31:17
between you and your God, Is 1:15
and your sins have hid his face from you
so that he does not hear.
3 For your hands are defiled with blood

59:1–21. The prophet is replying to complaints that the Lord's salvation is slow in coming. The power of God is as great as ever (v. 1); the sinfulness of men is the reason why salvation is delayed (vv. 2–8); people need to acknowledge their sins and turn back to God (vv. 9–15a). The Lord repays people according to their deeds; so, when the children of Jacob are converted, then will Zion be redeemed (vv. 15b–20). In v. 21 (which is in prose) God himself speaks, to confirm his everlasting Covenant with those who turn back to him. St Thomas Aquinas comments: "This passage explains the preparation needed for salvation: first, the need for salvation is set forth (vv. 1–15a), and then the preparation for it, *The Lord saw it* ... (vv.15b–21)" (*Expositio super Isaiam*, 59).

59:1. The prophet's reflections have led him to make this point which is a source of consolation for people whenever doubts cross their mind or they feel discouraged because God has apparently neglected them: "'The arm of the Lord has not been shortened' (Is 59:1). God is no less powerful today than he was in other times; his love for man is no less true. Our faith teaches us that all creation, the movement of the earth and the other heavenly bodies, the good actions of creatures and all the good that has been achieved in history,

sancto meo, / et vocaveris sabbatum delicias / et diem Domino sacrum gloriosum; / et glorificaveris eum relinquens vias tuas / et negotia tua et sermones tuos, / 14tunc delectaberis super Domino; / et vehi te faciam super altitudines terrae / et cibabo te hereditate Iacob patris tui. / Os enim Domini locutum est. **[59]** 1Ecce non est abbreviata manus Domini, / ut salvare nequeat, / neque aggravata est auris eius, / ut non exaudiat; / 2sed iniquitates vestrae diviserunt / inter vos et Deum vestrum, / et peccata vestra absconderunt faciem eius / a vobis, ne exaudiret. / 3Manus enim vestrae pollutae sunt sanguine,

j. Or *pursuing your own business*

and your fingers with iniquity;
your lips have spoken lies,
your tongue mutters wickedness.
Job 15:35 [4]No one enters suit justly,
Ps 7:15 no one goes to law honestly;
Jas 1:15 they rely on empty pleas, they speak lies,
they conceive mischief and bring forth iniquity.
Mt 3:7 [5]They hatch adders' eggs,
they weave the spider's web;
he who eats their eggs dies,
and from one which is crushed a viper is hatched.
[6]Their webs will not serve as clothing;
men will not cover themselves with what they make.
Their works are works of iniquity,
and deeds of violence are in their hands.
Prov 1:16 *Rom 3:15–17* [7]Their feet run to evil,
and they make haste to shed innocent blood;
their thoughts are thoughts of iniquity,
desolation and destruction are in their highways.
[8]The way of peace they know not,
and there is no justice in their paths;
they have made their roads crooked,
no one who goes in them knows peace.

Jer 8:15 Jn 8:12 Amos 5:18–20 [9]Therefore justice is far from us,
and righteousness does not overtake us;
we look for light, and behold, darkness,

---

in short everything, comes from God and is directed towards him" (St Josemaría Escrivá, *Christ Is Passing By*, 130).

59:4. "They conceive mischief and bring forth iniquity": a sapiential proverb, also found elsewhere (Job 15:35; Ps 7:14), showing that evil follows an inexorable course unless one takes action to stop it. It begins with being careless in little things and ends in committing grave sins that lead to eternal death (cf. Jas 1:15).

/ et digiti vestri iniquitate; / labia vestra locuta sunt mendacium, / et lingua vestra iniquitatem fatur. / [4]Non est qui invocet iustitiam, / neque est qui iudicet vere; / confidunt in nihilo et loquuntur vanitates: / conceperunt laborem et pepererunt iniquitatem. / [5]Ova aspidum rumpunt / et telas araneae texunt; / qui comederit de ovis eorum, morietur, / et, quod fractum est, erumpet in regulum. / [6]Telae eorum non erunt in vestimentum, / neque operientur operibus suis; / opera eorum opera iniquitatis, / et facinora violentiae in manibus eorum. / [7]Pedes eorum ad malum currunt / et festinant, ut effundant sanguinem innocentem; / cogitationes eorum cogitationes iniquitatis, / vastitas et contritio in viis eorum. / [8]Viam pacis nescierunt, / et non est iudicium in gressibus eorum; / semitae eorum incurvatae sunt eis: / omnis, qui calcat in eis, ignorat pacem. / [9]Propter hoc elongatum est iudicium a nobis, / et non apprehendit nos

and for brightness, but we walk in gloom.
[10] We grope for the wall like the blind, — Deut 28:29
we grope like those who have no eyes;
we stumble at noon as in the twilight,
among those in full vigor we are like dead men.
[11] We all growl like bears,
we moan and moan like doves;
we look for justice, but there is none;
for salvation, but it is far from us.
[12] For our transgressions are multiplied before thee, — Ps 51:5
and our sins testify against us; — Jer 14:7
for our transgressions are with us,
and we know our iniquities:
[13] transgressing, and denying the LORD,
and turning away from following our God,
speaking oppression and revolt,
conceiving and uttering from the heart lying words.
[14] Justice is turned back,
and righteousness stands afar off;
for truth has fallen in the public squares,
and uprightness cannot enter.
[15] Truth is lacking,
and he who departs from evil makes himself a prey.

The LORD saw it, and it displeased him
that there was no justice.
[16] He saw that there was no man, — Is 63:5
and wondered that there was no one to intervene;
then his own arm brought him victory,
and his righteousness upheld him.

---

iustitia; / exspectamus lucem, et ecce tenebrae, / splendorem, et in caligine ambulamus. / [10]Palpamus sicut caeci parietem / et quasi absque oculis attrectamus; / impegimus meridie quasi in crepusculo, / inter sanos quasi mortui. / [11]Rugimus quasi ursi omnes / et quasi columbae gementes gemimus; / exspectamus iudicium, et non est, / salutem, et elongata est a nobis. / [12]Multiplicatae sunt enim iniquitates nostrae coram te, / et peccata nostra respondent nobis; / quia scelera nostra nobiscum, / et iniquitates nostras cognovimus: / [13]peccare et mentiri contra Dominum / et recedere a Deo nostro, / loqui violentiam et transgressionem, / concipere et murmurare de corde verba mendacii. / [14]Et conversum est retrorsum iudicium, / et iustitia longe stat, / quia corruit in platea veritas, / et aequitas non potuit ingredi. / [15]Et facta est veritas in oblivionem, / et, qui recedit a malo, spoliatur. / Et vidit Dominus, et malum apparuit in oculis eius, / quia non est iudicium. / [16]Et vidit quia non est vir, / et aporiatus est, quia non est qui occurrat; / et salvavit sibi brachium suum, / et iustitia eius ipsa confirmavit eum. / [17]Indutus est iustitia ut lorica, / et galea salutis in capite eius; / indutus est

Wis 5:17–20 Eph 6:14–17 1 Thess 5:8

[17] He put on righteousness as a breastplate,
  and a helmet of salvation upon his head;
he put on garments of vengeance for clothing,
  and wrapped himself in fury as a mantle.
[18] According to their deeds, so will he repay,
  wrath to his adversaries, requital to his enemies;
  to the coastlands he will render requital.
[19] So they shall fear the name of the LORD from the west,
  and his glory from the rising of the sun;
for he will come like a rushing stream,
  which the wind of the LORD drives.

Is 41:14 *Rom 11:26–27* Is 55:3 2 Sam 23:2 Is 51:16 Jer 1:9

[20] "And he will come to Zion as Redeemer,
  to those in Jacob who turn from transgression, says the LORD.
[21] "And as for me, this is my covenant with them, says the LORD:
my spirit which is upon you, and my words which I have put in
your mouth, shall not depart out of your mouth, or out of the
mouth of your children, or out of the mouth of your children's
children, says the LORD, from this time forth and for evermore."

59:17. The salvific action of God is described here in terms of the "spiritual armour" that he wears. The same imagery occurs later in Wisdom 5:17–20; St Paul will use it in connexion with the spiritual battles that a Christian has to engage in; and it became a favourite image with spiritual writers: "Your baptism is a shield, faith is your helmet, love your lance, and patience your suit of armour. Your arsenal is made up of all the good works that will earn you your just reward" (St Ignatius of Antioch, *Ad Polycarpum*, 6).

vestimentis ultionis / et operuit se zelo quasi pallio. / [18]Secundum opera sic retribuet: / iram hostibus suis, / retributionem inimicis suis, / insulis vicem reddet. / [19]Et timebunt, qui ab occidente, nomen Domini, / et, qui ab ortu solis, gloriam eius, / cum venerit quasi fluvius violentus, / quem spiritus Domini cogit. / [20]Et veniet pro Sion redemptor / et eis, qui redeunt ab iniquitate in Iacob, / dixit Dominus. / [21]Hoc foedus meum cum eis, / dixit Dominus: / «Spiritus meus, qui est super te, / et verba mea, quae posui in ore tuo, / non recedent de ore tuo / et de ore seminis tui / et de ore seminis seminis tui, / dixit Dominus, amodo et usque in sempiternum».

2. THE GLORY OF JERUSALEM AND SALVATION FOR THE NATIONS*

Is 45:14
Rev 21:9–27

A radiant new Jerusalem

60 [1]Arise, shine; for your light has come,
and the glory of the LORD has risen upon you.

Is 45:15
Mic 4:2
Ex 24:16; Is 9:1

***60:1—64:11.** In the central section of Third Isaiah, the restored Jerusalem has a wonderful radiance; it is the dwelling place of the glory of the Lord, and from it all the nations will hear about God's salvation. These are chapters that shine with hope and joy. In the opening verses, Jerusalem, the Lord's spouse, is invited to leap with joy, for the glory of the Lord will light up the holy city, which will become a beacon for the nations (60:1–22). From there, too, the Lord's herald proclaims the good news of salvation to the poor, the oppressed and all who labour under some burden (61:1–11). The holy city will radiate righteousness for all the nations to see (62:1–12). Finally, the Lord, depicted as a conqueror, enthroned in a glorious Jerusalem, is proclaimed as the sovereign lord who will judge and reward and punish (63:1—64:11).

60:1–22. These verses are a magnificent hymn to Jerusalem, completely restored, idealized; the prophet does not need to identify it by name. The most remarkable feature of the city is its radiance, mentioned at the start and end of the poem (vv. 1–3 and 19–22): it stems from the glory of the Lord, who has made the city's temple his dwelling-place. The city acts as a magnet for all the nations, not only because it instructs them by means of the Law and by the word of God, as we heard at the start of the book (2:2–4; cf. Mic 4:1–3) but also because they are in awe of its splendour. The central verses of the poem rejoice in the pilgrimages that make their way to the holy city: first, those of Israelites, who had been scattered across the world: the pilgrims are most happy and they bear rich gifts for the Lord (vv. 4–9). Foreigners will come, too, and they will bring precious materials to reconstruct and embellish the city they previously destroyed. The obeisance they must do corresponds to the harm they did earlier (vv. 10–14). But the most important event is the arrival of the Lord who will bring gifts in abundance, the most precious being peace (vv. 15–10) and light (vv. 19–22). This picture of the new Jerusalem (one would expect) must have raised the spirits of those engaged in the final stages of the rebuilding of the temple.

This poem clearly has resonances with the eschatological description of the heavenly Jerusalem in the Revelation to John (cf. Rev 21:9–27). Some of the wording is virtually the same: cf. v. 3 with Rev 21:24 ("By its light shall the nations work; and the kings of the earth shall bring their glory into it"); v. 11

[60] [1]Surge, illuminare, quia venit lumen tuum, / et gloria Domini super te orta est. / [2]Quia ecce tenebrae operient terram / et caligo populos; / super te autem orietur Dominus, / et gloria eius in te

[2]For behold, darkness shall cover the earth,
and thick darkness the peoples;
but the LORD will arise upon you,
and his glory will be seen upon you.
Rev 21:24 [3]And nations shall come to your light,
and kings to the brightness of your rising.

Is 49:18–22 [4]Lift up your eyes round about, and see;
Bar 5:5–6 they all gather together, they come to you;
your sons shall come from far,
and your daughters shall be carried in the arms.
Ps 72:10 [5]Then you shall see and be radiant,
your heart shall thrill and rejoice;[k]
because the abundance of the sea shall be turned to you,
the wealth of the nations shall come to you.

---

with Rev 21:25–26 ("its gates shall never be shut by day—and there will be no night there"); v. 14 with Rev 3:9 ("I will make them come and bow down before your feet"); v. 19 with Rev 21:23 ("the city has no need of sun or moon to shine upon it, for the glory of God is its light, and its lamp is the Lamb") and 22:5 ("night shall be no more; they need no light of lamp or sun, for the Lord God will be their light, and they shall reign for ever and ever"). The hopes harboured by the early Christians (and the consolation to which the new people of God look forward) are in continuity with the hope felt by the ancient people of Israel. The message of Isaiah and that of the book of Revelation were each (in different historical contexts) calling for firm faith in the Saviour of all. The New Testament fills out the Old by openly declaring that God saves us through his Son, Jesus Christ.

60:4–9. The pilgrimage described here comes from all corners of the earth, and yet it is a familial one. It is made up of people who were scattered throughout the known world, and not just those exiled in Babylon. Those from the west come by sea (v. 5), bearing the sort of goods normally transported by sea, particularly by Greek and Phoenician merchants. Those from the east, from the Arabian peninsula (Kedar and Nebaioth) and further afield will travel in caravans bringing precious commodities typical of the area—silver, gold etc. (v. 6). The visit of the Magi, who came bearing presents to adore Jesus, is in line with the sort of commerce that was current at the time, and it is probably connected with this text

videbitur. / [3]Et ambulabunt gentes in lumine tuo, / et reges in splendore ortus tui. / [4]Leva in circuitu oculos tuos et vide: / omnes isti congregati sunt, venerunt tibi; / filii tui de longe veniunt, / et filiae tuae in ulnis gestantur. / [5]Tunc videbis et illuminaberis, / et palpitabit et dilatabitur cor tuum, / quia confluet

k. Heb *be enlarged*

[6]A multitude of camels shall cover you, Ex 2:15
the young camels of Midian and Ephah; 1 Kings 10:1
all those from Sheba shall come.
They shall bring gold and frankincense,
and shall proclaim the praise of the LORD.
[7]All the flocks of Kedar shall be gathered to you, Gen 25:13
the rams of Nebaioth shall minister to you;
they shall come up with acceptance on my altar,
and I will glorify my glorious house.

[8]Who are these that fly like a cloud,
and like doves to their windows?
[9]For the coastlands shall wait for me, Ps 48:8
the ships of Tarshish first, Is 55:5
to bring your sons from far,

---

of Isaiah. Certainly, when this passage is read in the liturgy on the Solemnity of the Epiphany, the implication is that those rich gifts brought to the temple in honour of the Lord prefigure those that the Magi offered to him who is truly the "Lord your God", "the Holy One of Israel" (v. 9). "Today, the wise man finds lying in a manger the One he had searched for as a brilliant light shining among the stars. Today, the wise man sees wrapped in swaddling clothes the One he long sought to find, unveiled, in the heavens. Today, to his great surprise, the wise man discerns in what he studies: heaven on earth, earth in the heavens, man in God, and God in man; what the whole universe could not contain inhabits the body of a child. And seeing all this, he believes and doubts no more; and he announces it to all, using his mystical powers: incense for God, gold for the King, and myrrh for the One who will die. Today, the Gentile who was once last is first, because the faith of the wise man sanctifies the belief of all the peoples" (St Peter Chrysologus, *Sermones*, 160). And Eusebius of Caesarea comments: "The conversion of the Gentiles glorifies the Church of God in a special way. The prophecy, *I will glorify my glorious house* [60:7], is fulfilled. This promise was made to the old Jerusalem, the mother of the new city, who, as has already been said, was the community of all among the ancient people who lived righteous lives—the prophets and patriarchs, all just men, those to whom the coming of Christ was first proclaimed" (*Commentaria in Isaiam*, 60, 6–7).

ad te multitudo maris, / fortitudo gentium veniet tibi; / [6]inundatio camelorum operiet te, / dromedarii Madian et Epha; / omnes de Saba venient, / aurum et tus deferentes / et laudem Domini annuntiantes. / [7]Omne pecus Cedar congregabitur tibi, / arietes Nabaioth ministrabunt tibi; / offerentur super placabili altari meo, / et domum gloriae meae glorificabo. / [8]Quae sunt istae, quae ut nubes volant, / et quasi columbae ad fenestras suas? / [9]Me enim insulae exspectabunt, / et in principio naves Tharsis, / ut adducant filios tuos de longe, / argentum eorum et aurum eorum cum eis, / nomini Domini Dei tui et

their silver and gold with them,
for the name of the LORD your God,
and for the Holy One of Israel,
because he has glorified you.

Is 49:17 10 Foreigners shall build up your walls,
and their kings shall minister to you;
for in my wrath I smote you,
but in my favour I have had mercy on you.
Rev 21:25–26 11 Your gates shall be open continually;
day and night they shall not be shut;
that men may bring to you the wealth of the nations,
with their kings led in procession.
12 For the nation and kingdom
that will not serve you shall perish;
those nations shall be utterly laid waste.
1 Kings 5:19–20 Is 35:2 13 The glory of Lebanon shall come to you,
the cypress, the plane, and the pine,
to beautify the place of my sanctuary;
and I will make the place of my feet glorious.
Is 1:26; 49:23 Rev 3:9 14 The sons of those who oppressed you
shall come bending low to you;
and all who despised you
shall bow down at your feet;
they shall call you the City of the LORD,
the Zion of the Holy One of Israel.

Is 62:4,12 15 Whereas you have been forsaken and hated,
with no one passing through,
I will make you majestic for ever,
a joy from age to age.
Is 49:23,26 16 You shall suck the milk of nations,
you shall suck the breast of kings;
and you shall know that I, the LORD, am your Saviour
and your Redeemer, the Mighty One of Jacob.

Sancto Israel, / quia glorificavit te. / 10Et aedificabunt filii peregrinorum muros tuos, / et reges eorum ministrabunt tibi; / in indignatione enim mea percussi te, / sed in beneplacito meo misertus sum tui. / 11Et aperientur portae tuae iugiter, / die ac nocte non claudentur, / ut afferatur ad te fortitudo gentium, / et reges earum adducantur. / 12Gens enim et regnum, quae non servierint tibi, peribunt, / et gentes vastitate vastabuntur. / 13Gloria Libani ad te veniet, / cupressus, ulmus et abies simul, / ad ornandum locum sanctuarii mei; / et locum pedum meorum glorificabo. / 14Et venient ad te curvi filii eorum, qui humiliaverunt te, / et adorabunt vestigia pedum tuorum omnes, qui detrahebant tibi, et vocabunt te Civitatem Domini, / Sion Sancti Israel. / 15Pro eo quod fuisti derelicta et odio habita, / et non erat qui

[17] Instead of bronze I will bring gold, Is 1:26
and instead of iron I will bring silver;
instead of wood, bronze,
instead of stones, iron.
I will make your overseers peace
and your taskmasters righteousness.
[18] Violence shall no more be heard in your land,
devastation or destruction within your borders;
you shall call your walls Salvation,
and your gates Praise.

[19] The sun shall be no more Rev 21:23; 22:5
your light by day,
nor for brightness shall the moon
give light to you by night;[l]
but the LORD will be your everlasting light,
and your God will be your glory.
[20] Your sun shall no more go down,
nor your moon withdraw itself;
for the LORD will be your everlasting light,
and your days of mourning shall be ended.
[21] Your people shall all be righteous; Is 57:13
they shall possess the land for ever,
the shoot of my planting, the work of my hands,
that I might be glorified.
[22] The least one shall become a clan,
and the smallest one a mighty nation;
I am the LORD;
in its time I will hasten it.

---

per te transiret, / ponam te in superbiam saeculorum, / gaudium in generationem et generationem; / [16]et suges lac gentium / et mamilla regum lactaberis / et scies quia ego Dominus salvator tuus, / et redemptor tuus Fortis Iacob. / [17]Pro aere afferam aurum / et pro ferro afferam argentum / et pro lignis aes / et pro lapidibus ferrum; / et ponam custodes tuos pacem / et praepositos tuos iustitiam. / [18]Non audietur ultra violentia in terra tua, / vastitas et contritio in terminis tuis; / et vocabis Salutem muros tuos / et portas tuas Laudem. / [19]Non erit tibi amplius sol ad lucendum per diem, / nec splendor lunae illuminabit te, / sed erit tibi Dominus in lucem sempiternam, / et Deus tuus in gloriam tuam. / [20]Non occidet ultra sol tuus, / et luna tua non minuetur, / quia erit tibi Dominus in lucem sempiternam, / et complebuntur dies luctus tui. / [21]Populus autem tuus omnes iusti; / in perpetuum hereditabunt terram, / germen plantationis meae, / opus manus meae ad glorificandum. / [22]Minimus erit in mille, / et parvulus in gentem fortem. / Ego Dominus in tempore eius subito faciam istud.

l. One ancient Ms Gk Old Latin Tg: Heb lacks *by night*

Is 11:2; 42:1
Mt 3:16
Lk 4:18–19

The herald of good tidings

61 [1]*The Spirit of the Lord GOD is upon me,
because the LORD has anointed me
to bring good tidings to the afflicted;[m]
he has sent me to bind up the brokenhearted,
to proclaim liberty to the captives,
and the opening of the prison[n] to those who are bound;

61:1–11. Into the air of great joy reflected in the previous hymn, the prophet inserts this very important oracle about the new messenger (vv. 1–3). The rest of the chapter is made up of three stanzas that celebrate the wonders of the holy city. These can be seen in profound, spiritual renewal (vv. 4–7), perfect fulfilment of the promises made to the ancient patriarchs (vv. 8–9), and joy-in-worship, comparable to that of bridegroom and bride, or that of the farmer on seeing a rich harvest (vv. 10–11).

The remarkable events and features of the city point to the time of the End, the time of the Lord's definitive, salvific intervention. In this context, these new things are ultimate and definitive. Because in the New Testament the Church is called "God's building" (1 Cor 3:9), erected on the foundation of the apostles (1 Cor 3:11), Christian tradition has seen the new, glorious Jerusalem as a symbol of the Church that makes its way through this world and will be made manifest at the end of time (cf. *Catechism of the Catholic Church*, 756–757).

61:1–3. This very compact oracle depicts the eschatological messenger speaking a soliloquy. It is one of the key passages in the book of Isaiah. It clearly has connexions with the songs of the Servant, especially the second song (49:1–6). The pouring out of the Spirit involves anointing, as in the case of the king (cf. 11:2) and in that of the Servant of the Lord (42:1). But the messenger is more than a king, more than a prophet, more than the community dwelling in the holy city in the latter days. His mission is a dual one—to be a messenger and a comforter. As a messenger, like a king's ambassador in times of war, he brings good tidings: he announces redemption for slaves, release for prisoners (cf. Jer 34:8, 17). His message proclaims a new order of things where there will be no need for repression, and where concord and well-being will prevail. The "year of the Lord's favour" (v. 2) is similar to the jubilee year (cf. Lev 25:8–19) or the sabbatical year (cf. Ex 21:2–11; Jer 34:14; Ezek 46:17) in the sense that it is a day chosen by the Lord, and different from any other; but here it means the point at which God shows himself to be most gracious and bestows definitive salvation (cf. 49:8). It is also called the day of vengeance

[61] [1]Spiritus Domini Dei super me, / eo quod unxerit Dominus me; / ad annuntiandum laeta mansuetis misit me, / ut mederer contritis corde / et praedicarem captivis liberationem / et clausis apertionem; /

m. Or *poor* **n.** Or *the opening of the eyes*: Heb *the opening*

[2]to proclaim the year of the LORD'S favour,
and the day of vengeance of our God;
to comfort all who mourn;
[3]to grant to those who mourn in Zion—
to give them a garland instead of ashes,
the oil of gladness instead of mourning,
the mantle of praise instead of a faint spirit;
that they may be called oaks of righteousness,
the planting of the LORD, that he may be glorified.

Lev 25:10
Mt 5:5

(v. 2) because on that day, essentially a day of good news, the wicked, too, will receive their just deserts.

As a comforter he will bind up hearts broken by illness or misfortune, and give encouragement to those who weep and revive those who mourn in Zion. When the comforter is the Lord or a messenger of his (cf. 40:1), one can expect him to re-establish his people, to set things right, (the way they were at the beginning), to renew the broken Covenant and re-establish institutions that had been dismantled, that is, bring about a situation where everything is in plentiful supply.

People who have reached rock bottom (the poor, prisoners etc.) will be given a place of honour on that day, and a wreath, perfume and a mantle of praise (v. 3). In sacred texts of the post-exilic period, the concept of the "poor" (or "afflicted": cf. note **m**) already went beyond the social category of those least well off: it had a religious connotation, meaning "the humble", those who saw themselves as having no value before God and who simply put their faith in his divine mercy. The final definition of the "poor" will emerge in the Beatitudes (Mt 5:3–12).

In Jesus' time, Jewish tradition, found in the targum or Aramaic translation of the Bible, considered the messenger described here to be a prophet (and for that reason it introduced this oracle with the words "Thus says the prophet"). So, when Jesus reads this passage in the synagogue of Nazareth he points out that "today the scripture has been fulfilled" (Lk 4:21) and that he is the prophet of whom Isaiah spoke. By doing so, he is saying that he is the Messiah, the Christ, the one anointed by the Holy Spirit (cf. Is 11:2), not so much as a king but as a prophet who proclaims salvation. Ever since then, Christian teaching sees Jesus as the last messenger sent by the Holy Spirit: "The prophet presents the Messiah as the one who comes in the Holy Spirit, the one who possesses the fullness of this Spirit in himself and at the same time for others, for Israel, for all the nations, for all humanity. The fullness of the Spirit of God is accompanied by many different gifts, the treasures of salvation, destined in a particular way for the poor and suffering, for all those who open their hearts to these gifts—sometimes through the painful experi-

[2]ut praedicarem annum placabilem Domino / et diem ultionis Deo nostro; / ut consolarer omnes lugentes, / [3]ut ponerem lugentibus Sion / et darem eis coronam pro cinere, / oleum gaudii pro luctu, /

Is 58:12 4They shall build up the ancient ruins,
they shall raise up the former devastations;
they shall repair the ruined cities,
the devastations of many generations.

Is 14:1 5Aliens shall stand and feed your flocks,
foreigners shall be your ploughmen and vinedressers;
Ex 19:6 6but you shall be called the priests of the LORD,
Is 66:21 men shall speak of you as the ministers of our God;
1 Pet 2:9 you shall eat the wealth of the nations,
Rev 1:6 and in their riches you shall glory.
7Instead of your shame you shall have a double portion,
instead of dishonour you[o] shall rejoice in your[p] lot;
therefore in your[p] land you[o] shall possess a double portion;
yours[q] shall be everlasting joy.

Is 55:3 8For I the LORD love justice,
I hate robbery and wrong;[r]
I will faithfully give them their recompense,
and I will make an everlasting covenant with them.

---

ence of their own existence—but first of all through that interior availability which comes from faith. The aged Simeon, the 'righteous and devout man' upon whom 'rested the Holy Spirit', sensed this at the moment of Jesus' presentation in the Temple, when he perceived in him the 'salvation … prepared in the presence of all peoples' at the price of the great suffering—the Cross—which he would have to embrace together with his Mother. The Virgin Mary, who 'had conceived by the Holy Spirit', sensed this even more clearly, when she pondered in her heart the 'mysteries' of the Messiah, with whom she was associated" (*Dominum et Vivificantem*, 16).

pallium laudis pro spiritu maeroris. / Et vocabuntur Terebinthi iustitiae, / plantatio Domini ad glorificandum. / 4Et aedificabunt deserta a saeculo / et ruinas antiquas erigent / et instaurabunt civitates desertas, / dissipatas in generatione et generatione. / 5Et stabunt alieni et pascent pecora vestra, / et filii peregrinorum agricolae et vinitores vestri erunt; / 6vos autem Sacerdotes Domini vocabimini, / Ministri Dei nostri dicetur vobis; / fortitudinem gentium comedetis / et in gloria earum superbietis. / 7Pro confusione eorum duplici / et ignominia laudabunt partem suam; / propterea in terra sua duplicia possidebunt, / laetitia sempiterna erit eis. / 8Quia ego Dominus diligens iudicium, / odio habens rapinam et iniquitatem; / et dabo opus eorum in veritate / et foedus perpetuum feriam eis. / 9Et scietur in gentibus semen eorum, / et germen eorum in medio populorum; / omnes, qui viderint eos, cognoscent illos, / quia isti sunt semen, cui benedixit Dominus. / 10Gaudens gaudebo in Domino, / et exsultabit anima mea in Deo meo, / quia induit me vestimentis salutis / et indumento iustitiae circumdedit me, / quasi sponsum decoratum corona / et quasi sponsam ornatam monilibus suis. / 11Sicut enim terra profert germen suum, / et sicut hortus semen suum germinat, / sic Dominus Deus germinabit iustitiam / et laudem coram universis gentibus.

o. Heb *they* **p.** Heb *their* **q.** Heb *theirs* **r.** Or *robbery with a burnt offering*

[9]Their descendants shall be known among the nations, Gen 12:2
and their offspring in the midst of the peoples;
all who see them shall acknowledge them,
that they are a people whom the LORD has blessed.

[10] I will greatly rejoice in the LORD, 1 Sam 2:1
my soul shall exult in my God; Lk 1:46
for he has clothed me with the garments of salvation, Rev 19:8; 21:2
he has covered me with the robe of righteousness,
as a bridegroom decks himself with a garland,
and as a bride adorns herself with her jewels.
[11] For as the earth brings forth its shoots, Is 45:8
and as a garden causes what is sown in it to spring up,
so the Lord GOD will cause righteousness and praise
to spring forth before all the nations.

Names of the new Jerusalem

62 [1]For Zion's sake I will not keep silent,
and for Jerusalem's sake I will not rest,
until her vindication goes forth as brightness,
and her salvation as a burning torch.

62:1–12. The new city of Jerusalem is now explicitly named; it is "Zion" (v. 1). It will be praised in this new hymn placed on the prophet's lips, in which he plays poetically with the names given the city. The depiction of Zion as the spouse of the Lord became popular among prophets from Hosea onwards.

The first stanza (vv. 1–9), addressed to the city, describes the new situation that awaits her in terms of a series of names: no one will any longer feel alone or unprotected, for God has shown Jerusalem the tenderness of a young husband (he calls her "My delight and "Married": v. 4). The advantages that derive from this spousal covenant can be seen (as in Hosea: cf. Hos 2:11–15) in metaphors to do with rich harvests (vv. 8–9).

The second stanza (vv. 10–12), spoken to those living in the city, is an exhortation to be prepared for when the Saviour will enter in glory in the last days (vv. 10–11; cf. 40:3). The poem ends (v. 12) with further plays on the names given the city and its inhabitants.

Since the sixth century, Christian tradition has used this poem in the liturgy of Christmas Day. The birth of Jesus has brought about the joyful union of God and mankind in a way that surpasses that described in terms of spousal union. A monk of the Middle Ages makes this beautiful comment:

[62] [1]Propter Sion non tacebo / et propter Ierusalem non / quiescam, / donec egrediatur ut splendor iustitia eius, / et salus eius ut lampas accendatur. / [2]Et videbunt gentes iustitiam tuam, / et cuncti reges

Is 56:5; 65:15 2The nations shall see your vindication,
and all the kings your glory;
and you shall be called by a new name
which the mouth of the LORD will give.
3You shall be a crown of beauty in the hand of the LORD,
and a royal diadem in the hand of your God.
Is 1:26; 60:15 Hos 2:11–15,25 4You shall no more be termed Forsaken,[s]
and your land shall no more be termed Desolate;[t]
but you shall be called My delight is in her,[u]
and your land Married;[v]
for the LORD delights in you,
and your land shall be married.
Is 65:19 5For as a young man marries a virgin,
so shall your sons marry you,
and as the bridegroom rejoices over the bride,
so shall your God rejoice over you.

Is 52:8 6Upon your walls, O Jerusalem,
I have set watchmen;
all the day and all the night
they shall never be silent.
You who put the LORD in remembrance,
take no rest,
7and give him no rest
until he establishes Jerusalem
and makes it a praise in the earth.

"*Like the bridegoom who comes out of his chamber* the Lord came down from heaven to dwell on earth and to become one with the Church through his incarnation. The Church was gathered together from among the Gentiles, to whom he gave his dowry and his blessings—his dowry, when God was made man; his blessings, when he was sacrificed for their salvation" (Fausto de Riez, *Sermo 5 in Epiphania*).

gloriam tuam; / et vocaberis nomine novo, / quod os Domini nominabit. / 3Et eris corona gloriae in manu Domini, / et diadema regni in manu Dei tui. / 4Non vocaberis ultra Derelicta, / et terra tua non vocabitur amplius Desolata; / sed vocaberis Beneplacitum meum in ea, / et terra tua Nupta, / quia complacuit Domino in te, / et terra tua erit nupta. / 5Nam ut iuvenis uxorem ducit virginem, / ita ducent te filii tui; / ut gaudet sponsus super sponsam, / ita gaudebit super te Deus tuus. / 6Super muros tuos, Ierusalem, constitui custodes; / tota die et tota nocte, in perpetuo non tacebunt. / Qui commonetis Dominum, ne taceatis / 7et ne detis silentium ei, / donec stabiliat et donec ponat Ierusalem / laudem in terra. / 8Iuravit Dominus in dextera sua / et in brachio fortitudinis suae: / «Non dabo triticum tuum ultra

s. Heb *Azubah* **t.** Heb *Shemamah* **u.** Heb *Hephzibah* **v.** Heb *Beulah*

[8]The LORD has sworn by his right hand Deut 28:30–33
and by his mighty arm:
"I will not again give your grain
to be food for your enemies,
and foreigners shall not drink your wine
for which you have laboured;
[9]but those who garner it shall eat it
and praise the LORD,
and those who gather it shall drink it
in the courts of my sanctuary."

[10] Go through, go through the gates, Is 49:22
prepare the way for the people;
build up, build up the highway,
clear it of stones,
lift up an ensign over the peoples.
[11] Behold, the LORD has proclaimed Is 40:10
to the end of the earth: Mt 21:5
Say to the daughter of Zion,
"Behold, your salvation comes;
behold, his reward is with him,
and his recompense before him."
[12] And they shall be called The holy people, Is 1:26; 60:14,15
The redeemed of the LORD;
and you shall be called Sought out,
a city not forsaken.

Victory at the End*

63 [1]Who is this that comes from Edom, Num 20:23
in crimsoned garments from Bozrah, Is 34:1–17
Rev 19:13

***63:1—64:12.** The previous oracle sang of the glory of the new Jerusalem and the prospect of its saviour's imminent arrival (cf. 62:11). Now at last the Lord comes as a conqueror and a Judge to dispense rewards and punishments. There are a number of oracles here to do with this theme, and they combine to create a long and beautiful apocalyptic poem. There are three stanzas in

/ cibum inimicis tuis, / neque bibent filii alieni / vinum tuum, in quo laborasti. / [9]Quia, qui collegerint illud, comedent / et laudabunt Dominum; / et, qui vindemiam fecerint, / illud bibent in atriis sanctuarii mei. / [10]Transite, transite per portas, / parate viam populo. / Sternite, sternite semitam, eligite lapides, / elevate signum ad populos». / [11]Ecce Dominus auditum fecit in extremis terrae: / «Dicite filiae Sion: / Ecce salus tua venit, / ecce merces eius cum eo, / et praemium eius coram illo. / [12]Et vocabunt eos Populus sanctus, / Redempti a Domino; / tu autem vocaberis Quaesita, / Civitas non derelicta». **[63]** [1]«Quis est iste, qui venit de Edom, / tinctis vestibus de Bosra? / Iste formosus in stola sua, /

he that is glorious in his apparel,
marching in the greatness of his strength?
"It is I, announcing vindication,
mighty to save."

2Why is thy apparel red,
and thy garments like his that treads in the wine press?
Jn 4:13 Rev 14:19–20 3"I have trodden the wine press alone,
and from the peoples no one was with me;
I trod them in my anger

---

it: the first (63:1–6) describes the Lord's victory over the Edomites, the epitome of a nation hostile to Israel; the second (63:7–14) celebrates the mercy of God and all he has done for his people; the third (63:15—64:12) is an entreaty full of confidence in the Lord, our Father.

God is twice invoked in urgent tones as the Father of Israel (63:16; 64:8). This is one of the most eloquent Old Testament passages about God's tender fatherly feelings towards his people. The author of the poem is fully confident that the Lord's fatherly heart will be sensitive towards everything his people suffer, even though they brought it on themselves (64:3–6). He beseeches God for help (63:17–19), even asking for a spectacular miracle (64:1).

The listing of the calamities that beset Israel continues in 64:1–12 in the same tone as 63:15–19: the prophet spells out why God should help his people.

63:1–6. The poem uses surprisingly strong, apocalyptic, language. It refers to a victory that appears to have two very different effects. On the one hand, victory is obtained after a very real and bloody struggle, symbolized by the treading of the wine-press, and it ends with the blood-stained clothes (v. 3). The conqueror works on his own, unaided (v. 5). On the other hand, his victory over the enemy means redemption for his people: the conqueror is, first and foremost, the redeemer (*goel*: v. 4; cf. 41:14).

Christian tradition has interpreted this passage as a prophecy about the Messiah. The Revelation to John combines it with Psalm 2 to describe Christ's battle with the beast and his eventual victory (Rev 19:11–21). The *Divine Office*, which offers the poem as an optional reading in Eastertide, suggests that these words of Isaiah apply to Jesus Christ, Judge of the living and the dead, who shed his blood during his passion. And just as the vine harvester does his heavy work on his own, with none to help him (v. 5), so too Jesus Christ was abandoned by his disciples and left alone on Calvary when he was redeeming the world.

gradiens in multitudine fortitudinis suae». / «Sum ego, qui loquor iustitiam, / potens ad salvandum». / 2«Quare ergo rubrum est indumentum tuum. / et vestimenta tua sicut calcantis in torculari?». / 3«Torcular calcavi solus, / et de gentibus non erat vir mecum; / calcavi eos in furore meo / et conculcavi

and trampled them in my wrath;
their lifeblood is sprinkled upon my garments,
and I have stained all my raiment.
4For the day of vengeance was in my heart,
and my year of redemption[w] has come.
5I looked, but there was no one to help; Is 59:16
I was appalled, but there was no one to uphold;
so my own arm brought me victory,
and my wrath upheld me.
6I trod down the peoples in my anger,
I made them drunk in my wrath,
and I poured out their lifeblood on the earth."

7I will recount the steadfast love of the LORD, Ps 89:2
the praises of the LORD,
according to all that the LORD has granted us,
and the great goodness to the house of Israel
which he has granted them according to his mercy,
according to the abundance of his steadfast love.
8For he said, Surely they are my people, Deut 32:5
sons who will not deal falsely;
and he became their Saviour.
9In all their affliction he was afflicted,[x]
and the angel of his presence saved them;
in his love and in his pity he redeemed them;
he lifted them up and carried them all the days of old.

10 But they rebelled Deut 32,15
and grieved his holy Spirit; Eph 4:30
therefore he turned to be their enemy,
and himself fought against them.
11 Then he remembered the days of old, Ex 2:1–10
of Moses his servant. Num 11:17
Neh 9:20

---

eos in ira mea. / Et aspersus est sanguis eorum super vestimenta mea, / et omnia indumenta mea inquinavi. / 4Dies enim ultionis in corde meo, / annus redemptionis meae venit. / 5Circumspexi, et non erat auxiliator, / miratus sum, et non fuit qui adiuvaret; / et salvavit mihi brachium meum, / et indignatio mea ipsa auxiliata est mihi. / 6Et conculcavi populos in furore meo / et contrivi eos in indignatione mea / et effudi in terram sanguinem eorum». / 7Miserationum Domini recordabor, / laudum Domini / super omnibus, quae reddidit nobis Dominus, / et super multitudinem bonorum domui Israel, / quae largitus est eis secundum misericordias suas / et secundum multitudinem miserationum suarum. / 8Et dixit: «Verumtamen populus meus est, / filii, qui non deludent»; / et factus est eis salvator. / 9In omni tribulatione eorum non legatus neque angelus, / sed ipse salvavit eos. / In dilectione sua et in

w. Or *the year of my redeemed* **x.** Another reading is *he did not afflict*

Where is he who brought up out of the sea
the shepherds of his flock?
Where is he who put in the midst of them
his holy Spirit,
Ex 14:5–31 12 who caused his glorious arm
to go at the right hand of Moses,
who divided the waters before them
to make for himself an everlasting name,
Is 51:10 13 who led them through the depths?
Like a horse in the desert,
they did not stumble.
Ps 77:21 14 Like cattle that go down into the valley,
the Spirit of the LORD gave them rest.
So thou didst lead thy people,
to make for thyself a glorious name.

Is 49:15; 64:7–11 15 Look down from heaven and see,
from thy holy and glorious habitation.
Where are thy zeal and thy might?
The yearning of thy heart and thy compassion
are withheld from me.
Is 41:14 16 For thou art our Father,
though Abraham does not know us
and Israel does not acknowledge us;
thou, O LORD, art our Father,
our Redeemer from of old is thy name.
17 O LORD, why dost thou make us err from thy ways
and harden our heart, so that we fear thee not?
Return for the sake of thy servants,
the tribes of thy heritage.
Deut 32:9 18 Thy holy people possessed thy sanctuary a little while;
our adversaries have trodden it down.

---

indulgentia sua / ipse redemit eos / et sustulit eos et portavit eos / cunctis diebus saeculi. / 10Ipsi autem
ad iracundiam provocaverunt / et afflixerunt spiritum sanctitatis eius; / et conversus est eis in inimicum
/ et ipse debellavit eos. / 11Et recordatus est dierum antiquorum, / Moysi et populi sui. / Ubi est qui
eduxit eos de mari / cum pastore gregis sui? / Ubi est qui posuit in medio eius / spiritum sanctitatis
suae? / 12Qui adduxit ad dexteram Moysi / brachium maiestatis suae, / qui scidit aquas ante eos, / ut
faceret sibi nomen sempiternum, / 13qui deduxit eos per abyssos / quasi equum per desertum, et non
impingebant? / 14Sicut armentum, quod descendit per vallem, / spiritus Domini fecit eos quiescere; /
sic conduxisti populum tuum, / ut faceres tibi nomen gloriae. / 15Attende de caelo et vide / de
habitaculo sancto tuo et gloriae tuae; / ubi est zelus tuus et fortitudo tua? / Commotio viscerum tuorum
et misericordiae tuae / super me continuerunt se. / 16Tu enim pater noster. / Abraham enim nescit nos,
/ et Israel ignorat nos; / tu, Domine, pater noster, / redemptor noster: a saeculo nomen tuum. / 17Quare
errare nos fecisti, Domine, de viis tuis, / indurasti cor nostrum, ne timeremus te? / Convertere propter
servos tuos, / tribus hereditatis tuae. / 18Brevi tempore hereditaverunt populum sanctum tuum, / hostes

[19] We have become like those over whom thou hast never ruled, Ps 144:5
like those who are not called by thy name. Rev 19:11

64 [1] O that thou wouldst rend the heavens and come down, Ps 18:8
that the mountains might quake at thy presence— Ps 50:3
[2y] as when fire kindles brushwood
and the fire causes water to boil—
to make thy name known to thy adversaries,
and that the nations might tremble at thy presence!
[3] When thou didst terrible things which we looked not for, 1 Cor 2:9
thou camest down, the mountains quaked at thy presence.
[4] From of old no one has heard
or perceived by the ear,
no eye has seen a God besides thee,
who works for those who wait for him.

64:1. The prophet's cry sums up very well the long years when Israel waited patiently for God to bring salvation; set in a messianic context, it expresses the hope in a Saviour that the chosen people maintained over the centuries. And in some way it is a cry that everyone utters to God when he or she begs to see their noble aspirations bear fruit. This centuries-long Advent, which in some way is being relived in our own days, finds its answer once again in the purpose of God the Father, who sent his Son, made Man, to bring about our Redemption, and who sent the Holy Spirit to enable human beings to share in his Love.

64:4. St Paul quotes from this verse when writing about the wisdom of God, and his love for those who love him, and the gifts he has in store for man: "As it is written, '*What no eye has seen, nor ear heard*, nor the heart of man conceived, what God has prepared for those who love him'" (1 Cor 2:9). Because these gifts will not be fully bestowed until the next life, the verse is often quoted in Christian spirituality to describe the happiness enjoyed in heaven. For example, St Robert Bellarmine says: "You promise to those who obey your commandments a reward more precious than gold and sweeter than honey from the comb. It is a great reward, as St James says: *The crown of life which the Lord has prepared for those who love him.* And what is the crown of life? It is a gift greater than any we can imagine or desire. St Paul

nostri conculcaverunt sanctuarium tuum. / [19]Facti sumus a saeculo, / cum non dominareris nostri, / neque invocaretur nomen tuum super nos. / Utinam dirumperes caelos et descenderes! / A facie tua montes defluerent. **[64]** [1]Sicut ignis succendit sarmenta, / aquam ebullire facit ignis, / ut notum facias nomen tuum inimicis tuis, / a facie tua gentes turbentur, / [2]cum feceris mirabilia, / quae non sperabamus. / Descendisti, et a facie tua montes defluxerunt. / [3]A saeculo non audierunt, neque aures perceperunt; / oculus non vidit Deum, absque te, / qui operaretur pro sperantibus in eum. / [4]Occurris

y. Ch 64:1 in Heb

Lev 15:19–20 [5]Thou meetest him that joyfully works righteousness,
those that remember thee in thy ways.
Behold, thou wast angry, and we sinned;
in our sins we have been a long time, and shall we be saved?[z]
[6]We have all become like one who is unclean,
and all our righteous deeds are like a polluted garment.
We all fade like a leaf,
and our iniquities, like the wind, take us away.
Is 29:16 [7]There is no one that calls upon thy name,
that bestirs himself to take hold of thee;
for thou hast hid thy face from us,
and hast delivered[a] us into the hand of our iniquities.

[8]Yet, O LORD, thou art our Father;
we are the clay, and thou art our potter;
we are all the work of thy hand.
[9]Be not exceedingly angry, O LORD,
and remember not iniquity for ever.
Behold, consider, we are all thy people.
[10]Thy holy cities have become a wilderness,
Zion has become a wilderness,
Jerusalem a desolation.
[11]Our holy and beautiful house,
where our fathers praised thee,
has been burned by fire,
and all our pleasant places have become ruins.
[12]Wilt thou restrain thyself at these things, O LORD?
Wilt thou keep silent, and afflict us sorely?

---

says, quoting the prophet Isaiah: *What no eye has seen, nor ear heard, nor the heart of man conceived, what God has prepared for those who love him*" (*De ascensione mentis in Deum*, first step).

laetanti, facienti iustitiam / et his, qui in viis tuis recordantur tui. / Ecce tu iratus es, et peccavimus; / in ipsis a saeculo nos salvabimur. / [5]Et facti sumus ut immundus omnes nos, / et quasi pannus inquinatus universae iustitiae nostrae; / et marcuimus quasi folium universi, / et iniquitates nostrae quasi ventus abstulerunt nos. / [6]Non est qui invocet nomen tuum, / qui consurgat et adhaereat tibi, / quia abscondisti faciem tuam a nobis / et dissolvisti nos in manu iniquitatis nostrae. / [7]Et nunc, Domine, pater noster es tu, / nos vero lutum; et fictor noster tu, / et opera manuum tuarum omnes nos. / [8]Ne irascaris, Domine, nimis / et ne ultra memineris iniquitatis; / ecce, respice: populus tuus omnes nos. / [9]Urbes sanctitatis tuae factae sunt in desertum, / Sion deserta facta est, / Ierusalem desolata est. / [10]Domus sanctitatis nostrae et gloriae nostrae, / ubi laudaverunt te patres nostri, / facta est in exustionem ignis, / et omnia desiderabilia nostra versa sunt in ruinas. / [11]Numquid super his continebis te, Domine, / tacebis et affliges nos vehementer?

z. Hebrew obscure **a.** Gk Syr Old Latin Tg: Heb *melted*

3. LAST THINGS*

The Lord's servants and enemies receive their deserts

65 [1]I was ready to be sought by those who did not ask for me; *Rom 10:20*
I was ready to be found by those who did not seek me.
I said, "Here am I, here am I,"
to a nation that did not call on my name.

***65:1—66:24.** This final section of the third and last part of the book has to do with events at the end of time, especially the judgment of God, who will repay people according to their merits, punishing the wicked and rewarding the good.

The principal theme is a vision of a happy future: after the Judgment, messianic peace will be established, with "new heavens and a new earth" (65:17); a new people will be born (66:7–14); and the nations will make their way to Jerusalem (66:18–24). The note of "newness" runs all the way through these chapters and an appeal not to dwell on past misfortunes, for that would only sap people's energies.

65:1–25. The plea in 64:1 ("O that thou wouldst rend the heavens and come down") is answered by God in this chapter, not without some paradoxes: those who did not seek God, find him (v. 1), and those to whom God makes himself known, choose to reject him, opting instead for idolatry (vv. 2–5). God will judge these ingrates and punish them for their iniquity (vv. 6–7). But he will also show mercy and not destroy the juice of the grape, the "remnant" of his true servants, the inheritors of Judah: to these he will provide flocks and folds and a banquet of plenty (vv. 8–16).

The salvation that God will bring about will be so generous that it will call for a new creation (vv. 17–25): "new heavens and a new earth" that will erase the memory of former things (v. 17); a new Jerusalem where there shall be no more weeping but only joy and delight (vv. 18–23). In that time God will respond immediately when the people invoke him (v. 24). Even wild animals will become meek—all except the serpent, to which the primeval curse will still apply (v. 25).

65:1–2. These verses carry a consoling message. God takes the initiative and he makes himself permanently available so that even those who never sought him and those who rebelled against him can find him. To the latter St Paul repeats these same words (Rom 10:20), when he denounces the fact that not everyone obeyed the Gospel. God's attitude of silent invitation is recalled in a beautiful sonnet found in a Spanish language edition of the *Divine Office*: "How many times has the angel said to me: Soul, go to the window and look out and you will see how much love

[65] [1]«Quaesitus sum ab his, qui non consulebant me, / inventus sum ab his, qui non quaerebant me. / Dixi: "Ecce ego, ecce ego!" / ad gentem, quae non invocabat nomen meum. / [2]Expandi manus meas

Rom 10:21 [2]I spread out my hands all the day
to a rebellious people,
who walk in a way that is not good,
following their own devices;
Deut 32:21 [3]a people who provoke me
to my face continually,
sacrificing in gardens
and burning incense upon bricks;
[4]who sit in tombs,
and spend the night in secret places;
who eat swine's flesh,
and broth of abominable things is in their vessels;
[5]who say, "Keep to yourself,
do not come near me, for I am set apart from you."
These are a smoke in my nostrils,
a fire that burns all the day.
[6]Behold, it is written before me:
"I will not keep silent, but I will repay,
yea, I will repay into their bosom
[7]their[b] iniquities and their[b] fathers' iniquities together,
says the LORD;
because they burned incense upon the mountains
and reviled me upon the hills,
I will measure into their bosom
payment for their former doings."

---

there is in quiet patience" (Lope de Vega, *Rimas castellanas*, Sonnet 18). And they are echoed by St Josemaría Escrivá in a comment on Simon of Cyrene's meeting with Jesus: "Simon's sons, Christians by then, will be known and held in high esteem among their brothers in the faith. And it all started with this unexpected meeting with the Cross. *I went to those who were not looking for me; I was found by those that sought me not* (Is 65:1). At times the Cross appears without our looking for it: it is Christ who is seeking us out. And if by chance, before this unexpected Cross which, perhaps, is therefore more difficult to understand, your heart were to show repugnance ..., don't give it consolations" (*The Way of the Cross*, fifth station).

tota die / ad populum rebellem, / qui graditur in via non bona / post cogitationes suas; / [3]populus, qui ad iracundiam provocat me / ante faciem meam semper, / qui immolant in hortis / et sacrificant super lateres, / [4]qui morantur in sepulcris / et in locis occultis pernoctant, / qui comedunt carnem suillam / et ius abominabile in vasis eorum, / [5]qui dicunt: "Recede! / Non appropinques mihi, quia sanctificarem te". / Isti fumus sunt in naribus meis, / ignis ardens tota die. / [6]Ecce scriptum est coram me; / non tacebo, sed retribuam, / et retribuam in sinum eorum / [7]iniquitates vestras et iniquitates patrum

b. Gk Syr: Heb *your*

Reward for the chosen of the Lord

8Thus says the LORD: Is 4:3
"As the wine is found in the cluster,
and they say, 'Do not destroy it,
for there is a blessing in it,'
so I will do for my servants' sake,
and not destroy them all.
9I will bring forth descendants from Jacob, Is 57:13
and from Judah inheritors of my mountains;
my chosen shall inherit it,
and my servants shall dwell there.
10 Sharon shall become a pasture for flocks,
and the Valley of Achor a place for herds to lie down,
for my people who have sought me.

11 But you who forsake the LORD,
who forget my holy mountain,
who set a table for Fortune
and fill cups of mixed wine for Destiny;
12 I will destine you to the sword, Is 50:2; 66:4
and all of you shall bow down to the slaughter; Jer 7:13
because, when I called, you did not answer,
when I spoke, you did not listen,
but you did what was evil in my eyes,
and chose what I did not delight in."

13 Therefore thus says the Lord GOD:
"Behold, my servants shall eat,
but you shall be hungry;
behold, my servants shall drink,
but you shall be thirsty;
behold, my servants shall rejoice,
but you shall be put to shame;

---

vestrorum / simul, dicit Dominus, / qui sacrificaverunt super montes / et super colles exprobraverunt
mihi; / et remetiar opus eorum primo / in sinu eorum». / 8Haec dicit Dominus: / «Quomodo si
inveniatur mustum in botro / et dicatur: "Ne dissipes illud, / quoniam benedictio est in eo", / sic faciam
propter servos meos, / ut non disperdam totum. / 9Et educam de Iacob semen / et de Iuda possidentem
montes meos; / et hereditabunt terram electi mei, / et servi mei habitabunt ibi. / 10Et erit Saron in pascua
gregum, / et vallis Achor in cubile armentorum / populo meo, qui quaesierunt me. / 11Vos autem, qui
derelinquitis Dominum, / qui obliviscimini montem sanctum meum, / qui ponitis Gad mensam / et
amphoram impletis Meni, / 12numerabo vos in gladio, / et omnes in caede corruetis; / pro eo quod
vocavi, et non respondistis, / locutus sum, et non audistis, / sed fecistis malum in oculis meis / et, quod
displicet mihi, elegistis». / 13Propter hoc haec dicit Dominus Deus: / «Ecce servi mei comedent, / et vos
esurietis; / ecce servi mei bibent, / et vos sitietis; / ecce servi mei laetabuntur, / et vos confundemini; /

[14] behold, my servants shall sing for gladness of heart,
but you shall cry out for pain of heart,
and shall wail for anguish of spirit.

Is 1:26; 56:5; 62:2
[15] You shall leave your name to my chosen for a curse,
and the Lord GOD will slay you;
but his servants he will call by a different name.
[16] So that he who blesses himself in the land
shall bless himself by the God of truth,
and he who takes an oath in the land
shall swear by the God of truth;
because the former troubles are forgotten
and are hid from my eyes.

Is 51:6; 66:22 Rev 21: 1–22:5 *2 Pet 3:13*

New heavens and a new earth

[17] "For behold, I create new heavens
and a new earth;

65:16. The *Catechism of the Catholic Church* offers an explanation of this verse: "In the book of the prophet Isaiah, we find the expression 'God of truth' (literally 'God of the Amen'), that is, the God who is faithful to his promises: 'He who blesses himself in the land shall bless himself by the God of truth (*amen*)' (Is 65:16). Our Lord often used the word 'Amen', sometimes repeated (cf. Mt 6:2, 5, 16; Jn 5:19), to emphasize the trustworthiness of his teaching, his authority founded on God's truth" (no. 1063). And a little further on, the *Catechism* expands on this: "Jesus Christ himself is the 'Amen' (Rev 3:14). He is the definitive 'Amen' of the Father's love for us. He takes up and completes our 'Amen' to the Father: 'For all the promises of God find their Yes in him. That is why we utter the Amen through him, to the glory of God' (2 Cor 1:20)" (no. 1065).

65:17–18. Here we have a clear and succinct description of the new state of affairs at the end of time—"new heavens and a new earth". As at the Creation, God in person, and he alone, will create them; but now they will have a heavenly form, for joy and gladness will be unceasing and eternal. This wording became very influential in Jewish religious thinking as can be seen from apocryphal texts (cf. 2 Ezra 6:16), and even more so in Christian tradition: in the Revelation to John, these are the opening words of the vision about the definitive and full establishment of the Kingdom of God (Rev 21:1—22:5). And the Second Letter of Peter urges the faithful to

[14]ecce servi mei laudabunt in exsultatione cordis, / et vos clamabitis prae dolore cordis / et prae contritione spiritus ululabitis. / [15]Et relinquetis nomen vestrum / in iuramentum electis meis: / "Interficiat te Dominus Deus"; / et servos suos vocabit nomine alio. / [16]Quicumque benedicit sibi in terra, / benedicet sibi in Deo Amen; / et, quicumque iurat in terra, / iurabit in Deo Amen; / quia oblivioni tradentur angustiae priores, / et quia abscondentur ab oculis meis. / [17]Ecce enim ego creo /

and the former things shall not be remembered
or come into mind.
18 But be glad and rejoice for ever Is 1:26
in that which I create;
for behold, I create Jerusalem a rejoicing,
and her people a joy.
19 I will rejoice in Jerusalem, Is 60:14
and be glad in my people;
no more shall be heard in it the sound of weeping
and the cry of distress.
20 No more shall there be in it
an infant that lives but a few days,
or an old man who does not fill out his days,
for the child shall die a hundred years old,
and the sinner a hundred years old shall be accursed.

---

transform this world in preparation for the coming of "new heavens and a new earth, in which righteousness dwells" (2 Pet 3:13). "At the end of time, the Kingdom of God will come in its fullness. After the universal judgment, the righteous will reign for ever with Christ, glorified in body and soul. The universe itself will be renewed: 'The Church … will receive her perfection only in the glory of heaven, when will come the time of the renewal of all things. At that time, together with the human race, the universe itself, which is so closely related to man and which attains its destiny through him, will be perfectly re-established in Christ' (*Lumen gentium*, 48). Sacred Scripture calls this mysterious renewal, which will transform humanity and the world, 'new heavens and a new earth' (2 Pet 13; cf. Rev 21:1). It will be the definitive realization of God's plan to bring under a single head 'all things in [Christ], things in heaven and things on earth' (Eph 1:10). In this new universe, the heavenly Jerusalem, God will have his dwelling among men. He will wipe away every tear from their eyes, and death shall be no more, neither shall there be mourning nor crying nor pain any more, for the former things have passed away' (Rev 21:4). […] The visible universe, then, is itself destined to be transformed, 'so that the world itself, restored to its original state, facing no further obstacles, should be at the service of the just' (St Irenaeus, *Adv. haer.* 5, 32, 1), sharing their glorification in the risen Jesus Christ" (*Catechism of the Catholic Church*, 1042–1044 and 1047).

caelos novos et terram novam, / et non erunt in memoria priora / et non ascendent super cor. / [18]Sed gaudebunt et exsultabunt usque in sempiternum / in his, quae ego creo, / quia ecce ego creo Ierusalem exsultationem / et populum eius gaudium. / [19]Et exsultabo in Ierusalem / et gaudebo in populo meo, / et non audietur in ea ultra / vox fletus et vox clamoris. / [20]Non erit ibi amplius infans dierum / et senex, qui non impleat dies suos. / Quoniam puer erit, / qui centenarius moriatur; / et, qui non attingat centum

Deut 28:30–33 Is 62:8 Jer 31:5 Amos 9:14

21 They shall build houses and inhabit them;
they shall plant vineyards and eat their fruit.
22 They shall not build and another inhabit;
they shall not plant and another eat;
for like the days of a tree shall the days of my people be,
and my chosen shall long enjoy the work of their hands.
23 They shall not labour in vain,
or bear children for calamity;[c]
for they shall be the offspring of the blessed of the LORD,
and their children with them.
24 Before they call I will answer,
while they are yet speaking I will hear.

Gen 3:14 Is 11:7,9

25 The wolf and the lamb shall feed together,
the lion shall eat straw like the ox;
and dust shall be the serpent's food.
They shall not hurt or destroy
in all my holy mountain, says the LORD."

1 Kings 8:27 Mt 5:34 *Acts 7:49–50*

The new temple and new form of worship

66 1 Thus says the LORD:
"Heaven is my throne
and the earth is my footstool;
what is the house which you would build for me,
and what is the place of my rest?

65:25. Here again we find the era of messianic peace being described in images similar to those used in the first part of the book (cf. 11:6–9), and the curse laid on the serpent is retained (cf. Gen 3:14). The messianic peace that mankind enjoys affects even the world of nature.

66:1–6. These oracles seem to contain echoes of the arguments that took place about the rebuilding of the temple after the return from exile. Physical rebuilding and external religious rites must take second place to genuine inner devotion, humility of heart and sincere acceptance of the word of the Lord.

annos, / maledictus erit. / [21]Et aedificabunt domos et habitabunt / et plantabunt vineas et comedent fructus earum. / [22]Non aedificabunt, ut alius habitet, / non plantabunt, ut alius comedat: / secundum enim dies ligni erunt dies populi mei, / et operibus manuum suarum diu fruentur electi mei. / [23]Non laborabunt frustra / neque generabunt in interitum repentinum, / quia semen benedictorum erunt Domini, / et nepotes eorum cum eis. / [24]Eritque: antequam clament, ego respondebo; / adhuc illis loquentibus, ego exaudiam. / [25]Lupus et agnus pascentur simul, / et leo sicut bos comedet paleas, / et serpenti pulvis panis eius. / Non nocebunt neque occident / in omni monte sancto meo», / dicit Dominus. **[66]** [1]Haec dicit Dominus: / «Caelum thronus meus, / terra autem scabellum pedum

c. Or *sudden terror*

[2]All these things my hand has made, Ps 24:1–2
and so all these things are mine,[d]
says the LORD.
But this is the man to whom I will look,
he that is humble and contrite in spirit,
and trembles at my word.

[3]"He who slaughters an ox is like him who kills a man;
he who sacrifices a lamb, like him who breaks a dog's neck;
he who presents a cereal offering, like him who offers swine's blood;
he who makes a memorial offering of frankincense, like him who blesses an idol.
These have chosen their own ways,
and their soul delights in their abominations;
[4]I also will choose affliction for them, Is 50:2; 65:15
and bring their fears upon them;

Verses 3–4 are written in a very condensed style, but the message is clear: they are an attack on sham religious practice by some of the people. They expose the lack of faith and emptiness found in religious practices by comparing four legitimate ritual practices with four idolatrous and abominable ones.

The voice of the Lord coming from the temple (v. 6; cf. 30:30; Joel 4:16; Ezek 1:24; Ps 29:3–9), symbolizing his strength and power, seems to be a source for what is said in Revelation 16:17, where the seventh angel proclaims punishment by pouring the contents of his bowl into the air: "and a great voice came out of the temple, from the throne, saying, 'It is done'."

In the new situation which looks to the messianic and eschatological era, the physical temple will cease to have importance; a spiritual form of worship will take over: "Woman, believe me, the hour is coming when neither on this mountain nor in Jerusalem will you worship the Father [...] But the hour is coming, and now is, when the true worshippers will worship the Father in spirit and truth, for such the Father seeks to worship him. God is spirit, and those who worship him must worship in spirit and truth" (Jn 4:21, 23–24).

meorum. / Quae ista domus, quam aedificabitis mihi, / et quis iste locus quietis meae? / [2]Omnia haec manus mea fecit, / et mea sunt universa ista, / dicit Dominus. / Ad hunc autem respiciam, / ad pauperculum et contritum spiritu / et trementem sermones meos. / [3]Qui immolat bovem, interficit virum; / qui sacrificat ovem, excerebrat canem; / qui offert oblationem, idemque sanguinem suillum; / qui adolet incensum, benedicit idolo. / Sicut isti elegerunt vias suas, / et in abominationibus suis anima eorum delectatur, / [4]sic ego eligam malam sortem eorum / et, quae timebant, adducam eis; / quia vocavi, et non erat qui responderet, / locutus sum, et non audierunt / feceruntque malum in oculis meis

d. Gk Syr: Heb *came to be*

because, when I called, no one answered,
when I spoke they did not listen;
but they did what was evil in my eyes,
and chose that in which I did not delight."

Jn 4:21,23–24 5Hear the word of the LORD,
you who tremble at his word:
"Your brethren who hate you
and cast you out for my name's sake
have said, 'Let the LORD be glorified,
that we may see your joy';
but it is they who shall be put to shame.

Is 30:30 Rev 16:17 6"Hark, an uproar from the city!
A voice from the temple!
The voice of the LORD,
rendering recompense to his enemies!

The new nation

Gen 2:23 Rev 12:5 7"Before she was in labour
she gave birth;
before her pain came upon her
she was delivered of a son.
8Who has heard such a thing?
Who has seen such things?

66:7–14. This last poem about the exaltation of Zion is built around the metaphor of motherhood. The opening verses (7–9) are a reflection full of rhetorical questions about the eschatological city that gives birth to an entire people in a spectacular, miraculous way. She is the new Eve, the mother of all the living (cf. Gen 2:23), who gives birth painlessly. This Zion, a thing of wonder, easy for God to create but impossible for men even to conceive, has been interpreted as a symbol of the Church who bears in her womb and gives birth to the members of the new people of God—and a symbol, too, of the Blessed Virgin Mary, who gave birth, without the loss of her virginity, to Jesus (cf. Rev 12:5). The end of the poem (vv. 10–14) also uses the analogy of Zion as a mother, although at one point, very boldly, it depicts God as

/ et, quod displicet mihi, elegerunt». / 5Audite verbum Domini, / qui tremitis ad verbum eius. / Dixerunt fratres vestri odientes vos / et abicientes vos propter nomen meum: / «Gloriam suam manifestet Dominus, / ut videamus laetitiam vestram»; / ipsi autem confundentur. / 6Vox clamoris de civitate, / vox de templo, / vox Domini / reddentis retributionem inimicis suis. / 7Antequam parturiret, peperit; / antequam veniret partus eius, peperit masculum. / 8Quis audivit umquam tale? / Et quis vidit huic simile? / Numquid oritur terra in die una, / aut parietur gens in momento? / Quia parturivit, iam peperit

Shall a land be born in one day?
 Shall a nation be brought forth in one moment?
For as soon as Zion was in labour
 she brought forth her sons.
9 Shall I bring to the birth and not cause to bring forth?
 says the LORD;
shall I, who cause to bring forth, shut the womb?
 says your God.

10 "Rejoice with Jerusalem, and be glad for her,
 all you who love her;
rejoice with her in joy,
 all you who mourn over her;
11 that you may suck and be satisfied
 with her consoling breasts;
that you may drink deeply with delight
 from the abundance of her glory."

12 For thus says the LORD: Rev 21:24
"Behold, I will extend prosperity to her like a river,
 and the wealth of the nations like an overflowing stream;

---

comforting his people like a mother giving suck to her children (v. 11). As we have seen, the second part of Isaiah is where the attributes of a mother are most often applied to God (cf. 42:14; 45:10; 49:15). "By calling God 'Father', the language of faith indicates two main things: that God is the first origin of everything and transcendent authority; and that he is at the same time goodness and loving care for all his children. God's parental tenderness can also be expressed by the image of motherhood (cf. Is 66:13; Ps 131:2), which emphasizes God's immanence, the intimacy between Creator and creature. The language of faith thus draws on the human experience of parents, who are in a way the first representatives of God for man. But this experience also tells us that human parents are fallible and can disfigure the face of fatherhood and motherhood. We ought therefore to recall that God transcends the human distinction between the sexes. He is neither man nor woman: he is God. He also transcends human fatherhood and motherhood (cf. Ps 27:10), although he is their origin and standard (cf. Eph 3:14; Is 49:15)" (*Catechism of the Catholic Church*, 239).

Sion filios suos. / 9«Numquid aperiam uterum et parere non faciam?», / dicit Dominus. / «Aut ego, qui parere facio, uterum claudam?», / ait Deus tuus. / 10Laetamini cum Ierusalem et exsultate in ea, / omnes, qui diligitis eam; / gaudete cum ea gaudio, / universi, qui lugebatis super eam, / 11ut sugatis et repleamini / ab ubere consolationis eius, / ut mulgeatis et deliciis affluatis / ex uberibus gloriae eius. / 12Quia haec dicit Dominus: / «Ecce ego dirigam ad eam quasi fluvium pacem / et quasi torrentem

and you shall suck, you shall be carried upon her hip,
and dandled upon her knees.
13 As one whom his mother comforts,
so I will comfort you;
you shall be comforted in Jerusalem.
Ezek 37:1–10 Jn 16:22 14 You shall see, and your heart shall rejoice;
your bones shall flourish like the grass;
and it shall be known that the hand of the LORD is with his servants,
and his indignation is against his enemies.

Punishment of the wicked

Mt 13:41–42 1 Thess 1:8 15 "For behold, the LORD will come in fire,
and his chariots like the stormwind,
to render his anger in fury,
and his rebuke with flames of fire.
16 For by fire will the LORD execute judgment,
and by his sword, upon all flesh;
and those slain by the LORD shall be many.

17 "Those who sanctify and purify themselves to go into the gardens, following one in the midst, eating swine's flesh and the abomination and mice, shall come to an end together, says the LORD.

66:15–17. The judgment of the Lord extends beyond the joy of the new Jerusalem, whose salvation is a great consolation and cause for rejoicing (66:10–14): those who have dishonoured the holiness of God will mourn when their time of punishment comes. The passage teaches that the Lord is just: the final elimination of all evil is part of the work of redemption.

The punishment by fire of evildoers is an image that is also used in the New Testament: "The Son of man will send his angels, and they will gather out of his kingdom all causes of sin and all evildoers, and throw them into the furnace of fire; there men will weep and gnash their teeth" (Mt 13:41–42; cf. 2 Thess 1:8).

inundantem gloriam gentium. / Sugetis, in ulnis portabimini, / et super genua blandientur vobis. / 13Quomodo si quem mater consolatur, / ita ego consolabor vos; / et in Ierusalem consolabimini. / 14Videbitis, et gaudebit cor vestrum, / et ossa vestra quasi herba germinabunt, / et manifestabitur manus Domini in servis eius, / et indignabitur inimicis suis. / 15Quia ecce Dominus in igne veniet, / et quasi turbo quadrigae eius, / reddere in indignatione furorem suum / et increpationem suam in flamma ignis; / 16quia in igne Dominus diiudicabit / et in gladio suo omnem carnem, / et multiplicabuntur interfecti a Domino. / 17Qui sanctificantur et purificantur, ut ingrediantur / in hortos post aliquem stantem in medio, / qui comedunt carnem suillam / et abominationem et murem, / simul consumentur, / dicit Dominus. 18Ego autem cognoscens opera eorum et cogitationes eorum veniam, ut congregem omnes gentes et linguas; et venient et videbunt gloriam meam. 19Et ponam in eis signum et mittam ex eis, qui salvati fuerint, ad gentes in Tharsis, Phut, Lud, Mosoch, Ros, Thubal et Iavan, ad insulas longinquas,

The nations in pilgrimage to Jerusalem

18"For I know[e] their works and their thoughts, and I am[f] coming to Ps 22:28; 86:9 Rev 15:4
gather all nations and tongues; and they shall come and shall see my
glory, 19and I will set a sign among them. And from them I will send
survivors to the nations, to Tarshish, Put,[g] and Lud, who draw the
bow, to Tubal and Javan, to the coastlands afar off, that have not heard
my fame or seen my glory; and they shall declare my glory among
the nations. 20And they shall bring all your brethren from all the Rom 15:16
nations as an offering to the LORD, upon horses, and in chariots, and
in litters, and upon mules, and upon dromedaries, to my holy
mountain Jerusalem, says the LORD, just as the Israelites bring their
cereal offering in a clean vessel to the house of the LORD. 21And some Ps 87:7
of them also I will take for priests and for Levites, says the LORD.

66:18–24. The book ends with a colophon, part in prose (vv. 18–21), part in verse (vv. 22–24). It begins by announcing that the glory of the Lord will be proclaimed to the nations, and they will respond by flocking in pilgrimage to the temple of the Lord.

Verses 18–21 are a sort of parallel to 2:2–4: both passages act as a kind of marker, one for the beginning and one for the end of the book. In other words, the exile in Babylon will come to be seen as divine punishment inflicted on the people for their sins, for their breaking the Covenant. There may be an oblique reference here to the expulsion of our first parents from the garden of Eden (Gen 1:23): Israel, too, was expelled from its land and from Zion, "the house of Jacob" (2:6). But God, in his mercy towards his people, will pardon them and have them come back to his "holy mountain", Jerusalem (v. 20), and this gathering will also involve "all nations and tongues" (v. 18). This return to Zion is a sign that their transgression is totally forgiven. In some ways, the book of Isaiah is an (imperfect) anticipation and account of salvation history which runs right through the Bible, from the expulsion from Paradise (Gen 3:23), to the vision of the "heavenly Jerusalem", in the "new heavens and the new earth" (v. 22 and Rev 21:1–27), at the centre of which will be found the "tree of life" (Rev 22:14).

Theodoret of Cyrus reads these words as an announcement of the universal salvation that stems from the Incarnation, and he comments that the prophet showed that Christ became "a slave not only to redeem the Jews but to bring salvation to all the nations" (*Commentaria in Isaiam*, 66,18). The Second Letter to the Corinthians attributed to St Clement of Rome also sees v. 18 as an announcement of the Second Coming of our Lord: "*I am coming to gather all nations and tongues:* this verse

ad eos, qui non audierunt de me et non viderunt gloriam meam, et annuntiabunt gloriam meam gentibus; 20et adducent omnes fratres vestros de cunctis gentibus oblationem Domino, in equis et in quadrigis et in lecticis et in mulis et in dromedariis, ad montem sanctum meum Ierusalem, dicit Dominus: quomodo si inferant filii Israel oblationem in vase mundo in domum Domini. 21Et assumam

e. Gk Syr: Heb lacks *know* **f.** Gk Syr Vg Tg: Heb *it is* **g.** Gk: Heb *Pul*

Is 51:6; 65:17 Rev 21:1–27 22 "For as the new heavens and the new earth
which I will make
shall remain before me, says the LORD;
so shall your descendants and your name remain.
23 From new moon to new moon,
and from sabbath to sabbath,
all flesh shall come to worship before me,
says the LORD.

Deut 16:17 24"And they shall go forth and look on the dead bodies of the
Mk 9:48 men that have rebelled against me; for their worm shall not die,
Sir 7:17 their fire shall not be quenched, and they shall be an abhorrence to
all flesh."

---

prophesies the last day, when Christ will come again to reward each man according to his deeds" (Pseudo-Clement, *Epistula II ad Corinthios*, 17, 4).

The nations mentioned in v. 19 are not easy to identify; but Tarshish is probably Spain; Put, Libya; Lud, Lydia; Tubal, Cilicia; and Javan, Ionia, Greece.

"And some of them also I will take for priests" (v. 21): this may mean (though one cannot be sure) that God will choose priests and Levites from among the pagans. Given the tenor of v. 22, it is more likely that "descendants" of Israel will hold the office of the holy priesthood; either interpretation fits in with the general newness and universalism that are a feature of chapters 65 and 66 (cf. 61:6).

The last oracle in the book of Isaiah is a call to an active, living hope (vv. 22–24). Verse 23, in its initial historical context, was addressed to the chosen people of the Old Testament, but it opens out to include all mankind; that is how the Fathers interpreted it. "There will be a new heaven and a new earth, where man will live forever united with God. Isaiah tells us that this new life will last forever: *For as the new heavens and the new earth which I shall make shall remain before me, says the Lord; so shall your descendants and your name remain* (Is 66:22)" (St Irenaeus of Lyons, *Adversus haereses*, 5, 36, 1).

Even so, a warning is issued about the punishment that awaits evildoers (v. 24). The harshness of the language here is in sharp contrast to the general tone of hope. The prophet may have chosen to strike this dark note in order to have the inhabitants of Zion (the saved) recognize God's sovereignty over those who reject him and have them appreciate the blessings bestowed in Zion, that is, in heaven. Jesus uses the metaphor of the worm that does not die to describe the punishment earned by the grave sin of scandal (cf. Mk 9:48).

ex eis in sacerdotes et Levitas, dicit Dominus. [22]Quia sicut caeli novi / et terra nova, quae ego faciam, / stabunt coram me, / dicit Dominus, / sic stabit semen vestrum et nomen vestrum. / [23]Et erit: unoquoque novilunio / et quovis sabbato / veniet omnis caro, ut adoret coram facie mea, / dicit Dominus. / [24]Et egredientur et videbunt cadavera virorum, / qui praevaricati sunt in me; / nam vermis eorum non morietur, / et ignis eorum non exstinguetur, / et erunt abominationi omni carni».

JEREMIAH

Introduction

Jeremiah is the second of the Major Prophets. In the Hebrew Bible and in the Vulgate Latin version his book comes after Isaiah and before Ezekiel. It focuses on the person and the preaching of the prophet Jeremiah, who lived in the last decades of the kingdom of Judah—a very important period, since it saw the collapse of the Assyrian empire, the rebirth of the Babylonian empire and the complete disappearance of the kingdom of Judah with the deportation of its leading families.

Jeremiah lived in Judah, during the time that the Neo-Babylonian empire began to constitute a threat to the Israelites (from 605 BC on) until eventually Jerusalem fell to the forces of Nebuchadnezzar (587 BC) and the deportation to Babylon took place. The prophet was well placed to see all these events and he was familiar with conditions in Judah after the deportation.

The text of Jeremiah has come down to us in two different versions. One of these has been transmitted through manuscripts written in Hebrew, and the other through Greek codexes. The Hebrew text is considerably longer than the Greek (it has some 2,700 more words) and in it the various oracles are arranged differently to the way they appear in the Greek. Still, the content of the two versions is virtually identical; they may well derive from two different stages in the editing process (which involved collecting and arranging the corpus of oracles and accounts attributed to Jeremiah or in which he figures as the protagonist). Christian preachers and commentators have used both Hebrew and Greek texts, depending on where they came from and where and when they lived; the Greek Fathers tended very much to use the Septuagint Greek text; the Vulgate (the Latin version most widely used in the Western Church) is more in line with the Hebrew than with the Greek version.

1. STRUCTURE AND CONTENT

Like the books of Isaiah and Ezekiel, this is a long book. It contains a large number of oracles deriving from a number of different periods; these are not arranged in chronological order; still, there is a certain, though not very well defined, logic to the order. This explains why the various editions of the Bible structure the book differently, one from another; that is, their system of headings and subheadings etc. varies.

Moreover, due to the considerable differences in text-arrangement in the Greek and Hebrew (referred to above), it is more difficult to "structure" the book of Jeremiah than other prophetical books. The most important difference has to do with the positioning of the "Oracles concerning the nations", which in the Greek appear after 23:13, thereby forming the central core of the book, whereas in Hebrew these come at the end, in chapters 46–51. The biblical translation made for the Spanish edition of the Navarre Bible is based on the Hebrew text and therefore has the "Oracles concerning the nations" at the end (as does the Revised Standard Version); hence the "structure" proposed and used in this edition: the book is divided into three parts, preceded by a prologue and followed by an epilogue.

PROLOGUE. THE CALLING AND THE MISSION OF JEREMIAH (1:1–19). A short heading or title (1:1–3) telling us when Jeremiah's preaching took place is followed by an account of his calling and of the mission given him by the Lord to preach his word (1:4–10). This in turn is followed by two symbolic visions seen by the prophet—the vision of the almond root (1:11–12) and the vision of the boiling pot (1:13–19).

1. ORACLES CONCERNING ISRAEL AND JUDAH (2:1—25:38). This is a substantial collection of the prophet's oracles on Israel and Judah over the course of his long career. The first section ties in somewhat with the theme of the vision of the root of almond, that is, the theme of vigilance, and it is a call to conversion addressed to the house of Israel and the house of Judah (2:1—4:4). The second section, connected with the vision of the boiling pot, is set in the framework of the threat posed to Judah and Jerusalem of military incursions by foreign powers. The prophet proclaims that the impending disaster can be attributed to the chosen people's infidelity to God (4:5—10:25). The third section focuses on the punishment awaiting Jerusalem and its cause (the breaking of the Covenant); all this is described in oracles and symbolic actions (11:1—20:18). And the last section of this part of the book enunciates divine judgment—exile—for which both kings and false prophets are to blame (21:1—25:38).

2. STORIES ABOUT THE LIFE OF JEREMIAH (26:1—45:5). The first part of the book consisted largely of oracles in verse, with occasional passages in prose. The reverse happens in the second part. It is mainly in prose and consists of accounts of Jeremiah's activity, focusing particularly on his oral preaching and his symbolic actions and their consequences. First we are told about clashes that he had with priests and false prophets (26:1—29:32). Then, after a description of the complicated situation that the prophet found himself in, comes a kind of parenthesis, the hope-filled "Book of Consolation" (30:1—33:26), with its promises of a rebuilding of Jerusalem and a renewal of the people, based on a New Covenant that will endure forever. This is followed by an account of the sufferings endured by Jeremiah over the course of his mission. The difficulties described in the first section of this part were

compounded by those that stemmed from his dealings with the kings of Judah (34:1—36:32). The persecution to which the prophet was subjected culminated in what could be called the "passion of Jeremiah", that is, all the various sufferings he underwent before and during the siege of Jerusalem by the Babylonians, and the great trials he experienced after the fall of the holy city (37:1—44:30).

3. ORACLES CONCERNING THE NATIONS (46:1—51:64). At this point, near the end of the book, the Hebrew manuscripts have a collection of oracles addressed not only to the the immediate neighbours of Israel and Judah but also to more distant countries—Egypt (46:2–28), the Philistines (47:1–7), Moab (48:1–47), the Ammonites (49:1–6), Edom (49:7–22), Damascus (49:23–27), Kedar and the kingdoms of Hazor (49:28–33), Elam (49:34–39) and Babylon (50:1—51:64); in other words, the oracles are arranged in such a way that they begin with Egypt, the ancient enemy, and end with Babylon, the invader that overpowered Judah. When the fall of Babylon is announced, reference is made to the imminent liberation of Jerusalem. Thus, the denunciation of the crimes of the pagans and the declaration of the punishments that will overtake them are a signal of the salvation that awaits Israel.

EPILOGUE. THE FALL OF JERUSALEM (52:1–34). The book ends with a concise account of the last days of the holy city; this is largely the same as the account found in the second book of Kings (cf. 2 Kings 24:18—25:30). The account covers the fall of Jerusalem to Nebuchadnezzar, the deportation that took place then, and the transfer to Babylon of the temple treasures. It ends with a short reference to the good treatment received in Babylon by the young King Jehoiachin, a proof that God protects the people even in most adverse circumstances.

Given the references to times etc. in the headings of many oracles, it is quite clear that they have not been arranged chronologically. What the compiler(s) did in fact was put most of the earlier oracles in the first sections of verse oracles addressed to Israel and Judah; and one can see a certain chronological order in the accounts of Jeremiah's prophetical activity that make up the second part of the book. Still, the material has basically been arranged by theme. It is significant, therefore, that at the centre of the book, as its theological core, so to speak, we find biographical accounts of Jeremiah's clashes with priests, false prophets and kings, being interrupted by a section that is largely a song of hope in the future restoration of Israel, the so-called "Book of Consolation".

2. COMPOSITION

Like most of the books of Holy Scripture, the book of Jeremiah went through a long and complex process of composition. The text itself tells us about the earliest and most important stages in this process. In chapter 36, Jeremiah tells us that, at the Lord's bidding, in the reign of Jehoiakim he saw to it that all the oracles he had spoken up to then were written down on a scroll. The prophet, who was under arrest at the time, called for Baruch, his secretary, and dictated this material to him. Once the scroll was written, Baruch took it to the temple and read it out, in line with Jeremiah's instructions. When the princes heard what was on the scroll, they decided to tell the king about it. The book was then read to the king who, as the reading progressed, cut off the sections just read and set fire to them in a brazier. So, the first copy of the book, all of it, was burned. At the Lord's instruction, Jeremiah dictated the text again to Baruch, who wrote it down, along with "many similar words" (36:32). This is as much as we know from the book itself.

It is also clear from the book that it contains at least two sorts of texts—one being verse oracles in which, when he speaks, Jeremiah uses the first person singular, just as if he were declaiming. Other passages are prose accounts, in which Jeremiah is normally spoken of in the third person: the prophet is the protagonist in narratives written by someone else.

It is likely possible that most of the original denunciation oracles spoken by Jeremiah—the first edition of the work, dictated to Baruch—are to be found among the verse oracles in the book that has come down to us. A good number of them would be in the first part (more specifically, in chapters 1–20), which includes the oracles about the house of Israel and the house of Judah. Later, that first collection of oracles would have been filled out with other oracles spoken by Jeremiah in various contexts and with various purposes in mind. There, too, other verse pieces would have been placed, scattered throughout chapters 11–20—heartfelt prayers offered in the presence of God. Baruch was probably responsible for the prose accounts; these set the oracles in a framework, record various symbolic actions performed by Jeremiah and narrate the difficulties that the prophet had to cope with as he strove to fulfil his mission from God. And these additions would have created a new edition of the book, one that would not be very different from its final form.

When Judah reached the nadir of its fortunes, with the fall of Jerusalem and the exile to Babylon, that collection of the oracles of Jeremiah would have helped to throw much light on the reasons for the calamitous situation in which the Jews found themselves. In the copies which may have been made at that time, these teachings were concluded in oracles composed in a markedly Deuteronomic style. Decades later, when Babylon fell to Cyrus the Great and the situation began to improve and hopes for the restoration of Israel were on the point of being realized, people were able to see in Jeremiah, in details of his oracles, things that had not seemed very important up to then; the restoration oracles, added at this time, had the effect of giving the whole book a more optimistic tone.

The differences in detail between the Hebrew and Greek editions of the book do not affect its canonicity: from the very beginning Jews and Christians saw it as part of the canon of Holy Scripture. As has been pointed out earlier, the Church has in fact used both the Greek and the Hebrew texts, venerating both as the word of God.

3. JEREMIAH AND HIS TIMES

The teachings contained in the book of Jeremiah stem primarily from the life and personality of the prophet himself; in other words, what he did and how he lived up to his calling in times of religious crisis carry a lesson that is always valid.

Jeremiah was born in Anathoth, a small town in the kingdom of Judah, to the north of Jerusalem, in the territory of the tribe of Benjamin (cf. Jer 1:1). He came from a priestly family and his work as a prophet lasted over forty years. His ministry began in the thirteenth year of Josiah, that is, 627 BC. During that king's reign, Jeremiah's ministry focused on the house of Israel; even though the kingdom of Israel no longer existed as such, the people could not easily forget it. The oracles that belong to this period contain denunciations of the apostasy and moral corruption of his fellow-citizens, calls to conversion, and warnings about an impending punishment due to the people's disregard for God. Five years after Jeremiah received his calling, in 622, King Josiah initiated a significant religious reform designed to bring the life of the kingdom into line with the Law of God. This stressed that the Lord was the only God, and sought to centralize religious worship at the temple in Jerusalem. Although Jeremiah must have been well aware of this reform movement, at no point does his book expressly mention it.

When Josiah died, his son Jehoahaz ruled for a short while and was succeeded by his brother Jehoiakim in 609. His accession meant a change of direction in religious policy, for the new king failed to enforce Josiah's reforms. The Law of God and the Covenant were transgressed more and more frequently. Jeremiah was preaching in Jerusalem during this period, his most notable address being a sermon in the temple against corrupt forms of worship; for this, he suffered imprisonment, but he continued his work as a prophet through his secretary, Baruch, inveighing against formalism in religious worship, any false reliance on religion, and idolatry and social injustice.

Shortly after the death of Jehoiakim, Nebuchadnezzar conquered Jerusalem (597), and made Judah a vassal kingdom; he took captive the young king Jehoiachin (who reigned for only a few months) and other leading citizens; these he brought to Babylon, leaving Zedekiah as king of Judah. This marked a new stage in the life of Jeremiah. He spoke out against those left behind in Judah; they considered that the deportees were exiled because their sins deserved that punishment; they claimed that they themselves were true to God—whereas for the most part the people in Jerusalem carried on much as they had done before, failing to realize that all these events were punishment for their own persistent infidelity to the Covenant. They kept trying to throw off the Babylonian yoke, through their own efforts or with the help of foreign allies. Jeremiah, for his part, urged them to accept the situation and submit to the Babylonians—and to become genuinely converted to the Lord. His preaching earned him the enmity of all—people, priests, prophets and kings—with the result that he was thrown into prison, where he stayed until the city fell to the Babylonians a second time, in 587 BC.

After this final defeat, which saw Zedekiah and many others being sent into exile, Jeremiah stayed in Jerusalem, which was now placed under the control of a governor, Gedaliah. Not long after his appointment, Gedaliah was assassinated, and the situation became so unstable that many of those left in Judah fled to Egypt, forcing Jeremiah to go with them. That is the last we hear of the prophet, whose career had begun forty years earlier.[1]

Jeremiah lived in Jerusalem for much of his life, and (as can be deduced from his recorded preaching, imbued as it is with images of ordinary life and freedom)[2] he must have been a man who liked to lead an ordinary, simple life; still, his divine mission made heavy demands on him. From the very start he discovered that his was no easy task and what he had to say was very unpopular; he was the butt of much criticism, and he made many enemies. This meant that his situation was often difficult, and sometimes painful. Yet, despite this, he stayed true to the Lord. The so-called "confessions"[3] in the book sum up the prophet's personality. He does not mince his words when he describes his inner feelings, his difficulties and sometimes his downheartedness, but at all times his faithfulness shines through.

4. MESSAGE

As already mentioned, the book of Jeremiah is thoroughly imbued with Deuteronomic thinking, which was very conscious of the importance of prophets and their message in the religious life of Israel. From the very start, when the book gives an account of Jeremiah's calling (1:4–10), the message is that the word of God, as placed on Jeremiah's lips, will certainly come true: what it says will happen—both the misfortunes and the salvation it predicts (Jer 1:10;18:7–8). The prophet is the authoritative interpreter of human events, the person commissioned to reveal the religious message that they contain. Time and again Jeremiah makes the point that the misfortunes that overtake Judah, including the exile, are the inevitable result of having broken the Covenant—and that God will send salvation and prosperity in a time to come.

1. According to a tradition first mentioned by Tertullian (*Scorpiace*, 8) his fellow citizens stoned him to death in Egypt. **2.** Cf. Jer 1:11–12; 1:13–19; 8:7; 17:11; 17:8; 14:4–6; 2:13. **3.** Cf. Jer 11:18—12:6; 15:10–21; 17:14–18; 18:18–23 and 20:7–18.

The Covenant

Like the other prophets, Jeremiah teaches that the God of Israel, the Lord, is the only true God. The other gods are idols, the product of human hands, lifeless bits of wood, stone or metal; there is nothing they can do for man (cf. 2:27–28; 10:3–5). But God is the creator of everything that exists—earth and heavens, sea and sky, wind and rain (cf. 10:12–13). He rules over everything; nothing escapes him (cf. 23:24), not even the innermost thoughts of the human heart (cf. 12:3; 18:23). He knows what happened to his people in the past, and their present circumstances—and what lies awaits them in the future (cf. 29:10–14; 33:3); and his judgment is just (cf. 11:10).

The prophet lays great stress on the Covenant as the bond linking God and his people. He uses Hosea's marriage-imagery to show that God's relationship with his people is one of love, and he describes very tenderly God's preferential love for Israel (2:1–13), a reciprocated love: "I remember the devotion of your youth" (2:2). He also follows Hosea in depicting God's love for Israel as that of a father for his child (3:19; 31:20). And he develops a form of words that makes clear that the Covenant has more to do with Love than with law. "I will be your God, and you shall be my people."[4] More than any other prophet, Jeremiah lamented the fact that the people broke the Covenant by their sins; and he again uses spousal imagery to make his point: "Surely, as a faithless wife leaves her husband, so have you been faithless to me, O house of Israel, says the Lord" (3:20). It pains him deeply to have to announce punishment and exile: "I said, 'Truly this is an affliction, and I must bear it.' My heart is destroyed, and all my cords are broken; my children have gone from me, and they are not" (10:19–20; cf. 3:13, 16, 19). In a mood of nostalgia, he laments the people's failure to mend their ways: "If you return, O Israel, says the Lord, to me you should return. If you remove your abominations [idols] from my presence …" (4:1).

Jeremiah's affection for God is most clearly to be seen in his "confessions", so called because they express the prophet's deepest feelings. In them he goes so far as to complain to the Lord, as a son would to his father, about the meagre results of his ministry: "I have not lent, nor have I borrowed, yet all of them curse me."

The "Book of Consolation" (30:1—33:26), which, as we have suggested, marks the climax of Jeremiah's theological message, hinges on the proclamation of the New Covenant: "Behold, the days are coming, says the Lord, when I will make a new covenant with the house of Israel and the house of Judah, not like the covenant which I made with their fathers when I took them by the hand to bring them out of the land of Egypt, my covenant which they broke, though I was their husband, says the Lord. But this is the covenant

4. Jer 7:23; 11:4; 30:22. Ezekiel, keen to lay the stress on the transcendence of God, retains only the first part of the phrase: "I am the Lord your God" (Ezek 20:7, 19, 20; 34:31).

which I will make with the house of Israel after those days, says the Lord: I will put my law within them, and I will write it upon their hearts; and I will be their God, and they shall be my people" (31:31–34). He joyfully proclaims that when man turns back to God, God will be merciful and save him. Not only that: God will enter into a New Covenant, which will be engraved on the human heart and will endure forever. Unlike what happened in the past, it will never be broken; there will be no more recrimination or punishment.

Salvation

Jeremiah had ample evidence that persistence in sin and neglect of God bred a stubborn and rebellious heart (cf. 5:23), one offering little hope of conversion: sin seemed to be etched with a pen of iron, to be engraved on the heart (cf. 17:1), staining it so badly that even lye could not remove it (cf. 2:21–22), no more than an Ethiopian could change the colour of his skin (cf. 13:23). All this rebelliousness could not be blamed on the Lord; it was entirely due to Israel's constant infidelity (cf. 11:10).

The people's sins were so great that they must inevitably lead to punishment and misfortune. But the last word that God speaks is not of destruction but of restoration. The book of Jeremiah contains many oracles that tell of a future, enduring salvation. Those who were taken into exile by hostile nations will be reunited and God will bring them back to their land (cf. 16:14–15 = 23:7–8). This return refers not just to a change of place, a return to Judah; primarily it means a change of heart. It does not come about by moral effort on the people's part: it is an unmerited gift from God; he will change their hearts and imbue them with a fear of the Lord that makes them forever faithful to the everlasting Covenant (cf. 32:36–41). Therefore, the New Covenant that the Lord will make with his people will be indelibly engraved on their hearts, so that it will endure forever (cf. 31:33).

In this new situation everything will be made new: Judah will be saved, and Israel will live in peace, and this is the name by which the God of Israel will be called: "The Lord is our righteousness" (23:5–6).

Messianic hope

Jeremiah does not explicitly say that a descendant of David will rule Israel. What he says, rather, is that God himself will guide and save his people by means of new shepherds: the shepherds of old caused havoc; the new shepherds will do what is right: "You have scattered my flock, and have driven them away, and you have not attended to them. Behold, I will attend to you for your evil doings, says the Lord. Then I will gather the remnant of my flock out of all the countries where I have driven them, and I will bring them back to their fold, and they shall be fruitful and multiply. I will set shepherds over them who will care for them, and they shall fear no more, nor be dismayed, neither shall any be missing, says the Lord" (23:2–4).

Even so, the book of Jeremiah does contain some oracles which could properly be described as messianic: "Behold, the days are coming, says the Lord, when I will raise up for David a righteous Branch, and he shall reign as king and deal wisely, and shall execute justice and righteousness in the land...."[5] Still, in this oracle the emphasis is placed not on the monarchy but on the Davidic inheritance of which the future Messiah will partake. Thus, we can say that Jeremiah was the last prophet to announce a Messiah who will be a descendant of David; however, this does not mean that the Messiah will be a king; he will be someone who, while inheriting a king's prerogatives, will perform his functions with perfection and justice; in addition to being a king, he will be the Saviour.

5. THE BOOK OF JEREMIAH IN THE LIGHT OF THE NEW TESTAMENT

In Old Testament tradition and in later Judaism, Jeremiah was regarded as one of the great prophets of Israel.[6] His name is scarcely mentioned in the New Testament (Mt 2:17; 16:14; 27:9)—as is true of most of the prophets—but it does contain more than ten direct quotations from his book and very many indirect references. But the main connexion between the book of Jeremiah and the New Testament is the fact that the prophet's announcement of a New Covenant between God and his people is borne out by the witness that the New Testament gives to the effect that that Covenant has been established by Jesus Christ. Thus, after the passion, death and resurrection of our Lord Jesus Christ, when the apostles reflected on what God had said through the prophets about the salvation to come, a salvation that did indeed come about through events they themselves witnessed, they realized that this was what the prophet had foretold: the New Covenant had been sealed with the blood that Jesus shed on the cross. The accounts of the institution of the Eucharist that are passed on by the Synoptics and by St Paul bear witness to the fact that Jesus "took a cup, and when he had given thanks he gave it to them, saying, Drink of it, all of you; for this is my blood of the new covenant, which is poured out for many for the forgiveness of sins."[7]

St Paul, writing to the Corinthians about his apostolic ministry, says that God "has qualified us to be ministers of a new covenant, not in a written code but in the Spirit" (2 Cor 3:6), meaning that the time of which Jeremiah spoke had come with Jesus. Similarly, the Letter to the Hebrews says that Christ is the mediator of a New Covenant that is greater than the one made by Moses

5. Jer 23:5–6; cf. Jer 33:15–16; 22:4; 17:23. **6.** Cf. Sir 49:8–9. The second book of Maccabees records a tradition about the advice the prophet gave to those sent into exile (2 Mac 2:1–12; 15:12–16). **7.** Mt 26:27–28; cf. Mk 14:23–24; Lk 22:20; 1 Cor 11:25.

(cf. Heb 8:6–13). It also draws a comparison between the priesthood of the Old Testament, which repeatedly offers sacrifices that can never take away sins, with that of the New Covenant, which can indeed do so (cf. Heb 10:11–18). And if Jeremiah proclaimed that the Law of this New Covenant would be written on people's hearts, St Paul teaches that the new law he referred to was the law of the grace of the Holy Spirit who dwells in the hearts of Christians through faith in Christ (cf. Jer 31:31–34 and Rom 8:1–13).

Also, the life and teachings of Jeremiah, when compared to the character of Christ as drawn by the Gospels, show Jeremiah to have been the Old Testament figure who most closely resembled Christ. When one sees just how misunderstood Jeremiah was, even as early as when he preached to the people of Anathoth, his native town (cf. Jer 11:21), one can more easily appreciate what Jesus said in Nazareth when his townsfolk reacted against him: "A prophet is not without honour except in his own country and in his own house" (Mt 13:57). Moreover, we can on occasions see in Jesus the same attitudes as Jeremiah had towards Jerusalem, the temple, religious worship, the Law and false prophets;[8] and in his preaching our Lord often uses the same similes and images as the prophet—for example, that of the barren fig tree and that of the fount of living water (Jer 8:13 and Mt 21:18; Jer 2:12 and Jn 4:10–15; 7:37–38). And in the case of both Jeremiah and Jesus, faithfulness to his mission led to misunderstanding and persecution.

For reasons such as these, Christian tradition sees Jeremiah as being a figure of Jesus Christ. St Jerome puts it very plainly: "All of the churches believe that what is said of Jeremiah refers also to the person of Christ";[9] and St Isidore confirms that: "in his words and sufferings Jeremiah prefigured the passion and death of the Lord our Saviour".[10] And so we find that the Fathers and ecclesiastical writers (most notably Origen, St Cyril of Alexandria, St Jerome, St Thomas Aquinas), as well as commenting and expanding on those aspects of Jeremiah's teaching that have most bearing on the New Testament and on Christology, often refer to this prophet as being a faithful interpreter of the Word of God and a figure of Jesus Christ.

8. Jer 19 and Mt 23:38; Jer 7:1–15 and Mt 21:12–13; 24:1–2; 26:60–61; Jer 7:21–26; 11:15 and Mt 23:6, 23–36; Jer 8:8–9 and Mt 14:3–6; Jer 23 and Mt 7:15–20. **9.** St Jerome, *Commentarii in Ieremiam propheta*, 2, 11. **10.** St Isidore of Seville, *Allegoriae quaedam*, 108.

PROLOGUE

THE CALL AND MISSION OF JEREMIAH* 2 Kings 2:26–7; 2 Kings 22:1

1 [1] The words of Jeremiah, the son of Hilkiah, of the priests who Josh 21:18
were in Anathoth in the land of Benjamin, [2]to whom the word
of the LORD came in the days of Josiah the son of Amon, king of Zeph 1:1
Judah, in the thirteenth year of his reign. [3]It came also in the days
of Jehoiakim the son of Josiah, king of Judah, and until the end of
the eleventh year of Zedekiah, the son of Josiah, king of Judah,
until the captivity of Jerusalem in the fifth month.

The Lord calls Jeremiah
[4]Now the word of the LORD came to me saying,
[5]"Before I formed you in the womb I knew you, Is 49:1,5
and before you were born I consecrated you; Lk 1:15 Rom 8:29
I appointed you a prophet to the nations." Gal 1:15

***1:1–19.** The book of Jeremiah is a collection of the prophet's oracles arranged more by subject than in chronological order and interspersed with stories about his life. The heading (vv. 1–3), as in most of the prophetical books, introduces the prophet and tells when he lived. Then, as an introduction to the book, comes an account of the call of Jeremiah (vv. 4–10) along with two visions that give a good description of the man (vv. 11–12 and 13–19).

1:1–3. Anathoth was a village in the kingdom of Judah about 5 km. (3 miles) north-east of Jerusalem. It was a Levite city (cf. Jos 21:18), to which Abiathar the priest was confined by order of King Solomon (1 Kings 2:26–27). Jeremiah's ministry as a prophet began in 627 BC, during the reign of Josiah (639–609) and lasted until the deportation to Babylon in 587, during the reigns of Jehoiakim (609) and Zedekiah (597–587). No mention is made here of the reigns of Jehoahaz (609) and Jehoiachin (597), probably because they were very short.

1:4–10. This account of the call of Jeremiah gives a very good idea of the mysterious nature of every divine call—a call from all eternity and involving no merit on the part of the person called, in which God makes known to a soul the why and wherefore of his or her life. No one comes into being by accident, for everything that happens is

[1] [1]Verba Ieremiae filii Helciae de sacerdotibus, qui fuerunt in Anathoth in terra Beniamin. [2]Quod factum est verbum Domini ad eum in diebus Iosiae filii Amon regis Iudae, in tertio decimo anno regni eius. [3]Et factum est in diebus Ioachim filii Iosiae regis Iudae, usque ad consummationem undecimi anni Sedeciae filii Iosiae regis Iudae, usque ad transmigrationem Ierusalem in mense quinto. [4]Et factum est verbum Domini ad me dicens: [5]«Priusquam te formarem in utero, novi te / et, antequam exires de

Ex 4:10 Is 6:8 [6]Then I said, "Ah, LORD GOD! Behold, I do not know how to speak,
for I am only a youth."* [7]But the LORD said to me,
"Do not say, 'I am only a youth';
for to all to whom I send you you shall go,
and whatever I command you you shall speak.
Ezek 2:6 [8]Be not afraid of them,
for I am with you to deliver you,
says the LORD."

---

part of God's providence (v. 5). God's action in creating a person is described graphically—"formed" you in the womb—a word used to describe what a potter does when he models something in clay. The Lord "knew" Jeremiah—a reference to his choosing him for a specific mission (cf. Amos 3:2; Rom 8:29); God has a plan for each person, and he endows each with talents that equip him or her to put that plan into effect. The passage also talks of a "consecration", that is, the earmarking of a person or thing for the service of God. God's plan for someone, made before the person is born, emerges in due course, when he or she is old enough to take on the assignments that God has been preparing him for. Glossing this passage, St John Chrysostom, has God say this: "I am the one who knit you together in your mother's womb. Your life is not a work of nature, nor the fruit of suffering. I am the origin and cause of all things: you should obey and offer yourself to me," and he adds: "It does not begin with *I consecrated you: first, I knew you; then, I consecrated you.* Thus is the original choice shown, and after the original choice, the particular calling" (*Fragmenta in Ieremiam*, 1).

When the mystery of a person's calling begins to be revealed, their initial reaction can be one of fear, because they are very conscious of their limitations and feel that they are not up to the tasks that the Lord entrusts them with. Jeremiah, for example, argues that he is too young (v. 6). We do not know how old he was at the time, for the word he uses to describe his age (*na'ar*) is imprecise. He was probably only an adolescent (cf. Gen 37:2; 1 Sam 2:18; 3:1–21). In responding to a vocation, one needs to listen, above all, to God who calls, who never leaves his chosen ones on their own, and who always gives them the wherewithal to carry out the mission he is charging them with (vv. 7–8).

The Lord's symbolic gesture of putting out his hand to touch Jeremiah's mouth, as if to fill it with divine words, is similar to other gestures found in accounts of the calling of prophets (cf. Is 6:7; Ezek 2:8—3:3; Dan 10:16). It is to tell the man not to be concerned: he can rest assured that God will give him the right words to express himself. It is

vulva, sanctificavi te / et prophetam gentibus dedi te». [6]Et dixi: «Heu, Domine Deus! Ecce nescio loqui, quia puer ego sum». [7]Et dixit Dominus ad me: «Noli dicere: "Puer sum", / quoniam, ad quoscumque mittam te, ibis / et universa, quaecumque mandavero tibi, loqueris. / [8]Ne timeas a facie eorum, / quia

[9]Then the LORD put forth his hand and touched my mouth; 2 Sam 23:2 Is 6:6–7; Is 59:1–3:21
and the LORD said to me, Ezek 2:8; 3:1–3
"Behold, I have put my words in your mouth. Dan 10:16 Mt 10:19–20
[10]See, I have set you this day over nations and over kingdoms, Jer 18:7; 31:28;
to pluck up and to break down, 45:4; Hos 6:5
to destroy and to overthrow,
to build and to plant."

Vision of the rod of almond

[11]And the word of the LORD came to me, saying, "Jeremiah, Is 55:10–11
what do you see?" And I said, "I see a rod of almond."[a] [12]Then Ezek 12:28
the LORD said to me, "You have seen well, for I am watching[b] Ezek 9:14
over my word to perform it."

---

a promise similar to that made by Jesus to his disciples: he assured them of the Holy Spirit's help when the time came for them to bear witness to him (cf. Mt 10:19–20).

The assignment given to Jeremiah implies a heavy responsibility; he will need fortitude if he is to carry it out (v. 10). It involves in the first place doing destructive things (plucking up, breaking down, destroying and overthrowing) and only then come constructive roles (building and planting). St Gregory the Great will apply the same idea to the attention that is called for in the pastoral care of the faithful: "One cannot build up if what disturbs the foundation has not been destroyed. In other words, the sweet words of good preaching are sown in vain if the thorns of self-love have not first been plucked from the hearts of the listeners" (*Regula pastoralis*, 3, 34).

1:11–12. In Hebrew, the almond tree is called *sheked*, meaning "watchful, alert", because it is the first to blossom when winter is on the way out: it is, so to speak, alert enough to sense that spring is coming, whereas other trees are still asleep, hibernating. The branch of an almond tree symbolizes the vigilance of the Lord; nothing that affects his people escapes him, even if they are forgetful of him. Therefore, God has chosen the prophet to warn his people about imminent misfortune. St Thomas Aquinas, explaining the significance of this branch, says: "The branch is the rod in the Lord's hand, and he stands ready to punish [...]. Others say that it is the rod carried by thieves who steal into a house through the windows and stand over those who lie sleeping within. The first interpretation seems more fitting" (*Postilla super Jeremiam*, 1, 4).

tecum ego sum, ut eruam te», / dicit Dominus. [9]Et misit Dominus manum suam et tetigit os meum; et dixit Dominus ad me: «Ecce dedi verba mea in ore tuo; / [10]ecce constitui te hodie super gentes et super regna, / ut evellas et destruas / et disperdas et dissipes / et aedifices et plantes». [11]Et factum est verbum Domini ad me dicens: «Quid tu vides, Ieremia?». Et dixi: «Virgam amygdali vigilantis ego video». [12]Et

a. Heb *shaqed* **b.** Heb *shoqed*

Vision of the boiling pot

Jer 4:5–31 [13]The word of the LORD came to me a second time, saying, "What
do you see?" And I said, "I see a boiling pot, facing away from the
Jer 4:6; 6:1–22 north." [14]Then the LORD said to me, "Out of the north evil shall
break forth upon all the inhabitants of the land. [15]For, lo, I am
calling all the tribes of the kingdoms of the north, says the LORD;
and they shall come and every one shall set his throne at the
entrance of the gates of Jerusalem, against all its walls round
about, and against all the cities of Judah. [16]And I will utter my
judgments against them, for all their wickedness in forsaking me;
they have burned incense to other gods, and worshipped the works
Jer 1:7–8 of their own hands. [17]But you, gird up your loins; arise, and say to
them everything that I command you. Do not be dismayed by
Jer 15:20 them, lest I dismay you before them. [18]And I, behold, I make you
this day a fortified city, an iron pillar, and bronze walls, against the
whole land, against the kings of Judah, its princes, its priests, and
the people of the land. [19]They will fight against you; but they shall
not prevail against you, for I am with you, says the LORD, to
deliver you."

1:13–19. Jeremiah is shown a pot that is beginning to boil over (v. 13). He is given to understand the meaning of the disquieting news that is reaching Jerusalem—rumours of advances by foreign armies that threaten the holy city from the north (vv. 14–15). These reports are a warning that God sends his people to encourage them to admit their unfaithfulness (v. 16). In this way the Lord is beginning to announce a future punishment, which we shall hear much more about as the book develops—a chastisement to be inflicted on the people of Judah and Jerusalem for failing to keep the Covenant.

It will be up to Jeremiah to speak to them, reproaching them for their sins and explaining the reasons for events (vv. 17–18)—not an easy task, but God will give him the strength to perform it (v. 19).

This passage outlines the framework, the setting, of the oracles and narratives contained in the book. God never forgets his people and, in a time of crisis, when the kingdom of Judah is

dixit Dominus ad me: «Bene vidisti, quia vigilo ego super verbo meo, ut faciam illud». [13]Et factum est verbum Domini secundo ad me dicens: «Quid tu vides?». Et dixi: «Ollam succensam ego video; et facies eius a facie aquilonis». [14]Et dixit Dominus ad me: «Ab aquilone pandetur malum / super omnes habitatores terrae; / [15]quia ecce ego convocabo / omnia regna aquilonis, / ait Dominus, / et venient et ponent unusquisque solium suum / in introitu portarum Ierusalem / et contra omnes muros eius in circuitu / et contra universas urbes Iudae; / [16]et loquar iudicia mea cum eis / super omnem malitiam eorum, / qui dereliquerunt me / et incensum obtulerunt diis alienis / et adoraverunt opus manuum suarum. / [17]Tu ergo accinge lumbos tuos / et surge et loquere ad eos omnia, / quae ego praecipio tibi; / ne timeas a facie eorum, / alioquin timere te faciam vultum eorum. / [18]Ego quippe dedi te hodie / in civitatem munitam / et in columnam ferream / et in murum aereum / contra omnem terram / regibus Iudae, principibus eius / et sacerdotibus et populo terrae; / [19]et bellabunt adversum te et non

PART ONE

Oracles concerning Israel and Judah*

1. CALL TO CONVERSION*

When Israel was devout, it had nothing to fear

Ex 13:17; 19:6
Jer 11:15
Hos 2:16–17
Rev 14:4

2 [1]The word of the LORD came to me, saying, [2]"Go and proclaim
in the hearing of Jerusalem, Thus says the LORD,

---

about to collapse, he chooses Jeremiah and sends him out on his mission. God means him to show the people the real reasons for all the distress they will meet and, once all the various disasters have come to pass, he intends Jeremiah to console them and assure them that God never abandons them.

***2:1—25:38.** Most of the oracles are in verse in this part of the book, but there are some prose passages. It is possible that the scroll containing the earliest oracles (which was burnt in 605 by order of King Jehoiakim: cf. 36:21–23) was made up largely of the poems found in this part (2:1—25:38). They would have been arranged in some sort of thematic order with an eye, too, on chronology.

In the first ten chapters, the oracles turn on the two great themes of the two introductory visions. Firstly, in connexion with the vision of the root of almond (1:11–12), we get a summary of the sins that the prophet has noticed in his role as watchman: Israel and Judah have forsaken the Lord; therefore they must be chastised. God has been faithful, but the people have rejected him; this wrong must be righted without delay—unless there is a genuine change of heart (2:1—4:4). Secondly, in connexion with the vision of the boiling pot facing away from the north (1:13–19), we get oracles threatening destruction from that quarter (4:5—10:25).

From chapter 11 on, prose passages appear with greater frequency, and Jeremiah's symbolic actions begin to have a higher profile. The prophet has personal experience of suffering, and his cries for help epitomize the way the people feel when they are struck down by misfortune in punishment for their sins (11:1—20:18). This part of the book ends with a severe indictment of those who ought to have given leadership but failed to do so (21:1—25:38).

All of this first part of the book is a severe warning to the people of Jerusalem and the entire kingdom of Judah. Even so, divine mercy can still be discerned: there is a prospect of forgiveness and salvation.

praevalebunt, / quia tecum ego sum, / ait Dominus, / ut eripiam te». **[2]** [1]Et factum est verbum Domini ad me dicens: [2]«Vade et clama in auribus Ierusalem dicens: / Haec dicit Dominus: / Recordatus sum

I remember the devotion of your youth,
  your love as a bride,
how you followed me in the wilderness,
  in a land not sown.

***2:1—4:4.** The oracles contained in this section were spoken early in Jeremiah's ministry, during the reign of Josiah, and possibly before that king set in train his religious reform (for nowhere does Jeremiah refer to it). This means that they would date from the period 627–622 BC. The difference is clearly drawn (3:6–11) between Israel, the Northern kingdom, whose capital was Samaria, and which had fallen to Assyria in 722, and Judah, the Southern kingdom, whose capital was Jerusalem. Assyria had been in control of Israel for some one hundred years, but now it was in decline; and Josiah, king of Judah, was trying to re-establish national unity on all levels—social, political and religious. His efforts would culminate in the great religious reform that began in 622 and which sought to centralize all ritual religious worship in Jerusalem.

The oracles in this section are set in this historical background. The earliest, those conserved in verse form, were spoken by Jeremiah himself and exude the vitality and pain of someone who was an eyewitness. The passages that now appear in prose may well have been added later, when the book was being re-written after the first manuscript was burned (cf. 36:21–23). These oracles are a warning about sin, about the punishment that it draws down, and about the need for personal conversion in order to attain salvation. The text as it now stands makes it clear that the misfortune that overtook the people of Israel was due to their unfaithfulness to God (2:1–37). Even so, the Lord calls all to conversion; if they respond, he will restore peace and unity to the people (3:1—4:4).

2:1–37. The oracles in this chapter follow the pattern of pleadings used in the ancient Middle East when pacts or alliances were broken. First, the accused party and the witnesses are apprised of the subject of the dispute used. Then the benefits enjoyed by the accused are spelt out; he, for his part, should have adhered to what he agreed in the covenant. This is followed by a list of charges, often couched in the form of questions; and then at the end comes a demand for immediate action to be taken to set things right. If no agreement is arrived at, a declaration of war inevitably follows.

The word of the Lord here is not that of a judge but of one of the two parties who made the Covenant and has been deceived by the unfaithfulness of the other. The prophet begins by reminding the people of all the benefits they received from God during the time that

tui, caritatis adulescentiae tuae / et amoris desponsationis tuae, / quando secuta es me in deserto, / in terra, quae non seminatur. / [3]Sanctus Domino Israel, / primitiae frugum eius; / omnes, qui devorabant eum, delinquebant; / mala veniebant super eos, / dicit Dominus. / [4]Audite verbum Domini, domus

[3]Israel was holy to the LORD,
the first fruits of his harvest.
All who ate of it became guilty;
evil came upon them, says the LORD."

Israel's unfaithfulness

[4]Hear the word of the LORD, O house of Jacob, and all the families
of the house of Israel. [5]Thus says the LORD:

Hos 4:1–3
2 Kings 17:15
Ps 115:8
Hos 9:10

---

they were faithful to him. In the early days, as they made their way through the wilderness, they had a loving relationship with the Lord, and he took care of them (vv. 1–3); he rescued them from Egypt and brought them to the land promised to them as their inheritance (cf. Hos 1–3). However, instead of staying true to the Lord, the Israelites forsook him and fell lower than other nations (symbolized here by the peoples of the Aegean, "the coasts of Cyprus", and the Arab lands, "Kedar": v. 10). Their religion centred on a personal God who took provident care of his followers, yet they turned their backs on him to worship Baal and other gods, who are quite worthless (vv. 6–7). They may form alliances with earthly powers in the hope of getting help, but to no avail.

Even the language that Jeremiah uses shows that Israel has been distancing itself from God (he is upbraiding *Israel*, to have *Judah* react). In the opening verses he addresses his people using the familiar form of the word "you" (vv. 2–3), then he changes to the formal "you" (vv. 4–10), and eventually uses the third person (vv. 11–15). Only in the second part of these oracles does the familiar form return, when he reproves the people, to get them to mend their ways (vv. 16–37).

The metaphor of the leaking cisterns (v. 13) conveys very well just how ineffective are Israel's pacts with foreign nations. In Jeremiah's time, there was a lot of debate about whether or not to make alliances with Assyria or Egypt to ensure survival in the face of hostile foreign powers. The prophet regards such pacts as being of no real use, but he also points to the danger of idolatry that may arise through contact with foreigners. Hence the sarcasm in vv. 16–18: Memphis and Tahpanhes, were two cities on the Lower Nile; "the Euphrates": literally, "River" (no definite article) in Hebrew. The people's fascination with the waters and lands of Egypt and Assyria indicates the pull exercised by those great powers on Israel. God had taken care of his people, he had given them a beautiful land of their own, yet Israel had turned away from him and gone after idols—infidelity leading to idolatry (vv. 4–27). Yet Israel will not acknowledge that it has done wrong, so the Lord accuses the people of their sins and warns them that if they don't change they will be brought low (vv. 28–37).

Iacob / et omnes cognationes domus Israel. / [5]Haec dicit Dominus: / Quid invenerunt patres vestri in me iniquitatis, / quia elongaverunt a me / et ambulaverunt post vanitatem / et vani facti sunt? / [6]Et non

"What wrong did your fathers find in me
that they went far from me,
and went after worthlessness, and became worthless?
Deut 8:14–16; 32:10–12 [6]They did not say, 'Where is the LORD
who brought us up from the land of Egypt,
who led us in the wilderness,
in a land of deserts and pits,
in a land of drought and deep darkness,
in a land that none passes through,
where no man dwells?'
Ex 3:8 Deut 8:7–10 [7]And I brought you into a plentiful land
to enjoy its fruits and its good things.
But when you came in you defiled my land,
and made my heritage an abomination.
Jer 8:8 Ezek 34:1 [8]The priests did not say, 'Where is the LORD?'
Those who handle the law did not know me;
the rulers[c] transgressed against me;
the prophets prophesied by Baal,
and went after things that do not profit.

[9]"Therefore I still contend with you, says the LORD,
and with your children's children I will contend.
Jer 18:13–16 [10]For cross to the coasts of Cyprus and see,
or send to Kedar and examine with care;
see if there has been such a thing.
Ex 24:16 Ps 106:20 Rom 1:23 [11]Has a nation changed its gods,
even though they are no gods?
But my people have changed their glory
for that which does not profit.
[12]Be appalled, O heavens, at this,
be shocked, be utterly desolate, says the LORD,

---

dixerunt: "Ubi est Dominus, / qui ascendere nos fecit de terra Aegypti, / qui traduxit nos per desertum,
/ per terram inhabitabilem et inviam, / per terram sitis et caliginis, / per terram, in qua non ambulavit
vir, / neque habitavit homo?". / [7]Et induxi vos in terram hortorum, / ut comederetis fructum eius et
optima illius; / et ingressi contaminastis terram meam / et hereditatem meam posuistis in
abominationem. / [8]Sacerdotes non dixerunt: / "Ubi est Dominus?". / Et tractantes legem nescierunt me,
/ et pastores praevaricati sunt in me, / et prophetae prophetaverunt in Baal / et, quae nihil prosunt, secuti
sunt. / [9]Propterea adhuc iudicio contendam vobiscum, / ait Dominus, / et cum filiis filiorum vestrorum
disceptabo. / [10]En transite ad insulas Cetthim et videte / et in Cedar mittite et considerate vehementer
/ et videte, si factum est huiuscemodi: / [11]si mutavit gens deos, / et certe ipsi non sunt dii; / populus vero
meus mutavit gloriam suam / in id, quod nihil prodest. / [12]Obstupescite, caeli, super hoc / et inhorrescite
supra modum, / dicit Dominus. / [13]Duo enim mala fecit populus meus: / me dereliquerunt fontem aquae
vivae, / ut foderent sibi cisternas, / cisternas dissipatas, / quae continere non valent aquas. / [14]Numquid

c. Heb *shepherds*

[13] for my people have committed two evils: Jn 4:1
they have forsaken me,
the fountain of living waters,
and hewed out cisterns for themselves,
broken cisterns,
that can hold no water.

[14] "Is Israel a slave? Is he a homeborn servant?
Why then has he become a prey?
[15] The lions have roared against him,
they have roared loudly.
They have made his land a waste;
his cities are in ruins, without inhabitant.
[16] Moreover, the men of Memphis and Tahpanhes Is 3:17; 7:20
have broken the crown of your head.

2:13. The image of the broken cisterns that cannot hold water is used again and again in Christian writing as an example of the condition of man when, instead of trusting in the Lord, he relies on himself or on earthly things. St Irenaeus of Lyons, for example, advises us to look for really solid support: "Where the Church is, there is the Spirit of God; and where the Spirit is, there is the Church and all grace. The Spirit is truth. Those who are not possessed of the Spirit are not suckled at their mother's breast to give them life, nor do they draw from the living waters that flow from the body of Christ: they *hewed out cisterns for themselves, broken cisterns*, and drink stagnant water. They abandon the faith of the Church and are no longer protected; they reject the Spirit and are not enlightened. Having departed from the way of truth, they are overcome by every error; they can find no sure footing. Their beliefs change from one moment to the next, and they never come to any conclusion because they would rather be the masters of words than followers of the truth. They do not build on rock, but on sand" (*Adversus haereses*, 3, 24, 1–2).

For his part, St John of the Cross applies the image to those who neglect God in their insatiable desire for possessions. "their appetite grows and their thirst increases the further they find themselves from the only source that can satisfy them, who is God. God himself said of them through Jeremiah his prophet: *they have forsaken me, the fountain of living waters, and hewed out cisterns for themselves, broken cisterns, that can hold no water*. What they drink in created things cannot satisfy their thirst, but only increases it. They sin in a thousand ways through their love for created things, and do themselves incalculable harm" (*Ascent of Mount Carmel*, 3, 19, 7).

servus est Israel / aut vernaculus? / Quare ergo factus est in praedam? / Super eum rugierunt leones / [15]et dederunt vocem suam;/ posuerunt terram eius in solitudinem: / civitates eius exustae sunt, / et non

Jer 4:18; 6:19 17 Have you not brought this upon yourself
by forsaking the LORD your God,
when he led you in the way?
Is 30:1–3 18 And now what do you gain by going to Egypt,
to drink the waters of the Nile?
Or what do you gain by going to Assyria,
to drink the waters of the Euphrates?
19 Your wickedness will chasten you,
and your apostasy will reprove you.
Know and see that it is evil and bitter
for you to forsake the LORD your God;
the fear of me is not in you, says the Lord GOD of hosts.

Deut 12:2; 23:19 20 "For long ago you broke your yoke
Jr 14:23 and burst your bonds;
Is 5:10; 6:9; 8:13 and you said, 'I will not serve.'
Ezek 16:16 Yea, upon every high hill
Mt 11:28:30 and under every green tree
you bowed down as a harlot.
21 Yet I planted you a choice vine,
wholly of pure seed.
How then have you turned degenerate
and become a wild vine?
22 Though you wash yourself with lye
and use much soap,
the stain of your guilt is still before me, says the Lord GOD.
23 How can you say, 'I am not defiled,
I have not gone after the Baals'?
Look at your way in the valley;
know what you have done—
a restive young camel interlacing her tracks,
24 a wild ass used to the wilderness,
in her heat sniffing the wind!

---

est qui habitet in eis. / [16]Filii quoque Mempheos et Taphnes / decalvabunt tibi verticem. / [17]Numquid non istud factum est tibi, / quia dereliquisti Dominum Deum tuum / eo tempore, quo ducebat te per viam? / [18]Et nunc quid tibi vis in via Aegypti, / ut bibas aquam Nili? / Et quid tibi cum via Assyriorum, / ut bibas aquam Fluminis? / [19]Arguet te malitia tua, / et aversio tua increpabit te; / scito et vide quia malum et amarum est / reliquisse te Dominum Deum tuum et non esse timorem mei apud te, / dicit Dominus, Deus exercituum. / [20]A saeculo confregisti iugum tuum, / rupisti vincula tua / et dixisti: "Non serviam". / In omni enim colle sublimi / et sub omni ligno frondoso / tu prosternebaris meretrix. / [21]Ego autem plantavi te vineam electam, / omne semen verum; / quomodo ergo conversa es / in palmites vineae alienae? / [22]Si laveris te nitro / et multiplicaveris tibi herbam fullonum, / maculata es in iniquitate tua coram me, / dicit Dominus Deus. / [23]Quomodo dicis: "Non sum polluta, / post Baalim non ambulavi"? / Vide viam tuam in convalle, / scito quid feceris: / camelus levis contorquens vias suas. / [24]Onager assuetus in solitudine / in desiderio animae suae attrahit aerem; / libidinem eius quis avertet?

Who can restrain her lust?
None who seek her need weary themselves;
in her month they will find her.
25 Keep your feet from going unshod
and your throat from thirst.
But you said, 'It is hopeless,
for I have loved strangers,
and after them I will go.'

Amos 2:4
Hos 2:7

26 "As a thief is shamed when caught,
so the house of Israel shall be shamed:
they, their kings, their princes,
their priests, and their prophets,
27 who say to a tree, 'You are my father,'
and to a stone, 'You gave me birth.'
For they have turned their back to me,
and not their face.
But in the time of their trouble they say,
'Arise and save us!'
28 But where are your gods
that you made for yourself?
Let them arise, if they can save you,
in your time of trouble;
for as many as your cities
are your gods, O Judah.

Deut 32:37–38
Jer 11:13

29 "Why do you complain against me?
You have all rebelled against me, says the LORD.
30 In vain have I smitten your children,
they took no correction;
your own sword devoured your prophets
like a ravening lion.

Amos 4:6
Mt 23:37

31 And you, O generation, heed the word of the LORD.
Have I been a wilderness to Israel,
or a land of thick darkness?
Why then do my people say, 'We are free,

Jer 2:23

/ Omnes, qui quaerunt eam, non deficient, / in menstruis eius invenient eam. / [25]Prohibe pedem tuum a nuditate / et guttur tuum a siti. / Et dixisti: «"Vanum est, nequaquam; / adamavi quippe alienos / et post eos ambulabo". / [26]Quomodo confunditur fur, quando deprehenditur, / sic confusi sunt domus Israel, / ipsi et reges eorum, principes / et sacerdotes et prophetae eorum / [27]dicentes ligno: "Pater meus es tu" et lapidi: "Tu me genuisti". / Verterunt ad me tergum et non faciem, / sed in tempore afflictionis suae dicent: / "Surge et libera nos!". / [28]Ubi sunt dii tui, quos fecisti tibi? / Surgant et liberent te in tempore afflictionis tuae; / secundum numerum quippe civitatum tuarum / facti sunt dii tui, Iuda. / [29]Quid vultis mecum iudicio contendere? / Omnes praevaricati estis in me, / dicit Dominus. / [30]Frustra percussi filios vestros: / disciplinam non receperunt. / Devoravit gladius vester prophetas vestros: / quasi leo vastator. / [31]O generatio, vos videte verbum Domini: / numquid solitudo factus sum Israeli / aut terra tenebrarum? / Quare

we will come no more to thee'?
32 Can a maiden forget her ornaments,
or a bride her attire?
Yet my people have forgotten me
days without number.

33 "How well you direct your course
to seek lovers!
So that even to wicked women
you have taught your ways.
Is 1:15 34 Also on your skirts is found
the lifeblood of guiltless poor;
you did not find them breaking in.
Yet in spite of all these things
35 you say, 'I am innocent;
surely his anger has turned from me.'
Behold, I will bring you to judgment
for saying, 'I have not sinned.'
36 How lightly you gad about,
changing your way!
You shall be put to shame by Egypt
as you were put to shame by Assyria.
37 From it too you will come away
with your hands upon your head,
for the LORD has rejected those in whom you trust,
and you will not prosper by them.

Israel, repudiated

Deut 24:1–4 3 1"If[d] a man divorces his wife
and she goes from him

3:1–5. In the last chapter the connexion between God and his people was referred to in terms of a loving relationship (cf. 2:2). The same marriage imagery is used here to describe God's rejection of Israel. Note the frequent use of the verb "to

ergo dixit populus meus: "Recessimus, / non veniemus ultra ad te"? / 32Numquid obliviscitur virgo ornamenti sui, / sponsa fasciae pectoralis suae? / Populus vero meus oblitus est mei / diebus innumeris. / 33Quam bene paras viam tuam / ad quaerendum amorem! / Et insuper in malum / docuisti vias tuas, / 34et in fimbriis tuis inventus est / sanguis animarum pauperum innocentium: / non effringentes invenisti eos; / sed in omnibus his / 35dixisti: "Innocens ego sum, / propterea aversus est furor eius a me". / Ecce ego iudicio contendam tecum, eo quod dixeris: "Non peccavi". / 36Quam leviter mutas vias tuas! / Et ab Aegypto confunderis, / sicut confusa es ab Assyria. / 37Nam et ab ista egredieris, / et manus tuae erunt super caput tuum, / quoniam obtrivit Dominus illos, quibus confisus es, / et nihil habebis prosperum in eis. **[3]** 1Si dimiserit vir uxorem suam, / et recedens ab eo / duxerit virum alterum, / numquid revertetur ad eam

d. Gk Syr: Heb *Saying, If*

and becomes another man's wife,
 will he return to her?
Would not that land be greatly polluted?
You have played the harlot with many lovers;
 and would you return to me? says the LORD.
[2]Lift up your eyes to the bare heights, and see! — Deut 12:2
 Where have you not been lain with? — Jer 2:20
By the waysides you have sat awaiting lovers
 like an Arab in the wilderness.
You have polluted the land
 with your vile harlotry.
[3]Therefore the showers have been withheld, — Lev 20:29; 26:19
 and the spring rain has not come; — Jer 5:24; 14:4
yet you have a harlot's brow,
 you refuse to be ashamed.
[4]Have you not just now called to me,
 'My father, thou art the friend of my youth—
[5]will he be angry for ever,
 will he be indignant to the end?'
Behold, you have spoken,
 but you have done all the evil that you could."

Ex 34:15–16
Lev 20:5
Deut 12:2; 31:16; Ezek 23
Hos 1:2; 4:12–14

Israel and Judah, two faithless sisters

[6]The LORD said to me in the days of King Josiah: "Have you seen
what she did, that faithless one, Israel, how she went up on every

---

return", both in a physical sense (return from exile) and in a moral one (conversion).

The precept about divorcing a wife (v. 1) refers to Deuteronomy 24:1–4, which lays down that if a wife is repudiated by her husband and then marries someone else, she can no longer go back to the first man—not even if the second husband repudiates her and gives her a bill of divorce. Jeremiah applies this situation to show that Israel is totally helpless because of her breaking the Covenant; having gone off and worshipped idols, she cannot return to her first love. She has no right to claim forgiveness from God, particularly since she shows no sign of repenting and no desire to change (v. 5). In a situation like this, the initiative has to be the Lord's.

3:6–11. This oracle, probably of a later date, is based on a comparison of the

---

ultra? / Numquid non polluta / et contaminata est terra illa? / Tu autem fornicata es cum amatoribus multis / et reverteris ad me?, / dicit Dominus. / [2]Leva oculos tuos ad colles et vide, / ubi non prostrata sis. / In viis sedebas exspectans eos / quasi Arabs in solitudine; / et polluisti terram / in fornicationibus tuis et in malitia tua. / [3]Quam ob rem prohibitae sunt stillae pluviarum, / et serotinus imber non fuit. / Frons mulieris meretricis facta est tibi; / noluisti erubescere. / [4]Nonne amodo vocas me: "Pater meus,

high hill and under every green tree, and there played the harlot?
7And I thought, 'After she has done all this she will return to me';
Deut 24:1 but she did not return, and her false sister Judah saw it. 8She saw
that for all the adulteries of that faithless one, Israel, I had sent her
away with a decree of divorce; yet her false sister Judah did not
fear, but she too went and played the harlot. 9Because harlotry was
so light to her, she polluted the land, committing adultery with
stone and tree. 10Yet for all this her false sister Judah did not
return to me with her whole heart, but in pretence, says the LORD."

11And the LORD said to me, "Faithless Israel has shown herself
less guilty than false Judah.

---

two kingdoms, Israel and Judah—two sisters, beloved by God, yet wicked and wayward. Ezekiel will use the same metaphor in some detail (Ezek 16 and 23). Judah should have learned from the misfortunes of the kingdom of Israel, which was wiped off the map almost a hundred years earlier. But she has committed exactly the same sins.

In many places in the Bible (Ex 34:15–16; Lev 20:5; Deut 31:16; Hos 1:2; 4:12–14; etc.) idolatrous acts were seen as a kind of prostitution or adultery against God, because the link established between man and God by the Covenant had the force of the bond of matrimony (see the note on 3:12–13). The stone and tree (v. 9) refer to the stone steles erected in honour of Baal for Canaanite rites; the tree-trunks marked out the perimeters of sites used for pagan worship or were set up in honour of the goddess Astarte.

Religious circles in Judah had been highly critical of Israel for its infidelity (they would have gone along with what the prophet said in the previous oracle) but they failed to see that things were no better in their own kingdom. Therefore Jeremiah reproaches them, arguing that Judah's return to God, under Josiah's reforms, was not truly sincere (v. 10). He calls on them not to defend their own sins while they are busy condemning those of others—much as in the New Testament Jesus taught the same message by using the simile of the speck and the beam in a man's eye. (cf. Mt 7:3–5).

/ dux adulescentiae meae tu es! / 5Numquid irascetur in perpetuum / aut perseverabit in finem?". / Ecce locuta es / et fecisti mala et praevaluisti». 6Et dixit Dominus ad me in diebus Iosiae regis: «Numquid vidisti, quae fecerit aversatrix Israel? Abiit sibimet super omnem montem excelsum et sub omni ligno frondoso et fornicata est ibi. 7Et dixi: "Cum fecerit haec omnia, ad me revertetur"; et non est reversa. Et vidit praevaricatrix soror eius, Iuda; 8et vidit quia pro eo quod moechata esset aversatrix Israel, dimisissem eam et dedissem ei libellum repudii, et non timuit praevaricatrix Iuda, soror eius, sed abiit et fornicata est etiam ipsa; 9et facilitate fornicationis suae contaminavit terram et moechata est cum lapide et ligno. 10Sed in omnibus his non est reversa ad me praevaricatrix soror eius Iuda in toto corde suo sed in mendacio», ait Dominus. 11Et dixit Dominus ad me: «Iustificavit animam suam aversatrix Israel comparatione praevaricatricis Iudae. 12Vade et clama sermones istos contra aquilonem et dices: Revertere, aversatrix Israel, / ait Dominus, / et non avertam faciem meam a vobis, / quia pius ego sum, / dicit Dominus, / et non irascar in perpetuum. / 13Verumtamen scito iniquitatem tuam, / quia in Dominum Deum tuum praevaricata es / et dispersisti vias tuas alienis / sub omni ligno frondoso; / et

Call to conversion

12 Go, and proclaim these words toward the north, and say,
'Return, faithless Israel, says the LORD.
I will not look on you in anger,
for I am merciful, says the LORD;
I will not be angry for ever.
13 Only acknowledge your guilt,
that you rebelled against the LORD your God
and scattered your favours among strangers under every green tree,
and that you have not obeyed my voice, says the LORD.
14 Return, O faithless children, says the LORD; Jer 31:32
for I am your master; Hos 2:19
I will take you, one from a city and two from a family, Rom 11:5
and I will bring you to Zion.
15 "'And I will give you shepherds after my own heart, who will Jer 23:4 Ezek 34:1
feed you with knowledge and understanding. 16 And when you Ex 25:8,10–22
have multiplied and increased in the land, in those days, says the 1 Kings 8:21
LORD, they shall no more say, "The ark of the covenant of the
LORD." It shall not come to mind, or be remembered, or missed; it
shall not be made again.* 17 At that time Jerusalem shall be called Is 1:26; 2:2; 45:14
the throne of the LORD, and all nations shall gather to it, to the Ezek 48:35

3:12–13. The call to conversion is probably addressed to Judah; it is the same call that is made in 3:14ff, but here it is in verse form. It seems to follow on from the parable of the two sisters: both need to show a change of heart; it is the only way to attain forgiveness and freedom. Although Israel's transgressions mean that she no longer has any rights under the Covenant (cf. 3:1–5), the Lord is always waiting for her with open arms. To express one's love for God, words are not enough: one has to show it with deeds and desist from anything that undermines the exclusivity of spousal love. But, still, God always forgives if he finds in man's heart a desire for conversion: "These are the beginning and the path of man's healing, and the necessary condition for him to recover what he could never attain by his own strength: God's friendship and grace, the supernatural life which alone can bring fulfilment to the deepest aspirations of the human heart" (John Paul II, *Incarnationis mysterium*, 2).

3:14–18. The fall of the city to the armies of Nebuchadnezzar and the

vocem meam non audistis, / ait Dominus. 14 Convertimini, filii, qui aversi estis a me, dicit Dominus, quia ego Dominus vester sum; et assumam vos unum de civitate et duos de cognatione et introducam vos in Sion; 15 et dabo vobis pastores iuxta cor meum, et pascent vos scientia et doctrina. 16 Cumque multiplicati fueritis et creveritis in terra in diebus illis, ait Dominus, non dicent ultra: "Arca testamenti Domini", neque ascendet super cor, neque recordabuntur illius, nec requiretur, nec fiet ultra. 17 In tempore illo vocabunt Ierusalem Solium Domini, et congregabuntur ad eam omnes gentes in nomine

presence of the LORD in Jerusalem, and they shall no more
Gen 13:14–15 stubbornly follow their own evil heart. [18]In those days the house
of Judah shall join the house of Israel, and together they shall
come from the land of the north to the land that I gave your fathers
for a heritage.

Conversion that will endure

Deut 1:31 [19] "'I thought
Ps 89:27 how I would set you among my sons,
and give you a pleasant land,
a heritage most beauteous of all nations.

---

deportations that followed (587 BC) marked the depth of Judah's misfortune; her repeated infidelity was the sole cause. Here, as in the previous oracle, the prophet says that God is ready to receive Israel and Judah back, provided they seek his forgiveness (3:12–13).

The oracle is full of hope; the future will never have any reason to hanker after the past. An entirely new situation will be created. Up to this, the ark of the Covenant was considered to be the foremost evidence of God's presence. According to the Bible, the ark was made in the wilderness on Moses' instructions, in line with the Lord's specifications; it was to be the centre-piece of the sanctuary (cf. Ex 25:10–22). The ark stayed with the people all the way to the land of Canaan and, after being kept in various places, it was solemnly placed by Solomon in the temple of Jerusalem. It contained the Covenant that the Lord made with Israel when he brought it out of the land of Egypt (cf. 1 Kings 8:21). With the fall of Jerusalem to Nebuchadnezzar and the looting of the temple, there is no further mention of the ark of the Covenant. That event marks the end of the old situation, Jeremiah's oracle seems to say. In the future it will be the whole city of Jerusalem that evidences the presence of God (vv. 16–17).

As is true of other oracles from Jeremiah, even though in the first instance they refer to the restoration of Judah after the exile, his words have a wider application, reaching out to the renewal that will take place when the Messiah comes. The Covenant to which the ark bore witness has been broken by Israel (cf. 11:6–8), and its place will be taken by a New Covenant to which the hearts of men shall bear witness (cf. 31:31–37) and which will have a new priesthood ("shepherds": v. 15).

3:19—4:4. These oracles repeat the call to conversion and could be an extension of the charges laid in 3:1–5. They are full of hope that when the Lord calls (3:22a), Israel will respond by acknowledging their fathers' sins and

Domini in Ierusalem; et non ambulabunt ultra post pravitatem cordis sui pessimi. [18]In diebus illis ibit domus Iudae ad domum Israel, et venient simul de terra aquilonis ad terram, quam dedi in hereditatem patribus vestris. [19]Ego autem dixi: Quomodo ponam te in filiis / et tribuam tibi terram desiderabilem, /

And I thought you would call me, My Father,
and would not turn from following me.
20 Surely, as a faithless wife leaves her husband,
so have you been faithless to me, O house of Israel,
says the LORD.'"

21 A voice on the bare heights is heard, Is 15:2
the weeping and pleading of Israel's sons,
because they have perverted their way,
they have forgotten the LORD their God.

---

their own (3:22b–25) and return to God (4:1–2). The simile of circumcision of the heart is used in connexion with a true "return" through sincere conversion (4:3–4). Circumcision was the sign of the Covenant between God and the people. The prophet is saying that nothing has any value unless it is accompanied by heartfelt fidelity (cf. Deut 10:16; 30:6). Conversion is sincere only if it leads to genuine inner change. It is not just a superficial act which somehow has automatic salvific effects: it is a true renewal involving a complete break with anything that could undermine it; it means a genuine change of heart. St Paul, too, talks about circumcision of the heart to describe obedience to the law of God "spiritual not literal" (Rom 2:25–29; cf. Acts 7:51).

When read after the deportation to Babylon, these oracles reminded people that the exiles' return to the land that God promised their forebears was dependent on personal conversion, personal "return" to God. In the light of the New Testament, the return to the promised land is seen as an anticipation of the pilgrimage to the everlasting home in heaven that God has promised to those who love him. Just as the exiles in Babylon were asked for deep conversion and a return to the Covenant, so too, after becoming slaves to sin, people need to return to God through a conversion of heart; Christ has made this possible. "The symbol of the heavens refers us back to the mystery of the covenant we are living when we pray to our Father. He is in heaven, his dwelling place; the Father's house is our homeland. Sin has exiled us from the land of the covenant (cf. Gen 3), but conversion of heart enables us to return to the Father, to heaven (Jer 3:19—4:1a; Lk 15:18, 21). In Christ, then, heaven and earth are reconciled (cf. Is 45:8; Ps 85:12), for the Son alone 'descended from heaven' and causes us to ascend there with him, by his cross, Resurrection and Ascension" (*Catechism of the Catholic Church*, 2795).

hereditatem praeclarissimam inter gentes? / Et dixi: Patrem vocabitis me / et post me ingredi non cessabitis. / [20]Sed, quomodo contemnit mulier amatorem suum, / sic contempsistis me, domus Israel», / dicit Dominus. / [21]Vox in collibus audita est, / ploratus et supplicatio filiorum Israel, / quoniam

[22] "Return, O faithless sons,
I will heal your faithlessness."
"Behold, we come to thee;
for thou art the LORD our God.
Ps 75:7; 121:1–2 Is 2:12–18 [23] Truly the hills are a delusion,
the orgies on the mountains.
Truly in the LORD our God
is the salvation of Israel.

[24] "But from our youth the shameful thing has devoured all for
which our fathers laboured, their flocks and their herds, their sons
and their daughters. [25] Let us lie down in our shame, and let our
dishonour cover us; for we have sinned against the LORD our God,
we and our fathers, from our youth even to this day; and we have
not obeyed the voice of the LORD our God."

4 [1] "If you return, O Israel, says the LORD,
to me you should return.
If you remove your abominations from my presence,
and do not waver,
Gen 12:3 [2] and if you swear, 'As the LORD lives,'
in truth, in justice, and in uprightness,
then nations shall bless themselves in him,
and in him shall they glory."

Deut 10:16; 30:6 Hos 10:12 Mt 13:22 Rom 2:25–29 [3] For thus says the LORD to the men of Judah and to the inhabitants of Jerusalem:
"Break up your fallow ground,
and sow not among thorns.

***4:5—10:25.** This section comprises oracles to do with Jeremiah's second vision (about the boiling pot: 1:13–19). As was true of the previous section, the early verse oracles contained in this new edition (written after the king burned the first: cf. 36:21–23) were supplemented with prose passages. Some of the latter are very short—for example, the reference in 5:18–19 to the exile that would take place in 597, or the paragraph of 9:12–14 insisting that transgression of the Covenant is the explanation for Israel's misfortunes;

iniquam fecerunt viam suam, / obliti sunt Domini Dei sui. / [22]«Convertimini, filii, qui aversi estis a me, / et sanabo aversiones vestras». / «Ecce nos venimus ad te; / tu enim es Dominus Deus noster. / [23]Vere mendaces erant colles / et tumultus montium; / vere in Domino Deo nostro / salus Israel. / [24]Confusio comedit laborem patrum nostrorum / ab adulescentia nostra, / greges eorum et armenta eorum, / filios eorum et filias eorum. / [25]Dormiemus in confusione nostra, / et operiet nos ignominia nostra, / quoniam Domino Deo nostro peccavimus / nos et patres nostri / ab adulescentia nostra usque ad hanc diem / et non audivimus vocem Domini Dei nostri». **[4]** [1]«Si converteris, Israel, / ait Dominus, / ad me convertere; / si abstuleris abominationes tuas a facie mea, / non effugies. / [2]Et iurabis: "Vivit Dominus!" / in veritate et in iudicio et in iustitia, / et benedicentur in ipso gentes / et in ipso gloriabuntur. / [3]Haec

[4]Circumcise yourselves to the LORD,
remove the foreskin of your hearts,
O men of Judah and inhabitants of Jerusalem;
lest my wrath go forth like fire,
and burn with none to quench it,
because of the evil of your doings."

Jer 21:12

2. INVASION FROM THE NORTH*

Jer 1:13–15

Threats of invasion

[5]Declare in Judah, and proclaim in Jerusalem, and say,
"Blow the trumpet through the land;
cry aloud and say,
'Assemble, and let us go
into the fortified cities!'

Jer 8:14; Joel 2:1

---

others, however, are longer—for example, 7:1—8:3, which deals with instances of idolatry.

4:5–31. As a complement to the exhortations to repentance in the previous section (2:1—4:4), we are now shown a very sombre scene, very much in line with the way things were in Jeremiah's time—a society constantly under threat of foreign invasion, until eventually Jerusalem fell to the Babylonians.

These oracles came from the early years of Jeremiah's preaching, and when they were spoken they could have applied to the threat posed by the Scythians (nomadic tribes located to the south-west of the Caspian Sea, who were pressing Judah from the north), as much as to the danger from Assyria, to whom Judah had been subject, to some extent, for decades. But the oracles would become relevant again around the year 605 BC when, coinciding with the decline of Assyria, Babylon was expanding rapidly. Whichever of these enemies the oracles refer to, the main point is that the Lord sends the prophet to paint this very explicit picture of what lies in store for Judah if the people don't repent (v. 14). Jeremiah tells his people that in the last analysis it is not the power of foreign nations they should fear, but the Lord, for he is behind their imminent defeat (v. 6b). The fault, he says, lies with the people, and the misfortunes that will overtake them are their just deserts, for they have rebelled against the Lord (vv. 17–18). The warning given by the prophet is expressed symbolically. Israel, the wife who has been unfaithful to the Lord,

enim dicit Dominus / viro Iudae et Ierusalem: / Novate vobis novale / et nolite serere super spinas. / [4]Circumcidimini Domino / et auferte praeputia cordium vestrorum, / viri Iudae et habitatores Ierusalem, / ne forte egrediatur ut ignis indignatio mea / et succendatur, et non sit qui exstinguat, / propter malitiam operum vestrorum. / [5]Annuntiate in Iuda / et in Ierusalem auditum facite; / et loquimini et canite tuba

6Raise a standard toward Zion,
flee for safety, stay not,
for I bring evil from the north,
and great destruction.
7A lion has gone up from his thicket,
a destroyer of nations has set out;
he has gone forth from his place
to make your land a waste;
your cities will be ruins
without inhabitant.

---

decks herself out in all her finery, thinking that she can use her charms to save herself; but it will not work (vv. 30–31). Even so, despite the desolate scene painted by Jeremiah, there is a ray of hope: there will be some survivors (v. 27).

Christian tradition has read what Jeremiah says about the destruction that awaits Judah as a reference to the destructive power of sin, which undermines the wise order stamped by God on creation and which undermines peace and stability. When man fails to acknowledge his God (v. 22), the earth falls back into the chaos and emptiness that marked the beginning of creation (cf. Gen 1:2), the lights of heaven go out, the mountains quake, and there is no trace of bird or man (vv. 23–26). Anyone who aspires no further than created things will only be disappointed, and can never have intimacy with God. "He who loves so low a creature", St John of the Cross comments, "is brought as low, and even lower, for love brings not only equality but makes the lover subject to what he loves. Therefore, if the soul falls in love with any thing, pure union with God and the transformation of the soul become impossible: the little worth of created things is further from the greatness of God than darkness is from light. As Jeremiah says, everything in the heavens and on the earth are as nothing when compared with God: *I looked on the earth, and lo, it was waste and void; and to the heavens, and they had no light* (v. 23). By saying that the earth is waste and void, he means that everything on earth is nothing, and that the earth itself is nothing. By saying that there is no light in the heavens, he means that, compared to God, the brightness of the stars is darkness. [...] Anyone who has only ever lived in darkness will not understand the light: the soul who has put his heart in created things cannot see God. Until he is purified, he will not be able to see clearly, nor can his soul be transformed by pure love" (*Ascent of Mount Carmel,* 1, 4, 3).

in terra, / clamate fortiter et dicite: / "Congregamini, et ingrediamur civitates munitas". / 6Levate signum in Sion, / fugite, nolite stare, / quia malum ego adduco ab aquilone / et contritionem magnam. / 7Ascendit leo de cubili suo, / et praedo gentium se levavit; / egressus est de loco suo, / ut ponat terram tuam in solitudinem: / civitates tuae vastabuntur, / remanentes absque habitatore. / 8Super hoc accingite

[8]For this gird you with sackcloth,
lament and wail;
for the fierce anger of the LORD
has not turned back from us."

[9]"In that day, says the LORD, courage shall fail both king and
princes; the priests shall be appalled and the prophets astounded."
[10]Then I said, "Ah, Lord GOD, surely thou hast utterly deceived Jer 14:13
this people and Jerusalem, saying, 'It shall be well with you';
whereas the sword has reached their very life."

[11]At that time it will be said to this people and to Jerusalem, "A Jer 51:2
hot wind from the bare heights in the desert toward the daughter
of my people, not to winnow or cleanse, [12]a wind too full for this
comes for me. Now it is I who speak in judgment upon them."
[13]Behold, he comes up like clouds,
his chariots like the whirlwind;
his horses are swifter than eagles—
woe to us, for we are ruined!
[14]O Jerusalem, wash your heart from wickedness,
that you may be saved.
How long shall your evil thoughts
lodge within you?
[15]For a voice declares from Dan
and proclaims evil from Mount Ephraim.
[16]Warn the nations that he is coming;
announce to Jerusalem,
"Besiegers come from a distant land;
they shout against the cities of Judah.
[17]Like keepers of a field are they against her round about,
because she has rebelled against me, says the LORD.
[18]Your ways and your doings
have brought this upon you.

---

vos ciliciis, / plangite et ululate, / quia non est aversa ira furoris Domini a nobis. / [9]Et erit in die illa, / dicit Dominus, / peribit cor regis / et cor principum, / et obstupescent sacerdotes, / et prophetae consternabuntur». / [10]Et dixi: «Heu, Domine Deus! / Ergo decepisti populum istum et Ierusalem / dicens: "Pax erit vobis"; / et ecce pervenit gladius usque ad animam». / [11]In tempore illo dicetur populo huic et Ierusalem: / «Ventus urens collium, qui sunt in deserto, / invadit filiam populi mei / non ad ventilandum et ad purgandum. / [12]Ventus plenior his veniet mihi, / nunc et ego loquar iudicia mea cum eis». / [13]Ecce quasi nubes ascendet, / et quasi tempestas currus eius; / velociores aquilis equi illius. / Vae nobis, quoniam vastati sumus! / [14]Lava a malitia cor tuum, / Ierusalem, ut salva fias; / usquequo morabuntur in te / cogitationes iniquae? / [15]Vox enim annuntiantis a Dan / et notam facientis calamitatem de monte Ephraim. / [16]Nuntiate gentibus. Ecce adsunt! / Auditum facite hoc super Ierusalem: / «Custodes venerunt de terra longinqua / et dederunt super civitates Iudae vocem suam; /

This is your doom, and it is bitter;
it has reached your very heart."

Jer 10:19 [19] My anguish, my anguish! I writhe in pain!
Oh, the walls of my heart!
My heart is beating wildly;
I cannot keep silent;
for I hear the sound of the trumpet,
the alarm of war.
Jer 10:20 [20] Disaster follows hard on disaster,
the whole land is laid waste.
Suddenly my tents are destroyed,
my curtains in a moment.
[21] How long must I see the standard,
and hear the sound of the trumpet?
Deut 32:6,28 Mic 7:3 [22] "For my people are foolish,
they know me not;
they are stupid children,
they have no understanding.
They are skilled in doing evil,
but how to do good they know not."
[23] I looked on the earth, and lo, it was waste and void;
and to the heavens, and they had no light.
[24] I looked on the mountains, and lo, they were quaking,
and all the hills moved to and fro.
[25] I looked, and lo, there was no man,
and all the birds of the air had fled.
[26] I looked, and lo, the fruitful land was a desert,
and all its cities were laid in ruins
before the LORD, before his fierce anger.
[27] For thus says the LORD, "The whole land shall be a desolation;
yet I will not make a full end.

---

[17]quasi custodes agrorum facti sunt super eam in gyro, / quia adversus me contumax erat», / dicit Dominus. / [18]Via tua et opera tua / fecerunt haec tibi; / ista malitia tua, quia amara, / quia tetigit cor tuum. / [19]Viscera mea, viscera mea! Doleo. / Parietes cordis mei! / Turbatur in me cor meum: / non tacebo, / quoniam vocem bucinae audivit anima mea, / clamorem proelii. / [20]Contritio super contritionem vocata est, / quoniam vastata est omnis terra, / repente vastata sunt tabernacula mea, / subito tentoria mea. / [21]Usquequo videbo vexillum, / audiam vocem bucinae? / [22]«Quia stultus populus meus: / me non cognoverunt; / filii insipientes sunt et vecordes: / sapientes sunt, ut faciant mala, / bene autem facere nesciunt». / [23]Aspexi terram, et ecce vacua erat et deserta; / et caelos, et non erat lux in eis. / [24]Aspexi montes, et ecce movebantur, / et omnes colles conturbati sunt. / [25]Aspexi, et ecce non erat homo, / et omne volatile caeli recesserat. / [26]Aspexi, et ecce hortus desertus, / et omnes urbes eius destructae sunt / a facie Domini et a facie irae furoris eius. / [27]Haec enim dicit Dominus: / «Deserta erit

28 For this the earth shall mourn,
and the heavens above be black;
for I have spoken, I have purposed;
I have not relented nor will I turn back."

Hos 4:3

29 At the noise of horseman and archer
every city takes to flight;
they enter thickets; they climb among rocks;
all the cities are forsaken,
and no man dwells in them.
30 And you, O desolate one,
what do you mean that you dress in scarlet,
that you deck yourself with ornaments of gold,
that you enlarge your eyes with paint?
In vain you beautify yourself.
Your lovers despise you;
they seek your life.
31 For I heard a cry as of a woman in travail,
anguish as of one bringing forth her first child,
the cry of the daughter of Zion gasping for breath,
stretching out her hands,
"Woe is me! I am fainting before murderers."

Is 3:16–24
Ezek 16:37–40;
23:22–29:40

Ps 48:7
Is 13:8
Jer 6:24; 13:21;
22:13; 50:43

Judah punished for its disobedience

5 [1]Run to and fro through the streets of Jerusalem,
look and take note!

Gen 18:16–33;
19: 24–25
Ps 14:1–3
Ezek 14:2
Mic 7:1,2

5:1–31. Having outlined the dangers that threaten Judah, Jeremiah goes on to explain that all this can be put down to their rebelliousness and their stubbornness in resisting the Lord.

The first scene (vv. 1–3) paints a grim picture of the iniquity of sin. The weakening of moral sense is described here in terms reminiscent of the episode in Genesis 18:23–32, where Abraham haggles with God to prevent him from punishing Sodom: a few just men should be enough to stay his hand. However, God does punish the city because of the widespread depravity (cf. Gen 19:24–25). The situation in

omnis terra, / sed tamen consummationem non faciam. / [28]Super hoc lugebit terra, / et maerebunt caeli desuper, / eo quod locutus sum, / statui et non paenitet me / nec avertar ab eo». / [29]A voce equitis et mittentis sagittam / fugit omnis civitas; / ingressi sunt silvas condensas / et ascenderunt rupes; / universae urbes derelictae sunt, / et non habitat in eis homo. / [30]Tu autem, vastata, quid facies? / Cum vestieris te coccino, / cum ornata fueris monili aureo, / et pinxeris stibio oculos tuos, / frustra componeris; / contempserunt te amatores tui, / animam tuam quaerent. / [31]Vocem enim quasi parturientis audivi, / angustias ut puerperae; / vox filiae Sion / intermorientis expandentisque manus suas: / «Vae mihi, quia defecit anima mea / propter interfectores!». **[5]** [1]Circuite vias Ierusalem / et aspicite et considerate / et quaerite in plateis eius, / an inveniatis virum, / an sit qui faciat iudicium et

Search her squares to see
  if you can find a man,
one who does justice
  and seeks truth;
that I may pardon her.

Jerusalem is somewhat similar. Great and small have been led astray by sins of all sorts, particularly those of lust (vv. 7–8), pride (vv. 12–13) and injustice (vv. 26–29), so much so that there is not one just man left (v.1). Instead of being converted and returning to the Lord, the people of Jerusalem feel quite self-sufficient and, to Jeremiah's mind, have no interest in God (v. 12). So, they deserve the foreign invasions that threaten (vv. 14–19). God does not want this punishment to befall them; it is not revenge on his part. In fact, he wants to prevent it from happening, if only the people would repent (vv. 1, 7). That is why the destruction that takes place will not be total (vv. 10, 18); the way will be left open for a conversion that will allow the people to be renewed and restored.

Despite this attitude on God's part, the prophet spells it out: the future does not look promising because the people are stubborn; it never even occurs to them there is anything wrong with their behaviour (cf. vv. 20–31). This is their big mistake: they fail to read the signs of the times, the reasons for all that is going on, the true causes. The prophet strives to get his listeners to reflect: if they look at the laws of nature, can they not see the purposes of God their Creator and protector (vv. 22–24)? Yet they seem determined not to change. God, who is righteousness and truth, stands in sharp contrast to the treachery and mendacity of his unfaithful people. They act like hunters, setting traps to take advantage of people (vv. 25–28).

The words of v. 21 are used by our Lord to reproach the apostles for their narrowminded views and lack of vision. They do not appreciate the scope of his mission or his power (cf. Mt 8:18).

Blindness to one's own faults and failure to mend one's ways are an obstacle to forgiveness; as long as the heart is closed, forgiveness cannot be granted: "Mercy in itself, as a perfection of the infinite God, is also infinite," John Paul II wrote. "Also infinite therefore and inexhaustible is the Father's readiness to receive the prodigal children who return to His home. Infinite are the readiness and power of forgiveness which flow continually from the marvelous value of the sacrifice of the Son. No human sin can prevail over this power or even limit it. On the part of man only a lack of good will can limit it, a lack of readiness to be converted and to repent, in other words persistence in obstinacy, opposing grace and truth, especially in the face of the witness of the cross and resurrection of Christ" (*Dives in misercordia*, 13).

quaerentem fidem, / et propitius ero ei. / [2]Quod si etiam «Vivit Dominus!» dixerint, / certe falso iurabunt. / [3]Domine, nonne oculi tui respiciunt fidem? / Percussisti eos, et non doluerunt, / attrivisti eos,

[2]Though they say, "As the LORD lives,"
yet they swear falsely.
[3]O LORD, do not thy eyes look for truth?
Thou hast smitten them,
but they felt no anguish;
thou hast consumed them,
but they refused to take correction.
They have made their faces harder than rock;
they have refused to repent.

Amos 4:6
Rev 16:9–11

[4]Then I said, "These are only the poor,
they have no sense;
for they do not know the way of the LORD,
the law of their God.
[5]I will go to the great,
and will speak to them;
for they know the way of the LORD,
the law of their God."
But they all alike had broken the yoke,
they had burst the bonds.

Ps 2:3
Jer 2:20
Mt 11:28–30

[6]Therefore a lion from the forest shall slay them,
a wolf from the desert shall destroy them.
A leopard is watching against their cities,
every one who goes out of them shall be torn in pieces;
because their transgressions are many,
their apostasies are great.

Hab 1:8
Zeph 3:3

[7]"How can I pardon you?
Your children have forsaken me,
and have sworn by those who are no gods.
When I fed them to the full,
they committed adultery
and trooped to the houses of harlots.
[8]They were well-fed lusty stallions,

Deut 32:15

---

et renuerunt accipere disciplinam: / induraverunt facies suas supra petram, / noluerunt reverti. / [4]Ego autem dixi: «Ecce pauperes illi stulte agunt, / quia ignorant viam Domini, / iudicium Dei sui. / [5]Ibo igitur ad optimates / et loquar eis; / ipsi enim noverunt viam Domini, / iudicium Dei sui». / Ecce hi simul confregerunt iugum, ruperunt vincula. / [6]Idcirco percussit eos leo de silva, / lupus deserti vastabit eos, / pardus vigilans super civitates eorum: / omnis, qui egressus fuerit ex eis, lacerabitur, / quia multiplicatae sunt praevaricationes eorum, / confortatae sunt aversiones eorum. / [7]«Super quo propitius tibi esse potero? / Filii tui dereliquerunt me / et iuraverunt in his, qui non sunt dii; / saturavi eos, et moechati sunt / et in domum meretricis gregatim confluebant. / [8]Equi impinguati et admissarii facti

each neighing for his neighbour's wife.
Jer 5:29; 9:8 [9]Shall I not punish them for these things? says the LORD;
and shall I not avenge myself
on a nation such as this?

Jer 2:21 [10]"Go up through her vine-rows and destroy,
but make not a full end;
strip away her branches,
for they are not the LORD's.
[11]For the house of Israel and the house of Judah
have been utterly faithless to me, says the LORD.
Ps 14:1 [12]They have spoken falsely of the LORD,
Is 28:15 and have said, 'He will do nothing;
Amos 9:10
Zeph 1:12 no evil will come upon us,
nor shall we see sword or famine.
[13]The prophets will become wind;
the word is not in them.
Thus shall it be done to them!'"

Jer 23:29 [14]Therefore thus says the LORD, the God of hosts:
Hos 6:5 "Because they[e] have spoken this word,
behold, I am making my words in your mouth a fire,
and this people wood, and the fire shall devour them.
Deut 28:49–52 [15]Behold, I am bringing upon you
Is 28:11 a nation from afar, O house of Israel, says the LORD.
Amos 6:14
It is an enduring nation,
it is an ancient nation,
a nation whose language you do not know,
nor can you understand what they say.
[16]Their quiver is like an open tomb,
they are all mighty men.

---

sunt: / unusquisque ad uxorem proximi sui hinniebat. / [9]Numquid super his non visitabo, / dicit Dominus, / et in gente tali non ulciscetur anima mea? / [10]Ascendite muros eius et dissipate, / consummationem autem nolite facere; / auferte propagines eius, / quia non sunt Domini. / [11]Praevaricatione enim praevaricata est in me / domus Israel et domus Iudae», / ait Dominus. / [12]Negaverunt Dominum / et dixerunt: «Non est ipse; / neque veniet super nos malum, / et gladium et famem non videbimus. / [13]Prophetae erunt in ventum, / et responsum non est in eis. / Haec ergo evenient illis». / [14]Propterea haec dicit Dominus, Deus exercituum: / «Quia locuti estis verbum istud, / ecce ego do verba mea in ore tuo in ignem / et populum istum in ligna, / et vorabit eos. / [15]Ecce ego adducam super vos gentem de longinquo, / domus Israel, / ait Dominus, / gentem robustam, / gentem antiquam, / gentem, cuius ignorabis linguam / nec intelleges quid loquatur. / [16]Pharetra eius quasi sepulcrum patens / universi fortes. / [17]Et comedet segetes tuas et panem tuum, / devorabit filios tuos et

e. Heb *you*

17 They shall eat up your harvest and your food;
they shall eat up your sons and your daughters;
they shall eat up your flocks and your herds;
they shall eat up your vines and your fig trees;
your fortified cities in which you trust
they shall destroy with the sword."

18"But even in those days, says the LORD, I will not make a full Is 4:3
end of you. 19And when your people say, 'Why has the LORD our Deut 4:27;
God done all these things to us?' you shall say to them, 'As you 28: 47–48; 29:23–24
have forsaken me and served foreign gods in your land, so you Jer 16:10ff;
shall serve strangers in a land that is not yours.'" 22:8

20 Declare this in the house of Jacob, Jer 8:18–23; 14
proclaim it in Judah:
21 "Hear this, O foolish and senseless people, Deut 29:3; Is
who have eyes, but see not, 6:10; Ezek 12:2; Mt 13:15
who have ears, but hear not. *Mk 8:18*
22 Do you not fear me? says the LORD; Job 38:8–11
Do you not tremble before me? Ps 104:9
I placed the sand as the bound for the sea,
a perpetual barrier which it cannot pass;
though the waves toss, they cannot prevail,
though they roar, they cannot pass over it.
23 But this people has a stubborn and rebellious heart;
they have turned aside and gone away. Gen 8:22
24 They do not say in their hearts, Deut 11:14
'Let us fear the LORD our God, 1 Sam 12:17 Job 29:23
who gives the rain in its season, Ps 147:8
the autumn rain and the spring rain, Jer 3:3
and keeps for us
the weeks appointed for the harvest.'

---

filias tuas, / comedet gregem tuum et armenta tua, / comedet vineam tuam et ficum tuam; / et conteret urbes munitas tuas, / in quibus tu habes fiduciam, gladio. / 18Verumtamen et in diebus illis, / ait Dominus, / non faciam in vobis consummationem». 19Quod si dixeritis: «Quare fecit nobis Dominus Deus noster haec omnia?», dices ad eos: «Sicut dereliquistis me et servistis diis alienis in terra vestra, sic servietis alienis in terra non vestra». 20Annuntiate hoc domui Iacob / et auditum facite in Iuda dicentes: / 21«Audi, popule stulte, qui non habes cor, / qui habentes oculos non vident, / et aures et non audiunt. / 22Numquid me non timebitis, / ait Dominus, / et a facie mea non trepidabitis? / Qui posui arenam terminum mari, praeceptum sempiternum, quod non praeteribit; / et commovebuntur et non poterunt, / et intumescent fluctus eius, et non transibunt illud». / 23Populo autem huic factum est cor contumax et rebelle; / recesserunt et abierunt / 24et non dixerunt in corde suo: / «Metuamus Dominum Deum nostrum, / qui dat nobis pluviam / temporaneam et serotinam in tempore suo, / hebdomadas

25 Your iniquities have turned these away,
and your sins have kept good from you.
26 For wicked men are found among my people;
they lurk like fowlers lying in wait.[f]
They set a trap;
they catch men.
27 Like a basket full of birds,
Is 1:23 Jer 7:6; 12,1 their houses are full of treachery;
therefore they have become great and rich,
Zech 7:10 28 they have grown fat and sleek.
They know no bounds in deeds of wickedness;
they judge not with justice
the cause of the fatherless, to make it prosper,
and they do not defend the rights of the needy.
Jer 5:9 29 Shall I not punish them for these things? says the LORD,
and shall I not avenge myself
on a nation such as this?"

30 An appalling and horrible thing
has happened in the land:
Is 10:3 31 the prophets prophesy falsely,
Jer 14:14 and the priests rule at their direction;
Ezek 13:2–6 Mic 2:11 my people love to have it so,
but what will you do when the end comes?

Imminent invasion

Jer 1:13–15 6 1 Flee for safety, O people of Benjamin,
Joel 2:1 from the midst of Jerusalem!

6:1–30. In the light of the rebellion that he has just denounced (cf. 5:1–31), Jeremiah makes another appeal to Jerusalem to save itself, for its destruction seems inevitable. He begins by rallying his fellow citizens, the Benjaminites (who perhaps sought refuge in Jerusalem because of the treat of invasion), to prepare to flee south, to Tekoa (vv. 1–3), and he announces to

statutas messis / custodientem nobis». / 25 Iniquitates vestrae declinaverunt haec, / et peccata vestra prohibuerunt bonum a vobis, / 26 quia inventi sunt in populo meo impii, / insidiantes quasi incurvati aucupes, / laqueos ponentes ad capiendos viros. / 27 Sicut decipula plena avibus, / sic domus eorum plenae dolo; / ideo magnificati sunt et ditati, / 28 incrassati sunt et impinguati: / et transgressi sunt terminos mali. / Causam non iudicaverunt, / causam pupilli, ut ipsi prospere agant, / et iudicium pauperum non iudicaverunt. / 29 Numquid super his non visitabo, / dicit Dominus, / aut super gentem huiuscemodi / non ulciscetur anima mea? / 30 Stupor et mirabilia / facta sunt in terra: / 31 prophetae prophetabant mendacium, / et sacerdotes applaudebant manibus suis, / et populus meus dilexit talia. / Quid igitur facietis in novissimo eius? **[6]** 1 Fugite, filii Beniamin, / de medio Ierusalem; / et in Thecua

f. Heb uncertain

Blow the trumpet in Tekoa,
and raise a signal on Beth-haccherem;
for evil looms out of the north,
and great destruction.
2The comely and delicately bred I will destroy,
the daughter of Zion.
3Shepherds with their flocks shall come against her; Jer 12:10
they shall pitch their tents around her,
they shall pasture, each in his place.
4"Prepare war against her;
up, and let us attack at noon!"

---

the people of Jerusalem that their enemies are eager to assault the city (vv. 4–6a); if they don't repent, the city will fall, immediately (vv. 6b–8). The passage goes on to show how desperate the situation is. Even a careful search has failed to produce a just man—who would be enough to change God's mind about Judah (cf. 5:1). Everyone—children, old people, prophets, priests—is full of wickedness and they do not want to see the danger (vv. 9–15); they won't repent despite all the Lord's efforts over the years to get them to do so, through his prophets ("watchmen": v. 17); there is no escape from the punishment that lies ahead. And so we find, at the end of the oracle, in the face of imminent danger (vv. 22–23), Jeremiah shows how pained he feels over Jerusalem and its obtuseness (vv. 24–28). His efforts to cleanse it of sin have proved useless (vv. 29–30).

The attitude of the leaders of the people condemned here by the prophet (v. 14) is quite surprising. Instead of alerting the people to the need to turn back to the Lord, they concentrate on pursuing their own interests (v. 13), as if everything were fine. St Jerome uses this passage to show what a nonsense it is to try to set people's minds at rest when a situation is in fact serious: "It is not noble to proclaim peace with sweet words and, at the same time, to destroy it by your deeds. You lay claim to one thing, and bring about its opposite. Your words say, 'We are in agreement', but afterwards you try to force the other to accept your line of argument. I, too, desire peace; and not only do I desire peace, I pray for it. Seek the peace of Christ, true peace, a peace that contains no trace of hostility, peace that does not carry within itself the seeds of war; not the peace that forces people to submit to one another, but the peace that unites them in friendship. Why do we call tyranny peace? Why do we not call things by their names? Where there is hatred, we say there is animosity. Only where there is love will there be peace" (*Epistolae*, 3, 82, 1–2).

clangite bucina / et super Bethcharem levate vexillum, / quia malum visum est ab aquilone / et contritio magna. / 2Speciosam et delicatam silere feci / filiam Sion. / 3Ad eam venient pastores et greges eorum, / figent in ea tentoria in circuitu; / pascet unusquisque partem suam. / 4«Sanctificate super eam bellum, / consurgite, et ascendamus in meridie; / vae nobis, quia declinavit dies, / quia longiores factae sunt

"Woe to us, for the day declines,
for the shadows of evening lengthen!"
5 "Up, and let us attack by night,
and destroy her palaces!"

6 For thus says the LORD of hosts:
"Hew down her trees;
cast up a siege mound against Jerusalem.
This is the city which must be punished;
there is nothing but oppression within her.
Is 57:20 Ezek 7:11 7 As a well keeps its water fresh,
so she keeps fresh her wickedness;
violence and destruction are heard within her;
sickness and wounds are ever before me.
8 Be warned, O Jerusalem,
lest I be alienated from you;
lest I make you a desolation,
an uninhabited land."

Deut 24:21; Is 46:3; Jer 2:21 9 Thus says the LORD of hosts:
"Glean[g] thoroughly as a vine
the remnant of Israel;
like a grape-gatherer pass your hand again
over its branches."
Jer 4:4 10 To whom shall I speak and give warning,
that they may hear?
Behold, their ears are closed,[h]
they cannot listen;
behold, the word of the LORD is to them an object of scorn,
they take no pleasure in it.
11 Therefore I am full of the wrath of the LORD;
I am weary of holding it in.

---

umbrae vesperi! / 5 Surgite, et ascendamus in nocte / et dissipemus domos eius». / 6 Quia haec dicit
Dominus exercituum: / «Caedite lignum eius / et fundite circa Ierusalem aggerem; / haec est civitas
visitationis, / omnis calumnia in medio eius. / 7 Sicut effluere facit cisterna aquam suam, / sic illa
effluere facit malitiam suam; / violentia et vastitas auditur in ea, / coram me semper afflictio et plaga.
/ 8 Erudire, Ierusalem, / ne forte recedat anima mea a te, / ne forte ponam te desertam, / terram
inhabitabilem». / 9 Haec dicit Dominus exercituum: / «Usque ad racemum colligent quasi in vinea /
reliquias Israel. / Converte manum tuam / quasi vindemiator ad palmites». / 10 Cui loquar et quem
contestabor, ut audiat? / Ecce incircumcisae aures eorum, / et audire non possunt; / ecce verbum
Domini factum est eis in opprobrium, / et non suscipient illud. / 11 Idcirco furore Domini plenus sum, /
laboravi sustinens. / «Effunde super parvulum foris / et super concilium iuvenum simul; / etiam vir cum

g. Cn: Heb *they shall glean* **h.** Heb *uncircumcised*

"Pour it out upon the children in the street,
  and upon the gatherings of young men, also;
both husband and wife shall be taken,
  the old folk and the very aged.
12 Their houses shall be turned over to others, Jer 8:10–12
  their fields and wives together;
for I will stretch out my hand
  against the inhabitants of the land," says the LORD.
13 "For from the least to the greatest of them, Is 56:11
  every one is greedy for unjust gain; Jer 14:18; 23:11
and from prophet to priest, Mic 3:11
  every one deals falsely.
14 They have healed the wound of my people lightly,
  saying, 'Peace, peace,'
  when there is no peace.
15 Were they ashamed when they committed abomination?
  No, they were not at all ashamed;
  they did not know how to blush.
Therefore they shall fall among those who fall;
  at the time that I punish them, they shall be overthrown,"
says the LORD.

16 Thus says the LORD: Jer 18:15
"Stand by the roads, and look, *Mt 11:29*
  and ask for the ancient paths,
where the good way is; and walk in it,
  and find rest for your souls.
But they said, 'We will not walk in it.'
17 I set watchmen over you, saying, Hos 9:8
  'Give heed to the sound of the trumpet!' Ezek 3:17
But they said, 'We will not give heed.'
18 Therefore hear, O nations,
  and know, O congregation, what will happen to them.

---

muliere capietur, / senex cum pleno dierum. / [12]Et transibunt domus eorum ad alteros, / agri et uxores pariter, / quia extendam manum meam / super habitantes terram», / dicit Dominus. / [13]A minore quippe usque ad maiorem / omnes avaritiae student, / et a propheta usque ad sacerdotem / cuncti faciunt dolum. / [14]Et curant contritionem populi mei in levitate / dicentes: «Pax, pax»; et non est pax. / [15]Confusi sunt, quia abominationem fecerunt; / quin potius confusione non sunt confusi / et erubescere nescierunt. / «Quam ob rem cadent inter ruentes; / tempore, quo visitavero eos, corruent», / dicit Dominus. / [16]Haec dicit Dominus: / «State super vias et videte / et interrogate de semitis antiquis, / quae sit via bona, et ambulate in ea / et invenietis refrigerium animabus vestris». / Et dixerunt: «Non ambulabimus!». / [17]Et constitui super vos speculatores: / «Audite vocem tubae». / Et dixerunt: «Non audiemus!». / [18]Ideo audite, gentes, / et cognosce, congregatio, / quanta ego faciam eis. / [19]Audi terra: «Ecce ego adducam mala super populum istum, / fructum cogitationum eorum, / quia verba mea non

Prov 1:29–31 [19] Hear, O earth; behold, I am bringing evil upon this people,
the fruit of their devices,
because they have not given heed to my words;
and as for my law, they have rejected it.
1 Kings 10:1 Ps 40:6 Jer 7:21 Amos 5:21 [20] To what purpose does frankincense come to me from Sheba,
or sweet cane from a distant land?
Your burnt offerings are not acceptable,
nor your sacrifices pleasing to me.
[21] Therefore thus says the LORD:
'Behold, I will lay before this people
stumbling blocks against which they shall stumble;
fathers and sons together,
neighbour and friend shall perish.'"

Jer 50:41–43 [22] Thus says the LORD:
"Behold, a people is coming from the north country,
a great nation is stirring from the farthest parts of the earth.
[23] They lay hold on bow and spear,
they are cruel and have no mercy,
the sound of them is like the roaring sea;
they ride upon horses,
set in array as a man for battle,
against you, O daughter of Zion!"
Jer 4:31; 20:10 [24] We have heard the report of it,
our hands fall helpless;
anguish has taken hold of us,
pain as of a woman in travail.
[25] Go not forth into the field,
nor walk on the road;
for the enemy has a sword,
terror is on every side.
Jer 25:34 Ezek 27:30 Amos 8:10 Zech 12:10 [26] O daughter of my people, gird on sackcloth,
and roll in ashes;

---

audierunt / et legem meam proiecerunt. / [20]Ut quid mihi tus, quod de Saba venit, / et calamus suave olens de terra longinqua? / Holocautomata vestra non sunt accepta, / et victimae vestrae non placent mihi». / [21]Propterea haec dicit Dominus: / «Ecce ego dabo in populum istum offendicula, / et offendent in eis patres et filii simul, / vicinus et proximus peribunt». / [22]Haec dicit Dominus: / «Ecce populus venit de terra aquilonis, / et gens magna consurget a finibus terrae; / [23]arcum et acinacem arripiet, / crudelis est et non miserebitur; / vox eorum quasi mare sonabit, / et super equos ascendent, / praeparati quasi vir ad proelium / adversum te, filia Sion». / [24]«Audivimus famam eius; / dissolutae sunt manus nostrae, / tribulatio apprehendit nos, / dolores ut parturientem». / [25]Nolite exire ad agros / et in via ne ambuletis, / quoniam gladius inimici, / pavor in circuitu. / [26]Filia populi mei, accingere cilicio / et volutare in cinere, / luctum unigeniti fac tibi, / planctum amarum, / quia repente veniet vastator super

make mourning as for an only son,
  most bitter lamentation;
for suddenly the destroyer
  will come upon us.

27 "I have made you an assayer and tester among my people,
  that you may know and assay their ways.
28 They are all stubbornly rebellious,
  going about with slanders;
they are bronze and iron,
  all of them act corruptly.
29 The bellows blow fiercely,
  the lead is consumed by the fire;
in vain the refining goes on,
  for the wicked are not removed.
30 Refuse silver they are called,
  for the LORD has rejected them."

Is 1:22
Jer 9:6
Ezek 22:17–22
Mal 3:2–3

False worship. Discourse concerning the temple

Jer 26:1–19

7 [1]The word that came to Jeremiah from the LORD: [2]"Stand in
the gate of the LORD'S house, and proclaim there this word,

7:1–20. Chapter 26 gives more detailed information about the situation covered in these verses, and what the outcome was. We are told there that Jeremiah made this speech in the temple "in the beginning of the reign of Jehoiakim the son of Josiah" (26:1), that is, in 608 BC. Shortly before that, Josiah had died in battle (2 Kings 23:29–30; 2 Chron 35:19–24), having done maintenance work on the temple and having introduced a programme of religious reform based on the centralization of worship in Jerusalem. Josiah was succeeded by Jehoahaz, whose reign lasted only three months (cf. Kings 23:31; 2 Chron 36:2), followed by Josiah's brother Jehoiakim. That latter reign saw a tolerance of the idolatrous practices that Josiah had striven to uproot.

The people of Judah felt sure that having the temple in their territory would guarantee divine favour and protection for them, and they became surer still after 601, when the Assyrian troops of Sennacherib turned back from the walls of Jerusalem without entering the holy city. The high profile that the temple received as a result of Josiah's

nos. / [27]Probatorem dedi te in populo meo; / et scies et probabis viam eorum. / [28]Omnes isti principes rebelles, / ambulantes fraudulenter. / Aes et ferrum, / omnia isti corrumpunt. / [29]Sufflavit sufflatorium in igne, / consumptum est plumbum; / frustra conflavit conflator, / scoriae enim non sunt separatae. / [30]Argentum reprobum vocate eos, / quia Dominus proiecit illos. **[7]** [1]Verbum, quod factum est ad Ieremiam a Domino dicens: [2]«Sta in porta domus Domini et praedica ibi verbum istud et dic: Audite

and say, Hear the word of the LORD, all you men of Judah who
enter these gates to worship the LORD. [3]Thus says the LORD of
hosts, the God of Israel, Amend your ways and your doings, and I
will let you dwell in this place. [4]Do not trust in these deceptive

---

reforms helps to explain the blind confidence felt by the people that they had nothing to fear if they stayed close to that sanctuary. So, at the time when Jeremiah was uttering these oracles, even though the temple was there in all its splendour, religious practice was far from being in line with what the Lord commanded. Hence the prophet's insistence on conversion, on true religion, which manifests itself in fidelity to the Lord, in charity and justice (vv. 5–7). Rites performed in the temple are of no avail if people don't listen to the Lord and if they continue to commit all sorts of sins. Naïve confidence in the temple is not enough (v. 4). To be safe and secure they must obey the Law of God (vv. 8–10). The temple has no magic power, and it will suffer the same fate as the shrine of Shiloh (v. 14), the famous centre of worship that housed the ark of the Covenant before it was moved to Jerusalem (Josh 18:1; Judg 21:19) and that was probably destroyed by the Philistines. Unless they mend their ways, the people of Jerusalem will be expelled, just like their brethren in the Northern kingdom, the Ephraimites (v. 15).

Despite his preaching, Jeremiah finds that they fail to repent. Not only do they not listen to him: they think that the temple guarantees their safety, yet they combine that belief with pagan rites in honour of Isthar, the "queen of heaven", the Assyrian goddess of fertility (vv. 16–18). God will surely punish them (vv. 19–20).

The expression "den of robbers" (v. 11), employed here to describe the temple when used by people who are very far from being obedient to the Lord, will occur again when Jesus expresses his pain at all the noise made by traders in the temple and at people's disrespect for that holy place (Mt 21:12–13 and par.). Jeremiah is not condemning religious worship in the temple of Jerusalem (nor does Jesus); he is saying that they have emptied it of meaning. In any event, after the coming of Christ, worship of the Lord is no longer confined to rites or external actions performed in some particular place; people can worship God in their hearts wherever they happen to be. Therefore St Jerome writes: "Those who say to themselves constantly, *This is the temple of the Lord, the temple of the Lord, the temple of the Lord*, should listen to what the Apostle says: *Do you not know that you are God's temple and that God's Spirit dwells in you?* (1 Cor 3:16). Are you in Jerusalem? Are you in Brittany? It does not matter. The heavenly Presence lies open before us always, for the kingdom of God is within us" (*Epistolae*, 2, 58, 2).

verbum Domini, omnis Iuda, qui ingredimini per portas has, ut adoretis Dominum. [3]Haec dicit Dominus exercituum, Deus Israel: Bonas facite vias vestras et opera vestra, et habitare vos faciam in loco isto. [4]Nolite confidere in verbis mendacii dicentes: "Templum Domini, templum Domini, templum

words: ‘This is the temple of the LORD, the temple of the LORD,
the temple of the LORD.’*
5 “For if you truly amend your ways and your doings, if you
truly execute justice one with another, 6 if you do not oppress the
alien, the fatherless or the widow, or shed innocent blood in this
place, and if you do not go after other gods to your own hurt,
7 then I will let you dwell in this place, in the land that I gave of
old to your fathers for ever.
8 “Behold, you trust in deceptive words to no avail. 9 Will you
steal, murder, commit adultery, swear falsely, burn incense to
Baal, and go after other gods that you have not known, 10 and then
come and stand before me in this house, which is called by my
name, and say, ‘We are delivered!’—only to go on doing all these
abominations? 11 Has this house, which is called by my name,
become a den of robbers in your eyes? Behold, I myself have seen
it, says the LORD. 12 Go now to my place that was in Shiloh, where
I made my name dwell at first, and see what I did to it for the
wickedness of my people Israel. 13 And now, because you have
done all these things, says the LORD, and when I spoke to you
persistently you did not listen, and when I called you, you did not
answer, 14 therefore I will do to the house which is called by my
name, and in which you trust, and to the place which I gave to you
and to your fathers, as I did to Shiloh. 15 And I will cast you out of
my sight, as I cast out all your kinsmen, all the offspring of
Ephraim.
16 “As for you, do not pray for this people, or lift up cry or
prayer for them, and do not intercede with me, for I do not hear
you. 17 Do you not see what they are doing in the cities of Judah
and in the streets of Jerusalem? 18 The children gather wood, the

Is 1:16–17
Jer 22:3
Ex 20:2
Deut 24:14
Jer 22:3; 13:10

Is 56:7
Mt 21:13 and par.

1 Sam 1:3;
4:10–12,12–22;
Ps 78:59–69

Josh 18:1
Judg 21:19
Is 50:2; 65:12;
66:4

Ezek 32:10
Jer 11:14;
14:11; 1 Jn 5:16

Jer 44:17–19

Domini est”. 5 Quoniam, si bene direxeritis vias vestras et opera vestra, si feceritis iudicium inter virum
et proximum eius, 6 advenae et pupillo et viduae non feceritis calumniam nec sanguinem innocentem
effuderitis in loco hoc et post deos alienos non ambulaveritis in malum vobismetipsis, 7 habitare vos
faciam in loco isto, in terra, quam dedi patribus vestris a saeculo usque in saeculum. 8 Ecce vos
confiditis vobis in sermonibus mendacii, qui non proderunt. 9 Quid? Furari, occidere, adulterari, iurare
mendaciter, incensum offerre Baal et ire post deos alienos, quos ignoratis; 10 et venitis et statis coram
me in domo hac, super quam invocatum est nomen meum, et dicitis: “Liberati sumus”, eo quod faciatis
omnes abominationes istas. 11 Numquid spelunca latronum facta est domus ista, super quam invocatum
est nomen meum in oculis vestris? Ecce, etiam ego vidi, dicit Dominus. 12 Ite ad locum meum in Silo,
ubi habitavit nomen meum a principio, et videte, quae fecerim ei propter malitiam populi mei Israel.
13 Et nunc, quia fecistis omnia opera haec, dicit Dominus, et locutus sum ad vos mane consurgens et
loquens, et non audistis, et vocavi vos, et non respondistis, 14 faciam domui huic, super quam invocatum
est nomen meum, et in qua vos habetis fiduciam, et loco, quem dedi vobis et patribus vestris, sicut feci
Silo; 15 et proiciam vos a facie mea, sicut proieci omnes fratres vestros, universum semen Ephraim. 16 Tu
ergo, noli orare pro populo hoc nec assumas pro eis deprecationem et orationem et non obsistas mihi,
quia non exaudiam te. 17 Nonne vides, quid isti faciant in civitatibus Iudae et in plateis Ierusalem? 18 Filii

fathers kindle fire, and the women knead dough, to make cakes for
the queen of heaven; and they pour out drink offerings to other
gods, to provoke me to anger. [19]Is it I whom they provoke? says
the LORD. Is it not themselves, to their own confusion? [20]Therefore
thus says the Lord GOD: Behold, my anger and my wrath will be
poured out on this place, upon man and beast, upon the trees of
the field and the fruit of the ground; it will burn and not be
quenched."

Jer 11:1–14 **The people's obstinacy**
Is 1:11 [21]Thus says the LORD of hosts, the God of Israel: "Add your burnt
Jer 6:20
Amos 5:21 offerings to your sacrifices, and eat the flesh. [22]For in the day that
Hos 8:13 I brought them out of the land of Egypt, I did not speak to your

---

7:21—8:3. Jeremiah called on the people to admit their sins and mend their ways, but his preaching fell on deaf ears (7:21–28). This leads him to intone a lament (v. 29), bemoaning the desolation that will be Judah (7:34). A day will come when the bones of those who practised idolatry will be disinterred and exposed to the elements that they worshipped in their lifetime. When that day comes, people will prefer death to life (7:30—8:3).

Topheth (7:31), which in Hebrew means "place of burning", was a "high place", that is, a slightly higher piece of ground used for idolatrous rites involving the sacrifice of children in honour of Baal-Molech (cf. 2 Kings 23:10). It was in the valley of Hinnom (also called *Gehenna*, according to a Greek transcription), a ravine to the south of Jerusalem which, much later on, and with an eye on passages in Jeremiah (cf. 19:1–15; 32:35), became synonymous with a place of torment (cf. Is 66:24; Mt 5:22, 29–30; 18:9; Mk 9:43; etc.).

The prophet's failure can be put down to the people's hardheartedness, that is, the insensitivity that prevents them from examining their consciences in a desire to change where necessary and thus be able to hear the voice of God. Holy Scripture calls this obstinacy "hardness of heart" or "stubbornness of heart" (7:24; cf. Ps 81:12; Mk 3:5). It is a kind of inner resistance, an imperviousness to the voice of conscience, but it can be traced back to free choices that people have made. "In our own time this attitude of mind and heart is perhaps reflected in the loss of the sense of sin, to which the Apostolic Exhortation *Reconciliatio et paenitentia*, 18 devotes

---

colligunt ligna, et patres succendunt ignem, et mulieres commiscent farinam, ut faciant placentas reginae caeli et libent diis alienis, ut me ad iracundiam provocent. [19]Numquid me ad iracundiam provocant, dicit Dominus, nonne semetipsos in confusionem vultus sui? [20]Ideo haec dicit Dominus Deus: Ecce furor meus et indignatio mea effunditur super locum istum, super homines et super iumenta et super lignum regionis et super fruges terrae et succendetur et non exstinguetur. [21]Haec dicit Dominus exercituum, Deus Israel: Holocautomata vestra addite victimis vestris et comedite carnes, [22]quia non sum locutus cum patribus vestris et non praecepi eis in die, qua eduxi eos de terra Aegypti, de verbo

fathers or command them concerning burnt offerings and
sacrifices. 23But this command I gave them, 'Obey my voice, and
I will be your God, and you shall be my people; and walk in all
the way that I command you, that it may be well with you.' 24But Jer 9:13
they did not obey or incline their ear, but walked in their own Ps 81:13
counsels and the stubbornness of their evil hearts, and went Mk 3:5
backward and not forward. 25From the day that your fathers came 2 Chron 36:15
out of the land of Egypt to this day, I have persistently sent all my Jer 25:4; 26:5; 29:19; 44:4
servants the prophets to them, day after day; 26yet they did not Ezek 3:4–7
listen to me, or incline their ear, but stiffened their neck. They did
worse than their fathers.

27"So you shall speak all these words to them, but they will not
listen to you. You shall call to them, but they will not answer you.
28And you shall say to them, 'This is the nation that did not obey Is 7:9
the voice of the LORD their God, and did not accept discipline;
truth has perished; it is cut off from their lips.

29 Cut off your hair and cast it away;
raise a lamentation on the bare heights, Jer 19:1–13
for the LORD has rejected and forsaken
the generation of his wrath.' 2 Kings 21:4–7

30"For the sons of Judah have done evil in my sight, says the Jer 32:34
LORD; they have set their abominations in the house which is Ezek 5:11; 7:20

---

many pages. Pope Pius XII had already declared that 'the sin of the century is the loss of the sense of sin' (*Radio Message*, 26 October 1946), and this loss goes hand in hand with the 'loss of the sense of God'. In the Exhortation just mentioned we read: 'In fact, God is the origin and the supreme end of man, and man carries in himself a divine seed. Hence it is the reality of God that reveals and illustrates the mystery of man. It is therefore vain to hope that there will take root a sense of sin against man and against human values, if there is no sense of offence against God, namely the true sense of sin' (no. 18) Hence the Church constantly implores from God the grace that integrity of human consciences will not be lost, that their healthy sensitivity with regard to good and evil will not be blunted" (John Paul II, *Dominum et Vivificantem*, 47).

holocautomatum et victimarum. 23Sed hoc verbum praecepi eis dicens: Audite vocem meam, et ero vobis Deus, et vos eritis mihi populus; et ambulate in omni via, quam mandaverim vobis, ut bene sit vobis. 24Et non audierunt nec inclinaverunt aurem suam, sed abierunt in voluntatibus et in pravitate cordis sui mali factique sunt retrorsum et non in ante 25a die, qua egressi sunt patres eorum de terra Aegypti, usque ad diem hanc. Et misi ad vos omnes servos meos prophetas, per diem consurgens diluculo et mittens; 26et non audierunt me nec inclinaverunt aurem suam, sed induraverunt cervicem suam et peius operati sunt quam patres eorum. 27Et loqueris ad eos omnia verba haec, et non audient te; et vocabis eos, et non respondebunt tibi; 28et dices ad eos: Haec est gens, quae non audivit vocem Domini Dei sui nec recepit disciplinam. Periit fides et ablata est de ore eorum. 29Tonde capillum tuum et proice / et sume in collibus planctum, / quia sprevit Dominus / et proiecit generationem furoris

Lev 18:21 Josh 18:16 2 Kings 23:10 Ps 106:38 Mt 5:22, 29–30; 18:9; Mk 9:43

Jer 19:6

Jer 16:4; 34:20

Jer 16:9; 25:10 Bar 2:23

called by my name, to defile it. 31And they have built the high
place[i] of Topheth, which is in the valley of the son of Hinnom, to
burn their sons and their daughters in the fire; which I did not
command, nor did it come into my mind. 32Therefore, behold, the
days are coming, says the LORD, when it will no more be called
Topheth, or the valley of the son of Hinnom, but the valley of
Slaughter: for they will bury in Topheth, because there is no room
elsewhere. 33And the dead bodies of this people will be food for
the birds of the air, and for the beasts of the earth; and none will
frighten them away. 34And I will make to cease from the cities of
Judah and from the streets of Jerusalem the voice of mirth and the
voice of gladness, the voice of the bridegroom and the voice of the
bride; for the land shall become a waste.

2 Kings 9:37; 21:3; Jer 16:4; 22:19; 25:3 Ezek 6:4–5

8 1"At that time, says the LORD, the bones of the kings of Judah,
the bones of its princes, the bones of the priests, the bones of
the prophets, and the bones of the inhabitants of Jerusalem shall
be brought out of their tombs; 2and they shall be spread before the
sun and the moon and all the host of heaven, which they have
loved and served, which they have gone after, and which they
have sought and worshipped; and they shall not be gathered or
buried; they shall be as dung on the surface of the ground. 3Death
shall be preferred to life by all the remnant that remains of this
evil family in all the places where I have driven them, says the
LORD of hosts.

Deceit and disobedience

4"You shall say to them, Thus says the LORD:
When men fall, do they not rise again?
If one turns away, does he not return?

8:4—9:16. Now begins a series of oracles (8:4—10:25) which bring to a close the chapters outlining the reasons for the punishment that will soon come from the north. The prophet has pointed out that the mere presence of the

sui. 30Quia fecerunt filii Iudae malum in oculis meis, dicit Dominus; posuerunt abominationes suas in domo, super quam invocatum est nomen meum, ut polluerent eam; 31et aedificaverunt excelsa Topheth, quae est in valle Benennom, ut incenderent filios suos et filias suas igni: quae non praecepi nec cogitavi in corde meo. 32Ideo ecce dies venient, dicit Dominus, et non dicetur amplius Topheth et vallis Benennom sed vallis Interfectionis; et sepelient in Topheth, eo quod non sit locus. 33Et erit morticinum populi huius in cibum volucribus caeli et bestiis terrae, et non erit qui abigat. 34Et quiescere faciam de urbibus Iudae et de plateis Ierusalem vocem gaudii et vocem laetitiae, vocem sponsi et vocem sponsae: in desolationem enim erit terra». **[8]** 1«In illo tempore, ait Dominus, eicient ossa regum Iudae et ossa principum eius et ossa sacerdotum et ossa prophetarum et ossa eorum, qui habitaverunt Ierusalem de sepulcris suis; 2et expandent ea ad solem et lunam et omnem militiam caeli, quae dilexerunt et quibus

i. Gk Tg: Heb *high places*

[5]Why then has this people turned away
in perpetual backsliding?
They hold fast to deceit,
they refuse to return.
[6]I have given heed and listened,
but they have not spoken aright;
no man repents of his wickedness,
saying, 'What have I done?'
Every one turns to his own course,
like a horse plunging headlong into battle.

---

temple is no guarantee of God's favour (cf. 7:1—8:3) and now he adds that neither is it enough to have the Law of the Lord: it offers no safeguard if one fails to obey it (cf. 8:8).

The sacred writer starts off by telling Judah that it is living a lie. Its people cannot see straight because they live by deceit and are deceiving themselves (8:4–7). That is why they cannot repent, that is, "return" to God which is the central idea in this short section; birds can tell the seasons and know when to migrate and when to return: God has provided all the markers (8:7), but the people of Jerusalem fail to read God's plans and behave in ways that are at odds with them. The prophet is not referring to those who back Josiah's reforms; he means those who misinterpret the Law of God and who reject his word as proclaimed by the prophet (8:8–9). These same people are denounced forthrightly in 8:10–12—verses not found in the Greek version, perhaps because they repeat 6:12–15.

We then find again the simile of the fruitless vine and fig trees. The citizens of Jerusalem have not produced the fruit expected of them (cf. Lk 13:7), so they will inevitably perish. The armies coming from the north are serpents, ready to attack them (8:13–17).

Jerusalem is in so grievous a situation that the prophet cannot but utter a further lament, perhaps also because the Lord has attacked them with a drought (cf. 14:1–6), and they fail to accept that "visitation" from God (cf. Amos 3:14; Hos 12:3; Is 13:11; etc.) as a possible cure (8:18–23). The prophet wishes he could leave them and flee to the desert (9:1). He would like to find some way to make them react, but he is at a loss; they pile evil upon evil, lying to one another and lying to God (9:2–8). So, all he can do is bemoan the affliction that is going to befall them (9:9–11) and which they deserve because they have forsaken God (9:12–15).

servierunt et post quae ambulaverunt et quae quaesierunt et adoraverunt; non colligentur et non sepelientur: in sterquilinium super faciem terrae erunt. [3]Et eligent magis mortem quam vitam omnes, qui residui fuerint de cognatione hac pessima in universis locis, ad quae eiecero eos, dicit Dominus exercituum. [4]Et dices ad eos: Haec dicit Dominus: / Numquid, qui cadit, non resurget, et, qui aversus est, non revertetur? / [5]Quare ergo aversus est populus iste, / Ierusalem aversione perpetua? / Apprehenderunt mendacium / et noluerunt reverti. / [6]Attendi et auscultavi: / nemo, quod bonum est,

Is 1:3 [7]Even the stork in the heavens
knows her times;
and the turtledove, swallow, and crane[j]
keep the time of their coming;
but my people know not
the ordinance of the LORD.*
Jer 2:8 [8]"How can you say, 'We are wise,
Mt 23 and the law of the LORD is with us'?
But, behold, the false pen of the scribes
has made it into a lie.
[9]The wise men shall be put to shame,
they shall be dismayed and taken;
lo, they have rejected the word of the LORD,
and what wisdom is in them?
Jer 6:12–15 [10]Therefore I will give their wives to others
Hos 12:3 and their fields to conquerors,

8:7. The image of the migratory birds is particularly apt here. It is a reminder that one should make a sincere effort to do what is right and not to try to justify one's self-seeking or idleness by appearing to be busy: "How pitiful the man who adorns himself with the foliage of a false apostolate, who has all the outward appearance of leading a fruitful life, but is not sincerely attempting to yield fruit! He seems to be using his time well. He seems to get around, to organize things, to be inventing new ways of solving all kinds of problems … but he has nothing to show for his efforts. No one will benefit from his works if they have no supernatural content. […] I'd like to remind you once more that we don't have much time left, *tempus breve est* (1 Cor 7:29), because life on earth is short, and also that, since we have the resources, all that's needed is our good-will to make use of the opportunities that God grants us. From the moment that our Lord came into this world, 'the acceptable time, the day of salvation' (2 Cor 6:2) commenced for us and for all men. May our Father God never have to cast upon us the reproach he spoke through the prophet Jeremiah: 'the kite, circling in the air, knows its time; turtle-dove can guess, and swallow, and stork, when they should return; only for my people the divine appointment passes unobserved'" (St Josemaría Escrivá, *Friends of God*, 51–52).

loquitur, / nullus est, qui agat paenitentiam / super malitia sua dicens: / "Quid feci?". / Omnes conversi sunt ad cursum suum, / quasi equus impetu vadens in proelio. / [7]Etiam ciconia in caelo / novit tempus suum; / turtur et hirundo et turdus / custodierunt tempus adventus sui; / populus autem meus non novit / iudicium Domini. / [8]Quomodo dicitis: "Sapientes nos sumus, / et lex Domini nobiscum est"? / Vere mendacium operatus est / stilus mendax scribarum. / [9]Confusi sunt sapientes, / perterriti et capti sunt; / verbum enim Domini proiecerunt, / et sapientia nulla est in eis. / [10]Propterea dabo mulieres eorum exteris, / agros eorum expugnatoribus, / quia a minimo usque ad maximum / omnes avaritiam

j. The meaning of the Hebrew word is uncertain

because from the least to the greatest
  every one is greedy for unjust gain;
from prophet to priest
  every one deals falsely.
11 They have healed the wound of my people lightly,
  saying, 'Peace, peace,'
  when there is no peace.
12 Were they ashamed when they committed abomination? Amos 3:14
  No, they were not at all ashamed;
  they did not know how to blush.
Therefore they shall fall among the fallen;
  when I punish them, they shall be overthrown, says the LORD.
13 When I would gather them, says the LORD, Is 5:1
  here are no grapes on the vine, Mt 21:18–22
  nor figs on the fig tree; Lk 13:6–9
even the leaves are withered,
  and what I gave them has passed away from them."[k]

14 Why do we sit still? Jer 4:5; 9:14
Gather together, let us go into the fortified cities
  and perish there;
for the LORD our God has doomed us to perish,
  and has given us poisoned water to drink,
  because we have sinned against the LORD.
15 We looked for peace, but no good came, Is 59:9
  for a time of healing, but behold, terror. Jer 14:19

16 "The snorting of their horses is heard from Dan; Jer 4:15
  at the sound of the neighing of their stallions
  the whole land quakes.
They come and devour the land and all that fills it,
  the city and those who dwell in it.

---

sequuntur, / a propheta usque ad sacerdotem / cuncti faciunt mendacium. / 11Et sanant contritionem / filiae populi mei in levitate / dicentes "Pax, pax", cum non sit pax. / 12Confusi sunt, quia abominationem fecerunt; / quin immo confusione non sunt confusi / et erubescere nescierunt, / idcirco cadent inter corruentes, / in tempore visitationis suae corruent, / dicit Dominus. / 13Congregans congregabo eos, / ait Dominus; / non est uva in vitibus, / et non sunt ficus in ficulnea, / folium defluxit, / et dabo eis gradientes super eos. / 14"Quare sedemus? / Convenite, et ingrediamur civitates munitas / et pereamus ibi, / quia Dominus Deus noster tradidit nos in interitum / et potum dedit nobis aquam fellis; / peccavimus enim Domino. / 15Exspectavimus pacem, et non est bonum, / tempus medelae, et ecce formido". / 16A Dan auditus est fremitus equorum eius, / a voce hinnituum fortium equorum eius / commota est omnis terra; / et venient et devorabunt terram et plenitudinem eius, / urbem et habitatores

k. Heb uncertain

Num 21:6 [17] For behold, I am sending among you serpents,
Deut 32:24 adders which cannot be charmed,
Sir 10:11
Jn 3:14–15 and they shall bite you," says the LORD.

[18] My grief is beyond healing,[l]
my heart is sick within me.
[19] Hark, the cry of the daughter of my people
from the length and breadth of the land:
"Is the LORD not in Zion?
Is her King not in her?"
"Why have they provoked me to anger with their graven images,
and with their foreign idols?"
[20] "The harvest is past, the summer is ended,
and we are not saved."
Jer 5:20–25 [21] For the wound of the daughter of my people is my heart wounded,
I mourn, and dismay has taken hold on me.

Gen 37:25; [22] Is there no balm in Gilead?
43:11 Is there no physician there?
Jer 46:11; 51:8 Why then has the health of the daughter of my people
not been restored?

9 [m] [1] O that my head were waters,
and my eyes a fountain of tears,
that I might weep day and night
for the slain of the daughter of my people!

9:1–6. Falsehood and deceit not only offend God and weaken the Covenant but seriously undermine social relationships. Social life can be truly peaceful only if there is mutual trust based on respect for truth. Being truthful involves honesty and discretion and giving people what is due to them in all justice. St Thomas Aquinas says that there is a moral duty to be truthful because "honesty demands that each man tell his neighbour the truth"

eius. / [17]Quia ecce ego mittam vobis / serpentes regulos, / quibus non est incantatio, / et mordebunt vos», / ait Dominus. / [18]Hilaritas mea facta est dolor in me, / cor meum maerens. / [19]Ecce vox clamoris filiae populi mei / de terra longinqua: / «Numquid Dominus non est in Sion? / Aut rex eius non est in ea?». / «Quare ergo me ad iracundiam concitaverunt in sculptilibus suis / et in vanitatibus alienis?». / [20]«Transiit messis, finita est aestas, / et nos salvati non sumus». / [21]Super contritione filiae populi mei / contritus sum et contristatus; / stupor obtinuit me. / [22]Numquid resina non est in Galaad? / Aut medicus non est ibi? / Quare enim non est obducta / cicatrix filiae populi mei? / [23]Quis dabit capiti meo aquam / et oculis meis fontem lacrimarum, / et plorabo die ac nocte / interfectos filiae populi mei? **[9]** [1]Quis dabit mihi in solitudine deversorium viatorum, / et de relinquam populum meum et recedam ab eis? / Quia omnes adulteri sunt, / coetus praevaricatorum. / [2]«Et tenderunt linguam suam quasi

l. Cn Compare Gk: Heb uncertain **m.** Ch 8:23 in Heb

[2][n]O that I had in the desert
a wayfarers' lodging place, Ps 12:1–5; 116:11
that I might leave my people
and go away from them!
For they are all adulterers,
a company of treacherous men.
[3]They bend their tongue like a bow; Gen 27:36
falsehood and not truth has grown strong[o] in the land; Jer 12:6 Hos 12:4
for they proceed from evil to evil, Mic 7:5
and they do not know me, says the LORD.

[4]Let every one beware of his neighbour,
and put no trust in any brother;
for every brother is a supplanter,
and every neighbour goes about as a slanderer.
[5]Every one deceives his neighbour,
and no one speaks the truth;
they have taught their tongue to speak lies;
they commit iniquity and are too weary to repent.[p]
[6]Heaping oppression upon oppression, and deceit upon deceit, Jer 6:29
they refuse to know me, says the LORD.

[7]Therefore thus says the LORD of hosts:
"Behold, I will refine them and test them,
for what else can I do, because of my people?
[8]Their tongue is a deadly arrow; Jer 5:9
it speaks deceitfully;

(*Summa theologiae*, 2, 100, a. 3). And he goes on: "Because he is a social being, every man has a duty to do everything in his power to preserve his society, for the sake of all who belong to it. Honesty and trust are fundamental elements of community; and in that sense, the virtue of truthfulness is a moral duty" (ibid., a. 3, ad 1).

arcum; / mendacium, et non veritas, invaluit in terra, / quia de malo ad malum egres si sunt / et me non cognoverunt, / dicit Dominus. / [3]Unusquisque se a proximo suo custodiat / et in omni fratre suo non habeat fiduciam, / quia omnis frater supplantat, / et omnis amicus fraudulenter incedit, / [4]et vir fratrem suum decipit, / et veritatem non loquuntur; / docuerunt enim linguam suam loqui mendacium, / inique egerunt, noluerunt converti. / [5]Iniuria super iniuriam, / dolus super dolum. / Renuerunt scire me», / dicit Dominus. / [6]Propterea haec dicit Dominus exercituum: / «Ecce ego conflabo et probabo eos; / quid enim aliud faciam filiae populi mei? / [7]Sagitta vulnerans lingua eorum; / dolum locuta est in ore suo: / pacem cum amico suo loquitur / et occulte ponit ei insidias. / [8]Numquid super his non visitabo eos,

n. Ch 9:1 in Heb **o.** Gk: Heb *and not for truth they have grown strong* **p.** Cn Compare Gk: Heb *your dwelling*

with his mouth each speaks peaceably to his neighbour,
  but in his heart he plans an ambush for him.
Hos 4:3 9 Shall I not punish them for these things? says the LORD;
  and shall I not avenge myself
  on a nation such as this?

Jer 34:22 10 "Take up[q] weeping and wailing for the mountains,
  and a lamentation for the pastures of the wilderness,
because they are laid waste so that no one passes through,
  and the lowing of cattle is not heard;
both the birds of the air and the beasts
  have fled and are gone.
Ps 107:43 11 I will make Jerusalem a heap of ruins,
Hos 14:9 a lair of jackals;
and I will make the cities of Judah a desolation,
  without inhabitant."

Ex 19:5 12 Who is the man so wise that he can understand this? To
whom has the mouth of the LORD spoken, that he may declare it?
Why is the land ruined and laid waste like a wilderness, so that no
Jer 7:24 one passes through? 13 And the LORD says: "Because they have
forsaken my law which I set before them, and have not obeyed my
Ps 80:6 Jer 8:14; 23:5 voice, or walked in accord with it, 14 but have stubbornly followed
Lam 3:15,19 their own hearts and have gone after the Baals, as their fathers
Deut 4:27; taught them. 15 Therefore thus says the LORD of hosts, the God of
28:36,64 Israel: Behold, I will feed this people with wormwood, and give
Rev 8:11 them poisonous water to drink. 16 I will scatter them among the
nations whom neither they nor their fathers have known; and I will
send the sword after them, until I have consumed them."

/ dicit Dominus, / aut in gente huiusmodi / non ulciscetur anima mea?». / 9 Super montes assumam fletum ac lamentum / et super pascua deserti planctum, / quoniam incensa sunt, / eo quod non sit vir pertransiens, / et non audiunt vocem gregis; / a volucre caeli usque ad pecora / transmigraverunt, recesserunt. / 10 «Et dabo Ierusalem in acervos arenae / et cubilia thoum, / et civitates Iudae dabo in desolationem, / eo quod non sit habitator». / 11 Quis est vir sapiens, qui intellegat hoc, / et ad quem verbum oris Domini fiat, / ut annuntiet istud: / Quare perierit terra, / exusta sit quasi desertum, / eo quod non sit qui pertranseat? 12 Et dixit Dominus: «Quia dereliquerunt legem meam, quam dedi eis, et non audierunt vocem meam et non ambulaverunt in ea; 13 et abierunt post pravitatem cordis sui et post Baalim, quos didicerunt a patribus suis». 14 Idcirco haec dicit Dominus exercituum, Deus Israel: «Ecce ego cibabo populum istum absinthio et potum dabo eis aquam fellis; 15 et dispergam eos in gentibus, quas non noverunt ipsi et patres eorum, et mittam post eos gladium, donec consumantur. 16 Haec dicit Dominus exercituum: / Attendite et vocate lamentatrices, et veniant; / et ad eas, quae sapientes sunt, mittite, et properent!». / 17 Festinent / et assumant super nos lamentum: / deducant oculi nostri lacrimas,

q. Gk Syr: Heb *I will take up*

Keening over the dead

17 Thus says the LORD of hosts:
"Consider, and call for the mourning women to come;
send for the skilful women to come;
18 let them make haste and raise a wailing over us,
that our eyes may run down with tears,
and our eyelids gush with water.

9:17–26. At this point Jeremiah cries out in anguish at the desolation that he sees around him. The situation is so pitiful that there is no one to call on for help—only the keening women who wail and moan (vv. 17–20). Death and destruction are everywhere to be seen (vv. 21–22). The personification of death in these verses influenced the depiction of death as a skeleton with a scythe. But God does not see it as that. He is the One who judges: there are things that man values (wisdom, power, riches) but there are more important things (mercy, justice and righteousness) which he comes to appreciate when he knows God (vv. 23–24). The important thing is not to rely on one's own strength but on God. St Paul says the same thing in 1 Corinthians 1:31 and 2 Corinthians 10:7 when he uses the words of vv. 23–24 to stress that effectiveness comes from the Lord: it makes no sense to glory in oneself or one's abilities. And St Clement of Rome also uses them to exhort people to be humble: "Therefore, my brothers, may we be humble, and leave aside all arrogance and vanity, foolishness and anger, and live as it was written—for the Holy Spirit said: *Let not the wise man glory in his wisdom* … —remembering above all the words spoken by Jesus in his teaching on kindness and patience" (*Ad Corinthios*, 13, 1).

Judah has become rudderless and, although it has kept up appearances in some areas, it really has nothing worthwhile. It is like the nations round about, who also practise circumcision but only as an external rite: its proper companion, inner conversion, is missing (vv. 25–26). Judah's fate will be no better than that of those nations (cf. the note on 25:15–38), promised all sorts of calamities in the oracles against the nations (cf. 46:1—51:64), as long as it fails to change on the inside and continues to rely on superficial religious practice. St Justin, explaining vv. 25–26 in the light of the New Testament, comments: "Do you see that this external circumcision, which God commanded as a sign, is not what God requires? The Egyptians and the sons of Moab and of Edom received no reward for it. However, any man, be he a Scythian or a Persian, who has come to know God and Jesus Christ and obeys the eternal law, is circumcised by the good and fruitful circumcision, and is loved by God, and God will be pleased by his gifts and offerings" (*Dialogus cum Tryphone*, 28, 4).

/ et palpebrae nostrae defluant aquis. / [18]Quia vox lamentationis audita est de Sion: / «Quomodo vastati sumus et confusi vehementer, / quia dereliquimus terram, / quoniam deiecta sunt tabernacula nostra».

19 For a sound of wailing is heard from Zion:
'How we are ruined!
We are utterly shamed,
because we have left the land,
because they have cast down our dwellings.'"

20 Hear, O women, the word of the LORD,
and let your ear receive the word of his mouth;
teach to your daughters a lament,
and each to her neighbour a dirge.
Jer 8:2 21 For death has come up into our windows,
it has entered our palaces,
cutting off the children from the streets
and the young men from the squares.
1 Cor 1:31 22 Speak, "Thus says the LORD:
2 Cor 10:17 'The dead bodies of men shall fall
Jas 1:9 like dung upon the open field,
like sheaves after the reaper,
and none shall gather them.'"

23 Thus says the LORD: "Let not the wise man glory in his
Jer 4:4 wisdom, let not the mighty man glory in his might, let not the rich
Rom 2:25 man glory in his riches; 24 but let him who glories glory in this,
that he understands and knows me, that I am the LORD who
practise steadfast love, justice, and righteousness in the earth; for
in these things I delight, says the LORD."*

25 "Behold, the days are coming, says the LORD, when I will punish all those who are circumcised but yet uncircumcised—26 Egypt,
Judah, Edom, the sons of Ammon, Moab, and all who dwell in the
desert that cut the corners of their hair; for all these nations are
uncircumcised, and all the house of Israel is uncircumcised in
heart."

/ 19 Audite ergo, mulieres, verbum Domini; / et assumant aures vestrae sermonem oris eius, / et docete filias vestras lamentum, / et unaquaeque proximam suam planctum. / 20 Quia ascendit mors per fenestras nostras, / ingressa est domos nostras, / disperdere parvulos deforis, / iuvenes de plateis. / 21 Loquere. Haec dicit Dominus: / «Et cadet morticinum hominis / quasi stercus super faciem regionis / et quasi manipulus post tergum metentis, / et non est qui colligat». / 22 Haec dicit Dominus: / «Non glorietur sapiens in sapientia sua, / et non glorietur fortis in fortitudine sua, / et non glorietur dives in divitiis suis; / 23 sed in hoc glorietur, qui gloriatur: / scire et nosse me, / quia ego sum Dominus, qui facio misericordiam / et iudicium et iustitiam in terra; / haec enim placent mihi, / ait Dominus. 24 Ecce dies veniunt, dicit Dominus, et visitabo super omnem, qui circumcisum habet praeputium, 25 super Aegyptum et super Iudam et super Edom et super filios Ammon et super Moab et super omnes, qui attonsi sunt in comam, habitantes in deserto, quia omnes gentes habent praeputium, omnis autem domus Israel incircumcisi sunt corde».

Uselessness of idols

Ps 115:4–8
Is 40:20
Is 44:25

10 [1]Hear the word which the LORD speaks to you, O house of
Israel.
[2]Thus says the LORD:
"Learn not the way of the nations,
nor be dismayed at the signs of the heavens
because the nations are dismayed at them,
[3]for the customs of the peoples are false.
A tree from the forest is cut down,
and worked with an axe by the hands of a craftsman.
[4]Men deck it with silver and gold;
they fasten it with hammer and nails
so that it cannot move.
[5]Their idols[r] are like scarecrows in a cucumber field,
and they cannot speak;
they have to be carried,

Is 40:19; 44:9–11; 45:20

Ps 115:5
Is 41:23

10:1–11. Scholars are of the view that, because their tone is different (there are no references here to the apostasy spoken of in the previous verses), these verses refer to the situation of those living in exile in Babylon. Nebuchadnezzar's victory over Judah was a severe shock to the' religious convictions of the Jews. Could it be that the Lord was less powerful than Marduk and the gods of Babylon, and had been unable to afford them protection? No, says the prophet, that military defeat cannot be put down to the weakness of the God of Judah, but rather to the people's repeated infidelity. That is why he ridicules the idolatry of the other nations here. Their gods are nothing—mere figurines made by craftsmen, bits of dead material, completely lifeless; whereas the Lord is the true God (vv. 6–7, 10). It is sheer madness to put any trust in idols. They will disappear, and the Lord alone will judge the nations. St Thomas Aquinas considers that this chapter "illustrates the dignity of the people, so that the justice of their grave guilt and terrible suffering will be clearly understood. [...] Their dignity is conveyed by means of comparison with other nations, through their adoration of the word of God; and they undergo punishment as an instrument of healing because they set aside the worship of God and turned to idols" (*Postilla super Jeremiam*, 10, 1).

The sentence that ends this passage (v. 11) is in Aramaic. It is a kind of set form of words that the exiles can speak

[10] [1]Audite verbum, quod locutus est Dominus super vos, domus Israel. / [2]Haec dicit Dominus: / «Iuxta vias gentium nolite discere / et a signis caeli nolite metuere, / quae timent gentes, / [3]quia leges populorum vanae sunt. / Quia lignum de saltu praecidit / opus manuum artificis in ascia, / [4]argento et auro decoravit illud, / clavis et malleis firmavit, / ut non moveatur; / [5]sicut formido in cucumerario sunt

r. Heb *They*

for they cannot walk.
Be not afraid of them,
for they cannot do evil,
neither is it in them to do good."

Ps 86:8 — 6 There is none like thee, O LORD;
Is 40:18; 42:8 — thou art great, and thy name is great in might.
Rev 15:4 — 7 Who would not fear thee, O King of the nations?
For this is thy due;
for among all the wise ones of the nations
and in all their kingdoms
there is none like thee.
8 They are both stupid and foolish;
the instruction of idols is but wood!
9 Beaten silver is brought from Tarshish,
and gold from Uphaz.
They are the work of the craftsman and of the hands of the goldsmith;
their clothing is violet and purple;
they are all the work of skilled men.
10 But the LORD is the true God;
he is the living God and the everlasting King.
At his wrath the earth quakes,
and the nations cannot endure his indignation.

Ps 96:5 — 11 Thus shall you say to them: "The gods who did not make the
Is 2:18 — heavens and the earth shall perish from the earth and from under
the heavens."[s]

The power of God, the Creator

Job 38
Ps 104 — 12 It is he who made the earth by his power,
Prov 8:27–31 — who established the world by his wisdom,
Jer 51:15–19 — and by his understanding stretched out the heavens.

---

out loud to show their faith in the true God, using language that the foreigners too can understand.

10:12–16. This poem, repeated in 51:15–19, is a sapiential reflection on God's lordship over all created things.

/ et non loquentur, / portantur, quia incedere non valent: / nolite ergo timere ea, / quia nec male possunt facere nec bene». / 6Non est similis tui, Domine; / magnus es tu, / et magnum nomen tuum in fortitudine. / 7Quis non timebit te, o rex gentium? / Te enim decet, / quoniam inter cunctos sapientes gentium / et in universis regnis earum nullus est similis tui. / 8Pariter insipientes et fatui sunt; / doctrina vanitatis eorum lignum est. / 9Argentum involutum, quod de Tharsis affertur, / et aurum de Ophaz, /

s. This verse is in Aramaic

[13] When he utters his voice there is a tumult of waters in the heavens, Ps 135:7
and he makes the mist rise from the ends of the earth.
He makes lightnings for the rain,
and he brings forth the wind from his storehouses.
[14] Every man is stupid and without knowledge;
every goldsmith is put to shame by his idols;
for his images are false,
and there is no breath in them.
[15] They are worthless, a work of delusion;
at the time of their punishment they shall perish.
[16] Not like these is he who is the portion of Jacob, Deut 32:9
for he is the one who formed all things, Jer 31:35
and Israel is the tribe of his inheritance;
the LORD of hosts is his name.

The Lord, who made the world by his power, will put to shame those who make idols and rely on them.

The words of vv. 14–15 show just how foolish it is to turn a material thing into a god. Extending this teaching, one could apply it to those who turn their activity into a god—a temptation that has always been there, and one that is easy enough to fall into. Hence the Second Vatican Council's warning: "In the course of history, the use of temporal things has been marred by serious vices. Affected by original sin, men have frequently fallen into many errors concerning the true God, the nature of man, and the principles of the moral law. This has led to the corruption of morals and human institutions and not rarely to contempt for the human person himself. In our own time, moreover, those who have trusted excessively in the progress of the natural sciences and the technical arts have fallen into an idolatry of temporal things and have become their slaves rather than their masters. The whole Church must work vigorously in order that men may become capable of rectifying the distortion of the temporal order and directing it to God through Christ" (*Apostolicam actuositatem*, 7).

opus artificis et manuum aurificis, / hyacinthus et purpura indumentum eorum; / opus artificum universa haec. / [10]Dominus autem Deus verus est, / ipse Deus vivens et rex sempiternus; / ab indignatione eius commovebitur terra, / et non sustinebunt gentes comminationem eius. [11]Sic ergo dicetis eis: «Dii, qui caelos et terram non fecerunt, pereant de terra et de his, quae sub / caelis sunt». / [12]Qui fecit terram in fortitudine sua, / firmavit orbem in sapientia sua / et prudentia sua extendit caelos. / [13]Ad vocem suam dat multitudinem aquarum in caelo / et elevat nebulas ab extremitatibus terrae; / fulgura in pluviam facit / et educit ventum de thesauris suis. / [14]Stultus factus est omnis homo absque scientia; / confusus est omnis artifex in sculptili, / quoniam falsum est, quod conflavit, / et non est spiritus in eis. / [15]Vana sunt et opus risu dignum; / in tempore visitationis suae peribunt. / [16]Non est his similis pars Iacob: / qui enim formavit omnia, ipse est, / et Israel tribus hereditatis eius, / Dominus exercituum nomen illi. / [17]Congrega de terra sarcinam tuam, / quae habitas in obsidione, / [18]quia haec dicit Dominus: / «Ecce ego longe proiciam habitatores terrae in hac vice / et tribulabo eos, ita ut inveniant me». / [19]Vae mihi

Imminent flight

Ezek 12:3 [17] Gather up your bundle from the ground,
O you who dwell under siege!
[18] For thus says the LORD:
"Behold, I am slinging out the inhabitants of the land
at this time,
and I will bring distress on them,
that they may feel it."

Jer 4:31 [19] Woe is me because of my hurt!
My wound is grievous.
But I said, "Truly this is an affliction,
and I must bear it."
Is 54:1–2 Jer 4:20 Ezek 34:1 [20] My tent is destroyed,
and all my cords are broken;
my children have gone from me,
and they are not;
there is no one to spread my tent again,
and to set up my curtains.
Ezek 34:2 [21] For the shepherds are stupid,
and do not inquire of the LORD;

10:17–25. The time of punishment has almost come. "Gathering one's baggage from the ground" is a clear allusion to exile. No longer is punishment being threatened: people are now being told that it is imminent (v. 22). Because their leaders ("shepherds": v. 21) have been so foolish, the Lord will soon uproot his people and send them away. This is meant not as vengeance but as a corrective, to get them to react (v. 18). Therefore the passage ends with an entreaty to the God of mercy, asking him to punish the enemy nations (v. 25), for the people are not entirely responsible for their actions (vv. 22–24).

Afflictions like those announced in these oracles can overtake people, but they are not sent by God to cause them pain; he allows them to happen in order to get men to reflect: "As a sinner, you must suffer the trials sent to you by God, so that after you have been corrected by punishment you may be saved. You punish a servant or a child, not because you take pleasure in tormenting him, but because you want to set him right; in the same way, God ordains suffering for those who have not taken care to listen to him and be converted by his word" (Origen, *Homilia in Jeremiam*, 12, 3).

super contritione mea, / pessima plaga mea! / Ego autem dixi: / «Plane haec infirmitas mea est, / et portabo illam». / [20]Tabernaculum meum vastatum est, omnes funiculi mei dirupti sunt; / filii mei exierunt a me et non subsistunt, / non est qui extendat ultra tentorium meum / et erigat pelles meas. / [21]Quia stulte egerunt pastores / et Dominum non quaesierunt; / propterea non prosperati sunt, / et omnis

therefore they have not prospered,
and all their flock is scattered.

22 Hark, a rumour! Behold, it comes!—
a great commotion out of the north country
to make the cities of Judah a desolation,
a lair of jackals.

23 I know, O LORD, that the way of man is not in himself, Prov 20:24
that it is not in man who walks to direct his steps.
24 Correct me, O LORD, but in just measure; Ps 6:2; 38:2
not in thy anger, lest thou bring me to nothing.

25 Pour out thy wrath upon the nations that know thee not, Ps 79:6–7 Is 9:11 Jer 30:16
and upon the peoples that call not on thy name;
for they have devoured Jacob;
they have devoured him and consumed him,
and have laid waste his habitation.

3. CAREER OF THE PROPHET JEREMIAH*

The Covenant broken

Jer 7:21–28

11 1The word that came to Jeremiah from the LORD: 2"Hear the
words of this covenant, and speak to the men of Judah and

***11:1—20:18.** This third section of the first part of the book contains quite an array of texts. The most important ones are what are called the "confessions" of Jeremiah (these occur in 11:18—12:6; 15:10–21; 17:14–18; 18:18–23 and 20:7–18), in which the prophet expresses his feelings very vehemently. To these are added oracles against Judah and Jerusalem, liturgical pieces, laments about the deportation of King Jehoiachin and the queen mother, as well as sapiential sayings. These are linked together by prose passages, which became steadily longer each time, about the prophet's ministry in Jerusalem.

11:1–17. This oracle can be dated to a little after 622 BC, the year that saw the

grex eorum dispersus est. / [22]Vox auditionis ecce venit / et commotio magna de terra aquilonis, / ut ponat civitates Iudae solitudinem / et habitaculum thoum. / [23]«Scio, Domine, quia non est hominis via eius, / nec viri est, ut ambulet et dirigat gressus suos. / [24]Corripe me, Domine, / verumtamen in iudicio et non in furore tuo, / ne forte ad nihilum redigas me». / [25]Effunde indignationem tuam super gentes, / quae non cognoverunt te, / et super cognationes, / quae nomen tuum non invocaverunt; / quia comederunt Iacob / et devoraverunt eum / et consumpserunt illum / et pascua eius dissipaverunt. **[11]** [1]Verbum, quod factum est ad Ieremiam a Domino dicens: [2]«Audite verba pacti huius et loquimini

Ex 19:1–20 Deut 27:26 the inhabitants of Jerusalem. 3You shall say to them, Thus says the
LORD, the God of Israel: Cursed be the man who does not heed the
Deut 4:20; 6:3; 7:12–13; 10:15; 11:9 words of this covenant 4which I commanded your fathers when I
brought them out of the land of Egypt, from the iron furnace,
saying, Listen to my voice, and do all that I command you. So shall
you be my people, and I will be your God, 5that I may perform the
oath which I swore to your fathers, to give them a land flowing
with milk and honey, as at this day." Then I answered, "So be it,
LORD."

6And the LORD said to me, "Proclaim all these words in the
cities of Judah, and in the streets of Jerusalem: Hear the words of

---

start of Josiah's religious reform. According to the biblical account (cf. 2 Kings 22:8–20), Josiah rent his garments and issued a call for penance and conversion when he heard what was in the book of the Law that had been found in the temple; he realized that what it laid down was not being done. Similarly, Jeremiah at that time is saying that the people's conduct means that they have broken the Covenant with God, and that they must return to him. He then calls on them to admit that they have reneged on the terms they agreed; they should become truly converted, ceasing to worship Baal and reverencing only the Lord. The passage sums up very well why the Lord should feel offended: they have broken the pact that they made with him.

Firstly, Jeremiah reminds the people that the Lord undertook, through the Covenant, to give them a rich land; he delivered on this, and even now they were enjoying that land (vv. 1–5). Having been set free from their Egyptian masters (Ex 19:1—20:21), the Israelites agreed to the terms of the Covenant, but they did not keep their commitment, despite all the warnings God sent them through the prophets. Some of the penalties laid down in the Covenant were put into effect (vv. 6–8). But still the people did not recognize their wrongdoing. At the time of Jeremiah's preaching, things had become so bad that it was no longer a matter of some precepts of the Covenant being broken: the Covenant itself had been broken; time and again the people had transgressed; infidelity was rife (vv. 9–17).

Commenting on these passages in a homily, Origen points out that what is being said here applies to people of all times, and asks himself: "Should not we also repent for the sins of *the men of Judah*, since we ourselves are *the men of Judah?* [...] These words are directed to us, and to all those among us who fall into sin" (*Homiliae in Jeremiam*, 9, 4).

---

ad viros Iudae et habitatores Ierusalem. 3Et dices ad eos: Haec dicit Dominus, Deus Israel: Maledictus vir, qui non audierit verba pacti huius, 4quod praecepi patribus vestris in die, qua eduxi eos de terra Aegypti, de fornace ferrea, dicens: Audite vocem meam et facite omnia, quae praecipio vobis, et eritis mihi in populum, et ego ero vobis in Deum; 5ut suscitem iuramentum, quod iuravi patribus vestris, daturum me eis terram fluentem lacte et melle, sicut est dies haec». Et respondi et dixi: «Amen, Domine». 6Et dixit Dominus ad me: «Vociferare omnia verba haec in civitatibus Iudae et in foris

this covenant and do them. 7For I solemnly warned your fathers
when I brought them up out of the land of Egypt, warning them
persistently, even to this day, saying, Obey my voice. 8Yet they did
not obey or incline their ear, but every one walked in the stubbornness of his evil heart. Therefore I brought upon them all the
words of this covenant, which I commanded them to do, but they
did not."

9Again the LORD said to me, "There is revolt among the men of
Judah and the inhabitants of Jerusalem. 10They have turned back Num 25:1–3
to the iniquities of their forefathers, who refused to hear my Hos 9:10
words; they have gone after other gods to serve them; the house of
Israel and the house of Judah have broken my covenant which I
made with their fathers. 11Therefore, thus says the LORD, Behold,
I am bringing evil upon them which they cannot escape; though
they cry to me, I will not listen to them. 12Then the cities of Judah Judg 10:14 Prov 1:28
and the inhabitants of Jerusalem will go and cry to the gods to Is 59:2; Ezek
whom they burn incense, but they cannot save them in the time of 8:18; Mic 3:4
their trouble. 13For your gods have become as many as your cities, Jer 2:28
O Judah; and as many as the streets of Jerusalem are the altars you
have set up to shame, altars to burn incense to Baal.

14"Therefore do not pray for this people, or lift up a cry or Jer 7:16
prayer on their behalf, for I will not listen when they call to me in Jer 7:1–15,22–28
the time of their trouble. 15What right has my beloved in my Jer 2:2
house, when she has done vile deeds? Can vows[t] and sacrificial

---

11:15–17. In a different style, perhaps because this passage was written later than the previous section, these verses condemn the shallow religious worship offered by the people—the fact that their day-to-day behaviour is at odds with their religious profession. This passage is a good example of the range of literary styles to be found in the book of Jeremiah.

Ierusalem dicens: Audite verba pacti huius et facite illa. 7Quia contestans contestatus sum patres vestros in die, qua eduxi eos de terra Aegypti, usque ad diem hanc; mane consurgens contestatus sum et dixi: Audite vocem meam. 8Et non audierunt nec inclinaverunt aurem suam, sed abierunt unusquisque in pravitate cordis sui mali; et induxi super eos omnia verba pacti huius, quod praecepi, ut facerent, et non fecerunt». 9Et dixit Dominus ad me: «Inventa est coniuratio in viris Iudae et in habitatoribus Ierusalem. 10Reversi sunt ad iniquitates patrum suorum priorum, qui noluerunt audire verba mea; et hi ergo abierunt post deos alienos, ut servirent eis: irritum fecerunt domus Israel et domus Iudae pactum meum, quod pepigi cum patribus eorum. 11Quam ob rem haec dicit Dominus: Ecce ego inducam super eos mala, de quibus exire non poterunt; et clamabunt ad me, et non exaudiam eos. 12Et ibunt civitates Iudae et habitatores Ierusalem et clamabunt ad deos, quibus sacrificant, et non salvabunt eos in tempore afflictionis eorum. 13Secundum numerum enim civitatum tuarum erant dii tui, Iuda, et secundum numerum viarum Ierusalem posuistis aras confusioni, aras ad sacrificandum Baal. 14Tu ergo noli orare pro populo hoc et ne assumas pro eis deprecationem et orationem, quia non exaudiam in tempore

t. Gk: Heb *many*

Ps 52:8 Is 5:1 flesh avert your doom? Can you then exult? [16]The LORD once called you, 'A green olive tree, fair with goodly fruit'; but with the roar of a great tempest he will set fire to it, and its branches will be consumed. [17]The LORD of hosts, who planted you, has pronounced evil against you, because of the evil which the house of Israel and the house of Judah have done, provoking me to anger by burning incense to Baal."

Jer 15:10 **Jeremiah's first "confession"**

[18] The LORD made it known to me and I knew;
then thou didst show me their evil deeds.

11:18—12:6. There are five passages in the book usually called the "confessions of Jeremiah" (cf. the note on 11:1—20:18)—trusting prayers in which the prophet opens his heart to the Lord and tells him his deepest feelings. They are given this name because they are reminiscent of St Augustine's well-known book with that title.

Some commentators think that this first "confession" goes back to the early years of the prophet's ministry when the priests of Anathoth opposed him because his preaching provided backing for Josiah's religious reform (the preceding passage, 11:1–17, would only go to show that). The reform went against the vested interests of those priests, because it sought to concentrate all formal religious worship in the temple of Jerusalem. In any event, Jeremiah complains to God about being persecuted by his fellow citizens and even by members of his own family (11:18–21; 12:6). That explains why Christian tradition has seen Jeremiah as a figure of Jesus Christ, who was also rejected by his own people (cf. Mt 13:57; Mk 6:4; Lk 4:24; Jn 7:3–5) and who was sacrificed as the Lamb of God to atone for the sins of men (11:19; cf. Is 53:7; Jn 1:29; 19:31). St Jerome, commenting on this passage, says: "All of the churches believe that what is said of Jeremiah refers also to the person of Christ" (*Commentarii in Ieremiam*, 2, 11).

The words of the prophet, similar to those found in Job and in the Psalms (cf. Job 21:7–13; Ps 37, 49, 73), express the pain, puzzlement and feelings of someone who sees the wicked prosper and is only too aware of his personal limitations when he tries to do what God asks of him (12:1–4). The Lord's answer seems very harsh: the opposition shown the prophet by his family is only the start: he needs to be more circumspect and to be ready to cope with even more difficult situations (12:5–6).

clamoris eorum ad me, in tempore afflictionis eorum. [15]Quid est dilectae meae, / ut in domo mea perficiat consilia mala? / Numquid vota et carnes sanctae / auferent a te malitias tuas, / in quibus glorieris?». / [16]Olivam uberem, pulchram, fructibus speciosam, / vocabit Dominus nomen tuum; / ad vocem strepitus grandis / succendit ignem in ea, / et combusti sunt rami eius. [17]Et Dominus exercituum, qui plantavit te, locutus est super te malum, pro malis domus Israel et domus Iudae, quae fecerunt sibi ad irritandum me, sacrificantes Baal. [18]Tu autem, Domine, demonstrasti mihi, et cognovi; / tunc

19 But I was like a gentle lamb
led to the slaughter.
I did not know it was against me
they devised schemes, saying,
"Let us destroy the tree with its fruit,
let us cut him off from the land of the living,
that his name be remembered no more."
20 But, O LORD of hosts, who judgest righteously,
who triest the heart and the mind,
let me see thy vengeance upon them,
for to thee have I committed my cause.

21 Therefore thus says the LORD concerning the men of
Anathoth, who seek your life, and say, "Do not prophesy in the
name of the LORD, or you will die by our hand"—22 therefore thus
says the LORD of hosts: "Behold, I will punish them; the young
men shall die by the sword; their sons and their daughters shall die
by famine; 23 and none of them shall be left. For I will bring evil
upon the men of Anathoth, the year of their punishment."

Ps 83:4
Is 53:7
Jer 18:18
Lam 3:60
Jn 1:29; 19:31

1 Kings 8:39
Ps 7:10; 44:22;
139:13; Prov
15:11; Jer
20:12; 17:10;
Wis 1:8
Acts 1:24

Deut 13:1–5
Is 30:10
Amos 2:12;
7:13; Mic 2:6

The fact that Jeremiah puts on record not only his inner complaint to God but also the uncompromising answer he is given, indicates that he accepted that answer; it invites us always to respond to God generously and bravely, and not to give importance to obstacles. Commenting on this passage, St John of the Cross has this to say to those who seem to want to serve God but who baulk at the effort entailed: "If you continue to satisfy the comfort and tastes of the flesh, your sensuality, and never arm yourself for battle or deny your body in anything, how will you ever desire to enter the troubled waters of the spiritual trials and works that lie deep within? O souls that desire to journey calmly and safely through the life of the Spirit! If only you knew that suffering is the source of true calm and safety, [...] you would never seek consolation from God or take comfort in created things. You would take up the cross, and be crucified, and drink the vinegar and gall (cf. Jn 19:29), and you would discover that by dying to this life and to yourself, you are brought to life in the joy of God" (*Flame of Living Love*, 2, 27–28).

ostendisti mihi opera eorum. 19 Et ego quasi agnus mansuetus, qui portatur ad victimam; et non cognovi quia super me cogitaverunt consilia: «Caedamus lignum in vigore eius et eradamus eum de terra viventium, et nomen eius non memoretur amplius». 20 Tu autem, Domine exercituum, / qui iudicas iuste et probas renes et corda: / videam ultionem tuam ex eis; / tibi enim revelavi causam meam. 21 Propterea haec dicit Dominus super viros Anathoth, qui quaerunt animam tuam et dicunt: «Non prophetabis in nomine Domini et non morieris in manibus nostris». 22 Propterea haec dicit Dominus exercituum: «Ecce ego visitabo super eos: iuvenes morientur in gladio, filii eorum et filiae eorum morientur in fame, 23 et reliquiae non erunt eis; inducam enim malum super viros Anathoth, annum visitationis eorum».

Ps 49; 73 Job 21:7–17 Jer 5:28 Hab 1:4,13 Mal 3:15

12 [1]Righteous art thou, O LORD,
when I complain to thee;
yet I would plead my case before thee.
Why does the way of the wicked prosper?
Why do all who are treacherous thrive?
[2]Thou plantest them, and they take root;
they grow and bring forth fruit;
thou art near in their mouth
and far from their heart.

Ps 5:11 Jer 11:19 Jas 5:5

[3]But thou, O LORD, knowest me;
thou seest me, and triest my mind toward thee.
Pull them out like sheep for the slaughter,
and set them apart for the day of slaughter.

Jer 5:20–25; 8:18–23; 14 Hos 4:3

[4]How long will the land mourn,
and the grass of every field wither?
For the wickedness of those who dwell in it
the beasts and the birds are swept away,
because men said, "He will not see our latter end."

Jer 15:10

[5]"If you have raced with men on foot, and they have wearied you,
how will you compete with horses?
And if in a safe land you fall down,
how will you do in the jungle of the Jordan?
[6]For even your brothers and the house of your father,
even they have dealt treacherously with you;
they are in full cry after you;
believe them not,
though they speak fair words to you."

Jer 7:14 Mt 23:38 Lk 13:35

The heritage of the Lord made a wilderness

[7]"I have forsaken my house,
I have abandoned my heritage;

12:7–17. These two oracles, one in verse (vv. 7–13) and the other in prose (vv. 14–17), both refer to Israel as being the "heritage" of God. The "heritage" was the land allocated to each family at the time the territory was

[12] [1]Iustus quidem tu es, Domine, si disputem tecum; / verumtamen de iudiciis loquar ad te. / Quare via impiorum prosperatur? / Bene est omnibus, qui praevaricantur et inique agunt. / [2]Plantasti eos, et radicem miserunt, / proficiunt et faciunt fructum; / prope es tu ori eorum / et longe a renibus eorum. / [3]Et tu, Domine, nosti me, vidisti me / et probasti cor meum tecum; / segrega eos quasi gregem ad victimam / et sanctifica eos in diem occisionis. / [4]Usquequo lugebit terra, / et herba omnis regionis siccabitur / propter malitiam habitantium in ea? / Consumptum est animal et volucre, / quoniam dixerunt: «Non videbit novissima nostra». / [5]«Si cum peditibus currens laborasti, / quomodo contendere

I have given the beloved of my soul
into the hands of her enemies.
[8]My heritage has become to me
like a lion in the forest,
she has lifted up her voice against me;
therefore I hate her.
[9]Is my heritage to me like a speckled bird of prey?
Are the birds of prey against her round about?
Go, assemble all the wild beasts;
bring them to devour.
[10]Many shepherds have destroyed my vineyard, Is 5:1,6; 63:18 Jer 6:3–5

---

divided up, as described in the book of Joshua (Josh 13:1—21:45) and which was passed on from father to son. The Lord himself gave Israel the land he had promised her forebears as a heritage, and the chosen people itself is God's "heritage", that is, his personal possession.

The first oracle (vv. 7–13) is a lament describing the pain it causes the Lord to hand his people over to its enemies (v. 7). Evil shepherds (v. 10)—prophets, priests, kings—allowed it to be pillaged, so it has become a wilderness. The oracle implies a reference to the situation that followed the death of King Josiah and about which the book has so much to say. We can see the harm done by pastors who refuse to listen to the word of God; and the oracle also shows how the land has suffered from successive enemy campaigns.

The second oracle (vv. 14–17) may refer to the incursions into Judah by Chaldeans, Syrians, Moabites and Ammonites that happened in the reign of Jehoiakim, around 600 BC, just prior to the fall of Jerusalem (cf. 2 Kings 24:2). The prophet lets it be known that the compassion of God has no limits. He can even save those nations, if they repent; but if they don't, they will perish.

Jesus evokes the words of v. 7 (cf. also 22:5) when, full of sorrow, he announces what the fate of Jerusalem will be (Mt 23:38; Lk 13:35), because of its opposition to God. Thus, this oracle is a permanent warning not to resist the will of God but to respond promptly to what he requires of us.

The Acts of the Apostles, in reporting St James' speech at the council of Jerusalem, quotes v. 15 as part of the evidence from Scripture that God chose to prepare a new people for himself—the Church—chosen from among all the nations (cf. Acts 15–16).

poteris cum equis? / Cum autem in terra pacis securus fueris, / quid facies in silva condensa Iordanis? / [6]Nam et fratres tui et domus patris tui, / etiam ipsi fraudulenter egerunt adversum te / et clamaverunt post te plena voce; / ne credas eis, cum locuti fuerint tibi bona». / [7]«Reliqui domum meam, / dimisi hereditatem meam; / dedi dilectam animae meae / in manu inimicorum eius. / [8]Facta est mihi hereditas mea / quasi leo in silva; / dedit contra me vocem, ideo odivi eam. / [9]Numquid avis discolor hereditas mea mihi? / Numquid aves in circuitu contra eam? / Venite, congregamini, omnes bestiae campi, / properate ad devorandum. / [10]Pastores multi demoliti sunt vineam meam, / conculcaverunt partem

they have trampled down my portion,
they have made my pleasant portion
a desolate wilderness.
11 They have made it a desolation;
desolate, it mourns to me.
The whole land is made desolate,
but no man lays it to heart.
12 Upon all the bare heights in the desert
destroyers have come;
for the sword of the LORD devours
from one end of the land to the other;
no flesh has peace.
Lev 26:16 13 They have sown wheat and have reaped thorns,
Deut 28:38 Mic 6:15 they have tired themselves out but profit nothing.
Hag 1:6 They shall be ashamed of their[u] harvests
because of the fierce anger of the LORD."

2 Kings 24:2 14Thus says the LORD concerning all my evil neighbours who
touch the heritage which I have given my people Israel to inherit:
"Behold, I will pluck them up from their land, and I will pluck up
Acts 15:16 the house of Judah from among them. 15And after I have plucked
them up, I will again have compassion on them, and I will bring
Is 45:14 them again each to his heritage and each to his land. 16And it shall
Jer 4:2 come to pass, if they will diligently learn the ways of my people,
to swear by my name, 'As the LORD lives,' even as they taught my
people to swear by Baal, then they shall be built up in the midst of
my people. 17But if any nation will not listen, then I will utterly
pluck it up and destroy it, says the LORD."

---

meam; / dederunt portionem meam desiderabilem / in desertum solitudinis. / 11Posuerunt eam in dissipationem; / lugetque coram me desolata, / vastata est omnis terra, / quia nullus est qui recogitet corde». / 12Super omnes colles in deserto venerunt vastatores, / quia gladius Domini devorat / ab extremo terrae usque ad extremum eius; / non est pax universae carni. / 13Seminaverunt triticum et spinas messuerunt, / laboraverunt, et non eis proderit; / confundemini a fructibus vestris / propter iram furoris Domini. 14Haec dicit Dominus adversum omnes vicinos meos pessimos, qui tangunt hereditatem, quam distribui populo meo Israel: «Ecce ego evellam eos de terra sua et domum Iudae evellam de medio eorum. 15Et erit: cum evulsero eos, convertar et miserebor eorum et reducam eos, virum ad hereditatem suam et virum in terram suam. 16Et erit: si eruditi didicerint vias populi mei, ut iurent in nomine meo: "Vivit Dominus!", sicut docuerunt populum meum iurare in Baal, aedificabuntur in medio populi mei. 17Quod si non audierint, evellam gentem illam evulsione et perditione», ait Dominus.

u. Heb *your*

The linen waistcloth entirely spoiled

13 [1]*Thus said the LORD to me, "Go and buy a linen waist- Acts 21:11
cloth, and put it on your loins, and do not dip it in water."
[2]So I bought a waistcloth according to the word of the LORD, and
put it on my loins. [3]And the word of the LORD came to me a
second time, [4]"Take the waistcloth which you have bought, which
is upon your loins, and arise, go to the Euphrates, and hide it there
in a cleft of the rock." [5]So I went, and hid it by the Euphrates, as

---

13:1–11. This is the first of Jeremiah's symbolic actions reported in the book. Actions of that sort, sometimes appearing to make sense, have the advantage of catching the audience's attention better than an oracle does.

It is not easy to imagine how Jeremiah, in the difficult circumstances of the time, could have twice gone to the Euphrates (about 1000 km. or 570 miles away). Therefore, scholars think that this symbolic action may have been something seen in a vision, or else they interpret it as containing a play on the words *Parah*, the name of a torrent near Anathoth (cf. Josh 18:23) and "*Perath*", the word used in Hebrew for the river Euphrates. Anyway, this symbolic action means that Judah, the Lord's decorative loincloth (of the sort worn by priests in the temple), will be corrupted by Babylonian influences and thereby destroyed.

God asked Jeremiah to buy a loincloth and put it on, to symbolize that, just as that garment fitted his waist exactly, God wanted the house of Israel and the house of Judah to cling to him (v. 11). The Lord wanted his people to trust in him completely: the word for "clinging" or adhesion often occurs in the book of Deuteronomy, too, to mean the fidelity due to God (cf. Deut 4:4; 10:20; 11:22; 13:5; 30:20). This "cleaving" to God comes about through faith. "Faith is first of all a personal adherence of man to God. At the same time, and inseparably, it is a *free assent to the whole truth that God has revealed.* As personal adherence to God and assent to his truth, Christian faith differs from our faith in any human person. It is right and just to entrust oneself wholly to God and to believe absolutely what he says. It would be futile and false to place such faith in a creature (cf. Jer 17:5–6; Ps 40:5; 146:3–4)" (*Catechism of the Catholic Church*, 150). Jeremiah's symbolic action may help us, then, to see that when someone forsakes God and puts all his trust in created things, be they other people or material things, it spoils that person's heart entirely. The passage also reminds us of what our Lord says in Matthew 5:13 about salt that has lost its taste being "good for nothing" (v. 10).

---

[13] [1]Haec dixit Dominus ad me: «Vade et posside tibi lumbare lineum et pones illud super lumbos tuos et in aquam non inferes illud». [2]Et possedi lumbare iuxta verbum Domini et posui circa lumbos meos. [3]Et factus est sermo Domini ad me secundo dicens: [4]«Tolle lumbare, quod possedisti, quod est circa lumbos tuos, et surgens vade ad Euphraten et absconde ibi illud in foramine petrae». [5]Et abii et

the LORD commanded me. 6And after many days the LORD said to
me, "Arise, go to the Euphrates, and take from there the
waistcloth which I commanded you to hide there." 7Then I went
to the Euphrates, and dug, and I took the waistcloth from the
place where I had hidden it. And behold, the waistcloth was
spoiled; it was good for nothing.
8Then the word of the LORD came to me: 9"Thus says the
Lev 26:19 LORD: Even so will I spoil the pride of Judah and the great pride
of Jerusalem. 10This evil people, who refuse to hear my words,
who stubbornly follow their own heart and have gone after other
Ex 19:5 gods to serve them and worship them, shall be like this waistcloth,
Deut 11:22; 30:20; Ps 76:11; which is good for nothing. 11For as the waistcloth clings to the
109:19 loins of a man, so I made the whole house of Israel and the whole
house of Judah cling to me, says the LORD, that they might be for
me a people, a name, a praise, and a glory, but they would not
listen.

The jar of God's wrath

12"You shall speak to them this word: 'Thus says the LORD, the
God of Israel, "Every jar shall be filled with wine."' And they will

---

13:12–14. The simile of the jar to be filled with wine certainly implies expectation of a joyful celebration. But Jeremiah speaks of the shock that the people will get when they find it full, not of wine, but of the Lord's wrath. Those who drink it will suffer terribly. He refers to the affliction that will overtake Jerusalem—which will happen very soon, when the holy city falls to Nebuchadnezzar, in 597.

The prophet puts very harsh words in the Lord's mouth (v. 14). Severe treatment is promised to those who endanger the safety of the entire people and who refuse to mend their ways. Origen explains this text by offering the following example: "Consider the doctor who, when he sees that the disease has spread or worsened, must decide to root out the cancer or to cauterize the wound. If he roots out the cancer or cauterizes the wound, he will cure the disease, but it may seem that he shows no mercy or compassion for the patient in his time of suffering" (*Homiliae in Jeremiam*, 12, 5).

absconditi illud ad Euphraten, sicut praeceperat mihi Dominus. 6Et factum est, post dies plurimos dixit Dominus ad me: «Surge, vade ad Euphraten et tolle inde lumbare, quod praecepi tibi, ut absconderes ibi». 7Et abii ad Euphraten et fodi et tuli lumbare de loco, ubi absconderam illud; et ecce, computruerat lumbare, ita ut nulli usui aptum esset. 8Et factum est verbum Domini ad me dicens: 9«Haec dicit Dominus: Sic putrescere faciam superbiam Iudae et superbiam Ierusalem multam; 10populus iste pessimus—qui nolunt audire verba mea et ambulant in pravitate cordis sui abieruntque post deos alienos, ut servirent eis et adorarent eos— erit sicut lumbare istud, quod nulli usui aptum est. 11Sicut enim adhaeret lumbare ad lumbos viri, sic agglutinavi mihi omnem domum Israel et omnem domum Iudae, dicit Dominus, ut esset mihi in populum et in nomen et in laudem et in gloriam, et non audierunt.

say to you, 'Do we not indeed know that every jar will be filled
with wine?' [13]Then you shall say to them, 'Thus says the LORD: Is 51:17
Behold, I will fill with drunkenness all the inhabitants of this land:
the kings who sit on David's throne, the priests, the prophets, and
all the inhabitants of Jerusalem. [14]And I will dash them one against
another, fathers and sons together, says the LORD. I will not pity or
spare or have compassion, that I should not destroy them.'"

God calls for conversion, but the people ignore him

[15] Hear and give ear; be not proud,
  for the LORD has spoken.
[16] Give glory to the LORD your God Amos 5:18 Jn 12:35–36

13:15–27. This oracle may have been uttered immediately after the first deportation to Babylon in 597 BC, since it seems to refer to the time when Jehoiakim and the royal family were taken from Jerusalem (v. 18; cf. 2 Kings 24:12–16), and to the plight that Judah found itself in at that time.

The opening verses (vv. 15–17) call for a change of heart, before something worse happens; the verses that follow (vv. 18–19) fit in with the deportation of the king and his family; and the final verses (vv. 20–27) are further thoughts on the exile: "Why have these things come upon me?" (v. 22). Jerusalem is depicted as being guilty of all sorts of crimes and of prostitution—a stereotypical depiction of an idolatrous and corrupt city.

The book of Jeremiah is strewn with remarks that imply profound pessimism as to Judah and Jerusalem's capacity to turn back to God. It evidently reflects the prophet's own experience: everything he said, all the examples and arguments he used, seemed to fall on deaf ears. God certainly expected more of his people, but he was deceived (cf. 8:13–15). Their sinfulness was so deep-rooted that nothing could wash it away (v. 23). They even failed to see that the travails of exile were the purification that could no longer be postponed (v. 27). "Suffering must serve *for conversion*, that is, *for the rebuilding of goodness* in the subject, who can recognize the divine mercy in this call to repentance. The purpose of penance is to overcome evil, which under different forms lies dormant in man. Its purpose is also to strengthen goodness both in man himself and in his relationships with others and especially with God" (John Paul II, *Salvifici doloris*, 12).

[12]Dices ergo ad eos sermonem istum: Haec dicit Dominus, Deus Israel: Omnis laguncula implebitur vino. Et dicent ad te: "Numquid ignoramus quia omnis laguncula implebitur vino?". [13]Et dices ad eos: Haec dicit Dominus: Ecce ego implebo omnes habitatores terrae huius et reges, qui sedent de stirpe David super thronum eius, et sacerdotes et prophetas et omnes habitatores Ierusalem ebrietate; [14]et collidam eos, virum in fratrem suum et patres et filios pariter, ait Dominus; non parcam et non concedam neque miserebor, ut non disperdam eos». [15]Audite et auribus percipite; nolite elevari, / quia Dominus locutus est. / [16]Date Domino Deo vestro gloriam, / antequam contenebrescat, / et antequam

before he brings darkness,
before your feet stumble
on the twilight mountains,
and while you look for light
he turns it into gloom
and makes it deep darkness.
17 But if you will not listen,
my soul will weep in secret for your pride;
my eyes will weep bitterly and run down with tears,
because the LORD's flock has been taken captive.

2 Kings 24:12–16
18 Say to the king and the queen mother:
"Take a lowly seat,
for your beautiful crown
has come down from your head."[v]
19 The cities of the Negeb are shut up,
with none to open them;
all Judah is taken into exile,
wholly taken into exile.

20 "Lift up your eyes and see
those who come from the north.
Where is the flock that was given you,
your beautiful flock?
Jer 4:30–31
21 What will you say when they set as head over you
those whom you yourself have taught
to be friends to you?
Will not pangs take hold of you,
like those of a woman in travail?
Is 3:17; 47:2–3; Jer 5:19; Lam 1:8; Hos 2:5; Nahum 3:5
22 And if you say in your heart,
'Why have these things come upon me?'
it is for the greatness of your iniquity
that your skirts are lifted up,
and you suffer violence.

---

offendant pedes vestri / ad montes caliginosos; / exspectabitis lucem, / et ponet eam in umbram mortis / et in caliginem. / [17]Quod si hoc non audieritis, / in abscondito plorabit anima mea / a facie superbiae; / plorans plorabit / et deducet oculus meus lacrimam, / quia captus est grex Domini. / [18]«Dic regi et dominatrici: / In humo sedete, / quoniam descendit de capite vestro / corona gloriae vestrae. / [19]Civitates austri clausae sunt, / et non est qui aperiat; / translata est omnis Iuda / transmigratione perfecta. / [20]Leva oculos tuos et vide / venientes ab aquilone: / Ubi est grex, qui datus est tibi, / pecus inclitum tuum? / [21]Quid dices, cum visitaverit te? / Tu enim ipsa docuisti eos adversum te, / amicos in caput tuum; / numquid non dolores apprehendent te / quasi mulierem parturientem? / [22]Quod si

v. Gk Syr Vg: Heb obscure

[23] Can the Ethiopian change his skin
or the leopard his spots?
Then also you can do good
who are accustomed to do evil.
[24] I will scatter you[w] like chaff
driven by the wind from the desert.
[25] This is your lot,
the portion I have measured out to you, says the LORD,
because you have forgotten me
and trusted in lies.
[26] I myself will lift up your skirts over your face,
and your shame will be seen.
[27] I have seen your abominations,
your adulteries and neighings, your lewd harlotries,
on the hills in the field.
Woe to you, O Jerusalem!
How long will it be
before you are made clean?"

Mt 7:16–19

Jer 2:20
Ezek 24:13

Oracles in a time of drought

14 [1]The word of the LORD which came to Jeremiah concerning the drought:

14:1—15:9. This highly dramatic passage is made up of poems and dialogues between God and Jeremiah. It paints a picture of anguish, hunger and death—a desperate attempt to provoke repentance. "The prophet includes here a prayer to God on behalf of his chosen people, so that having punished them he will also show them his mercy" (St Thomas Aquinas, *Postilla super Jeremiam*, 14, 1).

What Jeremiah had been saying about the evils that would befall Jerusalem was all coming true. After the attack on the city in 597 and the deportation that ensued, the situation was terrible. The affliction suffered by the city was compounded by a terrible drought which made its plight and that of all Judah even worse (14:1–6; cf. 8:18–23). In their extremity the people cry out to God, begging him not to treat

dixeris in corde tuo: / "Quare venerunt mihi haec?". / Propter multitudinem iniquitatis tuae / revelatae sunt laciniae tuae, / pollutae sunt plantae tuae. / [23]Numquid mutare potest Aethiops pellem suam / aut pardus varietates suas? / Tunc et vos poteritis benefacere, / cum didiceritis malum. / [24]Et disseminabo eos quasi stipulam, / quae raptatur in vento deserti. / [25]Haec sors tua parsque mensurae tuae a me, / dicit Dominus, / quia oblita es mei / et confisa es in mendacio. / [26]Unde et ego sublevabo lacinias tuas super faciem tuam, / et apparebit ignominia tua, / [27]adulteria tua et hinnitus tuus, / scelus fornicationis tuae. / Super colles in agro vidi abominationes tuas. / Vae tibi, Ierusalem! Non mundaberis; / usquequo adhuc?». **[14]** [1]Quod factum est verbum Domini ad Ieremiam de siccitate. / [2]Luget Iuda, / et portae

w. Heb *them*

Lam 1:4 2"Judah mourns
and her gates languish;
her people lament on the ground,
and the cry of Jerusalem goes up.
Lev 26:18–20 3Her nobles send their servants for water;
they come to the cisterns,
they find no water,
they return with their vessels empty;
they are ashamed and confounded
and cover their heads.
Jer 3:3 4Because of the ground which is dismayed,
Hos 4:3 since there is no rain on the land,
the farmers are ashamed,
they cover their heads.
5Even the hind in the field forsakes her newborn calf
because there is no grass.
6The wild asses stand on the bare heights,
they pant for air like jackals;

---

them like strangers (14:7–9). The Lord replies through his prophet, and despite Jeremiah's attempts to excuse his fellow citizens, he does not mince his words: all these disasters are due to the faults and sins of the people (14:10–12), who made the mistake of relying on false prophets who put their minds at ease with promises of peace and prosperity (14:13–16). Jeremiah is deeply distressed by the whole situation, and he again begs God not to punish Judah (14:17–19); and the people again entreat God, their only hope (14:20–22). But the Lord has already promulgated his sentence. He will not go back on it—not even if the nation's great mediators, Moses and Samuel, were to speak on its behalf (15:1–4; cf. Ex 32:11–14; 1 Sam 7:8–12). Its wickedness dates back a long time—certainly to the reign of Manasseh (698–642), the son of Hezekiah (15:4), who tolerated and even promoted impiety and idolatry (2 Kings 21:1–18). So, the Lord had no option but to carry out his sentence (15:5–9): Judah had "rejected" him (cf. 15:6). This last part of the oracle is very severe and shows the profound pain felt by the prophet, for there is nothing he can do to ward off this great misfortune.

The words of 15:2 (cf. 43:11) are quoted in the book of Revelation (13:10) with reference to the latter days, to exhort readers to accept the truth of God's message and bear persecution with endurance and faith.

eius languescunt / et contristatae iacent in terra, / et clamor Ierusalem ascendit. / 3Maiores eorum miserunt minores suos ad aquam: / venerunt ad cisternas, / non invenerunt aquam; / reportaverunt vasa sua vacua, / confusi sunt et afflicti / et operuerunt capita sua. / 4Propter terrae vastitatem, / quia non venit pluvia in terram, / confusi sunt agricolae, / operuerunt capita sua. / 5Nam et cerva in agro peperit et reliquit, / quia non erat herba. / 6Et onagri steterunt in collibus, / traxerunt aerem quasi thoes; /

their eyes fail
because there is no herbage.

7 “Though our iniquities testify against us, Is 59:12
act, O LORD, for thy name’s sake;
for our backslidings are many,
we have sinned against thee.
8 O thou hope of Israel, Jer 17:13
its saviour in time of trouble,
why shouldst thou be like a stranger in the land,
like a wayfarer who turns aside to tarry for a night?
9 Why shouldst thou be like a man confused, Deut 28:10
like a mighty man who cannot save? Jer 7:30; 15:16
Yet thou, O LORD, art in the midst of us,
and we are called by thy name;
leave us not.”

10 Thus says the LORD concerning this people: Hos 8:13
“They have loved to wander thus,
they have not restrained their feet;
therefore the LORD does not accept them,
now he will remember their iniquity
and punish their sins.”

11 The LORD said to me: “Do not pray for the welfare of this Jer 7:16
people. 12 Though they fast, I will not hear their cry, and though Is 1:15; 58:3
they offer burnt offering and cereal offering, I will not accept Jer 7:21
them; but I will consume them by the sword, by famine, and by Mal 3:4
pestilence.”
13 Then I said: “Ah, Lord GOD, behold, the prophets say to Jer 23
them, ‘You shall not see the sword, nor shall you have famine, but Jer 5:31; 27:10;
I will give you assured peace in this place.’” 14 And the LORD said 29:8–9

---

defecerunt oculi eorum, / quia non erat herba. / 7 «Si iniquitates nostrae testificantur adversus nos, / Domine, fac propter nomen tuum, / quoniam multae sunt aversiones nostrae, / tibi peccavimus. / 8 Exspectatio Israel, / salvator eius in tempore tribulationis, / quare quasi peregrinus es in terra / et quasi viator declinans ad pernoctandum? / 9 Quare es velut vir attonitus, / ut fortis, qui non potest salvare? / Tu autem in medio nostri es, Domine, / et nomen tuum invocatum est super nos; / ne derelinquas nos». 10 Haec dicit Dominus populo huic: «Ita diligunt vagari, pedes suos non prohibent et Domino non placent». Nunc recordatus est iniquitatum eorum et visitat peccata eorum. 11 Et dixit Dominus ad me: «Noli orare pro populo isto in bonum. 12 Cum ieiunaverint, non exaudiam preces eorum; et, si obtulerint holocautomata et oblationes, non suscipiam ea; quoniam gladio et fame et peste consumam eos». 13 Et dixi: «Heu, Domine Deus! Ecce prophetae dicunt eis: “Non videbitis gladium, et fames non erit in vobis, sed pacem veram dabit vobis in loco isto”». 14 Et dixit Dominus ad me: «Falso prophetae vaticinantur in nomine meo: non misi eos et non praecepi eis neque locutus sum ad eos; visionem

to me: "The prophets are prophesying lies in my name; I did not
send them, nor did I command them or speak to them. They are
prophesying to you a lying vision, worthless divination, and the
deceit of their own minds. 15Therefore thus says the LORD concerning the prophets who prophesy in my name although I did not
send them, and who say, 'Sword and famine shall not come on
this land': By sword and famine those prophets shall be
consumed. 16And the people to whom they prophesy shall be cast
out in the streets of Jerusalem, victims of famine and sword, with
none to bury them—them, their wives, their sons, and their
daughters. For I will pour out their wickedness upon them.

17 "You shall say to them this word:
'Let my eyes run down with tears night and day,
and let them not cease,
for the virgin daughter of my people is smitten with a great wound,
with a very grievous blow.
18 If I go out into the field,
behold, those slain by the sword!
And if I enter the city,
behold, the diseases of famine!
For both prophet and priest ply their trade through the land,
and have no knowledge.'"

Jer 8:15; 13:16 Amos 5:18 19 Hast thou utterly rejected Judah?
Does thy soul loathe Zion?
Why hast thou smitten us
so that there is no healing for us?
We looked for peace, but no good came;
for a time of healing, but behold, terror.
Ps 106:6 20 We acknowledge our wickedness, O LORD,
and the iniquity of our fathers,
for we have sinned against thee.

---

mendacem et divinationem et fraudulentiam et seductionem cordis sui prophetant vobis. 15Idcirco haec
dicit Dominus contra prophetas, qui prophetant in nomine meo, quos ego non misi, dicentes: "Gladius
et fames non erit in terra hac": In gladio et fame consumentur prophetae illi; 16et homines, quibus
prophetant, erunt proiecti in viis Ierusalem prae fame et gladio, et non erit qui sepeliat eos: ipsi et
uxores eorum, filii et filiae eorum, et effundam super eos malum suum. 17Et dices ad eos verbum istud:
/ Deducant oculi mei lacrimam / per noctem et diem, et non taceant, / quoniam contritione magna
contrita est / virgo filia populi mei, / plaga pessima vehementer. / 18Si egressus fuero ad agros, / ecce
occisi gladio; / et, si introiero in civitatem, / ecce attenuati fame; / propheta quoque et sacerdos /
abierunt per terram nescientes». / 19Numquid proiciens abiecisti Iudam, / aut Sion abominata est anima
tua? / Quare ergo percussisti nos, / ita ut nulla sit sanitas? / Exspectavimus pacem, et non est bonum,
/ et tempus curationis, et ecce turbatio. / 20Cognovimus, Domine, impietates nostras, / iniquitates

[21] Do not spurn us, for thy name's sake;
do not dishonour thy glorious throne;
remember and do not break thy covenant with us.
[22] Are there any among the false gods of the nations that can
bring rain?
Or can the heavens give showers?
Art thou not he, O LORD our God?
We set our hope on thee,
for thou doest all these things. 1 Sam 7:8–12

15 [1]Then the LORD said to me, "Though Moses and Samuel Ex 32:11
stood before me, yet my heart would not turn toward this Ps 99:6 Ezek 4:14,16
people. Send them out of my sight, and let them go! [2]And when Jer 43:11
they ask you, 'Where shall we go?' you shall say to them, 'Thus Rev 13:10
says the LORD:
"Those who are for pestilence, to pestilence,
and those who are for the sword, to the sword;
those who are for famine, to famine,
and those who are for captivity, to captivity."'
[3]"I will appoint over them four kinds of destroyers, says the LORD:
the sword to slay, the dogs to tear, and the birds of the air and the
beasts of the earth to devour and destroy. [4]'And I will make them 2 Kings 21:11,16,17;
a horror to all the kingdoms of the earth because of what 23:26; 24:3
Manasseh the son of Hezekiah, king of Judah, did in Jerusalem.

[5]"Who will have pity on you, O Jerusalem, Ex 34:6–7 Is 51:19
or who will bemoan you?
Who will turn aside
to ask about your welfare?
[6]You have rejected me, says the LORD, Hos 13:14
you keep going backward;
so I have stretched out my hand against you and destroyed you;—
I am weary of relenting.

---

patrum nostrorum, quia peccavimus tibi. / [21]Ne des nos in opprobrium propter nomen tuum, / ne facias contumeliam solio gloriae tuae; / recordare, ne irritum facias foedus tuum nobiscum. / [22]Numquid sunt in sculptilibus gentium, qui pluant, / aut caeli possunt dare imbres? / Nonne tu es Dominus Deus noster, / quem exspectamus? / Tu enim fecisti omnia haec. **[15]** [1]Et dixit Dominus ad me: «Si steterit Moyses et Samuel coram me, non est anima mea ad populum istum; eice illos a facie mea, et egrediantur. [2]Quod si dixerint ad te: "Quo egrediemur?", dices ad eos: Haec dicit Dominus: Qui ad mortem, ad mortem; / et qui ad gladium, ad gladium; / et qui ad famem, ad famem; / et qui ad captivitatem, ad captivitatem. [3]Et mandabo super eos quattuor species, dicit Dominus: gladium ad occisionem et canes ad lacerandum et volatilia caeli et bestias terrae ad devorandum et dissipandum. [4]Et dabo eos in commotionem universis regnis terrae, propter Manassem filium Ezechiae regem Iudae, super omnibus, quae fecit in Ierusalem. [5]Quis enim miserebitur tui, Ierusalem, / aut quis contristabitur pro te, / aut quis ibit ad rogandum de pace tua? / [6]Tu reppulisti me, / dicit Dominus, / retrorsum abiisti; / et extendi

[7]I have winnowed them with a winnowing fork
in the gates of the land;
I have bereaved them, I have destroyed my people;
they did not turn from their ways.
[8]I have made their widows more in number
than the sand of the seas;
I have brought against the mothers of young men
a destroyer at noonday;
I have made anguish and terror
fall upon them suddenly.
[9]She who bore seven has languished;
she has swooned away;
her sun went down while it was yet day;
she has been shamed and disgraced.
And the rest of them I will give to the sword
before their enemies, says the LORD."

Jer 1:4–10, 17–19

Jeremiah's second "confession"

Lk 2:34

[10]Woe is me, my mother, that you bore me, a man of strife and
contention to the whole land! I have not lent, nor have I borrowed,
yet all of them curse me. [11]So let it be, O LORD, [x]if I have not
entreated[y] thee for their good, if I have not pleaded with thee on

---

15:10–21. Jeremiah again opens his heart to the Lord. The mission God gave him has not proved easy. In vv. 10–11 he seems to share his thoughts with his mother, with himself and with God, and in vv. 15–21 he makes a prayerful complaint to God, who spells out what course he should take and offers hope of deliverance. Verses 12–14, which break the thread of the passage and are to be found again in 17:3–4, seem to stress the solidarity that exists between Jeremiah and the people.

Despite the fact that Jeremiah has sought only to serve the Lord and intercede with him even on behalf of enemies, wishing no one evil, he has been rejected and cursed and has become a source of discord. He tells the Lord how pained he feels (vv. 10–11) and he goes on to recall times when he

manum meam super te et interfeci te: / laboravi miserans. / [7]Et ventilavi eos ventilabro / in portis terrae; / orbavi et disperdidi populum meum: / a viis suis non sunt reversi. / [8]Multiplicatae sunt mihi viduae eius / super arenam maris, / induxi eis super matrem / militem vastatorem meridie, / misi super eam repente / perturbationem et terrorem. / [9]Infirmata est, quae peperit septem, / exhalavit animam suam; / occidit ei sol, cum adhuc esset dies, / confusa est et erubuit, / et residuos eorum in gladium dabo / in conspectu inimicorum eorum», / ait Dominus. / [10]Vae mihi, mater mea, / quoniam genuisti me virum rixae / et virum discordiae in universa terra! / Non feneravi, nec feneravit mihi quisquam; / omnes maledicunt mihi. / [11]Amen, Domine, ministravi tibi in bonum, / intercessi apud te in tempore

x. Gk Old Latin: Heb *the LORD said* **y.** Cn: Heb obscure

behalf of the enemy in the time of trouble and in the time of
distress! [12]Can one break iron, iron from the north, and bronze?
[13]"Your wealth and your treasures I will give as spoil, without Jer 17:3–4
price, for all your sins, throughout all your territory. [14]I will make
you serve your enemies in a land which you do not know, for in
my anger a fire is kindled which shall burn for ever."

[15] O LORD, thou knowest; Ps 69:8
remember me and visit me,
and take vengeance for me on my persecutors.
In thy forbearance take me not away;
know that for thy sake I bear reproach.
[16] Thy words were found, and I ate them, Jer 14:9
and thy words became to me a joy
and the delight of my heart;
for I am called by thy name,
O LORD, God of hosts.
[17] I did not sit in the company of merrymakers, Jer 16:8
nor did I rejoice;
I sat alone, because thy hand was upon me,
for thou hadst filled me with indignation.
[18] Why is my pain unceasing,
my wound incurable,

---

felt very happy in his relations with God (v. 16), and other times when he felt desolate because everyone rejected him (vv. 17–18). As in the first "confession" (11:18—12:6), the Lord's reply seems harsh, calling him to personal conversion (v. 19a). Because Jeremiah must preach conversion to others, he must begin with himself, by being true to the mission entrusted to him; he must shed any feelings of pessimism. Once he is cleansed, he will be well able to speak the word of the Lord and the people will heed him (vv. 19b–21).

Jeremiah's trusting dialogue with the Lord, and the reply he is given (v. 19), are a personal call to the reader of this passage: "This is meant for everyone, for God is always calling on us to return to him" (Origen, *Homiliae in Jeremiam*, 14, 18).

afflictionis / et in tempore tribulationis pro inimico. / [12]Numquid frangitur ferro / ferrum aquilonis et aes? / [13]«Divitias tuas et thesauros tuos / in direptionem dabo gratis, / propter omnia peccata tua, / in omnibus terminis tuis. / [14]Et servire te faciam inimicis tuis / in terra, quam nescis, / quia ignis succensus est in furore meo: / super vos ardebit». / [15]Tu scis, Domine; / recordare mei et visita me / et vindica me de his, qui persequuntur me; / noli in patientia tua abripere me, / scito quoniam sustinui pro te opprobrium. / [16]Inventi sunt sermones tui, et comedi eos, / et factum est mihi verbum tuum / in gaudium et in laetitiam cordis mei, / quoniam invocatum est nomen tuum super me, / Domine, Deus exercituum. / [17]Non sedi in concilio ludentium / et gloriatus sum; / a facie manus tuae solus sedebam,

refusing to be healed?
Wilt thou be to me like a deceitful brook,
like waters that fail?

Jer 1:9 [19] Therefore thus says the LORD:
"If you return, I will restore you,
and you shall stand before me.
If you utter what is precious, and not what is worthless,
you shall be as my mouth.
They shall turn to you,
but you shall not turn to them.
Jer 1:18–19 [20] And I will make you to this people
a fortified wall of bronze;
they will fight against you,
but they shall not prevail over you,
for I am with you
to save you and deliver you, says the LORD.
[21] I will deliver you out of the hand of the wicked,
and redeem you from the grasp of the ruthless."

Actions symbolic of the punishment to come

16 [1]The word of the LORD came to me: [2]"You shall not take a
wife, nor shall you have sons or daughters in this place.

16:1–21. The prophet's own life is a symbol of the misfortunes of his people. The Lord asks Jeremiah to impose three serious privations on himself in order to set an example that will make the people think: he should stay celibate (v. 2), and attend neither wakes (v. 5) nor festivities (v. 8). People may find each of these three things disconcerting. Celibacy practised for religious reasons was something seldom found among the people of Israel, for children were seen as a blessing from God and they would ensure that a person's memory lived on. And people would have found it very strange that someone should not offer condolences in a bereavement, or should refuse to take part in celebrations.

As usually happens, this account of the symbolic actions of the prophet includes an explanation of their

/ quoniam indignatione replesti me. / [18]Quare factus est dolor meus perpetuus, / et plaga mea desperabilis renuit curari? / Factus es mihi quasi rivus mendax, / aquae infideles. / [19]Propter hoc haec dixit Dominus: / «Si converteris, convertam te, / et ante faciem meam stabis; / et si separaveris pretiosum a vili, / quasi os meum eris; / convertentur ipsi ad te, / et tu non converteris ad eos. / [20]Et dabo te populo huic / in murum aereum fortem; / et bellabunt adversum te / et non praevalebunt, / quia ego tecum sum, / ut salvem te et eruam te, / dicit Dominus. / [21]Et liberabo te de manu pessimorum / et redimam te de manu fortium». **[16]** [1]Et factum est verbum Domini ad me dicens: [2]«Non accipies uxorem, et non erunt tibi filii et filiae in loco isto. [3]Quia haec dicit Dominus super filios et filias, qui

3For thus says the LORD concerning the sons and daughters who are born in this place, and concerning the mothers who bore them and the fathers who begot them in this land: 4They shall die of

Deut 28:26
Jer 8:2; 15:2;
25:33; 34:20

meaning. Here we are told that the prohibitions refer to the punishment that awaits Judah. The first one indicates that the punishment is imminent and devastating. Jeremiah is not to marry or have children because his wife and children would most certainly die (vv. 3–4). The other two prohibitions point to the scale of the disaster: so many will die that they cannot be given proper funerals (vv. 6–7), and the tribulation will be such that joy is nowhere to be found (v. 9). The real explanation for all this comes at the end. Something terrible is going to happen very soon because for generations the people have been rejecting the Lord. The time has come when God will leave Judah at the mercy of its enemies (vv. 10–13).

However, in the midst of these predictions of doom we find words of consolation for those who will be deported (vv. 14–15); these occur again at 23:7–8. They are a ray of hope in the midst of darkness. They seem to be saying that God, who has demanded of Jeremiah almost a death-in-life (16:1–8), is promising the people life in spite of their sins. When they forsake their evil ways, the Lord will show his power by bringing the exiles home in a way even more marvellous than he did when he delivered his people from bondage in Egypt. The exodus from Egypt was one of the mainstays of Israel's trust in the Lord, a point of reference for its entire religious life; and the return of the exiles will be seen as a second exodus, a new beginning for a new situation.

Verses 16–18 then link up with v. 13 to provide more predictions of disaster. Jeremiah uses the metaphor of fishermen and hunters (v. 16) to show how relentless the punishment will be. No one can escape it. But then, as in vv. 14–15, we find more words of consolation and hope, this time in a hymn of praise to God. After the pain and purification, even the pagans will acknowledge the Lord as their God (v. 19); they will come to see that idols, being man-made things, are quite worthless (vv. 20–21).

The "fishers" (v. 16) may refer to the Babylonians, who were famous for their skill at fishing (cf. Hab 1:15–17). We are told that they and the "hunters" will be instruments used by God to carry out his purposes in regard to Judah. The imagery of fishing and hunting implies the idea of exhaustiveness. In its literal and proper sense it refers to the Babylonians, who will trap *all* the Israelites, no matter where they hide. Christian writers, mindful of Jesus' use of the fishing analogy (cf. Lk 5:10), give this passage a spiritual interpretation, seeing Christians as people who should seek out everyone, wherever

generantur in loco isto, et super matres eorum, quae genuerunt eos, et super patres eorum, de quorum stirpe sunt nati in terra hac: 4Mortibus aegrotationum morientur, non plangentur et non sepelientur; in sterquilinium super faciem terrae erunt et gladio et fame consumentur, et erit cadaver eorum in escam

deadly diseases. They shall not be lamented, nor shall they be
buried; they shall be as dung on the surface of the ground. They
shall perish by the sword and by famine, and their dead bodies
shall be food for the birds of the air and for the beasts of the earth.
5"For thus says the LORD: Do not enter the house of mourning,
or go to lament, or bemoan them; for I have taken away my peace
from this people, says the LORD, my steadfast love and mercy.
6Both great and small shall die in this land; they shall not be
buried, and no one shall lament for them or cut himself or make
himself bald for them. 7No one shall break bread for the mourner,
to comfort him for the dead; nor shall any one give him the cup of
consolation to drink for his father or his mother. 8You shall not go
Jer 7:34; 25:10 into the house of feasting to sit with them, to eat and drink. 9For
thus says the LORD of hosts, the God of Israel: Behold, I will make
to cease from this place, before your eyes and in your days, the
voice of mirth and the voice of gladness, the voice of the
bridegroom and the voice of the bride.

---

they may be, to bring them closer to God: "'Behold, I will send many fishermen,' says the Lord, 'and I will catch those fishes (Jer 16:16).' That is his way of explaining the great task we have before us: we must become fishermen. The world is often compared, in conversation or in books, with the sea. It is a good comparison, for in our lives, just as in the sea, there are quiet times and stormy seasons, periods of calm and gusts of strong wind. One often finds souls swimming in difficult waters, in the midst of heavy waves. They travel through stormy weather, their journey one sad rush, despite their apparently cheerful expressions and their boisterousness. Their bursts of laughter are a cover for their discouragement and ill-temper. Their lives are bereft of charity and understanding. Men, like fish, devour each other. Our task as children of God is to get all men to enter, freely, into the divine net; to get them to love each other. If we are Christians, we must seek to become fishermen like those described by the prophet Jeremiah with a metaphor which Jesus also often used: 'Follow me and I will make you fishers of men' (Mk 4:19), he says to Peter and Andrew" (St Josemaría Escrivá, *Friends of God*, 259).

volatilibus caeli et bestiis terrae». 5Haec enim dixit Dominus: «Ne ingrediaris domum convivii neque vadas ad plangendum neque lugebis eos, quia abstuli pacem meam a populo isto, dicit Dominus, misericordiam et miserationes. 6Et morientur grandes et parvi in terra ista, non sepelientur neque plangentur, et non se incident, neque calvitium fiet pro eis. 7Et non frangent lugenti panem ad consolandum super mortuo et non dabunt ei calicem ad consolandum super patre suo et matre. 8Et domum convivii non ingredieris, ut sedeas cum eis et comedas et bibas. 9Quia haec dicit Dominus exercituum, Deus Israel: Ecce ego auferam de loco isto in oculis vestris et in diebus vestris vocem gaudii et vocem laetitiae, vocem sponsi et vocem sponsae. 10Et cum annuntiaveris populo huic omnia verba haec, et dixerint tibi: "Quare locutus est Dominus super nos omne malum grande istud? Quae

[10]“And when you tell this people all these words, and they say Deut 29:24
to you, ‘Why has the LORD pronounced all this great evil against Jer 5:19
us? What is our iniquity? What is the sin that we have committed
against the LORD our God?’ [11]then you shall say to them: ‘Because
your fathers have forsaken me, says the LORD, and have gone after
other gods and have served and worshipped them, and have
forsaken me and have not kept my law, [12]and because you have
done worse than your fathers, for behold, every one of you follows
his stubborn evil will, refusing to listen to me; [13]therefore I will Deut 4:26–28;
hurl you out of this land into a land which neither you nor your 28:36
fathers have known, and there you shall serve other gods day and Jer 17:4
night, for I will show you no favour.’

[14]“Therefore, behold, the days are coming, says the LORD, when Ex 20:2
it shall no longer be said, ‘As the LORD lives who brought up the Jer 23:7–8
people of Israel out of the land of Egypt,’ [15]but ‘As the LORD lives
who brought up the people of Israel out of the north country and
out of all the countries where he had driven them.’ For I will bring
them back to their own land which I gave to their fathers.

[16]“Behold, I am sending for many fishers, says the LORD, and Hab 1:15–17;
they shall catch them; and afterwards I will send for many hunters, Mt 4:19; Lk
and they shall hunt them from every mountain and every hill, and 5:10
out of the clefts of the rocks. [17]For my eyes are upon all their
ways; they are not hid from me, nor is their iniquity concealed
from my eyes. [18]And[z] I will doubly recompense their iniquity and Is 44:10
their sin, because they have polluted my land with the carcasses of Rev 18:6
their detestable idols, and have filled my inheritance with their
abominations.”

[19]O LORD, my strength and my stronghold, Ps 31:5
    my refuge in the day of trouble, Is 45:14

---

iniquitas nostra et quod peccatum nostrum, quod peccavimus Domino Deo nostro?”, [11]dices ad eos: Quia dereliquerunt me patres vestri, ait Dominus, et abierunt post deos alienos et servierunt eis et adoraverunt eos et me dereliquerunt et legem meam non custodierunt. [12]Sed et vos peius operati estis quam patres vestri: ecce enim ambulat unusquisque post pravitatem cordis sui mali, ut me non audiat. [13]Et eiciam vos de terra hac in terram, quam ignoratis, vos et patres vestri; et servietis ibi diis alienis, die ac nocte, quia non dabo vobis gratiam. [14]Propterea ecce dies veniunt, dicit Dominus, et non dicetur ultra: “Vivit Dominus, qui eduxit filios Israel de terra Aegypti!”, [15]sed: “Vivit Dominus, qui eduxit filios Israel de terra aquilonis et de universis terris, ad quas eieci eos!”. Et reducam eos in terram suam, quam dedi patribus eorum. [16]Ecce ego mittam piscatores multos, dicit Dominus, et piscabuntur eos; et post haec mittam eis multos venatores, et venabuntur eos de omni monte et de omni colle et de cavernis petrarum. [17]Quia oculi mei super omnes vias eorum: non sunt absconditae a facie mea, et non est occulta iniquitas eorum ab oculis meis. [18]Et reddam primum dupliciter iniquitates et peccata eorum,

z. Gk: Heb *And first*

to thee shall the nations come
from the ends of the earth and say:
"Our fathers have inherited nought but lies,
worthless things in which there is no profit.
Is 40:20 Is 42:8 20 Can man make for himself gods?
Such are no gods!"

21"Therefore, behold, I will make them know, this once I will
make them know my power and my might, and they shall know
that my name is the LORD."

God rewards people as they deserve

Prov 3:3; 7:3 Jer 31:33 Dan 7:10 **17** 1"The sin of Judah is written with a pen of iron; with a
point of diamond it is engraved on the tablet of their heart,

---

17:1–13. This passage includes a number of short oracles in the style of wisdom writing, graphically expressing themes that were constant in Jeremiah's preaching. Judah's sin of idolatry was quite obvious: anyone travelling the country could see people frequenting the places where Canaanite gods were worshipped; they were everywhere one went (vv. 1–3a). That is why the Lord will abandon the Israelites, who will be uprooted from their land and enslaved (vv. 3b–4).

Using words similar to those of Psalm 1, the prophet describes the misfortune that will befall those who trust in themselves, as against the prosperity of those who trust in God (vv. 5–8). St Thomas Aquinas' commentary on Psalm 1 fits in nicely with the simile here of the tree planted beside water (v. 8): "We are asked to consider three things in the image of the tree—its being well-rooted, its fruitfulness, and the sustaining of its life. To be well-rooted, the tree must be well-watered, otherwise it will dry up and wither away; thus, we are told that the tree is planted beside running waters, which symbolize the currents of grace. 'He who believes in me ... out of his heart shall flow rivers of living water' (Jn 7:38). The one whose roots draw on the living waters will bear much fruit in all the good works that he does, and fruitfulness is the second aspect of the image that we are asked to contemplate. 'But the fruit of the Spirit is love, joy, peace, patience, kindness, goodness, faithfulness', etc. (Gal 5:22). The tree does not wither away: it is sustained in life. Some trees lose their leaves, but others never lose their leaves; and thus it is with righteous

quia contaminaverunt terram meam in morticinis idolorum suorum et abominationibus suis impleverunt hereditatem meam». 19Domine, fortitudo mea et praesidium meum / et refugium meum in die tribulationis; / ad te gentes venient ab extremis terrae et dicent: / «Vere mendacium possederunt patres nostri, / vanitatem, quae nihil prodest». / 20Numquid faciet sibi homo deos, / et ipsi non sunt dii? / 21«Idcirco ecce ego ostendam eis per vicem hanc, / ostendam eis manum meam et virtutem meam, / et scient quia nomen mihi Dominus». **[17]** 1Peccatum Iudae scriptum est stilo ferreo, / in ungue

and on the horns of their altars, [2]while their children remember
their altars and their Asherim, beside every green tree, and on the
high hills, [3]on the mountains in the open country. Your wealth and
all your treasures I will give for spoil as the price of your sin[a]
throughout all your territory. [4]You shall loosen your hand[b] from
your heritage which I gave to you, and I will make you serve your
enemies in a land which you do not know, for in my anger a fire is
kindled which shall burn for ever."

Deut 12:2
Judg 3:7
Is 27:9
Jer 15:13–14

[5]Thus says the LORD:
"Cursed is the man who trusts in man
and makes flesh his arm,
whose heart turns away from the LORD.
[6]He is like a shrub in the desert,
and shall not see any good come.
He shall dwell in the parched places of the wilderness,
in an uninhabited salt land.

Ps 146:3–4

[7]"Blessed is the man who trusts in the LORD,
whose trust is the LORD.
[8]He is like a tree planted by water,
that sends out its roots by the stream,

Ps 1:3; 25:2; 40:5
Prov 11:28
Ps 1:3; 42:3
Jn 4:10

men [...]; they will not be forgotten by God even in their tiniest and least significant actions. 'The righteous will flourish like a green leaf' (Prov 11:28)" (*Postilla super Psalmos*, 1, 3).

God cannot be deceived; he sees right into a person's heart, and he will judge each on his merits (vv. 9–11). The hope of Israel is the Lord (vv. 12–13), the fount of water (cf. 2:13; Ps 42:2; Jn 4:10) without which none can live (cf. v. 8). To show that those who forsake God will be judged and condemned, Jeremiah uses an image (they "shall be written in the earth": v. 13) that is reminiscent of Jesus' gesture when he "judges" the men who accuse the woman caught in adultery (Jn 8:6). The wind will blow their names away: they will have no place in the book of life.

adamantino exaratum / super tabulam cordis eorum / et in cornibus ararum eorum, / [2]ut recordarentur filii eorum ararum suarum / et palorum suorum iuxta ligna frondentia / in collibus excelsis, / [3]montibus in campo. / «Divitias tuas, omnes thesauros tuos / in direptionem dabo, / excelsa tua propter peccata / in universis finibus tuis. / [4]Et relinques hereditatem tuam, / quam dedi tibi; / et servire te faciam inimicis tuis / in terra, quam ignoras, / quoniam ignem succendistis in naribus meis; / usque in aeternum ardebit». / [5]Haec dicit Dominus: / «Maledictus homo, qui confidit in homine / et ponit carnem brachium suum, / et a Domino recedit cor eius; / [6]erit enim quasi myricae in deserto / et non videbit, cum venerit bonum, / sed habitabit in siccitate in deserto, / in terra salsuginis et inhabitabili. / [7]Benedictus vir, qui confidit in Domino, / et erit Dominus fiducia eius; / [8]et erit quasi lignum, / quod

a. Cn: Heb *your high places for sin* **b.** Cn: Heb *and in you*

and does not fear when heat comes,
for its leaves remain green,
and is not anxious in the year of drought,
for it does not cease to bear fruit."

Mk 7:21 9 The heart is deceitful above all things,
and desperately corrupt;
1 Sam 16:7 Ps 62:13; who can understand it?
139:23 10 "I the LORD search the mind
Prov 17:3 and try the heart,
Jer 11:20; 32:19 to give to every man according to his ways,
Mt 16:27 according to the fruit of his doings."
Rom 8:27

11 Like the partridge that gathers a brood which she did not hatch,
so is he who gets riches but not by right;
in the midst of his days they will leave him,
and at his end he will be a fool.

12 A glorious throne set on high from the beginning
is the place of our sanctuary.
Ps 73:27 13 O LORD, the hope of Israel,
Is 1:28 all who forsake thee shall be put to shame;
Jer 2:13; 14:8 Lk 10:20 those who turn away from thee[c] shall be written in the earth,
Jn 8:6 for they have forsaken the LORD, the fountain of living water.

Jer 15:10 **Jeremiah's third "confession"**
Ps 6:3–4 14 Heal me, O LORD, and I shall be healed;
save me, and I shall be saved;
for thou art my praise.

17:14–18. In this third "confession", Jeremiah, under pressure from the people, has recourse to the Lord (cf. Ps 6:2–3; 5:10–11). He is predicting all sorts of calamities, but they do not come to pass; the people jeer and call his bluff (v. 15). Jeremiah has no wish for the "day of disaster", "day of evil",

transplantatur super aquas, / quod ad humorem mittit radices suas / et non timebit, cum venerit aestus; / et erit folium eius viride, / et in anno siccitatis non erit sollicitum / nec aliquando desinet facere fructum / 9 Dolosum est cor super omnia et insanabile; / quis cognoscet illud? / 10 Ego Dominus scrutans cor et probans renes, / qui do unicuique iuxta viam suam / et iuxta fructum operum suorum. / 11 Perdix fovit, quae non peperit, / ita faciens divitias sed non in iudicio. / In dimidio dierum suorum derelinquet eas / et in novissimo suo erit insipiens». / 12 Solium gloriae, altitudo a principio, / locus sanctificationis nostrae! / 13 Exspectatio Israel, Domine, / omnes, qui te derelinquunt, confundentur; / recedentes a te in terra scribentur, / quoniam dereliquerunt venam / aquarum viventium, Dominum. / 14 Sana me, Domine,

c. Heb *me*

15 Behold, they say to me,
"Where is the word of the LORD?
Let it come!"
16 I have not pressed thee to send evil,
nor have I desired the day of disaster,
thou knowest;
that which came out of my lips
was before thy face.

17 Be not a terror to me;
thou art my refuge in the day of evil.
18 Let those be put to shame who persecute me, Ps 5:11
but let me not be put to shame;
let them be dismayed,
but let me not be dismayed;
bring upon them the day of evil;
destroy them with double destruction!

---

to come (vv. 16–18); he has proclaimed it because God told him to; if the word of God is borne out, then Jeremiah will, of course, be justified. He feels safe because he has done what God asked him to, and in the midst of calamities he finds refuge in the Lord (v. 17).

Meditating on these words of Jeremiah, St John of Avila recommends praying for trust in God: "During my trials and tribulations, Lord, during my day of suffering, *be not a terror to me* (Jer 17:17); do not make me carry again the weight of your cross. I will go on, Lord; we will move forward in truth and in love. Take revenge on those who seek to destroy us: the persecution of the world, the temptations of the flesh, the war waged by the devil. Be what you once were, Lord, be not a terror to me" (*Sermones*, temporal cycle, 15, 210–216).

When the prophet shares his deepest feelings with God like this, ever-ready to try to be better, he helps us see what a truly contemplative conversation with God should be like: "My beloved brethren," St Bernard says, "the first stage of contemplation is to consider constantly what God desires, what he rewards, what is pleasing in his eyes. All of us fail often, and our pride collides with the purity of the will of God, and will neither accept nor yield to it. Let us humble ourselves before the powerful hand of Almighty God, and strive to draw his mercy down on our misery, saying: *Heal me, Lord, and I shall be healed; save me, and I shall be saved*" (*Sermones de diversis*, 5, 5).

et sanabor; / salvum me fac, et salvus ero, / quoniam laus mea tu es. / [15]Ecce ipsi dicunt ad me: / «Ubi est verbum Domini? Veniat». / [16]Et ego non institi pro malo apud te / et diem calamitatis non desideravi, / tu scis: quod egressum est de labiis meis, / rectum in conspectu tuo fuit. / [17]Non sis mihi tu formidini; / refugium meum tu in die afflictionis. / [18]Confundantur, qui me persequuntur, / et non confundar ego; / paveant illi, et non paveam ego; / induc super eos diem afflictionis / et duplici

Ex 20:8 **Sabbath observance**

Ex 20:8–11 19Thus said the LORD to me: "Go and stand in the Benjamin[d] Gate,
Deut 5:12–15 by which the kings of Judah enter and by which they go out, and
in all the gates of Jerusalem, 20and say: 'Hear the word of the
LORD, you kings of Judah, and all Judah, and all the inhabitants of
Jerusalem, who enter by these gates. 21Thus says the LORD: Take
heed for the sake of your lives, and do not bear a burden on the
sabbath day or bring it in by the gates of Jerusalem. 22And do not
Deut 9:13 carry a burden out of your houses on the sabbath or do any work,
Jer 7:26; 19:15 but keep the sabbath day holy, as I commanded your fathers. 23Yet
they did not listen or incline their ear, but stiffened their neck, that
they might not hear and receive instruction.

24"'But if you listen to me, says the LORD, and bring in no
burden by the gates of this city on the sabbath day, but keep the
1 Kings 10:1–13 sabbath day holy and do no work on it, 25then there shall enter by
2 Chron 9:1–12 the gates of this city kings[e] who sit on the throne of David, riding
Jer 22:4 in chariots and on horses, they and their princes, the men of Judah
Ezek 37:25 Joel 4:20 and the inhabitants of Jerusalem; and this city shall be inhabited
Zech 9:9 for ever. 26And people shall come from the cities of Judah and the

---

17:19–27. In denouncing Judah's infidelity to the Covenant, Jeremiah instances breaking the sabbath day (cf. Ex 20:8–11; Deut 5:12–15). The setting of this oracle is the Gate of the Sons of the People. This is the only reference in the Bible to a gate of this name. It may have been inside the temple precincts, or it could have been the Benjamin Gate (that is the RSV interpretation) or the Gate of the Fountains. The oracle urges the people of Jerusalem to keep to what the Covenant says about sabbath observance (vv. 19–23). It assures them that if they do so, they will rejoice at all the blessings God will send them (vv. 24–26). It will be like the days of Solomon, when rich caravans, like that of the queen of Sheba will be attracted by the splendour of the holy city (1 Kings 10:1–13; 2 Chron 9:1–12). But if they fail to keep the sabbath day holy, nothing will be able to protect them from punishment (v. 27).

contritione contere eos. 19Haec dixit Dominus ad me: «Vade et sta in porta Filiorum populi, per quam
ingrediuntur reges Iudae et egrediuntur, et in cunctis portis Ierusalem; 20et dices ad eos: Audite verbum
Domini, reges Iudae et omnis Iuda cunctique habitatores Ierusalem, qui ingredimini per portas istas.
21Haec dicit Dominus: Custodite animas vestras et nolite portare pondera in die sabbati nec inferatis
per portas Ierusalem; 22et nolite efferre onera de domibus vestris in die sabbati et omne opus non
facietis: sanctificate diem sabbati, sicut praecepi patribus vestris. 23Et non audierunt nec inclinaverunt
aurem suam; sed induraverunt cervicem suam, ne audirent me et ne acciperent disciplinam. 24Et erit:
si audieritis me, dicit Dominus, ut non inferatis onera per portas civitatis huius in die sabbati, et si
sanctificaveritis diem sabbati, ne faciatis in eo omne opus, 25ingredientur per portas civitatis huius reges
et principes sedentes super solium David et ascendentes in curribus et equis, ipsi et principes eorum,
viri Iudae et habitatores Ierusalem; et habitabitur civitas haec in sempiternum. 26Et venient de

d. Cn: Heb *sons of people* **e.** Cn: Heb *kings and princes*

places round about Jerusalem, from the land of Benjamin, from
the Shephelah, from the hill country, and from the Negeb, bringing
burnt offerings and sacrifices, cereal offerings and frankincense,
and bringing thank offerings to the house of the LORD. 27But if
you do not listen to me, to keep the sabbath day holy, and not to
bear a burden and enter by the gates of Jerusalem on the sabbath
day, then I will kindle a fire in its gates, and it shall devour the
palaces of Jerusalem and shall not be quenched.'"

Jeremiah in the potter's house

18 1The word that came to Jeremiah from the LORD: 2"Arise, Gen 2:7
and go down to the potter's house, and there I will let you Jer 19:1,2
hear my words." 3So I went down to the potter's house, and there
he was working at his wheel. 4And the vessel he was making of
clay was spoiled in the potter's hand, and he reworked it into
another vessel, as it seemed good to the potter to do.

18:1–12. Nothing extraordinary happens during Jeremiah's visit to the potter's workshop, but the prophet uses the potter's work as an image to illustrate aspects of his preaching. God is like a potter who has clay in his hands and hopes it will lend itself to be moulded to the shape he wants. The image of God as potter (cf. 1:5) reminds the reader of the Bible of the account in Genesis that describes God forming Adam out of dust from the ground (Gen 2:7), and it recalls other passages of the Old (Is 29:16; 45:9; 64:7) and the New Testaments (Rom 9:20–23) in which clay in the hands of a potter serves to show the omnipotence of God and the littleness of man. The Lord can do with Judah whatever he chooses (v. 6). And if God has authority over his people, then it means that he is able to make it anew and that, if he so wishes, he can destroy any nation or people (vv. 7–10). Just as the potter can change the shape of vessels he has formed out of soft clay, so God expects his people to let themselves be remade (v. 11). But Judah, in its obstinacy, has freely chosen to oppose God (v. 12).

In the potter's house Jeremiah reflects on the power of God and the wisdom of those who yield to his hands and put no obstacles in his way, and he causes others to do the same: "Lord, help me to be faithful and docile towards you, *sicut lutum in manu figuli*, like clay in the potter's hands. In this way it will not be I that live, but you, my Love, who will live and work in me" (St Josemaría Escrivá, *The Forge*, 875).

civitatibus Iudae et de circuitu Ierusalem et de terra Beniamin et de Sephela et de montuosis et a Nageb, portantes holocaustum et victimam et sacrificium et tus, et inferent oblationem laudis in domum Domini. 27Si autem non audieritis me, ut sanctificetis diem sabbati et ne portetis onus intrantes per portas Ierusalem in die sabbati, succendam ignem in portis eius, et devorabit domos Ierusalem et non exstinguetur». **[18]** 1Verbum, quod factum est ad Ieremiam a Domino dicens: 2«Surge et descende in domum figuli et ibi audies verba mea». 3Et descendi in domum figuli, et ecce ipse faciebat opus super

Is 29:16; 45:9 5Then the word of the LORD came to me: 6“O house of Israel,
Rom 9:21 can I not do with you as this potter has done? says the LORD.
Behold, like the clay in the potter’s hand, so are you in my hand,
Jer 1:10; O house of Israel. 7If at any time I declare concerning a nation or
26:13,19 a kingdom, that I will pluck up and break down and destroy it,
Ezek 18:21–24 8and if that nation, concerning which I have spoken, turns from its
Jon 3:10 evil, I will repent of the evil that I intended to do to it. 9And if at any
Jer 1:10 time I declare concerning a nation or a kingdom that I will build and
plant it, 10and if it does evil in my sight, not listening to my voice,
then I will repent of the good which I had intended to do to it. 11Now,
therefore, say to the men of Judah and the inhabitants of Jerusalem:
‘Thus says the LORD, Behold, I am shaping evil against you and
devising a plan against you. Return, every one from his evil way,
and amend your ways and your doings.’

Jer 2:25 12“But they say, ‘That is in vain! We will follow our own plans,
and will every one act according to the stubbornness of his evil
heart.’

Israel forgot the Lord and was laid waste

Jer 2:10–12 13“Therefore thus says the LORD:
Ask among the nations,
who has heard the like of this?
The virgin Israel
has done a very horrible thing.
14 Does the snow of Lebanon leave
the crags of Sirion?[f]
Do the mountain[g] waters run dry,[h]
the cold flowing streams?

18:13–17. The docility of the clay has led the prophet to reflect on the people’s resistance to God’s guidance (18:12). Now, using examples taken from nature (cf. 8:7), he shows that their forgetfulness of God goes against nature and is the only explanation of the misfortunes that will soon befall them.

rotam; 4et dissipatum est vas, quod ipse faciebat e luto manibus suis, et rursus fecit illud vas alterum, sicut placuerat in oculis eius, ut faceret. 5Et factum est verbum Domini ad me dicens: 6«Numquid sicut figulus iste non potero vobis facere, domus Israel?, ait Dominus. Ecce, sicut lutum in manu figuli, sic vos in manu mea, domus Israel. 7Repente loquar adversum gentem et adversum regnum, ut eradicem et destruam et disperdam illud; 8si paenitentiam egerit gens illa a malo suo, propter quod locutus sum adversus eam, agam et ego paenitentiam super malo, quod cogitavi ut facerem ei. 9Et subito loquar de gente et de regno, ut aedificem et plantem illud; 10si fecerit malum in oculis meis, ut non audiat vocem meam, paenitentiam agam super bono, quod locutus sum ut facerem ei. 11Nunc ergo, dic viro Iudae et habitatoribus Ierusalem dicens: Haec dicit Dominus: Ecce ego fingo contra vos malum et cogito

f. Cn: Heb *the field* **g.** Cn: Heb *foreign* **h.** Cn: Heb *Are … plucked up?*

15 But my people have forgotten me, Jer 2:32
they burn incense to false gods;
they have stumbled[i] in their ways,
in the ancient roads,
and have gone into bypaths,
not the highway,
16 making their land a horror, 1 Kings 9:8
a thing to be hissed at for ever. Jer 19:8
Every one who passes by it is horrified Lam 2:15–16
and shakes his head.
17 Like the east wind I will scatter them
before the enemy.
I will show them my back, not my face,
in the day of their calamity."

Jeremiah's fourth "confession" Jer 15:10
18 Then they said, "Come, let us make plots against Jeremiah, for Jer 2:8;5:13,31; 6:13; 11:19
the law shall not perish from the priest, nor counsel from the wise, Mt 22:15

18:18–23. Jeremiah feels hemmed in by his enemies when he proclaims the word of the Lord, and in this fourth "confession" he expresses how he feels. His situation causes him great pain. God called him to intercede for the people, and he has done so; but, although he has sought only their good, they plot against him (v. 18). These words have been interpreted as an announcement of how the Jewish authorities schemed against Jesus, seeking to arrest him (cf. Mt 22:15; Mk 12:13; Lk 20:20). And the resistance that Jeremiah encountered in his preaching is interpreted by St Jerome, in the light of the New Testament, as a prefiguring of the difficulties that Jesus would encounter from people "who spread calumnies and slander to frustrate the work of holy men. So that the truths that these disciples taught would be rejected as lies, they made the law and the plans of God the property of their priests and wise men and false prophets (cf. 18:18)" (*Commentarii in Ieremiam*, 4, 18).

contra vos cogitationem; revertatur unusquisque a via sua mala, et dirigite vias vestras et opera vestra». [12]Qui dixerunt: «Vanum est; post cogitationes enim nostras ibimus et unusquisque pravitatem cordis sui mali faciemus». [13]Ideo haec dicit Dominus: / «Interrogate gentes: / quis audivit talia horribilia, / quae fecit nimis virgo Israel? / [14]Numquid deficiet de petra agri / nix Libani, / aut arescent aquae erumpentes / frigidae et defluentes? / [15]Quia oblitus est mei populus meus, / vanitati sacrificantes / et impingentes in viis suis, / in semitis antiquis, / ut ambularent per calles / in itinere non trito, / [16]ut poneret terram eorum in desolationem / et in sibilum sempiternum: / omnis, qui praeterierit per eam, obstupescet / et movebit caput suum. / [17]Sicut ventus urens dispergam eos / coram inimico; / dorsum et non faciem ostendam eis in die perditionis eorum». [18]Et dixerunt: «Venite, et cogitemus contra Ieremiam cogitationes; non enim peribit lex a sacerdote, neque consilium a sapiente, nec sermo a

i. Gk Syr Vg: Heb *they made them stumble*

nor the word from the prophet. Come, let us smite him with the tongue, and let us not heed any of his words."

[19] Give heed to me, O LORD,
and hearken to my plea.[j]
Ps 35:7 [20] Is evil a recompense for good?
Yet they have dug a pit for my life.
Remember how I stood before thee
to speak good for them,
to turn away thy wrath from them.
Ps 5:11 [21] Therefore deliver up their children to famine;
give them over to the power of the sword,
let their wives become childless and widowed.
May their men meet death by pestilence,
their youths be slain by the sword in battle.
2 Kings 24:2–4 [22] May a cry be heard from their houses,
Jer 12:9 when thou bringest the marauder suddenly upon them!
For they have dug a pit to take me,
and laid snares for my feet.
Jer 11:20 [23] Yet, thou, O LORD, knowest
all their plotting to slay me.
Forgive not their iniquity,
nor blot out their sin from thy sight.
Let them be overthrown before thee;
deal with them in the time of thine anger.

The earthen flask is shattered, and Jeremiah receives a beating

19 [1]Thus said the LORD, "Go, buy a potter's earthen flask, and take some of the elders of the people and some of the senior

---

The harsh things that Jeremiah says in this prayer (vv. 21–23) are not so much a desire for vengeance on his part as an assertion of the respect that is owed to God and his word, which no one has a right to mock (cf. Ps 6; 79; 109).

propheta. Venite, et percutiamus eum lingua et non attendamus ad universos sermones eius». [19]Attende, Domine, ad me / et audi vocem adversariorum meorum. / [20]Numquid redditur pro bono malum, / quia foderunt foveam animae meae? / Recordare quod steterim in conspectu tuo, / ut loquerer pro eis bonum / et averterem indignationem tuam ab eis. / [21]Propterea da filios eorum in famem / et deduc eos in manus gladii; / fiant uxores eorum absque liberis et viduae, / et viri eorum interficiantur morte, / iuvenes eorum confodiantur gladio in proelio. / [22]Audiatur clamor de domibus eorum; / adduces enim super eos latronem repente, / quia foderunt foveam, ut caperent me, / et laqueos absconderunt pedibus meis. / [23]Tu autem, Domine, scis omne consilium eorum / adversum me in mortem; / ne propitieris iniquitati eorum, / et peccatum eorum a facie tua non deleatur. / Fiant corruentes in conspectu tuo; / in tempore furoris tui abutere eis. **[19]** [1]Haec dicit Dominus: «Vade et eme lagunculam figuli testeam et accipe

j. Gk Compare Syr Tg: Heb *my adversaries*

priests, 2and go out to the valley of the son of Hinnom at the entry Josh 18:16
of the Potsherd Gate, and proclaim there the words that I tell you. Neh 2:13; 3:14
3You shall say, 'Hear the word of the LORD, O kings of Judah and 1 Sam 3:11 2 Kings 21:12

19:1—20:6. This passage deals with another symbolic action of the prophet's —the breaking of an earthenware flask, whose shards fall on top of earlier rubble, symbolizing the fate that awaits Judah. The action takes place in two stages—at the Potsherd Gate (19:1–13) and then in the court of the temple (19:14–15). It leads to Jeremiah's imprisonment (20:1–6).

It is not clear where the Potsherd Gate was. It is usually identified with the Dung Gate (cf. Neh 2:13; 3:14; 12:31) of Jerusalem, to the south where the valleys of the Tyropeon and the Ben–Hinnon meet 409. As regards the Topheth and the valley of Slaughter, see the note on 7:21—8:3.

A little earlier, in connexion with Jeremiah's visit to the potter's house, (18:1–12), we saw the potter working the clay and being able to shape different sorts of vessels, and even to change the shape of a pot (in other words, the comparison gave hope of possible change); now we see a flask that has already been fired and whose shape cannot be altered. The die is cast. The hearts of the people have become hardened; they have refused to let themselves be changed by the word of God (19:15). And so the Lord tells the prophet to break the flask—as a sign of the misfortune that will soon befall them. Just as that jar is broken, so will God destroy the city and the people, rendering them as impure as Topheth (19:12). Nothing will escape destruction.

The image of the malleable clay and the fired clay was used early in Christian preaching in connexion with the need for conversion: "Let us do penance while we are in this world," writes an author in the second century; "we are the clay in the potter's hands. The potter can re-form the jar if it is deformed and broken, while the clay is still wet in his hands; once it has been placed in the oven it cannot be undone and remade. In the same way, we, while we are still in this world, have time to repent and to be converted from the bottom of our hearts, to renounce all the sins that we have committed while we wear this mortal flesh, so that the Lord may save us. Once we have left this world, and entered into eternity, we can neither confess our sins nor do penance" (Pseudo-Clement, *Epistula II ad Corinthios*, 8, 1–3).

For the first time, the book reports Jeremiah suffering corporal punishment (20:1–6). In the course of his ministry, he was dogged by difficulties; here we are given another instance. The Pashur mentioned here (who is different from the person with the same name in 21:1 and 38:1) was probably a priest charged with keeping order in the temple. The place where Jeremiah underwent this

---

de senioribus populi et de senioribus sacerdotum 2et egredere ad vallem Benennom, quae est iuxta introitum portae Fictilium, et praedicabis ibi verba, quae ego loquar ad te, 3et dices: Audite verbum Domini, reges Iudae et habitatores Ierusalem: Haec dicit Dominus exercituum, Deus Israel: Ecce ego

inhabitants of Jerusalem. Thus says the LORD of hosts, the God of
Israel, Behold, I am bringing such evil upon this place that the
ears of every one who hears of it will tingle. [4]Because the people
have forsaken me, and have profaned this place by burning
incense in it to other gods whom neither they nor their fathers nor
the kings of Judah have known; and because they have filled this
Lev 18:21 place with the blood of innocents, [5]and have built the high places
Deut 17:3 Jer 7:31–33 of Baal to burn their sons in the fire as burnt offerings to Baal,
which I did not command or decree, nor did it come into my
Josh 18:16 mind; [6]therefore, behold, days are coming, says the LORD, when
Jer 2:23; 23:10 this place shall no more be called Topheth, or the valley of the son
of Hinnom, but the valley of Slaughter. [7]And in this place I will
make void the plans of Judah and Jerusalem, and will cause their
people to fall by the sword before their enemies, and by the hand
of those who seek their life. I will give their dead bodies for food
to the birds of the air and to the beasts of the earth. [8]And I will
make this city a horror, a thing to be hissed at; every one who
passes by it will be horrified and will hiss because of all its
Lev 26:29 disasters. [9]And I will make them eat the flesh of their sons and
Deut 28:53–57 Ezek 5:10 their daughters, and every one shall eat the flesh of his neighbour
Lam 4:10 in the siege and in the distress, with which their enemies and those
who seek their life afflict them.'

[10]"Then you shall break the flask in the sight of the men who
go with you, [11]and shall say to them, 'Thus says the LORD of

---

punishment was a part of the temple, perhaps near the Benjamin Gate of the city, but not precisely there (cf. 2 Kings 15:35). The incident leads Jeremiah to denounce Pashur, not because the priest opposed him personally but because he resisted the word of God as spoken by the prophet. The name he gives Pashur ("Terror on every side": v. 3; cf. 20:10), is Magor-Misabib in Hebrew–a reference to the situation that Jeremiah predicts, in which the nobles of the city will be deported (that happened in 597 BC). Like all those who through hardness of heart failed to listen to the words of God, Pashur will be responsible for the misfortune that overtakes Jerusalem and its temple.

inducam afflictionem super locum istum, ita ut omnis, qui audierit illam, tinniant aures eius, [4]eo quod dereliquerint me et alienum fecerint locum istum et sacrificaverint in eo diis alienis, quos nescierunt ipsi et patres eorum et reges Iudae; et repleverunt locum istum sanguine innocentium; [5]et aedificaverunt excelsa Baal ad comburendos filios suos igne in holocaustum Baal: quae non praecepi nec locutus sum, nec ascenderunt in cor meum. [6]Propterea ecce dies veniunt, dicit Dominus, et non vocabitur amplius locus iste Topheth et vallis Benennom sed vallis Occisionis. [7]Et dissipabo consilium Iudae et Ierusalem in loco isto; et subvertam eos gladio in conspectu inimicorum suorum et in manu quaerentium animas eorum et dabo cadavera eorum escam volatilibus caeli et bestiis terrae. [8]Et ponam civitatem hanc in stuporem et in sibilum; omnis, qui praeterierit per eam, obstupescet et sibilabit super universa plaga eius. [9]Et cibabo eos carnibus filiorum suorum et carnibus filiarum suarum; et unusquisque carnem

hosts: So will I break this people and this city, as one breaks a
potter's vessel, so that it can never be mended. Men shall bury in
Topheth because there will be no place else to bury. 12Thus will I
do to this place, says the LORD, and to its inhabitants, making this
city like Topheth. 13The houses of Jerusalem and the houses of the
kings of Judah—all the houses upon whose roofs incense has been
burned to all the host of heaven, and drink offerings have been
poured out to other gods—shall be defiled like the place of
Topheth.'"

14Then Jeremiah came from Topheth, where the LORD had sent
him to prophesy, and he stood in the court of the LORD's house,
and said to all the people: 15"Thus says the LORD of hosts, the God Deut 9:13
of Israel, Behold, I am bringing upon this city and upon all its 2 Kings 23:12 Jer 7:26; 32:29
towns all the evil that I have pronounced against it, because they
have stiffened their neck, refusing to hear my words."

20 1Now Pashhur the priest, the son of Immer, who was chief 1 Chron 24:14
officer in the house of the LORD, heard Jeremiah prophesy- Jer 21:1; 29:26
ing these things. 2Then Pashhur beat Jeremiah the prophet, and put 2 Kings 15:35
him in the stocks that were in the upper Benjamin Gate of the
house of the LORD. 3On the morrow, when Pashhur released
Jeremiah from the stocks, Jeremiah said to him, "The LORD does
not call your name Pashhur, but Terror on every side. 4For thus
says the LORD: Behold, I will make you a terror to yourself and to
all your friends. They shall fall by the sword of their enemies
while you look on. And I will give all Judah into the hand of the
king of Babylon; he shall carry them captive to Babylon, and shall 2 Kings
slay them with the sword. 5Moreover, I will give all the wealth of 24:12–16; 25:13–17

---

amici sui comedet in obsidione et in angustia, in qua concludent eos inimici eorum et qui quaerunt animas eorum. 10Et conteres lagunculam in oculis virorum, qui ibunt tecum, 11et dices ad eos: Haec dicit Dominus exercituum: Sic conteram populum istum et civitatem istam, sicut conteritur vas figuli, quod non potest ultra instaurari; et in Topheth sepelientur, eo quod non sit alius locus ad sepeliendum. 12Sic faciam loco huic, ait Dominus, et habitatoribus eius, ut ponam civitatem istam sicut Topheth; 13et erunt domus Ierusalem et domus regum Iudae sicut locus Topheth, immundae: omnes domus, in quarum domatibus sacrificaverunt omni militiae caeli et libaverunt libamina diis alienis». 14Venit autem Ieremias de Topheth, quo miserat eum Dominus ad prophetandum, et stetit in atrio domus Domini et dixit ad omnem populum: 15«Haec dicit Dominus exercituum, Deus Israel: Ecce ego inducam super civitatem hanc et super omnes urbes eius universa mala, quae locutus sum adversum eam, quoniam induraverunt cervicem suam, ut non audirent sermones meos». **[20]** 1Et audivit Phassur filius Emmer sacerdos, qui constitutus erat princeps in domo Domini, Ieremiam prophetantem sermones istos; 2et percussit Phassur Ieremiam prophetam et misit eum in nervum, quod erat in porta Beniamin superiore in domo Domini. 3Cumque illuxisset in crastinum, eduxit Phassur Ieremiam de nervo; et dixit ad eum Ieremias: «Non Phassur vocavit Dominus nomen tuum sed Pavorem undique. 4Quia haec dicit Dominus: Ecce ego dabo te in pavorem, te et omnes amicos tuos, et corruent gladio inimicorum suorum, et oculi tui videbunt; et omnem Iudam dabo in manu regis Babylonis, et traducet eos in Babylonem et percutiet eos gladio. 5Et dabo universam substantiam civitatis huius et omnem laborem

the city, all its gains, all its prized belongings, and all the treasures
of the kings of Judah into the hand of their enemies, who shall
plunder them, and seize them, and carry them to Babylon. 6And
you, Pashhur, and all who dwell in your house, shall go into
captivity; to Babylon you shall go; and there you shall die, and
there you shall be buried, you and all your friends, to whom you
have prophesied falsely."

Jer 15:10 **Jeremiah's fifth "confession"**

7O LORD, thou hast deceived me,
and I was deceived;
thou art stronger than I,
and thou hast prevailed.

20:7–18. This last, very dramatic "confession" is one of the most impressive passages in prophetical literature. It (especially vv. 14–18) has features in common with Job 3:1–10. It could have been uttered around 605–604 BC when Jeremiah was being persecuted by King Jehoiakim. Despite all his efforts, Jeremiah feels that he has failed; he believes in God—but could it be that he never received a special call? It is a time of inner crisis for Jeremiah. He laments his vocation, for it has led to his persecution (vv. 7–9); then he makes an act of trust in God despite the harassment he is suffering (vv. 10–13); the passage ends with a series of imprecations (vv. 14–18).

The prophet confides his feelings to God and complains about his calling (v. 7a). It looks as if God has misled him (v. 7b): the prophet has made enemies on every side. When he proclaims the word of God no one listens: reproach and derision are the only response he gets (v. 10). He would like to walk away. Yet he cannot, for God is like a "burning fire" in his heart (v. 9). Despite all his difficulties, his zeal for the Lord wins the day: it only goes to prove that those who have experienced the love of God cannot contain their desire to make him known to others–to those who once knew him and have forgotten him, and to those who have never heard of him. That is the message that Theodoret of Cyrus takes from this passage, recalling the example of St Paul: "The same happened to St Paul as he stood in silence in Athens. His soul burned within him when he saw the terrible idolatry that was practised in that city (cf. Acts 17:16). The prophet had the same experience" (*Interpretatio in Jeremiam*, 20, 9). And when Origen reads this passage and asks himself whether God could ever deceive someone, he explains: "We are little children, and we must be treated as little children. God, therefore, entrances

eius omneque pretium et cunctos thesauros regum Iudae dabo in manu inimicorum eorum; et diripient
eos et tollent et ducent in Babylonem. 6Tu autem, Phassur et omnes habitatores domus tuae, ibitis in
captivitatem; et in Babylonem venies et ibi morieris ibique sepelieris, tu et omnes amici tui, quibus
prophetasti mendacium». 7Seduxisti me, Domine, et seductus sum; / fortior me fuisti et invaluisti. /

I have become a laughingstock all the day;
every one mocks me.
8For whenever I speak, I cry out,
I shout, "Violence and destruction!"
For the word of the LORD has become for me
a reproach and derision all day long.
9If I say, "I will not mention him,
or speak any more in his name,"
there is in my heart as it were a burning fire
shut up in my bones,

Job 32:19–20
Ps 39:4
Jer 23:29

---

us in order to form us, although we may not be aware of this captivation before the appropriate time comes. God does not deal with us as people who have already left childhood, who can no longer be led by sweet words but only by deeds" (*Homiliae in Jeremiam*, 19, 15).

In spite of everything, Jeremiah is sure that God will never forsake him (v. 11). From what he says, we can see that there is an inner tension between his experience of all kinds of sufferings (vv. 14–18) and the conviction that God will never leave him (vv. 12–13). What he says in v. 18 could suggest that he is utterly depressed, but what he is doing is baring his soul to someone whom he loves and trusts entirely, even in the midst of total darkness and a sense of powerlessness. Events will show this to be the case: Jeremiah did not give up his ministry but persevered in it to the end of his life. He admits his limitations but he stays true to God: this bears out what the Lord will tell St Paul when he feels the situation is beyond him: "My power is made perfect in your weakness" (2 Cor 12:9).

Meditating on this "confession" of Jeremiah, St John of the Cross concludes that sometimes God's purposes are impossible to understand: "It is very difficult to attempt to understand fully the words and deeds of God, or even to decide what they may be, without falling often into error or becoming very confused. The prophets who were entrusted with the word of God knew this well; their task of prophesying to the people was a daunting one, for the people could not always see what was spoken coming to pass. Therefore, they mocked and laughed at the prophets, as Jeremiah says: *I have become a laughingstock all the day; every one mocks me* (20:7). Although the prophet speaks as though resigned to his fate, in the voice of a weak man who is unable to bear any longer the vicissitudes of God, he makes clear the difference between the prophecy and its fulfilment and the common sense that the divine sayings contain, because he knows that the prophets were often taken as mischief-makers" (*Ascent of Mount Carmel*, 2, 20, 6).

Factus sum in derisum tota die, / omnes subsannant me. / 8Quia quotiescumque loquor, vociferor, / iniquitatem et vastitatem clamito; / et factus est mihi sermo Domini / in opprobrium et in derisum tota die. / 9Et dixi: «Non recordabor eius / neque loquar ultra in nomine illius». / Et factus est in corde meo

and I am weary with holding it in,
  and I cannot.
Ps 31:14; 10 For I hear many whispering.
41:10; 55:13 Terror is on every side!
"Denounce him! Let us denounce him!"
  say all my familiar friends,
  watching for my fall.
"Perhaps he will be deceived,
  then we can overcome him,
  and take our revenge on him."
11 But the LORD is with me as a dread warrior;
  therefore my persecutors will stumble,
  they will not overcome me.
They will be greatly shamed,
  for they will not succeed.
Their eternal dishonour
  will never be forgotten.
Jer 11:20 12 O LORD of hosts, who triest the righteous,
  who seest the heart and the mind,
let me see thy vengeance upon them,
  for to thee have I committed my cause.

13 Sing to the LORD;
  praise the LORD!
For he has delivered the life of the needy
  from the hand of evildoers.

Job 3:3 14 Cursed be the day
Jer 15:10 on which I was born!
Job 3:1–10 The day when my mother bore me,
  let it not be blessed!
Jer 1:5; 15:10 15 Cursed be the man
  who brought the news to my father,
"A son is born to you,"
  making him very glad.

---

quasi ignis exaestuans / claususque in ossibus meis: / et defeci, ferre non sustinens. / 10 Audivi enim contumelias multorum / et terrorem in circuitu: / «Denuntiate, et denuntiemus eum». / Omnes pacifici mei observabant lapsum meum: / «Forte decipietur, et praevalebimus adversus eum / et consequemur ultionem ex eo». / 11 Dominus autem mecum est quasi bellator fortis; / idcirco, qui persequuntur me, / cadent et infirmi erunt. / Confundentur vehementer, quia non prosperati sunt; / opprobrium sempiternum, quod numquam delebitur. / 12 Et tu, Domine exercituum, / probator iusti, qui vides renes et cor, / videam, quaeso, ultionem tuam ex eis; / tibi enim revelavi causam meam. / 13 Cantate Domino, laudate Dominum, / quia liberavit animam pauperis / de manu malorum. / 14 Maledicta dies, in qua natus sum; / dies, in qua peperit me mater mea, / non sit benedicta. / 15 Maledictus vir, qui annuntiavit

16 Let that man be like the cities
which the LORD overthrew without pity;
let him hear a cry in the morning
and an alarm at noon,
17 because he did not kill me in the womb;
so my mother would have been my grave,
and her womb for ever great.
18 Why did I come forth from the womb
to see toil and sorrow,
and spend my days in shame?

Gen 19:24–25

Job 3:1ff

Job 3:20

4. JUDGMENTS CONCERNING KINGS AND PROPHETS*

Reply to Zedekiah

21 1This is the word which came to Jeremiah from the LORD,
when King Zedekiah sent to him Pashhur the son of

2 Kings 24: 10–20; 25:18 Jer 38:1

***21:1—25:38.** This final section of the first part of the book contains oracles concerning kings and prophets with a prose introduction about Jeremiah's reply to messengers from Zedekiah in which he addresses the futility of opposing the Babylonians.

21:1–10. When the troops of Nebuchadnezzar took Jerusalem for the first time (in 597), and made Judah a vassal state, King Jehoiachin was deported and in his place the Babylonians installed his uncle, Mattaniah, changing his name to Zedekiah (cf. 2 Kings 24:10–17). The new name means "the Lord's justice" or "the Lord is Just", but the king was far from being a model of trust in God: he was no sooner on the throne than he began to plot against his sponsors; he rebelled against the king of Babylon (cf. 2 Kings 24:18–20), who lost no time in setting out to punish him. The scene dealt with in these verses occurred in 588 BC when the Babylonian army was nearing Jerusalem, and the panic-stricken king asked Jeremiah to plead with God, to see if he would protect Judah. It parallels the situation, a century earlier, when Isaiah persuaded God to save the city when it was being besieged by Sennacherib, the king of Assyria (cf. 2 Kings 18:1—19:37). The Pashur mentioned here is not the person who imprisoned Jeremiah in the

patri meo / dicens: «Natus est tibi puer masculus» / et gaudio laetificavit eum; / 16sit homo ille, ut sunt civitates, / quas subvertit Dominus / et non paenituit eum: / audiat clamorem mane / et ululatum in tempore meridiano, / 17qui non me interfecit a vulva, / ut fieret mihi mater mea sepulcrum, / et vulva eius conceptus aeternus. / 18Quare de vulva egressus sum, / ut viderem laborem et dolorem, / et consumerentur in confusione dies mei? **[21]** 1Verbum, quod factum est ad Ieremiam a Domino, quando misit ad eum rex Sedecias Phassur filium Melchiae et Sophoniam filium Maasiae sacerdotem

Malchiah and Zephaniah the priest, the son of Ma-aseiah, saying,
2“Inquire of the LORD for us, for Nebuchadnezzar king of Babylon
is making war against us; perhaps the LORD will deal with us
according to all his wonderful deeds, and will make him withdraw
from us.”
Deut 4:34 3Then Jeremiah said to them: 4“Thus you shall say to Zedekiah,
‘Thus says the LORD, the God of Israel: Behold, I will turn back
the weapons of war which are in your hands and with which you
are fighting against the king of Babylon and against the Chaldeans
who are besieging you outside the walls; and I will bring them
together into the midst of this city. 5I myself will fight against you
with outstretched hand and strong arm, in anger, and in fury, and
2 Chron 36:17 in great wrath. 6And I will smite the inhabitants of this city, both
Jer 37:17 man and beast; they shall die of a great pestilence. 7Afterward,

---

previous chapter (20:1–6); he appears again in 38:1.

In all the years up to this, Jeremiah kept calling the people to conversion in order to preserve Judah from being punished for its infidelity; but to no avail. According to this passage, the siege mounted by the Babylonians (whose kings were of Chaldean origin: v. 3) was not just a military incident: it was the punishment that God had warned he would send (vv. 3–7). King Zedekiah is now so terrified that he seeks the Lord’s help, but it is too late. The only way to salvation (cf. Deut 30:15, 19; Sir 15:18) lies in the acceptance of suffering as a means to conversion (that is, in surrender to the Babylonians: v. 9b); those who, relying on their resources, insist on putting up a fight, will surely die.

The king’s messengers to Jeremiah sought an easy way out by asking for a miracle (vv. 1–2). But that is not how God works. He works miracles when it suits his purposes and not just to accommodate people—particularly if in normal circumstances they have no time for God and only appeal to him when difficulties arise: “The Christian knows that God works miracles, that he did them centuries ago, that he continued doing them, and that he still works them now [...]. But miracles are a sign of the saving power of God, not a cure for incompetence nor an easy way to dodge effort” (St Josemaría Escrivá, *Christ Is Passing By*, 50).

dicens: 2«Interroga pro nobis Dominum, quia Nabuchodonosor rex Babylonis proeliatur adversum nos; si forte faciat Dominus nobiscum secundum omnia mirabilia sua, et recedat a nobis». 3Et dixit Ieremias ad eos: «Sic dicetis Sedeciae: 4Haec dicit Dominus, Deus Israel: Ecce ego convertam vasa belli, quae in manibus vestris sunt et quibus vos pugnatis adversum regem Babylonis et Chaldaeos, qui obsident vos in circuitu murorum; et congregabo eos in medio civitatis huius. 5Et debellabo ego vos in manu extenta et in brachio forti et in furore et in indignatione et in ira grandi 6et percutiam habitatores civitatis huius, homines et bestias: pestilentia magna morientur. 7Et post haec, ait Dominus, dabo Sedeciam regem Iudae et servos eius et populum eius, qui derelicti sunt in civitate hac a peste et gladio et fame, in manu Nabuchodonosor regis Babylonis et in manu inimicorum eorum et in manu

says the LORD, I will give Zedekiah king of Judah, and his
servants, and the people in this city who survive the pestilence,
sword, and famine, into the hand of Nebuchadnezzar king of
Babylon and into the hand of their enemies, into the hand of those
who seek their lives. He shall smite them with the edge of the
sword; he shall not pity them, or spare them, or have compassion.'
8"And to this people you shall say: 'Thus says the LORD: Deut 30:15
Behold, I set before you the way of life and the way of death. 9He Deut 30:15,19
who stays in this city shall die by the sword, by famine, and by Jer 38:2; 39:18
pestilence; but he who goes out and surrenders to the Chaldeans
who are besieging you shall live and shall have his life as a prize
of war. 10For I have set my face against this city for evil and not Lev 20:5
for good, says the LORD: it shall be given into the hand of the king Jer 34:2,22; 38:18; 44:11;
of Babylon, and he shall burn it with fire.' 52:13

Oracles concerning the mission of the king

11"And to the house of the king of Judah say, 'Hear the word of
the LORD, 12O house of David! Thus says the LORD:

"'Execute justice in the morning,
and deliver from the hand of the oppressor

21:11—22:9. These oracles blame the kings for the lamentable state of the country. They point the finger at the king of Judah, and at Jerusalem, and then at idolatry (and the breaking of the Covenant which it implies), as being the cause of the evils that beset the city. The prophet begins by addressing the king, denouncing him for his injustice (21:11–12), and then he condemns Jerusalem for its arrogance (21:13–14), symbolized by his reference to the "rock", for the city was built on a hill above the valleys of the Tyropeon and the Cedron (21:13). Then the oracle turns to the king again, spelling out the consequences of his transgression of the Law of Moses (22:3; cf. Ex 22:21; 23:29; Lev 19:33; Deut 10:18), and to Jerusalem, whose punishment will be terrible (22:6–7): the greatness of the city symbolized by Mount Lebanon and Gilead, places famed for their beauty and natural resources, will be reduced to nothing. The oracle ends by summarizing the reason for all this destruction: the people of Jerusalem forsook the Covenant (22:8–9).

quaerentium animam eorum; et percutiet eos in ore gladii et non flectetur neque parcet nec miserebitur. 8Et ad populum hunc dices: Haec dicit Dominus: Ecce ego do coram vobis viam vitae et viam mortis: 9qui habitaverit in urbe hac, morietur gladio et fame et peste; qui autem egressus fuerit et transfugerit ad Chaldaeos, qui obsident vos, vivet, et erit ei anima sua quasi spolium. 10Posui enim faciem meam super civitatem hanc in malum et non in bonum, ait Dominus: in manu regis Babylonis dabitur, et exuret eam igni. 11Et domui regis Iudae: / Audite verbum Domini, / 12domus David. Haec dicit Dominus: / Iudicate mane iudicium / et eruite vi oppressum de manu expoliantis, / ne forte egrediatur ut ignis indignatio mea / et succendatur, et non sit qui exstinguat, / propter malitiam operum

him who has been robbed,
lest my wrath go forth like fire,
and burn with none to quench it,
because of your evil doings.'"

13 "Behold, I am against you, O inhabitant of the valley,
O rock of the plain, says the LORD;
you who say, 'Who shall come down against us,
or who shall enter our habitations?'
Jer 50:32 14 I will punish you according to the fruit of your doings,
says the LORD;
I will kindle a fire in her forest,
and it shall devour all that is round about her."

22 1Thus says the LORD: "Go down to the house of the king of
Judah, and speak there this word, 2and say, 'Hear the word
of the LORD, O King of Judah, who sit on the throne of David,
you, and your servants, and your people who enter these gates.
Ex 22:21 3Thus says the LORD: Do justice and righteousness, and deliver
Lev 19:33 from the hand of the oppressor him who has been robbed. And do
Deut 10:18
Jer 7:6; 21:12 no wrong or violence to the alien, the fatherless, and the widow,

---

22:1–5. The prophet's criticisms of the rulers for their failure to give good government are a reminder that just rule is something that a society must have if it is to function properly. "In the political sphere, it must be noted that truthfulness in the relations between those governing and those governed, openness in public administration, impartiality in the service of the body politic, respect for the rights of political adversaries, safeguarding the rights of the accused against summary trials and convictions, the just and honest use of public funds, the rejection of equivocal or illicit means in order to gain, preserve or increase power at any cost—all these are principles which are primarily rooted in, and in fact derive their singular urgency from, the transcendent value of the person and the objective moral demands of the functioning of States. When these principles are not observed, the very basis of political coexistence is weakened and the life of society itself is gradually jeopardized, threatened and doomed to decay" (John Paul II, *Veritatis splendor*, 101).

vestrorum. / 13Ecce ego ad te, habitatricem vallis, / petram in planitie, / ait Dominus; / qui dicitis: "Quis invadet nos? / Et quis ingredietur domos nostras?". / 14Et visitabo super vos iuxta fructum operum vestrorum, / dicit Dominus; / et succendam ignem in saltu eius, / et devorabit omnia in circuitu eius». **[22]** 1Haec dicit Dominus: «Descende in domum regis Iudae et loqueris ibi verbum hoc 2et dices: Audi verbum Domini, rex Iudae, qui sedes super solium David, tu et servi tui et populus tuus, qui ingredimini per portas istas. 3Haec dicit Dominus: Facite iudicium et iustitiam et liberate vi oppressum de manu expoliantis et advenam et pupillum et viduam nolite affligere neque opprimatis inique et sanguinem

nor shed innocent blood in this place. [4]For if you will indeed obey Jer 17:25
this word, then there shall enter the gates of this house kings who
sit on the throne of David, riding in chariots and on horses, they,
and their servants, and their people. [5]But if you will not heed these
words, I swear by myself, says the LORD, that this house shall
become a desolation. [6]For thus says the LORD concerning the Jer 22:23
house of the king of Judah: Ezek 17:3

"'You are as Gilead to me,
as the summit of Lebanon,
yet surely I will make you a desert,
an uninhabited city.[k]
[7]I will prepare destroyers against you, Jer 21:13
each with his weapons;
and they shall cut down your choicest cedars,
and cast them into the fire.

[8]"'And many nations will pass by this city, and every man will 1 Kings 9:7–9
say to his neighbour, "Why has the LORD dealt thus with this great Jer 5:19
city?" [9]And they will answer, "Because they forsook the covenant Deut 28:25–26
of the LORD their God, and worshipped other gods and served
them.'"

22:10–12. Shallum is another name for Jehoahaz, the son of Josiah (cf. 2 Chron 3:15), who succeeded as king of Judah when Josiah died in 609 BC. He reigned for only a few months, being deposed by the pharaoh Neco and led captive to Egypt, where he died (cf. 2 Kings 23:29–34; 2 Chron 36:1–4).

Jeremiah makes it clear that there is no reason to mourn Josiah (cf. 2 Chron 35:24–25), who was a devout king and who died a short time earlier; but they should make lament for Jehoahaz, for he will be led into captivity and will never return. After the threats contained in the previous oracles, the fate of Jehoahaz signals that Judah's punishment is imminent and prefigures the deportation that will take place in a few years' time.

innocentem ne effundatis in loco isto. [4]Si enim facientes feceritis verbum istud, ingredientur per portas domus huius reges, sedentes de genere David super thronum eius et ascendentes currus et equos, ipsi et servi et populus eorum. [5]Quod si non audieritis verba haec, in memetipso iuravi, dicit Dominus, quia in solitudinem erit domus haec. [6]Quia haec dicit Dominus super domum regis Iudae: / Galaad tu mihi, / caput Libani, / verumtamen ponam te solitudinem, / urbes inhabitabiles, / [7]et sanctificabo super te / interficientem virum et arma eius, / et succident electas cedros tuas / et praecipitabunt in ignem. [8]Et pertransibunt gentes multae per civitatem hanc, et dicet unusquisque proximo suo: "Quare fecit Dominus sic civitati huic grandi?". [9]Et respondebunt: "Eo quod dereliquerint pactum Domini Dei sui et adoraverint deos alienos et servierint eis"». [10]Nolite flere mortuum / neque lugeatis super eum fletu;

k. Cn: Heb *cities*

2 Kings 23:29–30,34 2 Chron 35:24–25; 36:1–4

Oracles against Shallum

10 Weep not for him who is dead,
nor bemoan him;
but weep bitterly for him who goes away,
for he shall return no more
to see his native land.

11 For thus says the LORD concerning Shallum the son of Josiah,
king of Judah, who reigned instead of Josiah his father, and who
went away from this place: "He shall return here no more, 12 but in
the place where they have carried him captive, there shall he die,
and he shall never see this land again."

Lev 19:13 Deut 24:15 Is 5:18–23 Amos 6:8 Jas 5:4

Oracles against Jehoiakim

13 "Woe to him who builds his house by unrighteousness,
and his upper rooms by injustice;
who makes his neighbour serve him for nothing,
and does not give him his wages;
14 who says, 'I will build myself a great house
with spacious upper rooms,'
and cuts out windows for it,
paneling it with cedar,
and painting it with vermilion.

22:13–19. When Neco the pharaoh took Jehoahaz to Egypt, he made his brother Eliakim king, changing his name to Jehoiakim to show that he was his vassal (cf. 2 Kings 23:26—24:7). During his reign Jehoiakim indulged himself by building sumptuous residences, but he took no interest at all in the more important matters of justice and righteousness. Hence Jeremiah's harsh judgement of him—one of the prophet's severest denunciations. He contrasts him with his father, the pious King Josiah, who did reign justly and for whom things therefore went well (vv. 15–16). Jehoiakim did not follow his father's example; instead of honouring the Lord and keeping his Law, he trusted in his own resources, tolerated irreligion and acted unjustly. Therefore, a sad fate awaits him (cf. vv. 18–19): after his death he will be given "the burial of an ass" (v. 19)—meaning either that his tomb will be profaned by the Babylonians or else that the whole people will rejoice at his death.

/ plangite eum, qui egreditur, / quia non revertetur ultra / nec videbit terram nativitatis suae. 11 Quia haec
dicit Dominus ad Sellum filium Iosiae regem Iudae, qui regnavit pro Iosia patre suo: «Qui egressus est
de loco isto, non revertetur huc amplius, 12 sed in loco, ad quem transtulerunt eum, ibi morietur et
terram istam non videbit amplius». 13 Vae, qui aedificat domum suam in iniustitia / et cenacula sua non
in iudicio, / proximum suum servire facit gratis / et mercedem eius non reddet ei; / 14 qui dicit:
«Aedificabo mihi domum latam / et cenacula spatiosa»; / qui aperit sibi fenestras / et facit laquearia
cedrina / pingitque sinopide! / 15 Numquid regnabis, / quoniam gloriaris in cedris? / Pater tuus numquid

[15] Do you think you are a king
because you compete in cedar?
Did not your father eat and drink
and do justice and righteousness?
Then it was well with him.
[16] He judged the cause of the poor and needy;
then it was well.
Is not this to know me?
says the LORD.
[17] But you have eyes and heart
only for your dishonest gain,
for shedding innocent blood,
and for practising oppression and violence."

[18]Therefore thus says the LORD concerning Jehoiakim the son of Josiah, king of Judah: 1 Kings 13:30 2 Kings 24:6 Jer 34:5

"They shall not lament for him, saying,
'Ah my brother!' or 'Ah sister!'
They shall not lament for him, saying,
'Ah lord!' or 'Ah his majesty!'
[19] With the burial of an ass he shall be buried,
dragged and cast forth beyond the gates of Jerusalem." 2 Chron 36:5–6 Is 14:18–19 Jer 36:30

Oracles against Jehoiachin

[20] "Go up to Lebanon, and cry out,
and lift up your voice in Bashan;
cry from Abarim,

22:20–30. Coniah (v. 24) is a shortened form of Jeconiah, another name for Jehoiachin, the son of Jehoiakim, who succeeded when his father died and reigned for little over three months. Nebuchadnezzar conquered Jerusalem, deposed him and deported him to Babylon, where he eventually died (cf. the note on 13:15–27; 2 Kings 24:8–17). None of his sons or descendants would ever become king.

The oracle is preceded by verses about what is going to happen to Jerusalem (vv. 20–23). The highest mountains round about (those of Lebanon, to the north, Bashan to the north-east, and Abarim, which include Mount Nebo, to the south-east) will

non comedit et bibit? / Sed fecit iudicium et iustitiam, / tunc bene erat ei. / [16]Iudicavit causam pauperis et egeni, / tunc bene. / «Numquid non hoc est nosse me?», / dicit Dominus. / [17]Tui vero oculi et cor tuum nonnisi ad avaritiam / et ad sanguinem innocentem fundendum / et ad calumniam et ad oppressionem faciendam. [18]Propterea haec dicit Dominus ad Ioachim filium Iosiae regem Iudae: «Non plangent eum: / "Vae, frater meus!" et "Vae, soror!". / Non concrepabunt ei: / "Vae, domine!" et "Vae, inclite!". / [19]Sepultura asini sepelietur, / tractus et proiectus longe / extra portas Ierusalem». / [20]Ascende Libanum et clama / et in Basan da vocem tuam / et clama de Abarim, / quia contriti sunt omnes

for all your lovers are destroyed.
Jer 2:25,31; 3:25; 7:23; 11:7 21 I spoke to you in your prosperity,
but you said, 'I will not listen.'
This has been your way from your youth,
that you have not obeyed my voice.
22 The wind shall shepherd all your shepherds,
and your lovers shall go into captivity;
then you will be ashamed and confounded
because of all your wickedness.
Jer 4:31; 21:13; 22:6 23 O inhabitant of Lebanon,
nested among the cedars,
how you will groan[1] when pangs come upon you,
pain as of a woman in travail!"

Gen 38:18 24 "As I live, says the LORD, though Coniah the son of Jehoiakim,
2 Kings 24:6–8 king of Judah, were the signet ring on my right hand, yet I would
Is 49:18 tear you off 25 and give you into the hand of those who seek your
Jer 37:1 life, into the hand of those of whom you are afraid, even into the
Hag 2:23 hand of Nebuchadnezzar king of Babylon and into the hand of the
Chaldeans. 26 I will hurl you and the mother who bore you into

---

proclaim Jerusalem's misfortune. She will have no "lovers", no "shepherds" (vv. 20, 22), that is, no one to look after her, no leaders of the people, no allies. The prophecy as such begins with a forewarning about exile (vv. 24–27) and ends with the announcement of the end of the monarchy (vv. 28–29). By being compared to a broken pot (v. 28), Jehoiachin stands for the total destruction of Jerusalem. By describing him as "childless" (v. 30), the oracle is declaring that the Davidic monarchy in Judah is coming to an end.

This oracle against Jehoiachin brings to a close the series of oracles against the kings of Judah in chapters 21–22. The clear message they contain is that those kings were incapable of leading the people along the path marked out by the Lord. The people have been grossly neglected. Priests and prophets were self-serving (cf. 6:13)–nor were the kings the good shepherds that they needed.

amatores tui. / 21 Locutus sum ad te in securitate tua, / et dixisti: «Non audiam!». / Haec est via tua ab adulescentia tua, / quia non audisti vocem meam. / 22 Omnes pastores tuos pascet ventus, / et amatores tui in captivitatem ibunt, / quia tunc confunderis et erubesces / ab omni malitia tua. / 23 Quae sedes in Libano / et nidificas in cedris, / quomodo congemisces, / cum venerint tibi dolores / quasi dolores parturientis! 24 «Vivo ego, dicit Dominus, quia si fuerit Iechonias, filius Ioachim rex Iudae, anulus in manu dextera mea, inde evellam eum 25 et dabo te in manu quaerentium animam tuam et in manu, quorum tu formidas faciem, in manu Nabuchodonosor, regis Babylonis, et in manu Chaldaeorum; 26 et mittam te et matrem tuam, quae genuit te, in terram alienam, in qua nati non estis, ibique moriemini;

l. Gk Vg Syr: Heb *be pitied*

another country, where you were not born, and there you shall die.
[27]But to the land to which they will long to return, there they shall
not return."

[28] Is this man Coniah a despised, broken pot,
a vessel no one cares for?
Why are he and his children hurled and cast
into a land which they do not know?
[29] O land, land, land,
hear the word of the LORD!
[30] Thus says the LORD: Jer 36:30
"Write this man down as childless,
a man who shall not succeed in his days;
for none of his offspring shall succeed
in sitting on the throne of David,
and ruling again in Judah."

The future king 1 Sam 16:11

23 [1]"Woe to the shepherds who destroy and scatter the sheep Is 56:11
of my pasture!" says the LORD. [2]Therefore thus says the Jer 6:3; 10:21; 22:22
LORD, the God of Israel, concerning the shepherds who care for Ezek 34:1,2

23:1–8. The previous chapters (21:1—22:30) announced the exile to come, and come it did, on account of the kings' failure to keep the Covenant. The kings, in chronological order, were the subject of the various oracles. Now Jeremiah, looking to the future, uses the image of shepherds to proclaim a new era in which God himself will be the shepherd-ruler of his people (vv. 1–4); he will raise up a new king who will govern justly (vv. 5–6); and the new situation that will develop after the return from exile will be more glorious than that of the period after the exodus from Egypt (vv. 7–8). John Paul II refers to this oracle to stress that the new people of God, the Church, will always have pastors to guide it: "In these words from the prophet Jeremiah, God promises his people that he will never leave them without shepherds to gather them together and guide them: 'I will set shepherds over them [my sheep] who will care for them, and they shall fear no more, nor be dismayed' (Jer 23:4). The Church, the people of God, constantly experiences the reality

[27]et in terram, ad quam ipsi levant animam suam, ut revertantur, illuc non revertentur». [28]Numquid vas despectum et contritum, vir iste Iechonias? Numquid vas absque omni voluptate? Quare abiecti sunt, ipse et semen eius, et proiecti in terram, quam ignoraverunt? [29]Terra, terra, terra, audi sermonem Domini! [30]Haec dicit Dominus: «Scribite virum istum sterilem, virum, qui in diebus suis non prosperabitur; nec enim erit de semine eius vir, qui sedeat super solium David et potestatem habeat ultra in Iuda». **[23]** [1]«Vae pastoribus, qui disperdunt et dissipant gregem pascuae meae!, dicit Dominus. [2]Ideo haec dicit Dominus, Deus Israel, ad pastores, qui pascunt populum meum: Vos dissipastis gregem meum et eiecistis eos et non visitastis eos; ecce ego visitabo super vos malitiam

Is 4:3 · Jer 6:3; 10:21 · Jer 3:15 · Ps 72:3; Is 4:2; 9:7; 11:1; 32:1 · Jer 30:9; 33: 15–16; Zech 3:8; 6:12; 9:9 · Mt 2:2 · Deut 33:28

my people: "You have scattered my flock, and have driven them
away, and you have not attended to them. Behold, I will attend to
you for your evil doings, says the LORD. [3]Then I will gather the
remnant of my flock out of all the countries where I have driven
them, and I will bring them back to their fold, and they shall be
fruitful and multiply. [4]I will set shepherds over them who will care
for them, and they shall fear no more, nor be dismayed, neither
shall any be missing, says the LORD.
[5]"Behold, the days are coming, says the LORD, when I will
raise up for David a righteous Branch, and he shall reign as king
and deal wisely, and shall execute justice and righteousness in the
land. [6]In his days Judah will be saved, and Israel will dwell

---

of this prophetic message and continues joyfully to thank God for it. She knows that Jesus Christ himself is the living, supreme and definitive fulfillment of God's promise: 'I am the good shepherd' (Jn 10:11). He, 'the great shepherd of the sheep' (Heb 13:20), entrusted to the apostles and their successors the ministry of shepherding God's flock (cf. Jn 21:15ff; 1 Pet 5:2)" (*Pastores dabo vobis*, 1).

23:5–6. The promise of the new king is the key to understanding Jeremiah's thought. The passage is repeated (with slight variations) in 33:15–16. "The days are coming", a phrase often found in oracles of salvation, is a reference to the End time, but sometimes it can mean the return from exile. The "righteous branch", meaning the future king, will eventually become a technical term for the Messiah, in both Zechariah (Zech 3:8; 6:12) and the New Testament (cf. Lk 1:78): he is "righteous", he shall "execute ... righteousness" and he will be called "the Lord is our righteousness". All this insistence on justice and right indicates, firstly, that Jeremiah wants to justify the accession of Zedekiah, whose name means "justice of the Lord"; but he also wants to show that the future Messiah will be David's legal, legitimate descendant: the Lord guarantees this by calling him a "righteous", that is "legitimate", branch. And the main message, of course, is that in the new era justice will reign and there will be peace and security: it will be the time of definitive salvation.

Thus, Jeremiah is proclaiming the coming of a descendant of David who will bring about a new era of prosperity and salvation. Jeremiah is the last prophet, in order of time, to proclaim a Messiah King, an intermediary between God and his people. At the same time, he is also promising direct intervention by God.

---

operum vestrorum, ait Dominus. [3]Et ego congregabo reliquias gregis mei de omnibus terris, ad quas eiecero eos, et convertam eos ad rura sua, et crescent et multiplicabuntur. [4]Et suscitabo super eos pastores, et pascent eos; non formidabunt ultra et non pavebunt, et nullus quaeretur ex numero, dicit Dominus. [5]Ecce dies veniunt, / dicit Dominus, / et suscitabo David germen iustum; / et regnabit rex et sapiens erit / et faciet iudicium et iustitiam in terra. / [6]In diebus illis salvabitur Iuda, / et Israel

securely. And this is the name by which he will be called: 'The LORD is our righteousness.'

7"Therefore, behold, the days are coming, says the LORD, when men shall no longer say, 'As the LORD lives who brought up the people of Israel out of the land of Egypt,' 8but 'As the LORD lives who brought up and led the descendants of the house of Israel out of the north country and out of all the countries where he[m] had driven them.' Then they shall dwell in their own land."

Jer 3:18; 16: 14–15 1 Cor 1:30

Oracles against false prophets

9Concerning the prophets:
My heart is broken within me,
all my bones shake;
I am like a drunken man,
like a man overcome by wine,
because of the LORD
and because of his holy words.

Deut 13:2–6 Jer 14:13–16

23:9–40. This collection, which is given its own heading ("Concerning the prophets": v. 9), probably records some oracles stemming from Jeremiah's disputes with false prophets during the reigns of Jehoiakim and Zedekiah. In the second part of the book we are told in more detail about the difficulties that Jeremiah had with them at the start of the kings' reigns (cf. 26:7–11; 28:1–17).

The "prophets" often mentioned in the book are people who put themselves forward as being messengers from God; but they simply told the people what they wanted to hear. This meant that they were very popular. Jeremiah, on the other hand, denounced unfaithfulness to the Covenant and warned about catastrophes to come: the false prophets opposed him, naturally, and, very often, the people did too. The unifying feature of this collection is its denunciation of the sin of those prophets: their bad example led others to sin, and made it difficult for them to accept the word of God as spoken by the true prophet.

The oracles begin with a lament over the deplorable state of the country (vv. 9–12)—one of the main causes being that the priests and prophets, who should have guided the people, have sown wickedness even in the temple of Jerusalem (v. 11). The passage goes on to show that immorality has become worse in the South than it ever had been

habitabit confidenter; / et hoc est nomen, quod vocabunt eum: / Dominus iustitia nostra. 7Propter hoc ecce dies veniunt, dicit Dominus, et non dicent ultra: "Vivit Dominus, qui eduxit filios Israel de terra Aegypti!", 8sed: "Vivit Dominus, qui eduxit et adduxit semen domus Israel de terra aquilonis et de cunctis terris!", ad quas eieceram eos; et habitabunt in terra sua». 9Ad prophetas. / Contritum est cor meum in medio mei, / contremuerunt omnia ossa mea; / factus sum quasi vir ebrius / et quasi homo

m. Gk: Heb *I*

Is 1:9,10 Jer 5:7,8 10 For the land is full of adulterers;
because of the curse the land mourns,
and the pastures of the wilderness are dried up.
Their course is evil,
and their might is not right.

---

in the old Northern kingdom (Samaria) —and that there is a price that must be paid (vv. 13–15). Excuses will do no good. People cannot escape their personal responsibility; they should be able to work out whether the prophets are preaching a message that leads to God or away from him (vv. 16–17). They should hear not what they want to hear but what God is saying. Moreover, the false prophets have no time for the Lord and show him no reverence (vv. 18–24). They attribute to God things that are no more than dreams (vv. 25–32), and their dreams are completely at odds with the Word of God. The two things are as different as shadow and substance, falsehood and truth (vv. 28b–29). Therefore, not everyone who claims his words are "prophecy" is to be believed.

Jeremiah is making a play on the Hebrew word *massāh*, which has two meanings: it can mean something physical, a "weight", a "burden" (cf. v. 33; 17:21, 22, 24, 27), or it can have a sense found in prophetical writings—something that is "lifted up", meaning an "oracle", or "prophecy" (Is 13:1; 15:1; 17:1; Nah 1:1; Zech 9:1; etc.). Thus, the question in v. 33, "What is the *massāh* of the Lord?" could be read as, "What is the burden of the Lord?" The same applies in v. 38. Jeremiah is complaining about these deceivers who have abused the word of the Lord and who themselves have become a burden to the Lord. Therefore, they will be "lifted up" like a bale or burden, and borne away, deported from the country (vv. 33–39). Since individuals are responsible for their own actions, they will deserve punishment if they let themselves be deceived by those false prophets (v. 40).

The passage contrasts the deceitfulness of false prophets with the truthfulness of the Word of God. St Anthony of Padua refers to vv. 30–32 in the context of docility to the Holy Spirit: "Blessed is he who speaks as the Holy Spirit bids him and not as his heart desires! There are those who speak according to their own spirit; they steal the words of others and speak them as their own. Of those men, and of all men like them, the Lord says through the mouth of Jeremiah: *Behold, I am against the prophets, says the Lord*… . Let us speak then as the Holy Spirit bids us to speak, asking him humbly and devoutly to fill us with his grace" (*Sermones*, 1, 226). For the Word of God has extraordinary force if a person receives it with simplicity and a clean heart. With Jeremiah, St John of the Cross asks: "*Is not my word like fire?* These words, as [the Lord] says in the gospel of John, are *spirit and life*

madidus a vino, / a facie Domini / et a facie verborum sanctorum eius; / 10quia adulteris repleta est terra, / quia a facie maledictionis luxit terra, / arefacta sunt arva deserti, / factus est cursus eorum malus,

[11]"Both prophet and priest are ungodly; Jer 6:13
even in my house I have found their wickedness, says the LORD.
[12] Therefore their way shall be to them
like slippery paths in the darkness,
into which they shall be driven and fall;
for I will bring evil upon them
in the year of their punishment, says the LORD.
[13] In the prophets of Samaria Jer 2:8; 5:31
I saw an unsavory thing:
they prophesied by Baal
and led my people Israel astray.
[14] But in the prophets of Jerusalem Gen 19
I have seen a horrible thing: Is 1:9,10
they commit adultery and walk in lies; Jer 29:23 Ezek 13:22
they strengthen the hands of evildoers,
so that no one turns from his wickedness;
all of them have become like Sodom to me,
and its inhabitants like Gomorrah."
[15] Therefore thus says the LORD of hosts concerning the prophets: Jer 9:14
"Behold, I will feed them with wormwood,
and give them poisoned water to drink;
for from the prophets of Jerusalem
ungodliness has gone forth into all the land."

[16]Thus says the LORD of hosts: "Do not listen to the words of Num 16:28
the prophets who prophesy to you, filling you with vain hopes;
they speak visions of their own minds, not from the mouth of the
LORD. [17]They say continually to those who despise the word of the
LORD, 'It shall be well with you'; and to every one who stubbornly
follows his own heart, they say, 'No evil shall come upon you.'"

(Jn 6:64); let those who have ears to hear, souls who have been purified and are in love, hear them. But those who do not long to hear them, and have given themselves over to other things, will not rejoice in the spirit and life of his words; they will be filled only with disgust" (*Flame of Living Love*, 1, 5).

/ et fortitudo eorum iniustitia. / [11]«Propheta namque et sacerdos polluti sunt, / et in domo mea inveni malum eorum, / ait Dominus. / [12]Idcirco via eorum erit quasi lubricum; / in tenebras proicientur et cadent in eis; / afferam enim super eos mala, / annum visitationis eorum, / ait Dominus. / [13]Et in prophetis Samariae vidi fatuitatem: / prophetabant in Baal / et decipiebant populum meum Israel. / [14]Et in prophetis Ierusalem vidi horribilia: / adulterium faciunt et in mendacio ambulant; / et confortaverunt manus pessimorum, / ut non converteretur unusquisque a malitia sua: / facti sunt mihi omnes ut Sodoma, / et habitatores eius quasi Gomorra» [15]Propterea haec dicit Dominus exercituum ad prophetas: / «Ecce ego cibabo eos absinthio / et potabo eos felle; / a prophetis enim Ierusalem / egressa est pollutio super omnem terram. [16]Haec dicit Dominus exercituum: Nolite audire verba prophetarum, qui prophetant vobis et / decipiunt vos; visionem cordis sui loquuntur, non de ore Domini. / [17]Dicunt his,

1 Cor 2:16 18 For who among them has stood in the council of the LORD
to perceive and to hear his word,
or who has given heed to his word and listened?
Jer 30:23–24 19 Behold, the storm of the LORD!
Wrath has gone forth,
a whirling tempest;
it will burst upon the head of the wicked.
20 The anger of the LORD will not turn back
until he has executed and accomplished
the intents of his mind.
In the latter days you will understand it clearly.

21 "I did not send the prophets,
yet they ran;
I did not speak to them,
yet they prophesied.
Jer 28:9 22 But if they had stood in my council,
then they would have proclaimed my words to my people,
and they would have turned them from their evil way,
and from the evil of their doings.

1 Kings 8:27
Ps 94:7; 139:7–12 23 "Am I a God at hand, says the LORD, and not a God afar off?
Ps 139:7–12 24 Can a man hide himself in secret places so that I cannot see
him? says the LORD. Do I not fill heaven and earth? says the LORD.
Wis 1:7 Sir 16:37 25 I have heard what the prophets have said who prophesy lies in
Amos 9:2–3 my name, saying, 'I have dreamed, I have dreamed!' 26 How long
shall there be lies[n] in the heart of the prophets who prophesy lies,
Judg 3:7; 8:33–34 and who prophesy the deceit of their own heart, 27 who think to
make my people forget my name by their dreams which they tell

---

qui despiciunt me: / "Locutus est Dominus: Pax erit vobis"; / et omni, qui ambulat in pravitate cordis sui, / dixerunt: "Non veniet super vos malum". 18 Quis enim affuit in consilio Domini et vidit et audivit sermonem eius? Quis consideravit verbum illius et audivit? 19 Ecce turbo Domini, indignatio egressa est, / et tempestas erumpens super caput impiorum irruet. / 20 Non cessabit furor Domini, usque dum faciat / et usque dum compleat cogitationes cordis sui; / in novissimis diebus intellegetis consilium eius. / 21 Non mittebam prophetas, / et ipsi currebant; / non loquebar ad eos, / et ipsi prophetabant. / 22 Si stetissent in consilio meo, / nota fecissent verba mea populo meo / et avertissent utique eos a via sua mala / et ab operibus suis pessimis. / 23 Putasne Deus e vicino ego sum, / dicit Dominus, / et non Deus de longe? / 24 Si occultabitur vir in absconditis, / ego non videbo eum?, / dicit Dominus. / Numquid non caelum et terram ego impleo?, / dicit Dominus. 25 Audivi, quae dixerunt prophetae prophetantes in nomine meo mendacium atque dicentes: "Somniavi, somniavi". 26 Usquequo istud est in corde prophetarum vaticinantium mendacium et prophetantium seductionem cordis sui? 27 Qui volunt facere, ut obliviscatur populus meus nominis mei, propter somnia eorum, quae narrat unusquisque ad proximum suum, sicut obliti sunt patres eorum nominis mei propter Baal. 28 Propheta, qui habet

n. Cn Compare Syr: Heb obscure

one another, even as their fathers forgot my name for Baal? 28 Let
the prophet who has a dream tell the dream, but let him who has
my word speak my word faithfully. What has straw in common
with wheat? says the LORD. 29 Is not my word like fire, says the Jer 5:14; 20:9
LORD, and like a hammer which breaks the rock in pieces?
30 Therefore, behold, I am against the prophets, says the LORD,
who steal my words from one another. 31 Behold, I am against the
prophets, says the LORD, who use their tongues and say, 'Says the
LORD.' 32 Behold, I am against those who prophesy lying dreams,
says the LORD, and who tell them and lead my people astray by
their lies and their recklessness, when I did not send them or
charge them; so they do not profit this people at all, says the LORD.

33 "When one of this people, or a prophet, or a priest asks you, Is 13:1
'What is the burden of the LORD?' you shall say to them, 'You are Lam 2:14
the burden,[o] and I will cast you off, says the LORD.' 34 And as for Mal 1:1
the prophet, priest, or one of the people who says, 'The burden of
the LORD,' I will punish that man and his household. 35 Thus shall
you say, every one to his neighbour and every one to his brother,
'What has the LORD answered?' or 'What has the LORD spoken?'
36 But 'the burden of the LORD' you shall mention no more, for the
burden is every man's own word, and you pervert the words of the
living God, the LORD of hosts, our God. 37 Thus you shall say to the
prophet, 'What has the LORD answered you?' or 'What has the
LORD spoken?' 38 But if you say, 'The burden of the LORD,' thus
says the LORD, 'Because you have said these words, "The burden
of the LORD," when I sent to you, saying, "You shall not say, 'The
burden of the LORD,'" 39 therefore, behold, I will surely lift you up Hos 4:6
and cast you away from my presence, you and the city which I gave

---

somnium, narret somnium et, qui habet sermonem meum, loquatur sermonem meum vere. Quid paleis ad triticum?, / dicit Dominus. / 29 Numquid non verba mea sunt quasi ignis, / dicit Dominus, / et quasi malleus conterens petram? 30 Propterea ecce ego ad prophetas, ait Dominus, qui furantur verba mea unusquisque a proximo suo. 31 Ecce ego ad prophetas, ait Dominus, qui assumunt linguas suas et aiunt: "Dicit Dominus". 32 Ecce ego ad prophetantes somnia mendacii, ait Dominus, qui narraverunt ea et seduxerunt populum meum in mendaciis suis et in iactantia sua, cum ego non misissem eos nec mandassem eis; qui nihil profuerunt populo huic, dicit Dominus. 33 Si interrogaverit te populus iste vel propheta aut sacerdos dicens: "Quod est onus Domini", dices ad eos: Vos estis onus; proiciam quippe vos, dicit Dominus. 34 Et propheta et sacerdos et populus, qui dicit: "Onus Domini", visitabo super virum illum et super domum eius. 35 Haec dicetis unusquisque ad proximum et ad fratrem suum: "Quid respondit Dominus?" et "Quid locutus est Dominus?". 36 Sed "Onus Domini" ultra non memorabitis, quia onus erit unicuique sermo suus, et pervertitis verba Dei viventis, Domini exercituum, Dei nostri. 37 Haec dices ad prophetam: "Quid respondit tibi Dominus?" et "Quid locutus est Dominus?". 38 Si autem "Onus Domini" dixeritis, propter hoc haec dicit Dominus: Quia dixistis sermonem istum: "Onus Domini", et misi ad vos dicens: Nolite dicere: "Onus Domini"; 39 propterea, ecce ego tollam vos portans et proiciam vos et civitatem, quam dedi vobis et patribus vestris, a facie mea; 40 et dabo vos in

o. Gk Vg: Heb *What burden*

2 Kings 24 12–16 Jer 29:1–20 Mt 21:18–19 2 Kings 24:12 2 Chron 36:10 Jer 27:20 Amos 7:1,4; 8:1

to you and your fathers. 40And I will bring upon you everlasting
reproach and perpetual shame, which shall not be forgotten.'"

Vision of the two baskets of figs

24 1After Nebuchadnezzar king of Babylon had taken into
exile from Jerusalem Jeconiah the son of Jehoiakim, king

24:1–10. This passage has to do with another symbolic vision (similar to that in Amos 8:1–3, and with the same literary structure as those in 1:1–13—vision, question, and explanation); it reveals God's judgment on the inhabitants of Judah who remained there, and on those who were deported to Babylon. It refers to the situation after the first deportation, in 597 BC: Jeohiachin ("Coniah" cf. 22:20–30) and many nobles and craftsmen were led off into exile, and the Babylonians installed Zedekiah as king (cf. the note on 21:1–10; 2 Kings 24:10–17).

The vision of the baskets of good and bad figs is explained: contrary to what the people of Jerusalem might think, God looks more favourably on those who were exiled than on those left behind. So, the latter should not feel proud that they are still in the country. Those who are now in distant parts "shall return to me with their whole heart" (v. 7; cf. 32:39), and they will be the true people of God whom the Lord will protect when they return from exile (v. 6). But those who stayed in Judah and did not mend their ways are destined to disappear (vv. 8–10). St John Chrysostom comments: "'Because he disposes of everything that is evil, of anything in which he can find no trace of goodness, he will destroy all those who do not serve him, who live lives of impiety and never strive to be reconciled with God.' He calls them a basket of bad figs (cf. v. 8) because he can see no good in them" (*Fragmenta in Ieremiam*, 24).

25:1–14. The narrative at this point jumps back almost ten years in time—to the year 605 or 604 BC, with events that will give rise to the crisis soon after and culminate in the fall of Jerusalem and the devastation of the land of Judah. After the battle of Carchemish (605) in which Nebuchadnezzar defeated Neco II, pharaoh of Egypt, the power of Babylon began to spread right across the Near East. Jeremiah was at this time twenty-three years into his ministry, during which he had constantly preached a call to conversion that had fallen on deaf ears. Therefore, he announces that the disaster that will befall Judah at the hands of the Babylonians is a punishment from God (vv. 1–8; cf. 3:22; 7:20; 23:22).

As the first part of the book draws to a close, having provided an extensive

opprobrium sempiternum et in ignominiam aeternam, quae numquam oblivione delebitur». **[24]** 1Ostendit mihi Dominus, et ecce duo calathi pleni ficis positi ante templum Domini, postquam transtulit Nabuchodonosor rex Babylonis Iechoniam filium Ioachim regem Iudae et principes eius et fabrum et inclusorem de Ierusalem et adduxit eos in Babylonem. 2Calathus unus ficus bonas habebat

of Judah, together with the princes of Judah, the craftsmen, and
the smiths, and had brought them to Babylon, the LORD showed
me this vision: Behold, two baskets of figs placed before the
temple of the LORD. [2]One basket had very good figs, like first-ripe
figs, but the other basket had very bad figs, so bad that they could
not be eaten. [3]And the LORD said to me, "What do you see,
Jeremiah?" I said, "Figs, the good figs very good, and the bad figs
very bad, so bad that they cannot be eaten."

[4]Then the word of the LORD came to me: [5]"Thus says the Ezek
LORD, the God of Israel: Like these good figs, so I will regard as 11:14–21
good the exiles from Judah, whom I have sent away from this
place to the land of the Chaldeans. [6]I will set my eyes upon them Jer 1:10;
for good, and I will bring them back to this land. I will build them 12:15; 29:10
up, and not tear them down; I will plant them, and not uproot

---

collection of oracles spoken by Jeremiah at various times over the course of his ministry, great emphasis is placed on the fact that God is the Lord of human history. The train of events over these years is no accident; God has designed it (v. 8). He has chosen to use Nebuchadnezzar to punish Judah (vv. 9–11); it is as if God has uttered an anathema against Jerusalem (cf. Deut 2:24–37; 20:16–18; Josh 6:21; etc.). But at the same time as explaining the true reasons for the catastrophe, the passage contains grounds for hope, because the Lord has decreed that his people will be oppressed for only a limited time—seventy years (vv. 12–14).

This time-limit can be taken almost literally, running from 605, the first year of Nebuchadnezzar's reign (v. 1), to 539, the year when Babylon fell to the Persians—almost seventy years of Babylonian dominion. It can also be taken symbolically, because elsewhere we find the number seventy being used to mean a very high number (cf. Judg 1:7; 1 Sam 6:19; Mt 18:22, etc.)—that is, a long period of oppression. Still, given the depressing panorama, the fact that it will continue for only seventy years implies a promise that a restoration will take place. The same thing happened to the generation that experienced the exodus from Egypt; they died out before the entry into the promised land; but their descendants did take possession of the land. The generation that went into exile in Babylon will never see home again, but the fact that they die in exile does not mean that God will not keep his promise. The seventy years is mentioned also in 29:10 and 2 Chronicles 36:21, and it is the basis of the prophecy in Daniel 9:1–27.

---

nimis, ut solent ficus esse primi temporis; et calathus unus ficus habebat malas nimis, quae comedi non
poterant, eo quod essent malae. [3]Et dixit Dominus ad me: «Quid tu vides, Ieremia?». Et dixi: «Ficus,
ficus bonas, bonas valde, et malas, malas valde, quae comedi non possunt, eo quod sint malae». [4]Et
factum est verbum Domini ad me dicens: [5]«Haec dicit Dominus, Deus Israel: Sicut ficus hae bonae, sic
cognoscam transmigrationem Iudae, quam emisi de loco isto in terram Chaldaeorum, in bonum. [6]Et
ponam oculos meos super eos ad placandum et reducam eos in terram hanc et aedificabo eos et non

Jer 4:4; 31:31, 33–34; 32:39; 1 Jn 5:20
them. 7I will give them a heart to know that I am the LORD; and
they shall be my people and I will be their God, for they shall
return to me with their whole heart.
8"But thus says the LORD: Like the bad figs which are so bad
they cannot be eaten, so will I treat Zedekiah the king of Judah,
his princes, the remnant of Jerusalem who remain in this land, and
Deut 28:37; Jer 15:4; 26:6; 29:18; 42:18; 44:12
those who dwell in the land of Egypt. 9I will make them a horror[p]
to all the kingdoms of the earth, to be a reproach, a byword, a
taunt, and a curse in all the places where I shall drive them. 10And
I will send sword, famine, and pestilence upon them, until they
shall be utterly destroyed from the land which I gave to them and
their fathers."

Exile, a punishment from the Lord

2 Kings 24:1; Jer 35:1
25 1The word that came to Jeremiah concerning all the people
of Judah, in the fourth year of Jehoiakim the son of Josiah,
king of Judah (that was the first year of Nebuchadnezzar king of
Babylon), 2which Jeremiah the prophet spoke to all the people of
Judah and all the inhabitants of Jerusalem: 3"For twenty-three
years, from the thirteenth year of Josiah the son of Amon, king of
Judah, to this day, the word of the LORD has come to me, and I
Jer 7:25
have spoken persistently to you, but you have not listened. 4You
have neither listened nor inclined your ears to hear, although the
LORD persistently sent to you all his servants the prophets, 5saying,
'Turn now, every one of you, from his evil way and wrong doings,
and dwell upon the land which the LORD has given to you and
your fathers from of old and for ever; 6do not go after other gods

---

destruam et plantabo eos et non evellam. 7Et dabo eis cor, ut sciant me quia ego sum Dominus; et erunt
mihi in populum, et ego ero eis in Deum, quia revertentur ad me in toto corde suo. 8Et sicut ficus
pessimae, quae comedi non possunt, eo quod sint malae, haec dicit Dominus, sic dabo Sedeciam regem
Iudae et principes eius et reliquos de Ierusalem, qui remanserunt in terra hac et qui habitant in terra
Aegypti. 9Et dabo eos in vexationem afflictionemque omnibus regnis terrae, in opprobrium et in
proverbium et in derisum et in maledictionem in universis locis, ad quae eieci eos. 10Et mittam in eis
gladium et famem et pestem, donec consumantur de terra, quam dedi eis et patribus eorum».
[25] 1Verbum, quod factum est ad Ieremiam de omni populo Iudae in anno quarto Ioachim filii Iosiae
regis Iudae —ipse est annus primus Nabuchodonosor regis Babylonis— 2quod locutus est Ieremias
propheta ad omnem populum Iudae et ad universos habitatores Ierusalem dicens: 3«A tertio decimo
anno Iosiae filii Amon regis Iudae usque ad diem hanc, iste tertius et vicesimus est annus, factum est
verbum Domini ad me, et locutus sum ad vos de nocte consurgens et loquens, et non audistis. 4Et misit
Dominus ad vos omnes servos suos prophetas, consurgens diluculo mittensque; et non audistis neque
inclinastis aures vestras, ut audiretis, 5cum diceret: "Revertimini unusquisque a via sua mala et a
pessimis cogitationibus vestris, et habitabitis in terra, quam dedit Dominus vobis et patribus vestris, a
saeculo et usque in saeculum; 6et nolite ire post deos alienos, ut serviatis eis adoretisque eos, neque me
ad iracundiam provocetis in operibus manuum vestrarum, et non affligam vos. 7Et non audistis me, dicit

p. Compare Gk: Heb *horror for evil*

to serve and worship them, or provoke me to anger with the work
of your hands. Then I will do you no harm.' [7]Yet you have not
listened to me, says the LORD, that you might provoke me to anger
with the work of your hands to your own harm.

[8]"Therefore thus says the LORD of hosts: Because you have not
obeyed my words, [9]behold, I will send for all the tribes of the north,
says the LORD, and for Nebuchadnezzar the king of Babylon, my
servant, and I will bring them against this land and its inhabitants,
and against all these nations round about; I will utterly destroy
them, and make them a horror, a hissing, and an everlasting
reproach.[q] [10]Moreover, I will banish from them the voice of mirth
and the voice of gladness, the voice of the bridegroom and the
voice of the bride, the grinding of the millstones and the light of
the lamp. [11]This whole land shall become a ruin and a waste, and
these nations shall serve the king of Babylon seventy years.
[12]Then after seventy years are completed, I will punish the king of
Babylon and that nation, the land of the Chaldeans, for their
iniquity, says the LORD, making the land an everlasting waste. [13]I
will bring upon that land all the words which I have uttered
against it, everything written in this book, which Jeremiah prophesied against all the nations. [14]For many nations and great kings
shall make slaves even of them; and I will recompense them
according to their deeds and the work of their hands."

Deut 20:16–18
Josh 6:21
Josh 6:17
Is 44:28; 45:1
Jer 27:6; 43:10
Ezek 29:18–20
Jer 7:34; 16:9
Ezek 26:13
Rev 18:22
Is 23:15
Jer 27:6; 28:14
2 Chron 36:21–22
Is 23:15
Jer 27:7; 29:10
Dan 9:2
Zech 1:12; 7:5
Jer 46–51

The cup of wrath for the nations

[15]Thus the LORD, the God of Israel, said to me: "Take from my
hand this cup of the wine of wrath, and make all the nations to

Ps 75:8
Lam 4:21
Is 51:17
Rev 14:10,16

25:15–38. The oracles to do with Judah and Jerusalem are now followed by a collection concerning the other nations in the region. To introduce them, the text narrates a symbolic vision in which the prophet is given a cup containing God's wrath as a symbol of punishment (cf. Ps 11:6; 75:8; Is 51:17; Ezek 23:31–34), which he makes all the nations drink.

Dominus, ut me ad iracundiam provocaretis in operibus manuum vestrarum, in malum vestrum". [8]Propterea haec dicit Dominus exercituum: Pro eo quod non audistis verba mea, [9]ecce ego mittam et assumam universas cognationes aquilonis, ait Dominus, et Nabuchodonosor regem Babylonis, servum meum, et adducam eos super terram istam et super habitatores eius et super omnes nationes, quae in circuitu illius sunt; et interficiam eos et ponam eos in stuporem et in sibilum et in ruinas sempiternas. [10]Perdamque ex eis vocem gaudii et vocem laetitiae, vocem sponsi et vocem sponsae, vocem molae et lumen lucernae, [11]et erit universa terra haec in solitudinem et in stuporem, et servient omnes gentes istae regi Babylonis septuaginta annis. [12]Cumque impleti fuerint septuaginta anni, visitabo super regem Babylonis et super gentem illam, dicit Dominus, iniquitatem eorum et super terram Chaldaeorum; et

q. Gk Compare Syr: Heb *desolations*

whom I send you drink it. [16]They shall drink and stagger and be crazed because of the sword which I am sending among them."

[17]So I took the cup from the LORD'S hand, and made all the nations to whom the LORD sent me drink it: [18]Jerusalem and the cities of Judah, its kings and princes, to make them a desolation and a waste, a hissing and a curse, as at this day; [19]Pharaoh king

---

The Lord is not the God of a particular place, as the idols of the nations are; he is the only God, the God of all the earth. Therefore his word is addressed not only to Jerusalem and Judah but to all other nations as well, from south to north (vv. 19–26)—Egypt, with its diverse population; the land of Uz, where Job came from (Job 1:1), which may have been situated between Egypt and Edom; the land of the Philistines, including its main cities; the Israelites' traditional enemies to the south and in Transjordan (Edom, Moab, Ammon) and to the north (Tyre and Sidon); the islands of the Mediterranean and the semi-nomadic tribes in the desert of northern Arabia (cf. 9:25; Gen 10:7; 25:3); the kings of the unknown region of Zimri; more distant peoples of Babylonia (Elam and Media); and all the kings of the north. All will experience the wrath of God—including the king of Babylon (v. 26), probably mentioned in an encrypted way here, "Sheshach" (note r; cf. 51:41), by replacing each consonant of the Hebrew word *Babel* with the consonant that occupies the same place in the Hebrew alphabet (but beginning from the last letter).

Whether or not they want to drink the cup, drink it they must (vv. 27–29), for the Lord is ruler of all nations. Nothing escapes his just judgments. No crime, be it committed in Israel or elsewhere, will go unpunished by him. His judgments will reach every corner of the earth (vv. 30–38). The one who executes God's judgment will be like a lion (v. 38), like a tempest (v. 32) that will devour rulers and their subjects alike (vv. 34–36).

This section (vv. 15–38) summarizes the message underlying the prophet's oracles against each of the nations (cf. 46:1—51:64). In the Hebrew text of Jeremiah (followed by the New Vulgate and the RSV), this section is positioned here as an anticipation of those oracles, which appear at the end of the book. In the Greek text, vv. 15–38 form an epilogue to those oracles, which appear in the centre of the book, in reverse order to that in which they come in the Hebrew text—first Elam, then Egypt, Babylon, the Philistines, Edom, Ammon, the Arabs, Damascus and Moab (cf. the note on 46:1—51:64).

ponam illam in solitudines sempiternas. [13]Et adducam super terram illam omnia verba mea, quae locutus sum contra eam, omne, quod scriptum est in libro isto, quaecumque prophetavit Ieremias adversum omnes gentes. [14]Quia servient eis etiam illi, gentes multae et reges magni, et reddam eis secundum opera eorum et secundum facta manuum suarum». [15]Quia sic dicit Dominus, Deus Israel, ad me: «Sume calicem vini furoris huius de manu mea et propinabis de illo cunctis gentibus, ad quas ego mittam te; [16]et bibent et turbabuntur et insanient a facie gladii, quem ego mittam inter eos». [17]Et accepi calicem de manu Domini et propinavi cunctis gentibus, ad quas misit me Dominus, [18]Ierusalem et

of Egypt, his servants, his princes, all his people, 20and all the Job 1:1
foreign folk among them; all the kings of the land of Uz and all
the kings of the land of the Philistines (Ashkelon, Gaza, Ekron,
and the remnant of Ashdod); 21Edom, Moab, and the sons of
Ammon; 22all the kings of Tyre, all the kings of Sidon, and the
kings of the coastland across the sea; 23Dedan, Tema, Buz, and all
who cut the corners of their hair; 24all the kings of Arabia and all
the kings of the mixed tribes that dwell in the desert; 25all the
kings of Zimri, all the kings of Elam, and all the kings of Media;
26all the kings of the north, far and near, one after another, and all
the kingdoms of the world which are on the face of the earth. And
after them the king of Babylon[r] shall drink.

27"Then you shall say to them, 'Thus says the LORD of hosts,
the God of Israel: Drink, be drunk and vomit, fall and rise no
more, because of the sword which I am sending among you.'

28"And if they refuse to accept the cup from your hand to drink,
then you shall say to them, 'Thus says the LORD of hosts: You
must drink! 29For behold, I begin to work evil at the city which is 1 Pet 4:17
called by my name, and shall you go unpunished? You shall not go
unpunished, for I am summoning a sword against all the inhabitants
of the earth, says the LORD of hosts.'

30"You, therefore, shall prophesy against them all these words, Ps 68:5; Is 63:3–6; Joel 3:16; Amos 1:2
and say to them:

'The LORD will roar from on high,
    and from his holy habitation utter his voice;
he will roar mightily against his fold,
    and shout, like those who tread grapes,
    against all the inhabitants of the earth.

---

civitatibus Iudae et regibus eius et principibus eius, ut darem eos in solitudinem et in stuporem, in sibilum et in maledictionem, sicut est dies ista; 19pharaoni regi Aegypti et servis eius et principibus eius et omni populo eius; 20et omni vulgo promiscuo et cunctis regibus terrae Us et cunctis regibus terrae Philisthim et Ascaloni et Gazae et Accaroni et reliquiis Azoti, 21Edom et Moab et filiis Ammon; 22et cunctis regibus Tyri et universis regibus Sidonis et regibus terrae insularum, qui sunt trans mare; 23et Dedan et Thema et Buz et universis, qui attonsi sunt in comam; 24et cunctis regibus Arabiae et cunctis regibus vulgi promiscui, qui habitant in deserto, 25et cunctis regibus Zimri et cunctis regibus Elam et cunctis regibus Medorum, 26cunctis quoque regibus aquilonis de prope et de longe, unicuique post fratrem suum et omnibus regnis terrae, quae super faciem eius sunt; et rex Sesach bibet post eos. 27«Et dices ad eos: Haec dicit Dominus exercituum, Deus Israel: Bibite et inebriamini et vomite; et cadite neque surgatis a facie gladii, quem ego mittam inter vos. 28Cumque noluerint accipere calicem de manu tua, ut bibant, dices ad eos: Haec dicit Dominus exercituum: Bibentes bibetis; 29quia ecce in civitate, super quam invocatum est nomen meum, ego incipio affligere, et vos immunes eritis? Non eritis immunes; gladium enim ego voco super omnes habitatores terrae, dicit Dominus exercituum. 30Et tu prophetabis ad eos omnia verba haec et dices ad illos: / Dominus de excelso rugiet / et de habitaculo sancto suo dabit vocem suam; / rugiens rugiet super pascua sua, / celeuma quasi calcantium concinetur

r. Heb *Sheshach*, a cipher for Babylon

[31] The clamour will resound to the ends of the earth,
for the LORD has an indictment against the nations;
he is entering into judgment with all flesh,
and the wicked he will put to the sword, says the LORD.'

[32] "Thus says the LORD of hosts:
Behold, evil is going forth
from nation to nation,
and a great tempest is stirring
from the farthest parts of the earth!

Jer 8:2 [33]"And those slain by the LORD on that day shall extend from
one end of the earth to the other. They shall not be lamented, or
gathered, or buried; they shall be dung on the surface of the ground.

[34] "Wail, you shepherds, and cry,
and roll in ashes, you lords of the flock,
for the days of your slaughter and dispersion have come,
and you shall fall like choice rams.[s]
[35] No refuge will remain for the shepherds,
nor escape for the lords of the flock.
[36] Hark, the cry of the shepherds,
and the wail of the lords of the flock!
For the LORD is despoiling their pasture,
Is 32:18 [37]and the peaceful folds are devastated,
Lam 2:2 because of the fierce anger of the LORD.
[38] Like a lion he has left his covert,
for their land has become a waste
because of the sword of the oppressor,
and because of his fierce anger."

/ adversus omnes habitatores terrae. / [31]Pervenit sonitus usque ad extrema terrae, / quia iudicium Domino cum gentibus; / in iudicium venit ipse cum omni carne; / impios tradidit gladio, / dicit Dominus. / [32]Haec dicit Dominus exercituum: / Ecce afflictio egreditur de gente in gentem, / et turbo magnus surgit a summitatibus terrae». [33]Et erunt interfecti Domini in die illa a summo terrae usque ad summum eius; non plangentur et non colligentur neque sepelientur: in sterquilinium super faciem terrae erunt. [34]Ululate, pastores, et clamate; / et volutamini vos in pulvere, optimates gregis, / quia completi sunt dies vestri ad occisionem / et ad dispersionem vestram, / et cadetis quasi vasa pretiosa. / [35]Et peribit fuga a pastoribus, / et salvatio ab optimatibus gregis. / [36]Vox clamoris pastorum / et ululatus optimatium gregis, / quia vastavit Dominus pascua eorum. / [37]Et conticuerunt arva pacis / a facie irae furoris Domini. / [38]Dereliquit quasi leo umbraculum suum, / quia facta est terra eorum in desolationem, / a facie irae violentae / et a facie irae furoris Domini.

s. Gk: Heb *a choice vessel*

PART TWO

Stories about the life of Jeremiah*

1. CLASHES WITH THE PEOPLE AND WITH PRIESTS AND PROPHETS*

Jeremiah arraigned

26 [1]In the beginning of the reign of Jehoiakim the son of Josiah, king of Judah, this word came from the LORD, Mt 24; 26:59,66 Lk 19:41–44

---

*26:1—45:4. The first part of the book was a lengthy collection of oracles, usually in verse form, interspersed with narrative passages; this second part consists largely of prose narratives. It is very likely that most of them were written down by Baruch, Jeremiah's secretary, a person who was very close to him from the year 605 on (cf. 32:12, 16; 36:4–20; 45:15 and the Introduction to this book). They tell us about Jeremiah's preaching and about the difficulties he encountered in the fulfillment of his ministry. The entire account, only occasionally interrupted by the inclusion of oracles, culminates in the so-called "Sufferings of Jeremiah" (37:1—44:30), in which we are told in some detail about what Jeremiah underwent in the period after the first deportation to Babylon, in 597. It was not only that people misunderstood him; he was ill-treated by those still living in the land of Judah and eventually, after the second conquest and deportation in the year 587, he was forcibly taken to Egypt, where he died.

These pages describe his clashes—first with the people, priests and prophets (26:1—29:32) and then with the kings who occupied the throne during those years of turmoil (34:1—36:32). The episodes are not in chronological order, and they derive from a number of separate collections of documents. One collection contains narratives of events in the reign of Jehoiakim (chaps. 26; 35–36; and 45); another, events in the time of Zedekiah (chaps. 27–29). In the centre of this part comes what is called the "Book of Consolation" (30:1–33:26), highly poetic and theological pages.

*26:1—29:32. The connecting thread in the first section of prose accounts of the life of Jeremiah is the prophet's fidelity to the mission entrusted to him by the Lord, despite ever-increasing opposition from his fellow citizens.

26:1–24. This chapter deals with the same incident in the temple that was narrated in 7:1—8:3 (see note), and

[26] [1]In principio regni Ioachim filii Iosiae regis Iudae factum est verbum istud a Domino dicens: [2]«Haec dicit Dominus: Sta in atrio domus Domini et loqueris ad omnes civitates Iudae, de quibus

Jer 7:1–15 2“Thus says the LORD: Stand in the court of the LORD’s house, and
speak to all the cities of Judah which come to worship in the
house of the LORD all the words that I command you to speak to
Jon 3:10 them; do not hold back a word. 3It may be they will listen, and
every one turn from his evil way, that I may repent of the evil
Lev 26:14 Deut 28:15 which I intend to do to them because of their evil doings. 4You
Jer 44:10,23 shall say to them, ‘Thus says the LORD: If you will not listen to
Jer 7:12, 25– me, to walk in my law which I have set before you· 5and to heed
26; 11:7–8 the words of my servants the prophets whom I send to you
Jer 7:12 urgently, though you have not heeded, 6then I will make this house
like Shiloh, and I will make this city a curse for all the nations of
the earth.’”

---

which occurred in 608 BC. It contains a summary of what the prophet said on that occasion, and people’s reactions to it (vv. 7–24). The religious life of the nation hinged on the temple, whose importance had increased further as a result of Josiah’s recent reforms; but Jeremiah proclaims that the temple will be destroyed; it will be reduced to rubble, like the old shrine at Shiloh (vv. 2–6). This prophecy so angered people, priests and prophets that they called for Jeremiah’s death (vv. 7–9), but the authorities managed to calm them down and Jeremiah escaped with his life (vv. 10–19), probably because his sincerity impressed the rulers: he was a man ready to risk his life in order to be faithful to his prophetic mission. Although one cannot be sure where the New Gate (v. 10) was, the rulers’ intervention clearly had a judicial character to it, since legal proceedings took place at the city gates. The New Testament contains clear echoes of this account—in the deliberations of the Sanhedrin on what to do with Jesus after he was arrested (cf. Mt 26:5–68 and par.), in the sentence handed down by Pilate (cf. Lk 23:22), and also in the account of the martyrdom of St Stephen (cf. Acts 6:12–14).

This episode dramatically illustrates the sort of clashes that Jeremiah became involved in when carrying out his mission from the Lord. He has harsh things to say, and meets resistance from the people, who have even begun to think that nothing that offends their sensibilities or contradicts their desires can come from God. Even so, Jeremiah does not back down, for the Lord gives him the strength to stay true to his calling (cf. 1:7–10).

veniunt, ut adorent in domo Domini, universos sermones, quos ego mandavi tibi, ut loquaris ad eos:
noli subtrahere verbum, 3si forte audiant et convertantur unusquisque a via sua mala, et paeniteat me
mali, quod cogito facere eis propter malitiam operum eorum. 4Et dices ad eos: Haec dicit Dominus: Si
non audieritis me, ut ambuletis in lege mea, quam dedi vobis, 5ut audiatis sermones servorum meorum
prophetarum, quos ego misi ad vos de nocte consurgens et dirigens, et non audistis, 6dabo domum
istam sicut Silo et urbem hanc dabo in maledictionem cunctis gentibus terrae». 7Et audierunt sacerdotes
et prophetae et omnis populus Ieremiam loquentem verba haec in domo Domini. 8Cumque complesset
Ieremias loquens omnia, quae praeceperat ei Dominus, ut loqueretur ad universum populum,

7The priests and the prophets and all the people heard Jeremiah Acts 6:13
speaking these words in the house of the LORD. 8And when
Jeremiah had finished speaking all that the LORD had commanded
him to speak to all the people, then the priests and the prophets
and all the people laid hold of him, saying, "You shall die! 9Why
have you prophesied in the name of the LORD, saying, 'This house
shall be like Shiloh, and this city shall be desolate, without
inhabitant'?" And all the people gathered about Jeremiah in the
house of the LORD.

10When the princes of Judah heard these things, they came up Mt 26:65ff
from the king's house to the house of the LORD and took their seat
in the entry of the New Gate of the house of the LORD. 11Then the
priests and the prophets said to the princes and to all the people,
"This man deserves the sentence of death, because he has prophesied against this city, as you have heard with your own ears."

12Then Jeremiah spoke to all the princes and all the people,
saying, "The LORD sent me to prophesy against this house and this
city all the words you have heard. 13Now therefore amend your
ways and your doings, and obey the voice of the LORD your God,
and the LORD will repent of the evil which he has pronounced
against you. 14But as for me, behold, I am in your hands. Do with
me as seems good and right to you. 15Only know for certain that Mt 27:24–25
if you put me to death, you will bring innocent blood upon
yourselves and upon this city and its inhabitants, for in truth the
LORD sent me to you to speak all these words in your ears."

16Then the princes and all the people said to the priests and the Lk 23:22
prophets, "This man does not deserve the sentence of death, for he
has spoken to us in the name of the LORD our God." 17And certain
of the elders of the land arose and spoke to all the assembled
people, saying, 18"Micah of Moresheth prophesied in the days of Mic 1:1; 3:12

26:18–24. In the course of these exchanges, some of the elders bring up the case of the prophet Micah (quoting words from Micah 3:12), in order to save Jeremiah's life. However, the sacred writer recalls what happened in

apprehenderunt eum sacerdotes et prophetae et omnis populus dicens: «Morte moriaris! 9Quare prophetasti in nomine Domini dicens: "Sicut Silo erit domus haec, et urbs ista desolabitur, eo quod non sit habitator"?». Et congregatus est omnis populus adversus Ieremiam in domo Domini. 10Et audierunt principes Iudae verba haec et ascenderunt de domo regis in domum Domini et sederunt in introitu portae domus Domini Novae. 11Et locuti sunt sacerdotes et prophetae ad principes et ad omnem populum dicentes: «Iudicium mortis est viro huic, quia prophetavit adversus civitatem istam, sicut audistis auribus vestris». 12Et ait Ieremias ad omnes principes et ad universum populum dicens: «Dominus misit me, ut prophetarem ad domum istam et ad civitatem hanc omnia verba, quae audistis. 13Nunc ergo bonas facite vias vestras et opera vestra et audite vocem Domini Dei vestri, et paenitebit Dominum mali, quod locutus est adversum vos. 14Ego autem ecce in manibus vestris sum; facite mihi,

Hezekiah king of Judah, and said to all the people of Judah: 'Thus
says the LORD of hosts,

Zion shall be ploughed as a field;
Jerusalem shall become a heap of ruins,
and the mountain of the house a wooded height.'

2 Chron 32:26 19 Did Hezekiah king of Judah and all Judah put him to death? Did
he not fear the LORD and entreat the favour of the LORD, and did
not the LORD repent of the evil which he had pronounced against
them? But we are about to bring great evil upon ourselves."

20 There was another man who prophesied in the name of the
LORD, Uriah the son of Shemaiah from Kiriath-jearim. He
prophesied against this city and against this land in words like
those of Jeremiah. 21 And when King Jehoiakim, with all his
warriors and all the princes, heard his words, the king sought to
put him to death; but when Uriah heard of it, he was afraid and
Jer 36:12–25 fled and escaped to Egypt. 22 Then King Jehoiakim sent to Egypt
certain men, Elnathan the son of Achbor and others with him,
23 and they fetched Uriah from Egypt and brought him to King
Jehoiakim, who slew him with the sword and cast his dead body
into the burial place of the common people.

2 Chron 34,8 24 But the hand of Ahikam the son of Shaphan was with
Jer 36:10 Jeremiah so that he was not given over to the people to be put to
death.

---

the case of Uriah, who was put to death (vv. 17–24). These two prophets preached a message that was very similar to Jeremiah's. Because Hezekiah, the king, was very interested in religious reform, he listened to the prophet Micah. Jehoiakim, however, had a very different outlook; just as he killed Uriah, so he could kill Jeremiah. In other words, it could have gone either way for Jeremiah; fortunately, he was defended by a senior official of the late King Josiah, Ahikam, the father of Gedaliah, who would be governor of Judah after the last deportation (cf. 39:14; 2 Kings 25:22–26).

quod bonum et rectum est in oculis vestris. 15 Verumtamen scitote et cognoscite quod si occideritis me, sanguinem innocentem tradetis contra vosmetipsos et contra civitatem istam et habitatores eius; in veritate enim misit me Dominus ad vos, ut loquerer in auribus vestris omnia verba haec». 16 Et dixerunt principes et omnis populus ad sacerdotes et prophetas: «Non est viro huic iudicium mortis, quia in nomine Domini Dei nostri locutus est ad nos». 17 Surrexerunt ergo viri de senioribus terrae et dixerunt ad omnem coetum populi loquentes: 18 «Michaeas Morasthites fuit propheta in diebus Ezechiae regis Iudae et ait ad omnem populum Iudae dicens: "Haec dicit Dominus exercituum: Sion quasi ager arabitur, / et Ierusalem in acervum lapidum erit, / et mons domus in excelsa silvarum". 19 Numquid morte condemnavit eum Ezechias rex Iudae et omnis Iuda? Numquid non timuerunt Dominum et deprecati sunt faciem Domini, et paenituit Dominum mali, quod locutus fuerat adversum eos? Et nos facimus malum grande contra animas nostras!». 20 Fuit quoque vir prophetans in nomine Domini Urias filius Semei de Cariathiarim et prophetavit adversus civitatem istam et adversus terram hanc iuxta omnia verba Ieremiae. 21 Et audivit rex Ioachim et omnes potentes et principes eius verba haec, et

The thongs and yoke-bars

Jer 18:1

27 [1]In the beginning of the reign of Zedekiah[u] the son of
Josiah, king of Judah, this word came to Jeremiah from the
LORD. [2]Thus the LORD said to me: "Make yourself thongs and
yoke-bars, and put them on your neck. [3]Send word[v] to the king of
Edom, the king of Moab, the king of the sons of Ammon, the king
of Tyre, and the king of Sidon by the hand of the envoys who have
come to Jerusalem to Zedekiah king of Judah. [4]Give them this

---

27:1–22. This episode takes place in Jerusalem in the first years of Zedekiah's reign, probably in 594 or 593 BC (cf. 28:1). After the death of the pharaoh Neco II in 595, the accession of Psammetichus II (594–589 BC) raised hopes in the region that the Babylonians might be overthrown. The fact that envoys (v. 3) from countries at that time under the sway of Nebuchadnezzar (and who paid him heavy tribute) should meet at Jerusalem, and the symbolic action performed by Jeremiah, suggest that they were trying to form an alliance to throw off the Babylonian yoke.

Jeremiah's intervention, with the yoke and thongs around his neck, makes his message very clear. What he has to say is based not on political arguments but on the word of God. The king and his people should not try to throw off the Babylonian yoke; if they want to save themselves, they should submit to Nebuchadnezzar; that is the only way to have peace and well-being (vv. 2–11). The prophet sends the same message to king Zedekiah (vv. 12–15) and to the priests and people (vv. 16–22), exhorting them not to listen to the false prophets—for if they do, they will not only fail to recover what they have lost: they will lose even more. The defeat and deportation that had occurred a few years before will be mild compared with what will happen to them soon. Everything of value that had not been stripped from the temple the first time will be taken this time—a worse humiliation still (vv. 18–19).

For a description of the vessels etc. mentioned in v. 19, see 1 Kings 7:15–39. The looting of the temple by Nebuchadnezzar is narrated in 2 Kings 24:10–16.

The passage underlines God's absolute dominion over all created things. It shows that not only Israel but also every other nation is in the hands of God. The king of Babylon is merely a tool used by God to execute his plans.

quaesivit rex interficere eum; et audivit Urias et timuit fugitque et ingressus est Aegyptum. [22]Et misit rex Ioachim viros in Aegyptum, Elnathan filium Achobor et viros cum eo in Aegyptum; [23]et eduxerunt Uriam de Aegypto et adduxerunt eum ad regem Ioachim, et percussit eum gladio et proiecit cadaver eius in sepulcris filiorum vulgi. [24]Igitur manus Ahicam filii Saphan fuit cum Ieremia, ut non traderetur in manus populi, et interficerent eum. **[27]** [1]In principio regni Sedeciae filii Iosiae regis Iudae factum est verbum istud ad Ieremiam a Domino dicens: [2]«Haec dicit Dominus ad me: Fac tibi vincula et iuga et pones ea in collo tuo [3]et mittes ea ad regem Edom et ad regem Moab et ad regem filiorum Ammon et ad regem Tyri et ad regem Sidonis in manu nuntiorum, qui venerunt Ierusalem ad Sedeciam regem

u. Another reading is *Jehoiakim* **v.** Cn: Heb *send them*

charge for their masters: 'Thus says the LORD of hosts, the God of
Is 45:12 Dan 4:17 Israel: This is what you shall say to your masters: 5"It is I who by
my great power and my outstretched arm have made the earth,
with the men and animals that are on the earth, and I give it to
Lk 4:5–6 whomever it seems right to me. 6Now I have given all these lands
Rom 13:1 Rev 13:2–4 into the hand of Nebuchadnezzar, the king of Babylon, my
servant, and I have given him also the beasts of the field to serve
Deut 11:7 him. 7All the nations shall serve him and his son and his grandson,
Bar 3:16–17 until the time of his own land comes; then many nations and great
kings shall make him their slave.

8"'But if any nation or kingdom will not serve this Nebuchadnezzar king of Babylon, and put its neck under the yoke of the
king of Babylon, I will punish that nation with the sword, with
famine, and with pestilence, says the LORD, until I have consumed
Jer 14:14; 28:8–9 it by his hand. 9So do not listen to your prophets, your diviners,
your dreamers,[w] your soothsayers, or your sorcerers, who are
saying to you, 'You shall not serve the king of Babylon.' 10For it
is a lie which they are prophesying to you, with the result that you
will be removed far from your land, and I will drive you out, and
you will perish. 11But any nation which will bring its neck under
the yoke of the king of Babylon and serve him, I will leave on its
own land, to till it and dwell there, says the LORD.'"

Jer 28:1 12To Zedekiah king of Judah I spoke in like manner: "Bring
your necks under the yoke of the king of Babylon, and serve him
and his people, and live. 13Why will you and your people die by
the sword, by famine, and by pestilence, as the LORD has spoken
concerning any nation which will not serve the king of Babylon?
14Do not listen to the words of the prophets who are saying to you,

---

Iudae; 4et praecipies eis, ut ad dominos suos loquantur: Haec dicit Dominus exercituum, Deus Israel: Haec dicetis ad dominos vestros: 5Ego feci terram et hominem et iumenta, quae sunt super faciem terrae, in fortitudine mea magna et in brachio meo extento et dedi eam ei, qui placuit in oculis meis. 6Et nunc itaque ego dedi omnes terras istas in manu Nabuchodonosor regis Babylonis servi mei, insuper et bestias agri dedi ei, ut serviant illi; 7et servient ei omnes gentes et filio eius et filio filii eius, donec veniat tempus terrae eius etiam ipsius; et servient ei gentes multae et reges magni. 8Gens autem et regnum, quod non servierit Nabuchodonosor regi Babylonis, et quicumque non curvaverit collum suum sub iugo regis Babylonis, in gladio et in fame et in peste visitabo super gentem illam, ait Dominus, donec consumam eos in manu eius. 9Vos ergo nolite audire prophetas vestros et divinos et somniatores et augures et maleficos, qui dicunt vobis: "Non servietis regi Babylonis", 10quia mendacium prophetant vobis, ut longe vos faciant de terra vestra, et eiciam vos, et pereatis. 11Porro gens, quae subiecerit cervicem suam sub iugo regis Babylonis et servierit ei, dimittam eam in terra sua, dicit Dominus, et colet eam et habitabit in ea». 12Et ad Sedeciam regem Iudae locutus sum secundum omnia verba haec dicens: «Subicite colla vestra sub iugo regis Babylonis et servite ei et populo eius, et vivetis. 13Quare moriemini tu et populus tuus gladio, fame et peste, sicut locutus est Dominus ad gentem, quae servire noluerit regi Babylonis? 14Nolite audire verba prophetarum dicentium vobis:

w. Gk Syr Vg: Heb *dreams*

'You shall not serve the king of Babylon,' for it is a lie which they
are prophesying to you. [15]I have not sent them, says the LORD, but
they are prophesying falsely in my name, with the result that I will
drive you out and you will perish, you and the prophets who are
prophesying to you."

[16]Then I spoke to the priests and to all this people, saying, 2 Kings 24:13
"Thus says the LORD: Do not listen to the words of your prophets 2 Chron 36:7
who are prophesying to you, saying, 'Behold, the vessels of the
LORD's house will now shortly be brought back from Babylon,'
for it is a lie which they are prophesying to you. [17]Do not listen to
them; serve the king of Babylon and live. Why should this city
become a desolation? [18]If they are prophets, and if the word of the
LORD is with them, then let them intercede with the LORD of hosts,
that the vessels which are left in the house of the LORD, in the
house of the king of Judah, and in Jerusalem may not go to
Babylon. [19]For thus says the LORD of hosts concerning the pillars, 1 Kings 7:15–27f
the sea, the stands, and the rest of the vessels which are left in this 2 Kings 25:13
city, [20]which Nebuchadnezzar king of Babylon did not take away, 2 Kings
when he took into exile from Jerusalem to Babylon Jeconiah the 24:8–17
son of Jehoiakim, king of Judah, and all the nobles of Judah and
Jerusalem—[21]thus says the LORD of hosts, the God of Israel,
concerning the vessels which are left in the house of the LORD, in
the house of the king of Judah, and in Jerusalem:[22] They shall be
carried to Babylon and remain there until the day when I give
attention to them, says the LORD. Then I will bring them back and
restore them to this place."

Dispute with Hananiah

28 [1]In that same year, at the beginning of the reign of Jer 14:13–16; 23:9–14
Zedekiah king of Judah, in the fifth month of the fourth

28:1–17. The reaction of the prophets and priests to what they saw as impertinence on Jeremiah's part (27:1–22) is not slow in coming.

Hananiah, claiming that he too is a prophet with a message from the Lord, replies to Jeremiah by saying that very soon—within two years—the whole

"Non servietis regi Babylonis", quia mendacium ipsi loquuntur vobis. [15]Quia non misi eos, ait Dominus, et ipsi prophetant in nomine meo mendaciter, ut eiciam vos et pereatis, tam vos quam prophetae, qui vaticinantur vobis». [16]Et ad sacerdotes et ad populum istum locutus sum dicens: «Haec dicit Dominus: Nolite audire verba prophetarum vestrorum, qui prophetant vobis dicentes: "Ecce vasa domus Domini revertentur de Babylone nunc cito". Mendacium enim prophetant vobis. [17]Nolite ergo audire eos, sed servite regi Babylonis, ut vivatis. Quare datur haec civitas in solitudinem? [18]Et si prophetae sunt, et est verbum Domini in eis, occurrant Domino exercituum, ut non veniant vasa, quae derelicta fuerant in domo Domini et in domo regis Iudae et in Ierusalem, in Babylonem» [19]Quia haec dicit Dominus exercituum ad columnas et ad mare et ad bases et ad reliqua vasorum, quae remanserunt

year, Hananiah the son of Azzur, the prophet from Gibeon, spoke
to me in the house of the LORD, in the presence of the priests and
all the people, saying, [2]"Thus says the LORD of hosts, the God of
Israel: I have broken the yoke of the king of Babylon. [3]Within two

---

situation will change for the better (v. 3). Jeremiah, in turn, says that he would like nothing better (for he loves his land and his people); but earlier prophets predicted misfortunes, and they occurred; favourable predictions are proven to be the word of God only when and if they come true. Hananiah does not give way. His arrogance (vv. 10–11) leads Jeremiah to repeat his message (vv. 12–14). The onlookers may have taken different sides, but two months later (much less than two years) it will be easy to see who the false prophet was and who the true (vv. 15–17). And the threat contained in the book of Deuteronomy will be carried out: "But the prophet who presumes to speak a word in my name which I have not commanded him to speak, or who speaks in the name of other gods, that same prophet shall die. […] [W]hen a prophet speaks in the name of the Lord, if the word does not come to pass or come true, that is a word which the Lord has not spoken; the prophet has spoken it presumptuously, you need not be afraid of him" (Deut 18:20; cf. Deut 13:6).

This debate in the presence of the people illustrates a problem that often arises in Holy Scripture, and in a way it is a perennial one: How can one know whether someone is truly a prophet sent by the Lord, when a number of prophets preach messages that are mutually incompatible? In ancient Israel, if a prediction came true, then one knew that the prophet was speaking on God's behalf. In the new People of God, the Holy Spirit helps the Church to discern whether a person's message comes from God, that is, whether he or she has a true charism: "These charisms, whether they be the more outstanding or the more simple and widely diffused, are to be received with thanksgiving and consolation for they are perfectly suited to and useful for the needs of the Church. Extraordinary gifts are not to be sought after, nor are the fruits of apostolic labor to be presumptuously expected from their use; but judgment as to their genuinity and proper use belongs to those who are appointed leaders in the Church, to whose special competence it belongs, not indeed to extinguish the Spirit, but to test all things and hold fast to that which is good" (Vatican II, *Lumen gentium*, 12).

in civitate hac, [20]quae non tulit Nabuchodonosor rex Babylonis, cum transferret Iechoniam filium Ioachim regem Iudae de Ierusalem in Babylonem et omnes optimates Iudae et Ierusalem; [21]quia haec dicit Dominus exercituum, Deus Israel, ad vasa, quae derelicta sunt in domo Domini et in domo regis Iudae et Ierusalem: [22]«In Babylonem transferentur et ibi erunt usque ad diem visitationis eorum, dicit Dominus; et afferri faciam ea et restitui in loco isto». **[28]** [1]Et factum est in anno illo, in principio regni Sedeciae regis Iudae, in anno quarto in mense quinto, dixit ad me Hananias filius Azur propheta de Gabaon in domo Domini coram sacerdotibus et omni populo dicens: [2]«Haec dicit Dominus exercituum, Deus Israel: Contrivi iugum regis Babylonis. [3]Adhuc duo anni dierum, et ego referri

years I will bring back to this place all the vessels of the LORD's
house, which Nebuchadnezzar king of Babylon took away from
this place and carried to Babylon. 4I will also bring back to this
place Jeconiah the son of Jehoiakim, king of Judah, and all the
exiles from Judah who went to Babylon, says the LORD, for I will
break the yoke of the king of Babylon."

5Then the prophet Jeremiah spoke to Hananiah the prophet in
the presence of the priests and all the people who were standing in
the house of the LORD;6 and the prophet Jeremiah said, "Amen!
May the LORD do so; may the LORD make the words which you
have prophesied come true, and bring back to this place from
Babylon the vessels of the house of the LORD, and all the exiles.
7Yet hear now this word which I speak in your hearing and in the
hearing of all the people. 8The prophets who preceded you and me
from ancient times prophesied war, famine, and pestilence against
many countries and great kingdoms. 9As for the prophet who Deut 18:21–22
prophesies peace, when the word of that prophet comes to pass, Ezek 2:5; 33:33
then it will be known that the LORD has truly sent the prophet."

10Then the prophet Hananiah took the yoke-bars from the neck Deut 28:48
of Jeremiah the prophet, and broke them. 11And Hananiah spoke
in the presence of all the people, saying, "Thus says the LORD:
Even so will I break the yoke of Nebuchadnezzar king of Babylon
from the neck of all the nations within two years." But Jeremiah
the prophet went his way.

12Sometime after the prophet Hananiah had broken the yoke-
bars from off the neck of Jeremiah the prophet, the word of the
LORD came to Jeremiah: 13"Go, tell Hananiah, 'Thus says the
LORD: You have broken wooden bars, but I[x] will make in their

---

faciam ad locum istum omnia vasa domus Domini, quae tulit Nabuchodonosor rex Babylonis de loco isto et transtulit ea in Babylonem. 4Et Iechoniam filium Ioachim regem Iudae et omnem transmigrationem Iudae, qui ingressi sunt in Babylonem, ego convertam ad locum istum, ait Dominus; conteram enim iugum regis Babylonis». 5Et dixit Ieremias propheta ad Hananiam prophetam in oculis sacerdotum et in oculis omnis populi, qui stabat in domo Domini, 6et ait Ieremias propheta: «Amen, sic faciat Dominus! Suscitet Dominus verba tua, quae prophetasti, ut referantur vasa in domum Domini et omnis transmigratio de Babylone ad locum istum. 7Verumtamen audi verbum hoc, quod ego loquor in auribus tuis et in auribus universi populi: 8Prophetae, qui fuerunt ante me et ante te ab initio et prophetaverunt super terras multas et super regna magna de proelio et de afflictione et de peste; 9propheta, qui vaticinatur pacem, cum venerit verbum eius, scietur propheta, quem misit Dominus in veritate». 10Et tulit Hananias propheta iugum de collo Ieremiae prophetae et confregit illud; 11et ait Hananias in conspectu omnis populi dicens: «Haec dicit Dominus: Sic confringam iugum Nabuchodonosor regis Babylonis post duos annos dierum de collo omnium gentium». Et abiit Ieremias propheta in viam suam. 12Et factum est verbum Domini ad Ieremiam, postquam confregit Hananias propheta iugum de collo Ieremiae prophetae, dicens: 13«Vade et dices Hananiae: Haec dicit Dominus:

x. Gk: Heb *you*

Jer 27:6 place bars of iron. [14]For thus says the LORD of hosts, the God of
Israel: I have put upon the neck of all these nations an iron yoke
of servitude to Nebuchadnezzar king of Babylon, and they shall
serve him, for I have given to him even the beasts of the field.'"
[15]And Jeremiah the prophet said to the prophet Hananiah, "Listen,
Hananiah, the LORD has not sent you, and you have made this
Deut 13:6 people trust in a lie. [16]Therefore thus says the LORD: 'Behold, I
will remove you from the face of the earth. This very year you
shall die, because you have uttered rebellion against the LORD.'"
[17]In that same year, in the seventh month, the prophet Hananiah
died.

Letter to the exiles

Ezek 8:1 29 [1]These are the words of the letter which Jeremiah the
prophet sent from Jerusalem to the elders[y] of the exiles, and

29:1–32. This chapter reports further clashes between Jeremiah and the prophets (cf. 27:12–22), this time in connexion with the situation in Babylon. The chapter can be divided into two parts—Jeremiah's letter (vv. 1–23) and the consequences that flow from it (vv. 24–32). It is possible that Elasah, one of the bearers of the letter, was a brother of Ahikam (cf. 26:24).

Shortly after King Jeconiah (Jehoiachin) and some of the people were led away to exile (cf. the note on 13:15–27; 24:1), Jeremiah sent this letter to the exiles in Babylon. In it he tells them (as he had already told the people of Judah) that they should not expect an early return home, as some false prophets have been telling them (vv. 8–9); these prophets, moreover, were creating problems with the Babylonian authorities (vv. 21–23). Instead, he tells the exiles to live peaceably in the land to which they have been deported (vv. 6–7); for it will be only seventy years before they can return. In the meantime, they should nourish their hope and seek the Lord: they will find him if they approach him with a sincere heart (vv. 10–14). As an aside, prefacing the oracle about the tragic fate of the false prophets Ahab and Zedekiah (vv. 21–23), Jeremiah predicts the misfortunes that will overtake those left in Jerusalem: they will be punished for failing to listen to the words of the Lord (vv. 15–20).

Iuga lignea contrivisti et facies pro eis iuga ferrea. [14]Quia haec dicit Dominus exercituum, Deus Israel: Iugum ferreum posui super collum cunctarum gentium istarum, ut serviant Nabuchodonosor regi Babylonis, et servient ei; insuper et bestias terrae dedi ei». [15]Et dixit Ieremias propheta ad Hananiam prophetam: «Audi, Hanania! Non misit te Dominus, et tu confidere fecisti populum istum in mendacio. [16]Idcirco haec dicit Dominus: Ecce emittam te a facie terrae; hoc anno morieris, adversum enim Dominum praevaricationem locutus es». [17]Et mortuus est Hananias propheta in anno illo, mense septimo. **[29]** [1]Et haec sunt verba epistulae, quam misit Ieremias propheta de Ierusalem ad reliquias seniorum transmigrationis et ad sacerdotes et ad prophetas et ad omnem populum, quem traduxerat

y. Gk: Heb *the rest of the elders*

to the priests, the prophets, and all the people, whom Nebuchadnezzar had taken into exile from Jerusalem to Babylon. [2]This was 2 Kings 24:12–16

Jeremiah's message here is the same as what he said when he explained the symbolic vision of the baskets of figs (cf. 24:1–10): those deported have good reason to hope in the future, because they will be converted to the Lord, but those who remained in Judah will come to a bad end because they have refused to listen to the word of God. As against a superficial interpretation of events, the prophet explains that it is not really the king of Babylon who sent the people of Judah into exile, but the Lord himself (vv. 4, 20–22). Therefore it makes sense that the word of God should encourage them to rebuild their lives in the country where they are exiled, and that the same divine word should tell them that they will be returning home, purified, after undergoing the privations of exile. There is nothing irrevocable about what has happened to them, for the Lord desires the best for those who seek him (v. 11). He wants them to repent; if they do so, he will immediately respond (cf. 33:3): "He [God] did not come to condemn us, to accuse us of meanness and smallness. He came to save us, pardon us, excuse us, bring us peace and joy. If only we realize the wonderful way in which God deals with his children, our hearts *must* change. We will see opening up before us an absolutely new panorama, full of relief, depth and light" (St Josemaría Escrivá, *Christ Is Passing By*, 165).

The incidents recounted in vv. 21–32 provide further information about how Jeremiah was mistreated for his opposition to the false prophets. The passage reports in a rather confused way the prophecy about Shemaiah which is a reply to the letter that man had sent from Babylon asking Zephaniah (cf. 21:1; 37:3; 52:24) to imprison Jeremiah (vv. 26–27). Jeremiah predicts that Shemaiah himself will be punished for his false prophecy (cf. v. 32).

Taken as a whole, chapter 29 is saying that the only way the people can have life is by being obedient to the true prophetic word. That word calls them to repentance; it can never be gainsaid, despite the self-satisfaction and false hopes harboured by Jeremiah's shallow-minded generation. Zephaniah is judged severely because he prophesied without having a mission from the Lord and gave the people a false sense of security (cf. v. 31). False prophets like him often found favour because they said things that the people wanted to hear (cf. 29:8–9). This passage is reminiscent of what Jesus said about the difficulties his followers would encounter: they should not be surprised if they suffer persecution, for the prophets before them did (cf. Lk 6:23). Indeed, it would be surprising if people who don't listen to God, people who don't obey him, were to praise Christ's disciples. Those Israelites who were not devout were quite happy with the teaching that false prophets offered (cf. Lk 6:26).

Nabuchodonosor de Ierusalem in Babylonem, [2]postquam egressus est Iechonias rex et domina et eunuchi et principes Iudae et Ierusalem et faber et inclusor de Ierusalem, [3]in manu Elasa filii Saphan

after King Jeconiah, and the queen mother, the eunuchs, the
princes of Judah and Jerusalem, the craftsmen, and the smiths had
departed from Jerusalem. 3The letter was sent by the hand of
Elasah the son of Shaphan and Gemariah the son of Hilkiah,
whom Zedekiah king of Judah sent to Babylon to Nebuchadnezzar
king of Babylon. It said:4 "Thus says the LORD of hosts, the God
of Israel, to all the exiles whom I have sent into exile from
Jerusalem to Babylon:

5Build houses and live in them; plant gardens and eat their
produce. 6Take wives and have sons and daughters; take wives for
your sons, and give your daughters in marriage, that they may
Ezra 6:10 bear sons and daughters; multiply there, and do not decrease. 7But
seek the welfare of the city where I have sent you into exile, and
pray to the LORD on its behalf, for in its welfare you will find your
welfare. 8For thus says the LORD of hosts, the God of Israel: Do
not let your prophets and your diviners who are among you
deceive you, and do not listen to the dreams which they dream,[z]
9for it is a lie which they are prophesying to you in my name; I did
not send them, says the LORD.

Jer 25:11,12; 27:22; 33:14 10"For thus says the LORD: When seventy years are completed
for Babylon, I will visit you, and I will fulfil to you my promise
and bring you back to this place. 11For I know the plans I have for
you, says the LORD, plans for welfare and not for evil, to give you
a future and a hope. 12Then you will call upon me and come and
Deut 4:29–31 pray to me, and I will hear you. 13You will seek me and find me;
2 Chron 15:2–4 when you seek me with all your heart, 14I will be found by you,
Wis 6:12–13 says the LORD, and I will restore your fortunes and gather you
Is 55:6–9 from all the nations and all the places where I have driven you,
Amos 5:4 says the LORD, and I will bring you back to the place from which
I sent you into exile.

---

et Gamariae filii Helciae, quos misit Sedecias rex Iudae ad Nabuchodonosor regem Babylonis in Babylonem dicens: 4«Haec dicit Dominus exercituum, Deus Israel, omni transmigrationi, quam transtuli de Ierusalem in Babylonem: 5Aedificate domos et habitate et plantate hortos et comedite fructum eorum, 6accipite uxores et generate filios et filias et date filiis vestris uxores et filias vestras date viris, et pariant filios et filias, et multiplicamini ibi et nolite esse pauci numero. 7Et quaerite pacem civitatis, ad quam transmigrare vos feci, et orate pro ea ad Dominum, quia in pace illius erit pax vobis. 8Haec enim dicit Dominus exercituum, Deus Israel: Non vos seducant prophetae vestri, qui sunt in medio vestrum, et divini vestri, et ne attendatis ad somnia vestra, quae vos somniatis, 9quia falso ipsi prophetant vobis in nomine meo, et non misi eos, dicit Dominus. 10Quia haec dicit Dominus: Cum impleti fuerint in Babylone septuaginta anni, visitabo vos et suscitabo super vos verbum meum bonum, ut reducam vos ad locum istum. 11Ego enim scio cogitationes, quas ego cogito super vos, ait Dominus, cogitationes pacis et non afflictionis, ut dem vobis posteritatem et spem. 12Et invocabitis me et ibitis; et orabitis me, et ego exaudiam vos. 13Quaeretis me et invenietis, cum quaesieritis me in toto corde

z. Cn: Heb *your dreams which you cause to dream*

15“Because you have said, ‘The LORD has raised up prophets Jer 14:14
for us in Babylon,’—16Thus says the LORD concerning the king
who sits on the throne of David, and concerning all the people
who dwell in this city, your kinsmen who did not go out with you
into exile: 17‘Thus says the LORD of hosts, Behold, I am sending Jer 24
on them sword, famine, and pestilence, and I will make them like
vile figs which are so bad they cannot be eaten. 18I will pursue Deut 28:25
them with sword, famine, and pestilence, and will make them a Jer 15:4; 24:9; 26:6
horror to all the kingdoms of the earth, to be a curse, a terror, a
hissing, and a reproach among all the nations where I have driven
them, 19because they did not heed my words, says the LORD, Jer 7:25
which I persistently sent to you by my servants the prophets, but
you would not listen, says the LORD.’—20Hear the word of the
LORD, all you exiles whom I sent away from Jerusalem to
Babylon: 21‘Thus says the LORD of hosts, the God of Israel,
concerning Ahab the son of Kolaiah and Zedekiah the son of Ma-
aseiah, who are prophesying a lie to you in my name: Behold, I
will deliver them into the hand of Nebuchadnezzar king of
Babylon, and he shall slay them before your eyes. 22Because of Is 65:15
them this curse shall be used by all the exiles from Judah in Jer 24:9
Babylon: “The LORD make you like Zedekiah and Ahab, whom Dan 3:6
the king of Babylon roasted in the fire,” 23because they have
committed folly in Israel, they have committed adultery with their
neighbours’ wives, and they have spoken in my name lying words
which I did not command them. I am the one who knows, and I
am witness, says the LORD.’”

24To Shemaiah of Nehelam you shall say: 25“Thus says the
LORD of hosts, the God of Israel: You have sent letters in your

---

vestro. 14Et inveniar a vobis, ait Dominus, et reducam captivitatem vestram et congregabo vos de
universis gentibus et de cunctis locis, ad quae expuli vos, dicit Dominus; et reverti vos faciam ad locum,
de quo transmigrare vos feci. 15Quia dixistis: “Suscitavit nobis Dominus prophetas in Babylone”.
16Quia haec dicit Dominus ad regem, qui sedet super solium David, et ad omnem populum habitatorem
urbis huius, ad fratres vestros, qui non sunt egressi vobiscum in transmigrationem, 17haec dicit
Dominus exercituum: Ecce mittam in eis gladium et famem et pestem et ponam eos quasi ficus malas,
quae comedi non possunt, eo quod pessimae sint; 18et persequar eos in gladio et in fame et in pestilentia
et dabo eos in vexationem universis regnis terrae, in maledictionem et in stuporem et in sibilum et in
opprobrium cunctis gentibus, ad quas ego eieci eos, 19eo quod non audierint verba mea, dicit Dominus,
quae misi ad eos per servos meos prophetas, de nocte consurgens et mittens, et non audistis, dicit
Dominus. 20Vos ergo audite verbum Domini, omnis transmigratio, quam emisi de Ierusalem in
Babylonem. 21Haec dicit Dominus exercituum, Deus Israel, ad Achab filium Colaiae et ad Sedeciam
filium Maasiae, qui prophetant vobis in nomine meo mendaciter: Ecce ego tradam eos in manu
Nabuchodonosor regis Babylonis, et percutiet eos in oculis vestris; 22et assumetur ex eis maledictio
omni transmigrationi Iudae, quae est in Babylone, dicentium: “Ponat te Dominus sicut Sedeciam et
sicut Achab, quos frixit rex Babylonis in igne!”; 23pro eo quod fecerint stultitiam in Israel et moechati
sunt in uxores amicorum suorum et locuti sunt verbum in nomine meo mendaciter, quod non mandavi
eis. Ego enim scio et sum testis, dicit Dominus. 24Et ad Semeiam Nehelamiten dices: 25Haec dicit

name to all the people who are in Jerusalem, and to Zephaniah the
son of Ma-aseiah the priest, and to all the priests, saying, [26]'The
LORD has made you priest instead of Jehoiada the priest, to have
charge in the house of the LORD over every madman who
prophesies, to put him in the stocks and collar. [27]Now why have
you not rebuked Jeremiah of Anathoth who is prophesying to you?
[28]For he has sent to us in Babylon, saying, "Your exile will be
long; build houses and live in them, and plant gardens and eat
their produce."'

[29]Zephaniah the priest read this letter in the hearing of Jeremiah
the prophet. [30]Then the word of the LORD came to Jeremiah:
[31]"Send to all the exiles, saying, 'Thus says the LORD concerning
Shemaiah of Nehelam: Because Shemaiah has prophesied to you
when I did not send him, and has made you trust in a lie,
Deut 13:6 [32]therefore thus says the LORD: Behold, I will punish Shemaiah of
Jer 28:16 Nehelam and his descendants; he shall not have any one living
among this people to see[a] the good that I will do to my people,
says the LORD, for he has talked rebellion against the LORD.'"

2. THE BOOK OF CONSOLATION*

Distress and hope

30 [1]The word that came to Jeremiah from the LORD: [2]"Thus
says the LORD, the God of Israel: Write in a book all the

***30:1—33:26.** The second section of the second part of the book is traditionally called the "Book of Consolation" because both the oracles in verse and the prose passages interspersed among them carried a message of consolation for the people during their years in exile.

Although the section may seem to break the thread of the narrative, it does not really do so. Having dealt with the

Dominus exercituum, Deus Israel, pro eo quod misisti in nomine tuo epistulas ad omnem populum, qui est in Ierusalem, et ad Sophoniam filium Maasiae sacerdotem et ad universos sacerdotes dicens: [26]"Dominus dedit te sacerdotem pro Ioiada sacerdote, ut sis praefectus in domo Domini super omnem virum arrepticium et prophetantem, ut mittas eum in nervum et in vincula. [27]Et nunc quare non increpasti Ieremiam Anathothiten, qui prophetat vobis? [28]Quia super hoc misit ad nos in Babylonem dicens: Longum est; aedificate domos et habitate et plantate hortos et comedite fructum eorum"». [29]Legit ergo Sophonias sacerdos epistulam istam in auribus Ieremiae prophetae. [30]Et factum est verbum Domini ad Ieremiam dicens: [31]«Mitte ad omnem transmigrationem dicens: Haec dicit Dominus ad Semeiam Nehelamiten: Pro eo quod prophetavit vobis Semeias, et ego non misi eum, et fecit vos confidere in mendacio, [32]idcirco haec dicit Dominus: Ecce ego visitabo super Semeiam Nehelamiten et super semen eius; non erit ei vir sedens in medio populi huius, et non videbit bonum, quod ego faciam populo meo, ait Dominus, quia praevaricationem locutus est adversus Dominum». **[30]** [1]Verbum, quod factum est ad Ieremiam a Domino dicens: [2]«Haec dicit Dominus, Deus Israel,

a. Gk: Heb *and he shall not see*

words that I have spoken to you. [3]For behold, days are coming, says
the LORD, when I will restore the fortunes of my people, Israel and
Judah, says the LORD, and I will bring them back to the land which
I gave to their fathers, and they shall take possession of it."

Ezra 2:1 Jer 29:14; 31:23

---

difficulties met by Jeremiah in his attempts to dispel false hopes in an early return from exile, the book now records oracles about a future return to Judah. The central theme is hope in the restoration of Israel and Judah based on a "new covenant". This section could date from the end of Zedekiah's reign (587 BC) or a little later.

The oldest part of the section consists in verse oracles. In these we find recurring references to impending judgment and punishment (30:5–7, 12–15, 23–24), calls to hope (30:10–11, 16–17, 18–21; 31:2–14), laments (31:15, 18–19), and promises of better times to come (31:16–17; 31:20–22). The general tone is rather sombre. However, in the final form of the book these oracles are linked by prose passages beginning with the words "days are coming" (30:3; 31:27, 31, 38) and which have the effect of giving these chapters a hopeful tone.

The most important passage announces the "new covenant" that will replace the one broken by the people's repeated transgressions down the years (cf. 31:31–37). From very early on, Christian writers have drawn attention to this passage: "God announces that a new covenant shall be made, and it will be a light to all the nations. We believe in his proclamation; our conviction derives from the power of the name of Jesus Christ who was crucified. All the people will forsake idolatry and sin in order to draw closer to God; they will suffer death to pledge their belief in him and to fulfil the creed of their religion. It is clear from the history of events and the power that lies behind them that God's proclamation is fulfilled in the New Law and the New Covenant, in which all righteous men from all nations who desire God's goodness place their hope. We, who were led to God by Christ crucified, are the people of Israel in spirit and in truth, the people of Judah and Jacob and Isaac, and of Abraham, the one to whom God bore witness before the time of circumcision, who was blessed and called the father of many nations" (St Justin, *Dialogus cum Tryphone*, 11, 4–5).

30:1–24. The oracles that mark the start of the "Book of Consolation" include some in verse, which are designed mainly to nourish the hope of Israel, that is, the Northern kingdom. To these, others are added (they are usually in prose) which apply those promises of restoration to Judah. The former were probably composed by Jeremiah early in his ministry, in the reign of Josiah, when Assyrian power was on the wane and when religious reform in the Southern kingdom gave grounds for hope that the Israelites, who had borne

dicens: Scribe tibi omnia verba, quae locutus sum ad te, in libro; [3]ecce enim dies veniunt, dicit Dominus, et convertam sortem populi mei Israel et Iudae, ait Dominus, et convertam eos ad terram,

⁴These are the words which the LORD spoke concerning Israel
and Judah:
⁵Thus says the LORD:
We have heard a cry of panic,
of terror, and no peace.
Jer 5:19 ⁶Ask now, and see,
can a man bear a child?
Why then do I see every man
with his hands on his loins like a woman in labour?
Why has every face turned pale?

---

the brunt of Assyrian aggression, would come back into the fold. The later oracles were composed after Judah had suffered deportations. God is not forgetful of his followers, be they from North or South, and he promises to re-establish his people in their land.

In the first oracles a sharp contrast is drawn between the suffering and anguish that prevails in Israel (seemingly an insoluble situation: vv. 5–7, 12–15), and the Lord's promise that he will not abandon his people or allow them to be destroyed even though they are experiencing the punishment that their sins deserve (vv. 10–11, 16–24). Similarly, Jerusalem will be rebuilt, and after a period of religious and moral reform, it will flourish again (vv. 18–21). Just as the Lord will deliver Israel, so he will come to Judah's rescue in due course. He will lift the yoke that Babylon has placed on the Jews (cf. 27:1–22) and they will be able to serve God once more, under the rule of a descendant of David (vv. 8–9; cf. 23:5; Ezek 34:23; 37:24). The Septuagint version omits verse 22, which occurs again in 31:33. It is a wording of the Covenant valid for all times and situations (cf. 7:23; 11:4; 24:7; 32:38).

The grounds for hope are the same as appear right through the book: "I am with you" (v. 11; cf. 1:8; 1:19; 15:20; 30:11; 46:28). Despite the sins of men, God is merciful: his love endures: "sin too constitutes man's misery. The people of the Old Covenant experienced this misery from the time of the Exodus, when they set up the golden calf. The Lord himself triumphed over this act of breaking the covenant when he solemnly declared to Moses that he was a 'God merciful and gracious, slow to anger, and abounding in steadfast love and faithfulness' (Ex 34:6) It is in this central revelation that the chosen people, and each of its members, will find, every time that they have sinned, the strength and the motive for turning to the Lord to remind him of what he had exactly revealed about himself and to beseech his forgiveness" (John Paul II, *Dives in misericordia*, 4).

quam dedi patribus eorum, et possidebunt eam». ⁴Et haec verba, quae locutus est Dominus ad Israel et ad Iudam: ⁵«Quoniam haec dicit Dominus: / Vocem terroris audivimus, / formido et non est pax. / ⁶Interrogate et videte, si generat masculus; / quare ergo vidi omnis viri manum / super lumbum suum quasi parturientis, / et conversae sunt universae facies in auruginem? / ⁷Vae, quia magna dies illa, / nec

[7]Alas! that day is so great
there is none like it;
it is a time of distress for Jacob;
yet he shall be saved out of it.
[8]"And it shall come to pass in that day, says the LORD of hosts,
that I will break the yoke from off their neck,[b] and I will burst
their[b] bonds, and strangers shall no more make servants of them.[c*]
[9]But they shall serve the LORD their God and David their king,
whom I will raise up for them.
[10] "Then fear not, O Jacob my servant, says the LORD,
nor be dismayed, O Israel;
for lo, I will save you from afar,
and your offspring from the land of their captivity.
Jacob shall return and have quiet and ease,
and none shall make him afraid.
[11] For I am with you to save you, says the LORD;
I will make a full end of all the nations
among whom I scattered you,
but of you I will not make a full end.
I will chasten you in just measure,
and I will by no means leave you unpunished.

[12] "For thus says the LORD:
Your hurt is incurable,
and your wound is grievous.
[13] There is none to uphold your cause,
no medicine for your wound,
no healing for you.
[14] All your lovers have forgotten you;
they care nothing for you;
for I have dealt you the blow of an enemy,
the punishment of a merciless foe,

Joel 2:11
Jer 23:5
Ezek 34:23; 37:24
Hos 3:5
Is 41:8
Jer 46:27–28
Mic 4:4
Jer 4:27; 10:24
Amos 9:8
Is 1:5–6
Lam 1:2,19; 2:4; Jer 4:30

---

est similis eius, / tempusque tribulationis est Iacob, / et ex ipso salvabitur. [8]Et erit: in die illa, ait Dominus exercituum, conteram iugum eius de collo tuo et vincula tua dirumpam; et non dominabuntur ei amplius alieni, [9]sed servient Domino Deo suo et David regi suo, quem suscitabo eis. [10]Tu ergo ne timeas, serve meus Iacob, / ait Dominus, / neque paveas, Israel, / quia ecce ego salvabo te de terra longinqua / et semen tuum de terra captivitatis eorum; / et revertetur Iacob et quiescet / et securus erit, et non erit quem formidet; / [11]quoniam tecum ego sum, / ait Dominus, / ut salvem te. / Faciam enim consummationem in cunctis gentibus, / in quibus dispersi te; / te autem non faciam in consummationem, / sed castigabo te in iudicio / nec quasi innocenti parcam tibi. / [12]Quia haec dicit Dominus: / Insanabilis fractura tua, / pessima plaga tua; / [13]non est qui iudicet iudicium tuum; / sunt ulceri medicamina, / tibi vero cicatrix non obducitur. / [14]Omnes amatores tui obliti sunt tui, / te non quaerunt;

b. Gk Old Latin: Heb *your* **c.** Heb *make a servant of him*

because your guilt is great,
because your sins are flagrant.
15 Why do you cry out over your hurt?
Your pain is incurable.
Because your guilt is great,
because your sins are flagrant,
I have done these things to you.
Is 33:1 16 Therefore all who devour you shall be devoured,
and all your foes, every one of them, shall go into captivity;
those who despoil you shall become a spoil,
and all who prey on you I will make a prey.
Jer 33:6 Mal 4:6 17 For I will restore health to you,
and your wounds I will heal, says the LORD,
Is 62:4 because they have called you an outcast:
'It is Zion, for whom no one cares!'

Is 54:1–3 18 "Thus says the LORD:
Behold, I will restore the fortunes of the tents of Jacob,
and have compassion on his dwellings;
the city shall be rebuilt upon its mound,
and the palace shall stand where it used to be.
19 Out of them shall come songs of thanksgiving,
and the voices of those who make merry.
I will multiply them, and they shall not be few;
I will make them honoured, and they shall not be small.
20 Their children shall be as they were of old,
and their congregation shall be established before me;
and I will punish all who oppress them.
Ex 19:12; 33:20 21 Their prince shall be one of themselves,
their ruler shall come forth from their midst;
I will make him draw near, and he shall approach me,
for who would dare of himself to approach me? says the LORD.

/ plaga enim inimici percussi te / castigatione crudeli: / propter multitudinem iniquitatis tuae / dura facta sunt peccata tua. / 15 Quid clamas super contritione tua? / Insanabilis est dolor tuus. / Propter multitudinem iniquitatis tuae / et propter dura peccata tua feci haec tibi. / 16 Propterea omnes, qui comedunt te, devorabuntur, / et universi hostes tui in captivitatem ducentur, / et, qui te vastant, vastabuntur, / cunctosque praedatores tuos dabo in praedam. / 17 Obducam enim cicatricem tibi / et a vulneribus tuis sanabo te, / dicit Dominus, / quia Eiectam vocaverunt te, / Sion haec, quae non habebat requirentem. / 18 Haec dicit Dominus: / Ecce ego convertam sortem tabernaculorum Iacob / et tectis eius miserebor, / et aedificabitur civitas in ruinis suis, / et arx in loco suo fundabitur; / 19 et egredietur de eis laus voxque ludentium. / Et multiplicabo eos, et non imminuentur, / et glorificabo eos, et non attenuabuntur. / 20 Et erunt filii eius sicut a principio, / et coetus eius coram me permanebit, / et visitabo adversum omnes, qui tribulant eum. / 21 Et erit dux eius ex eo, / et princeps de medio eius procedet; et applicabo eum, et accedet ad me. / Quis enim iste est, qui pignori dabit cor suum, / ut appropinquet

22 And you shall be my people,
and I will be your God." Lev 26:12 Jer 24:7; 31:31 Ezek 11:20

23 Behold the storm of the LORD! Jer 23:19–20
Wrath has gone forth,
a whirling tempest;
it will burst upon the head of the wicked.
24 The fierce anger of the LORD will not turn back
until he has executed and accomplished
the intents of his mind.
In the latter days you will understand this.

Restoration promised

31 1"At that time, says the LORD, I will be the God of all the Jer 3:18
families of Israel, and they shall be my people."
2Thus says the LORD: Hos 2:16–17

31:1–14. The oracles in this chapter hinge on the promise that Israel will relive its experiences of earlier times, when it enjoyed the love and protection of God, its father and shepherd, as it made its way through the wilderness to find tranquillity in the promised land.

The prophet again predicts the happy return of the exiles (vv. 2–3) and the restoration of Israel and of the holy city, here given the glorious name of Zion (vv. 4–6). The people will return home rejoicing at the goodness of God (vv. 7–9), who will continue to shower blessings on them (vv. 10–14). The passage stresses the kindness shown by God. He reveals himself as "a father to Israel" (v. 9) and "shepherd" to his flock (v. 10), for he is faithful to the love he has for them (v. 3).

Referring to this and other passages in the prophetical books that speak of God's tender mercy, John Paul II points out that "it is significant that in their preaching the prophets link mercy, which they often refer to because of the people's sins, with the incisive image of love on God's part. The Lord loves Israel with the love of a special choosing, much like the love of a spouse (cf. e.g. Hos 2:21–25; Is 54:6–8), and for this reason he pardons its sins and even its infidelities and betrayals. When he finds repentance and true conversion, he brings his people back to grace (cf. Jer 31:20; Ezek 39:25–29). In the preaching of the prophets, mercy signifies a special power of love, which prevails over the sin and infidelity of the chosen people. […] Connected with

mihi?, / ait Dominus. / 22Et eritis mihi in populum, / et ego ero vobis in Deum. / 23Ecce turbo Domini, furor egrediens, / procella ruens; / in capite impiorum conquiescet. / 24Non cessabit ab ira indignationis Dominus, / donec faciat et compleat / cogitationes cordis sui; / in novissimo dierum intellegetis ea. **[31]** 1In tempore illo, / dicit Dominus, / ero Deus universis cognationibus Israel, / et ipsi erunt mihi in populum. / 2Haec dicit Dominus: / Invenit gratiam in deserto / populus, qui remanserat a gladio; / vadet ad requiem suam Israel». / 3De longe Dominus apparuit mihi: / «In caritate perpetua dilexi te; / ideo

“The people who survived the sword
found grace in the wilderness;
when Israel sought for rest,
Is 54:8 3 the LORD appeared to him[d] from afar.
Hos 11:1–9 Mal 1:2 Rom 11:28 I have loved you with an everlasting love;
therefore I have continued my faithfulness to you.
4 Again I will build you, and you shall be built,
O virgin Israel!
Again you shall adorn yourself with timbrels,
and shall go forth in the dance of the merrymakers.
Is 65:21–22 Amos 9:14 5 Again you shall plant vineyards
upon the mountains of Samaria;
the planters shall plant,
and shall enjoy the fruit.
Is 2:3 Jer 30:3 6 For there shall be a day when watchmen will call
in the hill country of Ephraim:
‘Arise, and let us go up to Zion,
to the LORD our God.’”

Is 4:3 7 For thus says the LORD:
“Sing aloud with gladness for Jacob,
and raise shouts for the chief of the nations;
proclaim, give praise, and say,
‘The LORD has saved his people,
the remnant of Israel.’
8 Behold, I will bring them from the north country,
and gather them from the farthest parts of the earth,

---

the mystery of creation is the mystery of the election, which in a special way shaped the history of the people whose spiritual father is Abraham by virtue of his faith. Nevertheless, through this people which journeys forward through the history both of the Old Covenant and of the New, that mystery of election refers to every man and woman, to the whole great human family. ‘I have loved you with an everlasting love, therefore I have continued my faithfulness to you’ (Jer 31:3)” (*Dives in misericordia*, 4).

attraxi te in misericordia. / 4 Rursumque aedificabo te, et aedificaberis, / virgo Israel; / adhuc ornaberis tympanis tuis / et egredieris in choro ludentium. / 5 Adhuc plantabis vineas in montibus Samariae; / plantabunt plantantes / et vindemiabunt. / 6 Quia erit dies, in qua clamabunt custodes / in monte Ephraim: / “Surgite, et ascendamus in Sion / ad Dominum Deum nostrum”. / 7 Quia haec dicit Dominus: / Exsultate in laetitia propter Iacob / et hinnite capiti gentium; / personate, canite et dicite: / “Salva, Domine, populum tuum, / reliquias Israel”. / 8 Ecce ego adducam eos de terra aquilonis / et congregabo eos ab extremis terrae; / inter quos erunt caecus et claudus, praegnans et pariens simul: /

d. Gk: Heb *me*

among them the blind and the lame,
the woman with child and her who is in travail, together;
a great company, they shall return here.
9 With weeping they shall come,
and with consolations[e] I will lead them back,
I will make them walk by brooks of water,
in a straight path in which they shall not stumble;
for I am a father to Israel,
and Ephraim is my first-born.

Ex 4:22
Ps 89:27; 126:5–6
Is 35:7; 40:3; 49:10; Jn 4:1
Rom 8:15
2 Cor 6:18

10 "Hear the word of the LORD, O nations,
and declare it in the coastlands afar off;
say, 'He who scattered Israel will gather him,
and will keep him as a shepherd keeps his flock.'
11 For the LORD has ransomed Jacob,
and has redeemed him from hands too strong for him.
12 They shall come and sing aloud on the height of Zion,
and they shall be radiant over the goodness of the LORD,
over the grain, the wine, and the oil,
and over the young of the flock and the herd;
their life shall be like a watered garden,
and they shall languish no more.
13 Then shall the maidens rejoice in the dance,
and the young men and the old shall be merry.
I will turn their mourning into joy,
I will comfort them, and give them gladness for sorrow.
14 I will feast the soul of the priests with abundance,
and my people shall be satisfied with my goodness, says the
LORD."

Jer 23:3
Ezek 34:1

Is 49:25
Jn 10:16
Lk 11:21–22
Is 35:10; 58:11
Ezek 17:23
Hos 3:5

Ps 30:12; 90:15
Jn 16:22

---

coetus magnus revertentium huc. / 9 In fletu venient, / et in deprecatione reducam eos / et adducam eos
per torrentes aquarum / in via recta, et non impingent in ea, quia factus sum Israeli pater, / et Ephraim
primogenitus meus est». / 10 Audite verbum Domini, gentes, / et annuntiate in insulis, quae procul sunt,
et dicite: / «Qui dispersit Israel, congregabit eum / et custodiet eum sicut pastor gregem suum». /
11 Redemit enim Dominus Iacob / et liberavit eum de manu potentioris. / 12 Et venient et laudabunt in
monte Sion / et confluent ad bona Domini / super frumento et vino et oleo / et fetu pecorum et
armentorum; / eritque anima eorum quasi hortus irriguus, / et ultra non esurient. / 13 Tunc laetabitur
virgo in choro, / iuvenes et senes simul. / «Et convertam luctum eorum in gaudium / et consolabor eos
et laetificabo a dolore suo. / 14 Et inebriabo animam sacerdotum pinguedine, / et populus meus bonis
meis adimplebitur», / ait Dominus. / 15 Haec dicit Dominus: / «Vox in Rama audita est / lamentationis,

e. Gk Compare Vg Tg: Heb *supplications*

Gen 29:9–30; 35:19; 48:7
Josh 18:25
1 Sam 10:2
Mt 2:18

Rachel's lament

15 Thus says the LORD:
"A voice is heard in Ramah,
lamentation and bitter weeping.
Rachel is weeping for her children;
she refuses to be comforted for her children,
because they are not."*

16 Thus says the LORD:
"Keep your voice from weeping,
and your eyes from tears;
for your work shall be rewarded, says the LORD,
and they shall come back from the land of the enemy.
17 There is hope for your future, says the LORD,
and your children shall come back to their own country.

31:15–17. Rachel was the favourite wife of the patriarch Jacob (cf. Gen 29:9–30) and the mother of Benjamin and of Joseph, who was in turn the father of Ephraim and Manasseh. Therefore, she can stand for all Israel—north (Ephraim and Manasseh) and south (Benjamin). Rachel's grieving, described in a highly lyrical poem, symbolizes the sadness of the exiles and prepares the way (by contrast) for the joy of their return (31:18–30). The reference to Ramah must be due to the fact that Rachel's tomb was near there. There is an Old Testament tradition that she was buried in Ramah, in the land of Benjamin, about 10 km. (6 miles) north of Jerusalem (cf. Josh 18:25; Judg 4:5; 1 Sam 10:2). And it was at Ramah that the deportees were assembled after the fall of Jerusalem (cf. 40:1). However, another tradition puts Rachel's tomb near Ephrath, on the road between Jerusalem and Bethlehem, some 4 km. (2.25 miles) from the latter town (cf. Gen 35:19; 48:7). It is thought nowadays that the most likely site is somewhere in the Benjaminite area.

Matthew 2:17–18 says that this passage in Jeremiah found fulfilment in the grieving that took place in Bethlehem and its environs after the massacre of the holy innocents by Herod: thus, Matthew seems to go along with the second tradition about the site of the tomb. The evangelist has Rachel weep again over the death of the innocents. As he sees it, Rachel's real weeping takes place in the Messiah's time, in the context of the "fulfilment" of the messanic prophecies in Jesus. That interpretation connects the events of Jesus' life and times with the ancient prophecies and the history of the people of God. Israel, the "son" of God, is a prefigurement of Jesus, the Son of God in the full sense, who, like Israel, was persecuted by the powers of this world.

luctus et fletus / Rachel plorantis filios suos / et nolentis consolari super eis, quia non sunt». / 16Haec dicit Dominus: / «Quiescat vox tua a ploratu, / et oculi tui a lacrimis, / quia est merces operi tuo, / ait Dominus, / et revertentur de terra inimici. / 17Et est spes novissimis tuis, / ait Dominus, / et revertentur

Repentance and mercy

18 I have heard Ephraim bemoaning, Ps 80:4 Hos 4:16
'Thou hast chastened me, and I was chastened,
like an untrained calf;
bring me back that I may be restored,
for thou art the LORD my God.
19 For after I had turned away I repented; Ezek 21:17; 36:31
and after I was instructed, I smote upon my thigh;

31:18–22. Ephraim has been chastened by punishment; it had turned away, but now it has been converted and has decided to return to the Lord (vv. 18–19). God is moved when he sees the people repent, he takes pity on them, and invites them to return to the land from which they were ejected (vv. 20–22).

St Ambrose reads these verses as a call to penance: "We blot out our sins by our good works; we are purified by our sorrow; the Lord our God hears our cries of distress as he once heard the tears of Ephraim: *I have heard Ephraim bemoaning*. Ephraim gives voice to his sorrow: *Thou hast chastened me, and I was chastened, like an untrained calf.* The calf is skittish and leaves the stable: Ephraim knows no better, nor can he learn any better, because he finds himself far from the stable of the Lord; like Jeroboam, he began to worship calves, servants of the master, not the master himself; his fate was prophesied by Aaron when he spoke of those among the chosen people who would be unfaithful. Therefore, when he repented, he said: *For after I had turned away I repented; ... I was ashamed, and I was confounded, because I bore the disgrace of my youth*. This passage shows us how we ought to do penance: sometimes in prayer, sometimes in tears. The day of sin is called the day of confounding, because all who deny Christ will be confounded" (*De poenitentia,* 2, 36–37).

The tenderness of God as described in vv. 20–21 reminds one of Hosea 11:1–9. The last lines of v. 22 have been interpreted in various ways. St Jerome went as far as to read them in a messianic sense, as a reference to the Blessed Virgin, in whose womb, "without the intervention of any man, the Son of Man [Jesus Christ] was brought to life" (*Commentarii in Ieremiam*, 4, 31). However, most commentators see them as either a reference to Israel (the woman) who returns to her husband (the Lord), or else as a reference to Genesis: in the new order after the return from exile, unheard-of things will happen: women will even take the initiative in proposing marriage (an idea that was out of the question in that era). Others add that the woman, far from being an occasion of sin as she was in Genesis 3:6, will be a source of protection and support. Married couples will be support for one another; neither party will have higher status than the other.

---

filii ad terminos suos. / 18Audiens audivi Ephraim transmigrantem: / "Castigasti me, et eruditus sum / quasi iuvenculus indomitus; / converte me, et convertar, / quia tu Dominus Deus meus. / 19Postquam

I was ashamed, and I was confounded,
because I bore the disgrace of my youth.'
Prov 3:12 Is 49:14–16 Hos 11:8–9 Rev 3:19
20 Is Ephraim my dear son?
Is he my darling child?
For as often as I speak against him,
I do remember him still.
Therefore my heart yearns for him;
I will surely have mercy on him, says the LORD.

Is 40:3; 57:14; 62:10 Jer 3:12
21 "Set up waymarks for yourself,
make yourself guideposts;
consider well the highway,
the road by which you went.
Return, O virgin Israel,
return to these your cities.
Hos 2:18–19
22 How long will you waver,
O faithless daughter?
For the LORD has created a new thing on the earth:
a woman protects a man."

Return of the exiles

Is 11:9
23 Thus says the LORD of hosts, the God of Israel: "Once more they
shall use these words in the land of Judah and in its cities, when
I restore their fortunes:

31:23–30. God, who is merciful, will not allow the chosen people to be burdened with misfortune indefinitely. Now it is announced that the exiles will be able to return home and join their brethren still living there. First comes a description of the way things will be in Judah under God's protection (vv. 23–25); then there is a verse (v. 26) which is difficult to interpret (it may be a comment written on the manuscript by a reader), followed by four verses (vv. 27–30) about God's protection and personal responsibility.

Verses 29–30 introduce the theme of personal responsibility for one's actions into the Bible for the first time. Contrary to the old proverb (v. 29), which also occurs in Ezekiel 18:2 (cf. Lam 5:7) it stresses that those who are living in exile will not have to pay for the sins of their ancestors: they will

enim convertisti me, / egi paenitentiam; / et postquam ostendisti mihi, / percussi femur meum; / confusus sum et erubui, / quoniam sustinui opprobrium adulescentiae meae". / [20]Estne filius honorabilis mihi Ephraim / aut puer delectabilis, / quia ex quo locutus sum de eo, / adhuc recordabor eius? / Idcirco conturbata sunt viscera mea super eum: / miserans miserebor eius», / ait Dominus. / [21]Statue tibi lapides, / pone tibi signa, / dirige cor tuum in iter, / viam, in qua ambulasti; / revertere, virgo Israel, / revertere ad civitates tuas istas. / [22]Usquequo vagaberis, / filia rebellis? / Quia creavit Dominus novum super terram: / femina circumdabit virum. [23]Haec dicit Dominus exercituum, Deus Israel: «Adhuc

'The LORD bless you, O habitation of righteousness,
O holy hill!'
24 And Judah and all its cities shall dwell there together, and the
farmers and those who wander[f] with their flocks. 25 For I will satisfy Sa 23:2–3
the weary soul, and every languishing soul I will replenish."
26 Thereupon I awoke and looked, and my sleep was pleasant
to me.
27 "Behold, the days are coming, says the LORD, when I will Ps 22:30
sow the house of Israel and the house of Judah with the seed of Is 49:19–20; 53:10; Hos
man and the seed of beast. 28 And it shall come to pass that as I have 2:23; Zech 2:8;
watched over them to pluck up and break down, to overthrow, 10:9; Jer 1:10
destroy, and bring evil, so I will watch over them to build and to Deut 24:16
plant, says the LORD. 29 In those days they shall no longer say: Ezek 18:2

---

have to answer to the Lord only for their own sins. This helps to show the personal character of the New Covenant that the text goes on to speak about (31:31–37). And the doctrine of personal retribution (cf. the note on Ezek 18:1–32) also becomes clearer. Moral responsibility is not a collective thing: rather, each person must answer to God for what he or she has done during life. "Sin, in the proper sense, is always a personal act, since it is an act of freedom on the part of an individual person and not properly of a group or community. This individual may be conditioned, incited and influenced by numerous and powerful external factors. He may also be subjected to tendencies, defects and habits linked with his personal condition. In not a few cases such external and internal factors may attenuate, to a greater or lesser degree, the person's freedom and therefore his responsibility and guilt. But it is a truth of faith, also confirmed by our experience and reason, that the human person is free. This truth cannot be disregarded in order to place the blame for individuals' sins on external factors such as structures, systems or other people. Above all, this would be to deny the person's dignity and freedom, which are manifested—even though in a negative and disastrous way—also in this responsibility for sin committed. Hence there is nothing so personal and untransferable in each individual as merit for virtue or responsibility for sin" (John Paul II, *Reconciliatio et paenitentia*, 16).

dicent verbum istud in terra Iudae et in urbibus eius, cum convertero sortem eorum: "Benedicat tibi Dominus, habitaculum iustitiae, mons sanctus". 24 Et habitabunt in eo Iudas et omnes civitates eius simul, agricolae et minantes greges. 25 Quia inebriavi animam lassam et omnem animam esurientem saturavi». 26 Ideo quasi de somno suscitatus sum et vidi, et somnus meus dulcis mihi. 27 «Ecce dies veniunt, dicit Dominus, et seminabo domum Israel et domum Iudae semine hominum et semine iumentorum. 28 Et sicut vigilavi super eos, ut evellerem et demolirer et dissiparem et disperderem et affligerem, sic vigilabo super eos, ut aedificem et plantem, ait Dominus. 29 In diebus illis non dicent ultra: / "Patres comederunt uvam acerbam, et dentes filiorum obstupuerunt", / 30 sed unusquisque in

f. Cn Compare Syr Vg Tg: Heb *and they shall wander*

'The fathers have eaten sour grapes,
and the children's teeth are set on edge.'
30But every one shall die for his own sin; each man who eats sour
grapes, his teeth shall be set on edge.

1 Cor 11:25
2 Cor 3:6
Heb 8:8–12;
10:16–18
Ex 19:1
Lk 22:20

The new Covenant

31*"Behold, the days are coming, says the LORD, when I will
make a new covenant with the house of Israel and the house of

31:31–37. The words of this oracle are central to Jeremiah's message, and they constitute the passage in the book that has had most impact on the New Testament and on Christian teaching. Most ancient and modern commentators consider these words to be original words of Jeremiah, and they generally attribute them to the early stages of his ministry, because they express support for King Josiah's religious reform.

The oracle is made up of two contrasting parts: the first (vv. 31–32) describes the Old Covenant, broken by the people's sins; the second (vv. 33–35) speaks very forcefully of the New Covenant which will endure forever.

The old Covenant is described in terms of three characteristic features: it carried the force of tradition because it was a pact made "with the fathers"; it was a sign of divine election, as can be seen from a phrase exclusive to Jeremiah: "when *I took them by the hand* to bring them out of the land of Egypt"; and it showed the Lord's authority over his people.

The new pact has three key features, too: it is *new*, it is something *interior*, and it is *heartfelt*, written upon their hearts. It is *new*, because prior to this the pact with God was never described in that way; that is, it is new not in terms of the previous covenant which has ceased to operate (cf. Heb 8:18–13) but in the sense that it is definitive and will not be superseded. When, at the Last Supper, Jesus said the words of consecration over the chalice: "This cup which is poured out for you is the new covenant" (Lk 22:20; 1 Cor 11:25), he brings Jeremiah's words to fulfilment. It is *interior* because it is etched in the heart of the people and of each individual. Its content did not change (it is the Law of God) but people will know it in a different way: the previous covenant was written on tablets of stone (Ex 31:38; 34:28ff), but this one will be written on the heart and soul of man. Therefore, it is part of a person's very being; it is not just an external obligation; people's well-formed consciences tell them what they ought to do; if they fail to live up to the demands of the Covenant, they lose their identity until they are converted and are redeemed from sin. In the Letter to the Hebrews it says, by way of explaining this passage, that in the New Covenant Christ has obtained forgiveness of sins for us through the cross,

iniquitate sua morietur; omnis homo, qui comederit uvam acerbam, / obstupescent dentes eius. 31Ecce dies veniunt, dicit Dominus, et feriam domui Israel et domui Iudae pactum novum; 32non secundum

Judah, 32not like the covenant which I made with their fathers when
I took them by the hand to bring them out of the land of Egypt, my
covenant which they broke, though I was their husband, says the
LORD. 33But this is the covenant which I will make with the house
of Israel after those days, says the LORD: I will put my law within

Jer 24:7; 32:39–40 Ezek 11:19; 36:26 2 Cor 3:3 *Heb 10:16–17*

---

and therefore the old sin offerings no longer have any effect: "Where there is forgiveness (of sins), there is no longer any offering for sin" (Heb 10:18). Finally, it is *heartfelt* because it is based on a loving relationship between God and his people. The wording that Jeremiah likes so much ("I will be their God, and they shall be my people" (Jer 31:33; cf. 7:23) implies bonds of fidelity and love. The nearest precedent for this is Hosea, who used the metaphor of marriage as the hinge of his preaching and who defined sin as estrangement from God, and punishment in terms of marital breakdown: "Call his name Not my people, for you are not my people and I am not your God" (Hos 1:9). Therefore, moral imperatives should not come via legal imposition from outside; they should arise from a person's heart—the aim being not so much perfect, guiltless behaviour as living in union with God: "All who keep his commandments abide in him, and he in them" (1 Jn 3:24).

The New Covenant has given its name to the "New Testament", on which the new people of God is founded, as the Second Vatican Council says: "At all times and in every race God has given welcome to whosoever fears him and does what is right. God, however, does not make men holy and save them merely as individuals, without bond or link between one another. Rather has it pleased him to bring men together as one people, a people that acknowledges him in truth and serves him in holiness. He therefore chose the race of Israel as a people unto himself. With it he set up a covenant. Step by step he taught and prepared this people, making known in its history both himself and the decree of his will and making it holy unto himself. All these things, however, were done by way of preparation and as a figure of that new and perfect covenant, which was to be ratified in Christ, and of that fuller revelation which was to be given through the Word of God Himself made flesh. 'Behold the days shall come saith the Lord, and I will make a new covenant with the House of Israel, and with the house of Judah. [...] I will give my law in their bowels, and I will write it in their heart, and I will be their God, and they shall be my people. [...] For all of them shall know Me, from the least of them even to the greatest, saith the Lord' (Jer 31:31–34). Christ instituted this new covenant, the new testament, that is to say, in his Blood, calling together a people made up of Jew and Gentile, making them one, not according to the flesh but in the Spirit" (*Lumen gentium*, 9).

---

pactum, quod pepigi cum patribus eorum in die qua apprehendi manum eorum, ut educerem eos de terra Aegypti, pactum, quod irritum fecerunt, et ego dominatus sum eorum, dicit Dominus. 33Sed hoc erit pactum, quod feriam cum domo Israel post dies illos, dicit Dominus: Dabo legem meam in

Hos 2:22
1 Jn 2:27

them, and I will write it upon their hearts; and I will be their God,
and they shall be my people. 34And no longer shall each man
teach his neighbour and each his brother, saying, 'Know the
LORD,' for they shall all know me, from the least of them to the
greatest, says the LORD; for I will forgive their iniquity, and I will
remember their sin no more."

Gen 1:14
Ps 136:7f
Is 51:15

The Lord's enduring protection

35 Thus says the LORD,
who gives the sun for light by day
and the fixed order of the moon and the stars for light by night,
who stirs up the sea so that its waves roar—
the LORD of hosts is his name:

Ps 148:6
Is 54:9
Jer 33:20

36 "If this fixed order departs
from before me, says the LORD,
then shall the descendants of Israel cease
from being a nation before me for ever."

37 Thus says the LORD:
"If the heavens above can be measured,
and the foundations of the earth below can be explored,
then I will cast off all the descendants of Israel
for all that they have done, says the LORD."

Neh 3:1,20; 12:39
Zech 14:10

The rebuilding of Jerusalem

38"Behold, the days are coming, says the LORD, when the city
shall be rebuilt for the LORD from the tower of Hananel to the

---

31:35–37. The Lord himself declares that his plans for his people endure forever. He assures Israel that his love and mercy towards them cannot change; they are as fixed as the stars in heaven, as immutable as the laws of nature. Nothing can change God's love for Israel.

31:38–40. In the new dispensation the holy city of Jerusalem plays a key role. Hence the promise that Jerusalem will

visceribus eorum et in corde eorum scribam eam; et ero eis in Deum, et ipsi erunt mihi in populum. [34]Et non docebit ultra vir proximum suum, et vir fratrem suum dicens: "Cognosce Dominum"; omnes enim cognoscent me, a minimo eorum usque ad maximum, ait Dominus, quia propitiabor iniquitati eorum et peccati eorum non memorabor amplius». [35]Haec dicit Dominus, / qui dat solem in lumine diei, / ordinem lunae et stellarum in lumine noctis, / qui turbat mare, et fremunt fluctus eius, / Dominus exercituum nomen illi: / [36]«Si defecerint leges istae coram me, / dicit Dominus, / tunc et semen Israel deficiet, / ut non sit gens coram me cunctis diebus». / [37]Haec dicit Dominus: / «Si mensurari potuerint caeli sursum, / et investigari fundamenta terrae deorsum, / et ego abiciam universum semen Israel / propter omnia, quae fecerunt, / dicit Dominus. [38]Ecce dies veniunt, dicit Dominus, et aedificabitur

Corner Gate. 39 And the measuring line shall go out farther,
straight to the hill Gareb, and shall then turn to Goah. 40 The whole
valley of the dead bodies and the ashes, and all the fields as far as
the brook Kidron, to the corner of the Horse Gate toward the east,
shall be sacred to the LORD. It shall not be uprooted or overthrown
any more for ever."

Ezek 41:13
Zech 2:5
Josh 6:17
Neh 3:28
2 Kings 14:13
2 Chron 23:15; 26:9
Jer 7:31
Zech 14:11
Rev 22:3

Jeremiah buys a field

32 1 The word that came to Jeremiah from the LORD in the
tenth year of Zedekiah king of Judah, which was the

2 Kings 25:1–2,8
Jer 37:5,11; 39:1; 52:4

---

be rebuilt and that it will be consecrated to the Lord; under the New Covenant the city limits will be inviolate. The tower of Hananel (cf. Zech 14:10; Neh 3:1; 12:39) was at the north-east end of the city. We know no more of Gareb and Goah than is mentioned here. The valley is that of Ben-Hinnom, where the Topheth was (cf. 7:21–8:3). The Corner Gate (Zech 14:10) was between the eastern hill and the temple esplanade (cf. Neh 3:20), and the Horse Gate was to the north-east (cf. 2 Kings 14:13; 2 Chron 26:9; Neh 3:28).

32:1–44. When the book of Jeremiah was being assembled, the report of this symbolic action of Jeremiah's (vv. 1–15) was included in the "Book of Consolation"; it is filled out with a prayer from Jeremiah (vv. 16–25) and the Lord's reply to it (vv. 26–44). It stresses the future restoration of Israel (cf. 31:38–40) in order to build up the hopes of those in exile. They should rest assured that God has not forsaken them and that they will indeed return home and will enjoy as happy a time as they ever had, linked to the Lord by a Covenant that will last forever.

The tenth year of Zedekiah (v. 1) was 587 BC. The king had rebelled against the Babylonians, and once again Nebuchadnezzar's army was at the gates of Jerusalem, determined to make of it an object lesson. Given the circumstances at the time, Jeremiah's purchase of a field demonstrates the prophet's strong faith. It seems to make no sense at all: Jeremiah himself was in prison, and Anathoth, his hometown, was behind enemy lines. Even so, Jeremiah bought the field, not because he was under any legal obligation to exercise his right of redemption (cf. the note on Ruth 2:18–23; 4:1–12), but because the Lord asked him to do so (vv. 6–8). The purchase of the field symbolizes the resurgence and prosperity of the area and, therefore, hope in a return from exile (vv. 13–15). This narrative passage contains interesting information about how real estate contracts were made at the time: there

---

civitas Domino a turre Hananeel usque ad portam Anguli, 39 et exibit ultra norma mensurae in conspectu eius super collem Gareb et vertetur in Goa, 40 et omnis vallis cadaverum et cineris et universa regio usque ad torrentem Cedron et usque ad angulum portae Equorum orientalis sanctum Domini; non evelletur et non destruetur ultra in perpetuum». **[32]** 1 Verbum, quod factum est ad Ieremiam a Domino in anno decimo Sedeciae regis Iudae; ipse est annus decimus octavus Nabuchodonosor. 2 Tunc

eighteenth year of Nebuchadnezzar. [2]At that time the army of the king of Babylon was besieging Jerusalem, and Jeremiah the prophet was shut up in the court of the guard which was in the palace of the king of Judah. [3]For Zedekiah king of Judah had

---

were two deeds of purchase, one sealed, the other open; the latter wrapped round the former, so that it could be read (vv. 9–12). The passage also contains the first mention of Baruch, giving his full name (v. 12).

Although Jeremiah does what the Lord asks him (v. 16), he does not fully understand what his action means and therefore he prays to the Lord about the danger that surrounds them (vv. 17–25). The Lord's reply confirms what he has told him already: the Lord directs human events, and the Babylonians are being used by him ("I am giving this city into (their) hands": v. 28) to punish Judah for its unfaithfulness (vv. 27–35; cf. the note on 7:21—8:3). This punishment, however, does not mean utter destruction, for peace and normality will later be restored (vv. 42–44). The people will be reborn forever (vv. 36–41; cf. 31:31–34).

In the circumstances, then, the purchase of the field bears witness to Jeremiah's hope. Even though Jerusalem will fall very soon, and more of its people will be deported as a penance for the sins of Judah, a time will come when the people will be brought back from wherever they have been scattered. The Lord will make a New Covenant with them; they will recover their lands, and happiness will reign. New Testament hope is based on this enduring providential help from God: "Through the prophets, God forms his people in the hope of salvation, in the expectation of a new and everlasting Convenant intended for all, to be written on their hearts (cf. Is 2:2–4; Jer 31:31–34; Heb 10:16). The prophets proclaim a radical redemption of the people of God, purification from all their infidelities, a salvation which will include all the nations (cf. Ezek 36; Is 49:5–6; 53:11). Above all, the poor and humble of the Lord will bear this hope. Such holy women as Sarah, Rebecca, Rachel, Miriam, Deborah, Hannah, Judith and Esther kept alive the hope of Israel's salvation" (*Catechism of the Catholic Church*, 64). Christians therefore should nourish their hope, convinced that God never ceases to watch over them: "With God enlightening our intellect, which seems to be inactive, we understand beyond any shadow of doubt that, since the Creator takes care of everyone, even his enemies, how much more will he take care of his friends! We become convinced that no evil or trouble can befall us which will not turn out to be for our good. And so, joy and peace become more firmly rooted in our spirit, and no merely human motives can tear them from us" (St Josemaría Escrivá, *Friends of God*, 305).

The Gospel of Matthew outlines some paraphrased words from Zechariah

exercitus regis Babylonis obsidebat Ierusalem, et Ieremias propheta erat clausus in atrio custodiae, qui erat in domo regis Iudae. [3]Clauserat enim eum Sedecias rex Iudae dicens: «Quare vaticinaris dicens:

imprisoned him, saying, "Why do you prophesy and say, 'Thus
says the LORD: Behold, I am giving this city into the hand of the
king of Babylon, and he shall take it; 4Zedekiah king of Judah Jer 34:3; 38:18;
shall not escape out of the hand of the Chaldeans, but shall surely 39:5–7; 52:9–11
be given into the hand of the king of Babylon, and shall speak
with him face to face and see him eye to eye; 5and he shall take
Zedekiah to Babylon, and there he shall remain until I visit him,
says the LORD; though you fight against the Chaldeans, you shall
not succeed'?"

6Jeremiah said, "The word of the LORD came to me: 7Behold, Mt 27:3–10
Hanamel the son of Shallum your uncle will come to you and say, Lev 25:25
'Buy my field which is at Anathoth, for the right of redemption by
purchase is yours.' 8Then Hanamel my cousin came to me in the
court of the guard, in accordance with the word of the LORD, and
said to me, 'Buy my field which is at Anathoth in the land of
Benjamin, for the right of possession and redemption is yours; buy
it for yourself.' Then I knew that this was the word of the LORD.

9"And I bought the field at Anathoth from Hanamel my cousin,
and weighed out the money to him, seventeen shekels of silver. 10I
signed the deed, sealed it, got witnesses, and weighed the money
on scales. 11Then I took the sealed deed of purchase, containing
the terms and conditions, and the open copy; 12and I gave the deed Jer 36:4; 43:3;
of purchase to Baruch the son of Neriah son of Mahseiah, in the 45:1
presence of Hanamel my cousin, in the presence of the witnesses
who signed the deed of purchase, and in the presence of all the
Jews who were sitting in the court of the guard. 13I charged

11:12–13 (cf. the note on Zech 11:4–17) with references to Jeremiah's purchase of the field (vv. 6–15) and his visit to the potter (cf. 18:2–3), to show that the Scriptures were fulfilled when the Jewish authorities used Judas' pieces of silver to buy the Potter's Field (Mt 27:3–10).

"Haec dicit Dominus: Ecce ego dabo civitatem istam in manu regis Babylonis, et capiet eam; 4et Sedecias rex Iudae non effugiet de manu Chaldaeorum, sed tradetur in manus regis Babylonis, et loquetur os eius cum ore illius, et oculi eius oculos illius videbunt; 5et in Babylonem ducet Sedeciam, et ibi erit, donec visitem eum, ait Dominus; si autem dimicaveritis adversum Chaldaeos, nihil prosperum habebitis"?». 6Et dixit Ieremias: «Factum est verbum Domini ad me dicens: 7Ecce Hanameel filius Sellum patruelis tuus veniet ad te dicens: "Eme tibi agrum meum, qui est in Anathoth; tibi enim competit ex propinquitate, ut emas". 8Et venit ad me Hanameel filius patrui mei secundum verbum Domini ad vestibulum custodiae et ait ad me: "Posside agrum meum, qui est in Anathoth in terra Beniamin, quia tibi competit hereditas, et tu propinquus es, ut possideas". Intellexi autem quod verbum Domini esset 9et emi agrum ab Hanameel filio patrui mei, qui est in Anathoth, et appendi ei argentum: septem et decem siclos argenteos. 10Et scripsi in libro et signavi et adhibui testes et appendi argentum in statera. 11Et accepi librum possessionis signatum, continentem stipulationes et rata, et apertum; 12et dedi librum possessionis Baruch filio Neriae filii Maasiae in oculis Hanameel patruelis mei et in oculis testium, qui obsignaverant in libro emptionis, et in oculis omnium Iudaeorum, qui

Baruch in their presence, saying, 14‘Thus says the LORD of hosts,
the God of Israel: Take these deeds, both this sealed deed of
purchase and this open deed, and put them in an earthenware
vessel, that they may last for a long time. 15For thus says the LORD
of hosts, the God of Israel: Houses and fields and vineyards shall
again be bought in this land.’

16“After I had given the deed of purchase to Baruch the son of
Neriah, I prayed to the LORD, saying: 17‘Ah Lord GOD! It is thou
who hast made the heavens and the earth by thy great power and
Ex 20:6; by thy outstretched arm! Nothing is too hard for thee, 18who
34:6–7 showest steadfast love to thousands, but dost requite the guilt of
fathers to their children after them, O great and mighty God
Ps 33:14–15 whose name is the LORD of hosts, 19great in counsel and mighty in
deed; whose eyes are open to all the ways of men, rewarding
every man according to his ways and according to the fruit of his
doings; 20who hast shown signs and wonders in the land of Egypt,
and to this day in Israel and among all mankind, and hast made
Deut 4:34 thee a name, as at this day. 21Thou didst bring thy people Israel
out of the land of Egypt with signs and wonders, with a strong
Ex 3:8 hand and outstretched arm, and with great terror; 22and thou
Deut 26:15 gavest them this land, which thou didst swear to their fathers to
Jer 26:4 give them, a land flowing with milk and honey; 23and they entered
and took possession of it. But they did not obey thy voice or walk
in thy law; they did nothing of all thou didst command them to do.
Therefore thou hast made all this evil come upon them. 24Behold,
the siege mounds have come up to the city to take it, and because
of sword and famine and pestilence the city is given into the hands
of the Chaldeans who are fighting against it. What thou didst
speak has come to pass, and behold, thou seest it. 25Yet thou, O Lord
GOD, hast said to me, “Buy the field for money and get witnesses”—
though the city is given into the hands of the Chaldeans.’”

---

sedebant in atrio custodiae. 13Et praecepi Baruch coram eis dicens: 14Haec dicit Dominus exercituum,
Deus Israel: Sume libros istos, librum emptionis hunc signatum et librum hunc, qui apertus est; et
pones illos in vase fictili, ut permanere possint diebus multis. 15Haec enim dicit Dominus exercituum,
Deus Israel: Adhuc possidebuntur domus et agri et vineae in terra ista. 16Et oravi ad Dominum,
postquam tradidi librum possessionis Baruch filio Neriae, dicens: 17Heu, Domine Deus, ecce tu fecisti
caelum et terram in fortitudine tua magna et in brachio tuo extento; non erit tibi difficile omne verbum,
18qui facis misericordiam in milibus et reddis iniquitatem patrum in sinum filiorum eorum post eos;
Deus magne, potens, Dominus exercituum nomen eius: 19magnus consilio et potens in operibus, cuius
oculi aperti sunt super omnes vias filiorum Adam, ut reddas unicuique secundum vias suas et secundum
fructum operum eius. 20Qui posuisti signa et portenta in terra Aegypti usque ad diem hanc et in Israel
et in hominibus; et fecisti tibi nomen, sicut est dies haec. 21Et eduxisti populum tuum Israel de terra
Aegypti in signis et in portentis et in manu robusta et in brachio extento et in terrore magno. 22Et dedisti
eis terram hanc, quam iurasti patribus eorum, ut dares eis, terram fluentem lacte et melle. 23Et ingressi
sunt et possederunt eam; et non oboedierunt voci tuae et in lege tua non ambulaverunt: omnia, quae

26The word of the LORD came to Jeremiah: 27"Behold, I am Jer 32:17 Zech 8:6
the LORD, the God of all flesh; is anything too hard for me? Lk 1:37
28Therefore, thus says the LORD: Behold, I am giving this city into
the hands of the Chaldeans and into the hand of Nebuchadnezzar
king of Babylon, and he shall take it. 29The Chaldeans who are
fighting against this city shall come and set this city on fire, and
burn it, with the houses on whose roofs incense has been offered
to Baal and drink offerings have been poured out to other gods, to
provoke me to anger. 30For the sons of Israel and the sons of Judah
have done nothing but evil in my sight from their youth; the sons
of Israel have done nothing but provoke me to anger by the work
of their hands, says the LORD. 31This city has aroused my anger
and wrath, from the day it was built to this day, so that I will
remove it from my sight 32because of all the evil of the sons of Jer 2:26; 8:1 Dan 9:2
Israel and the sons of Judah which they did to provoke me to
anger—their kings and their princes, their priests and their
prophets, the men of Judah and the inhabitants of Jerusalem.
33They have turned to me their back and not their face; and though
I have taught them persistently they have not listened to receive Jer 7:30–31
instruction. 34They set up their abominations in the house which
is called by my name, to defile it. 35They built the high places of Lev 18:21
Baal in the valley of the son of Hinnom, to offer up their sons and 1 Kings 16:19
daughters to Molech, though I did not command them, nor did it Jer 7:31
enter into my mind, that they should do this abomination, to cause
Judah to sin.

36"Now therefore thus says the LORD, the God of Israel, concerning this city of which you say, 'It is given into the hand of the

---

mandasti eis, ut facerent, non fecerunt; et occurrere fecisti eis omnia mala haec. 24Ecce munitiones
exstructae sunt adversum civitatem, ut capiatur, et urbs data est in manu Chaldaeorum, qui proeliantur
adversus eam, in gladio et fame et pestilentia; et quaecumque locutus es, acciderunt, ut tu ipse cernis.
25Et tu dicis mihi, Domine Deus: Eme agrum argento et adhibe testes, cum urbs data sit in manu
Chaldaeorum». 26Et factum est verbum Domini ad Ieremiam dicens: 27«Ecce ego Dominus, Deus
universae carnis; numquid mihi difficile erit omne verbum? 28Propterea haec dicit Dominus: Ecce ego
tradam civitatem istam in manus Chaldaeorum et in manus regis Babylonis, et capiet eam. 29Et venient
Chaldaei proeliantes adversum urbem hanc et succendent eam igni et comburent eam et domos, in
quarum domatibus sacrificabant Baal et libabant diis alienis libamina ad irritandum me. 30Erant enim
filii Israel et filii Iudae iugiter facientes malum in oculis meis ab adulescentia sua, filii Israel, qui usque
nunc exacerbant me in opere manuum suarum, dicit Dominus. 31Quia in furorem et in indignationem
meam facta est mihi civitas haec a die, qua aedificaverunt eam, usque ad diem istam, qua auferetur de
conspectu meo 32propter omnem malitiam filiorum Israel et filiorum Iudae, quam fecerunt, ad
iracundiam me provocantes, ipsi et reges eorum, principes eorum et sacerdotes eorum et prophetae
eorum, viri Iudae et habitatores Ierusalem. 33Et verterunt ad me terga et non facies, cum docerem eos
diluculo consurgens et erudiens, et nollent audire, ut acciperent disciplinam. 34Et posuerunt idola sua
in domo, super quam invocatum est nomen meum, ut polluerent eam; 35et aedificaverunt excelsa Baal,
quae sunt in valle Benennom, ut initiarent filios suos et filias suas Moloch; quod non mandavi eis, nec
ascendit in cor meum, ut facerent abominationem hanc et in peccatum deducerent Iudam». 36Et nunc

king of Babylon by sword, by famine, and by pestilence':
37Behold, I will gather them from all the countries to which I
drove them in my anger and my wrath and in great indignation; I
will bring them back to this place, and I will make them dwell in
Deut 6:24 safety. 38And they shall be my people, and I will be their God. 39I
Jer 24:7; will give them one heart and one way, that they may fear me for
31:31; 50:5 ever, for their own good and the good of their children after them.
Ezek 11:19; 16:60 40I will make with them an everlasting covenant, that I will not
Jer 31:31 turn away from doing good to them; and I will put the fear of me
Deut 30:9 in their hearts, that they may not turn from me. 41I will rejoice in
doing them good, and I will plant them in this land in faithfulness,
with all my heart and all my soul.
42"For thus says the LORD: Just as I have brought all this great
evil upon this people, so I will bring upon them all the good that I
promise them. 43Fields shall be bought in this land of which you
are saying, It is a desolation, without man or beast; it is given into
the hands of the Chaldeans. 44Fields shall be bought for money,
and deeds shall be signed and sealed and witnessed, in the land of
Benjamin, in the places about Jerusalem, and in the cities of
Judah, in the cities of the hill country, in the cities of the
Shephelah, and in the cities of the Negeb; for I will restore their
fortunes, says the LORD."

Grounds for hope

33 1The word of the LORD came to Jeremiah a second time,
while he was still shut up in the court of the guard: 2"Thus

33:1–13. The "Book of Consolation" closes by giving further reasons for hope: the promises of restoration will come true (cf. 32:15). The main ground for hope is the power of the Lord: he is the creator of all things (v. 2), he rules over them, and he is the source of salvation. He is good and he never

propter ista, haec dicit Dominus, Deus Israel, ad civitatem hanc, de qua vos dicitis quod tradatur in manus regis Babylonis in gladio et in fame et in peste: 37«Ecce ego congregabo eos de universis terris, ad quas eieci eos in furore meo et in ira mea et in indignatione grandi; et reducam eos ad locum istum et habitare eos faciam confidenter. 38Et erunt mihi in populum, et ego ero eis in Deum. 39Et dabo eis cor unum et viam unam, ut timeant me universis diebus, et bene sit eis et filiis eorum post eos. 40Et feriam eis pactum sempiternum et non desinam eis benefacere et timorem meum dabo in corde eorum, ut non recedant a me. 41Et laetabor super eis, cum bene eis fecero, et plantabo eos in terra ista in veritate, in toto corde meo et in tota anima mea. 42Quia haec dicit Dominus: Sicut adduxi super populum istum omne malum hoc grande, sic adducam super eos omne bonum, quod ego loquor ad eos, 43et possidebuntur agri in terra ista, de qua vos dicitis quod deserta sit, eo quod non remanserit homo et iumentum, et data sit in manu Chaldaeorum. 44Agri ementur pecunia et scribentur in libro, et imprimetur signum, et testes adhibebuntur in terra Beniamin et in circuitu Ierusalem, in civitatibus Iudae et in civitatibus montanis et in civitatibus Sephelae et in civitatibus, quae ad austrum sunt, quia convertam sortem eorum», ait Dominus. **[33]** 1Et factum est verbum Domini ad Ieremiam secundo,

says the LORD who made the earth,[g] the LORD who formed it to
establish it—the LORD is his name: 3Call to me and I will answer Jer 29:12
you, and will tell you great and hidden things which you have not
known. 4For thus says the LORD, the God of Israel, concerning the
houses of this city and the houses of the kings of Judah which
were torn down to make a defence against the siege mounds and
before the sword:[h] 5The Chaldeans are coming in to fight[i] and to
fill them with the dead bodies of men whom I shall smite in my
anger and my wrath, for I have hidden my face from this city
because of all their wickedness. 6Behold, I will bring to it health
and healing, and I will heal them and reveal to them abundance[j] of
prosperity and security. 7I will restore the fortunes of Judah and
the fortunes of Israel, and rebuild them as they were at first. 8I will Jer 31:31
cleanse them from all the guilt of their sin against me, and I will Ezek 36:25
forgive all the guilt of their sin and rebellion against me. 9And this Heb 9:13–14
city[k] shall be to me a name of joy, a praise and a glory before all
the nations of the earth who shall hear of all the good that I do for
them; they shall fear and tremble because of all the good and all
the prosperity I provide for it.

---

forgets those who have recourse to him; he is ever-merciful and never fully rejects them. All he is waiting for is the people's decision to turn back to him; then he will hearken to them and hasten to their aid: "Call to me and I will answer you" (v. 3).

Judah and Jerusalem will be rebuilt materially and spiritually (vv. 4–8). The world will be amazed to see what God has done for them (v. 9). The city will begin to function again, and so will the temple (vv. 10–11), and life in the countryside will be idyllic (vv. 12–13). Gratitude will fill their hearts (v. 11) and they will sing their thanks, using words found in Psalm 106:1 and 107:1, and which recur throughout Psalm 136 (cf. also 1 Chron 16:34; 2 Chron 7:3; Ezra 3:11; 1 Mac 4:24).

The Hebrew of v. 5 (cf. note **i**) is very obscure.

cum adhuc clausus esset in atrio custodiae, dicens: 2«Haec dicit Dominus, qui facturus est id, Dominus, qui formaturus est illud et paraturus, Dominus nomen eius: 3Clama ad me, et exaudiam te et annuntiabo tibi grandia et inaccessibilia, quae nescis. 4Quia haec dicit Dominus, Deus Israel, super domos urbis huius et ad domos regis Iudae, quae destructae sunt, pro munitionibus et pro gladio 5venientium, ut dimicent cum Chaldaeis et impleant eas cadaveribus hominum, quos percussi in furore meo et in indignatione mea, abscondens faciem meam a civitate hac propter omnem malitiam eorum. 6Ecce ego obducam ei cicatricem et sanitatem et curabo eos et revelabo illis abundantiam pacis et veritatis 7et convertam sortem Iudae et sortem Israel et aedificabo eos sicut a principio. 8Et emundabo illos ab omni iniquitate sua, in qua peccaverunt mihi, et propitius ero cunctis iniquitatibus eorum, in quibus deliquerunt mihi et spreverunt me; 9et erit mihi in nomen et in gaudium et in laudem et in exsultationem cunctis gentibus terrae, quae audierint omnia bona, quae ego facturus sum eis; et pavebunt et

g. Gk: Heb *it* **h.** Heb obscure **i.** Cn: Heb *They are coming in to fight against the Chaldeans* **j.** Heb uncertain **k.** Heb *and it*

10"Thus says the LORD: In this place of which you say, 'It is a
waste without man or beast,' in the cities of Judah and the streets
of Jerusalem that are desolate, without man or inhabitant or beast,
1 Chron 16:34 Ezekra 3:11 there shall be heard again 11the voice of mirth and the voice of
Ps 106:1; 107:1 gladness, the voice of the bridegroom and the voice of the bride,
Jer 25:10 the voices of those who sing, as they bring thank offerings to the
house of the LORD:

'Give thanks to the LORD of hosts,
for the LORD is good,
for his steadfast love endures for ever!'

For I will restore the fortunes of the land as at first, says the LORD.
Is 65:10 12"Thus says the LORD of hosts: In this place which is waste,
without man or beast, and in all of its cities, there shall again be
habitations of shepherds resting their flocks. 13In the cities of the
hill country, in the cities of the Shephelah, and in the cities of the
Negeb, in the land of Benjamin, the places about Jerusalem, and
in the cities of Judah, flocks shall again pass under the hands of
the one who counts them, says the LORD.
14"Behold, the days are coming, says the LORD, when I will
fulfil the promise I made to the house of Israel and the house of

---

33:14–26. These verses, which are not in the Septuagint and which may be a later addition, are a collection of messianic announcements based on the unchanging nature of the Lord's promise. He will keep the Davidic dynasty in being through a descendant of David (vv. 15–16; cf. 23:5–6; 2 Sam 7:12–16) and will ensure that there are always Levites to perform the functions of priests (vv. 17–18). This pact will be as fixed as the laws that govern the universe (vv. 19–26; cf. 33:2). The "two families" (v. 24) refer to Israel (Jacob) and Judah (David).

The New Testament shows that all the promises in the "Book of Consolation" find fulfilment in Jesus Christ, son of David (cf. Mt 1:1), the eternal high priest of the New Covenant (cf. Heb 8:1–13). "God is ever faithful, and he has placed himself in our debt, not because he has received anything from us, but through all the promises he has made to us. In his own eyes, the promises seem to be of little value; he

turbabuntur in universis bonis et in omni pace, quam ego faciam eis. 10Haec dicit Dominus: Adhuc audietur in loco isto, quem vos dicitis esse desertum, eo quod non sit homo et iumentum in civitatibus Iudae et foris Ierusalem, quae desolatae sunt absque homine et absque habitatore et absque pecore, 11vox gaudii et vox laetitiae, vox sponsi et vox sponsae, vox dicentium: "Confitemini Domino exercituum, quoniam bonus Dominus, / quoniam in aeternum misericordia eius"; et portantium vota in domum Domini; reducam enim sortem terrae sicut a principio, dicit Dominus. 12Haec dicit Dominus exercituum: Adhuc erit in loco isto deserto, absque homine et absque iumento, et in cunctis civitatibus eius habitaculum pastorum accubantium gregum. 13In civitatibus montuosis et in civitatibus Sephelae et in civitatibus, quae ad austrum sunt, et in terra Beniamin et in circuitu Ierusalem et in civitatibus Iudae adhuc transibunt greges ad manum numerantis, ait Dominus. 14Ecce dies veniunt, dicit Dominus,

Judah. 15In those days and at that time I will cause a righteous Is 4:2
Branch to spring forth for David;* and he shall execute justice and Jer 23:5–6
righteousness in the land. 16In those days Judah will be saved and
Jerusalem will dwell securely. And this is the name by which it 2 Sam 7:1; 1
will be called: 'The LORD is our righteousness.' Kings 2:4 Ps 89:4
17"For thus says the LORD: David shall never lack a man to sit Lk 1:32–33
on the throne of the house of Israel, 18and the Levitical priests Is 66:21
shall never lack a man in my presence to offer burnt offerings, to Zech 4:14 Rev 1:6
burn cereal offerings, and to make sacrifices for ever." Rom 12:1; 15:16
19The word of the LORD came to Jeremiah: 20"Thus says the Heb 7:17; 13:15
LORD: If you can break my covenant with the day and my covenant Ps 89:34–38 Jer 31:35–36
with the night, so that day and night will not come at their appointed
time, 21then also my covenant with David my servant may be 2 Sam 7:1
broken, so that he shall not have a son to reign on his throne, and
my covenant with the Levitical priests my ministers. 22As the host Gen 15:5
of heaven cannot be numbered and the sands of the sea cannot be
measured, so I will multiply the descendants of David my servant,
and the Levitical priests who minister to me."
23The word of the LORD came to Jeremiah: 24"Have you not
observed what these people are saying, 'The LORD has rejected the
two families which he chose'? Thus they have despised my people
so that they are no longer a nation in their sight. 25Thus says the
LORD: If I have not established my covenant with day and night
and the ordinances of heaven and earth, 26then I will reject the
descendants of Jacob and David my servant and will not choose
one of his descendants to rule over the seed of Abraham, Isaac,
and Jacob. For I will restore their fortunes, and will have mercy
upon them."

---

has put them in writing, a compendium of promises, so that we will be able to read them, one after another, as they come to pass. As has been said many times before, the prophetic era is made up of the days in which the Lord made his promises" (St Augustine, *Enarrationes in Psalmos*, 109, 1).

et suscitabo verbum bonum, quod locutus sum ad domum Israel et ad domum Iudae. 15In diebus illis et
in tempore illo germinare faciam David germen iustitiae, et faciet iudicium et iustitiam in terra. 16In
diebus illis salvabitur Iuda, et Ierusalem habitabit confidenter; et hoc est nomen, quod vocabit eam:
Dominus iustitia nostra. 17Quia haec dicit Dominus: Non interibit de David vir, qui sedeat super
thronum domus Israel; 18et de sacerdotibus Levitis non interibit vir a facie mea, qui offerat
holocautomata et incendat sacrificium et caedat victimas omnibus diebus». 19Et factum est verbum
Domini ad Ieremiam dicens: 20«Haec dicit Dominus: Si irritum potest fieri pactum meum cum die et
pactum meum cum nocte, ut non sit dies et nox in tempore suo, 21et pactum meum irritum esse poterit
cum David servo meo, ut non sit ex eo filius, qui regnet in throno eius, et cum Levitis sacerdotibus
ministris meis. 22Sicuti enumerari non possunt stellae caeli et metiri arena maris, sic multiplicabo
semen David servi mei et Levitas ministros meos». 23Et factum est verbum Domini ad Ieremiam
dicens: 24«Numquid non vidisti quid populus hic locutus sit dicens: "Duae cognationes, quas elegerat

3. CLASHES WITH THE KINGS OF JUDAH*

Jer 21:1–7;
32:1–5 **A message for Zedekiah**
2 Kings 25:1 **34** 1The word which came to Jeremiah from the LORD, when
Jer 39:1; 52:4 Nebuchadnezzar king of Babylon and all his army and all
the kingdoms of the earth under his dominion and all the peoples
were fighting against Jerusalem and all of its cities: 2"Thus says
the LORD, the God of Israel: Go and speak to Zedekiah king of
Judah and say to him, 'Thus says the LORD: Behold, I am giving
this city into the hand of the king of Babylon, and he shall burn it
2 Kings 25:7 Jer 39:7; 52:11 with fire. 3You shall not escape from his hand, but shall surely be
Ezek 12:13; captured and delivered into his hand; you shall see the king of
17:20 2 Chron 21:19 Babylon eye to eye and speak with him face to face; and you shall
Jer 2:18 go to Babylon.' 4Yet hear the word of the LORD, O Zedekiah king

---

***34:1—36:32.** After the "Book of Consolation" (30:1—33:26), the text picks up the thread of its account of the difficulties that Jeremiah encountered in his ministry as a prophet. From the start of chapter 34 it focuses more on his dealings with kings.

34:1–7. This passage may refer to the time when the ambitious pharaoh Hophra sent assistance to Judah, which had probably been under attack from early in 588 BC (cf. Ezek 17:15–18; Lam 4:17). Lachish (v. 6), which was 38 km. (23 miles) south-west of Jerusalem, and Azekah, about 30 km. (17 miles) west of the capital, were still holding out. The Babylonian army must at some point have lifted its siege to deal with the Egyptians (cf. 37:5–11). Given this situation, Jeremiah sends Zedekiah the same message as he had put in his letter to the exiles (cf. 29:1–20) and which had given rise to opposition from the false prophets: the king should not be trying to confront the Babylonians; rather, he should submit to them; he will not escape otherwise (vv. 1–7). However, the king ignores the message.

From the tenor of the promise in vv. 4–5, one might deduce that the king would die in peace, contrary to what other passages say happened (cf. 39:7; 52:11; 2 Kings 25:7; Ezek 12:13; 17:20). These words should be taken as a conditional promise: "If you do as I say ... ".

Dominus, abiectae sunt", et populum meum despexerunt, eo quod non sit ultra gens coram eis? 25Haec dicit Dominus: Si pactum meum inter diem et noctem et leges caelo et terrae non posui, 26equidem et semen Iacob et David servi mei proiciam, ut non assumam de semine eius principes seminis Abraham et Isaac et Iacob; reducam enim sortem eorum et miserebor eis». **[34]** 1Verbum, quod factum est ad Ieremiam a Domino, quando Nabuchodonosor rex Babylonis et omnis exercitus eius universaque regna terrae, quae erant sub potestate manus eius, et omnes populi bellabant contra Ierusalem et contra omnes urbes eius, dicens: 2«Haec dicit Dominus, Deus Israel: Vade et loquere ad Sedeciam regem Iudae et dices ad eum: Haec dicit Dominus: Ecce ego tradam civitatem hanc in manus regis Babylonis, et succendet eam igni; 3et tu non effugies de manu eius, sed comprehensione capieris et in manu eius traderis, et oculi tui oculos regis Babylonis videbunt, et os eius cum ore tuo loquetur, et Babylonem

of Judah! Thus says the LORD concerning you: 'You shall not die by the sword. [5]You shall die in peace. And as spices were burned for your fathers, the former kings who were before you, so men shall burn spices for you and lament for you, saying, "Alas, lord!"' For I have spoken the word, says the LORD."

[6]Then Jeremiah the prophet spoke all these words to Zedekiah king of Judah, in Jerusalem, [7]when the army of the king of Babylon was fighting against Jerusalem and against all the cities of Judah that were left, Lachish and Azekah; for these were the only fortified cities of Judah that remained.

Slaves set free

[8]The word which came to Jeremiah from the LORD, after King Zedekiah had made a covenant with all the people in Jerusalem to

---

34:8–22. We have no details of the historical circumstances of this episode, and whether it has to do with fulfilling something laid down in the Law. According to Exodus 21:2 and Deuteronomy 15:12–18, if someone could not pay a debt, it could be cancelled by his undertaking to work for the creditor for six years; in the seventh year the debtor would go free. It could be that in the case in point the decision to set the slaves free arose from the fact that owners were unable to maintain slaves due to the siege, or that the slaves were needed for the army. Later, during the truce when the Babylonian army withdrew temporarily (cf. 37:5), some people regretted releasing their slaves and subjected them once more. But by doing that (vv. 11, 16) the sometime owners broke their solemn pact with God (vv. 15, 18). They failed to keep their agreement, solemnized by walking through the parts of the sacrificed calf (v. 18), thereby profaning the name of God (vv. 15–16). And just as this action meant that the transgressor would also be cut in pieces (cf. Gen 15:10; 1 Sam 11:7), so too they will be destroyed by God for not being faithful to their commitment (vv. 19–22). Behind the importance given here to adhering to agreements lies the vital need to be faithful to the Covenant. It serves as a reminder to keep one's promises: "The virtue of faithfulness requires each man to do what he has promised to do" (St Thomas Aquinas, *Summa theologiae*, 2–2, 101, a. 3). And St Augustine, praising this virtue, comments: "Faithfulness is beautiful. [...] As gold shines brightly before our eyes, fidelity is bright before the eyes of our heart" (*Sermones*, 9, 16).

introibis. [4]Attamen audi verbum Domini, Sedecia rex Iudae. Haec dicit Dominus ad te: Non morieris in gladio, [5]sed in pace morieris et secundum combustiones patrum tuorum regum priorum, qui fuerunt ante te, sic comburent tibi et "Vae, domine!" plangent te, quia verbum ego locutus sum», dicit Dominus. [6]Et locutus est Ieremias propheta ad Sedeciam regem Iudae universa verba haec in Ierusalem; [7]et exercitus regis Babylonis pugnabat contra Ierusalem et contra omnes civitates Iudae, quae reliquae erant, contra Lachis et contra Azeca: hae enim supererant de civitatibus Iudae urbes munitae. [8]Verbum,

Lev 25:10, make a proclamation of liberty to them, [9]that every one should set
39,46 free his Hebrew slaves, male and female, so that no one should
enslave a Jew, his brother. [10]And they obeyed, all the princes and
all the people who had entered into the covenant that every one
would set free his slave, male or female, so that they would not be
enslaved again; they obeyed and set them free. [11]But afterward
they turned around and took back the male and female slaves they
had set free, and brought them into subjection as slaves. [12]The
Ex 20:2 word of the LORD came to Jeremiah from the LORD: [13]"Thus says
the LORD, the God of Israel: I made a covenant with your fathers
Deut when I brought them out of the land of Egypt, out of the house of
15:12–13 bondage, saying, [14]'At the end of six years each of you must set
free the fellow Hebrew who has been sold to you and has served
you six[l] years; you must set him free from your service.' But your
fathers did not listen to me or incline their ears to me. [15]You recently
repented and did what was right in my eyes by proclaiming liberty,
each to his neighbour, and you made a covenant before me in the
house which is called by my name; [16]but then you turned around
and profaned my name when each of you took back his male and
female slaves, whom you had set free according to their desire,
Jer 29:18 and you brought them into subjection to be your slaves. [17]Therefore,
thus says the LORD: You have not obeyed me by proclaiming
liberty, every one to his brother and to his neighbour; behold, I
proclaim to you liberty to the sword, to pestilence, and to famine,
says the LORD. I will make you a horror to all the kingdoms of the
earth. [18]And the men who transgressed my covenant and did not

---

quod factum est ad Ieremiam a Domino, postquam percussit rex Sedecias foedus cum omni populo in Ierusalem praedicans eis libertatem, [9]ut dimitteret unusquisque servum suum et unusquisque ancillam suam, Hebraeum et Hebraeam, liberos et nequaquam dominarentur eis, id est in Iudaeo et fratre suo. [10]Audierunt ergo omnes principes et universus populus, qui inierant pactum, ut dimitteret unusquisque servum suum et unusquisque ancillam suam liberos et ultra non dominarentur eis; audierunt igitur et dimiserunt. [11]Et conversi sunt deinceps et retraxerunt servos et ancillas suas, quos dimiserant liberos, et subiugaverunt in famulos et in famulas. [12]Et factum est verbum Domini ad Ieremiam a Domino dicens: [13]«Haec dicit Dominus, Deus Israel: Ego percussi foedus cum patribus vestris in die, qua eduxi eos de terra Aegypti de domo servitutis, dicens: [14]Cum completi fuerint septem anni, dimittat unusquisque fratrem suum Hebraeum, qui venditus est ei, et serviet tibi sex annis, et dimittes eum a te liberum, et non audierunt patres vestri me nec inclinaverunt aurem suam. [15]Et conversi estis vos hodie et fecistis, quod rectum est in oculis meis, ut praedicaretis libertatem unusquisque ad proximum suum; et inistis pactum in conspectu meo in domo, super quam invocatum est nomen meum. [16]Et reversi estis et commaculastis nomen meum et reduxistis unusquisque servum suum et unusquisque ancillam suam, quos dimiseratis, ut essent liberi et suae potestatis, et subiugastis eos, ut sint vobis servi et ancillae. [17]Propterea haec dicit Dominus: Vos non audistis me, ut praedicaretis libertatem unusquisque fratri suo et unusquisque amico suo; ecce ego praedico vobis libertatem, ait Dominus, ad gladium et pestem et famem et dabo vos in commotionem cunctis regnis terrae. [18]Et dabo viros, qui praevaricantur foedus

l. Gk: Heb *seven*

keep the terms of the covenant which they made before me, I will
make like[m] the calf which they cut in two and passed between its
parts—[19]the princes of Judah, the princes of Jerusalem, the eunuchs,
the priests, and all the people of the land who passed between the
parts of the calf; [20]and I will give them into the hand of their Jer 7:33; 16:4
enemies and into the hand of those who seek their lives. Their
dead bodies shall be food for the birds of the air and the beasts of
the earth. [21]And Zedekiah king of Judah, and his princes I will
give into the hand of their enemies and into the hand of those who
seek their lives, into the hand of the army of the king of Babylon
which has withdrawn from you. [22]Behold, I will command, says Jer 9:10
the LORD, and will bring them back to this city; and they will fight
against it, and take it, and burn it with fire. I will make the cities
of Judah a desolation without inhabitant."

Jeremiah visits the Rechabites

35 [1]*The word which came to Jeremiah from the LORD in the
days of Jehoiakim the son of Josiah, king of Judah: [2]"Go to 2 Kings 10:15

35:1–19. The episode narrated here took place in the reign of Jehoiakim (v. 1), that is, some years before the events of the previous chapter and no later than 598 BC; however, when the book of Jeremiah was being assembled, the piece was included here because of the light it sheds, by way of contrast, on the previous episode. Chapter 34:8–22 spoke of how the people of Jerusalem failed to keep commitments they had made; now we learn about how faithful and obedient the Rechabites were. The only information we have about these people is what Jeremiah says here, and it gave rise to a number of legends, which were collected in an apocryphal Christian book called the *History of the Rechabites*. We do know that they were Kenites (cf. 1 Chron 2:55), and descendants of Jonadab (also called Jehonadab); the latter appears in 2 Kings 10:15, 17 in connexion with King Jehu of Israel's campaign against Baal-worship. The Rechabites were very zealous for the Lord; they had the austere lifestyle of semi-nomads; they lived in tents and did not cultivate the

meum et non observaverunt verba foederis, quibus assensi sunt in conspectu meo, sicut vitulum, quem conciderunt in duas partes et transierunt inter divisiones eius, [19]principes Iudae et principes Ierusalem, eunuchi et sacerdotes et omnis populus terrae, qui transierunt inter divisiones vituli; [20]et dabo eos in manu inimicorum suorum et in manu quaerentium animam eorum, et erit morticinum eorum in escam volatilibus caeli et bestiis terrae. [21]Et Sedeciam regem Iudae et principes eius dabo in manus inimicorum suorum et in manus quaerentium animas eorum et in manus exercituum regis Babylonis, qui recesserunt a vobis. [22]Ecce ego praecipio, dicit Dominus, et reducam eos in civitatem hanc; et proeliabuntur adversus eam et capient eam et incendent igni; et civitates Iudae dabo in solitudinem, eo quod non sit habitator». **[35]** [1]Verbum, quod factum est ad Ieremiam a Domino in diebus Ioachim filii Iosiae regis Iudae dicens: [2]«Vade ad domum Rechabitarum et loquere eis; et introduces eos in domum

m. Cn: Heb lacks *like*

the house of the Rechabites, and speak with them, and bring them
to the house of the LORD, into one of the chambers; then offer
them wine to drink." 3So I took Ja-azaniah the son of Jeremiah,
son of Habazziniah, and his brothers, and all his sons, and the
whole house of the Rechabites. 4I brought them to the house of the
LORD into the chamber of the sons of Hanan the son of Igdaliah,
the man of God, which was near the chamber of the princes,
above the chamber of Ma-aseiah the son of Shallum, keeper of the
threshold. 5Then I set before the Rechabites pitchers full of wine,
2 Kings 10:15 and cups; and I said to them, "Drink wine." 6But they answered,
"We will drink no wine, for Jonadab the son of Rechab, our father,
commanded us, 'You shall not drink wine, neither you nor your
Ex 20:12 sons for ever; 7you shall not build a house; you shall not sow seed;
Eph 6:2–3 you shall not plant or have a vineyard; but you shall live in tents
all your days, that you may live many days in the land where you
sojourn.' 8We have obeyed the voice of Jonadab the son of Rechab,
our father, in all that he commanded us, to drink no wine all our
days, ourselves, our wives, our sons, or our daughters, 9and not to
build houses to dwell in. We have no vineyard or field or seed; 10but

---

soil. They disdained the comforts of urban life and settled farming; hence their abstinence from wine (v. 6).

In those years Nebuchadnezzar's troops were terrorizing the Judean countryside, with the result that many, including the Rechabites (v. 11), sought refuge within the walls of Jerusalem. However, the Rechabites did not want to give up their ancestral customs. Jeremiah brings the Rechabites to the temple, where he offers them wine (vv. 3–5). But they decline it (vv. 6–11) and the prophet praises them for this. Thus, the obedience of the Rechabites to the voice of their ancestor Jonadab serves to underline the disobedience of Judah. This little episode is not just an anecdote about sobriety, but a lesson about the faithfulness and obedience to be seen in their behaviour. The Rechabites will be blessed by the Lord (vv. 12–19), but the people of Jerusalem will be chastised because they disobeyed the word of God.

Domini in unam exedram et dabis eis bibere vinum». 3Et assumpsi Iezoniam filium Ieremiae filii Habsaniae et fratres eius et omnes filios eius et universam domum Rechabitarum; 4et introduxi eos in domum Domini ad exedram filiorum Hanan filii Iegdaliae hominis Dei, quod erat iuxta exedram principum super exedram Maasiae filii Sellum, qui erat custos vestibuli. 5Et posui coram filiis domus Rechabitarum scyphos plenos vino et calices et dixi ad eos: «Bibite vinum». 6Qui responderunt: «Non bibemus vinum, quia Ionadab filius Rechab pater noster praecepit nobis dicens: "Non bibetis vinum, vos et filii vestri, usque in sempiternum 7et domum non aedificabitis et sementem non seretis et vineas non plantabitis, nec habebitis, sed in tabernaculis habitabitis cunctis diebus vestris, ut vivatis diebus multis super faciem terrae, in qua vos peregrinamini". 8Oboedivimus ergo voci Ionadab filii Rechab patris nostri in omnibus, quae praecepit nobis, ita ut non biberemus vinum cunctis diebus nostris, nos et mulieres nostrae, filii et filiae nostrae, 9et non aedificaremus domos ad habitandum et vineam et agrum et sementem non habuimus, 10sed habitavimus in tabernaculis; et oboedientes fecimus iuxta

we have lived in tents, and have obeyed and done all that Jonadab
our father commanded us. [11]But when Nebuchadnezzar king of
Babylon came up against the land, we said, 'Come, and let us go
to Jerusalem for fear of the army of the Chaldeans and the army
of the Syrians.' So we are living in Jerusalem."

2 Kings 24: 1–2
Jer 46:2

[12]Then the word of the LORD came to Jeremiah: [13]"Thus says
the LORD of hosts, the God of Israel: Go and say to the men of
Judah and the inhabitants of Jerusalem, Will you not receive
instruction and listen to my words? says the LORD. [14]The
command which Jonadab the son of Rechab gave to his sons, to
drink no wine, has been kept; and they drink none to this day, for
they have obeyed their father's command. I have spoken to you
persistently, but you have not listened to me. [15]I have sent to you
all my servants the prophets, sending them persistently, saying,
'Turn now every one of you from his evil way, and amend your
doings, and do not go after other gods to serve them, and then you
shall dwell in the land which I gave to you and your fathers.' But
you did not incline your ear or listen to me. [16]The sons of Jonadab
the son of Rechab have kept the command which their father gave
them, but this people has not obeyed me. [17]Therefore, thus says
the LORD, the God of hosts, the God of Israel: Behold, I am
bringing on Judah and all the inhabitants of Jerusalem all the evil
that I have pronounced against them; because I have spoken to
them and they have not listened, I have called to them and they
have not answered."

2 Kings 17:13
Jer 7:13;
25:4–7

[18]But to the house of the Rechabites Jeremiah said, "Thus says
the LORD of hosts, the God of Israel: Because you have obeyed
the command of Jonadab your father, and kept all his precepts,
and done all that he commanded you, [19]therefore thus says the
LORD of hosts, the God of Israel: Jonadab the son of Rechab shall
never lack a man to stand before me."

---

omnia, quae praecepit nobis Ionadab pater noster. [11]Cum autem ascendisset Nabuchodonosor rex Babylonis ad terram, diximus: Venite, et ingrediamur Ierusalem a facie exercitus Chaldaeorum et a facie exercitus Syriae. Et mansimus in Ierusalem». [12]Et factum est verbum Domini ad Ieremiam dicens: [13]«Haec dicit Dominus exercituum, Deus Israel: Vade et dic viris Iudae et habitatoribus Ierusalem: Numquid non recipietis disciplinam, ut oboediatis verbis meis?, dicit Dominus. [14]Praevaluerunt sermones Ionadab filii Rechab, quos praecepit filiis suis, ut non biberent vinum, et non biberunt usque ad diem hanc, quia oboedierunt praecepto patris sui; ego autem locutus sum ad vos de mane consurgens et loquens, et non oboedistis mihi. [15]Misique ad vos omnes servos meos prophetas, consurgens diluculo mittensque et dicens: Convertimini unusquisque a via sua pessima et bona facite opera vestra et nolite sequi deos alienos neque colatis eos, et habitabitis in terra, quam dedi vobis et patribus vestris, et non inclinastis aurem vestram neque audistis me. [16]Firmaverunt igitur filii Ionadab filii Rechab praeceptum patris sui, quod praeceperat eis; populus autem iste non oboedivit mihi. [17]Idcirco haec dicit Dominus exercituum, Deus Israel: Ecce ego adducam super Iudam et super omnes habitatores Ierusalem universam afflictionem, quam locutus sum adversum illos, eo quod locutus sum ad illos, et non

2 Kings 22:8–20
2 Chron 34:14–28
Jer 25:1; 45:1

The scroll written by Jeremiah and burned by order of the king

36 [1]In the fourth year of Jehoiakim the son of Josiah, king of
Judah, this word came to Jeremiah from the LORD: [2]"Take
a scroll and write on it all the words that I have spoken to you
against Israel and Judah and all the nations, from the day I spoke
to you, from the days of Josiah until today. [3]It may be that the

---

36:1–32. This episode, like the previous one, took place in the reign of Jehoiakim. Earlier we learned of the difficulties Jeremiah encountered when he preached in the temple shortly after Jehoiakim became king (cf. 7:1—8:3; 26:1–24). Things got no better over time. The incident reported here took place in 605 and 604 (vv. 1, 9). The temple is out of bounds for Jeremiah (v. 5), probably on account of what happened earlier. The Lord asks Jeremiah to write down all his prophecies from the very start of his ministry, and to read them in public. This reading makes a good impression on the people and the princes or nobles (vv. 9–19) but not on the king (vv. 20–26).

The reading of the scroll in the presence of King Jehioakim was probably a very different affair from a similar event in his father Josiah's time. According to Kings and Chronicles, the scroll of the Law was discovered in the course of building work in the temple. The scroll was brought to the king and read out in his presence; and Josiah tore his garments and was moved to repentance. Moreover, he sent messengers out to ask the prophets for counsel as to the will of the Lord (cf. 2 Kings 22:8–20; 2 Chron 34:14–28). But Jehoiakim's reaction is very different from that of his father; not only is there no question of repentance: despite attempts to dissuade him (v. 25), the king has the scroll torn up and burned, in a futile attempt to silence the words of the Lord (vv. 22–24). But man cannot erase the word of God. The Lord protects the prophet, and Jeremiah not only dictates the same material again, but adds "many similar words" (vv. 27–28, 32). The message is clear: if Josiah's conversion led God to take pity on Judah, Jehoiakim deserved the punishment that the Lord had forewarned him about, a warning he ignored (vv. 29–31; cf. 22:18–19).

Scholars have learned much from this account about how this and other biblical books came to be written: they were drafted by a disciple of the prophet, and the text was changed and added to until eventually it received its final form. In this whole process the Holy Spirit was at work.

---

audierunt, vocavi illos, et non responderunt mihi». [18]Domui autem Rechabitarum dixit Ieremias: «Haec dicit Dominus exercituum, Deus Israel: Pro eo quod oboedistis praecepto Ionadab patris vestri et custodistis omnia mandata eius et fecistis universa, quae praecepit vobis, [19]propterea haec dicit Dominus exercituum, Deus Israel: Non deficiet vir de stirpe Ionadab filii Rechab stans in conspectu meo cunctis diebus». **[36]** [1]Et factum est in anno quarto Ioachim filii Iosiae regis Iudae, factum est verbum hoc ad Ieremiam a Domino dicens: [2]«Tolle volumen libri et scribes in eo omnia verba, quae locutus sum tibi adversum Israel et Iudam et adversum omnes gentes a die qua locutus sum ad te ex diebus Iosiae usque ad diem hanc, [3]si forte, audiente domo Iudae universa mala, quae ego cogito facere

house of Judah will hear all the evil which I intend to do to them,
so that every one may turn from his evil way, and that I may
forgive their iniquity and their sin."
4Then Jeremiah called Baruch the son of Neriah, and Baruch Jer 32:12;
wrote upon a scroll at the dictation of Jeremiah all the words of 33:1; 39:15; 45:1
the LORD which he had spoken to him. 5And Jeremiah ordered Jer 20:1–2
Baruch, saying, "I am debarred from going to the house of the
LORD; 6so you are to go, and on a fast day in the hearing of all the
people in the LORD'S house you shall read the words of the LORD
from the scroll which you have written at my dictation. You shall
read them also in the hearing of all the men of Judah who come
out of their cities. 7It may be that their supplication will come
before the LORD, and that every one will turn from his evil way,
for great is the anger and wrath that the LORD has pronounced
against this people." 8And Baruch the son of Neriah did all that
Jeremiah the prophet ordered him about reading from the scroll
the words of the LORD in the LORD's house.
9In the fifth year of Jehoiakim the son of Josiah, king of Judah, 2 Chron 20:3
in the ninth month, all the people in Jerusalem and all the people
who came from the cities of Judah to Jerusalem proclaimed a fast
before the LORD. 10Then, in the hearing of all the people, Baruch Jer 26:24
read the words of Jeremiah from the scroll, in the house of the
LORD, in the chamber of Gemariah the son of Shaphan the
secretary, which was in the upper court, at the entry of the New
Gate of the LORD's house.

36:4. This has interesting things to say about the role of a scribe. Using a roll, made up of sheets of papyrus (or sometimes parchment), he would write in ink to the author's dictation (v. 18). He wrote in fairly narrow parallel columns so that the reader, rolling with one hand and unrolling with the other had three or four columns in view at any one time. Among the materials a scribe used was a penknife for sharpening his pen (v. 23).

eis, revertatur unusquisque a via sua pessima, et propitius ero iniquitati et peccato eorum». 4Vocavit
ergo Ieremias Baruch filium Neriae; et scripsit Baruch ex ore Ieremiae omnes sermones Domini, quos
locutus est ad eum, in volumine libri. 5Et praecepit Ieremias Baruch dicens: «Ego impeditus sum nec
valeo ingredi domum Domini. 6Ingredere ergo tu et lege de volumine, in quo scripsisti ex ore meo
verba Domini, audiente populo in domo Domini, in die ieiunii; insuper et audiente universo Iuda, qui
veniunt de civitatibus suis, leges eis, 7si forte cadat oratio eorum in conspectu Domini, et revertatur
unusquisque a via sua pessima, quoniam magnus furor et indignatio est, quam locutus est Dominus
adversus populum hunc». 8Et fecit Baruch filius Neriae iuxta omnia, quae praeceperat ei Ieremias
propheta, legens ex volumine sermones Domini in domo Domini. 9Factum est autem in anno quinto
Ioachim filii Iosiae regis Iudae, in mense nono, praedicaverunt ieiunium in conspectu Domini omni
populo in Ierusalem et universae multitudini, quae confluxerat de civitatibus Iudae in Ierusalem.
10Legitque Baruch ex volumine sermones Ieremiae in domo Domini, in exedra Gamariae filii Saphan

11When Micaiah the son of Gemariah, son of Shaphan, heard
Jer 26:22 all the words of the LORD from the scroll, 12he went down to the
king's house, into the secretary's chamber; and all the princes
were sitting there: Elishama the secretary, Delaiah the son of
Shemaiah, Elnathan the son of Achbor, Gemariah the son of
Shaphan, Zedekiah the son of Hananiah, and all the princes.
13And Micaiah told them all the words that he had heard, when
Baruch read the scroll in the hearing of the people. 14Then all the
princes sent Jehudi the son of Nethaniah, son of Shelemiah, son of
Cushi, to say to Baruch, "Take in your hand the scroll that you
read in the hearing of the people, and come." So Baruch the son of
Neriah took the scroll in his hand and came to them. 15And they
said to him, "Sit down and read it." So Baruch read it to them.
16When they heard all the words, they turned one to another in
fear; and they said to Baruch, "We must report all these words to
the king." 17Then they asked Baruch, "Tell us, how did you write
all these words? Was it at his dictation?" 18Baruch answered them,
"He dictated all these words to me, while I wrote them with ink on
the scroll." 19Then the princes said to Baruch, "Go and hide, you
and Jeremiah, and let no one know where you are."

20So they went into the court to the king, having put the scroll
in the chamber of Elishama the secretary; and they reported all the
words to the king. 21Then the king sent Jehudi to get the scroll,
and he took it from the chamber of Elishama the secretary; and
Jehudi read it to the king and all the princes who stood beside the
Amos 3:15 king.22 It was the ninth month, and the king was sitting in the
winter house and there was a fire burning in the brazier before
him. 23As Jehudi read three or four columns, the king would cut

---

scribae in vestibulo superiore, in introitu portae Novae domus Domini, audiente omni populo.
11Cumque audisset Michaeas filius Gamariae filii Saphan omnes sermones Domini ex libro, 12descendit
in domum regis ad exedram scribae; et ecce ibi omnes principes sedebant: Elisama scriba et Dalaias
filius Semiae et Elnathan filius Achobor et Gamarias filius Saphan et Sedecias filius Hananiae et
universi principes. 13Et nuntiavit eis Michaeas omnia verba, quae audivit, legente Baruch ex volumine
in auribus populi. 14Miserunt itaque omnes principes ad Baruch Iudi filium Nathaniae filii Selemiae filii
Chusi dicentes: «Volumen, ex quo legisti audiente populo, sume in manu tua et veni». Tulit ergo Baruch
filius Neriae volumen in manu sua et venit ad eos. 15Et dixerunt ad eum: «Sede et lege haec in auribus
nostris»; et legit Baruch in auribus eorum. 16Igitur cum audissent omnia verba, obstupuerunt
unusquisque ad proximum suum; et dixerunt ad Baruch: "Nuntiare debemus regi omnes sermones
istos". 17Et interrogaverunt Baruch dicentes: «Indica nobis, quomodo scripsisti omnes sermones istos
ex ore eius». 18Dixit autem eis Baruch: «Ex ore suo loquebatur ad me omnes sermones istos, et ego
scribebam in volumine atramento». 19Et dixerunt principes ad Baruch: «Vade et abscondere, tu et
Ieremias, et nemo sciat, ubi sitis». 20Et ingressi sunt ad regem in atrium, porro volumen deposuerunt in
exedra Elisamae scribae; et nuntiaverunt audiente rege omnes sermones. 21Misitque rex Iudi, ut sumeret
volumen; qui, tollens illud de exedra Elisamae scribae, legit audiente rege et universis principibus, qui
stabant circa regem. 22Rex autem sedebat in domo hiemali in mense nono, et posita erat arula coram eo
plena prunis; 23cumque legisset Iudi tres pagellas vel quattuor, scidit eas scalpello scribae et proiecit in

them off with a penknife and throw them into the fire in the
brazier, until the entire scroll was consumed in the fire that was in
the brazier. 24Yet neither the king, nor any of his servants who
heard all these words, was afraid, nor did they rend their garments.
25Even when Elnathan and Delaiah and Gemariah urged the king
not to burn the scroll, he would not listen to them. 26And the king Jer 45:1–8
commanded Jerahmeel the king's son and Seraiah the son of Azriel and Shelemiah the son of Abdeel to seize Baruch the secretary
and Jeremiah the prophet, but the LORD hid them.

27Now, after the king had burned the scroll with the words
which Baruch wrote at Jeremiah's dictation, the word of the LORD
came to Jeremiah:28 "Take another scroll and write on it all the
former words that were in the first scroll, which Jehoiakim the
king of Judah has burned. 29And concerning Jehoiakim king of Jer 25:9
Judah you shall say, 'Thus says the LORD, You have burned this
scroll, saying, "Why have you written in it that the king of Babylon
will certainly come and destroy this land, and will cut off from it
man and beast?" 30Therefore thus says the LORD concerning Jer 22:30
Jehoiakim king of Judah, He shall have none to sit upon the throne
of David, and his dead body shall be cast out to the heat by day
and the frost by night. 31And I will punish him and his offspring
and his servants for their iniquity; I will bring upon them, and upon
the inhabitants of Jerusalem, and upon the men of Judah, all the evil
that I have pronounced against them, but they would not hear.'"

32Then Jeremiah took another scroll and gave it to Baruch the
scribe, the son of Neriah, who wrote on it at the dictation of
Jeremiah all the words of the scroll which Jehoiakim king of
Judah had burned in the fire; and many similar words were added
to them.

---

ignem, qui erat super arulam, donec consumeretur omne volumen igni, qui erat in arula. 24Et non
timuerunt neque sciderunt vestimenta sua rex et omnes servi eius, qui audierunt universos sermones
istos. 25Verumtamen Elnathan et Dalaias et Gamarias instanter rogaverunt regem, ne combureret
librum, et non audivit eos. 26Et praecepit rex Ierameel filio regis et Saraiae filio Azriel et Selemiae filio
Abdeel, ut comprehenderent Baruch scribam et Ieremiam prophetam; abscondit autem eos Dominus.
27Et factum est verbum Domini ad Ieremiam, postquam combusserat rex volumen et sermones, quos
scripserat Baruch ex ore Ieremiae, dicens: 28«Rursum tolle volumen aliud et scribe in eo omnes
sermones priores, qui erant in primo volumine, quod combussit Ioachim rex Iudae. 29Et super Ioachim
regem Iudae dices: Haec dicit Dominus: Tu combussisti volumen illud dicens: "Quare scripsisti in eo
annuntians: Certe veniet rex Babylonis et vastabit terram hanc et cessare faciet ex illa hominem et
iumentum?". 30Propterea haec dicit Dominus contra Ioachim regem Iudae: Non erit ex eo, qui sedeat
super solium David, et cadaver eius proicietur ad aestum per diem et ad gelu per noctem; 31et visitabo
contra eum et contra semen eius et contra servos eius iniquitates suas; et adducam super eos et super
habitatores Ierusalem et super viros Iudae omne malum, quod locutus sum ad eos, et non audierunt».
32Ieremias autem tulit volumen aliud et dedit illud Baruch filio Neriae scribae; qui scripsit in eo ex ore
Ieremiae omnes sermones libri, quem combusserat Ioachim rex Iudae igni; et insuper additi sunt multi

4. THE SUFFERINGS OF JEREMIAH*

2 Kings 24:17 **Imprisonment**
Jer 13:18–19; 22:20–30 37 1Zedekiah the son of Josiah, whom Nebuchadnezzar king
of Babylon made king in the land of Judah, reigned instead
2 Kings 24:17–20 of Coniah the son of Jehoiakim. 2But neither he nor his servants
nor the people of the land listened to the words of the LORD which
he spoke through Jeremiah the prophet.
2 Kings 25:18 3King Zedekiah sent Jehucal the son of Shelemiah, and
Zephaniah the priest, the son of Ma-aseiah, to Jeremiah the
prophet, saying, "Pray for us to the LORD our God." 4Now
Jeremiah was still going in and out among the people, for he had
Jer 34:21; 44:30 not yet been put in prison. 5The army of Pharaoh had come out of
Egypt; and when the Chaldeans who were besieging Jerusalem
heard news of them, they withdrew from Jerusalem.
6Then the word of the LORD came to Jeremiah the prophet:
7"Thus says the LORD, God of Israel: Thus shall you say to the

---

***37:1—44:30.** After the accounts of persecution suffered by Jeremiah from prophets, priests and kings, the narrative now reaches a climax with the events of the days prior to the destruction of Judah and Jerusalem and the subsequent deportation (587 BC), which involved many more people than the previous one. Jeremiah spent most of this time in confinement; but he was still able to work as a prophet. He went to Egypt after the fall of Jerusalem and, according to an ancient tradition, he was martyred there.

Jeremiah comes across as a man of great integrity, and a man faithful to God despite adverse circumstances. These chapters therefore are often read as a prefiguring of the passion of Christ. St Isidore of Seville comments that "in his words and through his sufferings, Jeremiah is a figure of the passion and death of the Lord our Saviour" (*Allegoriae quaedam*, 108). And St Thomas says that the passion of Jesus "was foretold by Jeremiah by words and signs, and explicitly foreshadowed in his sufferings" (*Summa theologiae*, 3, 27, a. 6c).

37:1–21. The narrative moves forward some years. The situation described here is similar to that dealt with in chapter 21, and this episode probably

sermones similes illis. **[37]** 1Et regnavit rex Sedecias filius Iosiae pro Iechonia filio Ioachim; quem constituit regem Nabuchodonosor rex Babylonis in terra Iudae. 2Et non oboedivit, ipse et servi eius et populus terrae, verbis Domini, quae locutus est in manu Ieremiae prophetae. 3Et misit rex Sedecias Iuchal filium Selemiae et Sophoniam filium Maasiae sacerdotem ad Ieremiam prophetam dicens: «Ora pro nobis Dominum Deum nostrum». 4Ieremias autem libere ambulabat in medio populi; non enim miserant eum in custodiam carceris. 5Igitur exercitus pharaonis egressus est de Aegypto, et audientes Chaldaei, qui obsidebant Ierusalem, huiuscemodi nuntium recesserunt ab Ierusalem. 6Et factum est verbum Domini ad Ieremiam prophetam dicens: 7«Haec dicit Dominus, Deus Israel: Sic dicetis regi Iudae, qui misit vos ad me interrogandum: Ecce exercitus pharaonis, qui egressus est vobis in auxilium,

king of Judah who sent you to me to inquire of me, 'Behold,
Pharaoh's army which came to help you is about to return to
Egypt, to its own land. [8]And the Chaldeans shall come back and
fight against this city; they shall take it and burn it with fire. [9]Thus
says the LORD, Do not deceive yourselves, saying, "The Chaldeans
will surely stay away from us," for they will not stay away. [10]For
even if you should defeat the whole army of Chaldeans who are
fighting against you, and there remained of them only wounded
men, every man in his tent, they would rise up and burn this city
with fire.'"

[11]Now when the Chaldean army had withdrawn from Jerusalem Jer 32:1
at the approach of Pharaoh's army, [12]Jeremiah set out from
Jerusalem to go to the land of Benjamin to receive his portion[n]
there among the people. [13]When he was at the Benjamin Gate, a

---

did not take place much later than then (cf. the note on 21:1–10 and 34:1–7). The Babylonians lifted the siege temporarily in order to deal with the Egyptians (v. 5), and Zedekiah, who already knew what the city's fate would be because of its failure to submit to the Babylonians (v. 3), sent messengers to the prophet in the hope of hearing better news. He seems to be still expecting a miracle along the lines of what happened in King Hezekiah's time (cf. the note on 21:1–10). However, Jeremiah only confirms his earlier message (vv. 6–10).

Jeremiah uses the situation to sort out some family affairs in his native town Anathoth (cf. vv. 11–12). His visit may have had to do with his purchase of a field (cf. 32:1–15). However, it was not at all clear what would happen in the war, and quite a number of people must have been trying to flee (cf. 38:19; 39:9). The prophet is accused of treason for wanting to visit territory held by the enemy, and he is eventually imprisoned in a private house which seems to have had cellars that could be used as a dungeon (v. 17). Despite being treated like this, the prophet stands up to the king; without taking back anything he said, he tells Zedekiah how unjustly he has treated him (vv. 18–21). The whole episode shows Jeremiah's nobility and integrity. He maintains his love for God and for the truth, regardless of what danger it may bring: "Don't be afraid of the truth, even though the truth may mean your death" (St Josemaría Escrivá, *The Way*, 34).

revertetur in terram suam in Aegyptum; [8]et redient Chaldaei et bellabunt contra civitatem hanc et capient eam et succendent eam igni. [9]Haec dicit Dominus: Nolite decipere animas vestras dicentes: "Euntes abibunt et recedent a nobis Chaldaei", quia non abibunt. [10]Sed et si percusseritis omnem exercitum Chaldaeorum, qui proeliantur adversum vos, et derelicti fuerint ex eis aliqui vulnerati, singuli de tentorio suo consurgent et incendent civitatem hanc igni». [11]Ergo cum recessisset exercitus Chaldaeorum ab Ierusalem propter exercitum pharaonis, [12]egressus est Ieremias de Ierusalem, ut iret in terram Beniamin et divideret ibi possessionem in conspectu populi. [13]Cumque pervenisset ad portam

n. Heb obscure

sentry there named Irijah the son of Shelemiah, son of Hananiah,
seized Jeremiah the prophet, saying, "You are deserting to the
Chaldeans." [14]And Jeremiah said, "It is false; I am not deserting
to the Chaldeans." But Irijah would not listen to him, and seized
Jeremiah and brought him to the princes. [15]And the princes were
enraged at Jeremiah, and they beat him and imprisoned him in the
house of Jonathan the secretary, for it had been made a prison.
[16]When Jeremiah had come to the dungeon cells, and remained
there many days, [17]King Zedekiah sent for him, and received him.
The king questioned him secretly in his house, and said, "Is there
any word from the LORD?" Jeremiah said, "There is." Then he
said, "You shall be delivered into the hand of the king of
Babylon." [18]Jeremiah also said to King Zedekiah, "What wrong
have I done to you or your servants or this people, that you have
put me in prison? [19]Where are your prophets who prophesied to
you, saying, 'The king of Babylon will not come against you and
against this land'? [20]Now hear, I pray you, O my lord the king: let
my humble plea come before you, and do not send me back to the
Jer 32:2; 38:9; house of Jonathan the secretary, lest I die there." [21]So King
52:6 Zedekiah gave orders, and they committed Jeremiah to the court
of the guard; and a loaf of bread was given him daily from the
bakers' street, until all the bread of the city was gone. So Jeremiah
remained in the court of the guard.

Jeremiah and the cistern of Malchiah

Jer 37:3; 21:1 **38** [1]Now Shephatiah the son of Mattan, Gedaliah the son of
Pashhur, Jucal the son of Shelemiah, and Pashhur the son of

38:1–28. Like the previous chapter, this one also contains an account concerning Jeremiah's arrest (vv. 1–13) and a conversation that he had with the king (vv. 14–28). Jeremiah keeps on urging submission to Babylon and

Beniamin, erat ibi custos portae nomine Ierias filius Selemiae filii Hananiae; et apprehendit Ieremiam prophetam dicens: «Ad Chaldaeos profugis». [14]Et respondit Ieremias: «Falsum est! Non fugio ad Chaldaeos». Et non audivit eum; sed comprehendit Ierias Ieremiam et adduxit eum ad principes. [15]Et irati sunt principes contra Ieremiam, quem caesum miserunt in carcerem, qui erat in domo Ionathan scribae; eam enim in carcerem fecerant. [16]Itaque ingressus est Ieremias in domum laci fornice tectam; et sedit ibi Ieremias diebus multis. [17]Mittens autem Sedecias rex tulit eum et interrogavit eum in domo sua abscondite et dixit: «Putasne est sermo a Domino?». Et dixit Ieremias: «Est»; et ait: «In manus regis Babylonis traderis». [18]Et dixit Ieremias ad regem Sedeciam: «Quid peccavi tibi et servis tuis et populo isti, quia misistis me in domum carceris? [19]Ubi sunt prophetae vestri, qui prophetabant vobis et dicebant: "Non veniet rex Babylonis super vos et super terram hanc"? [20]Nunc ergo audi, obsecro, domine mi rex; valeat deprecatio mea in conspectu tuo, et ne me remittas in domum Ionathan scribae, ne moriar ibi». [21]Praecepit ergo rex Sedecias, ut traderetur Ieremias in vestibulo custodiae, et daretur ei torta panis cotidie ex vico Pistorum, donec consumerentur omnes panes de civitate. Et mansit Ieremias in vestibulo custodiae. **[38]** [1]Audivit autem Saphatias filius Matthan et Godolias filius

Malchiah heard the words that Jeremiah was saying to all the
people, 2"Thus says the LORD, He who stays in this city shall die
by the sword, by famine, and by pestilence; but he who goes out
to the Chaldeans shall live; he shall have his life as a prize of war,

Jer 21:9; 39:18; 45:5 2 Kings 25:1–21

---

personal conversion; the princes, or nobles, will hear none of this. Wary, perhaps, about putting an envoy of God to death, they put him into a big water-tank, from which he is rescued by a court official, a foreigner. Having escaped in this way, the prophet manages to stay in the hall of the court guard without anyone observing him, it seems (v. 13). One ecclesiastical writer, Olympiodorus, interpreted Jeremiah's imprisonment as a prefigurement of Jesus' passion and death. Commenting on v. 6, he said: "The prophet becomes a figure of the mystery of Christ, who was handed over by Pilate to the Jews, descended into hell, and was raised from the dead. Jeremiah climbs out of the cistern he was cast into; Scripture often refers to hell as a cistern" (*Fragmenta in Jeremiam*, 38, 6).

In his conversation with the king, Jeremiah re-affirms his message (vv. 17–18); Zedekiah is afraid of what will happen if he surrenders (v. 19), but the prophet tells him he should trust in the Lord. If he fails to do so, his humiliation will be great; even the women will despise him (v. 22). Zedekiah will be stuck in the mire (v. 22)—and will suffer more than Jeremiah has suffered (v. 6).

Without saying why, the king asks the prophet not to reveal his prophecy (vv. 24–26); and so Jeremiah keeps quiet about it when the princes interrogate him about his interview with the king (v. 27). The prophet's response does not mean that he is deceiving them (they had no right to be party to Jeremiah's conversation with the king) or that he fears them; we know that his courage was never in question.

These verses show how very different in attitude Zedekiah and Jeremiah were. Zedekiah used all his ingenuity and political skill to save himself and Judah from their enemies: but he lost both life and land. Jeremiah, however, preached the word of God without diluting it in any way—even though people clamoured for his death (v. 4); and when the Babylonians won the day, he was released from prison and survived (v. 28). It is very much what Jesus taught: "Whoever would save his life will lose it, and whoever loses his life for my sake will find it" (Mt 16:25).

Most of this passage forms a reading in the *Divine Office* for the 23rd Sunday in Ordinary Time, and the response to that reading is a call to serve the Lord, no matter what trials that involves. It links some words from Judith 8:23 (Vg) with others from St Paul to do with predicaments he encountered that were similar to the prophet's: "as servants of God we commend ourselves in every way: through great endurance, in afflictions, hardships, calamities, beatings, imprisonments" (2 Cor 6:4–5a).

Phassur et Iuchal filius Selemiae et Phassur filius Melchiae sermones, quos Ieremias loquebatur ad omnem populum dicens: 2«Haec dicit Dominus: Quicumque manserit in civitate hac, morietur gladio

and live. [3]Thus says the LORD, This city shall surely be given into the hand of the army of the king of Babylon and be taken." [4]Then the princes said to the king, "Let this man be put to death, for he is weakening the hands of the soldiers who are left in this city, and the hands of all the people, by speaking such words to them. For this man is not seeking the welfare of this people, but their harm." [5]King Zedekiah said, "Behold, he is in your hands; for the king can do nothing against you." [6]So they took Jeremiah and cast him into the cistern of Malchiah, the king's son, which was in the court of the guard, letting Jeremiah down by ropes. And there was no water in the cistern, but only mire, and Jeremiah sank in the mire.

Jer 39:16 [7]When Ebed-melech the Ethiopian, a eunuch, who was in the king's house, heard that they had put Jeremiah into the cistern—the king was sitting in the Benjamin Gate—[8]Ebed-melech went from the king's house and said to the king,[9] "My lord the king, these men have done evil in all that they did to Jeremiah the prophet by casting him into the cistern; and he will die there of hunger, for there is no bread left in the city." [10]Then the king commanded Ebed-melech, the Ethiopian, "Take three men with you from here, and lift Jeremiah the prophet out of the cistern before he dies." [11]So Ebed-melech took the men with him and went to the house of the king, to a wardrobe of[o] the storehouse, and took from there old rags and worn-out clothes, which he let down to Jeremiah in the cistern by ropes. [12]Then Ebed-melech the Ethiopian said to Jeremiah, "Put the rags and clothes between your armpits and the ropes." Jeremiah did so. [13]Then they drew Jeremiah up with ropes and lifted him out of the cistern. And Jeremiah remained in the court of the guard.

---

et fame et peste; qui autem profugerit ad Chaldaeos, vivet, et erit anima eius quasi spolium et vivet. [3]Haec dicit Dominus: Certe tradetur civitas haec in manu exercitus regis Babylonis, et capiet eam». [4]Et dixerunt principes regi: «Rogamus, ut occidatur homo iste; de industria enim dissolvit manus virorum bellantium, qui remanserunt in civitate hac, et manus universi populi loquens ad eos iuxta verba haec; siquidem homo iste non quaerit pacem populo huic sed malum». [5]Et dixit rex Sedecias: «Ecce ipse in manibus vestris est; nequit enim rex vobis quidquam negare» [6]Tulerunt ergo Ieremiam et proiecerunt eum in lacum Melchiae filii regis, qui erat in vestibulo custodiae. Et submiserunt Ieremiam funibus. Et in lacu non erat aqua sed lutum; descendit itaque Ieremias in caenum. [7]Audivit autem Abdemelech Aethiops, vir eunuchus, qui erat in domo regis, quod misissent Ieremiam in lacum; porro rex sedebat in porta Beniamin. [8]Et egressus est Abdemelech de domo Regis et locutus est ad regem dicens: [9]«Domine mi rex, malefecerunt viri isti omnia, quaecumque perpetrarunt contra Ieremiam prophetam, mittentes eum in lacum, ut moriatur ibi fame; non sunt enim panes ultra in civitate». [10]Praecepit itaque rex Abdemelech Aethiopi dicens: «Tolle tecum hinc triginta viros et leva Ieremiam prophetam de lacu, antequam moriatur». [11]Assumptis ergo Abdemelech secum viris, ingressus est domum regis, in conclave, quod erat sub thesauro, et tulit inde pannos ex vestibus veteribus et scissis et submisit eos ad Ieremiam in lacum per funiculos. [12]Dixitque Abdemelech Aethiops ad Ieremiam: «Pone veteres pannos

o. Cn: Heb *to under*

[14]King Zedekiah sent for Jeremiah the prophet and received him at the third entrance of the temple of the LORD. The king said to Jeremiah, "I will ask you a question; hide nothing from me." [15]Jeremiah said to Zedekiah, "If I tell you, will you not be sure to put me to death? And if I give you counsel, you will not listen to
me." [16]Then King Zedekiah swore secretly to Jeremiah, "As the Is 57:16
LORD lives, who made our souls, I will not put you to death or Jer 37:17
deliver you into the hand of these men who seek your life."

[17]Then Jeremiah said to Zedekiah, "Thus says the LORD, the God of hosts, the God of Israel, If you will surrender to the princes of the king of Babylon, then your life shall be spared, and this city shall not be burned with fire, and you and your house shall live. [18]But if you do not surrender to the princes of the king of Babylon, then this city shall be given into the hand of the Chaldeans, and they shall burn it with fire, and you shall not escape from their hand." [19]King Zedekiah said to Jeremiah, "I am afraid of the Jews who have deserted to the Chaldeans, lest I be handed over to them and they abuse me." [20]Jeremiah said, "You shall not be given to them. Obey now the voice of the LORD in what I say to you, and it shall be well with you, and your life shall be spared. [21]But if you refuse to surrender, this is the vision which the LORD has shown to me: [22]Behold, all the women left in the house of the king of Judah were being led out to the princes of the king of Babylon and were saying,

'Your trusted friends have deceived you
  and prevailed against you;
now that your feet are sunk in the mire,
  they turn away from you.'

[23]All your wives and your sons shall be led out to the Chaldeans, and you yourself shall not escape from their hand, but shall be seized by the king of Babylon; and this city shall be burned with fire."

---

et haec scissa sub scapuli et postea funes». Fecit ergo Ieremias sic; [13]et extraxerunt Ieremiam funibus et eduxerunt eum de lacu. Mansit autem Ieremias in vestibulo custodiae. [14]Et misit rex Sedecias et tulit ad se Ieremiam prophetam ad ostium tertium, quod erat in domo Domini; et dixit rex ad Ieremiam: «Interrogo ego te sermonem, ne abscondas a me aliquid». [15]Dixit autem Ieremias ad Sedeciam: «Si annuntiavero tibi, numquid non interficies me? Et si consilium dedero tibi, non me audies». [16]Iuravit ergo rex Sedecias Ieremiae clam dicens: «Vivit Dominus, qui fecit nobis animam hanc, non occidam te et non tradam te in manu virorum istorum, qui quaerunt animam tuam». [17]Et dixit Ieremias ad Sedeciam: «Haec dicit Dominus exercituum, Deus Israel: Si profectus exieris ad principes regis Babylonis, vivet anima tua, et civitas haec non succendetur igni, et salvus eris tu et domus tua; [18]si autem non exieris ad principes regis Babylonis, tradetur civitas haec in manu Chaldaeorum, et succendent eam igni, et tu non effugies de manu eorum». [19]Et dixit rex Sedecias ad Ieremiam: «Sollicitus sum propter Iudaeos, qui transfugerunt ad Chaldaeos, ne forte tradar in manus eorum, et illudant mihi». [20]Respondit autem Ieremias: «Non te tradent; audi, quaeso, vocem Domini, quam ego loquor ad te, et bene tibi erit, et vivet anima tua. [21]Quod si nolueris egredi, iste est sermo, quem ostendit

[24]Then Zedekiah said to Jeremiah, "Let no one know of these
words and you shall not die. [25]If the princes hear that I have
spoken with you and come to you and say to you, 'Tell us what
you said to the king and what the king said to you; hide nothing
Jer 37:20 from us and we will not put you to death,' [26]then you shall say to
them, 'I made a humble plea to the king that he would not send me
back to the house of Jonathan to die there.'" [27]Then all the princes
came to Jeremiah and asked him, and he answered them as the king
had instructed him. So they left off speaking with him, for the
conversation had not been overheard. [28]And Jeremiah remained in
the court of the guard until the day that Jerusalem was taken.

2 Kings 25:1–4
Jer 52:1–34

Jeremiah is released after the fall of Jerusalem

39 [1]In the ninth year of Zedekiah king of Judah, in the tenth
month, Nebuchadnezzar king of Babylon and all his army

39:1—40:6. This passage goes into some detail about events in the aftermath of the fall and destruction of Jerusalem in August 589 BC, after a siege lasting a year and a half; it summarizes information available in 52:1–34 and 2 Kings 25:1–30. The tragic outcome of the king's attempt to flee with his family confirms what the prophet foretold. Zedekiah is taken to Riblah, in Syria, and, after being tortured, is brought to Babylon. Presumably he died there, for the Bible has nothing more to say about him (an indication, perhaps, of its disapproval of the last king of Judah). But Jeremiah is set free (39:11–14; 40:1–6), probably after having been included in the group of captives brought to Ramah on their way to exile (40:1; cf. 31:15–17). He decides to stay behind with Gedaliah, the nephew of Shaphan (secretary to the pious King Josiah) and the son of Ahikam, the prophet's protector. Gedaliah had been appointed governor of Judah by Nebuchadnezzar after the fall of Jerusalem (cf. 40:7) and had established himself at Mizpah, 13 km. (8 miles) north of the city.

The fate of Jerusalem and of Zedekiah is in sharp contrast to the salvation of the Ethiopian official

mihi Dominus: [22]Ecce omnes mulieres, quae remanserunt in domo regis Iudae, educentur ad principes regis Babylonis et ipsae dicent: "Seduxerunt te et praevaluerunt adversum te / viri pacifici tui; / demersi sunt in caeno pedes tui, / illi autem recesserunt a te". [23]Et omnes uxores tuae et filii tui educentur ad Chaldaeos, et non effugies manus eorum, sed in manu regis Babylonis capieris; et civitatem hanc comburet igni». [24]Dixit ergo Sedecias ad Ieremiam: «Nullus sciat verba haec, et non morieris. [25]Si autem audierint principes quia locutus sum tecum, et venerint ad te et dixerint tibi: "Indica nobis, quid locutus sis cum rege, ne celes nos, et non te interficiemus, et quid locutus est tecum rex", [26]dices ad eos: "Prostravi ego preces meas coram rege, ne me reduci iuberet in domum Ionathan, et ibi morerer"». [27]Venerunt ergo omnes principes ad Ieremiam et interrogaverunt eum, et locutus est eis iuxta omnia verba, quae praeceperat ei rex; et cessaverunt ab eo: nihil enim fuerat auditum. [28]Mansit vero Ieremias in vestibulo custodiae usque ad diem, quo capta est Ierusalem. Et factum est ut caperetur Ierusalem. **[39]** [1]Anno nono Sedeciae regis Iudae, mense decimo, venit Nabuchodonosor rex Babylonis et omnis

came against Jerusalem and besieged it; [2]in the eleventh year of
Zedekiah, in the fourth month, on the ninth day of the month, a
breach was made in the city. [3]When Jerusalem was taken,[p] all the 2 Kings 18:17;
princes of the king of Babylon came and sat in the middle gate: 25:4–12
Nergal-sharezer, Samgar-nebo, Sarsechim the Rabsaris, Nergal- Jer 38:17
sharezer the Rabmag, with all the rest of the officers of the king of
Babylon.[4] When Zedekiah king of Judah and all the soldiers saw
them, they fled, going out of the city at night by way of the king's
garden through the gate between the two walls; and they went
toward the Arabah. [5]But the army of the Chaldeans pursued them,
and overtook Zedekiah in the plains of Jericho; and when they had
taken him, they brought him up to Nebuchadnezzar king of
Babylon, at Riblah, in the land of Hamath; and he passed sentence
upon him. [6]The king of Babylon slew the sons of Zedekiah at
Riblah before his eyes; and the king of Babylon slew all the
nobles of Judah. [7]He put out the eyes of Zedekiah, and bound him Jer 34:2
in fetters to take him to Babylon. [8]The Chaldeans burned the
king's house and the house of the people, and broke down the
walls of Jerusalem. [9]Then Nebuzaradan, the captain of the guard,

---

(39:15–18) and the release of the prophet (40:1–6). Zedekiah, not trusting in God, had tried to save his life and he perished. The Ethiopian put his trust in God (witness his action in saving Jeremiah from death: 38:7–13) and was saved from the Babylonians and from his enemies (39:17). Jeremiah was set free because he was faithful to the word of the Lord that foretold the fall of Jerusalem. All these events, which are part of God's providence, bear out the truth of the message spoken by the prophet; despite all kinds of opposition, he never failed to speak out. When he clashed with Hananiah, there were those who were in doubt as to which of them was speaking the true word of God (cf. 28:1–17), but events have proved Jeremiah right. Once again, the biblical text points out that the word of God always comes true and that happiness lies in trusting God and being faithful to his word.

exercitus eius ad Ierusalem et obsidebant eam. [2]Undecimo autem anno Sedeciae, mense quarto, nona
mensis, aperta est civitas; [3]et ingressi sunt omnes principes regis Babylonis et sederunt in porta Media:
Nergelsereser Samegarnabu, Sarsachim princeps eunuchorum, Nergelsereser princeps magorum et
omnes reliqui principes regis Babylonis. [4]Cumque vidisset eos Sedecias rex Iudae et omnes viri
bellatores, fugerunt et egressi sunt nocte de civitate per viam horti regis et per portam, quae erat inter
duos muros, et egressi sunt ad viam Arabae. [5]Persecutus est autem eos exercitus Chaldaeorum; et
comprehenderunt Sedeciam in campestribus Iericho et captum adduxerunt ad Nabuchodonosor regem
Babylonis in Rebla, quae est in terra Emath; et locutus est ad eum iudicia. [6]Et occidit rex Babylonis
filios Sedeciae in Rebla in oculis eius, et omnes nobiles Iudae occidit rex Babylonis; [7]oculos quoque
Sedeciae eruit et vinxit eum compedibus, ut duceretur in Babylonem. [8]Domum quoque regis et domum
vulgi succenderunt Chaldaei igni; et murum Ierusalem subverterunt. [9]Et reliquias populi, quae

p. This clause has been transposed from the end of Chapter 38

carried into exile to Babylon the rest of the people who were left
in the city, those who had deserted to him, and the people who
remained. [10]Nebuzaradan, the captain of the guard, left in the land
of Judah some of the poor people who owned nothing, and gave
them vineyards and fields at the same time.

[11]Nebuchadnezzar king of Babylon gave command concerning
Jeremiah through Nebuzaradan, the captain of the guard, saying,
[12]"Take him, look after him well and do him no harm, but deal
with him as he tells you." [13]So Nebuzaradan the captain of the
guard, Nebushazban the Rabsaris, Nergal-sharezer the Rabmag,
2 Kings 25:22–25 and all the chief officers of the king of Babylon [14]sent and took
Jeremiah from the court of the guard. They entrusted him to
Jer 40:5–9: 11,16 Gedaliah the son of Ahikam, son of Shaphan, that he should take
him home. So he dwelt among the people.

Jer 45:1–5 [15]The word of the LORD came to Jeremiah while he was shut up
in the court of the guard: [16]"Go, and say to Ebed-melech the
Ethiopian, 'Thus says the LORD of hosts, the God of Israel:
Behold, I will fulfil my words against this city for evil and not for
good, and they shall be accomplished before you on that day.
[17]But I will deliver you on that day, says the LORD, and you shall
not be given into the hand of the men of whom you are afraid.
Jer 21:9; 38:2 [18]For I will surely save you, and you shall not fall by the sword;
but you shall have your life as a prize of war, because you have
put your trust in me, says the LORD.'"

40 [1]The word that came to Jeremiah from the LORD after
Nebuzaradan the captain of the guard had let him go from

40:7—41:18. This account of the failed attempt to re-establish order among those who had not been deported fills out what is reported in 2 Kings 25:22–26. However, the prophet is not mentioned. The Babylonian authorities

remanserant in civitate, et perfugas, qui transfugerant ad eum, et superfluos artificum, qui remanserant, transtulit Nabuzardan magister satellitum in Babylonem. [10]Et de plebe pauperum, qui nihil penitus habebant, dimisit Nabuzardan magister satellitum in terra Iudae; et dedit eis vineas et agros in die illa. [11]Praeceperat autem Nabuchodonosor rex Babylonis de Ieremia Nabuzardan magistro satellitum dicens: [12]«Tolle illum et pone super eum oculos tuos nihilque ei mali facias, sed, ut voluerit, sic facies ei». [13]Misit ergo Nabuzardan princeps satellitum et Nabusezban princeps eunuchorum et Nergelsereser princeps magorum et omnes optimates regis Babylonis [14]miserunt et tulerunt Ieremiam de vestibulo custodiae et tradiderunt eum Godoliae filio Ahicam filii Saphan, ut duceret domum. Et habitavit in populo. [15]Ad Ieremiam autem factus fuerat sermo Domini, cum clausus esset in vestibulo custodiae, dicens: [16]«Vade et dic Abdemelech Aethiopi dicens: Haec dicit Dominus exercituum, Deus Israel: Ecce ego inducam sermones meos super civitatem hanc in malum et non in bonum; et erunt in conspectu tuo in die illa. [17]Et liberabo te in die illa, ait Dominus, et non traderis in manus virorum, quos tu formidas; [18]sed eruens liberabo te, et gladio non cades, sed erit tibi anima tua quasi spolium, quia in me habuisti fiduciam», ait Dominus. **[40]** [1]Sermo, qui factus est ad Ieremiam a Domino, postquam dimissus est

Ramah, when he took him bound in chains along with all the
captives of Jerusalem and Judah who were being exiled to
Babylon. [2]The captain of the guard took Jeremiah and said to him, Deut 29:24–25
"The LORD your God pronounced this evil against this place; [3]the Jer 50:7
LORD has brought it about, and has done as he said. Because you
sinned against the LORD, and did not obey his voice, this thing has
come upon you. [4]Now, behold, I release you today from the chains
on your hands. If it seems good to you to come with me to
Babylon, come, and I will look after you well; but if it seems
wrong to you to come with me to Babylon, do not come. See, the
whole land is before you; go wherever you think it good and right

---

had left Gedaliah, a man of upright character (cf. 40:14–16), as governor of Judah, and those who, like Jeremiah, peaceably accepted Babylonian rule, tried to get back to some sort of normal life. However, there were others who despised this governor imposed by the foreigners. The king of Ammon, perhaps envious of Gedaliah, took advantage of this and encouraged Ishmael, a distant relative of the house of David (41:1), to assassinate the governor. Within two months (cf. 39:2 and 41:1), a promising situation had ended in tragedy. Ishmael sowed terror and slew almost an entire group of pilgrims from the north who, after the destruction of Jerusalem, were making their way to the city, displaying their grief, intent on offering sacrifices in the temple (41:4–7). It is not said why he killed them; it seems it was only plunder he was after (41:8), but he despised Mizpah. The cistern, built by Asa (cf. 1 Kings 15:22) and crucial to the survival of the city, was filled with dead bodies (41:9). Ishmael and his men took prisoner those who had been with Gedaliah in Mizpah; but, attempting to cross over to the Ammonites, they were cut off by Johanan, a short distance from there. Even so, the prisoners were afraid to return to Mizpah, fearing what the Babylonians would do when they learned of the assassination of Gedaliah; so they set off for Egypt. Jeremiah may have been in this group of prisoners, for he had meant to stay with Gedaliah (cf. 40:6); however, he is not mentioned in this account. Perhaps the editor of the book did not want to involve him in yet another disaster; or maybe he simply did not know where the prophet was at this time.

The anniversary of the assassination became a Jewish day of fasting (Zech 7:5; 8:19).

a Nabuzardan magistro satellitum de Rama, quando tulit eum vinctum catenis in medio omnium, qui migrabant de Ierusalem et Iuda et ducebantur in Babylonem. [2]Tollens ergo princeps satellitum Ieremiam, dixit ad eum: «Dominus Deus tuus locutus est malum hoc super locum istum [3]et adduxit; et fecit Dominus, sicut locutus est, quia peccastis Domino et non audistis vocem eius, et factus est vobis sermo hic. [4]Nunc ergo ecce solvi te hodie de catenis, quae sunt in manibus tuis. Si placet tibi, ut venias mecum in Babylonem, veni, et ponam oculos meos super te; si autem displicet tibi venire mecum in Babylonem, reside; ecce omnis terra in conspectu tuo est: quod elegeris et quo placuerit tibi ut vadas, illuc perge». [5]Cum nondum reverteretur, dixit: «Revertere ad Godoliam filium Ahicam filii Saphan,

2 Kings 25:22–25 to go. 5If you remain,[q] then return to Gedaliah the son of Ahikam,
son of Shaphan, whom the king of Babylon appointed governor of
the cities of Judah, and dwell with him among the people; or go
wherever you think it right to go." So the captain of the guard gave
him an allowance of food and a present, and let him go. 6Then
Jeremiah went to Gedaliah the son of Ahikam, at Mizpah, and
dwelt with him among the people who were left in the land.

Gedeliah the governor, and his assassination

2 Kings 25:23–24 7When all the captains of the forces in the open country and their
men heard that the king of Babylon had appointed Gedaliah the
son of Ahikam governor in the land, and had committed to him
men, women, and children, those of the poorest of the land who
had not been taken into exile to Babylon, 8they went to Gedaliah
at Mizpah—Ishmael the son of Nethaniah, Johanan the son of
Kareah, Seraiah the son of Tanhumeth, the sons of Ephai the
Netophathite, Jezaniah the son of the Ma-acathite, they and their
men. 9Gedaliah the son of Ahikam, son of Shaphan, swore to them
and their men, saying, "Do not be afraid to serve the Chaldeans.
Dwell in the land, and serve the king of Babylon, and it shall be
well with you. 10As for me, I will dwell at Mizpah, to stand for
you before the Chaldeans who will come to us; but as for you,
gather wine and summer fruits and oil, and store them in your
Is 4:3 vessels, and dwell in your cities that you have taken." 11Likewise,
when all the Jews who were in Moab and among the Ammonites
and in Edom and in other lands heard that the king of Babylon had
left a remnant in Judah and had appointed Gedaliah the son of
Ahikam, son of Shaphan, as governor over them, 12then all the
Jews returned from all the places to which they had been driven

---

quem praeposuit rex Babylonis civitatibus Iudae; habita ergo cum eo in medio populi vel quocumque
placuerit tibi ut vadas, vade». Dedit quoque ei magister satellitum cibaria et munuscula et dimisit eum.
6Venit autem Ieremias ad Godoliam filium Ahicam in Maspha et habitavit cum eo in medio populi, qui
relictus fuerat in terra. 7Cumque audissent omnes principes exercitus, qui dispersi fuerant per regiones,
ipsi et viri eorum, quod praefecisset rex Babylonis Godoliam filium Ahicam terrae et quod
commendasset ei viros et mulieres et parvulos et de pauperibus terrae, qui non fuerant translati in
Babylonem, 8venerunt ad Godoliam in Maspha; Ismael, inquam, filius Nathaniae et Iohanan et Ionathan
filii Caree et Saraia filius Thanehumeth et filii Ophi, qui erant de Netopha, et Iezonias filius Maachathi,
ipsi et viri eorum. 9Et iuravit eis Godolias filius Ahicam filii Saphan et comitibus eorum dicens: «Nolite
timere servire Chaldaeis; habitate in terra et servite regi Babylonis, et bene erit vobis. 10Ecce ego habito
in Maspha, ut stem coram Chaldaeis, qui veniunt ad nos; vos autem colligite vindemiam et messem
et oleum et condite in vasis vestris et manete in urbibus vestris, quas tenetis». 11Sed et omnes Iudaei,
qui erant in Moab et in filiis Ammon et in Edom et in universis regionibus, audito quod dedisset rex
Babylonis reliquias in Iudaea et quod praeposuisset super eos Godoliam filium Ahicam filii Saphan,
12reversi sunt, inquam, omnes Iudaei de universis locis, ad quae profugerant, et venerunt in terram

q. Syr: Heb obscure

and came to the land of Judah, to Gedaliah at Mizpah; and they gathered wine and summer fruits in great abundance.

13 Now Johanan the son of Kareah and all the leaders of the forces in the open country came to Gedaliah at Mizpah 14 and said to him, "Do you know that Baalis the king of the Ammonites has sent Ishmael the son of Nethaniah to take your life?" But Gedaliah the son of Ahikam would not believe them. 15 Then Johanan the son of Kareah spoke secretly to Gedaliah at Mizpah, "Let me go and slay Ishmael the son of Nethaniah, and no one will know it. Why should he take your life, so that all the Jews who are gathered about you would be scattered, and the remnant of Judah would perish?" 16 But Gedaliah the son of Ahikam said to Johanan the son of Kareah, "You shall not do this thing, for you are speaking falsely of Ishmael."

41 1 In the seventh month, Ishmael the son of Nethaniah, son of Elishama, of the royal family, one of the chief officers of the king, came with ten men to Gedaliah the son of Ahikam, at Mizpah. As they ate bread together there at Mizpah, 2 Ishmael the son of Nethaniah and the ten men with him rose up and struck down Gedaliah the son of Ahikam, son of Shaphan, with the sword, and killed him, whom the king of Babylon had appointed governor in the land. 3 Ishmael also slew all the Jews who were with Gedaliah at Mizpah, and the Chaldean soldiers who happened to be there.

4 On the day after the murder of Gedaliah, before any one knew of it, 5 eighty men arrived from Shechem and Shiloh and Samaria, with their beards shaved and their clothes torn, and their bodies gashed, bringing cereal offerings and incense to present at the temple of the LORD. 6 And Ishmael the son of Nethaniah came out

Deut 14:1
2 Kings 25:19

Iudae ad Godoliam in Maspha et collegerunt vinum et messem multam nimis. 13 Iohanan autem filius Caree et omnes principes exercitus, qui dispersi fuerant in regionibus, venerunt ad Godoliam in Maspha 14 et dixerunt ei: «Scito quod Baalis rex filiorum Ammon misit Ismael filium Nathaniae percutere animam tuam»; et non credidit eis Godolias filius Ahicam. 15 Iohanan vero filius Caree dixit ad Godoliam seorsum in Maspha loquens: «Ibo et percutiam Ismael filium Nathaniae, nullo sciente, ne interficiat animam tuam, et dissipentur omnes Iudaei, qui congregati sunt ad te, et peribunt reliquiae Iudae». 16 Et ait Godolias filius Ahicam ad Iohanan filium Caree: «Noli facere verbum hoc; falsum enim tu loqueris de Ismael». **[41]** 1 Et factum est in mense septimo, venit Ismael filius Nathaniae filii Elisama de semine regali et optimates regis et decem viri cum eo ad Godoliam filium Ahicam in Maspha; et comederunt ibi panes simul in Maspha. 2 Surrexit autem Ismael filius Nathaniae et decem viri, qui cum eo erant, et percusserunt Godoliam filium Ahicam filii Saphan gladio; et interfecerunt eum, quem praefecerat rex Babylonis terrae. 3 Omnes quoque Iudaeos, qui erant cum Godolia in Maspha, et Chaldaeos, qui reperti sunt ibi, et viros bellatores percussit Ismael. 4 Secundo autem die postquam occiderat Godoliam, nullo adhuc sciente, 5 venerunt viri de Sichem et de Silo et de Samaria, octoginta viri, rasi barba et scissis vestibus et incisi in cute, et munera et tus habebant in manu, ut offerrent in domo Domini. 6 Egressus ergo Ismael filius Nathaniae in occursum eorum de Maspha,

from Mizpah to meet them, weeping as he came. As he met them,
he said to them, "Come in to Gedaliah the son of Ahikam." [7]When
they came into the city, Ishmael the son of Nethaniah and the men
with him slew them, and cast them into a cistern. [8]But there were
ten men among them who said to Ishmael, "Do not kill us, for we
have stores of wheat, barley, oil, and honey hidden in the fields."
So he refrained and did not kill them with their companions.
1 Kings 15:16–22 [9]Now the cistern into which Ishmael cast all the bodies of the
men whom he had slain was the large cistern[r] which King Asa had
made for defence against Baasha king of Israel; Ishmael the son
of Nethaniah filled it with the slain. [10]Then Ishmael took captive
all the rest of the people who were in Mizpah, the king's daughters
and all the people who were left at Mizpah, whom Nebuzaradan,
the captain of the guard, had committed to Gedaliah the son of
Ahikam. Ishmael the son of Nethaniah took them captive and set
out to cross over to the Ammonites.
[11]But when Johanan the son of Kareah and all the leaders of the
forces with him heard of all the evil which Ishmael the son of
Josh 18:15 Nethaniah had done, [12]they took all their men and went to fight
2 Sam 2:13 against Ishmael the son of Nethaniah. They came upon him at the
great pool which is in Gibeon. [13]And when all the people who
were with Ishmael saw Johanan the son of Kareah and all the
leaders of the forces with him, they rejoiced. [14]So all the people
whom Ishmael had carried away captive from Mizpah turned
about and came back, and went to Johanan the son of Kareah.
[15]But Ishmael the son of Nethaniah escaped from Johanan with
eight men, and went to the Ammonites. [16]Then Johanan the son of
Kareah and all the leaders of the forces with him took all the rest

---

incedens et plorans ibat. Cum autem occurrisset eis, dixit ad eos: «Venite ad Godoliam filium Ahicam».
[7]Qui cum venissent ad medium civitatis, interfecit eos Ismael filius Nathaniae et proiecit in medium
laci, ipse et viri, qui erant cum eo. [8]Decem autem viri reperti sunt inter eos, qui dixerunt ad Ismael:
«Noli occidere nos, quia habemus thesauros in agro, frumenti et hordei et olei et mellis»; et cessavit et
non interfecit eos cum fratribus suis. [9]Lacus autem, in quem proiecerat Ismael omnia cadavera virorum,
quos percussit, est lacus magnus, quem fecit rex Asa propter Baasa regem Israel; ipsum replevit Ismael
filius Nathaniae occisis. [10]Et captivas duxit Ismael omnes reliquias populi, qui erant in Maspha, filias
regis et universum populum, qui remanserat in Maspha, quos commendaverat Nabuzardan princeps
satellitum Godoliae filio Ahicam; et cepit eos Ismael filius Nathaniae et abiit, ut transiret ad filios
Ammon. [11]Audivit autem Iohanan filius Caree et omnes principes bellatorum, qui erant cum eo, omne
malum, quod fecerat Ismael filius Nathaniae, [12]et, assumptis universis viris, profecti sunt, ut bellarent
adversum Ismael filium Nathaniae; et invenerunt eum ad aquas multas, quae sunt in Gabaon. [13]Cumque
vidisset omnis populus, qui erat cum Ismael, Iohanan filium Caree et universos principes bellatorum,
qui erant cum eo, laetati sunt. [14]Et omnis populus, quem ceperat Ismael in Maspha, reversus est et abiit
ad Iohanan filium Caree; [15]Ismael autem filius Nathaniae fugit cum octo viris a facie Iohanan et abiit
ad filios Ammon. [16]Tulit ergo Iohanan filius Caree et omnes principes bellatorum, qui erant cum eo,

r. Gk: Heb *he had slain by the hand of Gedaliah*

of the people whom Ishmael the son of Nethaniah had carried
away captive[s] from Mizpah after he had slain Gedaliah the son of
Ahikam—soldiers, women, children, and eunuchs, whom Johanan
brought back from Gibeon. [17]And they went and stayed at Geruth 2 Kings 25:26
Chimham near Bethlehem, intending to go to Egypt [18]because of Zech 7:5; 8:19
the Chaldeans; for they were afraid of them, because Ishmael the
son of Nethaniah had slain Gedaliah the son of Ahikam, whom the
king of Babylon had made governor over the land.

The flight to Egypt

42 [1]Then all the commanders of the forces, and Johanan the Jer 40:13
son of Kareah and Azariah[t] the son of Hoshaiah, and all the

---

42:1—43:7. Jeremiah appears again in this section; there seems to be no end to his travails. After the assassination of Gedaliah (a man whose policy was in line with that which Jeremiah himself had been proposing prior to the fall of Jerusalem: cf. 41:1–18), the prophet again meets with misunderstanding from his own people. Once again they seek his guidance, promising to obey the word of the Lord (42:1–6), but when he fails to convince them, they turn against him (43:1–4). They ask Jeremiah to intercede with God for them, and, after ten days, when perhaps the delay was inclining them towards flight, they receive a very unambiguous reply—one similar to the message that Jeremiah had been preaching for many years: namely, that they have nothing to fear if they stay where they are, but if they flee to Egypt, all sorts of calamities will overtake them (42:7–22). By taking the easy course, they will encounter suffering, whereas even though trusting in God seems to involve difficulty and danger, they will be safe. If they go to Egypt, they will meet death, not the sort of life they are looking for (42:22). However, once again the prophet suffers rejection; he is accused of spreading not the word of God but the word of man (that of Baruch, to be precise: 43:1–4); so, in disobedience to the Lord, they set out for the country of the Nile, forcing the prophet to go with them (43:5–7). They head for Tahpanhes, a city on the east of the delta, probably because it had a Jewish colony.

On the one hand, the episode reflects Jeremiah's prestige and the people's respect for his prophetic ministry: he

universas reliquias vulgi, quas reduxerat ab Ismael filio Nathaniae venientes de Maspha, postquam percussit Godoliam filium Ahicam, viros fortes ad proelium et mulieres et pueros et eunuchos, quos reduxerat de Gabaon. [17]Et abierunt et sederunt in Gherutchamaam, quae est iuxta Bethlehem, ut pergerent et introirent Aegyptum [18]a facie Chaldaeorum; timebant enim eos, quia percusserat Ismael filius Nathaniae Godoliam filium Ahicam, quem praeposuerat rex Babylonis in regione. **[42]** [1]Et accesserunt omnes principes bellatorum, scilicet Iohanan filius Caree et Iezonias filius Osaiae et universum vulgus, a parvo usque ad magnum, [2]dixeruntque ad Ieremiam prophetam: «Cadat oratio

s. Cn: Heb *whom he recovered from Ishmael* **t.** Gk: Heb *Jezaniah*

people from the least to the greatest, came near [2]and said to Jeremiah the prophet, "Let our supplication come before you, and pray to the LORD your God for us, for all this remnant (for we are left but a few of many, as your eyes see us), [3]that the LORD your God may show us the way we should go, and the thing that we should do." [4]Jeremiah the prophet said to them, "I have heard you; behold, I will pray to the LORD your God according to your request, and whatever the LORD answers you I will tell you; I will keep nothing back from you." [5]Then they said to Jeremiah, "May the LORD be a true and faithful witness against us if we do not act according to all the word with which the LORD your God sends you to us. [6]Whether it is good or evil, we will obey the voice of the LORD our God to whom we are sending you, that it may be well with us when we obey the voice of the LORD our God."

[7]At the end of ten days the word of the LORD came to Jeremiah. [8]Then he summoned Johanan the son of Kareah and all the commanders of the forces who were with him, and all the people from the least to the greatest, [9]and said to them, "Thus says the LORD, the God of Israel, to whom you sent me to present your

---

had, after all, been true to the Lord in the midst of all sorts of difficulties. But it also shows that the people were as unfaithful as ever. When God makes his will known to them, they stubbornly stick to their own analysis of the situation. There was nothing ambiguous about the word of the Lord: going to Egypt was not just a descent, geographically speaking; it meant a relapse into the state of slavery (a moral slavery, this time) from which God had rescued their ancestors.

The passage carries a lesson about not trying to bend the word of God to suit one's own preferences. What the Lord says may involve effort, but only good can come from it. Analogically, the scene tells us that, if we seek advice from those who are faithful and upright, we should be ready to take it, even if we find it difficult or not to our liking. "You've been told to do something which seems useless and difficult. Do it. And you will see that it is easy and fruitful" (St Josemaría Escriva, *The Way*, 623).

nostra in conspectu tuo, et ora pro nobis ad Dominum Deum tuum pro universis reliquiis istis, quia derelicti sumus pauci de pluribus, sicut oculi tui nos intuentur; [3]et annuntiet nobis Dominus Deus tuus viam, per quam pergamus, et verbum, quod faciamus». [4]Dixit autem ad eos Ieremias propheta: «Audivi. Ecce ego oro ad Dominum Deum vestrum secundum verba vestra; omne verbum, quodcumque responderit pro vobis, indicabo vobis nec celabo vos quidquam». [5]Et illi dixerunt ad Ieremiam: «Sit Dominus inter nos testis verax et fidelis, si non iuxta omne verbum, in quo miserit te Dominus Deus tuus ad nos, sic faciemus. [6]Sive bonum est sive malum, voci Domini Dei nostri, ad quem mittimus te, oboediemus, ut bene sit nobis, cum audierimus vocem Domini Dei nostri». [7]Cum autem completi essent decem dies, factum est verbum Domini ad Ieremiam; [8]vocavitque Iohanan filium Caree et omnes principes bellatorum, qui erant cum eo, et universum populum a minimo usque ad magnum [9]et dixit ad eos: «Haec dicit Dominus, Deus Israel, ad quem misistis me, ut prosternerem

supplication before him: [10]If you will remain in this land, then I Gen 6:6
will build you up and not pull you down; I will plant you, and not Deut 32:36 Jer 1:10; 18:8;
pluck you up; for I repent of the evil which I did to you. [11]Do not 24:6
fear the king of Babylon, of whom you are afraid; do not fear him,
says the LORD, for I am with you, to save you and to deliver you
from his hand. [12]I will grant you mercy, that he may have mercy
on you and let you remain in your own land. [13]But if you say, 'We
will not remain in this land,' disobeying the voice of the LORD
your God [14]and saying, 'No, we will go to the land of Egypt,
where we shall not see war, or hear the sound of the trumpet, or be
hungry for bread, and we will dwell there,' [15]then hear the word of
the LORD, O remnant of Judah. Thus says the LORD of hosts, the
God of Israel: If you set your faces to enter Egypt and go to live
there, [16]then the sword which you fear shall overtake you there in
the land of Egypt; and the famine of which you are afraid shall
follow hard after you to Egypt; and there you shall die. [17]All the Jer 44:14,28
men who set their faces to go to Egypt to live there shall die by the
sword, by famine, and by pestilence; they shall have no remnant
or survivor from the evil which I will bring upon them.

[18]"For thus says the LORD of hosts, the God of Israel: As my Jer 24:9
anger and my wrath were poured out on the inhabitants of Jerusalem,
so my wrath will be poured out on you when you go to Egypt. You
shall become an execration, a horror, a curse, and a taunt. You shall
see this place no more. [19]The LORD has said to you, O remnant of
Judah, 'Do not go to Egypt.' Know for a certainty that I have
warned you this day [20]that you have gone astray at the cost of your
lives. For you sent me to the LORD your God, saying, 'Pray for us
to the LORD our God, and whatever the LORD our God says declare

---

preces vestras in conspectu eius: [10]Si quiescentes manseritis in terra hac, aedificabo vos et non destruam, plantabo et non evellam; iam enim placatus sum super malo, quod feci vobis. [11]Nolite timere a facie regis Babylonis, quem vos pavidi formidatis; nolite metuere eum, dicit Dominus, quia vobiscum sum ego, ut salvos vos faciam et eruam de manu eius; [12]et dabo vobis, ut misericordiam inveniatis, et ipse miserebitur vestri et habitare vos faciet in terra vestra. [13]Si autem dixeritis vos: "Non habitabimus in terra ista", nec audieritis vocem Domini Dei vestri [14]dicentes: "Nequaquam, sed ad terram Aegypti pergemus, ubi non videbimus bellum et clangorem tubae non audiemus et famem non sustinebimus et ibi habitabimus", [15]propter hoc nunc audite verbum Domini, reliquiae Iudae: Haec dicit Dominus exercituum, Deus Israel: Si posueritis faciem vestram, ut ingrediamini Aegyptum, et intraveritis, ut ibi peregrinemini, [16]gladius, quem vos formidatis, ibi comprehendet vos in terra Aegypti, et fames, pro qua estis solliciti, adhaerebit vobis in Aegypto, et ibi moriemini. [17]Omnesque viri, qui posuerunt faciem suam, ut ingrediantur Aegyptum et peregrinentur ibi, morientur gladio et fame et peste: nullus de eis remanebit nec effugiet a facie mali, quod ego afferam super eos. [18]Quia haec dicit Dominus exercituum, Deus Israel: Sicut effusus est furor meus et indignatio mea super habitatores Ierusalem, sic effundetur indignatio mea super vos, cum ingressi fueritis Aegyptum, et eritis in exsecrationem et in stuporem et in maledictum et in opprobrium et nequaquam ultra videbitis locum istum». [19]Verbum Domini super vos, reliquiae Iudae: «Nolite intrare Aegyptum; scientes scietis quia obtestatus sum vos hodie, [20]quia

to us and we will do it.’ [21]And I have this day declared it to you,
but you have not obeyed the voice of the LORD your God in
anything that he sent me to tell you. [22]Now therefore know for a
certainty that you shall die by the sword, by famine, and by
pestilence in the place where you desire to go to live.”

43 [1]When Jeremiah finished speaking to all the people all
these words of the LORD their God, with which the LORD

43:8—44:30. Jeremiah’s preaching in Egypt, at the end of his ministry, begins with God’s charging him to perform another symbolic action, announcing imminent Babylonian victory over the Egyptians (43:8–9). The prophet has come to Egypt against his will—forced to do so by those who hoped that their remnant would be safe there from the Babylonians; but the prophet tells them it will do them no good, because that country, too, will be overrun by those same conquerors (43:10–13; cf. 46:13–26; Ezek 30). Flavius Josephus says that that is what happened, in 582 BC (*Antiquitates Iudaicae*, 10, 9, 7), though there is no other evidence to that effect. But there is evidence that Nebuchadnezzar II defeated the pharaoh Amasis, (568–526 BC) in the year 568, but did not succeed in conquering Egypt.

After the account of the symbolic action comes a condemnation of the idolatry into which the Jews had fallen in Egypt. The word of the Lord seems to be addressed to all the Israelites living in that country—those in the delta (Migdol, Tahpanhes and Memphis) and those in Upper Egypt (Pathros); those who had been settled there for some time and those just come from Judah. The capital of Pathros was Elephantine, where many documents have been found that attest to much religious syncretism among the Jews resident there.

The passage shows how different Jeremiah’s interpretation of events is as compared with that of the Jews born in Egypt (44:28). The Jewish community there were of the view that Josiah’s religious reform was to be blamed for everything that had gone wrong, and that therefore the thing to do was to go back to the way things were prior to the time of Josiah. In his discussions with them, Jeremiah says, rather, that idolatry is the root cause of all their troubles (44:1–14). He tells them that unless they give up their false gods, they will be destroyed just as Judah was. He fails to produce any reaction. Even the women, who needed their husbands’ consent to make any sort of pledge (cf. Num 30:4–17), are all in favour of idolatrous practices. The people report what their experience has

---

decepistis animas vestras. Vos enim misistis me ad Dominum Deum nostrum dicentes: “Ora pro nobis ad Dominum Deum nostrum et iuxta omnia, quaecumque dixerit tibi Dominus Deus noster, sic annuntia nobis, et faciemus”. [21]Et annuntiavi vobis hodie, et non audistis vocem Domini Dei vestri super universis, pro quibus misit me ad vos. [22]Nunc ergo scientes scietis quia gladio et fame et peste moriemini in loco, ad quem voluistis intrare et ibi peregrinari». **[43]** [1]Factum est autem, cum complesset Ieremias loquens ad populum universos sermones Domini Dei eorum, pro quibus miserat

their God had sent him to them, [2]Azariah the son of Hoshaiah and Johanan the son of Kareah and all the insolent men said to Jeremiah, "You are telling a lie. The LORD our God did not send you to say, 'Do not go to Egypt to live there'; [3]but Baruch the son of Neriah has set you against us, to deliver us into the hand of the Chaldeans, that they may kill us or take us into exile in Babylon." [4]So Johanan the son of Kareah and all the commanders of the forces and all the people did not obey the voice of the LORD, to remain in the land of Judah. [5]But Johanan the son of Kareah and all the commanders of the forces took all the remnant of Judah who had returned to live in the land of Judah from all the nations to which they had been driven—[6]the men, the women, the children, the princesses, and every person whom Nebuzaradan the captain of the guard had left with Gedaliah the son of Ahikam, son of Shaphan; also Jeremiah the prophet and Baruch the son of Neriah. [7]And they came into the land of Egypt, for they did not obey the voice of the LORD. And they arrived at Tahpanhes.

Oracles delivered in Egypt

[8]Then the word of the LORD came to Jeremiah in Tahpanhes: [9]"Take in your hands large stones, and hide them in the mortar in the pavement which is at the entrance to Pharaoh's palace in Tahpanhes, in the sight of the men of Judah, [10]and say to them,

---

been: tragedy overtook them (44:15–19) because they had given up their Canaanite gods (cf. 7:18). The prophet rejects this interpretation; he repeats his argument and predicts all sorts of woes (44:20–30). The Lord is "watching over them for ever" and their rebellion will not go unpunished (44:27). Because they are such sceptics, Jeremiah offers them a sign to prove the truth of his prediction (44:29): the pharaoh will suffer the same fate as Zedekiah did. The text says no more, but it is borne out by the fact that Hophra was murdered in 568 BC.

eum Dominus Deus eorum ad illos omnia verba haec, [2]dixit Azarias filius Osaiae et Iohanan filius Caree et omnes viri superbi dicentes ad Ieremiam: «Mendacium tu loqueris; non misit te Dominus Deus noster dicens: "Ne ingrediamini Aegyptum, ut illic peregrinemini", [3]sed Baruch filius Neriae incitat te adversum nos, ut tradat nos in manu Chaldaeorum, ut interficiant nos et traducant in Babylonem». [4]Et non audivit Iohanan filius Caree et omnes principes bellatorum et universus populus vocem Domini, ut manerent in terra Iudae. [5]Sed tollens Iohanan filius Caree et universi principes bellatorum universos reliquiarum Iudae, qui reversi fuerant de cunctis gentibus, ad quas fuerant ante dispersi, ut peregrinarentur in terra Iudae, [6]viros et mulieres et parvulos et filias regis et omnem animam, quam reliquerat Nabuzardan princeps satellitum cum Godolia filio Ahicam filii Saphan, et Ieremiam prophetam et Baruch filium Neriae, [7]et ingressi sunt terram Aegypti, quia non oboedierunt voci Domini; et venerunt usque ad Taphnas. [8]Et factus est sermo Domini ad Ieremiam in Taphnis dicens: [9]«Sume lapides grandes in manu tua et absconde eos in caemento, sub pavimento, quod est ad portam domus pharaonis in Taphnis, cernentibus viris Iudaeis; [10]et dices ad eos: Haec dicit Dominus exercituum, Deus Israel: Ecce ego mittam et assumam Nabuchodonosor regem Babylonis servum

Jer 25:9; 27:6 'Thus says the LORD of hosts, the God of Israel: Behold, I will
send and take Nebuchadnezzar the king of Babylon, my servant,
and he[u] will set his throne above these stones which I have hid,
Jer 15:2 and he will spread his royal canopy over them. 11He shall come
and smite the land of Egypt, giving to the pestilence those who are
doomed to the pestilence, to captivity those who are doomed to
captivity, and to the sword those who are doomed to the sword.
12He[v] shall kindle a fire in the temples of the gods of Egypt; and
he shall burn them and carry them away captive; and he shall
clean the land of Egypt, as a shepherd cleans his cloak of vermin;
and he shall go away from there in peace. 13He shall break the
obelisks of Heliopolis which is in the land of Egypt; and the
temples of the gods of Egypt he shall burn with fire.'"

Is 19:13
Jer 2:16; 46:14 **44** 1The word that came to Jeremiah concerning all the Jews
that dwelt in the land of Egypt, at Migdol, at Tahpanhes, at
Memphis, and in the land of Pathros, 2"Thus says the LORD of
hosts, the God of Israel: You have seen all the evil that I brought
upon Jerusalem and upon all the cities of Judah. Behold, this day
they are a desolation, and no one dwells in them, 3because of the
wickedness which they committed, provoking me to anger, in that
they went to burn incense and serve other gods that they knew not,
2 Chron 36:15 neither they, nor you, nor your fathers. 4Yet I persistently sent to
Jer 7:25 you all my servants the prophets, saying, 'Oh, do not do this
abominable thing that I hate!' 5But they did not listen or incline
their ear, to turn from their wickedness and burn no incense to
other gods. 6Therefore my wrath and my anger were poured forth
and kindled in the cities of Judah and in the streets of Jerusalem;

---

meum et ponam thronum eius super lapides istos, quos abscondi, et statuet solium suum super eos; 11veniensque percutiet terram Aegypti, quos in mortem, in mortem et, quos in captivitatem, in captivitatem et, quos in gladium, in gladium; 12et succendet ignem in delubris deorum Aegypti et comburet ea et captivos ducet illos et excutiet terram Aegypti, sicut pastor pediculis excutit pallium suum, et egredietur inde in pace; 13et conteret statuas domus Solis, quae sunt in terra Aegypti, et delubra deorum Aegypti comburet igni». **[44]** 1Verbum, quod factum est per Ieremiam ad omnes Iudaeos, qui habitabant in terra Aegypti, habitantes in Magdolo et in Taphnis et in Memphi et in terra Phatures, dicens: 2«Haec dicit Dominus exercituum, Deus Israel: Vos vidistis omne malum istud, quod adduxi super Ierusalem et super omnes urbes Iudae; et ecce desertae sunt hodie, et non est in eis habitator 3propter malitiam, quam fecerunt, ut me ad iracundiam provocarent et irent, ut sacrificarent et colerent deos alienos, quos nesciebant et illi et vos et patres vestri. 4Et misi ad vos omnes servos meos prophetas, de nocte consurgens mittensque et dicens: Nolite facere verbum abominationis huiuscemodi, quam odivi. 5Et non audierunt nec inclinaverunt aurem suam, ut converterentur a malis suis et non sacrificarent diis alienis; 6et effusa est indignatio mea et furor meus et succensa est in civitatibus Iudae et in plateis Ierusalem, et versae sunt in solitudinem et vastitatem secundum diem hanc. 7Et nunc haec dicit Dominus exercituum, Deus Israel: Quare vos facitis malum grande contra

u. Gk Syr: Heb *I* **v.** Gk Syr Vg: Heb *I*

and they became a waste and a desolation, as at this day. 7And Num 16:38
now thus says the LORD God of hosts, the God of Israel: Why do
you commit this great evil against yourselves, to cut off from you
man and woman, infant and child, from the midst of Judah,
leaving you no remnant? 8Why do you provoke me to anger with Is 4:3; Jer 42:18
the works of your hands, burning incense to other gods in the land
of Egypt where you have come to live, that you may be cut off and
become a curse and a taunt among all the nations of the earth?
9Have you forgotten the wickedness of your fathers, the wicked- 1 Kings
ness of the kings of Judah, the wickedness of their[w] wives, your 11:1,8; 15:13
own wickedness, and the wickedness of your wives, which they 2 Kings 11:1
committed in the land of Judah and in the streets of Jerusalem?
10They have not humbled themselves even to this day, nor have
they feared, nor walked in my law and my statutes which I set
before you and before your fathers.

11"Therefore thus says the LORD of hosts, the God of Israel:
Behold, I will set my face against you for evil, to cut off all Judah.
12I will take the remnant of Judah who have set their faces to come
to the land of Egypt to live, and they shall all be consumed; in the
land of Egypt they shall fall; by the sword and by famine they
shall be consumed; from the least to the greatest, they shall die by
the sword and by famine; and they shall become an execration, a
horror, a curse, and a taunt. 13I will punish those who dwell in the
land of Egypt, as I have punished Jerusalem, with the sword, with
famine, and with pestilence, 14so that none of the remnant of Judah
who have come to live in the land of Egypt shall escape or survive or
return to the land of Judah, to which they desire to return to dwell
there; for they shall not return, except some fugitives."

---

animas vestras, ut intereat ex vobis vir et mulier, parvulus et lactans de medio Iudae, nec relinquatur vobis quidquam residuum, 8provocantes me in operibus manuum vestrarum, sacrificando diis alienis in terra Aegypti, in quam ingressi estis, ut ibi peregrinemini, et dissipet vos, et sitis in maledictionem et in opprobrium cunctis gentibus terrae? 9Numquid obliti estis mala patrum vestrorum et mala regum Iudae et mala uxorum eius et mala vestra et mala uxorum vestrarum, quae fecerunt in terra Iudae et in plateis Ierusalem? 10Non sunt contriti usque ad diem hanc et non timuerunt et non ambulaverunt in lege mea et in praeceptis meis, quae dedi coram vobis et coram patribus vestris. 11Ideo haec dicit Dominus exercituum, Deus Israel: Ecce ego ponam faciem meam in vobis in malum et disperdam omnem Iudam. 12Et assumam reliquias Iudae, qui posuerunt facies suas, ut ingrederentur terram Aegypti et peregrinarentur ibi, et consumentur omnes in terra Aegypti: cadent in gladio et in fame et consumentur a minimo usque ad maximum, in gladio et in fame morientur; et erunt in exsecrationem et in stuporem et in maledictionem et in opprobrium. 13Et visitabo super habitatores terrae Aegypti, sicut visitavi super Ierusalem, in gladio et in fame et in peste: 14et non erit qui effugiat et sit residuus de reliquiis Iudaeorum, qui venerunt, ut peregrinarentur in terra Aegypti et reverterentur in terram Iudae, ad quam ipsi elevant animas suas, ut revertantur et habitent ibi; non revertentur, nisi qui

w. Heb *his*

[15]Then all the men who knew that their wives had offered
incense to other gods, and all the women who stood by, a great
assembly, all the people who dwelt in Pathros in the land of
Egypt, answered Jeremiah: [16]"As for the word which you have
spoken to us in the name of the LORD, we will not listen to you.
Jer 7:18 [17]But we will do everything that we have vowed, burn incense to
Hos 2:7 the queen of heaven and pour out libations to her, as we did, both
we and our fathers, our kings and our princes, in the cities of
Judah and in the streets of Jerusalem; for then we had plenty of
food, and prospered, and saw no evil. [18]But since we left off
burning incense to the queen of heaven and pouring out libations
to her, we have lacked everything and have been consumed by the
sword and by famine." [19]And the women said,[x] "When we burned
incense to the queen of heaven and poured out libations to her,
was it without our husbands' approval that we made cakes for her
bearing her image and poured out libations to her?"

[20]Then Jeremiah said to all the people, men and women, all the
Jer 3:16 people who had given him this answer: [21]"As for the incense that
you burned in the cities of Judah and in the streets of Jerusalem,
you and your fathers, your kings and your princes, and the people
of the land, did not the LORD remember it?[y] Did it not come into
his mind? [22]The LORD could no longer bear your evil doings and
the abominations which you committed; therefore your land has
become a desolation and a waste and a curse, without inhabitant,
Jer 26:4 as it is this day. [23]It is because you burned incense, and because
you sinned against the LORD and did not obey the voice of the

---

fugerint». [15]Responderunt autem Ieremiae omnes viri, scientes quod sacrificarent uxores eorum diis alienis, et universae mulieres, quarum stabat multitudo grandis, et omnis populus habitantium in terra Aegypti in Phatures, dicentes: [16]«Sermonem, quem locutus es ad nos in nomine Domini, non audiemus ex te, [17]sed facientes faciemus omne verbum, quod egressum est de ore nostro, ut sacrificemus reginae caeli et libemus ei libamina, sicut fecimus nos et patres nostri, reges nostri et principes nostri in urbibus Iudae et in plateis Ierusalem, et saturati sumus panibus et bene nobis erat malumque non vidimus. [18]Ex eo autem tempore, quo cessavimus sacrificare reginae caeli et libare ei libamina, indigemus omnibus et gladio et fame consumpti sumus. [19]Quod si nos sacrificamus reginae caeli et libamus ei libamina, numquid sine viris nostris fecimus ei placentas ad effingendum eam et libandum ei libamina?». [20]Et dixit Ieremias ad omnem populum, adversum viros et adversum mulieres et adversum universam plebem, qui responderant ei verbum, dicens: [21]«Numquid non sacrificium, quod sacrificastis in civitatibus Iudae et in plateis Ierusalem, vos et patres vestri, reges vestri et principes vestri et populus terrae, horum recordatus est Dominus, et ascendit super cor eius? [22]Et non poterat Dominus ultra portare propter malitiam operum vestrorum et propter abominationes, quas fecistis; et facta est terra vestra in desolationem et in stuporem et in maledictum, eo quod non sit habitator, sicut est dies haec. [23]Propterea quod sacrificaveritis et peccaveritis Domino et non audieritis vocem Domini et in lege et in praeceptis et in testimoniis eius non ambulaveritis, idcirco evenerunt vobis mala haec, sicut est dies

x. Compare Syr: Heb lacks *And the women said* **y.** Syr: Heb *them*

LORD or walk in his law and in his statutes and in his testimonies,
that this evil has befallen you, as at this day."
24Jeremiah said to all the people and all the women, "Hear the
word of the LORD, all you of Judah who are in the land of Egypt,
25Thus says the LORD of hosts, the God of Israel: You and your
wives have declared with your mouths, and have fulfilled it with
your hands, saying, 'We will surely perform our vows that we
have made, to burn incense to the queen of heaven and to pour out
libations to her.' Then confirm your vows and perform your vows!
26Therefore hear the word of the LORD, all you of Judah who Gen 22:16
dwell in the land of Egypt: Behold, I have sworn by my great Jer 31:28 Ezek 20:39
name, says the LORD, that my name shall no more be invoked by
the mouth of any man of Judah in all the land of Egypt, saying,
'As the Lord GOD lives.' 27Behold, I am watching over them for
evil and not for good; all the men of Judah who are in the land of
Egypt shall be consumed by the sword and by famine, until there
is an end of them. 28And those who escape the sword shall return
from the land of Egypt to the land of Judah, few in number; and
all the remnant of Judah, who came to the land of Egypt to live,
shall know whose word will stand, mine or theirs. 29This shall be
the sign to you, says the LORD, that I will punish you in this place,
in order that you may know that my words will surely stand
against you for evil: 30Thus says the LORD, Behold, I will give Jer 39:5;
Pharaoh Hophra king of Egypt into the hand of his enemies and 46:13,25
into the hand of those who seek his life, as I gave Zedekiah king Ezek 29:2–3; 30:20–21
of Judah into the hand of Nebuchadnezzar king of Babylon, who
was his enemy and sought his life."

---

haec». 24Dixit autem Ieremias ad omnem populum et ad universas mulieres: «Audite verbum Domini,
omnis Iuda, qui estis in terra Aegypti. 25Haec dicit Dominus exercituum, Deus Israel, dicens: Vos et
uxores vestrae locuti estis ore vestro et manibus vestris implestis dicentes: "Faciamus vota nostra, quae
vovimus, ut sacrificemus reginae caeli et libemus ei libamina". Implete vota vestra et opere perpetrate
ea. 26Ideo audite verbum Domini, omnis Iuda, qui habitatis in terra Aegypti: Ecce ego iuravi in nomine
meo magno, ait Dominus, quia nequaquam ultra vocabitur nomen meum ex ore omnis viri Iudae
dicentis: "Vivit Dominus Deus", in omni terra Aegypti. 27Ecce ego vigilabo super eos in malum et non
in bonum, et consumentur omnes viri Iudae, qui sunt in terra Aegypti, gladio et fame, donec penitus
consumantur. 28Et, qui fugerint gladium, revertentur de terra Aegypti in terram Iudae, viri pauci, et
scient omnes reliquiae Iudae, quae ingressae sunt terram Aegypti, ut peregrinarentur ibi, cuius sermo
compleatur, meus an illorum. 29Et hoc vobis signum, ait Dominus, quod visitem ego super vos in loco
isto, ut sciatis quia vere complebuntur sermones mei contra vos in malum. 30Haec dicit Dominus: Ecce
ego tradam pharaonem Ophree, regem Aegypti, in manu inimicorum eius et in manu quaerentium
animam illius, sicut tradidi Sedeciam regem Iudae in manu Nabuchodonosor regis Babylonis inimici
sui et quaerentis animam eius».

Jer 39:15–18

An oracle of comfort for Baruch

Jer 32:12; 36:1; 51:31–35

45 1The word that Jeremiah the prophet spoke to Baruch the
son of Neriah, when he wrote these words in a book at the
dictation of Jeremiah, in the fourth year of Jehoiakim the son of
Josiah, king of Judah: 2"Thus says the LORD, the God of Israel, to
you, O Baruch: 3You said, 'Woe is me! for the LORD has added
sorrow to my pain; I am weary with my groaning, and I find no
Is 5:5 rest.' 4Thus shall you say to him, Thus says the LORD: Behold,
Jer 1:10 what I have built I am breaking down, and what I have planted I
Jer 21:9; 38:2; 39:18 am plucking up—that is, the whole land. 5And do you seek great
things for yourself? Seek them not; for, behold, I am bringing evil
upon all flesh, says the LORD; but I will give you your life as a
prize of war in all places to which you may go."

45:1–5. As was pointed out in the note on 26:1—45:4, most of the narratives in this second part of the book of Jeremiah, which consists mainly of prose accounts, were probably written down by Baruch, Jeremiah's secretary. Signing off, as it were, Baruch transcribes an oracle spoken to him personally, years earlier. It was a sort of reward for all the work he had done in transcribing the words of Jeremiah in 605 (v. 1; cf. 36:1–4). Baruch complained, so to speak, about what it took out of him to render Jeremiah this assistance (v. 3) and the prophet replies by putting his mind at rest, telling him that God, too, "suffers" at having to break down what he has so lovingly built up (v. 4). Therefore, if the Master suffers, the servant should not be surprised if he, too, must suffer. But he should take heart, because the Lord himself will watch over him (v. 5). These words are reminiscent of what our Lord says when he tells his disciples that they will share in their Master's sufferings (cf. Jn 15:20), but that they can rest easy because they will be rewarded for it: "In the world you have tribulation; but be of good cheer, I have overcome the world" (Jn 16:33; cf. Mt 28:20).

[45] 1Verbum, quod locutus est Ieremias propheta ad Baruch filium Neriae, cum scriberet verba haec in libro ex ore Ieremiae, anno quarto Ioachim filii Iosiae regis Iudae, dicens: 2«Haec dicit Dominus, Deus Israel, super te, Baruch. 3Dixisti: "Vae misero mihi, quoniam addidit Dominus dolorem maerori meo; laboravi in gemitu meo et requiem non inveni". 4Haec dices ad eum: Sic dicit Dominus: Ecce, quod aedificavi, ego destruo et, quod plantavi, ego evello, universam terram hanc; 5et tu quaeris tibi grandia? Noli quaerere, quia ecce ego adducam malum super omnem carnem, ait Dominus, et dabo tibi animam tuam quasi spolium in omnibus locis, ad quaecumque perrexeris».

PART THREE

Is 19
Ezek 29:1–32:32

Oracles against the nations*

46 [1]The word of the LORD which came to Jeremiah the prophet Jer 25:13,15–25
concerning the nations.

Oracles against Egypt

[2]About Egypt. Concerning the army of Pharaoh Neco, king of 2 Kings 23:19
Egypt, which was by the river Euphrates at Carchemish and which 2 Chron 35:20

***46:1—51:64.** In the Hebrew Bible, which the new Vulgate and the RSV follow, this collection of oracles against nine foreign nations is placed at the end of the book of Jeremiah, just before the epilogue. However, it seems that originally they came at the end of the first part of the book, immediately before 25:13 (cf. the note on 25:15–38). That is where they appear in the Greek Septuagint text–which also gives them in reverse order to that of the Hebrew text. Most of these oracles were probably composed between 605 AD (the first oracle against Egypt) and 590 BC (the oracles against Edom, Ammon and Moab)—in other words, prior to the events recounted in 39:1—44:30.

Other prophetical books contain similar collections of oracles against the neighbouring countries—Amos (1:3—2:3); Isaiah (13:1—23:18) and Ezekiel (25:1—32:32). From a theological point of view the fact that the prophets of Israel should address and denounce these nations demonstrates Israel's belief that the Lord is the only God, the God of all nations, and that he has authority to judge them and often to condemn them severely. Moreover, the harsh treatment dealt out to foreign nations is very different from the favouritism shown to Israel, even though it too is punished.

46:2–28. In the final years of the kingdom of Judah, many favoured an alliance with Egypt in order to keep the Babylonians at bay. However, Jeremiah always opposed that policy, because he saw it as an attempt to avoid the right solution—conversion to the Lord and fidelity to the Covenant. Besides, there was always a risk that close relations with neighbouring countries might steer Judah into idolatry. The books of Isaiah (Is 19:1–15) and Ezekiel (Ezek 29:1—32:32) also contain oracles addressed to Egypt, although in the case of Isaiah they end by expressing hope of conversion: Is 19:16–25).

This passage includes two oracles against Egypt. The first (vv. 3–12) centres on pharaoh Neco's expedition against Babylon in 605 BC. King Josiah of Judah tried to block him but was

[46] [1]Quod factum est verbum Domini ad Ieremiam prophetam contra gentes. [2]Ad Aegyptum. Adversum exercitum pharaonis Nechao regis Aegypti, qui erat iuxta fluvium Euphraten in Charchamis,

Nebuchadnezzar king of Babylon defeated in the fourth year of Jehoiakim the son of Josiah, king of Judah:

---

fatally wounded in battle (2 Kings 23:29–30; 2 Chron 35:20–24). However, that same year the Babylonians defeated Neco at Carchemish; the oracle twice mentions the call to arms (vv. 3–4, 9) and the humiliating defeat inflicted on Neco on the banks of the Euphrates (vv. 5–6; 10–12). The might of Egypt (vv. 7–8) is defeated because of its pride, as evidenced by its claim, 'I will cover the earth'—things that only God could bring about, and its defeat is interpreted as a sacrifice of praise to the Lord (v. 10).

The second oracle (vv. 13–14) hinges on Nebuchadnezzar's campaign against Egypt. This is the only reference to this event that we know of. The oracle reports the Babylonian invasion as being something designed by God (vv. 15–16); the army strides forward (v. 18) against a pharaoh who promised more than he delivered (v. 17): this may be a reference to Hophra, who proved to be of no real help to the people of Judah when they were under siege from Babylon. The powerful invader will lay Egypt low (vv. 20–24).

Both oracles depict Egypt as defeated and in retreat–certainly not, then, a suitable ally in a time of need. The section ends on a hopeful note: there is a promise of restoration for Egypt (vv. 25–26) and a call to the house of Israel to trust in the Lord (vv. 27–28; cf. 30:10–11), even though he sends punishment. The prophet's message is that the God of Israel is a just God and the Lord of all nations. He punishes people for their sins in the hope that this will bring about a change of heart. "[P]unishment has a meaning not only because it serves to repay the objective evil of the transgression with another evil, but first and foremost because it creates the possibility of rebuilding goodness in the subject who suffers. This is an extremely important aspect of suffering. It is profoundly rooted in the entire Revelation of the Old and above all the New Covenant. Suffering must serve *for conversion*, that is, *for the rebuilding of goodness* in the subject, who can recognize the divine mercy in this call to repentance. The purpose of penance is to overcome evil, which under different forms lies dormant in man. Its purpose is also to strengthen goodness both in man himself and in his relationships with others and especially with God" (John Paul II, *Salvifici doloris*, 12).

"Your bull" (v. 15): this seems to have two meanings–both the bull Apis (a depiction of the god Ptah, the protector of Memphis) and the Egyptian army itself. The Hebrew word for "bull" also means "strong". The form is, perhaps, being used here to contrast the "strength of Egypt", the god Apis, and the "strength of Israel", the Lord, God of Israel (cf. Is 1:24; 49:26; 60:16; Ps 132:2, 5; Gen 49:24).

"Amon of Thebes" (v. 25) literally "Amon of No", the principal Egyptian deity, remembered especially in Thebes, the capital of Upper Egypt, which in Hebrew is called "No".

quem percussit Nabuchodonosor rex Babylonis in quarto anno Ioachim filii Iosiae regis Iudae. [3]«Praeparate scutum et clipeum / et procedite ad bellum. / [4]Iungite equos et ascendite, equites; / state

3"Prepare buckler and shield,
and advance for battle!
4Harness the horses;
mount, O horsemen!
Take your stations with your helmets,
polish your spears,
put on your coats of mail!
5Why have I seen it?
They are dismayed
and have turned backward.
Their warriors are beaten down,
and have fled in haste;
they look not back—
terror on every side! says the LORD.
6The swift cannot flee away,
nor the warrior escape;
in the north by the river Euphrates
they have stumbled and fallen.

2 Kings 23:29–30
2 Chron 35:20–24

Amos 2:14–16

7"Who is this, rising like the Nile,
like rivers whose waters surge?
8Egypt rises like the Nile,
like rivers whose waters surge.
He said, I will rise, I will cover the earth,
I will destroy cities and their inhabitants.
9Advance, O horses,
and rage, O chariots!
Let the warriors go forth:
men of Ethiopia and Put who handle the shield,
men of Lud, skilled in handling the bow.
10That day is the day of the Lord GOD of hosts,
a day of vengeance,
to avenge himself on his foes.
The sword shall devour and be sated,
and drink its fill of their blood.

Is 8:7–8
Jer 47:2
Dan 11:22

Is 34:6
Joel 1:15
Zeph 1:7

---

in galeis, polite lanceas, induite vos loricis. / 5Quid igitur? Vidi ipsos pavidos et terga vertentes, / fortes eorum caesos; / fugerunt conciti nec respexerunt: / terror undique, / ait Dominus. / 6Non fugiat velox, / nec salvari se putet fortis; / ad aquilonem iuxta flumen Euphraten / victi sunt et ruerunt. / 7Quis est iste, qui quasi Nilus ascendit, / et veluti fluviorum intumescunt gurgites eius? / 8Aegyptus Nili instar ascendit, / et velut flumina moventur fluctus eius, / et dixit: "Ascendens operiam terram, / perdam civitatem et habitatores eius". / 9Ascendite, equi, et irruite, currus; / et procedant fortes, / Aethiopia et Phut tenentes scutum et Ludii arripientes et iacientes sagittas. / 10Dies autem ille Domini, Dei exercituum, dies ultionis, / ut sumat vindictam de inimicis suis: devorat gladius, et saturatur, / et

For the Lord GOD of hosts holds a sacrifice
in the north country by the river Euphrates.
Jer 8:12 11 Go up to Gilead, and take balm,
O virgin daughter of Egypt!
In vain you have used many medicines;
there is no healing for you.
12 The nations have heard of your shame,
and the earth is full of your cry;
for warrior has stumbled against warrior;
they have both fallen together."

Jer 42:15–22; 43:8:13 13 The word which the LORD spoke to Jeremiah the prophet
about the coming of Nebuchadnezzar king of Babylon to smite the
land of Egypt:
Jer 44:1 14 "Declare in Egypt, and proclaim in Migdol;
proclaim in Memphis and Tahpanhes;
Say, 'Stand ready and be prepared,
for the sword shall devour round about you.'
Is 46:1–2 15 Why has Apis fled?[z]
Why did not your bull stand?
Because the LORD thrust him down.
16 Your multitude stumbled[a] and fell,
and they said one to another,
'Arise, and let us go back to our own people
and to the land of our birth,
because of the sword of the oppressor.'
17 Call the name of Pharaoh, king of Egypt,
'Noisy one who lets the hour go by.'

Josh 19:12; Jer 48:15; 51:57 18 "As I live, says the King,
whose name is the LORD of hosts,

---

inebriatur sanguine eorum; / victima enim Domini, Dei exercituum, / in terra aquilonis iuxta flumen
Euphraten. / 11Ascende in Galaad et tolle resinam, / virgo filia Aegypti; / frustra multiplicas
medicamina, / tibi vero cicatrix non obducitur. / 12Audierunt gentes ignominiam tuam, et ululatus tuus
replevit terram, / quia fortis impegit in fortem, / et ambo pariter conciderunt». 13Verbum, quod locutus
est Dominus ad Ieremiam prophetam super eo quod veniret Nabuchodonosor rex Babylonis
percussurus terram Aegypti. 14«Annuntiate Aegypto / et auditum facite in Magdolo, / et resonet in
Memphi et in Taphnis, / dicite: "Sta et praepara te, / quia devoravit gladius ea, / quae per circuitum
tuum sunt". / 15Quare deiectus est fortis tuus? / Non stetit, quoniam Dominus subvertit eum. /
16Multiplicavit ruentes, / ceciditque vir ad proximum suum, et dixerunt: "Surge, / et revertamur ad
populum nostrum / et ad terram nativitatis nostrae, / a facie gladii saevientis". / 17Vocate nomen
pharaonis regis Aegypti: / Tumultum, qui praetermisit tempus opportunum. / 18Vivo ego, inquit rex, /

z. Gk: Heb *Why was it swept away* **a.** Gk: Heb *He made many stumble*

like Tabor among the mountains,
and like Carmel by the sea, shall one come.
19 Prepare yourselves baggage for exile,
O inhabitants of Egypt!
For Memphis shall become a waste,
a ruin, without inhabitant.

20 "A beautiful heifer is Egypt,
but a gadfly from the north has come upon her.
21 Even her hired soldiers in her midst
are like fatted calves;
yea, they have turned and fled together,
they did not stand;
for the day of their calamity has come upon them,
the time of their punishment.

22 "She makes a sound like a serpent gliding away;
for her enemies march in force,
and come against her with axes,
like those who fell trees.
23 They shall cut down her forest, says the LORD,
though it is impenetrable,
because they are more numerous
than locusts;
they are without number.
24 The daughter of Egypt shall be put to shame,
she shall be delivered into the hand of a people from the north."

25 The LORD of hosts, the God of Israel, said: "Behold, I am
bringing punishment upon Amon of Thebes, and Pharaoh, and
Egypt and her gods and her kings, upon Pharaoh and those who
trust in him. 26 I will deliver them into the hand of those who seek
their life, into the hand of Nebuchadnezzar king of Babylon and
his officers. Afterward Egypt shall be inhabited as in the days of
old, says the LORD.

Ezek 30:14–16
Nahum 3:8

Is 19:22–25
Ezek 29:11–14

Dominus exercituum nomen eius, / quoniam sicut Thabor in montibus / et sicut Carmelus ad mare veniet. / [19]Vasa transmigrationis fac tibi, / habitatrix filia Aegypti, / quia Memphis in solitudinem erit / et destruetur et inhabitabilis erit. / [20]Vitula elegans atque formosa Aegyptus, / stimulus ab aquilone venit ei. / [21]Mercennarii quoque eius, / qui versabantur in medio eius quasi vituli saginati, / versi sunt et fugerunt simul / nec stare potuerunt, / quia dies interfectionis eorum venit super eos, / tempus visitationis eorum. / [22]Vox eius quasi serpentis sibilantis, / quoniam cum exercitu properabunt et cum securibus venient ei, / quasi caedentes ligna. / [23]Succiderunt saltum eius, / ait Dominus, / qui supputari non potest; / multiplicati sunt enim super locustas, / et non est eis numerus. / [24]Confusa est filia Aegypti / et tradita in manu populi aquilonis». [25]Dixit Dominus exercituum, Deus Israel: «Ecce ego visitabo

Jer 30:10–11 27 "But fear not, O Jacob my servant,
nor be dismayed, O Israel;
for lo, I will save you from afar,
and your offspring from the land of their captivity.
Jacob shall return and have quiet and ease,
and none shall make him afraid.
28 Fear not, O Jacob my servant, says the LORD,
for I am with you.
I will make a full end of all the nations
to which I have driven you,
but of you I will not make a full end.
I will chasten you in just measure,
and I will by no means leave you unpunished."

Josh 13;2
Jer 25:20
Ezek 25:15–17
Amos 1:6–8
Zeph 2:4–7

Oracles against the Philistines

47 1The word of the LORD that came to Jeremiah the prophet
concerning the Philistines, before Pharaoh smote Gaza.

47:1–7. The Philistines were a people who reached Canaan by sea towards the end of the second millennium BC and established themselves along the coast. Ashkelon and Gaza were among their main cities. The Philistines seem to have come from Crete, Caphtor ("Kaftor" in Hebrew), and were skilled in ironwork. In many passages of the Bible we find them opposing the Israelites, from the era of the Judges onwards, and during the period of the monarchy. The oracle may refer to the time when Neco II disengaged from his campaign to help the Assyrians in 609 BC (cf. 2 Kings 23:33); or to Hophra's campaign against the Syrians in 570. In both instances the enemy, descending from the north, defeated the Philistines. The Philistines' lamentations will continue (v. 5). They are also called the "remnant of the Anakim", because they occupied territory previously inhabited by the descendants of the giant Anak (cf. Josh 11:22); there is an indirect allusion here to Goliath, the Philistine giant. This is a short but very impressive oracle; unlike the oracle against Egypt, it does not end on a hopeful note.

super Amon de No et super pharaonem et super Aegyptum et super deos eius et super reges eius et super pharaonem et super eos, qui confidunt in eo; 26et dabo eos in manu quaerentium animam eorum et in manu Nabuchodonosor regis Babylonis et in manu servorum eius; et post haec habitabitur sicut diebus pristinis, ait Dominus. 27Et tu ne timeas, serve meus Iacob, / et ne paveas, Israel, / quia ecce ego salvum te faciam de longinquo / et semen tuum de terra captivitatis eorum; / et revertetur Iacob et requiescet, / securus erit, et non erit qui exterreat eum. / 28Et tu noli timere, serve meus Iacob, / ait Dominus, / quia tecum ego sum, / quia ego consumam cunctas gentes, ad quas eieci te; / te vero non consumam, / sed castigabo te in iudicio / nec quasi innocenti parcam tibi». **[47]** 1Quod factum est verbum Domini ad Ieremiam prophetam contra Philisthim, antequam percuteret pharao Gazam. 2Haec dicit Dominus: «Ecce, aquae ascendunt ab aquilone / et erunt quasi torrens inundans / et operient terram

2"Thus says the LORD:
Behold, waters are rising out of the north,
and shall become an overflowing torrent;
they shall overflow the land and all that fills it,
the city and those who dwell in it.
Men shall cry out,
and every inhabitant of the land shall wail.
3At the noise of the stamping of the hoofs of his stallions,
at the rushing of his chariots, at the rumbling of their wheels,
the fathers look not back to their children,
so feeble are their hands,
4because of the day that is coming to destroy — Gen 10:14
all the Philistines, — Josh 13:2
to cut off from Tyre and Sidon
every helper that remains.
For the LORD is destroying the Philistines,
the remnant of the coastland of Caphtor.
5Baldness has come upon Gaza, — Deut 2:10
Ashkelon has perished. — Josh 11:22
O remnant of the Anakim,[b]
how long will you gash yourselves?
6Ah, sword of the LORD!
How long till you are quiet?
Put yourself into your scabbard,
rest and be still!
7How can it[c] be quiet, — Ezek 14:17
when the LORD has given it a charge?
Against Ashkelon and against the seashore
he has appointed it."

---

et plenitudinem eius, / urbem et habitatores eius. / Clamabunt homines, / et ululabunt omnes habitatores terrae / 3a strepitu ungularum fortium equorum eius, / a commotione quadrigarum eius / et tumultu rotarum illius; / non respexerunt patres filios, manibus dissolutis, / 4pro adventu diei, in quo vastabuntur omnes Philisthim, / et dissipabitur Tyro et Sidoni omnis superstes auxiliator: / depopulatus est enim Dominus Philisthim, / reliquias insulae Caphtor. / 5Venit calvitium super Gazam, / conticuit Ascalon; / reliquiae Enacim, / usquequo incidetis vos? / 6O mucro Domini, / usquequo non quiesces? / Ingredere in vaginam tuam, / refrigerare et sile. / 7Quomodo quiescet, / cum Dominus praeceperit ei adversus Ascalonem / et adversus maritimas regiones / ibique condixerit illi?».

b. Gk: Heb *their valley* **c.** Gk Vg: Heb *you*

Num 20:23; 22:36
Judg 3:12–14
1 Sam 14:47
2 Sam 8:2
2 Kings 3:4–27
Is 15–16; 46:1–2
Amos 2:1–3
Ezek 25:8–11

Oracles against Moab

48 [1]Concerning Moab.
Thus says the LORD of hosts, the God of Israel:
"Woe to Nebo, for it is laid waste!
Kiriathaim is put to shame, it is taken;
the fortress is put to shame and broken down;
[2]the renown of Moab is no more.
In Heshbon they planned evil against her:
'Come, let us cut her off from being a nation!'
You also, O Madmen, shall be brought to silence;
the sword shall pursue you.

48:1–47. The oracles that follow are directed at Moab (vv. 1–47), the Ammonites (49:1–6) and Edom (49:7–22), the three nations east of the river Jordan and the Dead Sea where many Jews had sought refuge during the period of unrest prior to the fall of Jerusalem (some of these Jews began to make their way back when Gedaliah was appointed governor of Judah: cf. 40:11–12). Ever since Israel established itself in Canaan it had uneasy relations with these neighbouring peoples.

It is rather surprising how long the oracle against Moab is; it is the longest of all these oracles. Biblical and extrabiblical sources don't tell us much about this small country to Judah's east. The book of Judges has a reference to oppression of the Israelites by Eglon, king of Moab (Judg 3:12–14). The Moabites also fought against Saul (1 Sam 14:47) and David (2 Sam 8:2). For a while they were a vassal of Israel, but Mesha, king of Moab, rebelled and battled against Jehoram of Israel and Jehoshaphat of Judah (2 Kings 3:4–27). In Jeremiah's time, armed Moabite bands, partisans of Nebuchadnezzar, attacked Judah (2 Kings 24:2).

The national deity of Moab was Chemosh, in whose honour Solomon built a place of worship near Jerusalem (1 Kings 11:7, 33; 2 Kings 23:13).

Amos 2:1–3, Ezekiel 25:8–11 and particularly Isaiah 15:1—16:14 contain oracles against Moab. In fact some of the wording here is very like that in Isaiah (vv. 32–33 and Is 16:6–10; vv. 37–38 and Is 15:2b–3). The oracle portrays a region laid waste; all it can do is lament. Its destruction is predicted: it will fall city by city, working down from the north (vv. 1–12). It is for its pride that Moab will be punished (vv. 13–30). Its plight will be so pathetic that others will bemoan it (vv. 31–39). Nothing can fend off its punishment: its capital, Heshbon, the site of the palace of its sometime king, Sihon (cf. Num 21:28), will be destroyed and the inhabitants led off into captivity (vv. 40–46). The Lord has decreed that this should be, as punishment for Moab's arrogance (v. 42) and its trust in the god Chemosh (vv. 7, 13, 46). However, in

[48] [1]Ad Moab. / Haec dicit Dominus exercituum, Deus Israel: / «Vae super Nabo, quoniam vastata est et confusa! / Capta est Cariathaim, confusa est arx et tremuit. / [2]Non est ultra exsultatio in Moab; / in

[3]"Hark! a cry from Horonaim, Jer 22:20
'Desolation and great destruction!'
[4]Moab is destroyed;
a cry is heard as far as Zoar.[d]
[5]For at the ascent of Luhith Is 15:5
they go up weeping;[e]
for at the descent of Horonaim
they have heard the cry[f] of destruction.
[6]Flee! Save yourselves!
Be like a wild ass[g] in the desert!
[7]For, because you trusted in your strongholds[h] and your treasures,
you also shall be taken;
and Chemosh shall go forth into exile,
with his priests and his princes.
[8]The destroyer shall come upon every city,
and no city shall escape;

Num 21:29
1 Kings 11:7,33
2 Kings 23:13
Jer 43:12; 49:3

---

the case of Moab, too, a note of hope is struck at the end (v. 47). Once again we can see that the God of Israel is also the God of all nations.

Verse 10 (cf. Judg 5:23), which denounces those who fail in their zeal to carry out a divine command (in this instance, the destruction of the Moabites), is often given a spiritual interpretation in ascetical writings. Pope St Gregory the Great used it to stress the need for priests to take their ministry seriously and to exhort lay people not to slacken in their search for perfection (cf. *Regula pastoralis*, 3, 25). For example, commenting on the first part of the verse he said: "Great care must be taken to avoid the sins of indolence and deceit, as the prophet says: *Cursed is he who does the work of the Lord with slackness*. We must always bear in mind that indolence is born of lethargy and laziness, and deceit of self-love; too little love of God gives rise to the former, and too great a love of self, fired by our imagination, causes the latter. Anyone who takes too much pride in what he has done well, and seeks his reward in earthly things, deceives himself and God" (*Moralia in Iob*, 9, 34, 53).

Hesebon cogitaverunt malum contra eam: / "Venite et disperdamus eam de gente". / Tu quoque, Madmen, conticesces, sequeturque te gladius. / [3]Vox clamoris de Oronaim: / "Vastitas et contritio magna". / [4]Contrita est Moab, / auditum fecerunt clamorem usque ad Segor. / [5]Per ascensum enim Luith / plorans ascendit in fletu, / quoniam in descensu Oronaim / hostes ululatum contritionis audierunt: / [6]"Fugite, salvate animas vestras / et eritis quasi myricae in deserto". / [7]Pro eo enim quod habuisti fiduciam / in operibus tuis et in thesauris tuis, / tu quoque capieris; / et ibit Chamos in transmigrationem, / sacerdotes eius et principes eius simul. / [8]Et veniet praedo ad omnem urbem, et urbs nulla salvabitur; / et peribit vallis, et dissipabuntur campestria, / quoniam dixit Dominus. / [9]Date

d. Gk: Heb *her little ones* **e.** Cn: Heb *weeping goes up with weeping* **f.** Gk Compare Is 15:5; Heb *the distress of the cry* **g.** Gk Aquila: Heb *like Aroer* **h.** Gk: Heb *works*

the valley shall perish,
and the plain shall be destroyed,
as the LORD has spoken.

9 “Give wings to Moab,
for she would fly away;
her cities shall become a desolation,
with no inhabitant in them.
Judg 5:23 10 “Cursed is he who does the work of the LORD with slackness;
1 Sam 15:3,9 and cursed is he who keeps back his sword from bloodshed.
1 Kings 20:42

11 “Moab has been at ease from his youth
and has settled on his lees;
he has not been emptied from vessel to vessel,
nor has he gone into exile;
so his taste remains in him,
and his scent is not changed.
12 “Therefore, behold, the days are coming, says the LORD,
when I shall send to him tilters who will tilt him, and empty his
1 Kings 12:29 vessels, and break his[i] jars in pieces. 13 Then Moab shall be
Hos 10:5; 16:6 ashamed of Chemosh, as the house of Israel was ashamed of
Amos 5:5 Bethel, their confidence.

14 “How do you say, ‘We are heroes
and mighty men of war’?
15 The destroyer of Moab and his cities has come up,
and the choicest of his young men have gone down to slaughter,
says the King, whose name is the LORD of hosts.
16 The calamity of Moab is near at hand
and his affliction hastens apace.
Is 14:5 17 Bemoan him, all you who are round about him,
Jer 22:18 and all who know his name;

---

pennas ad volandum; / et civitates eius desertae erunt et inhabitabiles. / 10 Maledictus, qui facit opus Domini neglegenter, / et maledictus, qui prohibet gladium suum a sanguine. / 11 Securus fuit Moab ab adulescentia sua / et requievit in faecibus suis / nec transfusus est de vase in vas / et in transmigrationem non abiit; / idcirco permansit gustus eius in eo, / et odor eius non est immutatus. / 12 Propterea, ecce, dies veniunt, / dicit Dominus, / et mittam ei stratores laguncularum; / et sternent eum / et vasa eius exhaurient / et lagunculas eorum collident. 13 Et confundetur Moab a Chamos, sicut confusa est domus Israel a Bethel, in qua habebat fiduciam. 14 Quomodo dicitis: “Fortes sumus / et viri robusti ad proeliandum”? / 15 Vastata est Moab, / et ascenderunt civitates illius, / et electi iuvenes eius descenderunt in occisionem, / ait rex, Dominus exercituum nomen eius. / 16 Prope est interitus Moab ut veniat, / et malum eius velociter accurret nimis. / 17 Lugete super eum, / omnes, qui estis in circuitu eius;

i. Gk Aquila: Heb *their*

say, ‘How the mighty sceptre is broken,
the glorious staff.’

18 “Come down from your glory,
and sit on the parched ground,
O inhabitant of Dibon!
For the destroyer of Moab has come up against you;
he has destroyed your strongholds.
19 Stand by the way and watch,
O inhabitant of Aroer!
Ask him who flees and her who escapes;
say, ‘What has happened?’
20 Moab is put to shame, for it is broken;
wail and cry!
Tell it by the Arnon,
that Moab is laid waste.

21 “Judgment has come upon the tableland, upon Holon, and Num 33:46
Jahzah, and Mepha-ath, 22 and Dibon, and Nebo, and Beth- Josh 13:17–19
diblathaim, 23 and Kiriathaim, and Beth-gamul, and Beth-meon,
24 and Keri-oth, and Bozrah, and all the cities of the land of Moab,
far and near. 25 The horn of Moab is cut off, and his arm is broken,
says the LORD.

26 “Make him drunk, because he magnified himself against the Is 51:17
LORD; so that Moab shall wallow in his vomit, and he too shall be
held in derision. 27 Was not Israel a derision to you? Was he found Jer 2:26 Ezek 25:8–11
among thieves, that whenever you spoke of him you wagged your Zeph 2:8
head?

28 “Leave the cities, and dwell in the rock,
O inhabitants of Moab!
Be like the dove that nests
in the sides of the mouth of a gorge.

/ et universi, qui scitis nomen eius, / dicite: “Quomodo confracta est virga fortis, / baculus gloriosus?”.
/ 18 Descende de gloria et sede in siti, / habitatrix filia Dibon, / quoniam vastator Moab ascendit ad te, /
dissipavit munitiones tuas. / 19 Ad viam sta et prospice, / habitatrix Aroer; / interroga fugientem / et eam,
quae evasit. / Dic: “Quid accidit?”. / 20 Confusus est Moab, quoniam victus est. / Ululate et clamate; /
annuntiate in Arnon, / quoniam vastatus est Moab. 21 Et iudicium venit ad terram campestrem super
Helon et super Iasa et super Mephaath 22 et super Dibon et super Nabo et super Bethdeblathaim, 23 et
super Cariathaim et super Bethgamul et super Bethmaon 24 et super Carioth et super Bosra et super
omnes civitates terrae Moab, quae longe et quae prope sunt. 25 Abscissum est cornu Moab, / et brachium
eius contritum est, / ait Dominus. 26 Inebriate eum, quoniam contra Dominum erectus est; et allidet
manum Moab in vomitu suo, et erit in derisum etiam ipse. 27 Nonne in derisum tibi fuit Israel? Num
inter fures repertus est? Quotiescumque enim adversum illum loquebaris, caput movebas. 28 Relinquite

Is 16:6 29 We have heard of the pride of Moab—
he is very proud—
of his loftiness, his pride, and his arrogance,
and the haughtiness of his heart.
30 I know his insolence, says the LORD;
his boasts are false,
his deeds are false.
2 Kings 3:25 31 Therefore I wail for Moab;
Is 16:7 I cry out for all Moab;
for the men of Kir-heres I mourn.
32 More than for Jazer I weep for you,
O vine of Sibmah!
Your branches passed over the sea,
reached as far as Jazer;[j]
upon your summer fruits and your vintage
the destroyer has fallen.
Is 16:10 33 Gladness and joy have been taken away
Joel 1:10 from the fruitful land of Moab;
I have made the wine cease from the wine presses;
no one treads them with shouts of joy;
the shouting is not the shout of joy.

Is 15:4–5 34 "Heshbon and Ele-aleh cry out;[k] as far as Jahaz they utter
their voice, from Zoar to Horonaim and Eglath-shelishiyah. For
the waters of Nimrim also have become desolate. 35 And I will
bring to an end in Moab, says the LORD, him who offers sacrifice
Is 15:5 in the high place and burns incense to his god. 36 Therefore my
heart moans for Moab like a flute, and my heart moans like a flute
for the men of Kir-heres; therefore the riches they gained have
perished.

---

civitates et habitate in petra, / habitatores Moab, / et estote quasi columba nidificans / in parietibus apertae voraginis. / 29 Audivimus superbiam Moab, / superbus est valde; / sublimitatem eius et arrogantiam / et superbiam et altitudinem cordis eius. 30 Ego scio, ait Dominus, iactantiam eius, et quod non sint rectae fabulationes, nec recta fecerint. 31 Ideo super Moab eiulabo et super Moab universam clamabo, super viros Cirhareseth plorabitur. 32 Plus quam in planctu Iazer plorabo tibi, / vinea Sabama; / propagines tuae transierunt mare, / usque ad Iazer pervenerunt. / Super messem tuam et vindemiam tuam / praedo irruit. / 33 Ablata est laetitia et exsultatio / de horto et de terra Moab, / et vinum de torcularibus sustuli; / nequaquam calcator uvae / solitum celeuma cantabit. 34 De clamore Hesebon usque Eleale et Iasa dederunt vocem suam, a Segor usque ad Oronaim, ad Eglatselisiam; aquae quoque Nemrim pessimae erunt. 35 Et auferam de Moab, ait Dominus, offerentem in excelsis et sacrificantem diis eius. 36 Propterea cor meum ad Moab quasi tibia resonabit, et cor meum ad viros Cirhareseth dabit sonitum tibiarum; quia depositum, quod acquisierunt, periit. 37 Omne enim caput calvitium et omnis

j. Cn: Heb *the sea of Jazer* **k.** Cn: Heb *From the cry of Heshbon to Elealeh*

37"For every head is shaved and every beard cut off; upon all
the hands are gashes, and on the loins is sackcloth. 38On all the
housetops of Moab and in the squares there is nothing but
lamentation; for I have broken Moab like a vessel for which no
one cares, says the LORD. 39How it is broken! How they wail!
How Moab has turned his back in shame! So Moab has become
a derision and a horror to all that are round about him."

Lev 21:2–5
Is 15:2–8
Jer 47:5

40 For thus says the LORD:
"Behold, one shall fly swiftly like an eagle,
and spread his wings against Moab;
41 the cities shall be taken
and the strongholds seized.
The heart of the warriors of Moab shall be in that day
like the heart of a woman in her pangs;
42 Moab shall be destroyed and be no longer a people,
because he magnified himself against the LORD.
43 Terror, pit, and snare
are before you, O inhabitant of Moab! says the LORD.
44 He who flees from the terror
shall fall into the pit,
and he who climbs out of the pit
shall be caught in the snare.
For I will bring these things[l] upon Moab
in the year of their punishment, says the LORD.

Deut 28:49
Jer 49:22
Ezek 17:3,12

Is 24:17–18
Lam 3:47

45 "In the shadow of Heshbon
fugitives stop without strength;
for a fire has gone forth from Heshbon,
a flame from the house of Sihon;
it has destroyed the forehead of Moab,
the crown of the sons of tumult.

Num
24:17,28–29

---

barba rasa erit, in cunctis manibus incisiones et super lumbos cilicium. 38Super omnia tecta Moab et in plateis eius omnis planctus, quoniam contrivi Moab sicut vas, quod nemini placet, ait Dominus. 39Quomodo victa est, et ululaverunt? Quomodo vertit dorsum Moab et confusus est? Eritque Moab in derisum et in terrorem omnibus in circuitu suo. 40Haec dicit Dominus: Ecce quasi aquila volabit / et extendet alas suas ad Moab. / 41Capta sunt oppida, / et munitiones comprehensae sunt, / et erit cor fortium Moab in die illa / sicut cor mulieris parturientis. / 42Et cessabit Moab esse populus, / quoniam contra Dominum gloriatus est. / 43Pavor et fovea et laqueus super te, / o habitator Moab, / dicit Dominus. / 44Qui fugerit a facie pavoris, cadet in foveam, / et, qui conscenderit de fovea, capietur laqueo; / adducam enim super Moab / annum visitationis eorum, / ait Dominus. / 45In umbra Hesebon steterunt sine viribus fugientes, / sed ignis egressus est de Hesebon, / et flamma de medio Sehon, / et

l. Gk Syr: Heb *to her*

46 "Woe to you, O Moab!
The people of Chemosh is undone;
for your sons have been taken captive,
and your daughters into captivity.

Jer 46:26 47 Yet I will restore the fortunes of Moab
in the latter days, says the LORD."
Thus far is the judgment on Moab.

Num 20:23 Deut 2:19 Judg 3:13; 10:6–11:28 1 Sam 14:47 2 Sam 10:1–14 1 Kings 11:7,33 2 Kings 24:2 Jer 25:21; 40:14 Ezek 25:1–7 Amos 1:13–15 Zeph 2:8–11

Oracles against the Ammonites

49 [1]Concerning the Ammonites.
Thus says the LORD:
"Has Israel no sons?
Has he no heir?
Why then has Milcom dispossessed Gad,
and his people settled in its cities?

49:1–6. The second nation to the east that is addressed in these oracles is Ammon, an area north of Moab and Judah. The Ammonites were often hostile towards the Israelites; they allied themselves with Eglon of Moab against Israel (cf. Judg 3:13) and with the Philistines (Judg 10:6—11:28). They attacked Israel again in the time of Saul (1 Sam 14:47) and in that of David (2 Sam 10:1–14). In Jeremiah's time they formed alliances with Babylon, Syria and Moab against Judah (cf. 2 Kings 24:2); and it was an Ammonite king, Baalis,who instigated the assassination of Gedaliah (cf. 40:14). Molech and Milcom were gods of Ammon, for whom Solomon built a place of worship near Jerusalem, just as he built one to Chemosh of Moab (1 Kings 11:7, 33; 2 Kings 23:13). Rabbah (present-day Amman) was the capital.

Jeremiah announces impending punishment because this pagan people, symbolized by their god Milcom, has taken over territory that the Lord gave to the tribe of Gad (v. 1; cf. Num 32:34–37; Josh 13:24–28). Despite having plenty of water and being therefore difficult to conquer (v. 4), Ammon will fall into enemy hands (v. 5). The city of Ai (v. 3) is not the same place as was conquered by Joshua (cf. Josh 7:2—8:29). Heshbon is a city sometimes considered Ammonite, sometimes Moabite (cf. 48:2). In Amos 1:13–15 and Ezekiel 25:1–7 we find further oracles against the Ammonites. In Jeremiah alone is a note of hope struck (v. 6), but this doesn't appear in the Greek version, so it could be a later addition.

devoravit tempora Moab / et verticem filiorum tumultus. / [46]Vae tibi, Moab! / Periit populus Chamos, / quia comprehensi sunt filii tui / et filiae tuae in captivitatem. / [47]Et convertam sortem Moab in novissimis diebus», / ait Dominus. / Hucusque iudicia Moab. **[49]** [1]Ad filios Ammon. Haec dicit Dominus: / «Numquid filii non sunt Israel, / aut heres non est ei? / Cur igitur hereditate possedit Melchom Gad, / et populus eius in urbibus eius habitavit? / [2]Ideo ecce dies veniunt, / dicit Dominus, / et auditum faciam super Rabba filiorum Ammon / fremitum proelii; / et erit in tumulum dissipata, /

[2]Therefore, behold, the days are coming,
says the LORD,
when I will cause the battle cry to be heard
against Rabbah of the Ammonites;
it shall become a desolate mound,
and its villages shall be burned with fire;
then Israel shall dispossess those who dispossessed him,
says the LORD.

Is 11:14

[3]"Wail, O Heshbon, for Ai is laid waste!
Cry, O daughters of Rabbah!
Gird yourselves with sackcloth,
lament, and run to and fro among the hedges!
For Milcom shall go into exile,
with his priests and his princes.
[4]Why do you boast of your valleys,[m]
O faithless daughter,
who trusted in her treasures, saying,
'Who will come against me?
[5]Behold, I will bring terror upon you,
says the Lord GOD of hosts,
from all who are round about you,
and you shall be driven out, every man straight before him,
with none to gather the fugitives.
[6]But afterward I will restore the fortunes of the Ammonites,
says the LORD."

Jer 48:2

Jer 46:26

Oracles against Edom

[7]Concerning Edom.
Thus says the LORD of hosts:

Num 20:23
Ps 137:7
Ezek 25:12–24
Amos 1:11–12
Obad 1–9; Gen 25:19–28:9; 32:4–33:17

49:7–22. The third eastern nation that is the subject of oracles here is Edom, which was to the south of Moab. The Edomites or Idumeans were descendants of Esau, the brother of Jacob (cf. Gen 25:19—28:9; 32:4—33:17; Deut 23:8) and

filiaeque eius igni succendentur, / et possidebit Israel possessores suos, ait Dominus. / [3]Ulula, Hesebon, quoniam vastata es, ut sis in acervum lapidum; / clamate, filiae Rabba, / accingite vos ciliciis, plangite / et circuite per muros, / quoniam Melchom in transmigrationem ducetur, / sacerdotes eius et principes eius simul. / [4]Quid gloriaris in vallibus? / Copiose fluxit vallis tua, filia rebellis, / quae confidebas in thesauris tuis / et dicebas: "Quis veniet ad me?". / [5]Ecce ego inducam super te terrorem, / ait Dominus, Deus exercituum, / ab omnibus, qui sunt in circuitu tuo; / et dispergemini singuli in viam suam, / nec erit qui congreget fugientes. / [6]Et post haec convertam / sortem filiorum Ammon», / ait Dominus. [7]Ad Edom. Haec dicit Dominus exercituum: / «Numquid non ultra est sapientia in Theman? / Periit

m. Heb *valleys, your valley flows*

Deut 23:8 Jer 25:21 Ezek 25:12–14 Lam 4:21; Bar 3:22; Obad 8

"Is wisdom no more in Teman?
Has counsel perished from the prudent?
Has their wisdom vanished?

Mal 1:2–5

8Flee, turn back, dwell in the depths,
O inhabitants of Dedan!
For I will bring the calamity of Esau upon him,
the time when I punish him.

Obad 5–6

9If grape-gatherers came to you,
would they not leave gleanings?
If thieves came by night,
would they not destroy only enough for themselves?
10But I have stripped Esau bare,
I have uncovered his hiding places,
and he is not able to conceal himself.
His children are destroyed, and his brothers,
and his neighbours; and he is no more.
11Leave your fatherless children, I will keep them alive;
and let your widows trust in me."

Is 51:17 Jer 25:28–29 Obad 16

12For thus says the LORD: "If those who did not deserve to
drink the cup must drink it, will you go unpunished? You shall not

---

therefore were kinsmen of the Israelites. But they were also hostile towards them: in the book of Genesis, Esau (Gen 25:30; cf. Jer 49:10) is the twin brother of Jacob (Isaac) and his rival even from the womb (Gen 25:23–26). But because Esau sold his birthright to Jacob, the Israelites claimed superiority over the Idumeans. According to Obadiah 12, Edom rejoiced over the destruction of Jerusalem. Both Isaiah 34:1–17 and Ezekiel 25:12–14 and 35:1–15 also contain oracles against the Edomites; however, the ones closest to those in Jeremiah are in the book of Obadiah (cf. the notes on Obad 1–14).

These oracles predict the destruction of Edom. Its fabled wisdom will be of no avail (its reputation extended to Teman, in the south: cf. Job 2:11; 15:18; Obad 8; Bar 3:22). The Dedanites, a people to the south-east of Edom, will have to flee to avoid the destruction that will overtake Edom (v. 8). The Lord will punish the Idumeans including Bozrah, their capital, on account of their pride (v. 16). Edom will be destroyed and totally obliterated, like Sodom and Gomorrah (v. 18; cf. Gen 19:1–28). The eagle (v. 22) stands for Nebuchadnezzar, as can be seen from the ornate allegory in Ezekiel 17:3–6.

consilium a prudentibus, / inutilis facta est sapientia eorum. / 8Fugite, terga vertite, descendite in voraginem, / habitatores Dedan, / quoniam perditionem Esau adduxi super eum, / tempore quo visitavi eum. / 9Si vindemiatores veniunt super te, / non relinquent racemum; / si fures in nocte, / diripiunt, quod placet sibi. / 10Ego vero discooperui Esau, / revelavi abscondita eius, / et celari non poterit; / vastatum est semen eius / et fratres eius et vicini eius, et non erit. / 11Relinque pupillos tuos, ego faciam eos vivere; / et viduae tuae in me sperabunt. 12Quia haec dicit Dominus: Ecce quibus non erat iudicium,

go unpunished, but you must drink. [13]For I have sworn by myself,
says the LORD, that Bozrah shall become a horror, a taunt, a waste,
and a curse; and all her cities shall be perpetual wastes."

14 I have heard tidings from the LORD, Obad 1:4
and a messenger has been sent among the nations:
"Gather yourselves together and come against her,
and rise up for battle!"
15 For behold, I will make you small among the nations,
despised among men.
16 The horror you inspire has deceived you, Jer 51:13
and the pride of your heart, Amos 9:2 Hab 2:9
you who live in the clefts of the rock,[n]
who hold the height of the hill.
Though you make your nest as high as the eagle's,
I will bring you down from there,
says the LORD.

17 "Edom shall become a horror; every one who passes by it Jer 50:40
will be horrified and will hiss because of all its disasters. [18]As Gen 19:1–28
when Sodom and Gomorrah and their neighbour cities were
overthrown, says the LORD, no man shall dwell there, no man shall Job 9:19
sojourn in her. [19]Behold, like a lion coming up from the jungle of Wis 12:12 Jer 50:44–46
the Jordan against a strong sheepfold, I will suddenly make them[o]
run away from her; and I will appoint over her whomever I choose.
For who is like me? Who will summon me? What shepherd can
stand before me? [20]Therefore hear the plan which the LORD has
made against Edom and the purposes which he has formed against
the inhabitants of Teman: Even the little ones of the flock shall be
dragged away; surely their fold shall be appalled at their fate. [21]At
the sound of their fall the earth shall tremble; the sound of their
cry shall be heard at the Red Sea. [22]Behold, one shall mount up
and fly swiftly like an eagle, and spread his wings against Bozrah,
and the heart of the warriors of Edom shall be in that day like the
heart of a woman in her pangs."

---

ut biberent calicem, bibentes bibent; et tu quasi innocens relinqueris? Non eris innocens, sed bibens bibes. [13]Quia per memetipsum iuravi, dicit Dominus, quod in solitudinem et in opprobrium et in desertum et in maledictionem erit Bosra; et omnes civitates eius erunt in solitudines sempiternas». [14]Auditum audivi a Domino, / et legatus ad gentes missus est: / «Congregamini et venite contra eam / et consurgite in proelium». / [15]«Ecce enim parvulum dedi te in gentibus, / contemptibilem inter homines. / [16]Arrogantia tua decepit te, / et superbia cordis tui, / qui habitas in cavernis petrae / et tenes altitudinem collis; / cum exaltaveris quasi aquila nidum tuum, / inde detraham te, / dicit Dominus. [17]Et erit Edom in desolationem: omnis, qui transibit per eam, stupebit et sibilabit super omnes plagas eius. [18]Sicut subversa est Sodoma et Gomorra et vicinae eius, ait Dominus, non habitabit ibi vir, et non

n. Or *Sela* **o.** Gk Syr: Heb *him*

Oracle against Damascus

Is 17:1–3 Amos 1:3–5 Zech 9:1–2

23 Concerning Damascus.
"Hamath and Arpad are confounded,
for they have heard evil tidings;
they melt in fear, they are troubled like the sea[p]
which cannot be quiet.

Jer 4:31

24 Damascus has become feeble, she turned to flee,
and panic seized her;
anguish and sorrows have taken hold of her,
as of a woman in travail.

Is 21:13–17 Jer 25:23–24

25 How the famous city is forsaken,[q]
the joyful city![r]
26 Therefore her young men shall fall in her squares,
and all her soldiers shall be destroyed in that day, says the
LORD of hosts.

1 Kings 20:1 2 Kings 6:24 Is 21:13

27 And I will kindle a fire in the wall of Damascus,
and it shall devour the strongholds of Ben-hadad."

Oracles against Kedar and the kingdoms of Hazor

28 Concerning Kedar and the kingdoms of Hazor which Nebuchadnezzar king of Babylon smote.

49:23–27. After predicting calamity for the nations east of the Jordan, Jeremiah now looks northwards. Damascus was the capital of Syria, and at one time the centre of one of the great empires of ancient time, which included among its territories Hamath, about 200 km. (125 miles) north of Damascus, and Arpad, further north still, not far from present-day Aleppo. It was famous for its wealth, but here it is told that that will prove no use to it: for its fate will be anguish and destruction. Many kings of Damascus were called Ben-hadah (v. 27); so the reference here is to "royal strongholds". Amos 1:3–5 and Isaiah 17:1–3 also contain oracles against Damascus.

peregrinabitur in ea filius hominis. 19 Ecce quasi leo ascendet de silva condensa Iordanis ad prata semper virentia, quia subito currere faciam eos ex illa; et, qui erit electus, illum praeponam ei. Quis enim similis mei? Et quis vocabit me in iudicium? Et quis est iste pastor, qui resistat vultui meo? 20 Propterea audite consilium Domini, quod iniit de Edom, et cogitationes eius, quas cogitavit de habitatoribus Theman: Certe abstrahent parvulos gregis, / certe desolabuntur super eos pascua eorum. / 21 A voce ruinae eorum commota est terra, / clamor in mari Rubro auditus est ocis eius. / 22 Ecce quasi aquila ascendet et volabit / et expandet alas suas super Bosram; / et erit cor fortium Edom in die illa / quasi cor mulieris parturientis». 23 Ad Damascum. «Confusa est Emath et Arphad, / quia auditum pessimum audierunt; / turbati sunt in mari sollicitudinis, / quod quiescere non potuit. / 24 Dissoluta est Damascus, versa in fugam; / tremor apprehendit eam, / angustia et dolores tenuerunt eam / quasi parturientem. / 25 Quomodo non erit derelicta civitas laudabilis, / urbs laetitiae? / 26 Ideo cadent iuvenes eius in plateis eius, / et omnes viri proelii conticescent in die illa, / ait Dominus exercituum. / 27 Et

p. Cn: Heb *there is trouble in the sea* **q.** Vg: Heb *not forsaken* **r.** Syr Vg Tg: Heb *city of my joy*

Thus says the LORD:
"Rise up, advance against Kedar!
Destroy the people of the east!
29 Their tents and their flocks shall be taken,
their curtains and all their goods;
their camels shall be borne away from them,
and men shall cry to them: 'Terror on every side!'
30 Flee, wander far away, dwell in the depths,
O inhabitants of Hazor! says the LORD.
For Nebuchadnezzar king of Babylon
has made a plan against you,
and formed a purpose against you.

31 "Rise up, advance against a nation at ease,
that dwells securely, says the LORD,
that has no gates or bars,
that dwells alone.
32 Their camels shall become booty,
their herds of cattle a spoil.
I will scatter to every wind
those who cut the corners of their hair,
and I will bring their calamity
from every side of them, says the LORD.
33 Hazor shall become a haunt of jackals,
an everlasting waste;
no man shall dwell there,
no man shall sojourn in her."

49:28–33. The authority of the Lord reaches beyond the frontiers of Israel to the nomadic tribes of the desert, Kedar (cf. 2:10) and Hazor, maybe to the south-east and east of the land of Canaan. Destruction extends even to where there are no cities and where people live in tents. The power of God cannot be confined to well-known urban settlements: it reaches out to remote wildernesses. Nebuchadnezzar's campaign against the Arabs may have taken place in 605 BC, but we cannot be sure.

succendam ignem in muro Damasci, / et devorabit moenia Benadad». 28Ad Cedar et ad regna Asor, quae percussit Nabuchodonosor rex Babylonis. Haec dicit Dominus: / «Surgite, ascendite ad Cedar / et vastate filios orientis. / 29Tabernacula eorum et greges eorum capient; / tentoria eorum et omnia vasa eorum / et camelos eorum tollent sibi; / et vocabunt super eos formidinem in circuitu. / 30Fugite, abite vehementer, / in voraginibus sedete, / qui habitatis Asor, / ait Dominus; / iniit enim contra vos / Nabuchodonosor rex Babylonis consilium / et cogitavit adversum vos cogitationes. / 31Consurgite, et ascendite / ad gentem quietam et habitantem confidenter, / ait Dominus; / non ostia nec vectes eis: / soli habitant. / 32Et erunt cameli eorum in direptionem, / et multitudo iumentorum in praedam; / et dispergam eos in omnem ventum, qui sunt attonsi in comam, / et ex omni confinio eorum / adducam

Oracle against Elam

34The word of the LORD that came to Jeremiah the prophet concerning Elam, in the beginning of the reign of Zedekiah king of Judah.

Is 22:6 35Thus says the LORD of hosts: "Behold, I will break the bow of Elam, the mainstay of their might; 36and I will bring upon Elam the four winds from the four quarters of heaven; and I will scatter them to all those winds, and there shall be no nation to which those driven out of Elam shall not come. 37I will terrify Elam before their enemies, and before those who seek their life; I will bring evil upon them, my fierce anger, says the LORD. I will send the sword after them, until I have consumed them; 38and I will set my throne in Elam, and destroy their king and princes, says the LORD.

Jer 46:26 39But in the latter days I will restore the fortunes of Elam, says the LORD."

Is 13; 14; 47
Rev 18

Oracle against Babylon

50 1The word which the LORD spoke concerning Babylon, concerning the land of the Chaldeans, by Jeremiah the prophet:

49:34–39. Elam was further away from Babylon, on the outer limits of the known world in Jeremiah's time. Its capital was Susa. Despite all their reputation for skill at archery (v. 35), the Elamites will be laid waste, but there is hope for them too (v. 39). This oracle, which dates from around 597 BC (v. 34), is designed to show that God's edicts reach to the very ends of the earth. Jeremiah declares that the Lord will set his throne in Elam (v. 38): in other words, there is nowhere that does not come under the Lord's sway.

50:1—51:19. The oracles against the nations (46:1—51:64) opened with those addressed to one of the main empires of the time, Egypt. Now, the series closes with an oracle about Babylon. During Jeremiah's lifetime, Judah and Jerusalem lived under constant threat from that quarter, until eventually they succumbed.

interitum super eos, / ait Dominus. / 33Et erit Asor in habitaculum thoum, / deserta usque in aeternum; / non manebit ibi vir, / nec peregrinabitur in ea filius hominis». 34Quod factum est verbum Domini ad Ieremiam prophetam super Elam, in principio regni Sedeciae regis Iudae, dicens: 35«Haec dicit Dominus exercituum: / Ecce ego confringam arcum Elam, summam fortitudinem eorum; / 36et inducam super Elam / quattuor ventos a quattuor plagis caeli, / et ventilabo eos in omnes ventos istos, / et non erit gens, / ad quam non perveniant profugi Elam. / 37Et pavere faciam Elam coram inimicis suis / et in conspectu quaerentium animam eorum; / et adducam super eos malum / iram furoris mei, / dicit Dominus, / et mittam post eos gladium, / donec consumam eos. / 38Et ponam solium meum in Elam / et perdam inde regem et principes, ait Dominus. / 39In novissimis autem diebus / convertam sortem Elam», / dicit Dominus. **[50]** 1Verbum, quod locutus est Dominus de Babylone et de terra Chaldaeorum in manu Ieremiae prophetae: 2«Annuntiate in gentibus et auditum facite, / levate signum;

2"Declare among the nations and proclaim,
set up a banner and proclaim,
conceal it not, and say:

Is 46:1
Jer 51:44

So far, Babylon has come out of this book rather well: it has been depicted as the means used by God to punish the chosen people for their sins, and to get them to mend their ways. But now the tone changes: Babylon has gone too far; it has destroyed the temple and has failed to recognize the authority of the Lord. Therefore, in this long oracle it is roundly condemned; in it, too, we can find canticles expressing hope for the Jews exiled in Babylon. It begins (50:2–20) by saying that Babylon and its gods Bel and Merodach will be overthrown and that this will lead to the restoration of Israel (50:2–7). God will have mercy on the Jewish exiles in Babylon and, by contrast, he will humble the arrogance of the Babylonians by sending enemy armies to lay the city low (50:8–16). The text shows the solicitude of the Shepherd for his flock, Israel (50:6, 17), whom he will lead back home once she is cleansed and her oppressors have been punished (50: 18–20). Although the Medes could be the victorious invader, the text does not seem to be thinking in terms of any particular invader; rather, it seems to be speaking generically about some power that, as happened at other times, came from the north to act as the Lord's scourge (50:3).

The oracles then return (50:21–46) to the theme of imminent destruction. A destroyer will come from the north and will reach the very limits of the Babylonian empire, that is, to the south, to Merathaim (v. 21), where the Tigris and the Euphrates reach the sea, and to the frontier with Elam (Pekod) to the east. Those who sowed destruction wherever they went (Babylon was a "hammer": v. 23) will be destroyed; they will be cornered like a wild beast (50:23–24); their powerful men ("bulls": v. 27) will perish. Babylon's pride and idolatry are the reasons why she will suffer this fate (50:29–40). The severity and inescapability of this punishment can be seen from the imagery used and in the use of the repetition (the word "sword" is used four times). And, summing up as it were what has been said so far, the oracle makes it clear that God not only utters threats but carries them out (50:41–46).

Thirdly (51:1–19), expanding on what it has said earlier, the oracle teaches that Babylon's aggressor has been raised up by God, to avenge his spouse, Israel (51:5). The city that seduced other nations (v. 7) will find no cure for its pain no matter what it tries (51:7–9). Its wealth and power are of no avail against the power of the Lord (51:10–19). The name *Leb-quamal* (51:1; note **u**) is probably used instead of *Chaldea*; cf. how in 51:41, note **x** and 25:26 *Sheshach* is used to designate Babylon (see the note on 25:15–38). Pope St Gregory applies 51:9 in a spiritual sense to the soul of a Christian in a state of sin: "*We*

/ praedicate et nolite celare, dicite: / "Capta est Babylon, / confusus est Bel, / victus est Merodach. / Confusa sunt sculptilia eius, / superata sunt idola eorum". 3Quoniam ascendit contra eam gens ab

‘Babylon is taken,
Bel is put to shame,
Merodach is dismayed.
Her images are put to shame,
her idols are dismayed.’
3“For out of the north a nation has come up against her, which
shall make her land a desolation, and none shall dwell in it; both
man and beast shall flee away.

Ps 126:5–6 4“In those days and in that time, says the LORD, the people of
Jer 3:18; 31:9–18 Israel and the people of Judah shall come together, weeping as
Ezek 37:22 they come; and they shall seek the LORD their God. 5They shall
Zech 12:10 ask the way to Zion, with faces turned toward it, saying, ‘Come,
let us join ourselves to the LORD in an everlasting covenant which
will never be forgotten.’

Mt 9:36 6“My people have been lost sheep; their shepherds have led
Ezek 34:1 them astray, turning them away on the mountains; from mountain
Zech 11:5 to hill they have gone, they have forgotten their fold. 7All who
found them have devoured them, and their enemies have said, ‘We
are not guilty, for they have sinned against the LORD, their true
habitation, the LORD, the hope of their fathers.’

Is 48:20; 52:11 8“Flee from the midst of Babylon, and go out of the land of the
Jer 51:6,45 Chaldeans, and be as he-goats before the flock. 9For behold, I am
Rev 18:4 stirring up and bringing against Babylon a company of great
nations, from the north country; and they shall array themselves
against her; from there she shall be taken. Their arrows are like a
skilled warrior who does not return empty-handed. 10Chaldea

---

would have healed Babylon, but she was not healed: the soul, confounded by the sins it has committed, endures the suffering sent to chasten it, but still fails to return to the path of righteousness” (*Regula pastoralis*, 3, 13).

aquilone, quae ponet terram eius in solitudinem, et non erit qui habitet in ea ab homine usque ad pecus: et moti sunt et abierunt. 4In diebus illis et in tempore illo, ait Dominus, venient filii Israel ipsi et filii Iudae simul; ambulantes et flentes properabunt et Dominum Deum suum quaerent. 5De Sion interrogabunt, ad cuius viam facies eorum: “Venite, et apponamur ad Dominum foedere sempiterno, quod nulla oblivione delebitur”. 6Grex perditus factus est populus meus, pastores eorum seduxerunt eos feceruntque vagari in montibus; de monte in collem transierunt, obliti sunt cubilis sui. 7Omnes, qui invenerunt, comederunt eos, et hostes eorum dixerunt: “Non delinquimus, pro eo quod peccaverunt Domino, habitaculo iustitiae et exspectationi patrum eorum Domino”. 8Recedite de medio Babylonis / et de terra Chaldaeorum egredimini; / et estote quasi haedi ante gregem. / 9Quoniam ecce ego suscito et adducam in Babylonem / congregationem gentium magnarum / de terra aquilonis; / et praeparabuntur adversus eam, / et inde capietur: / sagitta eorum quasi bellatoris electi / non revertetur vacua. / 10Et erit

shall be plundered; all who plunder her shall be sated, says the
LORD.

11 "Though you rejoice, though you exult, Is 47:10
O plunderers of my heritage,
though you are wanton as a heifer at grass,
and neigh like stallions,
12 your mother shall be utterly shamed,
and she who bore you shall be disgraced.
Lo, she shall be the last of the nations,
a wilderness dry and desert.
13 Because of the wrath of the LORD she shall not be inhabited,
but shall be an utter desolation;
every one who passes by Babylon shall be appalled,
and hiss because of all her wounds.
14 Set yourselves in array against Babylon round about,
all you that bend the bow;
shoot at her, spare no arrows,
for she has sinned against the LORD.
15 Raise a shout against her round about, Is 59:18 Jer 51:6
she has surrendered;
her bulwarks have fallen,
her walls are thrown down.
For this is the vengeance of the LORD:
take vengeance on her,
do to her as she has done.
16 Cut off from Babylon the sower, 2 Kings 24:10 Is 43:14 Jer 51:34
and the one who handles the sickle in time of harvest;
because of the sword of the oppressor,
every one shall turn to his own people,
and every one shall flee to his own land.

Chaldaea in praedam; / omnes vastantes eam replebuntur», / ait Dominus. / [11]Dum exsultatis et magna loquimini / diripientes hereditatem meam / dum effusi estis sicut vituli super herbam / et hinnitis sicut equi fortes, / [12]confusa est mater vestra nimis, / et in opprobrium facta est, quae genuit vos; / ecce novissima erit in gentibus, / deserta, invia et arens. / [13]Ab ira Domini non habitabitur, / sed redigetur tota in solitudinem; / omnis, qui transibit per Babylonem, stupebit / et sibilabit super universis plagis eius. / [14]Praeparamini contra Babylonem per circuitum / omnes, qui tenditis arcum; / debellate eam, non parcatis iaculis, / quia Domino peccavit. / [15]Clamate adversus eam; / ubique dedit manum, / ceciderunt fundamenta eius, / destructi sunt muri eius, / quoniam ultio Domini est; / ultionem accipite de ea: / sicut fecit, facite ei. / [16]Disperdite satorem de Babylone / et tenentem falcem in tempore messis; / a facie gladii saevientis / unusquisque ad populum suum convertetur, / et singuli ad terram suam fugient. / [17]Ovis dispersa Israel; / leones eiecerunt eum. / Primus comedit eum rex Assyriae; / iste novissimus exossavit eum / Nabuchodonosor rex Babylonis. [18]Propterea haec dicit Dominus exercituum, Deus Israel: «Ecce ego visitabo regem Babylonis et terram eius, sicut visitavi regem

Jer 51:34 [17]"Israel is a hunted sheep driven away by lions. First the king
of Assyria devoured him, and now at last Nebuchadnezzar king of
Is 14:24–25 Babylon has gnawed his bones. [18]Therefore, thus says the LORD of
hosts, the God of Israel: Behold, I am bringing punishment on the
king of Babylon and his land, as I punished the king of Assyria.
[19]I will restore Israel to his pasture, and he shall feed on Carmel
and in Bashan, and his desire shall be satisfied on the hills of
Is 4:3 Ephraim and in Gilead. [20]In those days and in that time, says the
LORD, iniquity shall be sought in Israel, and there shall be none;
and sin in Judah, and none shall be found; for I will pardon those
whom I leave as a remnant.

[21] "Go up against the land of Merathaim[s],
and against the inhabitants of Pekod.[t]
Slay, and utterly destroy after them, says the LORD,
and do all that I have commanded you.
[22] The noise of battle is in the land,
and great destruction!
Is 14:4–6 Jer 51:8,20,41 [23] How the hammer of the whole earth
is cut down and broken!
How Babylon has become
a horror among the nations!
[24] I set a snare for you and you were taken, O Babylon,
and you did not know it;
you were found and caught,
because you strove against the LORD.
[25] The LORD has opened his armoury,
and brought out the weapons of his wrath,
for the Lord GOD of hosts has a work to do
in the land of the Chaldeans.
Josh 6:17 [26] Come against her from every quarter;
open her granaries;

Assyriae; [19]et reducam Israel ad pascua sua, et pascetur Carmelum et Basan, et in monte Ephraim et Galaad saturabitur anima eius. [20]In diebus illis et in tempore illo, ait Dominus, quaeretur iniquitas Israel et non erit, et peccatum Iudae et non invenietur, quoniam propitius ero eis, quos reliquero. [21]Super terram Merataim ascende / et super habitatores Phacud. / Dissipa et interfice persequens eos, / ait Dominus, / et fac iuxta omnia, quae praecepi tibi». / [22]Vox belli in terra / et contritio magna. / [23]Quomodo confractus est et contritus / malleus universae terrae? / Quomodo versa est in desolationem Babylon in gentibus? / [24]Illaqueavi te, et capta es, Babylon, / et nesciebas; / inventa es et apprehensa, / quoniam Dominum provocasti. / [25]Aperuit Dominus thesaurum suum / et protulit vasa irae suae, / quoniam opus est Domino Deo exercituum / in terra Chaldaeorum. / [26]Venite ad eam ab extremis finibus, / aperite horrea eius; / redigite eam in acervos lapidum quasi manipulos / et interficite eam, /

s. Or *Double Rebellion* **t.** Or *Punishment*

pile her up like heaps of grain, and destroy her utterly;
let nothing be left of her.
27 Slay all her bulls, Ps 22:13
let them go down to the slaughter. Is 34:7
Woe to them, for their day has come, Jer 46:21; 48:15
the time of their punishment.

28 "Hark! they flee and escape from the land of Babylon, to
declare in Zion the vengeance of the LORD our God, vengeance for
his temple.

29 "Summon archers against Babylon, all those who bend the Ex 21:25
bow. Encamp round about her; let no one escape. Requite her Ps 28:4
according to her deeds, do to her according to all that she has Is 14:13–14 Rev 18:6
done; for she has proudly defied the LORD, the Holy One of Israel.
30 Therefore her young men shall fall in her squares, and all her
soldiers shall be destroyed on that day, says the LORD.

31 "Behold, I am against you, O proud one,
says the Lord GOD of hosts;
for your day has come,
the time when I will punish you.
32 The proud one shall stumble and fall,
with none to raise him up,
and I will kindle a fire in his cities,
and it will devour all that is round about him.

33 "Thus says the LORD of hosts: The people of Israel are
oppressed, and the people of Judah with them; all who took them
captive have held them fast, they refuse to let them go. 34 Their Is 41:14;
Redeemer is strong; the LORD of hosts is his name. He will surely 43:14 Jer 10:16;
plead their cause, that he may give rest to the earth, but unrest to 51:10,36
the inhabitants of Babylon.

---

nec sit quidquam reliquum. / 27 Dissipate universos tauros eius, / descendant in occisionem. / Vae eis,
quia venit dies eorum, / tempus visitationis eorum! / 28 Vox fugientium / et eorum, qui evaserunt de terra
Babylonis, / ut annuntient in Sion / ultionem Domini Dei nostri, / ultionem templi eius. / 29 Convocate
in Babylonem sagittarios, / omnes, qui tendunt arcum; / consistite adversus eam per gyrum, et nullus
evadat: / reddite ei secundum opus suum, / iuxta omnia, quae fecit, facite illi, / quia contra Dominum
erecta est, / adversum Sanctum Israel. / 30 «Idcirco cadent iuvenes eius in plateis eius, / et omnes viri
bellatores eius conticescent in die illa, / ait Dominus. / 31 Ecce ego ad te, Superbia, / dicit Dominus,
Deus exercituum, / quia venit dies tuus, / tempus visitationis tuae. / 32 Et cadet Superbia et corruet, /
et non erit qui suscitet eam; / et succendam ignem in urbibus eius, / et devorabit omnia in circuitu eius».
33 Haec dicit Dominus exercituum: «Calumniam sustinent filii Israel et filii Iudae simul; omnes, qui
ceperunt eos, tenent, nolunt dimittere eos. 34 Redemptor eorum fortis, Dominus exercituum nomen eius,

35 "A sword upon the Chaldeans, says the LORD,
and upon the inhabitants of Babylon,
and upon her princes and her wise men!
36 A sword upon the diviners,
that they may become fools!
A sword upon her warriors,
that they may be destroyed!
Jer 51:13, 30,36 37 A sword upon her horses and upon her chariots,
and upon all the foreign troops in her midst,
that they may become women!
A sword upon all her treasures,
that they may be plundered!
38 A drought upon her waters,
that they may be dried up!
For it is a land of images,
and they are mad over idols.

Rev 18:2 39 "Therefore wild beasts shall dwell with hyenas in Babylon,
and ostriches shall dwell in her; she shall be peopled no more for
Jer 49:18; 51:26,37 ever, nor inhabited for all generations. 40 As when God overthrew
Sodom and Gomorrah and their neighbour cities, says the LORD, so
no man shall dwell there, and no son of man shall sojourn in her.

Jer 6:22–24; 51:27 41 "Behold, a people comes from the north;
a mighty nation and many kings
are stirring from the farthest parts of the earth.
42 They lay hold of bow and spear;
they are cruel, and have no mercy.
The sound of them is like the roaring of the sea;
they ride upon horses,
arrayed as a man for battle
against you, O daughter of Babylon!

---

iudicio defendet causam eorum, ut quietem det terrae et conturbet habitatores Babylonis. 35 Gladius ad Chaldaeos, / ait Dominus, / et ad habitatores Babylonis / et ad principes et ad sapientes eius! / 36 Gladius ad divinos eius, qui stulti erunt! / Gladius ad fortes illius, qui timebunt! / 37 Gladius ad equos eius et ad currus eius / et ad omne vulgus, quod est in medio eius; / et erunt quasi mulieres! / Gladius ad thesauros eius, qui diripientur! / 38 Siccitas super aquas eius erit, et arescent, / quia terra sculptilium est, / et in portentis insaniunt. 39 Propterea habitabunt dracones cum thoibus, et habitabunt in ea struthiones; et non inhabitabitur ultra usque in sempiternum nec exstruetur usque ad generationem et generationem. 40 Sicut subvertit Deus Sodomam et Gomorram et vicinas eius, ait Dominus, non habitabit ibi vir, et non peregrinabitur in ea filius hominis. 41 Ecce populus venit ab aquilone, et gens magna et reges multi consurgent a finibus terrae. 42 Arcum et acinacem apprehendent, crudeles sunt et immisericordes; vox eorum quasi mare sonabit, et super equos ascendent sicut vir paratus ad proelium contra te, filia Babylon. 43 Audivit rex Babylonis famam eorum, et dissolutae sunt manus eius; angustia apprehendit

43 "The king of Babylon heard the report of them,
and his hands fell helpless;
anguish seized him,
pain as of a woman in travail.

44"Behold, like a lion coming up from the jungle of the Jordan Jer 49:19–21
against a strong sheepfold, I will suddenly make them run away
from her; and I will appoint over her whomever I choose. For who
is like me? Who will summon me? What shepherd can stand
before me? 45Therefore hear the plan which the LORD has made
against Babylon, and the purposes which he has formed against
the land of the Chaldeans: Surely the little ones of their flock shall
be dragged away; surely their fold shall be appalled at their fate.
46At the sound of the capture of Babylon the earth shall tremble,
and her cry shall be heard among the nations."

51 1Thus says the LORD: 1 Pet 5:13
"Behold, I will stir up the spirit of a destroyer Rev 16:19; 17:5; 18:20–24
against Babylon,
against the inhabitants of Chaldea;[u]
2and I will send to Babylon winnowers, Is 41:16
and they shall winnow her, Jer 4:11; 15:7 Mt 3:12
and they shall empty her land,
when they come against her from every side
on the day of trouble.
3Let not the archer bend his bow, Josh 6:17
and let him not stand up in his coat of mail.
Spare not her young men;
utterly destroy all her host.
4They shall fall down slain in the land of the Chaldeans,
and wounded in her streets.

---

eum, dolor quasi parturientem. 44Ecce quasi leo ascendet de silva condensa Iordanis ad prata semper virentia, quia subito currere faciam eos ex illa et, qui erit electus, illum praeponam ei. Quis enim similis mei? Et quis vocabit me in iudicium? Et quis est iste pastor, qui resistat vultui meo?». 45Propterea audite consilium Domini, quod mente concepit adversum Babylonem, et cogitationes eius, quas cogitavit super terram Chaldaeorum: certe abstrahent parvulos gregis, certe desolabuntur super eos pascua eorum. 46A voce captivitatis Babylonis commota est terra, et clamor inter gentes auditus est. **[51]** 1Haec dicit Dominus: / «Ecce ego suscitabo super Babylonem / et super habitatores Chaldaeae / quasi ventum pestilentem; / 2et mittam in Babylonem ventilatores, / et ventilabunt eam / et demolientur terram eius, / quoniam venerunt super eam undique / in die afflictionis. / 3Non tendat, qui tendit arcum suum, / et non ascendat loricatus; / nolite parcere iuvenibus eius, / interficite omnem militiam eius». / 4Et cadent interfecti in terra Chaldaeorum / et vulnerati in plateis eius, / 5quoniam non est viduatus Israel et Iuda / a Deo suo, Domino exercituum; / terra autem eorum repleta est delicto / in conspectu

u. Heb *Leb-qamai*, a cipher for Chaldea

Is 54:5–6 [5]For Israel and Judah have not been forsaken
by their God, the LORD of hosts;
but the land of the Chaldeans[v] is full of guilt
against the Holy One of Israel.

Jer 50:8,15 Rev 18:4 [6]"Flee from the midst of Babylon,
let every man save his life!
Be not cut off in her punishment,
for this is the time of the LORD's vengeance,
the requital he is rendering her.

Is 51:17 Jer 25:15–29; 50:23 Rev 14:8; 17:4; 18:2,3 [7]Babylon was a golden cup in the LORD's hand,
making all the earth drunken;
the nations drank of her wine,
therefore the nations went mad.
[8]Suddenly Babylon has fallen and been broken;
wail for her!
Take balm for her pain;
perhaps she may be healed.
Jer 50:16 [9]We would have healed Babylon,
but she was not healed.
Forsake her, and let us go
each to his own country;
for her judgment has reached up to heaven
and has been lifted up even to the skies.
Jer 50:34 [10]The LORD has brought forth our vindication;
come, let us declare in Zion
the work of the LORD our God.

Is 13:17 [11]"Sharpen the arrows!
Take up the shields!
The LORD has stirred up the spirit of the kings of the Medes, because his purpose concerning Babylon is to destroy it, for that is the vengeance of the LORD, the vengeance for his temple.

Sancti Israel. / [6]Fugite de medio Babylonis, / et salvet unusquisque animam suam; / nolite perire in poena eius, / quoniam tempus ultionis est Domino: / vicissitudinem ipse retribuet ei. / [7]Calix aureus Babylon in manu Domini / inebrians omnem terram; / de vino eius biberunt gentes / et ideo insaniunt. / [8]Subito cecidit Babylon et contrita est. / Ululate super eam; / tollite resinam ad dolorem eius, / si forte sanetur. / [9]«Curavimus Babylonem, / et non est sanata. / Derelinquite eam, / et eamus unusquisque in terram suam, / quoniam pervenit usque ad caelos iudicium eius / et elevatum est usque ad nubes. / [10]Protulit Dominus iustitias nostras; / venite, et narremus in Sion / opus Domini Dei nostri». / [11]Acuite

v. Heb *their land*

12 Set up a standard against the walls of Babylon;
make the watch strong;
set up watchmen;
prepare the ambushes;
for the LORD has both planned and done
what he spoke concerning the inhabitants of Babylon.
13 O you who dwell by many waters, Jer 50:37–38
rich in treasures, Rev 17:1,15
your end has come,
the thread of your life is cut.
14 The LORD of hosts has sworn by himself:
Surely I will fill you with men, as many as locusts,
and they shall raise the shout of victory over you.

15 "It is he who made the earth by his power, Jer 10:12–16
who established the world by his wisdom,
and by his understanding stretched out the heavens.
16 When he utters his voice there is a tumult of waters in the Ps 135:7
heavens,
and he makes the mist rise from the ends of the earth.
He makes lightnings for the rain,
and he brings forth the wind from his storehouses.
17 Every man is stupid and without knowledge;
every goldsmith is put to shame by his idols;
for his images are false,
and there is no breath in them.
18 They are worthless, a work of delusion;
at the time of their punishment they shall perish.
19 Not like these is he who is the portion of Jacob,
for he is the one who formed all things,
and Israel is the tribe of his inheritance;
the LORD of hosts is his name.

---

sagittas, implete pharetras; / suscitavit Dominus spiritum regum Medorum, / et contra Babylonem mens eius est, ut perdat eam, / quoniam ultio Domini / est ultio templi sui. / [12]Super muros Babylonis levate signum, / augete custodiam, / ponite custodes, praeparate insidias, / quia cogitavit Dominus, / et facit quaecumque locutus est / contra habitatores Babylonis. / [13]Quae habitas super aquas multas, / locuples in thesauris, / venit finis tuus, / pedalis praecisionis tuae. / [14]Iuravit Dominus exercituum per animam suam: / «Quoniam, etsi replevero te hominibus quasi brucho, / super te celeuma cantabitur». / [15]Qui fecit terram in fortitudine sua, / praeparavit orbem in sapientia sua et prudentia sua extendit caelos; / [16]dante eo vocem, multiplicantur aquae in caelo; / qui levat nubes ab extremo terrae, / fulgura in pluviam facit / et producit ventum de thesauris suis. / [17]Stultus factus est omnis homo, absque scientia; / confusus est omnis conflator in sculptili, / quia mendax conflatio eius, / nec est spiritus in eis. / [18]Vana sunt opera et risu digna, / in tempore visitationis suae peribunt. / [19]Non sicut haec pars Iacob, / quia, qui fecit omnia, ipse est, / et Israel tribus hereditatis eius: / Dominus exercituum nomen eius. /

Jer 50:23 20 "You are my hammer and weapon of war:
with you I break nations in pieces;
with you I destroy kingdoms;
21 with you I break in pieces the horse and his rider;
with you I break in pieces the chariot and the charioteer;
22 with you I break in pieces man and woman;
with you I break in pieces the old man and the youth;
with you I break in pieces the young man and the maiden;
23 with you I break in pieces the shepherd and his flock;
with you I break in pieces the farmer and his team;
with you I break in pieces governors and commanders.

2 Kings 23:13 24 "I will requite Babylon and all the inhabitants of Chaldea
Is 13:2
Jer 50:15,29 before your very eyes for all the evil that they have done in Zion,
Zech 4:7 says the LORD.

25 "Behold, I am against you, O destroying mountain, says the LORD,
which destroys the whole earth;

51:20–58. The oracle elaborates (51: 20–26) on the analogy of the hammer, already used in 50:23. Babylon was the weapon that God used to punish other nations, but now it will be smashed to pieces just as it reduced the temple of Jerusalem to rubble (cf. 50:28).

But there are further threats against Babylon (51:27–44). It is not only the Medes that are invited to destroy Babylon, but other nations to the north, that had earlier been defeated by Babylon—nations in Armenia (Ararat) and around Lake Urmiah (Minni and Ashkenaz: 51:27). Babylon will become a place of desolation (51:29–33) because God is coming to avenge the holy city and its inhabitants (51:36–40), who like the prophet Jonah have been devoured by a monster and will then be thrown up by it (51:34–35, 44). There is nothing left to be done but make lament for the famous city (51:41–43), for even its world-famous walls will be tumbled down (51:41–43).

Finally, the oracle addresses those who are in exile (51:45–58). The prophet urges them to have faith, for the Lord will fulfil his promises. He will avenge the destruction of the temple and the actions of those who destroyed it, because he is a just Judge who rewards and punishes men according to their deeds.

[20]«Malleus tu mihi, vas belli: / et ego collisi in te gentes / et dispersi in te regna / [21]et collisi in te equum et equitem eius / et collisi in te currum et ascensorem eius / [22]et collisi in te virum et mulierem / et collisi in te senem et puerum / et collisi in te iuvenem et virginem / [23]et collisi in te pastorem et gregem eius / et collisi in te agricolam et iugales eius / et collisi in te duces et magistratus. [24]Et reddam Babyloni et cunctis habitatoribus Chaldaeae omne malum suum, quod fecerunt in Sion in oculis vestris, ait Dominus. [25]Ecce ego ad te, mons pestifer, / ait Dominus, / qui corrumpis universam terram; / et extendam manum meam super te / et evolvam te de petris / et dabo te in montem combustionis. / [26]Et

I will stretch out my hand against you,
    and roll you down from the crags,
    and make you a burnt mountain.
[26] No stone shall be taken from you for a corner   Jer 50:40
    and no stone for a foundation,
but you shall be a perpetual waste,
    says the LORD.

[27] "Set up a standard on the earth,
    blow the trumpet among the nations;
prepare the nations for war against her,
    summon against her the kingdoms,
    Ararat, Minni, and Ashkenaz;
appoint a marshal against her,
    bring up horses like bristling locusts.
[28] Prepare the nations for war against her,
    the kings of the Medes, with their governors and deputies,
    and every land under their dominion.
[29] The land trembles and writhes in pain,
    for the LORD'S purposes against Babylon stand,
to make the land of Babylon a desolation,
    without inhabitant.
[30] The warriors of Babylon have ceased fighting,   Is 19:16
    they remain in their strongholds;   Jer 50:37
their strength has failed,   Nahum 3:13
    they have become women;
her dwellings are on fire,
    her bars are broken.
[31] One runner runs to meet another,
    and one messenger to meet another,
to tell the king of Babylon
    that his city is taken on every side;
[32] the fords have been seized,
    the bulwarks are burned with fire,

---

non tollent de te lapidem in angulum / et lapidem in fundamenta, / sed perditus in aeternum eris», / ait Dominus. / [27]Levate signum in terra, / clangite bucina in gentibus, / sanctificate super eam gentes, / vocate contra illam regna / Ararat, Menni et Aschenez. / Constituite super eam scribas, / adducite equos quasi bruchum aculeatum. [28]Sanctificate contra eam gentes, reges Mediae, duces eius et universos magistratus eius cunctamque terram potestatis eius. [29]Et commovebitur terra et conturbabitur, / quia impletur contra Babylonem cogitatio Domini, / ut ponat terram Babylonis / desertam et inhabitabilem. / [30]Cessaverunt fortes Babylonis a proelio, / habitaverunt in praesidiis; / devoratum est robur eorum, / et facti sunt quasi mulieres; / incensa sunt tabernacula eius, / contriti sunt vectes eius. / [31]Currens obviam currenti veniet, / et nuntius obvius nuntianti, / ut annuntiet regi Babylonis / quia capta est civitas eius / a summo usque ad summum. / [32]Et vada praeoccupata sunt, / et paludes incensae sunt igni; / et

and the soldiers are in panic.
Is 17:5 33 For thus says the LORD of hosts, the God of Israel:
The daughter of Babylon is like a threshing floor
at the time when it is trodden;
yet a little while
and the time of her harvest will come."

Jer 50:17 34 "Nebuchadnezzar the king of Babylon has devoured me,
he has crushed me;
he has made me an empty vessel,
he has swallowed me like a monster;
he has filled his belly with my delicacies,
he has rinsed me out.
35 The violence done to me and to my kinsmen be upon Babylon,"
let the inhabitant of Zion say.
"My blood be upon the inhabitants of Chaldea,"
let Jerusalem say.
Jer 50:34 36 Therefore thus says the LORD:
"Behold, I will plead your cause
and take vengeance for you.
I will dry up her sea
and make her fountain dry;
Is 25:2 Jer 18:16; 50:39 37 and Babylon shall become a heap of ruins,
the haunt of jackals,
a horror and a hissing,
without inhabitant.

Jer 50:40 38 "They shall roar together like lions;
they shall growl like lions' whelps.
Ps 76:6 Jer 51:57 39 While they are inflamed I will prepare them a feast
and make them drunk, till they swoon away[w]
and sleep a perpetual sleep
and not wake, says the LORD.

---

viri bellatores conturbati sunt. / [33]Quia haec dicit Dominus exercituum, Deus Israel: / «Filia Babylonis quasi area tempore triturae eius; / adhuc modicum, et veniet tempus messionis eius». / [34]«Comedit me, devoravit me Nabuchodonosor; / rex Babylonis reddidit me quasi vas inane, / absorbuit me quasi draco, / replevit ventrem suum deliciis meis et eiecit me». / [35]«Iniquitas adversum me et caro mea super Babylonem!», / dicit habitatio Sion. / «Et sanguis meus super habitatores Chaldaeae!», / dicit Ierusalem. / [36]Propterea haec dicit Dominus: / «Ecce ego iudicabo causam tuam / et ulciscar ultionem tuam / et desertum faciam mare eius / et siccabo venam eius; / [37]et erit Babylon in tumulos, / habitatio thoum, / stupor et sibilus, / eo quod non sit habitator. / [38]Simul ut leones rugient, / frement veluti catuli leonum. / [39]In calore eorum ponam potus eorum / et inebriabo eos, ut sopiantur / et dormiant somnum

w. Gk Vg: Heb *rejoice*

40 I will bring them down like lambs to the slaughter,
like rams and he-goats.

41 "How Babylon[x] is taken, Jer 25:26; 49:25; 50:23
the praise of the whole earth seized!
How Babylon has become
a horror among the nations!
42 The sea has come up on Babylon;
she is covered with its tumultuous waves.
43 Her cities have become a horror,
a land of drought and a desert,
a land in which no one dwells,
and through which no son of man passes.
44 And I will punish Bel in Babylon, Jer 50:2
and take out of his mouth what he has swallowed.
The nations shall no longer flow to him;
the wall of Babylon has fallen.

45 "Go out of the midst of her, my people! Jer 50:8; 51:6
Let every man save his life
from the fierce anger of the LORD!
46 Let not your heart faint, and be not fearful Mt 24:6ff
at the report heard in the land,
when a report comes in one year
and afterward a report in another year,
and violence is in the land,
and ruler is against ruler.

47 "Therefore, behold, the days are coming
when I will punish the images of Babylon;
her whole land shall be put to shame,
and all her slain shall fall in the midst of her.

---

sempiternum et non consurgant, / dicit Dominus. / 40Deducam eos quasi agnos ad victimam, / quasi arietes cum haedis». / 41Quomodo capta est Babel, / et comprehensa est gloria universae terrae? / Quomodo facta est in stuporem / Babylon inter gentes? / 42Ascendit super Babylonem mare, / multitudine fluctuum eius operta est. / 43Factae sunt civitates eius in stuporem, / terra inhabitabilis et deserta, / terra, in qua nullus habitet, / nec transeat per eam filius hominis. / 44«Et visitabo super Bel in Babylone / et eiciam, quod absorbuerat, de ore eius; / et non confluent ad eum ultra gentes, / siquidem et murus Babylonis corruet. / 45Egredimini de medio eius, populus meus, / ut salvet unusquisque animam suam / ab ira furoris Domini. 46Et ne forte mollescat cor vestrum, et timeatis auditum, qui audietur in terra; et veniet in anno auditio, et post hunc annum auditio, et iniquitas in terra, et dominator super dominatorem. 47Propterea ecce dies veniunt, et visitabo super sculptilia Babylonis, et omnis terra

x. Heb *Sheshach*, a cipher for Babylon

Is 44:23 Jer 50:3 Rev 18:20; 19:1–2

48 Then the heavens and the earth,
and all that is in them,
shall sing for joy over Babylon;
for the destroyers shall come against them out of the north,
says the LORD.

49 Babylon must fall for the slain of Israel,
as for Babylon have fallen the slain of all the earth.

Ps 137:5

50 "You that have escaped from the sword,
go, stand not still!
Remember the LORD from afar,
and let Jerusalem come into your mind:
51 'We are put to shame, for we have heard reproach;
dishonour has covered our face,
for aliens have come
into the holy places of the LORD's house.'

52 "Therefore, behold, the days are coming, says the LORD,
when I will execute judgment upon her images,
and through all her land
the wounded shall groan.

Is 14:13 Jer 49:16

53 Though Babylon should mount up to heaven,
and though she should fortify her strong height,
yet destroyers would come from me upon her,
says the LORD.

54 "Hark! a cry from Babylon!
The noise of great destruction from the land of the Chaldeans!
55 For the LORD is laying Babylon waste,
and stilling her mighty voice.
Their waves roar like many waters,
the noise of their voice is raised;

---

eius confundetur, et universi interfecti eius cadent in medio eius. [48]Et laudabunt super Babylonem caeli et terra et omnia, quae in eis sunt, quia ab aquilone venient ei praedones, ait Dominus. [49]Et Babylon cadet, occisi in Israel, sicut pro Babylone ceciderunt occisi universae terrae. [50]Qui fugistis gladium, ite, nolite stare; recordamini procul Domini, et Ierusalem ascendat super cor vestrum. [51]"Confusi sumus, quoniam audivimus opprobrium; operuit ignominia facies nostras, quia venerunt alieni super sanctificationem domus Domini". [52]Propterea ecce dies veniunt, ait Dominus, et visitabo super sculptilia eius, et in omni terra eius gemet vulneratus. [53]Si ascenderit Babylon in caelum et firmaverit in excelso robur suum, a me venient vastatores eius», ait Dominus. [54]Vox clamoris de Babylone et contritio magna de terra Chaldaeorum, [55]quoniam vastavit Dominus Babylonem et perdidit ex ea vocem magnam; et sonabunt fluctus eorum quasi aquae multae, dedit sonitum vox eorum. [56]Quia venit super eam, id est super Babylonem, praedo; et apprehensi sunt fortes eius, et fractus est arcus eorum, quia Deus ultor Dominus reddens retribuet. [57]«Et inebriabo principes eius et sapientes eius et duces

[56] for a destroyer has come upon her,
upon Babylon;
her warriors are taken,
their bows are broken in pieces;
for the LORD is a God of recompense,
he will surely requite.
[57] I will make drunk her princes and her wise men, Jer 51:39
her governors, her commanders, and her warriors;
they shall sleep a perpetual sleep and not wake,
says the King, whose name is the LORD of hosts.

[58] "Thus says the LORD of hosts: Hab 2:13
The broad wall of Babylon
shall be leveled to the ground
and her high gates
shall be burned with fire.
The peoples labour for nought,
and the nations weary themselves only for fire."

Oracle proclaimed in Babylon

[59]The word which Jeremiah the prophet commanded Seraiah the
son of Neriah, son of Mahseiah, when he went with Zedekiah king

---

51:56. "[F]or the Lord is a God of recompense, he will surely requite." This is one of the truths about the nature of God that is revealed in different ways and continually clarified over the course of the Old and New Testaments. It is a keystone of the Christian faith. "Following in the steps of the prophets and John the Baptist, Jesus announced the judgment of the Last Day in his preaching (cf. Dan 7:10; Joel 3–4; Mal 3:19; Mt 3:7–12). Then will the conduct of each one and the secrets of hearts be brought to light (cf. Mk 12:38–40; Lk 12:1–3; Jn 3:20–21; Rom 2:16; 1 Cor 4:5). Then will the culpable unbelief that counted the offer of God's grace as nothing be condemned (cf. Mt 11:20–24; 12:41–42). Our attitude to our neighbour will disclose acceptance or refusal of grace and divine love (cf. Mt 5:22; 7:1–5). On the Last Day Jesus will say: 'Truly I say to you, as you did it to one of the least of these my brethren, you did it to me' (Mt 25:40)" (*Catechism of the Catholic Church*, 678).

eius et magistratus eius et fortes eius; et dormient somnum sempiternum et non expergiscentur», ait rex, Dominus exercituum nomen eius. [58]Haec dicit Dominus exercituum: «Murus Babylonis ille latissimus funditus suffodietur, / et portae eius excelsae igni comburentur; / et laboraverunt populi pro nihilo, / et gentes pro igni lassatae sunt». [59]Verbum, quod praecepit Ieremias propheta Saraiae filio Neriae filii Maasiae, cum pergeret cum Sedecia rege Iudae in Babylonem in anno quarto regni eius;

of Judah to Babylon, in the fourth year of his reign. Seraiah was
the quartermaster. [60]Jeremiah wrote in a book all the evil that
should come upon Babylon, all these words that are written
concerning Babylon. [61]And Jeremiah said to Seraiah: "When you
Jer 51:26 come to Babylon, see that you read all these words, [62]and say, 'O
LORD, thou hast said concerning this place that thou wilt cut it off,
so that nothing shall dwell in it, neither man nor beast, and it shall
be desolate for ever.' [63]When you finish reading this book, bind a
Rev 18:21 stone to it, and cast it into the midst of the Euphrates, [64]and say,
'Thus shall Babylon sink, to rise no more, because of the evil that
I am bringing upon her.'"[y]

Thus far are the words of Jeremiah.

51:59–64. As a kind of appendix, another symbolic action is reported here. Although there is no other source for this visit by Zedekiah to Babylon in the year 593 BC, it is very likely that the king of Judah had to present himself in the capital of the empire to do homage as Nebuchadnezzar's vassal. That this episode did indeed take place seems to be confirmed by the fact that Seraiah was a brother of Baruch, the redactor of the book.

On reading these words, particularly vv. 60–64 in the light of 51:1–19, the Christian reader cannot but be reminded of the announcement of the downfall of Babylon in the Revelation to John (cf. Rev 16:19; 17:5; 18:20–24; etc.). There Babylon refers not only to Rome (cf. 1 Pet 5:13) but also to any power that attempts to create a civilization without reference to God. It may, for a while, persecute the righteous, but in the end it will be punished for doing so.

Saraias autem erat princeps, qui mansionibus praeerat. [60]Et scripsit Ieremias omne malum, quod venturum erat super Babylonem, in libro uno, omnia verba haec, quae scripta sunt contra Babylonem. [61]Et dixit Ieremias ad Saraiam: «Cum veneris in Babylonem et videris et legeris omnia verba haec, [62]dices: "Domine, tu locutus es contra locum istum, ut disperderes eum, ne sit qui in eo habitet ab homine usque ad pecus, et ut sit perpetua solitudo". [63]Cumque compleveris legere librum istum, ligabis ad eum lapidem et proicies illum in medium Euphraten [64]et dices: "Sic submergetur Babylon et non consurget a facie afflictionis, quam ego adduco super eam, et dissolvetur"». Hucusque verba Ieremiae.

y. Gk: Heb *upon her. And they shall weary themselves*

EPILOGUE

2 Kings
24:18–25:30

THE FALL OF JERUSALEM

The lamentations of Jeremiah

52 [1]*Zedekiah was twenty-one years old when he became king; and he reigned eleven years in Jerusalem. His mother's name was Hamutal the daughter of Jeremiah of Libnah. [2]And he did what was evil in the sight of the LORD, according to all that Jehoiakim had done. [3]Surely because of the anger of the LORD things came to such a pass in Jerusalem and Judah that he cast them out from his presence.

And Zedekiah rebelled against the king of Babylon. [4]And in the Jer 39:1–2
ninth year of his reign, in the tenth month, on the tenth day of the month, Nebuchadnezzar king of Babylon came with all his army against Jerusalem, and they laid siege to it and built siegeworks against it round about. [5]So the city was besieged till the eleventh year of King Zedekiah. [6]On the ninth day of the fourth month the famine was so severe in the city, that there was no food for the
people of the land. [7]Then a breach was made in the city; and all Jer 39:4–10

52:1–34. The book of Jeremiah is rounded off by this account of the fall of Jerusalem showing that the prophecies in the book found fulfilment. The narrative is made up of passages from the second book of Kings (2 Kings 24:18—25:30) with scarcely any changes. The only omission is the passage about the short term of office of Gedaliah (2 Kings 25:22–26).

The Hebrew text of Jeremiah (but not the Greek) adds to the 2 Kings account (which is part of "Deuteronomic history") a summary giving the numbers of those taken to Babylon in the various deportations (52:28–30). These deportations took place in 597, 587 and 582–581 BC. The last deportation is reported only in the book of Jeremiah.

When Evil-merodach became king of Babylon in 561, King Jehoiachin was released from prison. In this way the book of Jeremiah ends on a note of hope, showing that in spite of all their travail the people are still being protected by God.

[52] [1]Filius viginti et unius anni erat Sedecias, cum regnare coepisset, et undecim annis regnavit in Ierusalem; et nomen matris eius Amital filia Ieremiae de Lobna. [2]Et fecit malum in oculis Domini iuxta omnia, quae fecerat Ioachim, [3]quoniam furor Domini erat in Ierusalem et in Iuda, usquequo proiceret eos a facie sua. Et recessit Sedecias a rege Babylonis. [4]Factum est autem in anno nono regni eius, in mense decimo decima mensis, venit Nabuchodonosor rex Babylonis, ipse et omnis exercitus eius, adversus Ierusalem; et obsederunt eam et aedificaverunt contra eam munitiones in circuitu. [5]Et fuit civitas obsessa usque ad undecimum annum regis Sedeciae. [6]Mense autem quarto, nona mensis, obtinuit fames in civitate, et non erant alimenta populo terrae. [7]Et dirupta est civitas, et omnes viri bellatores fugerunt exieruntque de civitate nocte per viam portae, quae est inter duos muros et ducit ad

the men of war fled and went out from the city by night by the
way of a gate between the two walls, by the king's garden, while
the Chaldeans were round about the city. And they went in the
Jer 39:4 direction of the Arabah. [8]But the army of the Chaldeans pursued
the king, and overtook Zedekiah in the plains of Jericho; and all
his army was scattered from him. [9]Then they captured the king,
and brought him up to the king of Babylon at Riblah in the land of
Hamath, and he passed sentence upon him. [10]The king of Babylon
slew the sons of Zedekiah before his eyes, and also slew all the
princes of Judah at Riblah. [11]He put out the eyes of Zedekiah, and
bound him in fetters, and the king of Babylon took him to
Babylon, and put him in prison till the day of his death.

[12]In the fifth month, on the tenth day of the month—which was
the nineteenth year of King Nebuchadnezzar, king of Babylon—
Nebuzaradan the captain of the bodyguard who served the king of
Babylon, entered Jerusalem. [13]And he burned the house of the
Lord, and the king's house and all the houses of Jerusalem; every
great house he burned down. [14]And all the army of the Chaldeans,
who were with the captain of the guard, broke down all the walls
round about Jerusalem. [15]And Nebuzaradan the captain of the
guard carried away captive some of the poorest of the people and
the rest of the people who were left in the city and the deserters
who had deserted to the king of Babylon, together with the rest of
the artisans. [16]But Nebuzaradan the captain of the guard left some
of the poorest of the land to be vinedressers and ploughmen.

[17]And the pillars of bronze that were in the house of the Lord,
and the stands and the bronze sea that were in the house of the
Lord, the Chaldeans broke in pieces, and carried all the bronze to
Babylon. [18]And they took away the pots, and the shovels, and the

---

hortum regis, Chaldaeis obsidentibus urbem in gyro, et abierunt per viam, quae ducit in Arabam.
[8]Persecutus est autem Chaldaeorum exercitus regem, et apprehenderunt Sedeciam in campestribus
Iericho, et omnis comitatus eius diffugit ab eo. [9]Cumque comprehendissent regem, adduxerunt eum ad
regem Babylonis in Rebla, quae est in terra Emath; et locutus est ad eum iudicia. [10]Et iugulavit rex
Babylonis filios Sedeciae in oculis eius, sed et omnes principes Iudae occidit in Rebla; [11]et oculos
Sedeciae eruit et vinxit eum compedibus et adduxit eum rex Babylonis in Babylonem et posuit eum in
domo carceris usque ad diem mortis eius. [12]In mense autem quinto, decima mensis, ipse est annus
nonus decimus Nabuchodonosor regis Babylonis, venit Nabuzardan princeps satellitum, qui stabat
coram rege Babylonis, in Ierusalem. [13]Et incendit domum Domini et domum regis; et omnes domos
Ierusalem et omnem domum magnam igni combussit; [14]et totum murum Ierusalem per circuitum
destruxit cunctus exercitus Chaldaeorum, qui erat cum magistro satellitum. [15]De pauperibus autem
populi et de reliquo vulgo, quod remanserat in civitate, et de perfugis, qui transfugerant ad regem
Babylonis, et superfluos artificum transtulit Nabuzardan princeps satellitum. [16]De pauperibus vero
terrae reliquit Nabuzardan princeps satellitum in vinitores et in agricolas. [17]Columnas quoque aereas,
quae erant in domo Domini, et bases et mare aereum, quod erat in domo Domini, confregerunt
Chaldaei et tulerunt omne aes eorum in Babylonem. [18]Et lebetes et vatilla et cultros et phialas et

snuffers, and the basins, and the dishes for incense, and all the
vessels of bronze used in the temple service; [19]also the small
bowls, and the firepans, and the basins, and the pots, and the
lampstands, and the dishes for incense, and the bowls for libation.
What was of gold the captain of the guard took away as gold, and
what was of silver, as silver. [20]As for the two pillars, the one sea,
the twelve bronze bulls which were under the sea,[z] and the stands,
which Solomon the king had made for the house of the LORD, the
bronze of all these things was beyond weight. [21]As for the pillars, 1 Kings 7:15
the height of the one pillar was eighteen cubits, its circumference
was twelve cubits, and its thickness was four fingers, and it was
hollow. [22]Upon it was a capital of bronze; the height of the one
capital was five cubits; a network and pomegranates, all of bronze,
were upon the capital round about. And the second pillar had the
like, with pomegranates. [23]There were ninety-six pomegranates on
the sides; all the pomegranates were a hundred upon the network
round about.

[24]And the captain of the guard took Seraiah the chief priest,
and Zephaniah the second priest, and the three keepers of the
threshold; [25]and from the city he took an officer who had been in 2 Kings 25:19
command of the men of war, and seven men of the king's council,
who were found in the city; and the secretary of the commander
of the army who mustered the people of the land; and sixty men
of the people of the land, who were found in the midst of the city.
[26]And Nebuzaradan the captain of the guard took them, and
brought them to the king of Babylon at Riblah. [27]And the king of
Babylon smote them, and put them to death at Riblah in the land
of Hamath. So Judah was carried captive out of its land.

---

mortariola et omnia vasa aerea, quae in ministerio fuerant, tulerunt; [19]et pelves et thymiamateria et
phialas et lebetes et candelabra et mortaria et cyathos, quotquot aurea aurea, et quotquot argentea
argentea, tulit magister satellitum; [20]columnas duas et mare unum et vitulos duodecim aereos, qui erant
subtus basi, quam fecerat rex Salomon domui Domini. Non erat pondus aeris omnium horum vasorum.
[21]De columnis autem, decem et octo cubiti altitudinis erant in columna una, et funiculus duodecim
cubitorum circuibat eam; porro grossitudo eius quattuor digitorum, et intrinsecus cava erat. [22]Et
capitella super utramque aerea: altitudo capitelli unius quinque cubitorum, et retiacula et malogranata
super capitellum in circuitu omnia aerea; similiter columnae secundae. [23]Et malogranata nonaginta sex
dependentia; omnia malogranata centum super retiacula in circuitu. [24]Et tulit magister satellitum
Saraiam sacerdotem primum et Sophoniam sacerdotem secundum et tres custodes vestibuli. [25]Et de
civitate tulit eunuchum unum, qui erat praepositus super viros bellatores, et septem viros de his, qui
videbant faciem regis, qui inventi sunt in civitate, et scribam principis militum, qui ex populo terrae
probabat tirones, et sexaginta viros de populo terrae, qui inventi sunt in medio civitatis. [26]Tulit autem
eos Nabuzardan magister satellitum et duxit eos ad regem Babylonis in Rebla; [27]et percussit eos rex

z. Heb lacks *the sea*

28This is the number of the people whom Nebuchadnezzar
carried away captive: in the seventh year, three thousand and
twenty-three Jews; 29in the eighteenth year of Nebuchadnezzar he
carried away captive from Jerusalem eight hundred and thirty-two
persons; 30in the twenty-third year of Nebuchadnezzar, Nebuzaradan
the captain of the guard carried away captive of the Jews seven
hundred and forty-five persons; all the persons were four thousand
and six hundred.

2 Kings 25:27–30 31And in the thirty-seventh year of the captivity of Jehoiachin
Jer 22:24–30; king of Judah, in the twelfth month, on the twenty-fifth day of the
37:1 month, Evil-merodach king of Babylon, in the year that he
became king, lifted up the head of Jehoiachin king of Judah and
brought him out of prison; 32and he spoke kindly to him, and gave
him a seat above the seats of the kings who were with him in
Babylon. 33So Jehoiachin put off his prison garments. And every
day of his life he dined regularly at the king's table; 34as for his
allowance, a regular allowance was given him by the king
according to his daily need, until the day of his death as long as he
lived.

Babylonis et interfecit eos in Rebla in terra Emath. Et translatus est Iuda de terra sua. 28Iste est populus,
quem transtulit Nabuchodonosor: in anno septimo, Iudaeos tria millia et viginti tres; 29in anno octavo
decimo Nabuchodonosor de Ierusalem animas octingentas triginta duas; 30in anno vicesimo tertio
Nabuchodonosor transtulit Nabuzardan magister satellitum animas Iudaeorum septingentas quadraginta
quinque; omnes ergo animae quattuor milia sescentae. 31Et factum est in tricesimo septimo anno
transmigrationis Ioachin regis Iudae, duodecimo mense vicesima quinta mensis, elevavit Evilmerodach
rex Babylonis, ipso anno regni sui, caput Ioachin regis Iudae; et eduxit eum de domo carceris. 32Et
locutus est cum eo bona et posuit thronum eius super thronos regum, qui erant secum in Babylone. 33Et
mutavit vestimenta carceris eius, et comedebat panem coram eo semper cunctis diebus vitae suae. 34Et
cibaria eius, cibaria perpetua dabantur ei a rege Babylonis statuta per singulos dies, usque ad diem
mortis suae, cunctis diebus vitae eius.

THE LAMENTATIONS OF JEREMIAH

Introduction

The book of Jeremiah is usually followed by those of Lamentations and Baruch in most modern Bibles. That is also where it occurs in the Vulgate — and in the New Vulgate, the Church's official Latin version.[1]

The book of Jeremiah closes with an epilogue about the last days of Jerusalem until the city fell into the hands of King Nebuchadnezzar, the more prominent citizens were deported, and the temple treasures were moved to Babylon (cf. Jer 52:1–34). The book of Lamentations is a collection of five poems bemoaning the desolation of the holy city—poems of great beauty and spiritual richness. Christian tradition reads it as a sort of second epilogue to the book of Jeremiah, sapiential and poetic in style, a natural extension of the Jeremiah epilogue.

St Cyril of Jerusalem, sometime around the year 350, included Lamentations among the prophetical books received by the Church: "Jeremiah, with Baruch, the Lamentations and the Letter: a book".[2] Similar references are to be found in documents of the first regional councils that drew up lists of sacred books: "Jeremiah, Baruch, Lamentations and the Letter", says the canon of the Council of Laodicea (360).[3] A little later, the *Decretum Damasi*, in the acts of the Council of Rome (382), says: "*Jeremiah*, along with *Quinot*, that is, his Lamentations: a book".[4] The relationship between Lamentations and the book of Jeremiah is regarded as so close that in later lists only Jeremiah is mentioned, the implication being that Lamentations is part of that book; that is also what happens in the canon of Holy Scripture identified authoritatively by the Councils of Florence[5] and Trent.[6]

However, in Jewish tradition these five laments form a separate book from that of Jeremiah, for reasons to do with the subject matter and with liturgical use. Lamentations is one of the five *megil.lot*, or manuscript rolls, read out in the synagogue on special days. This book, specifically, is read on the ninth day of the month of Ab, a day of mourning for the devastation suffered by Jerusalem; the name it is given is *'Eyka*,[7] the opening word of its text in Hebrew.

1. In the Greek codexes the order is usually Jeremiah, Baruch, Lamentations and the Letter of Jeremiah; however, in the Latin translations the book of Lamentations is switched to immediately after Jeremiah, and the Letter forms simply another chapter in Baruch. In the Hebrew Bible the books of Jeremiah and Lamentations are placed far apart—Jeremiah among the "Prophets" and Lamentations among the "Writings". **2.** *Catechesis,* 4, 35–36. **3.** Council of Laodicea, canon 60 (EB 12). **4.** Cf. Dz-Sch 179; see note 7 below. **5.** Cf. Dz-Sch 1335. **6.** Cf. Dz-Sch 1502. **7.** In the Talmud and other ancient Jewish writings it is also called *Quinot,* that is, "songs of mourning".

1. STRUCTURE AND CONTENT

The book has a simple and well-defined structure. It consists of five clearly identifiable poems, each occupying a chapter. The first, second and fourth are acrostics, that is, each has twenty-two verses (the number of letters in the Hebrew alphabet), and the initial letters of the verses follow alphabetical order. The third is also acrostic, but it has a more complex structure: each letter of the alphabet starts three successive verses. The fifth lamentation is not acrostic, although it does have twenty-two verses and therefore is reminiscent of the alphabet.

The content of the poems is fairly similar, one to another, and always has to do with the ruinous state of Jerusalem and the plight of its people. However, each lamentation tends to have a focus of its own:

1. THE DESOLATION OF JERUSALEM (1:1–22). The first lamentation gives a very vivid poetic impression of the desolate state of the holy city. First, it shows how it looks to an attentive observer (1:1–11). Then Jerusalem herself speaks and expresses her grief and makes entreaty to God (1:12–22).

2. ZION'S MISFORTUNE AND ITS CAUSES (2:1–22). Now that the lamentable condition of Jerusalem has been described, the question must be asked as to why all of this has happened. At the start and finish of the poem, we are left in no doubt: the principal cause of this devastation is the wrath of God (2:1 and 2:22). There is no point in investigating why the Babylonians invaded it: "The Lord has become like an enemy" (2:5); Jerusalem needed this purification.

3. PERSONAL LAMENT OVER THE FATE OF ISRAEL (3:1–66). This is the most poignant part of the book, and it occurs right in the middle, at its heart. No longer is the city's grief being described by others; in this poem she speaks for herself. She has lived through it all, and from what she says she has clearly learned the right lessons: the collapse of her world has taught her to be patient and to fix her sights on the Lord (3:1–39); and so she calls on others to study their own behaviour and be converted (3:40–41), so that she and they may acknowledge their sins and implore God's forgiveness in order to obtain salvation (3:42–66).

4. ZION'S MISFORTUNES AND THOSE RESPONSIBLE FOR THEM (4:1–22). The fourth lamentation reflects again on the ruinous state of the holy city; this time it considers not only the underlying reason for it, but the people responsible—the prophets and priests (cf. 4:13).

5. A DESOLATE PEOPLE PLEADS FOR MERCY (5:1–22). The book ends with an urgent cry to God for help.

2. COMPOSITION AND HISTORICAL BACKGROUND

The book of Lamentations does not give a detailed description of the fall of Jerusalem, but it vividly conveys the pain and grief of the city and its inhabitants. So, although it certainly gives the impression that all this devastation has been caused by the Babylonian army in the kingdom of Judah, it is not easy to say for sure which military campaign it refers to or exactly when it happened. But that is not what really matters: the book is designed primarily to make readers think and learn the appropriate lessons.

As regards when the text was composed, there is no doubt but that it was at some point after the fall of Jerusalem in the year 587 BC. Most scholars nowadays think that the traditional dating makes sense (it dates the book to quite soon after the fall of the city to Nebuchadnezzar).

However, what is not clear is who the author of these songs was; for, although, as we have said, Lamentations was often handed down as an appendix to the book of Jeremiah, that prophet does not seem to have been the author (no more than he seems to be the author of the other appendixes that became attached to the book that bears his name).

Songs of lamentation about destroyed cities and temples are to be found not infrequently in the literature of the Ancient East. The Sumerians, notably, left behind poems of this sort, lamenting the destruction of Ur, Sumer, Nippur, Eridu and Uruk, composed in the second millennium BC and often used in scribal schools of Babylonia as models for scholars' exercises. The custom of writing such songs endured up to when all Mesopotamia came under the control of the Seleucid Greeks—at which point Hellenistic culture came to dominate the entire region. So, there is nothing surprising in the laments being composed by pious Jews when they contemplated Jerusalem in ruins. These poems are indeed laments, but they are written by someone who regards the Lord as the master of human affairs; who tries to discover why things have come to this pass, and who has a deep trust in God and is convinced that he will answer prayer.

3. MESSAGE

Looked at superficially, Lamentations may appear to be a sad book, bemoaning misfortune, and expressing a dejection bordering on pessimism; and it is true that those were very hard times for the people of Israel; God seemed to have forgotten all his promises and turned his back on his elect. However, if one reads these poems thoughtfully, one is soon able to see the unshakeable faith that underlies the grief and entreaty that go to make up the book.

It may well be that the first lesson that a reader draws has to do with the seriousness of the sin that was the ultimate cause of all this misfortune—the people's vain search for safety and salvation through a policy of alliances with foreign powers, instead of relying entirely on God. That was why the Lord allowed all of this to happen (cf. 1:5, 14, 18; 3:42; 4:6; 5:16). But, although humanly speaking the people have no one to turn to in the midst of their tribulation, they do love God; and a strong note of trust in God comes across from these pages. All their suffering, all their anguish, is not vengeance on God's part for sins committed against him. Nor is the Lord a distant God, who has no interest in people's needs and is indifferent to what befalls them (cf. 3:22–26). Suffering has a cleansing quality to it, and it can open the way to optimism and hope—but one needs to face suffering with faith: that in turn will lead to a change of heart and enable one to see the redemptive value of pain and suffering.

The poems tell us about trust in God—and about the value of prayer (cf. 1:9b, 11b, 20; 2:20; 3:55–56; 5:1–22). If, only too well aware of their own limitations, people seek God's help, they do so because they know that they will be listened to by someone who has the power to come to their aid, for he is the Lord of the world and of all that happens in it.

God is a just judge, who can discern the gravity of sin and knows whether repentance is genuine; so, those reading Lamentations should be led to examine themselves and their own situation, and to seek the help of God's grace to become truly converted to him.

4. THE BOOK OF LAMENTATIONS IN THE LIGHT OF THE NEW TESTAMENT

As we have seen, the book of Lamentations is used in Jewish tradition to commemorate the sad plight of the city of Jerusalem and to help people reflect on the redemptive value of suffering; so, too, in the Christian tradition these texts are used to express consternation at the sufferings of our Lord during his passion and redemptive death. From the ninth century onwards it became customary to read from this book in the liturgy of Holy Week.[8] In the current edition of the *Divine Office*, a substantial part of the book is to be found in the office of readings for Holy Week (Year 2).

Also, a spiritual reading of the book and what it has to say about the havoc wrought by sin helps the reader to have a better appreciation of the value of suffering and of the need to be completely detached from earthly things if one is to have the right dispositions for meeting God. St John of the Cross says that, in these poems, the prophet "... brings to life all the passions of the soul while it is purified in the spiritual night"[9]

8. It is read in Night Prayer I during the Triduum of Holy Thursday, Good Friday and Holy Saturday, according to the *Ordo romanus XIIIA*. **9.** *Dark Night of the Soul*, 2, 7, 3.

First lament: The desolation of Jerusalem

1 [1] How lonely sits the city
that was full of people!
How like a widow has she become,
she that was great among the nations!
She that was a princess among the cities
has become a vassal.

Is 47:9
Ezekra 4:20
Bar 4:12

1:1–22. The first lamentation is a poem in two parts: in the first part, (vv. 1–11), the author very poignantly describes the desolation of Jerusalem; in the second the city herself speaks, first to register her grief (vv. 12–19) and then to entreat the Lord, confident that he will hear her (vv. 20–22).

The narrator begins by describing the plight of the city at the time (vv. 1–11): she is like a disconsolate widow (vv. 1–2, 8) who spends the night in tears as she compares the beauty (v. 6) and prosperity (v. 7) that were hers, with her present hunger (v. 11) and desolation—all her children have been taken captive, and she herself is despoiled of all her treasures (vv. 7, 10).

The various images overlap one another, in no apparent order, but the general course of events is clear: Jerusalem has been forsaken by all who claimed to be her friends (v. 2), and those who dwelt within her, all content and joyful, have been deported far beyond her walls (v. 3). If one reflects on it, one can see why all this came about: "The Lord has made her suffer for the multitude of her transgressions" (v. 5). Her misfortunes are not the result of the superior military strength of Babylon; nor can one say that the destruction of the city took place because God was unaware of the danger threatening his people or that he was taken by surprise when Judah was overthrown and its temple profaned (v. 10). On the contrary, the Lord knew all about it and he did nothing to prevent that whole train of events; Israel had sinned so grievously (v. 8) that she needed to be forced to take stock of her position and turn back to the Lord. She realizes that now and, therefore, set within these laments we find two prayers in which she presents her affliction and grief to the Lord (vv. 9, 11). Theodoret of Cyrus comments: "Lamentation is a sign of understanding and love. I believe that the prophet of God wrote down his lamentations as a spiritual aid to the men of his own time and all those who were to come after him, so that all would learn from the Scriptures that sin is the source of all evil" (*Interpretatio in Threnos*, 1).

In the second section of this first lamentation (vv. 12–22), Jerusalem herself, cast in the role of a disconsolate widow, bemoaning the loss of her children, and with tears as her only possession (vv. 15–16), appeals for compassion. She cannot contain her grief (v. 12).

[1] [1]ALEPH. Quomodo sedet sola / civitas plena populo! / Facta est quasi vidua / domina gentium; / princeps provinciarum / facta est sub tributo. / [2]BETH. Plorans plorat in nocte, / et lacrimae eius in

Ps 69:21
Jer 9:17; 30:14
Lam 2:18
Jn 13:18

[2]She weeps bitterly in the night,
tears on her cheeks;
among all her lovers
she has none to comfort her;
all her friends have dealt treacherously with her,
they have become her enemies.

[3]Judah has gone into exile because of affliction
and hard servitude;
she dwells now among the nations,
but finds no resting place;
her pursuers have all overtaken her
in the midst of her distress.

Is 3:26
Jer 14:2

[4]The roads to Zion mourn,
for none come to the appointed feasts;
all her gates are desolate,
her priests groan;

Still, from the depths of her sorrow she acknowledges that God always acts justly, so the lament ends with a prayer in which she recognizes her faults and asks God to undo her enemies (vv. 20–22).

For centuries the Church has used these words in her Holy Week liturgy; expressing, as they do, feelings of intense sorrow, they can give some inkling of what our Lord suffered in his passion, which he lovingly bore in order to redeem the world from its sins. Jeremiah, too, could see that there was never suffering to compare with this. It is not surprising that this passage, especially v. 12, is sometimes to be found on crucifixes and quoted in texts used for the Way of the Cross: "No sooner has Jesus risen from his first fall than he meets his Blessed Mother, standing by the wayside where he is passing. With immense love Mary looks at Jesus, and Jesus at his Mother. Their eyes meet, and each heart pours into the other its own deep sorrow. Mary's soul is steeped in bitter grief, the grief of Jesus Christ. *O all you that pass by the way, look and see, was there ever a sorrow to compare with my sorrow!* (Lam 1:12). But no one notices, no one pays attention; only Jesus. Simeon's prophecy has been fulfilled: *thy own soul a sword shall pierce* (Lk 2:35). In the dark loneliness of the Passion, our Lady offers her Son a comforting balm of tenderness, of union, of faithfulness; a 'yes' to the divine will" (St Josemaría Escrivá, *The Way of the Cross*, 4th station).

maxillis eius; / non est qui consoletur eam / ex omnibus caris eius: / omnes amici eius spreverunt eam / et facti sunt ei inimici. / [3]GHIMEL. Migravit Iudas prae afflictione / et multitudine servitutis; / habitat inter gentes / nec invenit requiem: / omnes persecutores eius apprehenderunt eam / inter angustias. /

her maidens have been dragged away,[a]
and she herself suffers bitterly.

5Her foes have become the head,
her enemies prosper,
because the LORD has made her suffer
for the multitude of her transgressions;
her children have gone away,
captives before the foe.

Deut 28:13,25,44
Ps 89:43
Jer 30:14–15
Lam 2:17

6From the daughter of Zion has departed
all her majesty.
Her princes have become like harts
that find no pasture;
they fled without strength
before the pursuer.

Ezek 10:18f; 11:22

7Jerusalem remembers
in the days of her affliction and bitterness[b]
all the precious things
that were hers from days of old.
When her people fell into the hand of the foe,
and there was none to help her,
the foe gloated over her,
mocking at her downfall.

8Jerusalem sinned grievously,
therefore she became filthy;
all who honoured her despise her,
for they have seen her nakedness;
yea, she herself groans,
and turns her face away.

Is 47:1,3
Ezek 16:37
Hos 2:10

4DALETH. Viae Sion lugent, / eo quod non sint qui veniant ad sollemnitatem; / omnes portae eius destructae, / sacerdotes eius gementes, / virgines eius afflictae, / et ipsa oppressa amaritudine. / 5HE. Facti sunt hostes eius in caput, / inimici eius in securitate, / quia Dominus afflixit eam / propter multitudinem iniquitatum eius; / parvuli eius ducti sunt captivi / ante faciem tribulantis. / 6VAU. Et egressus est a filia Sion / omnis decor eius; / facti sunt principes eius velut cervi / non invenientes pascua / et abierunt absque fortitudine / ante faciem persequentis. / 7ZAIN. Recordata est Ierusalem / dierum afflictionis suae et peregrinationis, / omnium desiderabilium suorum, / quae habuerat a diebus antiquis, / cum caderet populus eius in manu hostili, / et non esset auxiliator; / viderunt eam hostes / et deriserunt interitum eius. / 8HETH. Peccatum peccavit Ierusalem, / propterea abominabilis facta est; / omnes, qui glorificabant eam, spreverunt illam, / quia viderunt ignominiam eius: / ipsa autem gemens

a. Gk Old Latin: Heb *afflicted* **b.** Cn: Heb *wandering*

Lam 1:2

[9]Her uncleanness was in her skirts;
she took no thought of her doom;
therefore her fall is terrible,
she has no comforter.
"O LORD, behold my affliction,
for the enemy has triumphed!"

Deut 23:4
2 Kings 24:13
Ezek 44:7–9
Acts 21:28

[10]The enemy has stretched out his hands
over all her precious things;
yea, she has seen the nations
invade her sanctuary,
those whom thou didst forbid
to enter thy congregation.

Deut 28:51f

[11]All her people groan
as they search for bread;
they trade their treasures for food
to revive their strength.
"Look, O LORD, and behold,
for I am despised."

Dan 9:12; 12:1
Mt 24:21

[12]"Is it nothing to you,[c] all you who pass by?
Look and see
if there is any sorrow like my sorrow
which was brought upon me,
which the LORD inflicted
on the day of his fierce anger.

[13]"From on high he sent fire;
into my bones[d] he made it descend;
he spread a net for my feet;
he turned me back;
he has left me stunned,
faint all the day long.

/ conversa est retrorsum. / [9] TETH. Sordes eius in fimbriis eius, / nec recordata est finis sui; / deposita est vehementer, / non habens consolatorem. / «Vide, Domine, afflictionem meam, quoniam erectus est inimicus!». / [10]IOD. Manum suam misit hostis / ad omnia desiderabilia eius, / quia vidit gentes / ingressas sanctuarium suum, / de quibus praeceperas, / ne intrarent in ecclesiam tuam. / [11]CAPH. Omnis populus eius gemens / et quaerens panem; / dederunt pretiosa quaeque pro cibo / ad refocillandam animam. / «Vide, Domine, et considera, / quoniam facta sum vilis! / [12]LAMED. O vos omnes, qui transitis per viam, / attendite et videte, / si est dolor sicut dolor meus, / quem paravit mihi, / quo afflixit me Dominus / in die irae furoris sui. / [13]MEM. De excelso misit ignem, / in ossa mea immisit eum; /

c. Heb uncertain **d.** Gk: Heb *bones and*

[14]"My transgressions were bound[e] into a yoke;
by his hand they were fastened together;
they were set upon my neck;
he caused my strength to fail;
the Lord gave me into the hands
of those whom I cannot withstand.

Deut 28:48

[15]"The Lord flouted all my mighty men
in the midst of me;
he summoned an assembly against me
to crush my young men;
the Lord has trodden as in a wine press
the virgin daughter of Judah.

Is 63:3
Jer 8:16
Joel 4:13

[16]"For these things I weep;
my eyes flow with tears;
for a comforter is far from me,
one to revive my courage;
my children are desolate,
for the enemy has prevailed."

Lam 1:2

[17]"Zion stretches out her hands,
but there is none to comfort her;
the LORD has commanded against Jacob
that his neighbours should be his foes;
Jerusalem has become
a filthy thing among them.

Lam 1:8

[18]"The LORD is in the right,
for I have rebelled against his word;
but hear, all you peoples,
and behold my suffering;

---

expandit rete pedibus meis, / convertit me retrorsum: / posuit me desolatam, / tota die maerore
confectam. / [14]NUN. Vigilavit super iniquitates meas, / in manu eius convolutae sunt / et impositae collo
meo; / debilitavit virtutem meam: / dedit me Dominus in manu, / de qua non potero surgere. /
[15]SAMECH. Sprevit omnes fortes meos / Dominus in medio mei; / vocavit adversum me conventum, / ut
contereret iuvenes meos: / torcular calcavit Dominus / virgini filiae Iudae. / [16]AIN. Idcirco ego plorans,
/ et oculus meus deducens aquas, / quia longe factus est a me consolator / reficiens animam meam; /
facti sunt filii mei desolati, / quoniam invaluit inimicus». / [17]PHE. Expandit Sion manus suas, / non est
qui consoletur eam; / mandavit Dominus adversum Iacob / in circuitu eius hostes eius: / facta est
Ierusalem / quasi polluta menstruis inter eos. / [18]SADE. «Iustus est Dominus, / quia contra os eius
rebellis fui. / Audite, obsecro, universi populi, / et videte dolorem meum: / virgines meae et iuvenes

e. Cn: Heb uncertain

my maidens and my young men
  have gone into captivity.

Lam 1:2,11 19"I called to my lovers
  but they deceived me;
my priests and elders
  perished in the city,
while they sought food
  to revive their strength.

Job 30:27 Is 16:11 Jer 4:19,20; 9:20 20"Behold, O LORD, for I am in distress,
  my soul is in tumult,
my heart is wrung within me,
  because I have been very rebellious.
In the street the sword bereaves;
  in the house it is like death.

Amos 5:18 21"Hear[f] how I groan;
  there is none to comfort me.
All my enemies have heard of my trouble;
  they are glad that thou hast done it.
Bring thou[g] the day thou hast announced,
  and let them be as I am.

Jer 51:35 22"Let all their evil doing come before thee;
  and deal with them
as thou hast dealt with me
  because of all my transgressions;
for my groans are many
  and my heart is faint."

---

mei / abierunt in captivitatem. / 19 COPH. Vocavi amicos meos, / et ipsi deceperunt me; / sacerdotes mei et senes mei / in urbe consumpti sunt, / quia quaesierunt cibum sibi, / ut refocillarent animam suam. / 20RES. Vide, Domine, quoniam tribulor; / efferbuerunt viscera mea, / subversum est cor meum in memetipsa, / quoniam valde rebellis fui; / foris orbavit me gladius / et domi mors. / 21SIN. Audi, quia ingemisco ego, / et non est qui consoletur me; / omnes inimici mei audierunt malum meum, / laetati sunt quoniam tu fecisti. / Adduc diem, quem proclamasti, / et fient similes mei. / 22THAU. Ingrediatur omne malum eorum coram te, / et fac eis, / sicut fecisti mihi / propter omnes iniquitates meas; / multi enim gemitus mei, / et cor meum maerens».

f. Gk Syr: Heb *they heard* **g.** Syr: Heb *thou hast brought*

Second lament: Zion's misfortunes and their causes

2 [1]How the Lord in his anger
has set the daughter of Zion under a cloud!

2 Sam 1:19
1 Chron 28:2
Is 14:15
Ezek 43:7

2:1–22. The second lamentation begins and ends with explicit references to the main reason for all Zion's misfortunes—the anger of God (vv. 1 and 22), that is, his just indignation at the sins of the people. However, the main body of the poem is a meditation containing reflections on the prospects of conversion. St Thomas points out that there are two parts to the poem: "In the first part of the poem, the disgrace of the destruction is lamented (vv. 1–7); in the second part, the grace of God's mercy is implored" (*Postilla super Threnos*, 2).

The poem begins by describing the fall of Jerusalem (vv. 1–9). Using bold imagery, the author describes the defeat of the Jews and the destruction of the temple as something done not so much by the Chaldeans as by the Lord himself, who became "like an enemy" to Israel (v. 5), rejected the temple and its rites (vv. 6–7), and deprived the city of its defences (vv. 8–9). It then goes on to show the reader just how things were in the city at the time—no law, no princes, no prophets (v. 9), no food (vv. 11–12), nothing but silence and weeping (vv. 10–11). Such being the scene, the inspired writer reproaches Jerusalem on a number of counts (vv. 13–19)—the apathy of its prophets (v. 14), the city's failure to turn back to God; it has become the object of jeers and mockery. But it must not stay like that; it must be converted to the Lord, by making anguished prayer (vv. 18–19)—prayer like that of the sacred writer (vv. 20–22) which stresses that Israel is still the Lord's chosen people.

Jerusalem's plight, then, is a punishment from God. Still, the severest reproach of all is that addressed to the prophets. The false prophets lulled the people into a false sense of security instead of calling them to conversion (v. 14); as Olympiodorus glosses the text, "they do not tell you the truth by which you would recognize your sins and repent [...]. On the contrary, they read you false prophecies and use vain arguments to drive you further from God" (*Fragmenta in Lamentationes*, 2, 14). On the other hand, the true word of God has been borne out: it is not surprising that v. 17 should be quoted when reminding Church pastors of their responsibilities: "The good pastor should know when to keep silent through discretion and when it is important to speak, so that he will never speak of what should not be said nor fail to speak when it must be said. As indiscreet speech can lead to sin; imprudent silence can leave those who were in need of teaching to wallow in their sin. It often happens that imprudent pastors are afraid to tell the truth openly because they fear that they will lose the respect of their people. The pastor who is afraid to tell his people the truth turns his back on them by his silence. He

[2] [1]ALEPH. Quomodo obtexit caligine in furore suo / Dominus filiam Sion! / Proiecit de caelo in terram / gloriam Israel / et non est recordatus scabelli pedum suorum / in die furoris sui. / [2]BETH. Praecipitavit

He has cast down from heaven to earth
the splendour of Israel;
he has not remembered his footstool
in the day of his anger.

Deut 28:52 [2]The Lord has destroyed without mercy
all the habitations of Jacob;
in his wrath he has broken down
the strongholds of the daughter of Judah;
he has brought down to the ground in dishonour
the kingdom and its rulers.

Ps 75:5 [3]He has cut down in fierce anger
Lam 4:11 all the might of Israel;
he has withdrawn from them his right hand
in the face of the enemy;
he has burned like a flaming fire in Jacob,
consuming all around.

Jer 21:5,6; 30:4 [4]He has bent his bow like an enemy,
with his right hand set like a foe;
and he has slain all the pride of our eyes
in the tent of the daughter of Zion;
he has poured out his fury like fire.

Is 63:10 [5]The Lord has become like an enemy,
he has destroyed Israel;
he has destroyed all its palaces,
laid in ruins its strongholds;
and he has multiplied in the daughter of Judah
mourning and lamentation.

---

builds a wall for the house of Israel, to keep out those who would destroy the flock; but when the people have sinned, as is said elsewhere in Scripture: *Your prophets have seen for you false and deceptive visions; they have not exposed your iniquity to restore your fortunes* (Lam 2:14)" (St Gregory the Great, *Regula pastoralis*, 2, 4).

Dominus / nec pepercit omnia pascua Iacob; / destruxit in furore suo / munitiones filiae Iudae; / deiecit in terram, polluit / regnum et principes eius. / [3]GHIMEL. Confregit in ira furoris sui / omne cornu Israel; / avertit retrorsum dexteram suam / a facie inimici / et succendit in Iacob quasi ignem flammae / devorantis in gyro. / [4]DALETH. Tetendit arcum suum quasi inimicus, / firmavit dexteram suam quasi hostis / et occidit omne, / quod pulchrum erat visu, / in tabernaculo filiae Sion; / effudit quasi ignem indignationem suam. / [5]HE. Factus est Dominus velut inimicus, / deglutivit Israel, / deglutivit omnia

6He has broken down his booth like that of a garden,
laid in ruins the place of his appointed feasts;
the LORD has brought to an end in Zion
appointed feast and sabbath,
and in his fierce indignation has spurned
king and priest.

2 Chron 36:19
Is 1:13
Jer 52:13
Lam 1:4
Zeph 3:18

7The Lord has scorned his altar,
disowned his sanctuary;
he has delivered into the hand of the enemy
the walls of her palaces;
a clamor was raised in the house of the LORD
as on the day of an appointed feast.

Ezek 24:21

8The LORD determined to lay in ruins
the wall of the daughter of Zion;
he marked it off by the line;
he restrained not his hand from destroying;
he caused rampart and wall to lament,
they languish together.

2 Kings 21:13
Is 34:11
Jer 5:10

9Her gates have sunk into the ground;
he has ruined and broken her bars;
her king and princes are among the nations;
the law is no more,
and her prophets obtain
no vision from the LORD.

Deut 4:6,8; 28:36
2 Kings 25:7
Ps 74:9
Ezek 7:26

10The elders of the daughter of Zion
sit on the ground in silence;
they have cast dust on their heads
and put on sackcloth;
the maidens of Jerusalem
have bowed their heads to the ground.

Josh 7:6
Is 3:26
Jer 6:26

---

moenia eius, / dissipavit munitiones eius / et multiplicavit in filia Iudae / maerorem et maestitiam. / 6VAU. Et dissipavit quasi hortum saepem suam, / demolitus est tabernaculum suum; oblivioni tradidit Dominus in Sion festivitatem et sabbatum / et despexit in indignatione furoris sui / regem et sacerdotem. / 7ZAIN. Reppulit Dominus altare suum, / maledixit sanctuario suo; / tradidit in manu inimici / muros domorum eius: / vocem dederunt in domo Domini / sicut in die sollemni. / 8HETH. Cogitavit Dominus dissipare / murum filiae Sion; / tetendit funiculum, / non avertit manum suam a perditione; / et in luctum redegit antemurale et murum: / pariter elanguerunt. / 9 TETH. Defixae sunt in terra portae eius; / perdidit et contrivit vectes eius. / Rex eius et principes eius in gentibus; / non est lex, / et prophetae eius non invenerunt / visionem a Domino. / 10IOD. Sederunt in terra, / conticuerunt senes filiae Sion, / consperserunt cinere capita sua, / accincti sunt ciliciis; / abiecerunt in terram capita sua /

[11]My eyes are spent with weeping;
my soul is in tumult;
my heart is poured out in grief[h]
because of the destruction of the daughter of my people,
because infants and babes faint
in the streets of the city.

Lam 1:11 [12]They cry to their mothers,
"Where is bread and wine?"
as they faint like wounded men
in the streets of the city,
as their life is poured out
on their mothers' bosom.

Is 46:5 Jer 30:12 Lam 1:12 Ezek 26:3 [13]What can I say for you, to what compare you,
O daughter of Jerusalem?
What can I liken to you, that I may comfort you,
O virgin daughter of Zion?
For vast as the sea is your ruin;
who can restore you?

Jer 2:8; 5:31; 23:16; 29:8 Ezek 13:10 [14]Your prophets have seen for you
false and deceptive visions;
they have not exposed your iniquity
to restore your fortunes,
but have seen for you oracles
false and misleading.

Jer 19:8 Mt 27:39 [15]All who pass along the way
clap their hands at you;
they hiss and wag their heads
at the daughter of Jerusalem;

---

virgines Ierusalem. / [11]CAPH. Defecerunt prae lacrimis oculi mei, / efferbuerunt viscera mea; / effusum est in terra iecur meum / super contritione filiae populi mei, / cum deficeret parvulus et lactans / in plateis oppidi. / [12]LAMED. Matribus suis dixerunt: / «Ubi est triticum et vinum?», / cum deficerent quasi vulnerati / in plateis civitatis, / cum exhalarent animas suas / in sinu matrum suarum. / [13]MEM. Cui comparabo te vel cui assimilabo te, / filia Ierusalem? / Cui exaequabo te et consolabor te, virgo filia Sion? / Magna est enim velut mare contritio tua; / quis medebitur tui? / [14]NUN. Prophetae tui viderunt tibi falsa et stulta / nec aperiebant iniquitatem tuam, / ut converterent sortem tuam; / viderunt autem tibi oracula / mendacii et seductionis. / [15]SAMECH. Plauserunt super te manibus / omnes transeuntes per viam; / sibilaverunt et moverunt caput suum / super filiam Ierusalem: / «Haeccine est urbs, quam

h. Heb *to the ground*

"Is this the city which was called
the perfection of beauty,
the joy of all the earth?"

16 All your enemies
rail against you;
they hiss, they gnash their teeth,
they cry: "We have destroyed her!
Ah, this is the day we longed for;
now we have it; we see it!"

Jer 4:16
Amos 5:18

17 The LORD has done what he purposed,
has carried out his threat;
as he ordained long ago,
he has demolished without pity;
he has made the enemy rejoice over you,
and exalted the might of your foes.

Lev 26:16
Deut 28:15

18 Cry aloud[i] to the Lord!
O[j] daughter of Zion!
Let tears stream down like a torrent
day and night!
Give yourself no rest,
your eyes no respite!

Lam 1:2

19 Arise, cry out in the night,
at the beginning of the watches!
Pour out your heart like water
before the presence of the Lord!
Lift your hands to him
for the lives of your children,
who faint for hunger
at the head of every street.

---

vocabant perfectum decorem, / gaudium universae terrae?». / 16PHE. Aperuerunt super te os suum / omnes inimici tui; / sibilaverunt et fremuerunt dentibus / et dixerunt: «Devoravimus; / en ista est dies, quam exspectabamus: / invenimus, vidimus». / 17AIN. Fecit Dominus, quae cogitavit; / complevit sermonem suum, / quem praeceperat a diebus antiquis: / destruxit et non pepercit. / Et laetificavit super te inimicum / et exaltavit cornu hostium tuorum. / 18SADE. Clamet cor tuum ad Dominum / super muros filiae Sion; / deduc quasi torrentem lacrimas / per diem et noctem. / Non des requiem tibi, / neque taceat pupilla oculi tui. / 19 COPH. Consurge, lamentare in nocte / in principio vigiliarum, / effunde sicut aquam cor tuum / ante conspectum Domini; / leva ad eum manus tuas / pro anima parvulorum tuorum, / qui

i. Cn: Heb *Their heart cried* **j.** Cn: Heb *O wall of*

Deut 28:53 Jer 4:10; 19:9 Lam 4:10

20 Look, O LORD, and see!
With whom hast thou dealt thus?
Should women eat their offspring,
the children of their tender care?
Should priest and prophet be slain
in the sanctuary of the Lord?

2 Chron 36:17 Jer 6:11; 20:10

21 In the dust of the streets
lie the young and the old;
my maidens and my young men
have fallen by the sword;
in the day of thy anger thou hast slain them,
slaughtering without mercy.

Jer 20:10

22 Thou didst invite as to the day of an appointed feast
my terrors on every side;
and on the day of the anger of the LORD
none escaped or survived;
those whom I dandled and reared
my enemy destroyed.

Third lament: Personal lament over the fate of Israel

3 1 I am the man who has seen affliction
under the rod of his wrath;

Jn 8:12

2 he has driven and brought me
into darkness without any light;
3 surely against me he turns his hand
again and again the whole day long.

3:1–66. In the third lamentation, at the centre of the book, the sense of pathos reaches its peak, for now the person speaks from personal experience. The earlier poems were far from being a cold, detached report of what happened to the people in general and the holy city in particular; but now someone who has been through it all shares his feelings with the reader. The words of this heartbroken man could be placed on the lips of everyone who has experienced or even now experiences the deprivation caused by war, injustice or illness; they

defecerunt in fame / in capite omnium compitorum. / 20RES. «Vide, Domine, et considera, / cui feceris ita; / ergone comedent mulieres fructum suum, / parvulos diligenter fovendos? / Num occidetur in sanctuario Domini / sacerdos et propheta? / 21SIN. Iacuerunt in terra foris / puer et senex; / virgines meae et iuvenes mei / ceciderunt in gladio: / interfecisti in die furoris tui, / percussisti nec misertus es. / 22THAU. Vocasti quasi ad diem sollemnem, / qui terrerent me de circuitu, / et non fuit in die furoris Domini, / qui effugeret et relinqueretur: / quos fovi et enutrivi, / inimicus meus consumpsit eos». **[3]** 1ALEPH. Ego vir videns paupertatem meam / in virga indignationis eius. / 2ALEPH. Me minavit et

[4]He has made my flesh and my skin waste away,
and broken my bones;
[5]he has besieged and enveloped me
with bitterness and tribulation;

Ps 51:8
Job 16:8; 30:30
Is 38:13

---

are evidence of a deep faith in God and are interwoven with sentiments of complaint and hope.

The first verses (vv. 1–20) are a monologue in which the writer, using daring analogies, lists all the misfortunes he has suffered. His lament reaches its climax in v. 18, when his sense of loss leads him to say that he has even lost his hope in the Lord. But the tone suddenly changes when he turns from himself to the Lord and realizes that "the steadfast love of the Lord never ceases, his mercies never come to an end" (v. 22). Theodoret comments that it is as if the man were saying: "I have given up greater hopes, and though my soul is cast down when I recall my disgrace, still I turn to call on the Lord's mercy" (*Interpretatio in Threnos*, 3, 18). This leads the poem's speaker to list in detail the qualities of the Lord—his faithfulness and goodness (vv. 23–25), his compassion (v. 32), the fact that he knows all things and is almighty (vv. 34–39), etc. He then turns to his fellow-citizens (vv. 40–47), inviting them to see that all their misfortunes are due to their sins. What each should do is bewail his faults (vv. 48–51) and remember that in moments of crisis the Lord never forsakes him (vv. 52–57). This lamentation, like the previous ones, ends with a prayer to the Lord in which he asks God to requite his assailants for what they have done.

As has been mentioned in other notes, the sufferings described in the opening verses can be read in a spiritual sense as a reminder of the purification a soul needs in order to be united to God —not an easy thing, for it involves self-denial and self-surrender; as Origen points out, commenting on v. 6: "The darkness of the soul is caused by the temptations that plague it" (*Selecta in Threnos*, 3, 6). And St John of the Cross writes: "It is impossible to exaggerate what the soul suffers during this time; it is not unlike the sufferings of purgatory. I do not know how to express how great the bitterness is, nor how deep it runs, so I turn to the words of Jeremiah: *I am the man who has seen affliction* … Jeremiah says this, and goes on to say much more. As much as God strives to cleanse and cure the soul of all its ills, the soul suffers great sorrow in the cleansing and the cure" (*Flame of Living Love*, 1, 21) And St Gregory Nazianzen saw in the words of v. 34 an allusion to the difficulties a Christian encounters in trying to reach God. After describing things of the flesh as a sort of darkness, he writes: "We, who are *prisoners of the earth* as Jeremiah has said, bound by the weight of our bodies, we know

adduxit / in tenebras et non in lucem. / [3]ALEPH. Tantum in me vertit et convertit / manum suam tota die. / [4]BETH. Consumpsit pellem meam et carnem meam, / contrivit ossa mea. / [5]BETH. Aedificavit in gyro

[6]he has made me dwell in darkness
like the dead of long ago.

Job 3:23; 19:8 [7]He has walled me about so that I cannot escape;
he has put heavy chains on me;
[8]though I call and cry for help,
he shuts out my prayer;
[9]he has blocked my ways with hewn stones,
he has made my paths crooked.

Job 10:16 Hos 13:8 [10]He is to me like a bear lying in wait,
like a lion in hiding;
[11]he led me off my way and tore me to pieces;
he has made me desolate;
Job 16:12–13 [12]he bent his bow and set me
as a mark for his arrow.

[13]He drove into my heart
the arrows of his quiver;
Deut 28:37 Job 30:9 Ps 69:12,22 [14]I have become the laughingstock of all peoples,
the burden of their songs all day long.
Jer 20:7; 23:15 [15]He has filled me with bitterness,
he has sated me with wormwood.

[16]He has made my teeth grind on gravel,
and made me cower in ashes;
Jer 16:5 [17]my soul is bereft of peace,
I have forgotten what happiness is;

---

that no man, no matter how fast he moves, can overtake his own shadow, for his shadow moves further as he moves on; nor can a man see anything if no light shines to make it visible. Like fish out of water, that can neither live nor move, the soul of man in his body cannot embrace spiritual things in a pure way, completely beyond the bodily dimension" (*De theologia* [*Oratio* 28], 12).

meo / et circumdedit me felle et labore. / [6]BETH. In tenebrosis collocavit me / quasi mortuos sempiternos. / [7]GHIMEL. Circumaedificavit adversum me, ut non egrediar, / aggravavit compedem meum. / [8]GHIMEL. Sed et cum clamavero et rogavero, / exclusit orationem meam. / [9] GHIMEL. Conclusit vias meas lapidibus quadris, / semitas meas subvertit. / [10]DALETH. Ursus insidians factus est mihi, / leo in absconditis. / [11]DALETH. Semitas meas subvertit et confregit me, / posuit me desolatam. / [12]DALETH. Tetendit arcum suum et posuit me / quasi signum ad sagittam. / [13]HE. Misit in renibus meis / filias pharetrae suae. / [14]HE. Factus sum in derisum omni populo meo, / canticum eorum tota die. / [15]HE. Replevit me amaritudinibus, / inebriavit me absinthio. / [16]VAU. Et fregit in glarea dentes meos, /

[18] so I say, "Gone is my glory,
and my expectation from the LORD." Job 17:15

[19] Remember my affliction and my bitterness,[k]
the wormwood and the gall!
[20] My soul continually thinks of it
and is bowed down within me.
[21] But this I call to mind,
and therefore I have hope:

[22] The steadfast love of the LORD never ceases,[l] Ex 34:6–7
his mercies never come to an end;
[23] they are new every morning;
great is thy faithfulness.
[24] "The LORD is my portion," says my soul, Ps 16:6; 73:26
"therefore I will hope in him."

[25] The LORD is good to those who wait for him, Ps 40:2
to the soul that seeks him. Is 30:18
[26] It is good that one should wait quietly Jer 15:17
for the salvation of the LORD.
[27] It is good for a man that he bear
the yoke in his youth.

[28] Let him sit alone in silence
when he has laid it on him;
[29] let him put his mouth in the dust—
there may yet be hope;
[30] let him give his cheek to the smiter, Is 50:6
and be filled with insults. Mt 5:39

---

depressit me cinere. / [17]VAU. Et repulsa est a pace anima mea, / oblitus sum bonorum. / [18]VAU. Et dixi: «Periit splendor meus et spes mea a Domino». / [19] ZAIN. Recordare paupertatis et peregrinationis meae, / absinthii et fellis. / [20]ZAIN. Memoria memor est / et tabescit in me anima mea. / [21]ZAIN. Haec recolam in corde meo, / ideo sperabo. / [22]HETH. Misericordiae Domini, quia non sumus consumpti, / quia non defecerunt miserationes eius. / [23]HETH. Novae sunt omni mane, / magna est fides tua. / [24]HETH «Pars mea Dominus, dixit anima mea; / propterea exspectabo eum». / [25]TETH. Bonus est Dominus sperantibus in eum, / animae quaerenti illum. / [26]TETH. Bonum est praestolari cum silentio / salutare Domini. / [27]TETH. Bonum est viro, cum portaverit / iugum ab adulescentia sua. / [28]IOD. Sedebit solitarius et tacebit, / cum istud imponitur ei. / [29] IOD. Ponet in pulvere os suum, / si forte sit spes. / [30]IOD. Dabit percutienti se maxillam, / saturabitur opprobriis. / [31]CAPH. Quia non repellet in sempiternum / Dominus. / [32]CAPH. Quia si afflixit, et miserebitur / secundum multitudinem misericordiarum suarum. / [33]CAPH. Non enim

k. Cn: Heb *wandering* **l.** Syr Tg: Heb *we are not cut off*

[31] For the Lord will not
cast off for ever,
Is 54:8–9 [32] but, though he cause grief, he will have compassion
according to the abundance of his steadfast love;
Ezek 33:11 Heb 12:10 [33] for he does not willingly afflict
or grieve the sons of men.

[34] To crush under foot
all the prisoners of the earth,
[35] to turn aside the right of a man
in the presence of the Most High,
[36] to subvert a man in his cause,
the Lord does not approve.

Gen 1 Ps 33:9 [37] Who has commanded and it came to pass,
unless the Lord has ordained it?
Is 45:7 [38] Is it not from the mouth of the Most High
that good and evil come?
Mic 7:9 [39] Why should a living man complain,
a man, about the punishment of his sins?

Is 55:7 [40] Let us test and examine our ways,
and return to the LORD!
[41] Let us lift up our hearts and hands
to God in heaven:
[42] "We have transgressed and rebelled,
and thou hast not forgiven.

[43] "Thou hast wrapped thyself with anger and pursued us,
slaying without pity;
Deut 28:37 Lam 3:8 [44] thou hast wrapped thyself with a cloud
so that no prayer can pass through.

3:44. These words, too, have given rise to an allegorical interpretation about the purification a soul experiences in his or her search for God. St John of the Cross saw in them the sense of isolation a soul can sometimes have, despite its best

humiliat ex corde suo / et affligit filios hominum. / [34]LAMED. Conterere sub pedibus suis / omnes vinctos terrae. / [35]LAMED. Declinare iudicium viri / in conspectu vultus Altissimi. / [36]LAMED .Pervertere hominem in iudicio suo, / num Dominus haec ignorat? / [37]MEM. Quis est iste, qui dixit, et factum est? / Dominus non iussit? / [38]MEM. Ex ore Altissimi nonne egrediuntur / et mala et bona? / [39] MEM. Quid murmurabit homo vivens, / vir pro peccatis suis? / [40]NUN. «Scrutemur vias nostras et quaeramus / et revertamur ad Dominum. / [41]NUN. Levemus corda nostra cum manibus / ad Dominum in caelos. / [42]NUN. Nos inique egimus et rebelles fuimus; / idcirco tu inexorabilis fuisti. / [43]SAMECH. Operuisti in furore et

[45] Thou hast made us offscouring and refuse
among the peoples. 1 Cor 4:13
[46] "All our enemies
rail against us;
[47] panic and pitfall have come upon us,
devastation and destruction;
[48] my eyes flow with rivers of tears
because of the destruction of the daughter of my people.

[49] My eyes will flow without ceasing,
without respite,
[50] until the LORD from heaven Is 63:15
looks down and sees;
[51] my eyes cause me grief
at the fate of all the maidens of my city.

[52] "I have been hunted like a bird Ps 11:2; 35:19;
by those who were my enemies without cause; 69:5; Jer 37:16; 38:6,10

---

efforts to reach God through prayer: "This is another thing of which the soul may complain and which often leads him to lose hope: the dark night of the soul stops his powers and dampens all his loves, and leads him to conclude with Jeremiah: *thou hast wrapped thyself with a cloud so that no prayer can pass through* (Lam 3:44). This says again what Jeremiah had already said in a different way: *he has blocked my way with hewn stones, he has made my paths crooked* (3:9). And if at times the soul asks and prays, he asks and prays with so little strength and faith that he feels that God neither listens to him nor takes any notice of him, as Jeremiah also said: *though I call and cry for help, he shuts out my prayer* (3:8). In truth this is no time to talk to God, but a time to *put his mouth in the dust—there may yet be hope* (3:29), and to suffer his purification with patience and in silence. God does the work of the soul; therefore, the soul can do nothing. He can neither pray nor cooperate in the divine action; still less can he do in temporal, human affairs. He may become so estranged from himself that great gaps open up in his memory, and for long time he will not know what he thinks or what he does or what he wants to do, nor will he see any of the things that lie all around him" (*Dark Night of the Soul*, 2, 8, 1).

percussisti nos; / occidisti nec pepercisti. / [44]SAMECH. Opposuisti nubem tibi, / ne transeat oratio. / [45]SAMECH. In eradicationem et abiectionem posuisti nos / in medio populorum. / [46]PHE. Aperuerunt super nos os suum / omnes inimici nostri. / [47]PHE. Formido et fovea facta est nobis, / vastatio et contritio». / [48]PHE. Rivos aquarum deducit oculus meus / in contritione filiae populi mei. / [49] AIN. Oculus meus lacrimas effundit nec tacet, / eo quod non sit requies. / [50]AIN. Donec respiciat et videat / Dominus de caelis. / [51]AIN. Oculus meus affligit animam meam / prae cunctis filiabus urbis meae. / [52]SADE.

53 they flung me alive into the pit
and cast stones on me;
54 water closed over my head;
I said, 'I am lost.'

55 "I called on thy name, O LORD,
from the depths of the pit;
Ps 130:2 56 thou didst hear my plea, 'Do not close
thine ear to my cry for help!'[m]
57 Thou didst come near when I called on thee;
thou didst say, 'Do not fear!'

58 "Thou hast taken up my cause, O LORD,
thou hast redeemed my life.
59 Thou hast seen the wrong done to me, O LORD;
judge thou my cause.
Jer 11:19 60 Thou hast seen all their vengeance, all their devices against me.

61 "Thou hast heard their taunts, O LORD,
all their devices against me.
62 The lips and thoughts of my assailants
are against me all the day long.
Lam 3:14 63 Behold their sitting and their rising;
I am the burden of their songs.

Deut 25:19 64 "Thou wilt requite them, O LORD,
Ps 28:4 according to the work of their hands.
Jer 11:20; 51:56 65 Thou wilt give them dullness of heart;
2 Tim 4:14 thy curse will be on them.
66 Thou wilt pursue them in anger and destroy them
from under thy heavens, O LORD."[n]

Venatione venati sunt me quasi avem / inimici mei gratis. / [53]SADE. Perdiderunt in lacu vitam meam / et iecerunt lapides super me. / [54]SADE. Inundaverunt aquae super caput meum, / dixi: «Perii». / [55]COPH Invocavi nomen tuum, Domine, / de profunditate lacus. / [56]COPH Vocem meam audisti: «Ne avertas / aurem tuam a singultu meo et clamoribus». / [57]COPH Appropinquasti in die, quando invocavi te, / dixisti: «Ne timeas». / [58]RES. Iudicasti, Domine, causam animae meae, / redemisti vitam meam. / [59] RES. Vidisti, Domine, afflictionem meam; / iudica iudicium meum. / [60]RES. Vidisti omnem furorem eorum, universas cogitationes eorum adversum me. / [61]SIN. Audisti opprobrium eorum, Domine, / omnes cogitationes eorum adversum me. / [62]SIN. Labia insurgentium mihi et meditationes eorum / adversum me tota die. / [63]SIN. Sessionem eorum et resurrectionem eorum vide; / ego sum psalmus eorum. / [64]THAU. Reddes eis vicem, Domine, / iuxta opera manuum suarum. / [65]THAU. Dabis eis duritiam cordis, / exsecrationem

m. Heb uncertain **n.** Syr Compare Gk Vg: Heb *the heavens of the LORD*

Fourth lament: Zion's misfortunes and those responsible for them

4 [1]How the gold has grown dim, Jer 6:27–30
how the pure gold is changed!
The holy stones lie scattered
at the head of every street.

4:1–22. The fourth lamentation is similar in tone to the second. The scene of desolation in the country, all the afflictions it is suffering, leads the author to enquire who is to blame. The opening verses describe the situation in Jerusalem (vv. 1–12). He focuses on the famine it is experiencing: (cf. 1:11; 2:12, 19): the children have nothing to eat (v. 4); people accustomed to fine food forage in rubbish dumps and, even so, they are only skin and bone (vv. 5–8); some may even have resorted to cannibalism (v. 10; cf. 2:20). The author draws a depressing conclusion: not even the jackals do that; nor was Sodom's sin as great as Jerusalem's, for its punishment was milder. Then the narrator moves out of the city, following the route taken by those who were deported (vv. 14–21). These people, blind (v. 14), without an anointed king to guide them (v. 20), are shunned by everyone: they are quite powerless (vv. 18–19), and have no one to succour them (v. 17) and are jeered at by those whose paths they cross (v. 15).

How could they be in such dire straits? The narrator puts his finger on the reason—"the sins of her prophets, and the iniquities of her priests, who shed in the midst of her the blood of the righteous" (v. 13). Those who should have given the people leadership failed to do so and, instead of having recourse to the Lord, they sought refuge in political alliances, in the vain hope that other nations would come to their aid (cf. v. 17). Still, in the midst of all this affliction, the narrator offers consolation, a ray of hope: Zion's punishment is over; her exile will come to an end (cf. v. 22).

The fourth lamentation is, then, a rallying cry, a call to seek the Lord; his plans are inscrutable and only he can resolve the catastrophic situation that exile has created, in just punishment of the sins of the people and their rulers.

Verse 20 is often read as referring to the incarnation and passion of Christ. Origen, interpreting the "shadow" as the incarnation, comments: "Do you see how the prophet, moved by the Holy Spirit, tells us that the shadow of Christ gives life to the Gentiles? How could he not bring us to life, for when the Word was made flesh Mary was told: *The Holy Spirit will come upon you, and the power of the Most High will overshadow you*?" (*In Canticum Canticorum*, 3, 2, 3). And St Irenaeus, reading the verse as an announcement of the Passion, writes: "Scripture taught that though Christ is the Spirit of God, he would be made man and suffer death; the Passion that he would endure is revealed and heard with shock and

tuam. / [66]THAU. Persequeris in furore et conteres eos / sub caelis tuis, Domine. **[4]** [1]ALEPH. Quomodo obscuratum est aurum, / mutatum est obryzum optimum! / Dispersi sunt lapides sancti / in capite

Jer 19:1,11
2 Cor 4:7

2The precious sons of Zion,
worth their weight in fine gold,
how they are reckoned as earthen pots,
the work of a potter's hands!

Job 39:13–17

3Even the jackals give the breast
and suckle their young,
but the daughter of my people has become cruel,
like the ostriches in the wilderness.

Lam 2:11–12

4The tongue of the nursling cleaves
to the roof of its mouth for thirst;
the children beg for food,
but no one gives to them.

5Those who feasted on dainties
perish in the streets;
those who were brought up in purple
lie on ash heaps.

Gen 9; 19
Deut 7
2 Pet 2:6

6For the chastisement[o] of the daughter of my people has been
greater
than the punishment[p] of Sodom,
which was overthrown in a moment,
no hand being laid on it.[q]

---

awe because he is the one *in whose shadow it is said that we shall live*. The *shadow* means his body, for as a shadow is cast by the body, Christ's body was made by his Spirit. But the word *shadow* also stands for the humbling of his body and for how easily his body will be humbled. For as the shadow of every body is cast on the ground and trodden under their feet, Christ's body is thrown to the ground in the Passion and stamped upon" (*Demonstratio praedicationis apostolicae*, 71).

omnium platearum. / 2BETH. Filii Sion incliti / et ponderati auro primo, / quomodo reputati sunt in vasa testea, / opus manuum figuli! / 3GHIMEL. Sed et thoes nudaverunt mammam, / lactaverunt catulos suos; / filia populi mei crudelis / quasi struthio in deserto. / 4DALETH. Adhaesit lingua lactantis / ad palatum eius in siti; / parvuli petierunt panem, / et non erat qui frangeret eis. / 5HE. Qui vescebantur voluptuose, / interierunt in viis; / qui nutriebantur in coccinis, / amplexati sunt stercora. / 6VAU. Et maior effecta est iniquitas filiae populi mei / peccato Sodomae, / quae subversa est in momento, / et non laborabant in ea manus. / 7ZAIN. Candidiores nazaraei eius nive, / nitidiores lacte, / rubicundiores in corpore coralliis, / sapphirus aspectus eorum. / 8HETH Denigrata est super carbones facies eorum, / et non sunt cogniti in plateis: / adhaesit cutis eorum ossibus, / aruit et facta est quasi lignum. / 9 TETH. Melius fuit occisis

o. Or *iniquity* **p.** Or *sin* **q.** Heb uncertain

[7]Her princes were purer than snow,
whiter than milk;
their bodies were more ruddy than coral,
the beauty of their form[r] was like sapphire.[s]

[8]Now their visage is blacker than soot,
they are not recognized in the streets;
their skin has shrivelled upon their bones,
it has become as dry as wood.

[9]Happier were the victims of the sword
than the victims of hunger,
who pined away, stricken
by want of the fruits of the field.

[10]The hands of compassionate women
have boiled their own children;
they became their food
in the destruction of the daughter of my people.

Deut 28:56–57
1 Kings 3:26
Lam 2:20

[11]The LORD gave full vent to his wrath,
he poured out his hot anger;
and he kindled a fire in Zion,
which consumed its foundations.

Lam 2:3

[12]The kings of the earth did not believe,
or any of the inhabitants of the world,
that foe or enemy could enter
the gates of Jerusalem.

[13]This was for the sins of her prophets
and the iniquities of her priests,
who shed in the midst of her
the blood of the righteous.

Jer 5:31; 6:13
Ezek 7:23; 22:6
Zeph 3:4

---

gladio / quam interfectis fame, / quoniam isti extabuerunt consumpti / a sterilitate terrae. / [10]IOD. Manus mulierum misericordium / coxerunt filios suos: / facti sunt cibus earum / in contritione filiae populi mei. / [11]CAPH. Complevit Dominus furorem suum, / effudit iram indignationis suae; / et succendit ignem in Sion, / qui devoravit fundamenta eius. / [12]LAMED. Non crediderunt reges terrae / et universi habitatores orbis, / quoniam ingrederetur hostis et inimicus / per portas Ierusalem. / [13]MEM. Propter peccata prophetarum eius / et iniquitates sacerdotum eius, / qui effuderunt in medio eius / sanguinem iustorum. / [14]NUN. Erraverunt caeci in plateis, / polluti sunt in sanguine, / ita ut nemo posset attingere / lacinias

r. Heb uncertain **s.** Heb *lapis lazuli* **t.** Heb uncertain

Num 35:32–33 14 They wandered, blind, through the streets,
so defiled with blood
that none could touch
their garments.

Lev 13:45 15 "Away! Unclean!" men cried at them;
"Away! Away! Touch not!"
So they became fugitives and wanderers;
men said among the nations,
"They shall stay with us no longer."

16 The LORD himself has scattered them,
he will regard them no more;
no honour was shown to the priests,
no favour to the elders.

Jer 37:7 Ezek 29:6 17 Our eyes failed, ever watching
vainly for help;
in our watching[t] we watched
for a nation which could not save.

18 Men dogged our steps
so that we could not walk in our streets;
our end drew near; our days were numbered;
for our end had come.

19 Our pursuers were swifter
than the vultures in the heavens;
they chased us on the mountains,
they lay in wait for us in the wilderness.

2 Kings 25:5–6 Ezek 12:13; 19:4 20 The breath of our nostrils, the LORD's anointed,
was taken in their pits,
he of whom we said, "Under his shadow
we shall live among the nations."

---

eorum. / 15 SAMECH. «Recedite! Pollutus est», clamaverunt eis; / «Recedite, abite, nolite tangere!». / Cum fugerent et errarent, dixerunt inter gentes: / «Non addent ultra ut incolant». / 16 PHE. Facies Domini dispersit eos, / non addet ut respiciat eos; / facies sacerdotum non respexerunt / neque senum miserti sunt. / 17 AIN. Adhuc deficiunt oculi nostri / ad auxilium nostrum vanum? / In specula nostra respeximus / ad gentem, quae salvare non potest. / 18 SADE. Insidiati sunt vestigiis nostris, / ne iremus per plateas nostras. / «Appropinquavit finis noster, completi sunt dies nostri, / quia venit finis noster». / 19 COPH Velociores fuerunt persecutores nostri / aquilis caeli; / super montes persecuti sunt nos, / in deserto insidiati sunt nobis. / 20 RES. Spiritus oris nostri, unctus Domini, / captus est in foveis eorum, / de quo

[21]Rejoice and be glad, O daughter of Edom,
dweller in the land of Uz;
but to you also the cup shall pass;
you shall become drunk and strip yourself bare.

Gen 9:21
Ps 137:7
Is 40:2; 51:17
Jer 25:15–20
Hab 2:15

[22]The punishment of your iniquity, O daughter of Zion, is accomplished,
he will keep you in exile no longer;
but your iniquity, O daughter of Edom, he will punish,
he will uncover your sins.

Fifth lament: A desolate people pleads for mercy

5 [1]Remember, O LORD, what has befallen us;
behold, and see our disgrace!

Ps 89:50

5:1–22. The Vulgate calls the fifth and last lamentation the "Prayer of Jeremiah the Prophet"; and it is in fact an entreaty, full of faith, asking the Lord to intervene on behalf of his suffering people. The first three lamentations ended with a prayer to the Lord, but there is no such prayer at the end of the fourth poem. Now, this final supplication acts as the prayer of the previous lamentation and as the conclusion to the book. St Thomas says that "after many lamentations, [the prophet] takes comfort in prayer" (*Postilla super Threnos*, 5, 1). It begins by describing the plight of the people (vv. 1–6), and then it acknowledges past sins and infidelities and how undeserving the people are; all they can do is plead for mercy (vv. 7–18). Verses 11–14 list the worst sorts of suffering undergone by the people of Judah and Jerusalem; public order has broken down, for no longer are there elders who meet at the city gate to dispense justice (v. 14). Yet, in spite of everything, they beseech God to renew their lives; they cannot, but he can (vv. 19–22).

The core of this entreaty is very succinct and deeply theological: "Restore us to thyself, O Lord, that we may be restored" (v. 21). The Council of Trent refers to this passage when it says that, to be justified, a person needs the grace of God—and needs to co-operate with it: "The origin of justification in adults is the grace of God, which comes to us through Christ Jesus; that is, the source of righteousness is the vocation they have received, through no merit of their own. Those who strayed far from God through sin are encouraged and helped to convert, and led to righteousness, by His grace, if they respond to and cooperate with that grace" (*De iustificatione* decree, 6th session, chap. 5; Dz-Sch.

dicebamus: «Sub umbra sua / vivemus in gentibus». / [21]SIN. Gaude et laetare, filia Edom, / quae habitas in terra Us; / ad te quoque perveniet calix, / inebriaberis atque nudaberis. / [22]THAU. Completa est iniquitas tua, filia Sion, / non addet ultra ut transmigret te; / visitavit iniquitatem tuam, filia Edom, / discooperuit peccata tua. **[5]** [1]Recordare, Domine, quid acciderit nobis; / intuere et respice

[2]Our inheritance has been turned over to strangers,
our homes to aliens.
[3]We have become orphans, fatherless;
our mothers are like widows.
[4]We must pay for the water we drink,
the wood we get must be bought.
[5]With a yoke[u] on our necks we are hard driven;
we are weary, we are given no rest.
Jer 2:18; 50:15 [6]We have given the hand to Egypt,
and to Assyria, to get bread enough.
Ezek 18:2 [7]Our fathers sinned, and are no more;
and we bear their iniquities.
[8]Slaves rule over us;
there is none to deliver us from their hand.
[9]We get our bread at the peril of our lives,
because of the sword in the wilderness.
[10]Our skin is hot as an oven
with the burning heat of famine.
Is 13:16 [11]Women are ravished in Zion,
Zech 14:2 virgins in the towns of Judah.

1525). The *Catechism of the Catholic Church*, 1432, explains this teaching as follows: "The human heart is heavy and hardened. God must give man a new heart (cf. Ezek 36:26–27). Conversion is first of all a work of the grace of God who makes our hearts return to him: 'Restore us to thyself, O Lord, that we may be restored!' (Lam 5:21) God gives us the strength to begin anew. It is in discovering the greatness of God's love that our heart is shaken by the horror and weight of sin and begins to fear offending God by sin and being separated from him. The human heart is converted by looking upon him whom our sins have pierced (cf. Jn 19:37; Zech 12:10): 'Let us fix our eyes on Christ's blood and understand how precious it is to his Father, for, poured out for our salvation, it has brought to the whole world the grace of repentance' (St Clement of Rome, *Ad Cor.* 7, 4: PG 1, 224)."

opprobrium nostrum. / [2]Hereditas nostra versa est ad alienos, / domus nostrae ad extraneos. / [3]Pupilli facti sumus absque patre, / matres nostrae quasi viduae. / [4]Aquam nostram pecunia bibimus, / ligna nostra pretio comparamus. / [5]Iugum in cervicibus nostris minamur; / lassis non datur requies. / [6]Aegyptiis dedimus manum et Assyriis, / ut saturaremur pane. / [7]Patres nostri peccaverunt et non sunt, / et nos iniquitates eorum portamus. [8]Servi dominantur nostri; / non est qui redimat de manu eorum. / [9] Vitae nostrae periculo afferimus panem nobis / a facie gladii in deserto. / [10]Pellis nostra quasi clibanus exusta est / propter aestum famis. / [11]Mulieres in Sion humiliaverunt / et virgines in civitatibus Iudae. / [12]Principes manu eorum suspensi sunt; / facies senum honorem non habuerunt. / [13]Adulescentes molam portaverunt, / et pueri sub lignis corruerunt. / [14]Senes deficiunt de portis, / iuvenes de choro

u. Symmachus: Heb lacks *with a yoke*

12 Princes are hung up by their hands;
no respect is shown to the elders.
13 Young men are compelled to grind at the mill;
and boys stagger under loads of wood.
14 The old men have quit the city gate,
the young men their music.
15 The joy of our hearts has ceased;
our dancing has been turned to mourning.
16 The crown has fallen from our head;
woe to us, for we have sinned!
17 For this our heart has become sick,
for these things our eyes have grown dim,
18 for Mount Zion which lies desolate; Is 34:13–15
jackals prowl over it.

19 But thou, O LORD, dost reign for ever; Ps 9:7; 102:12,13; 145:13;146:10 Hab 1:12
thy throne endures to all generations.
20 Why dost thou forget us for ever,
why dost thou so long forsake us?
21 Restore us to thyself, O LORD, that we may be restored! Ps 80:3,7,19 Jer 31:18
Renew our days as of old!
22 Or hast thou utterly rejected us?
Art thou exceedingly angry with us?

---

psallentium. / 15 Defecit gaudium cordis nostri; / versus est in luctum chorus noster. / 16 Cecidit corona capitis nostri; / vae nobis, quia peccavimus! / 17 Propterea maestum factum est cor nostrum, / ideo contenebrati sunt oculi nostri, / 18 propter montem Sion, quia desolatus est: / vulpes ambulant in eo. / 19 Tu autem, Domine, in aeternum permanebis, / solium tuum in generationem et generationem. / 20 Quare in perpetuum oblivisceris nostri, / derelinques nos in longitudinem dierum? / 21 Converte nos, Domine, ad te, et convertemur; / innova dies nostros sicut a principio. / 22 Ergone proiciens reppulisti nos, / iratus es contra nos vehementer?

BARUCH

Introduction

Under the name of Baruch, two independent texts are to be found which, from the time of the Vulgate onwards, usually appear together—the book of Baruch and the Letter of Jeremiah. When in the thirteenth century the sacred writings were divided up into chapters, the Letter was accounted for as the sixth chapter of Baruch. However, in most of the Greek manuscripts of the Septuagint, the text of Baruch is placed immediately after the book of Jeremiah, and the Letter of Jeremiah appears as a continuation of Lamentations. In the Latin versions, Baruch and the Letter come after Jeremiah and Lamentations. That is the order adopted by the New Vulgate, by modern Catholic Bibles, and by the Revised Standard Version. Baruch and the Letter both deal with the situation of the exiles in Babylon, so it makes sense to put them after the book of Jeremiah, which deals with the causes of the exile, and before Ezekiel, a prophet who ministered during the Babylonian captivity.

The book of Baruch has come down to us only in Greek, but most modern scholars think that that text is a translation of a Hebrew original, now lost. Perhaps because the original Hebrew was not conserved, the book does not appear in the Jewish canon of Jamnia (*c.*90–100 AD).

Early Christian interpreters consider the book of Baruch, along with Lamentations, to be an appendix to the book of Jeremiah; for this reason it is not expressly mentioned in the lists of inspired books that were drawn up by some councils—not because they had doubts about its canonicity. From the fourth century onwards, we begin to see Baruch figuring as a book title independent of Jeremiah, particularly in the manuscripts and printed editions of the Vulgate Latin version. The Council of Trent includes the book of Baruch as such in its list of canonical books. Martin Luther and some Protestants include it in the apocrypha of the Old Testament, or simply omit it altogether.

1. STRUCTURE AND CONTENT

The book of Baruch can be divided into five sections of unequal length.

1. INTRODUCTION (1:1–14). This identifies the author, his reasons for writing the book, and where he was at the time, and it gives a brief description of the circumstances of the exiles in Babylon (1:1–9); it also tells of the dispatch of a letter to those left behind in Jerusalem, requesting them to offer sacrifices and prayers (1:10–14).

2. CONFESSION OF SINS AND PRAYER FOR FORGIVENESS (1:15—3:8). Written in prose, this section of the book consists of two confessions in which the people publicly acknowledge to God their past sins and the sad consequences of them (1:15—2:10 and 2:19–35); each of these confessions is followed by a prayer for forgiveness (2:11–18 and 3:1–8). The sins that they confess have brought down on them just punishment from God in the form of exile, and the people and their rulers are indeed in need of conversion.

3. ISRAEL AND WISDOM (3:9—4:4). Written in verse, this section is a poem in praise of Wisdom, so it is the section most akin to the wisdom books. Israel finds herself in the wilderness because she has forsaken the way of the Lord, the way of Wisdom (3:9–14). The pagan nations seek a purely human form of wisdom, which desires power and wealth (3:15–31)—not true Wisdom, which comes only from God (3:32–36). The Lord revealed Wisdom through his Law and gave it to Jacob-Israel, who should feel fortunate to posess the commandments of God (3:37–44).

4. CONVERSION TO GOD. JERUSALEM'S JOY (4:5—5:9). This section, which is in verse, contains alternating passages of lamentation and hope and encouragement. Jerusalem weeps for her scattered children, acknowledges that she is unable to succour them, and realizes that God is her only hope. One could say that this part is made up of a number of sections. The first rallies the people's spirits (4:5–8); it is followed by a lamentation by Jerusalem to "the neighbours of Zion" (4:9–16) and to her own children, giving them encouragement and calling them to conversion (4:17–29); then comes a song of rejoicing (4:30–37) and, finally, a summing-up and conclusion (5:1–9).

5. THE LETTER OF JEREMIAH (6:1–72). This is the letter that the prophet wrote to the exiles in Babylon. It is a long exhortation not to get involved in the worship of the gods in the pagan nations where the Israelites find themselves on account of their sins. Most of the letter is written in a satirical tone; it ridicules idolatry, contrasting it with the power of the Lord, who has worked and continues to work wonders in the heavens and on earth, all of which is evidence that he is the only God.

Although it has a simple structure to it, the book of Baruch includes a number of literary genres—letters (1:10–14; 6:1–72), entreaties (1:15–22; 2:11–18; 3:1–8), expressions of contrition (2:1–10, 19–26), songs of praise and consolation and sorrow (4:8—5:9), all intoned with the one theme of sin-exile-return. An outstanding feature, positioned at the centre of the book, is its reflection on wisdom, along with a song of exhortation, a sapiential admonition and a song to divine Wisdom (3:9—4:8).

2. COMPOSITION AND HISTORICAL BACKGROUND

The main source of information about Baruch himself is the book of Jeremiah, which features a Baruch as a scribe, helper and confidant of the prophet (cf. Jer 32:12, 16). Jeremiah charged Baruch with writing down his prophecies, so that he could read them out in the temple, in the presence of the people, including King Jehoiakim. The king ordered the scroll to be burned (cf. Jer 36:1–26), but Baruch wrote the prophecies down again, at Jeremiah's dictation (cf. Jer 36:27–32). In Jeremiah 51:59 there is mention of a man called Seriah, of the same family as Baruch and the quartermaster of King Zedekiah of Judah, who was charged with bringing to Babylon a text written by Jeremiah predicting misfortunes that would overtake that empire. Many interpreters think that Seriah and Baruch were brothers. If so, it would confirm that Baruch was a person of considerable social importance. After the fall of Jerusalem, Baruch accompanied his master, Jeremiah, into Egypt (cf. Jer 43:2–7).

We know very little about Baruch after this point, except that, according to Baruch 1:1–3, he was in Babylon in the fifth year after the fall of Jerusalem (587 BC). Flavius Josephus, the Jewish historian, says that, after the conquest of the holy city, Nebuchadnezzar invaded Egypt and deported to Babylon the Jews who had taken refuge there;[1] but, according to another rabbinical tradition attested to by St Jerome,[2] Baruch and Jeremiah died before Nebuchadnezzar's invasion of Egypt. Some rabbinical traditions make Baruch the teacher of Ezra, but there are no serious grounds for this. Almost everything to do with the book of Baruch is a subject of debate among scholars—who the author was, whether it was always a book (rather than originally a number of separate items), how it came to be written (its process of composition), when it was written, and what language it was originally written in. Speaking in general terms, we can say that the language and style of the book—its Semitical features, its affinities to the book of Jeremiah and to Lamentations and its literary unity—supports the attribution of the book to Baruch, Jeremiah's secretary; but it does not prove it. The book could easily be a very early instance of pseudepigraphy, for the attribution to Baruch appears in the heading of the book. Its various parts, with the exception of chapter 6 (the Letter of Jeremiah), are not so different from one another that the book could not have been written by a single author; the differences could be put down to the various parts being written in somewhat different historical situations—that is, when grief over the fall and destruction of Jerusalem was still very much alive, and then at a time when there was a danger of pagan influences dominating the Jews or when the wisdom of foreign countries was being assessed by them. These various features suggest that the book was written sometime after the Babylonian exile, but without being in any way specific, because circumstances similar to those of the Babylonian exile could have arisen in the Persian period (between 500 and 300 BC) or in the Hellenistic period (between 300 and 50 BC), that is,

1. Cf. *Antiquitates iudaicae*, 10, 181f. **2.** *Commentarii in Isaiam*, 30, 6f.

between the fifth and first centuries BC. At present, it is impossible to say anything more exact that that.

3. MESSAGE

Baruch is a sort of bridge between the prophetical books and the wisdom writings. It stresses themes much favoured by the prophets— the omnipotence, unicity and eternity of God, and the falsity of idols; acknowledgment of the sins committed by the chosen people; expectation of redemption, in the form of a restoration of Jerusalem and a return of the Jews who were scattered abroad. What it has to say about wisdom is of special importance: it says that its nature is divine, and it depicts Wisdom as a person, though not as clearly as the book of Wisdom does.

If one reads the book right through, one is led from painful contemplation of the afflictions of the people (caused by their sins) to joy at the prospect of future salvation—the pattern typical of the prophetical books.

4. THE BOOK OF BARUCH IN THE LIGHT OF THE NEW TESTAMENT

The book of Baruch is not explicitly quoted in the New Testament, although there are passages there that are reminiscent of phrases in Baruch.[3] It has received little commentary in the Tradition of the Church. The Fathers see it more as an appendix to the book of Jeremiah than as a book in its own right—as one can see from Aristides (*c.*130), Tertullian and, particularly, St Irenaeus. That may be why it is so seldom quoted, except for 3:36–38, a passage that the Fathers often interpret in a messianic sense, as an announcement of the Incarnation. It is only from the fourth century onwards that we find the book of Baruch being mentioned by name by some Fathers, such as St Athanasius, St Cyril of Jerusalem, Epiphanius, and others. However, it should be mentioned that Baruch 4:36–37 and 5:1–9 were used in connexion with discussions of eschatology; Baruch 3:12 in Trinitarian debates, and Baruch 4:20, 22 and 3:35–37 in Christological discussions.

In modern times, the book of Baruch, including the letter of Jeremiah, is cited very seldom, probably because most of its content is to be found, in one form or another, in the major prophets (Jeremiah, Daniel, Isaiah and Ezekiel), and in the Psalms and wisdom writings.

The Christian reader sees in the book of Baruch the providence of God at work in the chequered history of the chosen people, preparing the ground for the salvation that God will later send in the person of Jesus Christ.

3. Bar 1:1 and 1 Thess 2:2; Bar 3:29 and Jn 3:13; Rom 10:6; Bar 4:1 and Mt 5:18; Bar 4:7 and 1 Cor 10:20; Bar 4:35 and Rev 18:2; Bar 4:37 and Mt 8:11 and Lk 13:29; Bar 6:72 and 1 Jn 5:21.

1. INTRODUCTION*

The situation of the exiles in Babylon

1 [1]These are the words of the book which Baruch the son of Jer 32:12; 36:4
Neraiah, son of Mahseiah, son of Zedekiah, son of Hasadiah,

***1:1–14.** These opening verses act as an introduction to the whole book. First, Baruch is introduced as the author (vv. 1–2) and as the person who reads the book aloud (vv. 3–4) to the assembled exiles in Babylon—that is, King Jehoiachin (also known as Jeconiah) of Judah (whom Nebuchadnezzar deposed after a reign of three months and deported in the year 597 BC: cf. 2 Kings 24:8–17), the royal family, the leading men and the people in general. The assembly acknowledges its sins and repents (vv. 5–7; cf. 2 Kings 23:1–3; Neh 9:1–3).

The exiles make a collection to send to Jerusalem (vv. 6–13), to the priest Jehoiakim and those still left there (cf. Ezra 8:21–36), to fund atonement and other offerings—to turn away the anger of the Lord from the exiles. They also ask for prayers to be said for the ruling house of Babylon. The brevity of the account (vv. 10–13) and the fact that it contains some historical inaccuracies suggest that the author is not so much interested in recording historical events as in communicating a message—about humble admission of past and present sins, conversion to the Lord, and an attitude of reconciliation towards the pagan overlords. The approach is in line with that found in Jeremiah 29:4–14, Ezra 6:9–10, etc.; and centuries later, it will be perfected in Christ's teaching and example as regards love for one's enemies (cf. Lk 6:27–38; 23:34). St Paul will teach the same lesson (Rom 13:1–7; 1 Tim 2:1–3), and St Stephen (cf. Acts 7:59–60) and other Christian martyrs will make it their own.

1:1–9. The genealogy of Baruch (v. 1), whose name means "Blessed", is given here in the Judaic style typical of the prophetical books, but somewhat more elaborately than usual, perhaps to underline his prophetical role, because this book did not form part of the volume containing the minor prophets. Neraiah and Mahseiah, Baruch's father and grandfather, also appear in Jeremiah 32:12.

King Jeconiah (v. 3), according to the transcription in the Vulgate and in many modern versions, is the Jehoiachin of the Hebrew text (the son of Jehoiakim), and the Coniah who appears in Jeremiah 22:24–30. We know from the historical books (2 Kings 24:8–20) that Jeconiah/Jehoiachin reigned in Judah for only three months, until he was deposed by Nebuchadnezzar and deported. The latter installed Zedekiah (Jeconiah's uncle) as king of Judah in 597 BC and held Jehoiachin under some form of arrest in Babylon. Babylonian cuneiform tablets record that Jeconiah was allowed to establish a small court

---

[1] [1]Et haec verba, quae scripsit Baruch filius Neriae filii Maasiae filii Sedeciae filii Asadei filii Helciae in Babylone, [2]in anno quinto, in septima die mensis, in tempore quo ceperunt Chaldaei Ierusalem et

son of Hilkiah, wrote in Babylon, 2in the fifth year, on the seventh
day of the month, at the time when the Chaldeans took Jerusalem
2 Kings 24:8–17 and burned it with fire. 3And Baruch read the words of this book
in the hearing of Jeconiah the son of Jehoiakim, king of Judah,
Jer 22:24–30 and in the hearing of all the people who came to hear the book,
4and in the hearing of the mighty men and the princes, and in the
hearing of the elders, and in the hearing of all the people, small
2 Kings 23:1–3 and great, all who dwelt in Babylon by the river Sud.
Neh 9:1–3 5Then they wept, and fasted, and prayed before the Lord; 6and
Mt 6:1–18 Ezra 8:21–36 they collected money, each giving what he could; 7and they sent it

---

in Babylon. Later on, the king was allowed a degree of freedom by Evil-merodach, Nebuchadnezzar's successor. According to the historical books, Jehoiakim the priest mentioned here in v. 7 would have been a priest of second rank, and not the high priest Jehozadak, who held that position when Jerusalem was conquered in 587 and who was deported to Babylon (cf. 1 Chron 6:15).

Nebuchadnezzar was responsible for two deportations. The first, referred to in v. 9, took place in 597 and included King Jeconiah/Jehoiachin, along with his court, nobles and part of the general population (cf. 2 Kings 24:10–12). The second came later, in 587, when Zedekiah rebelled against the king of the Chaldeans: Jerusalem was taken and destroyed, Nebuchadnezzar had Zedekiah's sons killed before his eyes and then had the king himself blinded and brought in fetters to Babylon (cf. 2 Kings 25:1–7).

The river Sud (v. 4) is mentioned only in this passage of Baruch. It may have been one of the many channels of the Euphrates in the neighbourhood of Babylon.

1:5–6. The three verbs in v. 5 (wept, fasted, prayed) sum up the attitude of sorrow and repentance of the Jews in exile. These actions are rounded off by almsgiving, and they also sum up the author's entire purpose—to evince sorrow for sins committed, and to have people make expiation by self-denial, and turn to God in the hope of regaining his friendship. Following Jesus' teaching (Mt 6:1–18), Christian tradition identifies prayer, fasting and almsgiving as works of penance: "Prayer, almsgiving and fasting are elements of one movement and act, and each gives life to the others. Fasting is the soul of prayer, and almsgiving is the life of fasting. Let no man try to separate them, for they cannot be separated [...]. Prayer and almsgiving and fasting together make up one intercessor for us before God, a single call to the Lord, a trinity of petitions" (St Peter Chrysologus, *Sermones*, 43).

incenderunt eam igni. 3Et legit Baruch verba libri huius in aures Iechoniae filii Ioachim regis Iudae et in aures omnis populi venientis ad librum 4et in aures potentium et filiorum regum et in aures seniorum et in aures omnis populi a minimo usque ad maximum universorum habitantium in Babylonia, ad flumen Sud. 5Et flebant et ieiunabant et orabant in conspectu Domini. 6Et collegerunt argentum, prout poterant manus singulorum, 7et miserunt in Ierusalem ad Ioachim filium Helciae filii Salom sacerdotem

to Jerusalem to Jehoiakim the high priest,[a] the son of Hilkiah, son
of Shallum, and to the priests, and to all the people who were
present with him in Jerusalem. 8At the same time, on the tenth day
of Sivan, Baruch[b] took the vessels of the house of the Lord, which
had been carried away from the temple, to return them to the land
of Judah—the silver vessels which Zedekiah the son of Josiah,
king of Judah, had made, 9after Nebuchadnezzar king of Babylon 2 Kings 24:10–12:14; 25:1–7
had carried away from Jerusalem Jeconiah and the princes and the
prisoners and the mighty men and the people of the land, and
brought them to Babylon.

Letter from the exiles to those in Jerusalem

10And they said: "Herewith we send you money; so buy with the Ezra 6:9–10 Rom 13:1–7
money and incense, and prepare a cereal offering, and offer them
upon the altar of the Lord our God; 11and pray for the life of Dan 5:1–6:1

1:11. Belshazzar also appears in the book of Daniel (5:1–2, 13, 22) as the son of Nebuchadnezzar. In fact he was the son of Nabonid and the fifth successor (and then only co-regent) of Nebuchadnezzar. This inaccuracy can be put down to the compressed nature of this account and to the fact that it has a theological rather than historical purpose; the reign of Nebuchadnezzar lasted almost until 539 BC when the Persians invaded and put Belshazzar to death (cf. Dan 5:1—6:1).

***1:15—3:8.** The introduction over, the first section of the book proper begins at 1:15. It has to do mainly with a public confession of sins and an appeal to God for forgiveness. Although at first sight it seems somewhat untidy and repetitive, we can break it down as follows: First, 1:15—2:5. This is an impressive confession of guilt by the exiles: they humbly acknowledge that they have sinned against the Lord, have failed to believe in his word ever since the time of the exodus from Egypt, have done wrong and on that account have been punished by God, who has scattered them among the nations. It all bears out what God told Moses would happen (1:15–22). Second, 2:6–26. This passage parallels the previous one somewhat but pleads with God for compassion and forgiveness (2:13–16; cf. v. 29). Third, 2:27–35. The people recall God's promises that, once they are converted, he will bring them back

et ad sacerdotes et ad omnem populum, qui inventi sunt cum illo in Ierusalem, 8cum acciperet vasa domus Domini, quae ablata fuerant de templo, ut referret ea in terram Iudae, decima die mensis Sivan: vasa argentea, quae fecit Sedecias filius Iosiae rex Iudae, 9 postquam adduxit Nabuchodonosor rex Babylonis Iechoniam et principes et inclusores et potentes et populum terrae ex Ierusalem et induxit eos in Babylonem. 10Et dixerunt: «Ecce misimus ad vos pecuniam; emite ex ea pecunia holocausta et pro peccato et tus et facite oblationem et afferte super altare Domini Dei nostri; 11et orate pro vita Nabuchodonosor regis Babylonis et pro vita Balthasar filii eius, ut sint dies eorum, sicuti sunt dies caeli

a. Gk *the priest* **b.** Gk *he*

Jer 29:7 Nebuchadnezzar king of Babylon, and for the life of Belshazzar
1 Tim 2:1–2 his son, that their days on earth may be like the days of heaven.
Dan 5:2,13 [12]And the Lord will give us strength, and he will give light to our
eyes, and we shall live under the protection[c] of Nebuchadnezzar
king of Babylon, and under the protection[c] of Belshazzar his son,
and we shall serve them many days and find favour in their sight.
[13]And pray for us to the Lord our God, for we have sinned against
the Lord our God, and to this day the anger of the Lord and his
wrath have not turned away from us. [14]And you shall read this book
which we are sending you, to make your confession in the house of
the Lord on the days of the feasts and at appointed seasons.

2. CONFESSION OF SINS AND PRAYER FOR FORGIVENESS*

Admission of sin

Jer 7:19 [15]"And you shall say: 'Righteousness belongs to the Lord our
Dan 9:7–8 God, but confusion of face, as at this day, to us, to the men of
Bar 2:6 Judah, to the inhabitants of Jerusalem, [16]and to our kings and our
princes and our priests and our prophets and our fathers, [17]because

---

to the promised land, from which they will never again be expelled, and he will make an everlasting covenant with them. The last verses (2:29–30) summarize the oracles contained in Jeremiah 25:8–11 and 27:22. Fourth, 3:1–8. This is a further, very touching prayer of entreaty for God's salvation. It has features in common with Daniel 9:4–19, and with the style of Jeremiah and Deuteronomy 28–32.

1:15–22. This passage marks the start of a prayer of lamentation and contrition—themes that take up a large part of the book. Similar sentiments are to be found in Daniel 9:5–11. A chorus is repeated at three points: "We have not heeded the voice of the Lord" (cf. vv. 18, 19, 21; cf. 2:5). Three sins are singled out—disobedience to the Lord's commandments (v. 18); failure to listen to the message of the prophets sent by God (v. 21); and lapsing into idolatry (v. 22).

super terram; [12]et dabit Dominus virtutem nobis et illuminabit oculos nostros, et vivemus sub umbra Nabuchodonosor regis Babylonis et sub umbra Balthasar filii eius et serviemus eis multis diebus et inveniemus gratiam in conspectu eorum. [13]Et orate pro nobis ad Dominum Deum nostrum, quia peccavimus Domino Deo nostro, et non avertit se indignatio Domini et ira eius a nobis usque in hunc diem. [14]Et legetis librum hunc, quem misimus ad vos recitari in domo Domini, in die sollemni et in diebus constitutis, [15]et dicetis: Domino Deo nostro iustitia, nobis autem confusio faciei, sicut hodiernus dies homini Iudae et habitatoribus Ierusalem [16]et regibus nostris et principibus nostris et sacerdotibus nostris et prophetis nostris et patribus nostris: [17]peccavimus enim ante Dominum et non credidimus

c. Gk *in the shadow*

we have sinned before the Lord, [18]and have disobeyed him, and Tob 3:3,4 Dan 9:5–6
have not heeded the voice of the Lord our God, to walk in the Bar 2:10
statutes of the Lord which he set before us. [19]From the day when
the Lord brought our fathers out of the land of Egypt until today, Jer 17:25–26
we have been disobedient to the Lord our God, and we have been
negligent, in not heeding his voice. [20]So to this day there have Ex 3:8
clung to us the calamities and the curse which the Lord declared Lev 26:14–39
through Moses his servant at the time when he brought our fathers Deut 28:15–68 Dan 9:11
out of the land of Egypt to give to us a land flowing with milk and
honey. [21]We did not heed the voice of the Lord our God in all the Jer 7:24
words of the prophets whom he sent to us, but we each followed
the intent of his own wicked heart by serving other gods and
doing what is evil in the sight of the Lord our God.

2 [1]"So the Lord confirmed his word, which he spoke against us, Dan 9:12–13
and against our judges who judged Israel, and against our
kings and against our princes and against the men of Israel and
Judah. [2]Under the whole heaven there has not been done the like
of what he has done in Jerusalem, in accordance with what is
written in the law of Moses, [3]that we should eat, one the flesh of his Deut 28:53–57
son and another the flesh of his daughter. [4]And he gave them into Jer 19:9 Lam 2:20; 4:10
subjection to all the kingdoms around us, to be a reproach and a Deut 28:37
desolation among all the surrounding peoples, where the Lord has Jer 29:18

2:1–5. The lamentation continues, admitting the aberrations that occurred during the siege of Jerusalem, and is in response to the oracle in Jeremiah 19:9 (which reminds one of what happened earlier, when Samaria was under siege: cf. 2 Kings 6:24–31). Here again is a confession of disobedience to God and an acknowledgment that the calamities and misfortunes that befell the people were punishment that they deserved; so there is a theological message here about God's sovereignty over human affairs. The passage is a warning about what happens when man fails to listen to God: he is in danger of acting like a beast and becoming a slave to false gods and foreign enemies.

ei [18]et non audivimus vocem Domini Dei nostri, ut ambularemus in mandatis Domini, quae dedit ante faciem nostram. [19] A die qua Dominus eduxit patres nostros de terra Aegypti et usque ad hanc diem eramus contumaces in Dominum Deum nostrum et temere egimus, ne audiremus vocem eius, [20]et adhaeserunt nobis mala et maledictio, quam constituit Dominus Moysi servo suo in die, qua eduxit patres nostros de terra Aegypti dare nobis terram fluentem lac et mel, sicut hic dies. [21]Et non audivimus vocem Domini Dei nostri secundum omnia verba prophetarum, quos misit ad nos, [22]et abivimus unusquisque in sensu cordis nostri mali ad serviendum diis alienis, facientes mala sub oculis Dei nostri. **[2]** [1]Et statuit Dominus verbum suum, quod locutus est super nos et super iudices nostros, qui iudicabant Israel, et super reges nostros et super principes nostros et super omnem hominem Israel et Iudae, [2]ut induceret super nos mala magna, quae non sunt facta sub omni caelo, secundum quae fecit in Ierusalem, secundum ea quae scripta sunt in lege Moysi, [3]comedere nos unumquemque carnes filii sui et unumquemque carnes filiae suae. [4]Et dedit illos subditos omnibus regnis, quae in circuitu nostro

Deut 28:13:43 scattered them. [5]They were brought low and not raised up, because
we sinned against the Lord our God, in not heeding his voice.

Lamentation

Jer 27:22 Dan 9:7–8 [6]"'Righteousness belongs to the Lord our God, but confusion of
Bar 1:15 face to us and our fathers, as at this day. [7]All those calamities with
which the Lord threatened us have come upon us. [8]Yet we have
Jer 1:12; 31:28; 44:27 not entreated the favour of the Lord by turning away, each of us,
Dan 9:14 from the thoughts of his wicked heart. [9]And the Lord has kept the

---

2:6–26. Further admission of sin (vv. 6–10) is followed by a contrite prayer, beseeching God to look down from his holy temple in Jerusalem and show compassion (vv. 11–18). The people also draw hope from their memory of the wonderful things God did during the exodus from Egypt (v. 11). The prayer takes up a theme often found in the Old Testament (vv. 17–18): no praise is offered to God in the underworld (cf. Ps 6:5; 30:9; 88:5, 11–12; Is 38:18–19). The sacred text speaks of "Hades" but this should not be taken as a reference to the Beyond in Greek mythology; rather, it is the Hebrew Sheol, the place of the dead (cf. the note on Job 26: 5–14). It is the living that are able to praise God; but an important nuance is added here: the true worshippers of God are the weak and those who are afflicted, meaning the "poor of the Lord" (cf. Is 49:13; 66:2; Zeph 2:3).

In verses 19–26 the people acknowledge that they deserve the terrible treatment they have suffered at the hands of the Babylonians, and that it confirmed earlier prophecies. The mention of the threefold scourge of famine, sword and pestilence (v. 25; cf. Jer 14:12; 24:10; 38:2) shows just how complete the devastation was.

Verses 11–18, and 3:1–8, are cited by John Paul II as an authentic example of prayer for God's forgiveness: "Israel was, in fact, the people of the covenant with God, a covenant that it broke many times. Whenever it became aware of its infidelity—and in the history of Israel there was no lack of prophets and others who awakened this awareness—it appealed to mercy. In this regard, the books of the Old Testament give us very many examples. Among the events and texts of greater importance one may recall: the beginning of the history of the Judges (3:7–9), the prayer of Solomon at the inauguration of the Temple (1 Kings 8:22–53), part of the prophetic work of Micah (Mic 7:18–20), the consoling assurances given by Isaiah (Is 1:18; 51:4–16), the cry of the Jews in exile (cf. Bar 2:11—3:8), and the renewal of the covenant after the return from exile (cf. Neh 9)" (*Dives in misericordia*, 4).

sunt, in opprobrium et in desolationem in omnibus populis, qui in circuitu nostro sunt, quo dispersit illos Dominus, [5]et facti sunt subtus et non supra, quia peccavimus Deo nostro non oboediendo voci eius. [6]Domino Deo nostro iustitia, nobis autem et patribus nostris confusio faciei, sicut hic dies; [7]quae locutus est Dominus super nos, omnia mala haec venerunt super nos, [8]et non sumus deprecati faciem Domini, ut averteremur unusquisque a cogitationibus cordis nostri pessimi. [9] Et vigilavit Dominus

calamities ready, and the Lord has brought them upon us, for the
Lord is righteous in all his works which he has commanded us to
do. 10Yet we have not obeyed his voice, to walk in the statutes of Bar 1:18
the Lord which he set before us.

11"'And now, O Lord God of Israel, who didst bring thy people Deut 6:21–22
out of the land of Egypt with a mighty hand and with signs and Jer 32:20–21
wonders and with great power and outstretched arm, and hast Dan 9:15–16
made thee a name, as at this day, 12we have sinned, we have been Ps 106:6
ungodly, we have done wrong, O Lord our God, against all thy
ordinances. 13Let thy anger turn away from us, for we are left, few Amos 3:12
in number, among the nations where thou hast scattered us.
14Hear, O Lord, our prayer and our supplication, and for thy own Ps 25:11
sake deliver us, and grant us favour in the sight of those who have
carried us into exile; 15that all the earth may know that thou art the Deut 9:19
Lord our God, for Israel and his descendants are called by thy Jer 14:9
name. 16O Lord, look down from thy holy habitation, and consider Deut 26:15
us. Incline thy ear, O Lord, and hear; 17open thy eyes, O Lord, and Dan 9:19
see; for the dead who are in Hades, whose spirit has been taken Ps 6:6; 30:10; 88:6:12,13
from their bodies, will not ascribe glory or justice to the Lord, Is 38:18;
18but the person that is greatly distressed,[d] that goes about bent 49:13; 66:2
over and feeble, and the eyes that are failing, and the person that Zeph 2:3 Deut
hungers, will ascribe to thee glory and righteousness, O Lord. 28:65–67
19For it is not because of any righteous deeds of our fathers or our Ezek 36:22
kings that we bring before thee our prayer for mercy, O Lord our Dan 9:18
God. 20For thou hast sent thy anger and thy wrath upon us, as thou
didst declare by thy servants the prophets, saying: 21"Thus says Jer 27:12
the Lord: Bend your shoulders and serve the king of Babylon, and

---

super mala et induxit ea super nos, quia iustus est Dominus in omnibus operibus suis, quae mandavit
nobis. 10Et non oboedivimus voci eius, ut ambularemus in praeceptis Domini, quae dedit ante faciem
nostram. 11Et nunc, Domine, Deus Israel, qui eduxisti populum tuum de terra Aegypti in manu valida,
in signis et portentis et in virtute magna et in brachio excelso et fecisti tibi nomen, sicut hic dies,
12peccavimus, impie fecimus, inique egimus, Domine Deus noster, in omnibus iustificationibus tuis.
13Avertatur ira tua a nobis, quia derelicti sumus pauci in gentibus, quo dispersisti nos. 14Exaudi,
Domine, orationem nostram et deprecationem nostram et eripe nos propter te et da nobis gratiam ante
faciem eorum, qui nos abduxerunt, 15ut sciat omnis terra quia tu es Dominus Deus noster, et quia
nomen tuum invocatum est super Israel et super genus eius. 16Domine, prospice de domo sancta tua et
attende in nos; inclina, Domine, aurem tuam et audi. 17Aperi, Domine, oculos tuos et vide, quia non
mortui, qui in inferno sunt, quorum spiritus ablatus est a visceribus eorum, dabunt gloriam et
iustificationem Domino, 18sed anima, quae tristis est super magnitudinem, quae incedit curva et infirma,
et oculi deficientes et anima esuriens dabunt tibi gloriam et iustitiam, Domine. 19 Quia non in
iustificationibus patrum nostrorum et regum nostrorum nos prosternimus preces nostras ante faciem
tuam, Domine Deus noster; 20quia immisisti indignationem tuam et iram tuam super nos, sicut locutus
es in manibus puerorum tuorum prophetarum dicens: 21"Sic dicit Dominus: Inclinate umerum vestrum

d. The meaning of the Greek is uncertain

you will remain in the land which I gave to your fathers. 22But if
you will not obey the voice of the Lord and will not serve the king
Jer 7:34 of Babylon, 23I will make to cease from the cities of Judah and
from the region about Jerusalem the voice of mirth and the voice
of gladness, the voice of the bridegroom and the voice of the
bride, and the whole land will be a desolation without inhabitants."

Jer 8:1–2 24"'But we did not obey thy voice, to serve the king of
Babylon; and thou hast confirmed thy words, which thou didst
speak by thy servants the prophets, that the bones of our kings and
the bones of our fathers would be brought out of their graves;[e]
Jer 14:12; 24:10; 36:30; 38:2 25and behold, they have been cast out to the heat of day and the
frost of night. They perished in great misery, by famine and sword
and pestilence. 26And the house which is called by thy name thou
hast made as it is today, because of the wickedness of the house of
Israel and the house of Judah.

The exiles will be brought home. An everlasting Covenant

27"'Yet thou hast dealt with us, O Lord our God, in all thy
kindness and in all thy great compassion, 28as thou didst speak by
thy servant Moses on the day when thou didst command him to
Lev 26:39 write thy law in the presence of the people of Israel, saying, 29"If
you will not obey my voice, this very great multitude will surely

---

2:27–35. After punishment comes the promise of rehabilitation that is to be found so often in prophetic oracles. The text announces confidently that Israel will have a change of heart and will give glory to God—and that he will bring them home (v. 34) and cause them to increase; and will make an everlasting covenant with them (vv. 34–35). In the words of God recorded here there is an echo of what he laid down in Moses' time about rewards and penalties for those who kept or broke the Law (cf. Lev 26:39–45; Deut 30:1–10). On the new and everlasting covenant, cf. Jer 31: 31–33; Ezek 36:24–31; Ps 89:28–37.

et servite regi Babylonis et sedebitis super terram, quam dedi patribus vestris. 22Et si non audieritis vocem Domini, ut serviatis regi Babylonis, deficere faciam a civitatibus Iudae et a plateis Ierusalem 23vocem laetitiae et vocem iucunditatis et vocem sponsi et vocem sponsae, et erit omnis terra sine vestigio ab inhabitantibus". 24Et non audivimus vocem tuam, ut serviremus regi Babylonis; et statuisti verba tua, quae locutus es in manibus puerorum tuorum prophetarum, ut eicerentur ossa regum nostrorum et ossa patrum nostrorum de loco suo; 25et ecce sunt proiecta in calore diei et in gelu noctis, et mortui sunt in doloribus malis, in fame et in gladio et in peste. 26Et posuisti domum, super quam invocatum est nomen tuum, sicut hic dies propter malitiam domus Israel et domus Iudae. 27Et fecisti in nos, Domine Deus noster, secundum omnem moderationem tuam et secundum omnem miserationem tuam magnam, 28sicut locutus es in manu pueri tui Moysi in die, quo mandasti ei scribere legem tuam

e. Gk *their place*

turn into a small number among the nations, where I will scatter
them. [30]For I know that they will not obey me, for they are a stiff- Deut 9:13
necked people. But in the land of their exile they will come to Lev 26:44ff
themselves, [31]and they will know that I am the Lord their God. I Jer 4:4
will give them a heart that obeys and ears that hear; [32]and they Ezek 36:26
will praise me in the land of their exile, and will remember my
name, [33]and will turn from their stubbornness and their wicked Deut 30:1,9ff
deeds; for they will remember the ways of their fathers, who
sinned before the Lord. [34]I will bring them again into the land Lev 26:39–45
which I swore to give to their fathers, to Abraham and to Isaac and Deut 30:1–10 Ps 89:29–38
to Jacob, and they will rule over it; and I will increase them, and Jer 31:31–33
they will not be diminished. [35]I will make an everlasting covenant Ezek
with them to be their God and they shall be my people; and I will 36:24–31
never again remove my people Israel from the land which I have
given them."

Plea for forgiveness Deut 28–32

3 [1]"'O Lord Almighty, God of Israel, the soul in anguish and the Dan 9:4–19 Bar 2:18
wearied spirit cry out to thee. [2]Hear, O Lord, and have mercy, Ps 29:10;
for we have sinned before thee. [3]For thou art enthroned for ever, 44:23

3:1–8. These verses are a concluding prayer of entreaty by the exiles. Their claim to be heard is based on a) repentance for past faults (v. 1), which they blame on their fathers (vv. 4–5, 8); and b) on the fact that the Lord is "enthroned for ever", that is, rules over all things, whereas the exiles "are perishing for ever", their situation is so miserable (v. 3). The prayer draws this contrast in order to move God to compassion (similar arguments are used in Daniel 3:25–45; 9:4–19). Theodoret of Cyrus, glossing v. 1, comments: "You are an ocean of kindness and a sea of mercy: pour out your kindness upon us, for those who have sinned require mercy in the same measure as those who have repented of their sins" (*Interpretatio in Baruch*, 3, 1). What comes across clearly from this passage is the sense of solidarity with past generations, and the conviction that historical events are an expression of God's will.

coram filiis Israel [29] dicens: "Si non audieritis vocem meam, profecto turba haec magna et multa convertetur in parvam inter gentes, quo eos dispergam; [30]quia scivi quod me non audient, quia populus est dura cervice. Et convertentur ad cor suum in terra captivitatis suae [31]et scient quia ego Dominus Deus illorum, et dabo illis cor intellegens et aures audientes, [32]et laudabunt me in terra captivitatis suae et memores erunt nominis mei; [33]et avertent se a dorso suo duro et a nequissimis adinventionibus suis, quia memores erunt viae patrum suorum, qui peccaverunt coram Domino. [34]Et convertam eos in terram, quam iuravi patribus eorum, Abraham, Isaac et Iacob; et possidebunt eam et multiplicabo eos, et non minorabuntur; [35]et statuam illis testamentum aeternum, ut sim illis in Deum, et ipsi erunt mihi in populum, et ultra iam non movebo populum meum Israel a terra, quam dedi illis". **[3]** [1]Domine omnipotens, Deus Israel, anima in angustiis et spiritus anxius clamat ad te. [2]Audi, Domine, et miserere, quia peccavimus in conspectu tuo; [3]quia tu sedens es in aeternum, et nos pereuntes in aeternum.

and we are perishing for ever. [4]O Lord Almighty, God of Israel, hear
now the prayer of the dead of Israel and of the sons of those who
sinned before thee, who did not heed the voice of the Lord their God,
so that calamities have clung to us. [5]Remember not the iniquities of
Jer 31:33 our fathers, but in this crisis remember thy power and thy name. [6]For
thou art the Lord our God, and thee, O Lord, will we praise. [7]For
thou hast put the fear of thee in our hearts in order that we should
call upon thy name; and we will praise thee in our exile, for we have
put away from our hearts all the iniquity of our fathers who sinned
Prov 4:20–22 before thee. [8]Behold, we are today in our exile where thou hast
Bar 2:4 scattered us, to be reproached and cursed and punished for all the
iniquities of our fathers who forsook the Lord our God.'"

3. ISRAEL AND WISDOM*

Israel is in exile because it failed to heed wisdom

Prov 4:20–22 [9]Hear the commandments of life, O Israel;
give ear, and learn wisdom!
[10]Why is it, O Israel, why is it that you
are in the land of your enemies,
that you are growing old in a foreign country,
that you are defiled with the dead,

The exact meaning of the phrase "the dead of Israel" (v. 4) is a matter of debate among scholars. Does it mean prayers by the dead for their offspring, or the prayers offered by patriarchs and prophets in their lifetimes? It may simply be a hyperbolic expression: the "dead" are the exiles, whose plight is such that they might as well be in Sheol (cf. 3:10–11).

***3:9—4:4.** This section is a consideration and eulogy of the divine attribute of true Wisdom; at the same time, it is an exhortation addressed to Israel ("Listen, Israel": 3:9). This passage from Baruch is similar in style to many of the Wisdom writings in the Old Testament. True Wisdom was given to Israel, who forsook it (3:9–14). The pagan nations look for Wisdom where

[4]Domine omnipotens, Deus Israel, audi nunc orationem defunctorum Israel et filiorum eorum, qui peccaverunt in conspectu tuo, qui non audierunt vocem Domini Dei sui, et adhaeserunt nobis mala. [5]Noli memor esse iniquitatum patrum nostrorum, sed memor esto manus tuae et nominis tui in hoc tempore, [6]quia tu es Dominus Deus noster, et laudabimus te, Domine, [7]quia propter hoc dedisti timorem tuum in cor nostrum, ut invocaremus nomen tuum; et laudabimus te in captivitate nostra, quia avertimus a corde nostro omnem iniquitatem patrum nostrorum, qui peccaverunt in conspectu tuo. [8]Ecce nos hodie in captivitate nostra, quo nos dispersisti in opprobrium et in maledictum et in expiationem, secundum omnes iniquitates patrum nostrorum, qui discesserunt a Domino Deo nostro». [9] Audi, Israel, mandata vitae; / auribus percipite, ut sciatis prudentiam. / [10]Quid est, Israel? / Quid est

11 that you are counted among those in Hades?
12 You have forsaken the fountain of wisdom. Sir 1:5
13 If you had walked in the way of God, Is 48:18
you would be dwelling in peace for ever. Jer 2:13
14 Learn where there is wisdom,
where there is strength,
where there is understanding,

---

there is none, Wisdom in solely human terms: they believe that it is to be found in worldly power and wealth, and in control over natural resources and animals (3:15–31); they fail to seek the Wisdom that comes from God (3:32–36; cf. Job 28:12–28; Sir 1:1–10; Wis 7:7–14). The Lord revealed his Wisdom to Israel in the Law; they should consider themselves blessed for having been chosen to receive the commandments of the Lord (3:37—4:4). This is the part of the book that has been most frequently commented on by the Fathers (cf. 3:37–38). St Irenaeus, for example, sees a prophetic foreshadowing of the redemption of all mankind through the Incarnation of the Word in 3:29—4:1: "Whenever and wherever people believe in him and carry out his will and call on his name, Jesus draws near and stands by their side and responds to the petitions they make from the bottom of their heart. When we have been redeemed, we will give thanks to God every day, for in his great, unimaginable, Wisdom he saved us and proclaimed our salvation from the highest heavens: the proclamation was made in the visible coming of the Lord, that is, when he was made man. We have received the salvation that, left to ourselves, we could never have earned. But what is impossible to man is possible to God" (*Demonstratio praedicationis apostolicae*, 97).

3:9–14. Why was Israel deported to a foreign country? Because it forsook "the way of God" (v. 13). God is called the "fountain of Wisdom" (v. 12), thereby anticipating the reply to the question in 3:15. Wisdom is described (v. 14) by synonyms that show how multi-faceted it is: it is "strength", it is "understanding", it gives "length of days, and life" and "light for the eyes, and peace". Commenting on the gifts of understanding and prudence, St Bonaventure refers to v. 14: "Of all the things that guide man's understanding in everything that he does and strives to avoid doing, he should consider most of all the purpose of his life. By his nature, he must hope for something, some gain, from what he does. But if you satisfy yourself with earthly consolations, you will reap a terrible reward. The greatest pearl of all is eternal happiness. Therefore, listen to what is said in Baruch: *Learn where there is wisdom …* (3:14)" (*De septem donis Spiritus Sancti*, 8, 10).

quod in terra es inimicorum? / [11]Inveterasti in terra aliena, / coinquinatus es mortuis, / reputatus es cum eis, qui apud inferos sunt. / [12]Dereliquisti fontem sapientiae! / [13]Si in via Dei ambulasses, / habitasses in pace in aeternum. / [14]Disce, ubi sit prudentia, / ubi fortitudo, ubi sit intellectus, / ut scias simul, ubi

that you may at the same time discern
where there is length of days, and life,
where there is light for the eyes, and peace.

The fleetingness of life

Job 28:12–20 [15] Who has found her place?
And who has entered her storehouses?
Jer 27:6 [16] Where are the princes of the nations,
and those who rule over the beasts on earth;
[17] those who have sport with the birds of the air,
and who hoard up silver and gold,
in which men trust,
and there is no end to their getting;
[18] those who scheme to get silver, and are anxious,
whose labours are beyond measure?
[19] They have vanished and gone down to Hades,
and others have arisen in their place.

[20] Young men have seen the light of day,
and have dwelt upon the earth;
but they have not learned the way to knowledge,
nor understood her paths,
nor laid hold of her.
[21] Their sons have strayed far from her[f] way.

3:15–21. Unlike the true Wisdom of God, the source of life, all things human are quite impermanent. Nothing human—power, skill, wealth—lasts forever. Various social categories are mentioned—rulers of nations (such as Nebuchadnezzar, whose power was considered to be unlimited: cf. Jer 27:6; Deut 2:37–38); people skilled in the art of falconry; and rich people who hoard gold and silver. They all go down to Hades, and others come to take their places.

sit longiturnitas dierum et vita, / ubi sit lumen oculorum et pax. / [15]Quis invenit locum eius? / Et quis intravit in thesauros eius? / [16]Ubi sunt principes gentium / et qui dominantur bestiis, quae sunt super terram, / [17]qui in avibus caeli ludunt, / [18]qui argentum thesaurizant et aurum, / in quo confidunt homines, / neque est finis acquisitionis eorum; / qui argentum fabricant et solliciti sunt, / nec est inquisitio operum illorum? / [19] Exterminati sunt et ad inferos descenderunt, / et alii loco eorum surrexerunt. / [20]Iuvenes viderunt lumen et habitaverunt super terram; / viam autem disciplinae non cognoverunt / [21]nec intellexerunt semitas eius; / neque susceperunt eam filii eorum, / a via eorum longe

f. Other authorities read *their*

The nations have no wisdom

22 She has not been heard of in Canaan, Deut 2:10 Ezek 28:4–5 Zech 9:2
nor seen in Teman;
23 the sons of Hagar, who seek for understanding on the earth, Gen 25:12 Job 2:11
the merchants of Merran and Teman,
the story-tellers and the seekers for understanding,
have not learned the way to wisdom,
nor given thought to her paths.

3:22–28. Wisdom is greater than mortal men. If Israel has unlearned whatever Wisdom she knew, it is even more difficult to find Wisdom in the surrounding nations, despite their reputation for it. Four nations famous for their Wisdom are mentioned—Canaan, the Idumeans (Edomites), Nabateas and the merchants of Merran (location unknown; a variant reading is "Madian") and Teman. The Canaanites were the earlier settlers of the promised land, from whom the people of Israel learned agricultural and other skills. The people of Teman, a city of Edom on the banks of the Red Sea, are mentioned in Jeremiah 49:7 as a model of Wisdom; Eliphaz the Temanite, one of the three "wise" friends of Job (Job 2:11), came from there. From the sons of Hagar, the Ishmaelites, came the Nabateans, a semi-nomadic desert tribe, who were also merchants. These peoples had a complex mythology for explaining the generation of the gods and the origin of the world and of mankind.

But not only is Wisdom not to be found among other nations: even the giants (mentioned in Gen 6:2–4 and Num 13:32–33) did not possess it. These were the ancient inhabitants of the promised land, called giants (Nephelim), great warriors. The giants belong to a very ancient oral tradition that included elements from the mythologies of the neighbouring countries. For example, in Greek mythology we find the Titans who tried to assault Mount Olympus, the dwelling-place of the gods, seeking to supplant Zeus; but they were struck down by lightning shafts sent out by the god; the blood and ashes of the Titans, mixed with the soil of the earth, produced human beings. There is no reason to think that Baruch derived ideas from that source; what he says could come from one of many religious explanations of the origins of man, but he has cleansed it of polytheistic accretions. There are other passages in the Old Testament that refer to men of enormous size having lived in Canaan (cf. Deut 3:11, where there is mention of Og, king of Bashan, the last of the Rephaim, whose bedstead measured nine cubits by four; and 1 Samuel 17:4–7, where the giant Goliath was "six cubits and a span" tall).

facti sunt. / [22]Neque audita est in Chanaan / neque visa est in Theman. / [23]Filii quoque Agar, qui exquirunt sapientiam super terram, / negotiatores Merran et Theman / et fabulatores et inquisitores prudentiae: / viam autem sapientiae non cognoverunt / neque commemorati sunt semitas eius. / [24]O

[24]O Israel, how great is the house of God!
And how vast the territory that he possesses!
[25]It is great and has no bounds;
it is high and immeasurable.
Gen 6:4 Num 13:32–33 Deut 1:28; 2:10; 3:11 1 Sam 17: 4–7 1 Sam 16:7
[26]The giants were born there, who were famous of old,
great in stature, expert in war.
[27]God did not choose them,
nor give them the way to knowledge;
[28]so they perished because they had no wisdom,
they perished through their folly.

Wisdom can come only from God

Sir 24:4–7 Wis 9:4,9–11
[29]Who has gone up into heaven, and taken her,
and brought her down from the clouds?
[30]Who has gone over the sea, and found her,
and will buy her for pure gold?
Job 28:13–14
[31]No one knows the way to her,
or is concerned about the path to her.

The created world reflects true wisdom

Job 28:23 Sir 1:1–10 Wis 7:7–14
[32]But he who knows all things knows her,
he found her by his understanding.
He who prepared the earth for all time
filled it with four-footed creatures;
[33]he who sends forth the light, and it goes,
called it, and it obeyed him in fear;

3:29–31. The author concludes his argument by asking a number of rhetorical questions that are reminiscent of Wisdom texts (cf. Wis 9:9–11; Sir 24:4–7): on his own, man cannot attain Wisdom; he can obtain it only from God. It is a divine attribute. Glossing v. 31, Olympiodorus comments: "If someone thinks that he finally and fully knows something, he does not yet understand it as it should be understood" (*Fragmenta in Baruch*, 3, 31).

3:32–35. To avoid any danger of polytheism and pantheism that might result from the notion that Wisdom is

Israel, quam magna est domus Dei, / et ingens locus possessionis eius! / [25]Magnus est et non habet finem, / excelsus est et immensus. / [26]Ibi fuerunt gigantes nominati illi, qui ab initio fuerunt, / statura magna, scientes bellum. / [27]Non illos elegit Deus / neque viam disciplinae dedit illis; / [28]et perierunt, quia non habuerunt prudentiam, / perierunt propter insipientiam suam. / [29] Quis ascendit in caelum et accepit eam / et deduxit eam de nubibus? / [30]Quis transfretavit mare et invenit eam / et apportabit eam auro electo? / [31]Non est qui noverit viam eius, / neque qui cogitet semitam eius. / [32]Sed qui scit omnia, novit eam, / adinvenit eam prudentia sua; / qui composuit terram in aeternum tempus, / implevit eam iumentis quadrupedibus; / [33]qui mittit lumen et vadit, / vocavit illud, et oboedivit ei in tremore. /

[34]the stars shone in their watches, and were glad;
he called them, and they said, "Here we are!"
They shone with gladness for him who made them.
[35]This is our God; Job 38:35
no other can be compared to him! Ps 147:4
Is 40:23,26

Israel, the repository of wisdom

[36]He found the whole way to knowledge, Ps 147:19
and gave her to Jacob his servant Sir 24:8,10
and to Israel whom he loved. Pt 8:31
[37]Afterward she appeared upon earth Wis 9:10
and lived among men. Jn 1:14

---

something divine, the sacred writer reasserts his belief in the one God, and his notion of creation. The Creator must not be confused with his works—light and stars (cf. Job 9:9; 38:35).

3:36—4:4. The Lord revealed his Wisdom in the Law and gave it to Israel. As the book of Sirach (Ecclesiasticus) in particular makes clear (Sir 19:20–28; 24:1–47; etc.), Wisdom is not just an endowment from God to the people; it is in fact the Law of Moses; that is where man most clearly sees God.

3:36–37. Two things here are worth stressing: 1) as in the sapiential books, Wisdom is mentioned as a gift from God to the patriarchs and the people of Israel (v. 36; cf. Sir 24:8–12); 2) however, it belongs not only to Israel but "lives among men" (v. 36); so here is another instance of the Old Testament universalist outlook.

St Gregory of Nyssa read v. 37 as proof that God in his providence looks after mankind: "*He found the whole way to knowledge, and gave her to Jacob his servant* ... Thus man discovered fire and the tasks that need fire and need no fire, and the work that involves water, and a thousand more discoveries and a thousand ways of working, so that he would lack nothing that helps to sustain his life" (*De beneficentia*, 1).

As with other similar passages where Wisdom is personified (cf. Prov 8: 1–36; Wis 6:12–25; 9:10; Sir 15:2–6, etc.), some Fathers and commentators saw in v. 37 (cf. Wis 9:10; Prov 8:31) a glimpse of the incarnation of the Son of God (cf. Jn 1:14). St Irenaeus offered his interpretation first in his *Demonstratio* (cf. the note on 3:9—4:4). He gives the same interpretation in his most famous and profound work, *Against Heresies*: "This is his Word, our Lord Jesus Christ, who in the last days became a man among men, to unite the beginning and the end, that is, man and God. Thus the prophets, who received the gift of prophecy from God, foretold his

[34]Stellae autem splenduerunt in custodiis suis / et laetatae sunt. / [35]Vocavit eas, et dixerunt: "Adsumus"; / luxerunt cum laetitia ei, qui fecit eas. / [36]Hic est Deus noster, / non aestimabitur alter adversus eum. / [37]Invenit omnem viam disciplinae / et dedit eam Iacob puero suo / et Israel dilecto suo. / [38]Post haec

Prov 1:32–33; 8: 35–36 Sir 24:23 4 [1]She is the book of the commandments of God,
and the law that endures for ever.
All who hold her fast will live,
and those who forsake her will die.
Prov 6:23 [2]Turn, O Jacob, and take her;
walk toward the shining of her light.
[3]Do not give your glory to another,
or your advantages to an alien people.
Deut 4:8, 32–37 Wis 9:18 [4]Happy are we, O Israel,
for we know what is pleasing to God.

4. CONVERSION TO GOD. JERUSALEM'S JOY*

Is 4:2–6; 10:20–21; 50:1; 52:3 Jer 3:14 **Song of exhortation and consolation for the exiles**
[5]Take courage, my people,
O memorial of Israel!

---

coming in the flesh; and his coming has intensified the communion and union of God and man, in accordance with the will of the Father. The word of God said long ago that he would *appear*[*ed*] *upon earth and live*[*d*] *among men* (Bar 3:37), that he would speak with them, and talk to them about the work he would do to save them and gather them into himself" (*Adversus haereses*, 4, 20, 5). We can see v. 37 also in the following passage where St John Damascene, explaining that God is at work everywhere, quotes Baruch loosely: "The earth is his footstool (cf. Is 66:1), whereby being made flesh he came to live among men" (*Expositio fidei*, 1, 13).

Echoing the Fathers, the Second Vatican Council refers to this passage of Baruch: "Through this revelation, therefore, the invisible God (cf. Col 1:15; 1 Tim 1:17) out of the abundance of his love speaks to men as friends (cf. Ex 33:11; John 15:14–15) and lives among them (cf. Bar 3:38), so that he may invite and take them into fellowship with himself" (*Dei Verbum*, 2). In v. 37, where it says "she lived among men", the Greek uses the verb *synanestraphe*, which the Latin translates as *conversatus est*, implying a relationship of familiarity between God and man; that familiar or familial relationship finds its fullest expression in the incarnation of the Son of God.

*__4:5—5:9.__ This brings us to the fourth section of the book. Themes of lamentation, hope, conversion and consolation alternate here. The narrative concerns

super terram visa est / et inter homines conversata est. **[4]** [1]Ipsa est liber praeceptorum Dei / et lex, quae permanet in aeternum. / Omnes, qui tenent eam, ad vitam; / qui autem relinquunt eam, morientur. / [2]Convertere, Iacob, et apprehende eam; / perambula ad splendorem in lumine eius. / [3]Noli dare alteri gloriam tuam / et dignitates tuas genti alienae. / [4]Beati sumus, Israel, / quia, quae placent Deo, nobis nota sunt. / [5]Confide, popule meus, / memoria Israel: / [6]venumdati estis gentibus / non in perditionem,

[6]It was not for destruction
that you were sold to the nations,
but you were handed over to your enemies
because you angered God.
[7]For you provoked him who made you, Deut 32:17
by sacrificing to demons and not to God.
[8]You forgot the everlasting God, who brought you up, Deut 32:5,10,15
and you grieved Jerusalem, who reared you. Is 1:2

Jerusalem makes lamentation to the cities round about
[9]For she saw the wrath that came upon you from God,
and she said:
"Hearken, you neighbours of Zion,
God has brought great sorrow upon me;
[10] for I have seen the captivity of my sons and daughters,
which the Everlasting brought upon them.
[11] With joy I nurtured them,
but I sent them away with weeping and sorrow.

Jerusalem, who shares her sorrow with her children scattered among the nations, acknowledges her inability to help them, and confesses that her only hope is the Lord God of Israel. It begins (4:5–8) with words of consolation and encouragement. Then Jerusalem makes a lamentation to the cities of Judah (4:9–16) and to her own children, exhorting them to conversion (4:17–29). This is followed by a song of rejoicing (4:30–37) and an optimistic summing up of the whole book (5:1–9).

4:5–8. The chosen people will be punished for their unfaithfulness, but still there are grounds for hope: a remnant, a "memorial" (v. 5), will remain loyal and will return from exile. This goes to show that the punishment meted out by God does not imply the destruction of the people; it is meant as a corrective, and marks the start of a new people. The theme of the "remnant of Israel" appears often in the prophets (cf. Amos 5:15; Mic 4:7; Is 4:2–6; 10:20–21; Jer 3:14; 5:18; Ezek 14:22; etc.) and is a reminder that everything that happens is guided by the hand of God.

4:9–16. Now it is Jerusalem who speaks. She is depicted as a widow and mother who sees that her children have been led off into captivity: "Jerusalem is called a widow because she has been deprived of the divine care that was once

/ sed, quia irritastis Deum, / traditi estis adversariis. / [7]Exacerbastis enim eum, qui fecit vos, / sacrificantes daemonibus et non Deo. / [8]Obliti autem estis Deum, qui vos pavit, Deum aeternum, / et contristastis eam, quae vos enutrivit, Ierusalem. / [9] Vidit enim supervenientem vobis iram a Deo / et dixit: «Audite, vicinae Sion: / Superinduxit mihi Deus luctum magnum. / [10]Vidi enim captivitatem filiorum meorum et filiarum, / quam superinduxit illis Aeternus. / [11]Nutrivi enim illos cum iucunditate,

Lam 1:1–2 12 Let no one rejoice over me, a widow
and bereaved of many;
I was left desolate because of the sins of my children,
because they turned away from the law of God.
13 They had no regard for his statutes;
they did not walk in the ways of God's commandments,
nor tread the paths of discipline in his righteousness.
14 Let the neighbours of Zion come;
remember the capture of my sons and daughters,
which the Everlasting brought upon them.
Deut 28:49–50 15 For he brought against them a nation from afar,
Jer 5:15; 6:22–23 a shameless nation, of a strange language,
who had no respect for an old man,
and had no pity for a child.
16 They led away the widow's beloved sons,
and bereaved the lonely woman of her daughters.

Is 60:1–4; **Jerusalem calls on her children to be converted and to have hope**
63:7–9; 17 "But I, how can I help you?
66:10–11 18 For he who brought these calamities upon you
Jer 30:18–22 will deliver you from the hand of your enemies.
19 Go, my children, go;
for I have been left desolate.
20 I have taken off the robe of peace

---

given to her" (Theodoret of Cyprus, *Interpretatio in Baruch,* 4, 12). It is a lament for those who have gone, leaving her alone—an echo of the poetry of the book of Lamentations.

4:17–29. But the punishment imposed by God will not last forever; there is good reason to hope, based on the compassion and goodness of the Everlasting One; he will deliver them (v. 22). The return of the exiles is announced, and the joy of the holy city—in tones reminiscent of the last part of the book of Isaiah (cf. Is 60:1–4; 63:7–9; 66:10–11) and some of Jeremiah's oracles (cf. Jer 30:18–22). The passage is both a song of consolation and an exhortation to turn to the Lord.

/ dimisi autem illos cum fletu et luctu. / 12 Nemo gaudeat super me, viduam et derelictam a multis; / desolata sum propter peccata filiorum meorum, / quia declinaverunt a lege Dei. / 13 Iustificationes autem eius non cognoverunt / neque ambulaverunt in viis mandatorum Dei / neque semitas disciplinae in iustitia eius ingressi sunt. / 14 Veniant vicinae Sion; / et memores estote captivitatis filiorum meorum et filiarum, / quam superinduxit illis Aeternus. / 15 Superinduxit enim illis gentem de longinquo, / gentem improbam et alterius linguae, / qui non sunt reveriti senem / neque parvulorum miserti sunt / 16 et abduxerunt dilectos viduae / et a filiabus unicam desolaverunt». / 17 Ego autem, quid possum adiuvare vos? / 18 Qui enim superinduxit in vos mala, / eripiet vos de manu inimicorum vestrorum. / 19 Abite, filii, abite; / ego enim derelicta sum sola. / 20 Exui me stola pacis, / indui autem me cilicio obsecrationis

and put on the sackcloth of my supplication;
I will cry to the Everlasting all my days.
21"Take courage, my children, cry to God,
and he will deliver you from the power and hand of the enemy.
22For I have put my hope in the Everlasting to save you,
and joy has come to me from the Holy One,
because of the mercy which soon will come to you
from your everlasting Saviour.[g]
23For I sent you out with sorrow and weeping, Jer 31:12–13
but God will give you back to me with joy and gladness for ever.
24For as the neighbours of Zion have now seen your capture, Is 60:1–3
so they soon will see your salvation by God,
which will come to you with great glory
and with the splendour of the Everlasting.
25My children, endure with patience the wrath Is 51:23
that has come upon you from God.
Your enemy has overtaken you,
but you will soon see their destruction
and will tread upon their necks.
26My tender sons have travelled rough roads; Lam 2:22; 4:5
they were taken away like a flock carried off by the enemy.

27"Take courage, my children, and cry to God, Is 40:1
for you will be remembered by him who brought this upon you.
28For just as you purposed to go astray from God,
return with tenfold zeal to seek him.
29For he who brought these calamities upon you
will bring you everlasting joy with your salvation."

---

meae, / clamabo ad Aeternum in diebus meis. / 21Confidite, filii, clamate ad Deum, / et eripiet vos de
dominatione, de manu inimicorum. / 22Ego enim speravi ab Aeterno salutem vestram; / et venit mihi
gaudium a Sancto / super misericordia, quae veniet vobis cito / ab Aeterno, salutari vestro. / 23Emisi
enim vos cum luctu et fletu; / reddet autem mihi vos Deus / cum gaudio et laetitia in aeternum. / 24Nam,
sicut nunc viderunt vicinae Sion vestram captivitatem, / sic videbunt cito a Deo vestram salutem, / quae
superveniet vobis cum magna gloria et splendore Aeterni. / 25Filii, patienter sustinete iram, quae vobis
a Deo supervenit; / persecutus est te inimicus tuus, / sed cito videbis perditionem / in cervicem eorum
ascendentem. / 26Delicati mei ambulaverunt vias asperas, / ducti sunt ut grex direptus ab inimicis. /
27Confidite, filii, et clamate ad Deum; / erit enim vestra ab inductore memoria. / 28Nam sicut fuit mens
vestra, ut erraretis a Deo, / conversi decuplate studium quaerendi eum; / 29 qui enim induxit in vos mala,
/ inducet in vos aeternam iucunditatem cum salute vestra. / 30Confide, Ierusalem; / consolabitur enim

g. Or *from the Everlasting, your Saviour*

Song of rejoicing

Is 1:26; 60:14; 62:2–4 30 Take courage, O Jerusalem,
for he who named you will comfort you.
Jer 30:17; 33:16 31 Wretched will be those who afflicted you
and rejoiced at your fall.
32 Wretched will be the cities which your children
served as slaves;
wretched will be the city which received your sons.
33 For just as she rejoiced at your fall
and was glad for your ruin,
so she will be grieved at her own desolation.
34 And I will take away her pride in her great population,
and her insolence will be turned to grief.
Lev 16:8; 17:7 Is 34:9 35 For fire will come upon her from the Everlasting for many days,
and for a long time she will be inhabited by demons.

Is 60:4–5 36 Look toward the east, O Jerusalem,
and see the joy that is coming to you from God!
37 Behold, your sons are coming, whom you sent away;
they are coming, gathered from east and west,
at the word of the Holy One,
rejoicing in the glory of God.

4:30–37. The prophet lifts the spirits of Jerusalem with a song of rejoicing, for her children held captive in east and west will return (vv. 36–37), while punishment awaits their captors ("the city which received your sons": v. 32)—an indirect reference to Babylon and the other oppressors of Judah.

In v. 30, "naming" is the same as establishing ownership; someone given a name belongs to the person who named him. Jerusalem belonged to God, he gave her the name originally, and he will give it back to her after the exile (cf. Is 1:26; 60:14; 62:2–4; Jer 30:17; 33:16).

Verses 36–37 evoke, in summary form, the content of Isaiah 60:1–22.

te, qui te nominavit. / 31 Miseri, qui te nocuerunt / et qui exsultati sunt in casu tuo! / 32 Miserae civitates, quibus servierunt filii tui; / misera, quae accepit filios tuos! / 33 Sicut enim gavisa est in tua ruina / et laetata est in tuo casu, / ita contristabitur in sua solitudine. / 34 Et amputabo exsultationem multitudinis, / et laetitia eius erit in luctum. / 35 Ignis enim superveniet illi ab Aeterno / in dies longinquos, / et inhabitabitur a daemoniis plurimum temporis. / 36 Circumspice ad orientem, Ierusalem, / et vide iucunditatem, quae a Deo tibi superventura est. / 37 Ecce veniunt filii tui, quos emisisti, / veniunt congregati ab ortu usque ad occasum / verbo Sancti, gaudentes in Dei gloria.

A summing up, by way of conclusion

5 [1]Take off the garment of your sorrow and affliction, O Jerusalem, Is 52:1 Rev 21:1–4
and put on for ever the beauty of the glory from God.
[2]Put on the robe of the righteousness from God; Is 61:10
put on your head the diadem of the glory of the Everlasting.
[3]For God will show your splendour everywhere under heaven.
[4]For your name will for ever be called by God, Ps 126 Is 40:4–5; 49:18–22; 60:1–4
"Peace of righteousness and glory of godliness."

[5]Arise, O Jerusalem, stand upon the height Jer 30:15–22
and look toward the east,
and see your children gathered from west and east,
at the word of the Holy One,
rejoicing that God has remembered them.
[6]For they went forth from you on foot, Is 49:22; 60:4
led away by their enemies;

5:1–9. By way of recapitulation, the book ends with a new song of consolation, the fourth in the book. It promises everlasting happiness, and the tone is eschatological. The new Jerusalem will be given a symbolic name that indicates not only that she belongs to God but also her main features: she will be "peace of righteousness" and "glory of godliness", that is, just peace and glorious devotion. Olympiodorus offers a spiritual interpretation: "Christ is our peace and our justice and our glory, and the example of the piety with which we should live: we, too, will receive those names from him" (*Fragmenta in Baruch*, 5, 4).

This passage has many parallels in the prophetical and Wisdom books—Is 40:4–5; 49:18–22; 60:1–4; Jer 30:15–22; Ps 126; etc. But particularly intriguing is the connexion between vv. 1–9 and the vision of the messianic Jerusalem in the Revelation to John 21:1–4, which St Irenaeus noticed in his *Adversus haereses*, where he concludes: "No allegorical interpretation of this can be given: everything is true and clear and defined, and God desires that it be so for the glory of righteous men. God raises man from the dead and, when the Kingdom comes, man will be brought to life with incorruptibility and made strong, and he will welcome in the glory of the Father. When everything has been renewed, he will truly live in the city of God" (5, 35, 2).

[5] [1]Exue te, Ierusalem, stola luctus et vexationis tuae / et indue te decore eius, / quae a Deo tibi data est gloriae in aeternum. / [2]Circumda te diploide iustitiae, quae a Deo est, / et impone mitram capiti tuo gloriae Aeterni. / [3]Deus enim ostendet omni, quod sub caelo est, / splendorem tuum. / [4]Vocabitur enim nomen tuum a Deo in aeternum: / Pax iustitiae et Gloria culturae Dei. / [5]Surge, Ierusalem, et sta in excelso / et circumspice ad orientem et vide congregatos filios tuos / a solis ortu usque ad occasum / verbo Sancti, gaudentes in memoria Dei. / [6]Exierunt enim abs te pedites abducti ab inimicis; / inducet

but God will bring them back to you,
carried in glory, as on a royal throne.
Is 40:3,4 [7]For God has ordered that every high mountain
and the everlasting hills be made low
and the valleys filled up, to make level ground,
so that Israel may walk safely in the glory of God.
Is 41:19 [8]The woods and every fragrant tree
have shaded Israel at God's command.
[9]For God will lead Israel with joy,
in the light of his glory,
with the mercy and righteousness that come from him.

Wis 13–15
Is 40:19–20;
44:9–20;
46:1–7

5. THE LETTER OF JEREMIAH*

Warning against idolatry

Jer 29:1
6 [1] A copy of a letter which Jeremiah sent to those who were to be
taken to Babylon as captives by the king of the Babylonians, to
give them the message which God had commanded him.

***6:1–73.** The long Letter of Jeremiah is addressed, as its heading indicates, to "those who were to be taken to Babylon as captives by the king of the Babylonians". In the Septuagint it appears as a separate book coming after the Lamentations of Jeremiah. The Vulgate Latin appends it to the book of Baruch. When the sacred books were divided up into chapters, the Letter became the sixth chapter of Baruch; that is where it comes in the New Vulgate and many modern translations of the Bible. Basically, the letter is a satire about idols and pagan cults written to protect the Jews living in exile. It has similarities to Wisdom 13–15, though the latter contains more profound arguments. Some passages are similar to Is 40:19–20; 44:9–20; 46:1–7; Jer 10:1–16; Ps 115:4–8; etc.

The main cults referred to are Babylonian—the god Bel (that is, Marduk, v. 41), sacred prostitution rites (vv. 43–44) and measures taken in the repair and transport of idols (vv. 11–12, 22–26, 33, 72). That might imply that the Letter is an attack on the cult of the god Tammuz (cf. v. 32; Ezek 8:14–15), but, taken overall, it can apply to any sort of idolatry; the sort of circumstances mentioned also occurred in

autem illos ad te / portatos cum gloria sicut thronum regni; / [7]constituit enim Deus humiliare / omnem montem excelsum et rupes perennes / et convalles implere ad aequalitatem terrae, / ut ingrediatur Israel in securitate gloriae Dei. / [8]Obumbrabunt autem et silvae et omne lignum suavitatis / Israel ex praecepto Dei. / [9] Praeibit enim Deus Israel cum laetitia / in lumine maiestatis suae, / cum misericordia et iustitia, / quae est ab ipso. **[6]** Exemplum epistulae, quam misit Ieremias ad abducendos captivos in Babyloniam a rege Babyloniorum, ut nuntiaret illis secundum quod praeceptum est ei a Deo. [1]Propter peccata, quae peccastis ante Deum, abducemini in Babyloniam captivi a Nabuchodonosor rege

2Because of the sins which you have committed before God, Dan 9:24–25
you will be taken to Babylon as captives by Nebuchadnezzar, king
of the Babylonians. 3Therefore when you have come to Babylon Is 40:20
you will remain there for many years, for a long time, up to seven Jer 10:1–16
generations; after that I will bring you away from there in peace.
4Now in Babylon you will see gods made of silver and gold and
wood, which are carried on men's shoulders and inspire fear in the
heathen. 5So take care not to become at all like the foreigners or
to let fear for these gods[i] possess you, when you see the multitude
before and behind them worshipping them. 6But say in your heart, Ex 23:20
"It is thou, O Lord, whom we must worship." 7For my angel is
with you, and he is watching your lives. Ps 115:4–8; 135:15–18

---

the period of Greek hegemony. The *Catechism of the Catholic Church*, 2112, when explaining the first commandment of the Lord, quotes this entire Letter as an Old Testament source for the authority of revelation: "The first commandment condemns *polytheism*. It requires man neither to believe in, nor to venerate, other divinities than the one true God. Scripture constantly recalls this rejection of idols [...]."

The Letter can be divided into nine paragraphs, the conclusion of each being along the lines of "Therefore they evidently are not gods; so do not fear them" (cf. vv. 16, 23, 29, 40, 45, 52, 56, 65, 69). That refrain helps to convey the main idea that the writer wants to get across.

6:2–7. It is taken as read that the exile is going to last a long time (v. 3); therefore the Letter wants to warn about the temptations and threats that the elaborate processions of Babylonian idols may present to the exiles.

The "seven generations" in v. 3 are "seventy weeks" in Daniel 9:24–25. But Jeremiah 25:11 and 29:10 are more specific: the exile will last seventy years. The figure is meant to be, not exact, but symbolic: the number seven stands for fullness, completion.

In v. 7 it is God who is speaking. The reference to the "angel" is reminiscent of Exodus 23:20–24, where God promises his people that an angel will stay with them during their years in the wilderness and as they enter the promised land. It may mean an angel as such, or the more mysterious presence of God.

Babyloniorum. 2Ingressi itaque in Babylonem, eritis illic annis pluribus et tempus longum usque ad
generationes septem; post hoc autem educam vos inde cum pace. 3Nunc autem videbitis in Babylone
deos argenteos et aureos et ligneos in umeris portari, ostentantes metum gentibus. 4Cavete ergo, ne et
vos assimilati assimilemini alienigenis, et metus vos capiat in ipsis. 5Videntes turbam ante et retro
adorantem eos, dicite autem in corde vestro: «Te oportet adorare, Domine». 6Angelus enim meus
vobiscum est; ipse autem exquiret animas vestras. 7Nam lingua eorum polita a fabro; ipsa etiam

i. Gk *for them*

Wis 13:10–19
Is 40:19–20; 41:6–7; 44:9–20
Jer 10:1–16

Idols are of no avail

[8]Their tongues are smoothed by the craftsman, and they themselves are overlaid with gold and silver; but they are false and
cannot speak. [9]People[j] take gold and make crowns for the heads of
their gods, as they would for a girl who loves ornaments; [10]and
sometimes the priests secretly take gold and silver from their gods
and spend it upon themselves, [11]and even give some of it to the
harlots in the brothel. They deck their gods[k] out with garments
like men—these gods of silver and gold and wood, [12]which cannot
save themselves from rust and corrosion. When they have been
dressed in purple robes, [13]their faces are wiped because of the dust
from the temple, which is thick upon them. [14]Like a local ruler the
god[l] holds a sceptre, though unable to destroy any one who
offends it. [15]It has a dagger in its right hand and has an axe; but it
cannot save itself from war and robbers. [16]Therefore they evidently are not gods; so do not fear them.

Idols are useless things, the products of craftsmen

[17]For just as one's dish is useless when it is broken, so are the
gods of the heathen,[m] when they have been set up in the temples.

6:8–16. The fact that idols are man-made things devoid of any power is a point often made in Old Testament passages against idolatry. In the prophetical and Wisdom writings, these verses have parallels in, for example, the passages mentioned in the shoulder notes to v. 8 and in Ps 115:4–8; 135:15–18; and Wis 13:10–19. Here, drawing an implied contrast with the God of Israel who does speak to his people, the author shows that the idols of pagan nations are dumb (v. 8). And whereas the true God saves, the false gods are quite unable to save others or even themselves (vv. 14–15). Besides, the things that idolatrous priests do only proves that idols have no power whatsoever (vv. 9–12).

6:17–29. Satire is often brought into play in the case against idols. The

inaurata et inargentata falsa sunt et non possunt loqui. [8]Et sicut virgini ornatum amanti, accepto auro fabricantur [9] coronas super capita deorum suorum. Interdum autem accidit etiam, ut sacerdotes, subtrahentes a diis aurum et argentum, erogent illud in semetipsos [10]et dent ex ipso et prostitutis in lupanari. Et ornant illos ut homines vestimentis, deos argenteos et aureos et ligneos. [11]Hi autem non liberantur ab aerugine et tinea. [12]Opertis illis veste purpurea, extergunt faciem eorum propter pulverem domus, qui est plurimus super eos. [13]Et sceptrum habet ut homo, iudex regionis, qui in se peccantem non interficiet. [14]Habet etiam gladium in manu dextera et securim, se autem de bello et a latronibus non liberabit. Unde notum est quia non sunt dii; [15]non ergo timueritis eos. Sicut enim vas hominis confractum inutile fit, tales sunt dii eorum. [16]Collocatis illis in domo, oculi eorum pleni sunt pulvere ex pedibus introeuntium. [17]Et sicut alicui, qui regem offendit, circumsaeptae sunt aulae, tamquam ad

j. Gk *they* **k.** Gk *them* **l.** Gk *he* **m.** Gk *of them*

Their eyes are full of the dust raised by the feet of those who
enter. 18And just as the gates are shut on every side upon a man
who has offended a king, as though he were sentenced to death, so
the priests make their temples secure with doors and locks and
bars, in order that they may not be plundered by robbers. 19They
light lamps, even more than they light for themselves, though their
gods[n] can see none of them. 20They are[o] just like a beam of the
temple, but men say their hearts have melted, when worms from
the earth devour them and their robes. They do not notice 21when
their faces have been blackened by the smoke of the temple.
22Bats, swallows, and birds light on their bodies and heads; and so
do cats. 23From this you will know that they are not gods; so do Is 46:7
not fear them. Wis 13:16

24As for the gold which they wear for beauty—they will not
shine unless some one wipes off the rust; for even when they were
being cast, they had no feeling. 25They are bought at any cost, but

---

author emphasizes that they are as useless as broken dishes; and that they are guarded the way prisoners are, and precautions must be taken if they are stolen, for they cannot defend themselves; they cannot even protect themselves against worms, or scare animals away (vv. 15–23). He also makes the point that they cannot feel anything and are at the mercy of corrupt priests (vv. 24–28)—unlike what happens in Israel where worship is governed by strict rules (Lev 6–7). Minucius Felix, in his exposition of the Christian faith, uses this passage when he argues that Roman superstitions were foolish: "Even dumb animals instinctively understand a great deal about your gods! Mice and swallows and birds of prey all know that your gods are not alive: they move and sit among them; if they are not driven away, they will make their nests in the mouths of your gods. Spiders spin webs around their faces and cover their heads with cobwebs. You wash, clean and polish and protect and fear things that you have made with your own hands, without ever thinking that you should first know God before you worship him; instead, everyone devotes themselves to their ancestors, preferring to reach out to the error outside than to look within themselves, because they know nothing of [these gods] they fear" (*Octavio*, 24, 9–10).

mortem ducto, domus eorum muniunt sacerdotes ostiis et clausuris et seris, ne a latronibus exspolientur.
18Lucernas accendunt et quidem plures quam sibi ipsis, quarum nullam videre possunt. 19 Sunt autem
sicut trabes in domo; corda vero eorum dicunt elingere serpentes, qui de terra sunt; dum comedunt eos
et vestimentum eorum, non sentiunt. 20Nigrae fiunt facies eorum a fumo, qui in domo fit. 21Super
corpus eorum et super caput volitant noctuae et hirundines et aves, similiter et cattae. 22Unde scietis
quia non sunt dii; non ergo timueritis eos. 23Aurum enim, quod circa se habent ad speciem, nisi aliquis
exterserit aeruginem, non fulgebit; neque enim, cum conflabantur, sentiebant. 24Ex omni pretio empta
sunt, in quibus spiritus non est. 25Sine pedibus, in umeris portantur, ostentantes ignobilitatem suam

n. Gk *they* **o.** Gk *It is*

there is no breath in them. [26]Having no feet, they are carried on
men's shoulders, revealing to mankind their worthlessness. [27]And
Lev 12:4; 15:19; 20:18 those who serve them are ashamed because through them these
gods[n] are made to stand, lest they fall to the ground. If any one
sets one of them upright, it cannot move of itself; and if it is tipped
over, it cannot straighten itself; but gifts are placed before them
just as before the dead. [28]The priests sell the sacrifices that are
offered to these gods[p] and use the money; and likewise their wives
preserve some with salt, but give none to the poor or helpless.
[29]Sacrifices to them may be touched by women in menstruation or
at childbirth. Since you know by these things that they are not
gods, do not fear them.

Idols are quite powerless

Lev 21:5–10 [30]For why should they be called gods? Women serve meals for
Ezek 8:14–15 gods of silver and gold and wood; [31]and in their temples the

6:30–69. The writer mocks the fact that the idolatrous Chaldeans should allow women to take part in religious rites (v. 30)—which would scandalize the Jews—and that the fabrics used to dress idols are taken by the priests for themselves and their families (v. 33). Verses 31–32 refer to funeral rites that were forbidden by the Law (cf. Lev 21:5–10). Idols can do nothing to prevent such aberrations or rescue their devotees from misfortune (vv. 34–39) —unlike the God of Israel who can establish kings, bestow prosperity or poverty, call people to account for their vows, save a man from death or be merciful towards the weak (cf. 1 Sam 2:8; Prov 30:8; Deut 23:22; Ps 35:10; etc.).

Even the Chaldeans show disrespect to idols, because by asking them to work miracles that they cannot perform, they expose their powerlessness. They claim that something that cannot hear, the god Bel (Marduk), can cure a dumb man (vv. 41–42), whereas the good Israelite knows that only the Lord can make the dumb speak (cf. Is 35:6). The worst aspect of idolatry is that its rites include so-called sacred prostitution (vv. 43–44), which God strictly forbids (cf. Deut 23:18–19). Besides,

hominibus; confunduntur et, qui excolunt ea, [26]propter quod, ne forte cadat in terram, per ipsos erigetur. Neque, si quis illud erectum statuerit, per semetipsum movebitur neque, si inclinatum fuerit, erigetur; sed sicut mortuis munera illis apponuntur. [27]Hostias vero eorum sacerdotes eorum vendunt et abutuntur; similiter et uxores eorum, ex ipsis partes sale condientes, neque mendico neque infirmo aliquid impertiunt. De sacrificiis eorum menstruatae et fetae contingunt. [28]Scientes itaque ex his quia non sunt dii, ne timueritis eos. [29]Unde enim vocabuntur dii? Quia mulieres apponunt diis argenteis et aureis et ligneis, [30]et in domibus illorum sacerdotes sedent habentes tunicas scissas et capita et barbam rasam, quorum capita nuda sunt. [31]Rugiunt autem clamantes coram diis suis sicut in cena mortui. [32]A

p. Gk *to them*

priests sit with their clothes rent, their heads and beards shaved,
and their heads uncovered. [32]They howl and shout before their
gods as some do at a funeral feast for a man who has died. [33]The
priests take some of the clothing of their gods[q] to clothe their
wives and children. [34]Whether one does evil to them or good, they
will not be able to repay it. They cannot set up a king or depose
one. [35]Likewise they are not able to give either wealth or money; Ps 68:6;
if one makes a vow to them and does not keep it, they will not 146:7–8
require it. [36]They cannot save a man from death or rescue the
weak from the strong. [37]They cannot restore sight to a blind man;
they cannot rescue a man who is in distress. [38]They cannot take
pity on a widow or do good to an orphan. [39]These things that are
made of wood and overlaid with gold and silver are like stones

---

the fact that idols cannot come to man's rescue is another proof of their worthlessness. Idols are the products of lies; they are mere human inventions—objects made by artisans (vv. 45–51).

The author of the Letter knows that it is the God of Israel, the true God, who establishes kings (cf. e.g. 1 Sam 10:1–9; 16:1–13; etc.) and sends down rain (cf. e.g. Deut 11:14; Ps 147:8; etc.). It is useless for pagans to ask for such gifts from idols, because they cannot even put out a fire or oppose a king (vv. 53–56). Olympiodorus, in one of the fragments of his commentary on the Letter, pauses to remark on the allegorical meaning of the "crows" mentioned in v. 54. He interprets these unclean animals as a reference to the demons "who were cast down from heaven by God, and who are cast out by holy men on earth with the help of Christ" (*Fragmenta in epistulam Jeremiae*, 6, 53).

Idols serve no purpose whatsoever: they cannot prevent themselves from being stolen; a king is of more use, or a utensil, or any architectural feature of a house (vv. 57–59); even inanimate things or the elements (sun, moon, stars, lightning, winds, clouds) are worth more than idols; nor can idols decide legal cases or do any good for man (vv. 60–64).

Implied in the author's teaching is the sovereignty of the Lord over the whole universe; he ensures that all created beings perform their functions. But idols have no power over created things, kings, nations, the elements or wild beasts (vv. 66–68).

vestimento eorum auferunt sacerdotes et vestiunt uxores suas et filios suos. [33]Neque si quid mali
patiantur ab aliquo neque si bonum, poterint retribuere; neque constituere regem possunt neque auferre.
[34]Similiter neque divitias neque aes poterunt dare. Si quis illis votum voverit nec reddiderit, non
requirent. [35]De morte hominem non liberabunt neque infirmiorem a potentiore eripient. [36]Hominem
caecum ad visum non restituent, de necessitate hominem non liberabunt. [37]Viduae non miserebuntur
neque orphano benefacient. [38]Lapidibus de monte similes sunt, lignea et inaurata et inargentata; qui

q. Gk *them*

from the mountain, and those who serve them will be put to
shame. [40]Why then must any one think that they are gods, or call
them gods?

Besides, even the Chaldeans themselves dishonour them; [41]for
when they see a dumb man, who cannot speak, they bring him and
pray Bel[r] that the man may speak, as though Bel[s] were able to
understand, [42]Yet they themselves cannot perceive this and
abandon them, for they have no sense. [43]And the women with
cords about them, sit along the passageways, burning bran for
incense and when one of them is led off by one of the passers-by
and is lain with, she derides the woman next to her, because she
was not as attractive as herself and her cord was not broken,
[44]Whatever is done for them is false. Why then must any one think
that they are gods, or call them gods?

[45]They are made by carpenters and goldsmiths; they can be
nothing but what the craftsmen wish them to be. [46]The men that
make them will certainly not live very long themselves; how then
can the things that are made by them be gods? [47]They have left
only lies and reproach for those who come after. [48]For when war
or calamity comes upon them, the priests consult together as to
where they can hide themselves and their gods.[t] [49]How then can
one fail to see that these are not gods, for they cannot save
themselves from war or calamity? [50]Since they are made of wood
and overlaid with gold and silver, it will afterward be known that
they are false. [51]It will be manifest to all the nations and kings that
1 Sam 10:1–9; they are not gods but the work of men's hands, and that
16:1–13 there is no work of God in them. [52]Who then can fail to know that
Ps 147:8 they are not gods?[u]

---

autem excolunt illa, confundentur. [39] Quomodo ergo aestimandum aut dicendum est esse illos deos? [40]Adhuc etiam ipsi Chaldaei non honorant ea; qui cum viderint mutum non posse loqui, afferunt Bel postulantes illum loqui, [41]quasi ipse possit sentire. Et non possunt ipsi, cum intellexerint, relinquere ea; sensum enim non habent. [42]Mulieres autem circumdatae funibus in viis sedent succendentes furfurem; [43]cum autem aliqua ex ipsis, attracta ab aliquo transeunte, dormierit cum eo, proximae suae exprobrat quod ea non sit digna habita, sicut ipsa, neque funis eius diruptus. [44]Omnia autem, quae illis fiunt, falsa sunt; quomodo ergo aestimandum est aut dicendum illos esse deos? [45]A fabris et ab aurificibus facti sunt; nihil aliud erunt, nisi id quod volunt artifices. [46]Ipsi etiam, qui ea faciunt, non erunt multi temporis; itaque numquid possunt, quae ab ipsis fabricata sunt, esse dii? [47]Reliquerunt enim falsa et opprobrium postea futuris. [48]Nam cum supervenerit illis proelium et mala, cogitant apud se sacerdotes, ubi se abscondant cum illis. [49] Quomodo ergo non est sentiendum quia non sunt dii, qui nec liberant se de bello nec de malis? [50]Nam cum sint lignea et inaurata et inargentata, scietur postea quia falsa sunt; gentibus universis et regibus manifestum erit quia non sunt dii sed opera manuum hominum, et nullum Dei opus in illis est. [51]Cui ergo non notum est quod non sunt dii? [52]Regem enim regioni non suscitabunt

r. Or *they bring Bel and pray* **s.** Gk *he* **t.** Gk *them* **u.** The Greek text of this verse is uncertain

[53]For they cannot set up a king over a country or give rain to men. [54]They cannot judge their own cause or deliver one who is wronged, for they have no power; they are like crows between heaven and earth. [55]When fire breaks out in a temple of wooden gods overlaid with gold or silver, their priests will flee and escape, but the gods[v] will be burnt in two like beams. [56]Besides, they can offer no resistance to a king or any enemies. Why then must any one admit or think that they are gods?

[57]Gods made of wood and overlaid with silver and gold are not able to save themselves from thieves and robbers. [58]Strong men will strip them of their gold and silver and of the robes they wear, and go off with this booty, and they will not be able to help themselves. [59]So it is better to be a king who shows his courage, or a household utensil that serves its owner's need, than to be these false gods; better even the door of a house that protects its contents, than these false gods; better also a wooden pillar in a palace, than these false gods.

[60]For sun and moon and stars, shining and sent forth for service, are obedient. [61]So also the lightning, when it flashes, is widely seen; and the wind likewise blows in every land [62]When God commands the clouds to go over the whole world, they carry out his command. [63]And the fire sent from above to consume mountains and woods does what it is ordered. But these idols[w] are not to be compared with them in appearance or power. [64]Therefore one must not think that they are gods nor call them gods, for they are not able either to decide a case or to do good to men. [65]Since you know then that they are not gods, do not fear them.

---

neque pluviam hominibus dabunt. [53]Iudicium quoque eorum non discernent nec regiones liberabunt iniuriam patientes, quia nihil possunt sicut corniculae inter medium caeli et terrae. [54]Etenim cum inciderit in domum deorum ligneorum vel inauratorum vel inargentatorum ignis, sacerdotes quidem ipsorum fugient et liberabuntur; ipsi vero sicut trabes in medio comburentur. [55]Regi autem et hostibus non resistent. Quomodo ergo aestimandum est aut recipiendum quia dii sunt? [56]Neque a furibus neque a latronibus se liberabunt dii lignei et inaurati et inargentati; [57]quibus hi fortiores sunt, quia aurum et argentum et vestimentum, quo operti sunt, auferent illis et abibunt; nec illi sibi auxilium ferent. [58]Itaque melius est esse regem ostentantem virtutem suam aut vas in domo utile, quo uti potest is, qui possidet illud, quam falsi dii, aut etiam ostium in domo, quod custodit, quae in ea sunt, quam falsi dii, et columna lignea in regiis quam falsi dii. [59] Sol quidem et luna et sidera, cum sint splendida et emissa ad utilitates, oboediunt; [60]similiter et fulgur cum apparuerit, perspicuum est; eodem modo et spiritus in omni regione spirat; [61]et nubes, quibus cum imperatum fuerit a Deo perambulare universum orbem, perficiunt, quod imperatum est; [62]ignis etiam missus desuper, ut consumat montes et silvas, facit, quod praeceptum est: haec autem neque speciebus neque virtutibus uni eorum similia sunt. [63]Unde neque aestimandum est neque dicendum illos esse deos, quando non possunt neque iudicium iudicare neque benefacere hominibus. [64]Scientes itaque quia non sunt dii, ne timueritis eos. [65]Neque enim regibus maledicent neque benedicent. [66]Signa in caelo gentibus non ostendent neque ut sol lucebunt neque

v. Gk *they* **w.** Gk *these things*

[66]For they can neither curse nor bless kings; [67]they cannot show signs in the heavens and[x] among the nations, or shine like the sun or give light like the moon. [68]The wild beasts are better than they are, for they can flee to cover and help themselves. [69]So we have no evidence whatever that they are gods; therefore do not fear them.

Summary

[70]Like a scarecrow in a cucumber bed, that guards nothing, so are their gods of wood, overlaid with gold and silver. [71]In the same way, their gods of wood, overlaid with gold and silver, are like a thorn bush in a garden, on which every bird sits; or like a dead body cast out in the darkness. [72]By the purple and linen[y] that rot upon them you will know that they are not gods; and they will finally themselves be consumed, and be a reproach in the land. [73]Better therefore is a just man who has no idols, for he will be far from reproach.

6:70–73. Idols are useless (v. 70) because they are nothing (v. 71); in fact, they are a cause for shame for the country that has them (v. 72). The author seems to have kept his most bitter irony for the end: idols are scarecrows that scare no one (v. 70); they are like dead bodies in the darkness (v. 71). The conclusion is obvious: a just man has no idols (v. 73) "Human life finds its unity in the adoration of the one God. The commandment to worship the Lord alone integrates man and saves him from an endless disintegration. Idolatry is a perversion of man's innate religious sense. An idolater is someone who 'transfers his indestructible notion of God to anything other than God' (Origen, *Contra Celsum* 2, 40)" (*Catechism of the Catholic Church*, 2114).

illuminabunt sicut luna. [67]Bestiae meliores sunt illis, quae possunt, fugientes sub tegumentum, prodesse sibi. [68]Nullo itaque modo nobis est manifestum quia sunt dii; propter quod ne timueritis eos. [69] Nam sicut in cucumerario formido nihil custodit, ita sunt dii illorum lignei et inaurati et inargentati. [70]Eodem modo et in horto spinae albae, super quam omnis avis sedet; similiter et mortuo proiecto in tenebris similes sunt dii eorum lignei et inaurati et inargentati. [71]A purpura et bysso, quae super illos tineant, scietis quia non sunt dii; ipsa etiam postremo comeduntur, et erit opprobrium in regione. [72]Melior est ergo homo iustus, qui non habet simulacra, nam erit longe ab opprobriis.

x. Other ancient authorities omit *and* **y.** Cn: Gk *marble*, Syr *silk*

EZEKIEL

Introduction

Chronologically, the book of Ezekiel is the third of the books of the major prophets, after Isaiah and Jeremiah. In the first centuries of the Christian era, the Jewish canon placed it between those two books, taking account of the content of the oracles rather than the chronological order of the books: "First Jeremiah, who is all threats; then Ezekiel who begins with threats and ends with consolation; and finally Isaiah who is all consolation."[1] However, the Christian canon, which followed the order found in the Septuagint Greek version (already to be seen in Sirach: cf. Sir 49:7–8), arranged the prophetical books in the order with which we are familiar, putting the book of Ezekiel after Jeremiah—Lamentations—Baruch. The Jewish canon changed its arrangement later, to put Ezekiel after Jeremiah.

1. STRUCTURE AND CONTENT

This book is more carefully organized than the other prophetical books. Quite early on, Jewish and Christian commentators pointed out that it divides into two parts, of almost equal length. The first (chaps. 1–24) consists almost entirely of reproaches and threats addressed to Israel on account of the transgressions that lead to the disaster of the exile. It opens with the vision in Chebar and the call of the prophet (1:1—3:26) and includes symbolic gestures and oracles foretelling the siege of Jerusalem (chaps. 4–7), a theophany in the temple, with a denunciation of sins committed there (chaps. 8–11), and oracles denouncing Judah and Israel just prior to the Babylonian invasion (chaps 12–24). The second part (chaps. 25–48), which is quite different, seeks to console the exiles and raise their spirits, through oracles against the nations and visions filled with hope. Flavius Josephus went so far as to say that Ezekiel left two books—one of reproaches, one of hope.[2] Over the centuries scholars have retained this division into two parts, observing, however, that the chapters containing the oracles against the nations (chaps. 25–32) form an independent bloc. This has led them to divide the book into three symmetrical parts (A, B, A'), a pattern often found in other prophetical books: A. Judgment and condemnation of Israel (chaps. 1–24). B. Transition: judgment and condemnation of the nations (chaps. 25–32). A'. Hope and the restoration of Israel (chaps. 33–48). This three-part division is used in our edition.

1. Talmud, *Baba Batra*, 14, 6. **2.** *Antiquitates iudaicae*, 10, 79.

The book's structure shows, on the one hand, the prophet's personality and his role, and, on the other, the sovereign figure of the Lord and his active presence in the affairs of his people. The prophet has been established by God as "a watchman for the house of Israel" to speak the word of the Lord, be it a word of warning or of consolation. This idea of the prophet as watchman is conveyed in virtually the same words early in the first (3:16–21) and second (33:7–9) parts of the book. By virtue of his divine calling and mission, the prophet must answer to God rather than the people: if he faithfully passes on the word of God, he will have saved his life (3:21), but if fear causes him not to tell the people about God's warning he will be responsible for what happens to the evildoer (3:18; 33:9). Even so, he will not be to blame for the actions of his hearers, for everyone (just or wicked) must bear responsibility for what he or she does. What the prophet will be called to account for is his unfaithfulness or otherwise in the transmission of the message given him by God (cf. Ezek 3:17 and 33:7).

The figure of the Lord—particularly his presence in the midst of his people which shows itself in what the prophet terms "the glory of God"—is the key element in the structure of the book as we can see in the three great visions. In the first chapter, the glory of the Lord is manifested in an extraordinary way to Ezekiel when he is far away from the promised land, among the exiles of his people, by the river Chebar (1:4–28). So, from the very start of the book it is perfectly clear that the Lord has not abandoned his own when they are most in need of help; even though they are in a foreign, unclean country, he is there with them. In the middle of the first part (chaps. 8–11) comes a further, awesome vision: "the glory of the Lord" leaves the temple and the city because of the sins committed there by the people (cf. Ezek 10:18–22). Finally, in the last chapters of the book, comes a vision of the Lord's glory inaugurating the new temple and taking up its abode there: "The glory of the God of Israel came from the east ..., (and entered) the temple by the gate facing east" (43:1–4). Divine punishment (the destruction of the city and the deportation of the Jews) was the result of the glory of God forsaking Jerusalem and the temple; the restoration of Israel involves the return of that glory to the centre of the promised land.

2. COMPOSITION

Compared with other prophetical books, Ezekiel has many unusual (even paradoxical) features; even so, there is a clear internal logic to them. Many commentators think that the book was compiled by the prophet himself after he made his speeches, saw his visions or performed his symbolic gestures. In other words, whereas in Isaiah or Jeremiah it is possible to distinguish oracles spoken by the prophet himself or in his time from others that were inserted later, in the case of the book of Ezekiel efforts to identify strata laid on top of one another have failed, for the entire book (its ideas, structure, literary devices, etc.) is designed for a reader rather than for a listener. All the indications are that Ezekiel was the first prophet to record in writing the oracles and gestures of his prophetical career. At least that is a conclusion one can validly draw after studying the main features of the book.

Ezekiel makes many connexions with the prophets who preceded him. For example, he uses wordings reminiscent of earlier prophecy that are found in Elijah, Elisha and prophets noted for ecstacies. But the prophet with whom he has most in common is Jeremiah. Ezekiel never explicitly mentions Jeremiah but, time and again, he explains the exile as being punishment for sins and he uses turns of phrase that echo Jeremiah—for example, when denouncing false shepherds (Jer 23:1 and Ezek 34:1–10), or the phrase "they shall be my people, and I will be their God" (Jer 30:22 and Ezek 11:20), etc. Themes typical of Jeremiah (for example, the allegory of the two sisters) are taken up again in Ezekiel (cf. Jer 3:6–10 and Ezek 23:1–49). However, the writing style of Ezekiel is much more repetitive and ornate.

Like the prophets who preceded him, Ezekiel uses oracles, visions, threats, symbolic actions, etc., but in with these he mixes other less prophetical genres such as parables, allegories, sapiential proverbs, legal cases, poems, etc. A feature of his style is his use of a rich Hebrew vocabulary, some Aramaic and Babylonian words, and he has a penchant for ornate language. He uses lots of clichés, and repeats himself time and again. Sometimes he manages to put things very well, but the impact wears off the more he repeats the phrase. Literary methods of that sort can be put down to the fact that he was a priest and moved in priestly circles: priests were supposed to teach the Law to the people, and their teaching method relied a lot on repetition and learning by rote.

As has been said already, Ezekiel often uses metaphors, allegories, poems, etc. For example, he describes the history of Israel in terms of a wayward wife (chap. 16) and two married sisters (chap. 23); he composes little vignettes that are quite effective, such as that about the useless wood of the vine (15:1–8), the two eagles (17:1–10), the cedar of salvation (17:22–24), the lioness and her cubs (19:1–9), the forest ablaze (20:45–49), the pot on the fire (24:1–14), etc.; and passionate poems like that of the sword (21:8–16), inspired probably by an ancient Babylonian song; and he often has recourse to the language of legal disputation and controversy (cf. 18:1–3; 20:30–32; 33:10–11). Although in many respects his language is the same as that found in other prophetical books, he does use devices of his own—visions of heaven, frequent use of symbolic actions and the repetition of clichés and fixed forms of words that he feels are particularly effective.

a) The visions are the high points of the book. The vision at Chebar changes Ezekiel into a prophet and protector of the glory of God (1:1—3:15). The vision of the profaned temple abandoned by the Lord (chaps. 8–11) signals the destruction of Jerusalem. And the vision of the new temple (chaps. 40–48) raises people's sights to a new, enduring presence of the glory of the Lord, and heralds a new stage when the promised land will enjoy great prosperity.

b) The symbolic gestures are oracles acted out. Ezekiel interprets the death of his wife as a sign of the imminent danger threatening Jerusalem, and his restrained mourning for her symbolizes the demeanour that the deportees should have (42:15–27). Prior to this, Ezekiel symbolizes the siege and destruction of Jerusalem by drawing a picture on a brick, by lying down on his left side and then on his right, by eating and drinking tiny, measured portions, by shaving his head and scattering the hair in a kind of ritual, etc. (chaps. 4–5). Other instances are when he leaves home with an exile's baggage (12:1–16) to show the deprivation that the deportees will experience (12:17–20). Gestures such as clapping his hands and stamping his feet (6:11), setting his face against evildoers (6:1; 13:17; 21:2), and crying and wailing (21:11), show how striking a figure the prophet cut. Some commentators interpret these symbolic gestures as being merely literary devices; that is, they say that the prophet never actually performed them; others argue that he did. Few fail to interpret their message, even if they argue that the incidents never actually happened.

c) Fixed turns of phrase are common in the book and are a function of the teaching method of Ezekiel the priest. Some of these are merely stylistic devices used to introduce a vision ("As I looked, behold": as in 1:4 and 10:1) or an oracle ("The word of the Lord came to me": as in 6:1; 7:1; etc.). Others have greater doctrinal significance; of these we would mention two:

—"Son of man". This is a Semitic expression meaning "human being" (cf. Ps 80:17; Jer 50:40; 51:43 and [though this is not obvious in the RSV] Jer 49:18, 33). In general it can be taken as a courteous form of words, to avoid using a personal pronoun (cf. Dan 8:17). But in Ezekiel it appears 93 times and has much greater significance. For one thing, it shows that the prophet sees himself as one among many, an ordinary man, with no special privileges, even though he is God's spokesman. For another, it indicates that compared with the Lord, Almighty God, who allows him to glimpse his glory, Ezekiel is a mere man, a weak and insignificant creature—the message conveyed being that there is an impossible distance between God and man. Finally, it shows the prophet's solidarity with the rest of his people, for he is not in any way different from his fellow men just because he has been entrusted with the divine message; rather, he sees himself as simply another member of the Israelite community which God is addressing through him

—"You shall know that I am the Lord" (and variants such as "They shall know ..."). This is a form of words normally used to close an oracle, or introduced in connexion with some divine revelation. In Ezekiel it occurs 54 times. The second part of the phrase ("I am the Lord") conveys, as happens in priestly literature (cf. Lev 19), the supreme nature of God's authority: God always does what he says he will do; only he has the right to impose obligations on man that are not negotiable. In a way, this formula is an abbreviation of the wording used in Deuteronomic texts to introduce the Covenant: "I am the Lord, your God, who brought you out of the land of Egypt, out of the house of bondage" (Ex 20:2). The first part of the formula ("You shall know …) indicates that every intervention by God, be it by word or action, reveals something of his person. The Lord, who stands above the world, is not unconcerned about human affairs, for he wants all men to be saved and to know the truth (cf. 1 Tim 2:4). For Ezekiel, the most important truth of all, which everyone can and should acknowledge, is that God is the sovereign Lord of all creation and of the lives of men, and that he acts freely and is in control of all things. Every created being is subordinate to the Lord. All mankind will eventually acknowledge his authority and his will.

3. EZEKIEL'S PERSONALITY AND THE TIMES IN WHICH HE LIVED

The book that bears his name is our only source of information about Ezekiel himself, and about where he lived and what he did. No one is in any doubt nowadays about the fact that he did exist or about when he was active: he lived at the most critical period in the history of Israel, which saw the destruction of Jerusalem and the deportation of part of its population to Babylon. Ezekiel was a member of a priestly family (1:3). In the year 597, while still very young, he was among the first group of people deported by Nebuchadnezzar. In the fifth year of King Jehoiachin's exile, having reached the age of thirty, that is, the age when he was due to take up his office as a priest,[3] he had a vision by the river Chebar, near the Euphrates, which had a profound influence on his soul. It was at this point that his prophetical activity began, and, according to what he says about himself, he engaged in prophecy on a regular basis. He dates his oracles and visions in relation to the year when the king was deported–the sixth year (cf. 8:1), the seventh (cf. 20:1), the ninth (cf. 24:1), the tenth (cf. 29:1), the eleventh (cf. 26:1; 30:20; 31:1) and the twelfth (cf. 32:1; 32:17; 33:21), that is, from 592 to 586, the years when Zedekiah was king in Judah. Then, after a gap of twelve years, he gives the dates of other oracles—the twenty-fifth year and the twenty-seventh from the time that Jehoiachin was

3. That is the usual interpretation given to the reference to the "thirtieth year" at the start of the book (cf. Ezek 1:1).

sent into exile. His last oracle, therefore, can be dated 571 BC. We know that he was married to a wife whom he loved dearly (24:16) and who died unexpectedly. That is all that we know about his life and doings; we do not even know when he died. St Athanasius reports[4] a tradition to the effect that the prophet was put to death by a Jewish leader whom he had denounced for idolatry; but that tradition is not very reliable.

The content and style of the book of Ezekiel take us beyond the parameters of classical prophecy. They show him to have been a complex personality. Ezekiel is capable of being saddened to the point of depression by the death of his wife or the destruction of Jerusalem, and of being elated to the point of clapping his hands and crying out loud and jumping with joy on seeing what happens to the enemies of Israel. There are no serious grounds for the theory that he suffered from some form of mental disorder. On the contrary, it makes much more sense to think that he identified deeply with his contemporaries and threw himself into his ministry because that was the sort of person he was—highly sensitive, capable of intense joy and sadness, pain and hope, discouragement and enthusiasm.

Around the start of the twentieth century there were some who argued that Ezekiel had begun his ministry in Jerusalem and that it was there he spoke the oracles to be found in the first part of the book (chaps. 1–24), on the grounds that those chapters go into a lot of detail about religious affairs and about the politics of the city. Thus they argued that he was not deported to Babylon until 587, and it was there that the second stage of his ministry took place. However, there is insufficient proof for Ezekiel's ministry having had these two, separate stages to it, and nowadays almost all scholars will say that all his prophetical ministry took place in Babylon. The book's references to Jerusalem can be explained both by the prophet's age when he went to Babylon in 597 (he was around 26—so that he would have been familiar with current events) and by the fact that he was a priest—which would have made it easy for him to mix with the more educated and better informed exiles, who must have continued to take a keen interest in the situation in the holy city.

One unresolved question is whether Ezekiel devoted himself more to preaching than to writing. The book itself contains indications that the written word was beginning to be more appreciated: in the first vision the Lord gives the prophet a book and tells him to eat it (3:1–3); this symbolic action seems to indicate the importance attaching to the word of God transmitted in written form. Without denying that Ezekiel the prophet preached and performed symbolic gestures, the fact remains that his book, more than any of the other prophetical books, is the work of a single author,

4. PG 25, 160.

with only a few later additions. It could be that Ezekiel himself wrote down his visions, oracles and intimate experiences; equally, it could be that one of his closest disciples did this, under Ezekiel's guidance. This would explain the consistency of doctrine and language in a book that uses a variety of literary genres.

4. MESSAGE

The fact that Ezekiel was a prophet and a priest, and had to explain the apparent failure that the exile implied, helps us to see why his book contains the message it does. The three great themes that keep cropping up in the book are: God: his nature, his holiness, his transcendence; morality grounded on ritual purity and personal responsibility; and a hope in salvation, which modifies traditional messianic teaching.

The holiness of God, who stands above all things

In the opening theophany (1:1–28), Ezekiel contemplates "the glory of the Lord"—the Lord drawing near to his followers and, while retaining his majesty, allowing himself to be seen, albeit only partially. He is the sovereign lord of Israel; only he can judge, condemn or save. And he is also the sovereign lord of other nations, some of which he reproves (chaps. 25–32) and others, such as Babylon, which he uses to chastise Israel and other peoples (cf. 21:23–32). The form of words mentioned earlier, "You shall know that I am the Lord," makes it clear that everyone, Israelite and Gentile, must acknowledge the majesty of God.

God's holiness and the fact that he stands above all things can be seen also in a kind of theology of the "Name of God". A "name", as we know, identifies a person and, in Semitic culture, it has special importance because knowing someone's name is the same as having authority over that person (cf. Gen 2:19–20). In the Priestly tradition, profaning the Name of God (cf. Lev 18:21; 19:12; 20:3), singing its praises (cf. Ps 7:17; 9:2) or exalting it (Ps 34:3) are equivalent to profaning, praising or exalting God himself. In the teaching of Ezekiel, the "Name of God" is holy (cf. Ezek 20:39; 36:20; 43:7; etc.) and is a guarantee of the life and safety of the people; his name must not be in any way exposed to derision by the nations (cf. 36:5, 23) or ever be profaned. God will forgive his people; he will bring about their return to the promised land and will restore the temple and its institutions etc., not on account of his people's conversion or because they have earned it, but solely on account of the honour of his Name, to ensure that it is not profaned by the Gentiles. The members of the people of God cannot, on their own, bring about their conversion: it must be God who gives them a change of heart and puts a new spirit into them (cf. 11:17–21; 36:26–28).

Ritual purity and personal responsibility

In Ezekiel, sin is given two names, already used by previous prophets—prostitution and defilement (rendered in the RSV by the words "defilement" and "detestable things": 20:30; cf. Jer 7:30; 16:18; etc.). He uses the images of adultery and prostitution to denounce not only idolatry but also sins against religious worship and ritual precepts. He condemns religious services held in the "high places" (cf. 6:13; 20:28), failure to keep the sabbath (cf. 20:12, 24), and defilement of the sanctuary (cf. 23:37–38). Idols he described as *gillulim*,[5] a word connected with "excrement" and which conveys the revulsion a priest feels for any sort of uncleanness (cf. 4:12–15). He puts a greater emphasis than any other prophet on the need to obey the precepts and regulations laid down by the Lord.

Ezekiel teaches that the history of Israel has always been stained by sin: there was never a time when Israel was faithful; she was unfaithful in Egypt (cf. 20:7) and unfaithful in the wilderness (cf. 20:13). He calls the people a "rebellious house" (cf. 2:5–6, 8; 3:9) because time and again they rebelled against the Lord (cf. 20:8, 13, 21) by breaking his commandments. Sin, according to Ezekiel, is an act of pride against the sovereign Lord, rather than a lack of love; it is an act that shows disregard for the Lord's commands, rather than disloyalty. Sin, therefore, has legal rather than moral connotations, in the sense that Ezekiel puts the stress more on the transgression of precepts than on the offence to God.

Each generation is responsible for its own actions and must bear the chastisement that it deserves and against which there is no appeal (cf. 14:12–23). In fact, each individual must answer for his or her sins, not those of their ancestors (cf. 18:1–32; 33:10–20). That is how Ezekiel explains the exile: it happened not because of things their forebears did but because of the sins of the exiles themselves.

This doctrine of personal retribution involves a risk of diluting a person's solidarity with others, be they ancestors or contemporaries. Ezekiel deals with this danger by stressing, on the one hand, the mercy of God, who saves a remnant (cf. 14:22) when the day of destruction comes, and, on the other, God's faithfulness, which will lead him to re-establish the Covenant. When the people see this happen, then they will repent and be forgiven once more (cf. 16:59–63).

Messianic hope

Hope of salvation, already hinted at in some passages in the first part of the book, is the thread that runs through the oracles, visions and symbolic actions of the second part. God himself will shepherd his people, for those who guided

5. Translated in the RSV as "idols". Cf. Ezek 8:10; 18:6; etc.

them until this time have acted only in their own interests (cf. chap. 34). He will not give Israel a new king; instead he will give them a prince on whom he will bestow the heritage of David (cf. 34:24; 37:24) along with special privileges (cf. 44:3; 45:7–12). The reference to David does not mean that dynastic succession will be restored; Israel will have no more kings. What Ezekiel says is that the ideal prince will establish a covenant of peace, similar to that made with David, and the people will be content (cf. 34:23–25). So, Ezekiel modifies traditional messianic teaching, which placed its hopes in a king descended from David; instead, he fosters hope in God himself; it will be God who gives life to his people; this he will do himself or through his Spirit (cf. chap. 37).

5. THE BOOK OF EZEKIEL IN THE LIGHT OF THE NEW TESTAMENT

In Jesus' time, the book of Ezekiel was not given nearly the same importance as those of Isaiah and Jeremiah, probably because some of its contents could give rise to interpretations that clashed with the doctrinal climate of the period. The visions, particularly that of the fiery chariot (cf. 1:1–28), could have led people into strange flights of fancy (witness some apocryphal writings and, later, in the middle ages, texts associated with Jewish mystical circles called the Kabala). Also, some of the ritual precepts mentioned several times in the book do not square with those contained in Numbers and Leviticus. The Dead Sea scrolls in fact contain only tiny fragments of six copies of the book and have very few quotations from it or references to it. In rabbinical literature, there is virtually no mention of it; all that we hear about it are problems concerning its canonicity.[6]

This explains why there are no explicit quotations from Ezekiel in the New Testament, and few direct allusions. The New Testament does contain elements which are part of general biblical tradition and which are also to be found in Ezekiel; these include the simile of the vine (Jn 15:1–10 and Ezek 15), that of the good shepherd (Jn 10:11–18 and Ezek 34), and that of the spring of water (Jn 7:37–38 and Ezek 47:1–12). The Revelation to John contains further allusions, but usually only in the sense of borrowing some terms or imitating matters of style. Nor does Patristic tradition use Ezekiel to the degree that it does the other major prophets. Only Origen (from whom we have some fragments), Theodoret of Cyrus, and later on St Jerome, commented on the book at length.

As time went by, the book came to have more influence on theology and the liturgy: in the area of theology, the vision of the bones restored to life (cf.

6. Cf. Talmud, *Menahot* treatise.

chap. 37) has been interpreted as heralding the resurrection of the dead for the last judgment; that of the spring flowing out of the temple (cf. chap. 47) has been used to explain the fruitfulness of the water of Baptism. And in moral theology Ezekiel's teaching about personal responsibility and the need for a new heart (cf. 11:19) is sometimes read as an expression of hope in the gift of divine grace.

PART ONE

Israel is judged and found guilty

Introduction

Ezek 10; Rev 4
Ezek 8:3; 40:12
2 Kings
24:12,15

1 [1]In the thirtieth year, in the fourth month, on the fifth day of the
month, as I was among the exiles by the river Chebar, the

1:1–3. As is usual in the prophetical books, the heading identifies the author and indicates when and where he exercised his ministry. Ezekiel was a priest, and there is evidence of this throughout the book—for example, in the stress he puts on precepts to do with divine worship and in his frequent use of the teaching techniques used by people who held temple positions.

"The thirtieth year": this seems to provide the key to dating Ezekiel's ministry, but it is not easy to decide how this should be interpreted. It could be a reference to the prophet's age at the start of his mission, as if he were to say, "when I was thirty years old," or it could be a reference to when the theophany that he is about to describe (vv. 2–3) occurred. Since that in fact happened in 593 BC (see below), the thirty years would refer to the period of time that had elapsed since that event. He could mean that he had the visions thirty years after the finding of the book of Deuteronomy in 622 BC, in the time of King Josiah (cf. 2 Kings 22:1—23:30), or that he was thirty. From Origen onwards (*Homilae in Ezechielem*, 1, 4), most scholars take it that the reference is to the age of Ezekiel at the time. Thirty was an important age for a priest, because that was when he began to exercise a priest's duties in the temple (cf. Num 4:23, 30), and it is probable that that was the point when Ezekiel received the word of the Lord and began his prophetical ministry. Jesus, too, was "about thirty years of age" (Lk 3:23) when he began his public ministry; and the Fathers point out the parallel: "When he was thirty years old, the heavens were opened and Ezekiel the prophet saw visions of God on the banks of the river Chebar. When he was thirty years old, our Lord travelled to the Jordan; the heavens were opened and the Spirit descended in the form of a dove, and a voice cried out from heaven, saying: *This is my beloved Son, in whom I am well pleased*" (St Gregory the Great, *Homiliae in Ezechielem prophetam*, 1, 2, 5).

Verses 2–3 are in the third person, unlike the rest of the passage, which is in the first person singular. They specify the date of the start of Ezekiel's ministry, "the first year of the exile of King Jehoiachin", that is, 593 BC, for

[1] [1]Et factum est in tricesimo anno, in quarto mense, in quinta mensis, cum essem in medio captivorum iuxta fluvium Chobar, aperti sunt caeli, et vidi visiones Dei. [2]In quinta mensis, ipse est

heavens were opened, and I saw visions of God. 2On the fifth day
of the month (it was the fifth year of the exile of King Jehoiachin),
1 Kings 18:46 3the word of the LORD came to Ezekiel the priest, the son of Buzi,
Ezek 3:22; 8:1; 33:22; in the land of the Chaldeans by the river Chebar; and the hand of
37:1; 40:1 the LORD was upon him there.

1. THE LORD CALLS EZEKIEL*

Ex 19:16–20 **Ezekiel's vision of the glory of the Lord**
Ps 18:9–15 4As I looked, behold, a stormy wind came out of the north, and a
29:3–10 great cloud, with brightness round about it, and fire flashing forth

---

that first deportation took place in 597 (cf. 2 Kings 24:10–17). These two verses giving the prophet's name and the year when his ministry began were probably added by a later author.

The Chebar is a tributary of the Euphrates; archaeological remains have been discovered on its banks which show that there was a Jewish settlement there from the sixth century BC on. By mentioning the location twice, the text wants to make it clear that the theophany or vision took place outside the land of Israel, in Babylon, and that, therefore, the Lord had remained with his followers even when they were living among the Gentiles, in a pagan and unclean land.

The fact that Ezekiel has a prophet's role is conveyed by the use of two wordings. The first, "the word of the Lord came to (him)", occurs in many other prophetical books (Hos 1:1; Joel 1:1; etc.); the second, "the hand of the Lord was upon him" (cf. 3:22; 8:1; 33:22; 37:1; 40:1) is used more in connexion with the early non-writer prophets, specifically those in the time of Elijah (1 Kings 18:46). Thus, Ezekiel is being depicted as a person of great importance, a priest by descent, a true defender of the faith like Elijah, and a prophet like his immediate predecessors.

***1:4—3:27.** This fairly homogenous section introduces the two protagonists of the book—God and the prophet. God reveals himself in all his majesty in a remarkable theophany; Ezekiel is able to see the splendour of his glory (1:4–28). The prophet is depicted as the person entrusted with the Lord's words and charged with passing them on to the people (2:1—3:15). Ezekiel is made a watchman; he must warn the people and look out for them at all times, no matter what it takes: "What did Ezekiel do to prompt my admiration? Having been ordered to accuse Jerusalem of her sins, he set his heart wholly on obedience to the Lord's command and paid no heed to the persecution he might encounter because of his preaching" (Origen, *Homiliae in Ezechielem*, 6, 1).

annus quintus transmigrationis regis Ioachin, 3factum est verbum Domini ad Ezechielem filium Buzi, sacerdotem, in terra Chaldaeorum secus flumen Chobar, et facta est super eum ibi manus Domini. 4Et

continually, and in the midst of the fire, as it were gleaming
bronze. 5And from the midst of it came the likeness of four living
creatures.* And this was their appearance: they had the form of

Ex 25:18 Ezek 10:8–22 Rev 4:6–8

1:4–28. This is an awesome vision. The prophet watches in amazement as he sees the throne arrive (v. 26), on which is seated "a likeness as it were of a human form", which becomes "the likeness of the glory of the Lord" (v. 28). The "glory of the Lord" is something that cannot be described. What can one say? It is like "gleaming bronze" (v. 4), "like burning coals of fire, like torches" (v. 13), "like sapphire" (v. 26) etc.; human language is at a complete loss to describe the grandeur of God's glory. The account of the vision shows that God stands above everything; he is ineffable. St Cyril of Jerusalem puts it this way: "Do you want to know why it is impossible to understand the nature of God? […] Tell me about the cherubim […]. In so far as it is possible, the prophet Ezekiel offered a description of them: each one had four faces; the faces of a man, of a lion, of an eagle, and of a bull […]. If we cannot form a clear idea of the cherubim, even with the help of this prophetic description; if we cannot make out the image of the throne as the prophet has described it, how can we expect to understand the one seated on the throne, the invisible and ineffable God? It is impossible for us to comprehend who God is; but by seeing all his works, it is possible for us to praise and worship him" (*Catecheses ad illuminandos*, 9, 3).

The various elements in the account leave us in no doubt as to the splendour of the vision, but the details given about each are difficult to understand. Many commentators think that the details were added much later, in an attempt to adapt the vision to the traditions of divine worship—for example, to identify the throne of the glory of the Lord with the carriage that was used for bearing the ark of the Covenant in solemn processions. Certainly, each piece of the vision must have a meaning, though it may sometimes escape us.

Wind, cloud and fire (cf. v. 4) accompany great theophanies, such as that of Sinai (Ex 19:16–20; Ps 18:9–15; 29:3–10); here they serve to emphasize the heavenly nature of the vision ("the heavens were opened": v. 1).

"The likeness of four living creatures" (v. 5): the Hebrew word *hayot*, used for these, indicates that they are not domestic animals or wild beasts, but mythological beings of the sort often represented in Assyrian art. In Ezekiel the number four means fullness (the idea must derive from the four cardinal points—north, south, east, west): the four creatures have four wings each, and four faces, and each of them has a wheel so that they can move in any of four directions (vv. 15–17). These creatures are unlike any known creature, for sometimes they are treated as masculine, and sometimes as feminine;

vidi: et ecce ventus turbinis veniebat ab aquilone et nubes magna et ignis conglobatus, et splendor in circuitu eius, et de medio eius quasi species electri, id est de medio ignis; 5et ex medio eius similitudo

men, [6]but each had four faces, and each of them had four wings.
[7]Their legs were straight, and the soles of their feet were like the
sole of a calf's foot; and they sparkled like burnished bronze.

---

sometimes the verb is in the singular, sometimes in the plural. In some way, they symbolize all living things, humans and beasts, created to show, in what they are and what they do, the glory of God in all its splendour. Almost from the beginning, Christian exegesis (cf. St Irenaeus, *Adversus haereses*, 3, 11, 18) interpreted the four animals (cf. v. 10) as symbolizing the four evangelists: "Because he begins his Gospel with an account of the human genealogy [of the Lord], Matthew is symbolized by the man; Mark is symbolized by the lion becuase he begins with a loud cry in the desert; Luke is symbolized by the bull because his book begins with a sacrifice; John is the eagle because his first focus is on the divinity of the Word [...]: in trying to see into the heart of the divine he is like the eagle that stares into the sun" (St Gregory the Great, *Homiliae in Ezechielem prophetam*, 1, 4, 1).

The "wheels" (vv. 15–21) suggest a war chariot, but they have extraordinary features and operate as if they were alive: they are "full of eyes" (v. 18) and "the spirit of the living creatures was in (them)" (v. 20). They symbolize all inanimate creation—a dimension of creation which, like man, is designed to reveal the greatness of the glory of God. The "firmament" (v. 22), in Semitic cosmology, was a huge, solid plate separating the upper waters from those below; rain resulted when God opened trapdoors in this plate (cf. Gen 1:6–8). But the firmament also acted as a divide between heaven and earth; below it, creatures lived their lives; above it, God lived his. Therefore, the things depicted here as being above the firmament (vv. 24–28) have to do with God: the voice, the sapphire throne, the fire, etc. are all manifestations of divine majesty.

The "glory of God" forms the centre of the vision; all the other details are meant to underscore the splendour of that glory. In Ezekiel, as in the Priestly tradition (cf. Ex 13:22; 24:16; 40:35; Lev 9:23–24), the "glory of God" means the presence of God, who rules over all that he has created and is active among them. When the glory of God is present, the people are safe, and things go well; when it is withdrawn, it is a sign that the very worst will happen. Ezekiel records that the vision comes to him as a "likeness", *demût* (as in Genesis 1:26), of the glory of God. So, St Cyril of Jerusalem makes the point that "The prophet saw the likeness of the glory of God (Ezek 1:28); he did not see the Lord, but only the likeness of his glory; he did not even see the glory itself, as it really is, but only its likeness. And yet, though he saw only the likeness of the glory of the Lord, the prophet was so moved that he fell to the ground. If so great a man as the prophet falls to the ground and trembles

---

quattuor animalium, et hic aspectus eorum: similitudo hominis erat eis. [6]Quattuor facies uni et quattuor pennae uni; [7]pedes eorum pedes recti, et planta pedis eorum quasi planta pedis vituli, et scintillabant

8Under their wings on their four sides they had human hands. And
the four had their faces and their wings thus: 9their wings touched Ezek 10:11
one another; they went every one straight forward, without turning
as they went. 10As for the likeness of their faces, each had the face Rev 4:7
of a man in front;[a] the four had the face of a lion on the right side,
the four had the face of an ox on the left side, and the four had the
face of an eagle at the back.[b] 11Such were their faces. And their Is 6:2
wings were spread out above; each creature had two wings, each
of which touched the wing of another, while two covered their
bodies. 12And each went straight forward; wherever the spirit
would go, they went, without turning as they went. 13In the midst Ex 19:18
of[c] the living creatures there was something that looked like Ps 18:12–13 Rev 4:5
burning coals of fire, like torches moving to and fro among the
living creatures; and the fire was bright, and out of the fire went
forth lightning. 14And the living creatures darted to and fro, like a Ps 104:4
flash of lightning.

15Now as I looked at the living creatures, I saw a wheel upon Ezek 10:9–13
the earth beside the living creatures, one for each of the four of
them.[d] 16As for the appearance of the wheels and their construction:
their appearance was like the gleaming of a chrysolite; and the
four had the same likeness, their construction being as it were a
wheel within a wheel. 17When they went, they went in any of their Zech 4:10
four directions[e] without turning as they went. 18The four wheels Rev 4:8
had rims and they had spokes;[f] and their rims were full of eyes
round about. 19And when the living creatures went, the wheels

---

in the presence of the likeness of the Lord's glory, any man who tries to see God as he really is will surely die. And Scripture tells us so: *No man shall see* [the face of God] *and live*" (*Catecheses ad illuminandos*, 9, 1).

quasi aspectus aeris candentis. 8Et manus hominis erant sub pennis eorum in quattuor partibus. Facies autem et pennae illorum quattuor: 9iunctae erant pennae eorum altera ad alteram; non revertebantur, cum incederent, sed unumquodque ante faciem suam gradiebatur. 10Similitudo autem vultus eorum: facies hominis et facies leonis a dextris ipsorum quattuor, facies autem bovis a sinistris ipsorum quattuor et facies aquilae ipsorum quattuor. 11Et pennae eorum extentae desuper; duae pennae singulorum iungebantur, et duae tegebant corpora eorum. 12Et unumquodque coram facie sua ambulabat: ubi erat impetus spiritus, illuc gradiebantur nec revertebantur, cum ambularent. 13Et in medio animalium, aspectus quasi carbonum ignis ardentium, quasi aspectus lampadarum discurrentium in medio animalium; et splendor erat ignis, et de igne fulgur egrediens. 14Et animalia ibant et revertebantur in similitudinem fulguris coruscantis. 15Cumque aspicerem animalia, apparuit rota una super terram iuxta singula animalia. 16Et aspectus rotarum et opus earum quasi species chrysolithi, et una similitudo ipsarum quattuor; et aspectus earum et opera, quasi sit rota in medio rotae. 17Per quattuor partes earum euntes ibant et non revertebantur, cum ambularent. 18Canthis autem earum erat altitudo et horribilis aspectus; et canthi earum erant oculis pleni in circuitu ipsarum quattuor. 19Cumque

a. Cn: Heb lacks *in front* **b.** Cn: Heb lacks *at the back* **c.** Gk Old Latin: Heb *And the likeness of* **d.** Heb *of their faces* **e.** Heb *on their four sides* **f.** Cn: Heb uncertain

went beside them; and when the living creatures rose from the
Ezek 10:16 earth, the wheels rose. 20Wherever the spirit would go, they went,
and the wheels rose along with them; for the spirit of the living
creatures was in the wheels. 21When those went, these went; and
when those stood, these stood; and when those rose from the
earth, the wheels rose along with them; for the spirit of the living
creatures was in the wheels.

Gen 1:6–8 Ex 24:10 22Over the heads of the living creatures there was the likeness
Ezek 10:1 of a firmament, shining like crystal,[g] spread out above their heads.
Rev 4:6 23And under the firmament their wings were stretched out straight,
one toward another; and each creature had two wings covering its
Gen 17:1 body. *24And when they went, I heard the sound of their wings
Job 37:4 like the sound of many waters, like the thunder of the Almighty, a
Ps 29:3; 68:33 Ezek 10:5 sound of tumult like the sound of a host; when they stood still,
Rev 1:15 they let down their wings. 25And there came a voice from above
the firmament over their heads; when they stood still, they let
down their wings.

Mt 26:64 26And above the firmament over their heads there was the
Rev 4:2–3 likeness of a throne, in appearance like sapphire;[h] and seated
above the likeness of a throne was a likeness as it were of a human
Ezek 8:2 form. 27And upward from what had the appearance of his loins
Rev 4:3 I saw as it were gleaming bronze, like the appearance of fire
enclosed round about; and downward from what had the
Gen 9:13–15 appearance of his loins I saw as it were the appearance of fire, and
Ex 13:22; 24:16 there was brightness round about him.[i] 28Like the appearance of
Josh 5:14 the bow that is in the cloud on the day of rain, so was the
Ps 127:1 appearance of the brightness round about.

Ezek 8:4 Dan 8:17 Such was the appearance of the likeness of the glory of the
Acts 9:4 LORD.* And when I saw it, I fell upon my face, and I heard the
Rev 1:17 voice of one speaking.

---

ambularent animalia, ambulabant pariter et rotae iuxta ea; et cum elevarentur animalia de terra, elevabantur simul et rotae. 20Quocumque impellebat spiritus ut irent, ibant, et rotae pariter levabantur sequentes eum; spiritus enim animalium erat in rotis. 21Cum euntibus ibant et cum stantibus stabant; et cum elevatis a terra pariter elevabantur, et rotae sequentes ea, quia spiritus animalium erat in rotis.
22Et similitudo super capita animalium firmamenti quasi aspectus crystalli horribilis et extenti super capita eorum desuper. 23Sub firmamento autem pennae eorum rectae altera ad alteram; unumquodque duabus alis velabat corpus suum. 24Et audiebam sonum alarum quasi sonum aquarum multarum, quasi sonum Omnipotentis: cum ambularent, erat strepitus vehemens ut sonus castrorum; cumque starent, demittebantur pennae eorum. 25Nam cum fieret vox supra firmamentum, quod erat super caput eorum, stabant et submittebant alas suas. 26Et super firmamentum, quod erat imminens capiti eorum, quasi aspectus lapidis sapphiri similitudo throni; et super similitudinem throni similitudo quasi aspectus hominis desuper. 27Et vidi quasi speciem electri, velut aspectum ignis per circuitum ab aspectu lumborum eius et desuper; et ab aspectu lumborum eius usque deorsum vidi quasi speciem ignis

g. Gk: Heb *awesome crystal* **h.** Heb *lapis lazuli* **i.** Or *it*

The prophet's mission

2 [1]And he said to me, "Son of man, stand upon your feet, and I Dan 8:17; 10:11
will speak with you." [2]And when he spoke to me, the Spirit Ezek 3:24
entered into me and set me upon my feet; and I heard him

2:1—3:3. The vision by the river Chebar is all about the grandeur and glory of God, who is sovereign over all things; whereas the account given of the call of Ezekiel tells us about the prophet and about the people of Israel, for whom the message is meant. The prophet is described as a son of man, whom the Spirit moves, a prophet among the people; and they are a rebellious people. The account takes the form of an address by the Lord containing a command to pass his word on to the people (2:1–7) and a symbolic action in which Ezekiel eats the scroll given to him by God (2:8—3:3).

2:1. "Son of man": this title is used repeatedly in these opening chapters. It occurs later on, too, more than ninety times; but it has special significance here, which is the first time it is used. Because Ezekiel is living in exile in a foreign and therefore unclean country, he cannot be given grand titles. He is an ordinary mortal, one creature among many, on an infinitely lower level than the Lord; one more among his people, like them an exile, a person brought low, but also someone who has hope in his heart. St Gregory the Great explains the title like this: "He is brought up often into heaven and his soul rejoices at great and beautiful mysteries which remain invisible to us. But it is fitting that he be called *son of man* while he contemplates those hidden wonders, so that he will not forget who he is or glory in the splendour that has been revealed to him" (*Homiliae in Ezechielem prophetam*, 1, 12, 22).

2:2. "The Spirit set me upon my feet". In the vision of God's glory, the word "spirit" has three meanings. It is a natural thing—a stormy *wind*, breath, spirit (1:4; cf. 13:11). From this comes the second meaning: *spirit* is an inner, superhuman strength which guides the actions of living creatures and cherubim, deciding when they should move and where they should go (cf. 1:12, 20, 21). But in the account of the call of Ezekiel, "spirit" has a third meaning: it is life-force, reminiscent of the "breath of life" that God breathed into man at the moment of creation (cf. Gen 2:7); this meaning will be seen more clearly in the vision of the bones brought back to life (cf. 37:5, 6, 8, 10). As a life-force, every time that the spirit affects Ezekiel, it is to "set him on his feet" (cf. 2:1; 3:20), to "lift him up" (cf. 3:12, 14, 24), so that he is better able to hear the word of God and to see what is happening in the temple of Jerusalem (cf. 8:3; 11:1; 43:5) or in Babylon (cf. 11:24). It is therefore an inner energy

splendentis in circuitu. [28]Velut aspectus arcus, cum fuerit in nube in die pluviae: sic erat aspectus splendoris per gyrum. Haec visio similitudinis gloriae Domini. Et vidi et cecidi in faciem meam et audivi vocem loquentis. **[2]** [1]Et dixit ad me: «Fili hominis, sta super pedes tuos, et loquar tecum». [2]Et ingressus est in me spiritus, postquam locutus est mihi et statuit me supra pedes meos, et audivi

Deut 9:7,24 speaking to me. 3And he said to me, "Son of man, I send you to
the people of Israel, to a nation[j] of rebels, who have rebelled
against me; they and their fathers have transgressed against me to
Ezek 3:7 this very day. 4The people also are impudent and stubborn: I send

that transforms the prophet and helps him to hear or see things that he could not if left on his own, for he is a mere "son of man".

2:3. Israel is a "nation of rebels" or, as it is put a little further on in the text, a "rebellious house" (2:8). The book defines the people of Israel in this negative way (cf. 2:5, 6, 8; 3:9) because it sums up the sinful history of their forebears and their own hostility towards God. Their rebelliousness involves arrogance towards God, rejection of his commandments, and refusal to listen to what he says. It makes them stubborn: one can even see it in their faces. Time and again Ezekiel tells them that their sin is grave, for they have freely chosen to adopt this attitude. They "will not listen to you", the Lord says to Ezekiel, "for they are not willing to listen to me" (3:7). Precisely because sin requires a free act of the will, the prophet puts special emphasis on personal responsibility. Each individual will be punished for his or her sins, not for those of their forebears (cf. 18:1–32). Because the people are so rebellious, God wants the prophet to be especially docile: "Do not be rebellious" (2:8). The Lord asks him to listen carefully to the word of God and to accept it joyfully. The gesture of eating the scroll shows what docility requires. Even though the scroll contains "words of lamentation and mourning and woe" (2:10), the prophet will find it "sweet as honey" when he does what he is told.

2:4. "Thus says the Lord God": this makes it clear that the prophet is not speaking on his own behalf. It is usually termed a "messenger formula" (words a messenger uses to preface his message), and occurs often in other prophetical books, particularly Isaiah and Jeremiah. However, in Ezekiel, where it appears almost 130 times, the name of God is reinforced ("Lord God"), to signal the infinite majesty of the Lord who speaks with full authority. The people's stubbornness in rejecting God's word is an act of rebellion, and the docility shown by the prophet is an almost obligatory act of submission. Ezekiel never resists the voice of the Lord, never raises any personal objection or difficulty—unlike Isaiah and Jeremiah. On the contrary, knowing that he is passing on a divine message, not inventing one of his own, he must do this bravely, and never flag, even if the people refuse to listen (cf. 2:6–7; 3:11). "True prophets are those who say the words that God has spoken to them;

loquentem ad me 3et dicentem: «Fili hominis, mitto ego te ad filios Israel, ad gentes apostatrices, quae recesserunt a me; ipsi et patres eorum praevaricati sunt in me usque ad diem hanc. 4Et filii dura facie et obstinato corde sunt, ad quos ego mitto te; et dices ad eos: Haec dicit Dominus Deus. 5Ipsi sive

j. Syr: Heb *nations*

you to them; and you shall say to them, 'Thus says the Lord GOD.'
5And whether they hear or refuse to hear (for they are a rebellious Ezek 12:2; 33:33
house) they will know that there has been a prophet among them.
6And you, son of man, be not afraid of them, nor be afraid of their Jer 1:8,17
words, though briers and thorns are with you and you sit upon
scorpions; be not afraid of their words, nor be dismayed at their
looks, for they are a rebellious house. 7And you shall speak my Jer 1:7
words to them, whether they hear or refuse to hear; for they are a
rebellious house.

8"But you, son of man, hear what I say to you; be not rebellious Rev 10:9
like that rebellious house; open your mouth, and eat what I give

---

the prophet of God is the one who delivers the words of God to men who cannot or do not deserve to understand God himself" (St Augustine, *Quaestiones in Heptateuchum*, 2, 17).

2:5. "They will know that there has been a prophet among them": a formal confirmation that Ezekiel is indeed a prophet. At a time when there was no king (for he was the prisoner of Nebuchadnezzar) and no temple (for it had been profaned and destroyed) and no social or religious institutions among the Jews, prophets acquired increased status. The prophet was God's only representative among the people; he was the only one with authority to demand that they listen to his message.

2:8—3:3. The action of eating the scroll symbolizes to the people that the prophet is faithfully passing on the word of God, and therefore that they should not neglect to take on board anything he says or try to tone it down. It also shows the positive attitude of the prophet himself: he eagerly "fills his stomach" with the words of the Lord even though they are severe. Commenting on this passage, Pope St Gregory the Great points out: "The Holy Scriptures are food and drink to nourish us [...]. The obscure pages, which cannot be understood unless further explanation be provided, are food, because everything must be explained in order to be properly understood, just as everything must be chewed in order to be swallowed. We do not chew what we drink: when the teaching is clear, we swallow it whole, because we are in need of no further explanation. The prophet Ezekiel will hear difficult and obscure words, so he is told to eat the scroll, not to drink it, as if to say, 'Meditate on this teaching and understand it well'" (*Homiliae in Ezechielem prophetam*, 1, 10, 3).

A "written scroll" (2:9): in ancient times books were written on rolls of parchment or on papyrus (see also Jer 36:4).

audiant, sive contemnant—quoniam domus exasperans est—sciant tamen quia propheta fuerit in medio eorum. 6Tu ergo, fili hominis, ne timeas eos neque sermones eorum metuas, etsi cardui et spinae te circumdant, et cum scorpionibus habitas. Verba eorum ne timeas et vultus eorum ne formides, quia domus exasperans est. 7Loqueris ergo verba mea ad eos, sive audiant, sive contemnant, quoniam exasperantes sunt. 8Tu autem, fili hominis, audi, quaecumque loquor ad te, et noli esse exasperans, sicut

Jer 1:9
Ezek 3:1–3; 8:3; you." [9]And when I looked, behold, a hand was stretched out to
Dan 10:10 me, and, lo, a written scroll was in it; [10]and he spread it before me;
Rev 5:1; 10:2,10 and it had writing on the front and on the back, and there were
written on it words of lamentation and mourning and woe.
3 [1]And he said to me, "Son of man, eat what is offered to you;
Rev 10:9–10 eat this scroll, and go, speak to the house of Israel." [2]So I
opened my mouth, and he gave me the scroll to eat. [3]And he said
to me, "Son of man, eat this scroll that I give you and fill your
stomach with it." Then I ate it; and it was in my mouth as sweet as
honey.
Jer 7:27 [4]And he said to me, "Son of man, go, get you to the house of
Is 28:9–13; Israel, and speak with my words to them. [5]For you are not sent to
33:19; Jon 3 a people of foreign speech and a hard language, but to the house
Mt 12:38–42 of Israel—[6]not to many peoples of foreign speech and a hard
language, whose words you cannot understand. Surely, if I sent
you to such, they would listen to you. [7]But the house of Israel will
not listen to you; for they are not willing to listen to me; because
all the house of Israel are of a hard forehead and of a stubborn
heart. [8]Behold, I have made your face hard against their faces, and

---

3:4–11. This oracle shows how ill-disposed Ezekiel's hearers are to listen, the approach that the prophet has to adopt, and the tone of the message. His hearers are stubborn in their rejection of God and of the prophet (v. 7). Ezekiel needs to be forthright and more determined than they are (vv. 8–9). It is not that he must meet their obstinacy with greater obstinacy still; he must try to draw them out of their rebelliousness by dint of being insistent. The message he bears is a clear and pressing one because it comes from God himself. If the prophet were speaking on his own behalf, he would need to back up his statements with strong arguments; but because he is speaking in God's name, all he need do is to keep making the same point: "Thus says the Lord" (v. 11): "These words were written for me, and are intended for the ears of all those who would be teachers, that the fear of the Lord would run deeper within us: we should tremble at the sight of words written not by human hands, but by angels of God" (Origen, *Homiliae in Ezechielem*, 2, 3).

domus exasperatrix est; aperi os tuum et comede, quaecumque ego do tibi». [9]Et vidi: et ecce manus missa ad me, in qua erat involutus liber; et expandit illum coram me, qui erat scriptus intus et foris, et scriptae erant in eo lamentationes et gemitus et vae. **[3]** [1]Et dixit ad me: «Fili hominis, quodcumque inveneris, comede; comede volumen istud et vadens loquere ad filios Israel». [2]Et aperui os meum, et cibavit me volumine illo [3]et dixit ad me: «Fili hominis, venter tuus comedet, et viscera tua complebuntur volumine isto, quod ego do tibi». Et comedi illud, et factum est in ore meo sicut mel dulce. [4]Et dixit ad me: «Fili hominis, vade ad domum Israel et loqueris verba mea ad eos. [5]Non enim ad populum profundi sermonis et ignotae linguae tu mitteris, ad domum Israel; [6]neque ad populos multos profundi sermonis et ignotae linguae, quorum non possis audire sermones; et si ad illos mittereris, ipsi audirent te. [7]Domus autem Israel nolunt audire te, quia nolunt audire me; omnis quippe

your forehead hard against their foreheads. [9]Like adamant harder Is 50:7
than flint have I made your forehead; fear them not, nor be
dismayed at their looks, for they are a rebellious house."
[10]Moreover he said to me, "Son of man, all my words that I shall
speak to you receive in your heart, and hear with your ears. [11]And
go, get you to the exiles, to your people, and say to them, 'Thus
says the Lord GOD'; whether they hear or refuse to hear."
[12]Then the Spirit lifted me up, and as the glory of the LORD 1 Kings 18:12
arose[k] from its place, I heard behind me the sound of a great Ezek 8:3; 11:1–24;
earthquake; [13]it was the sound of the wings of the living creatures 43:5; Mt 4:1
as they touched one another, and the sound of the wheels beside Lk 2:13–14;
them, that sounded like a great earthquake. [14]The Spirit lifted me 4:1; Rev 1:10
up and took me away, and I went in bitterness in the heat of my
spirit, the hand of the LORD being strong upon me; [15]and I came to
the exiles at Tel-abib, who dwelt by the river Chebar.[l] And I sat
there overwhelmed among them seven days.

Ezekiel, a watchman for the house of Israel

[16]And at the end of seven days, the word of the LORD came to me: Is 21:6,8,11; 52:8; 56:10
[17]"Son of man, I have made you a watchman for the house of Jer 6:17

3:12–15. When the vision ends, the glory of God withdraws in the same thunderous and majestic way that it came (v. 13). The prophet is plunged into sadness; but he knows well that the spirit of God moves him and gives him strength.

The name of Telabib, a place close to Babylon, means in Chaldean "hill of the flood"—probably a reference to the river in the epic poem of Gilgamesh. That was where the deportees were living, to whom the message was addressed. Archaeology has found no traces of this city—which has no connexions to present-day Tel-Aviv, whose name in Hebrew means "hill of the springtime", and which is situated to the southeast of Jerusalem.

3:16–21. A "watchman for the house of Israel" (v. 17). A watchman was the

domus Israel dura fronte est et obstinato corde. [8]Ecce dedi faciem tuam valentiorem faciebus eorum et frontem tuam duriorem frontibus eorum; [9]ut adamantem et duriorem silice dedi faciem tuam: ne timeas eos neque metuas a facie eorum, quia domus exasperans est». [10]Et dixit ad me: «Fili hominis, omnes sermones meos, quos loquor ad te, assume in corde tuo et auribus tuis audi. [11]Et vade, ingredere ad transmigrationem, ad filios populi tui, et loqueris ad eos et dices eis: Haec dicit Dominus Deus; sive audiant, sive contemnant». [12]Et assumpsit me spiritus, et audivi post me vocem commotionis magnae, cum elevaretur gloria Domini de loco suo; [13]et vocem alarum animalium percutientium alteram ad alteram et vocem rotarum sequentium animalia et vocem commotionis magnae. [14]Spiritus quoque levavit me et assumpsit me; et abii amarus in indignatione spiritus mei: manus enim Domini erat super me gravis. [15]Et veni ad transmigrationem, ad Telabib, ad eos, qui habitabant iuxta flumen Chobar; et

k. Cn: Heb *blessed be the glory of the LORD* **l.** Heb *Chebar, and to where they dwelt*. Another reading is *Chebar, and I sat where they sat*

Ezek 33:1–9 Israel; whenever you hear a word from my mouth, you shall give
Ezek 18:18; them warning from me. 18If I say to the wicked, 'You shall surely
36:6,8; Jn 8:21 die,' and you give him no warning, nor speak to warn the wicked
from his wicked way, in order to save his life, that wicked man
shall die in his iniquity; but his blood I will require at your hand.
19But if you warn the wicked, and he does not turn from his
wickedness, or from his wicked way, he shall die in his iniquity;
Jer 6:21 but you will have saved your life. 20Again, if a righteous man
Ezek 14:3; 18:24; turns from his righteousness and commits iniquity, and I lay a
33:12–13 stumbling block before him, he shall die; because you have not
1 Jn 2:10 warned him, he shall die for his sin, and his righteous deeds which
2 Pet 2:21 he has done shall not be remembered; but his blood I will require

---

person charged with protecting the people by warning them of any sudden attack (cf. 2 Sam 18:24; Ps 127:1). The prophet, as a watchman (cf. Is 21:6; Hos 9:8; Hab 2:1), must keep guard and warn his hearers of impending danger (cf. Is 52:8; 56:10; Jer 6:17). If they fail to listen, it will be their own fault; but if the prophet keeps quiet, or delivers the wrong message, then he will be to blame for what happens. St Gregory Nazianzen applies this teaching to a pastor's readiness to obey the word of God: "If the pastor fears the responsibility of the task he has been entrusted with, the rule of obedience will be a help to him: God will reward his trust and perfect his work if the pastor places all his hope in Him. But if he is tempted to disobey, I know not who can help him or in what he can put his trust. We run the risk of hearing said of us, in relation to the people who have been entrusted to our care: *his blood I will require at your hand* (Ezek 3:18)" (*Apologetica* [*Oratio* 2], 113).

Later, at the start of the second stage of his ministry, in a passage which some term the "account of his new call", Ezekiel himself will stress the watchman theme (33:1–9). There, too, the doctrine of personal responsibility comes up. St Gregory the Great develops the idea of the preacher as watchman; he points out, among other things: "The life and work of a sentry should take place on high, and it should be prudent: on high, so that he may rise above earthly things; and prudent, so that he will not be struck down by the arrows of the enemy. Moreover, he must lead his listeners to high ground, and by his words set their hearts on the path of righteousness towards their heavenly homeland" (*Homiliae in Ezechielem prophetam*, 1, 11, 7).

sedi, ubi illi sedebant, et mansi ibi septem diebus obstupefactus in medio eorum. 16Cum autem pertransissent septem dies, factum est verbum Domini ad me dicens: 17«Fili hominis, speculatorem dedi te domui Israel; et audies de ore meo verbum et commonebis eos ex me. 18Si, dicente me ad impium: Morte morieris, non commonueris eum neque locutus fueris ei, ut avertatur a via sua impia et vivat, ipse impius in iniquitate sua morietur, sanguinem autem eius de manu tua requiram. 19Si autem tu commonueris impium, et ille non fuerit conversus ab impietate sua et a via sua impia, ipse quidem in iniquitate sua morietur, tu autem animam tuam liberasti. 20Sed et si conversus iustus a iustitia sua, fecerit iniquitatem, ponam offendiculum coram eo; ipse morietur, quia non commonuisti eum: in peccato suo morietur, et non erunt in memoria iustitiae eius, quas fecit; sanguinem vero eius de manu

at your hand. [21]Nevertheless if you warn the righteous man not to sin, and he does not sin, he shall surely live, because he took warning; and you will have saved your life."

Ezekiel is struck dumb

[22]And the hand of the LORD was there upon me; and he said to me, "Arise, go forth into the plain,[m] and there I will speak with you."
[23]So I arose and went forth into the plain;[m] and, lo, the glory of Ezek 1:28
the LORD stood there, like the glory which I had seen by the river

3:22–27. The scene that closes the account of the call of Ezekiel repeats some of its main features. First, the fact that the initiative comes entirely from the Lord: "the hand of the Lord was there upon me" (v. 22: cf. 1:3). Then, the theophany, "like the glory which I had seen by the river Chebar" (v. 23). This reference to his first vision of the glory (cf. 1:1, 3) will be repeated when the temple is profaned (cf. 10:12) and on the more significant occasion of the restoration (cf. 43:3). The third element is the very clear order from God to stay at home and stay silent (vv. 24–26); although this may have seemed a strange instruction at the time, it requires the prophet to have solidarity with his people, for he, like them, must suffer isolation, slavery and silence. Early commentators, reading the text literally, interpreted this instruction as signifying that Ezekiel had some physical or mental ailment; but nowadays all commentators see the episode as meaning that the prophet identifies with the deportees (who sought to lie low as long as Jerusalem and the temple were still standing), and that he is prepared to speak out only what the Lord wants him to say and when he wants him to do so. In fact, he will speak out again when the "fugitive" comes to him to confirm that Jerusalem has been destroyed (24:27; 33:22). This command certainly did not oblige Ezekiel never to speak a word, for in the chapters that follow we find many oracles by him. However, he only spoke within his house, where many of the exiles, particularly the elders, would go to listen to him (cf. 8:1; 14:1; 20:1, 3).

"I will make your tongue cleave to the roof of your mouth" (v. 26): a similar graphic phrase is found in Psalm 137:6; here it emphasizes that the prophet's dumbness is a further affliction, in addition to the adversity that he was already experiencing as an exile in Babylon; he is called to speak but won't be able to.

tua requiram. [21]Si autem tu commonueris iustum, ut non peccet iustus, et ille non peccaverit, vivens vivet, quia commonuisti eum et tu animam tuam liberasti». [22]Et facta est super me manus Domini, et dixit ad me: «Surgens egredere in campum, et ibi loquar tecum». [23]Et surgens egressus sum in campum, et ecce ibi gloria Domini stabat quasi gloria, quam vidi iuxta fluvium Chobar, et cecidi in

m. Or *valley*

Ezek 2:2 Chebar; and I fell on my face. 24But the Spirit entered into me,
and set me upon my feet; and he spoke with me and said to me,
"Go, shut yourself within your house. 25And you, O son of man,
Ps 137:6 behold, cords will be placed upon you, and you shall be bound
Ezek 24:27 with them, so that you cannot go out among the people; 26and I
will make your tongue cleave to the roof of your mouth, so that
Ezek 24:27; you shall be dumb and unable to reprove them; for they are a
29:21; 33:22 rebellious house. 27But when I speak with you, I will open your
Mt 11:15 mouth, and you shall say to them, 'Thus says the Lord GOD'; he
Rev 22:11 that will hear, let him hear; and he that will refuse to hear, let him
refuse; for they are a rebellious house.

2. SYMBOLIC ACTIONS AND ORACLES*

Jer 18:1 **The siege of Jerusalem foretold**

2 Kings 25:1 **4** 1"And you, O son of man, take a brick and lay it before you,
Jer 6:6 and portray upon it a city, even Jerusalem; 2and put siegeworks

---

***4:1—5:4.** Symbolic actions are gestures designed to convey a message. Here we are told of five episodes, one after the other, that herald the imminent blockade of Jerusalem imposed by Nebuchadnezzar. They are strange, almost childish, actions, but they clearly convey what the rigours of the siege will be like. More than one commentator has suggested that they may never have been actually performed, but are simply stories invented to communicate a message.

4:1–8. The actions that describe the siege of Jerusalem contain a good deal of information on preparations for battle in this period. In Sumeria and Babylon, archaeologists have unearthed maps of cities etched on clay tablets. Ezekiel could well have seen maps of that sort during his exile in Babylon.

All kinds of explanations have been offered for the 390 days that the prophet spent lying down and which correspond to 390 years of punishment for wrong-doing (v. 5). The Greek translation of the Septuagint changed the figure to 190, being the number of years that the people of the Northern kingdom (Israel) were scattered, from the fall of Samaria (722 BC) to the

faciem meam. 24Et ingressus est in me spiritus et statuit me super pedes meos et locutus est mihi et dixit ad me: «Ingredere et includere in medio domus tuae. 25Et tu, fili hominis, ecce data sunt super te vincula, et ligabunt te in eis, et non egredieris in medio eorum; 26et linguam tuam adhaerere faciam palato tuo, et eris mutus nec quasi vir obiurgans, quia domus exasperans est. 27Cum autem locutus fuero tibi, aperiam os tuum, et dices ad eos: Haec dicit Dominus Deus. Qui audit, audiat; et, qui contemnit, contemnat, quia domus exasperans est». **[4]** 1«Et tu, fili hominis, sume tibi laterem et pones eum coram te et describes in eo civitatem Ierusalem. 2Et ordinabis adversus eam obsidionem et

against it, and build a siege wall against it, and cast up a mound
against it; set camps also against it, and plant battering rams
against it round about. [3]And take an iron plate, and place it as an Ezek 12:6,11;
iron wall between you and the city; and set your face toward it, 24:24,27
and let it be in a state of siege, and press the siege against it. This
is a sign for the house of Israel.

[4]"Then lie upon your left side, and I will lay the punishment of Ezek 44:10,12
the house of Israel upon you[n]; for the number of the days that you
lie upon it, you shall bear their punishment. [5]For I assign to you a Num 14:34
number of days, three hundred and ninety days, equal to the
number of the years of their punishment; so long shall you bear
the punishment of the house of Israel. [6]And when you have
completed these, you shall lie down a second time, but on your
right side, and bear the punishment of the house of Judah; forty
days I assign you, a day for each year. [7]And you shall set your
face toward the siege of Jerusalem, with your arm bared; and you
shall prophesy against the city. [8]And, behold, I will put cords upon Ezek 3:25
you, so that you cannot turn from one side to the other, till you
have completed the days of your siege.

Severe shortages in the city

[9]"And you, take wheat and barley, beans and lentils, millet and Lev 19:19
spelt, and put them into a single vessel, and make bread of them. Deut 22:9

---

decree of Cyrus (530 BC). If one stays with the figure of 390, it could refer to the years of the monarchy from when Solomon's reign began (in approximately 970 BC) to 587 BC, when Jerusalem was besieged. Anyway, these figures are only meant to indicate that the Lord has fixed when events must happen. In this instance the point being made has to do with divine mercy: for each year of iniquity, God imposes only one day of punishment.

4:9–17. The siege of Jerusalem meant a period of terrible scarcity—no water, no bread, no fuel, nothing. Ezekiel

aedificabis munitiones et comportabis aggerem et dabis contra eam castra et pones arietes in gyro. [3]Et tu sume tibi sartaginem ferream et pones eam in murum ferreum inter te et inter civitatem; et obfirmabis faciem tuam ad eam, et erit in obsidionem, et circumdabis eam: signum est domui Israel. [4]Et tu recumbes super latus tuum sinistrum et pones iniquitates domus Israel super eo; numero dierum, quibus recumbes super illud, assumes iniquitatem eorum. [5]Ego autem dedi tibi annos iniquitatis eorum numero dierum trecentos et nonaginta dies, et portabis iniquitatem domus Israel. [6]Et cum compleveris haec, recumbes super latus tuum dextrum secundo et assumes iniquitatem domus Iudae quadraginta diebus; diem pro anno, diem, inquam, pro anno dedi tibi. [7]Et ad obsidionem Ierusalem convertes faciem tuam, et brachium tuum erit exsertum, et prophetabis adversus eam. [8]Ecce circumdedi te vinculis, et non te convertes a latere tuo in latus aliud, donec compleas dies obsidionis tuae. [9]Et tu sume tibi

n. Cn: Heb *you shall lay … upon it*

During the number of days that you lie upon your side, three
hundred and ninety days, you shall eat it. [10]And the food which
you eat shall be by weight, twenty shekels a day; once a day you
shall eat it. [11]And water you shall drink by measure, the sixth part
of a hin; once a day you shall drink. [12]And you shall eat it as a
Dan 1:8 barley cake, baking it in their sight on human dung." [13]And the
Hos 9:3 LORD said, "Thus shall the people of Israel eat their bread unclean,
Ex 22:30–31 among the nations whither I will drive them." [14]Then I said, "Ah
Lev 7:24; 17:15 Lord GOD! behold, I have never defiled myself; from my youth up
Deut 14:3–21 till now I have never eaten what died of itself or was torn by
Acts 10:14 beasts, nor has foul flesh come into my mouth." [15]Then he said to
Lev 26:26 me, "See, I will let you have cow's dung instead of human dung,
Ps 105:16 on which you may prepare your bread." [16]Moreover he said to me,
Ezek 12:18–19 "Son of man, behold, I will break the staff of bread in Jerusalem;

---

laments the rationing of bread and water (vv. 10–11), but what hurts him most is the fact that the most elementary rules concerning the purification of food have to be broken. It was forbidden to mix different seeds in the same field (cf. Lev 19:19; Deut 22:9); yet the prophet mixes vegetables and cereals to make a loaf (v. 9). Anything that had contact with excrement, particularly human excrement (cf. Deut 23:13–15), became unclean, and for that reason dung could not be used as a fuel, even though it was common among other peoples to use it for that purpose. But, during the siege, no other fuel was available; hence dung was used—even human excrement (v. 12). However, because of the prophet's scruples about eating unclean food, he is permitted to use animal dung instead (v. 15). The fact that once-forbidden fuels were now being used went to show that an important element in the religious practice of Israel was fast disappearing—the total separation between clean and unclean. The people were close to losing their identity as a nation.

"I will break the staff of bread" (v. 16): that is literally what the Hebrew says, meaning, I will cut off their food supply. Bread, made in the form of rings, was hung on poles (cf. Ps 105:16; Lev 26:26); breaking the poles or staffs meant reducing the store of bread in Jerusalem.

frumentum et hordeum et fabam et lentem et milium et far et mittes ea in vas unum et facies tibi panes numero dierum, quibus recumbes super latus tuum: trecentis et nonaginta diebus comedes illud. [10]Cibus autem tuus, quo vesceris, erit in pondere viginti stateres in die; a tempore usque ad tempus comedes illud. [11]Et aquam in mensura bibes, sextam partem hin; a tempore usque ad tempus bibes illud. [12]Et quasi subcinericium hordeaceum comedes illud; et stercore, quod egreditur de homine, coques illud in oculis eorum». [13]Et dixit Dominus: «Sic comedent filii Israel panem suum pollutum inter gentes, ad quas eiciam eos». [14]Et dixi: «Heu, Domine Deus, ecce anima mea non est polluta, et morticinum et laceratum a bestiis non comedi ab infantia mea usque nunc, et non est ingressa in os meum caro immunda». [15]Et dixit ad me: «Ecce dedi tibi fimum boum pro stercoribus humanis, et facies panem tuum in eo». [16]Et dixit ad me: «Fili hominis, ecce ego conteram baculum panis in Ierusalem, et

they shall eat bread by weight and with fearfulness; and they shall
drink water by measure and in dismay. 17I will do this that they Lev 26:39
may lack bread and water, and look at one another in dismay, and
waste away under their punishment.

The symbolic sword

5 1"And you, O son of man, take a sharp sword; use it as a 2 Sam 10:4–5
barber's razor and pass it over your head and your beard; then Is 7:20
take balances for weighing, and divide the hair. 2A third part you Ezek 21
shall burn in the fire in the midst of the city, when the days of the Rev 8:7
siege are completed; and a third part you shall take and strike with
the sword round about the city; and a third part you shall scatter to
the wind, and I will unsheathe the sword after them. 3And you
shall take from these a small number, and bind them in the skirts
of your robe. 4And of these again you shall take some, and cast
them into the fire, and burn them in the fire; from there a fire will
come forth into all the house of Israel.

5:1–4. The symbolic gesture of shaving with a sword, and the things Ezakiel is told to do with the hair, are reminiscent of the punishment meted out to Israel's oppressors, mentioned in the oracle of the Immanuel (Is 7:20). The whole action shows, moreover, the afflictions that will befall Jerusalem and the entire people—fire, the sword and being scattered to the wind (v. 2). Also, if one bears in mind that it was considered demeaning to lose one's hair and beard (cf. 2 Sam 10:4–5), the action reported here symbolizes a people brought low, decimated and deported. Of the actions required of the prophet, this is the only one that will be mentioned in the oracle heralding the destruction of Jerusalem (5:11).

Those who survive the destruction of Jerusalem will be like "the remnant" that seeks the warmth and protection of the "skirts" of the prophet's robe (v. 3). Verse 4 is unclear in the original text; it probably means that those who return from exile, too, will be judged by the Lord if they fail to live upright lives.

comedent panem in pondere et in sollicitudine et aquam in mensura et in desolatione bibent, 17ut, deficientibus pane et aqua, desoletur unusquisque cum fratre suo, et contabescant in iniquitatibus suis. **[5]** 1Et tu, fili hominis, sume tibi gladium acutum radentem pilos et assumes eum et duces per caput tuum et per barbam tuam et assumes tibi stateram ponderis et divides eos. 2Tertiam partem igne combures in medio civitatis, post completionem dierum obsidionis; et assumens tertiam partem, concides gladio in circuitu eius; tertiam vero aliam disperges in ventum, et gladium nudabo post eos. 3Et sumes inde parvum numerum et ligabis eos in summitate pallii tui; 4et ex eis rursum tolles et proicies eos in medio ignis et combures eos igne; ex eo egredietur ignis. Et dices ad omnem domum

Oracle against the city on account of its rebelliousness

Ezek 38:12 Mt 23:37 [5]Thus says the Lord GOD: This is Jerusalem; I have set her in the
center of the nations, with countries round about her. [6]And she has
wickedly rebelled against my ordinances[o] more than the nations,
and against my statutes more than the countries round about her,
by rejecting my ordinances and not walking in my statutes.
Ezek 16:47 Rom 2:14, 15,27 [7]Therefore thus says the Lord GOD: Because you are more
turbulent than the nations that are round about you, and have not
walked in my statutes or kept my ordinances, but have acted[p]
according to the ordinances of the nations that are round about

5:5–17. The oracles against Jerusalem are so carefully devised that they seem to have been originally conceived as written texts rather than spoken aloud. They begin in a surprising way: "This is Jerusalem" (v. 5)—words followed by three threats that are linked by a wording along the lines of "Therefore thus says the Lord God" (vv. 7, 8; cf. v. 11). The first is an accusation directed against Jerusalem for being worse than all the nations around it (v. 7). In the second we see the Lord very irate and determined to punish as he has never punished before (vv. 8–10). The third, a more studied literary piece, spells out the misfortunes that will befall Jerusalem (vv. 11–17).

In the formal announcement of the punishment, the prophet uses for the first time the phrase, "and they shall know that I, the Lord ..." (vv. 13–15), which will be repeated from now on. This is to put on record the fact that every divine action, including that leading to the siege and destruction of Jerusalem, is a form of Revelation, for it manifests who God is (the sovereign Being) and how he acts towards mankind—that is, freely and justly. The wording "You (they) shall know that I am the Lord", repeated more than fifty times, is rounded off here and in some other places, with the words "I, the Lord, have spoken". It solemnly guarantees that the oracle comes from God and therefore will certainly be fulfilled.

5:5. "This is Jerusalem": with an exile's nostalgia, Ezekiel sings the praises of his lost city, the "centre of the nations", and bewails the depth of depravity to which she has sunk—worse even than the nations that caused her ruin. The prophet's distress will echo in the pain that Jesus felt on his approach to the same city: "O Jerusalem, Jerusalem, killing the prophets and stoning those who are sent to you!" (Mt 23:37).

Israel: [5]Haec dicit Dominus Deus: Ista est Ierusalem! In medio gentium posui eam et in circuitu eius terras. [6]Et contempsit iudicia mea, ut plus esset impia quam gentes, et praecepta mea ultra quam terrae, quae in circuitu eius sunt: iudicia enim mea proiecerunt et in praeceptis meis non ambulaverunt. [7]Idcirco haec dicit Dominus Deus: Quia tumultuati estis magis quam gentes, quae in circuitu vestro sunt, et in praeceptis meis non ambulastis et iudicia mea non fecistis et iuxta iudicia gentium, quae in

o. Or *changed my ordinances into wickedness* **p.** Another reading is *and have not acted*

you; [8]therefore thus says the Lord GOD: Behold, I, even I, am Jer 1:16
against you; and I will execute judgments in the midst of you in Dan 9:12
the sight of the nations. [9]And because of all your abominations I Amos 3:2
will do with you what I have never yet done, and the like of which Lev 26:29,33
I will never do again. [10]Therefore fathers shall eat their sons in the Deut 28:53
midst of you, and sons shall eat their fathers; and I will execute Jer 19:9 Lam 2:20; 4:10
judgments on you, and any of you who survive I will scatter to all
the winds. [11]Wherefore, as I live, says the Lord GOD, surely, 2 Kings 16:10–15;21:7
because you have defiled my sanctuary with all your detestable Ezek 7:4; 8:18;
things and with all your abominations, therefore I will cut you 9:10; 24:14
down;[q] my eye will not spare, and I will have no pity. [12]A third Ezek 6:11–12
part of you shall die of pestilence and be consumed with famine Rev 6:8; 8:7
in the midst of you; a third part shall fall by the sword round about
you; and a third part I will scatter to all the winds and will
unsheathe the sword after them.

5:10. "Fathers shall eat their sons ... and sons shall eat their fathers": this does not mean that cannibalism actually took place; it is a literary exaggeration meant to show the dire straits of poverty and hunger in which the people will find themselves (cf. Lev 26:29; Lam 2:20; 4:10). Flavius Josephus very probably had these passages in mind when writing about the destruction of Jerusalem by Titus and when he recounts the anguished words of a mother to her child before killing him for food: "If you survive among the Romans, you will be a slave: famine is worse than slavery, and these invaders are more cruel than either starvation or slavery. Your story will form the body of my work; you will bear the brunt of your enemies' wrath; and your fate will provide a recurring message for the history of all mankind" (*De bello Iudaico*, 7, 8).

5:12. As an explanation of the symbolic action to do with the shaven hair (cf. 5:1–4), this verse foretells the afflictions that will decimate the victims of invasion—pestilence and famine for those in the rearguard, death by the sword for those who fight and fall, and deportation for the survivors. Such was the fate of those besieged in Jerusalem.

circuitu vestro sunt, non estis operati, [8]ideo haec dicit Dominus Deus: Ecce ego ad te et ipse ego faciam in medio tui iudicia in oculis gentium [9]et faciam in te, quae non feci et quibus similia ultra non faciam, propter omnes abominationes tuas. [10]Ideo patres comedent filios in medio tui, et filii comedent patres suos, et faciam in te iudicia et ventilabo universas reliquias tuas in omnem ventum. [11]Idcirco vivo ego, dicit Dominus Deus, vere pro eo quod sanctum meum violasti in omnibus offensionibus tuis et in omnibus abominationibus tuis, ego quoque radam, et non parcet oculus meus, et non miserebor. [12]Tertia tui pars peste morietur et fame consumetur in medio tui, et tertia tui pars in gladio cadet in circuitu tuo,

q. Another reading is *I will withdraw*

[13]"Thus shall my anger spend itself, and I will vent my fury
upon them and satisfy myself; and they shall know that I, the
LORD, have spoken in my jealousy, when I spend my fury upon
them. [14]Moreover I will make you a desolation and an object of
reproach among the nations round about you and in the sight of all
that pass by. [15]You shall be[r] a reproach and a taunt, a warning and
a horror, to the nations round about you, when I execute judgments on you in anger and fury, and with furious chastisements—
Deut 32:23–24 I, the LORD, have spoken—[16]when I loose against you[s] my deadly
arrows of famine, arrows for destruction, which I will loose to
destroy you, and when I bring more and more famine upon you,
Ezek 4:16 and break your staff of bread. [17]I will send famine and wild beasts
Rev 6:8 against you, and they will rob you of your children; pestilence and
blood shall pass through you; and I will bring the sword upon you.
I, the LORD, have spoken."

Oracles of the mountains of Israel

Ezek 19:9; 20:46; 21:2; 36:1; Lev 26:30–31

6 [1]The word of the LORD came to me: [2]"Son of man, set your
face toward the mountains of Israel, and prophesy against

6:1–14. After his denunciation of Jerusalem, the prophet turns to the "mountains of Israel". For a deportee stranded on the immense plains of Babylon, those hills came to epitomize the Israel for which he yearned. Now, as the country is being denounced, the diatribe is directed at its hills; and if consolation is to come, it will come from the sight of those hills (cf. 36:1–15). The mountains were always places of worship: the Canaanites built their temples there; and the Israelites who took them over used them for worship too—sometimes for idol worship, sometimes for the cult of Yahweh, the true God. But from the time of Josiah's reform onwards (2 Kings 22:1—23:25), the only worship of the Lord that was allowed was in the temple of Jerusalem, or Mount Zion. The other shrines on high ground, and sometimes in ravines and valleys, came to be associated exclusively with the

tertiam vero partem tuam in omnem ventum dispergam et gladium evaginabo post eos. [13]Et complebo furorem meum et requiescere faciam indignationem meam in eis et consolabor; et scient quia ego Dominus locutus sum in zelo meo, cum implevero indignationem meam in eis. [14]Et dabo te in desertum et in opprobrium in gentibus, quae in circuitu tuo sunt, in conspectu omnis praetereuntis; [15]et eris opprobrium et blasphemia, exemplum et stupor in gentibus, quae in circuitu tuo sunt, cum fecero in te iudicia in furore et in indignatione et in castigationibus irae. [16]Ego Dominus locutus sum. Quando misero sagittas famis pessimas in vos, quae erunt mortiferae, et quas mittam, ut destruam vos, et famem congregabo super vos et conteram vobis baculum panis; [17]et immittam in vos famem et bestias pessimas, et absque liberis facient te, et pestilentia et sanguis transibunt per te, et gladium inducam super te. Ego Dominus locutus sum». **[6]** [1]Et factus est sermo Domini ad me dicens: [2]«Fili hominis,

r. Gk Syr Vg Tg: Heb *And it shall be* **s.** Heb *them*

them, [3]and say, You mountains of Israel, hear the word of the Lord
GOD! Thus says the Lord GOD to the mountains and the hills, to
the ravines and the valleys: Behold, I, even I, will bring a sword
upon you, and I will destroy your high places. [4]Your altars shall 2 Kings 23:14,16
become desolate, and your incense altars shall be broken; and I
will cast down your slain before your idols. [5]And I will lay the Jer 8:1–2
dead bodies of the people of Israel before their idols; and I will
scatter your bones round about your altars. [6]Wherever you dwell Is 2:18
your cities shall be waste and your high places ruined, so that your Jer 10:14–15
altars will be waste and ruined,[t] your idols broken and destroyed, Mic 1:7
your incense altars cut down, and your works wiped out. [7]And the Is 4:3
slain shall fall in the midst of you, and you shall know that I am
the LORD.

[8]"Yet I will leave some of you alive. When you have among the Jer 44:18
nations some who escape the sword, and when you are scattered Ezek 12:16; 14:22

---

cult of idols. Nevertheless, for Ezekiel, the mountains retained their religious significance; they stand for greater closeness to God.

The oracle has three parts to it, each ending with the same form of words: "You shall know that I am the Lord" (vv. 7, 10, 14). The first (vv. 1–7) severely condemns the "high places": they will be destroyed (v. 4) or, what is worse, defiled with dead bodies (v. 5). The second (vv. 8–10) strikes a note of hope: a "remnant" will be left (v. 8) who will acknowledge their transgressions and will see that their punishment has not been in vain. The third part (vv. 11–14), which begins with an expression of joy as the prophet claps his hands and stamps his feet (v. 11), anticipates the exiles' joy when they come to realize that their exile has a salvific purpose. Afflictions sent by God are really meant to bring us to our senses, for "... God does not want us to endure suffering for its own sake; rather, he wants us to reflect on all these things in the light of the Lord's Wisdom [...], so that we will see that the punishments we suffer are worthy in God's eyes and do not defile his justice" (Origen, *Homiliae in Ezechielem*, 5, 1).

pone faciem tuam ad montes Israel et prophetabis ad eos [3]et dices: Montes Israel, audite verbum Domini Dei. Haec dicit Dominus Deus montibus et collibus, voraginibus et vallibus: Ecce ego inducam super vos gladium et destruam excelsa vestra; [4]et demoliar aras vestras, et confringentur delubra vestra, et deiciam interfectos vestros ante idola vestra. [5]Et dabo cadavera filiorum Israel ante faciem simulacrorum vestrorum et dispergam ossa vestra circum aras vestras; [6]in omnibus habitationibus vestris urbes desertae erunt, et excelsa demolientur, ut dissipentur et intereant arae vestrae, et confringantur et cessent idola vestra, et conterantur delubra vestra, et deleantur opera vestra. [7]Et cadet interfectus in medio vestri, et scietis quia ego Dominus. [8]Et relinquam in vobis eos, qui fugerint

t. Syr Vg Tg: Heb *and be made guilty*

Lev 26:40–41 Deut 30:1–2 Ezek 16; 23

through the countries, 9then those of you who escape will
remember me among the nations where they are carried captive,
when I have broken[u] their wanton heart which has departed from
me, and blinded their eyes which turn wantonly after their idols;
and they will be loathsome in their own sight for the evils which
they have committed, for all their abominations. 10And they shall
know that I am the LORD; I have not said in vain that I would do
this evil to them."

Ezek 25:6

11Thus says the Lord GOD: "Clap your hands, and stamp your
foot, and say, Alas! because of all the evil abominations of the
house of Israel; for they shall fall by the sword, by famine, and by
pestilence. 12He that is far off shall die of pestilence; and he that
is near shall fall by the sword; and he that is left and is preserved
shall die of famine. Thus I will spend my fury upon them. 13And
you shall know that I am the LORD, when their slain lie among
their idols round about their altars, upon every high hill, on all the
mountain tops, under every green tree, and under every leafy oak,
wherever they offered pleasing odor to all their idols. 14And I will
stretch out my hand against them, and make the land desolate and
waste, throughout all their habitations, from the wilderness to
Riblah.[v] Then they will know that I am the LORD."

Deut 12:2 Is 57:5 Jer 2:20

Ex 29:18 2 Kings 23:33; 25:6

Amos 5:18 Lam 4:18 Amos 8:2 Rev 7:1; 20:8

The day of the Lord

7 1The word of the LORD came to me: 2"And you, O son of man,
thus says the Lord GOD to the land of Israel: An end! The end

---

6:9. From Hosea onwards, God's relationship with his people is described in terms of marriage, and idolatry therefore is depicted as prostitution and adultery—"wanton heart", "eyes that turn wantonly ...". In this connexion, one should remember that idolatrous rites in Canaanite temples often used sacred prostitution to entreat the gods for fertility in the land, in livestock and even in human beings.

7:1–27. This oracle about the "day of the Lord" contains an announcement of

gladium in gentibus, cum dispersero vos in terris; 9et recordabuntur mei liberati vestri in gentibus, ad quas captivi ducti sunt, quia contrivi cor eorum fornicans et recedens a me, et oculos eorum fornicantes post idola sua; et displicebunt sibimet super malis, quae fecerunt in universis abominationibus suis, 10et scient quia ego Dominus non frustra locutus sum, ut facerem eis malum hoc. 11Haec dicit Dominus Deus: Plaude manu tua et percute pede tuo et dic: Heu ad omnes abominationes malas domus Israel, quia gladio, fame et peste ruituri sunt! 12Qui longe est, peste morietur; qui autem prope, gladio corruet; et, qui relictus fuerit et obsessus, fame morietur, et complebo indignationem meam in eis. 13Et scietis quia ego Dominus, cum fuerint interfecti eorum in medio idolorum suorum, in circuitu ararum suarum, in omni colle excelso, in cunctis summitatibus montium et subtus omne lignum nemorosum et subtus universam quercum frondosam, locum ubi obtulerunt tura redolentia universis idolis suis. 14Et

u. Syr Vg Tg: Heb *I have been broken* **v.** Another reading is *Diblah*

has come upon the four corners of the land. [3]Now the end is upon Ezek 7:8–9
you, and I will let loose my anger upon you, and will judge you
according to your ways; and I will punish you for all your
abominations. [4]And my eye will not spare you, nor will I have Ezek 5:11
pity; but I will punish you for your ways, while your abominations
are in your midst. Then you will know that I am the LORD.

[5]"Thus says the Lord GOD: Disaster after disaster! Behold, it Mt 24:3
comes. [6]An end has come, the end has come; it has awakened Rev 8:13; 9:12; 11:14

---

divine judgment (vv. 1–9) and all the terrible things it will bring with it. From the literary point of view, it marks the climax of the previous oracles, and all sorts of literary devices are used in it—repetition of striking words and phrases, vivid imagery, exaggeration, etc. Doctrinally, it repeats ideas that people were familiar with from Amos onwards (Amos 5:18–20) about the day of the Lord not being a day of consolation but of condemnation. Things said here in connexion with divine judgment were used and updated in Christian preaching as an exhortation to penance. Commenting in Rome on the book of Ezekiel at a time when the Lombards were making inroads in northern Italy, in the late sixth century AD, St Gregory the Great said: "We see our cities in ruins, our defences torn down, our fields torn up, and our churches destroyed; yet we still emulate our parents in their sins: we do not denounce the pride we saw in them. They sinned during days of feasting and joy; we sin on the day of punishment. But Almighty God, who judges all sinfulness, has lifted our souls up from the earth; he has established his tribunal of justice: he awaits our repentance and conversion" (*Homiliae in Ezechielem prophetam*, 1, 9, 9).

7:2–9. "An end! The end has come ...": the oracle starts in this dramatic way to warn people that the day of reckoning for the promised land is imminent. Amos was the first to use the phrase "The end has come for my people" (Amos 8:2), meaning the end of a stage of history, but registering, above all, the full gravity of divine judgment. Taking up this wording and reinforcing it (cf. v. 6) Ezekiel is making the point that divine judgment is imminent and inescapable—and, also, that it is a mournful thing, as can be seen in the parallel phrase in v. 5: "Disaster after disaster". Ezekiel is not referring to the end of the world, a frequent theme in the New Testament (cf. e.g. Mt 24:3; Rev 8:13), but his words imply that a definitive divine judgment is inexorable.

extendam manum meam super eos et faciam terram desolatam et destitutam a deserto usque Rebla in omnibus habitationibus eorum, et scient quia ego Dominus». **[7]** [1]Et factus est sermo Domini ad me dicens: [2]«Et tu, fili hominis, loquere. Haec dicit Dominus Deus terrae Israel: Finis venit, finis super quattuor plagas terrae; [3]nunc finis super te, et immittam furorem meum in te et iudicabo te iuxta vias tuas et ponam super te omnes abominationes tuas. [4]Et non parcet oculus meus super te, et non miserebor, sed vias tuas ponam super te, et abominationes tuae in medio tui erunt, et scietis quia ego Dominus. [5]Haec dicit Dominus Deus: Afflictio super afflictionem ecce venit. [6]Finis venit, venit finis;

against you. Behold, it comes. 7Your doom[w] has come to you, O
inhabitant of the land; the time has come, the day is near, a day of
Ezek 7:3–4 tumult, and not of joyful shouting upon the mountains. 8Now I
will soon pour out my wrath upon you, and spend my anger
against you, and judge you according to your ways; and I will
punish you for all your abominations. 9And my eye will not spare,
nor will I have pity; I will punish you according to your ways,
while your abominations are in your midst. Then you will know
that I am the LORD, who smite.

Jer 16:4 10"Behold, the day! Behold, it comes! Your doom[w] has come,
Ezek 7:3–4 injustice[x] has blossomed, pride has budded. 11Violence has grown
up into a rod of wickedness; none of them shall remain, nor their
abundance, nor their wealth; neither shall there be preeminence
among them.[y] 12The time has come, the day draws near. Let not
the buyer rejoice, nor the seller mourn, for wrath is upon all their
multitude. 13For the seller shall not return to what he has sold,
while they live. For wrath[z] is upon all their multitude; it shall not
turn back; and because of his iniquity, none can maintain his life.[a]

7:10–14. The verbs used in v. 10–11 do not have exact parallels in English; they indicate the life-cycle of a plant—germinating, growing, maturing and dying. Like the fruit in Amos' vision (cf. Amos 8:1–3), the people have reached maturity—which is a sign that the end is near.

7:15–25. "Sword ..., pestilience and famine"—another reference to the three catastrophes of war (cf. 5:11), symbolizing the worst misfortunes that can befall a nation. Verses 15–16 are reminiscent of Matthew 24:16–18.

The "knees as weak as water" (v. 17)—an analogy typical of Ezekiel (cf. 21:12), it is difficult to translate. The Hebrew text says: "The knees give in water." It is a good description of the fear and exhaustion felt by soldiers who see defeat looming; but it may mean literally that their knees buckle, or, even, that fear prevents them from controlling their bodily functions. "Baldness on all their heads" (v. 18): it

evigilavit adversum te, ecce venit. 7Venit contractio super te, qui habitas in terra; venit tempus, prope est dies turbationis et non iubilationis in montibus. 8Nunc de propinquo effundam iram meam super te et complebo furorem meum in te et iudicabo te iuxta vias tuas et imponam tibi omnia scelera tua; 9et non parcet oculus meus, nec miserebor, sed vias tuas imponam tibi, et abominationes tuae in medio tui erunt, et scietis quia ego sum Dominus percutiens. 10Ecce dies, ecce venit; egressa est contractio, floruit iniustitia, germinavit superbia; 11violentia surrexit, ut esset virga impietatis: non ex eis et non ex pompa eorum neque ex sonitu eorum; et non erit requies in eis. 12Venit tempus, appropinquavit dies: qui emit, non laetetur; et, qui vendit, non lugeat, quia ira super omnem pompam eius. 13Quia, qui vendit, ad id quod vendidit non revertetur, cum adhuc sit in viventibus vita eorum. Visio enim ad omnem pompam

w. The meaning of the Hebrew word is uncertain **x.** Or *the rod* **y.** The Hebrew of verse 11 is uncertain **z.** Cn: Heb *vision* **a.** Heb obscure

[14]"They have blown the trumpet and made all ready; but none goes to battle, for my wrath is upon all their multitude. [15]The sword is without, pestilence and famine are within; he that is in the field dies by the sword; and him that is in the city famine and pestilence devour. [16]And if any survivors escape, they will be on the mountains, like doves of the valleys, all of them moaning, every one over his iniquity. [17]All hands are feeble, and all knees weak as water. [18]They gird themselves with sackcloth, and horror covers them; shame is upon all faces, and baldness on all their heads. [19]They cast their silver into the streets, and their gold is like an unclean thing; their silver and gold are not able to deliver them in the day of the wrath of the LORD; they cannot satisfy their hunger or fill their stomachs with it. For it was the stumbling block of their iniquity. [20]Their[b] beautiful ornament they used for vainglory, and they made their abominable images and their detestable things of it; therefore I will make it an unclean thing to them. [21]And I will give it into the hands of foreigners for a prey, and to the wicked of the earth for a spoil; and they shall profane it. [22]I will turn my face from them, that they may profane my precious[c] place; robbers shall enter and profane it, [23]and make a desolation.[d]

"Because the land is full of bloody crimes and the city is full of violence, [24]I will bring the worst of the nations to take possession of their houses; I will put an end to their proud might, and their holy places shall be profaned. [25]When anguish comes, they will seek peace, but there shall be none. [26]Disaster comes upon disaster,

Deut 32:25
Lam 1:20
Mt 24:16–18

Ezek 21:12

Lev 21:5
2 Sam 10:4
Is 3:24
Amos 8:10

2 Kings 21:4
Ezek 8:5–16

2 Kings 21:16
Ezek 11:6

Is 29:14
Jer 4:20; 18:18
Lam 2:9
Mic 3:6

---

was considered shameful for men to lose their hair, whether through natural or other causes (cf. 2 Sam 10:4; Lev 21:5).

7:26–27. These verses mention the functions specific to office-holders in that society (cf. Jer 18:18). The

eius non regredietur, et unusquisque in iniquitate sua vitam suam non confortabit. [14]Canite tuba, praeparentur omnia, sed non est qui vadat ad proelium; ira enim mea super universam pompam eius. [15]Gladius foris, pestis et fames intrinsecus. Qui in agro est, gladio morietur; et, qui in civitate, fame et pestilentia devorabuntur. [16]Et salvabuntur, qui fugerint ex eis, et erunt in montibus quasi columbae convallium omnes gementes, unusquisque in iniquitate sua. [17]Omnes manus dissolventur, et omnia genua fluent aquis. [18]Et accingent se ciliciis, et operiet eos formido; et in omni facie confusio, et in universis capitibus eorum calvitium. [19]Argentum suum foras proicient, et aurum eorum in immunditiam erit; argentum eorum et aurum eorum non valebit liberare eos in die furoris Domini; animam suam non saturabunt, et ventres eorum non implebuntur, quia scandalum iniquitatis eorum factum est, [20]et ornamentum monilium suorum in superbiam posuerunt et imagines abominationum suarum et simulacrorum fecerunt ex eo; propter hoc dedi eis illud in immunditiam. [21]Et dabo illud in manus alienorum ad diripiendum et impiis terrae in praedam, et contaminabunt illud. [22]Et avertam faciem meam ab eis, et violabunt thesaurum meum absconditum; et introibunt in illud praedones et contaminabunt illud [23]et facient ex illo catenas; quoniam terra plena est iudicio sanguinum, et civitas

b. Syr Symmachus: Heb *Its* **c.** Or *secret* **d.** Cn: Heb *make the chain*

rumour follows rumour; they seek a vision from the prophet, but the law perishes from the priest, and counsel from the elders. 27The king mourns, the prince is wrapped in despair, and the hands of the people of the land are palsied by terror. According to their way I will do to them, and according to their own judgments I will judge them; and they shall know that I am the LORD."

3. VISION OF THE SINS OF ISRAEL*

Ezek 1:3; 14:1; 20

Theophany

8 1In the sixth year, in the sixth month, on the fifth day of the
month, as I sat in my house, with the elders of Judah sitting

---

prophet's office was to utter oracles and explain visions; words were his stock in trade. The priest's function was to instruct the people as regards the Law. The elders ("the wise" in the book of Jeremiah) gave counsel in public life and on private matters. The king was the governor; he was close to his subjects, rejoicing with them in times of victory, and mourning with them in times of misfortune. The prince, being the heir, imitated his father. Finally, the ordinary people ("the people of the land") were those who with their "hands" met the needs of all.

***8:1—11:25.** These four chapters form a literary unit hinging on the theophany in the temple, which has many similarities to the first vision, the one by the river Chebar (chaps. 1–3). The passage begins with a short account of how the vision began (8:1–3) and it concludes with some verses describing its conclusion (11:22–25). The body of the account consists in five detailed and awesome visions—the shameful abominations committed in the temple of Jerusalem (8:4–18), the massacre of the city's inhabitants on account of their sins (9:1–11), the burning and destruction of the temple, and the withdrawal of the glory of God (10:1–22). Then comes God's sentence against the rulers of Israel (11:1–13) and, finally, a ray of hope—the promise of restoration (11: 14–21). The entire vision is a poignant lament over the fact that "the glory of God" has left his temple and, on that account, destruction is inevitable.

8:1. "In the sixth year, in the sixth month, on the fifth of the month". According to the meticulous chronology

plena iniquitate. 24Et adducam pessimos de gentibus, et possidebunt domos eorum; et quiescere faciam superbiam potentium, et possidebunt sanctuaria eorum. 25Angustia superveniente, requirent pacem, et non erit. 26Calamitas super calamitatem veniet, et auditus super auditum; et quaerent visionem de propheta, et lex peribit a sacerdote, et consilium a senioribus. 27Rex lugebit, et princeps induetur horrore, et manus populi terrae conturbabuntur. Secundum viam eorum faciam eis et secundum iudicia eorum iudicabo eos, et scient quia ego Dominus». **[8]** 1Et factum est in anno sexto, in sexto mense, in quinta mensis, ego sedebam in domo mea, et senes Iudae sedebant coram me, et cecidit super me ibi

before me, the hand of the Lord GOD fell there upon me. 2Then I beheld, and, lo, a form that had the appearance of a man;[e] below what appeared to be his loins it was fire, and above his loins it was like the appearance of brightness, like gleaming bronze. 3He put forth the form of a hand, and took me by a lock of my head; and the Spirit lifted me up between earth and heaven, and brought me in visions of God to Jerusalem, to the entrance of the gateway of the inner court that faces north, where was the seat of the image of jealousy, which provokes to jealousy.

Ezek 1:26–28
Deut 32:21
2 Kings 21:7
Ezek 3:12; 5:11; Dan 5:5; 14:36
2 Cor 12:1–4

Sins committed against the temple

4And behold, the glory of the God of Israel was there, like the vision that I saw in the plain.

Ex 24:16
Ezek 1:28–29; 3:22

---

in the book, this would mean 17 or 18 September 592 BC. The preciseness of the date is a sign that the book has been very carefully put together.

The "elders of Judah" sitting in front of the prophet symbolize the entire people witnessing that the prophet is having visions and their eagerness to hear what he has to say (cf. 14:1; 20:1).

8:2–3. This description of the "form that had the appearance of man" purposely repeats things mentioned in the first vision beside the river Chebar (1:27). All of Ezekiel's great visions centre on the glory of God, that is, the glorious presence of God.

The "image of jealousy" is a reference to an idol which, given the fact that it stood at the very entrance to the temple, was a provocation to devout Israelites. We cannot be sure what this idol represented but it may have been an image of the Canaanite goddess Aserah which King Manasseh ordered to be set up in the temple of Jerusalem around the middle of the seventh century BC (cf. 2 Kings 21:7).

8:4–18. The vision goes on to describe the sins of idolatry committed within the temple—worship of reptiles and loathsome beasts, probably introduced by the pro-Egypt faction, since they resemble the gods of the Nile (vv. 10–13); women weeping for Tammuz, the Mesopotamian god of vegetation and fertility (vv. 14–15); and, the worst sign of depravity, twenty-five men, probably priests, worshipping the sun (vv. 16– 17). It is all so depraved that the Lord will certainly punish them. Commenting on the idolatrous paintings on the walls, St Jerome draws a moral lesson: "We too

manus Domini Dei, 2et vidi: et ecce similitudo quasi aspectus viri, ab aspectu lumborum eius et deorsum ignis, et a lumbis eius et sursum quasi aspectus splendoris ut visio electri. 3Emisit similitudinem manus et apprehendit me in cincinno capitis mei; et elevavit me spiritus inter terram et caelum et adduxit in Ierusalem, in visionibus Dei, iuxta ostium interius, quod respiciebat aquilonem, ubi erat statutum idolum zeli ad provocandam aemulationem. 4Et ecce ibi gloria Dei Israel secundum

e. Gk: Heb *fire*

[5]Then he said to me, "Son of man, lift up your eyes now in the
direction of the north." So I lifted up my eyes toward the north,
and behold, north of the altar gate, in the entrance, was this image
of jealousy. [6]And he said to me, "Son of man, do you see what
they are doing, the great abominations that the house of Israel are
committing here, to drive me far from my sanctuary? But you will
see still greater abominations."

[7]And he brought me to the door of the court; and when I looked,
behold, there was a hole in the wall. [8]Then said he to me, "Son of
man, dig in the wall"; and when I dug in the wall, lo, there was a
door. [9]And he said to me, "Go in, and see the vile abominations
that they are committing here." [10]So I went in and saw; and there,
portrayed upon the wall round about, were all kinds of creeping
Ex 24:1 Num 11:16 things, and loathsome beasts, and all the idols of the house of
2 Chron 34:8 Israel. [11]And before them stood seventy men of the elders of the

---

paint images of idols on the walls of our temple when we allow ourselves to be overcome by vice and sins, and carve out idols in our hearts" (*Commentarii in Ezechielem*, 8, 11). This moral finds its best expression in mystical writings, which use Ezekiel's imagery to describe the enemies that try to block the soul's access to God: "The images of unclean animals and creeping things that line the walls of the first alcove in the temple are the thoughts and ideas that the understanding has of all the low things and creatures of this earth; and they are painted in the temple of the soul when we fill our understanding with such thoughts and ideas. The women who stand further in within the temple, weeping for the god Adonis, are the appetites that make up the second power of the soul, the will. Those appetites, too, weep, when they are entranced by the foul images painted by the understanding. And the men who are found in the third room are the images and pictures of created things which inhabit and thwart the third part of the soul, the memory. They have turned their backs on the temple, for when the three powers of the soul have been seduced by creatures and created things, the soul has turned its back on God, who is the right reason of the soul and cannot be bound by any earthly thing" (St John of the Cross, *Ascent of Mount Carmel*, 1, 9, 6).

visionem, quam videram in campo; [5]et dixit ad me: «Fili hominis, leva oculos tuos ad viam aquilonis».
Et levavi oculos meos ad viam aquilonis, et ecce ab aquilone portae altaris hoc idolum zeli in introitu.
[6]Et dixit ad me: «Fili hominis, putasne vides tu, quid isti faciunt, abominationes magnas, quas domus
Israel facit hic, ut procul recedam a sanctuario meo? Et adhuc conversus videbis abominationes
maiores». [7]Et duxit me ad ostium atrii, et vidi: et ecce foramen unum in pariete. [8]Et dixit ad me: «Fili
hominis, fode parietem»; et cum perfodissem parietem, apparuit ostium unum. [9]Et dixit ad me:
«Ingredere et vide abominationes pessimas, quas isti faciunt hic». [10]Et ingressus vidi: et ecce omnis
similitudo reptilium et animalium abominatio et universa idola domus Israel depicta erant in pariete in
circuitu per totum; [11]et septuaginta viri de senioribus domus Israel, et Iezonias filius Saphan stabat in

house of Israel, with Ja-azaniah the son of Shaphan standing
among them. Each had his censer in his hand, and the smoke of the Lev 26:1
cloud of incense went up. 12Then he said to me, "Son of man, have Is 29:15
you seen what the elders of the house of Israel are doing in the dark, Ezek 9:9
every man in his room[f] of pictures? For they say, 'The LORD does
not see us, the LORD has forsaken the land.'" 13He said also to me,
"You will see still greater abominations which they commit."

14Then he brought me to the entrance of the north gate of the
house of the LORD; and behold, there sat women weeping for
Tammuz.* 15Then he said to me, "Have you seen this, O son of
man? You will see still greater abominations than these."

16And he brought me into the inner court of the house of the 1 Kings 6:36
LORD; and behold, at the door of the temple of the LORD, between Job 31:26
the porch and the altar, were about twenty-five men, with their Jer 2:27; 8:2; 32:33
backs to the temple of the LORD, and their faces toward the east, Ezek 11:1
worshipping the sun toward the east. 17Then he said to me, "Have
you seen this, O son of man? Is it too slight a thing for the house
of Judah to commit the abominations which they commit here,
that they should fill the land with violence, and provoke me
further to anger? Lo, they put the branch to their nose. 18Therefore
I will deal in wrath; my eye will not spare, nor will I have pity;
and though they cry in my ears with a loud voice, I will not hear
them."

8:17. "They put the branch to the nose" (v. 17)—some idolatrous gesture, the meaning of which is lost to us. It was probably in common use in Babylonian religious rites, but it was a blasphemous thing to do in the presence of the Lord in the temple: the transgression lay in treating the Lord as if he were a false god, and in not giving him due honour.

medio eorum stantium ante picturas, et unusquisque habebat turibulum in manu sua, et vapor nebulae de ture consurgebat. 12Et dixit ad me: «Certe vides, fili hominis, quae seniores domus Israel faciunt in tenebris, unusquisque in cubiculo simulacri sui; dicunt enim: "Non videt Dominus nos, dereliquit Dominus terram"». 13Et dixit ad me: «Adhuc videbis abominationes maiores, quas isti faciunt». 14Et duxit me ad ostium portae domus Domini, quod respiciebat ad aquilonem, et ecce ibi mulieres sedebant plangentes Thammuz. 15Et dixit ad me: «Certe vidisti, fili hominis; adhuc videbis abominationes maiores his». 16Et introduxit me in atrium domus Domini interius, et ecce in ostio templi Domini, inter vestibulum et altare, quasi viginti quinque viri dorsa habentes contra templum Domini et facies ad orientem, et adorabant ad ortum solis. 17Et dixit ad me: «Certe vidisti, fili hominis; numquid parum est hoc domui Iudae, ut facerent abominationes istas, quas fecerunt hic, quia replentes terram iniquitate iterum irritaverunt me et ecce applicant ramum ad nares suas. 18Ergo et ego faciam in furore: non parcet oculus meus, nec miserebor et, cum clamaverint ad aures meas voce magna, non exaudiam eos».

f. Gk Syr Vg Tg: Heb *rooms*

Punishment deserved by the Israelites

9 1Then he cried in my ears with a loud voice, saying, "Draw
near, you executioners of the city, each with his destroying
Ex 28:42 weapon in his hand." 2And lo, six men came from the direction of
Lev 16:4 Tob 5:4 the upper gate, which faces north, every man with his weapon for
Rev 1:13 slaughter in his hand, and with them was a man clothed in linen,
with a writing case at his side. And they went in and stood beside
the bronze altar.

9:1–11. The implications of the Lord's decision to "deal in wrath" (8:18) is spelt out in detail. The description of the massacre of the inhabitants of Jerusalem (v. 6) is more a piece of religious teaching than an exact account of what happened when the Babylonians invaded the city. There is intentional symbolism in the description, even if we don't always manage to see what it means. Thus, the executioners come from the north (v. 2), that is, the direction from which came Assyrian-Babylonian invasions capable of destroying the kingdom. There are seven of them, six with "weapons for slaughter in their hands" and one clothed in linen like a priest (cf. Ex 28:42; Lev 16:4)—seven in all, that is, a number indicating completeness; and the fact that there is a priest in charge implies that they are there by order of the Lord. What is being described, then, is absolute and utter destruction. If these men stand for the armies of Nebuchadnezzar, as they seem to do, Ezekiel is depicting those armies as being weapons in God's hands and not as wicked invaders.

The "glory of the God of Israel" (v. 3) goes up from the Holy of Holies to direct the plan of punishment, and, above all, as a sign that God is preparing to leave his dwelling-place, the temple. The "mark" (v. 4) is a tau, the last letter of the alphabet, which in ancient Hebrew had the form of a cross; it is reminiscent of the mark of Cain (Gen 4:15). All who bear the mark will escape death; but they will not escape punishment (cf. 7:16). The people who bear the mark may be the exiles, the prophet's companions. St Jerome records a nice interpretation by Origen: "When the people of Israel were asked what the taw means, some answered that because it is the last of the twenty-two letters of the alphabet it shows the perfection of those who remained to wail and lament the sins of the people. Others said it was a sign of those who had fulfilled the Law, which is *Torah* in Hebrew. And, finally, others said that it referred to those who believe in Christ, because the *taw* takes the form of a cross, the sign with which all Christians are marked at their baptism" (*Selecta in Ezechielem*, 9).

Defilement of the temple with the bodies of the slain (v. 7) was the very worst form of punishment, because it

[9] 1Et clamavit in auribus meis voce magna dicens: «Appro pinquaverunt visitationes urbis, et unusquisque vas interfectionis habet in manu sua». 2Et ecce sex viri veniebant de via portae superioris, quae respicit ad aquilonem, et uniuscuiusque vas interitus in manu eius; vir quoque unus in medio eorum vestitus lineis, et atramentarium scriptoris ad renes eius; et ingressi sunt et steterunt iuxta altare

[3]Now the glory of the God of Israel had gone up from the
cherubim on which it rested to the threshold of the house; and he
called to the man clothed in linen, who had the writing case at his
side. [4]And the LORD said to him, "Go through the city, through
Jerusalem, and put a mark upon the foreheads of the men who
sigh and groan over all the abominations that are committed in it."
[5]And to the others he said in my hearing, "Pass through the city
after him, and smite; your eye shall not spare, and you shall show
no pity; [6]slay old men outright, young men and maidens, little
children and women, but touch no one upon whom is the mark.
And begin at my sanctuary." So they began with the elders who
were before the house. [7]Then he said to them, "Defile the house,
and fill the courts with the slain. Go forth." So they went forth,
and smote in the city. [8]And while they were smiting, and I was left
alone, I fell upon my face, and cried, "Ah Lord GOD! wilt thou
destroy all that remains of Israel in the outpouring of thy wrath
upon Jerusalem?"
[9]Then he said to me, "The guilt of the house of Israel and Judah
is exceedingly great; the land is full of blood, and the city full of
injustice; for they say, 'The LORD has forsaken the land, and the

Ex 25:18 Ezek 1:28; 10:4,18

Gen 4:15 Ex 12:7,13 Rev 7:2–3; 9:4; 20:4

Ex 32:27 Num 25:5,8 Jer 25:29 Ezek 8:11 1 Pet 4:17 Rev 7:3; 9:4

Gen 18:16–32 Ex 32:11–14 Num 14:13–19 Jer 7:16; 12:3; 15:11; 17:14–18;18:20–21

Is 4:3; 6:11 Ezek 11:13; 24:9; Amos 7:2,5

Ps 10:11 Ezek 8:12

---

would force the Lord to withdraw. The destruction of the city (which has yet to happen) is a foregone conclusion, the inevitable outcome of this defilement.

9:8. Intercession was one of the essential duties of a prophet, as can be seen from Moses, the prophet par excellence (Ex 32:11–14; Num 14:13–19). Important prophets such as Amos (Amos 7:2–3) and Jeremiah in their "confessions" beseeched the Lord on their own behalf (Jer 12:3; 17:14–18; 18:20–21), on behalf of the people (Jer 7:16) and even on behalf of their enemies (Jer 15:11). But neither Jeremiah nor Ezekiel obtained what they prayed for, because God's decision to inflict punishment was by then irrevocable. We know, too, about Abraham's pleading for Sodom, and how the Lord refused him (Gen 18:16–32).

---

aereum. [3]Et gloria Dei Israel elevata est de cherub, super quem erat, ad limen domus; et vocavit virum, qui indutus erat lineis et atramentarium scriptoris habebat in lumbis suis. [4]Et dixit Dominus ad eum: «Transi per mediam civitatem in medio Ierusalem et signa thau super frontes virorum gementium et dolentium super cunctis abominationibus, quae fiunt in medio eius». [5]Et illis dixit, audiente me: «Transite per civitatem sequentes eum et percutite; non parcat oculus vester, neque misereamini: [6]senem, adulescentulum et virginem et parvulum et mulieres interficite usque ad internecionem; omnem autem, super quem videritis thau, ne occidatis, et a sanctuario meo incipite». Coeperunt ergo a viris senioribus, qui erant ante faciem domus. [7]Et dixit ad eos: «Contaminate domum et implete atria interfectis. Egredimini». Et egressi sunt et percutiebant eos, qui erant in civitate. [8]Et caede completa, remansi ego ruique super faciem meam et clamans aio: «Heu, Domine Deus! Ergone disperdes omnes reliquias Israel, effundens furorem tuum super Ierusalem?». [9]Et dixit ad me: «Iniquitas domus Israel et Iudae magna est nimis valde; et repleta est terra sanguinibus, et civitas repleta est iniustitia. Dixerunt

LORD does not see.' [10]As for me, my eye will not spare, nor will I
have pity, but I will requite their deeds upon their heads."
Rev 1:13 [11]And lo, the man clothed in linen, with the writing case at his
side, brought back word, saying, "I have done as thou didst
command me."

The glory of the Lord leaves the Temple

Ezek 1:22,26 Rev 4:3 **10** [1]Then I looked, and behold, on the firmament that was over
the heads of the cherubim there appeared above them

10:1–22. The siege of Jerusalem ended with a terrible fire that razed the temple, the royal palace and private houses (cf. 2 Kings 25:9). Ezekiel describes the event in theological language, and he describes it as happening when the glory of the Lord dramatically withdraws from the temple.

The first scene (vv. 1–7) shows the priest, dressed in linen, charged with taking coals from the very throne of God and flinging them on the city to set it ablaze. The war in Jerusalem is therefore being interpreted as a necessary purification, carried out on the express instructions of God. The glory of God (v. 4) manifests itself here in the midst of the cloud of smoke and in the brightness given off by the cleansing fire. That, too, is how it appears in the account of the call of Isaiah (cf. Is 6:6–7).

The second scene (vv. 8–17) describes in detail the throne of the glory of God. Many of the details given here fill out and help to explain what is described in chapter one. The "cherubim", mentioned as many as eighteen times here, are the same "living creatures" as appeared in that chapter (1:15); in addition to bearing the throne, they obey the Lord's commands, specifically that of giving the cleansing fire to the man clothed in linen (v. 7). They are fantastic characters; in Ezekiel, they symbolize all imaginable, exotic creatures, yet ones that are subject to the Lord, whom they serve and obey promptly and meticulously.

The last scene (vv. 18–22) is about the withdrawal of the glory of the Lord from the temple. It is a particularly forceful description precisely because it does not go into detail about the actual withdrawal, but focuses on the entourage of the divine glory and identifies each of the elements, all of which appeared already in the vision at the Chebar: there is the same glory of the God of Israel (v. 19), the same cherubim and living creatures (v. 20), with the same faces and wings. All these details betoken the seer's sense of loss and desolation, so deeply does he feel the absence of the God of Israel. Applying to his own times this nostalgia for God

enim: "Dereliquit Dominus terram, et Dominus non videt"; [10]igitur et meus non parcet oculus, neque miserebor: viam eorum super caput eorum reddam». [11]Et ecce vir, qui indutus erat lineis, qui habebat atramentarium in lumbis suis, respondit verbum dicens: «Feci, sicut praecepisti mihi». **[10]** [1]Et vidi: et ecce super firmamentum, quod erat super caput cherubim, quasi lapis sapphirus, quasi species

something like a sapphire, in form resembling a throne. [2]And he
said to the man clothed in linen, "Go in among the whirling
wheels underneath the cherubim; fill your hands with burning
coals from between the cherubim, and scatter them over the city."

Gen 19:24
Rev 8:5

And he went in before my eyes. [3]Now the cherubim were
standing on the south side of the house, when the man went in;
and a cloud filled the inner court. [4]And the glory of the LORD went
up from the cherubim to the threshold of the house; and the house
was filled with the cloud, and the court was full of the brightness
of the glory of the LORD. [5]And the sound of the wings of the
cherubim was heard as far as the outer court, like the voice of God
Almighty when he speaks.

Ex 24:16; 40:34–35
1 Kings 8:10–11; Is 6:6–7
Ex 19:19
Ps 29:3
Ex 1:24

[6]And when he commanded the man clothed in linen, "Take fire
from between the whirling wheels, from between the cherubim,"
he went in and stood beside a wheel. [7]And a cherub stretched
forth his hand from between the cherubim to the fire that was
between the cherubim, and took some of it, and put it into the
hands of the man clothed in linen, who took it and went out. [8]The
cherubim appeared to have the form of a human hand under their
wings.

Ezek 1:5–21
Ex 24:16
Ezek 1:28

[9]And I looked, and behold, there were four wheels beside the
cherubim, one beside each cherub; and the appearance of the
wheels was like sparkling chrysolite. [10]And as for their appearance,
the four had the same likeness, as if a wheel were within a wheel.
[11]When they went, they went in any of their four directions[g]

---

and for his glory, St Gregory the Great commented: "Since we can no longer see the likeness of the glory of the Lord in the spirit of prophecy, we should seek it continually and desire to contemplate it in Holy Scripture, in the teachings sent from heaven and in the doctrines of the spirit" (*Homilae in Ezechielem prophetam*, 1, 8, 32).

similitudinis solii apparuit super ea. [2]Et dixit ad virum, qui indutus erat lineis, et ait: «Ingredere in medio rotarum, quae sunt subtus cherub, et imple manus tuas prunis ignis, quae sunt inter cherubim, et effunde super civitatem». Ingressusque est in conspectu meo. [3]Cherubim autem stabant a dextris domus, cum ingrederetur vir, et nubes implevit atrium interius. [4]Et elevata est gloria Domini desuper cherub ad limen domus, et repleta est domus nube, et atrium repletum est splendore gloriae Domini. [5]Et sonitus alarum cherubim audiebatur usque ad atrium exterius, quasi vox Dei omnipotentis loquentis. [6]Cumque praecepisset viro, qui indutus erat lineis, dicens: «Sume ignem de medio rotarum, de medio cherubim», ingressus ille stetit iuxta rotam; [7]et extendit cherub manum de medio cherubim ad ignem, qui erat inter cherubim, et sumpsit et dedit in manus eius, qui indutus erat lineis; qui accipiens egressus est. [8]Et apparuit in cherubim similitudo manus hominis subtus pennas eorum, [9]et vidi: et ecce quattuor rotae iuxta cherubim; rota una iuxta cherub unum, et rota alia iuxta cherub unum, species autem rotarum erat quasi species lapidis chrysolithi, [10]et aspectus earum similitudo una illis quattuor, quasi sit rota in medio rotae. [11]Cumque ambularent in quattuor partes, gradiebantur et non

g. Heb *on their four sides*

without turning as they went, but in whatever direction the front
wheel faced the others followed without turning as they went.
[12]And[h] their rims, and their spokes,[i] and the wheels were full of
eyes round about—the wheels that the four of them had. [13]As for
the wheels, they were called in my hearing the whirling wheels.
[14]And every one had four faces: the first face was the face of the
cherub, and the second face was the face of a man, and the third
the face of a lion, and the fourth the face of an eagle.

[15]And the cherubim mounted up. These were the living
creatures that I saw by the river Chebar. [16]And when the cherubim
went, the wheels went beside them; and when the cherubim lifted
up their wings to mount up from the earth, the wheels did not turn
from beside them. [17]When they stood still, these stood still, and
when they mounted up, these mounted up with them; for the spirit
of the living creatures[j] was in them.

Hos 9:12 [18]Then the glory of the LORD went forth from the threshold of
the house, and stood over the cherubim. [19]And the cherubim lifted
up their wings and mounted up from the earth in my sight as they
went forth, with the wheels beside them; and they stood at the
door of the east gate of the house of the LORD; and the glory of the
God of Israel was over them.

[20]These were the living creatures that I saw underneath the God
of Israel by the river Chebar; and I knew that they were cherubim.
[21]Each had four faces, and each four wings, and underneath their
Ezek 1:10 wings the semblance of human hands. [22]And as for the likeness of
their faces, they were the very faces whose appearance I had seen
by the river Chebar. They went every one straight forward.

---

convertebantur ambulantes, sed ad locum, ad quem ire declinabat quae prima erat, sequebantur et ceterae nec convertebantur, cum ambularent. [12]Et omne corpus eorum et terga et manus et pennae et rotae plena erant oculis in circuitu illis quattuor; [13]et rotae istae vocatae sunt Volubiles, audiente me. [14]Quattuor autem facies habebat unumquodque: facies prima facies cherub, et facies secunda facies hominis, et tertia facies leonis, et quarta facies aquilae. [15]Et elevati sunt cherubim: ipsum est animal, quod videram iuxta fluvium Chobar. [16]Cumque ambularent, cherubim ibant pariter, et rotae iuxta ea; et cum elevarent cherubim alas suas, ut exaltarentur de terra, non convertebantur rotae, sed et ipsae iuxta erant. [17]Stantibus illis, stabant et cum elevatis elevabantur; spiritus enim animalium erat in eis. [18]Et egressa est gloria Domini a limine templi et stetit super cherubim; [19]et elevantes cherubim alas suas exaltata sunt a terra coram me, et, illis egredientibus, rotae quoque subsecutae sunt; et stetit in introitu portae domus Domini orientalis, et gloria Dei Israel erat super eos. [20]Ipsum est animal, quod vidi subter Deum Israel iuxta fluvium Chobar, et intellexi quia cherubim essent. [21]Quattuor per quattuor vultus unicuique, et quattuor alae unicuique, et similitudo manus hominis sub alis eorum; [22]et similitudo vultuum eorum, ipsi vultus quorum aspectum videram iuxta fluvium Chobar. Et singuli ante faciem

h. Gk: Heb *And their whole body and* **i.** Heb *spokes and their wings* **j.** Or *of life*

The rulers of the people are condemned*

11 [1]The Spirit lifted me up, and brought me to the east gate of Ezek 3:12; 8:16; 10:19
the house of the LORD, which faces east. And behold, at the
door of the gateway there were twenty-five men; and I saw among
them Ja-azaniah the son of Azzur, and Pelatiah the son of Benaiah,
princes of the people. [2]And he said to me, "Son of man, these are
the men who devise iniquity and who give wicked counsel in this
city; [3]who say, 'The time is not near[k] to build houses; this city is Jer 1:13
the cauldron, and we are the flesh.' [4]Therefore prophesy against Ezek 24:3,6, 1–14
them, prophesy, O son of man."
[5]And the Spirit of the LORD fell upon me, and he said to me,
"Say, Thus says the LORD: So you think, O house of Israel; for I

***11:1–21.** This chapter contains two contrasting oracles, but they complement each other; both have to do with divine judgment: the first (vv. 1–13), with the divine punishment of Jerusalem; the second, a message of hope for the exiles in Babylon. They are interrupted by the news of the death of Pelatiah, one of the leading men of Jerusalem, which leads Ezekiel to make an anguished plea to God: "Wilt thou make a full end of the remnant of Israel?" (v. 13).

11:1–13. The oracle against the people of Jerusalem shows just how far things have gone; they sin without restraint because they think the city can come to no harm. The twenty-five men, Ja-azaniah and Pelatiah among their leaders, stand for those who were guilty of excess and idolatry and who favoured (v. 2) an alliance with Egypt against Babylon.

"This city is the cauldron, and we are the flesh" (v. 3)—a proverb about peace and plenty: Jerusalem is a spacious, invulnerable place where the inhabitants enjoy well-being. But the Lord changes the meaning: the cauldron is full of the bodies of the slain, thanks to its rulers—and, though the latter think they are safe, they will be brought out of the city (v. 7) and put to death by foreigners. The simile of the cauldron will be used again to announce the imminent siege of Jerusalem (cf. 24:3–12).

The death of Pelatiah, whose name ironically means "the Lord saves", confirms that what the oracle says must come to pass, inexorably—a prospect so terrible that the seer himself makes an anguished plea to the Lord (v. 13).

suam gradiebantur. **[11]** [1]Et elevavit me spiritus et duxit me ad portam domus Domini orientalem, quae respicit solis ortum; et ecce in introitu portae viginti quinque viri, et vidi in medio eorum Iezoniam filium Azur et Pheltiam filium Banaiae, principes populi. [2]Dixitque ad me: «Fili hominis, hi sunt viri, qui cogitant iniquitatem et tractant consilium pessimum in urbe ista [3]dicentes: "Nonne dudum aedificatae sunt domus? Haec est lebes, nos autem carnes". [4]Idcirco vaticinare de eis; vaticinare, fili hominis». [5]Et irruit in me spiritus Domini et dixit ad me: «Loquere. Haec dicit Dominus: Sic locuti estis, domus Israel, et cogitationes cordis vestri ego novi. [6]Plurimos occidistis in urbe hac et implestis

k. Or *Is not the time near ...?*

know the things that come into your mind. 6You have multiplied
your slain in this city, and have filled its streets with the slain.
7Therefore thus says the Lord GOD: Your slain whom you have
laid in the midst of it, they are the flesh, and this city is the
cauldron; but you shall be brought forth out of the midst of it.
8You have feared the sword; and I will bring the sword upon you,
says the Lord GOD. 9And I will bring you forth out of the midst of
2 Kings it, and give you into the hands of foreigners, and execute
25:19,21 judgments upon you. 10You shall fall by the sword; I will judge
Jer 39:6; 52:10 you at the border of Israel; and you shall know that I am the LORD.
11This city shall not be your cauldron, nor shall you be the flesh in
Deut 12:29–30 the midst of it; I will judge you at the border of Israel; 12and you
shall know that I am the LORD; for you have not walked in my
statutes, nor executed my ordinances, but have acted according to
the ordinances of the nations that are round about you."
Ezek 9:8 13And it came to pass, while I was prophesying, that Pelatiah
the son of Benaiah died. Then I fell down upon my face, and cried
with a loud voice, and said, "Ah Lord GOD! wilt thou make a full
end of the remnant of Israel?"

Jer 24 **A promise of restoration**
Ezek 33:24 14And the word of the LORD came to me: 15"Son of man, your
brethren, even your brethren, your fellow exiles,[l] the whole house

---

11:14–21. The oracle addressed to the exiles, which is full of hope, counterposes the thinking of those who were left behind in Jerusalem and the plans that God has in mind. Those Jews thought that the deportees had been sent away on account of their sins; that is, exile was punishment for their forsaking the Lord, and in addition to exile they lost the right to inherit the land (v. 15). But the Lord assures them that he continues to be a sanctuary for those in exile (v. 16) and that, once the exile is over, he will give them the land of Israel forever (v. 17); he will also give them a new heart and a new spirit (v. 18).

"I have been a sanctuary for them" (v. 15): Ezekiel never tires of making the point that the Lord stays with the exiles; in this he follows a line started

vias eius interfectis. 7Propterea haec dicit Dominus Deus: Interfecti vestri, quos posuistis in medio eius, hi sunt carnes, et haec est lebes, et educam vos de medio eius. 8Gladium metuitis, et gladium inducam super vos, ait Dominus Deus. 9Et eiciam vos de medio eius daboque vos in manu hostium et faciam in vobis iudicia. 10Gladio cadetis, in finibus Israel iudicabo vos, et scietis quia ego Dominus. 11Haec non erit vobis in lebetem, et vos non eritis in medio eius in carnes: in finibus Israel iudicabo vos; 12et scietis quia ego Dominus, qui in praeceptis meis non ambulastis et iudicia mea non fecistis, sed iuxta iudicia gentium, quae in circuitu vestro sunt, estis operati». 13Et factum est cum prophetarem, Pheltias filius Banaiae mortuus est; et cecidi in faciem meam, clamans voce magna, et dixi: «Heu, Domine Deus,

l. Gk Syr: Heb *men of your kindred*

of Israel, all of them, are those of whom the inhabitants of
Jerusalem have said, 'They have gone far from the LORD; to us
this land is given for a possession.' 16Therefore say, 'Thus says the Lord GOD: Though I removed them far off among the nations, and though I scattered them among the countries, yet I have been a sanctuary to them for a while[m] in the countries where they have gone.' Ezek 36:19
17Therefore say, 'Thus says the Lord GOD: I will gather you from the peoples, and assemble you out of the countries where you have been scattered, and I will give you the land of Israel.' Deut 30:3–5 Ezek 20:41; 28:25; 34:13; 36:24–25
18And when they come there, they will remove from it all its

by Jeremiah: God is under no obligation to make himself present only in the temple (cf. Jer 7–8); he is present wherever his faithful followers are. The "for a while" in v. 16 shows that the exile will not last very long.

A "new heart" and a "new spirit": v. 19 is translated in various ways. The Greek and some manuscripts that the New Vulgate follows read "another heart". The text is making the point that there will be no differences of opinion between those who stayed on in Jerusalem and those who will return from exile. This wonderful solidarity is something that the New Testament celebrates when it depicts the early Christians as being "of one heart and soul" (Acts 4:32). The image of the heart of flesh, a human heart, replacing the "stony", insensitive heart graphically describes the complete inner and outer renewal (cf. 36:26–27) that the people will experience as a nation and as individuals (v. 21). And a very early Christian text comments: "It is said thus because he was to be made flesh and dwell among us. My brothers, the dwelling-place of our heart should be a holy temple for the Lord" (*Letter of Barnabas*, 6, 14–15).

When explaining that everything necessary for salvation must come from God, John Cassian mentions 11:19–20: "Even the fear of the Lord, which keeps us close to Him, is given to us by the Lord. [...] Ezekiel says: *I will give them a new heart, and put a new spirit within them*. This is a deep and clear teaching: our good will and dispositions are inspired by the Lord when he draws us towards salvation, directly or through the ministry of another, when we feel almost compelled to respond. It is he who grants us the perfection of virtue. It is left to us to respond to the Lord's promptings and help with either fortitude or negligence, and thus earn our reward or punishment" (*Collationes*, 3, 19).

consummationem tu facis reliquiarum Israel!». 14Et factum est verbum Domini ad me dicens: 15«Fili hominis, fratres tui, fratres tui, viri propinqui tui et omnis domus Israel, universi, quibus dixerunt habitatores Ierusalem: "Longe sunt a Domino; nobis data est terra in possessionem". 16Propterea haec dicit Dominus Deus: Quia longe feci eos in gentibus et quia dispersi eos in terris, ero eis in sanctificationem modicam in terris, ad quas venerunt. 17Propterea loquere: Haec dicit Dominus Deus: Congregabo vos de populis et adunabo de terris, in quibus dispersi estis, daboque vobis humum Israel. 18Et ingredientur illuc et auferent omnes offensiones cunctasque abominationes eius de illa. 19Et dabo

m. Or *in small measure*

Ps 51:10 Jer 32:39 detestable things and all its abominations. 19 And I will give them
Ezek 36:26 one[n] heart, and put a new spirit within them; I will take the stony
Acts 4:32 Deut 30:6–8 heart out of their flesh and give them a heart of flesh, 20 that they
Ps 51:12–14 may walk in my statutes and keep my ordinances and obey them;
Jer 4:4 Ezek 18:31; and they shall be my people, and I will be their God. 21 But as for
36:26; 44:7 those[o] whose heart goes after their detestable things and their
Jer 31:31 abominations, I will requite their deeds upon their own heads,
Ezek 36:27 Ex 24:16 says the Lord GOD."
Ezek 1:28 22 Then the cherubim lifted up their wings, with the wheels
2 Cor 3:3 beside them; and the glory of the God of Israel was over them.
23 And the glory of the LORD went up from the midst of the city,
and stood upon the mountain which is on the east side of the city.
Ezek 3:12 24 And the Spirit lifted me up and brought me in the vision by the
Spirit of God into Chaldea, to the exiles. Then the vision that I had
seen went up from me. 25 And I told the exiles all the things that
the LORD had showed me.

11:22–24. The vision ends by returning the two protagonists to their places: "the glory of the God of Israel", which dwelt in the temple (cf. 8:4), withdraws from both temple and city, and stops on the mountain to the east, that is, Mount Olivet, to wait there until the city has been cleansed by destruction (cf. 43:2–4) and it can re-enter it. Ezekiel, who had been carried by the Spirit to Jerusalem (cf. 8:3), is brought back by the same Spirit to where he lives with the other exiles in Chaldea (v. 24). There he can tell them "all the things that the Lord (showed him)" (v. 25). In communicating his message to the prophets, God uses words and visions; as the Letter to the Hebrews puts it, "in many and various ways God spoke of old to our fathers by the prophets" (Heb 1:1).

eis cor aliud et spiritum novum tribuam in visceribus eorum; et auferam cor lapideum de carne eorum et dabo eis cor carneum, 20 ut in praeceptis meis ambulent et iudicia mea custodiant faciantque ea et sint mihi in populum, et ego sim eis in Deum. 21 Quorum cor post offendicula et abominationes suas ambulat, horum viam in capite suo ponam», dicit Dominus Deus. 22 Et elevaverunt cherubim alas suas, et rotae cum eis, et gloria Dei Israel erat super eos; 23 et ascendit gloria Domini de medio civitatis stetitque super montem, qui est ad orientem urbis. 24 Et spiritus levavit me adduxitque in Chaldaeam ad transmigrationem in visione in spiritu Dei; et sublata est a me visio, quam videram. 25 Et locutus sum ad transmigrationem omnia verba Domini, quae ostenderat mihi.

n. Another reading is *a new* **o.** Cn: Heb *To the heart of their detestable things and their abominations their heart goes*

4. ORACLES CONCERNING IMMINENT INVASION*

2 Kings 25:8–11
Jer 18:1

The exiles' departure*

12 [1]The word of the LORD came to me: [2]"Son of man, you Is 6:10; 42:20
dwell in the midst of a rebellious house, who have eyes to Jer 5:21

***12:1—14:23.** Up to this point, the warnings to Jerusalem have been given by way of symbolic actions (chaps. 4–5) and chilling prophecies (chaps. 6–7), and the vision of the outrages committed in the temple (chaps. 8–11). However, neither the people living in Jerusalem nor the exiles seem to accept that a catastrophe is about to happen. In this section of the book Ezekiel speaks out against the people and their refusal to believe by announcing that King Zedekiah is to be deported forthwith (chap. 12) and then by condemning the false prophets who deceive the people by giving them false hopes (chap. 13); he also criticizes pagan beliefs (chap. 14). These oracles are designed to move the listeners' hearts and to get them to put all their trust in the Lord: he can help them in their exile. That is the import of the phrase that recurs in this passage: "You will know that I am the Lord."

***12:1–28.** The date of the last deportation, which happened in 587 BC (cf. 2 Kings 25:8–21), is announced by five oracles or symbolic gestures, each beginning with the wording, "The word of the Lord came to me" (vv. 1, 8, 17, 21, 26). The first two centre on the detention and deportation of King Zedekiah (vv. 1–16), the next one on the poor circumstances of the exiles (vv. 17–20), and the last two focus on how soon these two events will be brought about (vv. 21–28). The symbolic actions of the prophet are well designed to prove to his listeners the truth of what he says.

12:1–16. The first symbolic action (leaving with an exile's baggage) is calculated to provoke feelings of depression; the deportation that they fear will indeed take place. "Exile" is mentioned six times in five verses; "in their sight", five times; and "rebellious house" twice. The preparations are made in daylight; but the actual leaving is shameful: it takes place at night, the face veiled, without looking back at the city.

Ezekiel's symbolic action stands for what will happen to King Zedekiah (v. 10; cf. 2 Kings 25:2–7), who is not mentioned here by either name or title of king. He is called "the prince in Jerusalem", not "prince of Judah", to indicate that catastrophe will befall the city and its inhabitants.

"I will spread my net over him, and he shall be in my snare" (v. 13); the net metaphor indicates that deportation is a kind of enslavement. And the use of the first person underlines once again the

[12] [1]Et factus est sermo Domini ad me dicens: [2]«Fili hominis, in medio domus exasperantis tu habitas, qui oculos habent ad videndum et non vident, et aures ad audiendum et non audiunt, quia domus

Ezek 2:5–7 Mt 13:14 see, but see not, who have ears to hear, but hear not; [3]for they are
a rebellious house. Therefore, son of man, prepare for yourself an
exile's baggage, and go into exile by day in their sight; you shall
go like an exile from your place to another place in their sight.
Perhaps they will understand, though[p] they are a rebellious house.
[4]You shall bring out your baggage by day in their sight, as
baggage for exile; and you shall go forth yourself at evening in
their sight, as men do who must go into exile. [5]Dig through the
Is 8:18 wall in their sight, and go[q] out through it. [6]In their sight you shall
Jer 18:1 lift the baggage upon your shoulder, and carry it out in the dark;
you shall cover your face, that you may not see the land; for I have
made you a sign for the house of Israel."

[7]And I did as I was commanded. I brought out my baggage by
day, as baggage for exile, and in the evening I dug through the
wall with my own hands; I went forth in the dark, carrying my
outfit upon my shoulder in their sight.

[8]In the morning the word of the LORD came to me: [9]"Son of
man, has not the house of Israel, the rebellious house, said to you,
2 Kings 25:2–7 'What are you doing?' [10]Say to them, 'Thus says the Lord GOD:
This oracle concerns the prince in Jerusalem and all the house of
Israel who are in it.'[r] [11]Say, 'I am a sign for you: as I have done,
so shall it be done to them; they shall go into exile, into captivity.'
[12]And the prince who is among them shall lift his baggage upon

---

fact that it is the Lord himself who is the cause of the deportation. Insistence on this helps to strike a very positive note: if God is the cause of the punishment (exile), he too will deliver his people when their imprisonment comes to an end.

The importance of a remnant escaping (v. 16) lies in the fact that they will bear witness to their sins and punishment before pagan nations—so that the latter too may acknowledge the Lord. This positive interpretation of the exile is a feature of the book of Ezekiel.

exasperans est. [3]Tu ergo, fili hominis, fac tibi vasa transmigrationis et transmigrabis per diem coram eis; transmigrabis autem de loco tuo ad locum alterum in conspectu eorum, si forte aspiciant, quia domus exasperans est. [4]Et efferes foras vasa tua quasi vasa transmigrantis per diem in conspectu eorum; tu autem egredieris vespere coram eis, sicut egreditur migrans. [5]Ante oculos eorum perfode tibi parietem et efferes per eum; [6]in conspectu eorum in umeris portabis, in caligine efferes: faciem tuam velabis et non videbis terram, quia portentum dedi te domui Israel». [7]Feci ergo, sicut praeceperat mihi Dominus: vasa mea protuli quasi vasa transmigrantis per diem et vespere perfodi mihi parietem manu; et in caligine extuli in umeris portans in conspectu eorum. [8]Et factus est sermo Domini ad me mane dicens: [9]«Fili hominis, numquid non dixerunt ad te domus Israel, domus exasperans: "Quid tu facis?". [10]Dic ad eos: Haec dicit Dominus Deus: Super ducem onus istud, qui est in Ierusalem, et super omnem domum Israel, quae est in medio eius. [11]Dic: Ego portentum vestrum. Quomodo feci, sic fiet illis: in transmigrationem et in captivitatem ibunt. [12]Et dux, qui est in medio eorum, in umeris portabit, in

p. Or *will see that* **q.** Gk Syr Vg Tg: Heb *bring* **r.** Heb *in the midst of them*

his shoulder in the dark, and shall go forth; he shall dig[s] through
the wall and go[t] out through it; he shall cover his face, that he may
not see the land with his eyes. [13]And I will spread my net over Ex 17:20
him, and he shall be taken in my snare; and I will bring him to 2 Kings 25:7
Babylon in the land of the Chaldeans, yet he shall not see it; and Jer 32:5; 34:3; 39:7
he shall die there. [14]And I will scatter toward every wind all who Ezek 17:20
are round about him, his helpers[u] and all his troops; and I will Lev 26:33
unsheathe the sword after them. [15]And they shall know that I am
the LORD, when I disperse them among the nations and scatter
them through the countries. [16]But I will let a few of them escape Is 4:3
from the sword, from famine and pestilence, that they may Ezek 6:8; 14:22
confess all their abominations among the nations where they go,
and may know that I am the LORD."

Shortage of bread and water

[17]Moreover the word of the LORD came to me: [18]"Son of man, eat Ezek 4:16
your bread with quaking, and drink water with trembling and with
fearfulness; [19]and say of the people of the land, Thus says the
Lord GOD concerning the inhabitants of Jerusalem in the land of
Israel: They shall eat their bread with fearfulness, and drink water
in dismay, because their land will be stripped of all it contains, on
account of the violence of all those who dwell in it. [20]And the
inhabited cities shall be laid waste, and the land shall become a
desolation; and you shall know that I am the LORD."

12:17–20. The second symbolic action is a message for the ordinary people of Jerusalem who will run short of food and drink. The rulers suffer shame and dishonour, the rest experience hunger and thirst. But everyone, including those left in Jerusalem, will have to pay for their misdeeds (v. 19); all must learn to reverence the Lord (v. 20).

caligine, et egredietur; parietem perfodient, ut transitus fiat per eum; faciem suam operiet, ut non videat oculo terram. [13]Et extendam rete meum super illum, et capietur in tendicula mea; et adducam eum in Babylonem in terram Chaldaeorum, et ipsam non videbit ibique morietur. [14]Et omnes, qui circa eum sunt, praesidium eius et agmina eius, dispergam in omnem ventum; et gladium evaginabo post eos. [15]Et scient quia ego Dominus, quando dispersero illos in gentibus et disseminavero eos in terris. [16]Et relinquam ex eis viros paucos a gladio et fame et pestilentia, ut narrent omnia scelera eorum in gentibus, ad quas ingredientur, et scient quia ego Dominus». [17]Et factus est sermo Domini ad me dicens: [18]«Fili hominis, panem tuum in conturbatione comede; sed et aquam tuam in trepidatione et sollicitudine bibe. [19]Et dices ad populum terrae: Haec dicit Dominus Deus ad eos, qui habitant in Ierusalem in terra Israel: Panem suum in sollicitudine comedent et aquam suam in desolatione bibent, quia desolabitur terra a plenitudine sua propter violentiam omnium, qui habitant in ea; [20]et civitates, quae nunc habitantur, desolatae erunt, terraque deserta, et scietis quia ego Dominus». [21]Et factus est

s. Gk Syr: Heb *they* **t.** Gk Syr Tg: Heb *bring* **u.** Gk Syr Tg: Heb *his help*

False hopes

2 Pet 3:3–4 21And the word of the LORD came to me: 22"Son of man, what is
this proverb that you have about the land of Israel, saying, 'The
days grow long, and every vision comes to nought'? 23Tell them
therefore, 'Thus says the Lord GOD: I will put an end to this
proverb, and they shall no more use it as a proverb in Israel.' But
say to them, The days are at hand, and the fulfilment[v] of every
Lam 2:14 Ezek 13:23 vision. 24For there shall be no more any false vision or flattering
divination within the house of Israel. 25But I the LORD will speak
the word which I will speak, and it will be performed. It will no
longer be delayed, but in your days, O rebellious house, I will
speak the word and perform it, says the Lord GOD."
Amos 6:3 26Again the word of the LORD came to me: 27"Son of man,
behold, they of the house of Israel say, 'The vision that he sees is
for many days hence, and he prophesies of times far off.'
Jer 1:11–12 28Therefore say to them, Thus says the Lord GOD: None of my
words will be delayed any longer, but the word which I speak will
be performed, says the Lord GOD."

Jer 14:13–16; 23:9–40; 27:9–10, 16–18; 28

False prophets*

13 1The word of the LORD came to me: 2"Son of man,
prophesy against the prophets of Israel, prophesy[w] and say

12:21–28. The two popular proverbs ridicule those who make threats but never carry them out. Ezekiel discredits the false prophets whom he will denounce later on (chap. 13), and asserts that what the Lord is announcing refers not to something in the distant future; it is going to happen very soon (v. 25; cf. v. 28). When they see the predictions about the destruction of the temple and the deportation of the king come true, the exiles, too, will give credence to what Ezekiel tells them about grounds for hope.

***13:1–23.** There were men and women who claimed to be prophets and raised false hopes, assuring the people

sermo Domini ad me dicens: 22«Fili hominis, quod est proverbium istud vobis in terra Israel dicentibus: "In longum differentur dies, et peribit omnis visio"? 23Ideo dic ad eos: Haec dicit Dominus Deus: Quiescere faciam proverbium istud, neque vulgo dicetur ultra in Israel; et loquere ad eos quod appropinquaverint dies et sermo omnis visionis. 24Non enim erit ultra omnis visio vana neque divinatio ambigua in medio filiorum Israel, 25quia ego Dominus loquar; quodcumque locutus fuero verbum, et fiet: non prolongabitur amplius, sed in diebus vestris, domus exasperans, loquar verbum et faciam illud», dicit Dominus Deus. 26Et factus est sermo Domini ad me dicens: 27«Fili hominis, ecce domus Israel dicentium: "Visio, quam hic videt, in dies multos et in tempora longa iste prophetat"; 28propterea dic ad eos: Haec dicit Dominus Deus: Non differetur ultra omnis sermo meus; verbum, quod locutus fuero, complebitur», dicit Dominus Deus. **[13]** 1Et factus est sermo Domini ad me dicens: 2«Fili hominis, vaticinare ad prophetas Israel, qui prophetant; et dices prophetantibus de corde suo: Audite

v. Heb *word* **w.** Gk: Heb *who prophesy*

to those who prophesy out of their own minds: 'Hear the word of
the LORD!' 3Thus says the Lord GOD, Woe to the foolish prophets Jer 23:16
who follow their own spirit, and have seen nothing! 4Your Is 13:22 Jer 9:10;

that temple and city would come to no harm. They lulled good Israelites into a false sense of security by painting a distorted picture of the future, so that they failed to see the true scale of divine punishment, and therefore did not realize the need for conversion. As Jeremiah had done earlier (cf. Jer 23:16–32; 29:20–28), Ezekiel shows just how false those utterances are and condemns their divination. First he denounces the false prophets (vv. 1–16) and then he turns on the women who use magic arts to delude simple folk (vv. 17–23). The deception perpetrated by both these groups of people is a form of enslavement, whereas the word of God, even though it makes demands, serves to liberate people (vv. 20–23).

13:1–16. This oracle denounces false prophets because their visions have no substance to them, and their message is all lies.

They "follow their own spirit" (v. 3) and not that of the Lord. The essential feature of the true prophet is that he is moved by the spirit of God, as Ezekiel always was (cf. 2:2; 3:12; 8:3; 11:1, 24). False prophets, who "speak visions of their own mind" (Jer 23:16), speak without knowledge and utter oracles that have no validity.

"Like foxes among ruins" (v. 4)—a simile that shows what wretches they are: they prowl around, taking advantage of the people's misfortunes (cf. Is 13:22; Jer 9:10; 10:22; 51:37). The true prophet seeks only to do good: he is Israel's watchman who alerts the people to danger (cf. 3:16–21). St Gregory uses this passage to exhort pastors of the flock: "In times of peace, the mercenary may look after the flock as a good shepherd would; but when the wolf appears, his true spirit in the care of the flock will become clear. A wolf threatens the flock whenever a sinful tyrant oppresses the faithful and the lowly. He who seemed to be a good shepherd, but was not, will abandon the sheep and take to his heels, because he fears any danger to himself and is not strong enough to stand up to evil. He flees, not only to another place, but leaving the flock behind him untended and unguarded. He flees when he sees injustice and remains silent; he flees when he hides in silence. The prophet said of these bad shepherds: *You have not gone up into the breaches, or built up a wall for the house of Israel, that it might stand in battle in the day of the Lord* (Ezek 13:5)" (*Homiliae in Evangelia*, 1, 14, 2).

"They shall not be in the council of my people" (v. 9), that is, they cannot be accepted either as rulers or as ordinary people in the ranks of Israel. This barring order serves to show the Lord's special love for Israel, who is referred to as many as seven times in this chapter as "my people".

verbum Domini. 3Haec dicit Dominus Deus: Vae prophetis insipientibus, qui sequuntur spiritum suum et nihil vident! 4Quasi vulpes in ruinis prophetae tui, Israel, facti sunt. 5Non ascendistis confractiones

10:22; 51:37 Amos 5:18 · Jer 23:21 Ezek 12:24; 22:28

prophets have been like foxes among ruins, O Israel. 5You have
not gone up into the breaches, or built up a wall for the house of
Israel, that it might stand in battle in the day of the LORD. 6They
have spoken falsehood and divined a lie; they say, 'Says the
LORD,' when the LORD has not sent them, and yet they expect him
to fulfil their word. 7Have you not seen a delusive vision, and
uttered a lying divination, whenever you have said, 'Says the
LORD,' although I have not spoken?"
8Therefore thus says the Lord GOD: "Because you have uttered
delusions and seen lies, therefore behold, I am against you, says
the Lord GOD. 9My hand will be against the prophets who see
delusive visions and who give lying divinations; they shall not be
in the council of my people, nor be enrolled in the register of the
house of Israel, nor shall they enter the land of Israel; and you
shall know that I am the Lord GOD. 10Because, yea, because they
have misled my people, saying, 'Peace,' when there is no peace;
and because, when the people build a wall, these prophets daub it
with whitewash; 11say to those who daub it with whitewash that it
shall fall! There will be a deluge of rain of rain,[x] great hailstones
will fall, and a stormy wind break out; 12and when the wall falls,
will it not be said to you, 'Where is the daubing with which you

Ezra 2:59 Neh 7:5 Ps 69:28 · Jer 6:14; 8:15; 14:13; 23:17 Ezek 22:28 Mic 3:5 Mt 7:27; 23:27

"Peace, when there is no peace" (v. 10): this summarizes just how deluded the people are—so lulled into sleep that they cannot react. Jeremiah used the same form of denunciation (cf. Jer 6:14; 8:15; 14:13; 23:17) against false prophets who sought to ingratiate themselves with their hearers, with no concern for the truth or for the people's good.

"When the people build a wall, these prophets daub it with whitewash" (v. 10)—a metaphor exposing the falsity of these prophets. Jesus will use similar imagery to denounce the hypocrisy of some Pharisees who were "like white-washed tombs" (Mt 23:27). The true prophet, like the physician, never tries to disguise the disease; he must try to uproot it. Similarly, a spiritual guide

neque opposuistis murum pro domo Israel, ut staretis in proelio in die Domini. 6Vident vana et divinant mendacium dicentes: "Ait Dominus", cum Dominus non miserit eos; et exspectant, ut confirmet sermonem. 7Numquid non visionem cassam vidistis et divinationem mendacem locuti estis, et dicitis: "Ait Dominus", cum ego non sim locutus? 8Propterea haec dicit Dominus Deus: Quia locuti estis vana et vidistis mendacium, ideo ecce ego ad vos, ait Dominus Deus; 9et erit manus mea super prophetas, qui vident vana et divinant mendacium: in consilio populi mei non erunt et in scriptura domus Israel non scribentur nec in terram Israel ingredientur, et scietis quia ego Dominus Deus. 10Eo quod deceperint populum meum dicentes: "Pax", et non est pax; et ipse aedificabat parietem, illi autem liniebant eum calce. 11Dic ad eos, qui liniunt calce, quod casurus sit; erit enim imber inundans, et dabo lapides grandinis desuper irruentes et ventum procellae dissipantem. 12Siquidem ecce cecidit paries; numquid non dicetur vobis: "Ubi est litura, quam levistis?". 13Propterea haec dicit Dominus Deus: Et

x. Heb *rain and you*

daubed it?' [13]Therefore thus says the Lord GOD: I will make a
stormy wind break out in my wrath; and there shall be a deluge of
rain in my anger, and great hailstones in wrath to destroy it. [14]And
I will break down the wall that you have daubed with whitewash,
and bring it down to the ground, so that its foundation will be laid
bare; when it falls, you shall perish in the midst of it; and you
shall know that I am the LORD. [15]Thus will I spend my wrath upon
the wall, and upon those who have daubed it with whitewash; and
I will say to you, The wall is no more, nor those who daubed it,
[16]the prophets of Israel who prophesied concerning Jerusalem and
saw visions of peace for her, when there was no peace, says the
Lord GOD.

False prophetesses

[17]"And you, son of man, set your face against the daughters of Lev 20:27
your people, who prophesy out of their own minds; prophesy
against them [18]and say, Thus says the Lord GOD: Woe to the

---

must go further than simply identifying the sickness of the soul.

13:17–23. Severe though it is, this oracle shows a degree of understanding. The Lord does not condemn these women for sorcery (a form of idolatry, deserving of death: cf. Ex 22:18; Lev 20:27). He censures them for misleading simple folk. The prophet addresses them as "daughters of your people" and never refers to them as fortunetellers or by any other title that might be taken as an insult. By treating them in so mild a way, he seems to be more interested in their conversion that in condemning them.

"Handfuls of barley" (v. 19). Necessity does not justify what these women are doing, though in some way the prophet seems to excuse them. The false prophets will incur severe punishment: "You shall perish … and you shall know that I am the Lord" (v. 14). The only punishment meted out to these women will be to have no more visions, and they will come to know the Lord when he sets the people free from their deception (v. 23). "Let us pray that God will deliver us from those teachers, wherever they are to be found, who preach only what they think their listeners want to hear, who wound and divide the Church, who seek their own happiness more than they strive to love the Lord" (Origen, *Homiliae in Ezechielem*, 3, 6).

erumpere faciam spiritum tempestatum in indignatione mea, et imber inundans in furore meo erit, et
lapides grandinis in ira in consumptionem; [14]et destruam parietem, quem levistis calce, et adaequabo
eum terrae, et revelabitur fundamentum eius, et cadet, et consumemini in medio eius et scietis quia ego
sum Dominus. [15]Et complebo indignationem meam in pariete et in his, qui leverunt eum calce,
dicamque vobis: Non est paries, et non sunt qui leverunt eum; [16]prophetae Israel, qui prophetant ad
Ierusalem et vident ei visionem pacis, et non est pax, ait Dominus Deus. [17]Et tu, fili hominis, pone
faciem tuam contra filias populi tui, quae prophetant de corde suo, et vaticinare super eas [18]et dic: Haec
dicit Dominus Deus: Vae, quae consuunt fascias pro omni articulo manus et faciunt velamina pro capite

women who sew magic bands upon all wrists, and make veils for
the heads of persons of every stature, in the hunt for souls! Will
you hunt down souls belonging to my people, and keep other
1 Sam 9:7 souls alive for your profit? [19]You have profaned me among my
people for handfuls of barley and for pieces of bread, putting to
death persons who should not die and keeping alive persons who
should not live, by your lies to my people, who listen to lies.

[20]"Wherefore thus says the Lord GOD: Behold, I am against
your magic bands with which you hunt the souls,[y] and I will tear
them from your arms; and I will let the souls that you hunt go
free[z] like birds. [21]Your veils also I will tear off, and deliver my
people out of your hand, and they shall be no more in your hand
as prey; and you shall know that I am the LORD. [22]Because you
have disheartened the righteous falsely, although I have not
disheartened him, and you have encouraged the wicked, that he
should not turn from his wicked way to save his life; [23]therefore
you shall no more see delusive visions nor practise divination; I
will deliver my people out of your hand. Then you will know that
I am the LORD."

Ezek 8:1; 20:1–4; 33:31

Idolatry denounced

14 [1]Then came certain of the elders of Israel to me; and sat
before me. [2]And the word of the LORD came to me: [3]"Son

14:1–23. The two oracles in this chapter begin with the form of words we have seen already: "The word of the Lord came to me" (vv. 2, 12). The first one (vv. 2–11) condemns idolatry in all its forms, including that of the false prophet who makes predictions in the name of the Lord (v. 9). The second (vv. 12–23) answers a question raised by many Israelites in connexion with the fate of the city and the kingdom: Will the just have to pay for the sins of the wicked? And if there are good people still in Israel, will their righteousness not suffice

omnis staturae ad capiendas animas! Numquid capietis animas de populo meo et vivificabitis animas vobis? [19]Et violastis me ad populum meum pro pugillo hordei et fragmento panis, ut interficeretis animas, quae mori non deberent, et vivificastis animas, quae non deberent vivere, mentientes populo meo credenti mendaciis. [20]Propter hoc haec dicit Dominus Deus: Ecce ego ad fascias vestras, quibus vos capitis animas quasi volatilia, et disrumpam eas de brachiis vestris; et dimittam animas, quas vos cepistis, animas quasi volatilia, [21]et disrumpam velamina vestra et liberabo populum meum de manu vestra, neque erunt ultra in manibus vestris ad praedandum, et scietis quia ego Dominus. [22]Pro eo quod maerere fecistis cor iusti mendaciter, quem ego non contristavi, et confortastis manus impii, ut non reverteretur a via sua mala et viveret, [23]propterea vana non videbitis et divinationes non divinabitis amplius, et eruam populum meum de manu vestra, et scietis quia ego Dominus». **[14]** [1]Et venerunt ad me viri seniorum Israel et sederunt coram me. [2]Et factus est sermo Domini ad me dicens: [3]«Fili hominis, viri isti posuerunt idola sua in cordibus suis et scandalum iniquitatis suae statuerunt contra

y. Gk Syr: Heb *souls for birds* **z.** Cn: Heb *the souls*

of man, these men have taken their idols into their hearts, and set
the stumbling block of their iniquity before their faces; should I let Ezek 18;
myself be inquired of at all by them? [4]Therefore speak to them, 33:10–20

---

to ensure the deliverance of all? Ezekiel's reply is a vigorous assertion of his doctrine of personal responsibility, which he will repeat with other nuances in chapters 18 and 33.

The presence of the elders (v. 1), as in 8:1, serves to emphasize the solemn nature of these oracles.

14:1–11. Idolatry rears its head again among both the exiles and those left behind in the city. The worst aspect of it is that both groups want to combine it with their worship of the Lord, and they go so far as to seek his counsel. St John of the Cross interprets these verses in an intriguing way: "Thus Ezekiel prophesied in the name of the Lord; and God spoke, according to his spirit, through the mouth of one who sought to follow the path of the Lord: [The man who] *comes to a prophet to inquire for himself of me, I the Lord will answer him myself; and I will set my face against that man, I will make him a sign and a byword and cut him off from the midst of my people; and you shall know that I am the Lord. And if the prophet be deceived and speak a word, I, the Lord, have deceived that prophet.* He will lose the Lord's favour and be deceived. That is what is meant by *I the Lord will answer him myself; and I will set my face against that man:* that man will be deprived of God's grace and favour, which makes it clear that the deception is the result of God's withdrawal. Then the devil will speak and respond according to the man's will and desires, and because he is satisfied, and the sayings and messages that he hears suit him, he will allow himself to be greatly deceived" (*Ascent of Mount Carmel*, 2, 21, 13).

"Idols into their hearts" (vv. 3, 4, 7): the Hebrew word for idols, *gillulîm*, includes both the false gods of Canaan that the people of Jerusalem revered, and the Babylonian gods, worshipped by the exiles in Babylon. The term can refer to graven images, rites, etc. that drew the Israelites away from the true God and caused defilement (cf. 6:8–10; 20; 23). By talking about taking idols into their hearts and "setting up the stumbling block of iniquity before one's face", Ezekiel is lamenting and denouncing the sin of idolatry in general and the ritual defilement that results from it.

"That they may be my people and I may be their God" (v. 11)—a typical Priestly tradition way of referring to the Covenant (cf. Ex 6:7; Lev 26:12). It is also to be found in Jeremiah (cf. Jer 7:23; 11:4; 30:22; 32:38), but it is Ezekiel who uses it most (36:28; 37:27; etc.), in reference to the definitive restoration that will take place after the exile. It serves to underline the indissoluble nature of the Covenant; even if the people commit grave sins and deserve to be severely punished, the Covenant will still stand.

faciem suam; numquid interrogatus respondebo eis? [4]Propter hoc loquere eis et dices ad eos: Haec dicit

and say to them, Thus says the Lord GOD: Any man of the house
of Israel who takes his idols into his heart and sets the stumbling
block of his iniquity before his face, and yet comes to the prophet,
I the LORD will answer him myself[a] because of the multitude of
2 Thess 2:11–12 his idols, 5that I may lay hold of the hearts of the house of Israel,
who are all estranged from me through their idols.

6"Therefore say to the house of Israel, Thus says the Lord GOD:
Repent and turn away from your idols; and turn away your faces
from all your abominations. 7For any one of the house of Israel, or
of the strangers that sojourn in Israel, who separates himself from
me, taking his idols into his heart and putting the stumbling block
of his iniquity before his face, and yet comes to a prophet to
inquire for himself of me, I the LORD will answer him myself;
Lev 17:10 Num 26:10 8and I will set my face against that man, I will make him a sign
and a byword and cut him off from the midst of my people; and
you shall know that I am the LORD. 9And if the prophet be
deceived and speak a word, I, the LORD, have deceived that
prophet, and I will stretch out my hand against him, and will
Rev 4:7 destroy him from the midst of my people Israel. 10And they shall
bear their punishment—the punishment of the prophet and the
Ex 6:7 Lev 26:12 punishment of the inquirer shall be alike—11that the house of
Jer 7:23; 11:4; Israel may go no more astray from me, nor defile themselves any
30:22; 32:38 more with all their transgressions, but that they may be my people
Ezek 36:28; 37:27 and I may be their God, says the Lord GOD."

Individual responsibility. The righteous will be saved

Lev 26:26 12*And the word of the LORD came to me: 13"Son of man, when a
land sins against me by acting faithlessly, and I stretch out my

---

14:12–23. When Jerusalem is destroyed, the just will be saved, but they will not be able to help their relatives; the wicked will be condemned, but

Dominus Deus: Omnis homo de domo Israel, qui posuerit idola sua in corde suo et scandalum iniquitatis suae statuerit contra faciem suam et venerit ad prophetam interrogans per eum me, ego Dominus respondebo ei per me pro multitudine idolorum suorum, 5ut capiam domum Israel in corde suo, quo recesserunt a me in cunctis idolis suis. 6Propterea dic ad domum Israel: Haec dicit Dominus Deus: Convertimini et recedite ab idolis vestris et ab universis contaminationibus vestris avertite facies vestras. 7Quia omnis homo de domo Israel et de advenis, quicumque advena fuerit in Israel, si alienatus fuerit a me et posuerit idola sua in corde suo et scandalum iniquitatis suae statuerit contra faciem suam et venerit ad prophetam, ut interroget per eum me, ego Dominus respondebo ei per me; 8et ponam faciem meam contra hominem illum et faciam eum in exemplum et in proberbium et disperdam eum de medio populi mei, et scietis quia ego Dominus. 9Et propheta cum erraverit et locutus fuerit verbum, ego Dominus decepi prophetam illum et extendam manum meam contra eum et delebo eum de medio populi mei Israel. 10Et portabunt iniquitatem suam: sicut iniquitas interrogantis, sic et iniquitas

a. Cn Compare Tg: Heb uncertain

hand against it, and break its staff of bread and send famine upon Gen 6:9; 7:1;
it, and cut off from it man and beast, [14]even if these three men, 18:22–23
Noah, Daniel,* and Job, were in it, they would deliver but their Job 1:1 Ezek 28:3

their children will not. The teaching on personal responsibility in this oracle (cf. chaps. 18 and 33) uses sapiential techniques. Four similar cases are set out, in line with four misfortunes that epitomize the siege and destruction of Jerusalem—famine, the sword, wild beasts and pestilence. In each case the scene is set in the same way, and the argument develops in the same way and comes to the same conclusion. The moral is clearly drawn at the end: the Lord cannot but impose exemplary punishment on the Israelites, but a "remnant" will survive; God's promises will stay in place for them, and future generations will see that the Lord did not act without cause against Jerusalem (v. 23).

"Noah, Daniel, and Job": Noah is best known from the account of the great flood, where he is described as "righteous" (cf. Gen 7:1; 6:8); Daniel is probably the name of an ancient Canaanite king of the fourteenth century BC, famous for his uprightness and known to us from Ungarit writings. The book of Daniel, written after Ezekiel's time, borrowed the name on account of the man's proverbial probity. Job was also a legendary character, remembered in the book that bears his name as being "blameless and upright" (Job 1:1). All three had this reputation for uprightness, and all three were non-Israelites. By mentioning them here, it seems very likely that Ezekiel wants to give his teaching on personal responsibility a universal character; and he is acknowledging that people outside Israel are able to lead upright lives: "The covenant with Noah remains in force during the times of the Gentiles, until the universal proclamation of the Gospel. (cf. Gen 9:16; Lk 21:24; *Dei Verburn* 3). The Bible venerates several great figures among the Gentiles: Abel the just, the king-priest Melchisedek—a figure of Christ—and the upright 'Noah, Daniel, and Job' (Ezek 14:14). Scripture thus expresses the heights of sanctity that can be reached by those who live according to the covenant of Noah, waiting for Christ to 'gather into one the children of God who are scattered abroad' (Jn 11:52)" (*Catechism of the Catholic Church*, 58).

Still, the passage is a call to the faithful to fulfil commitments they made to the Lord: "Those righteous men, who were wholly just, could not free their own children from slavery: how shall we enter the Kingdom of God if we are not faithful to the pure, unstained baptism that we have received? Who will be our advocate if we have no righteous and holy deeds to our name?" (Pseudo-Clement, *Epistula II ad Corinthios*, 6, 9).

prophetae erit, [11]ut non erret ultra domus Israel a me neque polluatur in universis praevaricationibus suis, sed sit mihi in populum, et ego sim eis in Deum», ait Dominus Deus. [12]Et factus est sermo Domini ad me dicens: [13]«Fili hominis, terra cum peccaverit mihi, ut praevaricetur praevaricans, extendam manum meam super eam et conteram virgam panis eius et immittam in eam famem et interficiam de ea hominem et iumentum; [14]et si fuerint tres viri isti in medio eius, Noe, Danel et Iob, ipsi iustitia sua

own lives by their righteousness, says the Lord God. [15]If I cause
wild beasts to pass through the land, and they ravage it, and it be
made desolate, so that no man may pass through because of the
beasts; [16]even if these three men were in it, as I live, says the Lord
God, they would deliver neither sons nor daughters; they alone
Lev 26:25 would be delivered, but the land would be desolate. [17]Or if I bring
a sword upon that land, and say, Let a sword go through the land;
and I cut off from it man and beast; [18]though these three men were
in it, as I live, says the Lord God, they would deliver neither sons
nor daughters, but they alone would be delivered. [19]Or if I send a
pestilence into that land, and pour out my wrath upon it with
blood, to cut off from it man and beast; [20]even if Noah, Daniel,
and Job were in it, as I live, says the Lord God, they would deliver
neither son nor daughter; they would deliver but their own lives by
their righteousness.

Ezek 5:17; 33:27 [21]"For thus says the Lord God: How much more when I send
Rev 6:8 upon Jerusalem my four sore acts of judgment, sword, famine,
Ezek 6:8; evil beasts, and pestilence, to cut off from it man and beast! [22]Yet,
12:16 if there should be left in it any survivors to lead out sons and
daughters, when they come forth to you, and you see their ways
and their doings, you will be consoled for the evil that I have
brought upon Jerusalem, for all that I have brought upon it. [23]They
will console you, when you see their ways and their doings; and
you shall know that I have not done without cause all that I have
done in it, says the Lord God."

Ps 80:9–17 **The useless wood**

Is 5:1 Jer 2:21 Hos 10:1 15 [1]And the word of the Lord came to me: [2]"Son of man, how
does the wood of the vine surpass any wood, the vine

15:1–8. The vine (cf. 17:6–10), which is to be found all over Israel and the whole Mediterranean world, is used in the Bible as a metaphor for the chosen people. Isaiah has a lovely "song of the vineyard" (Is 5:1–7); other prophets

liberabunt animas suas, ait Dominus Deus. [15]Quod si et bestias pessimas induxero super terram, ut
absque liberis faciant eam, et fuerit deserta, in qua nullus pertranseat propter bestias, [16]tres viri isti si
fuerint in ea, vivo ego, dicit Dominus Deus, quia nec filios nec filias liberabunt, sed ipsi soli
liberabuntur, terra autem desolabitur. [17]Vel si gladium induxero super terram illam et dixero gladio:
Transi per terram, et interfecero de ea hominem et iumentum, [18]et tres viri isti fuerint in medio eius,
vivo ego, dicit Dominus Deus, non liberabunt filios neque filias, sed ipsi soli liberabuntur. [19]Vel si
pestilentiam immisero super terram illam et effudero indignationem meam super eam in sanguine, ut
auferam ex ea hominem et iumentum, [20]et Noe et Danel et Iob fuerint in medio eius, vivo ego, dicit
Dominus Deus, quia filium et filiam non liberabunt, sed ipsi iustitia sua liberabunt animas suas.
[21]Quoniam haec dicit Dominus Deus: Quod si et quattuor iudicia mea pessima, gladium et famem et
bestias malas et pestilentiam misero in Ierusalem, ut interficiam de ea hominem et pecus, [22]tamen

branch which is among the trees of the forest? [3]Is wood taken
from it to make anything? Do men take a peg from it to hang any
vessel on? [4]Lo, it is given to the fire for fuel; when the fire has
consumed both ends of it, and the middle of it is charred, is it
useful for anything? [5]Behold, when it was whole, it was used for
nothing; how much less, when the fire has consumed it and it is
charred, can it ever be used for anything! [6]Therefore thus says the Ps 80:8
Lord GOD: Like the wood of the vine among the trees of the Ezek 17:6; 19:10–14
forest, which I have given to the fire for fuel, so will I give up the
inhabitants of Jerusalem. [7]And I will set my face against them;
though they escape from the fire, the fire shall yet consume them;
and you will know that I am the LORD, when I set my face against
them. [8]And I will make the land desolate, because they have acted
faithlessly, says the Lord GOD."

---

have seen the luxuriant or barren vine as a symbol of the wealth or wretchedness of the chosen people (cf. Hos 10:1; Jer 2:21; Ps 80:8–16). All have made reference to its fruit, abundant or meagre, sweet or bitter. But this poem focuses on the plant itself, on the uselessness of its wood and on the fact that its branches become firewood. Jesus used the same metaphor to show that a person needs to be joined to him in order to have union with God: "If a man does not abide in me, he is cast forth as a branch and withers; and the branches are gathered, thrown into the fire and burned".

The first part of the poem (vv. 1–5) says that wood from the vine is of little use, and the second (vv. 6–8) applies this lesson to the city of David. Thus the poem is a vivid reflection on the doom announced in the previous chapters. Up to this, Ezekiel has used literary genres frequently used by the prophets—oracles, visions, symbolic gestures, etc.; now he provides a piece of poetry to make his hearers realize that destruction is imminent, and nothing can be done to avert it.

relinquetur in ea salvatio educentium filios et filias: ecce ipsi egredientur ad vos, et videbitis viam eorum et opera eorum et consolabimini super malo, quod induxi in Ierusalem in omnibus, quae importavi super eam. [23]Et consolabuntur vos, cum videritis viam eorum et opera eorum, et cognoscetis quod non frustra fecerim omnia, quae feci in ea», ait Dominus Deus. **[15]** [1]Et factus est sermo Domini ad me dicens: / [2]«Fili hominis, quid habet lignum vitis / prae omnibus lignis sarmentorum, / quae sunt inter ligna silvarum? / [3]Numquid tolletur de ea lignum, / ut fiat opus, / aut fabricabitur de ea paxillus, / ut dependeat in eo quodcumque vas? / [4]Ecce igni datum est in escam, / utramque partem eius consumpsit ignis, / et medietas eius adusta est; / numquid utile erit ad opus? / [5]Etiam cum esset integrum, / non erat aptum ad opus; / quanto magis cum ignis illud devoraverit et combusserit, / nihil ex eo fiet operis. / [6]Propterea haec dicit Dominus Deus: / Quomodo lignum vitis inter ligna silvarum, / quod dedi igni ad devorandum, / sic tradam habitatores Ierusalem. / [7]Et ponam faciem meam in eos: / de igne egressi sunt, / et ignis consumet eos. / Et scietis quia ego Dominus, / cum posuero faciem meam in eos / [8]et dedero terram inviam et desolatam, / eo quod praevaricatores exstiterint», / dicit Dominus Deus.

Is 1:21
Jer 2:2; 3:6
Ezek 23;
Hos 1:3
Mt 22:2–14;

Jerusalem, the unfaithful wife*

16 [1]Again the word of the LORD came to me: [2]"Son of man,
make known to Jerusalem her abominations, [3]and say, Thus

***16:1—19:14.** In these chapters Ezekiel announces the sentence passed on Israel and Judah on account of the transgressions and sins they have been piling up. He does this by imagining a formal trial (*rîb*) in which the charges are described by a series of allegories. First there is the story of the unfaithful and evil wife, who stands for Israel (chap. 16); then comes the allegory of the eagles, symbolizing the deportation: Nebuchadnezzar seems to destroy everything before him, but the Lord comes on the scene and sets about reassembling the broken pieces (chap. 17); thirdly, the metaphor of the father and son is used to reiterate teaching about personal responsibility (chap. 18); and, finally, comes the allegory of the lioness and her cubs—a lament over the plight of the exiles in Babylon (chap. 19).

***16:1–43.** The prophet Hosea was the first to use the metaphor of the wanton wife to charge Israel with her infidelity (Hos 1–3); Jeremiah uses the imagery of marriage to describe the Covenant and how Israel came to break it (Jer 2:2). Ezekiel, here and in chapters 20 and 23, is the one who develops the metaphor most. The wife is Jerusalem, depicted with negative features from her birth onwards (vv. 1–5) and then completely transformed into the most beautiful of princesses (vv. 6–14). However, she proved unfaithful and committed the most vile sins of adultery with the empires round about (vv. 15–34). All this, a mixture of fact and metaphor, paves the way for the sentence that must be passed: "I will judge you as women who break wedlock" (v. 38); she will become the prey of the nations that she adulated (vv. 35–41). But the end is not destruction (vv. 42–43), as one would have expected; it is the start of a new phase (cf. 16:59–63). Ezekiel, who is addressing the exiles, once again opens the door to hope in an ultimate restoration (vv. 42–43).

16:1–5. "Your father was an Amorite, and your mother a Hittite" (v. 3). Jerusalem had, in fact, belonged to the Canaanites until David conquered it; these would have included the Amorites, a Semitic people (cf. Num 21:13), and the Hittites, who had come from Asia Minor (cf. Gen 23:16). Ezekiel is not so much concerned about historical accuracy (cf. Deut 7:1 and par.) as in pointing out the pagan origins of the holy city, to make it clear that all its qualities and all its dignity derive solely from the Lord. The practices mentioned in v. 4 were ancient customs to do with the care of newborn babies. The point being made is that in addition to having an obscure origin, Jerusalem began life utterly alone.

---

[16] [1]Et factus est sermo Domini ad me dicens: [2]«Fili hominis, notas fac Ierusalem abominationes suas [3]et dices: Haec dicit Dominus Deus ad Ierusalem: Radix tua et generatio tua de terra Chanaan, pater

25:1–13;
says the Lord GOD to Jerusalem: Your origin and your birth are of Jn 3:29
the land of the Canaanites; your father was an Amorite, and your Eph 5:25–33 Rev 17; Is 1:21
mother a Hittite. 4And as for your birth, on the day you were born Jer 2:2; 3:6
your navel string was not cut, nor were you washed with water to Ezek 23 Hos 1:3
cleanse you, nor rubbed with salt, nor swathed with bands. 5No Rev 17
eye pitied you, to do any of these things to you out of compassion
for you; but you were cast out on the open field, for you were
abhorred, on the day that you were born.
6"And when I passed by you, and saw you weltering in your
blood, I said to you in your blood, 'Live, 7and grow up[b] like a Hos 2:5

16:6–34. The charge of infidelity against Jerusalem lies in the endowments it received from God (vv. 6–14) and its history of wickedness—evidence of the fact that it has persistently abused God's gifts (vv. 15–34). Although the charge has historical basis, the passage is not meant to be a detailed catalogue; the point being made is that the city had a history of sin and infidelity.

"I passed by you" (v. 6): when God passes by, he brings salvation; here he turns an abandoned child into the most beautiful of women, the envy of all her peers. St John of the Cross will apply this to what happens when the Lord passes by the soul (*Spiritual Canticle*, 23, 6) and the things said here help us to see the relationship between the soul and God as a love story. St Thérèse of Lisieux mentions Ezekiel in this connexion: "I was at the most troubling age for girls. But the Lord passed by, and did for me as he said he would do, in the words of the prophet Ezekiel: 'When he passed by me, Jesus saw that I was at the age for love. He pledged his troth to me, and I became *his* … He wrapped his cloak about me, and anointed me with perfume; he dressed me in embroidered cloth and silk, and gave me gold and silver and precious jewels to wear … He gave me fine flour and honey and oil to eat … and I grew more and more beautiful, until I was like a queen …' (cf. Ezek 16:6–13). Jesus did all these things for me. I could repeat, again, all the words that I have just written, and show how he has fulfilled each, one by one, in me. But all the graces that I have referred to elsewhere are proof enough" (*Autobiographical Writings*, 5, 47, r).

"You trusted in your beauty, and played the harlot" (v. 15): breaking away from God, particularly the sin of idolatry, was called prostitution by the

tuus Amorraeus et mater tua Hetthaea. 4Et quando nata es, in die ortus tui non est praecisus umbilicus tuus, et in aqua non es lota in emundationem nec sale salita nec involuta pannis. 5Non pepercit super te oculus, ut faceret tibi unum de his, miseratus tui, sed proiecta es super faciem terrae in abiectione animae tuae in die, qua nata es. 6Praeteriens autem te, vidi te palpitare in sanguine tuo et dixi tibi, cum esses in sanguine tuo: Vive. Dixi, inquam, tibi: In sanguine tuo vive. 7Crescentem quasi germen agri dedi te, et crevisti et grandis effecta es et pervenisti ad mundum muliebrem: ubera tua intumuerunt,

b. Gk Syr: *I made you a myriad*

Ex 19:1,5 Deut 23:1 Ruth 3:9

plant of the field.' And you grew up and became tall and arrived at
full maidenhood;[c] your breasts were formed, and your hair had
grown; yet you were naked and bare.
8"When I passed by you again and looked upon you, behold,
you were at the age for love; and I spread my skirt over you, and

---

prophets who used marriage as a metaphor for the Covenant (cf. Hos 2:18–25; Jer 2:2–3). Ezekiel accentuates the features of this sin by pointing out that, instead of being paid for her harlotry, Jerusalem took the initiative: she gave herself over to her lovers, that is, other gods, and, worse still, presented to them the finery that the Lord had bestowed on her (v. 33): that was how Jerusalem behaved towards Egypt (v. 26), Assyria (v. 28) and Babylon (v. 29). The prophet shows that, since Jerusalem's history could not have been worse, it would be difficult to devise a punishment fitted to such a crime. However, while spelling out the whole charge, Ezekiel is able to see the wonderful rehabilitation that will take place once her punishment is over. Some of the things he says have been read as a prophecy about Christ: "The Daughter of Sion did not repay the Lord for the gifts she received from his bounty. The Father washed her clean with his blood; she covered his son with spittle. He dressed her in the purple robes of kings; she wrapped him in a rag woven from jibes and jeers. He crowned her with glory; she crowned him with thorns. He gave her milk and honey to eat; she gave him gall to drink. He poured out pure wine for her; she handed him a sponge dipped in vinegar. He made her welcome in his cities; she cast him out into the wilderness. He clothed her feet in sandals; she made him limp barefoot to Golgotha. He gave her a sapphire brooch to wear on her breast; she pierced his side with a spear. When she committed outrages against the servants of God and killed the prophets, and endured exile in Babylon as a punishment, he led her home to freedom when the day of her chastisement was ended" (St Ephraem of Nisibi, *Commentarii in Diatessaron*, 18, 1). Pseudo-Macarius, for his part, applies this text of Ezekiel to every Christian soul that has been unfaithful to divine grace. After quoting and making a précis of 16:6–15, he exclaims: "Thus does the Spirit reprove the soul who, by his grace, had come to know God; the soul who had been forgiven all his past sins, and adorned with the precious gifts of the Holy Spirit, and given divine and heavenly food to eat; the soul who, in spite of his knowledge of the Lord, turned his back on righteous living, and was cast out of the life in which he had once rejoiced because his deeds were not just, and he was judged lacking in love for Christ, his heavenly spouse" (*Homiliae spirituales,* 15, 4).

et pilus tuus germinavit; sed eras nuda et confusione plena. 8Et transivi per te et vidi te; et ecce tempus tuum, tempus amantium. Et expandi amictum meum super te et operui ignominiam tuam; et iuravi tibi

c. Cn: Heb *ornament of ornaments*

covered your nakedness: yea, I plighted my troth to you and
entered into a covenant with you, says the Lord GOD, and you
became mine. 9Then I bathed you with water and washed off your
blood from you, and anointed you with oil. 10I clothed you also
with embroidered cloth and shod you with leather, I swathed you
in fine linen and covered you with silk. 11And I decked you with
ornaments, and put bracelets on your arms, and a chain on your
neck. 12And I put a ring on your nose, and earrings in your ears,
and a beautiful crown upon your head. 13Thus you were decked Deut 32:12
with gold and silver; and your raiment was of fine linen, and silk,
and embroidered cloth; you ate fine flour and honey and oil. You
grew exceedingly beautiful, and came to regal estate. 14And your Lam 2:15
renown went forth among the nations because of your beauty, for
it was perfect through the splendour which I had bestowed upon
you, says the Lord GOD.

15“But you trusted in your beauty, and played the harlot Deut 31:16; 32:15; Is 57:8
because of your renown, and lavished your harlotries on any Jer 2:2–3
passer-by. 16You took some of your garments, and made for Hos 2:18–25
yourself gaily decked shrines, and on them played the harlot; the Ex 32:2
like has never been, nor ever shall be. 17You also took your fair Hos 2:6,10
jewels of my gold and of my silver, which I had given you, and
made for yourself images of men, and with them played the
harlot; 18and you took your embroidered garments to cover them, Hos 2:8
and set my oil and my incense before them. 19Also my bread
which I gave you—I fed you with fine flour and oil and honey—
you set before them for a pleasing odour, says the Lord GOD.[d] Lev 18:21
20And you took your sons and your daughters, whom you had Jer 7:31 Ezek 20:26,31;
borne to me, and these you sacrificed to them to be devoured. 23:37

---

et ingressus sum pactum tecum, ait Dominus Deus, et facta es mea. 9Et lavi te aqua et emundavi
sanguinem tuum ex te et unxi te oleo; 10et vestivi te discoloribus et calceavi te calceis corii delphini
et cinxi te bysso et indui te serico. 11Et ornavi te ornamento et dedi armillas in manibus tuis et torquem
circa collum tuum; 12et dedi inaurem super os tuum et circulos auribus tuis et coronam decoris in capite
tuo. 13Et ornata es auro et argento et vestita es bysso et serico et multicoloribus. Similam et mel et
oleum comedisti et decora facta es vehementer nimis et apta ad regnum. 14Et egressum est nomen tuum
in gentes propter speciem tuam, quia perfecta eras in decore meo, quem posueram super te, dicit
Dominus Deus. 15Et habens fiduciam in pulchritudine tua fornicata es in nomine tuo et exposuisti
fornicationem tuam omni transeunti, quisquis fuerit. 16Et sumens de vestimentis tuis fecisti tibi excelsa
variegata et fornicata es super eis, sicut non est factum neque futurum est. 17Et tulisti vasa decoris tui
de auro meo atque argento meo, quae dedi tibi, et fecisti tibi imagines masculinas et fornicata es in eis.
18Et sumpsisti vestimenta tua multicoloria et operuisti illas et oleum meum et thymiama meum posuisti
coram eis. 19Et panem meum, quem dedi tibi, similam et oleum et mel, quibus enutrivi te, posuisti in
conspectu eorum in odorem suavitatis, et factum est, ait Dominus Deus. 20Et tulisti filios tuos et filias
tuas, quas generasti mihi, et immolasti eis ad devorandum. Numquid parva est fornicatio tua?

d. Syr: Heb *and it was, says the Lord GOD*

Were your harlotries so small a matter [21]that you slaughtered my
children and delivered them up as an offering by fire to them?
[22]And in all your abominations and your harlotries you did not
remember the days of your youth, when you were naked and bare,
weltering in your blood.

[23]"And after all your wickedness (woe, woe to you! says the
Deut 12:2 Lord GOD), [24]you built yourself a vaulted chamber, and made
yourself a lofty place in every square; [25]at the head of every street
you built your lofty place and prostituted your beauty, offering
Is 30; 31 yourself to any passer-by, and multiplying your harlotry. [26]You
also played the harlot with the Egyptians, your lustful neighbours,
multiplying your harlotry, to provoke me to anger. [27]Behold,
therefore, I stretched out my hand against you, and diminished
your allotted portion, and delivered you to the greed of your
enemies, the daughters of the Philistines, who were ashamed of
2 Kings 16:7–18; 21:1–18 your lewd behaviour. [28]You played the harlot also with the
Assyrians, because you were insatiable; yea, you played the harlot
2 Chron 28:16–21; 33:1–10 with them, and still you were not satisfied. [29]You multiplied your
harlotry also with the trading land of Chaldea; and even with this
Jer 2:18,36 you were not satisfied.

[30]"How lovesick is your heart, says the Lord GOD, seeing you
Is 1:21; 57:8 did all these things, the deeds of a brazen harlot; [31]building your
Jer 2:20; 3:2,6,20 vaulted chamber at the head of every street, and making your lofty
Ezek 23:3,8 place in every square. Yet you were not like a harlot, because you
Hos 1:2; 8:9 scorned hire. [32]Adulterous wife, who receives strangers instead of
her husband! [33]Men give gifts to all harlots; but you gave your
gifts to all your lovers, bribing them to come to you from every
side for your harlotries. [34]So you were different from other

---

[21]Immolasti filios meos et dedisti illos consecrans eis. [22]Et post omnes abominationes tuas et fornicationes non es recordata dierum adulescentiae tuae, quando eras nuda et confusione plena, palpitans in sanguine tuo. [23]Et accidit post omnem malitiam tuam—vae, vae tibi!, ait Dominus Deus— [24]et aedificasti tibi fornicem et fecisti tibi excelsum in cunctis plateis; [25]ad omne caput viae aedificasti locum elevatum tuum et abominabilem fecisti decorem tuum et divisisti pedes tuos omni transeunti et multiplicasti fornicationes tuas. [26]Et fornicata es cum filiis Aegypti vicinis tuis magnorum membrorum et multiplicasti fornicationem tuam ad irritandum me. [27]Ecce ego extendi manum meam super te et imminui portionem tuam et dedi te in animam odientium te, filiarum Palaestinarum, quae erubescunt in via tua scelerata. [28]Et fornicata es in filiis Assyriorum, eo quod necdum fueris expleta; et, postquam fornicata es, nec sic es satiata. [29]Et multiplicasti fornicationem tuam usque ad terram mercatorum Chaldaeam, et nec sic satiata es. [30]In quo mundabo cor tuum, ait Dominus Deus, cum faceres omnia haec opera mulieris meretricis et procacis? [31]Quia fabricasti fornicem tuum in capite omnis viae et excelsum tuum fecisti in omni platea; nec facta es quasi meretrix, quia sprevisti pretium. [32]Mulier adultera loco viri sui accipit alienos. [33]Omnibus meretricibus dantur mercedes, tu autem dedisti mercedes cunctis amatoribus tuis et donabas eis, ut intrarent ad te undique ad fornicandum tecum. [34]Factumque in te est contra consuetudinem mulierum in fornicationibus tuis, et post te non sunt fornicati; in eo enim quod dedisti mercedes et mercedes non accepisti, factum est in te contrarium.

women in your harlotries: none solicited you to play the harlot;
and you gave hire, while no hire was given to you; therefore you
were different.
35“Wherefore, O harlot, hear the word of the LORD: 36Thus says Ex 21:12
the Lord GOD, Because your shame was laid bare and your Lev 20:10; 24:17
nakedness uncovered in your harlotries with your lovers, and Deut 22:23–24
because of all your idols, and because of the blood of your
children that you gave to them, 37therefore, behold, I will gather Hos 2 12
all your lovers, with whom you took pleasure, all those you loved Rev 17:5–6,16
and all those you loathed; I will gather them against you from
every side, and will uncover your nakedness to them, that they
may see all your nakedness. 38And I will judge you as women
who break wedlock and shed blood are judged, and bring upon
you the blood of wrath and jealousy. 39And I will give you into the Rev 17:16
hand of your lovers, and they shall throw down your vaulted
chamber and break down your lofty places; they shall strip you of
your clothes and take your fair jewels, and leave you naked and Hos 2:5
bare. 40They shall bring up a host against you, and they shall stone Jn 8:5,7
you and cut you to pieces with their swords. 41And they shall burn 2 Kings 25:9 Jer 39:8;52:13

16:35–43. The law of retaliation or vengeance underlies the punishments announced in vv. 36–38: the peoples and gods to whom Jerusalem gave herself over, will be her executioners; the blood she spilt will bring down bloody retribution (cf. Ex 21:12; Lev 24:17); her adultery will be punished by stoning (Lev 20:10; Deut 22:23–24).

“All those you loved and all those you loathed” (v. 37): the use of opposites like this is a common Semitic way of indicating preference for the first-mentioned, while still accepting the second-mentioned, in this case those “loathed”. For example, Jacob “loves” Rachel but “hates” Leah (cf. Gen 29: 30–31); and Jesus will even say that a person who “does not hate his own father and mother … cannot be my disciple” (Lk 14:26).

“Have you not committed lewdness …” (v. 43): this translation follows the Hebrew, which presents difficulties and has suffered in transmission. The Greek and Latin say more or less “Still, I have not done to you all that your abominations deserve”; this fits well in the context and helps to show that God is merciful, even in the punishment he inflicts.

35Propterea, meretrix, audi verbum Domini. 36Haec dicit Dominus Deus: Quia effusum est aes tuum,
et revelata est ignominia tua in fornicationibus tuis ad amatores tuos et ad omnia idola abominabilia
tua, in sanguine filiorum tuorum, quos dedisti eis, 37ideo ecce ego congregabo omnes amatores tuos,
quibus iucunda fuisti, et omnes, quos dilexisti, cum universis, quos oderas; et congregabo eos super te
undique et nudabo ignominiam tuam coram eis, et videbunt omnem turpitudinem tuam. 38Et iudicabo
te iudiciis adulterarum et effundentium sanguinem et dabo te in sanguinem furoris et zeli. 39Et dabo te
in manus eorum, et destruent fornicem tuum et demolientur excelsa tua et denudabunt te vestimentis
tuis et auferent vasa decoris tui et derelinquent te nudam plenamque ignominia. 40Et convocabunt
contra te congregationem et lapidabunt te lapidibus et trucidabunt te gladiis suis. 41Et comburent domos

your houses and execute judgments upon you in the sight of many
women; I will make you stop playing the harlot, and you shall also
give hire no more. [42]So will I satisfy my fury on you, and my
jealousy shall depart from you; I will be calm, and will no more be
angry. [43]Because you have not remembered the days of your youth,
but have enraged me with all these things; therefore, behold, I will
requite your deeds upon your head, says the Lord GOD.

"Have you not committed lewdness in addition to all your
abominations?

Jerusalem and her sisters, Samara and Sodom

[44]Behold, every one who uses proverbs will use this proverb about
Ezek 16:3 you, 'Like mother, like daughter.' [45]You are the daughter of your
mother, who loathed her husband and her children; and you are
Gen 19:23–29 the sister of your sisters, who loathed their husbands and their
2 Kings children. Your mother was a Hittite and your father an Amorite.
17:5,17 Is 1:10 [46]And your elder sister is Samaria, who lived with her daughters
Rev 11:8 to the north of you; and your younger sister, who lived to the south

---

16:44–58. The allegory of members of a family is followed here, too, to draw a comparison between Jerusalem's conduct and that of Samaria (Israel) and Sodom, who are depicted as three sisters. Samaria was invaded by Assyria in punishment for her idolatry (2 Kings 17:5, 17), and, long before that, Sodom was engulfed by fire because of her perverse conduct (Gen 19:23–29). But Jerusalem has behaved far worse than her sisters (vv. 47–48), and therefore she must pay the price for her sins (v. 58; cf. v. 43). Ezekiel is using these allegories to make the point that Jerusalem's sins are particularly grievous because they are committed by the most beloved city of the Lord (cf. Is 49:14–16; 54:6–7; etc.).

Verse 49 points to the root cause of Sodom's vices: an easy life of luxury, careless of the needs of others, led her on to worse sins yet. Hence the ascetical tradition's stress on the avoidance of idleness as a means to preserve virtue. The *Roman Catechism* makes the same point when it shows the way to keep all aspects of the Sixth Commandment: "In the first place, we must flee from idleness, for, as Ezekiel wrote, it was through idleness that the people of Sodom succumbed and fell into the shameful evil of concupiscence" (3, 7, 10).

tuas igni et facient in te iudicia in oculis mulierum plurimarum; et faciam ut desinas fornicari, et mercedes ultra non dabis. [42]Et satiabo indignationem meam in te, et auferetur zelus meus a te; et quiescam nec irascar amplius. [43]Eo quod non fueris recordata dierum adulescentiae tuae et provocasti me in omnibus his, propterea et ego vias tuas in capite tuo dabo, ait Dominus Deus, et non feci iuxta scelera tua in omnibus abominationibus tuis. [44]Ecce omnis, qui dicit vulgo proverbium in te, assumet illud dicens: "Sicut mater, ita et filia eius". [45]Filia matris tuae es tu, quae sprevit virum suum et filios suos; et soror sororum tuarum es tu, quae spreverunt viros suos et filios suos. Mater vestra Hetthaea, et pater vester Amorraeus. [46]Et soror tua maior Samaria, ipsa et filiae eius, quae habitat ad sinistram tuam;

of you, is Sodom with her daughters. 47Yet you were not content
to walk in their ways, or do according to their abominations;
within a very little time you were more corrupt than they in all
your ways. 48As I live, says the Lord GOD, your sister Sodom and
her daughters have not done as you and your daughters have done.
49Behold, this was the guilt of your sister Sodom: she and her
daughters had pride, surfeit of food, and prosperous ease, but did
not aid the poor and needy. 50They were haughty, and did
abominable things before me; therefore I removed them, when I
saw it. 51Samaria has not committed half your sins; you have Gen 19
committed more abominations than they, and have made your Jer 3:11
sisters appear righteous by all the abominations which you have
committed. 52Bear your disgrace, you also, for you have made Rom 2:3
judgment favourable to your sisters; because of your sins in which
you acted more abominably than they, they are more in the right
than you. So be ashamed, you also, and bear your disgrace, for
you have made your sisters appear righteous.

53"I will restore their fortunes, both the fortunes of Sodom and
her daughters, and the fortunes of Samaria and her daughters, and
I will restore your own fortunes in the midst of them, 54that you
may bear your disgrace and be ashamed of all that you have done,
becoming a consolation to them. 55As for your sisters, Sodom and
her daughters shall return to their former estate, and Samaria and
her daughters shall return to their former estate; and you and your
daughters shall return to your former estate. 56Was not your sister
Sodom a byword in your mouth in the day of your pride, 57before
your wickedness was uncovered? Now you have become like her[e]
an object of reproach for the daughters of Edom[f] and all her

---

soror autem tua minor te, quae habitat a dextris tuis, Sodoma et filiae eius. 47Sed nec in viis earum
ambulasti neque secundum scelera earum fecisti; quasi parum fuisset, sceleratiora fecisti illis in
omnibus viis tuis. 48Vivo ego, dicit Dominus Deus, non fecit Sodoma soror tua, ipsa et filiae eius, sicut
fecisti tu et filiae tuae. 49Ecce haec fuit iniquitas Sodomae, sororis tuae: superbia, saturitas panis et
securum otium erat ei et filiabus eius, et manum egeni et pauperis non sustentabant; 50et elevatae sunt
et fecerunt abominationes coram me, et abstuli eas, sicut vidisti. 51Et Samaria dimidium peccatorum
tuorum non peccavit, sed vicisti eas sceleribus tuis et iustificasti sorores tuas in omnibus
abominationibus tuis, quas operata es. 52Ergo et tu porta confusionem tuam, quae absolvisti sorores tuas
peccatis tuis, sceleratius agens quam illae; iustificatae sunt enim a te. Ergo et tu confundere et porta
ignominiam tuam, quae iustificasti sorores tuas. 53Et convertam sortem earum, sortem Sodomorum cum
filiabus suis et sortem Samariae et filiarum eius; et convertam sortem tuam in medio earum, 54ut portes
ignominiam tuam et confundaris in omnibus, quae fecisti consolans eas. 55Et soror tua Sodoma et filiae
eius revertentur ad pristinum statum suum, et Samaria et filiae eius revertentur ad pristinum statum
suum, et tu et filiae tuae revertimini ad pristinum statum vestrum. 56Nonne fuit Sodoma, soror tua, in
fabulam in ore tuo in die superbiae tuae, 57antequam revelaretur malitia tua, sicut hoc tempore tu es

e. Cn: Heb uncertain **f.** Another reading is *Aram*

neighbours, and for the daughters of the Philistines, those round
about who despise you. [58]You bear the penalty of your lewdness
and your abominations, says the LORD.

Lk 15:11–32

Forgiveness and the Covenant

[59]"Yea, thus says the Lord GOD: I will deal with you as you have
Lev 26:42 done, who have despised the oath in breaking the covenant, [60]yet
Jer 31:3,31–34 Ezek 36:31 I will remember my covenant with you in the days of your youth,
Hos 2:16–25 and I will establish with you an everlasting covenant. [61]Then you
will remember your ways, and be ashamed when I[g] take your
sisters, both your elder and your younger, and give them to you as
daughters, but not on account of the covenant with you. [62]I will
establish my covenant with you, and you shall know that I am the

16:59–63. A promise of eventual restoration underlay the previous allegories. In these verses the prophet concentrates on assuring his people that the Lord will establish an everlasting Covenant (v. 60) with the city once she has been cleansed by chastisement. Ezekiel is the prophet who most clearly explains the cleansing effects of the exile. And what he says here is valid also for the Christian soul: "When we sin, we are weighed down with shame and confusion: let us ask God from the bottom of our hearts to give us the grace and strength to struggle to the end, to live in accordance with the truth with all the powers of our soul and body. And if our faith is put to the test—for just as gold is tried in a furnace, the mettle of our souls is tested through temptations and persecutions—may the occasion find us prepared for battle [...], for by our preparation and our struggle we prove the love we have for God in Christ Jesus" (Origen, *Homiliae in Ezechielem*, 10, 5).

"I will remember my covenant" (v. 60): the play on words—"remember the covenant", "remember your ways" (v. 61)—reinforces the message about forgiveness: when the people remember what they have done, they feel ashamed; the Lord takes the initiative, forgives them, renews the Covenant and, as a result, the people acknowledge their sins and repent. The same process is to be seen in the parable of the prodigal son, in which the father forgives his son prior to hearing him repent (Lk 15:11–32), though Jesus puts the emphasis more on the nature of fatherhood than on the Covenant, and more on the individual than on the people as a whole.

in opprobrium filiarum Syriae et cunctarum in circuitu tuo filiarum Palaestinarum, quae ambiunt te per gyrum? [58]Scelus tuum et ignominiam tuam tu portabis, ait Dominus. [59]Quia haec dicit Dominus Deus: Et faciam tibi, sicut fecisti, qui despexisti iuramentum, ut irritum faceres pactum. [60]Et recordabor ego pacti mei tecum in diebus adulescentiae tuae et suscitabo tibi pactum sempiternum. [61]Et recordaberis viarum tuarum et confunderis, cum receperis sorores tuas te maiores cum minoribus tuis, et dabo eas tibi in filias sed non ex pacto tuo. [62]Et suscitabo ego pactum meum tecum, et scies quia ego Dominus,

g. Syr: Heb *you*

LORD, [63]that you may remember and be confounded, and never Rom 3:19
open your mouth again because of your shame, when I forgive
you all that you have done, says the Lord GOD."

2 Kings 24:8–25:21 Jer 37:3–10

Allegory of the two eagles*

17 [1]The word of the LORD came to me: [2]*"Son of man, Judg 14:12
propound a riddle, and speak an allegory to the house of Jer 48:40

***17:1–24.** This chapter, a mixture of fact and allegory, is written in a simple style but it is full of meaning. It can be divided into three parts —the allegory of the two eagles (vv. 1–10); its application, written in prose (vv. 11–21); and the definitive restoration, symbolized by the lofty cedar (vv. 22–24, also in verse).

17:1–10. The early history of the chosen people prior to the monarchy was traced in the career of the unfaithful wife who was punished and then absolved by means of the everlasting Covenant. Now, recent history, covering the period from the first deportation in 597 BC to the second ten years later, is described by the allegory of the two eagles. The information contained in 2 Kings 24:8—25:21 enables us to identify what is happening here: the first eagle, "with long pinions" (v. 3), is Nebuchadnezzar; the cedar is Jerusalem, from which the Chaldean king took away only a part, the top, in the first deportation; the "topmost of its young wings" is King Jeohiachin, who is carried off to Babylon, "a city of merchants" (v. 4) and treated as a royal prisoner; the "seed of the land" is Zedekiah, Jeohiachin's uncle, set up on the throne of Jerusalem, the "low spreading vine" (v. 6), which began to reestablish itself and to bear fruit. So far, everything is positive.

The second eagle, "with great wings and much plumage" (v. 7), is the pharaoh of Egypt, either Psammetichus II or Hophra, with whom Zedekiah made a pact reneging on the one he made previously with Nebuchadnezzar (cf. Jer 37:3–10). Then comes an east wind (v. 10) that will destroy everything—the return of Nebuchadnezzar; he is the instrument of the Lord's wrath and will totally destroy the holy city.

17:2. "Propound a riddle, and speak an allegory": riddles and parables or allegories were an important element in the rich resources of Semitic Wisdom used by the prophets. A riddle was a sort of conundrum with moral resolution (cf. Judg 14:12; Hab 2:6), and a parable was a simple story also designed to impart a lesson. The prophets, particularly Ezekiel, use the term *māshāl,* "parable", to mean both a proverb (cf. 12:22–23; 16:44) and a short story or tale, as in this case and in 24:3. The Gospels, which inherited this

---

[63]ut recorderis et confundaris, et non sit tibi ultra aperire os prae confusione tua, cum placatus fuero tibi in omnibus, quae fecisti», ait Dominus Deus. **[17]** [1]Et factum est verbum Domini ad me dicens: [2]«Fili hominis, propone aenigma et narra parabolam ad domum Israel [3]et dices: Haec dicit Dominus

Israel; [3]say, Thus says the Lord GOD: A great eagle with great
wings and long pinions, rich in plumage of many colors, came to
Ezek 16:29 Lebanon and took the top of the cedar; [4]he broke off the topmost
of its young twigs and carried it to a land of trade, and set it in a
city of merchants. [5]Then he took of the seed of the land and
planted it in fertile soil; he placed it beside abundant waters. He
set it like a willow twig, [6]and it sprouted and became a low
spreading vine, and its branches turned toward him, and its roots
remained where it stood. So it became a vine, and brought forth
branches and put forth foliage.

[7]"But there was another great eagle with great wings and much
plumage; and behold, this vine bent its roots toward him, and shot
forth its branches toward him that he might water it. From the bed
where it was planted[8] he transplanted it[h] to good soil by abundant
waters, that it might bring forth branches, and bear fruit, and
become a noble vine. [9]Say, Thus says the Lord GOD: Will it
thrive? Will he not pull up its roots and cut off its branches,[i] so
that all its fresh sprouting leaves wither? It will not take a strong
Jer 4:11 arm or many people to pull it from its roots. [10]Behold, when it is
Ezek 19:2
Hos 13:15 transplanted, will it thrive? Will it not utterly wither when the east
wind strikes it—wither away on the bed where it grew?"

The allegory come true

2 Kings [11]Then the word of the LORD came to me: [12]"Say now to the
24:10–17 rebellious house, Do you not know what these things mean? Tell

---

pedagogical tradition, show us Jesus using riddles, proverbs, parables, etc. to catch the attention of his listeners.

17:11–21. This interpretation of the allegory spells out the parts that might not be so clear. In it, Ezekiel refers four times to the breach of the Covenant as the reason for the fall of Jerusalem and the exile that followed. King Zekediah failed to keep his pact with Nebuchadnezzar (vv. 13, 16, 18) and in failing to

Deus: / Aquila grandis / magnarum alarum, / longo pennarum ductu, / plena plumis et varietate, / venit ad Libanum / et tulit cacumen cedri; / [4]summitatem frondium eius avellit / et transportavit eam in terram Chanaan, / in urbem negotiatorum posuit illam. / [5]Et tulit de semine terrae / et posuit illud in terra pro semine, / super aquas multas, / quasi salicem posuit illud, / [6]ut germinaret et cresceret in vineam latiorem / humili statura, / respicientibus ramis eius ad illam, / et radices eius sub illa essent. / Facta est ergo vinea / et fructificavit in palmites / et emisit propagines. / [7]Et fuit aquila altera grandis, / magnis alis / multisque plumis; / et ecce vinea ista, / quasi mittens radices suas ad eam, / palmites suos extendit ad illam, / ut irrigaret eam abundantius / quam areolae, in quibus erat plantata. / [8]In terra bona / super aquas multas / plantata est, / ut faciat frondes / et portet fructum / et sit in vineam grandem. / [9]Dic: Haec dicit Dominus Deus: / Ergone prosperabitur? / Nonne radices eius evellet / et fructum eius distringet, / et marcescent omnia recentia germina eius, et arescet? / Et non opus erit brachio grandi

h. Cn: Heb *it was transplanted* **i.** Cn: Heb *fruit*

them, Behold, the king of Babylon came to Jerusalem, and took
her king and her princes and brought them to him to Babylon. 2 Kings 24:17
13And he took one of the seed royal and made a covenant with 2 Chron 36:13 Jer 37:1
him, putting him under oath. (The chief men of the land he had
taken away, 14that the kingdom might be humble and not lift itself
up, and that by keeping his covenant it might stand.) 15But he 2 Kings 24:20
rebelled against him by sending ambassadors to Egypt, that they
might give him horses and a large army. Will he succeed? Can a
man escape who does such things? Can he break the covenant and
yet escape? 16As I live, says the Lord GOD, surely in the place 2 Kings 25:7
where the king dwells who made him king, whose oath he
despised, and whose covenant with him he broke, in Babylon he
shall die. 17Pharaoh with his mighty army and great company will
not help him in war, when mounds are cast up and siege walls
built to cut off many lives. 18Because he despised the oath and 1 Chron 29:24
broke the covenant, because he gave his hand and yet did all these
things, he shall not escape. 19Therefore thus says the Lord GOD:
As I live, surely my oath which he despised, and my covenant
which he broke, I will requite upon his head. 20I will spread my Ezek 12:13; 29:35
net over him, and he shall be taken in my snare, and I will bring
him to Babylon and enter into judgment with him there for the
treason he has committed against me. 21And all the pick[j] of his
troops shall fall by the sword, and the survivors shall be scattered
to every wind; and you shall know that I, the LORD, have spoken."

---

do so he broke the Covenant with the Lord (v. 19). The prophet is showing the people that the Lord did not fail them, did not go back on his word. He did what was necessary to bring good from the sinful situation: he suspended the benefits and joys of the Convenant for a time, so that the Covenant would not be destroyed and lost forever.

neque populo multo, / ut evellat eam radicitus. / 10Ecce plantata est; ergone prosperabitur? / Nonne, cum tetigerit eam ventus urens, / siccabitur / et in areis, in quibus germinaverat, arescet?». 11Et factum est verbum Domini ad me dicens: 12«Dic ad domum exasperantem: Nescitis quid ista significent? Dic: Ecce venit rex Babylonis Ierusalem et assumpsit regem et principes eius et adduxit eos ad semetipsum in Babylonem; 13et tulit de semine regni pepigitque cum eo foedus et accepit ab eo iusiurandum, sed et fortes terrae sustulit, 14ut esset regnum humile et non elevaretur, sed custodiret pactum eius et servaret illud. 15Qui recedens ab eo, misit nuntios ad Aegyptum, ut daret sibi equos et populum multum. Numquid prosperabitur vel consequetur salutem, qui fecit haec? Et, qui dissolvit pactum, numquid effugiet? 16Vivo ego, dicit Dominus Deus, quoniam in loco regis, qui constituit eum regem, cuius fecit irritum iuramentum et solvit pactum, quod habebat cum eo, in medio Babylonis morietur. 17Et non in exercitu grandi neque in populo multo adiuvabit eum pharao in proelio, in iactu aggeris et in exstructione munitionum, ut interficiat animas multas. 18Spreverat enim iuramentum, ut solveret foedus, et ecce dedit manum suam et, cum omnia haec fecerit, non effugiet. 19Propterea haec dicit

j. Another reading is *fugitives*

Is 53:2 [22]Thus says the Lord GOD: "I myself will take a sprig from the
lofty top of the cedar, and will set it out; I will break off from the
topmost of its young twigs a tender one, and I myself will plant it
Mt 13:32 Mk 4:32 upon a high and lofty mountain; [23]on the mountain height of Israel
Lk 13:19 will I plant it, that it may bring forth boughs and bear fruit, and
Ps 113:7–9 become a noble cedar; and under it will dwell all kinds of beasts;[k]
Ezek 21:3 in the shade of its branches birds of every sort will nest. [24]And all
Mt 23:12 Lk 1:51–53; 23:31 the trees of the field shall know that I the LORD bring low the high

17:22–24. Chapters 15–17 contain a number of allegories. The special feature of the cedar tree allegory describing the eventual restoration is the way it puts the stress on God's action by explicitly repeating the first person singular: "I myself", "I the Lord will bring low", "I the Lord have spoken". Some commentators think that these verses might have been inserted in the text later, but the style and content of the oracle are perfectly in line with Ezekiel's thinking.

"In the shade of its branches birds of every sort will rest" (v. 23): the same words are used in the account of the flood about all sorts of birds entering Noah's ark. It points therefore to the eschatological nature of the oracle: after the exile, just as after the flood, everything will be completely new, although it will derive from something that already existed. Also, the reference to "birds of every sort" points to the catholic nature of the new Israel. It is no surprise therefore that our Lord should use similar imagery to describe the Kingdom of God: it is like a grain of mustard seed that grows and "becomes a tree, so that the birds of the air come and make nests in its branches" (Mt 13:32).

"I the Lord bring low the high tree" (v. 24): here again we see the Lord as the protagonist in the history of the chosen people. He is the author of life, which makes what is dry flourish, and of death, which withers the green tree. He has set his might against those who, in their arrogance, do not accept him (cf. 31:10–14). The New Testament will have much to say about the value of humility; for example: "whoever exalts himself will be humbled, and whoever humbles himself will be exalted" (Mt 23:12).

Dominus Deus: Vivo ego, quoniam iuramentum meum, quod sprevit, et foedus meum, quod praevaricatus est, ponam in caput eius [20]et expandam super eum rete meum, et comprehendetur tendicula mea, et adducam eum in Babylonem et iudicabo illum ibi in praevaricatione, qua praevaricatus est in me. [21]Et omnes electi eius in universo agmine suo gladio cadent; residui autem in omnem ventum dispergentur, et scietis quia ego Dominus locutus sum. [22]Haec dicit Dominus Deus: / Et sumam ego de cacumine cedri sublimis et ponam; / de vertice ramorum eius tenerum distringam / et plantabo super montem excelsum et eminentem. / [23]In monte sublimi Israel plantabo illud; / et erumpet in germen et faciet fructum / et erit in cedrum magnam; / et habitabunt sub ea omnes volucres, / et universum volatile sub umbra frondium eius nidificabit. / [24]Et scient omnia ligna regionis / quia ego Dominus / humiliavi lignum sublime / et exaltavi lignum humile / et siccavi lignum viride / et frondere

k. Gk: Heb lacks *all kinds of beasts*

tree, and make high the low tree, dry up the green tree, and make
the dry tree flourish. I the LORD have spoken, and I will do it."

Ex 34:6–7
Ezek 14:12;
33:10–20

Individual responsibility*

18 [1]The word of the LORD came to me again: [2]"What do you
mean by repeating this proverb concerning the land of

Jer 18:17;
31:29
Ezek 16:44

***18:1–32.** Here Ezekiel uses the father-son relationship as a key to this ongoing explanation of the catastrophe of the fall of Jerusalem and the exile. In the previous chapters he showed that the Lord did not give up on his special love for Israel; punish her he will, because she deserves it, but the broken Covenant will be re-established. Now he repeats a lesson that the exiles must learn: the Lord is not being very cruel or unjust towards them; nor is he whenever he allows people to suffer.

Traditional teaching put more emphasis on solidarity and unity among the people—in terms of both space (all its parts formed one Israel) and time (all generations made up the same people). Thus, it defined the Lord as just and merciful when he rewarded or punished successive generations for the things their forebears did (cf. Ex 34:6–7 and note). But Ezekiel breaks new ground by asserting the principle of individual retribution/responsibility: the exiles have been punished for their own sins, not those of their forebears. This explanation for suffering is a very considerable advance, but the focus is still a narrow one. The book of Job, too, tackles the question of the suffering of the blameless, and the answer it gives does not go far enough. Not until the New Testament will the full picture emerge in the light of Jesus' death on the cross. Christ suffers for the sins of men, he dies in order to redeem us, and he shows that suffering of every sort, even the suffering of the innocent, has a redemptive value: "When we consider once more the central mysteries of our faith, we are surprised to see how very human gestures are used to express the deepest truths: the love of God the Father who gives up his Son, and the Son's love which calmly leads him to Calvary. God does not approach us in power and authority. No, he 'takes the form of a servant, being born in the likeness of man'. Jesus is never distant or aloof, although sometimes in his preaching he seems very sad, because he is hurt by the evil men do. However, if we watch him closely, we will note immediately that his anger comes from love. It is a further invitation for us to leave infidelity and sin behind. '"Have I any pleasure in the death of the wicked," says the Lord God, "and not rather that he should turn from his way and live?"' These words explain Christ's whole life. They allow us to understand why he has come to us with a heart made of flesh, a heart like ours. This is a convincing proof of his love and a constant witness to the mystery

feci lignum aridum. / Ego Dominus locutus sum et feci». **[18]** [1]Et factus est sermo Domini ad me dicens: [2]«Quid est vobis quod vulgo dicitis proverbium istud in terra Israel dicentes: "Patres

Israel, 'The fathers have eaten sour grapes, and the children's teeth
Deut 24:16 are set on edge'? 3As I live, says the Lord GOD, this proverb shall
Jer 31:30 no more be used by you in Israel. 4Behold, all souls are mine; the
Ezek 18:20 soul of the father as well as the soul of the son is mine: the soul
that sins shall die.

---

of divine charity" (St Josemaría Escrivá, *Christ Is Passing By*, 162).

18:1–20. To counter the spiteful adage about the sour grapes and the teeth on edge (cf. Jer 31:29), Ezekiel offers a practical case involving three generations—a righteous father (vv. 5–9) who has a violent son (vv. 10–13), who in turn has a son who is righteous (vv. 14–20). The moral in each case is the same: "The soul that sins shall die" (v. 20; cf. v. 9); "the righteouness of the righteous shall be upon himself, and the wickedness of the wicked shall be upon himself" (v. 20; cf. 9). Any possible confusion about personal or communal guilt for sin is addressed by the Catechism in the following way: "God's threat to inflict his punishment unto the third and fourth generation should be understood not as proof that children will suffer for the sins of their parents, but that the need for penance and expiation is fundamental [...]. Therefore, there is no contradiction between this threat and the words of the prophet: *the soul that sins shall die* (Ezek 18:4). St Gregory, whose teaching follows in the line of what all the Fathers taught, tells us: 'Every man who sins as his father did shares in his father's guilt. But the man who has no part in his father's iniquity bears none of his fault. The evil son of the evil father will pay not only for his own sins, but for those of his father as well, because he added his own sins to his father's sins against the Lord; it is just, in the eyes of a strict judge, that he who followed in the footsteps of his evil father should pay for the sins of his father in this life'" (*Roman Catechism*, 3, 2, 31–32).

The sins listed here (idolatry, adultery, uncleanness, oppression, greed: vv. 6–8; 11–13; 15–17) are meant to include all the Lord's commandments, especially those written in what is known as the "Deuteronomic code" (Deut 12:1—26:15) and the "law of holiness" (Lev 17:1—26:46). In Ezekiel's time people were familiar with the Decalogue and with standard lists of virtues (cf. Ps 15:2–4; Is 33:15–16; Jer 22:3–5; Mic 6:8) and sins (cf. 22:6–12). The New Testament, too, uses similar lists (cf. 1 Cor 5:11; Eph 5:5) as a memory aid in moral instruction. So, one can see that Ezekiel was familiar with teaching methods that were in use in the temple. Following this tradition, the Church has always argued that the most effective means be used in catechetical teaching: "so that the faithful, according to their talents, ability and state in life, can learn Catholic doctrine most effectively and put it into practice" (*Code of Canon Law*, 779).

---

comederunt uvam acerbam, et dentes filiorum obstupescunt"? 3Vivo ego, dicit Dominus Deus, non
dicetis ultra hoc proverbium in Israel. 4Ecce omnes animae meae sunt: ut anima patris, ita et anima filii

[5]"If a man is righteous and does what is lawful and right—[6]if
he does not eat upon the mountains or lift up his eyes to the idols
of the house of Israel, does not defile his neighbour's wife or
approach a woman in her time of impurity, [7]does not oppress any
one, but restores to the debtor his pledge, commits no robbery,
gives his bread to the hungry and covers the naked with a garment,
[8]does not lend at interest or take any increase, withholds his hand
from iniquity, executes true justice between man and man, [9]walks
in my statutes, and is careful to observe my ordinances[l]—he is
righteous, he shall surely live, says the Lord GOD.

[10]"If he begets a son who is a robber, a shedder of blood,[m] [11]who
does none of these duties, but eats upon the mountains, defiles his
neighbour's wife, [12]oppresses the poor and needy, commits robbery,
does not restore the pledge, lifts up his eyes to the idols, commits
abomination, [13]lends at interest, and takes increase; shall he then
live? He shall not live. He has done all these abominable things; he
shall surely die; his blood shall be upon himself.

[14]"But if this man begets a son who sees all the sins which his
father has done, and fears, and does not do likewise, [15]who does
not eat upon the mountains or lift up his eyes to the idols of the
house of Israel, does not defile his neighbour's wife, [16]does not
wrong any one, exacts no pledge, commits no robbery, but gives
his bread to the hungry and covers the naked with a garment,
[17]withholds his hand from iniquity,[n] takes no interest or increase,
observes my ordinances, and walks in my statutes; he shall not die
for his father's iniquity; he shall surely live. [18]As for his father,

Ps 15:2–5; 24:3–4; Lev 18:19; Deut 4:19; 12:2
Ezek 6:13; 22:9
Mt 25:35ff

Ex 22:25
Lev 25:36
Deut 1:16
Jer 15:10

Ezek 22:12
Zech 8:16

---

mea est; anima, quae peccaverit, ipsa morietur. [5]Et vir, si fuerit iustus et fecerit iudicium et iustitiam,
[6]in montibus non comederit et oculos suos non levaverit ad idola domus Israel et uxorem proximi sui
non violaverit et ad mulierem menstruatam non accesserit [7]et hominem non afflixerit, pignus debitori
reddiderit, per vim nihil rapuerit, panem suum esurienti dederit et nudum operuerit vestimento, [8]ad
usuram non commodaverit et fenus non acceperit, ab iniquitate averterit manum suam, iudicium verum
fecerit inter virum et virum, [9]in praeceptis meis ambulaverit et iudicia mea custodierit, ut faciat
veritatem, hic iustus est, vita vivet, ait Dominus Deus. [10]Quod si genuerit filium latronem, effundentem
sanguinem et facientem unum de istis, [11]cum ipse haec omnia non fecerit, et etiam in montibus
comedentem et uxorem proximi sui polluentem, [12]egenum et pauperem affligentem, rapientem rapinas,
pignus non reddentem et ad idola levantem oculos suos, abominationem facientem, [13]ad usuram dantem
et fenus accipientem, numquid vivet? Non vivet. Cum universa detestanda haec fecerit, morte morietur;
sanguis eius in ipso erit. [14]Quod si genuerit filium, qui videns omnia peccata patris sui, quae fecit,
timuerit et non fecerit simile eis: [15]super montes non comederit et oculos suos non levaverit ad idola
domus Israel et uxorem proximi sui non violaverit [16]et virum non afflixerit, pignus non retinuerit et
rapinam non rapuerit, panem suum esurienti dederit et nudum operuerit vestimento, [17]ab iniuria
averterit manum suam, usuram et fenus non acceperit, iudicia mea fecerit, in praeceptis meis
ambulaverit, hic non morietur in iniquitate patris sui, sed vita vivet. [18]Pater eius, quia calumniatus est

l. Gk: Heb *has kept my ordinances to deal truly* **m.** Heb *blood, and he does any one of these things*
n. Gk: Heb *the poor*

because he practised extortion, robbed his brother, and did what is not good among his people, behold, he shall die for his iniquity.
[19]"Yet you say, 'Why should not the son suffer for the iniquity of the father?' When the son has done what is lawful and right, and has been careful to observe all my statutes, he shall surely
Deut 24:16 live. [20]The soul that sins shall die. The son shall not suffer for the
Is 3:10 Ezek 18:4 iniquity of the father, nor the father suffer for the iniquity of the son; the righteousness of the righteous shall be upon himself, and the wickedness of the wicked shall be upon himself.

The good effects of conversion
[21]"But if a wicked man turns away from all his sins which he has committed and keeps all my statutes and does what is lawful and

---

18:21–32. These verses reply to a question that may arise from the doctrine of personal retribution: If the sinner must live with the consequences of his sins, what is the purpose of repentance? Ezekiel takes the question very much to heart, and his reply includes one of the most beautiful summaries of divine mercy: "Have I any pleasure in the death of the wicked ..., and not rather that he should turn from his way and live?" (v. 23; cf. 33:11). It is true that the explanation of divine justice and punishment develops over a long period until the New Testament is reached; even so, from the very beginning of divine Revelation, there is never any doubt but that God is always ready to forgive. Over the centuries, Christian spirituality has written beautiful pages filled to overflowing with heartfelt trust in God's mercy. As an example, we will quote a prayer by a Christian writer of the Armenian Church: "You are the Lord of Mercy. Have mercy on me, a sinner, who beseeches you with sighs and tears. [...] O kind and merciful Lord! You are patient with sinners, for you have said: *if a wicked man turns away from all his sins which he has committed ... none of the transgressions which he has committed shall be remembered against him* (Ezek 18:21–22). Look, see how I have come before you and fallen at your feet: your guilty servant pleads for your mercy. Do not recall my sins, nor spurn me because of my wickedness. [...] You are the Lord of goodness and mercy; you forgive all sin" (John Mandakuni, *Oratio*, 2–3).

Of course, God's forgiveness is closely interwoven with personal conversion. Therefore, it is not surprising to find these verses of Ezekiel being quoted in connexion with the need for

---

et fecit rapinas nec bonum operatus est in medio populi sui, ecce mortuus est in iniquitate sua. [19]Et dicitis: "Quare non portavit filius iniquitatem patris?". Videlicet, quia filius iudicium et iustitiam operatus est, omnia praecepta mea custodivit et fecit illa, vivet vita. [20]Anima, quae peccaverit, ipsa morietur; filius non portabit iniquitatem patris, et pater non portabit iniquitatem filii. Iustitia iusti super eum erit, et impietas impii erit super eum. [21]Si autem impius egerit paenitentiam ab omnibus peccatis suis, quae operatus est, et custodierit universa praecepta mea et fecerit iudicium et iustitiam, vita vivet,

right, he shall surely live; he shall not die. 22None of the trans- Ezek 33:16
gressions which he has committed shall be remembered against Ezek 33:11 Wis 11:26
him; for the righteousness which he has done he shall live. 23Have Lk 15:7;
I any pleasure in the death of the wicked, says the Lord GOD, and 10:32; Jn 8:11; Rom 11:32
not rather that he should turn from his way and live? 24But when 1 Tim 2:4,6
a righteous man turns away from his righteousness and commits 2 Pet 3:9–20
iniquity and does the same abominable things that the wicked man Ezek 3:20; 33:12; Rev 2:5
does, shall he live? None of the righteous deeds which he has
done shall be remembered; for the treachery of which he is guilty
and the sin he has committed, he shall die.
25"Yet you say, 'The way of the Lord is not just.' Hear now, O
house of Israel: Is my way not just? Is it not your ways that are not
just? 26When a righteous man turns away from his righteousness
and commits iniquity, he shall die for it; for the iniquity which he
has committed he shall die. 27Again, when a wicked man turns

---

the sacrament of penance: "at all times, the practice of penance in order to obtain grace and attain righteousness was necessary for all those who fell into mortal sin, even those who sought to be washed clean by the waters of baptism, so that, when sinfulness had been purged and set to rights, they would detest any offence against God through their hatred of sin and the sorrow of their souls. Thus says the Prophet: *Repent and turn from all your transgressions, lest iniquity be your ruin* (Ezek 18:30)" (Council of Trent, Session 14, 1). There is also a need for genuine contrition: "Contrition, which is the most important element of penance, is a sorrow of the soul, a hatred of all the sins that have been committed, and a desire not to sin again in the future. This sense of contrition has always been a fundamental condition of forgiveness; the man who falls into sin after his baptism can only receive pardon if he is contrite, trusts in the mercy of God, and fulfills all the other conditions that are binding in this sacrament. This Council declares that contrition encompasses not only the end of sin and the beginning of new life, but the reparation of the old, sinful life, as it was written: *Cast away from you all the transgressions which you have committed against me, and get yourselves a new heart and a new spirit!* (Ezek 18:31)" (Council of Trent, Session 14, 4).

non morietur. 22Omnes iniquitates eius, quas operatus est, non memorabuntur ei; in iustitia sua, quam operatus est, vivet. 23Numquid voluntatis meae est mors impii, dicit Dominus Deus, et non ut convertatur a viis suis et vivat? 24Si autem averterit se iustus a iustitia sua et fecerit iniquitatem secundum omnes abominationes, quas operari solet impius, numquid vivet? Omnes iustitiae eius, quas fecerat, non recordabuntur; in praevaricatione, qua praevaricatus est, et in peccato suo, quod peccavit, in ipsis morietur. 25Et dixistis: "Non est aequa via Domini". Audite ergo, domus Israel: Numquid via mea non est aequa, et non magis viae vestrae pravae sunt? 26Cum enim averterit se iustus a iustitia sua et fecerit iniquitatem, morietur; in iniustitia, quam operatus est, morietur. 27Et cum averterit se impius ab impietate sua, quam operatus est, et fecerit iudicium et iustitiam, ipse animam suam vivificabit;

away from the wickedness he has committed and does what is
lawful and right, he shall save his life. [28]Because he considered
and turned away from all the transgressions which he had
Ezek 33:17 committed, he shall surely live, he shall not die. [29]Yet the house of
Israel says, 'The way of the Lord is not just.' O house of Israel, are
my ways not just? Is it not your ways that are not just?
Ezek 7:3; 33:20 [30]"Therefore I will judge you, O house of Israel, every one
Mt 3:2; 16:27 Rev 2:5 according to his ways, says the Lord GOD. Repent and turn from
Jer 4:4 all your transgressions, lest iniquity be your ruin.[o] [31]Cast away
Ezek 11:19 from you all the transgressions which you have committed against
Wis 1:13 me, and get yourselves a new heart and a new spirit! Why will you
Ezek 33:11; die, O house of Israel? [32]For I have no pleasure in the death of any
18:23; Mt 3:2 one, says the Lord GOD; so turn, and live."

Allegory of the lioness*

2 Sam 1:17–27 **19** [1]And you, take up a lamentation for the princes of Israel,
[2]and say:

***19:1–14.** Two allegories are used here to describe the collapse of Jerusalem. They are both in verse, and use the rhythm of Hebrew lamentation poetry (v. 1). Poetry of this type, made up of sad and sombre rhythms difficult to capture in translation, was used in funeral services. David composed a beautiful elegy in honour of Saul and Jonathan (2 Sam 1:17–27). Here we have a lament for Jerusalem, which is depicted as a lioness; she brings up two of her cubs but neither of them prospers: these are two kings, one of whom was deported to Egypt (v. 4), that is, Jehoahaz, the son of Josiah, who was taken to Egypt as a prisoner by the pharaoh Neco II (cf. 2 Kings 23: 32–33); the other was led in chains to Babylon (v. 9)—Jehoiachin (2 Kings 24:1–17). Both kings suffered the same punishment because both "did what was evil in the sight of the Lord" (2 Kings 23:32; 24:9). They were punished for their own sins, not those of their ancestors. Ezekiel bemoans their fate and that of Jerusalem.

The image of the transplanted and withered vine (vv. 10–14) is a favourite one of Ezekiel's (cf. 17:5–10), and an apt one in describing the ruin of Jerusalem.

[28]considerans enim et avertens se ab omnibus iniquitatibus suis, quas operatus est, vita vivet, non moritur. [29]Et dicunt domus Israel: "Non est aequa via Domini". Numquid viae meae non sunt aequae, domus Israel, et non magis viae vestrae pravae? [30]Idcirco unumquemque iuxta vias suas iudicabo, domus Israel, ait Dominus Deus. Convertimini et agite paenitentiam ab omnibus iniquitatibus vestris, et non erit vobis in scandalum iniquitatis. [31]Proicite a vobis omnes praevaricationes vestras, in quibus praevaricati estis, et facite vobis cor novum et spiritum novum. Et quare moriemini, domus Israel? [32]Quia nolo mortem morientis, dicit Dominus Deus. Revertimini et vivite. **[19]** [1]Et tu, assume planctum super principes Israel / [2]et dices: / Qualis erat mater tua leaena / inter leones! / Cubavit in

o. Or *so that they shall not be a stumbling block of iniquity to you*

What a lioness was your mother
among lions!
She couched in the midst of young lions,
rearing her whelps.
3And she brought up one of her whelps; 2 Kings 23:31
he became a young lion,
and he learned to catch prey;
he devoured men.
4The nations sounded an alarm against him; 2 Kings 23:33–34
he was taken in their pit;
and they brought him with hooks
to the land of Egypt.
5When she saw that she was baffled,[p] 2 Kings 23:34,36 2 Chron 36:5
that her hope was lost,
she took another of her whelps
and made him a young lion.
6He prowled among the lions;
he became a young lion,
and he learned to catch prey;
he devoured men.
7And he ravaged their strongholds,[q]
and laid waste their cities;
and the land was appalled and all who were in it
at the sound of his roaring.
8Then the nations set against him 2 Kings 24:2
snares[r] on every side;
they spread their net over him;

19:1–9. The lion was used in literature as a symbol of brave and skilful soldiers (Gen 49:9; Ps 22:13, 21); archaeology has discovered paintings etc. in which the lion is depicted in this way. But the allusion in the allegory is ironic: the power and valour of the kings of Judah, their ability to hunt prey and devour men (vv. 3, 6) was simply an illusion. The Fathers used this allegorical poem to make the point that human power and glory is a very impermanent thing.

medio leunculorum, / enutrivit catulos suos. / 3Et educavit unum de leunculis suis; / leo factus est / et didicit capere praedam, / homines devoravit. / 4Et convocaverunt contra eum gentes, / in fovea earum captus est; / et adduxerunt eum in circulis / in terram Aegypti. / 5Quae cum vidisset quoniam exspectaverat, / et perierat spes eius, / tulit alium de leunculis suis, / leonem constituit eum. / 6Qui incedebat inter leones, / factus est leo / et didicit praedam capere, / homines devoravit; / 7et fregit arces eorum / et civitates eorum vastavit. / Et obstupuit terra et plenitudo eius / a voce rugitus illius. / 8Et

p. Heb *had waited* **q.** Tg Compare Theodotion: Heb *knew his widows* **r.** Cn: Heb *from the provinces*

he was taken in their pit.
2 Kings 24:8–17 9With hooks they put him in a cage,
and brought him to the king of Babylon;
they brought him into custody,
that his voice should no more be heard
upon the mountains of Israel.

Is 5:1 10Your mother was like a vine in a vineyard[s]
Ezek 17:6–10 47:12; Ps 1:3 transplanted by the water,
fruitful and full of branches
by reason of abundant water.
Rev 22:1–2 11Its strongest stem became
a ruler's sceptre;
it towered aloft
among the thick boughs;
it was seen in its height
with the mass of its branches.
Jn 15:6 12But the vine was plucked up in fury,
cast down to the ground;
the east wind dried it up;
its fruit was stripped off,
its strong stem was withered;
the fire consumed it.
2 Kings 24:12–16 13Now it is transplanted in the wilderness,
in a dry and thirsty land.
Ezek 5:4 14And fire has gone out from its stem,
has consumed its branches and fruit,
so that there remains in it no strong stem,

19:10–14. The chequered career of the vine reflects very well what happened to the exiles of Israel, both kings and people: full of vigour, like a healthy vine (vv. 10–11), Israel suffered destruction and exile, like a vine ripped up in fury (v. 12); now, moved to an inhospitable country, it is like a vine transplanted to the wilderness (v. 14) where it cannot yield fruit.

convenerunt adversum eum gentes / undique de provinciis / et expanderunt super eum rete suum, / in fovea earum captus est. / 9Et miserunt eum in caveam in circulis / et adduxerunt eum ad regem Babylonis; / qui misit eum in carcerem, / ne audiretur vox eius ultra / super montes Israel. / 10Mater tua vineae assimilabatur / super aquam plantata. / Fructus eius et frondes eius creverunt / ex aquis multis; / 11et factae sunt ei virgae solidae / in sceptra dominantium, / et exaltata est statura eius / usque in nubes, / et apparuit in altitudine sua, / in multitudine palmitum suorum. / 12Et evulsa est in ira / in terramque proiecta, / et ventus urens siccavit fructum eius; / abrepta et arefacta est virga roboris eius, / ignis comedit eam. / 13Et nunc transplantata est in desertum, / in terra invia et sitienti. / 14Et egressus est ignis de virga ramorum eius, / qui fructum eius comedit; / et non fuit in ea virga fortis, / sceptrum

s. Cn: Heb *in your blood*

no sceptre for a ruler.
This is a lamentation, and has become a lamentation.

An account of Israel's infidelities*

Ezek 16:1

20 [1]In the seventh year, in the fifth month, on the tenth day of Ezek 14:1–5
the month, certain of the elders of Israel came to inquire of

---

***20:1—24:27.** The first part of the book of Ezekiel ends with passages confirming that Jerusalem must be chastised. Here we find a repetition of the charges already raised about unfaithfulness and the breach of the Covenant; some of the more vivid allegories, such as that of marriage, occur again (chapter 23 is an echo of chapter 16); and sentences of condemnation are handed down against which there can be no appeal. Even so, Ezekiel tries to raise the spirits of the exiles, so that when the prophecies about Jerusalem come true, they will realize that the prophet's oracles of hope will also be borne out; these oracles are to be found in the second part of the book. In his desire to explain why the exile has happened, the prophet will use himself, the cure of his dumbness and the death of his wife, as a symbol (24:27). From the time of the destruction of Jerusalem onwards, the prophet will speak only to console and to show the people that they have good reason to hope.

20:1–44. This short history of Israel is told with a didactic purpose in mind—to show that God is at work in the affairs of men, that he chose a people for himself, whom he punished when they were unfaithful and then restored to favour so that his name would not be brought into contempt. The account, expressed in the form of a legal investigation (*rîb*), consists of two parts: the first looks to the past, and Israel is found guilty because she acted wickedly (vv. 1–32); the second looks to the future and is full of hope (vv. 33–44). Some commentators have argued that the second part was a later addition, inserted to tone down the denunciation in the first part. However, the language and style are similar to that of the rest of the chapter. The Lord is the leading figure in all that happens; up to the exile he has punished the people severely, while leaving a "remnant" who can make a fresh start; and from the exile onwards, once the people are cleansed, a new stage begins in which they are offered the same gifts as were extended to those who were rescued from Egypt. Thus, Ezekiel is telling the exiles that past events are the best proof that God is always looking after his people; he does this even when he chastises them, but above all when he encourages them and promises them gifts that can never pass away. God reveals himself in the created universe, but he does so also by his intervention in the affairs of men: "Only God can answer the question about the good,

regni». Planctus est, et erit in planctum. **[20]** [1]Et factum est in anno septimo, in quinto mense, in decima mensis, venerunt viri de senioribus Israel, ut interrogarent Dominum, et sederunt coram me.

the LORD, and sat before me. [2]And the word of the LORD came to
me: [3]"Son of man, speak to the elders of Israel, and say to them,
Thus says the Lord GOD, Is it to inquire of me that you come? As
Ezek 16:2; 22:2; 23:36 I live, says the Lord GOD, I will not be inquired of by you. [4]Will
you judge them, son of man, will you judge them? Then let them
know the abominations of their fathers, [5]and say to them, Thus

---

because he is the Good. But God has already given an answer to this question: he did so *by creating man and ordering him* with Wisdom and love to his final end, through the law which is inscribed in his heart (cf. Rom 2:15), the 'natural law'. The latter 'is nothing other than the light of understanding infused in us by God, whereby we understand what must be done and what must be avoided. God gave this light and this law to man at creation'. He also did so *in the history of Israel*, particularly in the 'ten words', the *commandments of Sinai*, whereby he brought into existence the people of the Covenant (cf. Ex 24) and called them to be his 'own possession among all peoples', 'a holy nation' (Ex 19:5–6), which would radiate his holiness to all peoples (cf. Wis 18:4; Ezek 20:41). The gift of the Decalogue was a promise and sign of the *New Covenant*, in which the law would be written in a new and definitive way upon the human heart (cf. Jer 31:31–34), replacing the law of sin which had disfigured that heart (cf. Jer 17:1). In those days, 'a new heart' would be given, for in it would dwell 'a new spirit', the Spirit of God (cf. Ezek 36:24–28)" (John Paul II, *Veritatis splendor*, 12).

20:1–32. This section begins very formally by specifying the date and recording that the elders are present. The date is 593 BC, that is, two years after the date of Ezekiel's call (1:2) and one year after his great vision of the temple (8:1). The elders are the representatives of the exiles, and in that capacity they visit Ezekiel in his house to consult with the Lord. The account given here of the history of Israel is in fact an assessment by God of the way the chosen people have behaved, as can be seen from the fact that it is spoken in the first person. It is divided into five stages—the people who were released from bondage in Egypt (vv. 5–10), the first generation who lived in the wilderness (vv. 11–17), those who were born in the wilderness (vv. 18–26), those who lived in the times of the monarchy (vv. 27–29), and finally the exiles, to whom the oracle is addressed (vv. 30–32). In each stage we find the same sequence of events—their election and endowment, their sin of rebellion, God's determination to punish them, and then his decision not to do so, out of respect for his name.

20:5–10. The account of the first three stages is based on traditions about the

[2]Et factus est sermo Domini ad me dicens: [3]«Fili hominis, loquere senioribus Israel et dices ad eos: Haec dicit Dominus Deus: Num ad interrogandum me vos venistis? Vivo ego, quia non respondebo vobis, ait Dominus Deus. [4]Numquid iudicabis eos, numquid iudicabis, fili hominis? Abominationes patrum eorum ostende eis. [5]Et dices ad eos: Haec dicit Dominus Deus: In die qua elegi Israel et levavi

says the Lord GOD: On the day when I chose Israel, I swore to the Ex 3:14
seed of the house of Jacob, making myself known to them in the Deut 7:6
land of Egypt, I swore to them, saying, I am the LORD your God.
[6]On that day I swore to them that I would bring them out of the Ex 3:8
land of Egypt into a land that I had searched out for them, a land
flowing with milk and honey, the most glorious of all lands. [7]And Lev 18:3
I said to them, Cast away the detestable things your eyes feast on, Josh 24:14
every one of you, and do not defile yourselves with the idols of
Egypt; I am the LORD your God. [8]But they rebelled against me
and would not listen to me; they did not every man cast away the
detestable things their eyes feasted on, nor did they forsake the
idols of Egypt.

"Then I thought I would pour out my wrath upon them and
spend my anger against them in the midst of the land of Egypt.
[9]But I acted for the sake of my name, that it should not be Ezek 20:14; 36:22
profaned in the sight of the nations among whom they dwelt, in
whose sight I made myself known to them in bringing them out of
the land of Egypt. [10]So I led them out of the land of Egypt and Lev 18:5 Deut 4:8
brought them into the wilderness. [11]I gave them my statutes and Ezek 20:8 Neh 9:14

---

exodus, and it recalls how the chosen people came into being and the early years of their history. Here God's initiative and active presence are made plain for all to see. Making no reference to the age of the patriarchs, Ezekiel sets the origin of the chosen people in Egypt ("in the land of Egypt": v. 5) because it was there that God made himself known to them and made promises to them, and manifested his name to them by wondrous signs: "I am the Lord your God" (v. 5). As the *Catechism* teaches: "In the decisive moments of his economy God reveals his name, but he does so by accomplishing his work. This work, then, is realized for us and in us only if his name is hallowed by us and in us" (*Catechism of the Catholic Church*, 2808).

The people "rebelled"; they refused to listen to God, and disobeyed him (v. 8). He decided to punish them, but refrained from doing so "for the sake of my name" (v. 9). For the sake of the name of the Lord (cf. 20:9, 14, 22), which is holy (cf. 20:39), God's sentence was suspended.

20:11–17. The first generation in the wilderness have the same experience.

manum meam pro stirpe domus Iacob et apparui eis in terra Aegypti et levavi manum meam pro eis dicens: Ego Dominus Deus vester; [6]in die illa levavi manum meam pro eis, ut educerem eos de terra Aegypti in terram, quam provideram eis fluentem lacte et melle, quae est egregia inter omnes terras. [7]Et dixi ad eos: Unusquisque abominationes oculorum suorum abiciat, et in idolis Aegypti nolite pollui: ego Dominus Deus vester. [8]Et irritaverunt me nolueruntque me audire; unusquisque abominationes oculorum suorum non proiecit, nec idola Aegypti reliquerunt. Et dixi, ut effunderem indignationem meam super eos et consummarem iram meam in eis in medio terrae Aegypti. [9]Et feci propter nomen meum, ut non violaretur coram gentibus, in quarum medio erant, et inter quas apparui eis, ut educerem eos de terra Aegypti. [10]Eduxi ergo eos de terra Aegypti et duxi in desertum. [11]Et dedi eis praecepta mea

Ex 20:8; 31:13 showed them my ordinances, by whose observance man shall live.
Jer 17:19–27 12Moreover I gave them my sabbaths, as a sign between me and
Ex 14:11 them, that they might know that I the LORD sanctify them. 13But
the house of Israel rebelled against me in the wilderness; they did
not walk in my statutes but rejected my ordinances, by whose
observance man shall live; and my sabbaths they greatly profaned.
"Then I thought I would pour out my wrath upon them in the
Ex 32:12 wilderness, to make a full end of them. 14But I acted for the sake
Ezek 20:9 of my name, that it should not be profaned in the sight of the
Num 14:28–30 nations, in whose sight I had brought them out. 15Moreover I
Deut 1:34–35 swore to them in the wilderness that I would not bring them into
Ps 95:11 the land which I had given them, a land flowing with milk and
honey, the most glorious of all lands, 16because they rejected my
ordinances and did not walk in my statutes, and profaned my
sabbaths; for their heart went after their idols. 17Nevertheless my

---

The Lord gave them ordinances (vv. 11–12) and they rebelled (v. 13); so the Lord determined to make an end of them (v. 13), but "for the sake of his name" he drew back (v. 14). Still, the sins they committed in the wilderness were such that neither Moses nor anyone else who left Egypt entered the promised land.

The mention of the sabbaths (v. 12; cf. Jer 17:19–27) shows Ezekiel's keenness, as a priest (cf. 22:8, 26; 23:38), that the exiles should observe the sabbath precepts, as a way of maintaining their identity in the pagan environment of Babylon: "It is no mystery that of the days of the week God chose the seventh as his own, for he himself called this day a 'sign' in Exodus and Ezekiel [...]. The sabbath signifies to men the need to dedicate themselves to God above all else; to be, and to show themselves to be, holy in his sight on the day that is consecrated wholly to him in a special way; it is a sign of man's need for holiness and religion. The sabbath also commemorates the creation of the universe, which was made for the glory and praise of God. Finally, the sabbath is a reminder to the Jews of the wondrous marvels worked by God when he freed them from slavery in Egypt [...]. Moreover, the sabbath is a sign and a symbol of the spiritual, heavenly Sabbath—the holy and mystical repose of the soul" (*Roman Catechism*, 3, 4, 13–15).

---

et iudicia mea ostendi eis, quae faciat homo et vivat in eis. 12Insuper et sabbata mea dedi eis, ut essent signum inter me et eos, et scirent quia ego Dominus sanctificans eos. 13Et irritaverunt me domus Israel in deserto: in praeceptis meis non ambulaverunt et iudicia mea proiecerunt, quae faciens homo vivet in eis, et sabbata mea violaverunt vehementer. Dixi ergo, ut effunderem furorem meum super eos in deserto et consumerem eos. 14Et feci propter nomen meum, ne violaretur coram gentibus, de quibus eduxi eos in conspectu earum. 15Attamen ego levavi quoque manum meam super eos in deserto, ne inducerem eos in terram, quam dedi eis fluentem lacte et melle, praecipuam terrarum omnium; 16quia iudicia mea proiecerunt et in praeceptis meis non ambulaverunt et sabbata mea violaverunt, post idola enim sua cor eorum gradiebatur. 17Et pepercit oculus meus super eos, ut non interficerem eos; nec

eye spared them, and I did not destroy them or make a full end of
them in the wilderness.
[18]"And I said to their children in the wilderness, Do not walk in Josh 24:14
the statutes of your fathers, nor observe their ordinances, nor 1 Pet 1:18
defile yourselves with their idols. [19]I the LORD am your God; walk
in my statutes, and be careful to observe my ordinances, [20]and
hallow my sabbaths that they may be a sign between me and you,
that you may know that I the LORD am your God. [21]But the Lev 18:5
children rebelled against me; they did not walk in my statutes, and
were not careful to observe my ordinances, by whose observance
man shall live; they profaned my sabbaths.
"Then I thought I would pour out my wrath upon them and
spend my anger against them in the wilderness. [22]But I withheld Ezek 20:14
my hand, and acted for the sake of my name, that it should not be
profaned in the sight of the nations, in whose sight I had brought
them out. [23]Moreover I swore to them in the wilderness that I Deut 28:64
would scatter them among the nations and disperse them through
the countries, [24]because they had not executed my ordinances, but

---

20:18–26. The second wilderness generation went through the same process again: the Lord gave them his precepts and sabbaths (v. 20), they rebelled (v. 21), and he decided that they should feel his wrath and be blotted out (v. 21), but for the sake of his name he held off (v. 22). However, he imposed on them "ordinances by which they could not have life" (v. 25), including the sacrifice of their children to Moloch (v. 26). St Jerome (cf. *Commentarim in Ezechielem*, in loc.) explained that this Semitic way of putting things does not mean that the Lord made the Israelites engage in idolatrous and monstrous practices prevalent among the people of Canaan; rather, he let them follow their base instincts and did not prevent them from falling into the same aberrations as their neighbours (cf. 2 Kings 16:3; 17:17). St Paul also explains the evil practices of pagans by saying that God punished them by leaving them to their own devices: "Since they did not see fit to acknowledge God, God gave them up to a base mind and to improper conduct" (Rom 1:28).

consumpsi eos in deserto. [18]Dixi autem ad filios eorum in solitudine: In praeceptis patrum vestrorum
nolite incedere nec iudicia eorum custodiatis nec in idolis eorum polluamini. [19]Ego Dominus Deus
vester. In praeceptis meis ambulate et iudicia mea custodite et facite ea [20]et sabbata mea sanctificate,
ut sint signum inter me et vos, et sciatur quia ego Dominus Deus vester. [21]Et exacerbaverunt me filii;
in praeceptis meis non ambulaverunt et iudicia mea non custodierunt, ut facerent ea, quae cum fecerit
homo, vivet in eis, et sabbata mea violaverunt. Et comminatus sum, ut effunderem furorem meum super
eos et consummarem iram meam in eis in deserto. [22]Averti autem manum meam et feci propter nomen
meum, ut non violaretur coram gentibus, de quibus eduxi eos in oculis earum. [23]Iterum levavi manum
meam in eos in solitudine, ut dispergerem illos in nationes et ventilarem in terras, [24]eo quod iudicia
mea non fecissent et praecepta mea reprobassent et sabbata mea violassent et post idola patrum suorum

Lev 18:21 had rejected my statutes and profaned my sabbaths, and their eyes
Ps 81:12 Acts 7:42 were set on their fathers' idols. [25]Moreover I gave them statutes
that were not good and ordinances by which they could not have
Rom 1:24 life; [26]and I defiled them through their very gifts in making them
2 Thess 2:11 2 Kings 21:6 offer by fire all their first-born, that I might horrify them; I did it
Jer 32:35 that they might know that I am the LORD.

[27]"Therefore, son of man, speak to the house of Israel and say
to them, Thus says the Lord GOD: In this again your fathers blas-
Deut 12:2 phemed me, by dealing treacherously with me. [28]For when I had
brought them into the land which I swore to give them, then wherever they saw any high hill or any leafy tree, there they offered their
sacrifices and presented the provocation of their offering; there
they sent up their soothing odors, and there they poured out their
drink offerings. [29](I said to them, What is the high place to which
you go? So its name is called Bamah[t] to this day.) [30]Wherefore
say to the house of Israel, Thus says the Lord GOD: Will you defile
yourselves after the manner of your fathers and go astray after
their detestable things? [31]When you offer your gifts and sacrifice
your sons by fire, you defile yourselves with all your idols to this
day. And shall I be inquired of by you, O house of Israel? As I
live, says the Lord GOD, I will not be inquired of by you.

20:27–29. Once they reached the promised land, the situation did not change very much. Far from acknowledging that it was the Lord who had opened up Canaan to them, they let themselves be drawn into idolatry and took part in pagan rites in the "high places". There is no mention here of how they will be disciplined for this, probably because the exile in Babylon is the punishment. But the passage does ridicule these idolatrous cults.

20:30–32. The exiles who are listening to all of this are not victims for the sins of their fathers; they are guilty of the same transgressions and the same idolatry as their forebears: that is why they are being punished. In fact, they have fallen much lower than their ancestors because they are losing hope that the Lord will save them, and they see themselves condemned to be forever like the pagans—worshippers of "wood and stone" (v. 32).

fuissent oculi eorum. [25]Ergo et ego dedi eis praecepta non bona et iudicia, in quibus non vivent; [26]et pollui eos in muneribus suis, cum offerrent omne, quod aperit vulvam, ut horrorem eis incuterem, et sciant quia ego Dominus. [27]Quam ob rem loquere ad domum Israel, fili hominis, et dices ad eos: Haec dicit Dominus Deus: Adhuc et in hoc blasphemaverunt me patres vestri, cum sprevissent me contemnentes, [28]et induxissem eos in terram, super quam levavi manum meam, ut darem eis. Viderunt omnem collem excelsum et omne lignum nemorosum et immolaverunt ibi victimas suas et dederunt ibi irritationem oblationis suae et posuerunt ibi odorem suavitatis suae et libaverunt libationes suas. [29]Et dixi ad eos: Quid est excelsum, ad quod vos ingredimini? Et vocatum est nomen eius Excelsum usque ad hanc diem. [30]Propterea dic ad domum Israel: Haec dicit Dominus Deus: Certe in via patrum

t. That is *High Place*

[32]"What is in your mind shall never happen—the thought, 'Let
us be like the nations, like the tribes of the countries, and worship
wood and stone.'

Deut 4:28
2 Kings 19:18
Jer 44:17

A restoration that shall endure

[33]"As I live, says the Lord GOD, surely with a mighty hand and an
outstretched arm, and with wrath poured out, I will be king over
you. [34]I will bring you out from the peoples and gather you out of
the countries where you are scattered, with a mighty hand and an
outstretched arm, and with wrath poured out; [35]and I will bring
you into the wilderness of the peoples, and there I will enter into
judgment with you face to face. [36]As I entered into judgment with

Ex 6:6
2 Cor 6:17
Ex 3:18; 4:27; 17:7; 19:24
Num 14:21–23:28,29

20:33–44. Seeking to raise the exiles from their dejection, the Lord renews his great promise and announces a new stage of salvation history comparable only to that which began in Egypt. The story of Israel began with release from bondage in Egypt (20:6), and it will end in a similar way: now, too, the Lord, with his "outstretched arm", will gather his people from among the nations (vv. 33, 34; cf. Ex 6:6); he will bring them into the wilderness (v. 35; cf. Ex 3:18; 4:27), there he will resolve the differences between them (cf. Ex 17:7) and, eventually, as on Sinai (cf. Ex 19–24), he will make a new Covenant with them (v. 37). All these echoes of things that happened in the exodus underscore God's faithfulness: far from blotting his people out, he will rehabilitate them in a definitive way.

All these things that the Lord is going to do for his people are grounded on the two great planks that Ezekiel uses in his teaching—the holiness of the name of God (vv. 39, 40, 41) which will ensure that the repatriated exiles are purged of any infidelity, and a new form of worship involving the choicest of offerings (vv. 40–41). The Priestly tradition (and Ezekiel more so) is always at pains to defend the name of God: "In spite of the holy Law that again and again their Holy God gives them—'You shall be holy, for I the Lord your God am holy' (Lev 19:2)—and although the Lord shows patience for the sake of his name, the people turn away from the Holy One of Israel and profane his name among the nations (cf. Ezek 20:36). For this reason the just ones of the Old Covenant, the poor survivors returned from exile, and the prophets burned with passion for the Name" (*Catechism of the Catholic Church*, 2811).

vestrorum vos polluimini et post offendicula eorum vos fornicamini [31]et in oblatione donorum vestrorum, cum traducitis filios vestros per ignem; vos polluimini in omnibus idolis vestris usque hodie, et ego respondebo vobis, domus Israel? Vivo ego, dicit Dominus Deus, quia non respondebo vobis. [32]Neque cogitatio mentis vestrae fiet dicentium: "Erimus sicut gentes et sicut cognationes terrarum, ut colamus ligna et lapides". [33]Vivo ego, dicit Dominus Deus, quoniam in manu forti et brachio extento et in furore effuso regnabo super vos. [34]Et educam vos de populis et congregabo vos de terris, in quibus dispersi estis; in manu valida et brachio extento et in furore effuso. [35]Et adducam vos in desertum populorum et iudicio contendam vobiscum ibi facie ad faciem. [36]Sicut iudicio contendi adversum patres

your fathers in the wilderness of the land of Egypt, so I will enter
into judgment with you, says the Lord GOD. 37I will make you
Is 4:3 pass under the rod, and I will let you go in by number.[u] 38I will
purge out the rebels from among you, and those who transgress
against me; I will bring them out of the land where they sojourn,
but they shall not enter the land of Israel. Then you will know that
I am the LORD.

Ezek 16:59–63; 36:20; 43:8
39"As for you, O house of Israel, thus says the Lord GOD: Go
serve every one of you his idols, now and hereafter, if you will not
listen to me; but my holy name you shall no more profane with
your gifts and your idols.

Is 56:7; 60:7 Ezek 17:23; 44:20 Mal 3:8
40"For on my holy mountain, the mountain height of Israel,
says the Lord GOD, there all the house of Israel, all of them, shall
serve me in the land; there I will accept them, and there I will
require your contributions and the choicest of your gifts, with all
your sacred offerings. 41As a pleasing odor I will accept you,
when I bring you out from the peoples, and gather you out of the
countries where you have been scattered; and I will manifest my
holiness among you in the sight of the nations. 42And you shall
know that I am the LORD, when I bring you into the land of Israel,
the country which I swore to give to your fathers. 43And there you
shall remember your ways and all the doings with which you have
polluted yourselves; and you shall loathe yourselves for all the
Ezek 20:14 evils that you have committed. 44And you shall know that I am the
LORD, when I deal with you for my name's sake, not according to
your evil ways, nor according to your corrupt doings, O house of
Israel, says the Lord GOD."

---

vestros in deserto terrae Aegypti, sic iudicio contendam vobiscum, dicit Dominus Deus, 37et transire vos faciam sub baculo meo et inducam vos in vinculis foederis. 38Et segregabo de vobis transgressores et impios et de terra incolatus eorum educam eos, et terram Israel non ingredientur, et scietis quia ego Dominus. 39Et vos, domus Israel, haec dicit Dominus Deus: Singuli post idola vestra ambulate et servite eis. Sed postea nonne audietis me et nomen meum sanctum non polluetis ultra in muneribus vestris et in idolis vestris? 40In monte enim sancto meo, in monte excelso Israel, ait Dominus Deus, ibi serviet mihi omnis domus Israel: omnes, inquam, in terra, in qua placebunt mihi; et ibi quaeram donaria vestra et primitias oblationum vestrarum in omnibus sanctificationibus vestris. 41In odorem suavitatis suscipiam vos, cum eduxero vos de populis et congregavero vos de terris, in quas dispersi estis, et sanctificabor in vobis in oculis nationum. 42Et scietis quia ego Dominus, cum induxero vos ad terram Israel, in terram, pro qua levavi manum meam, ut darem eam patribus vestris. 43Et recordabimini ibi viarum vestrarum et omnium scelerum vestrorum, quibus polluti estis, et displicebitis vobis in conspectu vestro in omnibus malitiis vestris, quas fecistis. 44Et scietis quia ego Dominus, cum benefecero vobis propter nomen meum, non secundum vias vestras malas neque secundum scelera vestra pessima, domus Israel», ait Dominus Deus.

u. Gk: Heb *bring you into the bond of the covenant*

The sword of the Lord*

[45v]And the word of the LORD came to me: [46]"Son of man, set your Ezek 16:46
face toward the south, preach against the south, and prophesy
against the forest land in the Negeb; [47]say to the forest of the Ps 83:15 Is 9:17;
Negeb, Hear the word of the LORD: Thus says the Lord GOD, 10:17–19
Behold, I will kindle a fire in you, and it shall devour every green Jer 21:14
tree in you and every dry tree; the blazing flame shall not be Ezek 21:3 Lk 23:31
quenched, and all faces from south to north shall be scorched by
it. [48]All flesh shall see that I the LORD have kindled it; it shall not
be quenched." [49]Then I said, "Ah Lord GOD! they are saying of
me, 'Is he not a maker of allegories?'"

21 [1w]The word of the LORD came to me: [2]"Son of man, set Job 9:22
your face toward Jerusalem and preach against the sanc-

***20:45—21:32.** The Lord's severe sentence against Jerusalem continues in this bloc of oracles that use the imagery of fire and sword. The first four all begin in the same way: "The word of the Lord came to me" (20:45; 21:1, 8, 18); the last, which is not addressed to Jerusalem, begins with a different form of words, "And you shall prophesy and say" (21:28). The conclusion (vv. 21:30–32) celebrates the destruction, in turn, of the sword, the instrument of death (symbolizing Babylon): the exiles have good reason to hope.

This tapestry of oracles shows in various ways the sovereignty of the Lord; he is behind every movement the invader makes, and only he can save those who have borne the deprivations of the siege. The point is made that God seeks man's good, even though sometimes man may not see it quite that way: "We firmly believe that God is master of the world and of its history. But the ways of his providence are often unknown to us. Only at the end, when our partial knowledge ceases, when we see God 'face to face' (1 Cor 13:12), will we fully know the ways by which—even through the dramas of evil and sin—God has guided his creation to that definite *sabbath* rest (cf. Gen 2:2) for which he created heaven and earth" (*Catechism of the Catholic Church*, 314).

20:45—21:7. This passage contains two linked oracles. The first (20:45–49), the more allegorical of the two, is about a fire that runs from north to south and devours everything in its path. This stands for Babylon that invades from the north, razing everything it meets. The second (21:1–7) explains the allegory: the fire is now the sword—indicating that the disaster predicted is a military invasion, not some natural calamity. And its target is not the south in general but Jerusalem in particular (21:1). The green trees and the dry trees

[21] [1]Et factus est sermo Domini ad me dicens: [2]«Fili hominis, pone faciem tuam contra meridiem et stilla ad austrum et propheta ad saltum agri Nageb. [3]Et dices saltui Nageb: Audi verbum Domini. Haec

v. Ch 21:1 in Heb **w.** Ch 21:6 in Heb

tuaries; prophesy against the land of Israel 3and say to the land of
Israel, Thus says the LORD: Behold, I am against you, and will
draw forth my sword out of its sheath, and will cut off from you
both righteous and wicked. 4Because I will cut off from you both
righteous and wicked, therefore my sword shall go out of its
sheath against all flesh from south to north; 5and all flesh shall
know that I the LORD have drawn my sword out of its sheath; it
shall not be sheathed again. 6Sigh therefore, son of man; sigh with
Ezek 7:17 breaking heart and bitter grief before their eyes. 7And when they
say to you, 'Why do you sigh?' you shall say, 'Because of the
tidings. When it comes, every heart will melt and all hands will be
feeble, every spirit will faint and all knees will be weak as water.
Behold, it comes and it will be fulfilled,'" says the Lord GOD.

Hymn to the sword

8And the word of the LORD came to me: 9"Son of man, prophesy
and say, Thus says the Lord, Say:

---

are, in this explanation, the righteous and the wicked (21:3). Once again we can see Ezekiel's sense of solidarity with his people when he sighs at the dire prospect (21:6).

21:8–17. This passage celebrates the sword as the weapon that God uses to punish his people. It describes poetically the quality of the sword (vv. 8–11) and the fear it provokes (vv. 12–13); the prophet is depicted as celebrating the sword's efficiency as it carves its way to achieve its cruel aim (vv. 14–16); the Lord is happy that he has meted out this punishment (v. 17).

"Smite ... upon your thigh" (v. 12). Some ancient texts confirm that to express pain or grief Semitic peoples would beat their thighs—the equivalent of beating one's breast.

"Prophesy ...; clap your hands" (v. 14). The prophet is a sensitive man and, after his lament for the fate of Jerusalem, he must now show that he rejoices because the punishment decreed by God is complete. Underlying this passage is the idea that even though the exile is a punishment, it also has the effect of purifying the people. Likewise the sword: it is a weapon that delivers pain and death, but in God's hands it becomes an instrument of salvation. Similarly, in the new economy of salvation, the cross, which epitomized the most ignominious form of punishment,

---

dicit Dominus Deus: Ecce ego succendam in te ignem, et comburet in te omne lignum viride et omne
lignum aridum; non exstinguetur flamma succensionis, et comburetur in ea omnis facies ab austro
usque ad aquilonem. 4Et videbit universa caro quia ego Domínus succendi eam, nec exstinguetur». 5Et
dixi: «Heu, Domine Deus! Ipsi dicunt de me: "Numquid non per parabolas loquitur iste"». 6Et factus
est sermo Domini ad me dicens: 7«Fili hominis, pone faciem tuam ad Ierusalem et stilla ad sanctuaria
et propheta contra humum Israel. 8Et dices terrae Israel: Haec dicit Dominus Deus: Ecce ego ad te, et
eiciam gladium meum de vagina sua et occidam in te iustum et impium. 9Pro eo autem quod occidi in

A sword, a sword is sharpened
and also polished,
[10]sharpened for slaughter,
polished to flash like lightning!
Or do we make mirth? You have despised the rod, my son, with
everything of wood. [11]So the sword is given to be polished, that it
may be handled; it is sharpened and polished to be given into the
hand of the slayer. [12]Cry and wail, son of man, for it is against my Jer 31:19
people; it is against all the princes of Israel; they are delivered
over to the sword with my people. Smite therefore upon your
thigh. [13]For it will not be a testing—what could it do if you
despise the rod?" says the Lord GOD.

[14]"Prophesy therefore, son of man; clap your hands and let the
sword come down twice, yea thrice, the sword for those to be
slain; it is the sword for the great slaughter, which encompasses
them, [15]that their hearts may melt, and many fall at all their gates.
I have given the glittering sword; ah! it is made like lightning, it is
polished[x] for slaughter. [16]Cut sharply to right[y] and left where your
edge is directed. [17]I also will clap my hands, and I will satisfy my
fury; I the LORD have spoken."

Assault on Jerusalem

[18]The word of the LORD came to me again: [19]"Son of man, mark
two ways for the sword of the king of Babylon to come; both of

---

is celebrated as the source of salvation; witness the well-known liturgical hymn attributed to Venantius Fortunatus: "O faithful cross, most noble tree! Never has the forest paid higher tribute in bole and branch and leaf! Sweet nails! O noble tree, where life began in the sweet fruit that hung from thee!" (Hymn used in Good Friday liturgy).

21:18–27. The sword is now in the hands of the king of Babylon, who

te iustum et impium, idcirco egredietur gladius meus de vagina sua ad omnem carnem, ab austro ad aquilonem, [10]ut sciat omnis caro quia ego Dominus eduxi gladium meum de vagina sua irrevocabilem. [11]Et tu, fili hominis, ingemisce in contritione lumborum et in amaritudinibus ingemisce coram eis. [12]Cumque dixerint ad te: "Quare tu gemis?", dices: Pro auditu quia venit et tabescet omne cor, et dissolventur universae manus, et infirmabitur omnis spiritus, et per cuncta genua fluent aquae; ecce venit et fiet», ait Dominus Deus. [13]Et factus est sermo Domini ad me dicens: [14]«Fili hominis, propheta et dices: Haec dicit Dominus Deus: Loquere: Gladius, gladius exacutus est / et etiam limatus; / [15]ut caedat victimas exacutus est, / ut splendeat limatus est. / [16]Et datus est ad levigandum, / ut teneatur manu. / Iste exacutus est gladius et iste limatus, / ut sit in manu interficientis. / [17]Clama et ulula, fili hominis, / quia hic directus est in populum meum, / hic in cunctos duces Israel, / qui gladio traditi sunt cum populo meo. / [18]Idcirco plaude super femur, / quia probatio est, / dicit Dominus Deus. / [19]Tu ergo,

x. Tg: Heb *wrapped up* **y.** Gk Syr Vg: Heb *right, set*

them shall come forth from the same land. And make a signpost,
Jer 49:2 make it at the head of the way to a city; [20]mark a way for the
Ezek 25,4–5 sword to come to Rabbah of the Ammonites and to Judah and to[z]
Jerusalem the fortified. [21]For the king of Babylon stands at the
parting of the way, at the head of the two ways, to use divination;
he shakes the arrows, he consults the teraphim, he looks at the
Ezek 4:2–3 liver. [22]Into his right hand comes the lot for Jerusalem,[a] to open
the mouth with a cry,[b] to lift up the voice with shouting, to set
battering rams against the gates, to cast up mounds, to build siege
towers. [23]But to them it will seem like a false divination; they have
sworn solemn oaths; but he brings their guilt to remembrance, that
they may be captured.

2 Chron 36:13 [24]"Therefore thus says the Lord GOD: Because you have made
Jer 52:2 your guilt to be remembered, in that your transgressions are
uncovered, so that in all your doings your sins appear—because

---

must attack first Jerusalem and then the Ammonites. Nebuchadnezzar thought that his campaign was being planned by augury and according to opportunity (v. 21), but in fact it was the Lord who was deciding the turn that history should take. The Israelites thought that luck was against them (v. 23), but it was the Lord who was punishing them for their sins. Once again God's sovereignty towers above the course of human events.

The oracle mentions the three types of divination used by the Babylonians (v. 21)—picking arrows from a quiver, consulting the *penates* or household gods, and examining the entrails of animals offered in sacrifice to idols.

21:28–32. The time of judgment has come for the Ammonites also (vv. 28–29), and in fact their city (present-day Amman, in Jordan) was razed to the ground by Nebuchadnezzar some years after Jerusalem. That event was a further proof of the truth of Ezekiel's prophecies; but, above all, it sent a signal of hope to the exiles.

The last words in the chapter (vv. 30–32) confirm that the sword (Babylon) was merely a weapon that God used; in due course it will be destroyed. God is the only judge; he hands down judgment as regards Judah and Jerusalem—but also against pagan nations, as will become clear from later oracles (chaps. 25–29).

fili hominis, / propheta et percute manu ad manum. / Et duplicetur gladius, / ac triplicetur gladius
interfectorum: hic est gladius occisionis magnae, / qui eos circumdat, / [20]ut cor tabescat, / et
multiplicentur corruentes. / In omnibus portis eorum / dedi occisionem gladii: / eheu, facti acuti et
limati ad fulgendum, / politi ad caedem! / [21]"Exacuere, vade ad dexteram sive ad sinistram, /
quocumque acies tuae sunt destinatae". / [22]Quin et ego plaudam manu ad manum / et saturabo
indignationem meam, / ego Dominus locutus sum». [23]Et factus est sermo Domini ad me dicens: [24]«Et
tu, fili hominis, pone tibi duas vias, ut veniat gladius regis Babylonis: de terra una egrediantur ambae;
et indicem statue, in capite viae civitatis statue. [25]Viam pones, quo veniat gladius, ad Rabba filiorum

z. Gk Syr: Heb *in* **a.** Heb *Jerusalem, to set battering rams* **b.** Gk: Heb *with slaughter*

you have come to remembrance, you shall be taken in them.[c]
[25]And you, O unhallowed wicked one, prince of Israel, whose day
has come, the time of your final punishment, [26]thus says the Lord
GOD: Remove the turban, and take off the crown; things shall not
remain as they are; exalt that which is low, and abase that which
is high. [27]A ruin, ruin, ruin I will make it; there shall not be even Gen 40:19
a trace[d] of it until he comes whose right it is; and to him I will Is 40:4
give it.

Assault on the Ammonites

[28]"And you, son of man, prophesy, and say, Thus says the Lord Jer 25:21; 49:1
GOD concerning the Ammonites, and concerning their reproach; Ezek 25:2
say, A sword, a sword is drawn for the slaughter, it is polished to
glitter[e] and to flash like lightning—[29]while they see for you false
visions, while they divine lies for you—to be laid on the necks of
the unhallowed wicked, whose day has come, the time of their
final punishment. [30]Return it to its sheath. In the place where you
were created, in the land of your origin, I will judge you. [31]And I
will pour out my indignation upon you; I will blow upon you with
the fire of my wrath; and I will deliver you into the hands of brutal
men, skilful to destroy. [32]You shall be fuel for the fire; your blood
shall be in the midst of the land; you shall be no more remembered; for I the LORD have spoken."

The crimes of Jerusalem*

22 [1]Moreover the word of the LORD came to me, saying, [2]"And Ezek 20:4;
you, son of man, will you judge, will you judge the bloody 23:26

***22:1–31.** This chapter contains three oracles (with scarcely any use of metaphor or allegory) which expose the guilt of Jerusalem and justify the Lord's sentence against her. Each begins with the technical formula "The word of the

Ammon et ad Iudam in Ierusalem munitissimam. [26]Stat enim rex Babylonis in bivio in capite duarum viarum, divinationem quaerens, commiscens sagittas; interrogat teraphim, iecur consulit. [27]Ad dexteram eius facta est divinatio super Ierusalem, ut ponat arietes, ut aperiat os ad caedem, ut elevet vocem in ululatu, ut ponat arietes contra portas, ut comportet aggerem, ut aedificet munitiones. [28]Eritque quasi consulens frustra oraculum in oculis eorum, et iuramenta sanctissima sunt eis; ipse autem in memoriam revocabit iniquitatem ad capiendum. [29]Idcirco haec dicit Dominus Deus: Pro eo quod in memoriam revocastis iniquitatem vestram, et revelatae sunt praevaricationes vestrae, et apparuerunt peccata vestra in omnibus operibus vestris; pro eo, inquam, quod in memoriam revocati estis, manu capiemini. [30]Tu autem, profane, impie dux Israel, cuius venit dies in tempore iniquitatis finitae—[31]haec dicit Dominus Deus— auferatur cidaris, tollatur corona; hoc non erit amplius. Humile sublevetur, et sublime humilietur. [32]Ruinam, ruinam, ruinam ponam illud; et hoc non fiet, donec veniat, cuius est iudicium, et tradam ei. [33]Et tu, fili hominis, propheta et dic: Haec dicit Dominus Deus ad

c. Gk: Heb *with the hand* **d.** Cn: Heb *not even this* **e.** Cn: Heb *to contain*

city? Then declare to her all her abominable deeds. [3]You shall say,
Thus says the Lord GOD: A city that sheds blood in the midst of
her, that her time may come, and that makes idols to defile herself!
2 Kings 21:16 [4]You have become guilty by the blood which you have shed, and
defiled by the idols which you have made; and you have brought
your day near, the appointed time[f] of your years has come.
Therefore I have made you a reproach to the nations, and a
mocking to all the countries. [5]Those who are near and those who
are far from you will mock you, you infamous one, full of tumult.
Ezek 5:14; 18:5–9 [6]"Behold, the princes of Israel in you, every one according to
Ex 22:21–22 his power, have been bent on shedding blood. [7]Father and mother
Lev 19:13 are treated with contempt in you; the sojourner suffers extortion in
Deut 27:16 your midst; the fatherless and the widow are wronged in you.
Lev 19:30 [8]You have despised my holy things, and profaned my sabbaths.
Lev 19:16 [9]There are men in you who slander to shed blood, and men in you
Deut 12:12 who eat upon the mountains; men commit lewdness in your midst.

Lord came to me, saying" (vv. 1, 17, 23). The first spells out Jerusalem's crimes (vv. 1–16); the second (in more general terms) extends the denunciation to the whole country (v. 17–22); and the third (vv. 23–31) is aimed at the various strata of society—princes, priests, prophets and ordinary people.

22:1–16. The serious charge against the city is spelt out at the start: "a city that sheds blood in the midst of her" (v. 3); then three types of sins are mentioned (vv. 6–8; 9–11 and 12). The first has to do with "shedding blood" and the others with the precepts of the "code of holiness" (Lev 17–26). All these sins have been committed "in you" (vv. 6, 7, 9, 10, 11, 12), that is, in Jerusalem, the holy city. So, when the people are scattered (a terrible punishment), this will belittle God in the eyes of foreign nations (v. 16)—but it will also cleanse Israel once and for all.

filios Ammon et ad opprobrium eorum; et dices: Gladius, gladius est evaginatus ad occidendum, limatus ad consumendum, ut fulgeat, [34]cum tibi videntur vana, et divinantur mendacia, ut ponatur gladius ad colla profanorum impiorum, quorum venit dies in tempore iniquitatis finitae. [35]Revertatur ad vaginam suam. In loco, in quo creatus es, in terra nativitatis tuae iudicabo te. [36]Et effundam super te indignationem meam, in igne furoris mei sufflabo in te; daboque te in manus hominum insipientium et fabricantium interitum. [37]Igni eris cibus, sanguis tuus erit in medio terrae; oblivioni traderis, quia ego Dominus locutus sum». **[22]** [1]Et factum est verbum Domini ad me dicens: [2]«Et tu, fili hominis, num iudicas, num iudicas civitatem sanguinum? [3]Et ostendes ei omnes abominationes suas et dices: Haec dicit Dominus Deus: Civitas effundens sanguinem in medio sui, ut veniat tempus eius et, quae fecit idola contra semetipsam, ut pollueretur. [4]In sanguine tuo, qui a te effusus est, deliquisti; et in idolis tuis, quae fecisti, polluta es; et appropinquare fecisti dies tuos et adduxisti tempus annorum tuorum. Propterea dedi te opprobrium gentibus et irrisionem universis terris. [5]Quae iuxta sunt et quae procul a te, triumphabunt de te, sordibus famosa, grandis tumultu. [6]Ecce principes Israel singuli pro brachio suo fuerunt in te ad effundendum sanguinem. [7]Pater et mater contempti sunt in te, advena oppressus est in medio tui, pupillum et viduam afflixerunt apud te. [8]Sanctuaria mea sprevisti et sabbata mea profanasti. [9]Viri detractores fuerunt in te ad effundendum sanguinem et super montes comederunt in

f. Two Mss Gk Syr Vg Tg: Heb *until*

[10]In you men uncover their fathers' nakedness; in you they humble Lev 18:7–8,19
women who are unclean in their impurity. [11]One commits Lev 18:9,15,
abomination with his neighbour's wife; another lewdly defiles his 19,20
daughter-in-law; another in you defiles his sister, his father's
daughter. [12]In you men take bribes to shed blood; you take interest Lev 25:35–37
and increase and make gain of your neighbours by extortion; and Deut 27:25
you have forgotten me, says the Lord GOD.

[13]"Behold, therefore, I strike my hands together at the dis- Ezek 6:11
honest gain which you have made, and at the blood which has
been in the midst of you. [14]Can your courage endure, or can your
hands be strong, in the days that I shall deal with you? I the LORD
have spoken, and I will do it. [15]I will scatter you among the nations Lev 26:33
and disperse you through the countries, and I will consume your Deut 4:27
filthiness out of you. [16]And I[g] shall be profaned through you in the Ezek 24:11
sight of the nations; and you shall know that I am the LORD."

[17]And the word of the LORD came to me: [18]"Son of man, the Is 1:22,25
house of Israel has become dross to me; all of them, silver[h] and Jer 6:28–30
bronze and tin and iron and lead in the furnace, have become Mal 3:3
dross. [19]Therefore thus says the Lord GOD: Because you have all
become dross, therefore, behold, I will gather you into the midst
of Jerusalem. [20]As men gather silver and bronze and iron and lead
and tin into a furnace, to blow the fire upon it in order to melt it; Mal 3:2–3
so I will gather you in my anger and in my wrath, and I will put

22:17–22. The prophets often used the metaphor of the furnace where precious metals are refined (cf. Is 1:25; 48:10 Jer 6:29; etc.). Ezekiel does not lose sight of the final product (the refined metal) but he focuses on the core of the process: "You shall be melted in the midst of (the city)" (v. 22). So, even though the passage is all about the siege and destruction of Jerusalem, there is a note of hope to it, because what is happening is that the city is being purified of its dross.

te; scelus operati sunt in medio tui. [10]Verecundiora patris discooperuerunt in te, immunditiam menstruatae humiliaverunt in te; [11]et unus in uxorem proximi sui operatus est abominationem, et alter nurum suam polluit nefarie; frater sororem suam, filiam patris sui, oppressit in te. [12]Munera acceperunt apud te ad effundendum sanguinem, usuram et fenus accepisti et avare proximos tuos calumniabaris meique oblita es, ait Dominus Deus. [13]Ecce complosi manus meas super lucrum tuum, quod fecisti, et super sanguinem, qui effusus est in medio tui. [14]Numquid sustinebit cor tuum, aut praevalebunt manus tuae in diebus, quos ego faciam tibi? Ego Dominus locutus sum et faciam; [15]et dispergam te in nationes et ventilabo te in terras et deficere faciam immunditiam tuam a te: [16]et profanabo me in te in conspectu gentium, et scies quia ego Dominus». [17]Et factum est verbum Domini ad me dicens: [18]«Fili hominis, versa est mihi domus Israel in scoriam; omnes isti argentum et aes et stannum et ferrum et plumbum in medio fornacis, scoria facti sunt. [19]Propterea haec dicit Dominus Deus: Eo quod versi estis omnes in scoriam, propterea ecce ego congregabo vos in medio Ierusalem [20]congregatione argenti et aeris et ferri et plumbi et stanni in medio fornacis, ut succendatur in ea ignis ad conflandum: sic congregabo in

g. Gk Syr Vg: Heb *you* **h.** Transposed from the end of the verse. Compare verse 20

you in and melt you. 21I will gather you and blow upon you with
the fire of my wrath, and you shall be melted in the midst of it.
22As silver is melted in a furnace, so you shall be melted in the
midst of it; and you shall know that I the LORD have poured out
my wrath upon you."
23"And the word of the LORD came to me: 24"Son of man, say
to her, You are a land that is not cleansed, or rained upon in the
day of indignation. 25Her princes[i] in the midst of her are like a
roaring lion tearing the prey; they have devoured human lives;
they have taken treasure and precious things; they have made
many widows in the midst of her. 26Her priests have done violence
to my law and have profaned my holy things; they have made no
distinction between the holy and the common, neither have they
taught the difference between the unclean and the clean, and they
have disregarded my sabbaths, so that I am profaned among them.
27Her princes in the midst of her are like wolves tearing the prey,
shedding blood, destroying lives to get dishonest gain. 28And her

Ex 20:13–15; Deut 7:14–20; Zeph 3:3–4; 1 Pet 5:8
Ex 20:8–11; Lev 11:16; 17–22; 19:30; 23:3
Deut 16:18–20

22:23–31. All members of the chosen people are blameworthy, and all deserve the catastrophe that is looming. They have failed to live up to their obligations. The princes of the royal house and the king were supposed to take care of the people (cf. Deut 17:14–20), not enrich themselves at their expense (v. 25). Priests ought to have been scrupulous in observing the precepts to do with divine worship, especially the sabbath (v. 26). Secular leaders had a duty to dispense justice impartially (v. 27; cf. Deut 16:18–20). Prophets (cf. Deut 18:9–22) should speak only the word of God, not their own imaginings (v. 28). And, finally, the ordinary people should be peaceable and make sure they look after the needy. The final complaint about not being able to find a just man or intercessor (v. 30) is particularly poignant and is reminiscent (in a reverse way) of Abraham's pleading for Sodom (cf. Gen 18:22–33).

furore meo et in ira mea et ponam et conflabo vos 21et congregabo vos et succendam vos in igne furoris mei, et conflabimini in medio eius. 22Ut conflatur argentum in medio fornacis, sic conflabimini in medio eius; et scietis quia ego Dominus effuderim indignationem meam super vos». 23Et factum est verbum Domini ad me dicens: 24«Fili hominis, dic ei: Tu es terra, super quam non cecidit pluvia neque imber in die furoris, 25cuius duces in medio eius sicut leo rugiens capiensque praedam: animas devoraverunt, opes et pretium acceperunt, viduas eius multiplicaverunt in medio illius. 26Sacerdotes eius contempserunt legem meam et polluerunt sanctuaria mea, inter sanctum et profanum non habuerunt distantiam et inter pollutum et mundum non docuerunt distinguere et a sabbatis meis averterunt oculos suos, et coinquinabar in medio eorum. 27Principes eius in medio illius quasi lupi rapientes praedam ad effundendum sanguinem et perdendas animas et avare sectanda lucra. 28Prophetae autem eius liniebant eis omnia calce, videntes vana et divinantes eis mendacium, dicentes: "Haec dicit

i. Gk: Heb *a conspiracy of her prophets*

prophets have daubed for them with whitewash, seeing false Deut 18:9–22
visions and divining lies for them, saying, 'Thus says the Lord Ezek 13:10–16
GOD,' when the LORD has not spoken. [29]The people of the land
have practised extortion and committed robbery; they have
oppressed the poor and needy, and have extorted from the
sojourner without redress. [30]And I sought for a man among them Gen 18:22–33
who should build up the wall and stand in the breach before me Ps 106:23
for the land, that I should not destroy it; but I found none. Is 59:15–16
[31]Therefore I have poured out my indignation upon them; I have
consumed them with the fire of my wrath; their way have I
requited upon their heads, says the Lord GOD."

Lev 18:18
2 Kings 17:5–23

Allegory of the two sisters*

23 [1]The word of the LORD came to me: [2]"Son of man, there Jer 3:6–13
were two women, the daughters of one mother; [3]they Ezek 16:1

***23:1–49.** In this sequence of denunciations of Jerusalem and Israel, Ezekiel takes up again the marriage metaphor used in chapter 16. Here he links it more to historical events—condemning not so much idolatrous practices as dangerous alliances with pagan nations. In fact, even though it is at odds with Leviticus 18:18, the Lord is depicted as marrying two sisters, just as Jacob did, who symbolize the two kingdoms—that of Samaria, which was destroyed by the Assyrians in 721 (cf. 2 Kings 17:5–23) and that of Jerusalem which fell in 587.

The names given the two sisters may have some special meaning, but, if so, it escapes us. *Oholah*, etymologically, means "her tent", and *Oholibah*, "my tent [is] in her", meaning probably that the sanctuary, the tent, of Samaria was not a lawful one, whereas the cult at Jerusalem was the authentic worship of the Lord.

The unrefined language used in the passage helps to show that the behaviour of the two kingdoms cannot in any way be justified: it must needs bring catastrophe down upon them. The passage also shows the Lord's intense love for the people of both kingdoms.

23:1–10. The stage when the tribes still lived in Egypt is summed up in one cutting line: "they played the harlot in their youth" (v. 3; cf. 16:26). Prostitution (idolatry, and pacts with foreign nations) is the thread running through this chapter: far from giving it up once they settled in the promised land, Oholah (Samaria) engaged in it increasingly, until Assyria, who had been exacting

Dominus Deus", cum Dominus non sit locutus. [29]Populus terrae calumniabatur calumniam et rapiebat violenter; egenum et pauperem affligebant et advenam opprimebant absque iudicio. [30]Et quaesivi de eis virum, qui interponeret saepem et staret in confractione contra me pro terra, ne dissiparem eam, et non inveni. [31]Et effudi super eos indignationem meam, in igne irae meae consumpsi eos, viam eorum in caput eorum reddidi», ait Dominus Deus. **[23]** [1]Et factus est sermo Domini ad me dicens: [2]«Fili hominis, duae mulieres filiae matris unius fuerunt [3]et fornicatae sunt in Aegypto, in adulescentia sua

Ezek 20:7–8 played the harlot in Egypt; they played the harlot in their youth;
there their breasts were pressed and their virgin bosoms handled.
4Oholah was the name of the elder and Oholibah the name of her
sister. They became mine, and they bore sons and daughters. As
for their names, Oholah is Samaria, and Oholibah is Jerusalem.
5"Oholah played the harlot while she was mine; and she doted
on her lovers the Assyrians, 6warriors clothed in purple, governors
and commanders, all of them desirable young men, horsemen
riding on horses. 7She bestowed her harlotries upon them, the
choicest men of Assyria all of them; and she defiled herself with
all the idols of every one on whom she doted. 8She did not give up
her harlotry which she had practised since her days in Egypt; for
in her youth men had lain with her and handled her virgin bosom
and poured out their lust upon her. 9Therefore I delivered her into
the hands of her lovers, into the hands of the Assyrians, upon
whom she doted. 10These uncovered her nakedness; they seized
her sons and her daughters; and her they slew with the sword; and
she became a byword among women, when judgment had been
executed upon her.
11"Her sister Oholibah saw this, yet she was more corrupt than
she in her doting and in her harlotry, which was worse than that of

---

heavy tribute from her, eventually invaded and removed her from the map (vv. 9–10).

23:11–35. The crimes of Oholibah (Judah) are given in more detail: they are more serious because Judah could see what had happened to her sister kingdom, Israel—and also because Judah was God's favourite. Besides, Israel had made pacts with only one kingdom (Assyria), whereas Judah formed alliances with Assyria, Babylon and even Egypt.

The cup filled with liquor that becomes poisonous (vv. 32–34) is a metaphor often used to indicate a punishment that is very severe—something one has to drink to the dregs (cf. Jer 25:14–29). The Revelation to John refers to the "wine of God's wrath" (cf. Rev 14:10) when referring to the eschatological punishment that will befall those who worship the beast, that is, idolators.

fornicatae sunt; ibi subacta sunt ubera earum, et tactae sunt mammae virginitatis earum. 4Nomina autem earum Oolla maior et Ooliba soror eius; et habui eas, et pepererunt filios et filias: porro earum nomina Samaria Oolla et Ierusalem Ooliba. 5Fornicata est igitur Oolla discedens a me; et insanivit in amatores suos, in Assyrios: bellatores 6vestitos hyacintho, principes et magistratus, iuvenes desiderabiles universi, equites ascensores equorum. 7Et dedit fornicationes suas ad eos electos filiorum Assyriae universos; et apud omnes, in quos insanivit, in omnibus idolis eorum polluta est. 8Insuper et fornicationes suas, quas habuerat in Aegypto, non reliquit; nam et illi dormierunt cum ea in adulescentia eius, et illi tetigerant ubera virginitatis eius et effuderant fornicationem suam super eam. 9Propterea tradidi eam in manus amatorum suorum, in manus filiorum Assyriae, in quos insanivit; 10ipsi discooperuerunt ignominiam eius, filios et filias illius tulerunt et ipsam occiderunt gladio; et facta est

her sister. 12She doted upon the Assyrians, governors and commanders, warriors clothed in full armour, horsemen riding on
horses, all of them desirable young men. 13And I saw that she was
defiled; they both took the same way. 14But she carried her harlotry
further; she saw men portrayed upon the wall, the images of the
Chaldeans portrayed in vermilion, 15girded with belts on their
loins, with flowing turbans on their heads, all of them looking like
officers, a picture of Babylonians whose native land was Chaldea.
16When she saw them she doted upon them, and sent messengers 2 Kings
to them in Chaldea. 17And the Babylonians came to her into the 20:12–19
bed of love, and they defiled her with their lust; and after she was Is 57:9
polluted by them, she turned from them in disgust. 18When she
carried on her harlotry so openly and flaunted her nakedness, I
turned in disgust from her, as I had turned from her sister. 19Yet
she increased her harlotry, remembering the days of her youth,
when she played the harlot in the land of Egypt 20and doted upon
her paramours there, whose members were like those of asses, and
whose issue was like that of horses. 21Thus you longed for the
lewdness of your youth, when the Egyptians[j] handled your bosom
and pressed[k] your young breasts."

22Therefore, O Oholibah, thus says the Lord GOD: "Behold, I
will rouse against you your lovers from whom you turned in
disgust, and I will bring them against you from every side: 23the
Babylonians and all the Chaldeans, Pekod and Shoa and Koa, and
all the Assyrians with them, desirable young men, governors and
commanders all of them, officers and warriors,[l] all of them riding

---

famosa mulieribus, et iudicia perpetrarunt in ea. 11Quod cum vidisset soror eius Ooliba, plus quam illa
insanivit libidine et fornicatione sua super fornicationem sororis suae. 12In filios Assyriorum amore
exarsit: duces et magistratus, bellatores indutos veste pretiosa, equites, qui vectabantur equis,
adulescentes cuncti desiderabiles. 13Et vidi quod polluta esset: via una ambarum; 14et auxit
fornicationes suas. Cumque vidisset viros depictos in pariete, imagines Chaldaeorum expressas
sinopide, 15et accinctos balteis renes, et tiaras defluentes in capitibus eorum; aspectus essedariorum
omnibus, similitudo filiorum Babylonis, quorum patria Chaldaea. 16Et insanivit super eos
concupiscentia oculorum suorum et misit nuntios ad eos in Chaldaeam. 17Cumque venissent ad eam
filii Babylonis ad cubile amoris, polluerunt eam stupris suis; et, cum polluta esset ab eis, recessit anima
eius ab illis. 18Cum manifestasset fornicationes suas et discooperuisset ignominiam suam, recessit
anima mea ab ea, sicut recesserat anima mea a sorore eius. 19Multiplicavit autem fornicationes suas,
recordans dies adulescentiae suae, quibus fornicata est in terra Aegypti; 20et insanivit libidine in
amatores suos, quorum membra sunt ut membra asinorum, et sicut fluxus equorum fluxus eorum. 21Et
desiderasti scelus adulescentiae tuae, quando subacta sunt in Aegypto ubera tua, et tactae mammae
pubertatis tuae. 22Propterea, Ooliba, haec dicit Dominus Deus: Ecce ego suscitabo amatores tuos contra
te, de quibus recessit anima tua; et congregabo eos adversum te in circuitu, 23filios Babylonis et
universos Chaldaeos, Phacud et Sue et Cue, omnes filios Assyriorum cum eis, iuvenes desiderabiles,

j. Two Mss: Heb *from Egypt* **k.** Cn: Heb *for the sake of* **l.** Compare verses 6 and 12: Heb *called*

on horses. [24]And they shall come against you from the north[m]
with chariots and wagons and a host of peoples; they shall set
themselves against you on every side with buckler, shield, and
helmet, and I will commit the judgment to them, and they shall
judge you according to their judgments. [25]And I will direct my
indignation against you, that they may deal with you in fury. They
shall cut off your nose and your ears, and your survivors shall fall
by the sword. They shall seize your sons and your daughters, and
your survivors shall be devoured by fire. [26]They shall also strip
Ex 16:3; 17:3 you of your clothes and take away your fine jewels. [27]Thus I will
put an end to your lewdness and your harlotry brought from the
land of Egypt; so that you shall not lift up your eyes to the
Egyptians or remember them any more. [28]For thus says the Lord
GOD: Behold, I will deliver you into the hands of those whom you
hate, into the hands of those from whom you turned in disgust;
Rev 17:16 [29]and they shall deal with you in hatred, and take away all the fruit
of your labour, and leave you naked and bare, and the nakedness
of your harlotry shall be uncovered. Your lewdness and your
harlotry [30]have brought this upon you, because you played the
harlot with the nations, and polluted yourself with their idols.
Jer 25:15 Rev 16:1 [31]You have gone the way of your sister; therefore I will give her
Ps 75:9 cup into your hand. [32]Thus says the Lord GOD:
Is 51:17 "You shall drink your sister's cup
Jer 25:15–18 which is deep and large;
Rev 14:10 you shall be laughed at and held in derision,
for it contains much;
[33]you will be filled with drunkenness and sorrow.
A cup of horror and desolation,
is the cup of your sister Samaria;

---

duces et magistratus universos, essedarios et nominatos, ascensores equorum omnes. [24]Et venient super te instructi curru et rota, cum multitudine populorum; scuto et clipeo et galea armabuntur contra te undique, et dabo coram eis iudicium, et iudicabunt te iudiciis suis. [25]Et ponam zelum meum in te, quem exercent tecum in furore: nasum tuum et aures tuas praecident et, quae remanserint de te, gladio concident; ipsi filios tuos et filias tuas capient, et novissimum tuum devorabitur igni. [26]Et denudabunt te vestimentis tuis et tollent vasa gloriae tuae; [27]et cessare faciam scelus tuum de te et fornicationem tuam de terra Aegypti, nec levabis oculos tuos ad eos et Aegypti non recordaberis amplius. [28]Quia haec dicit Dominus Deus: Ecce ego tradam te in manu eorum, quos odisti, in manu, de quibus recessit anima tua; [29]et agent tecum in odio et tollent omnes labores tuos et dimittent te nudam et ignominia plenam, et revelabitur ignominia fornicationum tuarum, scelus tuum et fornicationes tuae. [30]Fecerunt haec tibi, quia fornicata es post gentes, inter quas polluta es in idolis earum. [31]In via sororis tuae ambulasti, et dabo calicem eius in manu tua. [32]Haec dicit Dominus Deus: / Calicem sororis tuae bibes / profundum et latum /—eris in derisum et in subsannationem—: / est capacissimus. / [33]Ebrietate et dolore repleberis, / calice stuporis et horroris, / calice sororis tuae Samariae, / [34]et bibes illum et epotabis usque

m. Gk: The meaning of the Hebrew word is unknown

34 you shall drink it and drain it out,
and pluck out your hair,[n]
and tear your breasts;
for I have spoken, says the Lord GOD. 35Therefore thus says the
Lord GOD: Because you have forgotten me and cast me behind
your back, therefore bear the consequences of your lewdness and
harlotry."

Judgment against the two sisters
36The LORD said to me: "Son of man, will you judge Oholah and
Oholibah? Then declare to them their abominable deeds. 37For
they have committed adultery, and blood is upon their hands; with

---

23:36–49. After the symbolic description of the crimes of the two kingdoms and how they will be punished, Ezekiel pronounces sentence once more, but in a more succinct form. This passage was probably added by the prophet or by a disciple of his after the book was drafted; it contains many phrases that are identical with things said in chapter 16; also, there are many changes of person (something seldom found in Ezekiel). The passage begins by speaking of the sister-kingdoms in the third person plural (vv. 36–40a); then it moves into second person singular (40b–41), then into third person singular (vv. 42–44), before ending in third person plural (v. 45).

The sins denounced are the same as before—adultery, injustice and idolatry; they are, it stresses, particularly serious because they have been "done to the Lord" (v. 38). The description given here of the women making themselves up does describe what courtesans did but Ezekiel's main point is that the sins committed were grave ones because the people concerned knew exactly what they were doing.

The penalty is that spelt out in the Law for women who committed adultery—death by stoning (cf. 16:38–40; Deut 22:24). However, Ezekiel once more stresses that the punishment has a positive purpose (that is, regeneration: "and you shall know that I am the Lord God": v. 49) and he is appealing to the exiles for a change of heart: "So that all who love him would be converted, he set forth his almighty will. May we, therefore, be obedient to his wonderful and glorious plan, and fall to our knees to beg for his mercy and clemency, and respond to the graces that he gives us, leaving aside all the foolish concerns, disputes and petty envies that lead to death" (St Clement of Rome, *Ad Corinthios*, 8, 5–9, 1).

ad faeces; / et fragmenta eius rodes / et ubera tua lacerabis, / quia ego locutus sum», / ait Dominus Deus. 35Propterea haec dicit Dominus Deus: «Quia oblita es mei et proiecisti me post tergum tuum, tu quoque porta scelus tuum et fornicationes tuas». 36Et ait Dominus ad me: «Fili hominis, numquid iudicas Oollam et Oolibam? Annuntia ergo eis scelera earum. 37Quia adulteratae sunt, et sanguis in

n. Compare Syr: Heb *gnaw its sherds*

their idols they have committed adultery; and they have even
offered up to them for food the sons whom they had borne to me.
Ezek 20:4; 22:2 38Moreover this they have done to me: they have defiled my
Lev 18:21 sanctuary on the same day and profaned my sabbaths. 39For when
they had slaughtered their children in sacrifice to their idols, on
the same day they came into my sanctuary to profane it. And lo,
this is what they did in my house. 40They even sent for men to
Lev 19:30 come from far, to whom a messenger was sent, and lo, they came.
For them you bathed yourself, painted your eyes, and decked
yourself with ornaments; 41you sat upon a stately couch, with a
table spread before it on which you had placed my incense and my
oil. 42The sound of a carefree multitude was with her; and with
men of the common sort drunkards[o] were brought from the
wilderness; and they put bracelets upon the hands of the women,
and beautiful crowns upon their heads.

43"Then I said, Do not men now commit adultery[p] when they
practise harlotry with her? 44For they have gone in to her, as men
go in to a harlot. Thus they went in to Oholah and to Oholibah to
Lev 20:10 commit lewdness.[q] 45But righteous men shall pass judgment on
Deut 22:21–22 them with the sentence of adulteresses, and with the sentence of
women that shed blood; because they are adulteresses, and blood
is upon their hands."

46For thus says the Lord GOD: "Bring up a host against them,
and make them an object of terror and a spoil. 47And the host shall
stone them and dispatch them with their swords; they shall slay
their sons and their daughters, and burn up their houses. 48Thus
will I put an end to lewdness in the land, that all women may take

---

manibus earum, et cum idolis suis fornicatae sunt; insuper et filios suos, quos genuerunt mihi,
obtulerunt eis ad devorandum. 38Sed et hoc fecerunt mihi: polluerunt sanctuarium meum in die illa et
sabbata mea profanaverunt. 39Cumque immolarent filios suos idolis suis et ingrederentur sanctuarium
meum in die illa, ut polluerent illud, ecce haec fecerunt in medio domus meae. 40Quin et miserunt ad
viros venientes de longe, ad quos nuntius missus erat; itaque ecce venerunt. Quibus te lavisti et
circumlevisti stibio oculos tuos et ornata es mundo muliebri; 41sedisti in lecto pulcherrimo, et mensa
ornata est ante te, thymiama meum et unguentum meum posuisti super eam. 42Et vox multitudinis
exsultantis erat apud eam et apud viros multitudo hominum, qui adducebantur de deserto; et posuerunt
armillas in manibus earum et coronas speciosas in capitibus earum. 43Et dixi de ea, quae attrita est in
adulteriis: Nunc fornicabitur in fornicatione sua etiam haec. 44Et ingressi sunt ad eam quasi ad
mulierem meretricem; sic ingrediebantur ad Oollam et ad Oolibam, mulieres nefarias. 45Viri ergo iusti
sunt; hi iudicabunt eas iudicio adulterarum et iudicio effundentium sanguinem, quia adulterae sunt, et
sanguis in manibus earum». 46Haec enim dicit Dominus Deus: «Adduc ad eas congregationem et trade
eas in terrorem et in rapinam; 47et lapidentur lapidibus congregationis et confodiantur gladiis eorum;
filios et filias earum interficiant et domos earum igne succendant. 48Et auferam scelus de terra, et

o. Heb uncertain **p.** Compare Gk: Heb obscure **q.** Gk: Heb *a woman of lewdness*

warning and not commit lewdness as you have done. [49]And your lewdness shall be requited upon you, and you shall bear the penalty for your sinful idolatry; and you shall know that I am the Lord GOD."

Allegory of the pot set on the fire

24 [1]In the ninth year, in the tenth month, on the tenth day of
the month, the word of the LORD came to me: [2]"Son of 2 Kings 25:1 Jer 39:1; 52:4
man, write down the name of this day, this very day. The king of
Babylon has laid siege to Jerusalem this very day. [3]And utter an Ezek 11:3–12

***24:1–27.** The siege of Jerusalem is imminent—"this very day" (v. 2); nothing can be done to prevent it; but, still, one can try to work out what God's ultimate purpose is. Ezekiel recites an allegorical poem about a pot of stew put on a fire (vv. 3–14) and then he goes on to explain the significance of the death of his own wife (what he does in connexion with this is the most deeply felt of all his symbolic actions: vv. 15–27).

But he prefaces all this by giving the exact date of the oracle—5 January 588 BC, scarcely two years since he began to utter the oracles of judgment against Jerusalem (20:1) and some four years since the time of his call (1:2). This dating of the siege lines up with that given in 2 Kings 25:1 and Jeremiah 52:4; but it is of special importance because, when the siege happens, it will show that he is a true prophet and it will confirm that what he says about future rehabilitation will also come true.

24:3–14. The pot full of meat, symbolizing abundance (cf. 11:3, 7), becomes in this poem-parable a symbol of the total destruction of Jerusalem. The good pieces and choice bones stand for the inhabitants of Jerusalem who thought that they were perfectly safe inside the holy city and who continued blithely to commit all sorts of sins (vv. 3–5); but every one of them, making up a gruesome stew, will be burned up and destroyed (vv. 9–10). The receptacle, symbolizing the city itself, stained with blood and rust (vv. 6–8), will need to become red-hot before it can be cleansed. The closing words (vv. 13–14) spell out the meaning of the metaphor, just in case there is any doubt about the siege and destruction of the city being necessary for its purification. In Ezekiel, purification involves more than just cleansing or even moral probity; as the code of holiness (Lev 17:1—26:46) and the Priestly tradition of the Pentateuch teach, it is all directed toward divine

discent omnes mulieres, ne faciant secundum scelus vestrum; [49]et dabunt scelus vestrum super vos, et peccata idolorum vestrorum portabitis et scietis quia ego Dominus Deus». **[24]** [1]Et factum est verbum Domini ad me in anno nono, in mense decimo, decima mensis, dicens: [2]«Fili hominis, scribe tibi nomen diei huius, in qua aggressus est rex Babylonis adversum Ierusalem hodie. [3]Et dices per proverbium ad domum irritatricem parabolam et loqueris ad eos: Haec dicit Dominus Deus: Pone

allegory to the rebellious house and say to them, Thus says the
Lord GOD:

Set on the pot, set it on,
pour in water also;
4put in it the pieces of flesh,
all the good pieces, the thigh and the shoulder;
fill it with choice bones.
Take the choicest one of the flock,
pile the logs[r] under it;
boil its pieces,[s]
seethe[t] also its bones in it.

6"Therefore thus says the Lord GOD: Woe to the bloody city, to
the pot whose rust is in it, and whose rust has not gone out of it!
Lev 17:13 Deut 12:16 Take out of it piece after piece, without making any choice.[u] 7For
Rev 18:24 the blood she has shed is still in the midst of her; she put it on the
bare rock, she did not pour it upon the ground to cover it with
Job 16:18 dust. 8To rouse my wrath, to take vengeance, I have set on the bare
rock the blood she has shed, that it may not be covered.
9Therefore thus says the Lord GOD: Woe to the bloody city! I also
will make the pile great. 10Heap on the logs, kindle the fire, boil
well the flesh, and empty out the broth,[v] and let the bones be
burned up. 11Then set it empty upon the coals, that it may become
hot, and its copper may burn, that its filthiness may be melted in

---

service, for only when sins and their traces have disappeared is it possible to render due worship to the Lord, the only God. It is easy, then, to apply the metaphor to the soul, which needs purification if it is to be pleasing to God: "The prophet says that to rid the soul of the sinful desires that taint and stain it, it is fitting and good that the soul should be, in a sense, overthrown and unmade, insofar as it has been defiled by its passions and imperfections" (St John of the Cross, *Dark Night of the Soul*, 2, 6, 5).

ollam; pone, inquam, / et mitte in ea aquam. / 4Congere frusta eius in ea, / omnem partem bonam, femur et armum, / electis ossibus imple eam, / 5pinguissimum pecus assume. / Compone quoque struem lignorum sub ea; / effervescant frusta eius, / et coque ossa illius in medio eius. / 6Propterea haec dicit Dominus Deus: / Vae civitati sanguinum, / ollae, cuius rubigo in ea est, / et rubigo eius non exivit de ea! / Per partes et per partes suas eice ex ea, / neque cadat super eam sors. / 7Sanguis enim eius in medio eius est, / super limpidissimam petram effudit illum; / non effudit illum super terram, / ut possit operiri pulvere; / 8ut superducerem indignationem meam / et vindicta ulciscerer, / dedi sanguinem eius / super petram limpidissimam, ne operiretur. / 9Propterea haec dicit Dominus Deus: / Vae civitati sanguinum, / cuius ego grandem faciam pyram! / 10Congere ligna, succende ignem, / coque carnes usque ad consumptionem / et effunde ius, / et ossa comburentur. / 11Relinque quoque eam super prunas vacuam, / ut incalescat, et ardescat aes eius, / et confletur in medio eius inquinamentum eius, / et

r. Compare verse 10: Heb *the bones* **s.** Two Mss: Heb *its boilings* **t.** Cn: Heb *its bones seethe*
u. Heb *no lot has fallen upon it* **v.** Compare GK: Heb *mix the spices*

it, its rust consumed. [12]In vain I have wearied myself;[w] its thick
rust does not go out of it by fire. [13]Its rust is your filthy lewdness.
Because I would have cleansed you and you were not cleansed
from your filthiness, you shall not be cleansed any more till I have
satisfied my fury upon you. [14]I the LORD have spoken; it shall Ezek 5:11
come to pass, I will do it; I will not go back, I will not spare, I will
not repent; according to your ways and your doings I will judge
you, says the Lord GOD."

Death of Ezekiel's wife Jer 18:1
[15]Also the word of the LORD came to me: [16]"Son of man, behold, 1 Kings 20:6
I am about to take the delight of your eyes away from you at a Lam 2:4
stroke; yet you shall not mourn or weep nor shall your tears run Lev 10:6 2 Sam 15:30
down. [17]Sigh, but not aloud; make no mourning for the dead. Bind Jer 16:5–7

24:15–27. The first part of the book ends here with this moving passage revealing the prophet's feelings about the death of his wife. All this—the sudden death of his wife, the fact that he does not publicly mourn her, his profound, silent grief—is the supreme symbol of what the siege of Jerusalem involved. Ezekiel's wife must have been still quite young, "the delight of your eyes" (v. 16; cf. Lam 2:4), and she must have died suddenly. She is a symbol of the temple, of which the people were so proud; no one could have imagined it would be destroyed. Mourning was a function of the person's social status and the regard in which he or she was held (cf. 2 Sam 1:2; 3:31; 14:2; 15:30, 32), but even the humblest in society would put on a veil and wear that sign of mourning at funeral meals, at the "bread of mourners" (v. 17). However, Ezekiel was not to weep for his wife; nor should the exiles show any public sign of grief; this would show that the misfortunes that befell Jerusalem were a private affair between themselves and God.

The mention of the prophet's name (v. 24), which has not appeared since the title of the book (1:3), gives these verses the stamp of his authority. The same is true of vv. 25–27 which tell the prophet that on the very day of his wife's death the fugitive will arrive reporting the destruction of Jerusalem, and Ezekiel will recover his power of speech (cf. 3:25–27 and 33:21–22).

consumatur rubigo eius. / [12]Multo labore sudatum est, / et non exibit de ea nimia rubigo eius, / neque per ignem. [13]Immunditia tua execrabilis, quia mundare te volui, et non es mundata a sordibus tuis; sed nec mundaberis prius, donec quiescere faciam indignationem meam in te. [14]Ego Dominus locutus sum; veniet et faciam: non indulgebo nec parcam nec placabor. Iuxta vias tuas et iuxta opera tua iudicabo te», dicit Dominus. [15]Et factum est verbum Domini ad me dicens: [16]«Fili hominis, ecce ego tollo a te delicias oculorum tuorum in plaga, et non planges neque plorabis, neque fluent lacrimae tuae. [17]Ingemisce tacens, mortuorum luctum non facies, corona tua circumligata sit tibi, et calceamenta tua

w. Cn: Heb uncertain

on your turban, and put your shoes on your feet; do not cover your
lips, nor eat the bread of mourners."[x] 18So I spoke to the people in
the morning, and at evening my wife died. And on the next
morning I did as I was commanded.

19And the people said to me, "Will you not tell us what these
things mean for us, that you are acting thus?" 20Then I said to
Jer 7:1–15 them, "The word of the LORD came to me: 21'Say to the house of
Lam 2:7 Ezek 7:20–22; Israel, Thus says the Lord GOD: Behold, I will profane my sanctuary,
23:47 the pride of your power, the delight of your eyes, and the desire of
your soul; and your sons and your daughters whom you left
behind shall fall by the sword. 22And you shall do as I have done;
you shall not cover your lips, nor eat the bread of mourners.[x]
Ezek 2:6 23Your turbans shall be on your heads and your shoes on your feet;
you shall not mourn or weep, but you shall pine away in your
Ezek 12:6–11 iniquities and groan to one another. 24Thus shall Ezekiel be to you
a sign; according to all that he has done you shall do. When this
comes, then you will know that I am the Lord GOD.'

25"And you, son of man, on the day when I take from them
their stronghold, their joy and glory, the delight of their eyes and
their heart's desire, and also their sons and daughters, 26on that
Ezek 3:26; day a fugitive will come to you to report to you the news. 27On
33:22 that day your mouth will be opened to the fugitive, and you shall
speak and be no longer dumb. So you will be a sign to them; and
they will know that I am the LORD."

---

pones in pedibus tuis nec amictu ora velabis nec cibos lugentium comedes». 18Locutus sum ergo ad populum mane, et mortua est uxor mea vespere; fecique mane, sicut praeceperat mihi. 19Et dixit ad me populus: «Quare non indicas nobis, quid ista significent, quae tu facis?». 20Et dixi ad eos: «Sermo Domini factus est ad me dicens: 21Loquere domui Israel: Haec dicit Dominus Deus: Ecce ego polluam sanctuarium meum, superbiam roboris vestri et delicias oculorum vestrorum et sollicitudinem animae vestrae. Filii vestri et filiae, quas reliquistis, gladio cadent. 22Et facietis, sicut feci: ora amictu non velabitis et cibos lugentium non comedetis, 23coronas habebitis in capitibus vestris et calceamenta in pedibus, non plangetis neque flebitis, sed tabescetis in iniquitatibus vestris, et unusquisque gemet ad fratrem suum. 24Eritque Ezechiel vobis in portentum: iuxta omnia, quae fecit, facietis, cum venerit istud, et scietis quia ego Dominus Deus. 25Et tu, fili hominis, ecce in die, quo tollam ab eis fortitudinem eorum et gaudium magnificentiae et delicias oculorum eorum et desiderium animae eorum, filios et filias eorum; 26in die illa, cum venerit fugiens ad te, ut annuntiet tibi, 27in die, inquam, illa aperietur os tuum cum eo, qui fugit; et loqueris et non silebis ultra erisque eis in portentum, et scient quia ego Dominus».

x. Vg Tg: Heb *men*

PART TWO

The nations are judged and found guilty*

Against the Ammonites

25 [1]The word of the LORD came to me: [2]"Son of man, set your
face toward the Ammonites, and prophesy against them.
[3]Say to the Ammonites, Hear the word of the Lord GOD: Thus

Is 13:23
Jer 46–51
Amos 1–2
Judg 3:13; 10:11
Deut 2:19
Jer 49:1–6
Ezek 21:33–37
Amos 1:13–15
Ezek 26:2
Rev 10:11

***25:1—32:32.** These chapters form the second part of the book of Ezekiel. "Oracles against the nations" form a substantial part of the more important prophetical books from Amos onwards. Amos was the first to proclaim them (Amos 1–2), and then Isaiah (Is 13–23) and Jeremiah (Jer 46–51). In those prophets the oracles very much reflect the thinking and doctrinal thrust of the entire book. In Ezekiel they have special features. They are placed more or less at the centre of the book, after the oracles of denunciation and before those to do with renewal. They are directed against *seven* nations, a significant number indicating completeness, totality; Amos, too, has seven. Ezekiel's oracles do not include Babylon (which is denounced in Isaiah and Jeremiah), whereas they do condemn the nations that were opposed to that great Chaldean superpower. This must be because he is implying that Babylon is acting as a weapon wielded by the Lord (which is not to say that Babylon's methods were not cruel). In the nations listed, the order is not so much chronological as thematic: the diatribe begins with four nations that divided Israel and celebrated her collapse (Ammon, Moab, Edom and the Philistines) and it concludes with those who considered themselves stronger than the rest and strove to oppose Babylon (Tyre, Sidon and, above all, Egypt).

The prophet's aim here is quite clear: he wants to show that God is sovereign lord over Israel and over all other nations; he steers the course of history. This sovereignty of God is entirely at odds with the polytheism of the time; he is always in charge, whereas the pagan gods (Marduk, Baal etc.) in which those nations put their trust are incapable of defending them. Ezekiel probably wants the exiles to draw a lesson of love from these oracles: the destruction of hostile nations shows that God never leaves Israel unprotected.

25:1–17. The four nations denounced in this chapter were overrun soon after the collapse of Judah, that is, in the period 586–570 BC; they bordered on Israel and had been its bitterest enemies from the beginning. Back in the times of the Judges we find the Ammonites opposing the Israelites (Judg 3:13; 10:11); they and the Moabites both

---

[25] [1]Et factus est sermo Domini ad me dicens: [2]«Fili hominis, pone faciem tuam contra filios Ammon et propheta de eis [3]et dices filiis Ammon: Audite verbum Domini Dei. Haec dicit Dominus Deus: Pro eo quod dixisti: "Euge!" super sanctuarium meum, quia pollutum est, et super terram Israel, quoniam

says the Lord GOD, Because you said, 'Aha!' over my sanctuary
when it was profaned, and over the land of Israel when it was
made desolate, and over the house of Judah when it went into
Num 24:21 exile; [4]therefore I am handing you over to the people of the East
for a possession, and they shall set their encampments among you
and make their dwellings in your midst; they shall eat your fruit,
and they shall drink your milk. [5]I will make Rabbah a pasture for
camels and the cities of the Ammonites[y] a fold for flocks. Then
you will know that I am the LORD. [6]For thus says the Lord GOD:
Because you have clapped your hands and stamped your feet and
rejoiced with all the malice within you against the land of Israel,
[7]therefore, behold, I have stretched out my hand against you, and
will hand you over as spoil to the nations; and I will cut you off
from the peoples and will make you perish out of the countries; I
will destroy you. Then you will know that I am the LORD.

---

derived from the incestuous union of Lot with his daughters (Gen 19:30–38), and in Judges 3:12–30 we find both these nations in conflict with the Israelites (cf. the note on Jer 48:1–47); the Edomites, descendants of Esau, come across as vengeful and debased (Gen 25:29; cf. Jer 49:7–22); there was permanent tension between them and the Israelites. All three nations had blood ties with the Israelites. The Philistines, on the other hand, who had come from Asia Minor and settled on the Mediterranean coast, were forever trying to make inroads into Israelite territory (cf. 2 Sam 5:17; 1 Kings 16:16); they were seen as foreigners, having a different ethnic background.

The oracles in this section all have the same sort of structure—a description of the nation's crime (vv. 3, 8, 12, 15) followed by the passing of a sentence that typically begins with the word "therefore" (vv. 4, 9, 13, 16). The oracles are brief, forthright and clear, and they end with the words "you will know that I am the Lord". The prophet, therefore, wants to make it clear that the misfortunes and disasters that befall these peoples occur because God wants to show that he rules supreme and desires them to acknowledge his dominion. Ezekiel's message looks beyond Israel to the wider world; there is a slight trace of this in these oracles.

desolata est, et super domum Iudae, quoniam ducti sunt in captivitatem, [4]idcirco ego tradam te filiis orientalibus in hereditatem, et collocabunt castra sua in te et ponent in te tentoria sua; ipsi comedent fruges tuas, et ipsi bibent lac tuum. [5]Daboque Rabba in pascua camelorum et filios Ammon in cubile pecorum, et scietis quia ego Dominus. [6]Quia haec dicit Dominus Deus: Pro eo quod plausisti manu et percussisti pede et gavisa es ex toto affectu super terram Israel, [7]idcirco ecce ego extendam manum meam super te et tradam te in direptionem gentium et interficiam te de populis et perdam de terris et conteram, et scies quia ego Dominus. [8]Haec dicit Dominus Deus: Pro eo quod dixerunt Moab et Seir:

y. Cn: Heb lacks *the cities of*

Against Moab

8“Thus says the Lord GOD: Because Moab[z] said, Behold, the
house of Judah is like all the other nations, 9therefore I will lay
open the flank of Moab from the cities[a] on its frontier, the glory of
the country, Beth-jeshimoth, Baal-meon, and Kiriathaim. 10I will
give it along with the Ammonites to the people of the East as a
possession, that it[b] may be remembered no more among the
nations, 11and I will execute judgments upon Moab. Then they
will know that I am the LORD.

Gen 19:30–38
Num 22:36
Judg 3:12–13
Is 15:1; Jer 48
Ezek 35:2
Amos 2:1–3
Zeph 2:8–11

Against Edom

12“Thus says the Lord GOD: Because Edom acted revengefully
against the house of Judah and has grievously offended in taking
vengeance upon them, 13therefore thus says the Lord GOD, I will
stretch out my hand against Edom, and cut off from it man and
beast; and I will make it desolate; from Teman even to Dedan they
shall fall by the sword. 14And I will lay my vengeance upon Edom
by the hand of my people Israel; and they shall do in Edom
according to my anger and according to my wrath; and they shall
know my vengeance, says the Lord GOD.

Gen 25:29f
Num 20:23
Ps 137:7
Is 21:13–14; 34:5; Jer 49: 7–22; Ezek 35;
Amos 1:11–12

Jer 49:7–22
Amos 9:12
Obad 18–21

Against the Philistines

15“Thus says the Lord GOD: Because the Philistines acted revengefully and took vengeance with malice of heart to destroy in never-
ending enmity; 16therefore thus says the Lord GOD, Behold, I will
stretch out my hand against the Philistines, and I will cut off the
Cherethites, and destroy the rest of the seacoast. 17I will execute
great vengeance upon them with wrathful chastisements. Then
they will know that I am the LORD, when I lay my vengeance upon
them.”

2 Sam 5:17f
1 Kings 16:16f
Is 14:29–32
Jer 25:20; 47:1
Joel 3:4
Zeph 2:4–7

“Ecce sicut omnes gentes domus Iudae!”, 9idcirco ecce ego aperiam latus Moab privans eam civitatibus, civitatibus, inquam, eius, a finibus eius, decore terrae: Bethiesimoth et Baalmeon et Cariathaim; 10filiis orientis cum filiis Ammon dabo eam in hereditatem, ut non sit memoria ultra filiorum Ammon in gentibus. 11Et in Moab faciam iudicia, et scient quia ego Dominus. 12Haec dicit Dominus Deus: Pro eo quod fecit Idumaea ultionem, ut se vindicaret de domo Iudae, peccavitque delinquens et vindictam expetivit de eis, 13idcirco haec dicit Dominus Deus: Extendam manum meam super Idumaeam et auferam de ea hominem et iumentum et faciam eam desertum; de Theman et usque Dedan gladio cadent. 14Et dabo ultionem meam super Idumaeam per manum populi mei Israel, et facient in Edom iuxta iram meam et furorem meum, et scient vindictam meam, dicit Dominus Deus. 15Haec dicit Dominus Deus: Pro eo quod fecerunt Palaestini in vindicta et ulti se sunt toto animo interficientes et implentes inimicitias sempiternas, 16propterea haec dicit Dominus Deus: Ecce ego extendam manum meam super Palaestinos et interficiam Cherethaeos et perdam reliquias maritimae regionis; 17faciamque in eis ultiones magnas, arguens in furore, et scient quia ego Dominus, cum

z. Gk Old Latin: Heb *Moab and Seir* **a.** Heb *cities from its cities* **b.** Cn: Heb *the Ammonites*

Against Tyre*

26 1*In the eleventh year, on the first day of the month, the
Is 23:1 word of the LORD came to me: 2“Son of man, because Tyre
Ezek 25:3 said concerning Jerusalem, ‘Aha, the gate of the peoples is broken,
it has swung open to me; I shall be replenished, now that she is
laid waste,’ 3therefore thus says the Lord GOD: Behold, I am
against you, O Tyre, and will bring up many nations against you,
as the sea brings up its waves. 4They shall destroy the walls of
Tyre, and break down her towers; and I will scrape her soil from
her, and make her a bare rock. 5She shall be in the midst of the sea
a place for the spreading of nets; for I have spoken, says the Lord
GOD; and she shall become a spoil to the nations; 6and her

***26:1—28:19.** Tyre was a city-state in northern Palestine, between the mountains of Lebanon and the sea. It was a Phoenician settlement, like Sidon, Byblos etc.; set on a rocky island, heavily fortified, its control extended on to the mainland of the continent. Because of its strategic position it became an important trading centre for the Middle East, doing business with merchants from other cities and towns in Asia Minor. Nebuchadnezzar never managed to conquer it, but his attacks on it took a heavy toll.

In Ezekiel’s oracles against Tyre we can see that he rejoices to see it defeated, is somewhat in awe of its influence and its defences, and has only disdain for its self-important king. But he leaves no doubt but that God is the only sovereign lord and Israel is his favourite nation.

26:1–21. At the start of these oracles against Tyre, Ezekiel is careful to give the exact date, that is, towards the end of the year 586, one year after the fall of Jerusalem. Then he criticizes the people of Tyre for rejoicing over the destruction of the Lord’s city (v. 2) and goes on to hand down a form of sentence, each part beginning with the words “thus says the Lord” (vv. 3, 7, 15, 19).

The first two parts (vv. 3–6 and 7–14) announce the destruction of a city that seemed impregnable yet which will be totally razed: it will become just “a place for the spreading of nets” (vv. 5, 14). The last two parts (vv. 15–18 and 19–21) are a kind of funeral lamentation over the disappearance of so fine a city. The chapter as a whole gives the impression that the prophet had a certain regard for or envy of Tyre’s strength, prosperity and influence.

dedero vindictam meam super eos». **[26]** 1Et factum est in undecimo anno, prima mensis, factus est
sermo Domini ad me dicens: 2«Fili hominis, pro eo quod dixit Tyrus de Ierusalem: “Euge, confracta
est / porta populorum! / Conversa est ad me; / quae erat plena, deserta est”, / 3propterea haec dicit
Dominus Deus: / Ecce ego super te, Tyre, / et ascendere faciam ad te gentes multas, / sicut ascendit
mare fluctuans; / 4et dissipabunt muros Tyri / et destruent turres eius, / et radam pulverem eius de ea,
/ et dabo eam in limpidissimam petram. / 5Siccatio sagenarum / erit in medio maris, / quia ego locutus
sum, / ait Dominus Deus; / et erit in direptionem gentibus. / 6Filiae quoque eius, quae sunt in agro, /

daughters on the mainland shall be slain by the sword. Then they
will know that I am the LORD.

7“For thus says the Lord GOD: Behold, I will bring upon Tyre Jer 1:14
from the north Nebuchadnezzar king of Babylon, king of kings, with Dan 2:37
horses and chariots, and with horsemen and a host of many soldiers.
8He will slay with the sword your daughters on the mainland; he will Ezek 4:1–3
set up a siege wall against you, and throw up a mound against you,
and raise a roof of shields against you. 9He will direct the shock of
his battering rams against your walls, and with his axes he will break
down your towers. 10His horses will be so many that their dust will
cover you; your walls will shake at the noise of the horsemen and
wagons and chariots, when he enters your gates as one enters a city
which has been breached. 11With the hoofs of his horses he will
trample all your streets; he will slay your people with the sword;
and your mighty pillars will fall to the ground. 12They will make Rev 18:21
a spoil of your riches and a prey of your merchandise; they will
break down your walls and destroy your pleasant houses; your
stones and timber and soil they will cast into the midst of the
waters. 13And I will stop the music of your songs, and the sound Is 24:8–9
of your lyres shall be heard no more. 14I will make you a bare Jer 25:10
rock; you shall be a place for the spreading of nets; you shall Rev 18:22
never be rebuilt; for I the LORD have spoken, says the Lord GOD.

15“Thus says the Lord GOD to Tyre: Will not the coastlands Rev 6:14
shake at the sound of your fall, when the wounded groan, when
slaughter is made in the midst of you? 16Then all the princes of the Is 23:8
sea will step down from their thrones, and remove their robes, and Jon 3:6
strip off their embroidered garments; they will clothe themselves
with trembling; they will sit upon the ground and tremble every
moment, and be appalled at you. 17And they will raise a lamentation Rev 18:9–19
over you, and say to you,

---

gladio interficientur, / et scient quia ego Dominus. / 7Quia haec dicit Dominus Deus: / Ecce ego
adducam ad Tyrum / Nabuchodonosor, regem Babylonis, / ab aquilone, regem regum, / cum equis et
curribus et equitibus / et coetu populoque magno. / 8Filias tuas, quae sunt in agro, / gladio interficiet,
/ et circumdabit te munitionibus / et comportabit aggerem in gyro / et levabit contra te clipeum / 9et
vineas et arietes temperabit in muros tuos / et turres tuas destruet in armatura sua. / 10Inundatione
equorum eius / operiet te pulvis eorum, / a sonitu equitum / et rotarum et curruum / movebuntur muri
tui, / dum ingressus fuerit portas tuas / quasi per introitus urbis dissipatae. / 11Ungulis equorum suorum
/ conculcabit omnes plateas tuas, / populum tuum gladio caedet, / et columnae tuae fortissimae / in
terram corruent. / 12Vastabunt opes tuas, / diripient negotiationes tuas / et destruent muros tuos / et
domos tuas praeclaras subvertent / et lapides tuos et ligna tua et pulverem tuum / in medio aquarum
ponent. / 13Et quiescere faciam tumultum canticorum tuorum, / et sonitus cithararum tuarum non
audietur amplius, / 14et dabo te in limpidissimam petram; / siccatio sagenarum eris, / nec aedificaberis
ultra, / quia ego locutus sum, / dicit Dominus Deus. 15Haec dicit Dominus Deus Tyro: Numquid non
a sonitu ruinae tuae et gemitu interfectorum tuorum, cum occisi fuerint in medio tui, commovebuntur
insulae? 16Et descendent de sedibus suis omnes principes maris et auferent pallia sua et vestimenta sua

'How you have vanished[c] from the seas,
O city renowned,
that was mighty on the sea,
you and your inhabitants,
who imposed your terror
on all the mainland![d]
18Now the isles tremble
on the day of your fall;
yea, the isles that are in the sea
are dismayed at your passing.'

Rev 17:6; 18:19 19"For thus says the Lord GOD: When I make you a city laid
waste, like the cities that are not inhabited, when I bring up the
Ezek 31:14; 32:18–32 deep over you, and the great waters cover you, 20then I will thrust
you down with those who descend into the Pit, to the people of
old, and I will make you to dwell in the nether world, among
primeval ruins, with those who go down to the Pit, so that you will
Rev 18:21 not be inhabited or have a place[e] in the land of the living. 21I will
bring you to a dreadful end, and you shall be no more; though you
be sought for, you will never be found again, says the Lord GOD."

Lamentation over the fall of Tyre

27 1The word of the LORD came to me: 2"Now you, son of
man, raise a lamentation over Tyre, 3and say to Tyre, who
dwells at the entrance to the sea, merchant of
the peoples on many coastlands, thus says the Lord GOD:
"O Tyre, you have said,
'I am perfect in beauty.'

27:1–36. The second oracle is a fine elegy on the destruction of Tyre, which Ezekiel depicts as a vessel that is shipwrecked. In the first part of it (vv. 1–11; in verse), he praises the wealth and splendour of a merchant ship built

varia abicient; et induentur stupore, in terra sedebunt et attoniti et tremefacti stupebunt super te. 17Et assumentes super te lamentum dicent tibi: "Quomodo peristi, quae habitas in mari, / urbs inclita, / quae fuisti fortis in mari / cum habitatoribus tuis, / quos formidabant universi! / 18Nunc stupebunt naves / in die ruinae tuae, / et turbabuntur insulae in mari / ob exitum tuum". 19Quia haec dicit Dominus Deus: Cum dedero te urbem desolatam sicut civitates, quae non habitantur, et adduxero super te abyssum, et operuerint te aquae multae, 20detraham te cum his, qui descendunt in lacum, ad populum pristinum et collocabo te in profundis terrae sicut ruinas a saeculo cum his, qui descendunt in lacum, ut non habiteris et consistas in terra viventium; 21in nihilum redigam te, et non eris et requisita non invenieris ultra in sempiternum», dicit Dominus Deus. **[27]** 1Et factum est verbum Domini ad me dicens: 2«Tu ergo, fili hominis, assume super Tyrum lamentum 3et dices Tyro, quae habitat in introitu maris, negotiatrici populorum ad insulas multas: Haec dicit Dominus Deus: O Tyre, tu dixisti: "Perfecti

c. Gk Old Latin Aquila: Heb *vanished, O inhabited one* **d.** Cn: Heb *her inhabitants* **e.** Gk: Heb *I will give beauty*

[4]Your borders are in the heart of the seas;
your builders made perfect your beauty.
[5]They made all your planks Deut 3:9
of fir trees from Senir;
they took a cedar from Lebanon
to make a mast for you.
[6]Of oaks of Bashan
they made your oars;
they made your deck of pines
from the coasts of Cyprus,
inlaid with ivory.
[7]Of fine embroidered linen from Egypt
was your sail,
serving as your ensign;
blue and purple from the coasts of Elishah
was your awning.
[8]The inhabitants of Sidon and Arvad
were your rowers;
skilled men of Zemer[f] were in you,
they were your pilots.
[9]The elders of Gebal and her skilled men were in you,
caulking your seams;
all the ships of the sea with their mariners were in you,
to barter for your wares.

---

with fine materials from the countries all around—cedar from Lebanon, oak from Bashan, linen from Egypt, etc. The second part (vv. 12–25; in prose) lists the goods in which Tyre traded and the cities they came from. The amount of detail becomes tedious, but the passage does convey a good idea of the prestige that Tyre enjoyed. The third part, the most poetic of all (vv. 25b–36) describes the sinking of the ship, and the reactions of the neighbouring peoples to the loss (vv. 28–36).

27:8–15. Arvad (vv. 8, 11) is a Phoenician island close to Tyre; the Greek and Latin versions give it as "Arad", but there is no known place of that name. In v. 15 the Septuagint and the Latin translations, and the RSV, read "Rhodes" instead of "Dedan" (cf. note **h** and Gen 10:4 which mentions the "Dodanim").

decoris ego sum!". / [4]In corde maris fines tui; / qui te aedificaverunt, impleverunt decorem tuum. / [5]Abietibus de Sanir exstruxerunt / tibi omnia tabulata; / cedrum de libano tulerunt, / ut facerent tibi malum; / [6]quercus de Basan / dolaverunt in remos tuos / et transtra tua fecerunt ex ebore / et cupressis de insulis Cetthim. / [7]Byssus varia texta de Aegypto / erat tibi in velum, / ut poneretur in malo, / hyacinthus et purpura de insulis Elisa / facta sunt operimentum tuum. / [8]Habitatores Sidonis et Aradii / fuerunt remiges tui; / sapientes tui, Tyre, / facti sunt nautae tui. / [9]Senes Gibli et prudentes eius fuerunt

f. Compare Gen 10:18: Heb *your skilled men, O Tyre*

Jer 46:9 10“Persia and Lud and Put were in your army as your men of
war; they hung the shield and helmet in you; they gave you
splendour. 11The men of Arvad and Helech[g] were upon your walls
round about, and men of Gamad were in your towers; they hung
their shields upon your walls round about; they made perfect your
beauty.
1 Kings 10:22 12“Tarshish trafficked with you because of your great wealth of
Is 23:1
Rev 18:13 every kind; silver, iron, tin, and lead they exchanged for your
Ezek 32:8 wares. 13Javan, Tubal, and Meshech traded with you; they
exchanged the persons of men and vessels of bronze for your
Ezek 38:6 merchandise. 14Beth-togarmah exchanged for your wares horses,
Ezek 25:13 war horses, and mules. 15The men of Rhodes[h] traded with you;
many coastlands were your own special markets, they brought you
in payment ivory tusks and ebony. 16Edom[i] trafficked with you
because of your abundant goods; they exchanged for your wares
emeralds, purple, embroidered work, fine linen, coral, and agate.
Judg 11:33 17Judah and the land of Israel traded with you; they exchanged for
your merchandise wheat, olives and early figs,[j] honey, oil, and
balm. 18Damascus trafficked with you for your abundant goods,
because of your great wealth of every kind; wine of Helbon, and
Gen 10:27 white wool, 19and wine[k] from Uzal they exchanged for your
wares; wrought iron, cassia, and calamus were bartered for your
Ezek 25:13 merchandise. 20Dedan traded with you in saddlecloths for riding.
21Arabia and all the princes of Kedar were your favoured dealers

---

27:17. Judah and Israel are mentioned as two countries with which Tyre traded; they are not given any particular political or religious importance.

in te, / ut sarcirent rimas tuas. / Omnes naves maris et nautae earum / fuerunt in te, ut mercarentur merces tuas. / 10Persae et Lud et Phut / erant in exercitu tuo, / viri bellatores tui. / Clipeum et galeam suspenderunt in te; / ipsi dederunt tibi splendorem. 11Filii Aradii cum exercitu tuo erant super muros tuos in circuitu, et Gammadii erant in turribus tuis. Clipeos suos suspenderunt in muris tuis per gyrum; ipsi compleverunt pulchritudinem tuam. 12Tharsis negotiatrix tua propter multitudinem cunctarum divitiarum; argentum, ferrum, stannum plumbumque dederunt pro mercibus tuis. 13Iavan, Thubal et Mosoch ipsi institores tui; mancipia et vasa aerea adduxerunt tibi in commutationem populo tuo. 14De domo Thogorma equos et equites et mulos adduxerunt pro mercibus tuis ad forum tuum; 15filii Rhodi negotiatores tui; insulae multae negotiatio manus tuae: dentes eburneos et ebenina reddiderunt tibi ut tributum. 16Edom negotiator tuus propter multitudinem operum tuorum; carbunculum, purpuram et scutulata et byssum et corallia et rubinum attulerunt pro mercibus tuis. 17Iuda et terra Israel ipsi institores tui; frumentum primum, balsamum et mel et oleum et resinam attulerunt tibi in commutationem. 18Damascenus negotiator tuus propter multitudinem operum tuorum, propter multitudinem diversarum opum; vinum de Helbon et lanam de Sahar 19et vinum de Uzal pro mercibus tuis dederunt; ferrum fabrefactum, cassia et calamus in commutatione tua erat. 20Dedan institores tui in tapetibus ad equitandum. 21Arabia et universi principes Cedar ipsi negotiatores manus tuae; cum

g. Or *and your army* **h.** Gk: Heb *Dedan* **i.** Another reading is *Aram* **j.** Cn: Heb *wheat of minnith and pannag* **k.** Gk: Heb *Vedan and Javan*

in lambs, rams, and goats; in these they trafficked with you. [22]The Gen 10:7
traders of Sheba and Raamah traded with you; they exchanged for 1 Kings 10:1
your wares the best of all kinds of spices, and all precious stones, Gen 11:31;
and gold. [23]Haran, Canneh, Eden,[l] Asshur, and Chilmad traded 12:1
with you. [24]These traded with you in choice garments, in clothes of
blue and embroidered work, and in carpets of colored stuff, bound
with cords and made secure; in these they traded with you.[m] [25]The
ships of Tarshish travelled for you with your merchandise.[n]

"So you were filled and heavily laden
in the heart of the seas.
[26]Your rowers have brought you out
into the high seas.
The east wind has wrecked you
in the heart of the seas.
[27]Your riches, your wares, your merchandise, Rev 18:17
your mariners and your pilots,
your caulkers, your dealers in merchandise,
and all your men of war who are in you,
with all your company
that is in your midst,
sink into the heart of the seas
on the day of your ruin.
[28]At the sound of the cry of your pilots
the countryside shakes,
[29]and down from their ships Rev 18:17
come all that handle the oar.
The mariners and all the pilots of the sea
stand on the shore
[30]and wail aloud over you, Rev 18:19
and cry bitterly.

---

agnis et arietibus et haedis, cum quibus erant negotiatores tui. [22]Venditores Saba et Regma, ipsi negotiatores tui, universa prima aromata et omnem lapidem pretiosum et aurum dederunt pro mercibus tuis. [23]Charran et Chenne et Eden negotiatores tui; Saba, Assyria et Chelmad venditores tui. [24]Ipsi negotiatores tui cum vestibus splendidis, involucris hyacinthinis et polymitis texturisque discoloribus, funibus obvolutis et cedris in negotiationibus tuis. [25]Naves Tharsis, principes tui / in negotiatione tua; / et repleta es et glorificata nimis / in corde maris. / [26]In aquis multis adduxerunt te / remiges tui; / ventus auster contrivit te / in corde maris. / [27]Divitiae tuae et thesauri tui et multiplices merces tuae, / nautae tui et gubernatores tui, / resarcientes rimas tuas et commutantes merces tuas, / omnes quoque viri bellatores tui, / qui sunt in te, / cum universa multitudine tua, / quae est in medio tui, / cadent in corde maris / in die ruinae tuae. / [28]A sonitu clamoris gubernatorum tuorum / conturbabuntur litora. / [29]Et descendent de navibus suis / omnes, qui tenebant remum; / nautae et universi gubernatores maris / in terra stabunt. / [30]Et eiulabunt super te voce magna / et clamabunt amare; / et superiacient pulverem

l. Cn: Heb *Eden the traders of Sheba* **m.** Cn: Heb *in your market* **n.** Cn: Heb *your travellers your merchandise*

They cast dust on their heads
and wallow in ashes;
31 they make themselves bald for you,
and gird themselves with sackcloth,
and they weep over you in bitterness of soul,
with bitter mourning.
Rev 18:18 32 In their wailing they raise a lamentation for you,
and lament over you:
'Who was ever destroyed[o] like Tyre
in the midst of the sea?
Rev 18:19 33 When your wares came from the seas,
you satisfied many peoples;
with your abundant wealth and merchandise
you enriched the kings of the earth.
34 Now you are wrecked by the seas,
in the depths of the waters;
your merchandise and all your crew
have sunk with you.
35 All the inhabitants of the coastlands
are appalled at you;
and their kings are horribly afraid,
their faces are convulsed.
36 The merchants among the peoples hiss at you;
you have come to a dreadful end
and shall be no more for ever.'"

Oracle against the king of Tyre

Gen 3:5 **28** 1 The word of the LORD came to me:
Is 14:13 2 "Son of man, say to the prince of Tyre, Thus says the Lord
Acts 12:22
2 Thess 2:4 GOD:

28:1–10. The oracle here is addressed to the king of Tyre ("the prince" in Ezekiel's language) but he stands for the whole country. The nation is denounced for its pride—most clearly to be seen in its king, who was rich and clever and so

capitibus suis, / in cinere volutabuntur. / 31 Et radent super te calvitium / et accingentur ciliciis / et plorabunt te in amaritudine animae / ploratu amarissimo; / 32 et assument super te congementes carmen lugubre / et plangent te: / "Quae est ut Tyrus, quae obmutuit / in medio maris? / 33 Cum venissent merces tuae de mari, satiasti populos multos; / in multitudine divitiarum tuarum et mercium tuarum / ditasti reges terrae. / 34 Nunc contrita es a mari / in profundis aquarum. / Opes tuae et omnis multitudo tua, / quae erat in medio tui, / ceciderunt. / 35 Universi habitatores insularum / obstupuerunt super te, / et reges earum horrore formidarunt vultu conturbato; / 36 negotiatores in populis sibilaverunt super te. / In horrorem facta es / et non eris usque in perpetuum"». **[28]** 1 Et factus est sermo Domini ad me

o. Tg Vg: Heb *like silence*

"Because your heart is proud,
  and you have said, 'I am a god,
I sit in the seat of the gods,
  in the heart of the seas,'
yet you are but a man, and no god,
  though you consider yourself as wise as a god—
3you are indeed wiser than Daniel; Ezek 14:14
  no secret is hidden from you; Zech 9:2
4by your wisdom and your understanding
  you have gotten wealth for yourself,
and have gathered gold and silver
  into your treasuries;
5by your great wisdom in trade
  you have increased your wealth,
  and your heart has become proud in your wealth—
6therefore thus says the Lord GOD:
"Because you consider yourself
  as wise as a god,
7therefore, behold, I will bring strangers upon you,
  the most terrible of the nations;
and they shall draw their swords against the beauty of your wisdom
  and defile your splendour.

---

influential in the region that he came to see himself as a god. He is given a severe sentence: he will die like any other man (v. 9); worse still, "he will die the death of the uncircumcised by the hand of foreigners" (v. 10). The prophet clearly regards pride as being almost as sinful as idolatry, for the gravity of every sin lies in desiring to be like a god. "Sin sets itself against God's love for us and turns our hearts away from it. Like the first sin, it is disobedience, a revolt against God through the will to become 'like gods' (Gen 3:5), knowing and determining good and evil. Sin is thus 'love of oneself even to contempt of God' (St Augustine, *De civ. Dei,* 14, 28). In this proud self-exaltation, sin is diametrically opposed to the obedience of Jesus, which achieves our salvation (cf. Phil 2:6–9)" (*Catechism of the Catholic Church*, 1850).

dicens: 2«Fili hominis, dic principi Tyri: Haec dicit Dominus Deus: Eo quod elevatum est cor tuum, / et dixisti: "Deus ego sum / et in cathedra deorum sedeo / in corde maris!", / cum sis homo et non Deus, / et dedisti cor tuum quasi cor Dei. / 3Ecce sapientior es tu Danel, / omne secretum non est absconditum a te, / 4in sapientia et prudentia tua / fecisti tibi opes / et acquisisti aurum et argentum / in thesauris tuis; / 5in multitudine sapientiae tuae et in negotiatione tua / multiplicasti tibi opes, / et elevatum est cor tuum in opibus tuis. / 6Propterea haec dicit Dominus Deus: Eo quod fecisti cor tuum quasi cor Dei, / 7idcirco ecce ego adducam super te / alienos violentissimos gentium; / et nudabunt gladios suos super

[8]They shall thrust you down into the Pit,
and you shall die the death of the slain
in the heart of the seas.
Is 31:3 [9]Will you still say, 'I am a god,'
in the presence of those who slay you,
though you are but a man, and no god,
in the hands of those who wound you?
Ezek 31:18; 32:19 [10]You shall die the death of the uncircumcised
by the hand of foreigners;
for I have spoken, says the Lord GOD."

Lamentation over the king of Tyre

[11]Moreover the word of the LORD came to me: [12]"Son of man,
raise a lamentation over the king of Tyre, and say to him, Thus
says the Lord GOD:

"You were the signet of perfection,[p]
full of wisdom
and perfect in beauty.

28:11–19. The oracles against Tyre culminate in this elegy which, in keeping with demands of the style, intersperse and in this case contrast the noblest of qualities with the most grevious of crimes. The poem contains clear allusions to the Genesis account of creation: like the first man, the king of Tyre was set in Eden, given riches of every kind and had a cherub as his protector (vv. 14–16). But he, too, sinned by committing crimes of violence (v. 16), and was expelled by the very angel appointed to be his guardian. The expulsion from Eden is the prototype of every divine punishment, as the *Catechism of the Catholic Church* explains, for it marked the move from a paradise of freedom to bondage in this world (cf. no. 2061)—whereas obeying the commandments of God is like having a garden of delights (cf. v. 13). An early Christian writer puts it this way: "If you discover the teachings [of the Word], and listen to them carefully, you will come to know what God desires for those who love him with a pure heart; your soul will become a garden of delights; you will find planted within yourself a great tree, always in flower, which bears many wonderful fruits of many different kinds" (*Epistula ad Diognetum*, 12, 1).

pulchritudinem sapientiae tuae / et polluent splendorem tuum. / [8]In fossam detrahent te, et morieris / interitu occisorum in corde maris. / [9]Numquid dicens loqueris: "Deus ego sum!" / coram interficientibus te, / cum sis homo et non Deus / in manu occidentium te? / [10]Morte incircumcisorum morieris / in manu alienorum, / quia ego locutus sum», / ait Dominus Deus. [11]Et factus est sermo Domini ad me dicens: «Fili hominis, leva planctum super regem Tyri [12]et dices ei: Haec dicit Dominus Deus: Tu signaculum perfectum, / plenus sapientia et perfectus decore; / [13]in deliciis paradisi Dei fuisti,

p. Heb obscure

[13]You were in Eden, the garden of God;
every precious stone was your covering,
carnelian, topaz, and jasper,
chrysolite, beryl, and onyx,
sapphire,[q] carbuncle, and emerald;
and wrought in gold were your settings
and your engravings.[r]
On the day that you were created
they were prepared.
[14]With an anointed guardian cherub I placed you;[s]
you were on the holy mountain of God;
in the midst of the stones of fire you walked.
[15]You were blameless in your ways
from the day you were created,
till iniquity was found in you.
[16]In the abundance of your trade
you were filled with violence, and you sinned;
so I cast you as a profane thing from the mountain of God,
and the guardian cherub drove you out
from the midst of the stones of fire.
[17]Your heart was proud because of your beauty;
you corrupted your wisdom for the sake of your splendour.
I cast you to the ground;
I exposed you before kings,
to feast their eyes on you.
[18]By the multitude of your iniquities,
in the unrighteousness of your trade
you profaned your sanctuaries;
so I brought forth fire from the midst of you;
it consumed you,
and I turned you to ashes upon the earth
in the sight of all who saw you.

Rev 17:4; 21:19

Gen 3:24
Ex 25:20
Is 14:13
Ezek 10:2

Ezek 10:2:7

/ omnis lapis pretiosus operimentum tuum: / sardius, topazius et iaspis, / chrysolithus et onyx et beryllus, / sapphirus et carbunculus et smaragdus, / aurum opus caelaturae in te; / in die, qua conditus es, praeparata sunt. / [14]Cum cherub extento et protegente te posui te, / in monte sancto Dei fuisti, / in medio lapidum ignitorum ambulasti, / [15]perfectus in viis tuis / a die conditionis tuae, / donec inventa est iniquitas in te. / [16]In multitudine negotiationis tuae repleta sunt interiora tua / iniquitate, et peccasti. / Et eieci te de monte Dei, / et perdidit te cherub protegens / de medio lapidum ignitorum. / [17]Elevatum est cor tuum in decore tuo; / perdidisti sapientiam tuam propter splendorem tuum: / in terram proieci te, / ante faciem regum dedi te, ut cernerent te. / [18]In multitudine iniquitatum tuarum / et iniquitate negotiationis tuae / polluisti sanctuaria tua; / producam ergo ignem de medio tui, / qui comedat te, / et dabo te in cinerem super terram / in conspectu omnium videntium te. / [19]Omnes, qui viderint te, in

q. Or *lapis lazuli* **r.** Heb uncertain **s.** Heb uncertain

[19]All who know you among the peoples
are appalled at you;
you have come to a dreadful end
and shall be no more for ever."

Oracle against Sidon

Is 23:4,12 Jer 25:22; 27:8 [20]The word of the LORD came to me: [21]"Son of man, set your face
toward Sidon, and prophesy against her [22]and say, Thus says the
Lord GOD:

"Behold, I am against you, O Sidon,
and I will manifest my glory in the midst of you.
And they shall know that I am the LORD
when I execute judgments in her,
and manifest my holiness in her;
[23]for I will send pestilence into her,
and blood into her streets;
and the slain shall fall in the midst of her,
by the sword that is against her on every side.
Then they will know that I am the LORD.

Num 33:55 Josh 23:13 [24]"And for the house of Israel there shall be no more a brier to
prick or a thorn to hurt them among all their neighbours who have
treated them with contempt. Then they will know that I am the
Lord GOD.

28:20–23. Sidon, another Phoenician city, tried to oppose Babylon and sought the support of Judah to do so (cf. Jer 27:3). This oracle marks the end of the divine edicts against the neighbours of Israel. Sidon's crime is not mentioned, and the penalty is not specified: it is simply pestilence and death. However, the passage does say that Sidon will have God's glory manifested to it and will "know that he is the Lord"—which is the purpose of oracles against the nations.

28:24–26. As an end-piece to these oracles, Ezekiel turns his thoughts to Israel to point out that the punishment meted out to the nations marks the start of Israel's rehabilitation. All these things—the defeat of the nations, the exile and definitive restoration—are being brought about by God himself

gentibus / obstupescent super te; / in horrorem factus es / et non eris in perpetuum». [20]Et factus est sermo Domini ad me dicens: [21]«Fili hominis, pone faciem tuam contra Sidonem et propheta de ea [22]et dices: Haec dicit Dominus Deus: Ecce ego ad te, Sidon, / et glorificabor in medio tui, / et scient quia ego Dominus, / cum fecero in ea iudicia / et sanctificatus fuero in ea. / [23]Et immittam ei pestilentiam / et sanguinem in plateis eius, / et corruent interfecti in medio eius gladio per circuitum, / et scient quia ego Dominus. [24]Et non erit ultra domui Israel stimulus amaritudinis et spina dolorem inferens undique per circuitum eorum, qui adversantur eis, et scient quia ego Dominus Deus. [25]Haec dicit Dominus Deus: Quando congregavero domum Israel de populis, in quibus dispersi sunt, sanctificabor in eis

25 “Thus says the Lord GOD: When I gather the house of Israel
from the peoples among whom they are scattered, and manifest
my holiness in them in the sight of the nations, then they shall
dwell in their own land which I gave to my servant Jacob. 26 And Ezek 37:25
they shall dwell securely in it, and they shall build houses and
plant vineyards. They shall dwell securely, when I execute
judgments upon all their neighbours who have treated them with
contempt. Then they will know that I am the LORD their God.”

Oracles against Egypt* Is 19; Jer 46

29 1 In the tenth year, in the tenth month, on the twelfth day of Ps 44:19
the month, the word of the LORD came to me: 2 “Son of Is 19:1; 27:1; 51:9

---

and are designed to reveal his holiness and have the whole world acknowledge his sovereignty.

***29:1—32:32.** Egypt was the great empire that gave asylum to the tribes of Jacob and then ill-treated them until eventually it saw them delivered by the hand of God. These traditions of the exodus are a paradigm of the chequered relationship between the two countries, Israel and Egypt. They were never easy neighbours. Whenever they formed an alliance, Israel always ended up the loser; even so, there was always some sort of pact on the point of being established between them. In the years immediately prior to the Babylonian invasion, kings Jehoahaz (2 Kings 23:31–35), Jehoiachin (2 Kings 24:8–17) and Zedekiah (2 Kings 24:18–20) paid dearly for their alignment with Egypt. Both Jeremiah and Ezekiel counselled against these treaties of friendship and interpreted them as a betrayal of the Lord.

In this section Ezekiel brings together seven oracles against Egypt, giving the date when each was uttered—the first (29:1–16) in the tenth year of Jehoiachin’s reign (588 BC); second (29:17–21), the twenty-seventh year (571), making it the latest of the oracles; third (30:1–19), the only one undated, probably uttered towards the end of 587 or the start of 586; fourth (30:20–26), the eleventh year (587); fifth (31:1–18), two months later; sixth (32:1–16), the twenty-second year (586); and the seventh (32:17–32) fifteen days after the sixth. The number seven indicates completeness. All these oracles were spoken in the early years of the exile, with the exception of the second (29: 17–21), which must date from sixteen years later and which is of special interest because it explains Egypt’s downfall.

In the rather heavy, baroque style of the whole book, the prophet emphasizes that, in bringing about the fall of the

coram gentibus, et habitabunt in terra sua, quam dedi servo meo Iacob; 26 et habitabunt in ea securi et aedificabunt domos plantabuntque vineas et habitabunt confidenter, cum fecero iudicia in omnibus, qui adversantur eis per circuitum, et scient quia ego Dominus Deus eorum». **[29]** 1 In anno decimo, in decimo mense, duodecima mensis, factum est verbum Domini ad me dicens: 2 «Fili hominis, pone

Jer 25:19; 44:30; 46:22 Ezek 32 Rev 12:3

man, set your face against Pharaoh king of Egypt, and prophesy
against him and against all Egypt; 3speak, and say, Thus says the
Lord GOD:

"Behold, I am against you,
Pharaoh king of Egypt,
the great dragon that lies
in the midst of his streams,
that says, 'My Nile is my own;
I made it.'[t]
4I will put hooks in your jaws,

---

great Egyptian empire, Babylon and its king Nebuchadnezzar were instruments in the Lord's hands: God decides the shape that history shall take; he determines exactly when a nation shall reach its peak and when it will be toppled. In the latest oracle (29:17–21), particularly, the prophet confronts a serious criticism: he had proclaimed the fall of Tyre (26: 3–14), whereas, in fact, Babylon succeeded only in exacting tribute from that city-state. Had the prophet made a mistake, or had the Lord failed to do what he had determined? The reply explains the matter: Tyre was punished; it lost its power and status; and Egypt was absorbed by Babylon. In explaining this, the prophet points out that the Lord rewarded Nebuchadnezzar with control of Egypt for the risks that he ran in his attacks on Tyre. Far from failing to chastise each nation, it is clear that the Lord controls events in such a way that his power and benevolence are always in evidence.

Finally, and this is his most important message, Ezekiel encourages the exiles to put all their trust in the Lord, who will eventually re-establish Israel and also Egypt, its ancestral enemy (29:13–16).

29:1–16. The haughtiness of the pharaoh and his country will be brought low, rendering them as helpless as a crocodile taken from the Nile and stranded on land to be the prey of vultures. Ezekiel is probably referring to the pharaoh Hophra who died in the year 569, shortly before Nebuchadnezzar invaded Egypt in 568–567 (cf. Jer 44:30). The depiction of the pharaoh as a crocodile, described in detail here, is in line with evidence in extrabiblical texts. The rehabilitation of Egypt (vv. 13–16) will take place some fifty years, that is, one generation, later. It will not be as complete as that of Israel, because it will never again become a great empire; but, still, the message of the oracle is one of hope and envisages a time of peace and prosperity for the country (cf. Is 19:16–25).

faciem tuam contra pharaonem, regem Aegypti, et prophetabis de eo et de Aegypto universa. 3Loquere et dices: Haec dicit Dominus Deus: Ecce ego ad te, pharao, / rex Aegypti, / draco magne, qui cubas / in medio fluminum tuorum / et dicis: "Meus est fluvius, / et ego feci memetipsum!". / 4Et ponam uncos in maxillis tuis / et agglutinabo pisces fluminum tuorum squamis tuis / et extraham te de medio

t. Syr Compare Gk: Heb *I have made myself*

and make the fish of your streams stick to your scales;
and I will draw you up out of the midst of your streams,
with all the fish of your streams
which stick to your scales.
5And I will cast you forth into the wilderness, Jer 8:2; 25:33
you and all the fish of your streams; Rev 6:8
you shall fall upon the open field,
and not be gathered and buried.
To the beasts of the earth and to the birds of the air
I have given you as food.

6"Then all the inhabitants of Egypt shall know that I am the 2 Kings 18:21
LORD. Because you[u] have been a staff of reed to the house of Is 36:6
Israel; 7when they grasped you with the hand, you broke, and tore Is 20:5; 30:3
all their shoulders; and when they leaned upon you, you broke, Jer 2:36
and made all their loins to shake;[v] 8therefore thus says the Lord
GOD: Behold, I will bring a sword upon you, and will cut off from
you man and beast; 9and the land of Egypt shall be a desolation
and a waste. Then they will know that I am the LORD.

"Because you[w] said, 'The Nile is mine, and I made it,' 10there- Ex 14:2
fore, behold, I am against you, and against your streams, and I
will make the land of Egypt an utter waste and desolation, from
Migdol to Syene, as far as the border of Ethiopia. 11No foot of
man shall pass through it, and no foot of beast shall pass through
it; it shall be uninhabited forty years. 12And I will make the land
of Egypt a desolation in the midst of desolated countries; and her
cities shall be a desolation forty years among cities that are laid
waste. I will scatter the Egyptians among the nations, and disperse
them among the countries.

13"For thus says the Lord GOD: At the end of forty years I will Is 19:23
gather the Egyptians from the peoples among whom they were Jer 46:26

---

fluminum tuorum, / et universi pisces tui squamis tuis adhaerebunt. / 5Et proiciam te in desertum / et omnes pisces fluminum tuorum. / Super faciem terrae cades; / non colligeris neque congregaberis. / Bestiis terrae et volatilibus caeli / dedi te ad devorandum. / 6Et scient omnes habitatores Aegypti / quia ego Dominus, / pro eo quod fuisti baculus arundineus / domui Israel: / 7quando apprehenderunt te manu, / confractus es et lacerasti omnem umerum eorum / et, innitentibus eis super te, / comminutus es / et dissolvisti omnes lumbos eorum. 8Propterea haec dicit Dominus Deus: Ecce ego adducam super te gladium et interficiam de te hominem et iumentum; 9et erit terra Aegypti in desertum et solitudinem, et scient quia ego Dominus. Pro eo quod dixeris: "Fluvius meus est, et ego feci!", 10idcirco ecce ego ad te et ad flumina tua, daboque terram Aegypti in solitudines, gladio dissipatam a Magdolo ad Syenen et usque ad terminos Chus. 11Non pertransibit eam pes hominis, neque pes iumenti gradietur in ea, et non habitabitur quadraginta annis; 12daboque terram Aegypti desertam in medio terrarum desertarum, et civitates eius in medio urbium subversarum erunt desolatae quadraginta annis, et dispergam Aegyptios in nationes et ventilabo eos in terras. 13Quia haec dicit Dominus Deus: Post finem quadraginta annorum

u. Gk Syr Vg: Heb *they* **v.** Syr: Heb *stand* **w.** Gk Syr Vg: Heb *he*

scattered; [14]and I will restore the fortunes of Egypt, and bring them back to the land of Pathros, the land of their origin; and there they shall be a lowly kingdom. [15]It shall be the most lowly of the kingdoms, and never again exalt itself above the nations; and I will make them so small that they will never again rule over the nations. [16]And it shall never again be the reliance of the house of Israel, recalling their iniquity, when they turn to them for aid. Then they will know that I am the Lord GOD."

Egypt given to Nebuchadnezzar

[17]In the twenty-seventh year, in the first month, on the first day of
Jer 25:9 the month, the word of the LORD came to me: [18]"Son of man,
Nebuchadnezzar king of Babylon made his army labour hard
against Tyre; every head was made bald and every shoulder was
rubbed bare; yet neither he nor his army got anything from Tyre to
Ezek 20:10, 24; 32:11 pay for the labour that he had performed against it. [19]Therefore
thus says the Lord GOD: Behold, I will give the land of Egypt to
Nebuchadnezzar king of Babylon; and he shall carry off its wealth[x]
Jer 43:10; 44:30; 46:26 and despoil it and plunder it; and it shall be the wages for his army.
[20]I have given him the land of Egypt as his recompense for which he
laboured, because they worked for me, says the Lord GOD.

[21]"On that day I will cause a horn to spring forth to the house
of Israel, and I will open your lips among them. Then they will
know that I am the LORD."

29:17–21. This brief oracle, the last one spoken by Ezekiel in 571 BC, is a theological explanation of the fall of Egypt: Nebuchadnezzar, the Lord's instrument, exposed himself to great danger by attacking the impregnable city of Tyre (cf. 28:1–10), and he is given Egypt by way of compensation. In this way, the proud country of the Nile was brought low, and rendered inferior to the more resilient Tyre, which, despite the battering it received during the Babylonian invasion, retained its independence.

congregabo Aegyptios de populis, in quibus dispersi fuerunt, [14]et convertam sortem Aegypti et collocabo eos in terra Phatures, in terra nativitatis suae; et erunt ibi in regnum humile. [15]Inter regna cetera erit humillima et non elevabitur ultra super nationes, et imminuam eos, ne imperent gentibus. [16]Neque erunt ultra domui Israel in confidentiam, in memoriam revocans iniquitatem, cum sequerentur eos, et scient quia ego Dominus Deus». [17]Et factum est in vicesimo et septimo anno, in primo, in una mensis, factum est verbum Domini ad me dicens: [18]«Fili hominis, Nabuchodonosor, rex Babylonis, servire fecit exercitum suum servitute magna adversus Tyrum; omne caput decalvatum et omnis umerus attritus est, et merces non est reddita ei neque exercitui eius de Tyro pro servitute, qua servivit adversum eam. [19]Propterea haec dicit Dominus Deus: Ecce ego dabo Nabuchodonosor, regi Babylonis, terram Aegypti, et accipiet opes eius et depraedabitur manubias eius et diripiet spolia eius, et erit merces exercitui illius, [20]ut stipendium eius, pro quo servivit adversum eam. Dedi ei terram Aegypti

x. Or *multitude*

The day of the Lord on Egypt

30 [1]The word of the LORD came to me: [2]"Son of man, prophesy, and say, Thus says the Lord GOD: Amos 5:18–20 Zeph 1:14–18

"Wail, 'Alas for the day!'
[3]For the day is near,
the day of the LORD is near;
it will be a day of clouds,
a time of doom for the nations.
[4]A sword shall come upon Egypt,
and anguish shall be in Ethiopia,
when the slain fall in Egypt,
and her wealth is carried away,
and her foundations are torn down.

Ezek 7:7 Joel 1:15; 2:1 Zeph 1:7

[5]Ethiopia, and Put, and Lud, and all Arabia, and Libya,[y] and the Jer 46:9
people of the land that is in league, shall fall with them by the
sword.

[6]"Thus says the LORD: Ezek 29:10
Those who support Egypt shall fall,
and her proud might shall come down;
from Migdol to Syene
they shall fall within her by the sword,
says the Lord GOD.

30:1–19. The "day of the Lord" is the day of judgment when the wicked will be condemned (cf. Amos 5:18–20; Zeph 1:14–18). Ezekiel recites the eschatological catastrophes described in the writings of previous prophets; he applies these to Egypt and refers to their impact on neighbouring countries. This oracle contains interesting information about the political geography of the time, though some of the cities mentioned are difficult to identify now. The listing of so many pagan cities serves to highlight the sovereignty of the Lord, to show that he controls all known nations. If God in his justice punishes them all, so will they all attain salvation once they acknowledge him (v. 19).

pro eo quod laboraverunt mihi, ait Dominus Deus. [21]In die illo germinare faciam cornu domui Israel, et tibi dabo apertum os in medio eorum, et scient quoniam ego Dominus». **[30]** [1]Et factum est verbum Domini ad me dicens: [2]«Fili hominis, propheta et dic: Haec dicit Dominus Deus: Ululate, vae diei, / [3]quia iuxta est dies, / et appropinquat dies Domini, / dies nubis; tempus gentium erit. / [4]Et veniet gladius in Aegyptum, / et erit pavor in Chus, / cum ceciderint vulnerati in Aegypto, / et ablatae fuerint opes illius, / et destructa fundamenta eius. / [5]Chus et Phut et Lud et omne vulgus promiscuum / et Chub et filii terrae foederis / cum eis gladio cadent. / [6]Haec dicit Dominus Deus: / Et corruent fulcientes Aegyptum, / et destruetur superbia potentiae eius; / a Magdolo usque ad Syenen gladio cadent in ea, /

y. Gk Compare Syr Vg: Heb *Cub*

[7]And she[z] shall be desolated in the midst of desolated countries
and her cities shall be in the midst of cities that are laid waste.
[8]Then they will know that I am the LORD,
when I have set fire to Egypt,
and all her helpers are broken.
[9]"On that day swift[a] messengers shall go forth from me to
terrify the unsuspecting Ethiopians; and anguish shall come upon
them on the day of Egypt's doom; for, lo, it comes!
[10]"Thus says the Lord GOD:
I will put an end to the wealth[b] of Egypt,
Ezek 29: by the hand of Nebuchadnezzar king of Babylon.
11–12 [11]He and his people with him, the most terrible of the nations,
shall be brought in to destroy the land;
and they shall draw their swords against Egypt,
and fill the land with the slain.
[12]And I will dry up the Nile,
and will sell the land into the hand of evil men;
I will bring desolation upon the land and everything in it,
by the hand of foreigners;
I, the LORD, have spoken.

Jer 43:12 [13]"Thus says the Lord GOD:
I will destroy the idols,
and put an end to the images, in Memphis;
there shall no longer be a prince in the land of Egypt;
so I will put fear in the land of Egypt.
Ezek 29:14 [14]I will make Pathros a desolation,
and will set fire to Zoan,
and will execute acts of judgment upon Thebes.
[15]And I will pour my wrath upon Pelusium,
the stronghold of Egypt,
and cut off the multitude of Thebes.

---

ait Dominus Deus. [7]Et dissipabuntur in medio terrarum desolatarum, et urbes eius in medio civitatum desertarum erunt; [8]et scient quia ego Dominus, cum dedero ignem in Aegyptum, et attriti fuerint omnes auxiliatores eius. [9]In die illa egredientur nuntii a facie mea in navibus ad conterendam confidentiam Chus, et erit pavor in eis in die Aegypti, quia veniet. [10]Haec dicit Dominus Deus: Cessare faciam pompam Aegypti in manu Nabuchodonosor, regis Babylonis. [11]Ipse et populus eius cum eo violentissimi gentium adducentur ad disperdendam terram; et evaginabunt gladios suos super Aegyptum et implebunt terram interfectis. [12]Et faciam alveos fluminum aridos et tradam terram in manu pessimorum et dissipabo terram et plenitudinem eius in manu alienorum. Ego Dominus locutus sum. [13]Haec dicit Dominus Deus: / Et disperdam simulacra / et cessare faciam idola de Memphi, / et dux de terra Aegypti / non erit amplius, / et dabo terrorem in terra Aegypti. / [14]Et disperdam terram Phatures / et dabo ignem in Tani / et faciam iudicia in No. [15]Et effundam indignationem meam super

z. Gk: Heb *they* **a.** Gk Syr: Heb *in ships* **b.** Or *multitude*

[16]And I will set fire to Egypt;
Pelusium shall be in great agony;
Thebes shall be breached,
and its walls broken down.[c]
[17]The young men of On and of Pibeseth shall fall by the sword;
and the women shall go into captivity.
[18]At Tehaphnehes the day shall be dark,
when I break there the dominion of Egypt,
and her proud might shall come to an end;
she shall be covered by a cloud,
and her daughters shall go into captivity.
[19]Thus I will execute acts of judgment upon Egypt.
Then they will know that I am the LORD."

Pharaoh's power broken

[20]In the eleventh year, in the first month, on the seventh day of the
month, the word of the Lord came to me: [21]"Son of man, I have
broken the arm of Pharaoh king of Egypt; and lo, it has not been
bound up, to heal it by binding it with a bandage, so that it may
become strong to wield the sword. [22]Therefore thus says the Lord
God: Behold, I am against Pharaoh king of Egypt, and will break
his arms, both the strong arm and the one that was broken; and I
will make the sword fall from his hand. [23]I will scatter the

30:20–26. Using repetition for the sake of effect, Ezekiel draws a contrast between the gradual collapse of the pharaoh's army and the growing strength of Babylon's.

"I will scatter the Egyptians among the nations" (v. 23). Egypt is the only nation that has to bear the same penalty as Israel—that of exile. Although the prophets, especially Jeremiah and Ezekiel, are very hard on Egypt, they do make it clear that there is a certain solidarity between Israel and Egypt, not only in misfortune but also in resurgence after exile (cf. 29:13–16).

Sin, robur Aegypti, et interficiam multitudinem No. [16]Et dabo ignem in Aegypto; quasi parturiens dolebit Sin, et in No scissura erit, et contra Memphin hostes plena die. [17]Iuvenes Heliopoleos et Bubasti gladio cadent, et ipsae captivae ducentur. [18]Et in Taphnis nigrescet dies, cum contrivero ibi sceptra Aegypti, et defecerit in ea superbia potentiae eius; ipsam nubes operiet, filiae autem eius in captivitatem ducentur. [19]Et faciam iudicia in Aegypto, et scient quia ego Dominus». [20]Et factum est in undecimo anno, in primo, in septima mensis, factum est verbum Domini ad me dicens: [21]«Fili hominis, brachium pharaonis, regis Aegypti, confregi, et ecce non est obvolutum, ut restitueretur ei sanitas, ut ligaretur pannis et farciretur linteolis, ut recepto robore posset tenere gladium. [22]Propterea haec dicit Dominus Deus: Ecce ego ad pharaonem, regem Aegypti, et comminuam brachium eius forte sed confractum et deiciam gladium de manu eius [23]et dispergam Aegyptum in gentibus et ventilabo eos in terris. [24]Et

c. Cn: Heb *and Memphis, distresses by day*

Egyptians among the nations, and disperse them throughout the
lands. 24And I will strengthen the arms of the king of Babylon,
and put my sword in his hand; but I will break the arms of Pharaoh,
and he will groan before him like a man mortally wounded. 25I
will strengthen the arms of the king of Babylon, but the arms of
Pharaoh shall fall; and they shall know that I am the Lord. When
I put my sword into the hand of the king of Babylon, he shall
stretch it out against the land of Egypt; 26and I will scatter the
Egyptians among the nations and disperse them throughout the
countries. Then they will know that I am the Lord."

Allegory of the cedar

31 1In the eleventh year, in the third month, on the first day of
the month, the word of the LORD came to me: 2"Son of
man, say to Pharaoh king of Egypt and to his multitude:
"Whom are you like in your greatness?
Is 17:9 3 Behold, I will liken you to[d] a cedar in Lebanon,
with fair branches and forest shade,
and of great height,

31:1–18. The cedar is a tree that achieves great height, with spreading branches that afford plenty of shade, and its timber is much in demand for building purposes, ships' masts, furniture, musical instruments, etc. The particular cedar to which the pharaoh is compared here is an exceptional specimen, not to be found in reality. Its features are exaggerated here to show the sheer scale of the pharaoh's collapse: great is his arrogance, and great the punishment it deserves. The passage begins with a poetic description of the cedar (vv. 3–9), spells out the divine judgment against Egypt (vv. 10–14), and tells what its repercussions were in the countries round about (vv. 15–18). Pride and arrogance are denounced, once more, as being very grave sins which God always punishes, as the *Magnificat* in the New Testament reminds us: "He has shown strength with his arm, he has scattered the proud in the imagination of their hearts, he has put down the mighty from their thrones, and exalted those of low degree" (Lk 1:51–52).

confortabo brachia regis Babylonis daboque gladium meum in manu eius; et confringam brachia pharaonis, et gemet gemitibus sicut transfixus coram facie eius. 25Et confortabo brachia regis Babylonis, et brachia pharaonis concident; et scient quia ego Dominus, cum dedero gladium meum in manu regis Babylonis, et extenderit eum super terram Aegypti. 26Et dispergam Aegyptum in nationes et ventilabo eos in terras, et scient quia ego Dominus». **[31]** 1Et factum est in anno unde cimo, in tertio, una mensis, factum est verbum Domini ad me dicens: 2«Fili hominis, dic pharaoni, regi Aegypti, et pompae eius: Cui similis factus es in magnitudine tua? / 3Ecce abies, quasi cedrus in Libano, / pulcher ramis et frondibus nemorosus / excelsusque altitudine, / et inter nubes elevatum est cacumen

d. Cn: Heb *Behold, Assyria*

its top among the clouds.[e]
4The waters nourished it,
the deep made it grow tall,
making its rivers flow[f]
round the place of its planting,
sending forth its streams
to all the trees of the forest.
5So it towered high Dan 4:11
above all the trees of the forest;
its boughs grew large
and its branches long,
from abundant water in its shoots.
6All the birds of the air Ezek 17:23
made their nests in its boughs; Mt 13:32
under its branches all the beasts of the field Mk 4:32
brought forth their young; Lk 13:19
and under its shadow
dwelt all great nations.
7It was beautiful in its greatness,
in the length of its branches;
for its roots went down
to abundant waters.
8The cedars in the garden of God could not rival it, Rev 2:7
nor the fir trees equal its boughs;
the plane trees were as nothing
compared with its branches;
no tree in the garden of God
was like it in beauty.
9I made it beautiful Gen 2:8
in the mass of its branches,
and all the trees of Eden envied it,
that were in the garden of God.

---

eius; / 4aquae nutrierunt illum, / abyssus exaltavit eum, / flumina eius manabant / in circuitu radicum
eius, / et rivos suos emisit / ad universa ligna campi. / 5Propterea elevata est altitudo eius / super omnia
ligna campi, / et multiplicata sunt arbusta eius, / et elevati sunt rami eius / propter aquas multas. /
6Cumque extendisset umbram suam, / in ramis eius fecerunt nidos / omnia volatilia caeli, / et sub
frondibus eius genuerunt / omnes bestiae campi, / et sub umbra illius habitabat / universa multitudo
gentium; / 7eratque pulcherrimus in magnitudine sua / et in dilatatione arbustorum suorum, / erat enim
radix illius / iuxta aquas multas. / 8Cedri non fuerunt pares illi / in paradiso Dei; / abietes non
adaequaverunt / ramos eius, / et platani non fuerunt / aequae frondibus illius; / omne lignum paradisi
Dei / non est assimilatum illi et pulchritudini eius, / 9quoniam speciosum feci eum / et multis
condensisque frondibus: / et aemulata sunt eum omnia ligna Eden, / quae erant in paradiso Dei.

e. Gk: Heb *thick boughs* **f.** Gk: Heb *going*

[10]“Therefore thus says the Lord GOD: Because it[g] towered high and set its top among the clouds,[h] and its heart was proud of its height, [11]I will give it into the hand of a mighty one of the nations; he shall surely deal with it as its wickedness deserves. I have cast it out. [12]Foreigners, the most terrible of the nations, will cut it down and leave it. On the mountains and in all the valleys its branches will fall, and its boughs will lie broken in all the watercourses of the land; and all the peoples of the earth will go from its shadow and leave it. [13]Upon its ruin will dwell all the birds of the air, and upon its branches will be all the beasts of the field. [14]All this is in order that no trees by the waters may grow to lofty height or set their tops among the clouds,[h] and that no trees that drink water may reach up to them in height; for they are all given over to death, to the nether world among mortal men, with those who go down to the Pit.

Num 16:33 [15]“Thus says the Lord GOD: When it goes down to Sheol I will
make the deep mourn for[i] it, and restrain its rivers, and many waters
shall be stopped; I will clothe Lebanon in gloom for it, and all the
Is 14:8–11,15 trees of the field shall faint because of it. [16]I will make the nations
Ezek 32:17–32 quake at the sound of its fall, when I cast it down to Sheol with those
who go down to the Pit; and all the trees of Eden, the choice and best of Lebanon, all that drink water, will be comforted in the nether world. [17]They also shall go down to Sheol with it, to those who are slain by the sword; yea, those who dwelt under its shadow among the nations shall perish.[j] [18]Whom are you thus like in glory and in greatness among the trees of Eden? You shall be brought down with the trees of Eden to the nether world; you shall lie among the uncircumcised, with those who are slain by the sword.

“This is Pharaoh and all his multitude, says the Lord GOD.”

---

[10]Propterea haec dicit Dominus Deus: Pro eo quod sublimatus est in altitudine et dedit summitatem suam usque in nubes, et elevatum est cor eius in altitudine sua, [11]tradam eum in manu potentis principis gentium; faciens faciet ei: iuxta impietatem eius eieci eum. [12]Et succident illum alieni, violentissimi nationum; et proicient eum super montes, et in cunctis convallibus corruent rami eius, et confringentur arbusta eius in universis voraginibus terrae, et recedent de umbra eius omnes populi terrae et relinquent eum. [13]Super ruinam eius habitabunt / omnia volatilia caeli, / et in ramis eius erunt / universae bestiae campi, / [14]ne eleventur in altitudine sua / omnia ligna aquarum neque ponant / sublimitatem suam inter nubes nec / stent apud eas in sublimitate sua / omnia, quae irrigantur aquis, quia / omnes traditi sunt in mortem / ad inferiora terrae, / in medio filiorum hominum, / ad eos, qui descendunt in lacum. [15]Haec dicit Dominus Deus: In die, quando descendit ad inferos, induxi luctum, operui propter eum abyssum et prohibui flumina eius et coercui aquas multas; obscuravi super eum Libanum, et omnia ligna agri concussa sunt. [16]A sonitu ruinae eius commovi gentes, cum deducerem eum ad infernum cum his, qui descendebant in lacum; et consolata sunt in inferioribus terrae omnia ligna Eden, egregia atque

g. Syr Vg: Heb *you* **h.** Gk: Heb *thick boughs* **i.** Gk: Heb *mourn for, I have covered* **j.** Compare Gk: Heb obscure

Lamentation over the fall of Pharaoh

32 [1]In the twelfth year, in the twelfth month, on the first day of Job 40:25–41:26
the month, the word of the LORD came to me: [2]"Son of Ezek 29:3–5
man, raise a lamentation over Pharaoh king of Egypt, and say to
him:

"You consider yourself a lion among the nations,
but you are like a dragon in the seas;
you burst forth in your rivers,
trouble the waters with your feet,
and foul their rivers.
[3]Thus says the Lord GOD: Ezek 31:12–16
I will throw my net over you
with a host of many peoples;
and I[k] will haul you up in my dragnet.
[4]And I will cast you on the ground,
on the open field I will fling you,
and will cause all the birds of the air to settle on you,
and I will gorge the beasts of the whole earth with you.
[5]I will strew your flesh upon the mountains,
and fill the valleys with your carcass.[l]

32:1–16. An elegy or dirge usually contains praise of the dead person, city or nation that has passed away. Here, however, the praise goes no further than to compare the pharaoh and Egypt to a lion (v. 2) and a mythological crocodile or dragon (cf. 29:3–5), while the rest of the piece is given over to describing the bloodshed and devastation. The elegy can be taken as having two parts to it—the first, describing the fate of the dragon (vv. 3–10); the second, applying that metaphor to the defeat of Egypt by Babylon (vv. 11–16). Like the previous oracles, the song is imbued with joy at God's victory over his enemies; yet, being an elegy it takes no pleasure from the catastrophe that befalls the country.

praeclara in Libano, universa, quae irrigabantur aquis. [17]Nam et ipsi cum eo descenderunt ad infernum ad interfectos gladio et auxiliatores eius, qui sederant sub umbra eius in medio nationum. [18]Cui assimilatus es, o inclite atque sublimis inter ligna Eden? Et ecce deductus es cum lignis Eden ad inferiora terrae; in medio incircumcisorum dormies cum his, qui interfecti sunt gladio. Ipse est pharao et omnis pompa eius», dicit Dominus Deus. **[32]** [1]Et factum est duodecimo anno, in mense duodecimo, in una mensis, factum est verbum Domini ad me dicens: [2]«Fili hominis, assume lamentum super pharaonem, regem Aegypti, et dices ad eum: Leo gentium peristi, / et eras sicut draco in mari; / et bulliebas in fluminibus tuis / et conturbabas aquas pedibus tuis / et turbida faciebas flumina earum. / [3]Haec dicit Dominus Deus: / Expandam super te rete meum / in coetu populorum multorum, / et extrahent te in sagena mea; / [4]et proiciam te in terram, / super faciem agri abiciam te / et habitare faciam super te omnia volatilia caeli / et saturabo de te bestias universae terrae; / [5]et dabo carnes tuas super montes / et implebo valles sanie tua. / [6]Et irrigabo terram paedore / sanguinis tui super montes, /

k. Gk Vg: Heb *they* **l.** Symmachus Syr Vg: Heb *your height*

[6]I will drench the land even to the mountains
with your flowing blood;
and the watercourses will be full of you.
Amos 8:9 Mt 24:29 Rev 6:12 [7]When I blot you out, I will cover the heavens,
and make their stars dark;
I will cover the sun with a cloud,
and the moon shall not give its light.
[8]All the bright lights of heaven
will I make dark over you,
and put darkness upon your land, says the Lord GOD.

[9]"I will trouble the hearts of many peoples, when I carry you
captive[m] among the nations, into the countries which you have not
known. [10]I will make many peoples appalled at you, and their
kings shall shudder because of you, when I brandish my sword
before them; they shall tremble every moment, every one for his
Jer 46:26 Ezek 14:17; 29:8–19 own life, on the day of your downfall. [11]For thus says the Lord
GOD: The sword of the king of Babylon shall come upon you. [12]I
will cause your multitude to fall by the swords of mighty ones, all
of them most terrible among the nations.

"They shall bring to nought the pride of Egypt,
and all its multitude shall perish.
[13]I will destroy all its beasts
from beside many waters;
and no foot of man shall trouble them any more,
nor shall the hoofs of beasts trouble them.
[14]Then I will make their waters clear,
and cause their rivers to run like oil, says the Lord GOD.
[15]When I make the land of Egypt desolate
and when the land is stripped of all that fills it,
when I smite all who dwell in it,
then they will know that I am the LORD.

---

et voragines implebuntur ex te; / [7]et operiam, cum exstinctus fueris, caelum / et nigrescere faciam stellas eius: / solem nube tegam, / et luna non dabit lumen suum; / [8]omnia luminaria caeli / maerere faciam super te / et dabo tenebras super terram tuam, / dicit Dominus Deus. [9]Et commovebo cor populorum multorum, cum induxero contritionem tuam in gentibus super terras, quas nescis. [10]Et stupescere faciam super te populos multos, et reges eorum horrore nimio formidabunt super te, cum volare coeperit gladius meus coram facie eorum, et obstupescet tremefactus unusquisque pro anima sua in die ruinae tuae. [11]Quia haec dicit Dominus Deus: Gladius regis Babylonis veniet tibi, [12]in gladiis fortium deiciam multitudinem tuam; / violentissimae gentium omnium hae / et vastabunt superbiam Aegypti, / et dissipabitur omnis pompa eius. / [13]Et perdam omnia iumenta eius, / quae erant super aquas plurimas, / et non conturbabit eas pes hominis ultra, / neque ungula iumentorum turbabit eas; / [14]tunc purissimas reddam aquas eorum / et flumina eorum quasi oleum adducam, / ait Dominus Deus. / [15]Cum dedero terram Aegypti desolatam, / deseretur autem terra a plenitudine sua, quando percussero omnes

m. Gk: Heb *bring your destruction*

[16]This is a lamentation which shall be chanted; the daughters of
the nations shall chant it; over Egypt, and over all her multitude,
shall they chant it, says the Lord GOD."

The death of Pharaoh bewailed

[17]In the twelfth year, in the first month,[n] on the fifteenth day of the
month, the word of the LORD came to me:[18] "Son of man, wail
over the multitude of Egypt, and send them down, her and the
daughters of majestic nations, to the nether world, to those who
have gone down to the Pit:

[19]"'Whom do you surpass in beauty?
Go down, and be laid with the uncircumcised.'

[20]They shall fall amid those who are slain by the sword,[o] and with
her shall lie all her multitudes.[p] [21]The mighty chiefs shall speak of

Ezek 31:16–18
Is 14:9–11

32:17–32. This lamentation is dated to the twenty-second year, that is, 586 BC, like the previous one (32:1). From a literary point of view, it relies on repetition (in almost exactly the same words) to describe the fate of famous nations of the past that have totally disappeared—Assyria and its capital Nineveh, Elam representing the Mesopotamian countries, Meshech and Tubal, early settlers in Asia Minor, and finally the Phoenicians and Edomites. The rhythm helps to give the impression that there is an inevitability about the whole process. If those nations ended up in Sheol (v. 21), in the depths of the earth ("the Pit": vv. 23, 24), Egypt, its pharaoh and his entire army will suffer the same fate.

The doctrinal and even the poetic thrust of the oracle comes from the rhetorical question it asks: "Whom do you surpass in beauty?", that is, in nobility (v. 19). And the reply is inarguable: "Go down and be laid with the uncircumcised" (v. 19). The worst aspect of Egypt's punishment is that she is put on a par with the very worst sort of people, the most cruel and most impious.

On hearing the fate that awaits these nations, the exiles would have been somewhat consoled and would have seen that the Lord was preserving them and that they could look forward to returning home and being completely rehabilitated.

habitatores eius, / scient quia ego Dominus. [16]Planctus est, et plangent eum; filiae gentium plangent eum, super Aegyptum et super omnem pompam eius plangent eum», ait Dominus Deus. [17]Et factum est in duodecimo anno, in quinta decima mensis, factum est verbum Domini ad me dicens: [18]«Fili hominis, cane lugubre super pompam Aegypti et detrahe eam, ipsam et filias gentium robustarum ad inferiora terrae cum his, qui descendunt in lacum. [19]Quo pulchrior es? / Descende et dormi cum incircumcisis. [20]In medio interfectorum gladio cadent; gladius datus est, attraxerunt eam et omnes populos eius. [21]Loquentur ei potentissimi robustorum de medio inferni, cum auxiliatoribus eius

n. Gk: Heb lacks *in the first month* **o.** Gk Syr: Heb *sword, the sword is delivered* **p.** Gk: Heb *they have drawn her away and all her multitudes*

them, with their helpers, out of the midst of Sheol: 'They have
come down, they lie still, the uncircumcised, slain by the sword.'
22"Assyria is there, and all her company, their graves round
about her, all of them slain, fallen by the sword; 23whose graves
are set in the uttermost parts of the Pit, and her company is round
about her grave; all of them slain, fallen by the sword, who spread
terror in the land of the living.
Jer 49:34–39 24"Elam is there, and all her multitude about her grave; all of
them slain, fallen by the sword, who went down uncircumcised
into the nether world, who spread terror in the land of the living,
and they bear their shame with those who go down to the Pit.
25They have made her a bed among the slain with all her multitude,
their graves round about her, all of them uncircumcised, slain by
the sword; for terror of them was spread in the land of the living,
and they bear their shame with those who go down to the Pit; they
are placed among the slain.
Is 66:19 Ezek 27:13; 26"Meshech and Tubal are there, and all their multitude, their
38:2,3; 39:1 graves round about them, all of them uncircumcised, slain by the
Is 14:18 sword; for they spread terror in the land of the living. 27And they
do not lie with the fallen mighty men of old[q] who went down to
Sheol with their weapons of war, whose swords were laid under
their heads, and whose shields[r] are upon their bones; for the terror
of the mighty men was in the land of the living. 28So you shall be
broken and lie among the uncircumcised, with those who are slain
by the sword.
29"Edom is there, her kings and all her princes, who for all their
might are laid with those who are slain by the sword; they lie with
the uncircumcised, with those who go down to the Pit.

---

descenderunt: "Tacent incircumcisi interfecti gladio!". 22Ibi Assyria et omnis multitudo eius, in circuitu illius sepulcra eius, omnes interfecti, qui ceciderunt gladio; 23quorum data sunt sepulcra in profundissimis laci, et facta est multitudo eius per gyrum sepulcri eius; universi interfecti, cadentes gladio, qui dederant quondam formidinem in terra viventium. 24Ibi Elam et omnis pompa eius per gyrum sepulcri sui; omnes hi interfecti ruentesque gladio, qui descenderunt incircumcisi ad inferiora terrae, qui dederant quondam formidinem suam in terra viventium et sustulerunt ignominiam suam cum his, qui descendunt in lacum. 25In medio interfectorum posuerunt cubile eius, in omni pompa eius, in circuitu eius sepulcra illius, omnes hi incircumcisi interfectique gladio; dederant enim terrorem suum in terra viventium et sustulerunt ignominiam suam cum his, qui descendunt in lacum, in medio interfectorum positi sunt. 26Ibi Mosoch, Thubal et omnis pompa eius, in circuitu illius sepulcra eius, omnes hi incircumcisi interfectique gladio, quia dederunt formidinem suam in terra viventium; 27et non dormient cum fortibus, qui ceciderunt a saeculo et descenderunt ad infernum cum armis suis et posuerunt gladios suos sub capitibus suis, et fuerunt scuta eorum super ossa eorum, quia terror fortium erat in terra viventium. 28Et tu ergo in medio incircumcisorum contereris et dormies cum interfectis gladio. 29Ibi Idumaea, reges eius et omnes duces eius, qui dati sunt in robore suo cum interfectis gladio

q. Gk Old Latin: Heb *of the uncircumcised* **r.** Cn: Heb *iniquities*

30"The princes of the north are there, all of them, and all the Sidonians, who have gone down in shame with the slain, for all the terror which they caused by their might; they lie uncircumcised with those who are slain by the sword, and bear their shame with those who go down to the Pit.

31"When Pharaoh sees them, he will comfort himself for all his multitude, Pharaoh and all his army, slain by the sword, says the Lord GOD. 32For he[s] spread terror in the land of the living; therefore he shall be laid among the uncircumcised, with those who are slain by the sword, Pharaoh and all his multitude, says the Lord GOD."

PART THREE

Hope and the restoration of Israel*

Ezekiel, the people's watchman*

33 1The word of the LORD came to me: 2"Son of man, speak to Ezek 3:17–21
your people and say to them, If I bring the sword upon a

***33:1—39:29.** After the destruction of Jerusalem in 587, Ezekiel changes the tone of his oracles: there will be no sign of threats in the third part of the book. From now on he will speak only about hope and renewal; about the life that the Lord will infuse into his people and each of its members. The novelty of this second stage of Ezekiel's ministry can be seen even in the literary style. By way of introduction, we hear again about the prophet's role as God's watchman and spokesman (chap. 33); then come oracles about the cleansing of the people and its institutions (chaps. 34–36), and finally those that herald the revival of the people (chap. 37), which even involves an eschatological battle against the powers of evil (chaps. 38–39).

et qui cum incircumcisis dormiunt et cum his, qui descenderunt in lacum. 30Ibi principes aquilonis omnes et universi Sidonii, qui deducti sunt cum interfectis in terrore suo, in sua fortitudine confusi; qui dormiunt incircumcisi cum interfectis gladio et sustulerunt confusionem suam cum his, qui descendunt in lacum. 31Videbit eos pharao et consolabitur super universa pompa sua. Interfecti sunt gladio pharaonis et omnis exercitus eius, ait Dominus Deus, 32quia dedi terrorem meum in terra viventium; et prostratus est in medio incircumcisorum cum interfectis gladio pharaonis et omnis pompa eius», ait Dominus Deus. **[33]** 1Et factum est verbum Domini ad me dicens: 2«Fili hominis, loquere ad filios populi tui et dices ad eos: Terra, cum induxero super eam gladium, et tulerit populus terrae virum unum

s. Cn: Heb *I*

land, and the people of the land take a man from among them, and
Joel 2:1 Jer 6:17 make him their watchman; 3and if he sees the sword coming upon
Amos 3:6 the land and blows the trumpet and warns the people; 4then if any
one who hears the sound of the trumpet does not take warning,

---

Now that the most dire oracles have been borne out by events, Ezekiel has the authority to assure his people of the benefits of divine mercy. Gone is their natural pride and false reliance on the temple: what needs to be done now is to build up their confidence in God, who has never turned his back on them. Ezekiel's message about God's steadfast love was a great help to those people, and it is valid for us also: "Keep your attention fixed on the goodness of God, which is always greater than all the sins we could commit. He does not remind us of our failure and ingratitude when we come to know ourselves and desire to become friends with him; nor does he dwell on the mercies he has already shown to chasten us. His merciful punishments served to forgive us more quickly, as people who, as it is written, were members of his household and had eaten of his bread. Remembering his words (Ezek 33:11), and all the things that he has done for me, since I tired of offending him, may His Majesty forgive me. He never tires of giving, nor does his mercy run out: may we never tire of receiving" (St Teresa of Avila, *Life*, 19, 15).

***33:1–33.** The responsibilities of the prophet in this period after the fall of Jerusalem do not change, but there are significant new nuances: he is, as he was before, the watchman charged with warning people about dangers that threaten the house of Israel (vv. 1–9; cf. 3:16–21); and he is very much aware of his personal responsibility towards his listeners: even if they fail to respond, he must still give them warning (vv. 10–20; 14:22–23 and 18:1–20). Moreover, and this is probably the most important thing at this stage, he must be especially eloquent, for God has given him back his power of speech (vv. 21–22) to enable him to explain that they indeed have a right to inherit the land (vv. 23–29), and to proclaim his message in the full confidence that he is speaking in God's name (vv. 30–33). Cf. 3:26–27; 24:27.

33:1–9. In this new account of his calling, Ezekiel uses the watchman metaphor to explain his role as a prophet. In chapter 3 (3:16–21) his duty to counsel his hearers was stressed; now he develops the metaphor of the watchman in a time of war (vv. 2–6), underlining that it is a heavy and far-reaching responsibility. In this new stage it is only the wicked that the prophet will have to admonish (vv. 7–9); seemingly, the just, who, along with the impious, received a warning in the oracle of chapter 3 and who are not mentioned here, will never again stray from their path.

de finibus suis et constituerit eum sibi speculatorem, 3et ille viderit gladium venientem super terram et cecinerit bucina et annuntiaverit populo; 4audiens autem quisquis ille est sonum bucinae, non se observaverit, veneritque gladius et tulerit eum: sanguis ipsius super caput eius erit; 5sonum bucinae

and the sword comes and takes him away, his blood shall be upon
his own head. 5 He heard the sound of the trumpet, and did not take
warning; his blood shall be upon himself. But if he had taken
warning, he would have saved his life. 6 But if the watchman sees
the sword coming and does not blow the trumpet, so that the
people are not warned, and the sword comes, and takes any one of
them; that man is taken away in his iniquity, but his blood I will
require at the watchman's hand.
7 "So you, son of man, I have made a watchman for the house Jer 1:18
of Israel; whenever you hear a word from my mouth, you shall Ezek 3:17–19
give them warning from me. 8 If I say to the wicked, O wicked
man, you shall surely die, and you do not speak to warn the
wicked to turn from his way, that wicked man shall die in his
iniquity, but his blood I will require at your hand. 9 But if you warn
the wicked to turn from his way, and he does not turn from his
way; he shall die in his iniquity, but you will have saved your life.

Individual responsibility

10 "And you, son of man, say to the house of Israel, Thus have you Ezek 14:12–20
said: 'Our transgressions and our sins are upon us, and we waste 18:21–30

33:10–20. The teaching about personal responsibility preached before the fall of Jerusalem (cf. 18:1–32) used the proverb of the sour grapes and the teeth set on edge to explain the exile. The teaching in this passage has to do with the possibility of conversion: the exiles have come to realize that their sins are the ultimate reason for their situation, but what can they do to extract themselves from it? The answer (the same as before) is set on the Lord's lips: "I have no pleasure in the death of the wicked, but that the wicked turn from his way and live" (v. 18; cf. 18:23). From this one can deduce that only the guilty endure punishment, but also (and more importantly) that the guilty can repent and change. Conversion is the first and primary purpose of the prophet's new message, and that holds true for the Church also: "We know that he does not accept the repentance of the dead or of those who are about to die and wish, at the very last moment, to redeem their souls by the remedy of his mercy. We are terrified by the thought that some might fall so far into sin that they will

audivit et non se observavit, sanguis eius in ipso erit. Si autem se custodierit, animam suam salvavit.
6 Quod si speculator viderit gladium venientem et non insonuerit bucina, et populus non se custodierit;
veneritque gladius et tulerit de eis animam: ille quidem in iniquitate sua captus est, sanguinem autem
eius de manu speculatoris requiram. 7 Te autem, fili hominis, speculatorem dedi domui Israel. Audiens
ergo ex ore meo sermonem, commonebis eos ex me. 8 Si, me dicente ad impium: Impie, morte morieris,
non fueris locutus, ut se custodiat impius a via sua, ipse impius in iniquitate sua morietur, sanguinem
autem eius de manu tua requiram. 9 Si autem commonueris impium, ut a viis suis convertatur, et ille non
fuerit conversus a via sua, ipse in iniquitate sua morietur, porro tu animam tuam liberasti. 10 Tu ergo,

2 Sam 14:14 away because of them; how then can we live?' [11]Say to them, As
Ezek 18:23 Lk 15:7, I live, says the Lord GOD, I have no pleasure in the death of the
10,32 wicked, but that the wicked turn from his way and live; turn back,
turn back from your evil ways; for why will you die, O house of
Israel? [12]And you, son of man, say to your people, The righteousness of the righteous shall not deliver him when he transgresses;
and as for the wickedness of the wicked, he shall not fall by it
when he turns from his wickedness; and the righteous shall not be
able to live by his righteousness[t] when he sins. [13]Though I say to
the righteous that he shall surely live, yet if he trusts in his
righteousness and commits iniquity, none of his righteous deeds
shall be remembered; but in the iniquity that he has committed he
shall die. [14]Again, though I say to the wicked, 'You shall surely
die,' yet if he turns from his sin and does what is lawful and right,
[15]if the wicked restores the pledge, gives back what he has taken
by robbery, and walks in the statutes of life, committing no
Ezek 18:22 iniquity; he shall surely live, he shall not die. [16]None of the sins
that he has committed shall be remembered against him; he has
done what is lawful and right, he shall surely live.

Ezek 18:29 [17]"Yet your people say, 'The way of the Lord is not just'; when
it is their own way that is not just. [18]When the righteous turns

---

despair of God's pity and mercy, believing that He cannot give succour to a man who turns to him at any time, or free him from the sin that weighs him down, from the burden he wishes were lifted from his shoulders. This would be nothing but another death suffered by the soul, killed by the cruel impossibility of ever being absolved and forgiven. But God is always ready to forgive, and he invites us to repent, making this promise: *if he turns from his sin and does what is lawful and right ... none of the sins that he has committed shall be remembered against him* (Ezek 33:14–16). God knows our hearts; he never refuses repentance or penance, no matter in what day or hour it comes" (Pope St Celestine I, *Cuperemus quidem*).

fili hominis, dic ad domum Israel: Sic locuti estis, dicentes: "Iniquitates nostrae et peccata nostra super nos sunt, et in ipsis nos tabescimus; quomodo ergo vivere poterimus?". [11]Dic ad eos: Vivo ego, dicit Dominus Deus; nolo mortem impii, sed ut revertatur impius a via sua et vivat. Convertimini, convertimini a viis vestris pessimis; et quare moriemini, domus Israel? [12]Tu itaque, fili hominis, dic ad filios populi tui: Iustitia iusti non liberabit eum in quacumque die praevaricatus fuerit; et impietas impii non nocebit ei in quacumque die conversus fuerit ab impietate sua; et iustus non poterit vivere in iustitia sua in quacumque die peccaverit. [13]Etiamsi dixero iusto quod vita vivat, et, confisus in iustitia sua, fecerit iniquitatem, omnes iustitiae eius oblivioni tradentur, et in iniquitate sua, quam operatus est, in ipsa morietur. [14]Sin autem dixero impio: Morte morieris, et egerit paenitentiam a peccato suo feceritque iudicium et iustitiam, [15]pignus restituerit ille impius rapinamque reddiderit, in mandatis vitae

t. Heb *by it*

from his righteousness, and commits iniquity, he shall die for it.
[19]And when the wicked turns from his wickedness, and does what
is lawful and right, he shall live by it. [20]Yet you say, 'The way of Ezek 18:30
the Lord is not just.' O house of Israel, I will judge each of you
according to his ways."

Ezekiel recovers his power of speech 2 Kings 25:2–11
[21]In the twelfth year of our exile, in the tenth month, on the fifth Jer 39:2; 52:5,6
day of the month, a man who had escaped from Jerusalem came Ezek 24:26–27
to me and said, "The city has fallen." [22]Now the hand of the LORD Ezek 3:26–27
had been upon me the evening before the fugitive came; and he
had opened my mouth by the time the man came to me in the
morning; so my mouth was opened, and I was no longer dumb.
[23]The word of the LORD came to me: [24]"Son of man, the Ezek 11:15
inhabitants of these waste places in the land of Israel keep saying,

---

33:21–33. At the end of the account of the call of Ezekiel we saw that the Lord imposed a period of silence on him, which was to last until a fugitive arrived with news of the fall of Jerusalem (cf. 3:22–27). That cure happened in the year 586, according to what it says here (v. 21), that is, one year after the collapse of the city. During that period of dumbness the prophet spoke the oracles contained in chapters 5–24 of the book; therefore the power of speech which he now recovers means that in addition to being able to utter those words that the Lord places in his mouth, he can also speak on his own account to console the exiles and raise their hopes.

First he addresses those who seek shelter in Jerusalem (vv. 23–29), thinking that they are the only heirs of the promise made to Abraham (cf. 11:14–21 and note). But Ezekiel's message is clear: all have sinned, and all must suffer the penalty. All, therefore, must submit to God's sentence and acknowledge him before anyone can set about claiming their rights.

Then the Lord warns the prophet himself (vv. 30–33) that even though the exiles have recourse to Ezekiel, it does not mean that they will listen readily to him; still, he must continue to speak, whether they listen or not (cf. 2:11).

"Like a love song" (v. 32; note **u**): this means that his listeners will often appreciate the beauty and even the depth of his message, but not live up to its demands.

ambulaverit nec fecerit quidquam iniustum, vita vivet et non morietur; [16]omnia peccata eius, quae peccavit, non imputabuntur ei: iudicium et iustitiam fecit, vita vivet. [17]Et dicunt filii populi tui: "Non est aequa via Domini"; et ipsorum via iniqua est. [18]Cum enim recesserit iustus a iustitia sua feceritque iniquitates, morietur in eis; [19]et cum recesserit impius ab impietate sua feceritque iudicium et iustitiam, vivet in eis. [20]Et dicitis: "Non est recta via Domini". Unumquemque iuxta vias suas iudicabo de vobis, domus Israel». [21]Et factum est in duodecimo anno, in decimo, in quinta mensis transmigrationis nostrae, venit ad me, qui fugerat de Ierusalem, dicens: «Vastata est civitas». [22]Manus autem Domini facta fuerat ad me vespere, antequam veniret qui fugerat; aperuitque os meum, donec veniret ad me mane, et, aperto ore meo, non silui amplius. [23]Et factum est verbum Domini ad me dicens: [24]«Fili

'Abraham was only one man, yet he got possession of the land;
Gen 9:4 but we are many; the land is surely given us to possess.'
Lev 1:5; 3:17; 17:10–14 25Therefore say to them, Thus says the Lord GOD: You eat flesh
Ezek 44:7 with the blood, and lift up your eyes to your idols, and shed blood;
Lev 18:20 shall you then possess the land? 26You resort to the sword, you
commit abominations and each of you defiles his neighbour's
Rev 2:23; 6:8 wife; shall you then possess the land? 27Say this to them, Thus
says the Lord GOD: As I live, surely those who are in the waste
places shall fall by the sword; and him that is in the open field I
will give to the beasts to be devoured; and those who are in
strongholds and in caves shall die by pestilence. 28And I will make
the land a desolation and a waste; and her proud might shall come
to an end; and the mountains of Israel shall be so desolate that
Rev 21:27 none will pass through. 29Then they will know that I am the LORD,
when I have made the land a desolation and a waste because of all
their abominations which they have committed.

30"As for you, son of man, your people who talk together about
you by the walls and at the doors of the houses, say to one
Ps 78:36 another, each to his brother, 'Come, and hear what the word is that
Is 29:13 comes forth from the LORD.' 31And they come to you as people
Mt 7:26; 13:22 Lk 8:21 come, and they sit before you as my people, and they hear what
you say but they will not do it; for with their lips they show much
Lk 7:32 love, but their heart is set on their gain. 32And, lo, you are to them
like one who sings love songs[u] with a beautiful voice and plays
well on an instrument, for they hear what you say, but they will
Deut 18:21 Ezek 2:5 not do it.33 When this comes—and come it will!—then they will
know that a prophet has been among them."

---

hominis, qui habitant in ruinosis his super humum Israel, loquentes aiunt: "Unus erat Abraham et
hereditate possedit terram; nos autem multi, nobis data est terra in possessionem". 25Idcirco dices ad
eos: Haec dicit Dominus Deus: Qui in sanguine comeditis et oculos vestros levatis ad idola vestra et
sanguinem funditis, numquid terram hereditate possidebitis? 26Stetistis in gladiis vestris, fecistis
abominationes, et unusquisque uxorem proximi sui polluit, et terram hereditate possidebitis? 27Haec
dices ad eos: Sic dicit Dominus Deus: Vivo ego, qui in ruinosis habitant, gladio cadent; et, qui in agro
est, bestiis tradetur ad devorandum; qui autem in praesidiis et in speluncis sunt, peste morientur. 28Et
dabo terram in solitudinem et desertum, et deficiet superba fortitudo eius, et desolabuntur montes Israel,
ita ut nullus sit qui per eos transeat; 29et scient quia ego Dominus, cum dedero terram desolatam et
desertam propter universas abominationes suas, quas operati sunt. 30Et tu, fili hominis, filii populi tui,
qui loquuntur de te iuxta parietes et in ostiis domorum et dicunt unus ad alterum, vir ad fratrem suum,
loquentes: "Venite et audite, qui sit sermo egrediens a Domino". 31Et veniunt ad te quasi si conveniat
populus, et sedent coram te populus meus; et audiunt sermones tuos et non faciunt eos, quia quasi
amatores loquuntur, et avaritiam suam sequitur cor eorum. 32Et es eis quasi carmen amatorum, quod
suavi voce et cum dulci chordarum sono canitur, et audiunt verba tua et non faciunt ea. 33Et cum
venerit, quod praedictum est—ecce enim venit—tunc scient quod prophetes fuerit inter eos».

u. Cn: Heb *like a love song*

1 Sam 17:34
1 Kings 22:17
Ps 23:1–6;
78: 70–72
Jer 2:8; 10:21;

Oracle against the shepherd of Israel*

34 [1]The word of the LORD came to me: [2]"Son of man,
prophesy against the shepherds of Israel,* prophesy, and

***34:1–31.** In some Sumerian and Egyptian texts the image of the shepherd is sometimes applied to leading men and gods. In the Bible it is often applied to kings (1 Kings 22:17), perhaps because David began life as a shepherd (1 Sam 17:34; Ps 78:70–72), and to the Lord (cf. Ps 23:1–6; 80:2–3). The prophets, particularly Jeremiah, use the image when talking about rulers, be they kings or priests (cf. Jer 2:8; 10:21; 25:34–36; Zech 11:4–17). In this first address to the exiles, Ezekiel talks about bad shepherds, that is, the evil rulers who led the people into the disaster of the exile (vv. 1–10) —and, by contrast, he speaks of the Lord, the supreme shepherd who takes over the reins of government to rule his people without intermediaries (vv. 11–22), and of the new messiah-ruler whom God himself will place at their head: he will be their new shepherd, David, who will lead his flock to the best pastures (vv. 23–31).

Jesus found this a very appropriate image for explaining his role as Messiah and Saviour (Jn 10:1–18) and as Judge at the end of time (cf. Mt 25:31–46). Moreover, he confirmed his words by actions. When, at the multiplication of the loaves, he gathers those who have followed him (they are "like sheep without a shepherd": Mk 6:34; cf. Ezek 34:5), and nourishes them with bread and with the word of his teaching, he is fulfilling this prophecy of Ezekiel which promises a new king, a true shepherd, and a new Covenant. Jesus is, then, the shepherd who assembles all mankind to lead it to salvation: "He is the one who has gathered together into one flock all the holy sheep from all the nations under heaven, without neglecting any of the peoples of the earth; he carries out every day what he once promised, when he said: *There are other sheep, that are not of this flock, and these too I will tend, and they will listen to my voice, and there will be one flock, and one shepherd*" (St Leo the Great, *Sermones*, 63, 7). And as John Paul II teaches: "The figure of Jesus Christ as shepherd of the Church, his flock, takes up and represents in new and more evocative terms the same content as that of Jesus Christ as head and servant. Fulfilling the prophetic proclamation of the Messiah and saviour joyfully announced by the psalmist and the prophet Ezekiel (cf. Ps 22–23; Ezek 34:11ff), Jesus presents himself as 'the good shepherd' (Jn 10:11, 14), not only of Israel but of all humanity (cf. Jn 10:16). His whole life is a continual manifestation of his 'pastoral charity'" (*Pastores dabo vobis*, 22).

34:1–10. As is usual in condemnatory oracles, the charges are mentioned first (vv. 2–6) and then comes the sentence, which begins with the usual "Therefore"

[34] [1]Et factum est verbum Domini ad me dicens: [2]«Fili hominis, propheta de pastoribus Israel, propheta et dices pastoribus: Haec dicit Dominus Deus: Vae pastoribus Israel, qui pascebant

23:1–6; 25:34–36 say to them, even to the shepherds, Thus says the Lord GOD: Ho,
Zech 11:4–17 Mt 18:12–14 shepherds of Israel who have been feeding yourselves! Should not
Lk 15:4–7 shepherds feed the sheep? 3You eat the fat, you clothe yourselves
Jn 10:1–18 with the wool, you slaughter the fatlings; but you do not feed the
1 Pet 5:2–4 sheep. 4The weak you have not strengthened, the sick you have
Rev 3:2 not healed, the crippled you have not bound up, the strayed you
have not brought back, the lost you have not sought, and with
Is 56:9–12 force and harshness you have ruled them. 5So they were scattered,
Zech 10:2 Mt 9:36 because there was no shepherd; and they became food for all the
1 Pet 2:25 wild beasts. 6My sheep were scattered, they wandered over all the
mountains and on every high hill; my sheep were scattered over
all the face of the earth, with none to search or seek for them.

Jude 12 7"Therefore, you shepherds, hear the word of the LORD: 8As I
live, says the Lord GOD, because my sheep have become a prey,
and my sheep have become food for all the wild beasts, since
there was no shepherd; and because my shepherds have not
searched for my sheep, but the shepherds have fed themselves,

---

(vv. 7–10). The rulers of the people (cf. 23:23–31), that is, the princes, priests, elders and professional prophets, have exploited the people and sought their own gain. What Ezekiel says here carries a message for those who hold office in Christian communites: "In the Church of Christ, everyone is obliged to make a tenacious effort to remain loyal to the teaching of Christ. No one is exempt. If the shepherds do not themselves strive to acquire a sensitive conscience and to remain faithful to dogma and moral teaching—which make up the deposit of faith and the inheritance of all—then the prophetic words of Ezekiel will be borne out: 'Son of man, prophesy against the shepherds of Israel, prophesy, and say to them, even to the shepherds, thus says the Lord God: Ho, shepherds of Israel who have been feeding yourselves! [...] This is a strong reproof, but the offence against God is even worse when those who have received the task of promoting the spiritual welfare of everyone abuse souls instead, depriving them of the crystal water of baptism, which regenerates the soul; of the soothing oil of confirmation, which strengthens it; of the tribunal which pardons; of the food which gives eternal life" (St Josemaría Escrivá, *Christ Is Passing By*, 81).

semetipsos! Nonne greges pascuntur a pastoribus? 3Lac comedebatis et lana operiebamini et, quod crassum erat, occidebatis, gregem autem non pascebatis; 4quod infirmum fuit, non consolidastis et, quod aegrotum, non sanastis; quod fractum est, non alligastis et, quod eiectum est, non reduxistis et, quod perierat, non quaesistis et super forte imperabatis cum violentia. 5Et dispersae sunt oves meae, eo quod non esset pastor; et factae sunt in devorationem omnium bestiarum agri et dispersae sunt. 6Erraverunt greges mei in cunctis montibus et in universo colle excelso, et super omnem faciem terrae dispersi sunt greges mei; et non erat qui requireret, non erat qui requireret. 7Propterea, pastores, audite verbum Domini: 8Vivo ego, dicit Dominus Deus, pro eo quod factus est grex meus in rapinam et oves meae in devorationem omnium bestiarum agri, eo quod non esset pastor, neque enim quaesierunt

and have not fed my sheep; [9]therefore, you shepherds, hear the
word of the LORD: [10]Thus says the Lord GOD, Behold, I am Ezek 3:18
against the shepherds; and I will require my sheep at their hand, Heb 13:17
and put a stop to their feeding the sheep; no longer shall the
shepherds feed themselves. I will rescue my sheep from their
mouths, that they may not be food for them.

The Lord, the shepherd of Israel

[11]"For thus says the Lord GOD: Behold, I, I myself will search for Lk 15:4
my sheep, and will seek them out. [12]As a shepherd seeks out his Jn 10:11 Is 66: 18–19
flock when some of his sheep[v] have been scattered abroad, so will Joel 2:2
I seek out my sheep; and I will rescue them from all places where Mt 24:31;
they have been scattered on a day of clouds and thick darkness. 25:32

34:11–22. Ezekiel says that God has made himself a shepherd for his people (v. 11); he always looks out for them (vv. 12–16), neglecting none. This solicitude includes the practice of justice (vv. 17–22); in this new stage it becomes clearer that divine love and mercy are compatible with condemnation of the wicked (v. 20): in fact, love can never exclude justice. This beautiful oracle resounds in our Lord's parable of the Good Shepherd who takes care of his sheep (cf. Jn 10:1–21), in what he says about the Father's joy on finding the lost sheep (cf. Mt 18:12–14; Lk 15: 4–7), and in things he has to say about the Last Judgment as reported by St Matthew (Mt 25:31–46). In a sermon on pastors, St Augustine comments: "He stands guard over us when we are awake and while we sleep. If an earthly flock is safe in the vigilant care of a human shepherd, how much more secure are we, who have God as our shepherd, not only because he desires to teach and help us, but because he is our creator. *As for you, my flock, thus says the Lord God: Behold, I judge between sheep and sheep, rams and he-goats* (Ezek 34:17). Why are he-goats to be found among God's flock? Goats who will be sent to the left, and sheep that will be called to the right side of God, are to be found in the same fields and by the same streams; and He tends together those who will later be separated. The meek patience of sheep is an imitation of the patience of God. He will separate the flock later, sending some to the right and some to the left" (*Sermones*, 47).

pastores mei gregem meum, sed pascebant pastores semetipsos et gregem meum non pascebant, [9]propterea, pastores, audite verbum Domini. [10]Haec dicit Dominus Deus: Ecce ego ipse super pastores requiram gregem meum de manu eorum et cessare eos faciam, ut ultra non pascant gregem nec pascant amplius pastores semetipsos; et liberabo gregem meum de ore eorum, et non erit ultra eis in escam. [11]Quia haec dicit Dominus Deus: Ecce ego ipse requiram oves meas et visitabo eas. [12]Sicut visitat pastor gregem suum in die, quando fuerit in medio ovium suarum dissipatarum, sic visitabo oves meas

v. Cn: Heb *when he is among his sheep*

[13]And I will bring them out from the peoples, and gather them
from the countries, and will bring them into their own land; and
I will feed them on the mountains of Israel, by the fountains, and
Ps 23:2 in all the inhabited places of the country. [14]I will feed them with
Jer 33:2 good pasture, and upon the mountain heights of Israel shall be
their pasture; there they shall lie down in good grazing land, and
on fat pasture they shall feed on the mountains of Israel. [15]I myself
will be the shepherd of my sheep, and I will make them lie down,
Is 40:11 says the Lord GOD. [16]I will seek the lost, and I will bring back the
Mal 4:6 strayed, and I will bind up the crippled, and I will strengthen the
Mt 18:11 Lk 15:4–7 weak, and the fat and the strong I will watch over;[w] I will feed
them in justice.

Mt 25:32–34 [17]"As for you, my flock, thus says the Lord GOD: Behold, I
judge between sheep and sheep, rams and he-goats. [18]Is it not
enough for you to feed on the good pasture, that you must tread
down with your feet the rest of your pasture; and to drink of clear
water, that you must foul the rest with your feet? [19]And must my
sheep eat what you have trodden with your feet, and drink what
you have fouled with your feet?

34:23–31. There are important fresh nuances in this messianic oracle about hope in a messiah-king when it is compared with the passage in Isaiah's "Book of Immanuel" (cf. Is 6–12). The messiah-king is called David (vv. 23–24) because he will have the qualities of that great king from Bethlehem; he will be a "prince", that is, not a king in the political sense; he will be God's "servant", coming in all humility, without pomp or ceremony. There will be a new flock (a new people), a new shepherd, messiah and a new Covenant, bringing the blessings contained in the "Code of holiness" (cf. Lev 26:3–13), and no danger will threaten or strike them (cf. Jer 23:5–6). Ezekiel does not mention the possibility of this new Covenant being broken; he sees it as inviolable. Not even the wicked, who will be outside it and gain no benefit from it, will be able to break it.

et liberabo eas de omnibus locis, in quibus dispersae fuerant in die nubis et caliginis. [13]Et educam eas de populis et congregabo eas de terris et inducam eas in terram suam et pascam eas in montibus Israel, in rivis et in cunctis sedibus terrae. [14]In pascuis uberrimis pascam eas, et in montibus excelsis Israel erunt pascua earum; ibi requiescent in herbis virentibus et in pascuis pinguibus pascentur super montes Israel. [15]Ego pascam oves meas et ego eas accubare faciam, dicit Dominus Deus. [16]Quod perierat, requiram et, quod eiectum erat, reducam et, quod confractum fuerat, alligabo et, quod infirmum erat, consolidabo et, quod pingue et forte, custodiam et pascam illas in iudicio. [17]Vos autem, grex meus, haec dicit Dominus Deus: Ecce ego iudico inter pecus et pecus, inter arietes et hircos. [18]Nonne satis vobis erat pascuam bonam depasci? Insuper et reliquias pascuarum vestrarum conculcastis pedibus vestris et, cum purissimam aquam biberetis, reliquam pedibus vestris turbabatis; [19]et oves meae his, quae conculcata pedibus vestris fuerant, pascebantur et, quae pedes vestri turbaverant, haec bibebant.

w. Gk Syr Vg: Heb *destroy*

[20]"Therefore, thus says the Lord GOD to them: Behold, I, I
myself will judge between the fat sheep and the lean sheep.
[21]Because you push with side and shoulder, and thrust at all the
weak with your horns, till you have scattered them abroad, [22]I will
save my flock, they shall no longer be a prey; and I will judge
between sheep and sheep.

A new shepherd, a new Covenant

[23]*And I will set up over them one shepherd, my servant David,
and he shall feed them: he shall feed them and be their shepherd.
[24]And I, the LORD, will be their God, and my servant David shall
be prince among them; I, the LORD, have spoken.

Jer 23:4–5 Ezek 37:27; 44:3 Jn 10:11,16 Rev 7:17

[25]"I will make with them a covenant of peace and banish wild
beasts from the land, so that they may dwell securely in the
wilderness and sleep in the woods. [26]And I will make them and
the places round about my hill a blessing; and I will send down
the showers in their season; they shall be showers of blessing.
[27]And the trees of the field shall yield their fruit, and the earth
shall yield its increase, and they shall be secure in their land; and
they shall know that I am the LORD, when I break the bars of their
yoke, and deliver them from the hand of those who enslaved them.
[28]They shall no more be a prey to the nations, nor shall the beasts
of the land devour them; they shall dwell securely, and none shall
make them afraid. [29]And I will provide for them prosperous[x]
plantations so that they shall no more be consumed with hunger in
the land, and no longer suffer the reproach of the nations. [30]And
they shall know that I, the LORD their God, am with them, and that
they, the house of Israel, are my people, says the Lord GOD. [31]And
you are my sheep, the sheep of my pasture,[y] and I am your God,
says the Lord GOD."

Is 11:6–9; 35:9; Jer 23:5–6 Hos 2:18,20 Ezek 37:26; 38:8; Lev 26:6

Is 60:21; 61:3

---

[20]Propterea haec dicit Dominus Deus ad eos: Ecce ego ipse iudico inter pecus pingue et macilentum;
[21]pro eo quod lateribus et umeris impingebatis et cornibus vestris ventilabatis omnia infirma pecora,
donec dispergerentur foras, [22]salvabo gregem meum, et non erit ultra in rapinam, et iudicabo inter
pecus et pecus. [23]Et suscitabo super eas pastorem unum, qui pascat eas, servum meum David; ipse
pascet eas et ipse erit eis in pastorem. [24]Ego autem Dominus ero eis in Deum, et servus meus David
princeps in medio eorum. Ego Dominus locutus sum. [25]Et faciam cum eis pactum pacis et cessare
faciam bestias pessimas de terra, et habitabunt in deserto securi et dormient in saltibus; [26]et ponam eos
et, quae sunt in circuitu collis mei, benedictionem et deducam imbrem in tempore suo: pluviae
benedictionis erunt. [27]Et dabit lignum agri fructum suum, et terra dabit germen suum, et erunt in terra
sua absque timore et scient quia ego Dominus, cum contrivero vectes iugi eorum et eruero eos de manu
imperantium sibi. [28]Et non erunt ultra in rapinam gentibus, neque bestiae terrae devorabunt eos, sed
habitabunt confidenter absque ullo terrore. [29]Et suscitabo eis germen nominatum, et non erunt ultra
imminuti fame in terra neque portabunt ultra opprobrium gentium; [30]et scient quia ego Dominus Deus

x. Gk Syr Old Latin: Heb *for renown* **y.** Gk Old Latin: Heb *pasture you are men*

Num 20:13 **Oracle against the mountains of Edom***
Deut 2:1,4,5 Is 21:11 35 1The word of the LORD came to me: 2"Son of man, set your
Jer 49:7–8 face against Mount Seir, and prophesy against it, 3and say
Ezek 25:12,18 to it, Thus says the Lord GOD: Behold, I am against you, Mount
Joel 3:19 Amos 1:11; Seir, and I will stretch out my hand against you, and I will make
Obad 1:21 you a desolation and a waste. 4I will lay your cities waste, and you
shall become a desolation; and you shall know that I am the LORD.
Obad 10–11 5Because you cherished perpetual enmity, and gave over the
people of Israel to the power of the sword at the time of their
Rev 16:6 calamity, at the time of their final punishment; 6therefore, as I live,
says the Lord GOD, I will prepare you for blood, and blood shall
pursue you; because you are guilty of blood,[z] therefore blood shall
pursue you. 7I will make Mount Seir a waste and a desolation; and
I will cut off from it all who come and go. 8And I will fill your
mountains with the slain; on your hills and in your valleys and in

---

***35:1—36:15.** The sacred text includes here an oracle against the Edomites (symbolized by "Mount Seir"), even though they were denounced already (cf. 25:12–14). What we have here are two contrasting oracles—the reproval of Edom (35:1–15) and the blessing of Israel (36:1–15): Mount Seir is cursed, the mountains of Israel praised.

35:1–15. The Edomites, descendants of Esau, were related to the Israelites, the descendants of Esau's brother, Jacob. But there was always tension between the two peoples, and sometimes war. This oracle, which uses the law of retaliation (the *lex talionis*) as a literary device, proclaims that the Edomites will die by the sword because they shed so much Jewish blood (vv. 5–9); they will be brought down because they sought to take over Israel and Judah (vv. 10–12); and they will be despised by the nations because they reviled Israel (vv. 13–15). Worst of all, they are guilty of blasphemy because they sought to control Israel and Judah "although the Lord was there" (v. 10); it was as if they had tried to defeat the Lord himself. Hence the severity of their punishment.

eorum cum eis, et ipsi populus meus domus Israel, ait Dominus Deus. 31Vos autem grex meus, grex pascuae meae vos, et ego Dominus Deus vester», dicit Dominus Deus. **[35]** 1Et factus est sermo Domini ad me dicens: 2«Fili hominis, pone faciem tuam adversum montem Seir et propheta de eo et dices illi: 3Haec dicit Dominus Deus: Ecce ego ad te, mons Seir; / et extendam manum meam super te / et dabo te desolatum atque desertum. / 4Urbes tuas demoliar, / et tu desertus eris / et scies quia ego Dominus. 5Eo quod fueris inimicus sempiternus et concluseris filios Israel in manus gladii in tempore afflictionis eorum, in tempore poenae extremae; 6propterea, vivo ego, dicit Dominus Deus, sanguini tradam te, et sanguis te persequetur et, cum sanguinem non oderis, sanguis persequetur te. 7Et dabo montem Seir desolatum atque desertum et auferam de eo euntem et redeuntem 8et implebo montes eius occisorum suorum, in collibus tuis et in vallibus tuis, atque in omnibus torrentibus tuis interfecti gladio cadent. 9In solitudines sempiternas tradam te, et civitates tuae non habitabuntur, et scietis quoniam ego

z. Gk: Heb *you have hated blood*

all your ravines those slain with the sword shall fall. [9]I will make
you a perpetual desolation, and your cities shall not be inhabited.
Then you will know that I am the LORD.

[10]"Because you said, 'These two nations and these two
countries shall be mine, and we will take possession of them,'—
although the LORD was there—[11]therefore, as I live, says the Lord
GOD, I will deal with you according to the anger and envy which
you showed because of your hatred against them; and I will make
myself known among you,[a] when I judge you. [12]And you shall
know that I, the LORD, have heard all the revilings which you
uttered against the mountains of Israel, saying, 'They are laid
desolate, they are given us to devour.' [13]And you magnified your- 1 Sam 2:3
selves against me with your mouth, and multiplied your words Rev 13:6
against me; I heard it. [14]Thus says the Lord GOD: For the rejoicing
of the whole earth I will make you desolate. [15]As you rejoiced
over the inheritance of the house of Israel, because it was desolate,
so I will deal with you; you shall be desolate, Mount Seir, and all
Edom, all of it. Then they will know that I am the LORD.

Blessing on the mountains of Israel

36 [1]"And you, son of man, prophesy to the mountains of
Israel, and say, O mountains of Israel, hear the word of the

36:1–15. This oracle of salvation follows the same pattern as the oracle denouncing the Edomites. It tells why Israel is being blessed, and then proclaims the blessing itself which begins with the usual "therefore" (vv. 3, 4, 5, 6, 14). But it is at pains to stress that it is the Lord, not the prophet, who utters the blessings, as can be seen from the repetition of the phrase "Thus says the Lord God" (vv. 2, 3, 4, 5, 6, 7, 13).

"I will do more good to you than ever before" (v. 11): a reference both to the origins of the people in the desert after the Covenant made at Sinai, when they enjoyed God's special protection and were provisioned by him, and to the origins of mankind, before the Fall.

Dominus. [10]Eo quod dixeris: "Duae gentes et duae terrae meae erunt, et hereditate possidebo eas!", cum Dominus esset ibi; [11]propterea, vivo ego, dicit Dominus Deus, faciam iuxta iram tuam et secundum zelum tuum, quem fecisti odio habens eos, et notus efficiar in eis, cum te iudicavero. [12]Et scies quia ego Dominus audivi universa opprobria tua, quae locutus es de montibus Israel dicens: "Deserti nobis ad devorandum dati sunt!". [13]Et insurrexistis super me ore vestro et vociferati estis vobis adversum me verba vestra; ego audivi. [14]Haec dicit Dominus Deus: Laetante universa terra, in solitudinem te redigam; [15]sicuti gavisus es super hereditatem domus Israel, eo quod fuerit dissipata, sic faciam tibi: dissipatus eris, mons Seir, et Idumaea omnis, et scient quia ego Dominus. **[36]** [1]Tu autem, fili hominis, propheta super montes Israel et dices: Montes Israel, audite verbum Domini. [2]Haec dicit

a. Gk: Heb *them*

Ezek 35:10 LORD. 2Thus says the Lord GOD: Because the enemy said of you,
'Aha!' and, 'The ancient heights have become our possession,'
3therefore prophesy, and say, Thus says the Lord GOD: Because,
yea, because they made you desolate, and crushed you from all
sides, so that you became the possession of the rest of the nations,
and you became the talk and evil gossip of the people; 4therefore,
O mountains of Israel, hear the word of the Lord GOD: Thus says
the Lord GOD to the mountains and the hills, the ravines and the
valleys, the desolate wastes and the deserted cities, which have
become a prey and derision to the rest of the nations round about;
Deut 4:24 5therefore thus says the Lord GOD: I speak in my hot jealousy
against the rest of the nations, and against all Edom, who gave my
land to themselves as a possession with wholehearted joy and utter
contempt, that they might possess[b] it and plunder it. 6Therefore
prophesy concerning the land of Israel, and say to the mountains
and hills, to the ravines and valleys, Thus says the Lord GOD:
Behold, I speak in my jealous wrath, because you have suffered
the reproach of the nations; 7therefore thus says the Lord GOD: I
swear that the nations that are round about you shall themselves
suffer reproach.

8"But you, O mountains of Israel, shall shoot forth your
branches, and yield your fruit to my people Israel; for they will
soon come home. 9For, behold, I am for you, and I will turn to
you, and you shall be tilled and sown; 10and I will multiply men

---

It all serves to highlight the benefits Israel will enjoy after the exile.

"You devour men" (v. 13): Canaan was known to be scarred by war even from before the time the Israelites settled there (cf. Num 13:32–33). Ezekiel mentions this to highlight the advantages of the new Israel; peace will reign there.

Dominus Deus: Eo quod dixerit inimicus de vobis: "Euge, altitudines sempiternae in hereditatem datae sunt nobis"; 3propterea vaticinare et dic: Haec dicit Dominus Deus: Pro eo quod desolati estis, et inhiaverunt vobis per circuitum, ut fieretis in hereditatem reliquis gentibus, et ascendistis super labium linguae et opprobrium populi; 4propterea, montes Israel, audite verbum Domini Dei: Haec dicit Dominus Deus montibus et collibus, torrentibus vallibusque et desertis dissipatis et urbibus derelictis, quae depopulatae sunt et subsannatae a reliquis gentibus per circuitum; 5propterea haec dicit Dominus Deus: In igne zeli mei locutus sum de reliquis gentibus et de Idumaea universa, quae dederunt terram meam sibi in hereditatem cum gaudio et toto corde et ex animo maligno, ut pascua eius depraedarentur. 6Idcirco vaticinare super humum Israel et dices montibus et collibus, torrentibus et vallibus: Haec dicit Dominus Deus: Ecce ego in zelo meo et in furore meo locutus sum, eo quod confusionem gentium sustinueritis; 7idcirco haec dicit Dominus Deus: Ego levavi manum meam: gentes, quae in circuitu vestro sunt, ipsae confusionem suam portabunt; 8vos autem, montes Israel, ramos vestros germinabitis et fructum vestrum afferetis populo meo Israel, prope est enim ut veniat. 9Quia ecce ego ad vos et convertar ad vos, et arabimini et accipietis sementem; 10et multiplicabo in vobis homines, omnem

b. One Ms: Heb *drive out*

upon you, the whole house of Israel, all of it; the cities shall be Is 61:4
inhabited and the waste places rebuilt; [11]and I will multiply upon Ezek 33:12 Amos 9:14
you man and beast; and they shall increase and be fruitful; and I
will cause you to be inhabited as in your former times, and will do
more good to you than ever before. Then you will know that I am
the LORD. [12]Yea, I will let men walk upon you, even my people
Israel; and they shall possess you, and you shall be their inheritance,
and you shall no longer bereave them of children. [13]Thus says the
Lord GOD: Because men say to you, 'You devour men, and you Num 13:32–33
bereave your nation of children,' [14]therefore you shall no longer
devour men and no longer bereave your nation of children, says the
Lord GOD; [15]and I will not let you hear any more the reproach of the
nations, and you shall no longer bear the disgrace of the peoples
and no longer cause your nation to stumble, says the Lord GOD."

1. THE RESTORATION OF ISRAEL*

Restoration; return from exile

[16]The word of the LORD came to me: [17]"Son of man, when the Lev 15: 19–27; 18:25–28
house of Israel dwelt in their own land, they defiled it by their

---

***36:16—39:29.** In this second to last section of the book, the prophet uses a series of metaphors to paint the scene of a restored Israel. The oracles have an eschatological dimension to them, particularly the latter ones (38:1—39:29).

Overall, what we are given here is a song celebrating hope; nothing is impossible to the Lord: he is able to renew Israel (36:16–38), by giving her a new heart and a new spirit (v. 25); he can make the people come back to life (37:1–14); and the unity between this new people and their Lord will be almost like the way things were in Eden (37:15–28)—so wonderful that it will astonish the nations (37:28). The final oracles (38:1—39:29) are a dramatic climax that convey an idea of the vicissitudes of the chosen people up to when their fortunes will be permanently restored. The empires seem to be those determining the course of events, but that is not the case: the Lord is always in control and, when the end comes, his victory will be so amazing

domum Israel, et habitabuntur civitates, et ruinosa instaurabuntur. [11]Et replebo vos hominibus et iumentis, et multiplicabuntur et crescent; et habitari vos faciam, sicut a principio bonisque donabo maioribus quam habuistis ab initio, et scietis quia ego Dominus. [12]Et adducam super vos homines, populum meum Israel, et hereditate possidebunt te, et eris eis in hereditatem et non addes ultra ut eos facias absque liberis. [13]Haec dicit Dominus Deus: Pro eo quod dicunt de vobis: "Devoratrix hominum es et faciens gentem tuam absque liberis"; [14]propterea homines non comedes amplius et gentem tuam non facies ultra absque liberis, ait Dominus Deus. [15]Nec auditam faciam in te amplius ignominiam gentium, et opprobrium populorum nequaquam portabis ultra et gentem tuam non facies amplius absque liberis», ait Dominus Deus. [16]Et factum est verbum Domini ad me dicens: [17]«Fili hominis,

ways and their doings; their conduct before me was like the
uncleanness of a woman in her impurity. [18]So I poured out my
wrath upon them for the blood which they had shed in the land,

---

that not only Israel but all other nations, too, will know that he truly is the Lord.

36:16–38. In these oracles, which continue the proclamation of Israel's restoration-purification, we can see the core of Ezekiel's teaching, namely, that the Lord, who is above all things, is the one who determines the election, punishment and restoration of his people. People have an obligation to accept the gifts that God offers; they must acknowledge that the Lord is sovereign and free, and render him due worship. This teaching can be seen in the announcement about restoration and a return to the promised land (vv. 16–24) and in the Lord's promise of inner renewal (vv. 25–38).

"They defiled it by their ways" (v. 17): the people's straying, their sins, defiled the promised land, the most precious of all the gifts God had given them. As Ezekiel explains it, their exile was a necessary punishment (v. 19), but it is also a condition for restoring to the land its lost honour.

"The holiness of my great name, which has been profaned among the nations" (v. 22): when the pagan nations saw the Israelites being deported, they thought that the God of Israel had been defeated or, at least, that he had failed to protect his people. In this sense the exile caused the name of the Lord to be profaned among the nations. The return of the people to the promised land was a necessary part of their deliverance (v. 24), but it was also needed to vindicate the name of the Lord (v. 22). This "theology" of the Name of God carries over into the New Testament, where we find it as a petition in the Our Father (cf. Mt 6:9; Lk 11:2), and from there it becomes part of the whole Christian tradition. The *Catechism* of the Council of Trent has this to say about these verses of Ezekiel: "Many people judge the truth of religion and of its Author by the deeds and lives of Christians. Those who truly profess their faith and put it into practice in their lives carry out the most valuable apostolate, provoking in others the desire to glorify the name of the heavenly Father" (*Roman Catechism*, 4, 10, 9).

"You shall be clean[sed]" (v. 25): Ezekiel views the renewal of Israel from the perspective of divine worship —sprinkling with water and other purification rites being a sign of inner change. This passage can be read as an announcement of the effects of Baptism: "Baptism, by the power of God, remits and pardons all sin—the original sin that we inherited from our first parents, and all our personal sins, no matter how grave and terrible they may seem to us, no matter how grave and terrible they were. This truth was foretold long ago by the prophet Ezekiel, through whom the Lord God spoke: *I will sprinkle*

domus Israel habitaverunt in humo sua et polluerunt eam in viis suis et in operibus suis; iuxta immunditiam menstruatae facta est via eorum coram me. [18]Et effudi indignationem meam super eos

for the idols with which they had defiled it. [19]I scattered them
among the nations, and they were dispersed through the countries;
in accordance with their conduct and their deeds I judged them.
[20]But when they came to the nations, wherever they came, they
profaned my holy name, in that men said of them, 'These are the
people of the LORD, and yet they had to go out of his land.' [21]But
I had concern for my holy name, which the house of Israel caused
to be profaned among the nations to which they came.

Is 52:5
Ezek 20:39
Rom 2:24

[22]"Therefore say to the house of Israel, Thus says the Lord
GOD: It is not for your sake, O house of Israel, that I am about to
act, but for the sake of my holy name, which you have profaned
among the nations to which you came. [23]And I will vindicate the
holiness of my great name, which has been profaned among the
nations, and which you have profaned among them; and the
nations will know that I am the LORD, says the Lord GOD, when
through you I vindicate my holiness before their eyes. [24]For I will
take you from the nations, and gather you from all the countries,
and bring you into your own land.

Ps 115:1
Is 48:11
Ezek 16:60–63
Mt 6:9
Ezek 11:17; 34:13

Inner renewal

[25]I will sprinkle clean water upon you, and you shall be clean
from all your uncleannesses, and from all your idols I will cleanse

Jn 3:5; 4:1
Heb 10:22

---

clean water upon you, and you shall be clean from all your uncleannesses (Ezek 36:25)" (ibid., 2, 2, 42).

"A new heart" and "a new spirit" (v. 26): renewal affects a person's disposition (heart) and motivation (spirit). The Israelites will have a completely new life-force: as a result, their conduct will be perfect (v. 27), the Covenant will never again be broken (v. 28), and the land, also cleansed of defilement, will be abundant in the fruit it yields (v. 30).

God's patent initiative in repatriating and renewing Israel is a proof of his disinterested love for his people. Jesus makes this very clear, for example, in his discourse on the bread of life: "No one can come to me unless the Father who sent me draws him" (Jn 6:44). "Our salvation flows from God's initiative of love for us, because 'he loved us and sent his Son to be the expiation for our sins' (Jn 4:10)" (*Catechism of the Catholic Church*, 620).

pro sanguine, quem fuderunt super terram, et in idolis suis polluerunt eam. [19]Et dispersi eos in gentes, et ventilati sunt in terras; iuxta vias eorum et iuxta opera eorum iudicavi eos. [20]Et ingressi sunt ad gentes, ad quas introierunt, et polluerunt nomen sanctum meum, cum diceretur de eis: "Populus Domini iste est, et de terra eius egressi sunt". [21]Et peperci nomini meo sancto, quod polluerat domus Israel in gentibus, ad quas ingressi sunt. [22]Idcirco dices domui Israel: Haec dicit Domihus Deus: Non propter vos ego faciam, domus Israel, sed propter nomen sanctum meum, quod polluistis in gentibus, ad quas intrastis; [23]et sanctificabo nomen meum magnum, quod pollutum est inter gentes, quod polluistis in medio earum, ut sciant gentes quia ego Dominus, ait Dominus Deus, cum sanctificatus fuero in vobis

Jer 4:4; 31:33; Ezek 11:19; 18:31; 2 Cor 3:3

you. [26]A new heart I will give you, and a new spirit I will put
within you; and I will take out of your flesh the heart of stone and

Jer 31:31; Ezek 37:14; Joel 2:28

give you a heart of flesh. [27]And I will put my spirit within you,
and cause you to walk in my statutes and be careful to observe my
ordinances. [28]You shall dwell in the land which I gave to your

Gal 5:22–25; 1 Jn 3:23–24; Lev 26:12

fathers; and you shall be my people, and I will be your God.
[29]And I will deliver you from all your uncleannesses; and I will
summon the grain and make it abundant and lay no famine upon
you. [30]I will make the fruit of the tree and the increase of the field
abundant, that you may never again suffer the disgrace of famine

Ezek 16:61–63

among the nations. [31]Then you will remember your evil ways, and
your deeds that were not good; and you will loathe yourselves for
your iniquities and your abominable deeds. [32]It is not for your
sake that I will act, says the Lord GOD; let that be known to you.
Be ashamed and confounded for your ways, O house of Israel.

[33]"Thus says the Lord GOD: On the day that I cleanse you from
all your iniquities, I will cause the cities to be inhabited, and the
waste places shall be rebuilt. [34]And the land that was desolate
shall be tilled, instead of being the desolation that it was in the

Is 51:3

sight of all who passed by. [35]And they will say, 'This land that was
desolate has become like the garden of Eden; and the waste and

Ps 126:2; Ezek 17:24; 22:14

desolate and ruined cities are now inhabited and fortified.' [36]Then
the nations that are left round about you shall know that I, the
LORD, have rebuilt the ruined places, and replanted that which was
desolate; I, the LORD, have spoken, and I will do it.

[37]"Thus says the Lord GOD: This also I will let the house of
Israel ask me to do for them: to increase their men like a flock.

---

coram eis. [24]Tollam quippe vos de gentibus et congregabo vos de universis terris et adducam vos in terram vestram; [25]et effundam super vos aquam mundam, et mundabimini ab omnibus inquinamentis vestris, et ab universis idolis vestris mundabo vos. [26]Et dabo vobis cor novum et spiritum novum ponam in medio vestri et auferam cor lapideum de carne vestra et dabo vobis cor carneum; [27]et spiritum meum ponam in medio vestri et faciam, ut in praeceptis meis ambuletis et iudicia mea custodiatis et operemini. [28]Et habitabitis in terra, quam dedi patribus vestris, et eritis mihi in populum, et ego ero vobis in Deum. [29]Et salvabo vos ex universis inquinamentis vestris et vocabo frumentum et multiplicabo illud et non imponam vobis famem. [30]Et multiplicabo fructum ligni et genimina agri, ut non portetis ultra opprobrium famis in gentibus. [31]Et recordabimini viarum vestrarum pessimarum operumque non bonorum, et displicebunt vobis iniquitates vestrae et scelera vestra. [32]Non propter vos ego faciam, ait Dominus Deus, notum sit vobis; confundimini et erubescite super viis vestris, domus Israel. [33]Haec dicit Dominus Deus: In die, qua mundavero vos ex omnibus iniquitatibus vestris et inhabitari fecero urbes et instauravero ruinosa, [34]et terra deserta fuerit exculta, quae quondam erat desolata in oculis omnis viatoris, [35]dicent: "Terra illa inculta facta est ut hortus Eden, et civitates desertae et destitutae atque destructae munitae inhabitantur". [36]Et scient gentes, quaecumque derelictae fuerint in circuitu vestro, quia ego Dominus aedificavi dissipata plantavique inculta; ego Dominus locutus sum et facio. [37]Haec dicit Dominus Deus: Adhuc in hoc exorabor a domo Israel, ut faciam eis: multiplicabo eos sicut gregem hominum, [38]ut gregem sanctum, ut gregem Ierusalem in sollemnitatibus

[38]Like the flock for sacrifices,[c] like the flock at Jerusalem during
her appointed feasts, so shall the waste cities be filled with flocks
of men. Then they will know that I am the LORD."

The dry bones

37 [1]The hand of the LORD was upon me, and he brought me Ezek 1:3; 3:12
out by the Spirit of the LORD, and set me down in the midst
of the valley;[d] it was full of bones.* [2]And he led me round among

---

37:1–14. This remarkable vision of the bones being brought back to life sets the scene for the climax of the resurgence of Israel, the unification of the two kingdoms (cf. 37:15–28). The dramatic contrast drawn here between death and life, bones and spirit, shows that the revitalization that God will bring about goes much further than material reconstruction or simply a return to the promised land; it implies, rather, a new beginning, both personal and social.

The vision itself (vv. 2–10) takes place on an immense plain (cf. 3:22–23) and it addresses the exiles' profound concern about their future: "Our bones are dried up, and our hope is lost" (v. 11). It is one of Ezekiel's most famous and most commented-on visions because it is very vivid and easy to understand. The prophet himself explains it as having to do with the destruction-restoration of Israel (vv. 11–14), though the Fathers of the Church see in it veiled references to the resurrection of the dead: "The Creator will revive our mortal bodies here on earth; he promises resurrection, the opening of sepulchres and tombs, and the gift of immortality [...]. And in all this, we see that he alone is God, who can do all things, the good Father who from his endless bounty will give life to the lifeless" (St Irenaeus, *Adversus haereses*, 5, 15, 1). St Jerome writes in similar terms: "The image of the resurrection would not have been used to describe the restoration of the people of Israel if the future resurrection of the dead had not been foreseen, because no one can be led to draw a conclusion from an idea that has no basis in reality" (*Commentarii in Ezechielem*, 37, 1ff.

"I will put my Spirit within you" (v. 14). The spirit of the Lord is, at least, the power of God (cf. Gen 2:7) performing an act of creation. It is also the principle of life causing man to "become a living being" (Gen 2:7); and, certainly, it is the principle of supernatural life. The same God that created all things can revitalize his demoralized people in Babylon and can allow humankind to partake of his own life. This promise,

eius; sic erunt civitates desertae plenae gregibus hominum, et scient quia ego Dominus». **[37]** [1]Facta est super me manus Domini et eduxit me in spiritu Domini et posuit me in medio campi, qui erat plenus ossibus, [2]et circumduxit me per ea in gyro: erant autem multa valde super faciem campi siccaque

c. Heb *flock of holy things* **d.** Or *plain*

them; and behold, there were very many upon the valley;[d] and lo,
they were very dry. 3And he said to me, "Son of man, can these
bones live?" And I answered, "O Lord GOD, thou knowest."
Rev 7:14 4Again he said to me, "Prophesy to these bones, and say to them,
Gen 2:7 O dry bones, hear the word of the LORD. 5Thus says the Lord GOD
Ps 104:30 to these bones: Behold, I will cause breath[e] to enter you, and you
Rev 11:11 shall live. 6And I will lay sinews upon you, and will cause flesh to
come upon you, and cover you with skin, and put breath[e] in you,
and you shall live; and you shall know that I am the LORD."

7So I prophesied as I was commanded; and as I prophesied,
there was a noise, and behold, a rattling; and the bones came
together, bone to its bone. 8And as I looked, there were sinews on
them, and flesh had come upon them, and skin had covered them;
Dan 7:2; 11:4 but there was no breath in them. 9Then he said to me, "Prophesy
Rev 7:1 to the breath, prophesy, son of man, and say to the breath,[f] Thus
says the Lord GOD: Come from the four winds, O breath,[f] and
Gen 2:7 breathe upon these slain, that they may live." 10So I prophesied as
Ps 104:30 Rom 8:11 he commanded me, and the breath came into them, and they lived,
Rev 11:11; 20:4 and stood upon their feet, an exceedingly great host.

Ps 102:3 11Then he said to me, "Son of man, these bones are the whole
Is 49:14 Ezek 33:10 house of Israel. Behold, they say, 'Our bones are dried up, and our
Lam 3:54 hope is lost; we are clean cut off.' 12Therefore prophesy, and say
Mt 27:52 Jn 5:28 to them, Thus says the Lord GOD: Behold, I will open your graves,

---

like others found in the prophets (cf. 11:19; Jer 31:31–34; Joel 3:1–5) will find its complete fulfilment at Pentecost, when the Spirit descends on the apostles: "According to these promises, at the 'end time' the Lord's Spirit will renew the hearts of men, engraving a new law in them. He will gather and reconcile the scattered and divided peoples; he will transform the first creation, and God will dwell there with men in peace" (*Catechism of the Catholic Church*, 715).

vehementer. 3Et dixit ad me: «Fili hominis, putasne vivent ossa ista?». Et dixi: «Domine, tu nosti». 4Et dixit ad me: «Vaticinare super ossa ista et dices eis: Ossa arida, audite verbum Domini. 5Haec dicit Dominus Deus ossibus his: Ecce ego intromittam in vos spiritum, et vivetis, 6et dabo super vos nervos et succrescere faciam super vos carnes et superextendam in vobis cutem et dabo vobis spiritum, et vivetis et scietis quia ego Dominus». 7Et prophetavi, sicut praeceperat mihi. Factus est autem sonitus, prophetante me, et ecce commotio; et accesserunt ossa ad ossa, unumquodque ad iuncturam suam. 8Et vidi: et ecce super ea nervi et carnes ascenderunt, et extenta est in eis cutis desuper, sed spiritum non habebant. 9Et dixit ad me: «Vaticinare ad spiritum; vaticinare, fili hominis, et dices ad spiritum: Haec dicit Dominus Deus: A quattuor ventis veni, spiritus, et insuffla super interfectos istos, ut reviviscant». 10Et prophetavi, sicut praeceperat mihi, et ingressus est in ea spiritus; et vixerunt steteruntque super pedes suos, exercitus grandis nimis valde. 11Et dixit ad me: «Fili hominis, ossa haec universa domus Israel est. Ipsi dicunt: "Aruerunt ossa nostra, et periit spes nostra, et abscissi sumus". 12Propterea vaticinare et dices ad eos: Haec dicit Dominus Deus: Ecce ego aperiam tumulos vestros et educam vos

e. Or *spirit* **f.** Or *wind* or *spirit*

and raise you from your graves, O my people; and I will bring you
home into the land of Israel. [13]And you shall know that I am the
LORD, when I open your graves, and raise you from your graves,
O my people. [14]And I will put my Spirit within you, and you shall Gen 1:26; 2:7
live, and I will place you in your own land; then you shall know 1 Thess 4:8
that I, the LORD, have spoken, and I have done it, says the LORD."

1 Kings 12:20–33 Jn 17:21

The reunification of the two kingdoms

[15]The word of the LORD came to me: [16]"Son of man, take a stick Num 17:2
and write on it, 'For Judah, and the children of Israel associated 2 Chron 11:12–16;15:9
with him'; then take another stick and write upon it, 'For Joseph
(the stick of Ephraim) and all the house of Israel associated with
him';[17] and join them together into one stick, that they may
become one in your hand. [18]And when your people say to you,
'Will you not show us what you mean by these?' [19]say to them, Zech 11:7,14
Thus says the Lord GOD: Behold, I am about to take the stick of
Joseph (which is in the hand of Ephraim) and the tribes of Israel
associated with him; and I will join[g] with it the stick of Judah, and

37:15–27. Unity will be the most obvious effect of the people's purification. By the symbolic action of the two sticks, Ezekiel shows that it is God himself who will bring about the unification of the tribes that made up the Southern kingdom (Judah) with those of the North (Joseph-Ephraim); it will be a union so strong that it will never again be broken (as it was broken after the death of Solomon: cf. 1 Kings 12:20–33). This unity is also a symbol of the oneness that Jesus wants the new people of God to have (cf. Jn 17:21) and which is essential for the success of his plans for mankind's salvation, "All men are called to be part of this catholic unity of the people of God which in promoting universal peace presages it. And there belong to or are related to it in various ways, the Catholic faithful, all who believe in Christ, and indeed the whole of mankind, for all men are called by the grace of God to salvation" (Vatican II, *Lumen gentium*, 13).

de sepulcris vestris, populus meus, et inducam vos in terram Israel; [13]et scietis quia ego Dominus, cum aperuero sepulcra vestra et eduxero vos de tumulis vestris, populus meus. [14]Et dabo spiritum meum in vobis, et vivetis, et collocabo vos super humum vestram, et scietis quia ego Dominus. Locutus sum et facio», ait Dominus Deus. [15]Et factus est sermo Domini ad me dicens: [16]«Et tu, fili hominis, sume tibi lignum unum et scribe super illud: Iudae et filiis Israel sociis eius. Et tolle lignum alterum et scribe super illud: Ioseph, lignum Ephraim, et cunctae domui Israel sociis eius. [17]Et adiunge illa unum ad alterum tibi in lignum unum; et erunt in unionem in manu tua. [18]Cum autem dixerint ad te filii populi tui loquentes: "Nonne indicas nobis, quid in his tibi velis?", [19]loqueris ad eos: Haec dicit Dominus Deus: Ecce ego assumam lignum Ioseph, quod est in manu Ephraim, et tribus Israel, quae iunctae sunt ei, et dabo eas pariter cum ligno Iudae et faciam eas in lignum unum, et erunt unum in manu mea.

g. Heb *join them*

make them one stick, that they may be one in my hand. [20]When
the sticks on which you write are in your hand before their eyes,
[21]then say to them, Thus says the Lord GOD: Behold, I will take
the people of Israel from the nations among which they have gone,
and will gather them from all sides, and bring them to their own
Jer 3:18; 50:4 land; [22]and I will make them one nation in the land, upon the
Ezek 34:24 mountains of Israel; and one king shall be king over them all; and
they shall be no longer two nations, and no longer divided into
Tit 2:14 two kingdoms. [23]They shall not defile themselves any more with
their idols and their detestable things, or with any of their
transgressions; but I will save them from all the backslidings in
which they have sinned, and will cleanse them; and they shall be
my people, and I will be their God.

[24]"My servant David shall be king over them; and they shall all
Is 60:21 Jer 17:25 have one shepherd. They shall follow my ordinances and be
Ezek 28:25,26; careful to observe my statutes. [25]They shall dwell in the land
36:28 Joel 3:20 where your fathers dwelt that I gave to my servant Jacob; they and
Jn 12:34 their children and their children's children shall dwell there for
Is 9:5 ever; and David my servant shall be their prince for ever. [26]I will
Jer 31:31 make a covenant of peace with them; it shall be an everlasting
Mt 5:9 Heb 13:20 covenant with them; and I will bless[h] them and multiply them, and

---

37:26. A "covenant of peace". The concluding words of the oracle (vv. 24–28) are messianic ones, as can be seen from the reference to David, king and shepherd (v. 24), and from the emphasis put on the fact that the nation will abide in the land "for ever" (v. 25) with the sanctuary in its midst (vv. 27, 28). Peace (cf. 34:25) is the greatest of the messianic gifts (cf. Is 9:5); it implies safety from external enemies but, above all, peace with God and neighbour. Jesus called peacemakers blessed, happy (cf. Mt 5:9). "[T]he peace of Christ radiates from God the Father. For by the cross the incarnate Son, the prince of peace reconciled all men with God. By thus restoring all men to the unity of one people and one body, he slew hatred in his own flesh; and, after being lifted on high by his resurrection, he poured forth the spirit of love into the hearts of men" (*Gaudium et spes*, 78).

[20]Erunt autem ligna, super quae scripseris, in manu tua in oculis eorum, [21]et dices ad eos: Haec dicit Dominus Deus: Ecce ego assumam filios Israel de medio nationum, ad quas abierunt, et congregabo eos undique et adducam eos ad humum suam [22]et faciam eos in gentem unam in terra, in montibus Israel; et rex unus erit omnibus imperans, et non erunt ultra duae gentes nec dividentur amplius in duo regna. [23]Neque polluentur ultra in idolis suis et abominationibus suis et in cunctis iniquitatibus suis, et salvos eos faciam de universis aversionibus suis, quibus peccaverunt, et mundabo eos, et erunt mihi populus, et ego ero eis Deus. [24]Et servus meus David rex super eos, et pastor unus erit omnium eorum; in iudiciis meis ambulabunt et mandata mea custodient et facient ea. [25]Et habitabunt super terram, quam

h. Tg: Heb *give*

will set my sanctuary in the midst of them for evermore. 27My
dwelling place shall be with them; and I will be their God, and
they shall be my people. 28Then the nations will know that I the Jn 1:14; 14:23
LORD sanctify Israel, when my sanctuary is in the midst of them 2 Cor 6:16
for evermore." Rev 7:15; 21:3

Escathological battle against Gog*

38 1*The word of the LORD came to me: 2"Son of man, set Gen 10:2 Ezek 27:13
your face toward Gog, of the land of Magog, the chief Rev 20:7–10

***38:1—39:29.** This is the most eschatological section of the book, for it has to do with the Last Judgment, when God condemns the guilty and saves the elect. Ezekiel depicts a huge onslaught against Israel, led by Gog, a character that symbolizes the wicked who make war on the chosen people. God will permit (or in biblical language "will ordain": in the Bible, events that God permits are actually attributed to him: cf. Ex 4:21; 8:17; 9:3; etc.) the mighty army of Gog and his allies to fall upon Israel, which is still weak from the effects of the exile. But when it seems that the chosen people are about to succumb to defeat, God himself will intervene and cause a cataclysm to befall Gog's and totally destroy it. This event will bring the nations to acknowledge God's sovereignty and know that he is holy (39:25–29).

The eschatological battle has four stages to it—the attack initiated by Gog (38:1–16), God's response to that onslaught (38:17–23), God's total victory over Gog (39:1–16), and the nations' and Israel's acknowledgment of God (39:17–29).

38:1–16. The most interesting thing here is the disconcerting way in which God acts: in spite of ordering Ezekiel to speak an oracle against Gog (v. 3), he uses Gog as a weapon against Israel (v. 7) and gives him a well-equipped army (v. 4). Although the attack seems to be of Gog's making (vv. 10, 14), the Lord leaves no doubt that he has planned everything "so that the nations may know me" (v. 16).

"Gog, of the land of Magog" (v. 2). No satisfactory explanation has been found as to who Gog is, or Magog, for that matter, who, according to Genesis 10:2, was a descendant of Japheth. Probably Ezekiel simply took two legendary-sounding names to symbolize all possible enemies of Israel; the land of Magog, of the stock of Japheth, would suit his purposes, because all the most vicious attacks on Israel had come from the north, particularly from Assyria and Babylon.

dedi servo meo Iacob, in qua habitaverunt patres vestri; et habitabunt super eam, ipsi et filii eorum et filii filiorum eorum usque in sempiternum, et David servus meus princeps eorum in perpetuum. 26Et percutiam illis foedus pacis, pactum sempiternum erit eis, et fundabo eos et multiplicabo; et dabo sanctuarium meum in medio eorum in perpetuum, 27et erit habitaculum meum in eis, et ero eis Deus, et ipsi erunt mihi populus; 28et scient gentes quia ego Dominus sanctificator Israel, cum fuerit sanctuarium meum in medio eorum in perpetuum». **[38]** 1Et factus est sermo Domini ad me dicens:

prince of Meshech and Tubal, and prophesy against him 3and say,
Thus says the Lord GOD: Behold, I am against you, O Gog, chief
Ezek 29:4 prince of Meshech and Tubal; 4and I will turn you about, and put
hooks into your jaws, and I will bring you forth, and all your
army, horses and horsemen, all of them clothed in full armour, a
great company, all of them with buckler and shield, wielding
Ezek 27:10 swords; 5Persia, Cush, and Put are with them, all of them with
Gen 10:2–3 shield and helmet; 6Gomer and all his hordes; Beth-togarmah
Ezek 27:14 from the uttermost parts of the north with all his hordes—many
Ezek 28:26; peoples are with you.
34:13 7"Be ready and keep ready, you and all the hosts that are
Jer 49:31 assembled about you, and be a guard for them. 8After many days
you will be mustered; in the latter years you will go against the
land that is restored from war, the land where people were
gathered from many nations upon the mountains of Israel, which
Is 28:2 had been a continual waste; its people were brought out from the
Jer 4:13 nations and now dwell securely, all of them. 9You will advance,
coming on like a storm, you will be like a cloud covering the land
you and all your hordes, and many peoples with you.
10"Thus says the Lord GOD: On that day thoughts will come
into your mind, and you will devise an evil scheme 11and say, 'I
will go up against the land of unwalled villages; I will fall upon
the quiet people who dwell securely, all of them dwelling without

---

"After many days" (v. 8): this vague reference to timing is the key, the symbol, that the entire oracle is eschatological, that is, it refers to a time in the future when God will intervene definitively both to condemn and to save. Similar expressions occur elsewhere in the oracle (cf. verses 10 and 16).

"At the centre of the earth" (v. 12). In the language of eschatology, places and dates are idealized and exaggerated; what is being referred to here is Jerusalem, *the* city of the messianic era. The Letter to the Hebrews and the book of Revelation will speak of a heavenly Jerusalem (cf. Heb 12:22; Rev 21:22).

2«Fili hominis, pone faciem tuam contra Gog, in terra Magog, principem summum Mosoch et Thubal, et vaticinare de eo 3et dices: Haec dicit Dominus Deus: Ecce ego ad te, Gog, principem summum Mosoch et Thubal, 4et circumagam te et ponam uncos in maxillis tuis et educam te et omnem exercitum tuum, equos et equites vestitos perfecte universos, multitudinem magnam cum scuto et clipeo arripientes gladium. 5Persae, Chus et Phut cum eis, omnes scutati et galeati; 6Gomer et universa agmina eius, domus Thogorma de extremo aquilone et totum robur eius, populi multi tecum. 7Praepara et instrue te et omnem multitudinem tuam, quae coacervata est ad te, et esto mihi in custodiam. 8Post dies multos evocaberis; in novissimo annorum venies ad terram, quae reversa est a gladio, congregata est de populis multis ad montes Israel, qui fuerunt deserti iugiter: haec de populis educta est, et habitant in ea confidenter universi. 9Ascendens autem quasi tempestas venies, quasi nubes, ut operias terram, tu et omnia agmina tua et populi multi tecum. 10Haec dicit Dominus Deus: In die illa ascendent sermones super cor tuum, et cogitabis cogitationem pessimam 11et dices: "Ascendam ad terram absque muro,

walls, and having no bars or gates'; [12]to seize spoil and carry off 1 Kings 10,1
plunder; to assail the waste places which are now inhabited, and
the people who were gathered from the nations, who have gotten
cattle and goods, who dwell at the center of the earth. [13]Sheba and Ezek 25:13
Dedan and the merchants of Tarshish and all its villages will say
to you, 'Have you come to seize spoil? Have you assembled your
hosts to carry off plunder, to carry away silver and gold, to take
away cattle and goods, to seize great spoil?'
[14]"Therefore, son of man, prophesy, and say to Gog, Thus says
the Lord GOD: On that day when my people Israel are dwelling
securely, you will bestir yourself[i] [15]and come from your place out
of the uttermost parts of the north, you and many peoples with
you, all of them riding on horses, a great host, a mighty army;
[16]you will come up against my people Israel, like a cloud covering Ex 14:4
the land. In the latter days I will bring you against my land, that
the nations may know me, when through you, O Gog, I vindicate
my holiness before their eyes.
[17]"Thus says the Lord GOD: Are you he of whom I spoke in
former days by my servants the prophets of Israel, who in those
days prophesied for years that I would bring you against them?
[18]But on that day, when Gog shall come against the land of Israel,
says the Lord GOD, my wrath will be roused. [19]For in my jealousy Hag 2:6–7 Lk 21:11
and in my blazing wrath I declare, On that day there shall be a Rev 6:12

38:17–23. God's intervention is described here in eschatological language—the expression "that day" (vv. 18, 19), the frequent use of the future tense, the way divine zeal is depicted in human terms, the use of the formula "in my blazing wrath" (v. 19) and the presence of earthquakes, torrential rains, etc.

veniam ad quiescentes habitantesque secure; hi omnes habitant sine muro, vectes et portae non sunt eis"; [12]ut diripias spolia et capias praedam, ut inferas manum tuam super deserta iterum inhabitata et super populum, qui est congregatus ex gentibus, qui acquisivit pecora et substantiam et habitat in umbilico terrae. [13]Saba et Dedan et negotiatores Tharsis et omnes principes eius dicent tibi: "Numquid ad sumenda spolia tu venis? Numquid ad diripiendam praedam congregasti multitudinem tuam, ut tollas argentum et aurum, auferas pecora atque substantiam et diripias manubias infinitas?". [14]Propterea vaticinare, fili hominis, et dices ad Gog: Haec dicit Dominus Deus: Numquid non in die illo, cum habitaverit populus meus Israel confidenter, consurges? [15]Et venies de loco tuo ab extremo aquilone, tu et populi multi tecum, ascensores equorum universi, coetus magnus et exercitus vehemens. [16]Et ascendes super populum meum Israel quasi nubes, ut operias terram. In novissimis diebus erit, et adducam te super terram meam, ut sciant gentes me, cum sanctificatus fuero in te in oculis eorum, o Gog. [17]Haec dicit Dominus Deus: Tu ergo ille es, de quo locutus sum in diebus antiquis in manu servorum meorum prophetarum Israel, qui prophetaverunt in diebus illis per annos, ut adducerem te super eos. [18]Et erit in die illa, in die adventus Gog super terram Israel, ait Dominus Deus, ascendet indignatio mea in furore meo. [19]Et in zelo meo, in igne irae meae locutus sum: In die illa erit commotio

i. Gk: Heb *will you not know*?

great shaking in the land of Israel; [20]the fish of the sea, and the
birds of the air, and the beasts of the field, and all creeping things
that creep on the ground, and all the men that are upon the face of
the earth, shall quake at my presence, and the mountains shall be
thrown down, and the cliffs shall fall, and every wall shall tumble
to the ground. [21]I will summon every kind of terror[j] against Gog,[k]
Is 66:16 says the Lord GOD; every man's sword will be against his brother.
Jer 25:31 [22]With pestilence and bloodshed I will enter into judgment with
Joel 3:2 Lk 21:11 him; and I will rain upon him and his hordes and the many
Rev 8:7; peoples that are with him, torrential rains and hailstones, fire and
14:10; 20:9 brimstone. [23]So I will show my greatness and my holiness and
Ezek 14:4; 36:23; make myself known in the eyes of many nations. Then they will
37:28; 39:7 know that I am the LORD.

Ezek 38:3–4

God's victory over Gog

39 [1]"And you, son of man, prophesy against Gog, and say,
Thus says the Lord GOD: Behold, I am against you, O Gog,

39:1–16. The fact that this oracle begins in the same way as that of the previous chapter (cf. 38:1–3) indicates that the same Lord who sent Gog to attack the people of Israel, now gets him to do the same thing in order to annihilate him; Gog's downfall is a sign that the new Israel will never again be attacked by another nation. The destruction of Gog takes place in three stages—first, his entire army is slain "upon the mountains of Israel" (v. 4); then all the weapons are burned, as a sign that an era of peace has come (vv. 9–10); finally, all the dead bodies are buried (vv. 11–16). The burial must be done exactly in line with the laws about uncleanness (cf. Num 9:11–16; Lev 21:1), to avoid defilement.

"For seven years" (v. 9): the number seven, both here and in v. 12, does not mean an exact period of time; it symbolizes the fact that the burning and burial must include everything.

"Valley of Hamon-gog" (v. 15): no place of this name has been identified; it must be Gog's multitude or in military terms a symbolic name, and ironic, too, given its etymology: it means "Gog's squadron". The city name, Hamonah (v. 16), means "squadrons", hordes, hosts.

magna super terram Israel, [20]et commovebuntur a facie mea pisces maris et volucres caeli et bestiae agri et omne reptile, quod movetur super humum, cunctique homines, qui sunt super faciem terrae; et subvertentur montes, et cadent rupes, et omnis murus in terram corruet. [21]Et convocabo adversus eum in cunctis montibus meis gladium, ait Dominus Deus; gladius uniuscuiusque in fratrem suum dirigetur. [22]Et iudicabo eum peste et sanguine et imbre vehementi et lapidibus grandinis; ignem et sulphur pluam super eum et super exercitum eius et super populos multos, qui sunt cum eo, [23]et magnificabor et sanctificabor et notus ero in oculis multarum gentium, et scient quia ego Dominus. **[39]** [1]Tu autem, fili hominis, vaticinare adversum Gog et dices: Haec dicit Dominus Deus: Ecce ego super te, Gog,

j. Gk: Heb *a sword to all my mountains* **k.** Heb *him*

chief prince of Meshech and Tubal; 2and I will turn you about and
drive you forward, and bring you up from the uttermost parts of
the north, and lead you against the mountains of Israel; 3then I will
strike your bow from your left hand, and will make your arrows
drop out of your right hand. 4You shall fall upon the mountains of Rev 19:17
Israel, you and all your hordes and the peoples that are with you; I
will give you to birds of prey of every sort and to the wild beasts to
be devoured. 5You shall fall in the open field; for I have spoken, says
the Lord GOD. 6I will send fire on Magog and on those who dwell
securely in the coastlands; and they shall know that I am the LORD.

7"And my holy name I will make known in the midst of my Ezek 38:23
people Israel; and I will not let my holy name be profaned any
more; and the nations shall know that I am the LORD, the Holy
One in Israel. 8Behold, it is coming and it will be brought about,
says the Lord GOD. That is the day of which I have spoken.

9"Then those who dwell in the cities of Israel will go forth and
make fires of the weapons and burn them, shields and bucklers,
bows and arrows, handpikes and spears, and they will make fires
of them for seven years; 10so that they will not need to take wood Is 14:2; 17:14;
out of the field or cut down any out of the forests, for they will 33:1
make their fires of the weapons; they will despoil those who
despoiled them, and plunder those who plundered them, says the
Lord GOD.

11"On that day I will give to Gog a place for burial in Israel, the
Valley of the Travellers[l] east of the sea; it will block the travellers,
for there Gog and all his multitude will be buried; it will be called
the Valley of Hamon-gog.[m] 12For seven months the house of Israel
will be burying them, in order to cleanse the land. 13All the people

---

principem summum Mosoch e Thubal; 2et circumagam te et seducam te et ascendere faciam de
extremo aquilone et adducam te super montes Israel. 3Et percutiam arcum tuum in manu sinistra tua et
sagittas tuas de manu dextera tua deiciam. 4Super montes Israel cades, tu et omnia agmina tua et populi,
qui sunt tecum; feris avibus, omni volatili et bestiis terrae dedi te devorandum: 5super faciem agri
cades, quia ego locutus sum, ait Dominus Deus. 6Et emittam ignem in Magog et in his, qui habitant
in insulis confidenter, et scient quia ego Dominus. 7Et nomen sanctum meum notum faciam in medio
populi mei Israel et non polluam nomen sanctum meum amplius, et scient gentes quia ego Dominus,
sanctus in Israel. 8Ecce venit et fit, ait Dominus Deus; haec est dies, de qua locutus sum. 9Et egredientur
habitatores de civitatibus Israel et succendent et comburent arma, clipeum et scutum, arcum et sagittas
et baculos, manus et contos, et succendent ea igne septem annis. 10Et non portabunt ligna de campis
neque succident de saltibus, quoniam arma succendent igne et depraedabuntur eos, quibus praedae
fuerant, et diripient vastatores suos, ait Dominus Deus. 11Et erit, in die illa dabo Gog locum nominatum
sepulcrum in Israel, vallem viatorum ad orientem maris, quae oppilat viam praetereuntibus; et sepelient
ibi Gog et omnem multitudinem eius, et vocabitur vallis Multitudinis Gog. 12Et sepelient eos domus
Israel, ut mundent terram septem mensibus; 13sepeliet autem eum omnis populus terrae, et erit eis

l. Or *Abarim* **m.** That is *the multitude of Gog*

of the land will bury them; and it will redound to their honour on
the day that I show my glory, says the Lord GOD. 14They will set
apart men to pass through the land continually and bury[n] those
remaining upon the face of the land, so as to cleanse it; at the end
of seven months they will make their search. 15And when these
pass through the land and any one sees a man's bone, then he shall
set up a sign by it, till the buriers have buried it in the Valley of
Deut 21:23 Hamon-gog. 16(A city Hamonah[o] is there also.) Thus shall they
cleanse the land.

Is 25:6–8 **Everlasting faithfulness to God**

Num 19:16 17"As for you, son of man, thus says the Lord GOD: Speak to the
Rev 19:17–18 birds of every sort and to all the beasts of the field, 'Assemble and
come, gather from all sides to the sacrificial feast which I am
preparing for you, a great sacrificial feast upon the mountains of
Israel, and you shall eat flesh and drink blood. 18You shall eat the

---

39:17–29. The scene in which all will acknowledge the Lord is set in a vast sacrificial feast at which all living creatures will partake of the sacrificed victim, the flesh and blood of the people's adversary, in the Lord's honour (vv. 17–20). The eschatological banquet symbolizes God's sovereignty over all the animals invited to fill themselves with the spoils taken from the enemy army (cf. Is 25:6–8).

The last section (vv. 21–29) sums up the reason for Israel's restoration announced in chapters 33–39—the glory and holiness of God. It proclaims the greatest gift to do with the renewal of Israel—the outpouring of the Spirit (v. 29). The New Testament allows us to read this as an announcement of the presence of the Holy Spirit who renews the new people of God, the Church, with his manifold gifts: "The Church, which the Spirit guides in the way of all truth and which he unified in communion and in works of ministry, he both equips and directs with hierarchical and charismatic gifts and adorns with his fruits. By the power of the Gospel he makes the Church keep the freshness of youth. Uninterruptedly he renews her and leads her to perfect union with her Spouse" (Vatican II, *Lumen gentium*, 4).

nominata dies, in qua glorificatus sum, ait Dominus Deus. 14Et viros iugiter constituent lustrantes terram, qui sepeliant eos, qui remanserant super faciem terrae, ut emundent eam; post menses autem septem quaerere incipient 15et circuibunt peragrantes terram; cumque viderint os hominis, statuent iuxta illud titulum, donec sepeliant illud pollinctores in valle Multitudinis Gog. 16Nomen quoque civitatis Amona, et mundabunt terram. 17Tu ergo, fili hominis, haec dicit Dominus Deus, dic volucri, universis avibus cunctisque bestiis agri: Convenite, properate, concurrite undique ad victimam meam, quam ego immolo vobis, victimam grandem super montes Israel, ut comedatis carnes et bibatis sanguinem. 18Carnes fortium comedetis et sanguinem principum terrae bibetis: arietes, agni et hirci taurique

n. Gk Syr: Heb *bury the travellers* **o.** That is *Multitude*

flesh of the mighty, and drink the blood of the princes of the
earth—of rams, of lambs, and of goats, of bulls, all of them
fatlings of Bashan. [19]And you shall eat fat till you are filled, and Is 23:18
drink blood till you are drunk, at the sacrificial feast which I am
preparing for you. [20]And you shall be filled at my table with
horses and riders, with mighty men and all kinds of warriors,' says
the Lord GOD.

[21]"And I will set my glory among the nations; and all the Ex 14:4
nations shall see my judgment which I have executed, and my
hand which I have laid on them. [22]The house of Israel shall know Deut 31:17
that I am the LORD their God, from that day forward. [23]And the
nations shall know that the house of Israel went into captivity for
their iniquity, because they dealt so treacherously with me that I
hid my face from them and gave them into the hand of their
adversaries, and they all fell by the sword. [24]I dealt with them
according to their uncleanness and their transgressions, and hid
my face from them.

[25]"Therefore thus says the Lord GOD: Now I will restore the
fortunes of Jacob, and have mercy upon the whole house of Israel;
and I will be jealous for my holy name. [26]They shall forget their
shame, and all the treachery they have practised against me, when
they dwell securely in their land with none to make them afraid,
[27]when I have brought them back from the peoples and gathered
them from their enemies' lands, and through them have vindicated
my holiness in the sight of many nations. [28]Then they shall know
that I am the LORD their God because I sent them into exile among
the nations, and then gathered them into their own land. I will Is 54:8
leave none of them remaining among the nations any more; [29]and Ezek 11:19;
I will not hide my face any more from them, when I pour out my 37:14
Spirit upon the house of Israel, says the Lord GOD." Joel 2:23

---

saginati de Basan sunt omnes; [19]et comedetis adipem in saturitatem et bibetis sanguinem in ebrietatem de victima, quam ego immolabo vobis. [20]Et saturabimini super mensam meam de equo et de iugali currus, de forti et de universis viris bellatoribus, ait Dominus Deus. [21]Et ponam gloriam meam in gentibus, et videbunt omnes gentes iudicium meum, quod fecerim, et manum meam, quam posuerim super eos; [22]et scient domus Israel quia ego Dominus Deus eorum a die illa et deinceps, [23]et scient gentes quoniam in iniquitate sua capta sit domus Israel, eo quod reliquerint me, et absconderim faciem meam ab eis et tradiderim eos in manus hostium suorum, et ceciderint in gladio universi. [24]Iuxta immunditiam eorum et scelera eorum feci eis et abscondi faciem meam ab illis. [25]Propterea haec dicit Dominus Deus: Nunc restituam Iacob et miserebor omnis domus Israel et assumam zelum pro nomine sancto meo. [26]Et portabunt confusionem suam et omnem praevaricationem, quam praevaricati sunt in me, cum habitaverint in terra sua confidenter; et nemo erit qui exterreat. [27]Et reduxero eos de populis et congregavero de terris inimicorum suorum et sanctificatus fuero in eis in oculis gentium plurimarum, [28]et scient quia ego Dominus Deus eorum, eo quod transtulerim eos in nationes et congregaverim eos super terram suam et non dereliquerim quemquam ex eis ibi. [29]Et non abscondam ultra faciem meam ab eis, eo quod effuderim spiritum meum super domum Israel», ait Dominus Deus.

2. THE NEW TEMPLE AND THE NEW FORM OF WORSHIP*

The new temple described

Ezek 1:3; 8:3; 32:21; 37:1 Rev 21:10

40 [1]*In the twenty-fifth year of our exile, at the beginning of
the year, on the tenth day of the month, in the fourteenth

***40:1—48:35.** The last vision in the book contains a detailed description of the new temple (chaps. 40–43), the regulations about the new form of worship (chaps. 44–46) and the division of land of the new Israel (chaps. 47–48). The literary style of these chapters is so different from that of the earlier ones that some commentators have suggested that they are the work of a later author. However, their arguments are not fully convincing. Besides, this awesome theophany rounds off that of the river Chebar (chaps. 1–3) and that of the profaned temple, when the glory of God leaves Jerusalem (chaps. 8–11), and it shows the solemn entry of God into the holy city and his taking possession of the new temple.

The central idea of this section was already present in the book—that is, the need for the people, institutions and even the land itself to be cleansed and renewed, for that is the only way that a proper relationship with God can be established. This renewal therefore is not so much a requirement deriving from the Covenant as a prerequisite for the people's relationship with the Lord. This is a message laden with joyful hope for the exiles and for the readers of this book: God, who is ever faithful to his word, never abandons his people, even though at times that may not seem to be the case.

40:1–47. This description of the new temple is so detailed that it is difficult to follow. However, it does convey the idea that it is a truly perfect building, as befits the abode of God the Most High.

"In the twenty-fifth year" (v. 1), that is, in 573 BC, probably in April, which was when the year began. It could be that Ezekiel is interpreting this version in a special religious sense. According to Leviticus 25:10, every fiftieth year was to be a jubilee, when liberty was proclaimed and everyone should go back to his property and his family. By noting that the vision took place in the twenty-fifth year after the first deportation, the prophet would be saying that the exiles were half-way on the road to liberation.

"In the visions of God" (v. 2): that is how the prophet's great visions begin (cf. 1:2; 8:3), but in this last vision people and actions figure less: the emphasis is on measurements, layouts and descriptions. However, because it is a prophetical vision, there is no point in expecting the description of the temple to agree with that of the temple of

---

[40] [1]In vicesimo et quinto anno transmigrationis nostrae, in exordio anni, decima mensis, quarto decimo anno, postquam percussa est civitas, in ipsa hac die facta est super me manus Domini et adduxit

year after the city was conquered, on that very day, the hand of the
LORD was upon me, 2and brought me in the visions of God into
the land of Israel, and set me down upon a very high mountain, on Ex 25:9–40
which was a structure like a city opposite me.[p] 3When he brought Ezek 42:16–19
me there, behold, there was a man, whose appearance was like Rev 11:1; 21:15

Solomon or with that rebuilt by Zerubbabel (cf. Ezra 5:24—6:18). All the data are symbolical and refer to an idealized temple.

"He set me down on a very high mountain" (v. 2), Mount Zion, where the temple would be sited. In fact, it is not very high, but Ezekiel is not referring to its real height but to its theological significance; cf. Isaiah 2:2: "the mountain of the house of the Lord shall be established as the highest of the mountains".

"The length of the measuring reed in the man's hand was six long cubits" (v. 5): if this is meant to convey an exact measurement, it is difficult to see how; in fact, some translations, attempting to translate the dimensions to metric ones, run into all sorts of problems. The RSV translation [and the Navarre Spanish] retain the old names (cubits etc.) which, besides, help to retain the symbolic air of the description. With apparent exactness, Ezekiel is describing an idealized temple—an enormous, rectangular, walled esplanade (vv. 1–27); at its centre, another space, also rectangular and walled, occupying about a tenth of the space of the esplanade (vv. 28–47). In the western part of this smaller space is the temple proper, rectangular in plan (40:48—41:26). Inside the temple is a vestibule, the nave (or sanctuary) and the "most holy place". In each of the walled areas and buildings, the gates are particularly important—their position, solidity and ornamentation. The dimensions for each area and room are given in detail but it is all very symbolic; there are many flights of seven steps going from one floor to another, and a flight of ten into the temple. These chapters lend themselves to allegorical interpretation. St Gregory's *Homilies on Ezekiel*, which contains some of his most brilliant intuitions about the interpretation of Holy Scripture, interpret the measuring reed as a symbol for Scripture: "The reed is a measuring reed, because in the holy word [of the Master], which was written down for our benefit, we can see his hidden plans" (*Homiliae in Ezechielem prophetam*, 2, 1, 11).

What we have here is a symmetrical building on three levels, a complex designed to give the impression of something perfect and complete—the most sublime building imaginable, for it is to house the only God and the true Lord of the universe.

me illuc. 2In visionibus Dei adduxit me in terram Israel et posuit me super montem excelsum nimis,
super quem erat quasi aedificium civitatis ad austrum. 3Et introduxit me illuc; et ecce vir, cuius erat
species quasi species aeris, et funiculus lineus in manu eius, et calamus mensurae in manu eius, stabat

p. Gk: Heb *on the south*

bronze, with a line of flax and a measuring reed in his hand; and
he was standing in the gateway. 4And the man said to me, "Son of
man, look with your eyes, and hear with your ears, and set your
mind upon all that I shall show you, for you were brought here in
order that I might show it to you; declare all that you see to the
house of Israel."

Ex 27:9–19; 5And behold, there was a wall all around the outside of the
38:9–20 2 Chron 3:3 temple area, and the length of the measuring reed in the man's
Rev 21:12 hand was six long cubits, each being a cubit and a handbreadth in
length; so he measured the thickness of the wall, one reed; and the
height, one reed. 6Then he went into the gateway facing east,
going up its steps, and measured the threshold of the gate, one
reed deep;[q] 7and the side rooms, one reed long, and one reed
broad; and the space between the side rooms, five cubits; and the
threshold of the gate by the vestibule of the gate at the inner end,
one reed. 8Then he measured the vestibule of the gateway, eight
cubits; 9and its jambs, two cubits; and the vestibule of the gate was
at the inner end. 10And there were three side rooms on either side
of the east gate; the three were of the same size; and the jambs on
either side were of the same size. 11Then he measured the breadth
of the opening of the gateway, ten cubits; and the breadth of the
gateway, thirteen cubits. 12There was a barrier before the side
rooms, one cubit on either side; and the side rooms were six cubits
on either side. 13Then he measured the gate from the back[r] of the
one side room to the back of the other, a breadth of five and twenty
cubits, from door to door. 14He measured also the vestibule,
twenty cubits; and round about the vestibule of the gateway was
the court.[s] 15From the front of the gate at the entrance to the end

---

autem in porta. 4Et locutus est ad me idem vir: «Fili hominis, vide oculis tuis et auribus tuis audi et
pone cor tuum in omnia, quae ego ostendam tibi, quia ut ostendantur tibi, adductus es huc; annuntia
omnia, quae tu vides, domui Israel». 5Et ecce murus forinsecus in circuitu domus undique, et in manu
viri calamus mensurae sex cubitorum, qui habebant cubitum et palmum; et mensus est latitudinem
aedificii calamo uno, altitudinem quoque calamo uno. 6Et venit ad portam, quae respiciebat viam
orientalem, et ascendit per gradus eius et mensus est limen portae calamo uno latitudinem 7et
cubiculum uno calamo in longum et uno calamo in latum et inter cubicula quinque cubitos et limen
portae iuxta vestibulum portae intrinsecus calamo uno. 8Et mensus est vestibulum portae 9octo
cubitorum et postem eius duobus cubitis; vestibulum autem portae erat intrinsecus. 10Porro cubicula
portae ad viam orientalem, tria hinc et tria inde, mensura una trium et mensura una postium ex utraque
parte. 11Et mensus est latitudinem ostii portae decem cubitorum et longitudinem portae tredecim
cubitorum, 12et saeptum ante cubicula cubiti unius utrimque; cubicula autem sex cubitorum erant hinc
et inde. 13Et mensus est portam a tecto cubiculi usque ad tectum eius a contra, latitudinem viginti et
quinque cubitorum, ostium contra ostium, (14)15et a facie ingressus portae usque ad faciem vestibuli

q. Heb *deep, and one threshold, one reed deep* **r.** Compare Gk: Heb *roof* **s.** Compare Gk: Heb *and he made the jambs sixty cubits, and to the jamb of the court was the gateway round about*

of the inner vestibule of the gate was fifty cubits. [16]And the 1 Kings 6:4,30
gateway had windows round about, narrowing inwards into their
jambs in the side rooms, and likewise the vestibule had windows
round about inside, and on the jambs were palm trees.

[17]Then he brought me into the outer court; and behold, there
were chambers and a pavement, round about the court; thirty
chambers fronted on the pavement. [18]And the pavement ran along
the side of the gates, corresponding to the length of the gates; this
was the lower pavement. [19]Then he measured the distance from
the inner front of[t] the lower gate to the outer front of the inner
court, a hundred cubits.

Then he went before me to the north, [20]and behold, there was a
gate[u] which faced toward the north, belonging to the outer court.
He measured its length and its breadth. [21]Its side rooms, three on
either side, and its jambs and its vestibule were of the same size as
those of the first gate; its length was fifty cubits, and its breadth
twenty-five cubits. [22]And its windows, its vestibule, and its palm
trees were of the same size as those of the gate which faced
toward the east; and seven steps led up to it; and its vestibule was
on the inside. [23]And opposite the gate on the north, as on the east,
was a gate to the inner court; and he measured from gate to gate,
a hundred cubits.

[24]And he led me toward the south, and behold, there was a gate
on the south; and he measured its jambs and its vestibule; they had
the same size as the others. [25]And there were windows round
about in it and in its vestibule, like the windows of the others; its
length was fifty cubits, and its breadth twenty-five cubits. [26]And

---

portae intrinsecus, quinquaginta cubitos. [16]Et erant fenestrae marginatae in cubiculis et in postibus intra
portam undique per circuitum; similiter autem erant et in vestibulo fenestrae per gyrum intrinsecus,
et ante postes pictura palmarum. [17]Et eduxit me ad atrium exterius, et ecce exedrae et pavimentum
stratum lapide in atrio per circuitum, triginta exedrae in circuitu pavimenti; [18]et pavimentum ad latus
portarum secundum longitudinem portarum; hoc erat pavimentum inferius. [19]Et mensus est latitudinem
a facie portae inferioris usque ad frontem portae interioris extrinsecus, centum cubitos. Sic oriens. Et
sic aquilo. [20]Portam quoque, quae respiciebat viam aquilonis atrii exterioris, mensus est, tam in
longitudine quam in latitudine; [21]et cubicula eius, tria hinc et tria inde, et postes eius et vestibulum eius
secundum mensuram portae prioris; quinquaginta cubitorum longitudo eius et latitudo viginti quinque
cubitorum. [22]Et fenestrae vestibuli eius et sculpturae palmarum secundum mensuram portae, quae
respiciebat ad orientem; et septem graduum erat ascensus eius, et vestibulum intrinsecus. [23]Et porta
atrii interioris contra portam aquilonis sicut in porta orientali; et mensus est a porta usque ad portam
centum cubitos. [24]Et duxit me ad viam australem, et ecce porta, quae respiciebat ad austrum; et mensus
est postes eius et vestibulum eius iuxta mensuras superiores. [25]Et fenestrae eius et vestibuli in circuitu
sicut fenestrae ceterae; quinquaginta cubitorum longitudo erat et latitudo viginti quinque cubitorum.
[26]Et in gradibus septem ascendebatur ad eam, et vestibulum erat intrinsecus, et caelatae palmae erant,

t. Compare Gk: Heb *from before* **u.** Gk: Heb *a hundred cubits on the east and on the north.*[20] *And the gate*

there were seven steps leading up to it, and its vestibule was on the
inside; and it had palm trees on its jambs, one on either side.
[27]And there was a gate on the south of the inner court; and he
measured from gate to gate toward the south, a hundred cubits.

[28]Then he brought me to the inner court by the south gate, and
he measured the south gate; it was of the same size as the others;
[29]its side rooms, its jambs, and its vestibule were of the same size
as the others; and there were windows round about in it and in its
vestibule; its length was fifty cubits, and its breadth twenty-five
cubits. [30]And there were vestibules round about, twenty-five cubits
long and five cubits broad. [31]Its vestibule faced the outer court, and
palm trees were on its jambs, and its stairway had eight steps.

[32]Then he brought me to the inner court on the east side, and he
measured the gate; it was of the same size as the others. [33]Its side
rooms, its jambs, and its vestibule were of the same size as the
others; and there were windows round about in it and in its
vestibule; its length was fifty cubits, and its breadth twenty-five
cubits. [34]Its vestibule faced the outer court, and it had palm trees
on its jambs, one on either side; and its stairway had eight steps.

[35]Then he brought me to the north gate, and he measured it; it
had the same size as the others. [36]Its side rooms, its jambs, and its
vestibule were of the same size as the others;[v] and it had windows
round about; its length was fifty cubits, and its breadth twenty-five
cubits. [37]Its vestibule[w] faced the outer court, and it had palm trees
on its jambs, one on either side; and its stairway had eight steps.

[38]There was a chamber with its door in the vestibule of the
gate,[x] where the burnt offering was to be washed. [39]And in the

---

una hinc et altera inde, in postibus eius. [27]Et porta erat atrio interiori in via australi, et mensus est a
porta usque ad portam in via australi centum cubitos. [28]Et introduxit me in atrium interius per portam
australem et mensus est portam iuxta mensuras superiores; [29]cubicula eius et postes eius, et vestibulum
eius eisdem mensuris; et fenestrae erant ei et vestibulo eius in circuitu. Quinquaginta cubitorum
longitudo erat et latitudo viginti quinque cubitorum. ([30])[31]Et vestibulum eius respiciebat ad atrium
exterius, et palmae in postibus eius, et octo gradus erant, quibus ascendebatur ad eam. [32]Et introduxit
me in atrium interius per viam orientalem et mensus est portam secundum mensuras superiores;
[33]cubicula eius et postes eius et vestibulum eius sicut supra; et fenestrae erant ei et vestibulo eius in
circuitu. Longitudo erat quinquaginta cubitorum et latitudo viginti quinque cubitorum. [34]Et vestibulum
eius respiciebat ad atrium exterius, et palmae caelatae in postibus eius hinc et inde et in octo gradibus
ascensus eius. [35]Et introduxit me ad portam, quae respiciebat ad aquilonem, et mensus est secundum
mensuras superiores [36]cubicula eius et postes eius et vestibulum eius; et fenestrae ei erant per
circuitum. Longitudo quinquaginta cubitorum erat et latitudo viginti quinque cubitorum. [37]Et
vestibulum eius respiciebat ad atrium exterius, et caelatura palmarum in postibus illius hinc et inde et
in octo gradibus ascensus eius. [38]Et erat exedra, cuius ostium in vestibulo portae; ibi lavabunt
holocaustum. [39]Et in vestibulo portae duae mensae hinc et duae mensae inde, ut mactetur super eas

v. One Ms Compare 29 and 33: Heb lacks *were of the same size as the others* **w.** Gk Vg Compare verses 26, 31, 34: Heb *jambs* **x.** Cn: Heb *at the jambs of the gates*

vestibule of the gate were two tables on either side, on which the
burnt offering and the sin offering and the guilt offering were to
be slaughtered. [40]And on the outside of the vestibule[y] at the
entrance of the north gate were two tables; and on the other side
of the vestibule of the gate were two tables. [41]Four tables were on
the inside, and four tables on the outside of the side of the gate,
eight tables, on which the sacrifices were to be slaughtered. [42]And
there were also four tables of hewn stone for the burnt offering, a
cubit and a half long, and a cubit and a half broad, and one cubit
high, on which the instruments were to be laid with which the
burnt offerings and the sacrifices were slaughtered. [43]And hooks,
a handbreadth long, were fastened round about within. And on the
tables the flesh of the offering was to be laid.

Lev 1:3,9–17; 5:6; Ezek 42:13; 44:17
2 Chron 4:6

[44]Then he brought me from without into the inner court, and
behold, there were two chambers[z] in the inner court, one[a] at the
side of the north gate facing south, the other at the side of the
south[b] gate facing north. [45]And he said to me, This chamber which
faces south is for the priests who have charge of the temple, [46]and
the chamber which faces north is for the priests who have charge
of the altar; these are the sons of Zadok, who alone among the
sons of Levi may come near to the LORD to minister to him. [47]And
he measured the court, a hundred cubits long, and a hundred
cubits broad, foursquare; and the altar was in front of the temple.

Num 3:27–32; 18:5
1 Kings 2:35
Ezek 42:13; 44:15

Interior of the temple

[48]Then he brought me to the vestibule of the temple and measured
the jambs of the vestibule, five cubits on either side; and the

1 Kings 6:3
2 Chron 3:4

40:48—41:26. The temple proper is also idealized, but there are three essential elements in it—the vestibule or hall (40:48–49), the nave, or sanctuary

holocaustum et pro peccato et pro delicto. [40]Et ad latus extra vestibulum ad ostium portae, quae respicit ad aquilonem, duae mensae; et ad la tus alterum vestibuli portae duae mensae. [41]Quattuor mensae hinc et quattuor mensae inde ad latus portae: octo mensae erant, super quas mactabunt. [42]aQuattuor autem mensae ad holocaustum de lapidibus quadris exstructae longitudine cubiti unius et dimidii et latitudine cubiti unius et dimidii et altitudine cubiti unius, [43]aet labia palmi unius reflexa intrinsecus per circuitum; [42]bsuper ista ponant vasa, quibus mactetur holocaustum et victima, [43]bsuper mensas autem carnes oblationis. [44]Et extra portam interiorem exedrae duae, in atrio interiori; una erat in latere portae respicientis ad aquilonem, et facies eius contra viam australem, et una ex latere portae australis, quae respiciebat ad viam aquilonis. [45]Et dixit ad me: «Haec est exedra, quae respicit viam meridianam; sacerdotum erit, qui excubant in custodiis templi. [46]Porro exedra, quae respicit ad viam aquilonis, sacerdotum erit, qui excubant ad ministerium altaris: isti sunt filii Sadoc, qui accedunt de filiis Levi ad Dominum, ut ministrent ei». [47]Et mensus est atrium longitudine centum cubitorum et latitudine centum cubitorum per quadrum. Altare autem erat ante faciem templi. [48]Et introduxit me in vestibulum templi;

y. Cn: Heb *to him who goes up* **z.** Gk: Heb *and from without to the inner gate were chambers for singers* **a.** Gk: Heb *which* **b.** Gk: Heb *east*

1 Kings 7:21 2 Chron 3:15–17

breadth of the gate was fourteen cubits; and the sidewalls of the
gate were three cubits[c] on either side. 49The length of the vestibule
was twenty cubits, and the breadth twelve[d] cubits; and ten steps
led up[e] to it; and there were pillars beside the jambs on either side.

(41:1–2), and the inner room, the Holy of Holies (41:3–4). The vestibule, *ulam* in Hebrew, was quite small, but flanked by square pillars or columns. At the entrance were two round columns like those made of bronze in Solomon's temple (cf. 1 Kings 7:31–41). The sanctuary, *hekal* in Hebrew, was a wide, rectangular nave, also known as "the Holy Place"; it was the sacred precinct to which only priests had access; there were to be found the table of the bread and the altar of incense. The "Holy of Holies", also known as *debir*, was a square room where the ark of the Covenant was housed. Only the high priest was allowed to enter it, and then only once a year, on the day of Atonement (cf. Lev 16:2); Ezekiel, an ordinary priest, does not enter it, but here for the first time he hears his guide speak, telling him "This is the most holy place" (v. 4). The plainness of the description of these three spaces indicates that the people listening to the prophet were familiar with their being the most sacred areas in the whole complex. When the (second) temple was rebuilt after the exile, the measurements given here were followed.

The description and dimensions of the temple walls and the side chambers etc. (41:5–16) symbolize that the buildings have all the necessary grandeur. The prophet goes into detail as regards the decoration and furniture of the various rooms, particularly the nave or sanctuary (41:17–26). The wooden table resembling an altar is given special mention (41:22–23). All the elements of the vision are idealized.

In the second volume of his *Homilies on Ezekiel*, St Gregory the Great uses the description of the temple as an image of the Church. The Church is one and universal (catholic), just as there is only one temple with many rooms (2, 3, 12); in it are the Fathers of the Old and New Testaments (2, 3, 16) and "it is alive in two dimensions—in time and in eternity; one suffering on earth, and the other rewarded in heaven; one earns its merits, the other rejoices in them. A sacrifice is offered in both—here below, the sacrifice of repentance; and in heaven, the sacrifice of praise [...]. Here below, the flesh is offered as a holocaust, but so that it shall attain eternal immortality in heaven, where no man shall say 'no', and no one will have to die; set aflame by the Love of God, each soul will offer Him eternal praise" (*Homiliae in Ezechielem*, 2, 10, 4).

et mensus est postes vestibuli quinque cubitis hinc et quinque cubitis inde et latitudinem portae
quattuordecim cubitorum et latera portae trium cubitorum hinc et trium cubitorum inde; 49longitudinem
autem vestibuli viginti cubitorum et latitudinem duodecim cubitorum, et decem gradibus ascendebatur

c. Gk: Heb *and the breadth of the gate was three cubits* **d.** Gk: Heb *eleven* **e.** Gk: Heb *and by steps which went up*

41 1Then he brought me to the nave, and measured the jambs; 1 Kings 6:3 2 Chron 3:5–7
on each side six cubits was the breadth of the jambs.[f] 2And 1 Kings 6:17
the breadth of the entrance was ten cubits; and the sidewalls of the
entrance were five cubits on either side; and he measured the
length of the nave forty cubits, and its breadth, twenty cubits. 3Then 1 Kings 6:20
he went into the inner room and measured the jambs of the entrance, 2 Chron 3:8–9
two cubits; and the breadth of the entrance, six cubits; and the
sidewalls[g] of the entrance, seven cubits. 4And he measured the length
of the room, twenty cubits, and its breadth, twenty cubits, beyond the
nave. And he said to me, This is the most holy place.

5Then he measured the wall of the temple, six cubits thick; and 1 Kings 6:5–6
the breadth of the side chambers, four cubits, round about the
temple. 6And the side chambers were in three stories, one over
another, thirty in each storey. There were offsets[h] all around the
wall of the temple to serve as supports for the side chambers, so
that they should not be supported by the wall of the temple. 7And
the side chambers became broader as they rose[i] from storey to
storey, corresponding to the enlargement of the offset[j] from storey
to storey round about the temple; on the side of the temple a
stairway led upward, and thus one went up from the lowest storey
to the top storey through the middle storey. 8I saw also that the
temple had a raised platform round about; the foundations of the
side chambers measured a full reed of six long cubits. 9The
thickness of the outer wall of the side chambers was five cubits;
and the part of the platform which was left free was five cubits.[k]
Between the platform[l] of the temple and the 10chambers of the

---

ad illud, et columnae erant in postibus, una hinc et altera inde. **[41]** 1Et introduxit me in templum et mensus est postes: sex cubitos latitudinis hinc et sex cubitos latitudinis inde. 2Et latitudo portae decem cubitorum erat, et latera portae quinque cubitis hinc et quinque cubitis inde; et mensus est longitudinem eius quadraginta cubitorum et latitudinem viginti cubitorum. 3Et introgressus intrinsecus, mensus est in poste portae duos cubitos et portam sex cubitorum et latitudinem laterum portae septem cubitorum hinc et septem cubitorum inde. 4Et mensus est longitudinem eius viginti cubitorum et latitudinem viginti cubitorum versus faciem templi. Et dixit ad me: «Hoc est Sanctum sanctorum». 5Et mensus est parietem domus sex cubitorum et latitudinem aedificii adiacentis quattuor cubitorum undique per circuitum domus; 6cubicula autem adiacentia, cubiculum super cubiculum, in tribus tabulatis. Et erant margines eminentes in pariete domus pro cubiculis adiacentibus per circuitum, ut essent fulcra, neque essent fulcra intra parietem domus, 7et latitudo ambitus sursum ascendens iuxta cubicula adiacentia, quia circumdata erat domus usque sursum circa domum; idcirco amplificata erat domus usque sursum, et de inferiore tabulato ascendebatur ad superius per medium. 8Et vidi in domo altitudinem per circuitum, fundamenta aedificii adiacentis mensura calami pleni, id est sex cubitorum, in altitudine. 9Et latitudo parietis aedificii adiacentis forinsecus erat quinque cubitorum. Et area vacua inter cubicula domui adiacentia, 10et inter exedras habebat latitudinem viginti cubitorum in circuitu domus undique.

f. Compare Gk: Heb *tent* **g.** Gk: Heb *breadth* **h.** Gk Compare 1 Kings 6:6: Heb *they entered* **i.** Cn: Heb *it was surrounded* **j.** Gk: Heb *for the encompassing of the temple* **k.** Syr: Heb lacks *five cubits* **l.** Cn: Heb *house of the side chambers*

court was a breadth of twenty cubits round about the temple on every side. [11]And the doors of the side chambers opened on the part of the platform that was left free, one door toward the north, and another door toward the south; and the breadth of the part that was left free was five cubits round about.

[12]The building that was facing the temple yard on the west side was seventy cubits broad; and the wall of the building was five cubits thick round about, and its length ninety cubits.

[13]Then he measured the temple, a hundred cubits long; and the yard and the building with its walls, a hundred cubits long; [14]also the breadth of the east front of the temple and the yard, a hundred cubits.

[15]Then he measured the length of the building facing the yard which was at the west and its walls[m] on either side, a hundred cubits.

The nave of the temple and the inner room and the outer[n]
1 Kings 6:15–18 vestibule [16]were panelled[o] and round about all three had windows
with recessed[p] frames. Over against the threshold the temple was
panelled with wood round about, from the floor up to the windows
(now the windows were covered), [17]to the space above the door,
even to the inner room, and on the outside. And on all the walls
round about in the inner room and the nave were carved like-
1 Kings 6:29–35; 7:36 nesses[q] [18]of cherubim and palm trees, a palm tree between cherub
and cherub. Every cherub had two faces: [19]the face of a man
toward the palm tree on the one side, and the face of a young lion
toward the palm tree on the other side. They were carved on the
whole temple round about; [20]from the floor to above the door
cherubim and palm trees were carved on the wall.[r]

---

[11]Et ostia aedificii adiacentis ad aream vacuam, ostium unum ad viam aquilonis et ostium unum ad viam australem; et latitudo muri areae vacuae quinque cubitorum in circuitu. [12]Et aedificium, quod erat ex adverso areae separatae versumque ad viam respicientem ad mare, latitudinis septuaginta cubitorum; paries autem aedificii quinque cubitorum latitudinis per circuitum et longitudo eius nonaginta cubitorum. [13]Et mensus est domus longitudinem centum cubitorum et areae separatae et aedificii et parietum eius longitudinem centum cubitorum; [14]latitudinem autem faciei domus et areae separatae contra orientem centum cubitorum. [15]Et mensus est longitudinem aedificii ex adverso areae separatae ad dorsum et parietum eius ex utraque parte centum cubitorum. Et templum interius et vestibulum exterius [16]strata erant ligno, et fenestrae marginatae et margines in circuitu triplices contra limen erant strato ligno per gyrum in circuitu, et a terra usque ad fenestras—et fenestrae poterant claudi—usque ad superiora ostii; [17]et usque ad domum interiorem et forinsecus et per omnem parietem in circuitu, intrinsecus et forinsecus, ad mensuram [18]fabrefacti cherubim et palmae, et palma inter cherub et cherub; duasque facies habebat cherub, [19]faciem hominis versam ad palmam ex hac parte et faciem leonis versam ad palmam ex alia parte: expressi per omnem domum in circuitu. [20]De terra usque ad

m. Cn: The meaning of the Hebrews term is unknown **n.** Gk: Heb *of the court* **o.** Gk: Heb *the thresholds* **p.** Cn Compare Gk 1 Kings 6:4: The meaning of the Hebrew term is unknown **q.** Cn: Heb *measures and carved* **r.** Cn Compare verse 25: Heb *and the wall*

[21]The doorposts of the nave were squared; and in front of the holy place was something resembling[22] an altar of wood, three cubits high, two cubits long, and two cubits broad;[s] its corners, its base,[t] and its walls were of wood. He said to me, "This is the table which is before the LORD." [23]The nave and the holy place had each a double door. [24]The doors had two leaves apiece, two swinging leaves for each door. [25]And on the doors of the nave were carved cherubim and palm trees, such as were carved on the walls; and there was a canopy of wood in front of the vestibule outside. [26]And there were recessed windows and palm trees on either side, on the sidewalls of the vestibule.[u]

Ex 30:1–3
1 Kings 6:20–21
Ezek 44:16
Mal 1:7,12
Rev 11:1

1 Kings 6:31–35

Outbuildings of the temple for the use of priests

42 [1]Then he led me out into the inner[v] court, toward the north, and he brought me to the chambers which were opposite the temple yard and opposite the building on the north. [2]The length of the building which was on the north side[w] was[x] a hundred cubits, and the breadth fifty cubits. [3]Adjoining the twenty cubits which belonged to the inner court, and facing the pavement which belonged to the outer court, was gallery[y] against gallery[y] in three stories. [4]And

42:1–20. The priests' rooms adjoining the temple were on three levels; a priest's rank and his temple duties determined where he went.

In the holy chambers (v. 13) the priests stored and ate the portions of the offerings allocated to them, specifically their portion of the cereal offerings (Lev 2:1–3) and sin offerings (Lev 6:17–23), which were considered to be "things most holy".

The description of the temple complex ends with the measurements of the outer perimeter. It is all very imposing; Ezekiel also observes that a separation wall divides secular buildings from the temple area (v. 20), to show that everything to do with the Lord and with his worship is very special.

superiora portae cherubim et palmae caelatae erant. In pariete templi [21]postes portae quadruplices, et coram sanctuario aspectus quasi aspectus [22]altaris lignei trium cubitorum altitudo, et longitudo eius duorum cubitorum, et anguli eius et bases eius et parietes eius lignei. Et locutus est ad me: «Haec est mensa coram Domino». [23]Et duo ostia erant templo et sanctuario [24]duo ostia. Ostiis erant duae valvae versatiles usque ad parietem, valvae duae ostio uni et valvae duae ostio alteri. [25]Et caelati erant in ipsis ostiis templi cherubim et sculpturae palmarum, sicut in parietibus quoque expressi erant; et tectum ligneum erat in vestibuli fronte forinsecus. [26]Et fenestrae marginatae et similitudo palmarum hinc atque inde in lateribus vestibuli et in cubiculis adiacentibus domus. **[42]** [1]Et eduxit me in atrium exterius per viam ducentem ad aquilonem; et duxit me ad exedram, quae erat contra aream separatam, et contra aedem ad aquilonem. [2]Longitudo erat centum cubitorum in latere aquilonis et latitudo quinquaginta cubitorum. [3]Contra viginti cubitos atrii interioris et contra pavimentum stratum lapide atrii exterioris elevabatur pars iuxta partem in tribus gradibus. [4]Et ante exedras deambulatio decem cubitorum

s. Gk: Heb lacks *two cubits broad* **t.** Gk: Heb *length* **u.** Cn: Heb *vestibule. And the side chambers of the temple and the canopies* **v.** Gk: Heb *outer* **w.** Gk: Heb *door* **x.** Gk: Heb *before the length* **y.** The meaning of the Hebrew word is unknown

before the chambers was a passage inward, ten cubits wide and a
hundred cubits long,[z] and their doors were on the north. 5Now the
upper chambers were narrower, for the galleries[y] took more away
from them than from the lower and middle chambers in the
building. 6For they were in three stories, and they had no pillars
like the pillars of the outer[a] court; hence the upper chambers were
set back from the ground more than the lower and the middle
ones. 7And there was a wall outside parallel to the chambers,
toward the outer court, opposite the chambers, fifty cubits long.
8For the chambers on the outer court were fifty cubits long, while
those opposite the temple were a hundred cubits long. 9Below
these chambers was an entrance on the east side, as one enters
them from the outer court, 10where the outside wall begins.[b]

On the south[c] also, opposite the yard and opposite the building,
there were chambers 11with a passage in front of them; they were
similar to the chambers on the north, of the same length and
breadth, with the same exits[d] and arrangements and doors. 12And
below the south chambers was an entrance on the east side, where
one enters the passage, and opposite them was a dividing wall.[e]

Lev 2:3; 6:16,26; 13Then he said to me, "The north chambers and the south
24:9; 2:3,10 chambers opposite the yard are the holy chambers, where the
priests who approach the LORD shall eat the most holy offerings;
there they shall put the most holy offerings—the cereal offering,
the sin offering, and the guilt offering, for the place is holy.
Lev 17:1 14When the priests enter the holy place, they shall not go out of it
into the outer court without laying there the garments in which

---

latitudinis, ad interiora respiciens, longitudinis centum cubitorum; et ostia eorum ad aquilonem.
5Exedrae superiores angustiores erant, quia gradus auferebant eis spatium, prae inferioribus et mediis
aedificii. 6Tristega enim erant et non habebant columnas, sicut erant columnae exteriorum; sic ergo in
gradibus de inferioribus, et de mediis a terra surgebat aedificium. 7Et murus exterior secundum exedras
erat in via atrii exterioris ante exedras, longitudo eius quinquaginta cubitorum, 8quia longitudo erat
exedrarum atrii exterioris quinquaginta cubitorum, quae erant ante faciem illarum, totum erat centum
cubitorum. 9Et erat subter exedras has introitus ab oriente ingredientibus in ea de atrio exteriori 10in
capite muri atrii. Contra viam meridianam in facie areae separatae, et erant exedrae ante aedificium,
11et via ante faciem earum iuxta similitudinem exedrarum, quae erant in via aquilonis; secundum
longitudinem earum et latitudinem earum, sic et omnes exitus earum et dispositiones et ostia earum.
12Et ad ostia exedrarum, quae erant in via respiciente ad notum, ostium in capite viae, quae via erat ante
murum protegentem per viam orientalem ingredientibus. 13Et dixit ad me: «Exedrae aquilonis et
exedrae austri, quae sunt ante aream separatam, hae sunt exedrae sanctae, in quibus vescuntur
sacerdotes, qui appropinquant ad Dominum sancta sanctorum: ibi ponent sancta sanctorum et
oblationem et pro peccato et pro delicto, locus enim sanctus est. 14Cum autem ingressi fuerint

z. Gk Syr: Heb *a way of one cubit* **a.** Gk: Heb lacks *outer* **b.** Cn: Compare Gk: Heb *in the breadth of the wall of the court* **c.** Gk: Heb *east* **d.** Heb *and all their exits* **e.** Cn: Heb *And according to the entrances of the chambers that were toward the south was an entrance at the head of the way, the way before the dividing wall toward the east as one enters them*

they minister, for these are holy; they shall put on other garments
before they go near to that which is for the people."
[15]Now when he had finished measuring the interior of the
temple area, he led me out by the gate which faced east, and
measured the temple area round about. [16]He measured the east
side with the measuring reed, five hundred cubits by the
measuring reed. [17]Then he turned and measured the north side, Ezek 45:2
five hundred cubits by the measuring reed. [18]Then he turned and
measured[f] the south side, five hundred cubits by the measuring
reed. [19]Then he turned to the west side and measured, five
hundred cubits by the measuring reed. [20]He measured it on the
four sides. It had a wall around it, five hundred cubits long and
five hundred cubits broad, to make a separation between the holy
and the common.

The glory of the Lord filling the temple

43 [1]Afterward he brought me to the gate, the gate facing east. Ezek 11:23
[2]And behold, the glory of the God of Israel came from the Rev 21:11; 18:1
east; and the sound of his coming was like the sound of many

43:1–12. This is the climax of the vision: "the glory of the Lord entered the temple by the gate facing east" (v. 4), that is, by the same route it took when it left the temple and the city (cf. 10:19; 11:22–23). The renewal of the temple and the rehabilitation of the people have been completed—so much so that there will never again be any defilement (vv. 7–9).

"I will dwell in their midst for ever" (v. 9). The presence of God is a guarantee of safety and effectiveness. Our Lord promised his disciples that he would be with them until the end of time (cf. Mt 28:20), and the Church develops in the world thanks to the presence of Jesus and the help of the Holy Spirit. "The God we seek is never far from us, because he dwells within

sacerdotes, non egredientur de sanctis in atrium exterius, sed ibi reponent vestimenta sua, in quibus ministrant, quia sancta sunt; vestienturque vestimentis aliis et sic procedent ad locum populi». [15]Cumque complesset mensuras interioris areae domus, eduxit me per viam portae, quae respiciebat ad viam orientalem, et mensus est ibi undique per circuitum. [16]Mensus est autem contra ventum orientalem calamo mensurae quingentos calamos in calamo mensurae per circuitum. [17]Et mensus est contra ventum aquilonis quingentos calamos in calamo mensurae per gyrum. [18]Et ad ventum australem mensus est quingentos calamos in calamo mensurae per circuitum. [19]Et conversus ad ventum occidentalem mensus est quingentos calamos in calamo mensurae. [20]Per quattuor ventos mensus est illud; murus ei erat undique per circuitum longitudine quingentorum cubitorum et latitudine quingentorum cubitorum, dividens inter sanctuarium et locum profanum. **[43]** [1]Et duxit me ad portam, quae respiciebat ad viam orientalem, [2]et ecce gloria Dei Israel ingrediebatur per viam orientalem, et vox erat ei quasi vox aquarum multarum, et terra splendebat a maiestate eius. [3]Et vidi visionem secundum speciem, quam videram, quando venit, ut disperderet civitatem, et species secundum

f. Gk: Heb *measuring reed round about. He measured*

Ezek 10: 18–19; 11:22–23 waters; and the earth shone with his glory. 3And[g] the vision I saw
was like the vision which I had seen when he came to destroy the
city, and[h] like the vision which I had seen by the river Chebar; and
I fell upon my face. 4As the glory of the LORD entered the temple
1 Kings 8:10–11 by the gate facing east, 5the Spirit lifted me up, and brought
Ezek 3:12 me into the inner court; and behold, the glory of the LORD filled
Rev 21:3,10 the temple.

6While the man was standing beside me, I heard one speaking
Ex 19:12; 25:8 to me out of the temple; 7and he said to me, "Son of man, this is
the place of my throne and the place of the soles of my feet, where
I will dwell in the midst of the people of Israel for ever. And the
house of Israel shall no more defile my holy name, neither they,
nor their kings, by their harlotry, and by the dead bodies[i] of their
kings, 8by setting their threshold by my threshold and their
doorposts beside my doorposts, with only a wall between me and
them. They have defiled my holy name by their abominations
which they have committed, so I have consumed them in my
Jn 16:13 anger. 9Now let them put away their idolatry and the dead bodies
of their kings far from me, and I will dwell in their midst for ever.

10"And you, son of man, describe to the house of Israel the
temple and its appearance and plan,[j] that they may be ashamed of
their iniquities. 11And if they are ashamed of all that they have
done, portray[k] the temple, its arrangement, its exits and its
entrances, and its whole form; and make known to them all its
ordinances and all its laws;[l] and write it down in their sight, so that
they may observe and perform all its laws and all its ordinances.

---

us if we are worthy of his presence. He lives in us as the soul inhabits the body, as long as we are holy members of his Body and dead to sin. Then he will truly dwell among us" (St Columbanus, *Instructiones*, 1, 3).

aspectum, quem videram iuxta fluvium Chobar; et cecidi super faciem meam. 4Et maiestas Domini ingressa est templum per viam portae, quae respiciebat ad orientem. 5Et levavit me spiritus et introduxit me in atrium interius; et ecce repleta erat gloria Domini domus. 6Et audivi loquentem ad me de domo, cum vir staret iuxta me, 7et dixit ad me: «Fili hominis, locus solii mei et locus vestigiorum pedum meorum, ubi habitabo in medio filiorum Israel in aeternum; et non polluent ultra domus Israel nomen sanctum meum, ipsi et reges eorum, in fornicationibus suis et in cadaveribus regum suorum in morte eorum, 8qui fabricati sunt limen suum iuxta limen meum et postes suos iuxta postes meos, et paries erat inter me et eos, et polluerunt nomen sanctum meum in abominationibus, quas fecerunt; propter quod consumpsi eos in ira mea. 9Nunc ergo repellant procul fornicationem suam et cadavera regum suorum a me, et habitabo in medio eorum semper. 10Tu autem, fili hominis, ostende domui Israel templum, et confundantur ab iniquitatibus suis et metiantur fabricam. 11Et si erubuerint ex omnibus, quae fecerunt,

g. Gk: Heb *And like the vision* **h.** Syr: Heb *and the visions* **i.** Or *the monuments* **j.** Gk: Heb *the temple that they may measure the pattern* **k.** Gk: Heb *the form of* **l.** Compare Gk: Heb *its whole form*

12This is the law of the temple: the whole territory round about upon the top of the mountain shall be most holy. Behold, this is the law of the temple.

3. THE NEW ALTAR

13"These are the dimensions of the altar by cubits (the cubit being a cubit and a handbreadth): its base shall be one cubit high,[m] and one cubit broad, with a rim of one span around its edge. And this shall be the height[x] of the altar: 14from the base on the ground to the lower ledge, two cubits, with a breadth of one cubit; and from

Ex 27:1–8
1 Kings 8:64
2 Chron 4:1; 7:7

43:13–27. The altar of sacrifice was one of the most important features of the temple. It was in the form of a pyramid and consisted of three ledges or platforms on top of one another, the ledge at the base being the largest. Though on a much smaller scale, it resembled the Babylonian towers or ziggurats, which must have greatly impressed the exiles.

The "altar hearth" (v. 15); the Hebrew term, *ari'el*, means a place where something is burned, in this case the "altar" where burnt offerings were made (where the victims were set ablaze); it symbolizes the way that man establishes contact with God. The prophet Isaiah applies this word *ari'el* to Jerusalem, although he takes the word to mean "lion of God" as its etymology also allows.

The rites prescribed here for the consecration of the altar (vv. 18–27) do not correspond exactly to those in Exodus (Ex 29:35–37) or Leviticus (Lev 8:10–15). Ezekiel is not so much concerned with specific ritual rules as with stressing the reverence that is due to divine worship and everything connected with it. Hence his insistence on atonement, purification and consecration (v. 26). For her liturgy the Church lays down many external rites, but that is not what really matters, for through them she manifests "the mystery of Christ and the real nature of the true Church [...], so that in her the human is directed toward and subordinated to the divine, the visible to the invisible, action to contemplation, and this present world to that city yet to come, the object of our quest" (Vatican II, *Sacrosanctum Concilium*, 2).

describe domum et supellectilem eius, exitus et introitus, et omnem figuram eius et universa praecepta eius et omnes leges eius ostende eis et scribes oculis eorum, ut custodiant omnem figuram eius et omnia praecepta illius et faciant ea. 12Ista est lex domus in summitate montis: omnes fines eius in circuitu sanctum sanctorum sunt; haec est ergo lex domus». 13Istae autem mensurae altaris in cubitis, cubitus habebat cubitum et palmum; fossae in circuitu eius erat cubitus in altitudine et cubitus in latitudine; et saepto eius ad marginem eius in circuitu palmus unus. Haec autem erat altitudo altaris: 14de fossa terrae usque ad crepidinem inferiorem duo cubiti, et latitudo cubiti unius; et a crepidine minore usque ad

m. Gk: Heb lacks *high* **x.** Gk: Heb *back*

the smaller ledge to the larger ledge, four cubits, with a breadth of
one cubit; 15and the altar hearth, four cubits; and from the altar
hearth projecting upward, four horns, one cubit high.[n] 16The altar
hearth shall be square, twelve cubits long by twelve broad. 17The
ledge also shall be square, fourteen cubits long by fourteen broad,
with a rim around it half a cubit broad, and its base one cubit
round about. The steps of the altar shall face east."

Consecration of the altar

Ex 29:36–37 18And he said to me, "Son of man, thus says the Lord GOD: These
Lev 1:5; 8:10–15 are the ordinances for the altar: On the day when it is erected for
1 Mac 4:52–46 offering burnt offerings upon it and for throwing blood against it,
Deut 17:9; 24:8 19you shall give to the Levitical priests of the family of Zadok,
Jer 33:18 Ezek 44:15 who draw near to me to minister to me, says the Lord GOD, a bull
for a sin offering. 20And you shall take some of its blood, and put
it on the four horns of the altar, and on the four corners of the
ledge, and upon the rim round about; thus you shall cleanse the
Ex 29:41 altar and make atonement for it. 21You shall also take the bull of
the sin offering, and it shall be burnt in the appointed place
belonging to the temple, outside the sacred area. 22And on the
second day you shall offer a he-goat without blemish for a sin
offering; and the altar shall be cleansed, as it was cleansed with
the bull. 23When you have finished cleansing it, you shall offer a
bull without blemish and a ram from the flock without blemish.
Lev 2:13 24You shall present them before the LORD, and the priests shall
sprinkle salt upon them and offer them up as a burnt offering to
Ex 29:35 the LORD. 25For seven days you shall provide daily a goat for a sin
Lev 8:33–35 offering; also a bull and a ram from the flock, without blemish,

crepidinem maiorem quattuor cubiti, et latitudo unius cubiti. 15Ipse autem focus quattuor cubitorum, et a foco usque sursum cornua quattuor. 16Et focus duodecim cubitorum in longitudine per duodecim cubitos latitudinis, quadrangulatum aequis lateribus. 17Et crepido quattuordecim cubitorum longitudinis per quattuordecim cubitos latitudinis in quattuor angulis eius; et saeptum in circuitu eius dimidii cubiti, et fossa eius unius cubiti per circuitum; gradus autem eius versi ad orientem. 18Et dixit ad me: «Fili hominis, haec dicit Dominus Deus: Hi sunt ritus altaris: in qua die fuerit fabricatum, ut offeratur super illud holocaustum, et effundatur sanguis, 19dabis sacerdotibus levitis, qui sunt de semine Sadoc, qui accedunt ad me, ait Dominus Deus, ut ministrent mihi, vitulum de armento pro peccato. 20Et assumens de sanguine eius, pones super quattuor cornua eius et super quattuor angulos crepidinis et super saeptum in circuitu et mundabis illud et expiabis. 21Et tolles vitulum, qui oblatus fuerit pro peccato, et combures illum in destinato loco domus extra sanctuarium. 22Et in die secunda offeres hircum caprarum immaculatum pro peccato, et expiabunt altare, sicut expiaverunt in vitulo. 23Cumque compleveris expians illud, offeres vitulum de armento immaculatum et arietem de grege immaculatum; 24et offeres eos in conspectu Domini, et mittent sacerdotes super eos sal et offerent eos holocaustum Domino. 25Septem diebus facies hircum pro peccato cotidie, et vitulum de armento et arietem de pecoribus immaculatos offerent. 26Septem diebus expiabunt altare et mundabunt illud et consecrabunt

n. Gk: Heb lacks *one cubit high*

shall be provided. [26]Seven days shall they make atonement for the
altar and purify it, and so consecrate it. [27]And when they have
completed these days, then from the eighth day onward the priests
shall offer upon the altar your burnt offerings and your peace
offerings; and I will accept you, says the Lord GOD."

Lev 9:1
Ezek 20:40
Rom 12:1
1 Pet 2:5

4. THE NEW FORM OF WORSHIP*

44 [1]Then he brought me back to the outer gate of the
sanctuary, which faces east; and it was shut. [2]And he said

***44:1–31.** The presence in the temple of the glory of the Lord determines the way in which members of the public will take part in divine worship: from now on, the prince can go as far as the eastern gate, without going through it (vv. 1–3); every Israelite may enter the temple, but no foreigner may (vv. 4–9); the Levites are temple ministers but they are not empowered to offer sacrifices (vv. 10–14); the priests, the sons of Zadok, do offer sacrifices and therefore they need to be especially observant of the rules of the liturgy. Because they must dedicate themselves entirely to religious worship, their upkeep will be funded by the other Israelites (vv. 15–31).

The pride of place that religious worship has in the new Israel shows the religious commitment of the people; in all that they do, the glory of God must be their aim. In the New Testament the teaching that is implicit here is spelt out—for example, in Jesus' sermon on the mount: "Seek first his kingdom and his righteousness, and all these things shall be yours as well" (Mt 6:33).

44:1–3. The eastern gate will always stay shut, as a sign that the glory of God, his presence, will never again leave the temple. The Fathers (cf. e.g. St Jerome, *Epistolae*, 48, 21) have interpreted this closed gate as a symbol of the virginity of Mary. The womb of Mary was the dwelling-place of the Son of God, who was born without breaking down the entrance gate: "Since the mysteries of the conception and incarnation of Christ are so many and so great, it is not surprising that divine Providence should foreshadow the event by wonderful signs and prophecies. The holy Doctors and Fathers have interpreted many passages of Scripture as referring to this mystery: we recall, from among the many examples, the sealed door that Ezekiel saw, the stone that fell from the mountain, the rod of Aaron ..." (*Roman Catechism*, 1, 4, 10).

---

illud. [27]Expletis autem diebus, in die octava et ultra facient sacerdotes super altare holocausta vestra et pacifica, et placatus ero vobis», ait Dominus Deus. **[44]** [1]Et convertit me ad viam portae sanctuarii exterioris, quae respiciebat ad orientem, et erat clausa; [2]et dixit Dominus ad me: «Porta haec clausa erit; non aperietur, et vir non transibit per eam, quoniam Dominus, Deus Israel, ingressus est per eam,

to me,[o] "This gate shall remain shut; it shall not be opened, and no one shall enter by it; for the LORD, the God of Israel, has entered by it; therefore it shall remain shut. 3Only the prince may sit in it to eat bread before the LORD; he shall enter by way of the vestibule of the gate, and shall go out by the same way."

Rules of admission to the temple

4Then he brought me by way of the north gate to the front of the temple; and I looked, and behold, the glory of the LORD filled the
Ezek 43:6–12 temple of the LORD; and I fell upon my face. 5And the LORD said to me, "Son of man, mark well, see with your eyes, and hear with your ears all that I shall tell you concerning all the ordinances of the temple of the LORD and all its laws; and mark well those who may be admitted to[p] the temple and all those who are to be excluded from the sanctuary. 6And say to the rebellious house,[q] to the house of Israel, Thus says the Lord GOD: O house of Israel, let there be an end to all your abominations, 7in admitting foreigners, uncircumcised in heart and flesh, to be in my sanctuary, profaning it,[r] when you offer to me my food, the fat and the blood. You[s] have broken my covenant, in addition to all your abominations. 8And you have not kept charge of my holy things; but you have set foreigners to keep my charge in my sanctuary.

Gen 17:10
Lev 17:8–9
Num 15:13–14
2 Chron 6:32–33
Jer 4:4
Ezek 22:26
Acts 21:28
Heb 13:10

44:4–9. According to some passages in the Peutateuch, pagans were allowed to make offerings to the Lord (cf. Lev 17:8–9; Num 15:13–14); and the book of Chronicles implies that God hearkens to foreigners who visit the temple to pray (cf. 2 Chron 6:32–33). Ezekiel is more rigorous than that: no one who is not a member of the chosen people is allowed to enter. These rules reflect a desire to preserve divine worship from any danger of defilement: no one "uncircumcised in heart and flesh" may enter.

eritque clausa. 3Princeps, ut princeps ipse sedebit in ea, ut comedat panem coram Domino; per viam vestibuli portae ingredietur et per eandem viam egredietur». 4Et adduxit me per viam portae aquilonis in conspectum domus; et vidi: et ecce implevit gloria Domini domum Domini, et cecidi in faciem meam. 5Et dixit ad me Dominus: «Fili hominis, pone cor tuum et vide oculis tuis et auribus tuis audi omnia, quae ego loquor ad te de universis caeremoniis domus Domini et de cunctis legibus eius; et pones cor tuum in introitu templi et in omni exitu sanctuarii 6et dices ad exasperantem me domum Israel: Haec dicit Dominus Deus: Sufficiant vobis omnes abominationes vestrae, domus Israel, 7eo quod induxistis alienigenas incircumcisos corde et incircumcisos carne, ut essent in sanctuario meo et polluerent domum meam, cum offertis panem meum, adipem et sanguinem; et dissolvistis pactum meum in omnibus abominationibus vestris 8et non explevistis ministerium sanctorum meorum et posuistis illos ministrantes mihi in sanctuario meo. Propterea 9haec dicit Dominus Deus: Omnis

o. Cn: Heb *the LORD* **p.** Cn: Heb *the entrance of* **q.** Gk: Heb lacks *house* **r.** Gk: Heb *it my temple* **s.** Gk Syr Vg: Heb *they*

[9]"Therefore[t] thus says the Lord GOD: No foreigner, uncir- Acts 21:28–29
cumcised in heart and flesh, of all the foreigners who are among
the people of Israel, shall enter my sanctuary.

The Levites Num 3:5–10
[10]But the Levites who went far from me, going astray from me Deut 18:1–18
after their idols when Israel went astray, shall bear their punishment. [11]They shall be ministers in my sanctuary, having oversight Num 16:9
at the gates of the temple, and serving in the temple; they shall
slay the burnt offering and the sacrifice for the people, and they
shall attend on the people, to serve them. [12]Because they ministered
to them before their idols and became a stumbling block of
iniquity to the house of Israel, therefore I have sworn concerning
them, says the Lord GOD, that they shall bear their punishment.
[13]They shall not come near to me, to serve me as priest, nor come Lev 2:3
near any of my sacred things and the things that are most sacred; but
they shall bear their shame, because of the abominations which they

44:10–14. According to the Priestly tradition, Levites were subordinate to the priests descended from Aaron (cf. Num 3:5–10), whereas the Deuteronomic tradition regarded them as equal (cf. Deut 18:1–18). After the exile, only priests descended from Zadok (v. 15), the priest who stayed loyal to David (cf. 1 Kings 2:26, 35), performed priestly functions; the other members of the tribe of Levi were subject to them, and had lesser roles. Ezekiel explains this arrangement by saying that the Levites proved unfaithful whereas the Zadokites did not go astray. Once again he puts the emphasis on ritual purity, especially in anything to do with the offering of sacrifices.

44:15–31. The priests who are charged with offering sacrifice and who are, on that account, close to God, must carefully observe the rules about dress (vv. 17–19), deportment (they must be well-groomed, and temperate: vv. 20–21), and choice of spouse (v. 22). They must be sure to observe the rules about contact with dead bodies, to avoid defilement (vv. 25–27). In addition to

alienigena incircumcisus corde et incircumcisus carne non ingredietur sanctuarium meum, omnis alienigena, qui est in medio filiorum Israel. [10]Sed Levitae, qui longe recesserint a me in errore filiorum Israel, qui erraverunt a me post idola sua, portabunt iniquitatem suam [11]et erunt in sanctuario meo aeditui et ianitores portarum domus et ministri domus: ipsi mactabunt holocausta et victimas populo et ipsi stabunt in conspectu eorum, ut ministrent eis. [12]Pro eo quod ministraverunt illis in conspectu idolorum suorum et facti sunt domui Israel in offendiculum iniquitatis, idcirco levavi manum meam super eos, dicit Dominus Deus; portabunt iniquitatem suam. [13]Et non appropinquabunt ad me, ut

t. Gk: Heb *for you*

have committed. 14 Yet I will appoint them to keep charge of the
temple, to do all its service and all that is to be done in it.

Num 18:1–19 **The priests**
Deut 10:8 15 "But the Levitical priests, the sons of Zadok, who kept the
1 Kings charge of my sanctuary when the people of Israel went astray
2:26,35 from me, shall come near to me to minister to me; and they shall
attend on me to offer me the fat and the blood, says the Lord GOD;
16 they shall enter my sanctuary, and they shall approach my table,
Ex 28:39,43; to minister to me, and they shall keep my charge. 17 When they
39:27 enter the gates of the inner court, they shall wear linen garments;
Ex 39:28 they shall have nothing of wool on them, while they minister at
Lev 6:3–4,10 the gates of the inner court, and within. 18 They shall have linen

---

offering sacrifices, they were responsible for religious education (v. 23) and could decide legal cases (v. 24). Their temple worship was their sole occupation (vv. 28–31) and they were not supposed to earn money elsewhere; in other words, sacred and profane were spheres to be kept apart.

For Ezekiel no effort was too great to preserve worship and the temple from any trace of defilement. All this helped to make people more aware of the greatness of God, who stands above all things and who is holy. Christian writers saw these passages in Ezekiel as a divine lesson on how to have a proper sense of who God is: "He gave instructions to the people about the building of the tabernacle and the temple, about the election of the Levites, the sacrifices and offerings, and all the purifications necessary for true worship. God has no need of any of these things [...]. But in laying down these many laws and prescriptions, he enlightened those who were always tempted to turn to the worship of idols, showing them the way and encouraging them to persevere in the service of God; that is, by listing the secondary details, he drew attention to the first principles: he showed the truth that lies behind images; the eternal in the temporal; the spiritual in the material; the heavenly in the earthly" (St Irenaeus, *Adversus haereses*, 4, 14, 3).

---

sacerdotio fungantur mihi, neque accedent ad omnia sancta mea, ad sanctissima, sed portabunt
confusionem suam et abominationes suas, quas fecerunt. 14 Et faciam eos ministros in omni ministerio
domus et in universis, quae facienda sunt in ea. 15 Sacerdotes autem levitae filii Sadoc, qui custodierunt
caeremonias sanctuarii mei, cum errarent filii Israel a me, ipsi accedent ad me, ut ministrent mihi, et
stabunt in conspectu meo, ut offerant mihi adipem et sanguinem, ait Dominus Deus. 16 Ipsi ingredientur
sanctuarium meum et ipsi accedent ad mensam meam, ut serviant mihi et custodiant ministerium
meum. 17 Cumque ingredientur portas atrii interioris, vestibus lineis induentur, nec ascendet super eos
quidquam laneum, quando ministrant in portis atrii interioris et in domo. 18 Vittae lineae erunt in

turbans upon their heads, and linen breeches upon their loins; they
shall not gird themselves with anything that causes sweat. 19And Ex 29:37; 30:29
when they go out into the outer court to the people, they shall put Ezek 46:20
off the garments in which they have been ministering, and lay
them in the holy chambers; and they shall put on other garments,
lest they communicate holiness to the people with their garments.
20They shall not shave their heads or let their locks grow long; Lev 21:5
they shall only trim the hair of their heads. 21No priest shall drink
wine, when he enters the inner court. 22They shall not marry a Lev 21:7–14
widow, or a divorced woman, but only a virgin of the stock of the
house of Israel, or a widow who is the widow of a priest. 23They Lev 10:10
shall teach my people the difference between the holy and the Ezek 22:26 Mal 2:7
common, and show them how to distinguish between the unclean Deut 17:8–9
and the clean. 24In a controversy they shall act as judges, and they Ezek 20:11
shall judge it according to my judgments. They shall keep my 12:16,19–20
laws and my statutes in all my appointed feasts, and they shall
keep my sabbaths holy. 25They shall not defile themselves by Lev 21:1–5
going near to a dead person; however, for father or mother, for son
or daughter, for brother or unmarried sister they may defile Num 19:11–12
themselves. 26After he is defiled,[u] he shall count for himself seven
days, and then he shall be clean.[v] 27And on the day that he goes
into the holy place, into the inner court, to minister in the holy Num 18:20–24
place, he shall offer his sin offering, says the Lord GOD. Deut 18:1–2
28"They shall have no[w] inheritance; I am their inheritance: and Josh 13:14
you shall give them no possession in Israel; I am their possession. Lev 6:14,
29They shall eat the cereal offering, the sin offering, and the guilt 17–29; 7:1–6; 27:21,28
offering; and every devoted thing in Israel shall be theirs. 30And Ex 13:2; 22:29 Num 15:20

---

capitibus eorum, et feminalia linea erunt in lumbis eorum, et non accingentur in sudore. 19Cumque egredientur atrium exterius ad populum, exuent se vestimenta sua, in quibus ministraverunt, et reponent ea in exedris sanctis et vestient se vestimentis aliis et non sanctificabunt populum in vestibus suis. 20Caput autem suum non radent neque comam nutrient, sed tondentes attondent capita sua. 21Et vinum non bibet omnis sacerdos, quando ingressurus est atrium interius. 22Et viduam et repudiatam non accipient sibi uxores sed virgines de semine domus Israel; sed et viduam, quae fuerit vidua a sacerdote, accipient. 23Et populum meum docebunt quid sit inter sanctum et profanum et inter mundum et immundum ostendent eis. 24Et cum fuerit controversia, stabunt ad iudicandum et in iudiciis meis iudicabunt; leges meas et praecepta mea in omnibus sollemnitatibus meis custodient et sabbata mea sanctificabunt. 25Et ad mortuum hominem non ingredientur, ne polluantur, nisi ad patrem et matrem et filium et filiam et fratrem et sororem, quae virum non habuit: in quibus contaminabuntur. 26Et postquam fuerit emundatus, septem dies numerabuntur ei, 27et in die introitus sui in sanctuarium ad atrium interius, ut ministret mihi in sanctuario, offeret pro peccato suo, ait Dominus Deus. 28Et erit eis in hereditatem: ego hereditas eorum; et possessionem non dabitis eis in Israel: ego enim possessio eorum. 29Oblationem et pro peccato et pro delicto ipsi comedent, et omne anathema in Israel ipsorum erit; 30et primitiva omnium primogenitorum et omnia libamenta ex omnibus, quae offertis, sacerdotum erunt; et

u. Syr: Heb *cleansed* **v.** Syr: Heb lacks *and then he shall be clean* **w.** Vg: Heb *as an*

the first of all the first fruits of all kinds, and every offering of all
kinds from all your offerings, shall belong to the priests; you shall
also give to the priests the first of your coarse meal, that a blessing
Lev 22:8 may rest on your house. [31]The priests shall not eat of anything,
whether bird or beast, that has died of itself or is torn.

How the land of Israel is to be allotted*

Josh 13:16 Ezek 42: 15–20; 44:30; 48:8–20

45 [1]"When you allot the land as a possession, you shall set
apart for the LORD a portion of the land as a holy district,
twenty-five thousand cubits long and twenty[x] thousand cubits
broad; it shall be holy throughout its whole extent. [2]Of this a
square plot of five hundred by five hundred cubits shall be for the
sanctuary, with fifty cubits for an open space around it. [3]And in
the holy district you shall measure off a section twenty-five
thousand cubits long and ten thousand broad, in which shall be the
Ezek 48:11–12 sanctuary, the most holy place. [4]It shall be the holy portion of the
land; it shall be for the priests, who minister in the sanctuary and

***45:1—46:24.** The new Israel that comes into being after the exile must have a new allocation of property (45:1–8), a new system of measurement for cereals and liquids (45:9–17), and new rites about offerings depending on the offerer and the status of the festival (45:18–25). Temple services are to be put on a new footing (46:1–15), as is the property of the prince (46:16–24). All these rules make tedious reading, but they all go to show the degree to which the old arrangements cease to apply for reasons to do with uncleanness, and, above all, they show the Lord's determination to establish new institutions and rules that are in keeping with his purity and holiness.

45:1–8. The allotment of the land that Ezekiel proposes would be impossible to carry out in practice, given the physical geography of Israel; but it does show that persons and institutions had greater status the closer they were to the temple and its religious services. That was the ideal. More distant, frontier, districts will be for the ordinary people. In the central part of the land of Israel there will be a huge tract which will belong to the priests, the Levites and the prince. This tract

primitiva farinae vestrae dabitis sacerdoti, ut reponat benedictionem domui tuae. [31]Omne morticinum et captum a bestia de avibus et de pecoribus non comedent sacerdotes. **[45]** [1]Cumque coeperitis terram dividere sortito, separate oblationem Domino sanctificatum de terra, longitudine viginti quinque milia et latitudine viginti milia: sanctificatum erit in omni termino suo per circuitum; [2]ex quo sanctuarium obtinebit quingentos per quingentos, quadrifariam per circuitum, et quinquaginta cubitos pascua eius per gyrum. [3]Et a mensura ista mensurabis longitudinem viginti quinque milium et latitudinem decem milium, et in ipso erit templum, Sanctum sanctorum. [4]Sanctificatum de terra erit sacerdotibus ministris sanctuarii, qui accedunt ad ministerium Domini; et erit eis locus in domos et in

x. Gk: Heb *ten*

approach the LORD to minister to him; and it shall be a place for
their houses and a holy place for the sanctuary. [5]Another section,
twenty-five thousand cubits long and ten thousand cubits broad,
shall be for the Levites who minister at the temple, as their
possession for cities to live in.[y]

[6]"Alongside the portion set apart as the holy district you shall
assign for the possession of the city an area five thousand cubits
broad, and twenty-five thousand cubits long; it shall belong to the
whole house of Israel.

[7]"And to the prince shall belong the land on both sides of the Ezek 44:3; 48:21
holy district and the property of the city, alongside the holy district
and the property of the city, on the west and on the east, corresponding in length to one of the tribal portions, and extending
from the western to the eastern boundary of the land. [8]It is to be Ezek 22:27; 48:1–7
his property in Israel. And my princes shall no more oppress my
people; but they shall let the house of Israel have the land
according to their tribes.

The justice system. Offerings to the prince

[9]"Thus says the Lord GOD: Enough, O princes of Israel! Put away Jer 22:3–5
violence and oppression, and execute justice and righteousness;
cease your evictions of my people, says the Lord GOD.

---

will extend from the Mediterranean Sea to the Jordan river, and the temple of Jerusalem will be at the centre of it.

45:9–17. The prince, that is, the ruler of the people (for the exile marked the end of the monarchy), has royal prerogatives, and it is his function to administer justice and righteousness (cf. Ps 72:1–2); he must act uprightly himself and never defraud his subjects by falsifying weights and measures (vv. 9–12). He should also set a good example with regard to divine worship, and be generous in providing offerings in line with his status.

The new system impinges directly on those in leadership positions; they must be just in all their dealings (v. 9). "Human society can be neither well-ordered nor prosperous unless it has some people invested with legitimate authority to preserve its institutions and to devote themselves as far as is necessary to work and care for the good of all" (*Catechism of the Catholic Church*, 1897).

pascua pecoribus. [5]Viginti quinque autem milia longitudinis et decem milia latitudinis erunt Levitis, qui ministrant domui; ipsis in possessionem, civitates ad habitandum. [6]Et possessionem civitatis dabitis quinque milia latitudinis et longitudinis viginti quinque milia, iuxta oblationem sacram; omni domui Israel erit. [7]Principi quoque ex utraque parte oblationis sacrae et possessionis civitatis, secundum oblationem sacram et possessionem urbis, a latere maris usque ad mare et a latere orientis versus orientem, longitudinem autem iuxta unamquamque partium, a termino occidentali usque ad terminum

y. Gk: Heb *twenty chambers*

Lev 19:35–37 10 “You shall have just balances, a just ephah, and a just bath.
Deut 25:14 Amos 8:5 11 The ephah and the bath shall be of the same measure, the bath
containing one tenth of a homer, and the ephah one tenth of a
Ex 30:13 homer; the homer shall be the standard measure. 12 The shekel
shall be twenty gerahs; five shekels shall be five shekels, and ten
shekels shall be ten shekels, and your mina shall be fifty shekels.[z]
Ex 30:13–16 13 “This is the offering which you shall make: one sixth of an
Mt 23:23 ephah from each homer of wheat, and one sixth of an ephah from
each homer of barley, 14 and as the fixed portion of oil,[a] one tenth
of a bath from each cor (the cor,[b] like the homer, contains ten
Lev 1:1; 2:1; 3:1 baths); 15 and one sheep from every flock of two hundred, from the
families[c] of Israel. This is the offering for cereal offerings, burnt
offerings, and peace offerings, to make atonement for them, says
Ex 23,14; 29:40 the Lord GOD. 16 All the people of the land shall give[d] this offering
Num 28:11 to the prince in Israel. 17 It shall be the prince’s duty to furnish the
Lev 14:19 burnt offerings, cereal offerings, and drink offerings, at the feasts,
the new moons, and the sabbaths, all the appointed feasts of the
house of Israel: he shall provide the sin offerings, cereal offerings,
burnt offerings, and peace offerings, to make atonement for the
house of Israel.

Feasts and offerings

Ex 12:1 18 “Thus says the Lord GOD: In the first month, on the first day of
the month, you shall take a young bull without blemish, and

45:18–25. In the rules about festivals one can also see Ezekiel’s concern for the purity of rites and those taking part in them. Only three feasts are mentioned—new year’s day, in spring (vv. 18–20); the Passover, on the fourteenth of the same month (vv. 21–24); and the feast of Tabernacles, in the seventh

orientalem. 8 Haec terra erit ei possessio in Israel, et non depopulabuntur ultra principes mei populum meum; sed terram dabunt domui Israel secundum tribus eorum. 9 Haec dicit Dominus Deus: Sufficiat vobis, principes Israel; violentiam et rapinas omittite et iudicium et iustitiam facite; auferte exactiones vestras a populo meo, ait Dominus Deus. 10 Statera iusta et ephi iustum et batus iustus sit vobis; 11 ephi et batus aequalia et unius mensurae sint, ut capiat decimam partem homer batus, et decimam partem homer ephi: iuxta mensuram homer sit aequa libratio eorum. 12 Siclus autem viginti gera habeat; quinque sicli sint quinque, et decem sicli sint decem, et quinquaginta sint vobis mina. 13 Haec est oblatio, quam offeratis: sextam partem ephi de gomor frumenti et sextam partem ephi de gomor hordei. 14 Praeceptum quoque de oleo—batus est mensura olei—: decimam partem bati offeratis de choro—decem bati homer faciunt, quia decem bati implent chorum—. 15 Et pecus unum de grege ducentorum, de pascuis irriguis Israel, in oblationem et in holocaustum et in pacifica ad expiandum pro eis, ait Dominus Deus. 16 Omnis populus terrae tenebitur ad hanc oblationem principi in Israel; 17 et super principem erunt holocausta et oblationes et libamina in diebus festis et in calendis et in sabbatis et in universis sollemnitatibus domus Israel; ipse faciet pro peccato et oblationem et holocaustum et pacifica

z. Gk: Heb *twenty shekels, twenty-five shekels, fifteen shekels shall be your mina* **a.** Cn: Heb *oil, the bath the oil* **b.** Vg: Heb *homer* **c.** Gk: Heb *watering places* **d.** Gk Compare Syr: Heb *shall be to*

cleanse the sanctuary. [19]The priest shall take some of the blood of
the sin offering and put it on the doorposts of the temple, the four
corners of the ledge of the altar, and the posts of the gate of the
inner court. [20]You shall do the same on the seventh day of the
month for any one who has sinned through error or ignorance; so
you shall make atonement for the temple.

[21]"In the first month, on the fourteenth day of the month, you Lev 23:5
shall celebrate the feast of the passover, and for seven days
unleavened bread shall be eaten. [22]On that day the prince shall
provide for himself and all the people of the land a young bull for
a sin offering. [23]And on the seven days of the festival he shall
provide as a burnt offering to the LORD seven young bulls and
seven rams without blemish, on each of the seven days; and a he-
goat daily for a sin offering. [24]And he shall provide as a cereal
offering an ephah for each bull, an ephah for each ram, and a hin
of oil to each ephah. [25]In the seventh month, on the fifteenth day Lev 23:34
of the month and for the seven days of the feast, he shall make the
same provision for sin offerings, burnt offerings, and cereal
offerings, and for the oil.

Offerings on the sabbath and on the day of the new moon Ex 20:8

46 [1]"Thus says the Lord GOD: The gate of the inner court that Num 28:9–14
faces east shall be shut on the six working days; but on the Ezek 45:17

---

month (v. 25). Pentecost is not mentioned, nor is there any reference to the events that each feast celebrates. However, Ezekiel goes into detail about the sacrifices to be offered, especially the sin offerings. The whole focus is on safeguarding the transcendence of God and the holiness of temple worship; other festival customs and traditions are of less importance.

46:1–15. In addition to the offerings to be made on the big feasts, sacrifices were prescribed in detail for each sabbath, each day of the new moon and even every day. Probably all the rules in

ad expiandum pro domo Israel. [18]Haec dicit Dominus Deus: In primo mense, una mensis, sumes vitulum de armento immaculatum et expiabis sanctuarium. [19]Et tollet sacerdos de sanguine hostiae pro peccato et ponet in postibus domus et in quattuor angulis crepidinis altaris et in postibus portae atrii interioris. [20]Et sic facies in septima mensis pro unoquoque, qui ignoravit et errore deceptus est, et expiabitis pro domo. [21]In primo mense, quarta decima die mensis, erit vobis Paschae sollemnitas; septem diebus azyma comedentur. [22]Et faciet princeps in die illa pro se et pro universo populo terrae vitulum pro peccato; [23]et in septem dierum sollemnitate faciet holocaustum Domino septem vitulos et septem arietes immaculatos cotidie septem diebus et pro peccato hircum caprarum cotidie; [24]et oblationem ephi per vitulum et ephi per arietem faciet et olei hin per singula ephi. [25]Septimo mense, quinta decima die mensis, in sollemnitate faciet, sicut supra dicta sunt, per septem dies, tam pro peccato quam pro holocausto et in oblatione et in oleo. **[46]** [1]Haec dixit Dominus Deus: Porta atrii interioris, quae respicit ad orientem, erit clausa sex diebus, in quibus opus fit; die autem sabbati aperietur, sed et

sabbath day it shall be opened and on the day of the new moon it
shall be opened. 2The prince shall enter by the vestibule of the
gate from without, and shall take his stand by the post of the gate.
The priests shall offer his burnt offering and his peace offerings,
and he shall worship at the threshold of the gate. Then he shall go
out, but the gate shall not be shut until evening. 3The people of the
land shall worship at the entrance of that gate before the LORD on
Num 28:9–10 the sabbaths and on the new moons. 4The burnt offering that the
prince offers to the LORD on the sabbath day shall be six lambs
Ezek 45:24 without blemish and a ram without blemish; 5and the cereal
offering with the ram shall be an ephah, and the cereal offering
with the lambs shall be as much as he is able, together with a hin
of oil to each ephah. 6On the day of the new moon he shall offer a
young bull without blemish, and six lambs and a ram, which shall
be without blemish; 7as a cereal offering he shall provide an ephah
with the bull and an ephah with the ram, and with the lambs as
much as he is able, together with a hin of oil to each ephah.
8When the prince enters, he shall go in by the vestibule of the
gate, and he shall go out by the same way.

Ex 23:14–17 9"When the people of the land come before the LORD at the
appointed feasts, he who enters by the north gate to worship shall
go out by the south gate; and he who enters by the south gate shall
go out by the north gate: no one shall return by way of the gate by
which he entered, but each shall go out straight ahead. 10When

---

this section are more an ideal than a reality, because the rules are very complex and the Israelites would have found it difficult to provide all the animals and other offerings. Still, these prescriptions go to show the important role played by religious rites in acknowledging God's sovereignty over all creation. "Creation was fashioned with a view to the sabbath and therefore for the worship and adoration of God. Worship is inscribed in the order of creation (cf. Gen 1:14). As the rule of St Benedict says, nothing should take precedence over 'the work of God', that is, solemn worship. This indicates the right order of human concerns" (*Catechism of the Catholic Church*, 347).

in die calendarum aperietur, 2et intrabit princeps per viam vestibuli portae deforis et stabit in poste
portae, et facient sacerdotes holocaustum eius et pacifica eius, et adorabit super limen portae et
egredietur; porta autem non claudetur usque ad vesperam. 3Et adorabit populus terrae ad ostium portae
illius in sabbatis et in calendis coram Domino. 4Holocaustum autem hoc offeret princeps Domino: in
die sabbati sex agnos immaculatos et arietem immaculatum 5et oblationem ephi per arietem, per agnos
autem oblationem, quantum dederit manus eius, et olei hin per singula ephi; 6in die autem calendarum
vitulum de armento immaculatum et sex agni et aries immaculati erunt 7et ephi per vitulum, ephi
quoque per arietem faciet oblationem, per agnos autem sicut invenerit manus eius, et olei hin per
singula ephi. 8Cumque ingressurus est princeps, per viam vestibuli portae ingrediatur et per eandem
viam exeat. 9Et cum intrabit populus terrae in conspectu Domini in sollemnitatibus, qui ingreditur per
portam aquilonis, ut adoret, egrediatur per viam portae meridianae; porro qui ingreditur per viam portae

they go in, the prince shall go in with them; and when they go out,
he shall go out.
[11]"At the feasts and the appointed seasons the cereal offering
with a young bull shall be an ephah, and with a ram an ephah, and
with the lambs as much as one is able to give, together with a hin
of oil to an ephah. [12]When the prince provides a freewill offering,
either a burnt offering or peace offerings as a freewill offering to
the LORD, the gate facing east shall be opened for him; and he
shall offer his burnt offering or his peace offerings as he does on
the sabbath day. Then he shall go out, and after he has gone out
the gate shall be shut.
[13]"He shall provide a lamb a year old without blemish for a Ex 29:38
burnt offering to the LORD daily; morning by morning he shall Num 28:3–4
provide it. [14]And he shall provide a cereal offering with it morning
by morning, one sixth of an ephah, and one third of a hin of oil to
moisten the flour, as a cereal offering to the LORD; this is the
ordinance for the continual burnt offering.[e] [15]Thus the lamb and
the meal offering and the oil shall be provided, morning by
morning, for a continual burnt offering.

Miscellaneous regulations

[16]"Thus says the Lord GOD: If the prince makes a gift to any of his
sons out of[f] his inheritance, it shall belong to his sons, it is their

46:16–24. The property of the prince (vv. 16–18) must not change hands. In fact, that holds good also for the property of private individuals, given that every fifty years, when the "year of liberty" is held, everything has to be given back to the original owner. The conviction that the land is a gift from God is a defence against avarice and a spur to cultivate the land and respect created things. The description of the temple kitchens (vv. 19–24), and how they are isolated from the other buildings, shows the care taken to ensure that the people would not come into contact with sacred things (the law prohibited that contact).

meridianae, egrediatur per viam portae aquilonis: non revertetur per viam portae, per quam ingressus est, sed e regione illius egredietur. [10]Princeps autem in medio eorum cum ingredientibus ingredietur et cum egredientibus egredietur. [11]Et in diebus festis et in sollemnitatibus erit oblatio ephi per vitulum et ephi per arietem, per agnos autem erit oblatio, quantum invenerit manus eius, et olei hin per singula ephi. [12]Cum autem fecerit princeps spontaneum holocaustum aut pacifica voluntaria Domino, aperietur ei porta, quae respicit ad orientem, et faciet holocaustum suum et pacifica sua, sicut facere solet in die sabbati, et egredietur, claudeturque porta, postquam exierit. [13]Et agnum anniculum immaculatum facies holocaustum cotidie Domino; semper mane facies illud. [14]Et oblationem facies super eo mane mane sextam partem ephi, et de oleo tertiam partem hin, ut conspergatur simila; oblatio Domino, legitimum iuge atque perpetuum. [15]Facient agnum et oblationem et oleum mane mane, holocaustum sempiternum.

e. Cn: Heb *perpetual ordinances continually* **f.** Gk: Heb *it is his inheritance*

Lev 25:10 property by inheritance. [17]But if he makes a gift out of his
inheritance to one of his servants, it shall be his to the year of
liberty; then it shall revert to the prince; only his sons may keep
a gift from his inheritance. [18]The prince shall not take any of the
inheritance of the people, thrusting them out of their property; he
shall give his sons their inheritance out of his own property, so
that none of my people shall be dispossessed of his property."

Ezek 42:1–9 [19]Then he brought me through the entrance, which was at the
side of the gate, to the north row of the holy chambers for the
priests; and there I saw a place at the extreme western end of
Lev 2; 2:4; 4–5 Ezek 40:39; 44:19 them. [20]And he said to me, "This is the place where the priests
shall boil the guilt offering and the sin offering, and where they
shall bake the cereal offering, in order not to bring them out into
the outer court and so communicate holiness to the people."

[21]Then he brought me forth to the outer court, and led me to the
four corners of the court; and in each corner of the court there was
a court—[22]in the four corners of the court were small courts[g],
forty cubits long and thirty broad; the four were of the same size.
[23]On the inside, around each of the four courts was a row of
masonry, with hearths made at the bottom of the rows round
about. [24]Then he said to me, "These are the kitchens where those
who minister at the temple shall boil the sacrifices of the people."

Gen 2:10–14 Ezek 41:1–2 Joel 3:18; 4:18 Zech 13,1; 14:8

The spring in the temple

47 [1]Then he brought me back to the door of the temple; and
behold, water was issuing from below the threshold of the

47:1–12. The vision of the spring flowing from the southern end of the temple and ending up in the Dead Sea, revitalizing everything it meets on its way, is one of the most striking images in the book. Its content is reminiscent

[16]Haec dixit Dominus Deus: Si dederit princeps donum alicui de filiis suis de hereditate sua, filiorum suorum erit; possidebunt illud hereditarie. [17]Si autem dederit legatum de hereditate sua uni servorum suorum, erit illius usque ad annum remissionis et revertetur ad principem; sola hereditas filiorum eius illorum erit. [18]Et non accipiet princeps de hereditate populi, ut expellat eos de possessione eorum, sed de possessione sua hereditatem dabit filiis suis, ut non dispergatur populus meus unusquisque a possessione sua». [19]Et introduxit me per ingressum, qui erat ex latere portae, in exedras sacras sacerdotum, quae respiciebant ad aquilonem, et erat ibi locus in extrema parte vergens ad occidentem; [20]et dixit ad me: «Iste est locus, ubi coquent sacerdotes pro delicto et pro peccato, ubi coquent oblationem, ut non efferant in atrium exterius, et sanctificetur populus». [21]Et eduxit me in atrium exterius et circumduxit me per quattuor angulos atrii, et ecce atriola singula per angulos atrii. [22]In quattuor angulis atrii atriola inclusa quadraginta cubitorum per longum et triginta per latum: mensurae unius quattuor erant. [23]Et paries per circuitum ambiens quattuor atriola, et culinae fabricatae erant subter parietes per gyrum. [24]Et dixit ad me: «Hae sunt domus culinarum, in quibus coquent ministri

g. Gk Syr Vg: The meaning of the Hebrew word is uncertain

temple toward the east (for the temple faced east); and the water was flowing down from below the south end of the threshold of the temple, south of the altar. [2]Then he brought me out by way of the north gate, and led me round on the outside to the outer gate, that faces toward the east;[h] and the water was coming out on the south side.

Jn 4:1; 7:38
Rev 22:1

[3]Going on eastward with a line in his hand, the man measured a thousand cubits, and then led me through the water; and it was ankle-deep. [4]Again he measured a thousand, and led me through the water; and it was knee-deep. Again he measured a thousand, and led me through the water; and it was up to the loins. [5]Again he measured a thousand, and it was a river that I could not pass through, for the water had risen; it was deep enough to swim in, a river that could not be passed through. [6]And he said to me, "Son of man, have you seen this?"

---

of the vision of the bones (37:1–14): there, it was the Spirit that gave life to the dry bones; here, the water refreshes the dead waters. The image of the river reminds one of how in paradise (Gen 2:10–14) the four branches of the river make the whole garden beautiful; here, a single river actually gives life. Although the vision contains references to actual places, such as the oasis of En-gedi (v. 10), the Dead Sea or the Arabah, it is symbolic and what it shows is that the renewal of the temple and its worship will bring all sorts of advantages to the whole people.

There is an echo of this vision in the New Testament in the words of Jesus recorded by St John: "If any one thirst, let him come to me and drink. He who believes in me, as the scripture has said, Out of his heart shall flow rivers of living water" (Jn 7:37). Early Christian tradition links this text of St John with Ezekiel's vision, seeing in the spring in the temple the waters of Baptism that flow from Christ who is life, or from Christ's side on the altar of the cross: "We go down to the water's edge steeped in our sins and impurity, and we walk out of the water, our hearts filled with grace, fear of the Lord and hope in Jesus" (*Epistula Barnabae* 11, 10).

domus Domini victimas populi». **[47]** [1]Et convertit me ad portam domus, et ecce aquae egrediebantur subter limen domus ad orientem; facies enim domus respiciebat ad orientem, aquae autem descendebant a latere templi dextro a meridie altaris. [2]Et eduxit me per viam portae aquilonis et convertit me ad viam foras ad portam exteriorem, quae respiciebat ad orientem; et ecce aquae exeuntes a latere dextro. [3]Cum egrederetur vir ad orientem, qui habebat funiculum in manu sua, mensus est mille cubitos et traduxit me per aquam usque ad talos. [4]Rursumque mensus est mille et traduxit me per aquam usque ad genua. [5]Et mensus est mille et traduxit me per aquam usque ad renes. Et mensus est mille; torrens, quem non potui pertransire, quoniam intumuerant aquae, aquae ad natandum; torrens, qui non poterat transvadari. [6]Et dixit ad me: «Certe vidisti, fili hominis»; et duxit me et convertit ad

h. Heb obscure

Then he led me back along the bank of the river. [7]As I went
back, I saw upon the bank of the river very many trees on the one
Deut 3:17; 4:49 side and on the other. [8]And he said to me, “This water flows
Zech 14:8 toward the eastern region and goes down into the Arabah; and
Rev 22:2 when it enters the stagnant waters of the sea,[i] the water will
Ex 15:25 become fresh. [9]And wherever the river[j] goes every living creature
which swarms will live, and there will be very many fish; for this
water goes there, that the waters of the sea[k] may become fresh; so
1 Sam 24:1 everything will live where the river goes. [10]Fishermen will stand
Is 15:8 beside the sea; from En-gedi to En-eglaim it will be a place for the
spreading of nets; its fish will be of very many kinds, like the fish
of the Great Sea. [11]But its swamps and marshes will not become
Ps 1:3 fresh; they are to be left for salt. [12]And on the banks, on both sides
Is 44:4 Jer 17:8 of the river, there will grow all kinds of trees for food. Their leaves
Ezek 19:10–11 will not wither nor their fruit fail, but they will bear fresh fruit
Rev 22:2 every month, because the water for them flows from the sanctuary.
Their fruit will be for food, and their leaves for healing.”

Gen 48:5 **The frontiers of the new Israel**

Num 34:1–12 Josh 1:4; 13: [13]Thus says the Lord GOD: “These are the boundaries by which
1–6; 17:14,17 you shall divide the land for inheritance among the twelve tribes

---

47:13–23. The new Israel will also have new borders. Once again Ezekiel mentions specific locations and takes account of the borders mentioned in ancient traditions (cf. Num 34:7–12), but he draws an idealized map that provides Israel with territory it never actually had.This ideal land will be distributed among the tribes of Israel, but without excluding foreigners (vv. 21–23). The fact that foreigners are given a place marks a great advance, particularly since they are actually given a share of the land. St Jerome sees that as something very remarkable: “In this passage we learn that there is no difference between the people of Israel and the Gentiles. If the land is divided among the people of Israel and Gentiles, it must be because the land is the inheritance of both Jew and Gentile, provided that they are converted and worship the one true God” (*Commentarii in Ezechielem*, 47, 21 ff).

ripam torrentis. [7]Cumque me convertissem, ecce in ripa torrentis ligna multa nimis ex utraque parte; [8]et ait ad me: «Aquae istae, quae egrediuntur ad regionem orientalem et descendunt ad Arabam, intrabunt mare, aquas salsas, et sanabuntur aquae: [9]et omnis anima vivens, quae movetur, quocumque venerit torrens, vivet, et erunt pisces multi satis, postquam venerint illuc aquae istae, et sanabuntur et vivent omnia, ad quae venerit torrens. [10]Et stabunt super mare piscatores; ab Engaddi usque ad Engallim siccatio sagenarum erit; plurimae species erunt piscium eius, sicut pisces maris Magni, multitudinis nimiae. [11]Palustria autem eius et stagna non sanabuntur, quia in salinas dabuntur. [12]Et

i. Compare Syr: Heb *into the sea to the sea those that were made to issue forth* **j.** Gk Syr Vg Tg: Heb *two rivers* **k.** Compare Syr: Heb lacks *the waters of the sea*

of Israel. Joseph shall have two portions. 14And you shall divide it
equally; I swore to give it to your fathers, and this land shall fall
to you as your inheritance.

15"This shall be the boundary of the land: On the north side, from
the Great Sea by way of Hethlon to the entrance of Hamath, and on
to Zedad,[l] 16Berothah, Sibraim (which lies on the border between
Damascus and Hamath), as far as Hazer-hatticon, which is on the
border of Hauran. 17So the boundary shall run from the sea to
Hazar-enon, which is on the northern border of Damascus, with the
border of Hamath to the north.[m] This shall be the north side.

18"On the east side, the boundary shall run from Hazar-enon[n]
between Hauran and Damascus;[m] along the Jordan between
Gilead and the land of Israel; to the eastern sea and as far as
Tamar.[o] This shall be the east side.

19"On the south side, it shall run from Tamar as far as the Num 34:3–5
waters of Meribath-kadesh, thence along the Brook of Egypt to Josh 15:1–4
the Great Sea. This shall be the south side.

20"On the west side, the Great Sea shall be the boundary to a
point opposite the entrance of Hamath. This shall be the west side.

21"So you shall divide this land among you according to the
tribes of Israel. 22You shall allot it as an inheritance for yourselves Ex 12:48
and for the aliens who reside among you and have begotten Lev 19:34
children among you. They shall be to you as native-born sons of
Israel; with you they shall be allotted an inheritance among the
tribes of Israel. 23In whatever tribe the alien resides, there you
shall assign him his inheritance, says the Lord GOD.

---

super torrentem orietur in ripis eius ex utraque parte omne lignum pomiferum; non defluet folium ex eo, et non deficiet fructus eius: per singulos menses afferet primitiva, quia aquae eius de sanctuario egredientur, et erunt fructus eius in cibum, et folia eius ad medicinam. 13Haec dicit Dominus Deus: Hic est terminus, in quo possidebitis terram in duodecim tribubus Israel, quia Ioseph duplicem funiculum habet; 14possidebitis autem eam, singuli aeque ut frater suus, super quam levavi manum meam, ut darem patribus vestris; et cadet terra haec vobis in possessionem. 15Hic est autem terminus terrae: ad plagam septentrionalem a mari Magno via Hethalon ad introitum Emath, 16Sedada, Berotha, Sabarim, quae est inter terminum Damasci et confinium Emath, usque ad Asarenon, quae est iuxta terminum Auran; 17erit ergo terminus a mari usque ad Asarenon, cum fines Damasci et fines Emath sint in aquilone; haec est plaga septentrionalis. 18Porro plaga orientalis de loco inter Auran et inter Damascum et in medio inter Galaad et terram Israel, Iordanis disterminans usque ad mare orientale, usque Thamar; haec est plaga orientalis. 19Plaga autem australis meridiana a Thamar usque ad aquas Meribathcades et torrentem usque ad mare Magnum; haec est plaga ad meridiem australis. 20Et plaga maris, mare Magnum a confinio per directum, donec venias Emath; haec est plaga maris. 21Et dividetis terram istam vobis per tribus Israel 22et mittetis eam in hereditatem, vobis et advenis, qui accesserint ad vos, qui genuerint filios in medio vestrum, et erunt vobis sicut indigenae inter filios Israel: vobiscum divident possessionem in medio tribuum Israel; 23in tribu autem quacumque fuerit advena, ibi dabitis

l. Gk: Heb *the entrance of Zedad, Hamath* **m.** Heb obscure **n.** Cn: Heb lacks *Hazar-enon*
o. Compare Syr: Heb *you shall measure*

Division of the land

Num 2:25–31 **48** [1]"These are the names of the tribes: Beginning at the
northern border, from the sea by way[p] of Hethlon to the
entrance of Hamath, as far as Hazar-enon (which is on the northern
border of Damascus over against Hamath), and[q] extending from
the east side to the west,[r] Dan, one portion. [2]Adjoining the
territory of Dan, from the east side to the west, Asher, one portion.
[3]Adjoining the territory of Asher, from the east side to the west,
Naphtali, one portion. [4]Adjoining the territory of Naphtali, from
the east side to the west, Manasseh, one portion. [5]Adjoining the
territory of Manasseh, from the east side to the west, Ephraim, one

---

48:1–29. The reorganization of the tribes is also idealized. Each receives the same amount of territory and they are spread out in an hierarchical order: the country will be divided into three great horizontal bands. Six tribes will be allocated the northern portion, with Judah's territory the closest to the holy portion. The middle band will be allocated to the Levites and priests and to the city which will spread on both sides of the temple, which will occupy the central square; and there will also be space for the prince and his family. The southernmost band will be occupied by the remaining five tribes, with the tribe of Benjamin, Jacob's favourite son, having the area nearest the temple.

By means of this distribution, Ezekiel shows that the most important place in the promised land is the temple, the dwelling-place of the glory of God. Alongside it, in addition to space reserved for the inhabitants of the city, will live those chosen to rule the people and attend to divine worship—priests and Levites, and the prince. Next, on each side come the tribes chosen by God—Judah to the north and Benjamin to the south. And then the other tribes.

Some Fathers of the Church explained this arrangement of the idealized holy land as being a symbol of the establishment of the messianic kingdom, where everything will be perfectly in order and all mankind will acknowledge and praise the true God, the centre of creation and of history. But for this to come about, evil must be shunned: "Because we are a holy people, we must live righteous lives, scorning calumny, immoral and impure relationships, drunkenness, rebelliousness and evil desires, and all adultery and pride" (St Clement of Rome, *Ad Corinthios*, 30, 1).

possessionem illi, ait Dominus Deus. **[48]** [1]Et haec nomina tribuum: in finibus aquilonis iuxta viam
Hethalon ad introitum Emath, Asarenon—fines Damasci ad aquilonem iuxta Emath—erit a plaga
orientali usque ad mare, Dan pars una. [2]Et iuxta terminum Dan a plaga orientali usque ad plagam maris,
Aser una. [3]Et iuxta terminum Aser a plaga orientali usque ad plagam maris, Nephthali una. [4]Et iuxta
terminum Nephthali a plaga orientali usque ad plagam maris, Manasse una. [5]Et iuxta terminum
Manasse a plaga orientali usque ad plagam maris, Ephraim una. [6]Et iuxta terminum Ephraim a plaga

p. Compare 47:15: Heb *by the side of the way* **q.** Cn: Heb *and they shall be his* **r.** Gk Compare verses 2–8: Heb *the east side the west*

portion. [6]Adjoining the territory of Ephraim, from the east side to
the west, Reuben, one portion. [7]Adjoining the territory of Reuben,
from the east side to the west, Judah, one portion.

[8]"Adjoining the territory of Judah, from the east side to the
west, shall be the portion which you shall set apart, twenty-five
thousand cubits in breadth, and in length equal to one of the tribal
portions, from the east side to the west, with the sanctuary in the
midst of it. [9]The portion which you shall set apart for the LORD Ezek 45:1–6
shall be twenty-five thousand cubits in length, and twenty[s]
thousand in breadth. [10]These shall be the allotments of the holy
portion: the priests shall have an allotment measuring twenty-five
thousand cubits on the northern side, ten thousand cubits in
breadth on the western side, ten thousand in breadth on the eastern
side, and twenty-five thousand in length on the southern side, with
the sanctuary of the LORD in the midst of it. [11]This shall be for the Ezek 44:15–16
consecrated priests, the sons[t] of Zadok, who kept my charge, who
did not go astray when the people of Israel went astray, as the
Levites did. [12]And it shall belong to them as a special portion
from the holy portion of the land, a most holy place, adjoining the
territory of the Levites. [13]And alongside the territory of the priests,
the Levites shall have an allotment twenty-five thousand cubits in
length and ten thousand in breadth. The whole length shall be
twenty-five thousand cubits and the breadth twenty[u] thousand.
[14]They shall not sell or exchange any of it; they shall not alienate Lev 27:10,
this choice portion of the land, for it is holy to the LORD. 28,33

[15]"The remainder, five thousand cubits in breadth and twenty-
five thousand in length, shall be for ordinary use for the city, for
dwellings and for open country. In the midst of it shall be the city;
[16]and these shall be its dimensions: the north side four thousand five Rev 21:15–17

---

orientali usque ad plagam maris, Ruben una. [7]Et iuxta terminum Ruben a plaga orientali usque ad plagam maris, Iudae una. [8]Et iuxta terminum Iudae a plaga orientali usque ad plagam maris oblatio, quam separabitis viginti quinque milibus latitudinis et longitudinis, sicuti singulae partes a plaga orientali usque ad plagam maris; et erit sanctuarium in medio eius. [9]Oblatio, quam separabitis Domino, longitudo viginti quinque milibus et latitudo viginti milibus. [10]His autem est oblatio sacra: sacerdotibus, ad aquilonem viginti quinque milia et ad mare latitudinis decem milia et ad orientem latitudinis decem milia et ad meridiem longitudinis viginti quinque milia; et erit sanctuarium Domini in medio eius. [11]Sacerdotibus consecratis erit, filiis Sadoc, qui custodierunt caeremonias meas et non erraverunt, cum errarent filii Israel, sicut erraverunt Levitae. [12]Et erit eis oblatio de oblatione terrae sanctum sanctorum iuxta terminum Levitarum; [13]sed et Levitis similiter secundum fines sacerdotum, viginti quinque milia longitudinis et latitudinis decem milia, totum in longitudine viginti et quinque milia et in latitudine viginti milia; [14]et non venumdabunt ex eo neque mutabunt, neque transferetur oblatio terrae, quia sanctificata est Domino. [15]Quinque milia autem, quae supersunt in latitudine per viginti quinque milia, profana erunt urbi in habitaculum et in pascua, et erit civitas in medio eius. [16]Et hae mensurae eius: ad

s. Compare 45:1: Heb *ten* **t.** One Ms Gk: Heb *of the sons* **u.** Gk: Heb *ten*

hundred cubits, the south side four thousand five hundred, the east side four thousand five hundred, and the west side four thousand and five hundred. 17And the city shall have open land: on the north two hundred and fifty cubits, on the south two hundred and fifty, on the east two hundred and fifty, and on the west two hundred and fifty. 18The remainder of the length alongside the holy portion shall be ten thousand cubits to the east, and ten thousand to the west, and it shall be alongside the holy portion. Its produce shall be food for the workers of the city. 19And the workers of the city, from all the tribes of Israel, shall till it. 20The whole portion which you shall set apart shall be twenty-five thousand cubits square, that is, the holy portion together with the property of the city.

21"What remains on both sides of the holy portion and of the property of the city shall belong to the prince. Extending from the twenty-five thousand cubits of the holy portion to the east border, and westward from the twenty-five thousand cubits to the west border, parallel to the tribal portions, it shall belong to the prince. The holy portion with the sanctuary of the temple in its midst, 22and the property of the Levites and the property of the city,[v] shall be in the midst of that which belongs to the prince. The portion of the prince shall lie between the territory of Judah and the territory of Benjamin.

23"As for the rest of the tribes: from the east side to the west, Benjamin, one portion. 24Adjoining the territory of Benjamin, from the east side to the west, Simeon, one portion. 25Adjoining the territory of Simeon, from the east side to the west, Issachar, one portion. 26Adjoining the territory of Issachar, from the east

---

plagam septentrionalem quingenti et quattuor milia et ad plagam meridianam quingenti et quattuor milia et ad plagam orientalem quingenti et quattuor milia et ad plagam occidentalem quingenti et quattuor milia. 17Erunt autem pascua civitatis ad aquilonem ducenti quinquaginta et ad meridiem ducenti quinquaginta et ad orientem ducenti quinquaginta et ad mare ducenti quinquaginta. 18Quod autem reliquum fuerit in longitudine iuxta oblationem sacram, decem milia ad orientem et decem milia ad occidentem, erunt iuxta oblationem sacram, et erunt fruges eius in panem his, qui serviunt civitati. 19Servientes autem civitati operabuntur ex omnibus tribubus Israel. 20Tota oblatio viginti quinque milium, per viginti quinque milia: in quadrum; separabitis oblationem sacram una cum possessione civitatis. 21Quod autem reliquum fuerit, principis erit, ex utraque parte oblationis sacrae et possessionis civitatis, e regione viginti quinque milium oblationis usque ad terminum orientalem, sed et ad mare e regione viginti quinque milium usque ad terminum maris secundum partes tribuum, principis erit. Et erit oblatio sacra et sanctuarium templi in medio eius, 22segregata a possessione Levitarum et a possessione civitatis in medio partium principis: inter terminum Iudae et inter terminum Beniamin erit possessio principis. 23Et reliquis tribubus: a plaga orientali usque ad plagam occidentalem, Beniamin una. 24Et iuxta terminum Beniamin a plaga orientali usque ad plagam occidentalem, Simeon una. 25Et iuxta terminum Simeonis a plaga orientali usque ad plagam occidentalem, Issachar una. 26Et iuxta terminum Issachar a plaga orientali usque ad plagam occidentalem, Zabulon una. 27Et iuxta terminum

v. Cn: Heb *and from the property of the Levities and from the property of the city*

side to the west, Zebulun, one portion. [27]Adjoining the territory of
Zebulun, from the east side to the west, Gad, one portion. [28]And
adjoining the territory of Gad to the south, the boundary shall run
from Tamar to the waters of Meribath-kadesh, thence along the
Brook of Egypt to the Great Sea. [29]This is the land which you
shall allot as an inheritance among the tribes of Israel, and these
are their several portions, says the Lord God.

The new Jerusalem

[30]"These shall be the exits of the city: On the north side, which is Jer 3:17
to be four thousand five hundred cubits by measure, [31]three gates, Joel 3:21 Zech 2:10
the gate of Reuben, the gate of Judah, and the gate of Levi, the Rev 2:13
gates of the city being named after the tribes of Israel. [32]On the Rev 21:12–13
east side, which is to be four thousand five hundred cubits, three
gates, the gate of Joseph, the gate of Benjamin, and the gate of
Dan. [33]On the south side, which is to be four thousand five
hundred cubits by measure, three gates, the gate of Simeon, the
gate of Issachar, and the gate of Zebulun. [34]On the west side,
which is to be four thousand five hundred cubits, three gates,[w] the
gate of Gad, the gate of Asher, and the gate of Naphtali. [35]The
circumference of the city shall be eighteen thousand cubits. And Is 1:26
the name of the city henceforth shall be, The Lord is there."

48:30–35. As a sort of appendix, Ezekiel depicts the city as being a perfect square with three gates on each side, one for each of the twelve tribes of Israel.

The new capital will have a new name. Ezekiel is probably playing with the sound of the words: *Yerusalaim*, which could be taken as meaning "City of the god Salem", will become *Yehu-Samah*, "The Lord is there", or else "here". Anyway, what is important is the meaning of the sentence that brings the book to a close: "The Lord is here", for it sums up Ezekiel's message: the glory of God, which left the temple and the city and stayed with the exiles in Babylon, will abide forever in the renewed and hallowed city.

Zabulon a plaga orientali usque ad plagam maris, Gad una. [28]Et iuxta terminum Gad ad plagam austri in meridiem, erit finis de Thamar usque ad aquas Meribathcades, ad torrentem usque ad mare Magnum. [29]Haec est terra, quam mittetis in sortem tribubus Israel, et hae partitiones earum, ait Dominus Deus. [30]Et hi egressus civitatis: a plaga septentrionali, cuius mensura quingenti et quattuor milia, [31]portae civitatis in nominibus tribuum Israel: portae tres a septentrione, porta Ruben una, porta Iudae una, porta Levi una. [32]Et ad plagam orientalem quingentorum et quattuor milium, portae tres: porta Ioseph una, porta Beniamin una, porta Dan una. [33]Et ad plagam meridianam, cuius mensura quingenti et quattuor milia, portae tres: porta Simeonis una, porta Issachar una, porta Zabulon una. [34]Et ad plagam occidentalem quingentorum et quattuor milium, portae tres: porta Gad una, porta Aser una, porta Nephthali una. [35]Per circuitum decem et octo milia, et nomen civitatis ex illa die: Dominus ibidem».

w. One Ms Gk Syr: Heb *their gates three*

DANIEL

Introduction

This book is called the "book of Daniel" because he is the protagonist in its narratives and because it contains visions that Daniel himself recounted or set down in writing (cf. Dan 7:1; 12:4). In this sense it is like other prophetical books that record the oracles of the prophet to whom the work is attributed (cf. Is 1:2; Jer 30:2; Ezek 24:3; etc.).

In the Christian Bible, the book of Daniel is the fourth of the major prophets. In Greek translations, where it actually appears (alongside Isaiah, Jeremiah and Ezekiel) depends on the particular version; in the Vulgate, it comes after Ezekiel, because Daniel is a prophet of the exile period. But in the Hebrew Bible, Daniel figures among the "Writings", coming after the book of Esther and before those of Ezra and Nehemiah. The reason for this is that when the book of Daniel was redacted, the group of books known as "the Prophets" had already been assembled and "closed"; that group included the earlier prophets, that is to say, those who recounted the history of the chosen people from the time that they entered the promised land up to the time of the exile (Joshua–Kings), and the later prophets, that is, Isaiah, Jeremiah, Ezekiel and the twelve minor prophets. However, in Jewish circles of the fourth century AD, Daniel was revered as a great prophet. And that is how he is seen in the New Testament (cf. Mt 24:15) and in the writings of Flavius Josephus.[1]

The Greek and Latin versions of the book give us a more extensive text than that in the Hebrew Bible: the former contain the psalm of Azariah and the song of the three young men in the fiery furnace (*3:1–68*), and the story of Susanna (chap. 13) and those of Bel and the dragon (chap. 14), figures whom the Babylonians regarded as living gods. Jews and Protestants consider those passages to be apocryphal, but the Catholic Church defined them as canonical at the Council of Trent; therefore, Catholics call them "deuterocanonical" parts of Daniel.

1. STRUCTURE AND CONTENT

The book of Daniel contains two distinct types of accounts—those in which a narrator tells a story about Daniel (chaps. 1–6; 13–14), and those in which Daniel himself reports or writes down his visions (chaps. 7–12). Given this

1. *Antiquitates iudaicae*, 10, 11, 7.

fact, and following the way the contents are arranged in the Greek codexes and in the Vulgate, the book can be divided into three parts:

1. DANIEL AND HIS COMPANIONS AT THE COURT OF BABYLON (1:1—6:28). The book opens with a chapter that acts as an introduction to the whole work (1:1–21) and that tells how Daniel and three companions enter the service of King Nebuchadnezzar but refrain from eating any food prepared for the king's table, and how God gives them great learning and understanding (Daniel, specifically, has the ability to interpret visions and dreams: cf. 1:17). Then, as if to confirm what chapter 1 has said, it records how Daniel interpreted Nebuchadnezzar's dream about the great image or statue (2:1–49). David knew the dream through divine inspiration and without the king telling him the content of it. Daniel interprets it as having to do with the end of time. (Curiously, from the start of 2:4b to the end of chapter 7, which contains Daniel's first vision, the text is in Aramaic.) The next story is about Daniel's companions (chaps. 3–4). Because they refuse to adore a golden statue put up by the king they are thrown into a fiery furnace, where they sing canticles of praise to the Lord, without coming to any harm; then the king acknowledges the God of the Jews. Later, Daniel interprets another dream of Nebuchadnezzar's about a tree hewn down; this dream has to do with the king and when the interpretation proves to be true, Nebuchadnezzar blesses and praises God the Most High (4:4–37). After this, at the court of Belshazzar (Nebuchadnezzar's son and successor according to this account), Daniel interprets the meaning of words written on the wall by a mysterious hand; as a reward, the king, who will die that very night, showers him with honours (chap. 5). Finally, when Darius the Mede (who, according to the book, succeeds Belshazzar to the throne), is thinking of putting Daniel in charge of the whole kingdom, the king's ministers urge their master to make a law that Daniel cannot obey—a law to worship no god other than the king himself. Daniel is thrown into a lions' den, but he emerges unscathed—and then Darius, too, acknowledges Daniel's God (5:31—6:28).

2. DANIEL'S DREAMS AND VISIONS (7:1—12:13). This part recounts four visions seen by Daniel. The first is introduced briefly by a narrator who sets it in the first year of Belshazzar's reign and says that Daniel himself set it down in writing (7:1). It is the vision of the four beasts that emerge from the sea, and in which "one like a son of man" comes and is given an everlasting dominion; the vision supplies its own interpretation: the four beasts stand for four empires, and in the end the saints of the Most High receive the kingdom (7:2–28). The second vision, narrated by Daniel himself, also took place in the reign of Belshazzar (8:1–27). The text reverts to Hebrew here, as it was at the start of the book, and it stays in Hebrew until the end of the visions. Daniel sees

a ram being attacked by a he-goat; the goat has a horn which, when it is broken, produces four more horns and a little horn (Antiochus IV) which wages war against God. Daniel is given the interpretation of this vision by Gabriel: the little horn will be destroyed, and then the end will come. The third vision, also narrated by Daniel, takes place in the time of Darius the Mede (9:1–27) and it comes to Daniel when he is studying the book of Jeremiah to discover how long the exile will last, and when he is praying to God to forgive the sins of the people. Gabriel tells him the meaning of the seventy years that Jeremiah spoke about: they are seventy weeks of years and they will come to an end after the city and sanctuary are destroyed and the "desolator" comes. The redactor of the book sets the fourth vision of the book in the third year of the reign of Cyrus the Persian (10:1). Daniel tells how he sees, first, a man clothed in linen who tells him what is going to happen in the wars between the kings of the north (the Seleucids) and those of the south (the Lagids), and how a "contemptible person" (Antiochus IV) will cause all sorts of affliction to the holy land, but that he, too, will meet his end—which will coincide with the coming of Michael to save the people of God, and with the resurrection of the dead. After this, Daniel sees two other persons: the man clothed in linen tells them when all the events in the vision will come to an end (chaps. 10–12).

3. OTHER STORIES CONCERNING DANIEL (13:1—14:42). These last two chapters, which are to be found only in the Greek versions (and later on in the Latin) contain three stories about Daniel told by a narrator, in which we see the prophet in action against wicked Jewish judges and against the idolatry practised by pagans. The first, which is not in its chronological place, is about Susanna who, because she does not yield to the lust of two old men, judges, is accused of adultery and condemned to death; but Daniel saves her by exposing the judges' deceit (chap. 13). The other two stories are set in Babylon in the time of Cyrus the Great. First, Daniel exposes the priests of Bel for making out that their idol eats the food set before it (14:1–22); then he slays a dragon, which the Babylonians venerated as a living God (14:23–27).

The Babylonians, angered by both these things, throw Daniel into the lions' den; when he is in the den, the prophet Habakkuk is carried from Judea by an angel, to bring him food (14:31–39); and when, after seven days, the king finds that Daniel is still alive, he takes him out of the den and praises the God of Daniel (14:40–42).

Thus, in the first part of the book we see Daniel, a devout Jew, endowed by God with insight enabling him to interpret visions and dreams that immediately come true; the second records the revelation received by Daniel about the End; and, in the third, he unmasks the evil intentions of men and the emptiness of idolatry—temptations that never seem to go away.

2. COMPOSITION AND HISTORICAL BACKGROUND

The final stages of the editing of the book saw the inclusion of material from different sources and periods concerning Daniel and his fellow exiles. This can be deduced from the variety of narrative forms (stories and visions), the fact that different episodes concentrate on different aspects of the prophet (interpreter of dreams, administrator, seer), and, of course, from the fact that the book has passages in three languages (Hebrew, Aramaic and Greek). It all leads one to ask: Who was Daniel, really, and how did the book come to be written?

Ezekiel mentions a wise and righteous man called Daniel (a name meaning "God is my judge") in the same breath as Job and Noah (cf. Ezek 14:14, 20); his wisdom is proverbial (Ezek 28:3). In an Ungarit text of the fourteenth century BC, there is a king called Daniel who judges the causes of widows and protects orphans. In ancient Israel we know of a number of people with the name—a son of David, according to 1 Chronicles 3:1; and one of the returned exiles (cf. Ezra 8:2; Neh 10:7). It is not easy, therefore, to identify through other sources the Daniel who is the protagonist of this book.

How the stories about Daniel came to be written (Daniel 1–6)

Set in Babylon during the period of the exile, these stories reflect the situation of the Jews in the eastern diaspora during the fifth to third centuries BC. In them we find an exhortation to the Jews to stay true to their religion and to worship their God and none other, even if there are obstacles in the way—even if it means their death. At the same time, these chapters show that it was possible and indeed desirable for Jews to be integrated into pagan society and to enter the service of the kings of other nations—and possible, too, for pagan kings to acknowledge and worship the God of Israel. In these stories, which could be called "moral tales", Daniel is depicted as a foreigner (in this case a Jew) who achieves success at the royal court. In this sense, it is the story of Joseph in Egypt (cf. Gen 41) all over again, or that of Esther at the court of King Ahasu-erus (Esther 2). The fact that the names of kings and the line of succession are given in the book of Daniel does not mean that the stories are meant to be historical; these references are there to set the scene. It was not in the third year of Jehoiakim (608–598), but rather in 597 that Nebuchadnezzar took Jerusalem, sacked the temple and led the king away into captivity. Daniel 5 says that Belshazzar was the son and successor of Nebuchadnezzar: he was in fact the son of that king's fourth successor, Nabonid (555–539) and never became king, but simply governor of Babylon before the country was conquered by Cyrus of Persia in 539. As regards Darius the Mede (mentioned in 6:1), no one knows who he was; in fact, when Cyrus conquered Babylon he had already overcome the Medes; in the book of Daniel, however, the empire of the Medes seems a continuation of the

Babylonian empire and to have come before the Persian empire, in such a way that, with the Greek empire that came later, we get four empires, symbolized by the four metals in the statue of Nebuchadnezzar's dream (cf. 2:31–45) or the four beasts in Daniel's vision (cf. 7:2–7). Besides, it could not be true that Daniel spent some seventy-five years at the court of Babylon—from the time of Nebuchadnezzar to "the first year of King Cyrus" (1:21). Therefore, there is every reason to think that the stories about Daniel at the court of Babylon are not specifically related to the actual kings mentioned: the author is relying on vague memories about kings in the distant past.

Each of the various stories is an independent item, even though they are linked in some way by the chronological sequence of the kings or by vague overlaps, cross-references and allusions between them (cf. 5:11–12 and 4:8–9). This implies that what interested the final redactor of the book was to show how God helped Daniel and his companions to have successful careers in those kingdoms and how their respective kings (Babylonian, Medean and Persian) came to acknowledge the God of Israel.

The writing up of the visions and revelations received by Daniel

It must have been later, availing of the same "Daniel", this time an interpreter of dreams (2:31–45) and a seer (chaps. 7–12), that the announcements of the coming of the kingdom of God and the end of time were composed. The interpretation of Nebuchadnezzar's dream about the statue obviously refers to the wars between the Lagids of Egypt and the Seleucids of Syria during the course of the third century BC. The visions in chapters 7–12 come to an end with the persecution of Anthiochus IV Epiphanes who profaned the temple of Jerusalem, set up a statue of Zeus Olympus there and proscribed Jewish religious rites (8:11–14; 9:26; 11:31–32). This indicates that the visions were written down sometime prior to the year 164 (the year when Judas Maccabeus recovered the temple and purified it, and the year, too, when Antiochus IV died: cf. 1 Mac 6:1–13; 2 Mac 9:1–29)—events which the book of Daniel does not mention. The four visions have to do with that period of violence and persecution, and announce its end; they belong to the literary genre of "apocalyptic writing" insofar as they contain the revelation (*apokalypsis*, in Greek) of secret plans of God, and of God's ultimate victory over the powers of this world at some point in the future; these powers will be toppled and the kingdom of God will be established.

"Apocalyptic writing" is really an extension of the oracular style used by the prophets, although it has unique features in terms of both language and content. These include: a) the use of pseudepigraphy, that is, making a famous person from the past the receiver and transmitter of the revelation—in this case, Daniel; b) going right back to the source of evils and showing the history of evil up to the present time in a schematic way: in the book of Daniel the story starts with the exile and then moves forward through four empires, each worse than its predecessor; c) the announcement of the end of the world and of time (which are dominated by evil forces) and the establishment of a kingdom of God in which the just will partake: according to Daniel's fourth vision, those who have already died will obtain a share in that kingdom by awaking to eternal life (cf. 2:31–45).

Each vision and its interpretation is structured more or less in the same way, but they are not a discrete linear series: they overlap one another. So, it is possible that there were originally a number of independent units. However, they all have Daniel as the seer, and all of them have to do with the same events—the end of the Seleucid period.

The connexion of the prophecies with the stories in the first part of the book is established by setting the prophecies in the times of the same four kings and in the same order—Nebuchadnezzar (2:31–45), Belshazzar (7:1), Darius the Mede (9:1) and Cyrus king of Persia (10:1). This suggests that the author or collector of the visions was aware of the Daniel stories, and arranged the visions in the same chronology in order to make the book more systematic. The sudden change from Hebrew to Aramaic in 2:4b, and the reversion to Hebrew in 8:1, does not break the continuity of the narrative, because the Aramaic section includes stories about Daniel as well as the first of the visions, and that vision is closely connected with the one that follows (which is in Hebrew). Both visions happen in the same reign (that of Belshazzar), and the first is referred to in the second (cf. 8:1). The best explanation available at present as to why these two languages are in the book is that the original nucleus of the book was in Aramaic (consisting of stories about Daniel and the first vision without any reference to Antiochus IV; cf. 7:8, 24–26), and that it was later filled out with the Hebrew parts and the first vision altered somewhat (retaining the Aramaic) to bring it into line with the content of the visions. Another explanation, that the entire book was written in Aramaic or Hebrew and that, later on, it was translated in part into the other language, is less convincing.

The sections in Greek

These sections show signs of having been composed at a later period, and they could have been added when the book was being translated into Greek, even though they already existed independently in Hebrew or Aramaic, as can be deduced from a linguistic analysis of the text. The Greek text of the Septuagint is markedly different from the Masoretic text, in *3:8*–6:27, and this suggests that there was another, different, Hebrew-Aramaic text in existence, which was used as the basis of that Greek translation; however, we have no way of knowing what that text might have contained.

There is a Greek text later than that of the Septuagint; this is known as the Theodotion text; it is much closer to the Masoretic text, and although it, too, contains the passages that are conserved only in Greek, it does not have them in the same order as that given in the Septuagint (which the Vulgate Latin follows). Thus, the Theodotion codexes put the story of Susanna at the start of the book, maybe because it has to do with the time when Daniel was a young man. There are interesting differences between the Theodotion and Septuagint versions: the latter is more severely critical of the elders; the former puts more emphasis on Susanna's integrity and her rescue. The last two stories in the Greek versions (Bel; the dragon) are a sort of satire on idolatry.

3. MESSAGE

The message of the book of Daniel is easier to read if one takes account of the situation of the Jews at the time when the book was being assembled. Although the exile was over and many Jews had returned to their homeland, Judea was under the control of foreign masters from the time of the Babylonians onwards. The Greeks replaced the Persians throughout the region, and the successors of Alexander the Great were active in trying to Hellenize their territories. The first Greek overlords of Judea were the Ptolemies of Egypt; these were replaced in 198 BC by the Seleucid Greeks (whose base was Syria). The Seleucid king Antiochus IV proscribed the practice of the Jewish religion and the persecution that took place during his reign produced many martyrs; some self-seeking Jews collaborated with the Seleucid authorities to achieve the Hellenization of Judea. Antiochus went as far as to erect a statue of Zeus in the temple of Jerusalem. Where, one might have asked, is the glory of the God of Israel? There was no sign of any change for the better: what was God doing for his people? Judea had been under foreign dominion for ages, and seemingly would go on being so: what were faithful Israelites supposed to do?

The author of the book of Daniel offers an answer to these questions. The stories about Daniel provide a theological insight into God's supremacy over the rulers of this world, and they show how God rewards those who are faithful. At the same time, the book enacts the meaning of Daniel's visions: the establishment of God's power and sovereignty over all the nations, for the sake of his chosen people, is set in the near future; this hope will sustain the commitment of those who have remained faithful. These are the most important aspects of the author's understanding of God, and of his teaching.

The God of Israel is the only God

Throughout the book, God is called the Most High, the God of heaven, and he is repeatedly found to have the destinies of men and nations in his hands, and to judge all things rightly.

In the stories of Daniel it is made clear that God bestows kingdoms on those whom he chooses and puts monarchs on their thrones, or removes them, as he so wills. This can be seen in the story of Nebuchadnezzar when the king loses his reason and is cast out and has to live among beasts until God restores his wits (cf. 4:28–37); we can see it, too, when Belshazzar unexpectedly dies as punishment for his pride (5:30). Moreover, by means of the dreams and visions that Daniel interprets, God reveals to kings that he is lord of all the world (cf. chaps. 2, 4 and 5). And he manifests his power by miraculously preserving from death those who trust in him, like the three young men in the furnace, and Daniel in the lions' den (cf. chaps. 3 and 6). These wondrous divine actions cause pagan kings to acknowledge and proclaim the God of the Jews as the Most High God, and to treat Daniel and his companions with honour and respect (cf. 2:46–49; *3:1–10*; 4:37; 5:23; 6:24–28).

These insights on the nature of God are combined and brought to life at crucial moments in the history of the persecution of the people as it is depicted in Daniel's visions. The succession of human empires is part of a grander divine plan to establish the kingdom of God. Although those empires have their power and glory, as symbolized in the metals of the statue in Nebuchadnezzar's dream (2:31–43) or by the ferocity of the beasts (7:4–7; 8:1–11), their dominance is something transitory that has its place in God's plans. Those plans will be implemented without man's help (cf. 2:44–45); it is God's express desire that dominion shall be given over to his saints (cf. 7:13–14, 27) and that powers hostile to him shall be destroyed (cf. 8:25; 11:45); he will save those who stay true to him by raising them from the dead to enjoy everlasting life (cf. 12:1–4).

At the end of the book (chap. 13), the story of Susanna makes it clear that no one will go unpunished for his wickedness, not even if he is a judge of Israel; for God is the Judge and Saviour of those who are treated unjustly and he will cause his justice to shine forth. Only he is the living God; idols are worthy of derision, as the stories of Bel and the dragon show (chap. 14).

God reveals his plans

In the stories about Daniel in the first part of the book, we see how, by giving Daniel the ability to interpret visions and dreams, God makes his purposes known to kings; everything he plans happens, inexorably, in regard both to Nebuchadnezzar (cf. 4:34) and to Belshazzar (5:30).

In Daniel's visions, which are designed to reveal God's intentions in times of crisis and persecution, God reveals what is going to happen in the end and how his word will find fulfilment. Now, divine revelation is given to Daniel not only by imbuing him with wisdom and understanding, but through heavenly mediators, angels such as Gabriel (7:16; 8:15–16; 9:21; 10:20; 12:5–13), who explain the meaning of the prophet's visions or inner experiences, as also the meaning of Scripture, specifically passages in the book of Jeremiah (cf. chap. 9). This range of testimonies—visions, angels, Scripture etc.—helps to show that divine revelation is reliable and that what it says about the future will be borne out by events. And yet the word of revelation is something mysterious; it has to be kept sealed, hidden, as it were (cf. 12:5–13), for it is accessible only through faith in God and in his power.

A message of hope

The strongest feeling that the book of Daniel provokes in the reader is one of hope in God. Even when the situation seems impossible, God comes to the rescue—for example, if someone is put into a fiery furnace (3:8–33) or a lions' den (6:17–29). This means that the persecution instigated by Antiochus, which has gone beyond all previous extremes, will come to an end: God will rescue his people (cf. 7:27; 8:23–26; 9:25–27; 12:1). God will bring deliverance by demolishing the powers of evil (symbolized by this king who makes war on God) and by establishing the kingdom of the saints. Daniel emphasizes the first aspect more (the suppression of the powers of evil) but he does allow us to glimpse ultimate victory: "seventy years are decreed … to finish the transgression, to put an end to sin, and to atone for iniquity, to bring in everlasting righteousness" (9:24).

Salvation will come not only to those who are alive when the end of time comes but also to those who died faithful to God (for example, Daniel himself), for at that time the dead will rise, "some to everlasting life, and some to shame and everlasting contempt" (12:2). This is a hope that the author of the book cherishes (cf. 12:13) and he wants the reader to have it, too.

The days of oppression and violence inflicted by tyrants are numbered, and the end is in sight: Daniel works it all out symbolically to show that in a short time it will all be over (cf. 9:27). This prospect of the end being near helps to increase a sense of hope. This hope is grounded in past events which are presented as prophecy (for example, the fall of the great empires; battles between Syrians and Greeks) that has been fulfiled.

A call to faithfulness

The conduct of Daniel and his companions at the court of Babylon provides a model for Jews living away from the promised land, in the diaspora. Daniel has no problem with working for the kings of the various empires, making available to them his God-given talents—the ability to interpret dreams and visions, his skill as an administrator, his wisdom and learning. And the kings appreciate him. But for Daniel and his companions the demands of their religion are the first priority—both the rules about which food is clean and which not (cf. 1:1–21) and the commandment to obey no god but the Lord, even if that means putting one's life at risk (cf. chaps. 2 and 6). Daniel's behaviour in Babylon sets an example also for Jews in Palestine when they encounter persecution. That persecution, the book says, did not happen because the people were unfaithful, but because the king in his pride took issue with God and suppressed the practice of the Jewish religion (cf. 8:10–12; 11:30, 36)—and he was abetted by some Jews who turned their back on the holy Covenant and let themselves be seduced by flattery (cf. 11:23, 32); the situation was similar to what happened to Daniel and his companions: envious fellow-citizens were largely responsible for the charges brought against them (cf. 3:8–12; 6:4–10).

Setting Daniel as a model, the book also calls on the reader to seek forgiveness for the people's transgressions against the Law of Moses (cf. 9:4–19); all are to blame, but particularly those who are more familiar with the Law, that is, the wise; these will suffer more in the persecution, but it will be a form of purification with a view to the end of time (cf. 11:33–35). This is the sort of faithfulness that the book of Daniel appeals for, rather than the armed rebellion that finds favour in the book of the Maccabees.

4. THE BOOK OF DANIEL IN THE LIGHT OF THE NEW TESTAMENT

In terms of when it was written, Daniel is the last prophetical book in the Old Testament, and therefore the closest to the New. In this sense we can say that Daniel focuses the hopes of the Jewish people towards Jesus Christ, and disposes them to welcome him as the Messiah who will definitively establish the kingdom of God.

Jesus, in fact, calls himself "the Son of man" (cf. Mk 8:31; 14:62), which is the title that Daniel gives the mediator of salvation (cf. Dan 7:13); and he proclaims that he has brought the Kingdom of God (cf. Mt 12:28), which is repeatedly promised in the book of Daniel (cf. 2:4; 7:27). Also, when Jesus speaks about the end of time he uses signs and expressions found in the book of Daniel: for example, see his reference to "the desolating sacrifice spoken of by the prophet Daniel" (Mt 24:15). Although Jesus speaks of the Kingdom of God as something already present, he also teaches (particularly in the parables of the sower etc.: Mt 13:1–43) that the Kingdom of God is a seed and it will grow over the course of time until it reaches its climax when the Son of man will judge the world (cf. Mt 25:31–46).

In the New Testament the book of Revelation is remarkably similar to that of Daniel, in the sense that future events are revealed in visions to the author, John, too—visions about the end of time (cf. Rev 1:1–2), which will see the complete establishment of God's kingdom, symbolized in the New Jerusalem that comes down from heaven (Rev 21–22). The book of Revelation uses much of the imagery and language of Daniel and develops it from a Christian perspective; one could say that it would be almost impossible to understand the Revelation to John if one did not take account of the Daniel background. Both books use the same literary genre ("revelation") to spread a message of hope;

in both we see God calling on his people to be faithful—at two different points in salvation history. The author of the book of Revelation, however, sets out from the death and resurrection of Christ—events whereby God's irreversible triumph over the forces of evil (symbolized by the Beast and his false prophet) and even over death has taken place already (cf. Rev 19:1–10).

The Gospel and Jesus' promise about his second coming shed a great deal of light on the book of Daniel and its imagery as regards the end of time and the Last Judgment. The risen Christ seated at the right of his Father is the Son of man to whom everlasting power and dominion has been given. At the end of time he will come again to judge the living and the dead. Meanwhile, the Church, by her preaching and her fidelity in the midst of trials, bears witness to the world about God's absolute sovereignty and about the kingdom of Christ, a kingdom of justice, truth and peace. That testimony will enable all to see God for who he is.

The book of Daniel has been referred to often in Christian tradition—witness how often Daniel is depicted in Christian art (especially Daniel in the lions' den), and in the writings of the Fathers. Commentaries by St Hippolytus, St Jerome, St Ephraem and Theodoret of Cyrus have come down to us; others we know of only through references—those of Cyril of Alexandria and Theodore of Mopsuestia. Due to its apocalyptic content, a whole range of interpretations of the book have been put forward. The Church's liturgy uses it, for example, in Cycle B at the end of the liturgical year (32nd Sunday in Ordinary Time) and on the Solemnity of Christ the King. And the Church recommends the canticle of the three young men (*3:35–68*) for thanksgiving to God, both in the Divine Office and after the celebration of Mass.

PART ONE

Daniel and his companions at the court of Babylon*

1. DANIEL AND HIS COMPANIONS IN THE SERVICE OF NEBUCHADNEZZAR*

2 Kings 24:1–2 **Arrival at the court**
2 Chron 36:5–7 1 [1]In the third year of the reign of Jehoiakim king of Judah,
Ezra 1:7 Gen 10:10 Nebuchadnezzar king of Babylon came to Jerusalem and
besieged it. [2]And the Lord gave Jehoiakim king of Judah into his

---

***1:1—6:29.** These chapters deal with Daniel at the court of the kings of Babylon—Nebuchadnezzar (1:1—4:37), Belshazzar (chap. 5) and Darius the Mede (chap. 6). These three reigns, arranged in a line as if they really followed one another, cover the entire period from the start of the Babylonian captivity to the arrival of Cyrus of Persia, who allowed the Jews to return to their homeland (cf. 1:21). The main themes running through these chapters are: 1) divine protection afforded Daniel and his companions; 2) the help that these young Jews render the kings; 3) their faithfulness to the Lord despite trials and ordeals; 4) the acknowledgment of the God of Israel by these pagan kings. In the overall context of the book, these first six chapters introduce the God of Israel and Daniel, who will later receive a revelation about the end of the world. They also provide the Jews of the Diaspora with a model of how a Jew in a pagan society ought to live. For that reason, the Church will read them with interest because she lives in the midst of the world and "realizes that she is truly linked with mankind and its history by the deepest of bonds" (Vatican II, *Gaudium et spes*, 1).

***1:1—4:37.** Nebuchadnezzar was the king who was responsible for the deportation of the Jews, and the most famous of the Babylonian kings. That may explain why he gets so much space in the book: Daniel interprets two dreams for him (2:1–49; 4:1–37), and the king three times acknowledges the God of Israel (2:46–49; 4:1–3; 4:37). Each episode in these chapters is an independent unit, and they all combine to show the qualities that Daniel and these other Jews had: they were accomplished people, successful in life; at the same time they stayed true to God, even when their religion was put to the test.

[1] [1]Anno tertio regni Ioachim regis Iudae venit Nabuchodonosor rex Babylonis Ierusalem et obsedit eam; [2]et tradidit Dominus in manu eius Ioachim regem Iudae et partem vasorum domus Dei, et

hand, with some of the vessels of the house of God; and he
brought them to the land of Shinar, to the house of his god, and
placed the vessels in the treasury of his god. 3 Then the king
commanded Ashpenaz, his chief eunuch, to bring some of the
people of Israel, both of the royal family and of the nobility,
4 youths without blemish, handsome and skilful in all wisdom,
endowed with knowledge, understanding learning, and competent
to serve in the king's palace, and to teach them the letters and
language of the Chaldeans. 5 The king assigned them a daily 2 Kings
portion of the rich food which the king ate, and of the wine which 25:29–30
he drank. They were to be educated for three years, and at the end
of that time they were to stand before the king. 6 Among these
were Daniel, Hananiah, Misha-el, and Azariah of the tribe of
Judah. 7 And the chief of the eunuchs gave them names: Daniel he
called Belteshazzar, Hananiah he called Shadrach, Misha-el he
called Meshach, and Azariah he called Abednego.

1:1–21. This chapter acts as an introduction to the whole book. It tells us who Daniel was and how he and his companions became members of Nebuchadnezzar's household. The dates given at the start and finish of the chapter (vv. 1, 21) show that Daniel was connected with the whole period of the exile.

1:1–7. The third year of the reign of Jehoiakim was 606 BC, but the siege and sack of Jerusalem by Nebuchadnezzar took place in 597. The sacred writer is content to use vague references like this; and it may well be that he is advancing the date of the deportation because that is more in line with seventy years—the length of the exile according to Jeremiah 25:11. The Hebrew word translated as "eunuch" (v. 3) is *sārîs*, which could refer to any palace officials or guards, not necessarily eunuchs. The country of Shinar is Babylonia, which is how the Greek version translates the name. It was quite common in the ancient East for a victorious king to appoint state officials from among the noblemen of subject peoples; Jewish officials, for example, could be very useful in dealings with Jewish communities.

1:8–16. The sacred writer extends Jewish regulations about food (cf. 1 Mac 1:62) to wine, to show that

asportavit ea in terram Sennaar in domum deorum suorum et vasa intulit in domum thesauri deorum
suorum. 3 Et ait rex Asfanaz praeposito eunuchorum suorum, ut introduceret de filiis Israel et de semine
regio et tyrannorum 4 pueros, in quibus nulla esset macula, decoros forma et eruditos omni sapientia,
cautos scientia et doctos disciplina, et qui possent stare in palatio regis, et ut docerent eos litteras et
linguam Chaldaeorum. 5 Et constituit eis rex annonam per singulos dies de cibis suis et de vino, unde
bibebat ipse, ut enutriti tribus annis postea starent in conspectu regis. 6 Fuerunt ergo inter eos de filiis
Iudae Daniel, Ananias, Misael et Azarias. 7 Et imposuit eis praepositus eunuchorum nomina: Danieli
Baltassar et Ananiae Sedrac, Misaeli Misac et Azariae Abdenago. 8 Proposuit autem Daniel in corde
suo, ne pollueretur de mensa regis neque de vino potus eius, et rogavit eunuchorum praepositum, ne

Royal fare—God's servants tested

Jud 12:2 8But Daniel resolved that he would not defile himself* with the
king's rich food, or with the wine which he drank; therefore he
asked the chief of the eunuchs to allow him not to defile himself.
9And God gave Daniel favour and compassion in the sight of the
Gen 39:4,21 Esther 2:9 chief of the eunuchs; 10and the chief of the eunuchs said to Daniel,
"I fear lest my lord the king, who appointed your food and your
drink, should see that you were in poorer condition than the
youths who are of your own age. So you would endanger my head
with the king." 11Then Daniel said to the steward whom the chief
of the eunuchs had appointed over Daniel, Hananiah, Misha-el,
Rev 2:10 and Azariah; 12"Test your servants for ten days; let us be given
vegetables to eat and water to drink. 13Then let our appearance
and the appearance of the youths who eat the king's rich food be
observed by you, and according to what you see deal with your
servants." 14So he hearkened to them in this matter, and tested
them for ten days. 15At the end of ten days it was seen that they
were better in appearance and fatter in flesh than all the youths
who ate the king's rich food. 16So the steward took away their rich
food and the wine they were to drink, and gave them vegetables.

---

keeping to the Jewish law was much better for the youths than eating the king's fare would have been. Besides, to eat and drink at the royal table would have involved eating and drinking things offered to the gods; it would have been a form of communing with pagan gods. As those young men saw it, being good Jews was not incompatible with the performance of duties for which they were trained. Similarly, "to remind a Christian that his life is meaningless unless he obeys God's will does not mean separating him from other men" (St Josemaría Escrivá, *Christ Is Passing By*, 21).

God can afford protection by making use of people's good dispositions; here he causes the chief eunuch to be well-disposed to the Jewish youths (v. 9). Thus, "though often unconscious collaborators with God's will, men can also enter deliberately into the divine plan by their actions, their prayers and their sufferings" (*Catechism of the Catholic Church*, 307).

contaminaretur. 9Dedit autem Deus Danieli gratiam et misericordiam in conspectu principis eunuchorum; 10et ait princeps eunuchorum ad Daniel: «Timeo ego dominum meum regem, qui constituit vobis cibum et potum; qui si viderit vultus vestros macilentiores prae ceteris adulescentibus coaevis vestris, condemnabitis caput meum regi». 11Et dixit Daniel ad custodem, quem constituerat princeps eunuchorum super Daniel, Ananiam, Misael et Azariam: 12«Tenta nos, obsecro, servos tuos diebus decem, et dentur nobis legumina ad vescendum et aqua ad bibendum; 13et videantur in conspectu tuo vultus nostri et vultus puerorum, qui vescuntur cibo regio, et, sicut videris, facies cum servis tuis». 14Qui, audito sermone huiuscemodi, tentavit eos diebus decem. 15Post dies autem decem apparuerunt vultus eorum meliores et corpulentiores prae omnibus pueris, qui vescebantur cibo regio. 16Porro custos tollebat cibaria

The wisdom of the three young men

[17]As for these four youths, God gave them learning and skill in all
letters and wisdom; and Daniel had understanding in all visions and
dreams. [18]At the end of the time, when the king had commanded
that they should be brought in, the chief of the eunuchs brought
them in before Nebuchadnezzar. [19]And the king spoke with them,
and among them all none was found like Daniel, Hananiah, Misha-
el, and Azariah; therefore they stood before the king. [20]And in
every matter of wisdom and understanding concerning which the
king inquired of them, he found them ten times better than all the
magicians and enchanters that were in all his kingdom. [21]And
Daniel continued until the first year of King Cyrus.

Gen 41:12
Dan 8:16; 9:23; 10:1,14; 5:12; 7:1

1 Kings 10:3–4

1:17–21. Athough Daniel and his companions are given a very good Chaldean education, their wisdom comes from God, not from that training (v. 17). It includes the understanding of all things human and, in Daniel's case, the ability to interpret dreams and visions. The king will soon see for himself that Daniel and the Jews have greater wisdom than others, but he does not yet know where it comes from (he will, later: cf. 2:47). But the Jewish or Christian reader of the book does know what the source of this true wisdom is: "God's truth is his wisdom, which commands the whole created order and governs the world (cf. Wis 13:1–9). God, who alone made heaven and earth (cf. Ps 115:15), can alone impart true knowledge of every created thing in relation to himself" (*Catechism of the Catholic Church*, 216).

Summing up the career of these Jewish youths in Babylon, and aware that their wisdom came from the Word of God, St Hippolytus of Rome comments: "It was the Word who gave them wisdom and made them faithful witnesses [to him] in Babylon, so that through them what was worshipped in Babylon would be scorned. Nebuchadnezzar was defeated by three young men whose faith was tested in the fires of the furnace; the holy woman Susanna was delivered from the jaws of death; and the terrible depth of ancient evil was laid bare. These were the victories won by four young men in Babylon; they were beloved of God and nurtured the fear of the Lord in their hearts" (*Commentarium in Danielem*, 1, 11).

et vinum potus eorum dabatque eis legumina. [17]Quattuor autem pueris his dedit Deus scientiam et disciplinam in omni scriptura et sapientia, Danieli autem intellegentiam omnium visionum et somniorum. [18]Completis itaque diebus, post quos dixerat rex, ut introducerentur, introduxit eos praepositus eunuchorum in conspectu Nabuchodonosor. [19]Cumque locutus eis fuisset rex, non sunt inventi de universis tales ut Daniel, Ananias, Misael et Azarias; et steterunt in conspectu regis. [20]Et omne verbum sapientiae et intellectus, quod sciscitatus est ab eis, rex invenit in eis decuplum super cunctos hariolos et magos, qui erant in universo regno eius. [21]Fuit autem Daniel usque ad annum primum Cyri regis.

Gen 41:1–36

2. DANIEL INTERPRETS THE DREAM OF THE STATUE*

The king's impossible demand

2 [1]In the second year of the reign of Nebuchadnezzar, Nebuchadnezzar had dreams; and his spirit was troubled, and his sleep
Dan 4:6; 5:7 left him. [2]Then the king commanded that the magicians, the
enchanters, the sorcerers, and the Chaldeans be summoned, to tell
the king his dreams. So they came in and stood before the king.

***2:1–49.** This whole episode is constructed very well from a literary point of view. Tension is first built up, and then gradually resolved. First, the writer describes a real quandary: the king asks for the impossible; he wants to be told what he dreamt and what the dream means (2:1–12). Daniel prays for God's help and is able to tell the king the content of the dream and its interpretation (2:13–45). Finally, the king acknowledges the God of Daniel (2:46–49). It is now clear that God has indeed given Daniel the power to interpret dreams (cf. 1:17); and by using this gift Daniel has saved the lives of the wise men of Babylon, and the king confesses the "God of gods".

The time given at the start of the chapter (2:1) does not tie in with what the previous chapter implied—about Daniel spending at least three years of Nebuchadnezzar's reign as a trainee before becoming one of the learned men of the kingdom (cf. 1:5, 18, 20). It implies that the author is not interested in historical detail and that he is probably making a collection of existing stories about Daniel as an interpreter of dreams.

2:1–12. In ancient times, dreams were thought to be a channel for divine messages about the future. This passage is reminiscent of the dreams that Joseph interpreted for the pharaoh of Egypt (cf. Gen 41:1–36). Daniel seems to be superior to Joseph, because not only does he interpret the dream but he discovers the dream's content by means of a divine revelation; as the Chaldeans put it, "not a man on earth" could meet the king's demand (2:10–11). "Chaldeans" is one of the many terms used to describe professional astrologers, magicians etc. Outside Babylon, the name was applied to itinerant Mesopotamian soothsayers who tried to make a living by their craft (in fact, the craft is supposed to have originated in that region). The magi admit that only the gods could meet the king's demands (v. 11): this is in fact a clue as to what is going to happen. The Chaldeans are acknowledging that man's intellectual capacity has its limits; cf. John Paul II, *Fides et ratio*, 42.

[2] [1]In anno secundo regni Nabuchodonosor vidit Nabuchodonosor somnium, et conterritus est spiritus eius, et somnus eius fugit ab eo. [2]Praecepit autem rex, ut convocarentur harioli et magi et malefici et Chaldaei et indicarent regi somnia sua; qui cum venissent, steterunt coram rege. [3]Et dixit ad eos rex: «Vidi somnium, et spiritus meus conterritus est, ut intellegat somnium». [4]Responderuntque Chaldaei

3And the king said to them, “I had a dream, and my spirit is
troubled to know the dream.” 4Then the Chaldeans said to the
king,[a] “O king, live for ever! Tell your servants the dream, and we
will show the interpretation.” 5The king answered the Chaldeans,
“The word from me is sure: if you do not make known to me the
dream and its interpretation, you shall be torn limb from limb, and
your houses shall be laid in ruins. 6But if you show the dream and
its interpretation, you shall receive from me gifts and rewards and
great honour. Therefore show me the dream and its interpretation.”
7They answered a second time, “Let the king tell his servants the
dream, and we will show its interpretation.” 8The king answered,
“I know with certainty that you are trying to gain time, because
you see that the word from me is sure 9that if you do not make the
dream known to me, there is but one sentence for you. You have
agreed to speak lying and corrupt words before me till the times
change. Therefore tell me the dream, and I shall know that you
can show me its interpretation.” 10The Chaldeans answered the
king, “There is not a man on earth who can meet the king’s
demand; for no great and powerful king has asked such a thing of
any magician or enchanter or Chaldean. 11The thing that the king Gen 41:16
asks is difficult, and none can show it to the king except the gods,
whose dwelling is not with flesh.”

12Because of this the king was angry and very furious, and
commanded that all the wise men of Babylon be destroyed.

---

regi Aramaice: «Rex, in sempiternum vive! Dic somnium servis tuis, et interpretationem eius indicabimus». 5Et respondens rex ait Chaldaeis: «Sermo recessit a me. Nisi indicaveritis mihi somnium et coniecturam eius, in frusta concidemini, et domus vestrae in sterquilinium ponentur; 6si autem somnium et coniecturam eius narraveritis, praemia et dona et honorem multum accipietis a me. Somnium igitur et interpretationem eius indicate mihi». 7Responderunt secundo atque dixerunt: «Rex somnium dicat servis suis, et interpretationem illius indicabimus». 8Respondit rex et ait: «Certe novi quia tempus redimitis, scientes quod recesserit a me sermo. 9Si ergo somnium non indicaveritis mihi, una est de vobis sententia. Et verbum fallax et deceptione plenum composuistis, ut loquamini mihi, donec tempus pertranseat; somnium itaque dicite mihi, ut sciam quod interpretationem eius loquamini mihi». 10Respondentes ergo Chaldaei coram rege dixerunt: «Non est homo super terram qui sermonem regis possit indicare; quapropter neque regum quisquam magnus et potens verbum huiuscemodi sciscitatur ab omni hariolo et mago et Chaldaeo. 11Sermo enim, quem tu quaeris, rex, gravis est, nec reperietur quisquam qui indicet illum in conspectu regis, exceptis diis, quorum non est cum hominibus conversatio». 12Quo audito, rex in furore et in ira magna praecepit, ut perirent omnes sapientes Babylonis. 13Et egressa sententia, ut sapientes interficerentur, quaerebantur Daniel et socii eius, ut perirent. 14Tunc Daniel interrogavit cum consilio et prudentia Arioch, principem militiae regis, qui egressus fuerat ad interficiendos sapientes Babylonis; 15respondens dixit ad Arioch, qui a rege potestatem acceperat, quam ob causam tam crudelis sententia a facie esset regis egressa. Cum ergo rem indicasset Arioch Danieli, 16Daniel ingressus rogavit regem, ut tempus daret sibi ad solutionem indicandam regi; 17et ingressus est domum suam Ananiaeque, Misaeli et Azariae sociis suis indicavit

a. Heb adds *in Aramaic*, indicating that the text from this point to the end of chapter 7 is in Aramaic

God explains the king's dream to Daniel

[13]So the decree went forth that the wise men were to be slain, and
they sought Daniel and his companions, to slay them. [14]Then Daniel
replied with prudence and discretion to Ari-och, the captain of the
kings guard, who had gone out to slay the wise men of Babylon;
[15]he said to Ari-och, the king's captain, "Why is the decree of the
king so severe?" Then Ari-och made the matter known to Daniel.
[16]And Daniel went in and besought the king to appoint him a
time, that he might show to the king the interpretation.

[17]Then Daniel went to his house and made the matter known to
Gen 24:7 Hananiah, Misha-el, and Azariah, his companions, [18]and told them
to seek mercy of the God of heaven concerning this mystery, so
that Daniel and his companions might not perish with the rest of
the wise men of Babylon. [19]Then the mystery was revealed to
Daniel in a vision of the night. Then Daniel blessed the God of
Neh 9:5 Ps 41:14; heaven. [20]Daniel said:
113,2; 115:18 "Blessed be the name of God for ever and ever.
Job 12:13 Prov 2:6 to whom belong wisdom and might.
Acts 1:7 [21]He changes times and seasons;
Rom 13:1 he removes kings and sets up kings;
Rev 5:12 he gives wisdom to the wise
and knowledge to those who have understanding;
Job 12:22 [22]he reveals deep and mysterious things;
Ps 139:11 1 Cor 2:10 he knows what is in the darkness,
and the light dwells with him.
[23]To thee, O God of my fathers,
I give thanks and praise,
for thou hast given me wisdom and strength,
and hast now made known to me what we asked of thee,
for thou hast made known to us the king's matter."

[24]Therefore Daniel went in to Ari-och, whom the king had
appointed to destroy the wise men of Babylon; he went and said
thus to him, "Do not destroy the wise men of Babylon; bring me
in before the king, and I will show the king the interpretation."

2:13–24. Although Daniel does not seem to have been consulted by the king, he and his companions are going to share the same fate as the Chaldean wise men. It does not make much sense; but what the author wants to show is that there is solidarity between Daniel and those magi, and to prepare the way for Daniel to intervene and save the lives of all of them. The tone of the story is ironic.

Daniel intervenes in three ways—first, with prudence and discretion (vv. 14–16); then, by prayer (vv. 17–23);

Daniel describes the king's dream
25Then Ari-och brought in Daniel before the king in haste, and
said thus to him: "I have found among the exiles from Judah a
man who can make known to the king the interpretation." 26The
king said to Daniel, whose name was Belteshazzar, "Are you able to
make known to me the dream that I have seen and its interpretation?" 27Daniel answered the king, "No wise men, enchanters,
magicians, or astrologers can show to the king the mystery which
the king has asked, 28but there is a God in heaven who reveals 1 Cor 2:10–11
mysteries, and he has made known to King Nebuchadnezzar what Rev 1:1,19; 4:1
will be in the latter days. Your dream and the visions of your head
as you lay in bed are these: 29To you, O king, as you lay in bed
came thoughts of what would be hereafter, and he who reveals
mysteries made known to you what is to be. 30But as for me, not
because of any wisdom that I have more than all the living has this
mystery been revealed to me, but in order that the interpretation
may be made known to the king, and that you may know the
thoughts of your mind.

---

and finally by revealing the dream to the king (vv. 27–45). Daniel acts prudently by going first to the captain of the guard, just as he had done earlier (cf. 1:8–16), and thereby gaining time.

The simple and humble prayer made by Daniel and his companions obtains what the human mind cannot. When God enlightens Daniel in this nocturnal vision he gives him the gift of prophecy, whereas all that the king sees in his dreams are mental pictures (cf. 2:28, 31). Daniel, conscious that he has received that gift, breaks into a prayer of thanksgiving, proclaiming God's sovereignty over the physical world and over the affairs of mankind, and his goodness in answering the prayer of those who believe in him (vv. 20–23). Light is used a symbol (v. 22) to indicate that there are no limits to God's knowledge; it extends even to what will happen in the future.

2:25–35. Daniel claims no personal credit for knowing the content of the king's dream; he makes it plain that God revealed the secret to him; only God knows what will happen in the "latter times" (vv. 27–28). We have entered the area of divine revelation, which is what this book is all about—the world of the End time, which as yet exists only in the mind of God. Our Lord himself will say that "of that day and hour no one knows ..." (Mt 24:36).

negotium, 18ut quaererent misericordiam a facie Dei caeli super sacramento isto et non perirent Daniel et socii eius cum ceteris sapientibus Babylonis. 19Tunc Danieli per visionem nocte mysterium revelatum est, et benedixit Daniel Deo caeli 20et locutus Daniel ait: «Sit nomen Dei benedictum / a saeculo et usque in saeculum, / quia sapientia et fortitudo eius sunt; / 21et ipse mutat tempora et aetates, / transfert atque constituit reges, / dat sapientiam sapientibus / et scientiam intellegentibus disciplinam: / 22ipse revelat profunda et abscondita / et novit in tenebris constituta, / et lux cum eo inhabitat, / 23Tibi,

31"You saw, O king, and behold, a great image. This image,
mighty and of exceeding brightness, stood before you, and its
Ps 118:22 appearance was frightening. 32The head of this image was of fine
Is 8:14 gold, its breast and arms of silver, its belly and thighs of bronze,
Mt 21:42–43 33its legs of iron, its feet partly of iron and partly of clay. 34As you
Lk 20:17–18 looked, a stone was cut out by no human hand, and it smote the
image on its feet of iron and clay, and broke them in pieces; 35then
Ps 1:4 the iron, the clay, the bronze, the silver, and the gold, all together
Rev 20:11 were broken in pieces, and became like the chaff of the summer
threshing floors; and the wind carried them away, so that not a
trace of them could be found. But the stone that struck the image
became a great mountain and filled the whole earth.

Daniel uses the opportunity to lead the king to the true God, the God of heaven, who knows all mysteries.

In line with the thread of the story, Daniel first tells the king about the content of his dream (2:31–35) and then interprets it (*3:13–22*). The king's vision is full of symbolism. In the Bible, statues connote idolatry, insofar as they are graven images (cf. Ex 32), even though the passage does not expressly say that the image is an idol. As one moves from head to feet, the metals used in the statue decrease in value. In contrast with the materials of the statue are the stone and the mountain, symbols of solidity and stability. The interpretation reads the metals as representative of the various kingdoms. This is a classical symbolic image: Hesiod, a Greek historian of the eighth-to-seventh century BC, in his book *Works and Days*, 199–201, had used the very same metals and in the same order to signify periods of history; something similar is to be found in Polybius (*Historia*, 38, 22) and other classical authors. Now, in Daniel's vision, the four metals all appear together, at the same time, so to speak—a sign that, for God, history is all of a piece.

The image with "feet of clay" (vv. 32–33) is often taken as a reminder that human nature is frail and that nevertheless it is endowed with precious gifts from God: "Our Lord and our God: how great you are! It is you who give our life supernatural meaning and divine vitality. For love of your Son, you cause us to say with all our being, with our body and soul: 'He must reign!' And this we do against the background of our weakness, for you know that we are creatures made of clay—and what creatures! Not just feet of clay, but heart and head too" (St Josemaría Escrivá, *Christ Is Passing By*, 181).

Deus patrum meorum, confiteor teque laudo, / quia sapientiam et fortitudinem dedisti mihi / et nunc ostendisti mihi, quae rogavimus te, / quia sermonem regis aperuisti nobis». 24Propterea Daniel, ingressus ad Arioch, quem constituerat rex, ut perderet sapientes Babylonis, sic ei locutus est: «Sapientes Babylonis ne perdas; introduc me in conspectu regis et solutionem regi enarrabo». 25Tunc Arioch festinus introduxit Danielem ad regem et dixit ei: «Inveni hominem de filiis transmigrationis Iudae, qui solutionem regi annuntiet». 26Respondit rex et dixit Danieli, cuius nomen erat Baltassar: «Putasne vere potes mihi indicare somnium, quod vidi, et interpretationem eius?». 27Et respondens

Daniel interprets the king's dream

[36]"This was the dream; now we will tell the king its interpretation.
[37]You, O king, the king of kings, to whom the God of heaven has Ezra 7:12; 1:2
given the kingdom, the power, and the might, and the glory, [38]and Jud 11:7
into whose hand he has given, wherever they dwell, the sons of Jer 27:6
men, the beasts of the field, and the birds of the air, making you

---

2:36–45. Daniel is not being sycophantic by addressing the king as he does in vv. 37–38; he is simply saying that the king has an impressive empire because he has been given it by God, who rules over all things; he wants the king to see that the power and glory that he enjoys are part of God's plans. The other metals (silver, bronze, iron), as one can deduce from the rest of the book, stand for the empires of the Medes, Persians and Greeks, though that interpretation is not perfectly clear because the silver could stand for the empire of the Medes and Persians together. The divided kingdom made of clay and iron is a reference to the Greek empire after the death of Alexander the Great (cf. 11:4) and to the political marriages made between the Seleucid and Lagid Greeks (Antiochus II marrying Bernice; Ptolemy V marrying Cleopatra: cf. 11:6, 17) that failed to bring about unity or union. This passage would have been composed when the Seleucids and Lagids were at loggerheads, and it was against the same background that the prophecy about the end of time seeing the establishment by God of an everlasting kingdom was made (God's action is symbolized by the stone that strikes the image; there is no sign of any human power at work). It does not say here who will be given the kingdom, but in the light of 7:26 and the fact that it says that the kingdom will not be left to another people (v. 44), the implication is that it will be given to faithful Israelites.

The symbol of the stone has a messianic dimension insofar as it is the means by which the everlasting kingdom will be established and the

---

Daniel coram rege ait: «Mysterium, quod rex interrogat, sapientes, magi et harioli et haruspices non queunt indicare regi; [28]sed est Deus in caelo revelans mysteria, qui indicavit tibi, rex Nabuchodonosor, quae ventura sunt in novissimis temporibus. Somnium tuum et visiones capitis tui in cubili tuo huiuscemodi sunt: [29]Tu, rex, cogitare coepisti in strato tuo quid esset futurum post haec; et, qui revelat mysteria, ostendit tibi, quae ventura sunt. [30]Mihi quoque non in sapientia, quae est in me plus quam in cunctis viventibus, sacramentum hoc revelatum est, sed ut interpretatio regi manifesta fieret, et cogitationes mentis tuae scires. [31]Tu, rex, videbas, et ecce statua una grandis: statua illa magna et statura sublimis stabat contra te, et intuitus eius erat terribilis. [32]Huius statuae caput ex auro optimo erat, pectus autem et brachia de argento, porro venter et femora ex aere, [33]tibiae autem ferreae, pedum quaedam pars erat ferrea, quaedam autem fictilis. [34]Videbas ita, donec abscissus est lapis sine manibus et percussit statuam in pedibus eius ferreis et fictilibus et comminuit eos; [35]tunc contrita sunt pariter ferrum, testa, aes, argentum et aurum, et fuerunt quasi folliculus ex areis aestivis, et rapuit ea ventus, nullusque locus inventus est eis; lapis autem, qui percusserat statuam, factus est mons magnus et implevit universam terram. [36]Hoc est somnium; interpretationem quoque eius dicemus coram te, rex. [37]Tu rex regum es, et Deus caeli regnum et fortitudinem et imperium et gloriam dedit tibi; [38]et omnia, in quibus habitant filii hominum et bestiae agri volucresque caeli, dedit in manu tua et te dominum

rule over them all—you are the head of gold. 39After you shall
arise another kingdom inferior to you, and yet a third kingdom of
Dan 7:7; bronze, which shall rule over all the earth. 40And there shall be a
8:5,21; 11:13 fourth kingdom, strong as iron, because iron breaks to pieces and
shatters all things; and like iron which crushes, it shall break and
crush all these. 41And as you saw the feet and toes partly of
potter's clay and partly of iron, it shall be a divided kingdom; but
some of the firmness of iron shall be in it, just as you saw iron
mixed with the miry clay. 42And as the toes of the feet were partly
iron and partly clay, so the kingdom shall be partly strong and

---

previous kingdoms destroyed. There are echoes here of images in other prophetical works and in the psalms. Isaiah speaks of God as a "stone of offence", a stumbling-block for Israel (cf. Is 8:14) and in Psalm 118:22 the people of God are compared to a stone which the builders have rejected and which has become the cornerstone. In the New Testament that stone is Christ, and the kingdom which he ushers in is the Kingdom of God which will be taken from Israel, to be given to another people that will produce fruit (cf. Mt 21:42–43); Christ also says that anyone who falls on that stone will be broken to pieces (cf. Lk 20:17–18). Using this Christological interpretation of the stone, some Fathers interpret the mountain from which the stone comes as being the Blessed Virgin, and the stone cut off "by no human hand" as an image of the conception of Jesus in the Virgin's womb without the involvement of a man: "When Daniel says that the one who inherits the eternal kingdom is *like a son of man*, who can he mean, if not the Lord himself? For he was born of a woman, *like a son of man*, but he showed that his life and power were not of human origin. To say that he is a stone that moves under no external force is a mysterious description: it means that Christ is not the fruit of the work and will of men; he is the fruit of the providence of God, the Father of the universe" (St Justin, *Dialogus cum Tryphone*, 76, 1).

The interpretation of the dream, the message it contains, would interest the reader of the book—but not Nebuchadnezzar, who died centuries earlier. It describes how, after the kingdoms of this world which succeed one another over the course of history, an everlasting kingdom will be established by God himself—a kingdom surpassing any that man could create. A Christian will read this as heralding the Kingdom of Christ, although that will not be an earthly, political kingdom, but a spiritual one, as Jesus will tell Pilate at his trial: "My kingship is not of this world" (Jn 18:36).

universorum constituit: tu es caput aureum. 39Et post te consurget regnum aliud minus te et regnum tertium aliud aereum, quod imperabit universae terrae. 40Et regnum quartum erit robustum velut ferrum; quomodo ferrum comminuit et domat omnia, et sicut ferrum comminuens conteret et comminuet omnia haec. 41Porro quia vidisti pedum et digitorum partem testae figuli et partem ferream, regnum divisum

partly brittle. 43As you saw the iron mixed with miry clay, so they
will mix with one another in marriage,[b] but they will not hold
together, just as iron does not mix with clay. 44And in the days of 2 Sam 7:16
those kings the God of heaven will set up a kingdom which shall Is 60:12 Ezek 4:3; 7:14
never be destroyed, nor shall its sovereignty be left to another Dan 3:90;
people. It shall break in pieces all these kingdoms and bring them 11:36; Mic 4:7
to an end, and it shall stand for ever; 45just as you saw that a stone Lk 1:33,37 1 Cor 15:24
was cut from a mountain by no human hand, and that it broke in Mt 21:42–44
pieces the iron, the bronze, the clay, the silver, and the gold. A
great God has made known to the king what shall be hereafter.
The dream is certain, and its interpretation sure."

The king acknowledges the true God

46Then King Nebuchadnezzar fell upon his face, and did homage
to Daniel, and commanded that an offering and incense be offered
up to him. 47The king said to Daniel, "Truly, your God is God of Lev 2:1; 6:8 Deut 10:17
gods and Lord of kings, and a revealer of mysteries, for you have Dan 3:90;
been able to reveal this mystery." 48Then the king gave Daniel 11:36
high honours and many great gifts, and made him ruler over the 1 Cor 14:25
whole province of Babylon, and chief prefect over all the wise
men of Babylon. 49Daniel made request of the king, and he
appointed Shadrach, Meshach, and Abednego over the affairs of
the province of Babylon; but Daniel remained at the king's court.

2:46–49. There is an important lesson in this scene. Nebuchadnezzar, "the king of kings" (2:37), does homage to Daniel, a person of no great importance, and treats him as if he were a messenger from God. The king acknowledges the absolute sovereignty of the God of Israel—which makes Nebuchadnezzar a model for all Gentiles—and, by confessing that God reveals mysteries to Daniel, he is saying that the wisdom that comes from God is incomparably greater than that of the wise men of Babylon. The implication is that the king himself realizes that soothsaying is of no use.

erit; et robur ferri erit ei, secundum quod vidisti ferrum mixtum testae ex luto. 42Et digitos pedum ex parte ferreos et ex parte fictiles, ex parte regnum erit solidum et ex parte contritum. 43Quod autem vidisti ferrum mixtum testae ex luto, commiscebuntur quidem humano semine, sed non adhaerebunt sibi, sicuti ferrum misceri non potest testae. 44In diebus autem regnorum illorum suscitabit Deus caeli regnum, quod in aeternum non dissipabitur, et regnum populo alteri non tradetur: comminuet et consumet universa regna haec, et ipsum stabit in aeternum. 45Secundum quod vidisti quod de monte abscisus est lapis sine manibus et comminuit testam et ferrum et aes et argentum et aurum, Deus magnus ostendit regi, quae ventura sunt postea; et verum est somnium et fidelis interpretatio eius». 46Tunc rex Nabuchodonosor cecidit in faciem suam et Danielem adoravit et hostias et incensum praecepit, ut sacrificarent ei. 47Loquens ergo rex ait Danieli: «Vere Deus vester Deus deorum est et Dominus regum et revelans mysteria, quoniam potuisti aperire sacramentum hoc». 48Tunc rex

b. Aramaic *by the seed of men*

3. THE THREE YOUNG MEN IN THE FIERY FURNACE*

Condemnation for those who will not worship the golden image

3 [1]King Nebuchadnezzar made an image of gold, whose height was sixty cubits and its breadth six cubits. He set it up on the plain of Dura, in the province of Babylon. [2]Then King Nebuchadnezzar sent to assemble the satraps, the prefects, and the

---

***3:1—4:3.** This story has a very different tone to that of the previous ones, though the scene is still the court of Babylon. It has to do with a confrontation between Jews, worshippers of the one true God, and Gentiles, who worship idols; a similar situation arises in chapter 6. Following the Greek version (which is what the Catholic Church follows and which is used in modern Catholic translations [including the RSVCE]), the passage can be divided into three parts: the first tells about the young men's refusal to worship the statue set up by the king; for this they are condemned to the fiery furnace (3:1–23); the second part, which does not exist in the Aramaic text, records the prayers that the young men say in the furnace (*3:1–68*: **notice the italic verse-numbering in chap. 3**); the third tells about the king's discovering that they are unscathed; as a result, he praises the God of Israel (3:24—4:3). The RSVCE notes on page 886 provide a concordance of verse numbers for this passage.

The entire passage shows that God can save from death those who are ready to die rather than worship idols. Early on, the king asks: "Who is the God that will deliver you out of my hands?" (3:15); he provides the answer himself when he says at the end: "Blessed be the God of Shadrach, Meshach, and Abednego, who has sent his angel and delivered his servants".

3:1–23. The Greek versions place the episode in the "eighteenth year of his [Nebuchadnezzar's] reign", which would be 587, the year in which the king sacked Jerusalem. So, the statue would be commemorating that event. However, the formal style of the narrative (the scene is the central plain of the empire, the Dura; the author makes a point of repeating the list of the office-bearers who attend the dedication of the statue, and the list of musical instruments, and the fact that the king's decree admits of no exceptions) suggests that the whole story is symbolic; the statue may symbolize idolatry as such, perhaps even Antiochus IV Epiphanes. Whatever about that, there

---

Danielem in sublime extulit et munera multa et magna dedit ei et constituit eum principem super omnes provincias Babylonis et principem praefectorum super cunctos sapientes Babylonis. [49]Daniel autem postulavit a rege et constituit super opera provinciae Babylonis Sedrac, Misac et Abdenago; ipse autem Daniel erat in foribus regis. **[3]** [1]Nabuchodonosor rex fecit statuam auream altitudine cubito rum sexaginta, latitudine cubitorum sex; et statuit eam in campo Dura in provincia Babylonis. [2]Itaque Nabuchodonosor rex misit ad congregandos satrapas, magistratus et iudices, duces et tyrannos et

governors, the counsellors, the treasurers, the justices, the
magistrates, and all the officials of the provinces to come to the
dedication of the image which King Nebuchadnezzar had set up.
3Then the satraps, the prefects, and the governors, the counsellors,
the treasurers, the justices, the magistrates, and all the officials of
the provinces, were assembled for the dedication of the image that
King Nebuchadnezzar had set up; and they stood before the image
that Nebuchadnezzar had set up. 4And the herald proclaimed Rev 5:9; 7:9;
aloud, "You are commanded, O peoples, nations, and languages, 13:7; 14:6; 17:15
5that when you hear the sound of the horn, pipe, lyre, trigon, harp, Rev 13:14–15
bagpipe, and every kind of music, you are to fall down and worship
the golden image that King Nebuchadnezzar has set up; 6and Jer 29:21–22
whoever does not fall down and worship shall immediately be cast *Mt 13:42,50*
into a burning fiery furnace." 7Therefore, as soon as all the peoples
heard the sound of the horn, pipe, lyre, trigon, harp, bagpipe, and
every kind of music, all the peoples, nations, and languages
fell down and worshipped the golden image which King
Nebuchadnezzar had set up.

---

is a counterposing here of the absolutism of imperial power (which wants to impose its religious agenda) and the faithfulness of these young Jewish men to their God. It is surprising that Daniel does not figure among them; maybe the reason is that this story was originally on its own, independent of the previous chapter—which would make sense because it does not seem right that Nebuchadnezzar who was depicted at the end of chapter 2 as confessing the God of Israel, should be adopting a hostile attitude to that same God here. Still, one needs to remember that the charge against the young men comes not from the king but from the Chaldeans, who had no problem about doing what the king ordered; as the author goes on to tell us, not without a certain irony, it will be those very Chaldeans who will be burned by the furnace (cf. 3:22; *3:23–24*).

The three young men stand up for the rights of conscience and for freedom of religion by offering passive resistance to an edict which exceeds the proper scope of the king's authority.

praefectos omnesque principes provinciarum, ut convenirent ad dedicationem statuae, quam erexerat Nabuchodonosor rex. 3Tunc congregati sunt satrapae, magistratus et iudices, duces et tyranni et optimates, qui erant in potestatibus constituti, et universi principes provinciarum ad dedicationem statuae, quam erexerat Nabuchodonosor rex. Stabant autem in conspectu statuae, quam posuerat Nabuchodonosor, 4et praeco clamabat valenter: «Vobis dicitur, populi, tribus et linguae: 5in hora, qua audieritis sonitum tubae et fistulae et citharae, sambucae et psalterii et symphoniae et universi generis musicorum, cadentes adorate statuam auream, quam constituit Nabuchodonosor rex. 6Si quis autem non prostratus adoraverit, eadem hora mittetur in fornacem ignis ardentis». 7Post haec igitur, statim ut audierunt omnes populi sonitum tubae, fistulae et citharae, sambucae et psalterii et symphoniae et omnis generis musicorum, cadentes omnes populi tribus et linguae adoraverunt statuam auream, quam constituerat Nabuchodonosor rex. 8Statimque et in ipso tempore accedentes viri Chaldaei accusaverunt

[8]Therefore at that time certain Chaldeans came forward and mali-
ciously accused the Jews. [9]They said to King Nebuchadnezzar,
"O king, live for ever! [10]You, O king, have made a decree, that
every man who hears the sound of the horn, pipe, lyre, trigon,
harp, bagpipe, and every kind of music, shall fall down and
worship the golden image; [11]and whoever does not fall down and
worship shall be cast into a burning fiery furnace. [12]There are
certain Jews whom you have appointed over the affairs of the
province of Babylon: Shadrach, Meshach, and Abednego. These
men, O king, pay no heed to you; they do not serve your gods or
worship the golden image which you have set up."

[13]Then Nebuchadnezzar in furious rage commanded that
Shadrach, Meshach, and Abednego be brought. Then they brought
these men before the king. [14]Nebuchadnezzar said to them, "Is it
true, O Shadrach, Meshach, and Abednego, that you do not serve
my gods or worship the golden image which I have set up? [15]Now
if you are ready when you hear the sound of the horn, pipe, lyre,
trigon, harp, bagpipe, and every kind of music, to fall down and
worship the image which I have made, well and good; but if you
do not worship, you shall immediately be cast into a burning fiery
furnace; and who is the god that will deliver you out of my hands?"

[16]Shadrach, Meshach, and Abednego answered the king, "O
Nebuchadnezzar, we have no need to answer you in this matter.

3:16–18. The young men's answer is a model of what people's attitude to God should be when tragedy strikes and particularly when martyrdom beckons: they should hope that God will come to their rescue, but even if he takes no action, they should stay true to him. "Because of their faith, they believe that they can escape death, but they say *if he does not deliver us out of your hand* so that the king will know that they may also die in the arms of the God they love" (St Cyprian, *Epistolae*, 58, 5). They do not seek to "compel" God to save them; they want to show that they obey his will, not the king's. That is the attitude our Lord had when his passion loomed: "Father, if thou art willing, remove this cup from me; nevertheless not my will, but thine, be done" (Lk 22:42).

Iudaeos [9]dixeruntque Nabuchodonosor regi: «Rex, in aeternum vive! [10]Tu, rex, posuisti decretum, ut
omnis homo, qui audierit sonitum tubae, fistulae et citharae, sambucae et psalterii et symphoniae et
universi generis musicorum, prosternat se et adoret statuam auream; [11]si quis autem non procidens
adoraverit, mittetur in fornacem ignis ardentis. [12]Sunt ergo viri Iudaei, quos constituisti super opera
provinciae Babylonis, Sedrac, Misac et Abdenago; viri isti te, rex, non honorant: deos tuos non colunt
et statuam auream, quam erexisti, non adorant». [13]Tunc Nabuchodonosor in furore et in ira praecepit,
ut adducerentur Sedrac, Misac et Abdenago; tunc viri illi adducti sunt in conspectu regis.
[14]Pronuntiansque Nabuchodonosor rex ait eis: «Verene, Sedrac, Misac et Abdenago, deos meos non
colitis et statuam auream, quam constitui, non adoratis? [15]Numquid estis nunc parati, quacumque hora
audieritis sonitum tubae, fistulae, citharae, sambucae, psalterii et symphoniae omnisque generis

17If it be so, our God whom we serve is able to deliver us from the Ps 37:39–40
burning fiery furnace; and he will deliver us out of your hand, O
king.[c] 18But if not, be it known to you, O king, that we will not serve
your gods or worship the golden image which you have set up."
19Then Nebuchadnezzar was full of fury, and the expression of
his face was changed against Shadrach, Meshach, and Abednego.
He ordered the furnace heated seven times more than it was wont
to be heated. 20And he ordered certain mighty men of his army to
bind Shadrach, Meshach, and Abednego, and to cast them into the
burning fiery furnace. 21Then these men were bound in their
mantles,[d] their tunics,[d] their hats, and their other garments, and
they were cast into the burning fiery furnace. 22Because the king's
order was strict and the furnace very hot, the flame of the fire slew
those men who took up Shadrach, Meshach, and Abednego. 23And
these three men, Shadrach, Meshach, and Abednego, fell bound Heb 11:34
into the burning fiery furnace.*

Prayers of the young men in the fiery furnace

1And they walked about in the midst of the flames, singing
hymns to God and blessing the Lord. 2Then Azariah stood Ezra 9:6–15
and offered this prayer; in the midst of the fire he opened his Dan 9:3–19
mouth and said:

3:1–68. As we have said, this section comes from the Greek versions and the New Vulgate translates it from Theodotion's version; it contains two pieces in verse: the first is a penitential piece, attributed to Azariah only (*3:3–22*); the second is a canticle of thanksgiving (*3:29–68*) sung by the three young men. Each piece is introduced by a prose description of the scene in the furnace (*3:1–2; 23–28*). The whole episode bears out the truth of what God told Israel in Isaiah 43:2: "When you walk through fire you shall not be burned."

musicorum, prosternere vos et adorare statuam, quam feci? Quod si non adoraveritis, eadem hora mittemini in fornacem ignis ardentis; et quis est deus, qui eripiat vos de manu mea?». 16Respondentes Sedrac, Misac et Abdenago dixerunt regi Nabuchodonosor: «Non oportet nos de hac re respondere tibi: 17Si enim Deus noster, quem colimus, potest eripere nos de camino ignis ardentis, et de manu tua, rex, liberabit. 18Quod si noluerit, notum sit tibi, rex, quia deos tuos non colimus et statuam auream, quam erexisti, non adoramus». 19Tunc Nabuchodonosor repletus est furore, et aspectus faciei illius immutatus est super Sedrac, Misac et Abdenago; et respondens praecepit, ut succenderetur fornax septuplum quam succendi consueverat; 20et viris fortissimis de exercitu suo iussit, ut ligarent Sedrac, Misac et Abdenago et mitterent eos in fornacem ignis ardentis; 21et confestim viri illi vincti, cum bracis suis et tiaris et calceamentis et vestibus missi sunt in medium fornacis ignis ardentis; 22itaque, quia iussio regis urgebat, et fornax succensa erat nimis, viros illos, qui miserant Sedrac, Misac et Abdenago, interfecit

c. Or *Behold, our God . . . king*. Or *If our God is able to deliver us, he will deliver us from the burning fiery furnace and out of your hand, O king* **d.** The meaning of the Aramaic word is uncertain **d.** The meaning of the Aramaic word is uncertain

Acts 5:30 — [3]*"Blessed art thou, O Lord, God of our fathers, and worthy of*
praise;
and thy name is glorified for ever.
1 Chron 29:10,20 — [4]*For thou art just in all that thou hast done to us,*
Ps 32 — *and all thy works are true and thy ways right,*
Neh 9:33 — *and all thy judgments are truth.*
Tob 3:2–6 — [5]*Thou hast executed true judgments in all that thou has brought*
Dan 4:34 — *upon us*
Rev 16:7; 19:2 — *and upon Jerusalem, the holy city of our fathers,*
for in truth and justice thou hast brought all this upon us
because of our sins
Dan 9:5–8 — [6]*For we have sinfully and lawlessly departed from thee,*
Bar 1:17f — *and have sinned in all things and have not obeyed thy*
commandments;
Neh 1:7 — [7]*we have not observed them or done them,*
Is 59:12–13 — *as thou hast commanded us that it might go well with us.*
Lev 26:14,38 — [8]*So all that thou hast brought upon us,*
Deut 28:15,63f — *and all that thou hast done to us,*
thou hast done in true judgment.
[9]*Thou hast given us into the hands of lawless enemies, most*
hateful rebels,
and to an unjust king, the most wicked in all the world.
[10]*And now we cannot open our mouths; shame and disgrace*
have befallen thy servants and worshippers.
Ex 32:11f — [11]*For thy name's sake do not give us up utterly,*
and do not break thy covenant,

3:3–22. As is conventional in penitential psalms, this begins by proclaiming that God is just in all his dealings, even when he punishes his people (vv. *3–5*; cf. Ps. 32). Then it accepts that the people's sins justify all that has befallen them (even giving them over to the most wicked king in all the earth, vv. *6–10*: perhaps a reference to Antiochus IV). Finally, it asks for God to take action on the grounds of the Covenant made with their ancestors (vv. *11–13*) and the fact

flamma ignis. [23]Viri autem tres, Sedrac, Misac et Abdenago, ceciderunt in medio camino ignis ardentis colligati. (*Quae sequuntur in Hebraeis voluminibus non repperi*). [24]Et ambulabant in medio flammae laudantes Deum et benedicentes Domino. [25]Stans autem Azarias oravit sic aperiensque os suum in medio ignis ait: [26]«Benedictus es, Domine, Deus patrum nostrorum, / et laudabilis et gloriosum nomen tuum in saecula, / [27]quia iustus es in omnibus, quae fecisti nobis, / et universa opera tua vera, et viae tuae rectae, / et omnia iudicia tua veritas. / [28]Iudicia enim vera fecisti / iuxta omnia, quae induxisti super nos / et super civitatem sanctam patrum nostrorum Ierusalem, / quia in veritate et in iudicio induxisti omnia haec / propter peccata nostra. / [29]Peccavimus enim et inique egimus recedentes a te / et deliquimus in omnibus; / [30]et praecepta tua non audivimus / nec observavimus / nec fecimus, sicut praeceperas nobis, / ut bene nobis esset. / [31]Omnia ergo, quae induxisti super nos, / et universa, quae fecisti nobis, / vero iudicio fecisti; / [32]et tradidisti nos in manibus inimicorum nostrorum / iniquorum

[12] *and do not withdraw thy mercy from us,*
for the sake of Abraham thy beloved 2 Chron 20:7 Is 41:8
and for the sake of Isaac thy servant Jas 2:23
and Israel thy holy one,
[13]*to whom thou didst promise*
to make their descendants as many as the stars of heaven Gen 15:2; 22:17
and as the sand on the shore of the sea.
[14]*For we, O Lord, have become fewer than any nation,*
and are brought low this day in all the world because of our sins. Deut 28:62 Jer 42:2
[15]*And at this time there is no prince, or prophet, or leader,*
no burnt offering, or sacrifice, or oblation, or incense, Hos 3:4 Lam 2:9
no place to make an offering before thee or to find mercy.
[16]*Yet with a contrite heart and a humble spirit may we be accepted,*
as though it were with burnt offerings of rams and bulls, Ps 25:3; 51:19 Hos 6:6
and with tens of thousands of fat lambs; Mic 6:7–8
[17] *such may our sacrifice be in thy sight this day,*
and may we wholly follow thee,
for there will be no shame for those who trust in thee.
[18]*And now with all our heart we follow thee,*
we fear thee and seek thy face.
[19]*Do not put us to shame,*
but deal with us in thy forbearance
and in thy abundant mercy.
[20]*Deliver us in accordance with thy marvellous works,*
and give glory to thy name, O Lord!
Let all who do harm to thy servants be put to shame;
[21] *let them be disgraced and deprived of all power and dominion,* Ps 35:26; 40:15
and let their strength be broken.
[22]*Let them know that thou art the Lord, the only God,*
glorious over the whole world." Ps 83:19

---

that the people have been brought so low and do repent their sins (vv. *14–18*); God's goodness and mercy must now be revealed; his very honour requires that he rescue them (vv. *19–22*).

et pessimorum praevaricatorumque / et regi iniusto et pessimo ultra omnem terram. / [33]Et nunc non possumus aperire os; / confusio et opprobrium facta sunt / servis tuis et his, qui colunt te. / [34]Ne, quaesumus, tradas nos in perpetuum / propter nomen tuum / et ne dissipes testamentum tuum / [35]neque auferas misericordiam tuam a nobis / propter Abraham dilectum tuum / et Isaac servum tuum / et Israel sanctum tuum, / [36]quibus dixisti / quod multiplicares semen eorum sicut stellas caeli / et sicut arenam, quae est in litore maris; / [37]quia, Domine, / imminuti sumus plus quam omnes gentes / sumusque humiles in universa terra / hodie propter peccata nostra; / [38]et non est in tempore hoc / princeps et propheta et dux / neque holocaustum neque sacrificium / neque oblatio neque incensum / neque locus primitiarum coram te, / ut possimus invenire misericordiam; / [39]sed in anima contrita et spiritu

Jn 5:44

[23]Now the king's servants who threw them in did not cease
feeding the furnace fires with naphtha, pitch, tow, and brush.
[24]And the flame streamed out above the furnace forty-nine cubits,
[25]and it broke through and burned those of the Chaldeans whom
Gen 16:7–11 *it caught about the furnace. [26]But the angel of the Lord came*
Ex 3:2 *down into the furnace to be with Azariah and his companions, and*
Tob 5:4; 12:15 *drove the fiery flame out of the furnace, [27]and made the midst of*
the furnace like a moist whistling wind, so that the fire did not
touch them at all or hurt or trouble them.

[28]Then the three, as with one mouth, praised and glorified and
blessed God in the furnace, saying:

Dan 3:26 *[29]"Blessed art thou, O Lord, God of our fathers,*
Acts 5:30 *and to be praised and highly exalted for ever;*
[30]And blessed is thy glorious, holy name
and to be highly praised and highly exalted for ever;

3:23–27. A contrast is drawn here between the harm that comes to the Chaldeans and the fact that the young men are saved by the action of the angel of the Lord. In other passages of the Old Testament the "angel of the Lord" stands for God's power and protection (cf. Gen 16:7–11; Ex 3:2; etc.); here he appears as a person alongside the three in the furnace, just as the angel who acts as Tobias' guide eventually reveals who he is (cf. Tob 12:15).

3:28–68. This magnificent hymn begins with praises addressed directly to God (vv. *29–34*); then it calls on others to join in (vv. *35–65*); and it ends by explaining why the three young men in particular should praise and thank God (vv. *66–68*). This means that attention is focussed first on God himself and his greatness, then on his creatures in heaven and on earth, and finally on the particular favours he does for those who fear him.

3:29–34. In prayers of praise, God is often called "God of our fathers" (cf. v. 3)—a way of acknowledging all the great things that God did in the past on behalf of his people. The references to the temple and the cherubim (vv. *31–32*) look beyond the temple of Jerusalem to heaven itself, the dwelling-place of God.

humilitatis suscipiamur / sicut in holocausto arietum et taurorum / [40]et sicut in milibus agnorum pinguium; / sic fiat sacrificium nostrum in conspectu tuo hodie, / et perfice subsequentes te, / quoniam non est confusio confidentibus in te. / [41]Et nunc sequimur te in toto corde / et timemus te et quaerimus faciem tuam; / [42]ne confundas nos, / sed fac nobiscum iuxta mansuetudinem tuam / et secundum multitudinem misericordiae tuae / [43]et erue nos in mirabilibus tuis / et da gloriam nomini tuo, Domine. / [44]Et confundantur omnes, qui ostendunt servis tuis mala; / confundantur absque ulla potentia, / et robur eorum conteratur. / [45]Sciant quia tu es Dominus, / Deus solus et gloriosus super orbem terrarum». [46]Et non cessabant, qui immiserant eos, ministri regis succendere fornacem naphta et stuppa et pice et malleolis, [47]et effundebatur flamma super fornacem cubitis quadraginta novem [48]et erupit et incendit, quos repperit iuxta fornacem de Chaldaeis. [49]Angelus autem Domini descendit cum Azaria et sociis eius in fornacem et excussit flammam ignis de fornace [50]et fecit medium fornacis quasi ventum roris flantem; et non tetigit eos omnino ignis neque contristavit nec quidquam molestiae intulit. [51]Tunc hi

[31]Blessed art thou in the temple of thy holy glory
and to be extolled and highly glorified for ever. Ps 150:1 Is 6:1
[32]Blessed are thou, who sittest upon cherubim and lookest upon the deeps, Ex 25:18 2 Sam 6:2
and to be praised and highly exalted for ever.
[33]Blessed art thou upon the throne of thy kingdom
and to be extolled and highly exalted for ever.
[34]Blessed art thou in the firmament of heaven
and to be sung and glorified for ever.
[35]"Bless the Lord, all works of the Lord,
sing praise to him and highly exalt him for ever: Ps 103:22;

3:35–68. These calls (similar to those in Psalm 148) are addressed first to all creation (v. 35), then to things in the heavens or firmament (vv. *36–51*), then to things earthly, culminating in man (vv. *42–60*) and finally to Israel and its different ranks of people (vv. *61–65*). The canticle ends with the three young men calling on themselves to praise and thank God forever for his mercy/ steadfast love, a word that sums up the Covenant (cf. its use as a chorus in Psalm 136). See the note on Ps 5:77.

The order and "hierarchy" in this canticle implies that, while all creatures in the heavens and on earth extol the glory of God by the sheer fact of their existence, it is through man and the praise that God's people and those who recite this hymn give to God, that the voice of this song in praise of God is found and God's glory is seen to be one with his everlasting mercy. His glory is acknowledged and seen to accord with his eternal mercy. The Second Vatican Council alludes to these verses (its only quotation from the book of Daniel) when it says: "Though made of body and soul, man is one. Through his bodily composition he gathers to himself the elements of the material world; thus they reach their crown through him, and through him raise their voice in free praise of the Creator" (*Gaudium et spes*, 14).

This canticle is called the "Benedicite" and is included in the Divine Office for Sundays and feast days. The Church also recommends it as a prayer for thanksgiving after Mass—Mass being the commemoration of Christ, the greatest manifestation of the glory of God.

tres, quasi ex uno ore, laudabant et glorificabant et benedicebant Deo in fornace dicentes: [52]«Benedictus es, Domine, Deus patrum nostrorum, / et laudabilis et superexaltatus in saecula; / et benedictum nomen gloriae tuae sanctum / et superlaudabile et superexaltatum in saecula. / [53]Benedictus es in templo sanctae gloriae tuae / et superlaudabilis et supergloriosus in saecula. / [54]Benedictus es in throno regni tui / et superlaudabilis et superexaltatus in saecula. / [55]Benedictus es, qui intueris abyssos sedens super cherubim, / et laudabilis et superexaltatus in saecula. / [56]Benedictus es in firmamento caeli / et laudabilis et gloriosus in saecula. / [57]Benedicite, omnia opera Domini, Domino, / laudate et superexaltate eum in saecula. / [58]Benedicite, caeli, Domino, / laudate et superexaltate eum in saecula. / [59]Benedicite, angeli Domini, Domino, / laudate et superexaltate eum in saecula. / [60]Benedicite, aquae omnes, quae super caelos sunt, Domino, / laudate et superexaltate eum in saecula. / [61]Benedicat omnis virtus Domino, / laudate et superexaltate eum in saecula. / [62]Benedicite, sol et luna, Domino, / laudate

145:10 Ps 103:20; *[36]Bless the Lord, you heavens*
148:2 *sing praise to him and highly exalt him for ever.*
[37]Bless the Lord, you angels of the Lord,
Ps 148:4 *sing praise to him and highly exalt him for ever.*
[38]Bless the Lord, all waters above the heaven,
sing praise to him and highly exalt him for ever.
[39]Bless the Lord, all powers,
Ps 103:21 *sing praise to him and highly exalt him for ever.*
[40]Bless the Lord, sun and moon,
Ps 148:3 *sing praise to him and highly exalt him for ever.*
[41]Bless the Lord, stars of heaven,
sing praise to him and highly exalt him for ever.
[42]Bless the Lord, all rain and dew, sing praise to him and highly
Ps 148:8 *exalt him for ever.*
[43]Bless the Lord, all winds,
sing praise to him and highly exalt him for ever.
[44]Bless the Lord, fire and heat,
sing praise to him and highly exalt him for ever.
[45]Bless the Lord, winter cold and summer heat,
sing praise to him and highly exalt him for ever.
[46]Bless the Lord, dews and snows,
sing praise to him and highly exalt him for ever.
[47]Bless the Lord, nights and days,
sing praise to him and highly exalt him for ever.
[48]Bless the Lord, light and darkness,
sing praise to him and highly exalt him for ever.
[49]Bless the Lord, ice and cold,
sing praise to him and highly exalt him for ever.
[50]Bless the Lord, frosts and snows,
sing praise to him and highly exalt him for ever.
[51]Bless the Lord, lightnings and clouds,
sing praise to him and highly exalt him for ever.

---

et superexaltate eum in saecula. / [63]Benedicite, stellae caeli, Domino, / laudate et superexaltate eum in saecula. / [64]Benedicite, omnis imber et ros, Domino, / laudate et superexaltate eum in saecula. / [65]Benedicite, omnes venti, Domino, / laudate et superexaltate eum in saecula. / [66]Benedicite, ignis et aestus, Domino, / laudate et superexaltate eum in saecula. / [67]Benedicite, frigus et aestus, Domino, / laudate et superexaltate eum in saecula. / [68]Benedicite, rores et pruina, Domino, / laudate et superexaltate eum in saecula. / [69]Benedicite, gelu et frigus, Domino, / laudate et superexaltate eum in saecula. / [70]Benedicite, glacies et nives, Domino, / laudate et superexaltate eum in saecula. / [71]Benedicite, noctes et dies, Domino, / laudate et superexaltate eum in saecula. / [72]Benedicite, lux et tenebrae, Domino, / laudate et superexaltate eum in saecula. / [73]Benedicite, fulgura et nubes, Domino, / laudate et superexaltate eum in saecula. / [74]Benedicat terra Dominum, / laudet et superexaltet eum in saecula. / [75]Benedicite, montes et colles, Domino, / laudate et superexaltate eum in saecula. / [76]Benedicite, universa germinantia in terra, Domino, / laudate et superexaltate eum in saecula. /

[52]*Let the earth bless the Lord;*
let it sing praise to him and highly exalt him for ever.
[53]*Bless the Lord, mountains and hills,*
sing praise to him and highly exalt him for ever. Ps 148:9
[54]*Bless the Lord, all things that grow on the earth,*
sing praise to him and highly exalt him for ever.
[55]*Bless the Lord, you springs,*
sing praise to him and highly exalt him for ever.
[56]*Bless the Lord, seas and rivers,*
sing praise to him and highly exalt him for ever.
[57]*Bless the Lord, you whales and all creatures that move in the waters,*
sing praise to him and highly exalt him for ever.
[58]*Bless the Lord, all birds of the air,*
sing praise to him and highly exalt him for ever.
[59]*Bless the Lord, all beasts and cattle,* Ps 148:10
sing praise to him and highly exalt him for ever.
[60]*Bless the Lord, you sons of men,*
sing praise to him and highly exalt him for ever.
[61]*Bless the Lord, O Israel,* Ps 135:19
sing praise to him and highly exalt him for ever.
[62]*Bless the Lord, you priests of the Lord,*
sing praise to him and highly exalt him for ever. Ps 134:1
[63]*Bless the Lord, you servants of the Lord*
sing praise to him and highly exalt him for ever.
[64]*Bless the Lord, spirits and souls of the righteous,*
sing praise to him and highly exalt him for ever.
[65]*Bless the Lord, you who are holy and humble in heart,*
sing praise to him and highly exalt him for ever. Zeph 2:3
[66]*Bless the Lord, Hananiah, Azariah, and Misha-el,*
sing praise to him and highly exalt him for ever;
for he has rescued us from Hades and saved us from the hand of death,

---

[77]Benedicite, maria et flumina, Domino, / laudate et superexaltate eum in saecula. / [78]Benedicite, fontes, Domino, / laudate et superexaltate eum in saecula. / [79]Benedicite, cete et omnia quae moventur in aquis, Domino, / laudate et superexaltate eum in saecula. / [80]Benedicite, omnes volucres caeli, Domino, / laudate et superexaltate eum in saecula. / [81]Benedicite, omnes bestiae et pecora, Domino, / laudate et superexaltate eum in saecula. / [82]Benedicite, filii hominum, Domino, / laudate et superexaltate eum in saecula. / [83]Benedic, Israel, Domino, / laudate et superexaltate eum in saecula. / [84]Benedicite, sacerdotes Domini, Domino, / laudate et superexaltate eum in saecula. / [85]Benedicite, servi Domini, Domino, / laudate et superexaltate eum in saecula. / [86]Benedicite, spiritus et animae iustorum, Domino, / laudate et superexaltate eum in saecula. / [87]Benedicite, sancti et humiles corde, Domino, / laudate et superexaltate eum in saecula. / [88]Benedicite, Anania, Azaria, Misael, Domino, /

and delivered us from the midst of the burning fiery furnace;
from the midst of the fire he has delivered us.
[67]*Give thanks to the Lord, for he is good,*
Ps 106:1; 136 *for his mercy endures for ever.*
Dan 6:27 [68]*Bless him, all who worship the Lord, the God of gods,*
sing praise to him and give thanks to him,
Dan 2:44; 4:31 *for his mercy endures for ever."**

The king acknowledges the God of the Jews
[24]Then King Nebuchadnezzar was astonished and rose up in haste.
He said to his counsellors, "Did we not cast three men bound into

3:24–30. At 3:24 the RSV in roman type links up again with the Aramaic text. The Greek translations introduce these verses by saying that the king heard the young men singing in the fiery furnace: hence his amazement; the Aramaic text simply says that he was astonished that they were alive (v. 24). Their deliverance reaches them in their place of torment, with the arrival of the angel to protect them. Nebuchadnezzar, looking down on the furnace, is able to see that they are safe. To someone like the king, a believer in all sorts of gods, the fourth person who looks like "a son of the gods" (v. 25) must have seemed a divine being; but the author makes it clear that he is simply an angel (v. 28). It is through the angel that God manifests his providence. The divine help given to the three young men, Novatian comments, "will not allow even their clothes to be singed by flame. This is just and right, for God sustains everything in the world in being and has power over all, each and every thing; therefore, he can furnish any thing or person with his help, since he is Lord of all" (*De Trinitate*, 8, 43).

The Fathers saw this "son of the gods" as meaning Christ. "Daniel knew the Son of God and saw the works of God. He saw the Son of God who cooled the fires of the furnace with dew. But when he says *Bless the Lord, all works of the Lord*, he does not include the Son among them, because he knows that He is not a creature, but the One through whom all creatures were made, and who should be praised and exalted in the Father" (St Athanasius, *Epistulae ad Serapionem*, 2, 6).

There is not a little irony in what the text says about the king's reaction: he praises the very fact that the young men disobeyed his orders, risking their lives

laudate et superexaltate eum in saecula; / quia eruit nos de inferno et salvos fecit de manu mortis / et liberavit nos de medio fornacis ardentis flammae / et de medio ignis eruit nos. / [89]Confitemini Domino, quoniam bonus, / quoniam in saeculum misericordia eius. / [90]Benedicite, omnes, qui timetis Dominum, Deo deorum; / laudate et confitemini ei, quia in saecula misericordia eius». (*Hucusque non habetur in Hebraeo et, quae posuimus, de Theodotionis editione translata sunt*). [91]([24])Tunc Nabuchodonosor rex obstupuit et surrexit propere; respondens ait optimatibus suis: «Nonne tres viros misimus in medium ignis compeditos?». Qui respondentes dixerunt regi: «Vere, rex». [92]([25])Respondit et ait: «Ecce ego video viros quattuor solutos et ambulantes in medio ignis, et nihil corruptionis in eis est, et species

the fire?" They answered the king, "True, O king." [25]He answered,
"But I see four men loose, walking in the midst of the fire, and
they are not hurt; and the appearance of the fourth is like a son of
the gods."

[26]Then Nebuchadnezzar came near to the door of the burning
fiery furnace and said, "Shadrach, Meshach, and Abednego,
servants of the Most High God, come forth, and come here!" Then
Shadrach, Meshach, and Abednego came out from the fire. [27]And
the satraps, the prefects, the governors, and the king's counsellors
gathered together and saw that the fire had not had any power over
the bodies of those men; the hair of their heads was not singed,
their mantles[d] were not harmed, and no smell of fire had come upon
them. [28]Nebuchadnezzar said, "Blessed be the God of Shadrach,
Meshach, and Abednego, who has sent his angel and delivered his
servants, who trusted in him, and set at nought the king's command, and yielded up their bodies rather than serve and worship
any god except their own God. [29]Therefore I make a decree: Any
people, nation, or language that speaks anything against the God Dan 6:27
of Shadrach, Meshach, and Abednego shall be torn limb from
limb, and their houses laid in ruins; for there is no other god who
is able to deliver in this way." [30]Then the king promoted Shadrach,
Meshach, and Abednego in the province of Babylon.

---

in the process, and he rewards them for doing so. The very people that the king ordered to worship the statue set up by himself, now benefit from a decree that commands that the God of the Jews is to be respected. The young men's heroism (their readiness to accept martyrdom) and their miraculous deliverance have completely changed the king's attitude.

quarti similis filio deorum». [93](26)Tunc accessit Nabuchodonosor ad ostium fornacis ignis ardentis et ait: «Sedrac, Misac et Abdenago, servi Dei excelsi, egredimini et venite». Statimque egressi sunt Sedrac, Misac et Abdenago de medio ignis. [94](27)Et congregati satrapae, magistratus et iudices et potentes regis contemplabantur viros illos, quoniam nihil potestatis habuisset ignis in corporibus eorum, et capillus capitis eorum non esset adustus, et sarabara eorum non fuissent immutata, et odor ignis non transisset per eos. [95](28)Et erumpens Nabuchodonosor ait: «Benedictus Deus eorum, Sedrac, Misac et Abdenago, qui misit angelum suum et eruit servos suos, qui crediderunt in eo, et verbum regis immutaverunt et tradiderunt corpora sua, ne servirent et ne adorarent omnem deum, excepto Deo suo. [96](29)A me ergo positum est decretum, ut omnis populus, tribus et lingua quaecumque locuta fuerit blasphemiam contra Deum Sedrac, Misac et Abdenago, in frusta concidatur, et domus eius in sterquilinium fiat, eo quod non est Deus alius, qui possit ita salvare». [97](30)Tunc rex promovit Sedrac, Misac et Abdenago in provincia Babylonis. [98](31)Nabuchodonosor rex omnibus populis, gentibus et linguis, quae habitant in universa terra: «Pax vobis multiplicetur. [99](32)Signa et mirabilia, quae fecit apud me Deus excelsus, placuit mihi praedicare: [100](33)Signa eius quam magna sunt, / et mirabilia eius quam fortia! / Et regnum eius regnum sempiternum, / et potestas eius in generationem et

d. The meaning of the Aramaic word is uncertain

4. DANIEL INTERPRETS THE DREAM OF THE TREE*

4 [e] 1*King Nebuchadnezzar to all peoples, nations, and lan-
Dan 2 guages, that dwell in all the earth: Peace be multiplied to you!
2It has seemed good to me to show the signs and wonders that the
Most High God has wrought toward me.
Dan 2:44; 4:31 3How great are his signs,
how mighty his wonders!
His kingdom is an everlasting kingdom,
and his dominion is from generation to generation.

The king's dream

4[f]I, Nebuchadnezzar, was at ease in my house and prospering in
my palace. 5I had a dream which made me afraid; as I lay in bed
the fancies and the visions of my head alarmed me. 6Therefore I
made a decree that all the wise men of Babylon should be brought
before me, that they might make known to me the interpretation

***4:1–37.** Most of chapter 4 is taken up with another dream of Nebuchadnezzar's and its interpretation—a theme like that of chapter 2. The passage begins with the king speaking and then telling Daniel about what he saw in the dream, for his magicians etc. have proved useless (vv. 4–19); then comes Daniel's interpretation (vv. 19–27); and, finally, events prove that the interpretation is true, and the king professes faith in the Most High (vv. 28–37). What this passage describes is somewhat like the malady suffered by Nabonid, the last king of Babylon before the Persian invasion. Among the scrolls found at Qumran was a work called *The Prayer of Nabonid* which blames idolatry for an illness that caused the king to be excluded from the court for seven years; but the king then repented his sins and was cured.

4:4–18. Once again the superiority of Daniel's wisdom is emphasized: he has "the spirit of the holy gods" (v. 8), which is how a pagan king would describe the spirit of prophecy. The Septuagint translation puts this episode in the eighteenth year of Nebuchadnezzar's reign (cf. the note on 3:1–23). The tree in the king's dream is like the

generationem». **[4]** 1Ego Nabuchodonosor quietus eram in domo mea et florens in palatio meo; 2somnium vidi, quod perterruit me, et cogitationes in stratu meo et visiones capitis mei conturbaverunt me. 3Et per me propositum est decretum, ut introducerentur in conspectu meo cuncti sapientes Babylonis, ut solutionem somnii indicarent mihi. 4Tunc ingrediebantur harioli, magi, Chaldaei et haruspices; et somnium narravi in conspectu eorum, et solutionem eius non indicaverunt mihi; 5donec denique ingressus est in conspectu meo Daniel, cui nomen Baltassar secundum nomen dei mei et qui habet spiritum deorum sanctorum in semetipso. Et somnium coram ipso locutus sum: 6«Baltassar,

e. Ch 3:31 in Aramaic **f.** Ch 4:1 in Aramaic

of the dream. [7]Then the magicians, the enchanters, the Chaldeans,
and the astrologers came in; and I told them the dream, but they
could not make known to me its interpretation. [8]At last Daniel
came in before me—he who was named Belteshazzar* after the Dan 5:11,14
name of my god, and in whom is the spirit of the holy gods[g]—and
I told him the dream, saying, [9]“O Belteshazzar, chief of the
magicians, because I know that the spirit of the holy gods[g] is in
you and that no mystery is difficult for you, here is[h] the dream
which I saw; tell me its interpretation. [10]The visions of my head as
I lay in bed were these: I saw, and behold, a tree in the midst of the Ezek 31:3–14
earth; and its height was great. [11]The tree grew and became strong,
and its top reached to heaven, and it was visible to the end of the Ezek 17:23; 31:6
whole earth. [12]Its leaves were fair and its fruit abundant, and in it was Mt 13:31–32 Mk 4:32
food for all. The beasts of the field found shade under it, and the Lk 13:19
birds of the air dwelt in its branches, and all flesh was fed from it.
[13]“I saw in the visions of my head as I lay in bed, and behold,
a watcher, a holy one,* came down from heaven. [14]He cried aloud
and said thus, ‘Hew down the tree and cut off its branches, strip
off its leaves and scatter its fruit; let the beasts flee from under it
and the birds from its branches. [15]But leave the stump of its roots
in the earth, bound with a band of iron and bronze, amid the
tender grass of the field. Let him be wet with the dew of heaven;
let his lot be with the beasts in the grass of the earth; [16]let his mind
be changed from a man’s, and let a beast’s mind be given to him;
and let seven times pass over him. [17]The sentence is by the decree
of the watchers, the decision by the word of the holy ones, to the Job 36:7
end that the living may know that the Most High rules the king- Jer 27:5

---

tree in Ezekiel’s oracle against the pharaoh, which likens the Egyptian king to a cedar of Lebanon that became so proud it was toppled (cf. Ezek 31). In the present dream, the emphasis is on the great size of the tree and its ability to give shelter (vv. 11–12), and on the fact that its ruin is designed to send out a message—that “the living may know that the Most High has power over all” (v. 17). The “watchman” and “holy one” in v. 13 must be an angel; the “seven times” in v. 16 means the fullness of time.

princeps hariolorum, quem ego scio quod spiritum deorum sanctorum habeas in te, et omne sacramentum non est impossibile tibi, visiones somnii mei, quas vidi, et solutionem eius narra. [7]Visio capitis mei in cubili meo: Videbam, et ecce arbor in medio terrae, / et altitudo eius nimia. / [8]Magna arbor et fortis, / et proceritas eius contingens caelum; / aspectus illius erat usque ad terminos universae terrae. / [9]Folia eius pulcherrima, / et fructus eius nimius, / et esca universorum in ea. / Subter eam habitabant bestiae agri, / et in ramis eius conversabantur volucres caeli, / et ex ea vescebatur omnis caro. / [10]Videbam in visione capitis mei super stratum meum, / et ecce vigil et sanctus de caelo

g. Or *Spirit of the holy God* **h.** Cn: Aramaic *visions of*

Dan 2:28 dom of men, and gives it to whom he will, and sets over it the
lowliest of men.' [18]This dream I, King Nebuchadnezzar, saw. And
you, O Belteshazzar, declare the interpretation, because all the wise
men of my kingdom are not able to make known to me the interpretation, but you are able, for the spirit of the holy gods[i] is in you."

The dream interpreted

[19]Then Daniel, whose name was Belteshazzar, was dismayed for
1 Sam 25:26 a moment, and his thoughts alarmed him. The king said,
2 Sam 18:32 "Belteshazzar, let not the dream or the interpretation alarm you."
Belteshazzar answered, "My lord, may the dream be for those
who hate you and its interpretation for your enemies! [20]The tree

4:19–27. Daniel's dismay when he hears about the dream (v. 19) arises from the fact that he realizes that the interpretation applies to the king; whereas the king seems to be quite at ease because he does not as yet know what the dream means. Daniel interprets it, applying every detail to the king himself, and he ends up telling him what he must do to avoid this terrible fate: he must practise righteousness and do works of mercy (v. 27). Daniel shows the king the path by which all those who do not know the true God can still attain salvation: "Nor does divine Providence deny the helps necessary for salvation to those who, without blame on their part, have not yet arrived at an explicit knowledge of God and with his grace strive to live a good life" (Vatican II, *Lumen gentium*, 16).

descendit. / [11]Clamavit fortiter et sic ait: / "Succidite arborem et praecidite ramos eius, / excutite folia eius et dispergite fructus eius. / Fugiant bestiae de sub ea, / et volucres de ramis eius. / [12]Verumtamen germen radicum eius in terra sinite / et in vinculo ferreo et aereo in herbis agri, / et rore caeli tingatur, / et cum feris pars eius in herba terrae. / [13]Cor eius ab humano commutetur, / et cor ferae detur ei, / et septem tempora mutentur super eum. / [14]In sententia vigilum decretum est, / et sermo sanctorum petitio, / ut cognoscant viventes / quoniam dominatur Excelsus in regno hominum / et, cuicumque voluerit, dabit illud / et humillimum hominem constituet super eo". [15]Hoc somnium vidi ego rex Nabuchodonosor. Tu ergo, Baltassar, interpretationem narra, quia omnes sapientes regni mei non queunt solutionem edicere mihi; tu autem potes, quia spiritus deorum sanctorum in te est». [16]Tunc Daniel, cuius nomen Baltassar, obstupuit quasi una hora, et cogitationes eius conturbabant eum. Respondens autem rex ait: «Baltassar, somnium et interpretatio eius non conturbent te». Respondit Baltassar et dixit: «Domine mi, somnium his, qui te oderunt, et interpretatio eius hostibus tuis sit. [17]Arborem, quam vidisti sublimem atque robustam, cuius altitudo pertingit ad caelum, et aspectus illius in omnem terram, [18]et rami eius pulcherrimi, et fructus eius nimius, et esca omnium in ea, subter eam habitantes bestiae agri, et in ramis eius commorantes aves caeli, [19]tu es, rex, qui magnificatus es et invaluisti, et magnitudo tua crevit et pervenit usque ad caelum, et potestas tua in terminos terrae. [20]Quod autem vidit rex vigilem et sanctum descendere de caelo et dicere: "Succidite arborem et dissipate illam; attamen germen radicum eius in terra dimittite, et vinculo ferreo et aereo in herbis agri, et rore caeli conspergatur, et cum feris sit pars eius, donec septem tempora mutentur super eum", [21]haec est interpretatio, rex, et sententia Altissimi, quae pervenit super dominum meum regem: [22]et eicient te ab hominibus, et cum bestiis feris erit habitatio tua, et fenum ut boves comedes et rore caeli infunderis; septem quoque tempora mutabuntur super te, donec scias quod dominetur Excelsus super

i. Or *Spirit of the holy God*

you saw, which grew and became strong, so that its top reached to
heaven, and it was visible to the end of the whole earth; [21]whose
leaves were fair and its fruit abundant, and in which was food for Mt 13:32
all; under which beasts of the field found shade, and in whose Mk 4:32
branches the birds of the air dwelt—[22]it is you, O king, who have Lk 13:19
grown and become strong. Your greatness has grown and reaches
to heaven, and your dominion to the ends of the earth. [23]And
whereas the king saw a watcher, a holy one, coming down from
heaven and saying, 'Hew down the tree and destroy it, but leave
the stump of its roots in the earth, bound with a band of iron and
bronze, in the tender grass of the field; and let him be wet with the
dew of heaven; and let his lot be with the beasts of the field, till
seven times pass over him'; [24]this is the interpretation, O king: It
is a decree of the Most High, which has come upon my lord the
king, [25]that you shall be driven from among men, and your
dwelling shall be with the beasts of the field; you shall be made to
eat grass like an ox, and you shall be wet with the dew of heaven,
and seven times shall pass over you, till you know that the Most
High rules the kingdom of men, and gives it to whom he will.
[26]And as it was commanded to leave the stump of the roots of the
tree, your kingdom shall be sure for you from the time that you
know that Heaven rules. [27]Therefore, O king, let my counsel be
acceptable to you; break off your sins by practising righteousness, Tob 12:9
and your iniquities by showing mercy to the oppressed, that there Sir 3:30
may perhaps be a lengthening of your tranquillity."

The dream and its interpretation come true

[28]All this came upon King Nebuchadnezzar. [29]At the end of
twelve months he was walking on the roof of the royal palace of
Babylon, [30]and the king said, "Is not this great Babylon, which I
have built by my mighty power as a royal residence and for the glory Rev 14:8
of my majesty?" [31]While the words were still in the king's mouth,
there fell a voice from heaven, "O King Nebuchadnezzar, to you it is
spoken: The kingdom has departed from you, [32]and you shall be
driven from among men, and your dwelling shall be with the beasts

---

regnum hominum et, cuicumque voluerit, det illud. [23]Quod autem praeceperunt, ut relinqueretur germen radicum eius, id est arboris, regnum tuum tibi manebit, postquam cognoveris potestatem caeli. [24]Quam ob rem, rex, consilium meum placeat tibi, et peccata tua eleemosynis redime et iniquitates tuas misericordiis pauperum; sic longitudo erit prosperitati tuae». [25]Omnia haec venerunt super Nabuchodonosor regem. [26]Post finem mensium duodecim in palatio regni Babylonis deambulabat; [27]responditque rex et ait: «Nonne haec est Babylon magna, quam ego aedificavi in domum regni, in robore fortitudinis meae et in gloria decoris mei?». [28]Cum adhuc sermo esset in ore regis, vox de caelo ruit: «Tibi dicitur, Nabuchodonosor rex: Regnum tuum transiit a te, [29]et ab hominibus te eicient, et cum

of the field; and you shall be made to eat grass like an ox; and seven
times shall pass over you, until you have learned that the Most High
rules the kingdom of men and gives it to whom he will."
33 Immediately the word was fulfilled upon Nebuchadnezzar. He was
driven from among men, and ate grass like an ox, and his body
was wet with the dew of heaven till his hair grew as long as
eagles' feathers, and his nails were like birds' claws.
34 At the end of the days I, Nebuchadnezzar, lifted my eyes to
Sir 18:1 heaven, and my reason returned to me, and I blessed the Most
Dan 2:44; 12:7;
Rev 4:9 High, and praised and honoured him who lives for ever;
for his dominion is an everlasting dominion,
and his kingdom endures from generation to generation;
35 all the inhabitants of the earth are accounted as nothing;
Is 40:22–34
Dan 2:28 and he does according to his will in the host of heaven
Job 9:12 and among the inhabitants of the earth;
Eccles 8:4
Is 45:9 and none can stay his hand
or say to him, "What doest thou?"
36 At the same time my reason returned to me; and for the glory of
Deut 32:4 my kingdom, my majesty and splendour returned to me. My
counsellors and my lords sought me, and I was established in my
kingdom, and still more greatness was added to me. 37 Now I,
Nebuchadnezzar, praise and extol and honour the King of heaven;
for all his works are right and his ways are just; and those who
walk in pride he is able to abase.

4:28–37. The story does not really say very much about what happened to Nebuchadnezzar. It simply records that the dream and its interpretation were borne out by subsequent events, and that the king came to acknowledge the one true God as a result of his misfortune. The narrator stresses the king's conversion by having him speak in the first person from v. 34 on: it is as if the king were making a personal confession. St Jerome comments: "If he had not lifted up his eyes to heaven, he could not have been restored to his former state. [...] Nebuchadnezzar understood that he had suffered for seven years and was humbled because he had raised his pride against God" (*Commentarii in Danielem*, 4, 31 and 34).

bestiis feris erit habitatio tua: fenum quasi boves comedes; et septem tempora mutabuntur super te, donec scias quod dominetur Excelsus in regno hominum et, cuicumque voluerit, det illud». 30 Eadem hora sermo completus est super Nabuchodonosor, et ex hominibus abiectus est et fenum ut boves comedit, et rore caeli corpus eius infectum est, donec capilli eius in similitudinem aquilarum crescerent, et ungues eius quasi avium. 31 «Igitur post finem dierum ego Nabuchodonosor oculos meos ad caelum levavi, et sensus meus redditus est mihi, et Altissimo benedixi et Viventem in sempiternum laudavi et glorificavi, quia potestas eius potestas sempiterna, / et regnum eius in generationem et generationem; / 32 et omnes habitatores terrae apud eum in nihilum reputati sunt: / iuxta voluntatem enim suam facit / tam in virtutibus caeli quam in habitatoribus terrae, / et non est qui resistat manui eius / et dicat ei:

5. BELSHAZZAR'S FEAST*

The hand writing on the wall

5 [1]King Belshazzar* made a great feast for a thousand of his Dan 7:1; 8:1
lords, and drank wine in front of the thousand.
[2]Belshazzar, when he tasted the wine, commanded that the
vessels of gold and of silver which Nebuchadnezzar his father had Ezra 5:14,15;

***5:1–30.** The structure here is similar to that of chapters 1 and 2, which focussed on Daniel as an interpreter of dreams; here it is not a dream but a vision. First comes an account of the king's vision (vv. 1–12), then Daniel's interpretation (vv. 13–28), and finally the king's reaction, and the events that prove Daniel right. The author uses considerable artistic licence in his references to the historical context: Belshazzar was not Nebuchadnezzar's son (v. 11), nor did Darius the Mede succeed Belshazzar (6:1); cf. "Introduction", pp. 794f, above. But by depicting Belshazzar as Nebuchadnezzar's son, the sacred writer creates a link with the previous chapter and is able to explain the disappearance, by divine decree, of the empire, that is, the statue's golden head (cf. 2:38). The dependence of this on the previous chapter, to which it refers (cf. 4:5 and 5:11–12, 18–21), suggests that it is designed to round off the earlier one by showing Daniel's connexion with the last king of Babylon (according to the book itself, that is—not in real life). The story illustrates, also, what was said in 1:17—that Daniel "had understanding in all visions and dreams". It is a gift that he makes available to the sacrilegious king, in the hope of changing his heart.

5:1–12. The sacrilege committed by the king and his court, and their idolatry, too, make this Belshazzar a sort of symbol of Antiochus Epiphanes, the king who sacked the temple and looted its sacred vessels (cf. 1 Mac 1:20–24; 2 Mac 5:11–16). The hand that writes on the wall, a sign of the living God (vv. 4–5), is something quite different from the pagan idols, which are incapable of movement. It is surprising that the king did not consult Daniel earlier (vv. 7–8), given that he was the official chief astrologer (v. 11). However, the sacred writer tells the story as he does, in order to highlight, once again, the superiority of Daniel's wisdom over that of all the wise men of Babylon and all their magic arts. Daniel's gift is seen by this polytheistic people as a spirit of a god which makes Daniel like the gods.

"Quid facis?". [33]In ipso tempore sensus meus reversus est ad me, et ad honorem regni mei maiestas mea et splendor meus reversa sunt ad me; et optimates mei et magistratus mei requisierunt me, et in regno meo constitutus sum, et magnificentia amplior addita est mihi. [34]Nunc igitur ego Nabuchodonosor laudo et magnifico et glorifico Regem caeli, quia omnia opera eius veritas, et viae eius iudicium, et gradientes in superbia potest humiliare». **[5]** [1]Balthasar rex fecit grande convivium optimatibus suis mille et coram his milibus vinum bibebat. [2]Balthasar ergo praecepit iam temulentus, ut afferrentur vasa aurea et argentea, quae asportaverat Nabuchodonosor pater eius de templo, quod fuit

6:5; 7:19 taken out of the temple in Jerusalem be brought, that the king and
his lords, his wives, and his concubines might drink from them.
3Then they brought in the golden and silver vessels[j] which had
Dan 1:2 been taken out of the temple, the house of God in Jerusalem; and
the king and his lords, his wives, and his concubines drank from
them. 4They drank wine, and praised the gods of gold and silver,
Rev 9:20 bronze, iron, wood, and stone.

5Immediately the fingers of a man's hand appeared and wrote
on the plaster of the wall of the king's palace, opposite the
lampstand; and the king saw the hand as it wrote. 6Then the king's
color changed, and his thoughts alarmed him; his limbs gave way,
and his knees knocked together. 7The king cried aloud to bring in
Esther 8:15 the enchanters, the Chaldeans, and the astrologers. The king said
Dan 2:2; 4:6; 5:16 to the wise men of Babylon, "Whoever reads this writing, and
shows me its interpretation, shall be clothed with purple, and have
a chain of gold about his neck, and shall be the third ruler in the
kingdom." 8Then all the king's wise men came in, but they could
not read the writing or make known to the king the interpretation.
9Then King Belshazzar was greatly alarmed, and his color
changed; and his lords were perplexed.

10The queen, because of the words of the king and his lords,
Dan 4:5 came into the banqueting hall; and the queen said, "O king, live
for ever! Let not your thoughts alarm you or your color change.
11There is in your kingdom a man in whom is the spirit of the holy
gods.[k] In the days of your father light and understanding and wisdom, like the wisdom of the gods, were found in him, and King

---

in Ierusalem, ut biberent in eis rex et optimates eius uxoresque eius et concubinae. 3Tunc allata sunt
vasa aurea, quae asportaverat de templo, quod fuerat in Ierusalem; et biberunt in eis rex et optimates
eius, uxores et concubinae illius: 4bibebant vinum et laudabant deos suos aureos et argenteos, aereos,
ferreos ligneosque et lapideos. 5In eadem hora apparuerunt digiti manus hominis et scripserunt contra
candelabrum in superficie parietis palatii regis; et rex aspiciebat articulos manus scribentis. 6Tunc regis
facies commutata est, et cogitationes eius conturbabant eum, et compages renum eius solvebantur, et
genua eius ad se invicem collidebantur. 7Exclamavit itaque rex fortiter, ut introducerent magos,
Chaldaeos et haruspices; et proloquens rex ait sapientibus Babylonis: «Quicumque legerit scripturam
hanc et interpretationem eius manifestam mihi fecerit, purpura vestietur et torquem auream habebit
in collo et tertius in regno meo dominabitur». 8Tunc ingressi sunt omnes sapientes regis et non
potuerunt nec scripturam legere nec interpretationem indicare regi; 9unde rex Balthasar satis
conturbatus est, et vultus illius immutatus est super eum, sed et optimates eius turbabantur. 10Regina
autem, sermonum regis optimatiumque eius causa, domum convivii ingressa est; et regina proloquens
ait: «Rex, in aeternum vive! Non te conturbent cogitationes tuae, neque facies tua immutetur. 11Est vir
in regno tuo, qui spiritum deorum sanctorum habet in se, et in diebus patris tui scientia et intellegentia
et sapientia quasi sapientia deorum inventae sunt in eo; nam et rex Nabuchodonosor pater tuus
principem magorum, incantatorum, Chaldaeorum et haruspicum constituit eum; pater tuus, o rex, 12quia
spiritus amplior et prudentia intellegentiaque et interpretatio somniorum et ostensio secretorum ac

j. Theodotion Vg: Aramaic *golden vessels* **k.** Or *Spirit of the holy God*

Nebuchadnezzar, your father, made him chief of the magicians, enchanters, Chaldeans, and astrologers,[l] 12because an excellent spirit, knowledge, and understanding to interpret dreams, explain riddles, and solve problems were found in this Daniel, whom the king named Belteshazzar. Now let Daniel be called, and he will show the interpretation."

Daniel interprets the handwriting

13Then Daniel was brought in before the king. The king said to Daniel, "You are that Daniel, one of the exiles of Judah, whom the king my father brought from Judah. 14I have heard of you that the spirit of the holy gods[k] is in you, and that light and understanding and excellent wisdom are found in you. 15Now the wise men, the enchanters, have been brought in before me to read this writing and make known to me its interpretation; but they could not show the interpretation of the matter. 16But I have heard that you can give interpretations and solve problems. Now if you can read the

---

5:13–28. The king is ready to believe in Daniel's supernatural powers, and offers him great rewards to use them on his behalf (vv. 14–16); but Daniel makes it clear that he never acts for personal gain. He is ready to interpret the writing on the wall, but he wants the king to acknowledge the Most High God, as his father had to do when misfortune overtook him (vv. 18–21). Therefore, he plainly tells the king what his sin has been (vv. 22–23) and reveals to him the sentence that God has passed—in other words, the meaning of the writing on the wall (vv. 24–28).

Four words were written by the mysterious hand according to the Masoretic text (which repeats the first word). They are the names of Eastern measures and coins—the mina, the shekel and the half-mina or paras. In his interpretation, Daniel links them to three verbs that sound like them—the verb *manah*, meaning to measure; *saqal*, to weigh; and *paras*, to divide. The last of the words in the Masoretic text is the plural (*parsim*), so that it sounds like "Persians" in Aramaic. And so, by this play on words, the end of the Babylonian empire and the arrival of the Persians is announced.

solutio ligatorum inventae sunt in eo, in Daniele, cui rex posuit nomen Baltassar. Nunc itaque Daniel vocetur et interpretationem narrabit». 13Igitur introductus est Daniel coram rege; ad quem praefatus rex ait: «Tu es Daniel de filiis captivitatis Iudae, quem adduxit rex pater meus de Iuda? 14Audivi de te quoniam spiritum deorum habeas, et scientia intellegentiaque ac sapientia ampliores inventae sint in te. 15Et nunc introgressi sunt in conspectu meo sapientes, magi, ut scripturam hanc legerent et interpretationem eius indicarent mihi et nequiverunt sensum huius sermonis edicere. 16Porro ego audivi de te quod possis obscura interpretari et ligata dissolvere; si ergo vales scripturam legere et interpretationem eius indicare mihi, purpura vestieris et torquem auream circa collum tuum habebis et

l. Aramaic repeats *the king your father* **k.** Or *Spirit of the holy God*

writing and make known to me its interpretation, you shall be
clothed with purple, and have a chain of gold about your neck,
and shall be the third ruler in the kingdom.
2 Kings 5:16 17 Then Daniel answered before the king, "Let your gifts be for
Dan 2:6 yourself, and give your rewards to another; nevertheless I will read
Acts 8:20 the writing to the king and make known to him the interpretation.
18 O king, the Most High God gave Nebuchadnezzar your father
kingship and greatness and glory and majesty; 19 and because of
the greatness that he gave him, all peoples, nations, and languages
trembled and feared before him; whom he would he slew, and
whom he would he kept alive; whom he would he raised up, and
whom he would he put down. 20 But when his heart was lifted up
and his spirit was hardened so that he dealt proudly, he was
deposed from his kingly throne, and his glory was taken from
him; 21 he was driven from among men, and his mind was made
Dan 4:22,33 like that of a beast, and his dwelling was with the wild asses; he
was fed grass like an ox, and his body was wet with the dew of
heaven, until he knew that the Most High God rules the kingdom
of men, and sets over it whom he will. 22 And you his son,
Belshazzar, have not humbled your heart, though you knew all
Job 12:10 this, 23 but you have lifted up yourself against the Lord of heaven;
Ps 135:15–17 and the vessels of his house have been brought in before you, and
Is 40:20 you and your lords, your wives, and your concubines have drunk

---

This sentence is passed on Belshazzar not only because he failed to glorify the God who gave him life (v. 23) but because he showed him disrespect through the sacrilegious use of the sacred vessels. Theodoret of Cyrus, commenting on v. 23, points out that Daniel "teaches them that they should worship the Lord God, not the things that they can see. Therefore, he denounces the vanity of the king, and tells him that the invisible God holds the high heavens in his sway. 'You,' he says to the king, 'you have not humbled your heart, nor seen the greatness of the heart of heaven, who is God and Lord of everything that is. If you had not been blinded by your pride, you would not have taken the vessels of the Lord from his temple'" *Interpretatio in Danielem*, 5, 23).

tertius in regno meo princeps eris». 17 Tunc respondens Daniel ait coram rege: «Munera tua sint tibi, et dona tua alteri da; scripturam autem legam tibi, rex, et interpretationem eius ostendam tibi. 18 O rex, Deus altissimus regnum et magnificentiam et gloriam et honorem dedit Nabuchodonosor patri tuo. 19 Et propter magnificentiam, quam dederat ei, universi populi, tribus et linguae tremebant et metuebant eum; quos volebat, interficiebat et, quos volebat, percutiebat et, quos volebat, exaltabat et, quos volebat, humiliabat. 20 Quando autem elevatum est cor eius, et spiritus illius obfirmatus est ad superbiam, depositus est de solio regni sui, et gloria eius ablata est ab eo; 21 et a filiis hominum eiectus est, sed et cor eius cum bestiis positum est, et cum onagris erat habitatio eius, fenum quoque ut boves comedebat, et rore caeli corpus eius infectum est, donec cognosceret quod potestatem haberet Deus altissimus in regno hominum et, quemcumque voluerit, suscitabit super illud. 22 Tu quoque filius eius, Balthasar, non

wine from them; and you have praised the gods of silver and gold, Dan 5:4
of bronze, iron, wood, and stone, which do not see or hear or
know, but the God in whose hand is your breath, and whose are all
your ways, you have not honoured.
[24]"Then from his presence the hand was sent, and this writing
was inscribed. [25]And this is the writing that was inscribed: MENE,
MENE, TEKEL, and PARSIN. [26]This is the interpretation of the matter:
MENE, God has numbered the days of your kingdom and brought
it to an end; [27]TEKEL, you have been weighed in the balances and
found wanting; [28]PERES, your kingdom is divided and given to the
Medes and Persians." 2 Kings 17:6 Dan 6:28

The interpretation is borne out

[29]Then Belshazzar commanded, and Daniel was clothed with
purple, a chain of gold was put about his neck, and proclamation
was made concerning him, that he should be the third ruler in the
kingdom.
[30]That very night Belshazzar the Chaldean king was slain.
[31]And Darius the Mede* received the kingdom, being about sixty- Dan 9:1
two years old.

5:29–30. The very abrupt end to the story shows the king keeping his promise to reward Daniel (cf. v. 16), so he must have believed the interpretation. But events quickly prove Daniel right (v. 30). There is no mention of the king's having a change of heart and praising the true God, as happens in the previous chapter and in the one that follows. Maybe there is an implication that the king's punishment was immediate, precisely because he did not seek forgiveness.

humiliasti cor tuum, cum scires haec omnia, [23]sed adversum Dominum caeli elevatus es, et vasa domus eius allata sunt coram te, et tu et optimates tui et uxores tuae et concubinae tuae vinum bibistis in eis; deos quoque argenteos et aureos et aereos, ferreos ligneosque et lapideos, qui non vident neque audiunt neque sentiunt, laudasti, porro Deum, qui habet flatum tuum in manu sua et omnes vias tuas, non glorificasti. [24]Idcirco ab eo missi sunt articuli manus, et scriptura haec exarata est. [25]Haec est autem scriptura, quae digesta est: mane, thecel, upharsin. [26]Et haec est interpretatio sermonis: mane, numeravit Deus regnum tuum et complevit illud; [27]thecel, appensus es in statera et inventus es minus habens; [28]phares, divisum est regnum tuum et datum est Medis et Persis». [29]Tunc, iubente Balthasar, indutus est Daniel purpura, et circumdata est torques aurea collo eius, et praedicatum est de eo quod haberet potestatem tertius in regno suo. [30]Eadem nocte interfectus est Balthasar rex Chaldaeorum. **[6]** [1]Et Darius Medus successit in regnum annos natus sexaginta duos. [2]Placuit Dario et constituit super regnum satrapas centum viginti, ut essent in toto regno suo, [3]et super eos principes tres, ex quibus Daniel unus erat, ut satrapae illis redderent rationem, et rex non sustineret molestiam. [4]Igitur ille Daniel superabat omnes principes et satrapas, quia spiritus Dei amplior erat in eo. Porro rex cogitabat constituere eum super omne regnum; [5]unde principes et satrapae quaerebant, ut invenirent occasionem Danieli ex latere regni, nullamque causam et suspicionem reperire potuerunt, eo quod fidelis esset, et omnis culpa et suspicio non inveniretur in eo. [6]Dixerunt ergo viri illi: «Non inveniemus Danieli huic

6. DANIEL IN THE LIONS' DEN*

Daniel sentenced to be put in the lions' den

Esther 1:1 6 [1]It pleased Darius to set over the kingdom a hundred and
twenty satraps, to be throughout the whole kingdom; [2]and over
them three presidents, of whom Daniel was one, to whom these
satraps should give account, so that the king might suffer no loss.
Dan 5:7,16,29 [3]Then this Daniel became distinguished above all the other
presidents and satraps, because an excellent spirit was in him; and

---

***6:1–28.** This passage, which is similar in parts to chapter 3, begins by showing how difficult it was for the Jews to stay true to their religion in the midst of a pagan society (vv. 1–18); then we see how God comes to their rescue (vv. 19–24); finally, the pagan king acknowledges the God of Israel (vv. 25–28). As in chapter 5, Daniel is center-stage; in fact, his companions are not even mentioned. The episode has no particular connexion with the previous ones; in fact, it seems to be a unit in its own right; it rounds off the part of the book dealing with Daniel at the court of Babylon. The fact that the story involves Darius the Mede, a king unknown to historical scholarship (see pp. 794f, above), reinforces the impression that this is a moral tale designed to get across the message that God helps those who strive to obey the precepts of the Jewish religion.

6:1–18. Daniel seems to be very much part of the social and political world of Babylon; thanks to his skill and loyalty, he is second only to the king. The plot against him may have been hatched out of jealousy, but the fact that he was a foreigner and a Jew probably did not help. His enemies set a sort of legal trap for Daniel. The king in his vanity issues a decree which, for a period of thirty days, makes him the only god there is. It is a decree that even he cannot revoke—much as he would wish to do so, in order to liberate Daniel from its penalty. Here Daniel the Jew is not being obliged to do something against his religion: he is being required to refrain from doing something that his religion enjoins—to pray to God facing towards Jerusalem (cf. 1 Kings 8:48). Daniel's opponents have managed to manipulate the king and change the law in such a way that they can accuse Daniel of breaking the law for religious reasons; he cannot be faulted on any other score.

When Daniel learned about the interdict, he did not change his standard pattern of prayer (v. 11); there is a lesson here for Christians, as the Fathers point out. Origen, for example, says: "The commandment to *pray without ceasing* (cf. Lk 18:1) can be understood and fulfilled only if we believe that the whole of man's life is a single, unbroken prayer. One part of this long prayer of life is what we call prayer, and we should pray no less than three times a day, as is made clear in the book of Daniel, who prayed three times a day even in the midst of great dangers" (*De oratione,* 12, 2).

the king planned to set him over the whole kingdom. 4Then the
presidents and the satraps sought to find a ground for complaint
against Daniel with regard to the kingdom; but they could find no
ground for complaint or any fault, because he was faithful, and no
error or fault was found in him. 5Then these men said, "We shall
not find any ground for complaint against this Daniel unless we
find it in connection with the law of his God."

6Then these presidents and satraps came by agreement[m] to the
king and said to him, "O King Darius, live for ever! 7All the
presidents of the kingdom, the prefects and the satraps, the counsellors and the governors are agreed that the king should establish an
ordinance and enforce an interdict, that whoever makes petition to
any god or man for thirty days, except to you, O king, shall be cast
into the den of lions. 8Now, O king, establish the interdict and sign
the document, so that it cannot be changed, according to the law of
the Medes and the Persians, which cannot be revoked." 9Therefore
King Darius signed the document and interdict. Esther 1:19

10When Daniel knew that the document had been signed, he
went to his house where he had windows in his upper chamber 1 Kings 8:44,48
open toward Jerusalem; and he got down upon his knees three Ps 5:7; 28:2;
times a day and prayed and gave thanks before his God, as he had 138:2
done previously. 11Then these men came by agreement[m] and
found Daniel making petition and supplication before his God. 1 Kings 8:44,48
12Then they came near and said before the king, concerning the Ps 5:8; 28:2;
interdict, "O king! Did you not sign an interdict, that any man 55:18; 138:2 Dan 3:49
who makes petition to any god or man within thirty days except to Acts 12:11
you, O king, shall be cast into the den of lions?" The king
answered, "The thing stands fast, according to the law of the

---

aliquam occasionem, nisi forte inveniamus adversus eum in lege Dei sui». 7Tunc principes et satrapae illi concurrerunt ad regem et sic locuti sunt ei: «Darie rex, in aeternum vive! 8Consilium inierunt cuncti principes regni, magistratus et satrapae, optimates et iudices, ut decretum regis promulget et edictum confirmet, ut omnis, qui petierit aliquam petitionem a quocumque deo et homine usque ad dies triginta, nisi a te, rex, mittatur in lacum leonum. 9Nunc itaque, rex, confirma sententiam et signa decretum, ut non immutetur iuxta legem Medorum et Persarum, quam praevaricari non licet». 10Porro rex Darius signavit edictum et decretum. 11Daniel autem, cum comperisset decretum signatum esse, ingressus est domum suam et, fenestris apertis in cenaculo suo contra Ierusalem, tribus temporibus in die flectebat genua sua et adorabat confitebaturque coram Deo suo, sicut et ante facere consueverat. 12Viri ergo illi accesserunt et invenerunt Danielem orantem et obsecrantem Deum suum. 13Tunc accesserunt et locuti sunt coram rege super edicto: «Rex, numquid non signasti decretum, ut omnis homo, qui rogaret quemquam de diis et hominibus usque ad dies triginta, nisi a te, rex, mitteretur in lacum leonum?». Respondens rex ait: «Verus est sermo iuxta decretum Medorum atque Persarum, quod praevaricari non licet». 14Tunc respondentes dixerunt coram rege: «Daniel de filiis captivitatis Iudae non curavit de te, rex, et de edicto, quod constituisti, sed tribus temporibus per diem orat obsecratione sua». 15Quod verbum cum audisset, rex satis contristatus est; et pro Daniele posuit cor, ut liberaret eum, et usque ad

m. Or *thronging*

Medes and Persians, which cannot be revoked." [13]Then they answered before the king, "That Daniel, who is one of the exiles from Judah, pays no heed to you, O king, or the interdict you have signed, but makes his petition three times a day."

[14]Then the king, when he heard these words, was much distressed, and set his mind to deliver Daniel; and he laboured till the sun went down to rescue him. [15]Then these men came by agreement[m] to the king, and said to the king, "Know, O king, that it is a law of the Medes and Persians that no interdict or ordinance which the king establishes can be changed."

[16]Then the king commanded, and Daniel was brought and cast into the den of lions. The king said to Daniel, "May your God, whom you serve continually, deliver you!" [17]And a stone was brought and laid upon the mouth of the den, and the king sealed it with his own signet and with the signet of his lords, that nothing might be changed concerning Daniel. [18]Then the king went to his palace, and spent the night fasting; no diversions were brought to him, and sleep fled from him.

Daniel's miraculous escape

[19]Then, at break of day, the king arose and went in haste to the den of lions. [20]When he came near to the den where Daniel was, he

---

6:19–24. Through divine intervention (once again by means of an angel: cf. 3:26), no harm comes to Daniel from the lions. It is as if Daniel is innocent in the sight of God—a point not lost on the king (v. 22) either; in fact, it spurs him to take control of the situation, assert his rights, and see that justice is done (vv. 23–24). Daniel's fidelity to his religion, and the fact that God protected him in his ordeal, expose the perversity of the king's edict, and cause the king to right the wrong he has done. The sacred writer points out why God intervened miraculously—because Daniel "trusted in his God" (v. 23). Daniel's rivals were punished in line with the customs of the time, that is, they were punished very severely.

St Augustine comments that the lions refrained from harming Daniel because he was faithful to God: "Submit to the one who has power over you, and you will be raised above those who once held you in thrall. In committing sin, man places above

---

occasum solis laborabat, ut erueret illum. [16]Viri autem illi accesserunt ad regem et dixerunt ei: «Scito, rex, quia lex Medorum est atque Persarum, ut omne decretum et edictum, quod constituit rex, non liceat immutari». [17]Tunc rex praecepit, et adduxerunt Danielem et miserunt eum in lacum leonum. Dixitque rex Danieli: «Deus tuus, quem colis semper, ipse liberet te». [18]Allatusque est lapis unus et positus est super os laci; quem obsignavit rex anulo suo et anulo optimatum suorum, ne quid fieret contra Danielem. [19]Et abiit rex in domum suam et dormivit incenatus, cibique non sunt illati coram eo; insuper et somnus recessit ab eo. [20]Tunc rex primo diluculo consurgens festinus ad lacum leonum perrexit;

cried out in a tone of anguish and said to Daniel, "O Daniel,
servant of the living God, has your God, whom you serve
continually, been able to deliver you from the lions?" 21Then
Daniel said to the king, "O king, live for ever! 22My God sent his
angel and shut the lions' mouths, and they have not hurt me, Heb 11:33
because I was found blameless before him; and also before you, O Tob 5:4
king, I have done no wrong." 23Then the king was exceedingly
glad, and commanded that Daniel be taken up out of the den. So
Daniel was taken up out of the den, and no kind of hurt was found
upon him, because he had trusted in his God. 24And the king
commanded, and those men who had accused Daniel were
brought and cast into the den of lions—they, their children, and
their wives; and before they reached the bottom of the den the
lions overpowered them and broke all their bones in pieces.

The king's profession of faith

25Then King Darius wrote to all the peoples, nations, and Ezra 1:3
languages that dwell in all the earth: "Peace be multiplied to you. Ruth 1:16
26I make a decree, that in all my royal dominion men tremble and Dan 3:29; 4:1
fear before the God of Daniel, 1 Pet 1:23
for he is the living God, Rev 4:9
enduring for ever;
his kingdom shall never be destroyed,
and his dominion shall be to the end.

himself what should always be beneath him; he submits to things that are less than him. [...] Acknowledge the one who has power over you, so that the things that are below you will see where you stand above them. For when Daniel acknowledged the power of the Lord God, the lions saw the superiority of Daniel over them and did not touch him" (*In epistolam Ioannis*, 8).

6:25–28. The king readily issues a decree that goes against his earlier one (cf. 6:9); the tenor of it is like that issued by Nebuchadnezzar in 4:1–3. So, both the Babylonian king and Darius the Mede acknowledged the God of the Jews as the one true God whose kingdom lasts forever; and they reached that point thanks to the wisdom that God gave the Jews (particularly Daniel) and to the exemplary fidelity of the Jews to their religion in the midst of trials.

[21]appropinquansque lacui Danielem voce lacrimabili inclamavit et affatus est Danielem: «Daniel, serve Dei viventis, Deus tuus, cui tu servis semper, putasne valuit liberare te a leonibus?». [22]Et Daniel regi respondens ait: «Rex, in aeternum vive! [23]Deus meus misit angelum suum et conclusit ora leonum, et non nocuerunt mihi, quia coram eo iustitia inventa est in me; sed et coram te, rex, delictum non feci». [24]Tunc rex vehementer gavisus est super eo et Danielem praecepit educi de lacu; eductusque est Daniel

Ezra 1:1,2; 4:5; 6:14 Dan 3:32 27He delivers and rescues,
he works signs and wonders
in heaven and on earth,
he who has saved Daniel
from the power of the lions."
28So this Daniel prospered during the reign of Darius and the
reign of Cyrus the Persian.

PART TWO

Daniel's dreams and visions*

1. VISION OF THE FOUR BEASTS AND OF THE SON OF MAN*

Dan 2; 5:1 Rev 13:1–18; 17:16; 19:19–21

Daniel's vision

7 1In the first year of Belshazzar king of Babylon, Daniel had a
dream and visions of his head as he lay in his bed. Then he

***7:1—12:13.** Up to the end of chapter 6, Daniel has been the interpreter of kings' dreams; now his own dreams are interpreted for him by an angel or heavenly being: the interpreter explains dreams (chaps. 7–8), the meaning of Scripture (chap. 9), and a vision (chaps. 10–12); and Daniel himself notes it all down.

Daniel had announced to Nebuchadnezzar the end of time as part of the interpretation of his dream (cf. 2:28); now Daniel is told when it will happen (cf. 12:5–12); for him (cf. 2:28); he is given a more specific revelation in which the figure of the tyrannical Antiochus IV (described here symbolically) is depicted as the epitome of evil and his death will mark the end of the present age (cf. 11:45—12:1). Earlier, Daniel's wisdom was seen as a divine gift to be used for the benefit of foreign kings; now it is depicted as coming from a revelation in which God speaks to Daniel through heavenly messengers and tells him about the

de lacu, et nulla laesio inventa est in eo, quia credidit Deo suo. 25Dixit autem rex, et adducti sunt viri illi, qui accusaverant Danielem, et in lacum leonum missi sunt, ipsi et filii eorum et uxores eorum, et non pervenerunt usque ad pavimentum laci, donec potirentur eis leones, et omnia ossa eorum comminuerunt. 26Tunc Darius rex scripsit universis populis, tribubus et linguis, habitantibus in universa terra: «Pax vobis multiplicetur! 27A me constitutum est decretum, ut in universo imperio regni mei tremescant et paveant Deum Danielis: ipse est enim Deus vivens / et permanens in saecula, / et regnum eius non dissipabitur, / et potestas eius usque in aeternum; / 28ipse liberator atque salvator / et faciens signa et mirabilia / in caelo et in terra. / Liberavit autem Danielem / de manu leonum». 29Porro Daniel prosperatus est in regno Darii et in regno Cyri Persae. **[7]** 1Anno primo Balthasar regis Babylonis

wrote down the dream, and told the sum of the matter. [2]Daniel
said, "I saw in my vision by night, and behold, the four winds of
heaven were stirring up the great sea. [3]And four great beasts came Rev 13:1; 17:12
up out of the sea, different from one another. [4]The first was like a

---

meaning of human history—a revelation that he must commit to writing, as a source of comfort and hope for the chosen people. "Revelation has set within history a point of reference which cannot be ignored if the mystery of human life is to be known. Yet this knowledge refers back constantly to the mystery of God which the human mind cannot exhaust but can only receive and embrace in faith. Between these two poles, reason has its own specific field in which it can enquire and understand, restricted only by its finiteness before the infinite mystery of God" (John Paul II, *Fides et ratio*, 14).

***7:1–28.** This chapter marks the end of the part of the book written in Aramaic; in it we again find elements seen in chapter 2 (where the Aramaic part began); these include: the arrangement of history into four periods (symbolized there by metals, here by beasts) and the establishment of an everlasting kingdom at the end. Thus, the chapter closes the Aramaic section and acts as a kind of introduction to the chapters (in Hebrew) in which Daniel receives and writes down divine revelations. Chapter 8 is written in Hebrew and it explains chapter 7; and this pattern continues: chapter 9 is explained by chapter 10; and 11 by 12. Daniel first outlines his dream or vision, and it is then interpreted by an angelic being. In this chapter the content of the dream is given in vv. 1–14, and its interpretation in vv. 15–28. Vision and interpretation constitute a single event, an account of which Daniel writes down, as he mentions at the start (cf. v. 1) and finish (cf. v. 28). Daniel's "signature" at beginning and end confirms the truth of his vision and the truthfulness of what he has written for the reader.

7:1–14. In chapter 5 the picture drawn of Belshazzar suggested that he stood figuratively for the sacrilegious King Antiochus IV. It is not surprising, then, that this dream of Daniel's is set in the first year of Belshazzar's reign, given that the climax of the prophecy (the little horn) concerns Antiochus IV. God is going to intervene definitively when irreligion is at its worst. There are two scenes in the vision—the beasts coming out of the sea (vv. 2–8) and the divine court and judgment (vv. 9–14).

7:2–8. The Great Sea (the Mediterranean: v. 2), out of which the beasts arise, stands for the world of gloom and chaos. Although earlier prophets did

Daniel somnium vidit et visionem capitis eius in cubili suo; tunc et somnium scripsit. Caput verborum, quae locutus est. [2]Respondit Daniel et dixit: «Videbam in visione mea nocte: et ecce quattuor venti caeli conturbabant mare Magnum, [3]et quattuor bestiae grandes ascendebant de mari diversae inter se. [4]Prima quasi leaena et alas habebat aquilae; aspiciebam, donec evulsae sunt alae eius; et sublata est de terra et super pedes quasi homo stetit, et cor hominis datum est ei. [5]Et ecce bestia alia, secunda, similis

Rev 13:2 lion and had eagles' wings. Then as I looked its wings were
plucked off, and it was lifted up from the ground and made to
stand upon two feet like a man; and the mind of a man was given
to it. 5 And behold, another beast, a second one, like a bear. It was
raised up on one side; it had three ribs in its mouth between its
Dan 8:8,22; teeth; and it was told, 'Arise, devour much flesh.' 6 After this I
11:3–4 looked, and lo, another, like a leopard, with four wings of a bird
on its back; and the beast had four heads; and dominion was given
Rev 13:1; 17:12 to it. 7 After this I saw in the night visions, and behold, a fourth
beast, terrible and dreadful and exceedingly strong; and it had
great iron teeth; it devoured and broke in pieces, and stamped the
residue with its feet. It was different from all the beasts that were
Rev 13:5 before it; and it had ten horns. 8 I considered the horns, and behold,
there came up among them another horn, a little one,* before
which three of the first horns were plucked up by the roots; and
behold, in this horn were eyes like the eyes of a man, and a mouth

---

use animals as symbols for empires (a crocodile for Egypt, cf. Ezek 32; an eagle or a monster for Babylon, cf. Ezek 17:3; Jer 51:34), the winged beasts of Daniel's vision are reminiscent of Mesopotamian statues. The lion with eagle's wings stands for Nebuchadnezzar; a proud man, he was brought low and later given back his reason (4:16, 34); the empire of the Medes is depicted as a bear ready to attack, and that of the Persians as a leopard, fleet of foot. The fourth beast resembles no animal, but its teeth of iron show it to be the Greek empire of Alexander the Great and his successors (cf. 2:40). Of those successors, (symbolized by the horns), attention is focused on Antiochus IV, the horn with eyes that speaks blasphemy (cf. vv. 8, 25). The gravity of those challenges to God's authority will be underlined in Revelation 13:5 in its description of the beast that is given power by the dragon. The worst sin of the powers of the world is their opposition to God and his laws. Interpreting the words of this passage as a prophecy in the strict sense, that is, as a prediction of something that will happen in the future, some Fathers read the last of the horns as being the Antichrist of whom the Revelation to John will have much to say (cf. Rev. 13:11–18; 17:16; 19:19–21).

urso in parte stetit, et tres costae erant in ore eius et in dentibus eius; et sic dicebant ei: "Surge, comede carnes plurimas". 6 Post hoc aspiciebam, et ecce alia quasi pardus et alas habebat avis quattuor super se, et quattuor capita erant in bestia; et potestas data est ei. 7 Post hoc aspiciebam in visione noctis, et ecce bestia quarta terribilis atque mirabilis et fortis nimis; dentes ferreos habebat magnos, comedens atque comminuens et reliqua pedibus suis conculcans; dissimilis autem erat ceteris bestiis, quas videram ante eam, et habebat cornua decem. 8 Considerabam cornua, et ecce cornu aliud parvulum ortum est de medio eorum, et tria de cornibus primis evulsa sunt a facie eius; et ecce oculi quasi oculi hominis erant in cornu isto, et os loquens ingentia. 9 Aspiciebam, / donec throni positi sunt, / et Antiquus dierum sedit. / Vestimentum eius quasi nix candidum, / et capilli capitis eius quasi lana munda; /

speaking great things. [9]As I looked,
throne were placed
and one that was ancient of days took his seat;
his raiment was white as snow,
and the hair of his head like pure wool;
his throne was fiery flames,
its wheels were burning fire.

Ezek 1:13–16
Rev 4:2; 20:4;
1:14; Mt 28:3
Mk 9:3

7:9–14. Divine judgment is passed on the kingdoms in this scene. God is depicted as being seated on a throne in heaven, his glory flashing out and angels all around. Judgment is about to take place, and it will be followed by execution of the sentence. The books (v. 10) contain all the actions of men (cf. Jer 17:1; Mal 3:16; Ps 56:8; Rev 20:12). The seer is shown history past (not laid out according to chronology: all the empires are included in one glance), and he notes that a more severe sentence is passed on the blasphemous horn than on the other beasts. They had their lives extended (v. 12), that is, their deprivation of power did not spell the end; but the little horn is destroyed forthwith. "Following in the steps of the prophets and John the Baptist, Jesus announced the judgment of the Last Day in his preaching (cf. Dan 7:10; Joel 3–4; Mal 3:19; Mt 3:7–12)" (*Catechism of the Catholic Church,* 678).

The one "like a son of man" who comes with the clouds of heaven and who, after the judgment, is given everlasting dominion over all the earth, is the very antithesis of the beasts. He has not risen from a turbulent sea like them; there is nothing ferocious about him. Rather, he has been raised up by God (he comes with the clouds of heaven) and he shares the human condition. The dignity of all mankind is restored through this son of man's triumph over the beasts. This figure, as we will discover later, stands for "the people of the saints of the Most High" (7:27), that is, faithful Israel. However, he is also an individual (just as the winged lion was an individual, and the little horn), and insofar as he is given a kingdom, he is a king. What we have here is an individual who represents the people. In Jewish circles around the time of Christ, this "son of man" was interpreted as being the Messiah, a real person (cf. *Book of the Parables of Enoch*); but it was a title that became linked to the sufferings of the Messiah and to his resurrection from the dead only when Jesus Christ applied it to himself in the Gospel. "Jesus accepted Peter's profession of faith, which acknowledged him to be the Messiah, by announcing the imminent Passion of the Son of Man (cf. Mt 16:23). He unveiled the authentic content of his messianic kingship both in the transcendent identity of the Son of Man 'who came down from heaven' (Jn 3:13; cf. Jn 6:62; Dan 7:13), and in his redemptive mission as the suffering Servant: 'The Son of Man came not to be served but to serve, and to give his life as a ransom for many' (Mt 20:28; cf. Is 53:10–12)" (*Catechism of the Catholic Church*, 440).

Ps 50:3; 56:9 Jer 17:1 Mal 3:16 Jn 5:22 Lk 2:13 Heb 1:14 Rev 5:11: 20:12

10A stream of fire issued
and came forth from before him;
a thousand thousands served him,
and ten thousand times ten thousand stood before him;
the court sat in judgment,
and the books were opened.

11I looked then because of the sound of the great words which
the horn was speaking. And as I looked, the beast was slain, and
Rev 19:20 its body destroyed and given over to be burned with fire. 12As for
the rest of the beasts, their dominion was taken away, but their
lives were prolonged for a season and a time. 13I saw in the night
visions,

Mt 24:30; 26:64 *Mk 13:26*; 14:62 *Lk 21:27*; 22:68 Jn 5:22 *Rev 1:7*; 14:14

and behold, with the clouds of heaven
there came one like a son of man,*
and he came to the Ancient of Days
and was presented before him.

Ps 2:6–7; 110:2 Dan 2:28,44 Mt 4:17; 8:20; 28:18 Lk 1:33 Heb 12:28 Rev 11:15; 22:5

14And to him was given dominion
and glory and kingdom,
that all peoples, nations, and languages
should serve him;
his dominion is an everlasting dominion,
which shall not pass away,
and his kingdom one
that shall not be destroyed.

When the Church proclaims in the Creed that Christ is seated at the right hand of the Father, she is saying that it was to Christ that dominion was given: "Being seated at the Father's right hand signifies the inauguration of the Messiah's kingdom, the fulfilment of the prophet Daniel's vision concerning the Son of man: 'To him was given domination and glory and kingdom, that all peoples, nations, and languages should serve him; his dominion is an everlasting dominion, which shall not pass away, and his kingdom one that shall not be destroyed' (Dan 7:14). After this event the apostles became witnesses of the 'kingdom [that] will have no end' (Nicene Creed)" (*Catechism of the Catholic Church*, 664).

thronus eius flammae ignis, / rotae eius ignis accensus. / 10Fluvius igneus effluebat / et egrediebatur a facie eius; / milia milium ministrabant ei, / et decies milies centena milia assistebant ei: / iudicium sedit, / et libri aperti sunt. 11Aspiciebam tunc propter vocem sermonum grandium, quos cornu illud loquebatur; et vidi quoniam interfecta esset bestia, et perisset corpus eius, et tradita esset ad comburendum igni; 12aliarum quoque bestiarum ablata esset potestas, et tempora vitae constituta essent eis usque ad tempus et tempus. 13Aspiciebam ergo in visione noctis: / et ecce cum nubibus caeli / quasi Filius hominis veniebat / et usque ad Antiquum dierum pervenit, / et in conspectu eius obtulerunt eum; / 14et data sunt ei potestas et honor et regnum; / et omnes populi, tribus et linguae / ipsi servierunt: / potestas eius potestas aeterna, / quae non auferetur, / et regnum eius, quod non corrumpetur. 15Horruit

The vision interpreted

[15]"As for me, Daniel, my spirit within me was anxious and the
visions of my head alarmed me. [16]I approached one of those who
stood there and asked him the truth concerning all this. So he told
me, and made known to me the interpretation of the things.
[17]'These four great beasts are four kings who shall arise out of the Mt 25:34
earth. [18]But the saints of the Most High shall receive the kingdom, Heb 12:28
and possess the kingdom for ever, for ever and ever.' Rev 20:4; 22:5

[19]"Then I desired to know the truth concerning the fourth beast,
which was different from all the rest, exceedingly terrible, with its
teeth of iron and claws of bronze; and which devoured and broke
in pieces, and stamped the residue with its feet; [20]and concerning Rev 13:5;
the ten horns that were on its head, and the other horn which came 17:12
up and before which three of them fell, the horn which had eyes
and a mouth that spoke great things, and which seemed greater
than its fellows. [21]As I looked, this horn made war with the saints, Dan 8:12,24;
and prevailed over them, [22]until the Ancient of Days came, and 11:31 Rev 11:7
judgment was given for the saints of the Most High, and the time Rev 13:7; 20:4
came when the saints received the kingdom.

7:15–28. The interpretation focuses on the protagonists in the period when the book of Daniel was written—those to whom the kingdom will be given, that is, faithful Jews or "saints of the Most High" (vv. 18, 27); and the horn that grows from the fourth beast, Antiochus IV, who blasphemes against God, persecutes those who keep the Law and suppresses sabbaths and feasts (v. 25; cf. 1 Mac 1:41–52). But the persecution will only go on for a certain time—three and a half "times", that is, half seven, which symbolizes completeness. The vision and its interpretation alarm Daniel on account of the sufferings that his people are undergoing and will undergo in the future; but he also says that "I kept the matter in my mind" (v. 28): his faith and hope are not affected.

spiritus meus: ego Daniel territus sum in his, et visiones capitis mei conturbaverunt me. [16]Accessi ad
unum de assistentibus et veritatem quaerebam ab eo de omnibus his; qui dixit mihi et interpretationem
sermonum edocuit me: [17]"Hae bestiae magnae quattuor, quattuor regna consurgent de terra; [18]suscipient
autem regnum sancti Dei altissimi et obtinebunt regnum usque in saeculum et saeculum saeculorum".
[19]Post hoc volui diligenter discere de bestia quarta, quae erat dissimilis valde ab omnibus his et terribilis
nimis, dentes ferrei et ungues eius aerei, comedens et comminuens et reliquias pedibus suis conculcans,
[20]et de cornibus decem, quae habebat in capite, et de alio, quod ortum fuerat ante, et ceciderant tria
cornua, de cornu illo, quod habebat oculos et os loquens grandia et maius erat ceteris. [21]Aspiciebam,
et ecce cornu illud faciebat bellum adversus sanctos et praevalebat eis, [22]donec venit Antiquus dierum
et iudicium dedit sanctis Excelsi, et tempus advenit, et regnum obtinuerunt sancti. [23]Et sic ait: "Bestia
quarta regnum quartum erit in terra, quod maius erit omnibus regnis et devorabit universam terram et
conculcabit et comminuet eam. [24]Porro cornua decem regni decem reges erunt; et alius consurget post
eos et ipse potentior erit prioribus et tres reges humiliabit [25]et sermones contra Excelsum loquetur et
sanctos Altissimi conteret et putabit quod possit mutare tempora et legem, et tradentur in manu eius
usque ad tempus et tempora et dimidium temporis; [26]et iudicium sedebit, et potentiam eius auferent, ut

23"Thus he said: 'As for the fourth beast,
there shall be a fourth kingdom on earth,
which shall be different from all the kingdoms,
and it shall devour the whole earth,
and trample it down, and break it to pieces.
Rev 17:12 24As for the ten horns,
out of this kingdom
ten kings shall arise,
and another shall arise after them;
he shall be different from the former ones,
and shall put down three kings.
1 Mac 1:41–52 Dan 8:14, 24–25; 11:36; 12:7,14 Rev 12:14 25He shall speak words against the Most High,
and shall wear out the saints of the Most High,
and shall think to change the times and the law;
and they shall be given into his hand
for a time, two times, and half a time.
26But the court shall sit in judgment,
and his dominion shall be taken away,
to be consumed and destroyed to the end.
Lk 12:32 Rev 11:15; 20:4 27And the kingdom and the dominion
and the greatness of the kingdoms under the whole heaven
shall be given to the people of the saints of the Most High;
their kingdom shall be an everlasting kingdom,
and all dominions shall serve and obey them.'

Daniel keeps silence

Lk 2:19 28"Here is the end of the matter. As for me, Daniel, my thoughts greatly alarmed me, and my color changed; but I kept the matter in my mind."

---

conteratur et dispereat usque in finem; 27regnum autem et potestas et magnitudo regnorum, quae sunt subter omne caelum, detur populo sanctorum Altissimi, cuius regnum regnum sempiternum est, et omnes reges servient ei et oboedient"». 28Hucusque finis verbi. Ego Daniel multum cogitationibus meis conturbabar, et facies mea mutata est in me; verbum autem in corde meo conservavi. **[8]** 1Anno tertio regni Balthasar regis visio apparuit mihi, ego Daniel, post id quod mihi apparuerat in principio. 2Vidi in visione, et factum est, dum viderem, eram in Susis castro, quod est in Elam provincia; vidi autem in visione esse me super rivum Ulai. 3Et levavi oculos meos et vidi: et ecce aries unus stabat ante rivum habens cornua et cornua excelsa et unum excelsius altero, et excelsius crescebat in postero. 4Vidi arietem cornibus ventilantem contra occidentem et contra aquilonem et contra meridiem, et omnes bestiae non poterant resistere ei neque liberari de manu eius; fecitque secundum voluntatem suam et magnificatus est. 5Et ego intellegebam: ecce autem hircus caprarum veniebat ab occidente super faciem totius terrae et non tangebat terram; porro hircus habebat cornu insigne inter oculos suos. 6Et venit usque ad arietem illum cornutum, quem videram stantem ante rivum, et cucurrit ad eum in impetu fortitudinis suae. 7Vidi eum appropinquantem prope arietem, et efferatus est in eum et percussit arietem et comminuit duo cornua eius, et non poterat aries resistere ei; cumque eum misisset in terram, conculcavit, et nemo quibat liberare arietem de manu eius. 8Hircus autem caprarum magnus factus est

2. VISION OF THE RAM AND THE HE-GOAT*

Daniel's vision

8 [1]In the third year of the reign of King Belshazzar a vision Dan 5:1; 7:1
appeared to me, Daniel, after that which appeared to me at the Rev 1:9
first. [2]And I saw in the vision; and when I saw, I was in Susa the Neh 1:1
Ezek 1:1–3

***8:1–27.** Daniel continues his account and now tells about another vision which, like the previous one, took place in the reign of King Belshazzar (8:1–14); and then he records the interpretation, provided this time by the angel Gabriel (8:15–27). This new vision, developing the last part of the previous one, shows the empire of the Medes and Persians being dislodged by the Greeks, and then the evil doings of Antiochus IV. The symbolism of the horned animals comes in again but the focus has shifted to when the end will come for Antiochus IV (cf. 8:13–14). This helps to strengthen the morale of those who are being persecuted.

8:1–14. The start is reminiscent of the vision that Ezekiel had on the banks of a river (cf. Ezek 1:1–3), although here (v. 2) it is not clear whether the vision takes place after Daniel is brought to Susa, or whether he simply sees himself in Susa during the vision (the latter is more likely). It is significant that prior to the fall of the Babylonian empire the vision relates to one of the cities where the Persian kings used to reside. That serves to accentuate the prophetical character of the vision which will go on to refer to the Persian period, for it begins with the fall of the Median-Persian empire. That is clearly the kingdom meant by the ram with the two horns; and the he-goat is the Greek empire; this will be confirmed by the interpretation (cf. 8:21). There is a theory (not very well founded) that these particular animals were chosen as symbols of those kingdoms because, according to a common belief, Persia was under the zodiacal sign of Aries, and Syria (the land of the Seleucid Greeks) under that of Capricorn. According to the Septuagint (but not the Hebrew, or the Theodotion text), the ram charges in all four directions (v. 4)—symbolizing its remarkable and rapid expansion. But it is from the west that Alexander the Great comes—a leader remarkable for his lightning conquests and his mighty army (v. 5): in the year 333 BC he defeated Xerxes at Issus.

Verse 8 clearly has to do with the death of Alexander and the division of his empire among four Greek generals, the Diadoches—Macedonia for Philip, Asia Minor for Antigonus, Syria for Seleucus and Egypt for Ptolemy. The passage then goes on to describe the doings of Antiochus IV Epiphanes (vv. 9–11), making clear references to his campaigns against Egypt, Persia and "the glorious land", that is, Israel (v. 9; cf. 11:16), and to his profanation of the temple, which took place in 176 BC (v. 12). Verses 10–11, however, can be interpreted as saying: 1) that, after

capital, which is in the province of Elam; and I saw in the vision,
Rev 13:11 and I was at the river Ulai. [3]I raised my eyes and saw, and behold,
a ram standing on the bank of the river. It had two horns; and both
horns were high, but one was higher than the other, and the higher
Dan 11:40 one came up last. [4]I saw the ram charging westward and north-
ward and southward; no beast could stand before him, and there
was no one who could rescue from his power; he did as he pleased
and magnified himself.

[5]As I was considering, behold, a he-goat came from the west
across the face of the whole earth, without touching the ground;
and the goat had a conspicuous horn between his eyes. [6]He came
to the ram with the two horns, which I had seen standing on the
Dan 11:11 bank of the river, and he ran at him in his mighty wrath. [7]I saw
him come close to the ram, and he was enraged against him and
struck the ram and broke his two horns; and the ram had no power
to stand before him, but he cast him down to the ground and
trampled upon him; and there was no one who could rescue the
ram from his power. [8]Then the he-goat magnified himself
exceedingly; but when he was strong, the great horn was broken,
and instead of it there came up four conspicuous horns toward the
four winds of heaven.

Dan 7:6; [9]Out of one of them came forth a little horn, which grew
11:16,41 exceedingly great toward the south, toward the east, and toward
Ezek 20:6,15 the glorious land. [10]It grew great, even to the host of heaven; and
Dan 12:3 some of the host of the stars it cast down to the ground, and
Zech 7:14

---

destroying the gods of other peoples, Antiochus dared to attack even the true God and his temple, or 2) that he attacked the people of Israel (whose members would be the "stars", as in 12:3), killing some of them, including the high priest Onias III in 171, for whose death Antiochus was held responsible (cf. 2 Mac 4:30, 38). This second interpretation comes from 8:24–25.

The number of evenings and mornings that all this persecution must still last (v. 14) is something that heaven is well aware of, for it is all laid down and discussed among the angels, here described as "holy ones" (cf. 12:6–7 and note **h**). The figure is somewhat puzzling. If "evenings and mornings" refers to the evening and morning sacrifices, then it becomes 1,150 days; but if evening-and-morning means a day, then it means 2,300 days. In neither case does the figure tie in with the three and a half "times" or years (which would be 1,260 days and whose symbolism is clear: cf. 7:25). Maybe the intention is to leave the reader vague as to when exactly the end will come (which is what happens in 12:11–12), or it may be saying that the period can be shortened.

trampled upon them. [11]It magnified itself, even up to the Prince of Rev 12:4
the host; and the continual burnt offering was taken away from Dan 11:31; 12:11
him, and the place of his sanctuary was overthrown. [12]And the
host was given over to it together with the continual burnt offering
through transgression;[n] and truth was cast down to the ground,
and the horn acted and prospered. [13]Then I heard a holy one Dan 12:6
speaking; and another holy one said to the one that spoke, "For Rev 6:10
how long is the vision concerning the continual burnt offering, the
transgression that makes desolate, and the giving over of the
sanctuary and host to be trampled under foot?"[o] [14]And he said to Dan 7:25
him,[p] "For two thousand and three hundred evenings and
mornings; then the sanctuary shall be restored to its rightful state."

The vision interpreted

[15]When I, Daniel, had seen the vision, I sought to understand it;
and behold, there stood before me one having the appearance of a
man. [16]And I heard a man's voice between the banks of the Ulai, Lk 1:11,26
and it called, "Gabriel, make this man understand the vision."

8:15–27. For Daniel (called here "son of man": v. 17; that is, a man) to be able to understand them, the two heavenly beings have the appearance of men and speak like men. And, when Revelation reaches its climax God will make himself truly man—amazing condescension on God's part, for "the words of God, expressed in human language, have been made like human discourse, just as the Word of the eternal Father, when he took to himself the flesh of human weakness, was in every way made like men" (Vatican II, *Dei Verbum,* 13).

The angel Gabriel appears in the Bible for the first time here; he is charged with making God's purposes known. This is his specific mission, as we will be told later in the book (cf. 9:21) and as is clear from the New Testament, when he delivers messages

nimis; cumque crevisset, fractum est cornu magnum, et orta sunt quattuor cornua loco illius per quattuor ventos caeli. [9]De uno autem ex eis egressum est cornu unum modicum et factum est grande contra meridiem et contra orientem et contra fortitudinem [10]et magnificatum est usque ad fortitudinem caeli et deiecit de fortitudine et de stellis et conculcavit eas; [11]et usque ad principem fortitudinis magnificatum est et ab eo tulit iuge sacrificium et deiecit locum sanctificationis eius. [12]Militia autem data est contra iuge sacrificium propter peccata, et prostrata est veritas in terra; cornu autem fecit et prosperatum est. [13]Et audivi unum de sanctis loquentem, et dixit unus sanctus alteri, nescio cui, loquenti: «Usquequo visio et iuge sacrificium et peccatum desolationis, quae facta est, et sanctuarium et fortitudo conculcabitur?». [14]Et dixit ei: «Usque ad vesperam et mane, dies duo milia trecenti; et mundabitur sanctuarium». [15]Factum est autem cum viderem ego Daniel visionem et quaererem intellegentiam, ecce stetit in conspectu meo quasi species viri; [16]et audivi vocem viri inter Ulai, et clamavit et ait: «Gabriel, fac intellegere istum visionem». [17]Et venit et stetit iuxta, ubi ego stabam;

n. Heb obscure **o.** Heb obscure **p.** Theodotion Gk Syr Vg: Heb *me*

Ezek 2:1
Dan 9:21–23; 10:15–19 Lk 1:19–26 Rev 1:17 [17]So he came near where I stood; and when he came, I was
frightened and fell upon my face. But he said to me, "Understand,
O son of man, that the vision is for the time of the end."
Rev 1:17 [18]As he was speaking to me, I fell into a deep sleep with my
Amos 5:18 face to the ground; but he touched me and set me on my feet. [19]He
said, "Behold, I will make known to you what shall be at the latter
end of the indignation; for it pertains to the appointed time of the

---

to Zechariah (Lk 1:11) and Mary (Lk 1:26). As regards angels (cf. the note on Ezek 23:20–33), St Gregory the Great says: "The word 'angel' refers to the function of the spiritual being, not its nature. All the holy spirits in heaven are spiritual beings, but they cannot always be called angels, because they are only angels when they perform the work of messengers" (*Homiliae in Evangelia*, 2, 34, 8). And St Jerome comments: "Gabriel is entrusted with this task because the vision concerns the battles and struggles among kings and the succession of kings, and Gabriel has charge of battles and disputes. The translation of 'Gabriel' is 'strength' or 'strong man of God'. Therefore, when the Lord was about to be born, to declare war on the devil and all evil spirits and to triumph over the whole world, the angel Gabriel was sent to Zechariah and Mary" (*Commentarii in Danielem*, 8, 16).

The interpretation of the vision adds nothing to what its symbolism tells us; however, it does reveal that it has an eschatological dimension, concerning the end of time (v. 17), and it does say that the death of the persecutor will be brought about by God, not by man (v. 25). This is in fact the aspect of the vision that has yet to come true. Until that time comes, the vision must be kept secret, that is, it is something that must be believed in (v. 26). The "many days" that have still to pass may mean that the ordeals that lie ahead are very severe, or else that no one knows exactly when the end will come. In any event, after hearing the interpretation and being overcome by it, Daniel returns to his normal duties, though still under some strain (v. 27). He knows what is going to happen, yet he does not abandon his post, for "the expectation of a new earth must not weaken but rather stimulate our concern for cultivating this one. For here grows the body of a new human family, a body which even now is able to give some kind of foreshadowing of the new age" (Vatican II, *Gaudium et spes*, 39).

cumque venisset, pavens corrui in faciem meam, et ait ad me: «Intellege, fili hominis, quoniam in tempore finis complebitur visio». [18]Cumque loqueretur ad me, collapsus sum pronus in terram, et tetigit me et statuit me in gradu meo [19]dixitque: «Ecce ego ostendam tibi, quae futura sint in novissimo maledictionis, quoniam in tempore erit finis. [20]Aries, quem vidisti habere cornua, reges Medorum est atque Persarum; [21]porro hircus caprarum rex Graecorum est, et cornu grande, quod erat inter oculos eius, ipse est rex primus. [22]Quod autem, fracto illo, surrexerunt quattuor pro eo, quattuor regna de gente eius consurgent sed non in fortitudine eius. [23]Et post regnum eorum, cum creverint iniquitate, consurget rex impudens facie et intellegens propositiones; [24]et roborabitur fortitudo eius sed non in viribus suis, et supra quam credi potest universa vastabit et prosperabitur et faciet et interficiet robustos et populum sanctorum, [25]et secundum sapientiam suam prosperabitur dolus in manu eius, et in corde suo

end. [20]As for the ram which you saw with the two horns, these are
the kings of Media and Persia. [21]And the he-goat[q] is the king of Dan 11:2,3
Greece; and the great horn between his eyes is the first king. [22]As
for the horn that was broken, in place of which four others arose,
four kingdoms shall arise from his[r] nation, but not with his power.
[23]And at the latter end of their rule, when the transgressors have
reached their full measure, a king of bold countenance, one who
understands riddles, shall arise. [24]His power shall be great,[s] and he Dan 7:18
shall cause fearful destruction, and shall succeed in what he does,
and destroy mighty men and the people of the saints. [25]By his Dan 2:34; 11:23
cunning he shall make deceit prosper under his hand, and in his
own mind he shall magnify himself. Without warning he shall Dan 12:4,9–13
destroy many; and he shall even rise up against the Prince of Rev 10,4; 19:9; 21:5;
princes; but, by no human hand, he shall be broken. [26]The vision 22:6
of the evenings and the mornings which has been told is true; but
seal up the vision, for it pertains to many days hence."

Daniel's reaction to the vision

[27]And I, Daniel, was overcome and lay sick for some days; then
I rose and went about the king's business; but I was appalled by
the vision and did not understand it.

3. THE PROPHECY OF THE SEVEN WEEKS*

Neh 1:5–11

Jeremiah's prophecy Bar 1–2; Dan 3:25–45; 6:1

9 [1]In the first year of Darius the son of Ahasu-erus, by birth a
Mede, who became king over the realm of the Chaldeans—[2]in Jer 25:12; 29:10

***9:1–27.** This time Daniel is given a revelation not through a vision but by reading a passage of prophecy from Jeremiah and having it interpreted for him by an angel. In the first three verses Daniel describes where he was at the time of the episode; the rest of the chapter has to do with his prayer on behalf of the people (vv. 4–19) and the angel's explanation of the words of

magnificabitur et in tranquillitate occidet plurimos et contra principem principum consurget et sine manu conteretur. [26]Et visio vespere et mane, quae dicta est, vera est; tu ergo signa visionem, quia post dies multos erit». [27]Et ego Daniel langui et aegrotavi per dies; cumque surrexissem, faciebam opera regis et stupebam ad visionem, et non erat qui intellegeret. **[9]** [1]In anno primo Darii filii Asueri de semine Medorum, qui imperavit super regnum Chaldaeorum, [2]anno uno regni eius, ego Daniel intellexi in libris numerum annorum, de quo factus est sermo Domini ad Ieremiam prophetam, ut complerentur

q. Or *shaggy he-goat* **r.** Theodotion Gk Vg: Heb *the* **s.** Theodotion and Beatty papyrus of Gk: Heb repeats *but not with his power* from verse 22

the first year of his reign, I, Daniel, perceived in the books the number of years which, according to the word of the LORD to Jeremiah the prophet, must pass before the end of the desolations of Jerusalem, namely, seventy years.

Jer 25:11–12; 29:10

3Then I turned my face to the Lord GOD, seeking him by prayer
and supplications with fasting and sackcloth and ashes.

Jeremiah (vv. 20–27). The passage in effect shows that to understand Scripture well, a person needs help from God; we can learn this lesson, too, from our Lord's interpretation of the Scriptures for the disciples he met on the road to Emmaus (cf. Lk 24:45).

9:1–3. The fact that this episode supposedly happens after the fall of the Babylonian empire and before the advent of the Persian empire (which will bring about the return of the exiles to their homeland) suggests that the circumstances of the Jews changed half way through the exile. This would make them more eager to know when it was going to end. This is what the author seems to mean by these references to historical events—references that do not correspond exactly with information from historical sources (Darius was not a Mede, but a Persian; he was not the son but, rather, the father of Xerxes that is, Ahasu-erus). The passage also follows the artificial chronology set out in the first part of the book (cf. 6:1). This inexactness may be intentional, to have the reader concentrate less on the actual circumstances of the exile and more on what it symbolizes. Once it is set down in writing, a prophecy has permanent validity and one can find in it the answer to one's questions (cf. 2 Mac 2:1–15), including those that arise after the return from exile, during the Seleucid persecution when this passage was written.

desolationes Ierusalem, septuaginta anni; 3et posui faciem meam ad Dominum Deum meum, ut
quaererem rogationem et deprecationem in ieiuniis, sacco et cinere. 4Et oravi Dominum Deum et
confessus sum et dixi: «Obsecro, Domine, Deus magne et terribilis, custodiens pactum et
misericordiam diligentibus eum et custodientibus mandata eius; 5peccavimus, inique fecimus, impie
egimus et recessimus et declinavimus a mandatis tuis ac iudiciis tuis; 6non oboedivimus servis tuis
prophetis, qui locuti sunt in nomine tuo regibus nostris, principibus nostris, patribus nostris omnique
populo terrae. 7Tibi, Domine, iustitia; nobis autem confusio faciei, sicut est hodie viro Iudae et
habitatoribus Ierusalem et omni Israel, his qui prope sunt et his qui procul in universis terris, ad quas
eiecisti eos propter iniquitates eorum, in quibus peccaverunt in te. 8Domine, nobis confusio faciei,
regibus nostris, principibus nostris et patribus nostris, quia peccavimus tibi; 9Domino autem, Deo
nostro, misericordia et propitiatio, quia recessimus a te. 10Et non audivimus vocem Domini Dei nostri,
ut ambularemus in lege eius, quam posuit nobis per servos suos prophetas; 11et omnis Israel praevaricati
sunt legem tuam et declinaverunt, ne audirent vocem tuam, et stillavit super nos maledictio et
detestatio, quae scripta est in libro Moysis servi Dei, quia peccavimus ei. 12Et statuit sermones suos,
quos locutus est super nos et super iudices nostros, qui iudicaverunt nos, ut superducerent in nos
magnum malum, quale numquam fuit sub omni caelo, secundum quod factum est in Ierusalem. 13Sicut
scriptum est in lege Moysis, omne malum hoc venit super nos, et non rogavimus faciem Domini Dei
nostri, ut reverteremur ab iniquitatibus nostris et cogitaremus veritatem tuam. 14Et vigilavit Dominus
super malitiam et adduxit eam super nos, quia iustus Dominus Deus noster in omnibus operibus suis,
quae fecit; non enim audivimus vocem eius. 15Et nunc, Domine Deus noster, qui eduxisti populum

Daniel's penitentional prayer

4I prayed to the LORD my God and made confession, saying, "O
Lord, the great and terrible God, who keepest covenant and
steadfast love with those who love him and keep his commandments, 5we have sinned and done wrong and acted wickedly and
rebelled, turning aside from thy commandments and ordinances;
6we have not listened to thy servants the prophets, who spoke in
thy name to our kings, our princes, and our fathers, and to all the
people of the land. 7To thee, O LORD, belongs righteousness, but to
us confusion of face, as at this day, to the men of Judah, to the
inhabitants of Jerusalem, and to all Israel, those that are near and
those that are far away, in all the lands to which thou hast driven
them, because of the treachery which they have committed against
thee. 8To us, O LORD, belongs confusion of face, to our kings, to
our princes, and to our fathers, because we have sinned against
thee. 9To the Lord our God belong mercy and forgiveness; because
we have rebelled against him, 10and have not obeyed the voice of
the LORD our God by following his laws, which he set before us by
his servants the prophets. 11All Israel has transgressed thy law and
turned aside, refusing to obey thy voice. And the curse and oath
which are written in the law of Moses the servant of God have
been poured out upon us, because we have sinned against him.

Ex 34:6
Lev 26:40
Deut 7:9,21
Neh 1:2,5
1 Kings 8:47
Neh 9:34
Jer 7:25–26;
44:21
Bar 1:15–17
Neh 9:34
Jer 7:25–26
Deut 28:64
Is 57:19
Bar 1:15–16
Neh 9:17
Deut 28:15
Jer 26:4
Lev 26:14–39
Deut 28:
15–68
Bar 2:1–2

9:4–19. This is a penitential prayer in which Daniel speaks in solidarity with his people and intercedes on their behalf. He acknowledges that God has acted justly in punishing the people by driving them out of the chosen land (vv. 4–8), but he reminds God that he is also forgiving and merciful (v. 9). They have been punished in line with the Law of Moses (v. 13), but God, who delivered them from Egypt (v. 15), will surely listen to his servants when they appeal to him, for his mercy is great (v. 18). If he forgives them, it will redound to the honour of God's name (vv. 17, 19). Commenting on v. 18, St Jerome observes: "Daniel expresses himself in human terms: when we are listened to, it seems as if God has inclined his ear to us; when he turns to look at us, it seems as if he has opened his eyes; and when he turns his face away, it is as if we are not worthy of being heard or to appear in his sight" (*Commentarii in Danielem*, 9, 18). St Basil, on another point, notes that Daniel's fasting prepares the ground for the revelation that follows: "Daniel would not have seen the vision if he had not first refined his soul by fasting" (*De jejunio*, 1, 9). For penitential prayers similar to this, see Ezra 9:6–15; Neh 9; Ps 51; Bar 1:15—3:8. Although Daniel's prayer is about the ordeal of exile, it is valid at all times. The Church, too, "embracing in her bosom sinners, at the same time holy and always in need of being purified, always follows the way of penance and renewal" (Vatican II, *Lumen gentium*, 8).

12 He has confirmed his words, which he spoke against us and
against our rulers who ruled us, by bringing upon us a great
calamity; for under the whole heaven there has not been done the
like of what has been done against Jerusalem. 13 As it is written in
the law of Moses, all this calamity has come upon us, yet we have
not entreated the favour of the LORD our God, turning from our
Neh 9:33 iniquities and giving heed to thy truth. 14 Therefore the LORD has
Jn 8:32; 1 Jn 3:19 kept ready the calamity and has brought it upon us; for the LORD
our God is righteous in all the works which he has done, and we
Deut 6:21 have not obeyed his voice. 15 And now, O LORD our God, who
Jer 32:20–21 didst bring thy people out of the land of Egypt with a mighty
hand, and hast made thee a name, as at this day, we have sinned,
Ps 44:14 we have done wickedly. 16 O LORD, according to all thy righteous
Rom 3:21 acts, let thy anger and thy wrath turn away from thy city
Jerusalem, thy holy hill; because for our sins, and for the iniquities
Ps 4:7 of our fathers, Jerusalem and thy people have become a byword
Bar 2:17 among all who are round about us. 17 Now therefore, O our God,
hearken to the prayer of thy servant and to his supplications, and
for thy own sake, O LORD,[t] cause thy face to shine upon thy
2 Kings 19:16 sanctuary, which is desolate. 18 O my God, incline thy ear and
Is 37:17; Lam 5:18 hear; open thy eyes and behold our desolations, and the city which
Bar 2:19 is called by thy name; for we do not present our supplications
before thee on the ground of our righteousness, but on the ground
Neh 9:19, 27,31 of thy great mercy. 19 O LORD, hear; O LORD, forgive; O LORD,
Ps 40:18 give heed and act; delay not, for thy own sake, O my God,
because thy city and thy people are called by thy name."

---

tuum de terra Aegypti in manu forti et fecisti tibi nomen secundum diem hanc, peccavimus, iniquitatem fecimus, 16 Domine, in omnem iustitiam tuam; avertatur, obsecro, ira tua et furor tuus a civitate tua Ierusalem et monte sancto tuo; propter peccata enim nostra et iniquitates patrum nostrorum Ierusalem et populus tuus in opprobrium sunt omnibus per circuitum nostrum. 17 Nunc ergo exaudi, Deus noster, orationem servi tui et preces eius et ostende faciem tuam super sanctuarium tuum, quod desertum est, propter temetipsum. 18 Inclina, Deus meus, aurem tuam et audi; aperi oculos tuos et vide desolationem nostram et civitatem, super quam invocatum est nomen tuum; neque enim in iustificationibus nostris prosternimus preces ante faciem tuam sed in miserationibus tuis multis. 19 Exaudi, Domine! Placare, Domine! Attende et fac! Ne moreris propter temetipsum, Deus meus, quia nomen tuum invocatum est super civitatem et super populum tuum». 20 Cumque adhuc loquerer et orarem et confiterer peccata mea et peccata populi mei Israel et prosternerem preces meas in conspectu Dei mei pro monte sancto Dei mei, 21 adhuc me loquente in oratione, ecce vir Gabriel, quem videram in visione principio, cito volans tetigit me in tempore sacrificii vespertini; 22 et docuit me et locutus est mihi dixitque: «Daniel, nunc egressus sum, ut docerem te, et intellegeres. 23 Ab exordio precum tuarum egressus est sermo; ego autem veni, ut indicarem, quia vir desideriorum es tu; ergo animadverte sermonem et intellege visionem. 24 Septuaginta hebdomades decretae sunt / super populum tuum et super urbem sanctam tuam, / ut consummetur praevaricatio, / et finem accipiat peccatum, / et deleatur iniquitas, / et adducatur iustitia sempiterna, / et impleatur visio et prophetes, / et ungatur Sanctus sanctorum. / 25 Scito ergo et animadverte: / ab exitu sermonis / ut iterum aedificetur Ierusalem / usque ad christum ducem, /

t. Theodotion Vg Compare Syr: Heb *for the Lord's sake*

The angel Gabriel explains the prophecy

20While I was speaking and praying, confessing my sin and the sin
of my people Israel, and presenting my supplication before the
LORD my God for the holy hill of my God; 21while I was speaking Ex 29:39
in prayer, the man Gabriel, whom I had seen in the vision at the Dan 8:15–18; 10:9–11
first, came to me in swift flight at the time of the evening sacrifice.
22He came[u] and he said to me, "O Daniel, I have now come out to
give you wisdom and understanding. 23At the beginning of your Dan 10:11,19
supplications a word went forth, and I have come to tell it to you,
for you are greatly beloved; therefore consider the word and
understand the vision.

9:20–27. According to the text, this passage is not about a vision but about an angelic message that is delivered on earth—not that there is much difference between the two: they are both ways of making a divine plan known to man. The word delivered by the angel comes from God, who answers Daniel's prayer even before he has finished it. God knows what we need even before we tell him (cf. Mt 6:8).

The seventy years that Jeremiah predicted that the exile would last (cf. Jer 25:11–14) are interpreted here (v. 24) as seventy weeks. Seventy, like seven, is a number symbolizing completeness, that is, the whole period of time involved (cf. 4:23). According to the angel, the seventy weeks refer to seventy weeks of years—the length of time between the start of the exile and the end which will follow the death of Antiochus IV. There is a lot of symbolism going on here. Seventy times seven or seventy weeks symbolizes total and definitive completion—when evil and sin will disappear, divine justice will take over, all the prophecies will come true, and the temple will be consecrated definitively (v. 24). The words "to anoint a most holy place" (v. 24) mark the climax of the passage; they refer to the fact that God will forever dwell in the midst of his people, in the temple. They could have to do with the high priesthood. The eschatological dimension of this passage can be seen from the light shed on it by the redemptive and sanctifying work of Christ "whom God put forward as an expiation by his blood, to be received by faith. This was to show God's righteousness, because in his divine forbearance he had passed over former sins" (Rom 3:25).

The anointed prince who comes at the end of the first seven weeks could be Cyrus: in Isaiah 45:1 he is described as the Lord's "anointed", that is, messiah; this would mean that the text is referring to the duration of the exile—forty-nine years from 587 (the year when Nebuchadnezzar took Jerusalem and when Jeremiah would have made his prophecy) to 538, the year when the exiles would have returned in obedience to Cyrus' edict. This "anointed prince" could also be Zerubbabel, the

u. Gk Syr: Heb *made to understand*

Neh 6:15–16; 12:27–43 24*“Seventy weeks of years are decreed concerning your
1 Chron 23:13 Is 53:11 people and your holy city, to finish the transgression, to put an end
Acts 10:38 Rom 3:24–26 to sin, and to atone for iniquity, to bring in everlasting right-
Mt 3:16 eousness, to seal both vision and prophet, and to anoint a most
Ezra 3:1–3 holy place.[v] 25Know therefore and understand that from the going
forth of the word to restore and build Jerusalem to the coming of
an anointed one, a prince, there shall be seven weeks. Then for
sixty-two weeks it shall be built again with squares and moat, but
2 Mac 4:34,38 in a troubled time. 26And after the sixty-two weeks, an anointed
1 Mac 1:45 one shall be cut off, and shall have nothing; and the people of the
Dan 11:31,36; prince who is to come shall destroy the city and the sanctuary. Its[w]
12:11 1 Mac 1:54 end shall come with a flood, and to the end there shall be war;
Mt 24:15 Mk 13:14 desolations are decreed. 27And he shall make a strong covenant

---

prince of David’s line, who returned to Judah with the repatriates and rebuilt the temple (cf. Ezra 5:2; 6:15). Some Fathers, however, see Jesus Christ in this Prince Messiah, and with good reason, for he was responsible for the liberation of the new people of God.

The sixty-two weeks that follow refer to the time after the return from exile, during which the walls of Jerusalem will be rebuilt (cf. Neh 6:15–16; 12:27–43) and which will see the beginning of the trials that were a feature of the author’s own time. The trials include the death of the anointed one who is “cut off” (v. 26), which would fit in with the death of the high priest Onias III in 171 BC (cf. 2 Mac 4:30–38).

After the seven and the sixty-two weeks, only one week remains to make up the seventy. This is the week in which all the grievous damage done by Antiochus IV will cease, for he will die. Antiochus’ time is the equivalent of half a week, that is, three and a half days. The passage shows how destructive that king has been: he has led many to adopt Greek ways and, worst of all, he has suppressed Jewish religious worship and installed a statue of Zeus in the temple. The reference to “abominations” in v. 27 is reminiscent of the ancient baals or Canaanite idols, which were regarded as unclean and fatal to their followers. The words “upon the wing of abominations shall come one who makes desolate”, which derive from the Greek version, seem to mean that the “desolating sacrilege” (cf. 1 Mac 1:54) will be placed in the wing of the temple. The New Testament (cf. Mt 24:15 and par.) uses the same wording. There is still a period of suffering ahead, the second half of the last week; but sentence has already been passed on the persecutor. These then are the words of hope that Daniel passes on from reading and scrutiny of Scripture (cf. 9:1). As St Paul will write: “All scripture is inspired by God and profitable for teaching, and reproof, for correction, and for training in righteousness, that the man of God may be complete, equipped for every good work” (2 Tim 3:16–17).

v. Or *thing* or *one* **w.** Or *his*

with many for one week; and for half of the week he shall cause sacrifice and offering to cease; and upon the wing of abominations shall come one who makes desolate, until the decreed end is poured out on the desolator."

4. THE LAST VISION*

Vision of the man clothed in linen

10 [1]*In the third year of Cyrus king of Persia a word was revealed to Daniel, who was named Belteshazzar. And the word was true, and it was a great conflict. And he understood the word and had understanding of the vision. Dan 9:23

***10:1—12:13.** The revelations received by Daniel culminate with this vision which displays all the features of a literary genre known as "angelic announcements"—the context in which the announcement occurred (10:1–4), the seer's reaction (10:5–9), the scene where the divine messenger introduces himself (10:10—11:1), revelation regarding what will happen in the future (11:2—12:4) and when and how it will happen (12:5–13). The emphasis here is on the message delivered to Daniel. The sole purpose of the vision is to introduce the people who will address Daniel. In chapters 2, 7 and 8, events were described by the use of symbols; now the text refers directly to the protagonists, the various kings who appear on the scene.

10:1–9. The third year of the reign of Cyrus (v. 1) was 536 BC, that is, after the king's proclamation, in the first year of his reign, allowing the exiles to return to Judah (cf. Ezra 1:1; 6:3; 2 Chron 36:22). So, the vision takes place after the years of exile and at the start

hebdomades septem. / Et hebdomades sexaginta duae erunt; / et rursum aedificabitur platea et muri / in angustia temporum. / [26]Et post hebdomades sexaginta duas / occidetur christus; / et nihil erit ei. / Et civitatem et sanctuarium dissipabit / populus ducis venturi, / et finis eius vastitas, / et usque ad finem belli / statuta desolatio. / [27]Confirmabit autem pactum multis / hebdomade una; / et in dimidio hebdomadi / deficiet hostia et sacrificium, / et erit super alam abominationis vastator, / et usquedum consummatio et decretum / effundantur super vastatorem». **[10]** [1]Anno tertio Cyri regis Persarum verbum revelatum est Danieli cognomento Baltassar, et verum verbum et acies magna; intellexitque sermonem, intellegentia enim fuit ei in visione. [2]In diebus illis ego Daniel lugebam tribus hebdomadis dierum, [3]panem desiderabilem non comedi, et caro et vinum non introierunt in os meum, sed neque unguento unctus sum, donec complerentur tres hebdomades dierum. [4]Die autem vicesima et quarta mensis primi eram iuxta fluvium magnum, qui est Tigris, [5]et levavi oculos meos et vidi: et ecce vir unus vestitus lineis, et renes eius accincti auro obryzo; [6]et corpus eius quasi chrysolithus, et facies eius velut species fulgoris, et oculi eius ut lampas ardens, et brachia eius et, quae deorsum sunt usque ad pedes, quasi species aeris candentis, et vox sermonum eius ut vox multitudinis. [7]Vidi autem ego Daniel solus visionem; porro viri, qui erant mecum, visionem non viderunt, sed terror nimius irruit super eos, et fugerunt in absconditum. [8]Ego autem relictus solus vidi visionem grandem hanc, et non remansit in me fortitudo, sed et species mea immutata est in me usque ad dissipationem, nec habui quidquam virium. [9]Et audivi vocem sermonum eius; et audiens vocem sermonum eius iacebam consternatus super faciem meam, et vultus meus haerebat terrae. [10]Et ecce manus tetigit me et erexit me super genua mea et super

Dan 9:3 2In those days I, Daniel, was mourning for three weeks. 3I ate
no delicacies, no meat or wine entered my mouth, nor did I anoint
myself at all, for the full three weeks. 4On the twenty-fourth day
of the first month, as I was standing on the bank of the great river,
Ezek 9:1–7; 10:2; Dan 8:2 that is, the Tigris, 5I lifted up my eyes and looked, and behold, a
Rev 1,13,15; 15:6; Ezek man clothed in linen, whose loins were girded with gold of
1:13–14,27 Uphaz. 6His body was like beryl, his face like the appearance of
Mt 28:3 Rev 1:14; lightning, his eyes like flaming torches, his arms and legs like the
2:18; 19:1–12 gleam of burnished bronze, and the sound of his words like the
noise of a multitude. 7And I, Daniel, alone saw the vision, for the
men who were with me did not see the vision, but a great trembling fell upon them, and they fled to hide themselves. 8So I was
left alone and saw this great vision, and no strength was left in me;
my radiant appearance was fearfully changed, and I retained no

---

of the Persian period, which is the period to which the message will refer (cf. 11:2).

As the author of the book sees it, the time from the third year of Jehoiakim (606 BC; cf. 1:1) to the third of Cyrus would be seventy years, a figure symbolizing that Daniel's ministry has now being fulfilled. Daniel prepared himself for this vision by prayer and fasting throughout the Passover and the week of the Azymes (that is what the text means when it says that the vision happened on the twenty-fourth day of the first month).

Daniel sees a heavenly being (v. 5), an extraordinary angel, with features reminiscent of those of one seen by Ezekiel. That prophet described the angel commissioned to organize the punishment inflicted on the Israelites as a "man clothed in linen" (cf. Ezek 9:1–7; 10:2) and he uses phrases that Daniel will borrow to describe the creatures who surround the throne of God like burning torches (Ezek 1:13–14, 27). So, what we have here links up with the prophecies of Ezekiel, just as in the previous chapter there was a link with those of Jeremiah.

Daniel is the only one who receives the revelation, though the people with him do sense that they are in the presence of the Divine (v. 7). The text says this to show that the vision is not something subjective, something dreamt up by the prophet: it actually happened; he did see a vision. (Something similar will happen when St Paul has a vision on the road to Damascus: cf. Acts 9:7.) The vision, which only Daniel sees, drains him of energy; it is too much for him (vv. 7–8). He has a reverential fear of the angel, which makes sense because "as purely *spiritual* creatures angels have intelligence and will: they are personal and immortal creatures, surpassing in perfection all visible creatures, as the splendor of their glory bears witness (cf. Pius XII, *Humani generis*; Lk 20:36; Dan 10:9–12)" (*Catechism of the Catholic Church*, 330).

strength. [9]Then I heard the sound of his words; and when I heard Dan 8:16–18
the sound of his words, I fell on my face in a deep sleep with my
face to the ground.

10:9—11:1. Daniel is called "man greatly loved" (10:11, 19), as he was earlier in 9:23; this is a reference to his prophetical calling and mission. Given that the angel here is the bearer of the word, we may take it that he is Gabriel, the angel of 9:23. His greeting, "Fear not", already carries a message (that God is well disposed) and it is typical of the language of angelic announcements (cf. Lk 1:13, 30). The vision that he is going to reveal to Daniel is one for which the ground was being prepared ever since the Babylonians attacked Jerusalem; Habakkuk had already said: "For still the vision awaits its time … If it is slow, wait for it" (Hab 2:3). If the angel took twenty-one days to come (the equivalent of the three weeks in 10:2), the reason was that the angel protector of Persia held him back, trying to prevent the revelation about the end from reaching Israel. The background to this passage is the belief that every nation has an angel of its own to protect it. In a world that believed in a plurality of gods, this angel would have been a god; for the monotheistic Jew, this protector becomes an angel. As well as conveying an idea of God's providence towards every nation, this passage allows us to glimpse that what happens on earth is also happening at the same time in the sphere of heaven; or, to put it another way, that it is in heaven that the destinies of nations are decided. Michael, being Israel's angel protector, is the only one who helps the revelation angel, Gabriel, to carry on with his assignment to announce salvation to the chosen people (10:21). According to Jewish tradition, Michael, whose name means, "Who is like God?", belongs to the highest rank of angels; he, along with Uriel, Raguael and Gabriel, did battle with the fallen angels and overcame them. In Jude 9, which mentions a dispute between Michael and the devil over the body of Moses, he is called "archangel"; and he is also mentioned in Revelation 12:7. "Michael means 'Who is like God?' […] Therefore, Michael is the angel sent when a mission or task requires special power, for by his name and his actions he reveals that no one else can do what God alone can do" (St Gregory the Great, *Homiliae in Evangelia*, 2, 34, 9). The Church, the new people of God, also has the archangel Michael as her protector.

The angel touches Daniel's lips (10:15–19), rather like what happened to Isaiah (Is 6:7) and Jeremiah (Jer 1:9), except that now the gesture is aimed at enabling Daniel to speak with the angel and receive the revelation, whereas in the other prophets it was to prepare them to speak to the people.

The revelation that Daniel will receive concerns God's purposes in regard to the tide of human events; these are plans that cannot be altered, for they are written in the book of truth (v. 21). The idea of a book in which

An angel appears

Dan 9:21–23 Rev 1:17; [10]And behold, a hand touched me and set me trembling on my
9:23; 10:19 hands and knees. [11]And he said to me, "O Daniel, man greatly
beloved, give heed to the words that I speak to you, and stand
upright, for now I have been sent to you." While he was speaking
Lk 1:13,30 this word to me, I stood up trembling. [12]Then he said to me, "Fear
not, Daniel, for from the first day that you set your mind to
understand and humbled yourself before your God, your words
Dan 12:1 have been heard, and I have come because of your words. [13]The
Jude 9 Rev 12:7 prince of the kingdom of Persia withstood me twenty-one days;
but Michael, one of the chief princes, came to help me, so I left
Gen 49:1 him there with the prince of the kingdom of Persia[x] [14]and came to
Dan 8:26 make you understand what is to befall your people in the latter
days. For the vision is for days yet to come."
Is 6:7 [15]When he had spoken to me according to these words, I turned
Jer 1:9 Dan 7:13 my face toward the ground and was dumb. [16]And behold, one in
the likeness of the sons of men touched my lips; then I opened my
mouth and spoke. I said to him who stood before me, "O my lord,
by reason of the vision pains have come upon me, and I retain no
strength. [17]How can my lord's servant talk with my lord? For now
no strength remains in me, and no breath is left in me."
[18]Again one having the appearance of a man touched me and
strengthened me. [19]And he said, "O man greatly beloved, fear not,

---

God has written down the actions of men, to be read through on Judgment Day, occurs often in the Old Testament (cf. Ex 32:32–33; Ps 56:8) and is also to be found in the New (cf. Rev 20:12); but here the book has a different purpose: it deals with God's plans for the future. It is a way of saying that the future is already predetermined in the mind of God.

10:19. The Vulgate Latin translates "man greatly beloved" as "man of desires" (*vir desideriorum*). "The man

palmas manuum mearum, [11]et dixit ad me: «Daniel, vir desideriorum, intellege verba, quae ego loquor ad te, et sta in gradu tuo; nunc enim sum missus ad te». Cumque dixisset mihi sermonem istum, steti tremens. [12]Et ait ad me: «Noli metuere, Daniel, quia ex die primo, quo posuisti cor tuum ad intellegendum et ad humiliandum te in conspectu Dei tui, exaudita sunt verba tua; et ego veni propter sermones tuos. [13]Princeps autem regni Persarum restitit mihi viginti et uno diebus; et ecce Michael, unus de principibus primis, venit in adiutorium meum; et ego remansi ibi iuxta regem Persarum. [14]Veni autem, ut docerem te, quae ventura sunt populo tuo in novissimis diebus, quoniam adhuc visio in dies». [15]Cumque loqueretur mihi huiuscemodi verbis, deieci vultum meum ad terram et tacui. [16]Et ecce quasi similitudo filiorum hominis tetigit labia mea; et aperiens os meum locutus sum et dixi ad eum, qui stabat contra me: «Domine mi, in visione angustiae venerunt super me, et nihil in me remansit virium. [17]Et quomodo poterit servus domini mei loqui cum hoc domino meo? Nihil enim in me remansit virium, et halitus meus non remansit in me». [18]Rursum ergo tetigit me quasi visio hominis et confortavit me [19]et dixit: «Noli timere, vir desideriorum; pax tibi, confortare et esto robustus». Cumque

x. Theodotion Compare Gk: Heb *I was left there with the kings of Persia*

peace be with you; be strong and of good courage." And when he
spoke to me, I was strengthened and said, "Let my lord speak, for
you have strengthened me." [20]Then he said, "Do you know why I Dan 8:21
have come to you? But now I will return to fight against the prince
of Persia; and when I am through with him, lo, the prince of
Greece will come. [21]But I will tell you what is inscribed in the Jude 9
book of truth: there is none who contends by my side against these Rev 12:7
11 except Michael, your prince. [1]And as for me, in the first year Dan 9:1
of Darius the Mede, I stood up to confirm and strengthen
him.

5. REVELATION CONCERNING WARS AND THE END TIME*

Wars between Persians and Greeks, Lagids and Seleucids

[2]"And now I will show you the truth. Behold, three more kings
shall arise in Persia; and a fourth shall be far richer than all of

---

who prays and mortifies his flesh and fasts because he wants to know what the future holds and the mysteries of God is rightly called a *man of desires*" (St Jerome, *Commentarii in Danielem*, 10, 19). The translation is a little free, but it has given rise to interesting developments in Christian ascetical writing. St Josemaría Escrivá also uses this expression from Daniel, applying it to the apostolic zeal of Christians: "Allow your soul to be consumed by desires for loving, for forgetting yourself, for sanctity, for Heaven. Do not stop to wonder whether the time will come to see them accomplished, as some pseudo-adviser might suggest. Make them more fervent every day, for the Holy Spirit says that he is pleased with 'men of desires'. Let your desires be operative and put them into practice in your daily tasks" (*Furrow*, 628).

***11:2—12:4.** The revelation made to Daniel includes past (11:2–20), present (11:21–39) and future (11:40—12:4) in

loqueretur mecum, convalui et dixi: «Loquere, domine mi, quia confortasti me». [20]Et ait: «Numquid scis, quare venerim ad te? Et nunc revertar, ut proelier adversum principem Persarum. Et ego egrediar, et ecce princeps Graecorum veniens. [21]Verumtamen annuntiabo tibi, quod expressum est in scriptura veritatis; et nemo est adiutor meus adversus hos, nisi Michael princeps vester. **[11]** [1]Ego autem ab anno primo Darii Medi astabam ei, ut confortaretur et roboraretur. [2]Et nunc veritatem annuntiabo tibi: Ecce adhuc tres reges stabunt pro Perside, et quartus ditabitur opibus nimis super omnes et, cum invaluerit divitiis suis, concitabit omnia adversum regnum Graeciae. [3]Surget vero rex fortis et dominabitur dominatione multa et faciet, quod placuerit ei; [4]et cum steterit, conteretur regnum eius et dividetur in quattuor ventos caeli, sed non in posteros eius neque secundum potentiam illius, qua dominatus est; lacerabitur enim regnum eius etiam ad alios, exceptis his. [5]Et confortabitur rex austri, et unus de principibus eius praevalebit super eum et dominabitur dominatione super dominationem eius. [6]Et post finem annorum foederabuntur; filiaque regis austri veniet ad regem aquilonis facere

one uninterrupted sequence. It is all couched in the future tense as if it were a prophecy about future events. In this way, the reader, who can see that the prophecy came true in the events before his time, can be confident that the predictions about the future will also be borne out by events. This type of prophecy, known as "prophecy after the event", shows that there is a unity running through God's plans for mankind, and that God is faithful to himself and does what he says he will do.

11:2–20. The first thing to be revealed is (v. 2) the line of succession of the kings of Persia (the fourth would be Xerxes the Great who led his army against Greece in 480 BC); then the arrival of Alexander the Great and his successors (vv. 3–4). The "king of the south" or Egypt (v. 5) is Ptolemy I Soter, and the prince who will become stronger than him is Seleucus I Nicator (304–281), who, after carving out his own empire in Syria and Babylon, became Ptolemy's ally and captain. The alliance mentioned in v. 6 is the one made by the "king of the north" or Syria, the Seleucid Antiochus II Theos, with Ptolemy II Philadelphus in 252 BC. A daughter of Ptolemy's, Berenice, became Antiochus' wife, but his previous wife, Laodice, avenged herself; she poisoned Antiochus and killed Berenice and her child by the king. The branch referred to in v. 7 is Ptolemy III Euergetes, Berenice's brother, who rose up against the king of the north (Seleucus II Callinicus, 247–226 BC, the son of Laodice), invaded Syria and was able to carry off much booty, thereby avenging the death of his sister (vv. 7–8). Seleucus II's counterattack on Egypt in 242–240 BC failed, and he had to withdraw to his own territory (v. 9). His sons, Seleucus III Soter, and Antiochus III the Great, continued to wage war on Egypt (v. 10), but the king of Egypt, Ptolemy IV Philopator defeated Antiochus III at the battle of Raphia in 217 BC (vv. 11–12).

Antiochus III continued to try to defeat Egypt; with the help of allies, (including some Jews), and taking advantage of internal strife in Egypt and possibly the rebellious in Palestine, he attacked the next king of Egypt, Ptolemy V Epiphanes in a war that lasted from 204 to 197 (vv. 13–14). In 204 he conquered Gaza (v. 15), and in 198 Sidon and Palestine, the "glorious land" (v. 16). He also sought to control Egypt by marrying his daughter Cleopatra to Ptolemy V; but this did not turn out to his advantage (v. 17). Despite this, he tried to extend his domains by conquering some Greek cities in Asia Minor and others in Egypt, but the Romans, under Lucius Cornelius Scipio, defeated him in the year 189 near Magnesia (v. 18). Revolts in the eastern reaches of his empire (Babylon and Persia) took Antiochus III in that direction and it was during his attempt to sack the temple of Bel in Elymais (Persia) he was killed by the temple's priests (v. 19; cf. 2 Mac 1:11–17, where the temple of Artemis at Nanaea is mentioned). Antiochus III was succeeded by Seleucus IV Philopator, the king who sent his first minister, Heliodorus, to

them; and when he has become strong through his riches, he shall
stir up all against the kingdom of Greece. [3]Then a mighty king Dan 7:6; 8:5–8,21
shall arise, who shall rule with great dominion and do according
to his will. [4]And when he has arisen, his kingdom shall be broken
and divided toward the four winds of heaven, but not to his
posterity, nor according to the dominion with which he ruled; for
his kingdom shall be plucked up and go to others besides these.

[5]"Then the king of the south shall be strong, but one of his
princes shall be stronger than he and his dominion shall be a great
dominion. [6]After some years they shall make an alliance, and the
daughter of the king of the south shall come to the king of the north
to make peace; but she shall not retain the strength of her arm, and
he and his offspring shall not endure; but she shall be given up, and
her attendants, her child, and he who got possession of[y] her.

[7]"In those times a branch[z] from her roots shall arise in his
place; he shall come against the army and enter the fortress of the
king of the north, and he shall deal with them and shall prevail.
[8]He shall also carry off to Egypt their gods with their molten
images and with their precious vessels of silver and of gold; and
for some years he shall refrain from attacking the king of the
north. [9]Then the latter shall come into the realm of the king of the
south but shall return into his own land.

[10]"His sons shall wage war and assemble a multitude of great
forces, which shall come on and overflow and pass through, and

---

plunder the temple of Jerusalem (cf. 2 Mac 3), only to be assassinated by the latter soon after, in 175. (v. 20).

The sacred writer goes into all this detail about the history of the time because the historical context helps to explain what follows—Antiochus IV's campaign against Egypt and the impossibility, in human terms, of Syria and Egypt ever making peace.

amicitiam. Et non obtinebit fortitudinem brachii, nec stabit brachium eius; et tradetur ipsa, et qui adduxerunt eam, et adulescens eius, et qui confortabat eam in temporibus. [7]Et stabit de germine radicum eius plantatio loco eius et veniet ad exercitum et ingredietur oppidum regis aquilonis; et faciet adversus eos et confortabitur. [8]Insuper et deos eorum cum sculptilibus eorum et vasis pretiosis argenti et auri captivos ducet in Aegyptum: ipse per aliquot annos praevalebit adversus regem aquilonis. [9]Et intrabit in regnum regis austri et revertetur ad terram suam. [10]Filii autem eius provocabuntur et congregabunt multitudinem exercituum plurimorum; et veniet properans et inundans et revertetur et concitabitur et congredietur usque ad oppidum eius. [11]Et provocabitur rex austri et egredietur et pugnabit adversus eum, adversus regem aquilonis; et praeparabit multitudinem nimiam, et dabitur multitudo in manu eius. [12]Et tolletur multitudo, et exaltabitur cor eius, et deiciet multa milia, sed non praevalebit. [13]Revertetur enim rex aquilonis et praeparabit multitudinem maiorem quam prius; et in fine temporum annorumque veniet properans cum exercitu magno et opibus nimis. [14]Et in temporibus illis multi consurgent adversus regem austri, filii quoque praevaricatorum populi tui extollentur, ut impleant visionem, et corruent. [15]Et veniet rex aquilonis et comportabit aggerem et capiet urbem munitissimam;

y. Or *supported* **z.** Gk: Heb *from a branch*

again shall carry the war as far as his fortress. [11]Then the king of
the south, moved with anger, shall come out and fight with the
king of the north; and he shall raise a great multitude, but it shall
be given into his hand. [12]And when the multitude is taken, his
heart shall be exalted, and he shall cast down tens of thousands,
but he shall not prevail. [13]For the king of the north shall again
raise a multitude, greater than the former; and after some years[a] he
shall come on with a great army and abundant supplies.

[14]"In those times many shall rise against the king of the south;
and the men of violence among your own people shall lift
themselves up in order to fulfil the vision; but they shall fail.
[15]Then the king of the north shall come and throw up siegeworks,
and take a well-fortified city. And the forces of the south shall not
stand, or even his picked troops, for there shall be no strength to
Dan 8:9; stand. [16]But he who comes against him shall do according to his
11:41–42 own will, and none shall stand before him; and he shall stand in
the glorious land, and all of it shall be in his power. [17]He shall set
his face to come with the strength of his whole kingdom, and he
shall bring terms of peace[b] and perform them. He shall give him
the daughter of women to destroy the kingdom;[c] but it shall not
stand or be to his advantage. [18]Afterward he shall turn his face to
the coastlands, and shall take many of them; but a commander
shall put an end to his insolence; indeed[d] he shall turn his
2 Mac 1:11–17 insolence back upon him. [19]Then he shall turn his face back
toward the fortresses of his own land; but he shall stumble and
fall, and shall not be found.

[20]"Then shall arise in his place one who shall send an exactor
of tribute through the glory of the kingdom; but within a few days
he shall be broken, neither in anger nor in battle.

Antiochus IV Epiphanes

[21]In his place shall arise a contemptible person to whom royal
majesty has not been given; he shall come in without warning and

---

11:21–39. Seleucus IV was succeeded by Antiochus IV Epiphanes, the "contemptible person" of v. 21, who usurped the throne of Demetrius, Seleucus' son. Antiochus asserted his control by a mixture of force and intrigue; he even orchestrated the death of Onias III, who may be the "prince of the covenant" mentioned in v. 22. He soon locked horns with the king of Egypt, Ptolemy VI. In the years 170–169 he organized a campaign against Egypt that resulted in the capture of Ptolemy (in this he was apparently helped by the treachery of

a. Heb *at the end of the times years* **b.** Gk: Heb *upright ones* **c.** Heb *her* or *it* **d.** Heb obscure

obtain the kingdom by flatteries. 22Armies shall be utterly swept
away before him and broken, and the prince of the covenant also.
23And from the time that an alliance is made with him he shall act
deceitfully; and he shall become strong with a small people.
24Without warning he shall come into the richest parts[e] of the
province; and he shall do what neither his fathers nor his fathers'
fathers have done, scattering among them plunder, spoil, and
goods. He shall devise plans against strongholds, but only for a
time. 25And he shall stir up his power and his courage against the

---

Egyptian ministers: cf. vv. 25–26). Although he pretended to treat Ptolemy in a kindly way (he was, after all, Antiochus' nephew), he plundered Egypt and made no effort to bring about peace, which can come about only at the time foreseen by God, that is, "the end" (v. 27). It was on Antiochus' return from that first campaign in Egypt that he took Jerusalem by storm and sacked the temple (cf. 2 Mac 5:1–21), perhaps on the excuse of imposing order when Jason and Menelaus were fighting over the high priesthood. After that, he returned to the city of Antioch. In 168 he set out on his second Egyptian campaign; although he was initially successful, he had to withdraw due to the intervention of the Romans (called in the text "Kittim": v. 30; cf. the note on Is 23:1–18). Enraged by this, he fell on Jerusalem again on his way back, plundered whatever was left in the temple, banned the daily sacrifices and erected an altar to Zeus (vv. 30–31). Some Jews collaborated with him, attracted by the splendour of Greek culture and by the king's bribes (v. 32); some stayed true to their religion and encouraged others to do the same, even at the cost of martyrdom and persecution (v. 33); others, like the Maccabees, revolted (v. 34). Martyrdom suffered out of fidelity to the Law does make sense: it serves as a form of purification in preparation for "the time of the end" (v. 35), which is predetermined. As the book sees it, the prospect of that moment, and not the force of armed struggle, is the reason why people should be hopeful and courageous.

Antiochus IV's impiety reached its zenith when he put himself forward as a god (hence his nickname Epiphanes, which is linked to the "epiphany" or manifestation of a god), and coined money which depicted him as having the features of Zeus. The author reads such irreligion as a sign that the end is near, for God will not be able to tolerate it any longer (v. 36). Also, Antiochus gave up the cult of Apollo, a deity revered by his ancestors, replacing it with that of Jupiter Capitolinus, or the god of fortresses. He respected neither the true God nor the traditional gods of his people (vv. 37–39).

et brachia austri non sustinebunt, et populo electorum eius non erit fortitudo ad resistendum. 16Et faciet
veniens super eum iuxta placitum suum, et non erit qui stet contra faciem eius; et stabit in terra inclita,
et consumptio in manu eius. 17Et ponet faciem suam, ut veniat ad tenendum universum regnum eius, et

e. Or *among the richest men*

king of the south with a great army; and the king of the south shall
wage war with an exceedingly great and mighty army; but he shall
not stand, for plots shall be devised against him. 26Even those who
eat his rich food shall be his undoing; his army shall be swept
away, and many shall fall down slain. 27And as for the two kings,
their minds shall be bent on mischief; they shall speak lies at the
same table, but to no avail; for the end is yet to be at the time
2 Mac 5:1–21 appointed. 28And he shall return to his land with great substance,
but his heart shall be set against the holy covenant. And he shall
work his will, and return to his own land.

29"At the time appointed he shall return and come into the
south; but it shall not be this time as it was before. 30For ships of
Kittim shall come against him, and he shall be afraid and withdraw, and shall turn back and be enraged and take action against
the holy covenant. He shall turn back and give heed to those who
Dan 8:11; 9:27; 12:11 forsake the holy covenant. 31Forces from him shall appear and
Mt 24:15 profane the temple and fortress, and shall take away the continual
Mk 13:14 burnt offering. And they shall set up the abomination that makes
desolate. 32He shall seduce with flattery those who violate the
covenant; but the people who know their God shall stand firm and
Dan 12:3,8 take action. 33And those among the people who are wise shall
make many understand, though they shall fall by sword and flame,
by captivity and plunder, for some days. 34When they fall, they
shall receive a little help. And many shall join themselves to them
Dan 12,10 with flattery; 35and some of those who are wise shall fall, to refine
and to cleanse them[f] and to make them white, until the time of the
end, for it is yet for the time appointed.

---

recta faciet cum eo et filiam feminarum dabit ei, ut evertat illud; et non stabit nec illius erit. 18Et
convertet faciem suam ad insulas et capiet multas, et cessare faciet princeps opprobrium eius, et
opprobrium eius convertetur in eum. 19Et convertet faciem suam ad oppida terrae suae et impinget et
corruet, et non invenietur. 20Et stabit in loco eius, qui mittat exactorem in decus regni; et in paucis
diebus conteretur, non in furore nec in proelio. 21Et stabit in loco eius despectus, et non tribuetur ei
honor regius; et veniet clam et obtinebit regnum in fraudulentia. 22Et brachia pugnantis expugnabuntur
a facie eius et conterentur; insuper et dux foederis. 23Et post amicitias, cum eo faciet dolum et ascendet
et superabit in modico populo. 24In prosperitate uberes urbes ingredietur et faciet, quae non fecerunt
patres eius et patres patrum eius: rapinas et praedam et divitias eorum dissipabit et contra oppida
cogitationes inibit, et hoc usque ad tempus. 25Et concitabitur fortitudo eius et cor eius adversum regem
austri in exercitu magno; et rex austri provocabitur ad bellum multis auxiliis et fortibus nimis, et non
stabit, quia inibunt adversus eum consilia. 26Et comedentes panem cum eo conterent illum;
exercitusque eius opprimetur, et cadent interfecti plurimi. 27Duorum quoque regum cor erit, ut
malefaciant et ad mensam unam mendacium loquentur et non proficient, quia adhuc finis in aliud
tempus. 28Et revertetur in terram suam cum opibus multis, et cor eius adversum testamentum sanctum;
et faciet et revertetur in terram suam. 29Statuto tempore revertetur et veniet ad austrum, et non erit priori
simile novissimum. 30Et venient super eum trieres, Romani; et percutietur et revertetur et indignabitur
contra testamentum sanctum et faciet reverteturque et cogitabit adversum eos, qui dereliquerunt

f. Gk: Heb *among them*

36“And the king shall do according to his will; he shall exalt Dan 2:47; 8:19
himself and magnify himself above every god, and shall speak 2 Thess 2:4
astonishing things against the God of gods. He shall prosper till Jude 16
the indignation is accomplished; for what is determined shall be Rev 13:5
done. 37He shall give no heed to the gods of his fathers, or to the
one beloved by women; he shall not give heed to any other god,
for he shall magnify himself above all. 38He shall honour the god
of fortresses instead of these; a god whom his fathers did not
know he shall honour with gold and silver, with precious stones
and costly gifts. 39He shall deal with the strongest fortresses by the
help of a foreign god; those who acknowledge him he shall
magnify with honour. He shall make them rulers over many and
shall divide the land for a price.

Last battles and final deliverance

40“At the time of the end the king of the south shall attack[g] him; Dan 8:9; 11:16
but the king of the north shall rush upon him like a whirlwind,

---

***11:40—12:4.** Up to 11:40 the revelation made to Daniel has considered historical events; it now moves on to describe the time of the End, which will come when the persecutor has fallen (11:40–45) and the people are raised up, when those who have been faithful are delivered (12:1–4). This is what the prophecy is primarily about, because it refers to a period after the sacred author's own time. To grasp the message here, one needs to focus not so much on the detail of what will happen as on the fact that it will happen. How it will come about can be seen by projecting on to the end time what happened in the past and what is happening now.

11:40–45. The time of the End will come when the power of evil (symbolized here by Antiochus IV) disappears. The death of the king is described in a continuation of the earlier narrative that reports another campaign against Egypt in which he has great success (vv. 40–42); but he has to turn and withdraw (not for the first time) because of news reaching him from his own country; as he makes his way back, he will have to pass through the land of Israel and there he will meet his end (vv. 44–45). What will happen is similar to what had happened before, but it happens for the last time. As he makes his way south towards Egypt, Antiochus IV will

testamentum sanctum. 31Et brachia ex eo stabunt et polluent sanctuarium fortitudinis et auferent iuge
sacrificium et dabunt abominationem vastatoris. 32Et impios in testamentum errare faciet fraudulenter;
populus autem scientium Deum suum obtinebit et faciet. 33Et docti in populo docebunt plurimos; et
ruent in gladio et in flamma et in captivitate et in rapina per dies. 34Cumque corruerint, sublevabuntur
auxilio parvulo, et applicabuntur eis plurimi fraudulenter. 35Et de eruditis ruent, ut aliqui eorum
conflentur et purgentur et dealbentur usque ad tempus praefinitum, quia adhuc aliud tempus erit. 36Et
faciet iuxta voluntatem suam rex et elevabitur et magnificabitur adversus omnem deum et adversus
Deum deorum loquetur magnifica et prosperabitur, donec compleatur iracundia; perpetrata quippe est

g. Heb *thrust at*

with chariots and horsemen, and with many ships; and he shall
come into countries and shall overflow and pass through. 41He
shall come into the glorious land. And tens of thousands shall fall,
but these shall be delivered out of his hand: Edom and Moab and
the main part of the Ammonites. 42He shall stretch out his hand
against the countries, and the land of Egypt shall not escape. 43He
shall become ruler of the treasures of gold and of silver, and all the
precious things of Egypt; and the Libyans and the Ethiopians shall
follow in his train. 44But tidings from the east and the north shall
alarm him, and he shall go forth with great fury to exterminate and
utterly destroy many. 45And he shall pitch his palatial tents
between the sea and the glorious holy mountain; yet he shall come
to his end, with none to help him.

1 Mac 6:1–16
2 Mac 9:1–29

12 1"At that time shall arise Michael, the great prince who has
charge of your people. And there shall be a time of trouble,
such as never has been since there was a nation till that time; but

Jer 30:7; Dan 10:3; Joel 2:2 Mt 24:21p Jude 9; Rev 3:5; 7:14; 12:7; 13:8; 16:18; 20:12

---

attack Judea again, but her neighbouring countries will not be touched, perhaps because these traditional enemies of the Jews are Antiochus' allies (v. 41). When he is established in Egypt, Libyans and Ethiopians, that is, peoples from east and south of Egypt, will flock to him (v. 43). On his homeward journey he will flaunt his power by pitching his tents in front of the temple. Death will overtake him there (v. 45). When evaluating the prophecy, it is not very relevant that Antiochus IV in fact died elsewhere (in Persia) of a terrible disease (cf. 1 Mac 6:1–16; 2 Mac 9:1–29), because what we are really being told about here is the connexion between the death of the persecutor and the salvation God grants to his people. The setting for Antiochus' death here is symbolic: death claims him in the land of Israel, from where God is going to rule the everlasting kingdom that he will soon establish.

12:1–4. The prophecy ends by announcing the deliverance of the people of God through the mediation of Michael, the angel protector of Israel. The names written in the book symbolize those

definitio. 37Et deos patrum suorum non reputabit neque concupiscentiam feminarum nec quemquam deorum curabit, quia super universa magnificabit se; 38deum autem oppidorum in loco suo venerabitur et deum, quem ignoraverunt patres eius, colet auro et argento et lapide pretioso rebusque pretiosis 39et faciet adversus oppida munita cum deo alieno; qui cognoverit eum, multiplicabit gloriam eius et dabit eis potestatem in multis et terram dividet pretio. 40Et in tempore praefinito proeliabitur adversus eum rex austri, et quasi tempestas veniet contra illum rex aquilonis in curribus et in equitibus et in classe magna, et ingredietur terras et conteret et pertransiet. 41Et introibit in terram gloriosam, et multae corruent; hae autem solae salvabuntur de manu eius: Edom et Moab et principium filiorum Ammon. 42Et mittet manum suam in terras, et terra Aegypti non effugiet; 43et dominabitur thesaurorum auri et argenti et in omnibus pretiosis Aegypti, et Libyes et Aethiopes in vestigia eius transibunt. 44Et fama turbabit eum ab oriente et ab aquilone; et veniet in ira magna, ut conterat et interficiat plurimos, 45et figet tabernacula palatii sui inter maria super montem sanctum decoris; et veniet usque ad summitatem eius, et nemo auxiliabitur ei. **[12]** 1In tempore autem illo consurget Michael, princeps magnus, qui

at that time your people shall be delivered, every one whose name 2 Mac 7:9
shall be found written in the book. [2]And many of those who sleep in Ezek 37:10 Jn 5:29
the dust of the earth shall awake, some to everlasting life, and some Is 66:24
to shame and everlasting contempt. [3]And those who are wise shall Mt 13:43
shine like the brightness of the firmament; and those who turn many 1 Cor 15:41–42
to righteousness, like the stars for ever and ever. [4]But you, Daniel, Dan 8:26; 10:5
shut up the words, and seal the book, until the time of the end. Many Amos 8:12 Rev 10:4
shall run to and fro, and knowledge shall increase."

---

who are truly the people of God—those whom God regards as his people because they have stayed faithful to him. There is no mention now of the everlasting kingdom on earth that we heard of in 2:44 and 7:14, but one presumes that there will be one, for those who were dead will rise, either to have a share in that kingdom or else to suffer the punishment they deserve. The new situation in which the good and the wicked find themselves will never change again: it will be forever. Those who will shine brightest are those who knew and taught the Law—those who "turn many to righteousness" (v. 3), not the martyrs. The book of Daniel goes further than the prophets Isaiah and Ezekiel went. They spoke symbolically of a resurgence of the people in terms of a resurrection (cf. Is 26:19; Ezek 37); in Daniel as in 2 Maccabees 7:14, 29 the resurrection is real, not symbolic: "God reveals the resurrection of the dead to his people progressively. Hope in the bodily resurrection of the dead established itself as a consequence intrinsic to faith in God as creator of the whole man, soul and body. The creator of heaven and earth is also the one who faithfully maintains his covenant with Abraham and his posterity. It was in this double perspective that faith in the resurrection came to be expressed" (*Catechism of the Catholic Church*, 992).

Moreover, Daniel proclaims the resurrection not only of martyrs (as happens in 2 Maccabees) but of all, for that is what the word "many" (v. 2) means. The Church, too, in the light of Jesus' teaching, believes that "all the dead will rise, 'those who have done good, to the resurrection of life, and those who have done evil, to the resurrection of judgment' (Jn 5:29; cf. Dan 12:2)" (ibid., 998).

stat pro filiis populi tui, et erit tempus angustiae, quale non fuit ab eo, quo gentes esse coeperunt, usque ad tempus illud. Et in tempore illo salvabitur populus tuus, omnis, qui inventus fuerit scriptus in libro. [2]Et multi de his, qui dormiunt in terra pulveris, evigilabunt: alii in vitam aeternam, et alii in opprobrium sempiternum. [3]Qui autem docti fuerint, fulgebunt quasi splendor firmamenti; et, qui ad iustitiam erudierint multos, quasi stellae in perpetuas aeternitates. [4]Tu autem, Daniel, claude sermones et signa librum usque ad tempus finis; pertransibunt plurimi, et multiplex erit scientia». [5]Et vidi ego Daniel: et ecce duo alii stabant, unus hinc super ripam fluminis, et alius inde ex altera ripa fluminis. [6]Et dixit viro, qui indutus erat lineis, qui stabat super aquas fluminis: «Usquequo finis horum mirabilium?». [7]Et audivi virum, qui indutus erat lineis, qui stabat super aquas fluminis, cum levasset dexteram et sinistram suam in caelum et iurasset per Viventem in aeternum: «Quia in tempus, tempora et dimidium temporis; et cum completa fuerit dispersio manus populi sancti, complebuntur universa haec». [8]Et ego audivi et non intellexi et dixi: «Domine mi, quid erit finis horum?». [9]Et ait: «Vade, Daniel, quia clausi sunt signatique sermones usque ad tempus praefinitum. [10]Purificabuntur et dealbabuntur et probabuntur

The time of the End

5 Then I Daniel looked, and behold, two others stood, one on this
Dan 8:15; 10:5 bank of the stream and one on that bank of the stream. 6 And I[h]
said to the man clothed in linen, who was above the waters of the
Sir 18:1 Dan 4:31; 7:25; stream, "How long shall it be till the end of these wonders?" 7 The
8:14 man clothed in linen, who was above the waters of the stream,
Rev 10:5–6 raised his right hand and his left hand toward heaven; and I heard
him swear by him who lives for ever that it would be for a time,
two times, and half a time; and that when the shattering of the
power of the holy people comes to an end all these things would
be accomplished. 8 I heard, but I did not understand. Then I said,
"O my lord, what shall be the issue of these things?" 9 He said,
"Go your way, Daniel, for the words are shut up and sealed until
Dan 11:35 the time of the end. 10 Many shall purify themselves, and make
Rev 22:11 themselves white, and be refined; but the wicked shall do
wickedly; and none of the wicked shall understand; but those who
Mt 24:15 *Mk 13:14* are wise shall understand. 11 And from the time that the continual
burnt offering is taken away, and the abomination that makes

12:5–13. Now that he has been told what is going to happen, the next passage of the revelation is about the timing of events. The revealer is the same remarkable angel that appeared at the start of the vision (cf. 10:5–6), and the location is the same (cf. 10:4). The message is not communicated directly to Daniel (as the previous one was); it is given to another angel (cf. RSV note **h**) because it is a mystery that is known only in heaven but to which Daniel is privy. The words "a time, two times, and half a time" (v. 7) imply that the time is short (cf. 7:25). And although Daniel would like to know exactly what the last thing to happen before the end will be, the only answer he is given is a clear call to be faithful in the midst of persecution (vv. 9–10). Still, he is told about two periods of time. The first, of 1290 days, from the date of the profanation of the temple, is one month longer than the three times (years) and a half (1260 days), and this may be saying that, although the time to the end is limited, it will be longer than he thinks. The second period, of 1335 days, mentioned in the context of a beatitude about patience or waiting, involves a month and a half more than the previous one; thus there is a stress on the need for perseverance in this waiting, even if the end is slow in coming. It is possible that mentions of these periods were later additions made to the text after the death of Antiochus IV, because he had died and yet the end had not come. In any case, those who die faithful, as Daniel will, do so hoping in ultimate resurrection. St Irenaeus says that these words were spoken to Daniel "so that he would understand that the promise made to him before (cf. 7:27) referred not to this life, but to eternity" (*Adversus haereses*, 5, 34, 2).

h. Gk Vg: Heb *he*

desolate is set up, there shall be a thousand two hundred and ninety
days. [12]Blessed is he who waits and comes to the thousand three
hundred and thirty-five days. [13]But go your way till the end; and you Dan 7:25
shall rest, and shall stand in your allotted place at the end of the days."

PART THREE

Other stories concerning Daniel*

1. THE STORY OF SUSANNA*

The two corrupt elders

13 *[1]There was a man living in Babylon whose name was
Joakim. [2]And he took a wife named Susanna, the daughter
of Hilkiah, a very beautiful woman and one who feared the Lord.
[3]Her parents were righteous, and had taught their daughter
according to the law of Moses. [4]Joakim was very rich, and had a

---

***13:1—14:42.** These chapters which, as we have said, are to be found only in the Greek manuscripts, form an end-piece to the book of Daniel that has been passed down to the Church. It fits in with the rest of the book because it, too, has Daniel as the main protagonist; but here he is not an interpreter of dreams or a seer of visions: he is a judge raised up by God to save the innocent (chap. 13), a wise man who shows how ridiculous it is to worship idols, as pagans do (chap. 14). Taken together, these two chapters set at the end of the book show that life goes on and that God ensures that justice is done, and that he exposes idols for what they are.

***13:1–64.** The episode of Daniel in the lions' den, and this story of Susanna, with its well-drawn characters and scenarios, are the two most popular passages in the book of Daniel. The Susanna story is set in a Jewish community, and it forms an independent narrative; it probably existed on its own originally, independent of the other stories in the book. The version of Theodotion puts it at the start of the book, to act as an introduction to

multi, et impie agent impii, neque intellegent omnes impii; porro docti intellegent. [11]Et a tempore, cum ablatum fuerit iuge sacrificium, et posita fuerit abominatio vastatoris, dies mille ducenti nonaginta. [12]Beatus, qui exspectat et pervenit usque ad dies mille trecentos triginta quinque. [13]Tu autem vade ad finem et requiesce; et stabis in sorte tua in fine dierum». *(Hucusque Daniel in Hebraeo volumine legimus. Cetera, quae sequuntur usque ad finem libri, de Theodotionis editione translata sunt).* **[13]** [1]Et erat vir habitans in Babylone, et nomen eius Ioachim; [2]et accepit uxorem nomine Susannam, filiam Helciae, pulchram nimis et timentem Dominum; [3]parentes enim illius, cum essent iusti, erudierunt filiam suam secundum legem Moysis. [4]Erat autem Ioachim dives valde, et erat ei pomerium

spacious garden adjoining his house; and the Jews used to come to him because he was the most honoured of them all.

[5]In that year two elders from the people were appointed as judges. Concerning them the Lord had said: "Iniquity came forth from Babylon, from elders who were judges, who were supposed to govern the people." [6]These men were frequently at Joakim's house, and all who had suits at law came to them.

[7]When the people departed at noon, Susanaa would go into her husband's garden to walk. [8]The two elders used to see her every day, going in and walking about, and they began to desire her. [9]And they perverted their minds and turned away their eyes from looking to Heaven or remembering righteous judgments. [10]Both were overwhelmed with passion for her, but they did not tell each other of their distress, [11]for they were ashamed to disclose their lustful desire to possess her. [12]And they watched eagerly, day after day, to see her.

[13]They said to each other, "Let us go home, for it is mealtime." [14]And when they went out, they parted from each other. But turning back, they met again; and when each pressed the other for the reason, they confessed their lust. And then together they arranged for a time when they could find her alone.

Daniel, whose name in fact means "God is my judge". There are notable differences between the Septuagint and Theodotion texts; in the latter, the emphasis is put on Susanna's innocence; in the former, it is on the wickedness of the two elders. Throughout the book of Daniel we have been shown that Daniel knows the secrets about the End; in the story of Susanna we see that he can read men's hearts and judge accordingly.

Some Fathers of the Church read this story as an allegory. St Hippolytus, for example, writes: "Susanna suffered at the hands of the elders what we still suffer today from the kings of Babylon. Susanna is a figure of the Church; Joakim, of Christ. The garden beside their house is an image of the dwelling-place of the faithful, who are planted like fruitful trees in the Church. Babylon is the power of this world. The two elders stand for the two enemies of the Church—the Jews and the pagans. The words, [they] *were judges, who were supposed to govern the people*, mean that they handed down unjust sentences against the just" (*Commentarium in Danielem*, 1, 15).

13:1–14. This passage describes the context of the story—a well-to-do Jewish family, all God-fearing people. Susanna could be taken as a symbol of Israel. And then there are two wicked judges, who are supposed to give the

vicinum domui suae; et ad ipsum confluebant Iudaei, eo quod esset honorabilior omnium. [5]Et constituti sunt de populo duo senes iudices in anno illo, de quibus locutus est Dominus quia egressa est iniquitas

Susanna condemned to death

[15]Once, while they were watching for an opportune day, she went in as before with only two maids, and wished to bathe in the garden, for it was very hot, [16]And no one was there except the two elders, who had hid themselves and were watching her. [17]She said to her maids, "Bring me oil and ointments, and shut the garden doors so that I may bathe." [18]They did as she said, shut the garden doors, and went out by the side doors to bring what they had been commanded; and they did not see the elders, because they were hidden.

---

people leadership. These two elders may have some link with the two false prophets who committed adultery and who are denounced in Jeremiah 29:21–23. The point is clearly made that what leads them astray is lust. A work attributed to St John Chrysostom comments on this passage: "If no passion undermines and corrupts it, the soul will remain clean and unstained. But if he does not guard his eyes, and looks at whatever he wants around him in the world, [...] the poison of desire will enter through a man's sight and strike to the bottom of his heart; and he who was once a sober and modest man will be overwhelmed by a whirlwind of passions" (*De Susanna*, col. 591).

13:15–44. The dramatic tension reaches its climax with the sentence passed on Susanna. Faced with the dilemma of saving her life by sinning against the Lord, or dying by staying faithful to her husband and to God, Susanna opts for the second course of action. She is a model for the people in the trials they have to endure. She cannot prove her innocence to the people, but she can certainly assert it to God, who knows all hidden things; and then she waits (v. 42). "How often does the trickery of those moved by envy and intrigue force many noble Christians into the same corner? They are offered only one choice—offend God or ruin their reputation. The only acceptable and upright solution is, at the same time, highly painful. Yet they must decide: 'Let me rather fall into your power through no act of mine, than commit sin in the Lord's sight'" (St Josemaría Escrivá, *Christ Is Passing By*, 68).

de Babylone a senibus iudicibus, qui videbantur regere populum. [6]Isti frequentabant domum Ioachim, et veniebant ad eos omnes, qui habebant iudicia. [7]Cum autem populus revertisset per meridiem, ingrediebatur Susanna et deambulabat in pomerio viri sui. [8]Et videbant eam duo senes cotidie ingredientem et deambulantem et facti sunt in concupiscentia eius [9]et everterunt sensum suum et declinaverunt oculos suos, ut non viderent caelum neque recordarentur iudiciorum iustorum. [10]Erant ergo ambo vulnerati amore eius nec indicaverunt sibi vicissim dolorem suum; [11]erubescebant enim indicare concupiscentiam suam, volentes concumbere cum ea. [12]Et observabant cotidie sollicitius videre eam. Dixitque alter ad alterum: [13]«Eamus domum, quia prandi hora est». Et egressi recesserunt a se. [14]Cumque revertissent, venerunt in unum et, sciscitantes ab invicem causam, confessi sunt concupiscentiam suam; et tunc in commune statuerunt tempus, quando eam possent invenire solam. [15]Factum est autem, cum observarent diem aptum, ingressa est aliquando sicut heri et nudiustertius cum duabus solis puellis voluitque lavari in pomerio, aestus quippe erat. [16]Et non erat ibi quisquam, praeter duos senes absconditos et contemplantes eam. [17]Dixit ergo puellis: «Afferte mihi oleum et smegmata et ostia pomerii claudite, ut laver». [18]Et fecerunt, sicut praeceperat; clauseruntque ostia pomerii et

19 When the maids had gone out, the two elders rose and ran to
her, and said: 20 "Look, the garden doors are shut, no one sees us,
and we are in love with you; so give your consent, and lie with us.
21 If you refuse, we will testify against you that a young man was
with you, and this was why you sent your maids away."
22 Susanna sighed deeply, and said, "I am hemmed in on every
Lev 20:10 side. For if I do this thing, it is death for me; and if I do not, I shall
Deut 22:22 not escape your hands, 23 I choose not to do it and to fall into your
Jn 8:4–5 hands, rather than to sin in the sight of the Lord."
24 Then Susanna cried out with a loud voice, and the two elders
shouted against her. 25 And one of them ran and opened the garden
doors. 26 When the household servants heard the shouting in the
garden, they rushed in at the side door to see what had happened to
her. 27 And when the elders told their tale, the servants were greatly
ashamed for nothing like this had ever been said about Susanna.
Lev 20:10 Deut 22:22 28 The next day, when the people gathered at the house of her
Jn 8:4–5 husband Joakim, the two elders came, full of their wicked plot to
Num 5:18–22 have Susanna put to death, 29 They said before the people, "Send
for Susanna, the daughter of Hilkiah, who is the wife of Joakim"
30 So they sent for her. And she came, with her parents, her
children, and all her kindred.
Deut 8:7 31 Now Susanna was a woman of great refinement, and
Esther 2:7 beautiful in appearance. 32 As she was veiled, the wicked men
ordered her to be unveiled, that they might feast upon her beauty.
33 But her family and friends and all who saw her wept.
Lev 24:14 34 Then the two elders stood up in the midst of the people, and
laid their hands upon her head. 35 And she, weeping, looked up
toward heaven, for her heart trusted in the Lord. 36 The elders said,

---

egressae sunt per posticium, ut afferrent, quae iusserat; nesciebantque senes intus esse absconditos.
19 Cum autem egressae essent puellae, surrexerunt duo senes et accurrerunt ad eam et dixerunt: 20 «Ecce
ostia pomerii clausa sunt, et nemo nos videt, et in concupiscentia tui sumus; quam ob rem assentire
nobis et commiscere nobiscum. 21 Quod si nolueris, dicemus testimonium contra te, quod fuerit tecum
iuvenis et ob hanc causam emiseris puellas a te». 22 Ingemuit Susanna et ait: «Angustiae sunt mihi
undique: si enim hoc egero, mors mihi est; si autem non egero, non effugiam manus vestras; 23 sed
melius mihi est absque opere incidere in manus vestras quam peccare in conspectu Domini» 24 Et
exclamavit voce magna Susanna; exclamaverunt autem et senes adversus eam, 25 et, cum cucurrisset
unus, aperuit ostia pomerii. 26 Cum ergo audissent clamorem in pomerio famuli domus, irruerunt per
posticam, ut viderent quidnam esset ei. 27 Postquam autem senes locuti sunt sermones suos, erubuerunt
servi vehementer, quia numquam dictus fuerat sermo huiuscemodi de Susanna. Et factum est die
crastina, 28 cum venisset populus ad virum eius Ioachim, venerunt et duo presbyteri pleni iniqua
cogitatione adversum Susannam, ut interficerent eam; 29 et dixerunt coram populo: «Mittite ad
Susannam, filiam Helciae, quae est uxor Ioachim»; et miserunt. 30 Et venit cum parentibus et filiis et
universis cognatis suis. 31 Porro Susanna erat delicata nimis et pulchra specie. 32 At iniqui illi iusserunt,
ut discooperiretur—erat enim cooperta—ut satiarentur decore eius. 33 Flebant igitur sui et omnes, qui
videbant eam. 34 Consurgentes autem duo presbyteri in medio populi, posuerunt manus super caput
eius; 35 quae flens suspexit ad caelum: erat enim cor eius fiduciam habens in Domino. 36 Et dixerunt

"As we were walking in the garden alone, this woman came in
with two maids, shut the garden doors, and dismissed the maids.
37Then a young man, who had been hidden, came to her and lay
with her. 38We were in a corner of the garden and when we saw
this wickedness we ran to them 39We saw them embracing, but we
could not hold the man, for he was too strong for us, and he
opened the doors and dashed out. 40So we seized this woman and
asked her who the young man was, but she would not tell us.
These things we testify."

41The assembly believed them because they were elders of the
people and judges; and they condemned her to death.

42Then Susanna cried out with a loud voice, and said, Ps 33:13–15
"O eternal God, who dost discern what is secret, who art aware of Prov 15:11 Heb 4:13
all things before they come to be, 43thou knowest that these men
have borne false witness against me. And now I am to die! Yet I
have done none of the things that they have wickedly invented
against me!" Dan 4:5; 5:11,14

44The Lord heard her cry.

Daniel intervenes

45And as she was being led away to be put to death, God aroused
the holy spirit of a young lad named Daniel; 46and he cried with
a loud voice, "I am innocent of the blood of this woman."

13:45–64. Nothing can be hidden from God ("He is a great eye, ever watchful: nothing that happens in the world can be hidden from him": St Hippolytus, *Commentarium in Danielem*, 1, 33) and his judgments are just and true. Here he acts by rousing the spirit of prophecy (here called "the holy spirit") in Daniel, who as a young man is very different to the elders. Daniel criticizes the people for being taken in so easily by the elders, and he convinces them to reopen the case. He tries to discover the truth, without being overawed by the seniority of the two judges. He uses a simple trick to divine the truth. All come to see that Susanna is a virtuous woman, true to her husband. She thus becomes a symbol of Israel's faithfulness to her God. In the earlier part of the book Daniel was esteemed by foreign kings; now the text shows that his own people, too, hold him in high regard. This is a further reason for accepting the revelations made through him.

presbyteri: «Cum deambularemus in pomerio soli, ingressa est haec cum duabus puellis et clausit ostia pomerii et dimisit puellas; 37venitque ad eam adulescens, qui erat absconditus, et concubuit cum ea. 38Porro nos cum essemus in angulo pomerii, videntes iniquitatem cucurrimus ad eos et vidimus eos commisceri. 39Et illum quidem non quivimus comprehendere, quia fortior nobis erat et, apertis ostiis, exilivit. 40Hanc autem cum apprehendissemus, interrogavimus, quisnam esset adulescens, et noluit indicare nobis. Huius rei testes sumus». 41Credidit eis multitudo quasi senibus populi et iudicibus, et condemnaverunt eam ad mortem. 42Exclamavit autem voce magna Susanna et dixit: «Deus aeterne, qui

[47]All the people turned to him, and said, "What is this that you
have said?" [48]Taking his stand in the midst of them, he said, "Are
you such fools, you sons of Israel? Have you condemned a
daughter of Israel without examination and without learning the
facts? [49]Return to the place of judgment. For these men have
borne false witness against her."

[50]Then all the people returned in haste. And the elders said to
him, "Come, sit among us and inform us, for God has given you
Wis 4:8–9 that right." [51]And Daniel said to them, "Separate them far from
each other, and I will examine them."

[52]When they were separated from each other, be summoned
one of them and said to him, "You old relic of wicked days, your
sins have now come home, which you have committed in the past,
Ex 23:7 [53]pronouncing unjust judgments, condemning the innocent and
letting the guilty go free, though the Lord said, "Do not put to
death an innocent and righteous person" [54]Now then, if you really
saw her, tell me this: Under what tree did you see them being
intimate with each other?" He answered, "Under a mastic tree."[a]
[55]And Daniel said, "Very well! You have lied against your own
head for the angel of God has received the sentence from God and
will immediately cut[a] you in two."

[56]Then he put him aside, and commanded them to bring the
other. And he said to him, "'You offspring of Canaan and not of
Judah, beauty has deceived you and lust has perverted your heart.
[57]This is how you both have been dealing with the daughters of
Israel, and they were intimate with you through fear; but a

---

absconditorum es cognitor, qui nosti omnia antequam fiant, [43]tu scis quoniam falsum contra me tulerunt testimonium; et ecce morior, cum nihil horum fecerim, quae isti malitiose composuerunt adversum me». [44]Exaudivit autem Dominus vocem eius. [45]Cumque duceretur ad mortem, suscitavit Deus spiritum sanctum pueri iunioris, cuius nomen Daniel; [46]et exclamavit voce magna: «Innocens ego sum a sanguine huius». [47]Et conversus omnis populus ad eum dixit: «Quis est iste sermo, quem tu locutus es?». [48]Qui cum staret in medio eorum, ait: «Sic fatui, filii Israel? Non iudicantes neque, quod verum est, cognoscentes, condemnastis filiam Israel! [49]Revertimini ad iudicium, quia falsum testimonium locuti sunt adversum eam». [50]Reversus est ergo omnis populus cum festinatione, et dixerunt ei senes: «Veni et sede in medio nostrum et indica nobis, quia tibi dedit Deus honorem senectutis». [51]Et dixit ad eos Daniel: «Separate illos ab invicem procul, et diiudicabo eos». [52]Cum ergo divisi essent alter ab altero, vocavit unum de eis et dixit ad eum: «Inveterate dierum malorum, nunc venerunt peccata tua, quae operabaris prius, [53]iudicans iudicia iniusta, innocentes opprimens et dimittens noxios, dicente Domino: "Innocentem et iustum non interficies". [54]Nunc ergo, si vidisti eam, dic sub qua arbore videris eos loquentes sibi». Qui ait: «Sub schino». [55]Dixit autem Daniel: «Recte mentitus es in caput tuum; ecce enim angelus Dei, accepta sententia a Deo, scindet te medium». [56]Et amoto eo, iussit adduci alium et dixit ei: «Semen Chanaan et non Iudae, species decepit te, et concupiscentia subvertit cor tuum. [57]Sic faciebatis filiabus Israel, et illae timentes loquebantur vobis, sed non filia Iudae sustinuit iniquitatem vestram. [58]Nunc ergo dic mihi sub qua arbore comprehenderis eos colloquentes sibi». Qui ait: «Sub

a. The Greek words for *mastic tree* and *cut* are so similar that the use of *cut* is ironic wordplay

daughter of Judah would not endure your wickedness. 58Now
then, tell me: Under what tree did you catch them being intimate
with each other?" He answered, "Under an evergreen oak."[b] 59And
Daniel said to him, "Very well! You also have lied against your
own head, for the angel of God is waiting with his sword to saw[b]
you in two, that he may destroy you both."

60Then all the assembly shouted loudly and blessed God, who
saves those who hope in him. 61And they rose against the two
elders, for out of their own mouths Daniel had convicted them of
bearing false witness; 62and they did to them as they had wickedly Deut 19:16–21
planned to do to their neighbour; acting in accordance with the
law of Moses, they put them to death. Thus innocent blood was
saved that day.

63And Hilkiah and his wife praised God for their daughter
Susanna, and so did Joakim her husband and all her kindred,
because nothing shameful was found in her. 64And from that day
onward Daniel had a great reputation among the people.

2. TWO STORIES ABOUT IDOLS*

The idol called Bel

14 *1When King Astyages was laid with his fathers, Cyrus the
Persian received his kingdom. 2And Daniel was a companion of the king, and was the most honoured of his friends.

***14:1–42.** This chapter continues two popular tales—the story of the idol called Bel (14:1–22) and that of the dragon held to be a god (14:23–27), followed by another, similar to the one in chapter 6, about Daniel thrown into the lions' den (14:28–42). The whole chapter is designed to show just how ridiculous idolatry is—the complete opposite of the salvation brought by the true God, the God of Israel. "Scripture constantly recalls this rejection of 'idols, [of] silver and gold, the work of men's hands. They have mouths, but do

prino». 59Dixit autem ei Daniel: «Recte mentitus es et tu in caput tuum; manet enim angelus Dei, gladium habens, ut secet te medium et interficiat vos». 60Exclamavit itaque omnis coetus voce magna et benedixerunt Deo, qui salvat sperantes in se. 61Et consurrexerunt adversum duos presbyteros—convicerat enim eos Daniel ex ore suo falsum dixisse testimonium—feceruntque eis, sicut male egerant adversum proximum, 62ut facerent secundum legem Moysis; et interfecerunt eos, et salvatus est sanguis innoxius in die illa. 63Helcias autem et uxor eius laudaverunt Deum pro filia sua Susanna, cum Ioachim marito eius et cognatis omnibus, quia non esset inventa in ea res turpis. 64Daniel autem factus est magnus in conspectu populi a die illa et deinceps. **[14]** 1Et rex Astyages appositus est ad patres suos,

b. The Greek words for *evergreen oak* and *saw* are so similar that the use of *saw* is ironic wordplay

[3]Now the Babylonians had an idol called Bel and the dragon
called Bel, and every day they spent on it twelve bushels of fine flour
and forty sheep and fifty gallons of wine. [4]The king revered it and
went every day to worship it. But Daniel worshipped his own God.
[5]And the king said to him, "Why do you not worship Bel?" He
answered, "Because I do not revere man-made idols, but the living
God, who created heaven and earth and has dominion over all flesh."
[6]The king said to him, "Do you not think that Bel is a living
God? Do you not see how much he eats and drinks every day?"
[7]Then Daniel laughed, and said, "Do not be deceived, O king; for
this is but clay inside and brass outside, and it never ate or drank
anything."

---

not speak; eyes, but do not see.' These empty idols make their worshippers empty: 'Those who make them are like them; so are all who trust in them' (Ps 115:4–5, 8; cf. Is 44:9–20; Jer 10:1–16; Dan 14:1–30; Bar 6; Wis 13:1—15:19). God, however, is the 'living God' who gives life and intervenes in history (Josh 3:10; Ps 42:3; etc.)" (*Catechism of the Catholic Church*, 2112).

14:1–22. The Septuagint gives this episode the title "From the prophecy of Habakkuk son of Joshua of the tribe of Levi", perhaps to show that the various elements in the chapter link up together (cf. 14:33). The narrator sets this passage in the court of King Cyrus the Persian, who did in fact annex Media after he had defeated King Astyages in 550 BC. The point he is making really is that Daniel was an important man at court, irrespective of who the reigning king was. The main thing that emerges from the story is Daniel's belief in the one true God and his shrewdness in exposing how pagan priests misled the people into believing that their idols consumed food and drink. "He does not want to triumph by reasons and arguments, but by deeds" (St John Chrysostom, *Interpretatio in Danielem prophetam*, 14). No divine intervention takes place; human wisdom on its own is able to show that this is not the true God. However, one can say, as St Cyprian does, that when Daniel speaks he is inspired by the Spirit of God and therefore that "he acted full of faith and with complete freedom" (*Epistolae*, 58, 5).

et suscepit Cyrus Perses regnum eius. [2]Erat autem Daniel conviva regis et honoratus super omnes amicos eius. [3]Erat quoque idolum nomine Bel apud Babylonios, ct impendebantur in eo per dies singulos similae artabae duodecim et oves quadraginta vinique metretae sex. [4]Rex quoque colebat eum et ibat per singulos dies adorare eum; porro Daniel adorabat Deum suum. Dixitque ei rex: «Quare non adoras Bel?». [5]Qui respondens ait ei: «Quia non colo idola manufacta sed viventem Deum, qui creavit caelum et terram et habet potestatem omnis carnis». [6]Et dixit ad eum rex: «Non tibi videtur esse Bel vivens deus? An non vides, quanta comedat et bibat cotidie?». [7]Et ait Daniel arridens: «Ne erres, rex; iste enim intrinsecus luteus est et forinsecus aereus, neque comedit neque bibit aliquando». [8]Et iratus rex vocavit sacerdotes eius et ait eis: «Nisi dixeritis mihi, quis est qui comedat impensas has, moriemini; [9]si autem ostenderitis quoniam Bel comedat haec, morietur Daniel, quia blasphemavit in Bel». Et dixit Daniel regi: «Fiat iuxta verbum tuum». [10]Erant autem sacerdotes Bel septuaginta,

[8]Then the king was angry, and he called his priests and said to them, “If you do not tell me who is eating these provisions, you shall die. [9]But if you prove that Bel is eating them, Daniel shall die, because he blasphemed against Bel.” And Daniel said to the king, “Let it be done as you have said.”

[10]Now there were seventy priests of Bel, besides their wives and children. And the king went with Daniel into the temple of Bel. [11]And the priests of Bel said, “Behold, we are going outside; you yourself, O king, shall set forth the food and mix and place the wine, and shut the door and seal it with your signet. [12]And when you return in the morning, if you do not find that Bel has eaten it all, we will die; or else Daniel will, who is telling lies about us.” [13]They were unconcerned, for beneath the table they had made a hidden entrance, through which they used to go in regularly and consume the provisions. [14]When they had gone out, the king set forth the food for Bel. Then Daniel ordered his servants to bring ashes and they sifted them throughout the whole temple in the presence of the king alone. Then they went out, shut the door and sealed it with the king’ s signet, and departed. [15]In the night the priests came with their wives and children, as they were accustomed to do, and ate and drank everything.

[16]Early in the morning the king rose and came, and Daniel with him. [17]And the king said, “Are the seals unbroken, Daniel?” He answered, “They are unbroken, O king.” [18]As soon as the doors were opened the king looked at the table, and shouted in a loud voice, “You are great, O Bel; and with you there is no deceit, none at all.”

[19]Then Daniel laughed, and restrained the king from going in, and said, “Look at the floor, and notice whose footsteps these are.” [20]The king said, “I see the footsteps of men and women and children.”

---

exceptis uxoribus et parvulis et filiis. Et venit rex cum Daniele in templum Belis. [11]Et dixerunt sacerdotes Belis: «Ecce nos egredimur foras; et tu, rex, affer escas et vinum miscens pone et claude ostium et signa anulo tuo; [12]et, cum ingressus fueris mane, nisi inveneris omnia comesta a Bel, morte moriemur, vel Daniel, qui mentitus est adversum nos». [13]Contemnebant autem, quia fecerant sub mensa absconditum introitum et per illum ingrediebantur semper et devorabant ea. [14]Factum est igitur, postquam egressi sunt illi, et rex posuit cibos ante Bel; et praecepit Daniel pueris suis, et attulerunt cinerem et cribraverunt per totum templum coram rege solo et egressi clauserunt ostium et signantes anulo regis abierunt. [15]Sacerdotes autem ingressi sunt nocte iuxta consuetudinem suam et uxores et filii eorum et comederunt omnia et biberunt. [16]Surrexit autem rex primo diluculo, et Daniel cum eo; [17]et ait rex: «Salvane sunt signa, Daniel?». Qui respondit: «Salva, rex». [18]Statimque cum aperuisset ostium, intuitus rex mensam, exclamavit voce magna: «Magnus es, Bel, et non est apud te dolus quisquam». [19]Et risit Daniel et tenuit regem, ne ingrederetur intro, et dixit: «Ecce pavimentum; animadverte, cuius vestigia sunt haec». [20]Et dixit rex: «Video vestigia virorum et mulierum et infantium». Et iratus est rex.

[21]Then the king was enraged and he seized the priests and their wives and children; and they showed him the secret doors through which they were accustomed to enter and devour what was on the table. [22]Therefore the king put them to death, and gave Bel over to Daniel, who destroyed it and its temple.

The dragon thought to be the living God

[23]There was also a great dragon, which the Babylonians revered. [24]And the king said to Daniel, "You cannot deny that this is a living god; so worship him." [25]Daniel said "I will worship the Lord my God, for he is the living God. [26]But if you, O king, will give me permission, I will slay the dragon without sword or club." The king said, "I give you permission."

[27]Then Daniel took pitch, fat, and hair, and boiled them together and made cakes, which he fed to the dragon. The dragon ate them, and burst open. And Daniel said, "See what you have been worshipping!"

Daniel condemned and rescued

[28]When the Babylonians heard it, they were very indignant and conspired against the king, saying, "The king has become a Jew; he has destroyed Bel, and slain the dragon, and slaughtered the priests."[29] Going to the king, they said, "Hand Daniel over to us,

---

14:23–27. Unlike the idol Bel, a thing made by human hands, the dragon does eat and drink, and the king takes this to mean that it is a living god; Daniel kills the dragon without sword or club, showing up just how credulous the king was. There is no evidence of there having been a cult of the dragon in Babylon, but the Babylonians did depict gods in the form of animals; that may be the background to this little tale, which provides further evidence of Daniel's shrewdness and wisdom.

14:28–42. It is ironic that instead of realizing that they have been victims of deceit, the Babylonians react against Daniel, who has removed the wool that had been pulled over their eyes. Their behaviour shows how blind idolatry can

[21]Tunc apprehendit sacerdotes et uxores et filios eorum, et ostenderunt ei abscondita ostiola, per quae ingrediebantur et consumebant, quae erant super mensam. [22]Occidit ergo illos rex et tradidit Bel in potestate Danieli, qui subvertit eum et templum eius. [23]Et erat draco magnus, et colebant eum Babylonii. [24]Et dixit rex Danieli: «Non potes dicere quia iste non sit deus vivens; adora ergo eum». [25]Dixitque Daniel: «Dominum Deum meum adoro, quia ipse est Deus vivens. [26]Tu autem, rex, da mihi potestatem, et interficiam draconem absque gladio et fuste». Et ait rex: «Do tibi». [27]Tulit ergo Daniel picem et adipem et pilos et coxit pariter; fecitque massas et dedit in os draconis et, cum comedisset, diruptus est draco. Et dixit: «Ecce quae colebatis». [28]Cum audissent Babylonii, indignati sunt vehementer et congregati adversum regem dixerunt: «Iudaeus factus est rex; Bel destruxit, draconem interfecit et sacerdotes occidit». [29]Et dixerunt, cum venissent ad regem: «Trade nobis Danielem; alioquin interficiemus te et domum tuam». [30]Vidit ergo rex quod irruerent in eum vehementer et,

or else we will kill you and your household,"30 The king saw that
they were pressing him hard, and under compulsion he handed
Daniel over to them.
31They threw Daniel into the lions' den, and he was there for
six days. 32There were seven lions in the den, and every day they
had been given two human bodies and two sheep; but these were
not given to them now, so that they might devour Daniel.
33Now the prophet Habakkuk was in Judea. He had boiled
pottage and had broken bread into a bowl, and was going into the
field to take it to the reapers. 34But the angel of the Lord said to
Habakkuk, "Take the dinner which you have to Babylon, to
Daniel, in the lions' den." 35Habakkuk said, "Sir, I have never seen
Babylon, and I know nothing about the den." 36Then the angel of
the Lord took him by the crown of his head, and lifted him by his
hair and set him down in Babylon, right over the den, with the
rushing sound of the wind itself.
37Then Habakkuk shouted, "Daniel! Daniel! Take the dinner
which God has sent you." 38And Daniel said, "Thou hast remembered me, O God, and hast not forsaken those who love thee."
39So Daniel arose and ate. And the angel of God immediately
returned Habakkuk to his own place.

---

make people—and they even force the king to go against his better judgment. The lions' den episode is a repeat of that in chapter 6, though the story here is more lurid (with its human bodies as fodder, and the lions starved in anticipation of Daniel's arrival), and we see God come to his rescue in a very unexpected way. We know nothing about the prophet Habakkuk other than what it says here. The man happens to have the same name as the prophet of the book of Habakkuk. Maybe he is brought in here to highlight the prophetical status of Daniel, but the episode seems in fact to be inspired by Ezekiel 8:3. It shows how God can use some people to put his plans for the salvation of others into effect—even in the exceptional ways that are described in this story.

necessitate compulsus, tradidit eis Danielem. 31Qui miserunt eum in lacum leonum, et erat ibi diebus
sex. 32Porro in lacu erant septem leones, et dabantur eis cotidie duo corpora et duae oves; et tunc non
data sunt eis, ut devorarent Danielem. 33Erat autem Abacuc propheta in Iudaea et ipse coxerat
pulmentum et intriverat panes in alveolo et ibat in campum, ut ferret messoribus. 34Dixitque angelus
Domini ad Abacuc: «Fer prandium, quod habes, in Babylonem Danieli, qui est in lacu leonum». 35Et
dixit Abacuc: «Domine, Babylonem non vidi et lacum nescio». 36Et apprehendit eum angelus Domini
in vertice eius et portavit eum capillo capitis sui posuitque eum in Babylone supra lacum in impetu
spiritus sui. 37Et clamavit Abacuc dicens: «Daniel, Daniel, tolle prandium, quod misit tibi Deus». 38Et
ait Daniel: «Recordatus es enim mei, Deus, et non dereliquisti diligentes te». 39Surgensque Daniel

[40]On the seventh day the king came to mourn for Daniel. When
he came to the den he looked in, and there sat Daniel. [41]And the
king shouted with a loud voice, "Thou art great, O Lord God of
Daniel, and there is no other besides thee." [42]And he pulled
Daniel[a] out, and threw into the den the men who had attempted his
destruction, and they were devoured immediately before his eyes.

---

comedit. Porro angelus Dei restituit Abacuc confestim in loco suo. [40]Venit ergo rex die septima, ut
lugeret Danielem; et venit ad lacum et introspexit, et ecce Daniel sedens. [41]Et exclamavit rex voce
magna dicens: «Magnus es, Domine, Deus Danielis, et non est alius praeter te». [42]Porro illos, qui
perditionis eius causa fuerant, intromisit in lacum; et devorati sunt in momento coram eo.

a. Gk *him*

Explanatory Notes

These Notes appear in the Revised Standard Version Catholic Edition. An asterisk *in* the biblical text as distinct from the Navarre Bible headings refers the reader to the Notes given here. N.B. In these Notes Vulgate additions are quoted in the Douay Version.

ISAIAH

Isaiah, the greatest of all the prophets, lived at a critical time in Israel's history. The very existence of the people was threatened by the king of Assyria in the latter part of the eight century BC. The well-known and beautiful Immanuel prophecies (chapters 6–12) were uttered on occasions of great national danger when Judah was ruled by an unworthy king—Ahaz. Under his successor, Hezekiah, a good and prudent king, Isaiah, who was himself of noble birth, occupied a position of influence in promoting religious reform, and many of his prophecies are to be ascribed to this period. He was by now a national figure with a large following. He appears last of all in the great crisis of 701 BC when, as he had promised, Jerusalem was saved from destruction by the Assyrians.

His prophecies are distinguished both for their poetical quality and for the elevation of their thought. The monotheism of Isaiah is declared in eloquent terms. Likewise, his Messianic predictions attain a clarity that has induced some to give him the title of "evangelist". The second part of the book (chapters 40–55), quite different from the first and perhaps even more sublime, is generally held now not to be by Isaiah himself but by a later prophet writing at the time of the Exile, doubtless a member of the Isaian school and following in his tradition. These chapters are remarkable for the words of comfort and encouragement they contain and perhaps even more for the remarkable "Servant Songs", prophecies about the Messiah to come, foretelling his sufferings. The remaining chapters (56–66) contain a varied selection of prophecies of different dates.

2:2–4: Note the universalism of this prophecy.

5:1–7: This moving allegory may be compared with similar passages in the New Testament, e.g., Mt 21:33–41; Jn 15:1–2.

6:1–13: This vision stresses the solemnity of the prophet's calling. The *Holy, holy, holy* is fittingly included in the Mass. The vision also serves to introduce the Immanuel prophecies.

7:14, *young woman*: The Hebrew word *'almah* is not more explicit. The Greek translates this as *parthenos*, virgin, and may be regarded as a witness to later Jewish tradition as to the meaning of the prophecy. The virginal conception is, of course, unequivocally stated in the Gospel where this prophecy is quoted (Mt 1:23; cf. also Lk 1:35).

9:6: Passage selected for the Introit of the Mass of Christmas Day, showing that the Church regards these words as being fulfilled in Jesus Christ.

11:1–3: cf. 61:1–2 and Lk 4:18–19.

11:2: The enumeration of the "gifts of the Holy Spirit" is taken from this passage.

40:1: Here begins the "Book of the Consolation of Israel", as it has been beautifully called. It was written to comfort and console the people in their exile in Babylonia.

42:1–4: The "Servant of Yahweh" is here introduced. This and three other prophecies (49:1–6; 50:4–9; 52:13—53:12) depict the Mesiah in a new light, giving details of his meekness and suffering.

53:4–6: The doctrine of vicarious atonement is the unique characteristic of this prophecy. We find it in the New Testament in all its fullness.

56–end: These prophecies were probably uttered in the difficult days of the return from exile, about the year 538 BC.

61:1–4: cf. Lk 4:18–19.

Explanatory Notes

JEREMIAH

Jeremiah, known to most people as the prophet of doom, lived at the most tragic period of Israel's history, during which Jerusalem was destroyed by Nebuchadnezzar and the people carried off into captivity. He was of a priestly family and he makes it clear in his book that he obeyed God's call to prophesy most reluctantly. It was his task, under the circumstances, to preach repentance and prophesy destruction if repentance was not forthcoming. But his words fell on deaf ears. In so far as people heard at all, it was only to resent what he said and make him suffer for it. As the prophet was of a specially sensitive and affectionate nature, his sufferings were all the more acute.

He did not always prophesy doom. Thus in 31:31–34, he foretells the new covenant in terms that remind us of passages in the prophet Isaiah. His words may not have had much effect during his lifetime, but after his death his influence was considerable, as was the case with other prophets also; cf. Mt 23:29–30. Not all the prophecies in the book are from Jeremiah himself, but some have been inserted later. An important feature of the book is the quantity of biographical material, which tells us a great deal about the prophet.

1:6: Typically, Jeremiah is reluctant to accept an office for which he feels himself ill suited, and which, he foresees, can bring nothing but suffering and disappointment.

3:16: The ark must have been destroyed at the same time as the temple in 586 BC. In the Messianic times the presence of the Lord will not be restricted to the ark of the covenant; cf. Rev 21:22.

7:4: Trust in the temple's presence without true service of God and observance of his commands is vain, just as earlier a similar trust in the presence of the ark was fruitless without moral observance; cf. 1 Sam 4:3.

8:7: cf. Is 1:3.

9:23–24: The basis of true religion.

13:1–11: Note here and elsewhere the use of symbolic action throughout Jeremiah's ministry.

30:8: The new covenant and the restoration.

31:15: Quoted by Matthew and applied to the Holy Innocents (Mt 2:18).

31:31–34: The new covenant; cf. Mt 26:28.

33:15: cf. Is 11:1: "a shoot from the stump of Jesse".

35: This chapter is our chief source of information about the little-known sect of Rechabites; cf. 2 Kings 10:15–16, 23. They obeyed what they felt to be a call to serve God in the wilderness and desert places. The ancient nomad life during the Exodus was always looked back to as the time of the greatest fidelity to God.

52: Historical supplement which recapitulates and enlarges on 2 Kings 24:18—25:30. Cf. Is 36–39, which was added in the same way.

LAMENTATIONS

This book is traditionally ascribed to Jeremiah but is probably not all by him. It seems rather to have been composed by more than one author, though at about the same period of the siege and exile. The poems, written in the rhythm known as *qinah*, were probably composed for the liturgical services that continued to be held on the site of the temple.

BARUCH

This book, one of the deuterocanonical books, is not extant in Hebrew and is placed here after Lamentations in the Latin Vulgate. It is said to have been composed by Baruch at Babylon during the Exile, but in fact the evidence indicates rather that some of it was composed about the second or even first century BC. The material may well have been composed at different periods, and the final editing have taken place towards the time of Christ. The particular value of the book is that it gives an insight into Jewish life in the Dispersion.

EZEKIEL

The beginning of Ezekiel's ministry overlapped the end of that of Jeremiah and the prophet is concerned with the same evils. But his style and matter are very different. Ezekiel was a priest and mainly concerned with the temple worship and the observance of the law. His description of the future temple should be compared with that in Revelation 21. Ezekiel performs a great variety of symbolic actions—as did Jeremiah on a smaller scale. Ezekiel's visions make one think of apocalyptic writing, e.g., Daniel and Revelation. He does not enlarge greatly on Messianic themes. He speaks of a new covenant (16:60) and, like Jeremiah, of personal responsibility (chapter 18). Above all, he insists on the need for interior renewal, and thus prepares the way for the teaching of Christ.

1:5, *four living creatures*: The description recalls the Assyrian *karibu*: statues of animals with human heads guarding the palace at Nineveh. Here these creatures are pressed into the service of Yahweh. They are met again in Revelation 4:6–8. The point of the vision is that Yahweh is not tied to Jerusalem and could follow his people into exile.

1:23: cf. the cherubim over the ark (Ex 25:20–22; Sam 4:4).

1:28, *the glory of the Lord*: The luminous cloud, or shekinah (Ex 24:16), that normally dwelt in the temple.

8:14, *weeping for Tammuz*: A vegetation god known as Adonis to the Phoenicians. He was supposed to die in the summer and come to life again in the spring. Women wept at the time of his departure to the underworld.

14:12–23: The Lord stresses individual responsibility rather than collective responsibility. It had been taken for granted that some just men would have to suffer in a group or city with the guilty majority.

14:14, *Daniel*: It is possible that this refers to Danel, an ancient Phoenician sage known to us from the Ras Shamara literature. It is unlikely that Ezekiel would have been speaking of Daniel the prophet, as the other names in this passage are both of more ancient personages. Moreover, the spelling of the name in the book of Ezekiel is different from the spelling used in the book of Daniel.

17:2–24: The Messiah, "a shoot from the stump of Jesse". Cf. Is 11:1, and also the parable of the mustard seed (Mt 13:31–32).

26: The city of Tyre, in those days an island and one of the richest cities in the East, was regarded as impregnable from the landward side. In this instance the siege lasted thirteen years but remained indecisive, as Nebuchadnezzar had no fleet. We must, therefore, regard the prophet's language here as rhetorical rather than historical; cf. 29:18.

34:2, *shepherds of Israel*: cf. Jn 10:1–30.

34:23–31: The Messiah and his kingdom.

37:1, *full of bones*: This vision foretells the restoration of Israel after the Exile (v. 12). It has sometimes been thought, wrongly, to foretell the resurrection of the body.

38–39: Gog and Magog. Gog—an obscure name probably meaning "darkness"—here represents the forces of evil. He is destroyed by Yahweh. Magog probably means no more than "land of Gog". The names appear to be used here as ciphers for Nebuchadnezzar and Babylon.

40–48: In these chapters Ezekiel describes the new temple and its worship. The passage is not meant to be taken historically and, in fact, the later builders of the temple made no attempt to take it literally. The prophet is referring to the Messianic times in symbolic language.

DANIEL

The book is composed of two distinct parts. In the first, there are stories about Daniel in the time of the Babylonian empire; in the second, there are a number of apocalyptic visions ascribed to Daniel and foretelling the future. The stories of the first part may be based on original material dating from the time of Daniel but must have been written down later, as they betray an unfamiliarity with the history of the period. Likewise, the visions of the second part are predominantly concerned with the Greek empire and it is unlikely that they were composed before that time. Their literary form, too, corresponds to the apocalyptic style of literature common in the second century BC. The Greek version has some portions not in the Hebrew or Aramaic and these are accepted as canonical by the Catholic Church. They are: the Prayer of Azariah and the Song of the Three Young Men (*3:1–68*); Susanna (chapter 13); Bel and the Dragon (chapter 14). In the rest of the book there are some parts written in Aramaic, thus suggesting a rather late date.

In the first part of the book, the main purpose is to exalt the God of Israel over the gods of the pagans through the experiences of the prophet Daniel. In the second part, the aim is equally to exalt the God of Israel, but this time it is done through a series of visions in which many prophecies are made—the chief of which is the seventy weeks of years until the coming of the Messiah (9:24). The author aims at sustaining the faith of the people of God during difficult times culminating in the persecution of Antiochus Epiphanes.

Explanatory Notes

1:8, *would not defile himself*: When the Greek persecution broke out, the king tried to get the Jews to break their laws about food and drink, and such breaches of the law were taken to be apostasy; cf. 2 Mac 6:18—7:42.

3:23: After this verse the section (sixty-eight verses) printed in italics is contained only in the Greek. It is here translated. It is here translated from Theodotion's version.

Concordance of verse numberings:

RSV	Vulgate	RSV	Vulgate
1–28	24–51	*37*	58
29–30	52	*38–45*	60–67
31	53	*46*	68–69
32	55	*47*	71
33	54	*48*	72
34	56	*49–50*	70
35	57	*51–68*	73–90
36	59		

3:68: The reader will notice that the roman figures used for the remaining verses of this chapter take up again the numbering of the protocanonical text. Verses 24–30 are numbered 91–97 in the Greek and Vulgate; they are written in Aramaic, not Hebrew.

4:1–3: These verses correspond to 3:31–33 in the Aramaic and to 3:98–100 in the Greek and Vulgate. The chapter is considerably longer in the Greek than in the Aramaic.

4:8, *Belteshazzar*: The name given to Daniel means "May Bel protect his life."

4:13, *a watcher, a holy one*: An angel, so called because he is ever watchful to serve God. In Ezekiel 1:18 the wheels representing angels are said to be full of eyes.

5:1, *Belshazzar*: He was the son of Nabonidus and was never in fact king.

5:31, *Darius the Mede*: Nothing is known in history of this person. The Persians, moreover, had already conquered the Medes before taking Babylon.

7:8, *another horn, a little one*: Antiochus Epiphanes, who originally was of no importance.

7:13, *a son of man*: The title with which God addressed Ezekiel. Here it means someone who is more than human.

9:24–27: Prophecy of the seventy weeks. The prophecy, made to encourage the Jews in time of persecution, looks to the future Messianic age in the time of the end; cf. 12:9. The seventy weeks are seventy seven-year periods, i.e., 490 years. But we can hardly take it as an exact historical period. Its immediate application seems to be the period 170–163 BC, i.e., from the beginning of the persecution of the Jews by Antiochus Epiphanes to the purification of the temple and the death of Antiochus.

10–12: Summary of the history of the Persian and Greek periods down to Antiochus Epiphanes and thence to the time of the end.

13:1: The story of Susanna, here translates from the Greek of Theodotion, is accepted by the Catholic Church as canonical Scripture and placed among the deuterocanonical writings. It is prefixed to the book of Daniel in the Septuagint Greek but in the Vulgate Latin it is placed here as chapter 13.

14:1: Bel and the Dragon. These stories, here translated from the Greek of Theodotion, are added at the end of Daniel by both Greek and Vulgate. The latter treats the appendix as chapter 14, but attaches verse 1 to the preceding chapter as 13:65.

Sources quoted in the Commentary

1. DOCUMENTS OF THE CHURCH

Council of Trent

De iustificatione: *Sessio VI: Decree De iustificatione*, 13 January 1547, DS 1520–1583.

Second Vatican Council

Ad gentes: Decree on the Church's missionary activity, 7 December 1965, AAS 58 (1966) 947–990.

Apostolicam actuositatem: Decree on the apostolate of lay people, 18 November 1995, AAS 58 (1966) 837–864.

Dei Verbum: Dogmatic Constitution on divine Revelation, 18 November 1995, AAS 58 (1966) 817–835.

Gaudium et spes: Pastoral Constitution on the Church in the modern world, 21 November 1964, AAS 57 (1965) 5–71.

Sacrosanctum Concilium: Constitution on the Sacred Liturgy, 4 December 1963, AAS 56 (1964) 5–71.

Pius XII

Haurietis aquas: Encyclical Letter on devotion to the Sacred Heart of Jesus, 15 May 1956, AAS (1956) 309–740.

Paul VI

Gaudete in Domino: Apostolic Exhortation on Christian Joy, 9 May 1975, AAS 67 (1975) 289–342.

John Paul II

Dies Domini: Apostolic Letter on the sanctification of the Lord's Day, 31 May 1998, AAS 90 (1998) 713–766.

Dives in misercordia: Encyclical Letter on the mercy of God, 30 November 1980, AAS 72 (1980) 1177–1232.

Dominum et Vivificantem: Encyclical Letter on the Holy Spirit in the life of the Church and of the world, 18 May 1986, AAS 78 (1986) 809–900.

Fides et ratio: Encyclical Letter on the relationship between faith and reason, 14 September 98, AAS 91 (1999) 5–88.

Incarnationis mysterium: Bull convoking the Great Jubilee of the year 2000, 29 November 1998, AAS 91 (1999) 129–147.

Novo incipiente: Letter to priests, 8 April 1979, AAS 71 (1979) 393–417.

Pastores dabo vobis: Apostolic Exhortation on the formation of priests, 25 March 1992, AAS 84 (1992) 657–804.

Reconciliatio et paenitentia: Apostolic Exhortation on reconciliation and penance, 2 December 1984, AAS 77 (1985) 185–275.

Salvifici doloris: Apostolic Letter on the meaning of Christian suffering, 1 February 1984, AAS 76 (1984) 201–250.

Veritatis splendor: Encyclical Letter on certain fundamental questions of the Church's moral teaching, 6 August 1993, AAS 85 (1993) 1133–1228.

OTHER

Roman Catechism

Catechism of the Catholic Church, New York, 1994

Code of Canon Law: *Codex Iuris Canonici auctoritate Ioannis Pauli PP II promulgatus*, Vatican City 1983.

2. LITURGICAL TEXTS

Roman Missal: *Missale Romanum*, editio typica altera, Vatican City, 1975

Divine Office: *Liturgia Horarum iuxta Ritum Romanum*, editio typica altera, Vatican City, 1987.

Sources quoted in the Commentary

3. THE FATHERS, ECCLESIASTICAL WRITERS AND OTER AUTHORS

Anon.
Epistula ad Diognetum in F.X. Funk (ed.), *Patres Apostolici*, vol. 1, Tübingen, 1901.
Letter of Barnabas: *Epistula Barnabae*: in F.X. Funk (ed.), *Patres Apostolici*, vol. 1, Tübingen, 1901.
Augustine, St
De civitate Dei libri XXII, PL 41, 13–804.
Enarrationes in Psalmos, PL 36–37
In epistolam Ioannis ad Parthos tractatus X, PL 35, 1977–2062.
Sermones, PL 38–39.
Quaestiones in Heptateuchum, PL 34, 547–824.
Ambrosiaster
Commentaria in epistolam ad Romanos, PL 17, 47–184.
Commentaria in epistolam ad Corinthios, PL 17, 183–338.
Ambrose, St
De poenitentia libri II, PL 16, 465–524.
Anselm, St
De processione Spiritus Sancti contra Graecos, PL 158, 285–326.
Anthony of Padua, St
Sermones: *Sermones dominicales y festivos*, ed. V. Terradillos, Murcia, 1995.
Athanasius, St
Epistulae quattuor ad Serapionem, PG 26, 529–648.
Balwin of Canterbury
De salutatione angelica, PL 204, 467–478.
Basil, St
Enarratio in Isaiam, PG 30, 117–668.
Bernard, St
Sermones in Cantica Canticorum, PL 183, 785–1198.
Sermones de diversis, PL 183, 35–56.
Boniface, St
Epistolae, PL 89, 687–804.
Bonaventure, St
De septem donis Spiritus Sancti
Celestine I, St
Epistola Cuperemus quidem ad episcopos provinciarum Viennensis et Narbonensis, PL 50, 429–436.
Cyprian, St
Epistolae, PL 4, 193–452.
Cyril of Alexandria, St
Commentarius in Isaiam prophetam, PG 70, 9ff.
Cyril of Jerusalem, St
Catecheses ad illuminandos, PG 33, 331–1180.
Clement of Rome, St
Epistula Clementis ad Corinthios I: F.X. Funk (ed.), *Patres Apostolici*, vol. 1, Tübingen, 1901.
Columbanus, St
Instructiones variae, PL 80, 229–260.
Ephrem of Nisibi, St
Commentarii in Isaiam: L. Leloir (ed.), *Commentaire de l'Evangile concordant: version arménienne*, CSCO Scriptores armeniaci 137 and 145, Louvain, 1953–4.
Eusebius of Caesarea
Commentaria in Isaiam, PG 24, 77–526.
Faustus of Riez
Sermo 5 in Epiphania, PLS3, 560–562.
Flavius Josephus
The Jewish War
Jewish Antiquities
Francis de Sales, St
Treatise on the Love of God
Gregory the Great, St
XL homiliarum in Evangelia libri II, PL 76, 1075–1312.
Homiliarum in Ezechielem prophetam libri II, PL 76, 785–1072.
Moralium libri sive expositio in librum Beati Iob, PL 75, 509–576, 782.
Liber regula pastoralis, PL 77, 9–149.
Gregory Nazianzen, St
Apologetica (Oratio 2), PG 35, 408–513.
De theologia (Oratio 28), PG 36, 25–72.
Gregory of Nyssa, St
De beneficentia (De pauperibus amandis), PG 46, 453–489.
Oratio in diem natalem Christi, PG 46, 1128–1149.
Hippolytus, St
Commentarium in Danielem, PG 10, 637–700.
Ignatius of Antioch, St
Ad Polycarpum: in F.X. Funk (ed.), Patres Apostolici, vol. 1, Tübingen 1901.
Irenaeus of Lyons, St
Adversus haereses
Demonstratio praedicationis apostolicae
Isidore of Seville, St
Allegoriae quaedam de Sacrae Scripturae, PL, 83, 99–130.
Jerome, St
Commentarii in Isaiam, PL 24, 9–678.
Commentarii in Ieremiam, PL 24, 679–900.
Commentarii in Ezechielem, PL 25, 15–490.
Commentarii in Danielem, PL 25, 491–584.
Epistolae, PL 30, 13–307.
Josemaría Escrivá, St
Friends of God
The Way
Christ Is Passing By
The Forge
Furrow

Sources quoted in the Commentary

The Way of the Cross
John Baptist Mary Vianney, St
Sermon on Holy Communion
John Cassian
Collationes: Vigintiquatuor collationes, PL 49, 477–1328.
John Chrysostom, St
Interpretatio in Isaiam prophetam, PG 56, 11–94.
Fragmenta in Ieremiam: Homilia in locum Jeremiae, PG 56, 153–162.
De Susanna sermo, PG 56, 586–594.
Interpretatio in Danielem prophetam, PG 56, 193–246.
John Damascene, St
Expositio accurate fidei orthodoxae, PG 94, 789–1228.
John of Avila, St
Sermones
John of the Cross, St
Flame of Living Love
Dark Night of the Soul
Ascent of Mount Carmel
Justin, St
Dialogus cum Tryphone
Leo the Great, St
Sermones, PL 54, 137–468.
Minucius Felix
Octavio, in V. Sanz (ed.), *Minucius Felix: Octavio,* Madrid, 2000
Novatian
De Trinitate liber, PL 3, 885–952.
Olimpiodorus
Fragmenta in Jeremiam, PG 93, 628–725.
Fragmenta in Lamentationes, PG 93, 725–761.
Fragmenta in Baruch, PG 93 762–773.
Fragmenta in epistulam Jeremiae, PG 93, 773–780.
Origen
Contra Celsum libri VIII, PG 11, 637–1632.
Libellus de oratione, PG 11, 415–562.
Homiliae in visiones Isaiae, PG 13, 217–252.
Homiliae in Jeremiam
Homiliae in Ezechielem, PG 13, 665–763.
In Canticum Canticorum, PG 13, 253–288.
Selecta in Ezechielem, PG 13, 763–825.
Selecta in Threnos, PG 12, 605–661.
Peter Chrysologus, St
Sermones, PL 52, 183–680.
Proclus of Constantinople, St
Sermo de Nativitate Domini PG 65, 843–846.
Pseudo-Clement
Epitula II ad Corinthos: in F.X. Funk (ed.), *Patres Apostolici*, vol. 1, Tübingen 1901.
Pseudo-Macarius
Homiliae spirituales, PG 34, 449–822.
Robert Bellarmine, St
De ascensione mentis in Deum
Teresa of Avila, St
Life
Thérése of the Child Jesus, St
Autobiographical Writings
Theodoret of Cyrrhus
Commentaria in Isaiam: in J.N. Guinot (ed.), *Théodoret de Cyr. Commentaire sur Isaïe* (276, 295, 315), Paris 1980–1984.
Interpretatio in Jeremiami, PG 81, 215–760.
Interpretatio in Thremos Jeremiae, PG 81, 780–805.
Interpretatio in Baruch, PG 81, 760–780.
Interpretatio in Danielem, PL 81, 1256–1546.
De incarnatione Domini, PG 75, 1419–1478.
Tertullian
Adversus Marcionem libri V, PL 2, 239–524.
Thomas Aquinas, St
Expositio super Isaiam
Postilla super Jeremiam
Postilla super Threnos
Summa theologiae
Thomas à Kempis
De imitatione Christi

Headings added to the Biblical Text

ISAIAH

Title 1:1

Part One 1:2

1. ORACLES ADDRESSED TO ISRAEL AND JUDAH 1:2

A. THE LORD COMPLAINS THAT THE PEOPLE HAVE FORSAKEN HIM 1:2
General denunciation 1:2
A sinful nation 1:4
Religion without soul 1:10
Call to conversion 1:16
The people must decide—obedience or rebellion 1:18
Infidelity and injustice 1:21
Punishment and purification 1:24

B. IDOLATRY CONDEMNED 2:1
The glory of Zion and peace among the nations 2:1
The day of the Lord 2:6
Downfall of Judah and Jerusalem 3:1
A warning to the women of Jerusalem 3:16
A holy remnant in Jerusalem 4:2

C. FAILURE TO RESPOND TO THE LORD 5:1
The song of the vineyard 5:1
Laments about sinners 5:8
The Lord calls Isaiah 6:1

D. THE BOOK OF IMMANU-EL 7:1
The sign of Immanu-el 7:1
Threat of invasions 7:18
Assyria conspires against Israel and Judah 8:1
Anguish caused by early defeats 8:21
The prince of Peace 9:1
The pride of the people of Ephraim 9:8
Assyria condemned 10:5
The remnant of Israel 10:20
The new descendant of David 11:1
The return of the exiles 11:10

2. ORACLES CONCERNING FOREIGN NATIONS 13:1
Oracle against Babylon 13:1
Oracle against Assyria 14:24
Oracle against the Philistines 14:28
Oracle against Moab 15:1
Oracle against Damascus and Ephraim 17:1
Oracle against Ethiopia 18:1
Oracle against Egypt 19:1
Isaiah, a sign against Egypt and Ethiopia 20:1
Oracle concerning the fall of Babylon 21:1
Oracle concerning Dumah 21:11
Oracle concerning Arabia 21:13
Oracle concerning the valley of vision 22:1
Oracle concerning Shebna 22:15
Oracle concerning Tyre 23:1

3. THE APOCALYPSE OF ISAIAH 24:1
The earth shall be laid waste 24:1
Hymn of thanksgiving 25:1
The Lord's banquet 25:6
Songs of salvation 25:9
The righteous call on the Lord 26:7
The Lord hands down judgment 26:20

4. OBDURACY OF ISRAEL AND JUDAH 28:1
Lamentation concerning the rulers of the people 28:1
Lamentation over Ariel 29:1
Against those who hide from the Lord 29:15
Lamentation over rebellious children 30:1
Lamentation over those who put their trust in Egypt 31:1
Lamentation concerning destroyers and traitors 33:1

5. VENGEANCE AND SALVATION PROMISED 34:1
Oracle against Edom 34:1
Promise of redemption 35:1

6. HEZEKIAH IN THE FACE OF A THREAT FROM ASSYRIA 36:1
Sennacherib's first embassy 36:1
Isaiah is insulted 37:1
Sennacherib's second embassy 37:9
Isaiah's oracle concerning Sennacherib 37:21
Death of Sennacherib 37:36
Illness and cure of Hezekiah 38:1
Embassy from the king of Babylon 39:1

Part Two 40:1

1. THE BOOK OF THE CONSOLATION OF ISRAEL 40:1
Prologue: promise of deliverance 40:1
God, Creator and ruler of all 40:12
The Lord will raise up a deliverer 41:1
God's special love for his people 41:8
The Lord is mightier than idols 41:21
First song of the Servant of the Lord 42:1
A new song 42:10

Headings added to the Biblical Text

Further acts of salvation by the Lord 42:14
The Lord's tender care of Israel 43:1
Announcement of a new exodus 43:14
God is faithful, despite Israel's sin 44:1
There is no God but the Lord. Rejection of idols 44:6
The Lord chooses Cyrus to effect his will 44:24
Cyrus' mission 45:1
The Lord rules over all 45:14
The Lord topples false gods 46:1
Oracle concerning the downfall of Babylon 47:1
Exhortation to heed the Lord 48:1
A lesson about history 48:17
The order is given for a new exodus 48:20

2. ZION RESTORED TO GLORY 49:1
Second song of the Servant of the Lord 49:1
The Lord's aid to the returning exiles 49:7
The restoration of Zion 49:14
Third song of the Servant of the Lord 50:4
Prophetic exhortation 50:10
An exhortation by the Servant 51:1
Appeal to the Lord 51:9
An urgent call addressed to Jerusalem 51:17
A new call to Zion 52:1
The messenger of peace 52:7
Fourth song of the Servant of the Lord 52:13
A glorious new Jerusalem 54:1
Epilogue: Invitation to partake of the banquet of the Lord's Covenant 55:1

Part Three 56:1

1. PROSPECT OF SALVATION FOR THE WHOLE WORLD 56:1
Worship open to all 56:1
Unworthiness of the rulers of Israel 56:9
Idolatry denounced 57:1
Salvation for the humble 57:14
Misguided fasting denounced 58:1
Salvation for those who admit their sin 59:1

2. THE GLORY OF JERUSALEM AND SALVATION FOR THE NATIONS 60:1
A radiant new Jerusalem 60:1
The herald of good tidings 61:1
Names of the new Jerusalem 62:1
Victory at the End 63:1

3. LAST THINGS 65:1
The Lord's servants and enemies receive their deserts 65:1
Reward for the chosen of the Lord 65:8
New heavens and a new earth 65:17
The new temple and new form of worship 66:1
The new nation 66:7
Punishment of the wicked 66:15
The nations in pilgrimage to Jerusalem 66:18

JEREMIAH

Prologue: The call and mission of Jeremiah 1:1

The Lord calls Jeremiah 1:4
Vision of the rod of almond 1:11
Vision of the boiling pot 1:13

Part One: Oracles concerning Israel and Judah 2:1

1. CALL TO CONVERSION 2:1
When Israel was devout, it had nothing to fear 2:1
Israel's unfaithfulness 2:4
Israel, repudiated 3:1
Israel and Judah, two faithless sisters 3:6
Call to conversion 3:12
Conversion that will endure 3:19

2. INVASION FROM THE NORTH 4:5
Threats of invasion 4:5
Judah punished for its disobedience 5:1
Imminent invasion 6:1
False worship. Discourse concerning the temple 7:1
The people's obstinacy 7:21
Deceit and disobedience 8:4
Keening over the dead 9:17
Uselessness of idols 10:1
The power of God, the Creator 10:12
Imminent flight 10:17

3. CAREER OF THE PROPHET JEREMIAH 11:1
The Covenant broken 11:1
Jeremiah's first "confession" 11:18
The heritage of the Lord made a wilderness 12:7
The linen waistcloth entirely spoiled 13:1
The jar of God's wrath 13:12
God calls for conversion, but the people ignore him 13:15
Oracles in a time of drought 14:1
Jeremiah's second "confession" 15:10
Actions symbolic of the punishment to come 16:1
God rewards people as they deserve 17:1
Jeremiah's third "confession" 17:14
Sabbath observance 17:19
Jeremiah in the potter's house 18:1
Israel forgot the Lord and was laid waste 18:13
Jeremiah's fourth "confession" 18:18

Headings added to the Biblical Text

THE LAMENTATIONS OF JEREMIAH

BARUCH

Headings added to the Biblical Text

The nations have no wisdom 3:22
Wisdom can come only from God 3:29
The created world reflects true wisdom 3:32
Israel, the repository of wisdom 3:36

4. CONVERSION TO GOD. JERUSALEM'S JOY 4:5
Song of exhortation and consolation for the exiles 4:5
Jerusalem makes lamentation to the cities round about 4:9
Jerusalem calls on her children to be converted and to have hope 4:17
Song of rejoicing 4:30
A summing up, by way of conclusion 5:1

THE LETTER OF JEREMIAH
Warning against idolatry 6:1
Idols are of no avail 6:8
Idols are useless things, the products of craftsmen 6:17
Idols are quite powerless 6:30
Summary 6:70

EZEKIEL

Part One: Israel is judged and found guilty 1:1

Introduction 1:1

1. THE LORD CALLS EZEKIEL 1:4
Ezekiel's vision of the glory of the Lord 1:4
The prophet's mission 2:1
Ezekiel, a watchman for the house of Israel 3:16
Ezekiel is struck dumb 3:22

2. SYMBOLIC ACTIONS AND ORACLES 4:1
The siege of Jerusalem foretold 4:1
Severe shortages in the city 4:9
The symbolic sword 5:1
Oracle against the city on account of its rebelliousness 5:5
Oracles of the mountains of Israel 6:1
The day of the Lord 7:1

3. VISION OF THE SINS OF ISRAEL 8:1
Theophany 8:1
Sins committed against the temple 8:4
Punishment deserved by the Israelites 9:1
The glory of the Lord leaves the Temple 10:1
The rulers of the people are condemned 11:1
A promise of restoration 11:14

4. ORACLES CONCERNING IMMINENT INVASION 12:1
The exiles' departure 12:1
Shortage of bread and water 12:17
False hopes 12:21
False prophets 13:1
False prophetesses 13:17
Idolatry denounced 14:1
Individual responsibility. The righteous will be saved 14:12
The useless wood 15:1
Jerusalem, the unfaithful wife 16:1
Jerusalem and her sisters, Samara and Sodom 16:44
Forgiveness and the Covenant 16:59
Allegory of the two eagles 17:1
The allegory come true 17:11
Individual responsibility 18:1
The good effects of conversion 18:21
Allegory of the lioness 19:1
An account of Israel's infidelities 20:1
A restoration that shall endure 20:33
The sword of the Lord 20:45
Hymn to the sword 21:8
Assault on Jerusalem 21:18
Assault on the Ammonites 21:28
The crimes of Jerusalem 22:1
Allegory of the two sisters 23:1
Judgment against the two sisters 23:36
Allegory of the pot set on the fire 24:1
Death of Ezekiel's wife 24:15

Part Two: The nations are judged and found guilty 25:1

Against the Ammonites 25:1
Against Moab 25:8
Against Edom 25:12
Against the Philistines 25:15
Against Tyre 26:1
Lamentation over the fall of Tyre 27:1
Oracle against the king of Tyre 28:1
Lamentation over the king of Tyre 28:11
Oracle against Sidon 28:20
Oracles against Egypt 29:1
Egypt given to Nebuchadnezzar 29:17
The day of the Lord on Egypt 30:1
Pharaoh's power broken 30:20
Allegory of the cedar 31:1
Lamentation over the fall of Pharaoh 32:1
The death of Pharaoh bewailed 32:17

Part Three: Hope and the restoration of Israel 33:1

Ezekiel, the people's watchman 33:1

Individual responsibility 33:10
Ezekiel recovers his power of speech 33:21
Oracle against the shepherd of Israel 34:1
The Lord, the shepherd of Israel 34:11
A new shepherd, a new Covenant 34:23
Oracle against the mountains of Edom 35:1
Blessing on the mountains of Israel 36:1

1. THE RESTORATION OF ISRAEL 36:16
Restoration; return from exile 36:16
Inner renewal 36:25
The dry bones 37:1
The reunification of the two kingdoms 37:15
Escathological battle against Gog 38:1
God's victory over Gog 39:1
Everlasting faithfulness to God 39:17

2. THE NEW TEMPLE AND THE NEW FORM OF WORSHIP 40:1
The new temple described 40:1
Interior of the temple 40:48
Outbuildings of the temple for the use of priests 42:1
The glory of the Lord filling the temple 43:1

3. THE NEW ALTAR 43:13
Consecration of the altar 43:18

4. THE NEW FORM OF WORSHIP 44:1
Rules of admission to the temple 44:4
The Levites 44:10
The priests 44:15
How the land of Israel is to be allotted 45:1
The justice system. Offerings to the prince 45:9
Feasts and offerings 45:18
Offerings on the sabbath and on the day of the new moon 46:1
Miscellaneous regulations 46:16
The spring in the temple 47:1
The frontiers of the new Israel 47:13
Division of the land 48:1
The new Jerusalem 48:30

DANIEL

Part One: Daniel and his companions at the court of Babylon 1:1

1. DANIEL AND HIS COMPANIONS IN THE SERVICE OF NEBUCHADNEZZAR 1:1
Arrival at the court 1:1
Royal fare—God's servants tested 1:8
The wisdom of the three young men 1:17

2. DANIEL INTERPRETS THE DREAM OF THE STATUE 2:1
The king's impossible demand 2:1
God explains the king's dream to Daniel 2:13
Daniel describes the king's dream 2:25
Daniel interprets the king's dream 2:36
The king acknowledges the true God 2:46

3. THE THREE YOUNG MEN IN THE FIERY FURNACE 3:1
Condemnation for those who will not worship the golden image 3:1
Prayers of the young men in the fiery furnace *3:1*
The king acknowledges the God of the Jews 3:24

4. DANIEL INTERPRETS THE DREAM OF THE TREE 4:1
The king's dream 4:4
The dream interpreted 4:19
The dream and its interpretation come true 4:28

5. BELSHAZZAR'S FEAST 5:1
The hand writing on the wall 5:1
Daniel interprets the handwriting 5:13
The interpretation is borne out 5:29

6. DANIEL IN THE LIONS' DEN 6:1
Daniel sentenced to be put in the lions' den 6:1
Daniel's miraculous escape 6:19
The king's profession of faith 6:25

Part Two: Daniel's dreams and visions 7:1

1. VISION OF THE FOUR BEASTS AND OF THE SON OF MAN 7:1
Daniel's vision 7:1
The vision interpreted 7:15
Daniel keeps silence 7:28

2. VISION OF THE RAM AND THE HE-GOAT 8:1
Daniel's vision 8:1
The vision interpreted 8:15
Daniel's reaction to the vision 8:27

3. THE PROPHECY OF THE SEVEN WEEKS 9:1
Jeremiah's prophecy 9:1
Daniel's penitentional prayer 9:4
The angel Gabriel explains the prophecy 9:20

4. THE LAST VISION 10:1
Vision of the man clothed in linen 10:1
An angel appears 10:10

Headings added to the Biblical Text

5. REVELATION CONCERNING WARS AND THE END TIME 11:2
Wars between Persians and Greeks, Lagids and Seleucids 11:2
Antiochus IV Epiphanes 11:21
Last battles and final deliverance 11:40
The time of the End 12:5

Part Three: Other stories concerning Daniel 13:1

1. THE STORY OF SUSANNA 13:1
The two corrupt elders 13:1
Susanna condemned to death 13:15
Daniel intervenes 13:45

2. TWO STORIES ABOUT IDOLS 14:1
The idol called Bel 14:1
The dragon thought to be the living God 14:23
Daniel condemned and rescued 14:28